MW01106412

THE SOLDIER'S WORDS

First-Hand Accounts of What the Confederate Soldiers Actually Wore & Interesting Anecdotes of the Civil War Years

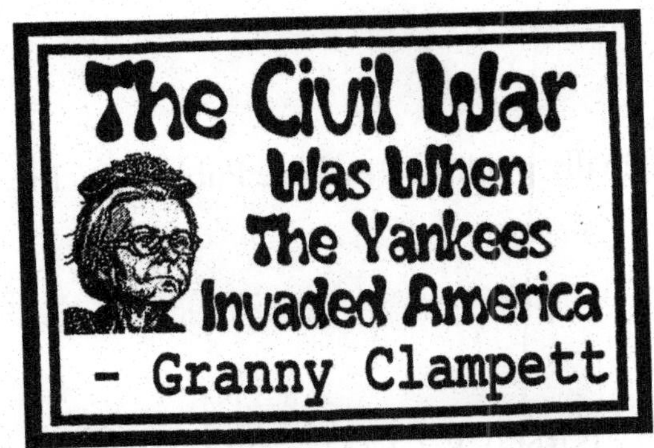

The Civil War
Was When
The Yankees
Invaded America
- Granny Clampett

Compiled By

KENN WOODS

First Edition

PAGE PUBLISHING, INC.
New York, NY

First originally published by Page Publishing, Inc. 2015

ISBN 978-1-63417-729-0 (pbk)
ISBN 978-1-63417-730-6 (digital)
ISBN 978-1-68139-569-2 (hardcover)

Printed in the United States of America

MW01106412

THE SOLDIER'S WORDS

First-Hand Accounts of What the Confederate Soldiers Actually Wore & Interesting Anecdotes of the Civil War Years

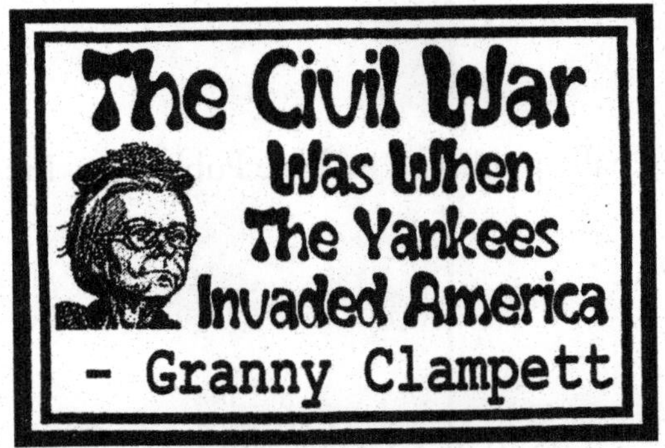
The Civil War
Was When
The Yankees
Invaded America
- Granny Clampett

Compiled By

KENN WOODS

First Edition

PAGE PUBLISHING, INC.
New York, NY

First originally published by Page Publishing, Inc. 2015

ISBN 978-1-63417-729-0 (pbk)
ISBN 978-1-63417-730-6 (digital)
ISBN 978-1-68139-569-2 (hardcover)

Printed in the United States of America

CONTENTS

ACKNOWLEDGEMENTS

I'd first like to thank my family for their support while I was researching and typing this manuscript. Also Ms. Gloria Cannon for assistance and advice when I had computer difficulties (which was often and severe) and for help editing. The staff/archivists of the Samuels Library, Frostburg State Library, Hanley Library and the Confederate Museum for their invaluable help in researching their repective archive. Numerous people gave me access to their family genealogical material, letters and diaries, that had reference to my subject. Virtually every librarian and achivest that I met during my research unselfishly and cheerfully assisted me, going above and beyond the call of duty. I'd like to take this opportunity to thank them all.

1861

INTRODUCTION

The Author Terry Lowry wrote one of the best reasons the Southern men flocked to the colors in 1861, "Most of the soldiers didn't understand the full implications of their presence at Scary (Creek; or any where else in the various military camps springing up all over the South)-All that mattered was that a northern aggressor was invading their state and as such it was utterly necessary for them to defend their families and property.

This introduction is a general overview of conditions of the Rebel soldiers through first-hand accounts. I wanted to present the soldiers/civilians observations through diaries, letters and memoirs. I have kept my comments to a minimum as I wished to show the actuality of the Confederate uniform from the actual words of the people who were there. I have been a Confederate re-enactor since 1988 and have heard the two schools of thought. 1 The Confederate Army was never very ragged, that was just a romantic myth presented after the war. 2 The Rebels were generally ragged throughout the war, wearing anything they could get their hands on. I haven't tried to make any point or prove either school of thought. I present the data verbatim-quotes-and will let the reader decide. Due to the publications of records of uniform articles issued and upon a certain date and from a certain depot, I have avoided using these records-I want the soldiers' words to stand for themselves. I have learned considerable regarding Victorian clothing articles and their prevalence in the Confederate Army despite the vitual destitution of clothing/uniforms; articles of clothing we'd consider superfluous-cravats, ties, vest, shawls, and other things I had never heard of (you'll see). I have also included anecdotes-good and bad- and some other items included as they were rather unknown or ignored. I have uncovered several "firsts" as I will point out in my comments as we go through the war.

What follows this section is first-hand accounts that flow chronilogically through the war years, form the spring of 1861and the excitement of succession, through the final months of 1865 and final surrender. I've arrange the entries by day, month, year and also by section-East, Middle South and Trans-Mississippi.

1861

General

The Young Lions-Confederate Cadets at War by James Lee Conrad Stackpole Books 1997

Pg. 20 "Cadet uniforms were patterned after those of the U.S. Military Academy. The dress jacket, or coatee, was the same gray wool garment adopted by West Point in honor of General Winfield Scott's similiarly dressed victorius troops at the War of 1812 Battle of Chippewa, Canada. The buttons were the main difference. Those of West Point were spherical, brass "bullet buttons," while those of the state schools were often flat and usually had the state coat of arms stamped on them. The forty or more buttons on this uniform were its most distinguishing feature, leading South Carolina cadets to refer to the coatees as their "buttons." The tails were another unique feature of this waist length, tight-fitting jacket. Seeing the University of Alabama cadets wearing them reminded on wag of winged insects. The name he used caught on, and the cadets were quickly dubbed "Katydids."

Fatigue jackets were worn by all cadets for day-to-day duties. The Alabama cadet wore an eight-button, gray wool fatigue jacket with a standing collar year round. In the winter he wore gray wool pants with a black stripe on the outer seam, and in the summer a white vest with white trousers. A "light cap of blue cloth" completed the Alabama Cadtes fatigue uniform. The VMI and GMI fatigue uniforms were similar to Alabama's except their cadets wore a nine-button fatigue jacket of brown, unbleached Russian drilling, and a blue, visored fatigue cap while they drilled in the summer. South Carolina cadets were outfitted with gray wool uniforms for winter and, at least during the war, a cotton uniform of "white, with a dark stripe," made of "very flimsy material," for summer wear. At some point prior to 1863, VMI authorized the wearing of a white fatigue jacket as part of the summer uniform. However, cadtes were authorized to wear this fatigue uniform on post only. For trips outside of school limits, the coat was worn-with one exception-VMI first classmen were permitted to wear a more compfortable, eleven-button "furlough" jacket of dark blue cloth when they visited off-post. Between November and April cadets wore a gray "surtout," a long overcoat with a cape extending to the coat's cuffs.

Until 1860, when it was replaced by the standard military-issue forage cap, the VMI fatigue cap was a visored, gray Mexican War-pattern dragoon cap, with "VMI" embroidered on the hatband. South Carolina cadets sported a blue fatigue cap with a patent leather visor. For dress parades, a tall black dress hat or or shako (a "tar bucket" in West Point slang,)was worn with the coatee. The front of the dress hat bore the school insignia: an engineer corps castle for VMI; a wreath embracing the letters ACC (Alabama Cadet Corps) for Alabama; the Georgie state seal, surmounted by a flying eagle, for the Marietta school; and a "brass tulip, shell and flame, with a brass palmetto tree in front" for the South Carolina Military

Academy. The shako was topped with ablack cloth "pom-pom" for privates and NCOs, and a black ostrich plume for officers. For dress parades and guard mounting the coatee and shako were worn, with white belts supporting a small cartridge box for enlisted, or a maroon or crimson sash and belt-carried saber for officers...."

Website THE LIBERY RIFLES The Bloody Thirty-First Reflections on the 31st Regiment of Virginia Volunteers Jason C. Spellman

"With initial constaints on issued clothing and equipment at the formation of the regiment, the men of the 31st were compelled to furnish their own goods from home although, no doubt, many of the initial weapons would have been replaced by December 1861...John Robinson of Company H describes the Confederate forces at Alleghany Mountain as equipped with "a scanty supply of blankets and rations." ...In a December 9th letter to his wife, Henry H Dedrick asks "Dear Lissa I wrote to you to send me some pants the first chance you get and the rest of them that I wrote for as I am nearly out of Pants." ...In January 1862 Second Lieutenant James B Galvin of Company I wrote to the Lutheran Sabbath School Association to thank the institution for providing them with fifty pairs of drawers. He writes "The boys were very much in need of the kind considerations of the benevolent Augusta county. The Lewis Rangers will long remember the kind esteem and gift."

"With the absence of military clothing, civilian dress was no doubt influenced by occupation. Staistics gathered by John Ashcroft provide some insight on the men of the regiment from a 322-man sample. It was found that 68% were farmers, 4% attorneys, and 3% students. (three largest groups)...the author does recommend overalls, thick, water-proof boots, red flannel shirts, etc...."

WOMEN OF THE SOUTH IN WAR TIME-Compiled by Matthew Page Andrews pub by The Norman Remington Co. 1923

"Genius of the Southern Women" Pg. 26 "Supplies of clothing of all kinds rapidly diminished as the war continued. Neatly trimmed thorns were often used in place of pins, and it was discovered that persimmon seeds made excellent buttons when thoughly dried and pierced with necessary holes for needle and thread, which, in their turn, became alarmingly scarce, so the the loss of a sewing needle became a household calamity. Buttons were also made outr of gourds, cut into molds and covered with cloth of any color or kind. Corn shucks, palmetto, and many kinds of grasses were woven into hats and bonnets. Every variety of dye was homemade. When the dyes failed to hold their respective colors, the articles were "redipped" again and again. When hat trimmings were worn "too long a time," the hats were reshaped and dyed another color.

All girls and women learned to card and spin and knit, if not previously aquainted with these arts. Every woven stocking was of especial value. When the feet were entirely worn out, the upper part was carefully unraveled and the thread first twisted on the spinning wheel and then knitted into new stockings or into gloves or mitts. All woven wearing apparel was treated in the same way. Leather became very scarce and the providing of shoes a big problem. Women learned, in time, to make their own uppers and all of their bedroom and house slippers. Soles for outdoor use proved to be the greatest difficulty. Sometimes they were made of wood,-and again-well, there were times when there were no shoes available!"

Pg. 426 "Sewing by Hand" "In the narrative of Mrs. Hadley, reference has been made to the possession and use of a sewing machine. Comparatively few of the Southern women had this great aide in the making of clothes. Mrs. John D. Weeden of Huntsville, Alabama, writes the experience of her mother, Mrs. Robert M. Patton, of Florence: "we kept a number of garments to make at home. I was just through college, and I made, together with my mother and a serving woman she had employed, uniforms, underwear, and several overcoats so heavy that we had to work on them while lying on a table. Every stitch was done with our fingers. We had no machines until 1869, when my father bought me one."

PLAIN FOLK'S FIGHT ed by Gary W. Gallagher pub by Univ N.C. Press 2005

Pg. 106 "...Women of the soldier's Aid Society in Pulaski County (N.C.) rolled up the carpets and rugs from their floors and sent them to Virginia to put something between the cold ground of winter camp quarters and the bodies of their men. Prominent planters like George Walker III served as local agents for the Battlefield Relief Association and collected supplies for companies at the front. Such attempts to equip and comfort the troops were public acts of Southern nationalism.

Early in the war the need for domestic labor was most pressing to meet the demand for uniforms and personal items. During the summer of 1861 women were called on to produce the winter clothing needed to keep soldiers from a humid, subtropical climate warm in northern Virginia. Each household was expected to supply two pairs of heavy brown or gray-mixed jeans lined with domestic cloth; one army jacket of the same material reaching four inches below the waistband and large enough for a shirt or vest to be worn underneath; one vest of jeans or linsey; an overshirt; and one or two pairs of drawers, heavy woolen socks, an overcoat or hunting shirt with belt; one good blanket. Gray and blue flannel shirts were preferred over red, as red shirts "present(ed) an excellent target for the enemy." In addition, families were required to provide their soldiers with a comb, pocketknife, small tin cup, iron spoon knife and fork. The ability of households to meet these demands depended largely on the spinning, weaving, sewing and knitting skills of women...Homespun cloth was critical for uniforms in 1861, before the Confederate quartermaster department could clothe the hastily organized regiments. Governor Brown's call for the creation of a homespun revolution to meet this need may have fallen on deaf ears among some elite white women, but no revolution was necessary among plain folk, only increased production....According to the "Georgia Journal and Messenger" in October, 1861, Telfiar women emulated the female patriots of 1776 by setting "an example of patriotism worthy of all imitation" in domestic cloth production.The mothers, sisters and wives of ninety-one men in one company forwarded to each a complete winter out fit consisting of an overcoat, vest, pants, drawers, and shirt. The only parts of the uniform not made in Telfair were the buttons..."

SOUTH GEORGIA REBELS -26th Regiment Georgia Volunteer Infantry by & pub by Alton T. Murray 1976

Pg.8 South Georgia Prepares for War-"...In the beginning, the uniforms were supplied by the soldiers themselves and these were not critical items until later. Shoes, hats, and other items of clothing were mostly brought from home and had not yet been worn out or lost..."

HISTORY OF THE FOURTH REGIMENT SOUTH CAROLINA VOLUNTEERS FROM THE COMMENCEMENT OF THE WAR UNTIL LEE'S SURRENDER J.W. Reid Shannon &Co. Printers & Stationers Morningside Bookshop 1975

Pg. 42 "...I would be glad if you would send me by mail my gloves and a good big needle, as I have to do my own patching and ironing. The ironing, however, goes minus..."

RECOLLECTIONS FROM 1861-1865 by John H. Lewis ex-Leiutenant in Huger's & R.H. Anderson's & Pickett's Division, Army of Northern Virginia pub. by Peak & Co. 1895 (1983)

Pg. 25 "...Memory goes back to the days of '61, and when I compare it to the later days of the war I smile at the pomp and splendor of our soldiers of that day; to see the officers with their new regulation coats of glittering gold lace it seemed that our Secretary of War was under the impression that gold lace and splendid uniforms would frighten the Yankees into submission, and close the war. At this time a single officer had more gold lace on the sleeves of his coat than would in after days have designated all the officers of a whole brigade, and I have no doubt that a second lieutenant with his gold lace felt himself or more importance and carried a greater weight of responsibility on his laced arms than five brigadiers later on in the war..."

CIVIL WAR SOLDIERS Reid Mitchell Viking Peguin 1988

Pg. 108 "According to local slave narratives, white farm wives and plantation mistresses played important roles in domestic cloth production before and during the war. One former slave recalled that after the fighting started and supplies of foreign cloth dried up at Hawkinsville, thread "had to be spun at home...by the negro women" who were "supervised by the mistress." When women of plantation households did not possess knowledge of textile production, white women taught these at "sewing frolics." Similar to quilting bees, these gatherings took place from time to time to instruct white and black women in domestic textile production."

The Lower Shenandoah Valley in the Civil War-The Impact of War on the Civilian Population and Upon Civil Institutions by Edward H. Phillips The Civil War Battles and Leaders Series 1993

Pg 31 mobilization, 1861 "Individuals took it upon themselves to recruit companies. Men volunteered to pay part of the expenses of equipping a company. Merchants contributed cotton goods, sheeting, flannel, and other things from their stock. Householders contributed from their surplus and frequently from a stock that wasn't surplus. Former Senator James M. Mason of Winchester, prior to his departure upon his European mission, directed that the family silver be donated to the public treasury to be melted down for coin. For the most part, people contributed time and labor. Women worked endlessly turning out articles for loved ones, for local companies, and for the army of the Shenandoah. The making of a Havelock was intimate and personal-it would be a gift to a brother or lover. Sewing circles and knitting circles turned out socks, jackets, caps, bandages, lint, flags, and mattresses. Early in May, a Winchester newspaper reported that the ladies of the town had sent hundreds of mattresses to the army at Harper's Ferry. Few had the hardihood to remain idle. The young and those unaccustomed to labor tried to do their part. Years later, old veterans grew sentimental over the drops of blood shed by dainty tender fingers pricked by the needle as they struggled with rough, heavy cloth. In the excitement for doing, a flighty young miss of fourteen undertook to fathom the mysteries of knitting. After nearly four years of intermittent work, she at last furtively slipped her first and last sock, a misshapen monstrosity, in a box bound for the army in the hope it would be of service to some one-legged soldier.

When counties purchased large quantities of cloth it was apparently women volunteers who, working singly or in circles in countless homes, transformed it into material of war. Much that could not be made from such by volunteers was nonetheless manufactured locally.... Even Clarke County, which was almost entirely agricultural and rural, and whose manufacturing establishments, according to the publisher census summaries, included only a few blacksmith shops, flour and grist mills, wagon and carriage shops, and a few small establishments for the manufacture of boots and shoes, was able to produce wagons and harness for local companies. Much of the woolen goods and possibly some of the cotton goods used in the Lower Shenandoah Valley in the production of the material of war were of local manufacture. There were many small woolen mills scattered throughout the countryside in this region which produced large quantities of cloth-coarse woolens and linsey woolsey-grey, drab stuff used principally for making the blankets and winter clothing of slaves of laboring people generally, but sometimes worn by frugal members of other classes. Material from these mills appears to have been widely used for the uniforms made locally, not merely because it was available, but also because, being coarse and durable, it was suitable. Andrew Hunter of Charlestown claimed that cloth from the mills of the four counties of the lower valley "contributed very largely toward clothing the army," during the winter 1861-1862.

THE HISTORY OF THE CONFEDERACY 1832-1865 by Clifford Dowdy pub by Barnes & Noble Books 1955

Pg. 103 "At Harper's Ferry in those spring days, the volunteers were as innocent of the organization as of discipline or standard uniform. The Confederacy, as a central government of the separate states, had little or nothing to do with the outfittingof volunteers. This was an affair of the states, and as there were neither time nor facilitiesfor large-scale manufacture, the Southern states never provided uniforms for their soldiers. The men were allowed an allotment with which to purchase their own uniforms wherever they could, though in most of the first companies (all of the old militia units) the men bought their own. Frequently men bought cadet-grey cloth and had it tailored. Ladies sewed on the braid and the frogs which decorated the privale as well as the general. In some of the cases where a rich man raised a company or battalion, he outfitted the whole lot of them, thus insuring has election as captain or major.

In this way, each company was caparisoned as grandly as a Graustarkian palace guardand, as each was different from the others, the total resembled an international assemblage of "corps de'elite.'

Their knapsacks, frequently packed by ladies, were things of wonder. In one of the fancier Virginia companies, the knapsack contained several pairs of white gloves, several changes of underwear, several white shirts (sometimes starch-bosomed, or as they said, "b'iled."), linen collars, neckties, white vest, socks, handkerchiefs, a fatigue jacket, writing paper and-what the men came to prize most-a needle case, with thread, buttons, and various-size needles. Outside the knapsack were extra shoes, an oilcloth, and-in Viginia for the coming summer!-two blankets. The lightest knapsack weighed thiry pounds and the heaviest fifty. If a little impractical for the field, the knapsack certainly accoutered the men superbly for the camp and its attendant social functions.

In addition to this equipment, most of the new soldiers, whether issued an old flintlock musket or nothing, carried in their belts revolvers and bowie knives. These weapons, which they confidently expected to use, were about the only warlike things among these militiamen."

THE LIFE OF JOHNNY REB. Bell Irvin Wiley La. State Univ. Press 1970

Pg. 323 "Alabama had a number of companies consisting almost wholly of foreigners. Company I of the Eighth Alabama Regiment, known as the "Emerald Guards," listed 104 men (from a total of 109) who named Ireland as their birthplace. The uniforms in which this company went to war was dark green, and the banner showed on the one side the

Confederate colors with Washington in the center, and on the other a harp enwreathed with shamrock and flashing the inscription "Erin-go-Bragh."

Website 16th TENNESSEE VOLUNTEER INFANTRY REGIMENT:

Clothing, Arms and Equipment: Part 1 Clothing "...when in 1861 officers applied to Montgomery, the Capitol at this time, for uniforms they were informed that "volunteers shall furnsh their own clothes." Regimental Commanders were also instructed to "draw from the military store cloth, linings, trimmings, and thread for uniforming..." most of the cloth produced was jean cloth and cassimere. "...These materials were either grey or brownish-grey produced by natural dyes such as sweet gum bark, logwood, and sumac, although thes dyes faded due to exposure from the sun producing a variety of brownish-earth toned tones..."

Whilst at Camp Trousdale, May 1861, the regiment were issued uniforms, a member of the 8th Tennessee, a sister unit camped with them, stated that the uniforms "ranged from butternut jeans to the finest articles of French cloth." But another member of the 8th about the same time said "we are now receiving our uniform and the State is going to uniform all the troops alike. Color of the uniform will be gray, and it looks very nice, and when the sixteen thousand troops here are all uniformed alike, we will present as fine looking front as any troops in the world."

May 29 1861 A private in the 8th Tennessee wrote: "We are now receiving our uniform and the State is going to uniform all the troops alike. Color of the uniform will be gray." Officers of the Regiment in June 1861 (as well as officers of other regiments) were described as wearing "dark blue frock coat with light-colored trim around the bottom of the collar only, plain sleeves." On the 29 June 1861 a private of the 14th Tennessee wrote "We will draw our regimental uniform this evening We drawed our company uniform on the 14th of this month but it is no comparison. We have more clothes than we can carry."

UNIFORMS OF THE CIVIL WAR by Robin Smith & Ron Field Lyons Press 2001

LOUISIANA-Pg. 202 "...The first uniform chosen by the Chasseurs a pied, or Louisiana Foot Rifles, was described by ths New Orleans Daily Crescent as being 'finer and much neater fitting than that of the famed French soldiers...Their vwery small caps, perched on top of their heads; their tight fitting, dark colored, short tailed coats, with their slender redfringes and green epaulettes; their enormous mouse colored breeches, falling in loose folds below their knees, their tight yellow leggings and their white gaiters-all these new things in military dress in this country, combined to give this new company a very novel and picturesque appearance'.By early 1861 this battalion had adopted a blue uniform with white gaiters.

The Orleans Guard Battalion, which was designated the 13th Louisiana Battalion, wore a dark blue frock and pants, and red forage cap for full dress. By February 1861 they had a fatigue uniform composed of 'dark blue kepis...jackets or short coats and pants of the same color, all trimmed with red, black belts and caotouche boxes'. During the Battle og Corinth (Miss) on 3-4 October 1862, the 6th Kentucky, at the sight of this'blue uniform brought out from New Orleans', mistook the Orleans Guard Battalion for the enemy and fired on them, killing two men! Thereafter, they were ordered to 'turn their uniform wrong side outwards, thus giving them the appearance of going to a masquerade ball'.

The Legion Francaise, formed among the French citizens of New Orleans, adopted a copy of the French infantry dress which consisted of a horizon-blue coat, and red pants and cap. The Confedertate Guards Response Battalion paraded in 'gray frock coats, caps and white pants'. The Garibaldi Legion, expanded from a volunteer militia company called the Garibaldi Guards, wore a 'black cocked hat, with a black plume on the cocked side, the stem of the plume…being covered with little feathers of red, green and white, (the colors of Italy) and the whole secured witrh a Pelican button. A red jacket, tight fitting to the waist but spreading out at the hips; a black belt around the waist, with cartouche-box behind, and the jacket buttoned up to the chin with Pelican buttons. Gray trousers, of the largest Zouave style, bulging out as low on the knee; and then buff leather leggings, stapped and buckles the rest of the way down to the gaiters…

The British Guard under Captain Shannon wore a suit 'white flannel with blue and silver facings'. The Belgian Guards' uniform was composed of 'dark green frock coats, trimmed with yellow, and pants and cap of same'. That worn by the Orleans Rifles was in imitation of '… the Kentucky or frontier Riflemen, consisting of broad brimmed black hats cocked on one side, loose hunting shirts of green with black fringes; pants yellow to the knee and below that black in imitation of yellow buckskin and leggings; and small carouche boxes slung at the side'.

The Louisiana Guerillas wore 'a velvet hunting jacket, mi tasses, or leggings, similar to those worn by Indians, cotton pantaloons and an otter skin cap'.

The 1st Special Battalion, or or 2nd Louisiana Infantry Battalion, raised by Chatham Roberdeau wheat, who had seen military service in Mexico, Cuba, Nickaragua, and Italy, was composed of a mixture of 'Irish roustabouts and riff-raff' of New Orleans, Filibusters, and the sons of wealthy planters. Some members of this unit had taken part in the Lopez expedition, and, until they had acquired uniforms, still wore their 'off-white drill pants or breeches with gaiters or boots, red flannel shirt, and broad-brimmed hat….' The Tiger Rifles, Co. B., initially decorated their hats with 'pictures of tigers in attitudes and slogans'. Their Zouave uniform was paid for by A. Keene Richards, a wealthy citizen of New Orleans…"

"A number of individual Louisiana volunteer, militia, and cadet companies are believed to have worn full or partial Zuoave dress. The Hope Guard paraded in 'Zouave jackets ands pants, of dark blue, neatly trimmed, white belts and blue kepis. …' The young Cadtets, also called the Louisiana Cadets, attached to the Orleans Rifle Battalion, wore a 'neat and elegant Zuoave uniform of light blue, with black caps. The Home Sentinels, a militia company of Iberville Parish which did not enlist into Confederate service, 'wore a Zuoave-like uniform with close-fitting jacket and red striped pants.…Another company from New Orleans, called the

Monroe Guards, had a vivandiere called Leona Neville who wore a 'nicely fitting black alpaca uniform.... TYhe 4th and 5th regiments also received theirs (uniforms) during September. On 19 August 1861, Lieutenant-Colonel Charles de Choisel wrote: I am getting made new fatigue uniforms, for the entire command, of a light blue heavy cloth, a very pretty and serviceable uniform indeed.' A member of the same regiment wrote on 1 October 1861: 'the new uniform is now all here complete, and I can assure you to see 1000 men all dressed alike makes for a different impression on a spectator than a variety of colors, caps and hats, coats and jackets, and such like mixtures.' ...May 1862 The uniforms received by the 8th Louisiana revealed the problems the State Penetentiary workshops experienced producing cloth of standard quality and color. Some of the clothing was in appearance as 'absyrd as a harlequin dress, the body and sleeves being of diverse colors and materials'... Typical was that received by the 3rd Louisians Infantry in Missouri during September. Each man was given'one red flannel shirt, one cotton shirt, one pair of plain linsey or flannel drawers, one pair of heavy woolen jeans pants and a long jacket, lined inside with linsey, and padded on the shoulders to carry the gun with ease'. This was elsewhere described as being 'of substantial marerial known as jeans, being grayish-blue in color, with the exeption of Co. K, (Pelican Rifles) which is of dark brown"

LIFE IN THE CONFEDERATE ARMY by Arthur P. Ford and Marion Johnstone Ford pub by The Neale Pub. Co. 1905

Pg. 11 "During the early period of the war a great many of the private soldiers in the Confederate Army had their own Negro servants in the field with them, who waited on their masters, cleaned their horses, cooked their meals, etc. Attached to our company (Palmetto Guards, Seventeenth Regiment South Carolina Militia, stationed at Charleston, S.C.) there were probably twenty-five such servants. This system continued during the first year or two of the war on the Carolina coast, but later on, as the service got harder and rations became scarcer, these negro servants were gradually sent back home, and the men did their own work, cooking, etc. As a rule, these negroes liked the life exceedingly. The work exacted of them was necessarily very light. They were never under fire, unless they chose to go there of their own accord, which some of them did, keeping close to their masters. And they spent much of their time foraging around the neighboring country. Although often on the pickett line, night as well as day with their masters, I never heard of an instance where one of these army servantsdeserted to the enemy."

THE CIVIL WAR INFANTRYMAN, In Camp, on the March, and in Battle by Gregory A. Coco Thomas publications, Gettysburg, Pa

Pg.39 Perry Mayo, even as early as 1861, saw through his field glasses four Rebels near a fort "...poorly clothed,...all of them having holes in the seat of their pants and in a ragged condition generally."

Sergeant John Worsham, 21st Virginia, was very descriptive of his fellow Confederates in July, 1863. He wrote: At this time our army was in a sad plight as to clothing. Hundreds had no shoes. Thousands were as ragged as they could be-some with the bottoms of their pants in long frazzles; others with their knees out, others out at the elbows, and their hair sticking through holes in their hats. Some of the men patched their clothing, and it was usually done with any material they could get. One man had the seat of his pants patched with bright red, and his knees patched with black. Another had used a piece of grey or brown blanket. There were, however, so few patches and so many holes that, when a Pennsylvania girl on the side of the road saw us pass and asked her mother how the officers were distinguished from the privates the mother replied that it was easy enough: the officer's pants were patched, and the private's pants were not.

Scores of Confederates, even whole regiments, eventually resorted to confiscating and wearing captured Union clothing and equipment. After the Battle of Shiloh in 1862, Lieutenant James Williams, who commanded Company A, 21st Alabama in that engagement, wrote his wife, Lizzie on several occasions. In these letters he spoke of his "immense pair of Yankee shoes," together with a captured blanket, haversack and canteen, which he had covered over with "reddish grey cloth." Just prior to the battle Williams requested that she make him a blue coat to complete his regular uniform. But after seeing the Federal troops at close quarters he explained to her: Since the battle I have regretted that I ever ordered a blue uniform-it is just like that of the enemy and it is feared that in the confusion of battle some of our officers were killed by men of our own side-I will never go into battle with my blue coat on that account but will wear my old grey jacket…(I will) observe what you say about appearing on the field in the fatal blue uniform; I have no desire to be killed by my own friends in mistake though many of our officers wear the blue coats all the time. He still liked his blue coat, as it was fancy and he could use it for evening dress parade. Later, on May 3, he received a new sword, socks and a hat turned up on one side, and fastened with a gold star and a black silken loop and tassle, the hat was greatly admired by everyone.

Pg 39 Sergeant Worsham remembered that by the close of the war, "…nearly all equipment in the Army of Northern Virginia were articles captured from the Yankees…most of the blankets were those marked "US" and also the rubber blankets or clothes. The very clothing that the men wore was mostly captured, for we were allowed to wear their pants, underclothing, and overcoats. As for myself, I purchased only one hat, one pair of shoes, and one jacket after 1861."

LIFE AND CAMPAIGNS OF LEIUT.-GEN. THOMAS J. JACKSON by Prof. R.L. Dabney, D.D. Sprinkle Pub. 1883 (1866)

Pg. 207 "The traveler who left the town of Alexandria, upon the Potomac, to go southwestward into the interior of Virginia, at the distance of twenty-five miles, found the Manassa's Gap

Railroad dividing itself on the right hand from the main stem, and turning westward towards the peaks of the Blue Ridge, which are visible in the horizon. This road sought a passage through those mountains at Manassa's Gap, a depression which received its name from an obscure Jew merchant named Manassa, who, years ago, had fixed his home in the gorge of the ravine. From this the roalroad was called the Masnass's Gap Road, and the junction with the Alexandria Railroad the Manassa's Junction. Thus the name of an insignificant Israelite has associated itself with a spot, which will never ceased to be remembered, while liberty and heroism have votaries in the world."

NORTHERN VIRGINIA'S OWN -THE 17TH INF. REGIMENT CONFEDERATE STATES ARMY by William M. Glascow Jr. Col. U.S. Army Ret.

Pg. 8, "Formed in 1856-"At their units organizational meeting, the charter members of the Alex. Riftlemen initially adopted the name "Alexandria Sharp Shooters," a green uniform with a forage cap, and a motion to place their units' initials on their cartridge boxes. Having made these decisions and elected their officers, the meeting was adjorned.

After the meeting, some of the units members gathered on the sidewalk in front of the exchange building to discuss the evenings events. It soon dawned on someone of their group that the display of the units initials on an item of equipment worn on the soldier's backsides would not be too appropriate. This induced Capt. Marye to yell for the men to reassemble. A quorum soon was obtained, and the units name rapibly was changed to Alexandrie Riflemen, since the men did not want to advertise in a particularly appropriate place that they were donkeys.

Pg. 9 "Members of the Mount Vernon Guards initially wore a uniform similar to the one worn by the U.S. Marine Corps in 1834. It consisted of a green tail coat with buff casimere facings, deep blue trousers with a buff casimere stripe down the outside seams, and a leather bell crown cap." The Guards after the John Brown Raid-"The Mount Vernon Guards new uniform was gray, but its coat was of the same design as the units previous green one. It had three rows of brass buttons down its front and tails similar to those of present-day West Point dress uniforms. The sleeves of the Mount Vernon Guards' coats were trimmed with silver lace, and the outside seam of the trousers had cord of the same color. This uniform was topped off with a shako that had a black pompom and a brass wreath that enclosed the letters "M.V.G."

Since the members of the Alex. Riflemen could not allow their older sister unit to get ahead of them, they also adopted a new uniform. It had a gray frock coat and trousers, and this uniform was also topped off with a shako that had a small ball-type green pompom."

OK, here's our first reference "pompoms" on the soldier's hat (or shako). What is the attraction of pompoms for these men?

Pg. 13 The Warrenton Riflemen originated in 1859. "This units uniform consisted of gray fatigue-type jacket and gray trousers. Its cap was high with an attached rain neck cloth similar to those worn by French North African troops."

1860-"At their organizational meeting, the young men of Alexandria's newest unit named it the "Old Dominion Rifles." They also adopted a uniform of traditional militia gray that one of the units members called "Virginia made cadet cloth." This uniform consisted of a jacket patterned after those worn by Hungarian Riflemen and trousers of a baggy zuoave design similar to those worn by French North African troops. Green trim placed emphasis on the uniform's pocket and trouser seams, and uniform buttons bore the seal of the Commonwealth of Virginia."

It was also decided at the units initial meeting that the Old Dominion Rifles out fit would be topped off with a French-style forage cap and bottomed out with black boots, but later pictures of the unit's uniform show that the forage cap was replaced by a brimmed felt hat which was more practical for field use."

Pg. 19 Warren Rifles, formed in 1861: At the time of its organization, The Warren Rifles became a younger sister to the Warren Blues. This unit had a history going back at least to 1840s, and its existence probably accounted for both of Front Royals infantry companies, initially wearing Regular Army-type dark blue uniforms at the start of the War Between the States."

Here'e a unit that wore their blue uniforms to Manassas, thereby contributing to the confusion

THE BATTLE OF SCARY CREEK by Terry Lowry pub by Pictorial Histories Pub Co. 1982

Pg.6 Early 1861 "The (Kanawha) Riflemen were composed of a fluctuating membership of some 75 to 100 men, and had an excellent brass band led by an English cornetist, but they were best remembered by veterans and residents of the area alike for their flashy uniforms which Patton (Captain George S. Patton) designed for them. Slightly varying descriptions were recalled, but it basically consisted of brass buttons stamped with the Virginia coat of arms on a uniform of "dark (olive) green broad-cloth, matching overcoats, broad gold (some veterans claimed black) stripes down the pantaloons, a fancy headgear which consisted of black hats with ostrich feathers dangling from a wide brim with a gold KR on the front of the cap, the entire headdress covered with oilcloth in bad weather, and white (cotton) Berlin gloves." The "coats were long, with epaulettes of gold braid...and a short shoulder cape that graced the coat."

"...When the Kanawha Riflemen were later mustered in to the Confederate sevice as Company H, 22nd Virginia Infantry, the authorities ordered them to dispose of the gaudy uniforms, resulting in an apparent change to "light blue jackets and dark gray trousers with yellow trimmings…"

"…The Kanawha (or Charleton) Sharpshooters…This unit dressed in their gray uniforms, could often be found practicing maneuvers in a field belonging to the Welch family…"

THE REBEL BOAST by Manly Wade Wellman pub. By Henry Holt & Co. N.Y. 1956

Pg48 1861 Fayetteville Observer article IMPORTANT TO SOLDIERS-RULES FOR HEALTH

"Sun-stroke may be prevent by wearing a silk hankerchief in the hat

A bullet through the abdomen (belly or stomach) is more certainly fatal than if aimed at the head or the heart….

Let the beard grow, but not longer than some three inches. This strengthens and thickens its growth and thus makes a more perfect protection for the lungs against dirt, and of the throat against the winds and cold in winter…

Twelve men are hit in battle, dressed in red, where there are only five, dressed in a blueish grey, a difference of more than two to one; green, seven; brown, six…defenders at Yorktown

"Field uniforms to replace the blue parade gear were maddengly slow in arriving from supply depots, and so Cary had written to Enfield, asking his older brother Lawrence to procure clothes there. Cay's cousin, First Lieutenant Montgomery Whitaker, dug into his own pocket to equip the troops."

Pg. 81 Enfield Blues, "Passed by the medical examiners, the two newcomers drew their uniforms. There had been no such wealth of equipment at Camp Ellis or at Yorktown. Suppy clerks gave each of them a dress uniform, a suit of fatigues, an overcoat, two shirts, two pairs of drawers, and two pairs of shoes…"

A dress uniform? Before I started their research I had no idea there was such in the Confederate Army.

16th TENNESSEE VOLUNTEER INFANTRY REGIMENT: Clothing, Arms and Equipment (website)

Part 1 Clothing: "…Whilst at Camp Trousdale, 1861 the regiment were issued uniforms, a member of the 8th Tennessee, a sister Regiment encamped with them, stated that the uniforms "ranged from butternut jeans to to the finest articles of French cloth." But another member of the 8th about the same time said "we are now receiving our uniform and the State is going to uniform all of the troops alike. Color of the uniform will be grey, and it looks very nice, and when the sixteen thousand troops here are all uniformed alike, we will present as fine looking front as any troops in the world…"

FOOTPRINTS OF A REGIMENT A Recollection of the 1st Georgia Regulars by W.H. Andrews Longstreet Press Atlanta Ga. 1992

Pg. 10 Savannah, Ga. 1861 "On arriving at Savannah we marched through the city and pitched our tents on the commons, where we drew new uniforms, shoes, caps, and overcoats. All having previously had their measures taken by a tailor. Our uniforms were of Confederate grey, single-breasted frock coats with Georgia buttons, black cords down the outer seams of the pants. Caps were grey. Overcoats extending to the knees,with large capes. Altogether we were nicely fitted up. Besides, we had a fatigue uniform consisting of jacket and pants.The regulars were armed with muskets, and drilled in Hardee's tactics for heavey infantry."

Here's another mention of a uniform with a "fatigue" uniform. This didn't last long

LIFE AND LETTERS OF WILDER DWIGHT: LIEUT. COL. SECOND, MASS INF. VOLS. Ticknor & Co. 1891

Pg. 349 Harper's Ferry 1861 "…Our men shot up at them and took them in the head and breast. The woods are torn and shivered by musketry and cannon. Thirty men in Confederate homespun, shot in the head, lie in this wood…"

THE SOUTH REPORTS THE CIVIL WARed by J.Cuttler Andrews pub byUniv. Of Pittsbough Press 1970

pg. 113, Savannah Republican 1861 Alexander

"As for the Commissary Department, he pointed out: "the hides taken from the cattle slaughtered for the use of the army will shoe the army; the tallow will light the army, while the oil from the feet is sufficient to keep all the harness, wagons and artillery in good order. As it is, not half the hides are saved in proper condition while four-fifths of the tallow and all the oil is wasted. In the meantime, the Government is paying large sums for shoes, harness and candles."

The reason for this was the difficulty collecting and caring for these items while with an army that's constantly on the move. The transport & manpower system also wouldn't support it, though its an excellent idea

GENERAL LEE'S ARMY-FROM VICTORY TO COLLAPSE by Joseph T. Glatthaar pub by Free Press a div. of Simon and Schuster

Pg. 209 "…Early in the war, for the most part, active men thought of soldiering as a lazy life, in which they received regular if suspect rations and performed occasional duty. "We are as fat as hogs and lazy as a dog," comented a Georgia privatein 1861, "When the sun shines hot the gress (grease) biles out my socks." McLaws informes his bride that his brother "Hugh is so fat that he has had to cut open his pants for five or six inches in the back…."

Clothing tended to be a more troublesome concern that first year of war. After four months of service, shoes and boots began to wear, and initial replacements arrived slowly. A colonel complained through official channels that some seventy men of the 2nd Virginia Cavalry were barefoot. Virginia Col. E.T.H. Warren noted four days later, "The truth is ¼ of our men are bearfooted half of them cannot hide their nakedness but are raged (ragged) as they can be." Fortunately these were the dog days of summer, when soldiers fighting on the defensive required only modest clothing and could function satisfactorily without shoes. A South Carolinian who fought at first Manassas joked with a friend that he needed new pants, "for I have patched these Old ones until they are more holy than righteous."

As the spring campaigns of 1862 opened, military officials redoubled their efforts to supply the army. High-ranking officers pressured their superiors and government officials for proper provisions, and wherever shoes or clothing became available, lower-ranking officers acted aggressively to secure them. An officer in Trimble's brigade diccovered a stockpile of shoes in a warehouse, and the brigade quartermaster directed his subordinate to sieze at least five hundred pairs. "Many of the men of the regiments of this brigade are absolutely barefooted & should it be necessary you will make the strongest representation to the Quartermaster having them in charge," he directed, "The shoes must be had."

"As the brisk fall weather transformed into the bitter cold of winter, soldiers shifted their concern to clothing. The Maryland Campaign merely showcased the problem of inadequate footwear and clothing, it did not solve it. The hardship affected everyone, regardless of background or wealth. As Pvt. James Thompson of the 11th Georgia, himself from a well-to-do family, commented to his parents and siblings, "Thir is plenty of lawyers and doctors hear barefooted and nearly necked that used to ware broad cloth and wouldn't hardly speek to a common man."

Here's afact worth noting, after four months the soldier's uniforms were wearing out and they were looking for replacements.

Pg. 425 "From their perspective, Union soldiers felt indignant when they recovered bodies of their comrades, stripped of shoes and clothing, under flags of truce. It gave Yankees the feeling that Rebels did not respect their dead…" After the battle of the Crater, "After Confederates stripped the bodies (of black troops as well as white) for usable items, those black soldiers who were taken prisoner buried the dead."

CIVIL WAR SOLDIERS Reid Mitchell Viking Peguin 1988

Pg. 25 Union beliefs regarding the "enemy" "the first New York Mounted Rifles heard that when two of their men were surounded and taken prisoner, the rebels took their coats and jackets and then kicked them…The surgeon of a New Jersey regiment, a colonel, believed, as "a fact beyond desput," that the Confederates refused to bury the Union dead at Bull Run, and delighted in boiling the meat from corpses and making utensils out of the skulls and bones. "one of these vessels was found with the inscription on it: This is the skull of a fine Yankee." Then followed the motto of Virginia: "Sic simper tyrannis."…A more puzzling Northern belief was that the Confederacy violated the rules of civilized warfare by using black troops against them. Francis Boland wrote that there had been two black regiments involved in the battle of Seven Pines. "They advanced against us. They mutilated our dead and stripped them naked. They bayoneted our wounded and cut their throats in cold blood." He concluded: "It is wrong to bring negroes into battlefields."

More research needs be done—by real researchers- regarding black troops inConfederateservice. I readanarticlewrittenby anarmchair researcher statingthatthe eyewitnesses were mistaken, thatthetroops they thought were black were really Hispanic or Italion; yeah, there were so many of those in the Army of Northern Virginia it woulldv'e been hard to keep them differtiated.

LETTERS OF JOHN BRATTON TO HIS WIFE Elizabeth Porcher Bratton Privately Pub. 1942

Pg. 1 1861? I of course would not send you a picture that you might not recognize, besides you wanted it in full uniform, and mine was so scuffed and abused that I could not have made a decent appearance…"

This is a good example of why I b eleive the photo-graphs, ambrotypes & Daguerotypes of the period are not a good example of the everyday dress of the Conferate soldier. If the soldier is to go to the trouble & expense of having his likeness taken, to send to the folks at home, he wouldn't do it in a ragged, mismatched uniform.

MILITARY COLLECTOR AND HISTORIAN-Journal of the Company of Military Historians Vol. XLI Fall, 1989 Enlisted Uniforms of the Maryland Confederate Infantry A Case Study, Part 1 by Ross M. Kimmel

Pg.99 uniform of Pvt. E. Courney Jenkins of Clarke's Company, Weston's Battalion 1st Maryland Infantry "Jenkin's jacket and trousers, in the Museum of the Confederacy, Richmond, are made of matching, heavy satinet. Satinet is a cotton warp, woolen fill twill cloth woven in such a way as to show the wool on the cloth face and the cheaper cotton on the under side. A sort of poor man's broadcloth, satinet saw extensive use in medium quality Confederate uniforms. Although Jenkin's uniform is now light brown, James McHenry Howard, who had a Kent, Paine uniform, remembered they "were of coarse gray, but very durable.

Of particular interest in Cpl. Francis Higdon's portrait [ambriotype] (the jacket of which is identical to Pvt. Jenkins) is his long Phrygian-style cap, which appears to match his jacket. (it looks like a two-foot long stocking cap-ed.). While such headgear was not unusual among Confederate troops early in the war, no other source confirms that the rest of Robertson's company, or other Richmond companies, wore them. Perhaps Higdon's reflects his personal whim, (or a studio prop) kepis being the presumed norm."

Pg. 100 Jane Claudia Johnson, the wife of Bradley T. Johnson, Major of the consolidated 1st Maryland Infantry. A native of North Carolina and daughter of a prominent democratic politition, Romulus M. Sanders, this intrepid lady went to her home state and secured from Governor John Willis Ellis 500 or 600 (accounts vary), M1841 "Mississippi" rifles, with "necessary equipments," and 10,000 rounds of ammunition. Bayonets were not included. She went next to Petersburg and Richmond where she secured donations of money from ardent secessionist citizens, and kettles, axes, ans other camp equipment from the Virginia Governor John Letcher. Delivering all the paraphanalia to the Harper's Ferry companies, she returned to Richmond, where, her husband reported:

She secured cloth for uniforms...by purchasing it from the mills where it was manufactured for the State of Virginia, and she paid for making it up into uniforms. Shoes, blankets and underclothes were supplied by Col. Larkin Smith, quarter-master general; and the tents had been ordered on her way back from North Carolina. On June 29th [1861] she started back to camp with forty-one tents, and uniforms, underclothes and shoes for five hundred men. She had paid out ten thousand dollars, the contribution of enthusiastic North Carolinians and Virginians.

Johnson elsewhere described the new uniform of the Harper's Ferry companies as consisting of "a French kepi (a little gray cap), a natty gray roundabout, collar and sleeves bound with black braid, and a similar stripe down the gray trousers.

Thus, by July 1861, the 1st Maryland Infantry mustered eight companies, completely clothed and very nearly completely equipped. For the most part, all the men were uniformly clothed. They wore gray jackets and trousers trimmed with black braid (with some diffences in braid pattern between the jackets of the Richmond and Harpers Ferry companies.) Harpers Ferry companies wore kepis, while the Richmond companies, or at least Roberson's company, may have worn Phrygian caps…"

Pg. 101 "…James McHenry Howard, reported that, as the result of the march from Winchester to Piedmont Station, where the regiment had taken the rails, and then from Manassas Junction to the battlefield, "the shoes were very nearly worn off my feet." In the heat of the march, he related, some of the men "threw off their jackets …[and]…lost them forever…"

A good example of how soldier's carelessness causes the loss of valuable equipment.

HANDLEY LIBRARY ARCHIVES-James A. Miller Collection correspondence C.W. era misc. New Market, Va.

Dear Shultz,…" I have been helping to make tents the last 4 or 5 days …We are making about 60 coats, pants & shirts for the Irish, we have their haversacks and blankets made, they are making their hats at Fidler's, (?) is making the knapsacks…I am sorry you did not take more clothes with you, you ought to have another coat &c.…" Your Affectionate Wife, Julia

THE CONFEDERATE VETERAN VOL.1

April 1893 Pg. 104 Harper's Ferry in 1861 by F.M. Burrows, Co. B, Thirteenth Virginia Infantry "After the battles of Bull Run and Manassas, it was the writer's priviledge to stand picket at the farm-house of good old Mrs. taylor, a few miles east of Fairfax Station. It was there I learned the true meaning of the word Manassas, and how it originated. A faithful old Negro man belonging to Mrs. Taylor met a neighboring brother and addressed him about as follows: "Uncle Willis, kin yer tell me how de got dis name Manassas fer dis place down der war dey has all dem big guns?" "I dunno, Brer Ephriam, cep'ing tis we is de man, and dem Yankees war cum down here is de asses; dats how we get de name Manassas, I speck."

Well said

THE CONFEDERATE VETERAN VOL. XIV 1906

Pg. 304 July 1906 Handcuffs on Manassas Battlefield by George G. Bryson "I cannot tell you much about the handcuffs seen on the First Manassas Battlefield. I saw them in barrels on the slope of the hill between the Henry House and the spring.... There were several boxes, still unopened, on which was written: "To be opened on the streets of Richmond."..."

"What Confederate command was it which went into that battle (Shiloh) armed with pikes? I suppose they were called pikes. They had a wooden handle ten or twelve feet long, on one end of which was an iron or steel spear, and also a curved knife. I saw perhaps a dozen, some lying on the ground and others hanging in trees. I also saw on this battlefield dead Federals having on coats made with breastplates in them."

Another Account Of Handcuffs by Mrs. E.A. Merriwether "Some years ago my husband's cousin, Capt. Robert Walker Lewis, of Albemarle, Va., wrote to him (Col. Minor Merriwether) of being in that First Manassas battle, and that he and his men captured a wagon loaded with handcuffs and shackles. Some of the Union prisoners captured at the same time stated that these instruments were intended to be used on the Rebels they expected to make prisoners, and intended to march them into Washington in that shackled condition. I now have hanging in my hall one of these shackles. It is made of two strong iron rings, with lock and key, to be fastened on the ankles. These rings were fastened together by a strong iron chain seventeen inches long."

Before doing this research, I had only heard second & third hand rumors of handcuffs at First Manassas. Here's some eyewitness accounts proving they were there. I wonder what was done with all of them?

THE CONFEDERATE VETERAN VOL. VII Jan 1899 Pg. 6

Early 1861 "...Alabama Light Dragoons, a company organized for state service by Capt. Theodore O'Hara, the talented author of the immortal poem "The Bivouac of the Dead." The proud-spirited O'hara had as a striking portion of the equipment a showy helmet with a long horsehair plume hanging down the backs of his troopers..."

A HISTORY OF THE SOUTHERN CONFEDERACY Clement Eaton pub, by The MacMillan Co. 1954Spring 1861

Pg. 84 "...The observant Northern reporter was much impressed with the contrast in appearance and manner between officers and privates in the Confederate army. The privates wore homespun suits of grey or butternut; some were wrapped in blankets of rag carpet, some had shoes of rough, untanned hide, others were in Federal blouses, and a few sported beaver hat. They were brown, brawny and wiry, "intense, fierce and animal." The officers, on the other hand, were "young, atheletic fellows, dressed in rich grey cassimere, trimmed in black and wearing soft black hats adorned with black ostrich feathers. Their spurs were strapped to elegantly fitting boots, and they looked as far above the needy, seedy privates as lords above their vassels." They appeared to be strongly animated by state pride...."

Eyewitnes accounts of the "multiform" in the Conferate Army.

Pg. 90 "...Confederate soldiers, if they conformed to army regulations, wore a gray double-breasted coat which extended halfway between the thighs and the knees, and trousers of sky-blue. Actually, they wore a variety of uniforms, including homespun shirts, dyed a yellowish or butternut hue with walnut hulls and copperas, and often captured Federal blue uniforms. Instead of the army regulation cadet cap or kepi they frequently wore a wide-brimmed slouch hat. A toothbrush was carried in the buttonhole....Probably the most serious deficiency of the Confederate armies was the lack of shoes, which forced many of the men to go barefoot even in the winter. There were times when numerous barefoot soldiers in both Lee's army and the Army of Tennessee would try to protect their feet from sharp stones and frozen ground by tying burlap cloth around them. Yet it must be noted that some Confedertaes were accustomed to going barefoot during the summer monthes; and they would at times remove their heavy army shoes to walk more comfortably. Although the Confederate government imported 550,000 pairs of shoes and boots from Europe, the supply did not meet the demand. Indeed, Lee may have suffered a check at Antietam because of the tremenduous amount of straggling in his army, which undoubtedly was caused in part by lack of shoes.

The frequent lack of soap and changes of clothing took away some of the glammer of a soldier's life. Aexander Donelson Coffee, an officer in Zolicofffer's army in East Tennessee, described a Confederate regiment as follows: "They were the hardest roughest looking set you ever saw, and I don't think there could have been a clean shirt in the reg. for a month." The manuscript journal of the Shaker community at Pleasant hill, Kentucky, describes the soldiers of Humphrey Marshall's Confederate brigade passing through their settlement as "ragged, greasy, and dirty, and some barefoot and looked more like the bipeds of pandemonium than beings of this earth...they surrounded our wells like the locusts of Egypt and struggled with each other for the water as if perishing with thirst, and they thronged our kitchen doors and windows, begging for bread like hungry wolves...They tore the loaves and pies into fragments and devoured them. Some even threatened to shoot others, if they did not divide with them...notwithstanding such a motley crew, they abstained from any violence or depredations and appeared exceedingly gratefull. During Longstreet's retreat from Suffolk, Viginia, Clifford Lanier, (brother of Sidney) wrote to his father: we are all well but very dirty-expect to bathe in the Nottaway River this evening tell Ma." Unwashed soldiers in closed railroad pessenger or box cars gave off a very annoying odor. Confederate foot soldiers did their own washing, and soap was often a luxury. Thus gray lice-graybacks-became the bane of both armies...."

THE CONFEDERATE VETERAN VOL. XXII 1914

Pg. 202 Rank & File In The Confederate Armies by Miss Hortense Herman "Volunteer infantrymen forced to furnish their own outfits in many cases had them grotesquely complete, ranging from toilet articles of lightest weight to heavy knapsack, blankets and clothing. Weapons of all kinds accompanied these belongings-Bowie knives, revolvers, pistols, sabers, long or short rifles, one man sometimes having two or three of the list. At first dress varied as much as the personal outfit, and was not until the short, serviceable gray jacket came into regular use that the Confederate rank and file could be said to have a uniform.

But it was not long before accessories were discarded both through necessity and choice, and the Confederate soldier reduced his equipment to something like the following minimum: One hat, one set of underwear, one pair of shoes (generally "brogans" with low heels), one pair of socks, one rubber or oilcloth and one woolen or "carpet" blanket and one haversack, containing probably tobacco and pipe, a small piece of soap, and temporary additions of food.

The clothing issued by the government was often poor in quality if sometimes abundant in quantity. The men wore out jackets in two or three monthes, pantaloons in one. They were coarse, stiff, and flimsy, the cut being worst of all-anybody could put them on, but nobody would they fit. In winter, when scarcely a particle of flannel was to be had, cotton pants were offered the soldiers. Shoes were scarce, blankets curiosities, and overcoats (except those stolen from the enemy) a positive phenomenon. Tents were rarely seen, two men ordinarily sleeping under blanket and oilcloth. Occassionally blankets were made of old carpets with gay colors, having a hole in the middle through which the soldier inserted his head when the weather was cool or rainy....The things need principally by the soldiers and found hardest to supply were shoes, socks and blankets, though underwear, shirts and pants were gladily accepted. The contributions were often coarse clothes made of a yellowish-brown homespun..."

OK, another fact to remember, men wore out jackets in two or three monthes, pants in one. The shoddier the goods, of course, the sooner they would wear out.

THE COMPANY OF MILITARY HISTORIANS www.military-historians.org

Pg.1 Leslie D. Jensen "...Perhaps, too, we are too easily lulled by an appealing image of the "ragged rebel," and therefore naively accept the concept of Johnny Reb being supplied indefinitely by the folks at home, convenientely ignoring the fact that no army, however resourceful, wages war very long if it doesn't develop a workable supply system..."

Wow, if this writer had done any research at all, he would have apologized rto all of us for even thinking this. As you read on, you will see just how ignorant this writer was.

Pg. 3 "…W.W.Blackford, who served on General J.E.B. Stuart's staff, noted:

"…In books written since the war, it seems to be the thing to represent the Confederate soldier as being in a chronic state of starvation and nakedness. During the last year of the war this was partially true, but previous to that time it was not any more than falls to the lot of all soldiers in an active campaign. Thriftless men would get barefooted and ragged and waste their rations to some extent anywhere, and thriftlessness is found in armies as well as at home.

When the men came to houses, the tale of starvation, often told, was the surest way to succeed in foraging…"

An elitist statement by an elitest officer in a prima donna unit. We will see in these pages how accurate this very judgemental statement proves to be.

Website Uniforms and Equipage of Georgia-early Civil War Uniforms

"The Bank's County Guards were formed on the fourth day of July, 1860, and elected Captain D.G. Chandler…Their uniforms were not very costly but consisted of bullet buttons and six yards of blue cotton jeans with a yellow strip down the pants about three inches wide…" (the article doesn't say whether they were cavalry or infantry-ed.)

Daily Constitutionalist, Augusta, Ga. March 24, 1861 Edgefield Rangers-"This company of mounted men paraded near Hamburg yesterday afternoon. Their uniform is of gray cloth, with black trimmings-the hat surmounted with a blue pompon (sic)…"

THE CONFEDERATE VETERAN VOL. XXXI 1923

Pg. 295 August 1923 Picuresque Soldiery by J.W. Minnich "Now a short history of Coppen's 1st Louisiana Zouaves, the "Zoo-Zoos" …Our caps were not of the high fez type. They were soft flannel, and close fitting, more like the old-fashiond night cap of our great granddaddies. The tassel was of a deep blue, and hung down behind instead of on the side, and our gingerbread trimmings on jacket and vest, of dark blue, were of red tape instead of yellow. Our leggings were of black leather, with three buckles, and an outside extension or flap to permit the fitting to any sized calf, of which we had quite a variety in shape and sizes, black shoes, connecting with the overlapping leggings by white gaiters…"

LIGHTENING STRIKE Carl Smith Osprey books 2001

Spring 1861Pg.25 "…They accepted hunger, endered the cold and wet, and scrounged equipment from the dead or from that discarded on the battlefield by fleeing Union soldiers. Confederate soldiers in tattered butternut wore a motley array of Union shoes, trousers, overcoats blankets and web gear (and thus sometimes could be subject to friendly fire because other Confederate troops could not rescognize them as fellow soldiers).

Confederate infantry wore grey, substituted by butternut when dye became in short supply as the war continued. They wore shorter sack coats, partly because this allowed better freedom of movement and partly because they conserved material by having shorter skirts. In the middle of the war many Southern supply began providing shell jackets with between seven and nine buttons. Although brogan shoes were supposed to be the standard issue, in the summer many men went shoeless, since shoes were in short supply. Unit specifics varied according to state and whether they were regular Confederate troops as opposed to state troops or militia. Ingeneral, though kepis were worn, slouch hats were by far the most widely used headwear. This is because in the hot and rainy South, men learned the value of face and neck protectionoffered by the wide brims, and a wide brim provided shade for the eyes when aiming a rifle. Shades of grey varied, as did the trousers, which were sometimes grey, sometimes light blue, sometimes light grey,and often butternut or brown by late in the war. Although uniforms prescribed blue pants, as shortages increased, depots found it expedient to cut pants and jackets from the same material. Backing colors for collars, cuffs, and enlisted stripes were medium blue for infantry, red for artillery, loden grey-green for medical, mustard yellow for cavalry, and buff-medium khaki for staff officers.

The cavalry usually wore snappy shell jackets, boots.and reinforced trousers. Many cavalry and artillerymen wore similar shell jackets (With different facing colors) as the South often lacked the ability to mass-produce the variety of coats as the war wore on. As with the Union, brogan shoes with heavy socks often replaced boots. Leggings were rarely issued to Southern troops, and if a unit was fortunate enough to have them, they were rarly worn after 1st Manassas, when the regular soldier learned to differentiate which equipment was essential and which was merely heavy. Southerners favored blanket rolls and haversacks with canteens instead of backpacks, although some units who had backpacks retained them…"

The knapsack/blanketroll choice seems to have been a personal one.

WIKIPEDIA Spring 1861

"…While on the march or in parade formation, Confederate Armies often displayed a wide variety of dress, ranging from faded, patched-together regulation uniforms; rough, homespun uniforms colored with homemade dyes such as butternut (a yellow-brown color), and even soldiers in a hodgepodge of civilian clothing. After a successful battle, it was not unusual for victorious Confederate troops to procure Union Army uniform parts from captured supplies and dead Union soldiers…"

Sartorial chaos

A LETTER FROM CHARLES EDWARD JORDAN TO HIS FAMILY AND FRIENDS Library of the Univ. of Va. 1952

Pg.16 Spring 1861 "...Springfield muskets arrived and "our boys," with neat gray uniforms and tall caps with pompons, were ready for the fray. It was truly an inspiring sight, especially to the writer and other youngsters who watched and practiced all the drills. Indeed, the village boys formed a little company, and with our wooden guns and "uniforms of many colors"-as our Irish friend expressed it-we felt that we, too, were ready to meet the Yankees and would gladly have marched to war with the Prince William Rifles..."

THEY TOOK THEIR STAND by Manly Wade Wellman pub by G.P. Putnam's Sons 1959

Pg. 47 Spring 1861 Charlston, S.C."... The Washington Light Infantry, in shakos and crossbelts decorated with badges of leopard skin, was the honor company..."
Pg. 141 Spring 1861 Richmond Va. "Southern rhetoric, at least, remained plentiful in the Confederacy, and sonorous names were spoken for the arriving units. There were fencibles, hussars, voltigeurs, dragoons, guards, Zouaves, rangers, and flying artillery. These wore all sorts and colors of uniforms, or no uniforms at all.

From its depot of mobilization at Corinth, in Mississippi, the Sixth Alabama Regiment rode across the country in boxcars. It field officers had donned frock coats of green cloth, as though they meant to march in a St. Patrick's Day parade..."

Pg. 142 Spring 1861 Richmond, Va. "...The officers engaged ladie's sewing circles to make gray field jackets and pantaloons to replace the dressy but impractical uniforms of the various companies..."

LETTERS FROM LEE'S ARMY by Susan Leigh Blackford and Charles Minor Blackford pub by Scribner Pub 1947

Pg. 1 "During the first three weeks after the John Brown Raid, as it was always called, a cavalry compant was organized in Lynchburg (Va) called "The Wise Troop," a name selected in honor of Henry A. Wise, then Governor of Virginia and ever active in encouraging the formation of military companies. The uniform of this troop seems now to me, who saw it many times afterwards so differently costumed, as very singular, even partaking of the absurd. It consisted of bright blue pantaloons with a gold cord down the sides, the brightest scarlet horsehair tufts hanging down behind them. The papers made great fun of them and pretended to think the British had invaded our homes again. The gay attire was, however; only a holiday dress; when the company was really equipped for the field, as it was two years afterwards, the Confederate gray was adopted and the red coats disappeared-either seeking the dye-pot to appear in some more somber hue or being relegated to some colored camp-follower who rejoiced in the startling tint....

Directly after Lincoln's call for troops the whole course of our ordinary life was changed. All our usual avocations at an end, and a new life began for women as well as men. The sound of the drum and fife could be heard from morning till night. The men were drilling and equipping themselves for war, while the women, with tearful eyes and saddened hearts, spent their time making coats, pantaloons, shirts, haversacks, and every kind of work that could make their men more comfortable or healthy in the field..."

THE WAR-Stonewall Jackson- His Campaigns and Battles. The Regiment as I Saw Them. by James H. Wood Capt. Co. "D" 37th Va. Infantry Regiment pub by the Eddy Press Corp. Cumb. Md. 1984

Pg19 Spring 1861 "Companies and regiments began at once to arrive, undrilled and undisciplined, raw and without arms, except in instances where the individual had given play to his own imagination as to what would be useful in battle, and pursuant thereto had brought the squirrel rifle, the shotgun, the butcher's knife and the pistol, some of the latter of the old pepperbox type. A few thought the savage, the daredevil mein the true indice of the soldier, hence the red hunting shirt, the coon skin cap, the unkempt hair and beard were popular insignia. How ludicrous was it all in the light of after experience! Yet the manifestations were not to be condemned. It is a chapter in their history that ought to give pride to their sons and daughters, because these were the promptings of purest patriotism."

Maybe this accounts for the scarcity of pepperbox pistols today. They must've been one of the first articles dropped by the wayside due to their weight.

ED. For those readers who are unfamiliar with the "pepperbox" pistol, I found an excellent description of its peculiarties and habits. The following is from "Roughing It" by Mark Twain: "...George Bemis was our fellow traveler. We had never seen him before. He wore in his belt an old original "Allen" revolver, such as irreverent people called a "pepperbox." Simply drawing the trigger back, cocked and fired the pistol. As the trigger came back, the hammer would begin to rise and the barrel turn over, and presently down would drop the hammer, and away would speed the ball. To aim along the turning barrel and hit the thing aimed at was a feat that was probably never donewith an "Allen" in the world. But George's was a reliable weapon, nevertheless, because, as one of the stage drivers afterward said, "If she didn't get what she went after, she would fetch something else." And so she did. She went after a deuce of spades nailed against a tree once, and fetched a mule standing about thirty yards to the left of it. Bemis did not want the mule; but the owner came out with a double-barreled shotgun and persuaded him to buy it anyhow. It was a cheerful weapon-the "Allen."

Sometimes all its six barrels would go off at once, and then there was no safe place in the region roundabout but behind it."

A NORTHERN WOMAN IN THE CONFEDERACY Magaret Sumner McLean Harper & Brothers 1914

Pg. 441 spring 1861 "...The uniform of the Confederacy is to be grey with insignia of rank on the collar and sleeves. The ornaments are well enough, but I fancy a whole army in grey will look lugubrious (connected with mourning; mournful-Webster's Third New International Dictionary-ed.)..."

CLEAR THE CONFEDERATE WAY!-The Irish in the Army of N. Va. By Kelly J. O'Grady, Savas pub. Co. 2000

Pg. 47 "In the spring of 1861, Richmond's Irish community celebrated St. Patrick's Day and succession with equal enthusiasum. On Mar 17th Richmond's Irish Militia Company, the Montgomery Guard paraded through the capitol city in high spirits in honor of the patron saint of Ireland. The Guard carried the stars and stripes on a green flag that featured an Irish harp. One month later, on April 17th, Virginia, the south's leading state and the cradle of American liberty, succeeded from the union. Almost immediately, the city's Irish soldiers took up the Confederate cudgel. As a long-standing state militia company, the Guard had marched for years each St. Patrick's Day adorned in bottle green uniforms, with buttons sporting the Va. State seal and hat brass insignia encircled by shamrocks. Now the Irish Company pledged it's allegiance to the south and proclaimed itself a Confederate Army unit."

HOW A ONE-LEGGED REBEL LIVES The Story of the Campaigns of of Stonewall Jackson John S. Robinson New Materials Copywright Butternut Press 1984

Pg. 8 "...The volunteer of 1861 was a very elaborate in stitution, and entertained the idea that he was little, if any inferior to Napoleon, in his capacity and possibilities, and he of the South was very sure that he was a match, in the field, for any five Yankees in the United States; an idea which was, to a certain extent, eliminated along with other erroneous ones which, at the outbreak of the disturbance, were entertained.

In his preparation for the campaign the Confederate soldiers were forced to depend upon home resources, and in the first place he thought big boots, the higher the better, were essential to his military appearance; but he learned after awhile that a broad bottomed shoe was very much lighter to carry and easier on his ankles.

He also thought he must wear a very heavy padded coat, with long tails and many buttons, but this too proved an error, and a very short experience induced him to lay aside the coat and substitute a short-waisted, single-breasted jacket, which transformation gave the "Rebs" the universal title of "Gray Jackets" by the neighbors over the way-the Yankees.

We went in heavy on fancy caps, wavelocks and other cockady and stately headgear, but these early gave way to the comfortable slouch hat, and to this day the Confederate veterans are much mystified when they read of the French and Prussian wearing the little caps and heavy helmets on the march and in the field, but the volunteer of '61 was a fearfully and wonderfully gotten up representative of the Sons of Mars in the first flush of his war-fever. He carried more baggage then than a major-general carried afterwards, and many of these "high privates" were followed by their own faithful body-servants, who did their cooking, washing, and foraging, blacked those imposing boots, dusted his clothes, and bragged to other negroes what a noble soldier and gentleman "Massa Tom" or "Massa Dick" was.

The knapsack was a terror, loaded with thirty to fifty pounds of surplus baggage, consisting of all manner of extra underwear, towels, combs, brushes, blacking, looking glasses, needles, thread, buttons, bandages, everything thought of as necessary, and strapped on the outside were two heavy blankets and a gum or oil-cloth. His haversack too, hung on his shoulder, and always had a good stock of provisions, as though a march across the Sahara might at any time be imminent. The inevitable canteen, with contents more or less, was also slung from the shoulder, and most of the boys thought a bold soldier's outfit for the war was absolutely incomplete unless he was supplied with long gloves. In fact the volunteer of '61 made himself a complete beast of burden, and was so heavily clad, weighted and cramped that a march was absolute torture, and the wagon trains of mess-chests and camp equipage were so immense in proportion to the number of men that it would have been impossible to guard them in an enemy's country, or anywhere else, against enterprizing cavalry. However, wisdom is born of experience, and before many campaigns had been worried through the private soldier, reduced to the minmum, consisted of one man, one hat, one jacket, one pair pants, one pair draws, one pair socks, one pair shoes,and his baggage was one blanket, one gum-cloth and one haversack, while the wonderfully-constructed mess-chests, with lids convertible into cozy dining tables, and with numerous divisions and sub-divisions in nooks and cases for the holding of all imaginable necesseties and luxuries, of tea and coffee, spices and condiments, dishes, cups, vases and spoons, were stored nevermore to see the light in the army again, and the company property consisted of two or three skillets or frying pans, which didn't take up much wagonroomfor the infantryman generally preferred to to stick the handle of the mess frying pan into the barrel of a musket and thus be sure of having it at a given point on the march when the minimum weight soldier got there, for the wagon got to be very unreliable for the transportation of anything but ammunition; but sometimes they carried a small quantity of commissary store, generally for the use of the train quartermaster and his staff...."

Pg. 12 "...The Confederate soldier held on to his haversack, not to carry food in it as is popularly supposed, but it was the ever-present receptacle for tobacco, pipe, strings, buttons and the like, and very often, when, with great display and bluster, by the commissaries, three days rations were issued to the men, they would cook and eat the whole lot at one meal, which was decidedly the most convient way of carrying it, and besides it was usually the case that they had been without food for from two to five meals, and it was not much of an exploit to consume the small quantity issued for what was termed "three days rations," and after eating it, they would trust to luck and strategy for meals, or go hungry, as usual, till the next ration day...."

A very good general overview. The servants that accompanied their masters to the field in the early part of the war were mostly sent home later, as the army-which did initially issue rations for servants, later on couldn't support them, plus their labor was increasingly needed at home.

DETAILED MINUTINAE OF SOLDIER LIFE by Carlton McCarthy pub by Collector's Library of the Civil War 1982 from the 1882 edition

Pg. 16 "The volunteer of 1861 made extensive preparations for the field. Boots, he thought, were an absolute necessity, and the heavier the soles and the longer the tops the better. His pants were stuffed inside the tops of his boots, of course. A double-breasted coat, heavily wadded, with two rows of big brass buttons and a long shirt were considered comfortable. A small stiff cap, with a narrow brim, took the place of the comfortable "felt" or the shining and towering tile worn in civil life.

Then over all was a huge overcoat, long and heavy with a cape reaching nearly to the waist. On his back he strapped a knapsack containing a full stock of underwear, soap, towels, comb, brush, looking glass, photographs, smoking and chewing tobacco, pipes, twine string and cotton strips for wounds and other emergencies, needles and thread, buttons, knife, fork, spoon, and many other things as each man's idea of what he was to encounter varied. On the outside of the knapsack, solidly folded, were two great blankets and a rubber or oil-cloth. This knapsack etc. weighed from fifteen to twenty-five pounds, sometimes even more. All seemed to think it was impossible to have on too many or too heavy clothes, or to have too many conveniences, and each had an idea that to be a good soldier he must provide against any possible emergency.

In addition to the knapsack, each man had a haversack, more or less costly, some of cloth and some of fine morocco, and stored with provisions always, as though he expected any moment to receive orders to march across the Great Desert, and supply his own wants along the way. A canteen was considered indespensible and at the outset it was thought prudent to keep it full of water. Many, expecting terrific hand-to-hand encounters, carried revolvers and even Bowie knives. Merino shirts (and flannel) were thought to be the right thing, but experiences demonstrated the contrary. Gloves were thought to be very necessary and goods things to have in winter time, the favorite style being buck gauntlets with long cuffs."

WEBSITE-16TH TENNESSEE VOLUNTEER INFANTRY REGIMENT: CLOTHING, ARMS AND EQUIPMENT

Pg. 1 "Another Southerner wrote 'I wore a cartridge box and bayonet holder on my belt. Extra cartridges were placed in pockets. Around my shoulder hung my wool blanket and a captured Yankee gum (poncho) in which I wrapped my few belongings…I also had a haversack in which my plate, knife, spoon and fork rested and what few meager rations we received. I tied my coffee boiler to my canteen to be ready to scoop up water at the first well or creek we passed."

I can't for the life of me imagine paper cartridges, placed in pockets, remained intact. Obviously I'missing something as there are numerous accounts of cartridges being carried in pockets.

CONFEDERATE VETERAN DEC. 1893 Vol. I No. 12

Pg. 367 Typical Confederate Soldier by G.B. Baskette, Nashville, Tenn.

"Nearly thiry-three years have passed since the alarm of war called from their peaceful pursuits the citizens who were to make name and fame as Confederate soldiers. The stirring scenes and the dreadful carnage of a memorable conflict have been removed by the lapse of time into the hazy past, and a new generation, however ready it may be to honor those who fought the battles of the South, is likely to form its idea of their appearance from the conventional military type. The Confederate soldier was not an ordinary soldier, either in appearance or character. With your permission I will undertake to draw a portrait of him as he really appeared in the hard service of privation and danger.

A face browned by exposure and heavily bearded, or for some weeks unshaven, begrimed with dust and sweat, and marked here and there with the darker stains of powder-a face whose stolid and even melancholy composure is easily broken into ripples of good humor or quickly flushed in the ferver and abandon of the charge; a frame tough and sinewy, and trained by hardship to amazing powers of endurance; a form, the shapelinessof which is hidden by its encumberments, suggesting in its careless and unaffected pose a languorous indisposition to exertion, yet a latent, lion-like strength and a terrible energy of action when aroused. Around the upper part of the face is a fringe of unkempt hair, and above this an old wool hat, worn and weather-beaten, the flaccid brim of which falls limp upon the shoulders behind, and is folded back in front against the elongated and crumpled crown. Over a soiled shirt which is unbuttoned and buttonless at the collar, is a ragged gray jacket that does not reach to the hips, with sleeves some inches too short. Below this trousers of a nondescript color, without form and almost void are held in place by a leather belt, to which is attached the cartridge box that rests behind the right hip, and the bayonet scabbard that dangles on the left. Just above the ankles each trouser leg is tied closely to the limb-a la Zouave-and beneath reaches of dirty socks disappear in a pair of badly used and curiously contorted shoes. Between the jacket and the waistband of the trousers, or the supporting belt, there appears a puffy display of cotton shirt which works out further with every hitch made by Johnny Reb in his effort to keep his pantaloons in place. Across his body frm his left shoulder there is a roll of threadbare blanket, the ends tied together resting or falling below the right hip. This blanket is Johnny's bed. Whenever he arises he takes up his bed and walks. Within this roll is a shirt, his only extra article of clothing. In action the blanket roll is thrown further back, and the cartridge box is drawn forward, frequently in front of the body. From the right shoulder, across the body, pass two staps, one cloth the other leather, making a cross with blanket roll on breast and back. These straps support respectively a greasy cloth haversack and a flannel-covered canteen, captured from the Yankees. Attached to the haversack strap is a tin cup, while in addition to other odds and ends of camp trumpery, there hangs over his back a frying pan, an invaluable utensil with which the soldier would be loth to part.

With his trusty gun in hand-an Enfield rifle, also captured from the enemy and substituted for the old flint-lock musket or the shot-gun with which he was originally armed-Johnny Reb, thus imperfectly sketched, stands in his shreds and patches a marvelous ensemble-picturesque, grotesque, unique- the model citizen soldier, the military hero of the nineteenth century. There is none of the tinsel or the trappings of the professional about him. From an esthetic military point of view he must appear a sorry looking soldier. But Johnny is not one of your dress parade soldiers. He doesn't care a copper whether anybody likes his looks or not. He is the most independent soldier that ever belonged to an organized army. He has repect for authority and cheerfully submits to discipline, because he sees the necessity of organization to effect the best results, but he maintains his individual autonomy, as it were, and never surrenders his sense of personal pride and responsibility. He is thoroughly tractable if properly officered, and is always ready to obey necessary orders, but he is quick to resent any official incivility, and it is a high private who feels, and is, every inch as good as a general. He may appear ludicrous enough on a display occasion of the holiday pomp and splendor of war, but place him where duty calls, in the immenent deadly breach or the perilous charge, and none in all the armies of the earth can claim a higher rank or prouder record. He may be outré and ill-fashioned in dress, but he has sublimated his povery and rags. The worn and faded gray jacket, glorified by valor and stained with the life-blood of its wearer, becomes,in its immortality of association, a more splendid vestment than mail of medieval knight or the rarest robe of royalty. The old, weather-beaten sloched hat, seen as the ages will see it, with its halo of fire, through the smoke of battle, is a kinglier covering than a crown. Half clad, half armed, often half fed, without money and without price, the Confederate soldier fought against the resources of the world. When at last his flag was furled and his arms were grounded in defeat, the cause for which he had struggled was lost, but he had won the fadless victory of soldiership."

Notice in the beginning of this quote, how the author mentions that the new generation of Southerners were forming the idea of finely uniformed soldiers, not the "ragged Rebels" that is closer to the reality and he wants to set the record straight. This is a blow to the historians who state that the ragged rebel was the presented ideal after the warand not reality. This is undoubtedly the best general overviewof the Rebel Soldier.

CONFEDERATE VETERAN MAY, 1895 Vol. III, No. 5

Pg. 134 R.I.Ridley's Journal "...And now I will try to while away a few hours of the armistice by transcribing some of the Nomenclature of our Southern Armies:

The North Carolinians are called "Tar Heels;" South Carolinians "Rice Birds;" Georgians "Goober Grabbers;" Alabamians "Yaller Hammers;" Texans "Cow Boys;" Tenneseans "Hog Drivers;" Louisianians "Tigers;" Floridians "Gophers;" Virginians "Tobacco Worms;" Arkansians "Tooth-Picks;" Missourians "Border Ruffians;" Kentuckians "Corn Crackers;" and Mississippians "Sand Lappers"...The Confederate soldier, in spite of his rags and lack of rations, was aways on the qui-vie for fun, and his sense of humor was alwaye appealed to when a column marched in sight of men whom they called "flag floppers." (signal men) It was hard for them to refrain such good-natured inquires as, "Mister, is the flies abotherin of you?":Say,is mosquitoes plentiful around here?"

CONFEDERATE VETERAN VOL. XX APRIL 1912

Pg. 157 "Confederate Gray Uniform (From the Roanoke (Va.) Times

"Again we have indignant protests against the reported purpose of the Tennessee authorities to adopt Confederate gray as the uniform for penitentiary convicts. We think it very unlikely that the report is true.

In the first place, it is very hard to define what is Confederate gray. At the beginning of the War of the States the Confederate soldiers and officers wore cadet gray, the same that is used at West Point, a kind of dark silver shade. Really-it was the most attractive and becoming uniform in the world-finer even than the British scarlet and much better adapted for the purposes of war. Most of the first soldiers of the Confederacy were stalwart young country men with broad shoulders, trim waists, and deep chests; and when a reigiment or brigade of them in their gray uniforms were drawn up in line, they made probably the handsomest array of fighting and efficient men ever gathered on earth.

Toward the last the Confederate soldiers wore anything they could get to cover them, whatever they could buy or pick up or capture from the enemy. Probably the clothing in most general use in the ranks was butternut homespun dyed at home with butternut or walnut shells.

We surmise that the gray it is proposed to adopt for the Tennessee convicts is a very coarse, rough, light gray, long used in the English prisons and marked with the broad arrow indicating that the wearer is the propery of the government. Aside from other considerations, and very sacred associations, the expense alone would prevent the Tennessee officials form using the real Confederate or cadet gray as garb for convicts. It is a costly and fine fabric, usually, we believe, made especially to order."

While I'd like to believe that the choice of gray for convict's uniforms was a coincidence, I don't put anything petty and/or vengeful past them Yankees.

SOLDIERS BLUE AND GRAY by James I. Robertson Jr. pub by Univ of S.C. Press 1988

Pg. ix "The men naturally denounced their officers. They fidgeted at long delays on a march, when everyone stood still while knapsacks and equipment bore down with increasing weightiness. They complained about the woolen uniformsthey wore year round-uniforms that, in the dryness of summer, were veritable ovens and that, in rainy weather, became colder, heavier, and wetter until most soldiers would have preferred nakedness

Equipment-Union vs. Confederate Cavalry by John M. Galloway

Pg. 153 "...The Confederate (cavalry) trooper had issued to him a saddle, a haversack, a canteen, a part of a bridle, an English carbine, a nondescript saber. A new recruit was always advised to throw away or not draw any of these things, but wait until a battle gave him a chance to get "something worth totin." The saddle ruined a horse's back, the canteen leaked, the haversack of cotton cloth was no protection, the English carbine was muzzle-loading and would not carry a ball fifty yards accurately....It was a certain sign of a new recruit to see him with any article of Confederate equipment about him...The Confederates had no tent, no fly cloths, and very little clothes except what he got from home...."

THE CIVIL WAR SOLDIER-A Historical Reader by Michael Barton & Larry M. Logue pub by N.Y. Univ Press 2002

Pg. 109 "The Confederate private envisioned by Richmond authorities in 1861 was a nattily dressed person....

But there was considerable difference between the clothing designated and that actually worn by the soldiers. This descrepancy first came from the inability of the Confederate Government to provide uniforms for the men who were called to arms. Captains who wrote into Montgomery to inquire about equipment for companies in process of organization were informed that "volunteers shall furnish their own clothes." The reason was obvious: Jeff Davis and company had none in stock, nor were any to be forthcoming until contracts with Southern manufacturers should bear fruit, or purchasing operations in Europe could be completed; and this was to require a long time.

In the meantime volunteer companies did the best they could. Some received issues of clothing from state authorities, though these were faced with problems of supply very much like those of the central government.

A procedure widely followed during the early months of he war was for captains to take funds appropriated by local authorities or donated by philanthropists-who sometimes were the captains themselves-or contributed by the recruits, to purchase cloth from whatever source it might be obtained, and to have the uniforms made up by the local tailors or seamstresses. In many cases the volunteers arranged individually for the fabrication of their outfits.

Women of the South responded nobly to the difficulties by organizing sewing clubs and knitting societies. As a general rule the aid rendered by the volunteer seamstresses was both timely and valuable, though there were numerous instances where coats, pants, and socks turned out by the ladies indicated considerably more zeal than skill.

The inevitable result of these devious sources and methods of supply was a miscellany that made mockery of the Richmond regulations. This is not to imply that the regalia worn by early volunteers were of poor quality. On the contrary, many of the companies were resplendently clothed. Captain Alexander Duncan of the Georgia Hussars, a regiment hailing from Savannah, boasted that $25,000 was spent for that organizations intial outfit.

In not a few instances, regiments went into Confederate service garbed in the flashy suits which they had worn for parade purposes as militia organizations. The Orleans Guard Battalion of New Orleans arrived at Shiloh while the battle was in progress, and went into the thick of the fight wearing blue dress uniforms. Fellow Rebels mistook the newcomers for Yankees and began to shoot at them. When the Guards realized the cause of their plight, they hastily turned their coats inside out so as to present a whitish color instead of the blue, and thus they went through the battle.

But blue was just one of many colors worn by soldiers of '61 and '62. The Emerald Guards of Mobile went to Virginia in dark green, a color adopted in honor of old Ireland, the land from which most of the members came. Captain Patterson's company of East Tennesseans dressed themselves in suits of yellow to give meaning to their previously adopted designation of "yellow jackets." The Granville Rifles of North Corolina sported uniforms featuring black pants and flaming red flannel shirts that must have made easy targets for Yankees considerably removed. Some of the Maryland companies who espoused the cause of the Confederacy were clothed in uniforms of blue and orange....

As the war went into the second and third years clothing became simpler and less diverse. Contributuing to this change was the increasing ability of the quartermaster general to meet requisitions made upon the government for uniforms. By the end of 1862 Caleb Huse's purchasing operations had yielded substantial returns in trousers and cloth for coats. Contracts with domestic manufacturers were also beginning, after heart-breaking delays, to achieve a partial degree of fulfillment. In recognition of these developments Congress, on October 8, 1862, passed an act which moditfied the prior policy of allowing cash payments of fifty dollars a year for soldiers who clothed themselves, and announced the intention of the government to provide the uniform prescribed by regulations...

Company officers were required to keep a record of clothing dispensed-two general issues a year were contemplated, one of winter uniforms in the fall, and the other of summer outfits in the spring-and soldiers who did not draw the full amount allowed were to be credited on the pay roll with the value of articles due them; on the other hand, those who overdrew their allowances were to be charged in like manner with items received in excess of the quantities authorized.

Notwithstanding the intention expressed by the act of October 8, 1862, the clothing issued by government quartermasters deviated considerably from Army Regulations. Blue trousers, for instance, seemed to have been the rare exception rather than the rule. Certainly the impression derived from soldier correspondence is that gray was the standard color for trousers as well as coats, and this impression is corroborated by wartime uniforms on display in various Confederate museums. Butr the cadet gray of 1861 and 1862 gradually gave way, as the blockade drove the South to an increasing dependenvce on her own resources, to a yellowish-brown resulting from the use of dye made of copperas and walnut hulls. This peculiar tint was dubbed butternut, and so wide was its use for uniforms that Confederate soldiers were rather generally referred to by both Yanks and Sotherners as "butternuts."

In a few instances, at least, undyed outfits were issued by the government. The Second Texas Regiment was the recipient of such an issue a few days before leaving Corinth for Shiloh. When the men beheld the whitish-looking garments exclamations of the most unorthodox character went up on every hand such as "Well I'll be Damn!" "Don't them things beat hell?" "Do the generals expect us to be killed and want us to wear our shrouds?" After the battle a Federal prisoner was said to have inquired: "Who were them hell cats that went into battle dressed in their graveclothes?"..."

Another good overview. As we will see, the government was only able to sporatically uniform the troops, also, blue trousers appeared to have been issued off & on, whether captured or contractor manufactured isn't clear. I suppose any cloth that could be made into clothing wouldv'e been pressed into service.

DAILY LIFE IN CIVIL WAR AMERICA by Dorothy Deneen Volo & James M. Volo

Pg 170 "Confederate soldiers acquired so much Federal equipment that it was difficult to distinguish between friend and foesimply by uniform. "A Rebel Captain and some of his men were clothed in our uniform," wrote a frustrated Federal officer, "a growing pactice so reprehensible that it should be met with condign (well deserved) punishment, as the deception engendered is always apt to cost lives and disasters." In winter, large contingents of Southern troops were seen sporting sky-blue federal trousers and greatcoats. Federal commanders insisted that Southern troops captured wearing federal equipment be treated as spies. The South countered that such items were legitimate objects of capture under the rules of war, to be used at the pleasure of the captors, leaving a dispute that was never resolved.

A resident of Winchester, Virginia, Cornelia McDonald, described the uniform of a fallen Southern gallant with the rank of major in 1862. "He was dressed in a beautiful new uniform, gray and buff, a splendid red silk scarf was around his waist." As the officer was dead, "his sword was lying by his side...not a drop of blood stained his clothing." He was a young man with "fine soft hair" and a "long jet-black beard" through which he had received a death wound, shot in the chin..."

A RISING THUNDER by Richard Wheeler oub by Harper Collins 1994

Pg. 164 "There was much rushing to and fro...the masculine portion of humanity engaged in making hot speeches, much drilling, also much anxiety about the fit of their new uniforms... and great solicitude concerning the brightness of their arms...upon which Pomp, John Tom, Cuffee, and a host of other ...darkies were kept at work polishing...The feminine portion busied themselves about making many needful things conducive to the comfort of these same helpless men-helpless in regard to the things which only a woman's quick intuition and deft fingers can supply...There was a shimmer of bright ribbons, silk, beads, glosssey satin, and downy velvet; and willing fingers soon transformed these delecate materials into smoking caps, slippers, tobacco pouches, cigar cases and portfolios [for writing paper and envelopes]

In many sections of the South, groups of women set up small factories,with uniforms the chief product. As recalled by Mrs. Jane Evans of Northern Viginia:

"In our little town...the courthouse was the place of meeting and thither all the ladies resorted to pass the the day at work. Some would cut out garments, others work the machines, while still others would finish them off. Coats, overcoats, pantaloons, and havelocks were made in great numbers. Ladies who had never done harder work than with a cambric needle now stitched industriously on coarse cloth, making heavy garments. They seemed to find nothing too hard for them. Besides this, they knit quantities of socks of the coarsest yarn; and so engrossed were they in their work, that when they went to visit their friends they would take their knitting, some even knitting as they walked or drove, and plying their needles as they discussed the all-absorbing topic, the war....

Troops continued to pour into Richmond ...without the necessary uniform or equipments to send them to the field. Our ladies engaged to preparethem properly for the work which they were committed to enter. Sewing societies were multiplied and those who had formerly devoted themselves to gaity and fashionable amusement found their only real pleasure in obedience to the demands made upon their time and talents in providing proper habiliments for the soldier...

"they very soon became adepts in the manufacture of the different articles which compose the rough and simple wardrobe of the soldier. To these...they took delight in adding various other articles...there were very few of the soldiers who were not furnished with a neat thread-case supplied with everything necessary to repair his clothing when absent from a friendly pair of hands which would do it for him; a visor to shield his face from the too fierce heat of the summer sunor to protect him from the cold of winter; a warm scarf and a Havelock.

"The sewing operations were varied by the scraping of lint [the preparation of cotton], the rolling of bandages, and the manufacture of cartridges, and many things unnecessary to mention, but which were the work of the women...They employed themselves cheerfully upon anything necessary to be done. Heavy tents of cumberous sailcloth, overcoats, jackets and pantaloons of stiff, heavy material, from the sewing on which they were frequently found with stiff, swollen, bleeding fingers, were neverthe less perseveringly undertaken..."

The bandages spoken of in this quote probably rewferred to a band to be worn around the waist, about kidney height, to ward off chills and/or diarrehea when sleeping on the ground.

RELIVING THE CIVIL WAR-A Reenactor's Handbook by Rilee Hadden pub by Stackpole Books1996

Pg. 36 "Standard Confederate Army uniforms were gray jackets or frock coats with either light blue or gray kersey wool trousers. This was the ideal, but many of the uniforms that were issued fell far short. Defining colors is tricky at best, and the grays used by Cofederate troops varied quite a bit and had different names. Some were more colorfast than others."

Pg. 37 "In the North, factories under contract to the state or federal government made the uniforms. Confederate uniforms, on the other hand, were often made at home and by hand, and often showed differences in style and in the skill of the women who made them. One account from North Carolina states that the ladies' Aid Society sewed nearly 120 uniforms for the men from their county:

The company had to be equipped, the uniforms for nearly one hundred and twenty men to be made; the tents that were to shelter them, the haversacks that were to hold their rations. All this was done by our society of ladies, and more, such as military blouses and covering the canteens for the men; this was all done by the ladies lovingly and cheerfully with their own fingers, for there was not a sewing machine at that time in all this county; all the heavy stitching of military suits, tents, and canteens was done by our fingers…In fall of 1861 we made nearly all the overcoats for the company…"

During the rest of the war, states, homes and counties supplied their men as best they could. Uniform cloth, materials, and patterns were likely similar among companies, at least until near the end of the war. Uniform style and quality often varied from company to companyin a regiment, however. The uniformity the federal government achieved in outfitting its soldiers was never accomplished by the South.

Trousers were of heavy wool or of a wool and cotton blend, sometimes called "jeans cloth' although it was not denim. There were no summer uniform pants of a lighter material. During the 1860s, all trousers, both civilian and military, were similar. The pants were high waisted, coming up almost to the navel or the lowest rib, and reached down to the instep of the boot. The area covering the fly buttons was narrow and as inconspicuous as possible. The pants were not worn snug or tight, since that would mean pulling out the suspender buttons every time the soldier leaned over or sat down, but were loosely worn and had a lot of give when sitting or squatting. For reasons of modesty the male form, like the female, was to be draped, not outlined in public. Loose trousers also acted as wicks by absorbing sweat from the legs and allowed the legs to be cooled by evaporation. Also, they left enough room for the long underwear that was worn year-round. *(I don't care what they say, wool trousers are HOT!, whether tight or loose!*

The army had four sizes of uniforms. Many soldiers wrote that there was really only two sizes: too big or too small. A common joke was to say the army had put a number one man in a number four suit. Anyone who was not one of these standard sizes had to do some sewing to make the uniform fit.

Late war Confederate gear included civilian items, captured Yankee equipment, worn or make-do clothing and equipment, and the butternut uniform, which was civilian clothing dyed with shells from butternuts. This process was far from consistent, and colors ranged from light beige to dark, rich, brown. Previously dyed materials dumped in the butternut dye kettle had results that were sometimes amazing. Bright plaids dyed butternut came out with mixed results, to say the least."

This study will demonstrate there was more civilian clothing- issued- than usually supposed.

East

INTRODUCTION

These are the recollections/memoirs of what it was like in the South in those beginning daysafter succession through when the war began. They detail the enthusiastic chaos that dominated the people in their rush to prepare their men for war. As the soldiers were supposed to uniform themselves, most every town and county had uniforms made up to suit their captain's fancy, though sometimes the men themselves voted for the color and style. There were few overall guidelines and the people were in a rush with the first wild enthusiasm of the upcoming war. No time could be lost in outfitting the troops with uniforms and the gear considered necessary for a soldier's comfort, as (many feared) the conflict would be over before they had a chance to show their mettle. Most of the officers were inexperienced with no idea exactly what should be taken and the men were even more inexperienced, looking at the whole thing as a grand expedition. They tended to take anything and everything they could think of for comfort in the upcoming campaign. Many volunteers showed up in their everyday clothes or Sunday best, expecting to be given uniforms (sometimes they were). We will then go through the year 1861, examing the effect of army life and campaigns as applies to uniforms in the participants own words.

OUR WOMEN IN THE WAR-A Series of Papers Written by Southern Ladies-S.C. News & Courier 1884-1885 Arranged by Miss Hattie Kilmore 1998 Old Confederate ways by Miss Claudine Rhett, Charlestown, S.C.

Pg. 17 Spinning and Weaving Under Difficulties "...We now had to consider how we were to provide clothing for our laborers, as it began to be difficult to obtain "English plains," a heavy cloth which they had always worn in cold weather, so we determined to have cloth made on the plantation. Have you any idea, my friend, the magnitude of this undertaking? I will describe the process. A special house was dedicated to the purpose, and a spinning wheel was procured. Old Mark and Cinda were detailed to card the wool, which had been shorn from our sheep Sappho and Phoebe, spun, and our cook Rosetta, who was a thrifty soul, was appointed dyer of the yarn. A large iron pot was set up in the yard, and such a mixing and stirring with a long handled paddle, of all sorts of barks and copperas and other ingredients went on that one might have thought it was a witches' cauldron. But the worst part of the operation was yet to come-a hand loom had to be obtained and where was it to come from? We were not to be daunted, however, and after making diligent inquiries in all directions we at last heard of one, which belonged to an Indian woman. So we forthwith dispatched Lymus, our head carpenter, to inspect it, and in a few week's time he constructed a similar one for us; Keziah, the Indian, was sent for to teach Rhyna how to work it and oh!

Triumph, our jeans was woven, and the negroes had strong, warm cloth. But it was slow work. A tolerably expert weaver could not make more than three yards a day, and there were ninety-five persons to be provided for. I have often sat with the workers and tried to card and to spin, but it is a difficult art to acquire. The droning sound of the spinning wheel is rather pleasant, and it is not arduous labor, but the weaving is a most tedious occupation…"

OUR WOMEN IN THE WAR-A Series of Papers Written by Southern Ladies-S.C. News & Courier 1884-1885 Arranged by Miss Hattie Kilmore 1998 Old Confederate ways by Miss Claudine Rhett, Charlestown, S.C.

Pg. 36 How The Arsenal Was Taken by: Mrs. Eliza B. Stenson Mecklinburg Co. N.C. "… The women were as anxious as the men, and there was plenty for them to do. The volunteers were to be fitted out, and there were miles of sewing to be done, to get all the needed garments put together. But before we got well started with our needles Governor Ellis sent orders to General Draughan, who commanded the county militia, to call out his men and take possession of the Arsenal, before authorities in Washington could send reinforcements. Ah! Then there was hurrying to and fro. Monday was the day appointed for the undertaking. I have forgotten the exact date, but it was about the middle of April (1861) the ladies had been at work fixing up hats for the volunteers. It had been decided that all the superfluous ornaments should be removed from the coats of the old members of the companies, and these garments put on a war footing. They were now to be put to a different use from that for which they were originally made. The fanciful helmets, with their bright colored plumes, were to be exchanged for soft hats. But we thought that soldiers must have a plume in their hats, so it was decided that a black feather would be the correct thing with which to go into real war, and there was a call for a contribution of feathers, which came in from ladies in abundance. It was in the midst of this decoration of hats that the order for our men to take their first march up to the cannon's mouth was given. It was necessary to go to work after service Sunday to get all the hats ready in time for next day's work. Cartridges too, could be made by the women, and all hands were busy…"

THE CIVIL WAR: THE SOUTH ed. by Thomas Streissguth Greehaven Press 2001

Pg. 74 Anymous account from "Blackwood's Edinburgh Magazine" in Dec. 1861 regarding a visit to the South in the spring of 1861. "…Neccessity has tought the South thjat she must rely upon herself for many things she cannot do without, and which, in former times, it was cheaper to import than to manufacture large numbers of hand-looms and spinning wheels are are seen in the country districts, which the population are rapidly learning to make good use of; and we met one planter who showed us enough cloth for the uniforms of fifty men, that had been entirely made on his own property.

Again, before the war, leather was so little manufactured in the South, that hides were seldom saved, and tan-yards were almost unknown. Shoemaking, saddlery, and many other industrial employments, are now being quickly brought into operation; and all the country appears to want is the machinery to adapt its boundless natural productions to the wants of man…Pg. 75 We saw a poor negro servant actually shedding tears because his master, on being told off to dig a trench around a battery, would not allow him to "lend a hand."

"Twill nebber do, massa," he said, "I go 'tarnal mad wid dem darn'd Yankees."

One day we heard a lad boasting to one of a different regiment of the number of gentlemen in his company who had thousands of dollars at their command. The latter replied, "Oh, of course they fight; but we have some in ours who have not got a cent!" The Washington Artillery, comprising many batteries, is composed of the best blood in New Orleans. The gunners, dressed in light blue uniforms, are all men of independent means…"

OUR WOMEN IN THE WAR-A Series of Papers Written by Southern Ladies-S.C. News & Courier 1884-1885 Arranged by Miss Hattie Kilmore 1998 Old Confederate ways by Miss Claudine Rhett, Charlestown, S.C.

Pg. 232 Hospital Scenes-The Story of General Lee's Socks by Miss Emily V. Mason Lexington, Va. "…Speaking of General Lee's socks-an "institution" peculiar to our hospitals- I must explain its origin and uses. Besides that, Mrs. Lee spent most of her time in making gloves and socks for the soldiers. She gave me at one time several pair of General Lee's old socks, so darned that we saw they had been well worn by our hero. We kept those to apply to the feet of those laggard "old soldiers" who were suspected of preferring the "luxury" of hospital life to the activity of the field. And such was the effect of the application of these war-like socks that even the threat of it had the effect of sending a man to his regiment who had been lingering months in inactivity. It came to be a standing joke in the hospital infinitely enjoyed by the men. If a poor wretch was out of his bed over a week he would be threatened with "General Lee's Socks," and through this means some of the most obstinate chronic cases were cured. Four of the most determined rheumatic patients, who had resisted scarifying of the limbs, and what was worst, the smallest and thinnest of diets, were sent to their regiments and did good service afterwards. With these men the socks had to be left on for several hours amidst shouts of laughter from the "assistants," showing that though men may resist pain and starvation they succumb directly to ridicule…"

THE CONFEDERATE VETERAN VOL. XXXII 1924

Pg. 469 Dec. 1924 Memories of Stonewall Jackson by John K. Hitner "He was resigned and submissive to the privations and hardships of his campaigns. Some visitors making complaints of the body pests-cooties, as familiarly called in camp-the General said: "Yes, we all have to endure them, for it is the mark or proof of a real soldier and, as someone has said, they are marked on their backs with the letters I.F.W. (in for the war), so we are just in for it!"

RICHMOND VOLUNTEERS 1861-1865 by Louis H. mandarin & Lee A. Wallace pub. by Richmond Civil War Centennial Committee Westover Press 1969

Pg. 214 15th Regiment Virginia Infantry Company B Virginia Life Guard "...The Virginia Life Guard was organized in January 1861 as a uniformed company of the line...The company's uniform, manufactured by the Crenshaw Woolen Mills of Richmond, consisted of blue flannel cloth hunting shirts with blue fringe and Virginia buttons, blue cloth caps, black pants and white gloves. In April the company numbered seventy-one and was equipped with Enfield rifles..."

I like the idea of lining the shirts with fringe.

DEAR SISTER-Civil War Letters to a Sister in Alabama by Frank Anderson Cappell pub by Brach Springs Publishing 2002

Pg. 32 Montgomery Jan.24,1861 My dear Sister, "...We have had given us blue jackets coats and slick caps. They are feeding us on sponge bread and dry ham..."

UNIFORMS OF THE CIVIL WAR by Robin Smith & Ron Field Lyons Press 2001

Pg. 228 "The Botetourt Dragoons, raised at Fincastle (Va.) during January 1861 under Captain Andrew L. Pitzer, adopted a 'blue cloth suit trimmed with yellow.'...During July 1861, the Boston Courier reported the seizure of 'a coat and cap belonging to the Old Dominion Dragoons (Co. B. 3rd Virginia Cavalry).'...They were described as follows:'The material from which they are manufactured is heavy blue satinet, far superior in quality to the material of the clothing of our troops. The coat is strongly, though not handsomely, made..."

NORFOLK BLUES-The Civil War Diary of the Norfolk Light Artillery Blues by Ken Wiley Bard St. Press 1997

Pg. 4 "...Jan. 1861-The uniform of the blues at this time differed only in slight details from that which had been adopted by the Co. when it was formed in 1829. It consisted of a dark blue wool jacket and trouser, generously trimmed with gold cord lace and adorned with 3 rows of 20 brass buttons. White crossed belts, black cartridge and cap boxes, and a tall, bell-shaped hat were reminiscent of the Napoleonic or "tin soldier" state of any uniform in use during the war with Mexico in 1846. On Jan. 12 1860 the Blues voted to update their uniform slightly by adopting a fatigue cap of the type then becoming popular. This was the French hat or "kepi" which would soon be in widespread use, The Blues adorned their version with crossed cannon barrels and #4 on the front, denoting the 4th Va. Regt.of Militia to which the Co was assigned. Each man in the company was responsible for buying his own uniform, and since many of the men had only recently enlisted, most of the uniforms at this time would have been practically new. As late as March 1861, the Blues placed an order with a clothing supplier in N.Y. for matching blue overcoats or "greatcoats"...."

THE CONFEDERATE VETERAN VOL. XXXII 1924

Pg. 420 Nov. 1924 The Edisto Rifles (S.C.) by Miss Marion Sally-"The uniform adopted was gray coat and trousers trimmed with black, and a gray cap. Each man paid for his own uniform. The company made a very handsome appearance when fully equipped and formed in line."

THE STORY OF THE CONFEDERACY Robert Selph Henry Grossett & Dunlap Pub. 1936

Pg. 27 Inauguration Day Feb. 11, 1861 "...In the middle of the morning the Columbus Guards marshed into the triangular space before the Exchange Hotel and "entertained thousands of our citizens by the display of their skill in military evolutions"- the sort of fancy drill that was then considered adequate training for the war.

Before noon, upon the firing of a signal gun, the procession formed-"red jackets, bottle-green jackets, and gray jackets formed a mingled ground, above which the brazon epaulets, gleaming swords and bristling bayonets flashed in the sunlight."

Once again, sartorial chaos

THE CORRESPONDENCE OF THOMAS READE ROOTES COBB 1860-1862 Southern History Association 1907

Pg. 80 Letter from Thomas Reade Rootes Cobb to Marion Lumpkin Cobb Feb. 18, 1861 Montgomery, Dearest Marion, (ceremonies of inauguration)"...At the head of the procession was Capt. Semme's Columbus Guards in a beautiful uniform of skyblue pants and bright red coats carrying a banner with the Georgia Coat of Arms..."

I'd like to have seen that parade

THE VIRGINIA MAGAZINE OF HISTORY AND BIOGRAPHY, Vol. 60, No. 4 Oct. 1952

PG. 600 "In the Spring of '61, when the whole South was in a fever of excitement owing to the fact that the troops were ordered out to be ready at any moment to report for duty,. It became necessary that the gray uniforms be speedily made. This would have been impracticable had not every woman and girl, now thrilling with patriotism, volunteered her services which were gladly accepted.

A large room was procured and every one who had a sewing machine cheerfully brought it forth, and those who had none rendered willing service.

A tailor in the village was engaged to cut the garments and with willing hands and devoted hearts the work was begun and steadily progressed until every volunteer was the proud possessor of a suit of gray."

THE ANSON GUARDS-Co. C 14th Regiment North Carolina Volunteers 1861-1865 by Maj. W.S.Smith Stone Pub. Co. 1914

Pg. 7 spring, 1861 "...Our old uniforms would no longer serve us, and "Little" Billy Patrick took our measure for a suit of gray, were to be made and forwarded. Our mothers and sisters had made for us uniforms of white linen pants and red flannel shirts, and each man had a heavy pair of shoes for stout service. We made a fine appearance and were ready for marching to the front...."

FOOTPRINTS OF A REGIMENT-A Recollection of the 1st Ga. Regulars 1861-1865 by W.H. Andrews First Sargeant, Co. M Longstreet Press Atlanta Ga. 1992

March 1861-Ogalthorpe Barracks, Ga. "In the way of uniforms we drew blue flannel shirts. And for bedding, a blanket for each man."

FOUR VALIANT YEARS In The Lower Shenandoah Valley 1861-1865 by Laura Virginia Hale Shen. Pub. House inc. Strasburg, Va. 1968

April 1861 a Winchester lady wrote: "I saw the students of the University of Virginia gaily marching through town." They were "in their red shirts and black trousers, utterly unprovided with such sordid things as overcoats and blankets, but full of ardor at the prospect of encountering the Yankees."

CIVIL WAR SOLDIERS Reid Mitchell Viking Peguin 1988

Pg. 65 April 1861 Oglethorp Light Infantry marching through the streets of Petersburg, Va "...indeed, we all looked like boys," one wrote his mother," with our handsome blue uniforms & smooth faces."

UNIFORMS OF THE CIVIL WAR 1861-65 BY Phillip Haythornewaite pub by Macmillan Color Series Macmillan Pub Co. Inc. 1975

Pg. 131 South Carolina-"...British war correspondent William H. Russell wrote on April 12,1861""There is an endless variety-often of ugliness- in dress and equipment and nomenclature among these companies...the tunic is of different cuts, colors, facings and materials-green with gray and yellow, gray with orange and black and white, blue with white and yellow facings, roan brown, burnt sienna and olive-jackets frocks, tunics, blouses, cloth, linen, tweed, flannel. Head-dress were generally some type of kepi, though straw and felt hats were common, while 'some men wore leather helmets, either the crested dragoon type or the Prussian spike type'. It is interesting to learn that some of these leather helmets 'probably dated back to the War of 1812 era', which does not rule out the possibility of their being of the Britsh fur-creasted 'Terleton' pattern; whilst others wore more modern 'pickelhaube' spiked helmets. 'Corsican' caps were also used, these being peaked cloth forage caps with a hanging bag and tassel at one side..."

"14th Virginia Cavalry, Co. 'H' (Rockbridge Dragoons) wore leather helmets, probably of an 1812 vintage, in the early stages of the war..."

Website THE STONEWALL BRIGADE—Stonewall Brigade-1861 Impression Guidelines by Bret Sumner, 4th Virginia http://www.stonewallbrigade.com/articles

Pg 1 Article from the Vindicator, April 26,1861 "Augusta Riflemen...Capt. Harman's company has appeared in full dress parade, presenting an attractive and truly soldierly appearance. The soldiers themselves are not only Augusta men, but the cloth from which their uniforms were made was manufactured at the Wollen Factory of Messrs. Crawford & Co. at this place. The county court made an appropriation of $3,000 to equip the company, but the actual costs will not amount to more than from $300 to $500. Such an example of economy is worthy of imitation."

Pg. 2 Memoir of John Newton Lyle First Lieutenant from Rockbridge County "The ladies of Rockbridge County...sent word that they would equip and send us forth as their special knights to do battle for their dear old Mother, Virginia....And right royally did our ladies fair prepare us for the camp and march. Each lad was provided with everything a fond mother might dream her son might need, even to a needlebook, buttons and thread, linen gaiters, a Havelock to screen his neck from the rays of the sun, and a red flannel waistband to wear next to the skin to keep off the diarrhea..."

FOUR YEARS IN REBEL CAPITOLS-An Inside view of Life in the Southern Confederacy, from birth to death from original notes collated in the years 1861-1865. by T.C. De Leon, Mobile, Al. the Gossip Printing Co. 1892

Pg. 96 Spring 1861 "Varied indeed were the forms one met on every street and road about Richmond. Here the long-haired Texan, sitting his horse like a centaur, with high-peaked saddle and jingling spurs, dashed by-a pictured "gaucho". There the western mountaineer, with bearskin shirt, fringed leggings, and the long, deadly rifle, carried one back to the days of Boone and the "dark and bloody ground". The dirty grey and tarnished silver of the muddy-complexioned Carolinian, the dingy butternut of the lank, muscular Georgian, with its green trimmings and full skirts; and the Alabamians from the coast, nearly all in blue of a cleaner hue and neater cut; while the Louisiana troops were, as a general thing, better equipped and more regularly uniformed than any others in the motley throng"

An amazingly chaotic composition of soldiers

Pg.96 "But the most remarked dress that flashed among these varied uniforms was the blue and orange of the Md. Zuoaves."

THE THIRTY-SEVENTH NORTH CAROLINA TROOPS-Tar heels in the Army of Northern Virginia by Michael C. Hardy pub. By McFarland & Co. 2003

Pg. 20 spring 1861 "…The companies had been given tents for sleeping quarters, but still wore their clothes from home and carried their hunting rifles and shotguns. When the individual companies offered their services to the state, they were accepted, provided they could arm themselves. While the men expected to receive uniforms from the state, they were oftentimes slow in arriving. Private Tugman wrote home again commenting on the lack of attire: I want you to make me a pair of pants and a shirt(.) if we could get our uniforms this winter I would not need them…"

I WILL GIVE THEM ONE MORE SHOT" RAMSEY'S 1st REGIMENT GEORGIA VOLUNTEERS by Goerge Winston Martin Mercer Univ. Press 201

Pg. 31 Camp Oglethorpe spring 1861 "…The reporter (Lennox) was amused by the dizzying array of uniforms worn by the volunteers: "(T)o a stranger or spectator just now presents an interesting scene, with the red shirts, blue shirts, gray shirts, and shirts without order and indescribable to an unpractised eye in such descriptions."

Visitors to the camps beheld a confusing hodgepodge of dress and fatigue uniforms. The Quitman Guards of Monroe County wore short gray jacket with three rows of buttons, with red epaulettes adorning their shoulders. Their headgear was trimmed in red with the letters "QG" and the Georgia coat of arms fastened on front, and adorned with a yellow plume. Their accouterments hung from white cross-belts.

Atlanta's Gate City Guardsmen were clothed in "dark blue Prince Albert coats, red breast, with three rows of brass buttons and cross bars of gold lace; light blue pants with red stripes, and dark beavers with nodding plumes of red and white." The Guards fatigue uniforms were of gray material. The Bainbridge Independents came "uniformed in coarse flannel shirts, and pantaloons of the coarsest negro cloth," while the Washington Rifles arrived garbed in green service jackets.

The uniform of the Oglethorpe Infantry was Federal blue, dark for their single-breasted frock coats and light for their trousers. Silver epaulettes festooned their shoulders. Dressed in a gray coatee adorned with three rows of buttons and black piping on their collars and sleeves, the Newnan Guards wore gray shakos topped by a red and white pompon, with the letters "NG" surrounded by a wreath, and like the color trousers highlighted with black stripes. Blue frock coats were worn by the Newnan officers, with the pompon fastened to a blue cap. Soldiers of the Southern Rights Guard sported drooping yellow plumes on their felt hats and wore dress blue frock coats trimmed with silk lace. A white stripe ran down the sides of their blue pants. The Guards fatigue uniform was a gray single-breasted frock coat with black trim…"

When I first got into re-enacting, (1988) I was told that no Southern troops had any brass numbers, letters wreaths, etc., that anything like that had to have been taken from the yankees

I WILL GIVE THEM ONE MORE SHOT" RAMSEY'S 1st REGIMENT GEORGIA VOLUNTEERS by George Winston Martin Mercer Univ. Press 201

Pg. 52 Spring 1861 Pensacola, Fl "For three months the ladies of this place have met daily and worked for the soldiers. They will do anything a soldier want-make uniforms, cap covers, shirts, drawers, mend clothing…."

A SCYTHE OF FIRE-THE CIVIL WAR STORY OF THE EIGHTH GEORGIA INFANTRY REGIMENT Warren Wilkinson & Steven E. Woodworth William Morrow Pub. 2002

Pg. 12 spring 1861 "…The next day the Light Guards marched jauntily down to the railroad station, cutting a fine figure in their tailor-made uniforms, each gray coat marked with ten horizontal black stripes across the front, and each stripe having a bright brass button at each end and in the middle. Elaborate patterns of gilt embroidery trimmed their collars and cuffs, along with still more brass buttons, and large epaulets sat on their shoulders fringed with even more gilt thread, while their gray trousers had a wide black stripe running down each outside leg seam. Topping off the outfit was a jaunty gray forage cap…"

"Loading the train took time, for the Light Guards were not traveling light. Most of the young men had a trunk or two each, in which they had packed fatigue uniforms, spare clothes, "any quantity of fine linen," and such necessities as silverware, so they could live like civilized gentlemen when they were in camp. Then, as they prepared to depart, sweethearts gave them such parting gifts as they thought would be useful to soldiers in the field: "embroidered slippers and pin-cushions and needlebooks, and all sorts of little et ceteras." They also loaded the departing young men with parcels of food to eat on the trip. Then at last the tearful goodbyes were said, and the soldiers and the young slave men who accompanied them as personal servants-one observer thought that nearly every member of the company had one-all got aboard the cars..."

A SCYTHE OF FIRE-THE CIVIL WAR STORY OF THE EIGHTH GEORGIA INFANTRY REGIMENT Warren Wilkinson & Steven E. Woodworth William Morrow Pub. 2002

Pg.14 Spring, 1861"... The Oglethorpe Light Infantry hailed from Savannah and made a striking appearance as they paraded in their long blue frock coats with fancy gilt embroidery on the collars and cuffs and buff-colored bib fronts secured by two vertical rows of nine big brass buttons each. Heavy gilt-and-fringe epaulets sat on each shoulder. Trousers were blue, trimmed with a broad buff stripe up each outer seam. Crowning the whole uniform, and making the wearer look larger than he really was, perched a tall shako topped with a plume of white feathers and sporting front and center a brass nameplate whereon a large wreath encircled the letters "OLI" in old English script. Buff-colored waist and cross belts and white gloves completed the outfit. The company was indeed a sight to behold...Stories also had it that although Bartow was captain of the blue uniformed OLI, it was he who successfully advocated gray as the standard color of Confederate military uniforms. Perhaps, but more likely Davis had the deciding say on that question..."

A SCYTHE OF FIRE-THE CIVIL WAR STORY OF THE EIGHTH GEORGIA INFANTRY REGIMENT Warren Wilkinson & Steven E. Woodworth William Morrow Pub. 2002

Pg. 19 spring 1861 Oglethorpe Light Infantry "...The Grays (Atlanta Grays) made a striking contrast to the OLI, for their uniforms were as simple as the Oglethorpe's were elaborate. They wore gray trousers and a nine-button, tight-fitting gray shell jacket with dark blue edging around the stand-up collar and three more brass buttons on each cuff. Instead of a jaunty forage cap or tall shako, the Grays wore a plain broad-brimmed slouch hat..."

UNDER BOTH FLAGS- Personal Stories of Sacrifice And Struggle During the Civil War ed by Tim Goff pub by The Lyons Press 1896

Pg. 301 The First Gun in Virginia in 1861 by William L. Sheppard spring 1861 Glouchester Point, Va. (all the article states is a battery from Richmond) after an engagement with a

Federal steamer, "It being apparent that the fight was over for the time being, we were allowed to break ranks and resume our preparations for dinner, and found, on coming somewhat to our normal selves, that we were very hungry. We were not long in discovering that whilst we had been occupied in upholding our honor at the front, we had had an enemy in the rear. Our camp had been raided by the pigs, our mess-kettles and frying pans overturned, and everything eatable within reach either consumed or spoiled. There was nobody to interfere with the pigs, as our attention was, of course, engrossed elsewhere, and every negro and non-combatant had retired to the bluff, out of sight.

I think from this incident sprang our future uncontrollable desire to kill a pig wherever we encountered him, especially if the provost-guard was not around."

THE STORY OF THE CONFEDERACY Robert Selph Henry Grossett & Dunlap Pub. 1936

Pg. 43 "but in the gay and joyous spring of 1861 all that was yet to be. There were men in the South of course, who saw just what Lieutenant McPherson foretold, but their forebodings were drowned in the rush of enthusiasm to get ready for the war. While in the North there were regimental camps, the South was dotted at first with the encampments of little companies. The courthouses, the schoolhouses, the scattered cross-roads villages became recruiting centers, Every county had its company, many more than one. There were the old social-military organizations brilliant companies with their bright and shining uniforms-tail coats, braided trousers, cross-belts, shakos and busbies and fancy head-gear, buttons of gilt, white gloves on drill and duty; there were the new organizations commanded by young lawyers and planters and merchants, with no uniforms, no guns, nothing but martial ardor. There were inumerable companies of "Grays"-not all of whom, by any means, wore gray; there were companies of "Rifles," not nearly all of whom had rifles; there were "Guards" of all sorts, and "Invinceables"; there were "Volunteers" and "Game Cocks" and "Tigers." The name of "Washington" was a great favorite for the companies, and after the affairs in Charleston Harbor, there were the "Beaugards" and "Sumpters." There were fancy names and plain names, and some fancy names that, by inspiration of the moment, became plain. Young Captain John B. Gordon-he was to become one of Lee's Lieutenant Generals-thought to call his Georgia company the "Mountain Rifles," but a mountaineer in the ranks with a coonskin cap beat him to the christening, and they were the Racoon Roughs."

SOUTH CAROLINA WOMEN IN THE CONFEDERACY vol. 1 MEMOIR OF A.S. ARNOLD

Pg.179 Spring1861"...Now the roll of the drum was heard daily. The blue cockaded "Minute Men" were organizing into companies; the women into "Soldier's Aid Societies." One day every week, for four years, these societies met to do anything they could for the soldiers. While at home they were still first in our thoughts-study of anything personal came afterwards.

We made tents, uniforms, caps, underwear, knit socks, gloves, comforters, all with our fingers, and often spun and wove the thread and cloth from which they were manufactured. Lessons were learned at night when the days work was done; or, we memorized lessons and poetry as we walked to and fro at the spinning wheel drawing out the soft thread for soldier's jeans. We conned French, Latin and English grammer as we carded the cotton into heavy rolls; read Shakespeare, Scott and other standard authors while we plaited palmetto to fashion into hats. Even as we walked in the gloaming, the busy needles clocked, knitting for the soldiers, and those who stayed at home were also in active service for our country.

My mother was the Treasurer and Secretary of our Aid Society; therefore, our home was the depot for the supplies sent through that channel. As the war continued, we scraped lint, rolled bandages, scoured the country for old, soft cloth, packed boxes of vegetables and dainties for the hospital service, and collected for the comfort of the wounded whatever we could find...."

THE LIBERTY HALL VOLUNTEERS-Stonewall's College Boys W.G. Bean Univ. Press of Va. 1964

Pg. 10 Spring 1861 "To supply the needs of the volunteers, the ladies of the county formed a sewing society, using one of the public halls of the town (Lexington, Va.) as a workshop Soon linen gaiters to cover the ankles and havelocks to protect the necks were hurriedly turned out; for making blouses and pants, gray cloth was secured from a woolen factory on Whistle Creek, west of Lexington (Va). Muskets and caps on which the initials of the company "L.H.V.," were emblazoned in brass letters were secured from V.M.I. Each member of the company was furnished a needle book, thread, and buttons. Reminising thirty years later, John Newton Lyle, one of the volunteers, wrote:

Thus tricked out in his white waist belt and cross belts fastened with a big brass buckle, his ankles and calves gleaming in white gaiters and his head adorned with a snowy havelock, (each volunteer) was a nobby soldier calculated to smash a maiden's heart..."

"Those were good times we were having in old Lexington, with no studies and plenty of leisure from military duties to gallant the girls. The only thing to mar the pleasure was the fear the war would soon be over and the boys who had gone ahead would be soon returning before we got off."

Pg. 14 Down the Valley Turnpike, en route to Manassas "...On another occasion, the company passed a militia company drilling near the turnpike. The college boys teased the militia captain unmercifully for his gorgeous uniform and his cocked hat with a gold band and a star, calling upon him "to come out of that hat"..."

FROM BULL RUN TO APPOMATTOX-A Boys View by L.W. Hopkins of Gen. J.E.B. Stuarts Cav. 6th Va. Regt. C.S.A. Flat-McGinley Co. Balt. Md. 1908

Pg. 23 "...(spring 1861) Now let us take a peep into the Virginia homes. What were the women doing? Ah, they were as busy as bees. These boys must be equipped not only with munitions of war, but each boy must take with him as many home comforts as could possibly be compressed into a bundle small enough to be carried. When he was at home, it took a good- sized room to holds these things; now he must put them into his pocket or on his back, and it took all of a mother's skill to gather these things up in to the least possible space, that her boy might have in the camp life all that a mother's love could give him. The Government would furnish the guns, the powder, the lead, the can teen and knapsack and haversack; the tinshop, the tincup; the shoemaker, the boots; the bookstore, the Bible (every boy must carry a Bible), but all the clothing, all the little necessary articles for comfort and health, must be manufactured in the home. Did you ever open the outside casing of one of these large patent beehives and see the bees at work inside? What rushing and pushing and confusion! Every bee, so far as human eye can see, seems busy. This beehive was but a replica of a Virginia home in the spring of 1861..."

Good analogy

U.S. ARMY HERITAGE & EDUCATION CENTER B. Coffman Letters, Co. H 33rd Virginia Infantry Regiment

Spring 1861 "Since my arrival here we have had 6 Generals-17 Colonels-15 Sr, Cols. And 18 Majors sent us from Tenn.-It was a very interesting sight to see them and even now they are the subjects of much witticisms and laughter-dressed in their snuff colored jeans with stars in number according to rank...Many of them were without good money and many of them had not changed their linen for three weeks..."

HANDLEY LIBRARY ARCHIVES-Hugh O. Pierce Papers Co F. 51st Virginia Militia

Pg. 8 spring 1861 Winchester, Va. "Some were in favor of choosing a uniform but others opposed it. Whereupon a fiery young fellow exclaimed, "If we don't have uniform I'll resign!" He had not been elected an officer, had no commission and consequently had nothing to resign. The Opequon Company was never organized; those determined to fight had to join the "Boomerangs."

THE CONFEDERATE REGULAR ARMY by Richard P. Weinert, Jr. pub by White Mane Pub Co 1991

Pg. 18 Spring, 1861 "Clothing presented a problem in the early days. Uniforms were not available despite the fact that they were minutely described in Army Regulations. A temporary uniform was devised and each regular recruit arriving at a depot was to receive a forage cap, a blue shirt as a blouse or sack coat, gray overalls and the necessary underclothing. Despite the fact that recruits began to gather in March 1861, even this makeshift clothing issue does not appear to be available until the end of April. Since many of the men were literally swept off the streets, it was often necessary for the recruiting officers to spend money not only for their food and transportation, but also for enough clothing to get them to the depots..."

First mention of overalls. I'd like to see or to at least get a description of these "gray overalls." The description of period overalls that I have is that they were oversized pants, designed to go over the regular pants.

FIRST & SECOND MD. INF. C.S.A. Robert J. Driver Jr. Willow Bend Books 2003

Pg.7 Spring 1861 "...Only Co.A was armed, and they had Hall's carbines, a weapon already discarded by the Federal army. One account states that the Marylanders were unarmed. However, Booth recorded that "the arms issued us were the old flint-lock musket type, which had been altered to percussion. Not a cartridge box was in the command, and taken altogether, we presented a sorry sight compared with troops of other states." The men were without uniform and equipment and stood in their "boots." They were also without tents, camp equipage, axes, hatchets, skillets and camp kettles. They could draw rations but did not know how to cook them."...

A VIRGINIA SCENE or Life in Old Prince William Alice Maude Ewell pub. by J.P. Bell Co. Inc. 1931

Pg. 55 spring 1861 "...About this time the ladies of our neighborhood began to be very busy making uniforms for our soldiers. With my sister-in-law, Mrs. Alice Ewell, I went to "Evergreen" the home of Colonel Edmund Berkeley, to assist in this work. We found Mrs. Berkeley, Mrs. Josiah Carter, and others engaged in cutting out the gray flannel fatigue shirts, which, trimmed with green, formed the first uniform of the "Evergreen Guards," the company of then Captain Berkeley, afterwards Colonel of the Eighth Virginia Regiment..."

THE CONFEDERATE VETERAN VOL.XI 1903

Pg. 351 August 1903 Gay to Grave in the Army of Northern Virginia "Then began the assemblying of that Southern manhood and boyhood who were to go "sounding down the ages" as the Confederate army. Among the first to enroll themselves under its banner were the Valley Rangers, a volunteer cavalry company composed of the very best of the young men living along the eastern side of Augusta County, (Va.), who, under their first captain, the brave Patrick, (who later as major of the Seventeenth Battalion was to die gloriously on the plains of Second Manassas), met in historic Waynsboro to go to the front. It was then the comedy parts in the great opening drama commenced. How excercised we were about our uniforms, how we had to send off for the material, and get just the right shade of color, and the exact buttons, braid, etc.! How we watched the making of them and how impatient we got; and, at length when finished and donned, how we did strut, and how gorgeous we were with our wide yellow (the cavalry color) striped trousers and braided coats and bright brass buttons (a gross of them, more or less); and our hats, great with wide-brimmed slouches, with plume and gilt cord and tassel; and what a sight was the little fellow in his over-large clothes!

THE CONFEDERATE VETERAN VOL XXXVI

Nov. 1928 Pg. 425 With The Louisiana Zouaves by J.W.Minnich "De Gourney's Battalion was organized in New Orleans in March,1861, as the fifth company of Copen's Battalion of Louisiana Zouaves, copied after the French "Zouaves d' Afrique," and were quite objects of interest and curiosity wherever we went or were seen during those early days. Only a year or so before Ellworth's Zouaves had created a furore throughout the country in their parade from Chicago to New York and Boston-if not mistaken. Copens determined to go Ellsworth one better by organizing a battalion on strictly French lines, a French corps in every detail. The official language was French, uniforms and all accouterments, from gaiters to skull caps with blue tassels and shaven forelock, and very baggy trousers, veritable "Red, white and blues," but the white was not conspicuous, only showing on the gaiters. Black shoes and leather leggings-yes, we were a sight and a wonder all along the route from Penscacola to Richmond and Yorktown…"

THE CONFEDERATE VETERAN VOL. XVII 1909

Pg. 24 Jan. 1909 The Washington Artillery Of Augusta, Ga. By W.A. Pickering "…April, 1861, we were ordered to Pensacola, Fla…Our officers believed in making a fine appearance. We went in with a fine dress uniform; but as it was of dark and light blue, it had to be changed to gray…"

Another mention of a dress uniform

A Confederate Chroncle-The life of a Civil War Survivor by Pamela Chas Hain Univ. of Missouri Press 2005

Pg. 20 April, 1861 The Ogelthorpe Light Infantry (Georgia) "Dressed their smart, new, blue-black uniforms, they were greeted as heroes along the three-day trip from Savannah, through Charleston, to Richmond: The Oglethorpe Light Infantry…made a striking appearance as they paraded in their long blue frock coats with fancy gilt embroidery on the collar and cuffs and buff-colored bib fronts secured by two vertical rows of nine big brass buttons each. Heavy gilt-and-fringe epaulets sat on each shoulder. Trousers were blue, trimmed with a broad buff stripe, up each outer seam. Crowning the whole uniform, and making the wearer look larger than he really was, perched a shako topped with a plume of white feathers and sporting front-and-center a brass nameplate whereon a large wreath encircled the letters "OLI" in old Englsh script. Buff-colored waist and cross belts and white gloes completed the outfit. The company was indeed a sight to behold….In early July, Thomas Wragg complained to his father that his "clothes are all worn out," and, in another short note, that they had received new uniforms."

THE CONFEDERATE VETERAN VOL. XXII 1914

Pg. 399 Sept. 1914 The Sons Of Liberty by Frank S. Robertson "In April, 1861, the above-named company, formed of students then attending the University of Virginia…Uniforms were ordered from Baltimore. The Sons of Liberty (named by Professor Holcombe) wore red shirts, trimmed with black velvet and well bespangled with brass buttons, black doeskin trousers, dark blue caps, and white cross belts with huge brass buckles. The other company, the Southern Guard, was distinguished by blue shirts and light-blue caps."

PRIVATE SOLDIERS AND PUBLIC HEROES ed. By Milton Bagby Ruledge Hill Press 1998April 1861

James Madison Conway first went off to war-"He wore a brass-buttoned grey frock coat trimmed in blue and black, a feathered hat, and leather guantelets."

THE CONFEDERATE VETERAN VOLXL

Sept. 1932 Pg. 256 University of Virginia Companies by Capt. John M. Payne April 1861 "…The Southern Guards wore black pants and a light blue shirt, while the Sons of Liberty had red shirts. The Governor let us have muskets, and we soon made a handsome appearance on the lawn of the University as accurately drilled companies…"

PRESONAL REMINISCENCES OF THE WAR OF 1861-5 W.H. Morgan J.P. Bell co. Inc. 1911

Pg. 34 April 1861 "...they made canteens, home-made haversacks of cotton cloth or cheap oilcloth, home-made knapsacks of poor material and very cumbersome, the latter packed full of clothes, hair-brushes and shoe-brushes, needle-cases, and many other little tricks which mothers, wives and sweethearts made for their soldier boys. Many of these things were superfluous and were not carried after the first year of the war; for the next three years about all a Confederate soldier carried was his gun, cartridge and cap box, a blanket, an oilcloth captured from the Yankees, and an extra shirt-very often not the latter.

Many a Confederate soldier has taken off his shirt, washed it, hung it on a bush, lying in the shade until it was dry. He also carried a haversack which was often empty..."

THE BLUE AND THE GRAY-Vol.1 by Henry Steele Commager the Bobb-Merrill Co. Inc. N.Y. 1950

Pg 62-63 April 1861"Then we began preparing our soldiers for the war. The ladies were all summoned to public places, to halls and lecture rooms, and sometimes to churches, and everybody who had sewing machines was invited to send them; they were never demanded because the mere suggestion was all-sufficient. The sewing machines were sent to these places and ladies that were known to be experts in cutting out garments were engaged in that part of the work, and every lady in town was turned into a seamstress and worked as hard as anybody could work; and the ladies not only worked themselves but they brought colored seamstresses to these places, and these halls and public places would be just filled with busy women all day long...."

"The young men carried dress suits with them and any quantity of fine linen...

Every soldier, nearly, had a servant with him, and a whole lot of spoons and forks, so as to live comfortably and elegantly in camp, and finally to make a splurge in Washington when they should arrive there, which they expected would be very soon indeed. That is really the way they went off; and their sweethearts gave them embroidered and pin-cushions and needle-books, and all sorts of little et ceteras..."

"DEAR MARTHA..." The Confederate War Letters Of A South Carolina Soldier Alexander Faulkner Fewell compiled and edited by Robert Harley Mackintosh, Jr. The R.L. Bryan Co. 197617th South Caroline Inf. Company E

Pg. 4 "In Columbia and Charleston, material was purchased for uniforms for the company and soon they were completed. They were gray jackets and black pants with blue stripes on the outside seam of the pants. When they wore out, wives or mothers at home made any necessary clothes for the soldiers."

Here's the first mention of resupply from the home folks vs. the government.

HISTORY OF CARPENTER'S BATTERY OF THE STONEWALL BRIGADE 1861-1865 C.A. Fonerden Henkel & Co. Printers 1911 April 1861

Pg. 6 "Upon assembling of a few thousand half armed, and less uniformed boy soldiers at Harper's ferry, the 1st Virginia Brigade was formed, consisting of the 2nd, 4th, 5th, 27th, and 33rd Virginia regiments, having for its first commander Colonel Thomas J. Jackson, subsequently the renowned "Stonewall Jackson."

A CAROLINIAN GOES TO WAR-The Civil War narrative of Arthur Middleton Manigault Brig. General C.S.A. Univ. S.C. Press 1983 10th S.C. Volunteers

Pg. 6 April 1861"...Capt. Plowden C.J. Weston, who had joined the Georgetown Rifle Guards as a private, typified those patriotic and wealthy Southern planters who willingly sacrificed everthing for the cause of their state and the Southern Confederacy. From his own purse, he provided company A of the 10th with 155 English Enfield rifles, accouterments and knapsacks, and material for both summer and winter uniforms. As a crowning touch, he "had uniformed and attached to his company a pioneer corps composed of four of his most able-bodied and trusted servants, by name: Flanders, Ceaser, Cooper, and Cudjoe, who, armed with picks, axes and spade, moved in advance of the company when on the march to clear its path of obstructions..."

FOUR YEARS ON THE FIRING LINE by James Cooper Nisbet-Captain Company C, 21st Georgia Regiment McCoat-Mercer Press 1963

Pg. 9 April 1861"...The uniforms of grey, made to order, had been shipped by E. Winship, Macon, Georgia, for which I paid. The bowie knives, scabbards and belts had been finished in Col. Ben Easley's shops at his expense and presented to the company..."

Pg 11 "...,Each man was armed with the aforesaid bowie knives, worn in leather scabbards. The men, uniformed in grey, presented a good appearance. The lieutenants were uniformed in homemade blue jeans. My uniform was of regular United States Army blue, tailor-made, a present (with my sword and belt) from my sister, Mrs. George H. Hazelhurst, of Macon Georgia, who was spending that summer on Lookout Mountain..."

Pg. 17 (writing about their "drill" sergeant) "He was a big, fine looking fellow from Louisville, Kentucky, on to his job, and a strict disciplinarian.

My country boys held him in great awe. Afterwards, when they had become veterans of many campaigns and heroes of a hundred fightsI heard them say that never at any time did they feet half as scared of the "Yanks" as they were of that redoubtable sergeant who would slap a raw recruit on the stomach with his sword, did the raw recruit stick out that member instead of his chest, at the commant: "Right dress! Assume the position of a soldier!"

He stuck hay and straw in the mouths of their brogans, that they might not mistake the right foot for the left, in marking time. Instead of ordering: "Mark time! Right Left Hep, hep!" he'd say: "mark time! Hay-foot!, straw-foot!" Hep, hep, ketch the step!" and woe to the poor fellow who lost it and kicked a front rank man in the shins. And oh, the fierceness of his eye when he cought a man in the ranks slyly scratching and knocking mosquitoes off his nose. It is almost impossible to give a fine military deportment to a company of country plow boys. Their work fixes their carriage; their muscles "gang their ain gait"; they have yokel postures. But they submit to discipline, learn to drill, and, in fact, make the best soldiers on the march and in the fight."

I WROTE YOU WORD- The Poignant Letters of Private Holt-John Lee Holt 1829-1863 ed by James A. Mumper printed by H.E. Howard, 1991

Pg.31 April1861 trip through Columbia, S.C. "...the ladies presented us with a great many Rosettes made of Palmetto... The Rosettes are to be worn on the hat or cap as an ornament of uniform..."

Same letter "...After I had commenced my letter yesterday we received a box containing our clothes I got my 2 pair drawers & a pair of gaiters & like them first rate The gaiters are the very things I wanted & thank you with all my heart for them I should have written you word to have made me some But I knew you had so much to do that I thought of buying them if I really needed them But I am truly glad you made them as they are much better ones than I could have bought without paying a very extravagant price for them & the drawers are also all that I could wish them to be & Oh how it makes my heart swell with emotion to think I have someone at home that is looking so much after my comfort and happiness..."

The choice of gaiters also seems a personal one.

Under Both Flags-Personal Stories of Sacrifice and Struggle During the Civil War ed by Tim Goff pub by Lyons Press 1896

Pg 359 April 1861 How North Carolina Went Into the War by Col. H.C. Graham The Warren County (NC) Guards at their first camp of instruction at Raleigh, N.C. "When this company arrived at Raleigh and came into camp (which was commanded by D.H. Hill, brother-in-law of Stonewall Jackson and afterward one of the ablest lieutenant-generals in the Confederate army), it came with a train of wagons which would have sufficed, a few years later on, to transport the baggage of Stonewall Jackson's corps, and the quality of the baggage was remarkable. There were banjoes, guitars, violins, huge camp chests, bedsteads, and other material startling in amount and unique as to quality, while the soldiers, a number of them large-landed proprieters, were uniformed in a style of magnificence, as to gold lace, plumes, and epaulletes, that would have required the genius of Sir Walter Scott to describe with proper effect. There was something really pathetic in the nonchalance and naivete exhibited by these Warren cavaliers, who could see no incongruity between camp life and the luxuries of home…These same fine Warren County soldiers soon learned the sad realities of war and nobily performed their duty. The handsome gold-laced uniforms were soon exchanged for the regulation gray blouse…"

VIRGINIANS AT WAR-The Civil War experiences of Seven young Confederates by John G. Shelby A Scholarly Resource Inc. In print Wil. Del. 2002

April 1861 Richmond Militia "…F Company was known as much for its uniform as its personnel. Members were required to purchase a gray frock coat, gray pants with black stripes along the outer seam, a gray cap "trimmed with black braid," a black cloth overcoat, white gloves, and buttons made of "Virginia fire-gilt." (Much of this uniform became the standard for the Confederate outfits) Gear was carried in expensive knapsacks, "imported from Paris, made of calfskin tanned with hair on, the color being red and white."

THE CONFEDERATE VETERAN VOL.1

May, 1893 Mortally Wounded-"Among the thrilling incidents, hair-breath escapes and deeds of valor that have been published, I have never seen where any old vet has acknowledged how bad he was scared "durin" the war, so I come to the front and tell my truthful story. How ignorant we were in the beginning about war! I fully believed I could whip five Yanks before breakfast and was afraid the war would be over before I could try my hand. Whole regiments were armed with long shop-made knives and old "pepper box" pistols, expecting a hand-to-hand fight…."

As an enthusiastic scholar of pepperbox firearms, I'd have loved to have followed this regiment during their first few days march. I can imagine that these heavy pistols were soon discarded along the way, what a wonderful chance for a collector! Mayber I'd need a cart.

A REBEL OF '61 by Jos. R. Stonebraker Wynkoop, Hallenbeck, Crawford Co., Printers 1899

Pg.91 April 1861 "…a Mrs. Webb, just south of the Court House (in Powhatan Co.). She and several daughters were busily engaged making plaids for dress goods, hats from corn husks, and window shades from dried grass….They made buttons from Persimmon seeds. When on the children's clothes they were more durable than pearl or porcelain. Shoe blacking from China berries. Home-made dyes from bark of trees- sassafras produced a yellow, laurel a drab, willow produced slate color in cotton and blue black in wool and linen; red oak a chocolate brown, white oak a lead color.

Clothed in their home-made "Butternut," a brigade of Confederate soldiers possessed all the above colors, multiplied by the different shades, presenting a queer sight to one not accustomed to their presence...."

Absolutely ingenious use of what's available.

A REBEL WAR CLERK'S DIARY AT THE CONFEDERATE CAPITOL John Beauchamp Jones Lippincott & Co. 1866

Pg. 392 April 1861 "...The ladies are postponing all engagements until their lovers have fought the Yankees. Their influence is great. Day after day they go to the Fairgounds where the 1st S.C. Vols. are encamped, showering them with their smiles, and all the delecacies the city affords. They wine them and cake them...and they deserve it. They are just from taking Fort Sumpter, and have won heroic distinction. I was introduced to several of the privates by their captain, who told me they were worth from $100,000 to half a million dollars each. The Tribune thought all these men would want to be captains! But that is not the only hallucination that the North labors under, judging from present appearances; by closing our ports it is thought that we can be subdued by the want of accustomed luxuries. These rich young men were dressed in coarse grey homespun! We have the best horsemen and the best marksmen in the world, and these are the qualities that will tell before the end of the war..."

SOUTH GEORGIA REBELS 26th Regiment Georgia Volunteer Infantry Lawton-Gordon-Evans Brigade by Alton J. Murray &pub. 1976

Pg 6 April 1861 "...Before the last companies were called up to form what later became the 26th Georgia, the men were told that they must furnish their own hunting rifles or double-barreled shotguns, or they would not be called...In the beginning, the uniforms were supplied by the soldiers themselves and these were not critical items until later. Shoes, hats, and other items of clothing were mostly brought from home and had not yet been worn out or lost..."

To Gettysburg "...The first little branch that we came to every man was trying to walk the foot-logs, when General Gordon jumped off his horse and waded the branch back and forth, to show the boys how to wade." (Note: the "boys" were probably trying to keep from ruining new shoes.)

The Lower Shenandoah Valley in the Civil War-The Impact of War on the Civilian Population and Upon Civil Institutions by Edward H. Phillips The Civil War Battles and Leaders Series 1993

Pg. 25 April 1861 "While the militia was dying, an army was slowly coming into being. It was no easy thing to mold inept militiamen and individualistic civilians into a fighting force. The carnival atmosphere at the camps, which remained more camps of assemblage than training centers, did not die easily with the appearance of the professionals, Colonel Jackson and Brigadier General Joseph E. Johnson. Harper's Ferry, Winchester, and Camp Lee, located at an important Potomac crossing, were as noteworthy for their very active social life as for military activity. Processions of ladies and gentlemen visited camp to see friends and relatives and to view the panoply of war. Parades were frequent and resplendent, for the brilliant militia uniforms still predominated. A flood of luxuries-baskets of choice food and wines-poured in from the neighborhood and from as far away as Alabama. Gentlemen privates who could afford it took for granted that they should have their servants. Personal baggage accumulated without thought of what could be carried or transported when the army should move. The folks at home busied themselves producing haversacks and knapsacks, havelocks, tents, and a host of other things considered indispensable to the well equipped soldier. Contributing to the unreality was the persistent talk of peace, a widespread expectation, which persisted into June, that there would really be no war, that the north would come to its senses, and reach an accommodation with the South."

Liberty Hall Volunteers-Stonewall Jackson's Boys by W.G. Bean The un iv. Press of Va. Charlottesville 1964

April 1861 "Finally the company was formed in in early April under the captaincy of Professor Alexander L. Nelson. It took the name "Liberty Hall Volunteers" from a similar organization which had been formed at the Liberty Hall Academy, one of Washington College's antecedents, during the American Revolution and which had marched under William Graham, rector of the institution, to Rockfish Gap to repel a threatened invasion by the British general Banastrew Tarleton. For several weeks after the beginning of the war on April 17, the company "played military." But in early June, when the faculty declared the session at an end and awarded degrees to the seniors, the campus was turned into a military camp, the drilling took on serious intent, and recruits who had no connection to the Washington College were accepted. The West Point-trained rector of Grace Episcopal Church in Lexington, William Nelson Pendleton, drilled the company until he assumed command of the Rockbridge Artillery. Then Cadet W.H. Morgan of V.M.I. took over and soon had the company in a high state of proficiency.

A MEMOIR OF CAPTAIN C. SETON FLEMING of the Second Florida Infantry C.S.A. by Francis P. Fleming pub by Times-Union Pub House 1881

April 1861 St. Augustine, Fl. "…The writer cannot pass this period without a grateful tribute to the ladies of St. Augustine. They were untiring in their offices of kindness; and with their own fair hands made up a complete uniform for the company, of the hunting-shirt pattern, the material of which was provided by the generous bounty of Captain Starke…"

FROM THE FLAME OF BATTLE TO THE FIERY CROSS-The Third Tennessee Infantry by James Van Eldik pub by Yucca Tree press 2001

Pg. 33 April 1861 "It would be doing violence to the feelings of a gallant company of soldiers not to make especial mention of the noble part taken by the ladies of Mount Pleasant in providing a neat and comfortable outfit of clothing,etc.

The citizens, the ladies taking the most active part, neatly uniformed the company and furnished it with good, substantial tents…Among the older citizens too [were those] who were conspicuous for their liberality in donating means to uniform and equip the company, and provide for the support of such as would leave their families in a destitute condition."

WITH STONEWALL JACKSON IN THE ARMY OF NORTHERN VIRGINIA by James Power Smith, captain & ADC an artillery corporal and the general's aid Va. Historical Society 1882

Pg.6 April 1861 "And one morning from the good home, with the tears and blessings of loving friends, a young student went out in a new uniform of Confederate grey, with red artillery cords. A new white haversack hung at his side filled with things our housekeeper knew well how to prepare. In one inside pocket was a Testament and in another a toothbrush. What more did a Confederate soldier ever want?"

Gives me goosepimples to read this, can you imagine, he was probably only seventeen, leaving for a different world.

A REBEL'S RECOLLECTION by George Cary Eggleston, Indiana Univ. Press Bloomington, 1959

Pg. 65 April 1861 "All the men wore epaulets of a gorgeousness rarely equaled except in portraits of field marshals and every man was a hero in immediate prospect."

I wonder how long those epaulettes lasted

HISTORY OF THE 9TH VA. CAV. IN THE WAR BETWEEN THE STATES by R.L.T. Beale rich. 1899

April 1861 "Sixty-five men in Westmoreland Co., Va. Banded together into a mounted troop they called "Lee's Light Horse." As they embarked for the camps of instruction, one of their number confessed, "there was nothing very martial in the appearance of the company. The officers and men were clad in the citizen's dress, and their horses caparisoned with saddles and bridles of every description used in the country. Their only arms were sabres and double-barreled shotguns collected from the homes of the people."

ONE OF JACKSON'S FOOT CAVALRY by John H. Worsham Collector's Library of the Civil War 1982 from 1912 edition

Pg. 53? April 1861 F Company of Richmond 1861 "This company had a fine cadet gray uniform, consisting of a frock coat, which had a row of Virginia fire-gilt buttons on its front; around the cuff of the sleeve, a band of gold braid, and two small fire-gilt buttons; on the collar the same gold braid so arranged that it looked very much like the mark of rank for a first lieutenant which was afterward adopted by the Confederacy. The pants had a black stripe about one and a quarter inches wide along the outer seams. The cap was made of the same cadet grey cloth, trimmed with black braid and two small fire-gilt buttons, and on its front the letter F. The non-commissioned officers had their mark of rank worked on the sleeves of their coats with black braid. The difference between the uniforms of the officers and the privates was in these particulars: the officer's coats were a little longer and their sleeves were highly ornamented with gold braid, something like that of the Confederate uniform; they had gold braid down the seams of their pants, and their caps were trimmed with gold braid. Each sergeant carried, besides his gun, a sword attached to his belt. When on duty every man was required to wear white gloves. He carried in his knapsack a jacket made of cadet grey cloth. He had black cloth overcoats, the skirt reaching a little below the knee, the capes a little below the elbows and the buttons were of Virginia fire-gilt.

Our knapsacks were a speciality, they were imported from Paris, made of calfskin with the hair on, the color being red and white, the skin was fitted around a box frame. Inside, they were divided into partitions; and outside, there were openings into some of these so that one could handle articles inside of them without opening the whole knapsack, and there were straps on the outside for blanket, overcoat, oilcloth, and shoes, and other straps and some hooks handy for attaching any article we wished to carry. We also imported our canteens"

Every man was required to wear gloves when on duty? I wonder how long this absolute splendor of F Company lasted.

RECOLLECTIONS-Postwar Reminiscences of Richmond Margeret Loughborough, Margaret 1861

April 1861 "…Tailors were crowded with work. Ladies would go to the tailors, get clothing that was cut out and make it for the soldiers. I made one suit (for one special soldier) beautifully, only I put button holes on the right side as I had always done for ladies. This soldier said it made no difference as in buttoning his coat on the right side he would always think of the maker; in later and more truthful days I found he always did think of the maker, but not always in a Christian manner…"

I have owned a jacket with buttons placed as described in this quote. It is more of a pain than you might imagine.

THE GUILFORD GRAYS Co. B 27th North Carolina Regiment by John A. Sloan R.O. Polkinhorn Printer 1883

Pg. 5 "…Early in April (1861) we received our arms, consisting of fifty stand of old flint-and-steel, smooth-bore muskets., a species of ordinance very effective at the breech. They were supposed to have descended from 1776, and to have been wrested by order of the Governor from the worms and rust of the Arsenal at Fayetteville. By the first of May we had received our handsome gray uniforms from Philadelphia. These uniforms, which we so gaily donned and proudly wore, consisted of a frock coat, single breasted, with two rows of state buttons, pants to match, with black stripe, waist belt of black leather, cross belt of white webbing, gray cap with pompon…"

WEBSITE: LOUISIANA IN THE CIVIL WAR: Grand Review of Troops

Pg. 3 April 29, 1861 The Daily Picayune,New Orleans, La. "…The Bienville Guards [Co. C, 5th La.], Bienville Rifle Co. [Co. B, 8th La.], and a splendid looking body of men from Algiers (whose title we did not learn) Appeared in citizen's dress their uniforms being not ready though they had their kepis and guns and they were none the less admireable for want of their uniforms. But for the want of their uniforms numerous other new companies would have been out to swell the already large splendid display."

WEBSITE-richmond.edu

Richmond Daily Dispatch:April 15, 1861
Ordinance Department
State of Virginia

"Commanding officers of foot and mounted troops, who have procured arms from elsewhere than the armory at Richmond, will please send to this Department the size of their bullets, in order that ammunition may be prepared for them when needed. It would be best to send one or two bullets, a cap or two, the size of the cone, and the name of the maker of the piece. Charles Dimmock." *What a logistical n ightmare!*

Richmond Daily Dispatch April 18, 1861 Armory R.L.I. Blues Richmond, April 17, 1861

"The Committee appointed to purchase the blue uniform from the members of the Company,will be at the Armory of the corps on Thursday Evening, 18th inst. from 8 o'clock to 10 o'c;lock to purchase the same. The members will attend promptly with the uniform. The Committee on Uniforms requests that all members of the Company will obtain the new uniform forthwith of Mr. Wm. Ira Smith, undress shirts of Kent, Paine & Co., and the caps of Hasse & Co., on 9th street. There must be no delay in this matter."

Richmond daily Dispatch April 18, 1861 Hdqs. Co. "a" 33rd Regt. April 18th, 1861

"Meet at your Drill Room this Evening, to have your measures taken for your pants, and also to receive your pants tonight. Sergeants, summon your squads."

Richmond Daily Dispatch April 18th, 1861 The 179th Regiment of Virginia Militia."...They are now number about 70 men, 55 of whom are already uniformed. On Tuesday evening last they assembled at their armory in full uniform, and were inspected by Col. J.H. Richardson, assisted by the staff of his regiment, preparatory to issueing arms and accouterments. The corps deserved to be well-sustained, as they were the first to introduce the feature of a cheap but comfortable uniform for the ordinary militia companies of the city...."

Richmond Daily Dispatch April 20, 1861 Headq's 33rd Regiment

"...Each volunteer will immediately provide himself with 1 knapsack, 1 canteen, at least 1 heavy single blanket, and a change of clothing. Woolen undergarments are strongly recommended..."

Richmond Daily Dispatch April 20, 1861 Haedquarters, Va. Life Guard, oreder No. 2

"The command will assemble at the headquarters of the 179th Regiment, (Bosher's Hall) on this (Saturday) morning at 9 o'clock, in full uniform-shirt, cap, black pants, and white gloves-to draw arms and accouterments."

Richmond Daily Dispatch April 22, 1861 [regimental orders] Headqr's 19th reg't. Va. Militia Order No. 2

"The officers and men of the 19th Regiment will, when ordered out, assemble on Franklin street, between 4th and 5th, armed with Guns, Pistols, Swords or any weapon they can secure."

I'd have loved to have seen this assembly

Richmond Daily Dispatch April 25, 1861 From the Valley of Virginia
Harrisonburg, Va. April 19, 1861

"Today, previous to the departure of one of our cavalry companies, the Union Cavalry, by a unanimous vote, of the company, struck off the "U" which stood for Union, and went with only a "C" on their caps. It is now the Se-(C)-session Cavalry. Strong disposition exists hereabouts to strike the "U" out of the dictionary, as we are nor for the Union, nor unwilling to fight those who are." *That's the spirit!!*

Richmond Daily Dispatch April 25, 1861 Troops from the Southwest

"Three more companies are expected to-day, viz: One from Pulaski, one from Montgomery, and one from Grayson. The corps from the last named county are said to be perfect nondescrips-they call themselves "Dare Devils" and deep in leggings, moccasins, and other back-woods appliances. There is not a man in the company who is not over six feet in height. Such men are valuable indeed."

Richmond daily Dispatch April 27, 1861 Albemarle County
The Chalottesville Review, of yesterday, has the following:

When our friend, Lieut. Cochran, of the Albermarle Rifles, was starting to Harper's Ferry, he suggested to Tarlton, a family servant, who was going with him, that he would want "a suit of clothes." Tarlton, we understand, protested against it, remarking that "he would kill a Yankee and strip him, if his clothes were fit for a gentleman to wear."

MY DIARY NORTH AND SOUTH by William Howard Russell pub by Alfred A. Knopf 1988

Pg. 79 April 16, 1861 "The Carolinians are capable of turning out a fair force of cavalry. At each stopping place I observed saddle horses tethered under the trees and light driving vehicles drawn by wiry muscular animals, not remarkable for size but strong lokking and active. Some farmers in blue jackets, and yellow braid and facings, handed round their swords to be admired by the company. A few blades had flashed in obscure Mexican skirmishes-one, however, had been bourne against "the Britishers."

Pg. 83 April 17, 1861 Chareston, S.C. "After breakfast I went down to the quay, with a party of the General's staff to visit Fort Sumpter. The senators and governors turned soldiers wore blue military caps, with "palmetto" trees embroidered theron; blue frockcoats with upright collars, and shoulder straps edged with lace and marked with two silver bars to designate their rank of captain; gilt buttons with the palmetto in relief; blue trousers with gold lace cord, and brass spurs-no straps…"

Pg. 85 April 17, 1861 Morris Island S.C. "…The sandbag batteries and an ugly black parapet, with guns peering through portholes as if from a ship's side, lay before us. Around them men were swarming like ants, and a crowd in uniform were gathered on the beach to receive us as we landed from the boat of the steamer, all eager for news, and provisions, and newspapers of which an immense flight immediately fell upon them. A guard with bayonets crossed in a very odd sort of manner, prevented any unauthorized person from landing. They wore the universal coarse gray jacket and trousers with worsted braid and yellow facings, uncouth caps, lead buttons stamped with the palmetto tree. Their unbronzed firelocks were covered with rust…"

I can imagine the guns rusting if not scrubbed daily due to the salt air.

THE CONFEDERATE VETERAN VOL. XV 1907

Pg. 353 August 1907 History Of The Prince William Cavalry by Mrs. M.R. Barlow "The cavalry was ordered into service on April 17, 1861, and was a fine and soldierly-looking lot of men, numbering some sixty to seventy members. It was uniformed with gray cloth made at Kelly's Mills, in Culpeper County. The uniform consisted of a frock coat with one row of buttons up the front and one on each side, connecting at the top with a gold lace V. Pants with yellow stripes, black hats with black plumes on the left side held up with crossed sabers, and a shield with the letters "P.W.C." in front-a plain but neat uniform in which the most insignificant must look his best; and as that trotted off by fours with the fine-looking genial captain and his kinsmen at their head, there was none but admiring eye and but few dry ones in the old town which had known and loved most of them from childhood to manhood."

STONEWALL IN THEVALLEY by Robert G. Tanner pub by Doubleday & Co. Inc. 1961

Pg. 31 April 18, 1861 Harper's ferry Va. "The Yankees, after all, were to be thrashed with ease. One grand victory should finish the war, and it would not do to miss any of this romantic adventure. Nor should one attend in less than immaculate dress. Many Valley men reported for duty wearing garish buff and yellow uniforms. Captain Jim Edmondson sent home from Harper's Ferry for striped calico shirts; white ones got dirty too fast. He also requested a pair of pants in a shade he specified as blue caramel. One rebel wrote: "[M]any of the privates brought with them their personal servants, while the officers were equipped with all that was necessary for elaborate enterainment." John Imboden believed the "fuss and feathers" displayed around Harper's Ferry could match the Champs Elysees on a pleasant afternoon. It was a splendid frolic and confirmed the universal opinion that the soldier's whole duty was to posture heroically." *Wow, if only!*

VA. REGT.HIST. SERIES OF THE VA. INF by Benjamin H. Trask

"...Capt. John C. Owens "Portsmouth Rifle Co." formerly of the 3rd Va. Regt. Of Vol. formed Co. G of the 9th Va.- The Rifles had organized in 1792 as a militia co. On April 20 1861, the unit mustered anew for the defense of Va. and encamped at Pig Point Battery at Nansendmond Co. The Portsmouth unit sported blue flannel uniforms with green trim. The Co. Quartermaster issued 100 Miss. Rifles, twenty deficient cap boxes, twelve haversacks, nineteen tents and twelve canteens..."

THE CONFEDERATE VETERAN VOL.XXV 1917

Pg. 120 March 1917 In The Year 1861 complied by John C. Stiles Vol. IV "Official Records" "Powder Flasks- A Virginia Colonel reported to Gen. Marchall that his men were poorly armed and carried their powder in horns, gourds, and bottles. And this only a few years from the magazine rifle!"

THE RANDOLPH HORNETS IN THE CIVIL WAR-A History & Roster of Co. M, 22ndNORTH Carolina Regiment by Wallace E. Jerrell pub. by McFarland & Co. 2004

Pg. 11 "...On 20 April 1861, Adjudant General J.F. Hoke issued a pronouncement which read, in part:

The following constitute a complete outfit necessary for a company of volunteers, in order to be able to take the field for a campaign, vis:

For the Company-Tents, Cooking Utensils, Mess Furniture vis: Water Buckets, Knives and Forks, tin Plates, Cups and Pans, Strong Bags for Rations, Axes ans Spades,(Ten Each), six Hatchets.

For each man-Two pair Pants (very loose) two Sack Coats, two Flannel Shirts, and as few Drawers, Socks and under shirts as possible. One Felt Hat, if not suppied with Caps, two pair Shoes, no Boots except for mounted service, one Blanket, one Knapsack, one Haversack, one canteen to be covered with cloth or leather, one Gutta Percha or Rubber Overcoat, if it can be procured.

Where the generous patriotism of the community offers to supply the wants of Companies, it is recommended that the above articles be procured as far as practicable.

The State will endeavor to supply the deficiencies when the Legislature shall have made the necessary appropriation.

At first, the men had no tents to protect them from the elements. Joshua Bain was a blacksmith, associated with several others in that work. This was probably a fairly large blacksmith operation with a barn big enough to accommodate the troops until tents could be made. Secoundly and equally significant was the fact that the troops would need some blacksmith work done to make some of the equipment and hardware for the months ahead. Sergeant Turner was with the company being paraded with the regiment when they arrived in Richmond, Virginia. He said, "I thought myself that we were nice looking, for we were uniformed and our new guns and bowie knives hanging by our sides, made us look dangerous and I thought that the Yankees would run at the first sight of us." Bowie knives, though sometimes issued, were generally brought from home. It may be that the blacksmith shop also manufactured these knives for Company M…The men chose to designate their company the "Randolph Hornets." According to Sergeant Turner, the company remained in camp at Joshua Bain's for about three weeks, then moved to Middletown Accademy, a school organized by the Horney and Makepeace families and located halfway between Cedar Falls and Franklinsville. It may be that by this time they had tents and needed a more spacious area to set up a camp. Also, this camp would have been more central to the county and nearer the home of Captain Odell, allowing better communication with the people he contracted to make uniforms and equipment. During the week or so that they were here, they were also fitted with their new uniforms.

Captain John M. Odell was diligent in seeing that the men were provided for. He obtained the materials locally, much of it through George Makepeace, superintendant of the Cedar Falls Company. Makepeace was a fervent supporter of the war effort and, according to attorney and local historian L. McKay Whately, practically outfitting the company, ordering the supplies through the Cedar Fall Company Store. Services of Cedar Falls Mill employees and other area craftsmen were obtained to make uniforms, shoes, blankets, knapsacks, cooking utensils, and other necessary goods. Many of Odell's detailed records of purchases still exist today in the state archives at Raleigh. The exact design of the uniforms Company M took to war are unknown, but are thought to be on the pattern of the N.C. state regulation uniform, which consisted of a long-skirted sack coat with a lay-down collar and black epaulettes on the shoulders. It is known that the material was jeans wool, a combination of wool and cotton. Captain Odell described it as Salem jeans. The shirts were described in his account as being Plaid Linsey. After being wounded and taken to a hospital in Petersburg after the battle of Mechanicsville on 26 June 1862, Sergeant John Turner described their shoes: "Our shoes were made of cloth and over the toes and around the heels there was a strip of leather. The leather part was shined up. The bottoms were made of wood…"

This the first quote on cloth shoes I didn't know they were used this early in the war.

THE CONFEDERATE VETERAN VOL XL

May 1932 Pg. 171 April 21, 1861 In The Junior Reserves by William Franklin Elkins "On April 21, 1861, Sunday morning, at five o'clock, the fife and drum aroused the citizens to get ready to march with the boys to the depot to see them off for the seat of war. These companies were commanded by men who had organized military companies prior to the war. One known as the Cabarrus Guards (N.C.) was commanded by Capt. Nelson Slough who had served in the war against Mexico, 1846-48. He had a fine military turn of mind. It will be interesting to know just what was the uniform of the men in his company, which was dark blue dress coats, with light blue pants, all belt trimmings white, and caps that were topped with red, white, and blue plumes. Each man looked full six feet with his plumes. The combined uniform was the most attractive I have ever seen." *More blue uniforms*

VOICES FROM COMPANY D Diaries by the Greensboro Guards, fifth Alabama Infantry Regiment, Army of Northern Virginia ed. By G. Ward Hubbs Univ. of Georgia Press 2003

Pg. 3 1861 April 22 "...Jas. D. Webb Esq. is the jolliest man in the company. He marches around in his little blue jacket and gray pants and looks like a little boy..."

SOLDIER OF SOUTHWESTERN VA. The Civil War Letters of Capt. John Peston Sheffy ed. By James I. Robertyson Jr. La. State Univ. Press 2004

Pg. 23-War Clouds and Love showers Marion Va. April 23-24, 1861 "...Today we organized the company of "Smyth Dragoons." I was elected Second Lieutenant, the only office to which I aspired, a post of high honor in such a Company. Our dress uniform will be black cassimere pants with yellow stripe, black cloth jockey coats for the men, frock coats for the officers, helmets with black plumes, sword-proof for the men, and felt hats with larger black plumes for the officers. The commissioned officers, Capt., 1st and 2nd Lieutenants, only have epaulets."

RICHMOND VOLUNTEERS 1861-1865 by Louis H. mandarin & Lee A. Wallace pub. by Richmond Civil War Centennial Committee Westover Press 1969

Pg. 104 Thomas Artillery organized on April 25, 1861 "...The company was named for James Thomas, a wealthy citizen of Richmond, who fully equipped and uniformed it in gray at a cost of $2,000..."

Culpeper-A Virginia County's History through 1920-the Culpeper Historical Society by Eugene M. Scheel Culpeper Va. 1982

Pg. 174 April 28, 1861 The Little Fork Rangers "Their first uniforms would have made excellent targets for Yankee bullets: Blue caps, red cut-away jackets with yellow striped across the front (designating their branch of service, cavalry) and white trousers. Their winter uniform specified black trousers with a red stripe. But when Virginia seceded, thirty citizens of the Oak Shade and Jeffersonton neighborhoods raised $292 to purchase gray cloth made at Swartz's woolen mills at Waterloo. The ladies met at Mrs. Henry Kirby's at Jeffersonton to sew uniforms, for Mrs. Kirby knew best how to put the suits together (ed. an anecdotal source states that the original uniforms were brought to Manassas with the Little Fork Rangers in order to wear them in the triumphal parade into Washington, D.C.) *Oh, Yeah, what an event that would have been!*

THE BATTLE OF SCARY CREEK by Terry Lowry pub by Pictorial Histories Pub Co 1982

"Company Orders for the Kanwha Riflemen Kanawhwa Valley Star, April 30, 1861
Company Orders # 1
April 26, 1861

1. In compliance with the requisition of a Proclamation of the Governor of Virginia dated at Richmond the 19th of April 1861, this command will hold itself in readinessfor marching orders.
2. In case such orders shall arrive, each one must provide himself with the following articles at least in addition to dress and fatigue uniforms, to wit: two shirts, four collars, two pair of socks, two pair of drawers, one blacking box and brush (to any two files), two pair white Berlin gloves, one quart tin cup, one white cotton haversack, one case knife, fork and spoon, two towels, two handkerchiefs, comb and brush, and toothbrush. Some stout linen thread, a few buttons, paper of pins and a thimble, in a small buckskin or cloth bag.
3. There being no knapsack in the possession of the company one ordinary sized carpetsack will be allowed to every two men, for the purpose of holding such of the above articles as are not in constant use. The knife, fork, spoon, haversack and tin cup, must be worn about the person, the first three and the last articles to the waist belt. Immediately after the receipt and promulgation of marching orders, the carpet sacks, duly packed, must be delivered to the Quartermaster Sergeant, neatly marked with the names of the two owners. Each file will procure a comfortable blanket and upon the receipt of orders, send the same to the Quartermaster Sergeant, shaped into a neat and compact bundle conspicuously marked with his name.
4. It is earnestly recommended that all under clothes should be woolen, especially the socks, as cotton socks are utterly unfit for marching in, and all files should wear woolen undershirts. Shoes, sewed soles, and fitting easily, but not too loosely to the foot, coming up over the ankle, are infinitely preferable to boots, and should be made strong and serviceable.
5. By the liberality and patriotism of the residents of Charleston, (one of them a lady), flannel cloth (gray) has been furnished for fatigue jackets, and provision

made for cutting them, all members of the company are hereby required at once to have their measures taken and jackets cut by Mr. James B. Noyes, tailor. Many ladies have kindly undertaken to make them up. All members of the company are required to have their jackets finished by Wednesday afternoon next at the latest. By the liberality of another resident, cloth for haversacks has been procured, and they have been cut out by another lady. They will be delivered to the Quartermaster Sergeant, and they must be finished by the same evening."

A BOTHERHOOD OF VALOR-the common soldiers of the Stonewall Brigade C.S.A and the iron brigade U.S.A. by Jeffry D. West Simon and Shuster NY NY 1999

Spring-summer 1861 At the time of the inspection, Jackson commanded nearly 8 thousand volunteers from Va., Al., Miss., & Ky. These unprecedented numbers, combined with the thousands of troops stationed near Manassas, east of the Blue Ridge, rapidly drained Virginia's supply of arms and equipment. At Harpers Ferry, rare was the company that had adequate accourtrements-cartridge boxes, belts, bayonets, knapsacks, haversacks, and canteens. While on drill or guard duty, the men carried their ammo in their trouser pockets. Uniforms embraced an array of colors. In the 2nd Va., for instance, one company wore the dark blue of the U.S. army; another yellow and grey cloth, and a 3rd, dark green.

Pg. 27 "Gen. Jackson sent wagons laden with the men's unnecessary clothing and luxuries to Charlestown. The latter directive moved one valley recruit to grumble that Jackson "considered a gum cloth, a blanket, a tooth brush and 40 rounds of cartridges as the full equipment of a gentleman soldier."

28th Va. INF. VA. REGIMENTAL HISTORIES SERIES by Frank F. Fields Jr. H.E. Howard

"Mountain rifles drilled there through April and May 1861 The units had no uniforms. Instead, the men wore "linsey shirts and big black hats, tucked up on one side with a rosette of green ribbon."

WAR DIARIES-The 1861 Kanawha Valley Campaigns by David L. Phillips & Rebecca L. Hill-chief reasearcher- pub by Gauley Mountain Press 1990

Pg. 46 "By the end of May…Captain William F. Bahlman of the 22nd Virginia wrote after the war:

"Our uniforms were a thing of beauty and a joy forever. They consisted of light blue flannel jackets and dark gray pants. Although we were infantry they put cavalry trimmings on us. The jackets had yellow stripes on the breasts and the pants had yellow stripes down the legs. They put sergeant cheverons on the officers and original markings on the sergeants. Nobody knew anything about the matter and those who thought they knew the most were mistaken…we had no knapsacks but long narrow sacks called pokes…"

There was a great deal of confusion regarding uniforms during the early days of the war. Colonel Beuhring Jones recruited a company in Fayette County which was later mustered into Confederate service at Kanawha falls and became part of the 60th Virginia, but he was initially the commander of the "Dixie Rifles" and later wrote about his experience with his taylor:

"I had just returned from Lewisburg, and sported a gray jacket gotten up by a tailor of that place, who, by the way of securing the job, had assured me he was perfectly "Au fait" in all the minutiae pertaining to the decoration of military rank.

I was quite proud of my up-buttoned, close fitting 'jacket of gray' and felt all the importance of the commander, until I was startled from my dream of consequentiality by being addressed by an old soldier as "Corporal Jones". My "Knight of the Shears", equally ignorant with myself had braided me as a corporal. My mortification was excessive, nor did I recover my composure until spasmodically I tore off the libeloius braid, and cast it disdainfully upon the ground."

THE CIVIL WAR: THE SOUTH ed. by Thomas Streissguth Greenhaven Press Inc. 2001

Pg. 77 A Month with "The Rebels"—from an anonymous English observer in the summer of 1861 "…From the reports we had heard in the North, we expected to find ragged and half-clad regiments; instead of which we failed, during many rides throught he various camps to see one man who was not clad in serviceable attire. It was expected that winter clothing would be served out before the 1st of November, and that dress would become more uniform…"

The Brit was kindly stating that uniformity was lacking.

THE MARYLAND LINE IN THE CONFEDERATE STATES ARMY W.W. Goldsborough-Major in the C.S.A. Kelly Piet & Co. 1869

Pg. 12 Summer 1861 "The regiment numbered over seven hundred men, and was second to none in the Confederate army. But two companies were uniformed at the time of its organization,(those from Richmond), but soon after, through the exertions of Mrs. Bradley T.Johnson, the whole command was dressed in neat, well-fitting gray uniforms…"

THEY TOOK THEIR STAND by Manly Wade Wellman pub by G. P. Putnam's Sons 1959

Pg. 151 Richmond Va. "A gay tale came…It concerned an adventure of one of those frantic ladies' sewing circles-it had cut out only the right legs of trousers to uniform a regiment of

Maryland volunteers. The embarrassed seamstresses had to scramble for more gray cloth, to make the left legs and complete the garments…"

Remember the description of supplying the Maryland Volunteers previous? OK, picture this-the gray cloth for the right & left legs were probably of a different hue-wouldn't that look resplendent on parade or in a re-enactment!

A PAIR OF BLANKETS War-time history in Letters to the Young People of the South by William H. Stewart Broadfoot Pub. Co. 1911

Pg. 32 summer 1861 "…the largest number formed formed the nucleus for an infantry company, which soon after organized at Pleasant Grove Baptist Church in the Southern part of the county, under the name of "Jackson Grays." It was named for the brave Jackson who killed Ellsworth at Alexandria.…The county having appropriated $12 each for equipping her soldiers, cloth was purchased for our uniforms, and the ladies of the neighborhood assembled every day in a near-by mansion house to make them up. It was not long before my men were dressed in gray with glittering Virginia buttons…"

Diary of A Confederate Sharpshooter-The Life of James Corad Peters Pictorial Histories Pub. Co. Charleston, W.Va. 1997

Summer 1861 "The men went into camp and began to collect their equipment and to drill. It was probably during this time that James received the items that he listed in his diary. With no other explanation he listed these in his diary:

Received of the Southern Confederacy
1 cap 1 pair pants
2 shirts 1 coat
1 overcoat 2 pair drawers
1 blanket 1 oil cloth
1 saddle blanket
1 haversack 1 nose bag
1 pair boots 1 pair spurs
1 cartridge box & cap box & belt
1 curry comb & brush
1 canteen 1 curcingle
1 bridle & martingale
1 tin cup 1 plate
1 shot gun

Berry Benson's Civil War Book-Memiors of a Confederate Scout and Sharpshooters ed. by Susan William Benson Univ. of Georgia Press 1992

Pg. 2 Summer 1861 Morris Island- Cimming's Point, S.C. A one-gun battery was about to be built not far above Cumming's Point to be commanded by Col. Tom Lamar of Edgefield District, and I was was one of eight taken from the Regiment to man it. And now we worked hard, often by night as well as by day, shoveling sand and rolling with barrows up plank inclines, and many a time we were wet through by rain, not being allowed to stop. Once having no dry garment to sleep in, I took a cotton sack, and cutting a hole in the bottom for my head and a hole in each side for my arms, I had a sleeveless shirt. Taking another sack, I cut two holes in the bottom, thrust my legs through, and tying the mouth of the sack about my waist, I had a pair of drawers…"

Ingenious

LIFE IN THE CONFEDERATE ARMY by John P. Ford pub by The Neale Pub Co. 1905

Pg. 23 Summer 1861 The Palmetto Guards of the Seventeenth Regiment South Carolina Militia stationed around Charleston, S.C. "…During this summer our shortness of rations began, and continued rather to intensify until the end. For the period of about two monthes it consisted of only one small loaf of baker's bread and a gill of sorghum syrup daily. For that time we had not a particle of fresh or salt meat. If we had not been where we could obtain plenty of fish, we would have suffered seriously. The quartermaster's department was as badly crippled as the commissary's and most of us could get no new shoes and several of our men were actually barefooted in consequence; but it being summer and on a sandy coast there was not much suffering as might have been otherwise…."

A REBEL'S RECOLLECTIONS by George Cary Eggleston, C.W. Centennial Series, Ind. Univ. Press, Bloomington

"During the spring and early summer of 1861, the men did not dream that they were to be paid anything for their in-services, or even that the government was to clothe them. They had bought their own uniforms, and whenever these wore out they ordered new ones to be sent, by the first opportunity, from home. I remember the very first time the thought of getting clothing from the government entered my mind. I was serving in Stuart's cavalry, and the summer of 1861 was nearly over. My boots had worn out, and as there happened at the time to be a strict embargo upon all visiting on the part of non-military people, I could not get a new pair from home. The spurs of my comrades had made uncomfortable impressions on my bare feet every day for a week, when someone suggested that I might possibly buy a pair of boots from the quartermaster, who was for the first time in possession of some government property of that description. When I returned with the boots and reported that the official had refused my proffered cash, contenting himself with charging the amount against me as a debit to be deducted from the amount of my "pay and clothing allowance", there was great merriment in the camp. The idea that there was anyone in back of us in this war-anybody who could, by any ingenuity of legal quibbling, be supposed to be indebted to us for our voluntary services in our own cause- was too ridiculous to be treated seriously. "Pay money" became the standing subject for jests. The card-playing with which the men amused themselves suffered a revolution at once; euchre gave place to poker, played for "pay money," the winnings to fall due when pay-day should come-a huge joke which was heartily enjoyed.

From this the reader will see how little was done in the beginning of the war toward the organization of an efficient quartermaster's department, and how completely this ill-organized and undisciplined mob of plucky gentlemen was left to prosecute the war as best it could, trusting to luck for clothing and even for food..."

This is just an amazing mindset, no wonder they achieved so much with so little

WASH.& LEE UNIV. Archives, Lexington, Va.Letters of Bethel J. Davidson Camp near Guienie's Station

Summer 1861 Dear Mother "...Until yesterday we had only tent flies, then as both ends to sleep under, but we succeeded in getting those tents yesterday.

The men are quite comfortable having blankets and plenty of clothes. There are still some who are rather bad off for shoes, but they will soon be supplied..."

I WILL GIVE THEM ONE MORE SHOT" RAMSEY'S 1st REGIMENT GEORGIA VOLUNTEERS by Goerge Winston Martin Mercer Univ. Press 201

Pg 125 summer 1861 "Encamped at McDowell Va, the 1st Georgia was in terrible condition. Almost all of their equipment-tents, blankets, cook pots, and more-had been lost during the retreat from Laurel Hill. Uniforms were in tatters, and clothing of any description was in desperately needed..."

Pg. 228 May, 1861 Lynchburg "...Here are all prisoners, recently captured, except officers, who are locked up in the city. Our guards are mostly citizens, boys and old men, equipped by themselves or with such guns as the provost could pick up. Most of them are impressed and drilled by invalid soldiers. I observed one man about fifty, very corpulent, good naturedly inclined, dressed in common citizens' coat and pants, white vest, white stove pipe hat, with a weed, armed with a shotgun, pacing his beat..."

Notes of A Private by John Milton Hubbard Co. E, 7th TN. Regt. Forrest's Cavalry Corps., C.S.A. pub. By R.P. Sharkelford Bolivar, TN 1973 from 1911&13 ed.

Pg. 11Summer 1861 "No page in the old school histories had told us how little a soldier must get along on, and there was no experienced campaigner to tell us. Some of us thought that a white shirt or two would be essential. Razors, combs, brushes and hand glasses were in our outfits. It bothered us to reduce these things to a small package that we could handle easily. We had many details to settle. Saddle bags? They had all been appropriated by the "early birds"-the fellows who were afraid the war would be over before they could get to it. We resorted to the use of the old-fashioned wallet, an article fashioned after the similitude to a pillow-slip, closed at both ends and with a slit in the middle. Made of stout sandburs, it proved to be a sufficient receptacle. But the "wallet" was not tidy enough for the "trim soldier," and in case of rain the contents were drenched. All this was remedied afterward by experience in packing, necessity for economy, and by spoils captured on the field. We, too, got to using McClellan saddles with large pockets, rubber cloths and regulation blankets. Indeed, later on, if Grant had met one of us, he would have pronounced us "correct" from halter to spur, if only he could have been blinded to the suit of grey or butternut. There came a time when we had new Yankee guns and were constantly on the lookout for cartridges of the right caliber. You see, we "paid some attention to details," if we did some times leave in a hurry."

History of Hampshire W.Va. by H.U. Maxwell & H.L. Swisher pub. by Mcclain Printing Co. 1972

Pg. 622 The Hampshire Guards "…It was called into service in May, 1861, to go to the front, and on the eighteenth of that month left Romney for Harper's Ferry. The trip down the south branch to the Baltimore and Ohio Railroad at Green Spring was made in buggies, carriges, on horseback, and in wagons, many citizens accompanying that far on their journey. The baggage train was enormous, the prevailing opinion seeming to be that the trip was a combined excursion and picnic, and that enough provisions and sufficient changes of clothing should be taken along to render life enjoyable."

A MARYLAND BOY IN LEE'S ARMY by George Wilson Booth pub by Univ. of Nebraska Press 2000

Pg. 10 May 1861 Harper's Ferry "…at this time I had nothing but the clothes on my back… The most picturesque were the Kentuckians under Col. Blanton Duncan, who occupied the Maryland Heights. Their uniform was after the frontier hunting pattern, fancifully trimmed and very attractive; most conspicuous in their equipment was the "bowie"…

Several Virginia regiments were neatly uniformed in gray, while the arriving troops from the more remote South were clad in homespun butternut suits, soon to be so familiar…

Not a cartridge box was in the command, and, taken altogether, we presented a sorry sight as compared with troops from other states; relief from this unfavorable condition was brought about through the personal efforts of a noble woman, Mrs. Bradley T. Johnson, who interceded with Governor Ellis of North Carolina, with such success as to secure some 600 Mississippi rifles, an excellent arm for those days, and by the purchase in Richmond of uniforms and clothing, which made us presentable…"

7TH VIRGINIA CAVALRY by Richard L. Armstrong-The Virginia Regimental Histories Series 1992

Pg. 4 May 1861 "…The companies were described in the early days of the war as being:…" poorly uniformed, armed and equipped for military service. Many of them still wore civilian clothes or uniforms made of gray, without regularity of color or make, and were armed with double-barreled shotguns, rifles or pistols of all makes. Few of them had sabres or swords, and all rode the citizen's saddle, and carried their clothes in the old-time-saddle-bags or rolled in bundles, which were attached in every kind of manner to their saddles…"

UNIFORMS OF THE CIVIL WAR by Robin Smith & Ron Field pub by Lyons Press 2001

Pg. 246 NORTH CAROLINA "…Troops organizing for war in 1861 found a great variety of clothing available for purchase in cities such as Raliegh and Wilmington. E.L. Harding, in the capitol, advertised "military goods just received from Richmond, Virginia," which included "Gray flannel shirts for soldiers," and "Mixed cassimere…"

An anonymousletter to the Raliegh North Carolina Standard, published on 1 May, 1861, urged the units organizing for war to buy uniforms of North Carolina's gray cassimere. "Its advantages," it was argued, was that it "…is cheap, that it will last well, and as experiments made by the Frensh Emporer prove that gray is the most difficult color to take sight upon, hence is less often hit. Again, it is the product of our own soil. I have lately seen a company uniformed in blue broadcloth and Northern blue cassimere. Now, that is just the uniform of the regular U. S. troops, further it is of Northern make and very expensive. If a man expects to go into service there is no sense in his wearing his ball-room clothes, no more than there is in his going into a pig-pen with them…"

MY DEAR EMMA-The War letters of Col. James K. Edmonson 1861-8165 ed.by Charles W. Turner PhD Pub By McClure Press 1978

Pg.8 May 1861 "…The weather here has been exceedingly cold for the season. I sent by S.J. Cambell for a heavy pair of blue carnite military pants and a military buff vest to be furnished by Mr. Garing. I would like also to have those calico shirts you spoke of…"

LIFE IN THE CONFEDERATE ARMY: BEING PRESONAL EXPERIENCES OF A PRIVATE SOLDIER IN THE CONFEDERATE ARMY by Arthur P. Ford and Marion Johnstone Ford pub by The Neale Pub Co. 1905

Pg.11 May 1861 "At this period of the war the Confederate Government allowed each soldier a certain sum yearly for his uniform, and each company decided for it…"

SOLDIER OF SOUTHWESTERN VA. The Civil War Letters of Capt. John Peston Sheffy ed. By James I. Robertyson Jr. La. State Univ. Press 2004

Pg.29 same chapter Marion, May 1st, 1861 "…We will find great difficulty in procuring arms and uniforms. Our agents inform us that no cloth can be procured in Richmond. We will be compelled to apparel ourselves in Thomas Jeans. It will perhaps be better than anything else for service. So might it be. Gay border lads we'll be, any how…"

THE CONFEDERATE ARMY 1861-1865 FLORIDA, ALA-BAMA, GEORGIA by Ron Field

Pg. 36 May 1, 1861 "…Following his visit to Fort Pulaski on Cockspur Island, Fla. May 1, 1861, London Times Correspondent William Howard Russell described members of the First Georgia regiment on guard duty at the landing as: tall, stout young fellows, in various uniforms or rude mufti (civilian clothes), in which the Garibaldian red shirt and felt slouched hat predominated. They are armed with smoothbore muskets (date 1851) quite new; and their bayonets, barrels and locks were quite bright and clean. The officer on duty was dressed in a blue frock coat with brass buttons emblazoned with the coat of arms of the state, and red silk sash and glazed kepi, and straw colored gauntlets…"

WEBSITE-richmond.edu

Richmond Daily Dispatch

May 1, 1861 Advice to volunteers-How to prepare for the campaign

A writer, who signs himself "An Old Soldier," gives the following advice to young soldiers

1. Remember that in a campaign more men die from sickness than from the bullet.
2. Line your blanket with one thickness of of brown drilling. This adds but four ounces in weight, and doubles the warmth.
3. Buy a small India-rubber blanket-only $1.50 to lay on the ground, or to throw over your shoulders when on guard duty during a rainstorm.

4. The best military hat in use is the light-colored soft felt, the crown being sufficiently high to allow space for air over the brain. You can fasten it up as a continental in fair weather, or turn it down when it is wet or very sunny.
5. Let your beard grow, so as to protect the throat and lungs.
6. Keep your entire person clean. This prevents fevers and bowel complaints in warm climates. Wash your each day, if possible. Avoid strong coffee and oily meat. Gen. Scott said that the too free use of these, together with neglect in keeping the skin clean, cost many a soldier his life in Mexico.
7. A sudden check of perspiration by chilly or night air often causes fever and death. When thus exposed, do not forget your blanket.

Richmond Daily Dispatch May 2, 1861 From Petersburg

"Considerable amusement was caused by several of the troops appearing in line minus their military hats. They had, unfortunetally, lost them on their journey here, by having them blown off their heads while looking out of the windows of thew cars when in rapid motion. The losses were soon restored, however, and new ones furnished by some of oue citizens."

Richmond Daily Dispatch May 3, 1861-Arrival of soldiers

"A company of infantry, numbering 108 men, under command of Capt. Robert Saunders, arrived yesterday via Danville Railroad from Yellow Branch, Campbell County, Virginia. The men were dressed in black jackets and gray pants, with black stripes, were armed with rifles, and looked very well."

Richmond Daily Dispatch-May 9, 1861 How to Guard against the heat

"As the heat of Sothern sun is one of the hardships our boys will have to encounter, permit an old soldier to state in what way the French army in Algiers guard themselves during the day, when on the march or standing sentry. Take a yard of thin, white flannel, fold it together once, and sew up one end; a ribbon or tape may be inserted to draw it around the neck-this thrown over the cap or shake, and falling behind, completely shields the head and shoulders from the rays of the sun. Woolen is preferable to linen or cotton, is equally light, costs less than the former, and is easier washed and kept clean."

This sounds like a glorifieds Havelock, but I bet it works.

VMI MS# 282

Robert Henry Cambel of Lexington, Va. Rockbridge Rifles Harper's Ferry May 4/1861 Dear Mother I wish you would send me some paper collars if you can get them, they are better than the linen collars. I can wear one of them a week and then you do not have the trouble of washings …"

Paper collars? I mean, he is in the field, why would he be wearing collars? Victorian clothing etiquette, I suppose

Richmond Daily Dispatch May 9, 1861 Ready for duty

"The Henrico Guard...tendered their services to the State, which were accepted.The men were clothed with gray pants, black stripes, gray shirts, and armed with improved muskets..."

May 9, 1861 India-Rubber blankets

"A lady correspondent in Williamsburg, having heard there is some difficulty in procuring India-rubber blankets for the soldiers who are going into camp and will greatly need them, proposes to the ladies of Richmond and elsewhere, to give their India-rubber piano covers for that purpose. They will answer as well. And each cover, by being cut, will make two or three blankets.

Our correspondent says she is sure that the ladies will be sufficiently patriotic to give up a useless, or at least unnecessary part of the parlor furniture, which may probably save the life of many a gallant soldier. We dare say that by communicating with any of the officers having charge of the proper department, very valuable service might be rendered."

Ingenious. I would gladly huddle under a piano cover rather than lay out in the rain

CONFEDERATE LETTERS AND DIARIES ed. by Walbrook D. Swank, colonel, USAF, Ret pub. by Papercraft Printing & Design 1992 Letters Pertaining to John Taylor Anderson Co. C, 13th Virginia Infantry

Pg. 89 May 6, 1861 Harper's Ferry (Va) Dear Sister, "...Sister I received the close you sent I am very much obliged to you they will be of great use to me, we have a very good barracks now..."

MY DIARY NORTH AND SOUTH by William Howard Russell pub by Alfred A. Knopf 1988

Pg. 129 May 7, 1861 "...On my way I passed a company of volunteers, one hundred and twenty artillerymen, and three field pieces, on their way to the station for Virginia, followed by a crowd of "citizens" and negroes of both sexes, cheering vociferously. The band was playing that excellent quick-step "Dixie." The men were stout, fine fellows, dressed in coarse gray tunics with yellow facings and French caps. They were armed with smoothbore muskets and their backpacks were unfit for marching, being waterproof bags slung from their shoulders. The guns had no caissons, and the shoeing of the troops was certainly deficient in soling…" *Already problems with shoes. This gets infinetely worse as the war progresses.*

Pg. 139 May 11, 1861 Fort Gaines, Mobile, Al. "Inside the work was crammed with men, some of whom slept in the casements-others in tents on the parade grounds and enceinte of the fort. They were Alabama Volunteers, and a sturdy lot of fellows as ever shouldered a musket; dressed in homespun coarse gray suits, with blue and yellow worsted facings and stripes-to European eyes not very respectful to their officers, but very obedient, I am told, and very peremptorily ordered about as I heard."

Pg. 153 May 16th, 1861 Fort Pickens, Fla. "The working parties, as they were called-volunteers from Mississippi and Alabama, great long bearded fellows in flannel shirts and slouched hats, uniformless in all save brightly burnished arms and resolute purpose…"

MY DEAR EMMA-The War letters of Col. James K. Edmonson 1861-8165 ed.by Charles W. Turner PhD Pub By McClure Press 1978

Pg. 9 Virginia Heights Division Head Quarters Harper's Ferry May 9 1861 My Dear Wife "…I have written to Joseph G. Steele for several things, an overcoat etc. which I suppose he will attend to and send by the first opportunity. I have also sent a memorandum by S.J. Campell for a pair of military pants and a military buff vest. I suppose he will have it attended to, if not, it makes no difference. I do not stand in need of them very much…"

CADET GRAY & BUTTERNUT BROWN Thomas M. Arlikas Thomas Pub 2006

Pg. 5 "Near Waldren, North Carolina, May 11, 1861 "…The 2nd North Carolina Troops stationed at this point…have no arms, and most of their uniforms, if they may be so-called, are as varied as their faces. Some of the officers wear red flannel sashes and yellow flannel epaulets. A few mount the French chapeau, and now and then, a full dressed individual relieves the general monotony of the (common) homespun…."

"After the surrender of Fort Donelson in February 1862, the men of the captured 14th Mississippi Infantry mingled with Federal soldiers who commented on their clothing: "They looked like all the rest, a motley looking set of men in various uniforms. I saw one or two regiments who wore blankets made of pieces of carpeting…"

A field editor for the Memphis Daily Appeal, on assignment with the Confederate Army of Mississippi in Septrember, 1862, described for its readers one of the more famous regiments in Confederate survice, Terry's Texas Rangers of the 8th Texas Cavalry: "They were shabby, dirty, ragged, and try to clothe themselves as best they can. The only badge they wore was a red star on the front of their hats or caps. One of them had a whole suit of bearskins, and several have pants of the same material. They are armed with short double-barreled shotguns, revolvers, and Bowie knives...."

This quote contains a great statement regarding Confederate uniformity: "most of their uniforms, if they may be so called, are as varied as their faces."

JAMES BRADFIELD DIARY Co. H, 17th Virginia Infantry

Pg. 3 May 15th 1861 "Leave Camp Christian about 4 o'clock in the morning and march seven miles nearer Richmond raining hard all day my feet are very painful having no shoes or boots for a day."

LETTERS OF MAJOR THOMAS ROWLAND, C.S.A. FROM NORTH CAROLINA 1861 and 1862 William and Mary College1916

Pg 37 Hd. Quarters, Cavalry Camp, Ashland Va. May 15, 1861 "...I am writing from the adjudant's office of the Cavalry Camp, which is now my office, so my letter is dated accordingly. I have been appointed by Col. Ewell adjudant of the Cavalry Camp, which now comprises six companies. It is soon to be increased by four more, making a full regiment. I have no uniform and no sabre yet and do not like to get one until I am sure that I will be able to pay for it myself. I conduct dress parade in my grey pants and borrow a sabre from someone on the sick list. If we should receive marching orders, I can probably obtain a horse and a sabre in this way and march with the regiment..."

HISTORY OF THE BEDFORD LIGHT ARTILLERY 1861-1865 by Rev. Joseph A. Graves pub by Press of the Bedford Democrat

Pg. 11 May 15, 1861 Bedford City, Va. "They made a fine appearance in their beautiful uniform, which is made of dark blue material, the coat buttoning straight up the front, fastened at the waist by a belt, with a short skirt below it. The pants and coat are trimmed with red, which is the style for artillery suits, and above all, is a cap to match, mounted with two brass cannon crossed obliquely.

After the manner of the times, many of these uniforms have been given to the Company by liberal and patriotic citizens. At the word of command, they march to the depot, followed by fathers, mothers, brothers and sisters. At noon the train moves off for Lynchburg, amid goodbyes, the waving of handkerchiefs, and the cheers of the enthusiastic and approving crowd..."

UPSHUR BROTHERS OF THE BLUE AND THE GRAY Betty Hornbeck McClain Printing Co., Parsons, W.Va. 1967

Pg 14 May 16th, 1861 regarding Confederate units forming in Western Va. "...There are other companies forming in the surrounding counties, but all without arms or uniformed (This would include the Upshur Grays.) This force, when received, will not for some months be more effective than undisciplined militia..."

Pg. 21 "What could one expect of undisciplined troops of both the North or South, who voted for their own officers and were told to furnish their own uniforms?..."

Pg. 25 June 3rd, retreat from Phillipi, Southwestern Va. "Poe formed the company and had the baggage loaded in two-horse wagon he had impressed at Fetterman. The baggage consisted of small gripsacks, containing the soldiers' Sunday-best outfits. Cornetius Carder was the driver and owner of the wagon and horses. Poe directed Carter to go eastward along the Beverly Pike and await futher orders..."

MY DEAR EMMA-The War letters of Col. James K. Edmonson 1861-8165 ed.by Charles w. Turner PhD McClure Press 1978

Pg. 12 Harper's Ferry May 17 1861 My Dear Emma "...If I get my overcoat and the things you all were so kind to send me, I do not think that I will want anything else for a while. I did not understand whether there were any calico shirts in the bundle you have sent me or not. I would like to have about two striped calico shirts for I will have stopped wearing white shirts. It is so hard to have them washed and they get dirty so quick..."

RICHMOND VOLUNTEERS 1861-1865 by Louis H. mandarin & Lee A. Wallace pub. by Richmond Civil War Centennial Committee Westover Press 1969

Pg. 44 Hampden Artillery was organized early in May 1861...On May 18 1861 the Richmond Dispatch reported the unit stationed at the Baptist College, and added: "The company numbers seventy-four men, are uniformed in grey cloth, and are armed with four 6 pounders."

THE MISSISSIPPI BRIGADE OF BRIG. GEN. JOSEPH R. DAVIS by T.P. Williams pub by Morningside Books 1999

Pg.32 May 19, Lynchburg, Va. the 11th and 2nd Mississippi Infantry-report of Lt. Col. George Deas, inspecter general of the Confederate army:

"The two regiments from Mississippi have with them their tents and camp equipage, but are not satisfied with their arms, which are chiefly of the old flint-lock musket altered into percussion. As usual with troops of this description, they all want rifles...One of these regiments (the Eleventh) under the command of Colonel Moore, is very superior to the other (the Second) under Colonel Faulkner. The latter is badly clothed and careless in its appointments. The officers are entirely without military knowledge of any description and the men have a slovenly and unsoldier-like appearance.

The clothing of the troops is not abundant, and, in the regiment from Mississippi, under Colonel Faulkner, almost every necessity is wanting. They seem to have come away from home without making proper preparations in this respect, and, indeed, it would seem that they expected to receive on their arrival in Virginia all the appointments of a soldier. Fortunately the approach of warm weather will obviate the necessity of a full suppy of clothing for these men; otherwise they could not enter upon a campaign in their present condition."

THE MITTELDORFER LETERS

May 22, 1861 Glouchester Point, Va. Dear Parents; "...I wish you would send me a pair of blue uniform pants with red braid for stripes...

Same camp after Manassas, Dear Sister;"...Tell Ma I thank her for that haversack and drawers we had a small haversack when we went to Yorktown but nothing to put in it..."

THE 33RD VIRGINIA INFANTRY by Lowell Reidenbaugh The Va. Regimental History Series, 1887

Pg. 3 Capt. F.W.M. Holliday of the Mountain Rangers wrote to Col. Francis B. Jones, an aide to Col. Thomas J. Jackson, the post commander at Harper's Ferry on May 26 1861 "My men want shoes very badly; the county has furnished the uniforms, beds, knapsacks, blankets, canteens, & haversacks. But my men are without shoes. I applied to the Quartermaster in this place, (Col. Wilson) and he informed me that he could not furnish them without authority from Col. Jackson. He says he can get them in town without any inconvenience, and as cheap as they can be had anywhere. Will you be kind enough to get the order at once and send it to me? Send it by return mail or bearer. Can I get arms &c when I get to the Fort? My men want Minnie rifles, as it is a rifle company."

WEBSITE confederateuniforms.org

Daily Advocate (Baton Rouge, La) May 26, 1861 "...with the "Crescent Blues" I am very little acquainted, and consequentaly know scarcely anything of the history of the organization. The company presents a very fine appearance, and is well drilled and orderly. Although called the "Blues," they are so only in name, for the old uniform has been exchanged for a suit of light gray, similar to that used by the Maryland troops…"

THE BLUES IN GRAY-The Civil War Journal of William David Dixon & The Rebel Blues Daybook ed by Roger S. Durham pub by Univ of TN Press 2000

Pg. 12 May 27, 1861 Fort Pulaski, Fl. "The subject of adopting a suitable hat for service having been introduced Private H[arry] G. Ward moved that the corps adopt a gray…or drab hat whichever could be more easily procured which motion was carried and Captain Anderson requested Sergt. [William D.] Davis to ascertain if the requisite kind and numbers could be obtained…"

MY DEAR EMMA-The War letters of Col. James K. Edmonson 1861-8165 ed.by Charles w. Turner PhD McClure Press 1978

Pg. 17 Martinsburg (Va.) May 30 1861 My dear Wife "…The box you and Rebecca etc. sent me by D.E. Ruff was very acceptable indeed. The eatables are already gone, the clothing of great use to me and came in very good time, the bandages will, I think, be of service to me. I am wearing one now, it feels very comfortable…."

Here are those bandages, cloth strips about 4-5 inches wide and padded to be worn above the waist, kidney height, to ward off kidney trouble & diarrhea.

A SCYTHE OF FIRE-THE CIVIL WAR STORY OF THE EIGHTH GEORGIA INFANTRY REGIMENT Warren Wilkinson & Steven E. Woodworth William Morrow Pub. 2002

Pg. 22 May 30, 1861 "…Two days later the Rome Light Guards marched into camp (Howard's Grove) in their natty gray uniforms. On the last day of May came the Oglethorpe Rifles, from Oglethorpe County, in the uniform of "gray Cassimere," a point of pride to some, though Private W.H. Maxey, in the ranks of the Oglethorpe Rifles, thought they were "not fit for a dog to look at."…"

UNIFORMS OF THE CIVIL WAR by Robin Smith & Ron Field Lyons Press 2001

Pg. 229 "…The Richmond Zouaves, who organized under Captain Edward McDonald Jr during May 1861. Their uniforms were made by the ladies of the Monumental Episcopal Church, and were probably based on a typical colorful Zouave pattern, of a blue jacket and orange baggy trousers….A complete zouave uniform, which possibly belonged to an officer of the Richmond zouaves, survives in the collection of the Chicago Historical Society. The navy blue jacket is edged with interwoven gold braid, and is fastened together at the neck by two small buttons or studs secured through a small gold edged tab. The sleeves are decorated with white clover-leaf design outlined with gold braid, and are slashed and buttoned at the underseam by six small brass buttons bearing the Virginia State seal. The scarlet pants with gold braid seam & stripes are in the chasseur-style, being gathered at the waist with pleats, and below the knee with narrow cuffs fastened by buckles or buttons. The chasseur-pattern forage cap is scarlet with gold piping and Hungarian knot on the crown. The blue wool cummerbund has a short scarlet fringe....They "also adopted leggings of white ducking..."

Website THE STONEWALL BRIGADE—Stonewall Brigade-1861 Impression Guidelines by Bret Sumner, 4th Virginia http://www.stonewallbrigade.com/articles

Pg. 3 Company Reports from the supplement to the Official Records of the Confederate Army, Harper's Ferry, May, 1861

1. Mountain Guards- April 19, 1861- "The company left home with only a fatigue uniform (red flannel shirt and grey pants)." "we were armed with the Deringer rifle. Shortly after arriving at Harper's Ferry, we exchanged them for the Mississippi rifle, Model 1842, altered to minie. We had forty-five of these rifles, no bayonets, eighty cartridge boxes without belts, twenty cap boxes, no bayonet scabbards."
2. Southern Guard- "Came into service with grey uniform, (illedgeble) coat and pants and United States Navy cap and blue flannel Jackets. Have new checked shirt. All the uniform furnished by the company and Augusta County."
3. West View Infantry-April 29, 1861- "The company uniform consists of one suit viz: grey pants and fatigue jacket."
4. Augusta Greys-"Uniforms in bad condition of grey woolen goods....Sixty-three percussion muskets, sixty-three cartridge boxes, sixty-three cap boxes, fifty-three bayonet scabbards, and sixty-three belts purchased by the captain."
5. Staunton Rifles- "Substantial uniform furnished by Augusta County. Has sixty-nine Minnie rifles and complete accouterments. The company has knapsacks and belts furnished by Augusta County."
6. Rockbridge Rifles-"Clothing in comfortable [illegible]. Most of the outfit of the company is quite good, sixty-five Minnie rifles ands accouterments complete. Tents furnished by the county of Rockbridge."
7. Ready Rifles of Augusta County-"Fifty-one rifles, forty-eight catridge boxes, no company equipage except cooking utensils, no cap boxes, no bayonets, no bayonet scabbards and no tents.'

8. Montgomery Highlanders-"It is armed with the Mississippi rifle and saber bayonet, which together with its accouterment on hand are in good condition. No bayonet scabbards nor full supply of camp boxes have ever been furnished them."
9. Grayson Daredevils-"It is armed with the Harper's Ferry rifle and saber bayonet, which with their accouterments are in good condition.'
10. Rockbridge Grays-"The uniform and general out fit of this company was originally very good, but is now greatly worn. The service it has performed has been exceedingly hard upon the men, clothing, and equipment. No tents have been furnished or sheltrer, just such as they could put up for themselves. It is armed with cadet muskets. No bayonet scabbards or cap boxes. They have old cadet and cartridge box which is totally inadequate to hold a sufficient supply of ammunition. The arms are in good order."
11. Liberty Hall Volunteers-"June 18, 1861-"Its uniforms and clothing are very poor, [illedgeble] furnished it and has been much exposed therefrom. It is [illedgeable] musket which is in good condition. Has no bayonet, scabbards, and no cap boxes were furnished. The captain furnished them to the company at his own expenseof --. The cartridge boxes are old and indifferent."

All these companies were soon formed into the regiments that comprised the first Brigde under General Jackson at Manassas

Grayson Daredevils- 2 descriptions by the Richmond Daily Whig they were a volunterr company from the backwoodsmountains of Viginia, became Company F. of the 4th Virginia. "The "Daredevils" from Grayson County arrived on Tuesday. Their unform consists of red hunting shirts, but they will change to grey before going into service. The men are unfailing marksmen with the rifle,and, if the opportunity offers, will perforate many of that band who so vauntingly swear that the havoc a home and country shall leave us no more."

"The corps from (Grayson) County are said to be perfect nondescripts-they call themselves the "Daredevils" and deep in leggings, moccasins, and other back-woods appliances. There is not a man in the company who is not over six feet in height."

THE BATTLE OF SCARY CREEK by Terry Lowry pub by Pictorial Histories Pub Co 1982

Pg. 22 May 11, 1861 Lt.Col. John McCausland ran a "recruitment ad" in the Kanawha Valley Star "The Captain will see that each man is provided with a uniform, one blanket and haversack, one extra pair of shoes, two flannel shirts (to be worn in place of the ordinary shirts), one comb and brush, one toothbrush, two pairs of drawers, four pairs of woolen socks, four handkerchiefs, two pairs of white gloves, one pair of rough pantaloons for fatigue duty, needles, thread, wax, buttons, secured in a small buckskin bag. The whole (excepting the blanket) will be placed in a bag, this will be placed on the blanket, rolled up, and secured to the back of each man by two straps."

Pg. 29 May 23 1861 "On May 23, Col. Christopher Q. Tompkins, who had apparently arrived at Camp Buffalo, reported his total strength there as "350 men comprising of five companies."...and also reiterated the now well known fact of the complete lack of material for uniforms..."

Pg. 33 "So as the month of May, for the year 1861, drew to a close, the Virginia volunteer forces retained full possession of the Kanawha Valley with a force somewhere between 350 and 500 in number, ill-equiped with outdated weapons and meager supplies, few uniforms, and poorly trained..."

THE RICHMOND DAILY DISPATCH-

June 16, 1861 "A company from Abbeville district (S.C.) arrived in this city on Wednesday night ...their uniform is a red frock and dark pants..."

A red frock coat? Oh, How I'd have loved to seen them on parade.

U.S. ARMY HERITAGE & EDUCATION CENTER

James T. Binion, Co. F 10th Georgia Infantry Regiment in a letter to his brother, summer (June) 1861 "...I want you to tell sister to make me some calico shirts and let me no when she get them done and I send for them get the cloth for his (brother) ...'

CIVIL WAR SOLDIERS Reid Mitchell Viking Peguin 1988

Pg. 106 Georgia- "In June 1861 he (Governor Brown) challenged its women to match the Revolutionary War record of their female ancestors by producing one homemade uniform of any kind of color."... "Women of the Soldier's Aid Society in Pulaski County rolled up the carpets and rugs from their floors and sent them to Virginia to put something between the cold ground of winter camp quarters and the bodies of their men. Prominent planters like George Walker III served as local agents for the Battlefield Relief Association and collected supplies for companies at the front. Such attepts to equip and comfort the troops were public acts of Southern Nationalism.

Early in the war the need for domestic labor was most pressing to meet the demand for uniforms and personal items. During the summer of 1861 women were called on to produce the winter clothing needed to keep soldiers from a humid, subtropical climate warm in northern Virginia. Each household was expected to supply two pairs of heavy brown or grey-mixed jeans lined with domestic cloth; one army jacket of the same materialreaching four inches below the waistband and large enough for a shirt or vest to be worn underneath; one vest of jeans or linsey; an overshirt; and one or two pairs of drawers, heavy woolen socks, an overcoat or hunting shirt with belt; and one good blanket. Gray and blue flannel shirts were preferred over red, as red shirts "present(ed) an excellent target for the enemy." In addition, families were required to provide their soldier with a comb, pocketknife, small tin cup, iron spoon, knife, and fork. The ability of households to meet these demands depended largely on the spinning, weaving, sewing and knitting skills of women. There were also financial incentives early in the war for families to make homespun clothing for their soldiers. In a circular issued on May 18, 1861, A.C.Wayne, Georgia's adjutant general, announced a Confederate commutation to reimburse soldiers who clothed themselves. The commutation was sent to their captain, who served as company agent and purchased the clothing "from home."

Some studies of elite Southern women suggest that their participation in domestic cloth production "seems to have been actually of very limited scope." Privileged women's "traditional identities," notes one historian, "conflicted with the campaign for home textile production." A decline in home manufacturing in planter households, the lack of a textile-producing tradition among elite women, and the association of such work with slaves are among the reasons cited to explain why a "homespun revolution" did not materialize. But most Southern women were not members of the privileged and educated slaveholding class. They were plain folk, especially in white belt neighborhoods, where they formed the overwhelming majority of households. Plain folk regardless of gender knew their economic independence depended on the hands of white family members, whereas planter households could rely more on slave labor."

THE CONFEDERATE VETERAN VOL.VI

Jan. 1898 Pg. 25 "Patriotic deed of Roger Chew-Mrs. Viginia C. East, Charlestown, W.Va., writes that in June, 1861, it became known that the troops under J.E.Johnston, stationed at Winchester, Va. were in sore need of ammunition. Powder was abundant, caps were being rapidly manufactured, but lead was exceedingly scarce. This urgent need coming to the notice of Mr. Roger Chew, a farmer residing near Charlestown, he communicated with Gen. T.J.Jackson, who had just succeeded Gen Johnson in command of the valley troops, and he sent a squad of soldiers and four wagons to dig and convey to camp one-fourth mile of lead piping, used to convey water to the house and grounds. That Sabbath day was a busy one. Finding the task beyond their powers, the labors and wagons of the neighborhood were pressed into service. The precious metal was conveyed into camp and hurriedly molded. This same ammunition served a great purpose in turning the tide of battle at first Manassas. It was used when Gen. T.J.Jackson was seen to stand as a "stone wall."

HURRAH FOR MR. ROGER CHEW!

THE PERSONAL MEMIORS OF J.T. SCHARF OF THE FIRST MARYLAND ARTILLERY ed by Tom Kelley pub by Butternut and Blue 1992

Pg 7 June1861. "...We got orders to leave for Manassas, and we prepared to move that night with all the guns and started to the station. We stayed there some time and went back on our horses to camp and slept all night without blankets or anything but my best Sunday clothes-light spring gray pants and vest, and fancy blue coat with scotch cap and patent leather shoes; all belonging to a soldier, for I was now a soldier. In the morning I arose and roamed about camp, and finally got a new uniform such as was worn by the company..."

The Loyal, True and Brave- American Civil War Soldiers by Steven E. Woodworth A Scholarly Resources Inc. Imprint, 2002

Pg. 6 June 3, 1861 Eighth Georgia, Company I at Harper's Ferry Va. Lt. Reed's account "Col. Francis Batrow..." The Sanvanah boys, Bartow's own company, with their perfect drill, neat uniforms and city ease and polish-to use a backwoods saying-took the shine off all the other companies. Savannah, Atlanta and Macon each furnished a company, Rome-or more correctly Floyd County-three, Meriwether, Pulaski, Oglehtorpe and Greene Counties each one-the regiment consisting of ten in all. Every company had a uniform conspicuously different from that of the rest-homespun being largely present even then. None of the officers but a few from the cities had respectable side-arms, and though their dress was somewhat more pretentious than the men's it was actually a burlesque of what it should have been. I never did get a decent sword or a Confederate uniform. As a whole, we were in appearance fantastic citizens playing soldiers. We never acquired any holiday gloss and show, but we did soon learn to march and fight..."

Notice the comment-"homespun being largely present even then."

Charlotte's Boys-civil War letters of the branch Family ed.by Mauriel Phillips Joslyn Rockbridge Pub. Co. 1996 John, Sanford & Hamilton Branch

Pg. 14 Capt. G. Chandler to Charlotte Branch Brunswick Ga. June 3, 1861 Mrs. Charlotte S. Branch & others Dear friends, "Your highly esteemed favors of a box of clothing reached us yesterday for which you will please accept our sincere thanks. The present was the more acceptable on account of the scarcity of such articles here. Many will not procure such conveniences here from the fact that they are not in this market..."

Pg. 21 Charlotte Branch to Adj. John L. Branch June 13 1861 My Dear John, "I rec. a letter from Capt. C(h) andler of the Banks Co. Guards in acknowledgement of a box of clothes I sentr to Brunswick, he is very grateful..."

Pg. 23 Charlotte Branch to Pvt. Hamilton Branch June 17, 1861 My Dear Child, "…We met at Mrs. Bartows on Saterday in answer to a call from her in the newspapers, the business before us was to see who would make clothes (&) uniforms for the OLI (Ogilthorpe Light Inafntry). There was a very large meeting all appeared to be anxious to do what they could. I shall make four suits, one a piece for each of you, one for a young man by the name of Carolin (James E. Carolin) whom I am interested in and the other is for a man I don't know, a stranger Francis Lunts or Lents (Lentz, a Swiss grocery clerk who was boarding in Savannah). You know these 2 men have no friends and so some body must make for them-…I have so busy all the morning attending to the uniform that I can't write more now…"

Pg. 25 Charlotte Branch to Sanford and Hamilton Branch June 20 61 My Dear Santy & Hammie "…How are you both off for clothes…The uniforms have been sent. I hope they will do service. I do not think them very pretty. Santy I commenced to put the chevrons on your sleeves but changed my mind as I did not know how many to put on so put braid and thread in your inside pocket, so that you could have it put on yourself…"

Pg. 30 Pvt. Hamilton Branch to Charlotte Branch My Dear, Dear, Mother June 27/61 Winchester Va. "P.S. Make my uniform to fit. Have you my measure. What color is it. Hammie…"

NORTHERN VIRGINIA'S OWN -THE 17TH INF. REGIMENT CONFEDERATE STATES ARMY by William M. Glascow Jr. Col. U.S. Army Ret.

Pg 57 With the army at Manassas, June 6, 1861 "We are very actively engaged in fortifying Camp Pickens." Sergeant Buck, of the Warren Rifles, wrote home on June 8, "Your most welcome letter with the bag of provisions and clothing was received, and I tell you that they were acceptable. The pants came just in time for my others were almost gone…Richard Timberlake and myself have a bunk together. He is a very nice fellow and very kind to me. His mother and father came down to see him and brought him a large box of provisions which we keep on our bunk…I wish you would send that money down as soon as you can get it changed as I have none at all and owe D. Spangler a dollar. I hope my pants are not of that heavy goods…we still have our knives."

Pg.58 When their uniforms suffered from the toll of constructing field fortifications under a hot Virginia summer son, the Warren ladies made new ones for the Alexandrians from "cadet grey cloth."

Supply from home folks

HISTORY OF THE FORTY-NINTH VA. INFANTRY C.S.A. "Extra Billy Smith's Boys" by Laura Virginia Hale & Stanley S. Phillips 1981

June 17, 1861 "The men remained in town for a month to recruit and drill, some boarding at the hotels," wrote Robert Daniel Funkhouser, upon whose memoirs most of this history is based. "We soon learned the drill, the manual of arms, and camp minutia." Meanwhile the ladies of Warren County were busy, at home or assembled in town, making uniforms and "overcoats of the military pattern." The cloth, furnished by the County, was bought at the reputed woolen factory of Thomas P. Mathews near Middletown, Frederick County, Va., and the coats and pants were cut by Jim Anderson, a local tailor."

RECOLECTIONS OF A Md. CONFEDERATE SOLDIER AND STAFF OFFICER UNDER JOHNSON, JACKSON AND LEE by McHenry Howard Press of Morningside Bookshop 1975

June 1861 "The French Zouave was the model soldier of that period, according to Am. Ideas, and the Md. Guard uniform was patterned on his. The full dress was a dark blue jacket, short and close fitting and much embroidered with yellow; a blue flannel shirt with a close row of small round gilt buttons (for ornament merely) down the front, between yellow trimming; blue pantaloons, very baggy and gathered below the knee and falling over the tops of long drab gaiters; a small blue cap, of the kepi kind, also trimmed in yellow; and finally, a wide red sash, or band rather, kept wide by hooks and eyes on the ends, completed this gaudy dress, which made a very brilliant effect on street parade but was totally unsuited for any active service. To fully adjust it, a man almost required the services of a valet- or a sister or sweetheart. The fatigue (undress) uniform substituted a more generous blue jacket and ordinary black pantaloons and left off the gaiters and sash, and was therefore the more sensible or less absurd..."

Pg. 19 June 1961 "It appeared that our party, some of us being in Md. Guard uniform which we had worn since starting from George Thomas's had been taken for Yankees landing from a prowling gunboat. We received a warm apology from both the colonel and the ladies of his family..."

Heathsville-"Two companies of infantry were stationed or organizing here, having a picket thrown out on the road, whose sentinel brought his bayonet to charge at the sight of this formidable invasion of strange and very gaudy uniforms, but recognizing Dr. Smith, he allowed us to pass, with an expression of much doubt and astonishment..."

Pg. 26"One evening I remained in Richmond until after dark and was sent out to camp by Mrs. Robert F. Morris in her carriage; when it stopped at the gate, the officer on duty took me for some one of high rank, an impression much strengthened when I stepped out in the moonlight in the blue and yellow Md. Guard uniform, turned out the guard and received me with presented arms and the respect due a general officer."

Pg. 46 FFX Courthouse-" With many of us, pantaloons and shoes had suffered severely from the briars, mud and water and stone road and presented a very sorry appearance as we marched through the main street. My own pantaloons hung in tatters from the knee down and my shoes were so dilapidated that it was with difficulty I could keep them on my feet as I shuffled along, and I noticed many of the citizens looking down at my legs and feet with mingled compassion and amusement."

LEXINGTON AND ROCKBRIDGE COUNTY IN THE CIVIL WAR The Va. Battles and Leaders Series by Robert J. Drivers Jr. H.E. Howard Inc. Lynchburg, Va.

June 1861-"I suppose there has no company left the county better or more thoroughly equipped, every man in complete uniform with coats and pants of grey cloth and most of them with two fatigue shirts, knapsacks, haversacks, canteens, bed sacks, and double tents-with new shoes and socks for all."

Collections of the Manuscript Division, Library of Congress

June, 1861 memior of a visiting English officer "The camp was about two miles out of town on the Charleston (SC) Fair Grounds, and a battalion drill was in progress when we drove into camp…and witnessed the regimental dress parade which succeeded the drill. I thought the Confederates, considering the lack of uniformity in their dress, made a very creditable appearance. Very few in the ranks were well dressed, the majority were like farmers of laborers…"

"I thanked him heartily and accompanied him out of the hotel and across the street to the drinking saloon. As we entered I saw a group of soldiers drinking at the bar. Among them was a little old man in blue jean overalls and checked shirt, with an old-fashioned, very narrow brim, stovepipe hat. I was greatly astonished when I was led up to this odd-looking character and he was introduced to me as the commanding colonel."

Seriously, that is a great uniform.

THE OLD DIMINION RIFLES

Camp Ashland June 1861 Dear Father, "…I wish the next opportunity you see you would tell mother to send me another pair of pants to rough it in & about three handkerchiefs. My saddle bags are in such a bad fix that I send by John Ned to get me a pair in town the tops won't keep out any water scarcely…" From Your Son S.S. Stringer

RICHMOND VOLUNTEERS 1861-1865 by Louis H. mandarin & Lee A. Wallace pub. by Richmond Civil War Centennial Committee Westover Press 1969

Pg. 284 Richmond Zouaves "...The uniforms for the Richmond Zouaves were made by the ladies of the Monumental Episcopal Church, and the following extract from an article, which appeared in the Richmpond Whig on June 10 (1861), suggests that the company was outfitted in a typical colorful Zouave pattern uniform, consisting of a blue jacket and orange baggy trousers: At drill hours our Armory (Corinthian Hall) presents quite an animated scene, and uniforms other than the blue and orange, mingle cum toga civile. To-night, two of the Zouaves Francais were present and expressed themselves well pleased with our appearance and movements. All thanks to the courteous Frenchmen, whether we deserve the compliments or not...

The two Frenchmen were apparently from Lieutenant Colonel Geoge Augute Gaston Coppen's Battalion of Louisiana Zouaves, which had arrived in Richmond on July 7. The Battalion, comprised of many nationalities, was uniformed in a red fez, blue jacket with gold braid trim, and red baggy trousers with white gaiters. It seems unlikely that members of this already notorious command would have praised the Richmond Zouaves had the Virginians been wearing anything other than the Zouave pattern uniforms. We do know that during June white canvas leggings were made for Captain McConnell's company by contract with a Mr. F. Thomas of Richmond. The Zouaves were equipped with a unique knapsack, which could be unfolded to serve as a raincoat or small tent. It was patented in the Confederate States by a Mr. Reith, a salesman for Messrs. Kent, Paine & Co., a dry goods firm in Richmond...By November 3 the Richmond Zouaves, still at Camp Bartow, had dwindled from three officers and fifty enlisted men present for duty in late August, to two officers and thiry-four enlisted men present for duty. The company at this time had received some clothing, and it is doubtful that much of their Zouave clothing was still in evidence..."

I'd like to see that knapsack.

RICHMOND VOLUNTEERS 1861-1865 by Louis H. mandarin & Lee A. Wallace pub. by Richmond Civil War Centennial Committee Westover Press 1969

Pg. 89 Richmond Fayette Artillery"...At the end of June 1861, the battery, equipped as light artillery, with four brass 6 pounders, was reported as being "well uniformed in blue flannel, & well equipped; discipline: good; drill: excellent..."

Pg. 183 1st Regiment Virginia Infantry Company I "...At the end of June 1861, the aggregate strength of company I was forty-seven. The company, rated as being poorly uniformed and equipped, was armed with altered smoothbore percussion muskets, which were considered as being "very unreliable." In the fall of 1861, however, the company was rearmed with

Springfield muskets "in good order." Also, by this time an adequate supply of clothing had been procured…"

16th TENNESSEE VOLUNTEER INFANTRY REGIMENT: Clothing, Arms and Equipment (website)

Savannah Republican Georgia 6 June, 1861 "…The coat is to be a short grey tunic of cadet grey cloth, double-breasted, with two rows of buttons down the breast, two inches apart at the waist, and widening toward the shoulders.-The pantaloons are to be made sky blue cloth, full in the lags. The buttons to be of plain gilt, convex form, three-quarters of an inch in diameter…the trimmings blue for infantry…"

Willy Dame, Richmond Howitzers, Army of Northern Virginia, wrote"…each man had one blanket, one small haversack, one change of underclothes, a canteen cup and plate of tin, a knife and fork, and the clothes in which he stood. When ready to march, the blanket, rolled lengthwise, the ends brought together and strapped, hung from the left shoulder across the right arm; the haversack, furnished with towel, soap, comb, knife and fork in various pockets, a change of underclothes in the main division, and whatever rations we happened to have in the other-hung on the left hip; the canteen, cup and plate, tied together, hung on the right; toothbrush at will, stuck in two buttonholes of jacket or in haversack; tobacco bag hung on to a breast button, pipe in pocket."

Another Southerner wrote "I wore a cartridge box and bayonet holder pon my belt. Extra cartridges were placed in pockets. Around my shoulder hung my wool blanket and a captured Yankee gum (poncho) in which I wrapped my few belongings. …I also had a haversack in which my plate, knife, spoon and fork rested with what few meager rations we received. I tied my coffee boiler to my canteen to be ready to scoop up water at the first well or creek we passed…"

During the Peninsular Campaign, May, June, July 1862, the Army of Northern Virginia was reported as "Some were wrapped in blankets of rag-carpet, and others wore shoes of rough, untanned hide. Others were without either shoes or jackets, and their heads were bound in red handkerchiefs. Some appeared in red shirts; some in stiff beaver hats; some attired in shreds and patches of cloth; and a few wore the soiled garments of civilian gentlemen; but the mass adhered to homespun suits of grey, or "butternut," and the coarse blue kersey common to slaves…"

In other words, multiform.

CONFEDERATE LETTERS AND DIARIES ed by Walbrook D. Swank Colonel USAF Retired pub by Papercraft Printing & Design 1992

Letters Pertainig to John Taylor Anderson Private, Co. C 13th Virginia Infantry Pg. 91June 7 1861 Harper's Ferry, Va Dear Sister, "…Sallie don't put yourself to any trouble about my clothes. I reckon that Mr. Parrott will come over that way before he comes back and if you have not got the clothes ready you will have other chances to send them…"

Website THE STONEWALL BRIGADE—Stonewall Brigade-1861 Impression Guidelines by Bret Sumner, 4th Virginia http://www.stonewallbrigade.com/articles

Pg. 2 Staunton newspaper June 7, 1861 "The following is a list of articles necessary to a soldier's comfort bring all of them you can, or the best substitute you can obtain: Two flannel overshirts, 2 woolen undershirts, 2 pair white cotton drawers, 2 pair woolen socks, 2 pair cotton socks, 2 colored handkerchiefs, 2 pair stout shoes, 3 towels, one blanket (hole in the middle), 1 blanket for cover, 1 broad brim hat, 1 pound castile soap, 2 pounds bar soap, one belt knife, some stout linen thread, large needles and a bit of beeswax; some buttons and some paper of pins, all in a small buckskin or stout cloth bag, 1 overcoat, 1 painted canvas cloth, 7 feet 4inches long and 5 feet wide."

Now, how in the Hell is one soldier gonna carry all that? A horse couldn't carry that load!

JAMES MADISON UNIV. ARCHIVES

June 8, 1861 Letter of Pvt. Rueben A. Scott Co. B, 10th Regiment Virginia Infantry Harper's Ferry Dear Mollie: "…We have a great many Negroes here not many companies that have less than three or four and some more they are a lowed to carry weapons when they are moving from one place to another not long since I saw two come in with a company of cavalry armed like the men riding fine horses I doubt if there ever was one so much honored in the north unless he happened to have money and the Yankees love that almighty dollar that is their Idol and think that the south would sell their rights for the same but a sad mistake on their part…"

Ok, another reference to African Americans in Southern ranks

NORTHERN VIRGINIA'S OWN -THE 17TH INF. REGIMENT CONFEDERATE STATES ARMY by William M. Glascow Jr. Col. U.S. Army Ret.

Pg. 58 In another letter on June 12, he wrote: "I intend wearing the pants you sent me before until they give out, as they are not so thick as the others. How warm those uniform pants are.

A great many of the boys had to pull their's off they were so warm. I think it was a very bad selection. I will send my old blue uniform pants up. Please fix them for me."

Uniform repair from the home folks

THE PAINFUL NEWS I HAVE TO WRITE-Letters and Diaries of Four Hite Brothers of Page County in the Service of the Confederacy Army of Northern Virginia Series Stonewall Brigade ed.by Harlan R. Jessup Butternut& Blue 1998

Pg. 10 John Hite To sister Bettie Winchester Frederick Va. June 12th 61 "...Some of us have our knapsacks. I have mine, and got all in it but blanket and pants..."

U.S. ARMY HERITAGE AND EDUCATION CENTER

June 14, 1861 Henry I. 4th Alabama Infantry Regiment Richmond Va.

Dear Ma, "...You said if I wanted anything let you know, as you would have several chances of sending them to me. I will certainly have to have more shirts and handkerchiefs for I either left my dirty ones at home or they taken from my trunk on the route for it was checked through to this place. I have not got more than six handkerchiefs & two or three shirts are missing. I don't care about the sleeve buttons much but if you want to give me something, you may send me the value of the buttons in tobacco from Lonny Hamilton & Co at 80 cents per pound. I think send it in plug & do not get that twisted tobacco..."

VMI MS 1864 # 282

Camp at Rosse's Ferry June 15, 1864 Dear Mother "...Jane kindly lent me a blanket, as I had nothing but a very small one with me and the weather here now is as cold as it is seen in November. I would like very much to have my coat, as I am in my shirt sleeves. Send it to me if you can..."

THE BATTLE OF SCARY CREEK by Terry Lowry pub by Pictorial Histories Pub Co 1982

Pg. 54 June16 1861 Letter to Lt. Welch (probably from his wife) "...I had heard you had lost your uniform-As the boat was detained I found just enough flannel in town to make you a jacket. I shall make it tomorrow and send it down with your pants. I should have done it sooner but they told me I would have to get some flannel dyed first..."

Pg. 56 June 17 Kan. C.H. June 17th, 1861
Lt. J.C. Welch

Dear Sir,

Your note in relation to Patrick's "Dudds" is received. I will send them first opportunity. Could have sent them yesterday if I had known the "Maffitt" was going down. Also have more guns (muskets) to send you. Also haversacks. I regret to have to say to your men that it has been impossible so far to get material for uniforms. We tried several persons going & sending down to get material anywhere it could be found from Gallipollis to Cinn. Least all efforts have failed so far. It is now impossible, as you know, to get anything from tailors. We are now trying to get it from the East. Hope we may succeed. Please explain to your men fully the reasons why the uniforms have not been forthcoming, as they may, without explanation think we have neglected the matter or are not trying to get it...."

Respectfully,
J.P. Hale
Capt. Kan. Artillery

MY DIARY NORTH AND SOUTH by William Howard Russell pub by Alfred A. Knopf 1988

Pg. 199 June 17th, 1861 Grand Junction, Tn. "These men were as fanciful in their names and dress as could be. In the train which preceded us there was a band of volunteers armed with rifled pistols and enomous Bowie knives, who called themselves "The Toothpick Company."

But these fellows were, nevertheless, the material for fighting and for marching after proper drill and with good officers, even though there was too large a proportion of old men and young lads in the ranks. To judge from their dress, these recruits came from the laboring and poorest classes of whites. The officers affected a French cut and bearing with indifferent success, and in the luggage vans there were three foolish young women with slop-dress imitation clothes of the Vivandie're type, who with disheveled hair, dity faces, and dusty hats and jackets, looked sad, sorry, and absurd. Their notions of propriety did not justify them in adopting straps, boots, and trousers, and the rest of the tawdry ill-made costume looked very bad indeed." *And just who asked for your snooty opinion?*

Pg. 203 Memphis, Tn. June 18th, 1861 "...The volunteers who were lounging about were dressed in different ways and had no uniform..."

Pg. 204 "The volunteers were mostly engaged at drill in distinct companies, but by order of the General some 700 or 800 of them were formed in line for inspection. Many of these men were in their shirt sleeves, and the awkwardness with which they handled their arms showed that, however good they might be as shots, they were bad hands at manual platoon exercise; but such great strapping fellows, that, as I walked down the ranks there were few whose shoulders were not above the level of my head, excepting here and there a weedy old man or a growing lad. They were armed with old patterned percussion muckets, no two clad alike, many very badly shod, few with knapsacks, but all provided with a tin water-flask and a blanket. These men have been only five weeks enrolled, and were called out by the State of Tennessee in anticipation of the vote of sucession"

VMI MS# 0331

Ervine Berkely Co. June the 18th, 1861 Dear Ellen, "...Tell Father I want him to get me some goods for pants as my pants is getting somewhat worn& will not last me very long time the legs below with something strong as they worn out through with the styrups leather..."

U.S. ARMY HERITAGE AND EDUCATION CENTER

June 18, 1861 I.C.M. Luce? S.C. Infantry Richmond Va. My Dear Kate: "...I have a request to make of you, that is to work me a flower palmetto to wear in my cap in front. It should be worked on blue cloth, about 2 inches or thereabouts in length. But if you have not the material, or do not feel well enough, you must not trouble about it..."

LEE'S TIGERS-The La. Inf. In the Army of Northern Va. by Terry L. Jones Univ. of La. Press

Pg. 16 June 20, 1861, passing through Petersburg on their way to Richmond, H.B. Cowles, Jr. wrote to an unknown friend: "...The greatest sight I have yet seen in the way of military was a body of about 600 Louisiana Zouaves, uniformed and drilled it was aid, in the true French Zouave style. Most of them were of foreign extraction-the French predominant-but there were Irish, Italians, Swiss, etc., etc. Their uniforms consisted of loose red flannel pants tied above the ankles, blue flannel jackets, and for headgear a kind of red flannel bag large enough at one end to fit the head and tapering to a point at the other where it was generally decorated with a piece of ribbon. This end fell behind. In this cap which, you see, did not protect their faces from the sun in the least they had been wasting for a month or two in the burning sun of Pensacola, and of course were as brown as they could well get-browner than I ever saw a white man. Add to their costume and complexion that they were hard specimens before they left the "cresent city" as their manner indicated and you may perhaps imagine what sort of men they were. In fact they were the most savage-looking crowd I ever saw..."

WELCOME THE HOUR OF CONFLICT-WILLIAM COWAN McCLELLAN & THE 9TH ALABAMA ed by John C. Carter Univ Al. Press 2007

Pg. 28 June 23 1861 Richmond William McClellan to Matilda McClellan Dear Sister, "...It is very hot here. I wish you would send me 2 pairs of cheap pants as they asked 2 prices for everything in Richmond..."

"DEAR MOTHER: DON'T GRIEVE ABOUT ME. IF I GET KILLED, I'LL ONLY BE DEAD." Ed. by Mills Lane The Beehive Press 1977

Pg. 19 Charles Norton to his Mother Camp Winchester, Virginia June 23 1861 "…Our orders last night were to leave our tents standing and only carry our blankets. I have fixed up a strap with a sort of a collar by which I can carry quits easily both my blanket and rubber. I am also fixing hook and eyes to the rubber, so as to make a shelter tent. We are fixed up smartly. For instance, Jim Johnson, Dick and I are all seated around a rough plank table, on which we spread an oilcloth. Stretched over it on four posts is a bed tick which is of no use, as straw is not always convienent and it's humbug anyhow. The ground is good enough…"
Theyr'e learning to rough it.

Dear Irvie, Dear Lucy-The Civil War Letters of Capt. Irving A. Buck, General Cleburne's AAG & Family pub. by Buck Pub. Co. 2002

Pg. 31 June 24, 1861 Camp Pickens, Va. Dear Ma. "Your note was handed me this morning- I was advised by the officers not to send my valise up until my knapsack came, so I kept it- my box goes up today…"

Pg. 34 Aug. 11,1861 Head Quarters Dear Lucy, "…I put my clothes in a carpet bag of Benton's and will send them up this evening…"

I had never heard of Confederate troops carrying their gear in either a valise or carpet bag, but it makes sense.

LETTERS FROM THE STONEWALL BRIGADE Ted Barcay, Liberty Hall Volunteers by Charles W. Turner Rockbridge Pub. Co. 1992

Pg. 20 Berkly Co. W. Va. June 25, 1861 "…Ma, I wish you to have me a pair of shoes made like the ones I have, Deaver has my measure. The ones I have are not worn out, but I ought to have a pair by the time they do. Have them made and send them to me by the first one that comes to the Fourth Regiment of Virginia Volunteers. There are three companies from Rockbridge in it and someone comes down almost every day…"

FIRST & SECOND MD. INF. C.S.A. Robert J. Driver Jr. Willow Bend Books 2003

Pg. 15 "…When the regiment returned from Harper's Ferry on June 25, one of the members of Murray's company shouted "Look out for your baggage, boys, the Plug Uglies (a notorious crowd of rowdies in the "Know Nothing" days in Baltimore") are coming.' and lifting our eyes, there was to be seen winding over the hill one of the sorriest, raggedest crowds we had ever beheld, which turned out to be the six (sic) companies which had organized at Harper's ferry…havind seen what was thought at that time to be some rather rough service, they were poorly clad and presented an "unkempt and unwashed appearance," recalled Mc Henry Howard…."

"I WILL GIVE THEM ONE MORE SHOT"-Ramsey's 1st Regiment Georgia Volunteers by George Wiston Martin pub by Mercwer Univ. Press 2010

Pg. 124 June 26, 1861 "Encamped at McDowell, (Shanendoah Vally, Va.) the 1st Georgia was in terrible condition. Almost all of their equipment-tents, blankets, cook pots, and more-had been lost during the retreat from Laurel Hill. Uniforms were in tatters, and clothing of any description was desparately needed…"

THE 33RD VIRGINIA INFANTRY by Lowell Reidenbaugh The Va. Regimental History Series, 1887

Pg. 3 "The two companies marched 45 miles to Winchester in three days, arriving on June 27 (1861). There the Guards received their supplies from Springfield which had been purchased by public subscription. These consisted of knapsacks, blankets, cartridge boxes, canteens and tents."

THE BATTLE OF SCARY CREEK by Terry Lowry pub by Pictorial Histories Pub Co 1982

Pg. 74 June 27 1861 Charleston, Western Va. Camp Two Mile "…Lewis (a Federal spy) said (of McClausland's men) "considering the lack of uniformity in their dress, made a very creditable appearance. Very few in the ranks were well dressed, the majority were like farmers or laborers."…"

DIARIES, LETTERS AND RECOLLECTION OF THE WAR BETWEEN THE STATES Vol III Winchester, Frederick Co. Historical Society Papers 1955

The Nimrod Hunter Steel Diary and Letters lieutenant of the Newtown Artillery, 16th brigade, Battery C, 3rd Virginia Division of the Confederate Army-Pg. 48 Friday, June 28, 1861 : Received six tents today, very good ones with flies, put them up out in the field…"

JAMES MADISON UNIV. Letter of Enoch V. Kaufman Camp Skinkers Rock Dear Uncle: "...Tell ASng. That I have got an over coat at last I drew one the other day from the Quarter Master it cost me $18.00 it is very low according to the way everything that is selling here..."

THE BATTLE OF SCARY CREEK by Terry Lowry pub by Pictorial Histories Pub Co 1982

Pg. 70 Letter from Col. Mccausland to V.M.I. Superintendant Francis Smith "...I am in hope that you will be able to send me 10 cadets soon. If you could only see our soldiers-rough-undisciplined-and badly uniformed-in fact, with their everyday clothes, amounting to nothing at all..."

VMI MS# 282

Harper's Ferry June 30 1861 Dear Mother "...I wish to tell Father to get Mr. Vanderslice to make me a pair of Sergeants Sheverons, tell him to make them like the cadet's are made. I cannot get a bit of lace here or I would get them made here, if he cannot get the lace at the Institute, go to Mr. James S. Smiths' jewelry store, and tell him to let him have that lace that belongs to sergeant Boude, tell him that Boude told me to send for it. Send it the first opportunity that you have as I wish to have them put on my coat...Some time ago you said that if John Donald wanted some check shirts that you would make them for him, he says that he will be very much obliged to you for them as he has nothing but his white shirts...I got two pairs of drawers and two shirts at Switzer's, a pea jacket at Young's worth $2.75 & a pair of buckskin gloves at Capt. Baker's, a pair of boots at Tom Daniel's worth $6.50, and a silk handkerchief at George White's..."

A pea jacket? What color?

LETTERS FROM LEE'S ARMY Compiled by Susan Leigh Blackford Annotated by her husband, Charles Minor Blackford, Charles Scribner's & Sons 1947Company B of the Second Virginia Cavalry- Charles Blackford was first lieutenant, later captain.

Pg. 20 Centerville, June 30th, 1861 "I must trouble you to send me as soon as you can the following articles: one small oven, two heavy blankets, dark if possible, some pipes and stems, a bottle of ink, two camp stools and a camp bed, the latter I want made according to the most approved pattern, such as they are now making in Richmond, the principle object being to get them as light as possible, so made that they will fold up and occupy very little room."

Wow, he doen't want much, does he?

MY DEAR EMMA-The War letters of Col. James K. Edmonson 1861-8165 ed.by Charles w. Turner PhD McClure Press 1978

Pg. 26 Camp Stevens near Winchester (Va.) June 30 1861 My dear Wife '...Rebecca has been very kind to me since you have been away. She has sent me several very useful articles, to wit a cap linen and a calico shirt beautifully embroidered, which is not only handsome but very comfortable, a Havelock, which is very comfortable but did not reach me soon enough to keep my skin from turning. Since that however a young lady in these parts has presented me with another one so I have now two Havelocks and two caps which I wear alternately. Rebecca is also (so Annie Lewis says in a letter to Bill) making me a haversack. I bought one however the other day in Martinsburg but I expect Rebecca's to be much the best. My dear wife, you are so kind. I know you would work by the midnight lamp, if it was necessary to provide clothes for the comfort of your husband but it is not necessary. I have as much clothing as I can possibly take care of ..."

THE BATTLE OF SCARY CREEK by Terry Lowry pub by Pictorial Histories Pub. C0. 1982

Pg. 46 July 1861 Western Va. "...The Fayetteville Riflemen, who when first organized in Fayette County (Va.), had uniforms made that, if not practical, were certainly pleasant to look at. The "jackets were made of blue flannel with yellow stripes across the breast like the European hussars...pants were of dark gray jeans with a wide yellow stripe on each leg."..."

THE MD. LINE IN THE CONFEDERATE ARMY1861-1865 by W.W. Goldsborough, pub. For the benefit of the Md. Line Confederate Soldier's Home. Pikesville, Md., under authority of the board of governors of the association of the Md. Line 1900.

Pg. 19 July 25, 1861 1st Md. Infantry, summer of 1861 after Manassas "The regiment numbered some seven hundred men, but only 2 of the companies were uniformed-those those of Murray and Dorsey from Richmond. The rest were clad in the garb in which they had left home, but it was sadly changed. Sleeping out in the mud and rain had despoiled the citizen's dress, and worn it threadbare, and in many cases it was in tatters. ...They were yeoman's sons, brave and warm-hearted; many of them were men of education and refinement; they never murmured or complained, and they went cheerfully to the call to their various camp duties."

THE MEN-49TH REGIMENT VIRGINIA VOLUNTEERS C.S.A.

"Requisition by Capt. M.T. Wheately, for the Warren blues, Co. E July 26, 1861:

12 common tents
2 wall tents
6 axes w/helves
6 camp hatchets
6 camp kettles
6 camp pans
9 spades
6 shovels
2 picks w/helves
1 drum complete 90 blankets
(no record of completion)

THE BATTLE OF SCARY CREEK by Terry Lowry pub by Pictorial Histories Pub Co 1982

Pg. 79 July 6 1861 Ripley Western Va.Letter from Henry Wise to Col. Thompkins "Please tell my son Richard to send up to me immediately his valis, with three shirts, ½ doz. Collars, a pair of drawers, my flannel under waistcoat & flannel undershirt & one pair of socks, my blue sack coat, my black thick pants, the gray summer coat in the box of things I bought from Jew ships stock, and some two twists of tobacco & also my boots and leggings…."

Southern Histrorical Society Papers With Stonewall Jackson

Pg. 9 July 1861 Rockbridge Artiilery- "…He was a slight figure in gray, with a few red trimmings, the young canoneer, but he wore a cheerful face and there was strong purpose behind it. On the caisson, until it was lost in battle, he carried a knapsack with a few articles of clean underclothing, strapped with a gray blanket. And stealthily stowed away in some limber chest was a little store of stationary for home letters, and a paperback book, to be read by all in turn and sometimes aloud…"

THIRD ALABAMA!-Civil War Memior of Brigadier General Cullen Andrews Boulle CSA ed by Brandon H. Beck pub by Univ Alabama Press 2000

Pg. 9 July 1861 "…The drum-corps had no equal. Hartman, of the Cadets, usually called Zou because he wore a French Zouave uniform, was the leader…"

LETTERS FROM LEE'S ARMY Compiled by Susan Leigh Blackford Annotated by her husband, Charles Minor Blackford, Charles Scribner's & Sons 1947 Company B of the Second Virginia Cavalry- Charles Blackford was first lieutenant, later captain.

Pg.34 July 1861 after the Battle of First Manassas "We bivouacked in the field and without tents or ant shelter but the oilcloths, a vast supply supply of which we had laid in from those upon which our foes had slept the night before. They were of the very best material and we gladly abandoned ours or kept them to throw over our saddles in the rain...."

NORTHERN VIRGINIA'S OWN -THE 17TH INF. REGIMENT CONFEDERATE STATES ARMY by William M. Glascow Jr. Col. U.S. Army Ret.

Pg.61 July1861 "During their almost two-month stay at Camp Pickens, the men of the 17th Va. Became fully trained in the art of soldiering in the field. In due course, they received two-man "pup tents" from the State Quartermaster, and they learned to lighten their loads after their first training march. Overcoats and knapsacks were discarded, and the men thereafter depended on a single blanket roll that readily could be carried on one shoulder slaunchwise across the body. Woolen underwear also went the route of overcoats, because cotton was easier to clean in the field."

LEE'S TIGERS-The La. Inf. In the Army of Northern Va. by Terry L. Jones Univ. of La. Press

Pg. 28 "...During their first year in Virginia, the Tigers could attribute little homesickness to shortages in food and clothing. Unlike later times, when the Confederate soldier was usually ill-clothed and poorly fed, the Louisianians enjoyed a fairly comfortable rookie year. In July, 1861, the four companies from Caddo Parish received $1500 each to buy supplies, and that autumn the 9th Louisiana received several large shipments of goods. One such delivery contained 12 cases of blankets, 872 pairs of drawers, 400 flannel shirts, 400 jackets, 400 pairs of pants, and 22 dozen pairs of socks. Along with these regimental supplies were numerous bundles addressed to individual soldiers. Typical of these was the one received by R.L. Tanner, containing three towels, two blankets, one pillow, a pair of pants, a pocketknife, a necktie, a cake of soap, a comb, and a bottle of medicine..." *A necktie?*

DESTRUCTION AND RECONSTRUCTION by Richard Taylor pub by Collector's Library of the Civil War 1983 reprinted from the 1879 edition

Pg. 40 July 30, 1861 Louisiana troops preparing to march to the Vally;"...As our next move, hourly expected, would take us beyond the reach of the railways, I have reduced the brigade to light marching order. My own kit, consisting of a change of underwear, and a tent "fly',could be carried on my horse. A fly can be put up in a moment, and by stopping the weather end with boughs a comfortable hut is made. The men carried each his blanket, an extra shirt and drawers, two pairs of socks (woolen) and a pair of extra shoes. These, with arms and ammunition, were asufficient load for strong marching. Tents, especially in a wooded country, are not only a nuisance, involving much transportation, the bane of armies, but are detrimental to health. In cool weather they are certain to be tightly closed, and the number of men occupying them breeds a foul atmosphere. The rapidity with which the men learn to shelter themselves, and their ingenuity in accomplishing it under unfavor able conditions are surprising. My people grumbled no little at being "stripped," but soon admitted they were better for it, and came to despise useless "impedimenta."

Pg. 49 Entering camp at New Market (Va) "…Over three thousand strong, neat in fresh clothing of gray with white gaiters, bands playing at the heads of their regiments, not a straggler, but every man in his place, stepping jauntily as on parade, though it had marched twenty miles and more, in open column with arms at "right shoulder shift," and rays of the declining sun flaming on polished bayonets, the brigade moved down the broad, smooth pike, and wheeled on its camping ground. Jackson's men, by thousands, had gathered on either side of the road to see us pass. Indeed, it was a martial sight, and no man with a spark of sacred fire in his heart but would have striven hard to prove worthy of such a command…"

THE PAINFUL NEWS I HAVE TO WRITE-Letters and Diaries of Four Hite Brothers of Page County in the Service of the Confederacy Army of Northern Virginia Series Stonewall Brigade ed.by Harlan R. Jessup Butternut& Blue 1998

Pg. 12 William Hite to his Parents Camp E.K. Smith near Winchester July 2nd 1861 "… There are 6 or 8 Regiments North and West of Winchester. some from the South. I have been in them. There is a great difference in the appearance of the men. The 10th Georgia Reg. was the cleanest and the Tennesse Regiments were the dirtyest and most Ragged that I saw…"

U.S. ARMY HERITAGE & EDUCATION CENTER Letters of James Griffin

Jarrat Hotel Petersburg, Va Hd Qrtrs Hampton Legion July2, 1861 My Darling Leila "…I will give you an account of a dozen daring Baltimorians. They took passage in boat, leaving Baltimore for Philidelphia. Some of them dressed as ladies, all were well armed, but arms concealed. As soon as the boat cleared the City, they dropped their hooped skirts, drew their repeaters and demanded a surrender-which was acceded to. They took charge of the steamer, turned her about and made for Fredericksburg. On their way the captured three Schooners, one loaded with ice, one with Coffee, and the other with coal.They landed them safely, and carried the Prisoners (thirty-eight in number) to Richmond yesterday…"

Repeaters? In 1861? Does he mean revolvers?

Charlotte's Boys

Pg. 34 Pvt Hamilton Btranch to Charlotte Branch Winchester July 2/61 My Dear, Dear, Mother "…I got my uniform yesterday. The white shirts came just in time."

Pg. 39 Pvt Hamilton Branch to Charlotte Branch July 15th 61 My Dear Mother, "…(P.S.) John and santy are well. Write to Cousin Eleanor (Hull) and ask her to get me a large size State of Florida button with the Coat of arms on it and Ma pleas send it to me. I want to put it on my coat. I have a Maryland, Mississippi, Alabama & Virginia button on my coat. I am going to try and get one from each of the C.S. Hammie…" *I've seen re-enactors (including my brother & myself) do this.*

Pg. 40 Charlotte Branch to Cpl. Sanford Branch July 15th 61 My Own Dear Son, "…I sent 4 pr. of socks with your uniformdid you not get them.…You did not say what you think of the clothes. I do not like them but suppose they will be useful. I had no hand in choosing the material…"

Pg. 41 Charlotte Branch to Adj. John Branch July 17th, 1861 My Dear, Dear, Son "…I have been very busy getting off the box of shirts, if you want any of the check shirts take them, as I furnished half the material although they were made for the OLI.…Hammie the black valise is yours in it is a box for Capt. (Joseph J.) West and 7 shirts which a lady sent for the use of the sick…"

LEE& JACKSON'S BLOODY TWELTH-Letters of Irby Goodwin Scott- First Lieutenant Co. G Putnam Light Infantry Twelth Ga. Vol. Inf. Ed. by Johnnie Perry Pearson Univ. Tn. Press 2010

Richmond, Va. July 5, 1861 Dear father, "…Richmond Reid has the appointment of Commissary for the regiment. He had our things placed in a house where they will be safe, I think, and he says he will have them sent to us if we need them…I had to leave the cloths you sent me and Nick because we could not carry them in our knapsacks…"

That's better than having to throw them away during a march.

31st REGIMENT VIRGINIA MILITIA Coln. R.F. Baldwin 31st Regt. V.M. R.E. Secverb Adj. Win. Va. Transcribed, Edited & indexed by David G. "Sammy" Copenhaver 2006

Pg. 36

Sepcial Order}
No.28 }

Headquaretrs 31st Regt V.M.
Winchester July 8th/61

The officer of the day & officer of the guard are hereby notified that on and after this 9th day of July, will be required to wear their Swords & Sashes while on duty.

By order of
Robt. F Baldwin
Col. 31stRegt…
WMP Fuller C

I WILL GIVE THEM ONE MORE SHOT" RAMSEY'S 1st REGIMENT GEORGIA VOLUNTEERS by Goerge Winston Martin Mercer Univ. Press 201

Pg. 85 "The uniforms that had so impressed Colonel Taliaferro were suffering as well. An officer in the Washington Rifles described his company's straits in a letter on 10 July (1861). He wrote, "On the march the men divested themselves of all the clothing but what was indespensable. Many brought but one suit. This they have worn all the time, rain or shine, in sleeping as well as waking hours. They have worn considerably. Men who prided themselves on neatness at home, go about in almost tatters and rags, and it is impossible to get clothes here for any price. When we were at home we intended and did order a new uniform made; but some of our citizens persuaded us that they would do that for us and make the cloths and send them on at their expense. I regret that I yielded to this-will wait till suffering come in on the men, if we wait till they raise the money to buy the cloth by taxing the county." The officer begged for a shipment of new uniforms.

Other necessities were solicited in addition to uniforms. "WANTED" read an advertisement in the Sandersville Central Georgian, "200 PAIRS HOME-KNIT SOCKS, for the Washington Rifles. They will be gratefully received by the Ladies volunteer Aid Association, as donations from the patriotic ladies at Washington County, by leaving them at the store of Youngblood, Newman & Co."

A MEMOIR OF CAPTAIN C. SETON FLEMING of the Second Florida Infantry C.S.A. by Francis P. Fleming pub by Times-union Pub House 1881

PG. 12 1861 A letter from their Father- Hibernia (Fl.) My dear Seton and Frank: "…I gave Frank a bundle with two pairs of woolen socks; you will find them most comfortable in damp weather.

Before you leave I must give you a little of my experience in campaigning (Col. Fleming had seen active service during the Florida Indian War). On the march, in the morning, eat but a slight meal; never drink anything stronger than coffee, water is best; when you eat but little you will not suffer from thirst. At night make your best meal and wash your feet in cold water and put on dry socks. You will find tea very refreshing and easy to make…"

VOICES FROM COMPANY D Diaries by the Greensboro Guards, fifth Alabama Infantry Regiment, Army of Northern Virginia ed. By G. Ward Hubbs Univ. of Georgia Press 2003

Pg. 14 July 12 (near Richmond) JHC: "…The drum beat reveille this morning before day light, which caused every one to think it was the long roll, and such jumping, pitching, tumbling and shuffling was never seen. Some got on pants of others a foot too short, others ran out without coats, and a good tale is told on Bob Jefferies, who it is said put on Gilliam James pants for a coat. …"

SOUTHERN INVINCIBILITY by Wily Sword St. Martin's Press 1999

Pg. 49 Near Winchester "our baggage has been reduced to a mere change of clothing, our tents have been now discarded and sent away, our meals are badly cooked, and we are suffering the privations of a soldier's life… July 14, 1861 "Nat Dawson confided how how was becoming "exceedingly lazy" about his army career. "My spare time is spent in studying tactics, and reading (news) papers." Only the purchase of natty new uniforms for the company-gray pants with a black stripe, close-fitting gray-flannel jackets with a black collar and wristbands, and gray caps with linen havelocks-seemed to briefly replenish the unit's sagging esprit de corps

GEORGIA BOYS WITH STONEWALL JACKSON by Aurelia Austin Univ. of Georgia Press 1967

Pg 3 July 17th, 1861, the 11th Georgia "…A short time after sunrise on the 17th, we began our first march, on foot, to Winchester (from Strasburg), a distance of eighteen miles; and a wearying, disagreeable tramp it was. The sun shone warmly, and the cruel government had provided us with no umberellas; clouds of floating dust almost stifled our breathing, and certainly succeeded in soiling our clean clothes and faces, and the hard, macadamized road wore ugly blisters on our tender feet; but night found us at the point of destination, and requited our toils with deep and peaceful slumbers…"

Did he really expect the government to provide umbrellas?

CIVIL WAR MEMOIRS OF TWO REBEL SISTERS Mollie Hansford, 7 miles north of Winchester & Victoria Hansford Kanawha Valley-Coalsmouth-now St. Albans, W.Va. ed. by William D. Wintz Pictorial History Pub. Co. 1989

Pg. 26 (from Victoria to Mollie) July 17, 1861 "...Nobody who has not seen a retreat of an army (although in no haste at all) can conceive any idea of it. We were standing out in front of my uncle's house looking down on the turnpike watching them go by. The cavalry and baggage wagons went by with the artillery near the last. I remember seeing five or six fine looking officers riding the finest horses I ever saw. They made a splendid appearance in their dark gray uniforms with brass buttons. They wore hats with plumes which they took off and rode with them in hand until they were completely by our group of waving, weeping women. One I noticed in particular was a very tall handsome man who rode a beautiful large black horse. Inquiring who they were, I was told they were officers of Chapman's Battery from Monroe County..."

A SCYTHE OF FIRE-THE CIVIL WAR STORY OF THE EIGHTH GEORGIA INFANTRY REGIMENT Warren Wilkinson & Steven E. Woodworth William Morrow Pub. 2002

Pg. 56 July 17, 1861 march towards Manassas "...Lt. John Reed believed that many of the men had decided the three days' rations weighed too heavy in their haversacks during the grueling march of July 18 and had lightened their loads by throwing food away. If so, it was a habit they would soon learn to break. At any rate, the boys were very hungry that morning.

As they marched along they came in time to a large, imposing brick plantation house with a long veranda across the front. A broad circular drive curved down to dual carriage gats on the road along which the troops were marching. A black house servant wearing a white apron stood beside the nearer gate. With "intense earnestness" he was saying again and again, "Misses says come up for breakfast. Come right up." This brought hoots and laughter from the men of the two leading companies, A and B, the Rome Light Guards and the Oglethorpe Light Infantry. Their uniforms were the showiest in the regiment, and even included epaulets. "The fool thinks we are officers," shouted one of them, to renewed laughter.

The slave, however, remained steadfast, and the boys decided it was worth a try. So the head of the column turned in at the gate and marched up the long circular drive. As they got near the house they saw a refined-looking lady standing on the front veranda. "Glad to see you, dear boys," she said, "just pass around the house to the dining room." They passed, with much doffing of kepis and shakos, and the very thought of what they found in that dining room was still making some of their mouths water fifty years later: "biscuits by the bushel, sliced bread and ham in stacks two feet high, cakes and donuts of all sizes and shapes, and on each side of the exit door innumerable tubs and cans of hot coffee." One after the other, gray-jacketed Rome Light Guards and Oglethorpes in their tall white-plumed shakos stopped as they entered and gazed at the feast before them. At least half a dozen ladies stood at various posts around the room ready to serve out the eatables to the salivating soldiers. "They literally passed us along, at the same time stuffing our haversacks as we proceeded," recalled a soldier. "You haven't time to stop and eat," they admonished the men, you are going to Manassas to help Beauregard; the Yankees attacked him yesterday and were repulsed. You must get there to help him."…"

SUNDAY IN CENTERVILLE-The Battle of Bull Run, 1861 by G. Allen Foster pob. By David White Inc. N.Y. 1971

July 21, 1861"McDowell, in violation of acceptable military tactics of the time, ordered Griffin's and Rickett's batteries placed in advance of the infantry line for more effective shelling of the area around the Henry House. Ricketts objected strenuously and demanded infantry support. But he was a Regular army man, long accustomed to obeying unpleasant orders, and he advanced his guns.

Then, just south of the artillery position, a regiment appeared in grey uniforms. Major Barry, McDowell's chief of artillery, who was with Griffin's and Rickett's batteries, insisted they were Union troops coming to support the batteries. Ricketts contended that they were Rebels, ordered his guns swung around and loaded with double canister. Barry was angry and called Rickett's attention to the flag. It was a stifling day and there was no breeze. The flag hung limp but at a distance there appeared to be red and white stripes and a blue field. Ricketts swung his gun s back to play on the Henry house.

At this point in the war, the Confederacy had not yet adopted what became its familiar battle flag. The Confederate flag at Bull Run had three broad stripes, red, white and red and a blue field with the stars of the eleven Confederate states. Hanging limp, it was almost impossible to distinguish from the United States flag. Now the troops in grey entered the woods on the east side of the turnpike as if they were going to skirmish with Beauregard's left. The two batteries kept up their incessant shelling of the Confederate line. Then a regiment in grey emerged from the woods at the same point where one in grey had entered. The flag still hung limp. Major Barry naturally took it for granted that this was the same regiment he had seen enter the woods. It looked the same in every detail. The regiment marched down the turnpike toward the two batteries as though it were in a Fourth of July parade. Then it wheeled and halted. The colonel walked up and down the ranks talking to the men. He stepped aside and raised his sword. The rifles came up and the colonel's sword came down. There was a blinding volley and nearly every man in the two batteries was dead. The regiment was the advance guard of Johnson's last brigade out of the valley. The brigade had detrained where the Manassas Gap Railroad crossed the Turnpike and run all the way."

Here's a good example of nonuniformity causing fatalities. Fortunately it turned out well for the Rebels.

REMINISCENCES OF BIG I by Lieutenant William Nathanial Wood Monicello Guard Company "A" 19th Virginia Regiment C.S.A. McCowat-Mercer Press 1959

Pg.1 July 21th, 1861 at Manassas "On the 20th I was ordered by Captain W.B. Mallory to take my turn in thowing up breastworks. Putting on a pair of buck gloves I worked most earnestly for a few minutes, but the July sun was so intense that I welcomed the "relief" most cordially. All my life I had been small for my age-sparely built and not strong, and weighed at this time 127 pounds, though twenty-one years old. My white shirt, standing collar, and hair parted behind gave the boys a target for good-humored jests which were as good-humoredly received.... There I was, however, a soldier only in position-in all else, possibly, the greenest of the awkward squad. I wore a brown frock coat, and a pair of black cassimere pants, and save a miserably sunburning cap, wore nothing of a soldier's garb..."

"DEAR MOTHER: DON'T GRIEVE ABOUT ME. IF I GET KILLED, I'LL ONLY BE DEAD." Ed. by Mills Lane The Beehive Press 1977

Pg. 30 John Fort to his Mother Piedmont, Va. July 20, 1861 outside of Paris, Va. On their way to Manassas "...Last night a hard rain bust suddenly upon us, and I arose up very wet. But soon our fire was made up, and the men along the whole line of troops might be seen standing silently and gloomy around their campfires looking with their white blankets on like beings of another world..."

White blankets? I guess it was more than the uniforms that were many colors.

WITH HONOR UNTARNISHED-The Story of the 1st Arkansas Infantry Regiment C.S.A. by Capt. John Hammock, USN (ret.) pub by Pioneer Press 1961

Pg. 31 July 21st 1861 Battle of Manassas "Then, two or three miles from its destination-the battle line- the brigade was halted by orders of General Johnston himself. Walker's battery unlimbered and opened up, as the infantrymen took position in a protective ring.

Soon there came an explanation of the sudden halt. A large body of troops in blue uniforms had been observed crossing Bull Run in the sector in which the brigade had just abandoned. If they were Federals, the path to the supply base at Manassas Junction was wide open to them, and Holme's Brigade would mark time until the stranger's identity became known.

It turned out the group under suspicion was a Confederate brigade wearing blue uniforms, which had previously crossed over the creek and was now returning to the west bank. Uniforms worn by the soldiers on both sides in the First Battle of Manassas were varigated in color and design. There were the old-line military companies, quasi-social in nature before the war, who appeared on the field in their distinctive uniforms, some gray, some blue, and some of many hues-as that of the Zouaves. At least one Federal artillery battery was wiped out because it permitted the close approach of some blue-clad infantry whom they mistook to be friendly. Both armies lost no time after this battle in standardizing their uniforms-blue for the North and gray for the South. In later years, with dyes in short supply, many Confederate uniforms would be stained a yellowish-brown from the juice of walnut shells, and this came to be called "butternut."

LEE& JACKSON'S BLOODY TWELTH-Letters of Irby Good-win Scott First Lieutenant Co. G Putnam Light Infantry Twelth Ga. Vol. Inf. Ed. by Johnnie Perry Pearson Univ. Tn. Press 2010

Pg. Highland Co. Va. July 21st, 1861 Dear Father and Family, "…You wished to know how my clothing held out. It holds out first rate so far. I will have plenty until fall unless some accident should happen and I should lose it. I do not know what I will need. I will let you know as soon as I can what I need, how to have it made, and so on. I will need as warm cloths as I can get for it is cool here now at night….We have had the good luck to have our knapsacks carried in a wagon so far. If we have to carry them on our backs over these mountains we will have to trhrow away some of our things. I should like to be stationed at some place to stay, this one difficulty in our way about cloths we move so much that unless our knapsacks are hauled we cannot carry them…"

DIARIES, LETTERS AND RECOLLECTION OF THE WAR BETWEEN THE STATES Vol III Winchester, Frederick Co. Historical Society Papers 1955

Pg. 51 Union retreat at 1st Manassas, July 21, 1861 "…Our boys got as much of their plunder as they could carry, guns, pistols, swords, knives, dirks, trunks, knapsacks, haversacks, canteens, overcoats, and everthing else they left behind them…"

Supply from the Yankees.

VMI Ms# 0476

James A. Hardin Papers near Strasburg July 22 1861 My Darling Sister "…I have changed shirts but once since I left Staunton & some garments I haven't changed at all. I have but one change along and they are dirty & I can neither get the chance nor time to get them washed…"

VOICES FROM COMPANY D Diaries by the Greensboro Guards, Fifth Alabama infantry Regiment, Army of Northern Virginia ed. by G.Ward Hubbs Univ. of Ga. Press 2003

Diarists: JHC John Henry Cowin
SP Samuel Pickens
JP James Pickens
JST John S. Tucker
VET Veteran from Co. D, 5th Alabama Regiment
HB Henry Beck

Pg. 25 July 24,1861 Manassas JHC "...The company is now in need of a uniform, but I do not know when we will get it...."

Pg. 28 July 26 JHC (Battalion drill) "...We were going at double quick, when I stepped on a very rough rock, bruising my foot badly. My shoes being worn out, the rock had fair play. I am now nearly barefoot, and the next march will put me entirely so. Have however sent to Richmond for a pair of shoes, but know not when I will get them..."

Shoes are already starting to wear out

Pg. 29 July 30, 1861 JHC "Father was at the Junction (Manassas) today, and says he never saw so much plunder, as was taken from the Yankees. We captured more guns, than we started the campaign with. Says there is a little of everything. It was the best equipped army that ever started out. The boys have gotten a great many things from the battle field, such as canteens, haversacks, &c. They have better ones than we. Their canteens are made of blacktin which keep the water cool longer than the common tin..."

RECOLECTIONS OF A MD. CONFEDERATE SOLDIER AND STAFF OFFICER UNDER JOHNSON, JACKSON AND LEE by McHenry Howard Press of Morningside Bookshop 1975

Pg. 46 "Next morning, July 24, I went by permission, to the tavern or house in the village to breakfast and ate ravenously, and I don't think an Indian, of whose capacity we read so much, would have surpassed me. For half a dollar I bought a very good pair of boots, although not new and several sizes too large for me-which I suspect came from the feet of some fallen soldier-and having borrowed a pair of pantaloons, my appearance and comfort were considerably improved...."

DEFEND THE VALLEY Margarette Barton Colt Crown Pub. 1994

Pg. 87 Frank Jones was on Jaskson's staff camped near the battlefield Letter of Frank B. Jones to Susan C. Jones July 25 1861 "…I was glad to see brother Strother on Tuesday, he left a coat with me which will supply to some extent my oil cloth & Havelock which I lost on the field of battle. Brother James is here & he promises to send me an oil cloth to wrap my blanket in which will be of great comfort to me…"

Sons Of Priveledge-The Charleston Light Dragoons In The Civil War by Eric Emerson pub by Univ of SC Press 2005

Pg. 19 "On July 26, 1861, it served as an honor guard for the bodies of Charlestonians who had been killed at the battle of Bull Run. Emma Holmes wrote that: "The Dragoons in their summer uniforms of pure white" and other militia companies met the bodies at the depot and escorted them to the city hall. During the procession the Dragoons were in the place of honor as the lead unit…"

This is the first I've ever heard of "summer uniforms of pure white," must be a dress uniform.

From Selma to Appomattox-The History of the Jeff Davis Artillery by Lwrence R. Laboda pub. by Owford Univ. Press 1994

Pg. 4 July 27, 1861 "The uniforms worn by the men of the newly formed battery no doudt varied greatly in style, with some trimmed in red (for artillery) and others with no special markings at all. At the time, though, the outfits worn by the members of the battery did contain distinctive unit insignia. As Private Wilber F. Claughton remembered, "We had no buttons (of one particular style) but wore letters on our hats or caps. Our letters were "J.D.M.A." for Jeff Davis Mounted Artillery…"

Once again, multi form

HISTORY OF THE FOURTH REGIMENT SOUTH CAROLINA VOLUNTEERS FROM THE COMMENCEMENT OF THE WAR UNTIL LEE'S SURRENDER J.W. Reid Shannon &Co. Printers & Stationers Morningside Bookshop 1975

Pg. 27 Stone Bridge Battlefield, Prince William County, July 28, 1861 "…There were a great many narrow escapes during the fight; a great many had holes shot in their clothing and some at several places. A young man of my company named Matthew Parker had two balls to go through his hat. It was an old-fashioned bee-gum hat, like the one that I wore off. We both swapped off our bee-gum hats that evening. We had a choice amongst thousands. We are now wearing nice low-crowned hats, but we don't know what they cost or who paid for them, neither do we care…"

Through Some Eventful Years—Diary of Susan Bradford Eppes Press of the J.W. Burke Co. 1926

Pg. 378 July 28th, 1861 "Colonel Robert Howard Gamble is organizing "Gambles Artillery," and Charley Hokins has enlisted in that company and so have many others from Tallahassee. Aunt Sue brought a beautiful piece of French opera flannel and asked me to make Charley two shirts. I am a little doubtful as to my ability but if I find it too difficult I can get my Lulu to finish them for me; she sews so neatly and she makes all my clothes, under Mother's direction. These shirts are blue and they are to have real silver buttons, which Aunt Sue has had made at the jewelers. She says silver will not tarnish as common metal buttons might do. Mr. Pratorious is making Charley's uniform. I suppose I will learm all the different uniforms after awhile. The infantry is grey, trimmed with blue, the buttons are of brass and the officers have gold lace on their sleeves, a chevron they call the design on the sleeves; a captain has three gold bars on his collar; the privates do not have any gold lace. Charley is in an artillery company and they wear a little red, but the uniform is grey, too. Cousin William Bradford is in a cavalry regiment and his gray uniform is trimmed with corn- color. They all look fine to me and I grow more patriotic all the time, but sister Mag says that is because I am not married…"

LEE& JACKSON'S BLOODYTWELTH-Letters of Irby Goodwin Scott First Lieutenant Co. G Putnam Light Infantry Twelth Ga. Vol. Inf. Ed. by Johnnie Perry Pearson Univ. Tn. Press 2010

Pg.14 Pocohantas Co. Top of aleghany (Alleghany) Mountain July 29th, 1861 Dear Father, "…I am going to get an overcoat from the Government which will come out of the pay I would receive for my services. It costs eight dollars. I do not know what to write about the cloths you spoke in your letter. In the first place I hope we will not be here in the winter, in the next if we were stationed I could take them and keep them but as it is if we move much I will have to throw away some I have now for we will have to carry them in our knapsacks on our backs. I will need some shoes or boots in the fall and winter if you come you can bring them. I have a pair of boots at home which are very good as far as I can recollect. I don't know what to say about the matter. I am completely puzzeled as to what is best. I don't know what the others are going to do about theirs, are you all fixing up cloths for us or not. I will wait a while and see what we are going to do and try and let you know in time. I should like for you to let me know when you expect to come on so that I may let you know in time what to do in the matter. I have plenty until winter…"

Already the government cannot supply the troops, but also cannot furnish transportation or storage of the extra clothing

LETTERS FROM LEE'S ARMY Compiled by Susan Leigh Blackford Annotated by her husband, Charles Minor Blackford, Charles Scribner's & Sons 1947 Company B of the Second Virginia Cavalry- Charles Blackford was first lieutenant, later captain.

Pg. 38 July 30 1861 "…Get me a pair of grey pantaloons and bring them down with you. I want enough Confederate grey cloth to make me a dress uniform. Send it to Page (Co.) to be made according to Confederate State regulations for a first lieutenant of cavalry…."

A SOLDIER'S RECOLLECTIONS—Leaves From The Diary of a Confederate by Randolph H. Kim pub. by Zenger Pub. Co. 1911

Pg 38 Fairfax Co. H., July 30, 1861 My Dear Mother (Referring to the yankee rout at First Manassas)"…I have a splendid overcoat gotten from a number they left behind…"

THE MITTELDORFER LETTERS

Same camp, August 27? "…I wish you would send me a pair of common shoes no.7 Send (?) by the first man that you can and also send me some writing paper and some ink…"

16th TENNESSEE VOLUNTEER INFANTRY REGIMENT: Clothing, Arms and Equipment (website)

Daniel Rouse, 7th Tennessee,14 August 1861 wrote "our clothes are beginning to give out and the worst of it is we cannot get anymore."

A SOLDIER'S RECOLLECTIONS-LEAVES FROM THE DIARY OF A YOUNG CONFEDERATE-Randolph H. McKim, late 1st Leiutenant & ADC 3rd Brigade, Johnson's division, ANV Longmans, Green & Co. 1911

Pg. 44 Fairfax Co H, August, 1861 "…I would here point out that our Maryland men faced from the start some of the hardships and limitations that came to many Southern regiments at a later stage of the war. In some commands the private soldiers had their trunks with them. It is related to a young Richmond gentleman, private in the howitzers, that he had as part of his outfit a dozen face towels besides bath towels, and that when orders were issued that all trunks should be sent back to Richmond, the elegant young dandy took offense and sent to the captain his "resignation"!

Neddless to say, our Maryland boys had neither trunks, nor cooks, nor woodchoppers... The first hard washing of my clothes which I did, burned off the skin from my arms dreadfully. (ed. note- he does'nt state whether he burnt himself by heating the water or using strong lye soap.)...Immediately after the victory we were marched back to Manassas (some six miles) and stayed there all Monday in a drenching rain, without tents, blankets or overcoats..."

The misery of soldier life b egins

SOUTHERN HISTORICAL SOCIETY PAPERS Volume XVI ed. by R.A. Brock 1888

Pg. 117 August, 1861 "...The following letter from the regimental quartermaster may be of interest, as showing the preparation which soldiers were then required to make for service: Camp Hagood, Summerville, S.C. Captain J. G. Pressley, Kingstree Postoffice, South Carolina:

Dear Sir,-I write to inform you that it will be well for each of your men to bring his blanket with him, otherwise he will have to supply himself out of the money allowed him to buy his clothes.

It is also adviseable for each of the officers to come prepared with all his camp equipage except tents, axes, hatchets and spades, as these are the only articles allowed them. Yours truly, etc., G.B. Lartigue ..."

Here they are planning to be supplied from the home folks.

THE STONE WALL The Story of a Confederate soldier by Brad Smiley Zebra Communications, Woodstock, Ga. 1998

Pg.35 August 1861 "...On a balmy August morning after I had taken breakfast I slipped into a new butternut-colored uniform Mama had made for me using a brownish dye she had extracted from walnuts..."

RECOLLECTIONS OF A CONFEDERATE STAFF OFFICER by G.Moxley Sorrel pub by Bantam Books 1995

Pg. 22 Aug. 1861 "Not long after the battle (1st Manassas) I set out on a visit to my father's country place, Ireland, fiteen miles from out camp (Centreville)...We were made very welcome, as fresh from the glorious battlefield, and the day was a happy one. The girls had made a captain's coat for me out of homespun cloth; but such a fit! Big enough for two captains of my thickness, it hung at all angles and flapped furiously in high winds. But love had prompted its making and I would never suffer any ugly remarks about it..."

Pg. 29 Aug. 1861 Fairfax Courthouse "Colonel Duncan McRae, Fifth North Carolina, had just received from Richmond a handsome new Confederate uniform and outfit. Alas! It soon came to grief. The colonel, in taking a high fence, lost his seat and came down very hard, splitting his fine coat in the back, from collar to waist.

A word here as to uniform and insignia. So fast does the memory of things pass that perhaps it may be well to make a note of what was the Confederate uniform. It was designed and settled on by a board of officers of the war department.

For all officers, a close-fitting double-breasted gray tunic.

For generals, all staff and field officers, dark blue trousers.

The arm of service was shown by collar and cuff-Generals and staff officers, buff; Cavalry, yellow; Artillery, red; Infantry, blue; medical Department, Black.

Dark blue trousers had broad gold stripes on outer seams, except generals, who wore two narrower and slightly apart.

Trousers for all line officers under rank of major were light blue with broad cloth stripe, color of service arm.

Rank was shown on collar and sleeve.

Generals wore on collar a gold wreath enclosing three stars in line, the middle one slightly larger. On the sleeves was the ornamental Hungarian knot of four braids width. They usually wore their buttons in groups of twos of threes. There was no difference in the uniform or rank mark among the several grades of general officers.

Colonels wore three stars in line, same size; lieutenant colonels, two, and majors, one. The knot on the sleeve was three braids wirth for the three grades of field officers-colonel, lieutenant colonel, and major.

For captains, rank was shown by three short bars lateral on front of collar; first lieutenant, two bars, and second lieutenant, one bar. Captains wore on sleeve Hungarian knot of two braids width, and first and second lieutenants, one boaid.

For headgear the French "kepi," color of service richly embroidered, was first provided, but the felt hat, black or any color that could be had, speedily pushed it aside almost before it had an existence.

The intention of the board of officers to adopt the tunic like the short, close-fitting, handsome Austrian garment, but it went completely by default. The officers would have none of it. They took to the familiar cut of frock coat with a good length of tail.

This is the ideal uniform regs

Confederate uniforms were in great number at the flag presentations a little later, of which I have already spoken. We were then bravely dressed in bright and handsome Confederate Gray." (Here he is speaking of the post-war assemblies-ed.)

Pg. 36 "It was always grarifiying to me to note the good equipment in which the troops from every state were sent to the front for the Confederacy. Governor Brown was thorough in doing the best for them that the blockade of the coast and his factories permitted. They came forward with good clothing, shoes and underwear, which, although of home make, were warm, comfortable and serviceable."

And were probably mostly of civilian cut

THE CIVIL WAR INFANTRYMAN, In Camp, on the March, and in Battle by Gregory A. Coco Thomas publications, Gettysburg, Pa

Pg.36-37 Regarding uniform prices, which varied widely in Confederate service, Lieutenant Charles Denoon, 41st Virginia, voiced that government shoes sold for eight to ten dollars, and the short waisted jackets, called "round abouts" or conversions, ran 12 to 14 dollars. According to the young officer it took a soldier four months' wages to buy a suit of clothes. Another Virginian, John L. Holt calculated in August 1861 that his uniform would cost $33.00, and he expected to receive "round about coats" as they took less cloth in construction than frock coats. He requested from home an overcoat and a pair of "oversocks," and he wanted the wool for his overcoat to be mixed, "about ¾ black to ¼ white (which) will make it about the proper color…" He asked his wife Ellen to make for him "some yarn drawers just single wove yarn cloth (which) will be nearly equal to flannel." Holt then informed Ellen that he could get calico for 25 cents per yard, and that the company had just drawn new uniforms at $7.50 apiece, which were "good ones made of heavy woolen goods." *Yarn drawers were knitted-like a sweater-pair of pants*

Even early in the war homemade military items were common in the South where no one really enforced the standing regulations. A 1st Georgia non-commissioned officer, Sergeant Walter Clark, remarked on an unusual style of cloth not often utilized in Confederate clothing. On December 8, 1861 in Winchester Virginia, a supply of blankets had arrived for the company from the citizens of Augusta:

"One of the contributors had no blankets, and in lieu of them donated a handsome crumb-cloth, which, like Joseph's coat, was of many colors, red and green being the prevailing tints. In the distribution this fell to Elmore Dunbar, the wag of the company. Not needing it as a blanket he took it to a tailor in Winchester, had it transformed into a full suit, cap, coat and pants, and donning it had an inumerable company of gamins, white and black, following in his wake all over town."

In 1861 there were many infantry companies completely undecided as to what colors should be used in ther uniforms. A 5th Texas soldier, John Stevens, recalled in his memoirs that after someone in his unit suggested that soldiers should have uniforms, no one could decide on a shade. Even the captain remained silent as each man gave his opinion. Finally it was proposed and agreed upon, "that each man get just what suited his fancy and have it made up in any style he chose-jes' so it was uniform."

Of course, infantry uniforms soon became austere and fairly standardized, but still came in an assortment of colors ranging from dark cadet grey to almost a white grey, to browns and tans, and yellow and white, and even dark blue closely resembling Union clothing. Valerius C. Giles, 4th Texas, verified that "(I)t was sometime after the war began that the Confederacy adopted any particular style of uniform. The color was universally grey, but the cut of the cloth varied materially." He recorded, "we were a motley-looking set, but as a rule comfortably dressed. In my company we had about four different shades of grey, but the trimmings were all of black braid."

Giles and his comrades even attempted to waterproof their outfits, using hot goose grease. He concluded that, "it penetrated the felt and leather like benzine…(but) stayed with us like a brother. Our hair,faces and hands were covered with it, and wouldn't wash off. So we went through that campaign as slick as goose grease could make us." By late 1862 Pvt. Giles added-As of December of that year many of his comrades were looking pretty ragged; he described one man in particular, Private John Griffith: "John was reduced to a flannel shirt of a very thin texture, a pair of cotton pants with one leg off at the knee, an old slouched wool hat, and one cheesecloth blanket." Griffith had no shoes but eventually made a pair of moccasins out of fresh cut beef hide and rawhide strips.

VOICES FROM COMPANY D Diaries by the Greensboro Guards, fifth Alabama Infantry Regiment, Army of Northern Virginia ed. By G. Ward Hubbs Univ. of Georgia Press 2003

Pg. 30 August 1 JHC "…Sent to Richmond a few days ago for a pair of shoes, by a lieutenant in the regiment. Today they came, and no more fitted for the army than no shoes at all, low-quartered bad leather, in fact, they were made for negro women for Sunday shoes. Had to take them in self defense…."

Already shoes were so hard toget that he had to take these. I wonder how long it took to wear them out?

HANDLEY LIBRARY ARCHIVES, WINCHESTER, VA Letters of Henry Jennings Co.A 5th Regiment Va Volunteers Jackson's Brigade

Aug 1st, 1861 Camp Harmon Dear Aunt, "…Tell Uncle James that if he is able I wish he would go to town and go to Mr. Funks and get the carpet sack and comfort and also John Dawes overcoat if it is there when he goes I am very glad of my boots tell the maker that they fit I want you to speak a good word to them from me…"

August the 14th, 1861 Dear Aunt, "Yours of the 9th came to hand today and found me well I received the clothes you sent me by Mr. Harteson but not those you sent by Fugit…I want him (Uncle James) to go to town and get my Minnie musket and my shawl and the things I roped up in it he will find them at Mrs. Hamilton just above the Southern church I want him to take them home for me the boots that I wrote to him about I do not want them too heavy so that they will be bad to march in I want them to have high legs…I left the quilt and carpet sack at the barrack and they have not been brought yet it might…and find them and bring them home…"

Doing this research was the first time I heard a shawl mentioned as an article of men's clothing, but there are many references throughout this book.

August the 14th 61 Dear Uncle +Aunt, "…I want you to send me my other red shirt and white one I want you uncle James to have me a good pair of boots made and send them down by the same conveyance that Vance Bell gets his he is going to have a pair made himself and will be sent in about a week the shoes furnished us by the government are so indifferent that we can not are them the things we but we have to pay a dollar for 20cts worth…the things you send me you can just take them down to Daweses and send them with Johns if you have the boots made by my old ones and get a business to do it …"

THE BATTLE OF SCARY CREEK by Terry Lowry pub by Pictorial Histories Pub Co 1982

Pg. 148 After the Battle and subsequent retreat, "…Wise did mention to Cooper that his men "have marched and countermarched incessantly, and fought well at Scary, and have scouted the enemy to their teeth, and are now without shoes…"

The shoe shortage is getting worse.

BROTHERS IN GRAY-The Civil War Letters of the Pierson Family ed. by Thomas W. Cutrer & t. Michael Parrish La. State Univ. Press 1997 Ninth Louisiana

Pg. 35 Rueben Allen Pierson to Mary Catherine Pierson, Camp Bienville, Va. Aug. 5th, 1861 Miss M.C. Pierson, "It is very difficult for us to procure shoes and we have to pay nearly three prices for them when we get them. For such shoes as Ben Stall makes, we have to pay from six to eight dollars a pair. My shoes that I started with is still serving me, but they are beginning to give way and I know not where I will get the next. Tell Father to send me a pair of good strong water proof boots of Stall's make if he has an opportunity before winter. And you must knit and send me 2 good strong pair of wool socks and one or 2 pair of homespun jean pants. I see in the banner that the ladies societies are to make and send us clothing for winter and Mr. Thurmond I understand agrees to bring them to us."

Footnote 54 Pg. 36 "...Catler G. Thurmond was a mount Lebanon Postmaster, councilman and merchant-the owner and proprietor of G.C. Thurmond and Company. On July 25, 1861, he wrote to the Louisiana Baptist, advising that "the ladies organize and form themselves into sewing societies" in order to make "drawers, shirts, socks, vests, pants coats and blankets, line them well, pay particular attention to the stability of the material and the substantial manner in which they are made." Thurmond concluded by stating that he would "take pleasure in carrying them my self"...Let Claiborne and Bienville forget not their valiant sons, let none be forgotten."..."

Pg. 50 Rueben Allen Pierson to William H. Pierson Camp Bienville, Va. August 17th, 1861 Dear Father, "I have already written you to order me a pair of strong water proof boots and several other articles of dress. I want a good double breasted homespun jeans vest. It will be of more service to me than any other garment in this cold climate where the mornings look very much like it would frost in August. Be sure to have my boots made full large so I can put them on either in wet or dry weather and also to wear course (sic) woolen socks with them. If you can procure them send me a large heavy pair of buckskin gloves. Send me two pair of coarse cotton drawers, a pair of Gumelastic leggin(g)s, if you can get them conveniently. I have a good waterproof coat which I bought at Grand Junction, Tenn.

I do not know how we will manage about moving with all our clothes in winter; we have been supplied with baggage wagons to move from Manassas up here; which is four miles. We did not even have to carry our knapsacks upon our backs."

Pg. 49 Rueben Allen Pierson to William H. Pierson Camp Bienville, Va. Sept. 18th, 1861 Dear Father, "If you have an opportunity send me my overcoat as such an article will be quite comfortable in the hard cold climate of Va. Mark everything that you send with my name so that I will be sure to get my own things."

Pg. 62 Rueben Allen Pierson to William H. Pierson, Camp Florida, Va., Nov. 12th, 1861 "My clothes are the very thing for this climate and they came to hand in good time."

Pg. 67 Rueben Allen Pierson to William H. Pierson, Camp Florida, Va. Decr. 3rd, 1861 Dear Father, "You wrote to me to state in my next letter whether I had received my bundle of goods or not. I have received them all and also the $25.00 sent by Mr. Candler. I have as many clothing as could do me any service through winter. I have a splendid overcoat which cost me in a trading way ($5.75) five dollars and six bits. I have as much money as I want and will have more than I started with when we draw."

"DEAR MOTHER: DON'T GRIEVE ABOUT ME. IF I GET KILLED, I'LL ONLY BE DEAD." Ed. by Mills Lane The Beehive Press 1977

Pg. 42 A.F. Boyd to his Father Big Shanty, (Georgia) August 1, 1861 Dear Father: We are well. We are now preparing to go to Virginia. We will leave some time next week. As Mr. McAfee has got a furlough to go home, I will send for some things by him. I want you to send me a pair of suspenders and two shirts. Have them made of good strong cloth, out of something that won't show dirt. I want them to wiat (wear?) over my other shirts. The other boys are getting them. Now is the time to get them, for when we get to Virginia they will not be easily gotten. I will thank you if you will speed this thing. Mr. McAfee will show you what kind of material to get ..."

"DEAR MOTHER: DON'T GRIEVE ABOUT ME. IF I GET KILLED, I'LL ONLY BE DEAD." Ed. by Mills Lane The Beehive Press 1977

Pg. 43 Shepard Pryor to his Wife Allegheny Mountain, Virginia, August 6, 1861 My Dear Nep: "...Some more news: John Wilson and myself has been patching the seat of our britches. This morning John puckered his patch bad. I got mine on finely as good as a heap of women would do that has a house full of children. You know I am a jack at all trades and good at none, but I think I made a pretty good patcher. I can beat anybody that I've seen attempt it yet in camp...."

Here they're already patching their uniforms

LETTERS FROM THE STONEWALL BRIGADE Ted Barcay, Liberty Hall Volunteers by Charles W. Turner Rockbridge Pub. Co. 1992

Pg. 28 August 6, 1861 Camp Harmon, near Centreville, Va. My Dear Mother, "...I do not need any clothes yet except a pair of shoes. The other pair you sent me I had tied to my baggage and some gentleman who perhaps thought that I had a good pair kindly helped himself without leave or license from me. The pair which I have will last some time yet., though they have a small hole in the side. One pair of my pants have a hole in them which I will mend today or at least try to mend..."

WELCOME THE HOUR OF CONFLICT-WILLIAM COWAN McCLELLAN & THE 9TH ALABAMA ed by John C. Carter pub. by Univ of Al Press 2007

Pg. 45 August the 7th, 1861 Manassas Junction,Va William McClellan to Robert McClellan Dear Bob,"...I want you to send me an Indian rubbercoat and one pair of pants of a gray color and a yellow stripe, a good bottle of brandy..."

Pg. 50 August the 12th, 1861 Manassas Junction William McClellan to Matilda McClellan Dear Sister,"...I wrote to you to send me a pair of pants and india rubber coat, a bottle of Brandy which I want to drink for my health..."

Pg. 51 Aug. 13, 1861 Manassas Junction William McClellan to Robert McClellan Dear Bob "...I have no pistols yet. I am allowed to carry it any where I please, though if I were home I would not start with one, it is a good deal of trouble to carry it...My coat is as good as ever I have worn it much, pants also....I would like to have the india rubber overcoat I wrote for it if it can be sent in any way..."

Pg. 55 Aug. 22, 1861 Athens Ga. Matilda McClellan to William McClellan Dear Brother, "...The ladies everywhere are making clothing for the soldiers. Mother will make you a gray suit and trim in yellow, also two pair of linsey drawers & two flannel shirts, which she wants you to put on as soon as compatible with cmfort. She will send you all you need. Your shoes I expect are wearing out..."

Pg. 59 Aug. 31, 1861 Broad Run(Va) William McClellan to Matilda McClellan Dear Sister, "...I will send the bundle you sent me home by Mr. Brass as the weather has got too cool to wear them I need a thicker pair of pants. Tell Father the next time he goes to Athens to get a pair, it does not make much difference what color they are so they have a yellow stripe down the leg. [If] I had some some rather they were gray. I have worn my Houston pants all the time they are very good pants yet, my coat is very good also. Tell Peck to get me a good long India rubber overcoat. It is of more service to a soldier than all the rest of his apparel, put them in a box and stuff the crevices with envelopes and paper, a pound of smoking tobacco ..."

I couldn't find out what "Houston pants" were.

Far, Far From Home—The Wartime Letters of Dick and Tally Simpson, 3rd South Carolina Volunteers ed by Guy R. Everson & Edward W. Simpson Jr. pib by Oxford Univ Press 1994

Pg. 48 Aug. 8, 1861 Richard Simpson to Anna Simpson Vienna Va. Dear Sister Anna, "... Tell Ma Cousin Jim says he can not wear woolen socks but would like to have some home knit cotton socks. I and Buddie wish the same..."

Pg. 56 Aug. 12 1861 Richard Simpson to Caroline Miller Vienna Va. Dear Aunt, "...Our position there was close to a house. In there I heard a piano so I concluded I would leave my companion and go in and hear some of the sweet melody. I did so, and in I walked, rifle in hand (For on guard I am not to lay down that article), and made a bland smile to the old man and said I thought I heard a piano and would his daughter play some for me. He said yes. I went into the parlor and here she came. I pulled off my hat and made a bow, but I forgot I had not combed my hair that day, also that I was in my shirt sleeves and my breeches were worn out behind…"

Pg. 60 Aug. 12, 1861 Tally Simpson to Mary Simpson Near Vienna, Va Dear Sister "…Buddie says send him 2 flannel drawers, a pr. of homemade gloves, and a thick pr. of Rock Island pants. Send me that what I wrote for before. Send me a pr. of gloves, substantial ones…"

I couldn't find out what "Rock Island pants" were either.

Pg. 61 Aug. 17th, 1861 Richard Simpson to Caroline Miller Vienna Va. Dear Aunt "I have been hard at work all day sewing up a fly to go over our tent and keep out the rain. We had two bed ticks that we generally filled with straw, but the rain came so thick through our tent that we came to the conclusion to cut them up and make a fly as I said. We have finished it now and are waiting anxiously for it to rain to see how we have succeeded…"

Pg. 64 Aug. 22, 1861 Richard Simpson to Anna Simpson Vienna, Va. Dear Sister Anna, "About sending Mose (slave). We must have a boy whether he takes the measles or not. So if you don't send him by Sloan, send him with anyone who will be coming on. Give him a suit of clothes just like our uniforms for it is of great importance (we now have a frock coat), a couple of blankets, and an oil cloth. He must have everything comfortable…Osh is the only one near me and says give you all his love. We sent by Dr. Gunnels for our uniforms. Osh says Aunt Jane made our pants and the coats will be made. We told Dr. G to have them made by (a) tailor and we would pay for them. How Aunt J came to make them I don't know…"

"DEAR MOTHER: DON'T GRIEVE ABOUT ME. IF I GET KILLED, I'LL ONLY BE DEAD." Ed. by Mills Lane The Beehive Press 1977

Pg. 48 William Butt to his Wife Richmond, Virginia, August 9, 1861 "…I do not want any overshoes. I wear my old shoes when it is muddy. I have bought me a pair of shoes, paid $3 a large shawl and a small camp cot for $5. My socks had better be dyed dark. Do not send me more than three pairs, I reckon I will need two check shirts this winter…"

Here's another reference to a shawl.

HISTORY OF THE FOURTH REGIMENT SOUTH CAROLINA VOLUNTEERS FROM THE COMMENCEMENT OF THE WAR UNTIL LEE'S SURRENDER J.W. Reid Shannon &Co. Printers & Stationers Morningside Bookshop 1975

Pg. 34 Camp Pettus, Fairfax Co. Va. August 11th, 1861 "…Prince Jerome-Bonaparte has visited our country, and on last Friday reviewed our army. We were marched to Centreville, which is about one and a half miles from here, on Friday, the 9th inst., and was reviewed by him. But, by the way, I thought it the warmest day that I had ever seen; it was perfectly suffocating. A great many men gave out and stopped before we got there, and a great many broke ranks after we got there. There were two men I know of who fainted. I came very near giving out myself. What made things worse, we had our thick woolen uniforms on, and our coats buttoned up. It was almost suffocating…As it happens I am again on guard to-day, writng on a Yankee drum head, one that we took at Stone Bridge. I this morning put on my new blue flannel shirt that I took from Uncle Sam on the day after the battle. It is a perfect fit; made on purpose for me. The reason that I put it on is this: my other shirts are wet; I had them washed yesterday…"

"DEAR MOTHER: DON'T GRIEVE ABOUT ME. IF I GET KILLED, I'LL ONLY BE DEAD." Ed. by Mills Lane The Beehive Press 1977

Pg. 50 Henry Graves to his Mother Sewell's Point (Virginia) August 11, 1861 "…Tell Ella the cap she made me is a splendid night cap. I put it clear over my head and face, leaving nothing but my mouth out, to breathe, and am thus protected effectively from the mosquitoes and sandflies, which varmints trouble us a great deal…."

CONFEDERATE CAPTAIN UJANIRTIS ALLEN'S LETTERS TO HIS WIFE ed. By Kandall Allen and Keith S. Bohannon La. State Univ. Press 1998

Pg. 20 Richmond Va. Aug. 14th 1861 "… How thoughtful you were in sending me my cap and pillow and other things. I did not need the knit drawers having supplied myself with good woolen ones. I have some good woolen undershirts. I do not know that I will need the flanell shirt you spoke of unless it is your desire that I should have it. Make it; send it on anyhow. It is said by good authority that we will have a winter campaign…."

"DEAR MOTHER: DON'T GRIEVE ABOUT ME. IF I GET KILLED, I'LL ONLY BE DEAD." Ed. by Mills Lane The Beehive Press 1977

Pg. 50 Shepard Pryor to his Wife Traveller's Rest, Virginia August 15 1861 My Dear Nep: I take the opportunity this morning to write you a few lines principally for the purpose of giving you a list of clothes that I shall want this winter….Now I will write you about my clothes. First thing is one pair of shoes, number eight. Barot and Harris in Americus (Ga.) has my measure. I want them made out of thick, heavy leather, high around the ankle and very thick, heavy bottoms. Have them pegged with tolerable broad heel(s) and not very high. Next is two pairs of good flannel drawers. My pants and coat I wrote you about. But for fear you did not get it, I'll describe them in this. They are to be made of black or some dark goods, something substantial and warm that will do good service. The pants I want lined with flannel, and the pants cut them them a fraction longer for the purpse of wearing suspenders, and one pair of suspenders. My coat you can get Cohen to cut a little larger so I can wear my overshirts with it in comfort. I want lined and padded. Two overshirts made of flannel or some other worsted goods. Two pair of woolen socks, one hand towel small and my overcoat. My coat, get the Georgia button for it and don't put any trimming only three stripes on the arm, if you can get the stuff to do it with. If not, it don't make any difference whether you have any at all or not....And last and most important is blankets. You must send me two good blankets. I know that blankets is scarce there and maybe you can get some in the country. I think Gus has a good blanket or two. I know if he has you can get them for me. Those big blankets they have to wear around them will be first rate. Be sure to send me two good blankets, for it will be cold here by the time they get here. There hasn't been many nights since I got in Virginia that I haven't slept under a blanket..."

BROTHERS IN GRAY-The Civil War Letters of the Pierson Family ed. by Thomas W. Cutrer & t. Michael Parrish La. State Univ. Press 1997 Ninth Louisiana

Pg. 43 Ruebin Allen Pierson to William H. Pierson Camp Bienville, Va. August 17th, 1861 Dear Father "...I have already written to you to order me a pair of strong water proof boots and several other articles of dress. I want a good double breasted homespun jeans vest. It will be of more service to me than any other garment in this cold climate where the mornings look very much like it would frost in August. Be sure to have my boots made full large so that I can put them on in wet or dry weather and also to wear course (sic) woolen socks with them. If you can procure them send me a large, heavy pair of buckskin gloves. Send me two pair of coarse cotton drawers, a pair of Gumelastic leggin(g)s, if you can get them conveniently. I have a good waterproof coat which I bought at Grand Junction, Tenn...."

RICHMOND DAILY DISPATCH-

August 17, 1861 "Maryland Artillery-"Their uniform in color is a light gray, almost white, from which it can hardly be distinguished at a distance-kepi, jacket and trousers being all the same color-releived by scarlet trimmings."

This is the firat reference to undyed wool uniforms or "drab" as they were called.

WRITING & FIGHTING FROM THE ARMY OF NORTHERN VIRGINIA ed. by William B. Styple Belle Grove Pub. 2003

Pg. 48 3rd Battalion Ga. Vol. Inf. Camp Davis Lynchburg Aug. 18 1861 "...There are some of the "Tigers" in the city, and inconsequence of leaving Manassas without leave, they were all ordered to be arrested. One of our corporals went into the city, an having a red shirt and Zouave cap, was forthwith halted and ordered to go to the "Bars." On inquiring the reason, the reply was, that they had orders to arrest all "Tigers," and our corporal protested that he was no Tiger, never saw a Tiger, didn't resemble one in the least, in short, hadn't the remotest idea what a Tiger was. It was no go-a scuffle ensued, and in the scuffle our corporal proved a real live Tiger, for he gained his liberty, and, I am happy to state, is now quite tame, and is still of the opinion that he never fought a Tiger but once, and then "lost every red."

U.S. ARMY HERITAGE AND EDUCATION CENTER

18 Aug. 1861 Lt. Stanley S. Challendish Co. G, 4th South Carolina Volunteer Infantry German town, Va. My Dear EWife: "...The coming winter in this climate I think the best things you ladies could send us would be some good woolen socks & shirts & Drawers & undershirts & also coarse towels & handkerchiefs as those things are always getting lost. The clothes I left home with and a few articles picked up from the Yankees have lasted me so far very well. Put in some Needles & Thread & Pins..."

VOICES FROM COMPANY D Diaries by the Greensboro Guards, Fifth Alabama infantry Regiment, Army of Northern Virginia ed. by G.Ward Hubbs Univ. of Ga. Press 2003

Diarists: JHC John Henry Cowin
SP Samuel Pickens
JP James Pickens
JST John S. Tucker
VET Veteran from Co. D, 5th Alabama Regiment
HB Henry Beck

Pg. 36 Aug. 18, `1861 Manassas JHC "...Today reminds me of Sunday on the plantation at home. All have our clean clothes on, faces washed and hair combed just like the negroes. If we were only as well off as they I would be satisfied for they have warm and dry houses to stay in, plenty to eat and good warm clothes, we of course have plenty to eat and wear, but not the houses..."

GRANDFATHER'S JOURNAL (Franklin Lafayette Riley) Company B Sixteenth Mississippi Infantry Volunteers Harris' Brigade Mahone's Division Hill's Cops, A.N.V. May 27, 1861-July 15, 1865 Austin C. Dobbins Morningside 1988

Pg. 33 Sunday-Monday, Aug. 18-19, 1861 Camp near Centreville"...Wrote Edward to send me 2 pairs of fresh trousers(woolen), 2 pair flannel drawers, 2 pairs socks and an overshirt by Southern (old Adams) Express. Cotton clothing isn't suitable for Va. Weather..."

Charlotte's Boys

Pg. 68 Charlotte Branch to Pvt. Hamilton Branch Bristo (Va.) Aug. 1861 My Dear Hammie, "I have looked daily and hourly for you ever since I have been here, I do wish you could come. You sayed in your last that there was very few clothes of John's. (John had been killed at 1st Manassas) where are his cloak and his shawl. He had 2 dozen shirts when he left home and plenty of drawers and 4 flannel shirts, several pr. of white pants a new pr. of blue cloth uniform pants and a pr. of light ones. I do wish if you cant come you would write to me for I am most desolate and lonely."

WRITING & FIGHTING FROM THE ARMY OF NORTHERN VIRGINIA ed. by William B. Styple Belle Grove Pub. 2003

Pg. 48 Eleventh Ga. Regiment Camp Bartow, 31/2 miles North-East of Manassas Junction, Aug. 20, 1861 "…Tents have been furnished which, added to the remnant forwarded us from Winchester, together with a few pressed into our service and given us, render our hill-side home less desolate than before. The hygiene of the regiment is my daily study; for upon this depends, in a great measure, the efficiencey of the men. Yet all this can effect but little so long as they are forces to sleep in their miserable wedges of tents furnished us by the Governor before leaving Georgia. They are low, narrow, pinned tightly to the ground, without flies and made of ordinary osnaburgs. Under such bolting cloths, who can expect to keep dry? The heavy dews we are now having penetrate them like a sieve; indeed moisture seems to have been woven into their very texture-in a word, they are unfit to shelter half a dozen ordinary cabbages from an October frost. Straw, ditching, daily airing, everything devised and furnished cannot improve them, and so long as men are forced to burrow in such kennels, disease and death will be constantly with us. Notwithstanding all this, with other pests, such as incessant rains, &c., general good cheer prevails…

A few suggestions to citizens of counties from which companies have been formed, and I am done. The winters in Northern Virginia are exceedingly severe, sudden in approach and of long duration. I would urge the necessity of refitting each company with all their wants, such as clothing, caps, woolen undershirts, shoes, socks &c., and above all, a new supply of tents-large with wall and fly, so as to make then at least comfortable. Let each county then, call a meeting, raise the funds, make the article, pack and ship them to Quarter-Master General Foster in Atlanta, and they will be transported free of charge…"

U.S. ARMY HERITAGE AND EDUCATION CENTER

August 20, 1861 C.M. Amoss- Cobb's Legion of Georgia Volunteers Co. C Richmond Va. My Dear Georgia:"…I am getting along very well on one blanket and shall need nothing more in that line. Please get my clothes as soon as you can and send them by express to Richmond…"

LETTERS AND PAPERS OF AN ARTILLERY OFFICER A.N.V. IN THE WAR FOR SOUTHERN INDEPENDENCE 1861-1865 Capt. John Hampden Chamberlain-Virginian Dietz Printing Co. Pub. 1932

Pg. 30 Valley Mountain, Va. Aug. 21st, 1861Dear Mother "…Arrived in camp we were almost too tired to eat. However I rubbed myself warm with a towel, put on dry clothes & was comfortably asleep in no time. All yesterday was pleasantly spent in drying clothes & resting…I left my silk shirts at home to avoid weight, bringing two, quite enough. I have bought a pair of yarn socks & hope to buy more but if you can in any way get a chance, please send me some & a pair of such silk or silk yarn drawers as I wear. Spence knows. V. would like such a gray flannel overshirt as I have & two heavy flannel undershirts…"

CONFEDERATE CENTENIAL STUDIES #24 Confederate Publications Co. Inc, 1963

Pg. 37 Sewell's Point (Va) Aug. 21, 1861, Dear Father, "I wish Ma would send me a coat; let her make it out of that gray woolen cloth she once made me a hunting coat from, or something of the same color. The cloth was furnished to us in Macon and it only cost 3 dollars for me to have a suit made. I had the pants made but not enough money for the coat. Ma can fit it by any of my coats. It must be a jacket, buttoning all the way up in front, military fashion, with a short collar designed to stand up; buttons either brass of silver, oval shape, nearly half inch in diameter; put a short piece of white tape ¼ inch wide upon the shoulder, running from front to back. Let it be warm; pockets inside and on both sides.

I wrote to Aunt Libbie to make Knox make me a pair of shoes. Please send them at the same time. An uncooked ham or two would also be very acceptable…"

HAM CHAMBERLAYNE-VIRGINIAN Letters and Papers of an Artillery Officer in the War for Independence 1861-1865 with introduction, notes and index by his son C.G.Chamberlayne Richmond, Va. Press of the Dietz Printing Co. Publishers 1932

Pg. 31 J.H. Chamberlayne to Lucy Parke Chamberlayne (Valley Mountain) Thursday (Aug.) 22nd (1861) 9 a.m. My Dear Sister, "…Let the Chn. Ass. Know that there is now great & by winter will be frightful need of clothing. Not in F., but in most of the Cos. Of all the Regts. In this division; many Cos. Of the 21st are extremely destitute of clothing having no overcoats…."

"DEAR MOTHER: DON'T GRIEVE ABOUT ME. IF I GET KILLED, I'LL ONLY BE DEAD." Ed. by Mills Lane The Beehive Press 1977

Pg.56 John Ellis to his Wife Greenbrier River, Virginia August 22, 1861 Dear Lovey, "...If this should reach you before Lieutenant Stubbs leaves Macon and you have any chance to send me anything, I will tell you what I want: two pair of thick woolen socks, that is about the only thing in the clothing line that I stand in need of at present. And then send me a good lot of writing paper and envelopes. That is the scarcest article in camp at present...."

FORGET-ME-NOTS OF THE CIVIL WAR: A ROMANCE Laura Elizabeth Press of A.R. Fleming Printing Co. 1909

Pg. 355 Letter from Walter Lee, Manassas Junction, August 23, 1861 My Dear Mother: "... This morning was very cool and chilly. It begins to feel as winter is fast approaching. You spoke of sending us some winter clothing. We would be very glad to have a good supply, as we shall suffer if not well clothed in this cold country. I can almost imagine how cold it will be on top of these high hills when the winter winds come whistling around them. The following list of clothes will be as many as we shall need and can take care of convieniently. Two pairs of thick woolen shirts each, such as can be worn either next to the skin or over other shirts; two pairs of red flannel drawers each, and some woolen socks. That is everything we shall need for the present. You can send them by express and we shall get them..."

GRANDFATHER'S JOURNAL (Franklin Lafayette Riley) Company B Sixteenth Mississippi Infantry Volunteers Harris' Brigade Mahone's Division Hill's Cops, A.N.V. May 27, 1861-July 15, 1865 Austin C. Dobbins Morningside 1988

Pg. 34 Friday-Saturday, Aug. 23-24, 1861 Camp near Centreville "Weather: cold, wet, windy, a night fit for neither man nor beast. Yet 60 of us, 20 at a time, stood guard for 24 hours; then we were relieved for 4. Outside we wore blankets to keep out the rain. Inside we snuggled under the same blankets to try to keep warm. We desperately need oilcloths. If this is Aug., what will it be in Dec.?"

DEAR SISTER-CIVIL WAR LETTERS TO A SISTER IN ALABAMA Frank Anderson Chappell pub. by Branch Springs Pub. 2002 (Third Alabama Regiment)

Pg. 40 Entrenched Camp near Drewery's Bluff, Va. Aug. 24, 1861 Dear Sister "...The clothing sent here by the LRL (Ladies Relief) does very well but the hats were not fit for a negro, there was but one of them taken out of the box. It was soon groaned out of sight and I have not seen them since. We are having a new uniform made that will cost between $15 and $20, but we are going to get money from the government to pay for. I reckon we will get them next week.

You asked me to let you know what I need in the way of clothing. I started a letter to Richmond last Monday by private Convey. I asked him to send me my overcoat if he met with an opportunity. I am tolerably well supplied with clothing with the exception of shoes and blankets. The weather is getting cool already and I know we are to (deal) with the cold…I have not bought anything in the clothing line except my uniform and cap that cost me $8.10…" J.Z.Branscomb

VOICES FROM COMPANY D Diaries by the Greensboro Guards, Fifth Alabama Infantry Regiment, Army of Northern Virginia ed. By G. Ward Hubbs Univ. of Georgia Press 2003

Pg. 39 August 25 JHC "…Sunday has come again and once more the company looks decently dressed in our red flannel shirts and kersey pants, sent by the citizens of Greensboro. They are very comfortable…"

VOICES FROM COMPANY D Diaries by the Greensboro Guards, fifth Alabama Infantry Regiment, Army of Northern Virginia ed. By G. Ward Hubbs Univ. of Georgia Press 2003

Pg. 40 August 26 JHC "…This afternoon our whole company turned out on drill in their new kersey pants and red flannel shirts, we looked well and drilled finely…"

JAMES MADISON UNIVERSITY ARCHIVES

Aug. 25, 1861Letter form James C. Ingram, 12th North Carolina Regiment to his mother, Priscella Ingram Camp Bee 12th Reg. Nco Dear Mother: "…I sent all of (shoes) by Mr Lund You Say You have Never (gotten) my clothes from Mr. Blackwell I left Coat Pants Vest (&) Hat there (&) my Shoes at Mr. Frank's (store) Mr Peanix promised to (Carry) them home for me but I suppose he forgot them…"

A LIFE FOR THE CONFEDERACY-AS RECORDED IN THE POCKET DIARIES OF PRIVATE ROBERT A. MOORE, Co. g, 17th Miss. Regt. Confederate guards, Holy Springs, Mississippi ed. by James w. Silver McCowat-Mercer Press 1959

Pg. 54 Monday, Aug. 26th, 1861 camp near Leesburg "…We were paid $21 for clothing but the Cpt. Had it put in the treasury to purchase clothes for the winter. Some of the boys were very mad & would not take the money for their wages because they could not get the other…"

"DEAR MOTHER: DON'T GRIEVE ABOUT ME. IF I GET KILLED, I'LL ONLY BE DEAD." Ed. by Mills Lane The Beehive Press 1977

Pg. 59 Henry Morton to Ira Foster Putnam County, Georgia August 26, 1861 Dear Sir: My Wife, Mrs. Sarah A. Morton, has made fifty shirts and knit thirty pairs of socks at her own expense, and she has been informed by her son, Leiutenant Talbot in Dr. Belt's company from Bulloch County, 9th Georgia Regiment, that you would send them to the soldiers free of expense, if she would send them to you now. If so, please let me know by return mail where to send them and how to direct them. Direct your letter to Eatonton, Putnam, Georgia. Yours Truly..."

Website www.libertyrifles.org/research/31stvahtml

Pg 3 "Requisition for Clothing and Company Equipage" written on 26 Aug. 1861 provides some insight on the general deficit of materials for the regiment. Reported Clothing amongst the troops was as follows:

- I. Hats or caps-8 on hand 652 required
- II. Coats-11 on hand, 649 required
- III. Pants (pairs)-24 on hand, 636 required
- IV. Drawers (pairs)-51 on hand, 1269 required
- V. Flannel Shirts-6 on hand, 1314 required
- VI. B;lankets-625 on hand, 695 required
- VII. Stockings (pairs)-0 on hand, 1980 required
- VIII. Shoes (pairs)-1 on hand, 1319 required
- IX. Great Coats-12 on hand, 648 required
- X. Knap Sacks-268 bon hand, 392 required
- XI. Haver Sacks-237 on hand, 423 required
- XII. Canteens and Straps-245 on hand, 417 required

Camp and garrison equipment reported as follows:

- I. Axes & Hatchets-5 on hand, 93 required
- II. Picks & Handles-0 on hand, 68 required
- III. Spades-0 on hand, 68 required
- IV. Camp Kettles-24 on hand, 74 required
- V. Common Tents-102 on hand, 0 required
- VI. Common Tent Poles or Pins-102 on hand, 0 required

Good Lord, did these guys have anything?

GRANDFATHER'S JOURNAL (Franklin Lafayette Riley) Company B Sixteenth Mississippi Infantry Volunteers Harris' Brigade Mahone's Division Hill's Cops, A.N.V. May 27, 1861-July 15, 1865 Austin C. Dobbins Morningside 1988

Pg. 35 Tuesday, Aug. 27, 1861 Page's land, Prince William County, Va. "Leaving Centreville around 9, we marched to Page's Land by 2P.M. The rods were good, bad, and horrible. For a fourth of the distance they were paved with rocks of all sizes, all sharp, all uncomfortable. Most of us developed stone bruises and blisters. We carried at least forty pounds of equipment (musket, knife, ammunition, haversack, knapsack, rations, blankets, extra clothes). No wonder our feet hurt!"

A SOUTH CAROLINIAN IN THE FIRST SOUTH CAROLINA VOLUNTEERS (HAGOOD'S REGIMENT) by Maj. John G. Pressely of the Eutaw Batallion, South Carolina Volunteers

Pg. 117 August 27, 1861 Camp Hagood, Summerville, S.C.
Captain J.G. Pressey,

Kingstree Post Office, South Carolina:

Dear Sir,-I write to inform you that it will be well for each of your men to bring his blanket with him, otherwise he will have to supply himself out of the money allowed him to buy his clothes.

It is also advisable for each of the officers to come prepared with all his camp equipage except tents, axes, hatchets, and spades, as these are the only articles allowed them.

Yours Truly, etc, G.B. Lartigue

A LIFE FOR THE CONFEDERACY-As Recorded in the Pocket Diaries of Pvt. Robert A. Moore Co. G, 17th Mississippi Regiment Confederate Guards Holly Springs, Miss. ed. by James W. Silver McCowat-Mercer Press Inc. 1959

Pg 54 Aug. 28th, 1861 camp near Leesburg "…Nearly all of the boys had their measures taken for a uniform to-day. Some of the boys will not have a uniform…"

I wish he'd stated why they didn't want a uniform.

"DEAR MOTHER: DON'T GRIEVE ABOUT ME. IF I GET KILLED, I'LL ONLY BE DEAD." Ed. by Mills Lane The Beehive Press 1977

Pg. 60 Alfred Dorman to his Parents Williamsburg, Virginia August 29, 1861 Pa and Ma: I received your presents by John B. My coat came to hand safe, my gloves from Aunt Carrie came safe, my handkerchief and quince likewise…"

LEE& JACKSON'S BLOODY TWELTH-Letters of Irby Goodwin Scott First Lieutenant Co. G Putnam Light Infantry Twelth Ga. Vol. Inf. Ed. by Johnnie Perry Pearson Univ. Tn. Press 2010

Pg 19 Camp Bartow Pochahontas Co. Va. Aug. 29th, 1861 Dear Father "...Give my best love to Grandma and my thanks for the blankets which I would like to bring home with me if I am so fortunate to get back remember me to all friends..."

UNDER THE STARS AND BARS—A History of the Surry Light Artillery pub by Press of Morningside Bookshop 1975

Pg. 310 "At the end of August 1861 all but a few of the Surry Light Artillery had uniforms, which were, presumably, the products of George S. Waite, an English-born tailor who had a shop at Surry Court House. A photograph of Servetus McQueen Williams, who enlisted in July, 1861, indicates the company wore gray jackets and trousers with the traditional scarlet trim of the artillery. The buttons on the jacket appear to be plain rather than the brass Virginia seal pattern commonly worn by the volunteers at this time..."

WAR DIARIES: The 1861 Kanawha Valley Campaign by David L. Phillips and Rebecca L. Hill, Cief Reseatcher Gauleu Mount Press 1990

Pg. 247 Major Isaac Smith of the Kanawha Riflemen Fall 1861 "I have just finished making a haversack-cut it out, sewed it entirely by myself and it is a good effort. Made it out of a piece of torn linen. Am delighted with my success in this new business."

A SCYTHE OF FIRE-THE CIVIL WAR STORY OF THE EIGHTH GEORGIA INFANTRY REGIMENT Warren Wilkinson & Steven E. Woodworth William Morrow Pub. 2002

Pg. 114 fall 1861 "...The cold winds finally came, and the men began to feel keenly their lack lack of adequate clothing for the season. They had not left home equipped for a winter in Virginia, and what they had taken with them had suffered a great deal from eight months hard service. By the end of October the crisp autum nights had prompted the Atlanta Grays, Co. F, to appeal to the people of Atlanta to provide them with new uniforms. "The coat should be a heavy frock, with military capes attached," read their notice in the "Atlanta Daily Intelligencer, "out of any kind of material, so that it is warm...."

At this point, they're not worried about any kind of uniformity, just as long as it covered the troops.

WAR DIARIES: The 1861 Kanawah Valley Campaigns by David L. Phillips Leesburg, Va. 1990

Pg. 46 Fall 1861 "Few of the units had any type of uniform. The Sandy Rangers were dressed in red hunting shirts.

The Fayetteville Rifles and the Mountain Cove Guards were especially grand by comparison. The Fayette County court had appropriated $5000 to clothe the two companies and the ladies of the area met at the Methodist Church in Fayetteville to sew uniforms for the men…"

LEAVES FROM THE DIARY OF A YOUNG CONFEDERATE-Randolph H. McKim, late 1st Leiutenant & ADC 3rd Brigade, Johnson's division, ANV Longmans, Green & Co. 1911

Pg. 46 fall, 1861 "…The first hard washing of my clothes which I did, burned off the skin from my arms dreadfully.…Immediately after the victory we were marched back to Manassas (some six miles) and stayed there all Monday in a drenching rain, without tents, blankets, or overcoats…"

16th TENNESSEE VOLUNTEER INFANTRY REGIMENT: Clothing, Arms and Equipment (website)

Jas Morrison Skelton, 11th Tennessee Infantry: "Fix up my overcoat in as small bundle as possible…and send it to me…tell Ma to send me a pair of linsey drawers…tell Lon to send me a pair of thick gloves…"

FRENCH HARDING Civil War Memoirs Ed. By Victor L. Thacker McClain Printing Co. Inc., Parsons W.Va. 2001

Pg.19 Fall 1861 scouting in Western Va. "…We were armed, and dressed in our usual clothing.…"

OK, does he mean their uniform or civilian clothing?

FOOTPRINTS OF A REGIMENT A Recollection of the 1st Georgia Regulars by W.H. Andrews Longstreet Press Atlanta Ga. 1992

Pg.22 Camp Rocky Run, Va. Fall 1861, "The Regulars has drawn new tents, known as the bell or Sibley tent, mounted on a tripod in the center where we can have a fire in the middle of the tent, the smoke going out at the top. Fifteen men can occupy one tent."… "The boys have to turn out for parade in apple pie order, shoes blacked, brasses brightened and white gloves on. …"

This trend won't last.

THE STONE WALL The Story of a Confederate soldier by Brad Smiley Zebra Communications, Woodstock, Ga. 1998

Pg. 48 fall 1861camp outside of Richmond Va. "Finally we began to receive some basic equipment. We were issued a hat, one shirt, a pair of pants, a pair of drawers, one blanket, a gun cloth, an oil cloth to wrap our blanket in or use as a ground cloth, a haversack and a strong tin cup. Tents were still scarce and issued only to every other soldier until the commissariat ran out…."

A REBEL CAVALRYMAN WITH LEE, STUART AND JACKSON by John N. Opu pub by W.B. Conkey Co. 1899

Pg. 58 Fall `1861 Valley of Virgina "…While we were at this camp, I witnessed a very amusing incident. Not far from our camp was a flour mill, above which was a large dam. On this occasion, I saw an Irishman seated on the groud, smoking his pipe and arranging the cartridges in his box. Presently, having fixed the catridges to his satisfaction, he arose, and pushing his cartridge box back into place, started to walk away. When he had gotten about fifty yards from the dam, there was an explosion in his rear. The astounded man looked around in all directions, to acertain from whence it came, when another explosion occurred, whereupon he realized that his cartridge box was on fire; and, instead of unbuckling his belt and dropping it, he made for the mill dam, leaping high in the air at every explosion, until, finally, reaching the bank he made one terrific plunge and disappeared beneath the surface of the water. Finally he reappeared upon the surface and I assisted him to the shore. I had hysterics for a week…"

UNIFORMS OF THE CIVIL WAR Lord, Wise, A.S. Barnes & Co. 1970

Pg. 16 From Lynchburg, Virginia, Late Fall, 1861 "…The (spectacle) which a regiment presents on parade is remarkable to the eye of the European. Many are comprised of companies who have uniforms of different colors; but in these cases is always some distinctive badge by which their Corps can easily be told. This defect…is being quickly remedied, as we saw numerous regiments which had arrived lately, whose dress was all the Horse Guards could desire…"

The writer doesn't say which regiments were so well-equipped or where they were from.

CONFEDERATE CAPTAIN UJANIRTIS ALLEN'S LETTERS TO HIS WIFE ed. By Kandall Allen and Keith S. Bohannon La. State Univ. Press 1998

Pg. 36 Fairfax Co. Sept. 1861 "…I would be glad if you would get me about four good blankets and send them to me when the uniforms are sent to the boys. Or just so I can get them by winter. I do not mean fine blankets; but good heavy fellows. An India ruber blanket would be of good service if I could get one but I know I can not. It would be good to spread down to make my pallet on. The blanket next to the ground is wet every morning from dew or moisture rising from the ground…."

DIARY OF A SOUTHERN REFUGEE DURING THE WAR by Judith White Brockenbrough McGuire J.W. Randolph & English1889

Pg 360 Sept. Northern Va. 1861 "… After we reached this place, we were ordered to explore the surrounding country in quest of fugitives. We took eighteen prisoners, and got back just at night, very wet. You never saw such a collection of property as was left in their flight. Hundreds of muskets, gun-carridges, wagon horses, Thousands of knapsacks, oil-cloths and blankets, hogsheads of sugar, barrels of pork, beans, etc.; in short, everything you can conceive. We found to-day over five hundred splendid army overcoats.

The men are amusing themselves reading letters, of which there were thousands left on the field. Some of them were directed to Mr. so-and-so, expected at Manassas Junction. Some asked for a piece of the floor of the house in which Ellsworth was killed, with blood on it, while others confidently express the belief that Beauregard's scalp was to be carried to Washington. When I tell you to-night we supped on Yankee crackers, Yankee coffee, and a nice beef-tongue, actually left on the hearth of one of the officer's quarters, in a kettle, ready to be set on the fire- that this is written with a Yankee pencil, given me by one of the men, and on Yankee paper, taken from their wagons, and that I am sitting on a Yankee camp-stool, and writing by a Yankee candle, you can form some idea of the utter rout. I have a pincushion for L., picked up on the field, a needle-case for K., and a sword taken from a Vermont volunteer, for W…"

This is extreme resupply from the Yan kees-I guess he's writng about the aftermath of First Manassas.

A REBEL CAVALRYMAN WITH LEE, STUART AND JACKSON by John N. Opu pub by W.B. Conkey Co. 1899

Pg. 50 Sept 1861 Valley of Virgina "…We then marched on towards Winchester, without interruptions, and, overtaking a one-horse wagon, of which we took possession, proceeded on our way. At a tollgate not far from the town was a picket composed of a militia company armed with flintlock muskets. These halted us and the Captain informed us that General Jackson had ordered him not to let a single soldier pass. We warned him that General Jackson and all H--- could not keep us out of Winchester, attempting at the same time to pass on, when the Captain and several of his men seized our horse. We sprang out of the wagon, loaded and capped our muskets, fixed bayonets, came to a charge, four abreast, with cocked guns. The militia company fled from the road, and thus we captured Winchester. The difference between us and the militia was, that we had been in the first battle of Manassas.

The next morning we sent out a young lady scout, who reported that the General had ordered the arrest of all thje soldiers in the town. In a short while, about eighty of us got together, formed a company, elected a Captain and marched up and down the town, defying the militia, who were afraid to tackle us.

On this occasion, some wag dubbed the militia "Shoe Heels," meaning that they substituted shoe heels for flints to their fire-locks, the inference being that they could not shoot..."

HISTORY OF THE FOURTH REGIMENT-From the Com-mencement of the War Until Lee's Surrender by J.W. Reid pub by Shannon & Co. Printers & Stationers 1975

Pg. 26 Sept. 1, 1861 Dear Father, "...I would be glad if you would send me by mail my gloves and a good big needle, as I have to do my own patching and ironing. The ironing, however, goes minus..."

A LIFE FOR THE CONFEDERACY-As Recorded in the Pocket Diaries of Pvt. Robert A. Moore Co. G, 17th Mississippi Regiment Confederate Guards Holly Springs, Miss. ed. by James W. Silver McCowat-Mercer Press Inc. 1959

Pg. 56 Sept. 2nd, 1861 camp near Leesburg "...Mr. (John) Bradley & Lieutenant Jackson left yesterday to purchase for the Reg. goods for a uniform. They will take them back to the homes of the different companies to have the goods made up..."

WRITING & FIGHTING FROM THE ARMY OF NORTHERN VIRGINIA ed. by William B. Styple Belle Grove Pub. 2003

Pg. 55 Sixth Alabama Inf. Sangster's Crossroads, Va. Sept. 2, 1861 "...And here let me say a word to those who are coming to join the army, in relation to what they should bring with them. There are but few who come into the army, that do not bring superfluous arms, clothing, &c., and the consequence is, the government being deficientin baggage wagons, and the men having more than they can carry upon their backs, are compelled to throw them away.

In the first place bring no side arms, infantry particularly, as they are totally useless, and money expended for them is thrown away. A soldier who will do full justice in using a musket or rifle in battle has no earthly use for side arms, as the instances are very rare, where opposing forces cross bayonets, or are near enough to effectually use small arms, besides the weight of repeating pistols of size sufficient to do execution any distance, and a large bowie knife, is an item of no inconsiderable importance I assure you, when a man is to foot it and carry besides his gun, pistol and knife, knapsack, wearing apparel, blankets, canteen and provisions sometimes for several days, to say nothing of the difficulties men are liable to get into, particularly those who are young and inexperienced, when they have side arms convenient to use upon each other on the slightest provocation. I have seen enough of those things in the army to authorizing me to advise all young men coming here to leave pistols and bowie knives at home. A good substantial pocket knife, is all the weapon an infantry soldier needs, besides his rifle or musket.

A man has no use for clothing, but that of the most durable and substantial kind, and just as little of that as is actually necessary. He will need two pair of pants, one coat, two heavy flannel shirts, two hickory shirts, two pair drawers, two pair woolen socks, and a good substantial hat or cap. These, with his blankets and an oil cloth to protect him from rain, will be about as much as any one will be able and willing to carry on his back..."

MY DEAR EMMA-The War letters of James K. Edmonson 1861-1865 ed.by Charles w. Turner PhD McClure Press 1978

Pg. 47 Camp Harman near Centerille (Va.) Sept. 3 1861 My dear Wife "...I do not need anything now in the shape of clothing, but when the weather gets colder I shall probably need more. I need a comfort or quilt, but I have sent home for one by Jim Holly..."

LEE& JACKSON'S BLOODY TWELTH-Letters of Irby Good-win Scott First Lieutenant Co. G Putnam Light Infantry Twelth Ga. Vol. Inf. Ed. by Johnnie Perry Pearson Univ. Tn. Press 2010

PG. 19 Camp Bartow, Sept. 5th, 1861 Pochahontas Co. Va. Dear Father & Family "...I wrote you last Thursday and as I have a chance to send a letter by Lieunt. Marshall who leaves here this evening for home I thought I would not let this opportunity slip and not write you. He comes home on business for the regeiment such as cloths, shoes, hats,&c. I expect he will remain about a month or more. As it will be no little trouble for him to get all the cloths & for every company from the different counties being scattered as they are...."

SOUTHERN HISTORICAL SOCIETY PAPERS Volume XVI ed. by R.A. Brock 1888

Pg. 119 The Wee Nee Volunteers of Williamsburg District fall 1861 "...Upon their arrival in Charleston, the men were embarked on a steamboat at a point near the Northeastern Railroad depot, and were landed at Fort Johnson on James Island.

On the 7th of September I wrote a letter, from which I extract the following: "...One of my men is without shoes, but I have sent to Charlston to buy him a pair. There are a good many of them who will suffer this winter, unless the people of Williamsburg will do their duty and supply them with clothing suitable for cold weather...My company is getting on very well, improving very fast in drill, and are a very quiet, obedient set. I do not think that I shall have much trouble with them. A good many of them are poorly provided with clothing, and I hope the ladies who are at work will remember them. I think four-fifths of them are making great sacrifices to serve their country..."

"DEAR MOTHER: DON'T GRIEVE ABOUT ME. IF I GET KILLED, I'LL ONLY BE DEAD." Ed. by Mills Lane The Beehive Press 1977

Pg. 61 Sheperd Pryor to his Wife Camp Bartow, Virginia September 7, 1861 Dear Nep: "...I got the daguerreotypes and shirt. I don't know how to express my feelings when I got them. I am more than thankful that you sent the pictures.It done me a deal of good. And the shirt, I could not have pleased myself half as well. With such cloth as it is made of I can keep warm in any sort of weather. To put on an undershirt, homespun shirt and overshirt, common coat and overcoat-that will do for anybody to wear. The shirt, I think, is extra (well) made..."

HANDLEY LIBRARY ARCHIVES, WINCHESTER, VA Letters of Henry Jennings Co. A 5th Regiment Va Volunters Jackson's Brigade

Sep. 8th 1861 Camp Harmon near Centreville (Va) Dear Aunt,"...I want you to send me some tobacco one pair woolen socks my cotton socks are good yet they hurt my feet when I march I want you to send me some paper and my lead pencil if you have my carpet sack I also don't care if you send me a handful to eat if it is convenient we do not drill on the seventh day in order to give us a chance to wash our clothes I have two shirts one pair of drawers and my cotton pants tell Lizzy she need not laugh about my washing for when I had washed and boiled my dirty drawers they are as white as if she had a done it..."

U.S. ARMY HERITAGE ABD EDUCATION CENTER

Sept. 8, 1861 C.M. Amoss-Cobb's Legion of Georgia Volunteers Richmond Va. Dear Georgia: "...If you have not already sent the suit oif clothing you spoke of sending please get a good stout overcoat for me. If we stay up here this winter I shall need something of the kind. Send a good pair of gloves and the other shirt you spoke of making. I would like to have two more linen shirts if you have them with you. If you do not have them with you, do not buy others. If you have sent the suit already Henry can bring the other things with him..."

PRIEST-HENRICKAND OTHER KIN-compiled by Miss Sydney M. Artz

Pg. 47 Woodstock, Va. Sept. 9th 1961 Dear Son, "...Your blanket and two pairs of socks, sweet oil, sand paper, tacks no.6 Some small change if you wish to pay any postage....I intend having you an oil-cloth overcoat made if I can have it lined so as to make it warm unless you would rather have another kind of one, if you would, let me know...you may send the socks that you have if they are worn out..."

I guess they needed the yarn if they're asking for his old socks back.

WELCOME THE HOUR OF CONFLICT—WILLAM COWAN McCLELLAN & THE 9TH ALABAMA ed by John C. Carter Univ of Al. Press 2007

Pg. 64 Spt. 6 1861 Manassas Junction William McCLellan to Thos. J. McCellan Dear Father, "...Tell Mother I will be very much obliged to her for the suit of clothes she spoke of sending me

Pg. 64 Sept. the 9th, 1861 Athens Ga. Sarah Anne McClellan Davis to William McClellan MyDear Brother,"...Things are going on about as they were when you left, everybody is working for the soldiers all of the time, you will believe this when I tell you that Kittie is hard at work knitting socks. (I did not think anyone could induce her to work). She has knit more than any one lady in the neighborhood except Matila...Hobbs Company will soon have good warm clothes sent them..."

Pg. 70 Late Sept.-this was written on a board a foot long and 6 inches wide-Manassas Junction William McClellan to Thos. J. McClellan Dear Father,'...My pants are about worn out. I will patch them in a day or so so they will do to wear some some time yet. I suppose our uniforms will be here in a few days. Tell Mother to send me the home spun suit she spoke of sending. I have got a pair of new shoes..."

Pg. 80 Sept 26 61 Camp at Centreville, Va William McClellan to Matilda McClellan Dear Sister, "...Write to me tell Mother I will soon need her warm drawers and shirts..."

Pg. 81 Sept 28th, 1861 Limestone Creek Robert McClellan to William McClellan Dear Will "...We have some good clothes to send you by the first chance. Warren Phillips is going on before long with Captain Hobbs Co[mpany's] clothes but I reckon we will send you yours he goes. Venable starts in a few days for the Alabama Volunteers on the Potomac. You will be certain to get your clothes soon..."

THE PAINFUL NEWS I HAVE TO WRITE-Letters and Diaries of Four Hite Brothers of Page County in the Service of the Confederacy Army of Northern Virginia Series Stonewall Brigade ed.by Harlan R. Jessup Butternut & Blue 1998

Pg. 48 Ambrose Shenk to William Hite (cousin Billy) Camp Harmon Sep 11th/61 "...We are now getting along tolerably well & the men seem to be better satisfied now as the(y) have rec. their Coats, Tents & part of the money for their services...."

YANKEE IN GRAY-The Civil war Memoirs of Henry E. Handerson The Press of Western Reserve Univ. 1962

Pg. 90 Camp Bienville, Sept. 11th, 1861 My Dear Father; "...I have some little funds now in the captain's hands, which will furnish me with some little necessaries for the winter, and, by the aid of Mother and my kind friends in Rapides, who insist upon sending me on some winter clothing, I trust I shall be able to wrestle pretty successfully with old Boreas, should the campaign last even until the spring. There will be, however, an immense amount of suffering in our camps this winter, should the war last as long as it now promises to do..."

GRANDFATHER'S JOURNAL (Franklin Lafayette Riley) Company B Sixteenth Mississippi Infantry Volunteers Harris' Brigade Mahone's Division Hill's Cops, A.N.V. May 27, 1861-July 15, 1865 Austin C. Dobbins Morningside 1988

Pg. 39 Thursday-Saturday, Sept. 12-14 1861 Near Fairfax Courthouse "...to find a package waiting for me. I now have a pair of woolen trousers, 3 pairs of socks, and an extra blanket, which I really don't need. Last week- for $1.25 apiece- I bought 2 blankets left by the Yankees at Manassas. The Blanket substitutes for the drawers I asked for, I guess..."

"DEAR MOTHER: DON'T GRIEVE ABOUT ME. IF I GET KILLED, I'LL ONLY BE DEAD." Ed. by Mills Lane The Beehive Press 1977

Pg. 62 Henry Graves to his Sister Norfolk, Virginia September 13, 1861 Dear Sis: "...It would be perhaps a strange sight for you to see me fixed up for acting the sentinel in my "bobtail" uniform, armed with a pistol, musket, bayonet, &c. Take me all in all, I imagine I present a decidedly fierce and formidable appearance...."

I guess "bobtail" refers to a roundabout jacket.

I WROTE YOU WORD- The Poignant Letters of Private Holt-John Lee Holt 1829-1863 ed by James A. Mumper print by H.E. Howard, 1991

The Charlotte Greys, 56th Va. Inf. Regt. Garnett's Brigade, Picketts Div. Longstreet's Corps. A.N.V.

New Fair Ground, Richmond, Va. Sept. 13th, 1861 "...My Dearest Ellen I forgot to tell you anything about my clothes in my other letters Pa said he would let you have wool to make them. I (want) you to mix the wool black and white together make them a tolerably dark grey & if you want anything diestuffs or anything else tell Pa to get it for you & I & he will settle it.

Same camp Sept. 22nd 1861 "...My Dearly beloved Wife...I do not know what to tell you about my clothes yet. I understand there is some doubt whether we can have them made at home or not. Maj. Green said he had named it to the Col. & he said he would see about it and let him know some time this week so I hope I can inform you fully about it the next time I write I expect we will have roundabout coats (short coats or jackets) & if we do it will not take so much cloth as frocks would (frock coats were double-breasted with wide skirts). I want you to fix my overcoat as I directed in my last & send it to me the first opportunity you have I want you to make the sleeves smartly larger You might take some of my old cloth coats or pants for the purpose if they will do or black yarn cloth either & line it well If you can get it I would like to have it lined with Lindsey or some other woolen goods anything you want to buy tell Pa to get it for you & he will do it you may if you get the chance knit me a coarse pair of oversocks. I know your situation (condition) is such that you can not do much for me..."

Richmond Va. Sept. 26th 1861 "...My Dearest Ellen, I wrote you word in my last that I would inform you more particularly about my clothes in this But as Maj. Green & Lieut. Henry are both at home I have not yet found out any more about it. If you think you cant conveniently make them I want you to let me know in your next & I must buy them but I had much rather have a good home made suit if I can get it than a suit that would cost me $15.00 here... We are now under immediate marching orders to join Floydes (Floyd's) Brigade near Lewisburg in Green Briar County (in what is now West Va.) ...My overcoat I wrote about you need not send if you have not already done so as I have bought me one. I thought it would be best to get one to take right on with me as I expect it is quite cold out there now & I did not know when I could get that one...."

Same camp Sept.29th, 1861 "...About my clothes I have (not) been informed certainly about them yet & you can go on with them as I have no idea but what they will answer as well as any or better mix the wool about ¾ black to ¼ white will make it about the proper color I expect we will have the coats roundabouts & if we do it wont take so much cloth...."

Same camp Sept 30th 1861 "...My Dearly beloved Wife Col. Stewart (Stuart, W.D.) intends to inspect everything we have tomorrow & see if we like (lack) anything or will need any more clothes for the winter & give us all the points about our clothes so Major Green informed us tonight I will then inform you what I want. He may think our present uniforms sufficient & if he does there will be no need of your making me any more at present…"

LETTERS OF JOHN BRATTON TO HIS WIFE by Elizabeth Porcher Bratton Privately Pub. 1942

Pg. 33 Letter from John Bratton to Bettie Bratton Spt. 15,. 1861 Camp near Germantown Va Dear Bettie,"…I sent a letter by Hollis yesterday and one by mail from Centreville in which I mentioned I wanted several things to keep me warm. As this is certain conveyance I will mention a part of my list. A pair of boots, wide sole. If Cramer can fit me. A uniform suit of Rock Island goods or some heavy materials as much like the Buckhead Uniform as possible. Jackson has my measure. He had to alter the coat to make it fit and ought to be warned to cut it according to alterations and not the original pattern. The pants ought to be full about the legs, and old McCarley never misses a fit for me in pants. Flannel shirts and drawers. The same for Lewis. By the by, I would like a warm winter cap, that will stand rain and keep my ears warm, for I am told it is common in this country for frost to bite ears.…I said something about gaiters but you need not trouble yourself about them. If you do, however, make them, send a pair of stout shoes along wioth them. I can change from boots to shoes with gaiters without taking a cold. Creight can bring these things back if they are not to be had.…"

Letter from John Bratten, 1861? "…he was visiting at the Citadel (Charleston, S.C.) and came up to me there, saying he had to take a second look to know me I was so much more sunburnt and bronzed than he supposed. I of course would not send you a picture that you might not recognize, besides you wanted it in full uniform, and mine was so scuffed and abused that I could not have made a decent appearance…"

A good quote to make my point about soldiers only posing for their likeness in a new uniform.

THE PAINFUL NEWS I HAVE TO WRITE-Letters and Diaries of Four Hite Brothers of Page County in the Service of the Confederacy-Army of Northern Virginia Series Stonewall Brigade ed.by Harlan R. Jessup Butternut & Blue 1998

Pg. 52 William Hite to John Hite Sunday Morning Luray Sept 15th 1861 "…I am having my winter clothes cut by the tailor to be made up this week. Overcoat and pants.…"

DEAR IRVIE, DEAR LUCY-The Civil War Letters of Capt. Irving A. Buck, General Cleburne's AAG & Family pub. by Buck Pub. Co. 2002

Pg. 39 Sept. 15, 1861 Head Quarters Fairfax Court House, Va. Dear Nellie (sister), "…The provisions and clothes all came o.k. I do not know what arrangement about sending things backwards and forwards now (the family lived in Frnt Royal, about 50 miles away). I suppose we will have to watch our opportunity....

I will try to send the basket, and our clothes up by Hamp (for laundry?-ed.) if I can get them over to the station- in regard to our keeping the boxes sent us, all that we neglected to return were two small paper boxes I left in Manassa and would have set them up last time but did not have room in the basket...

If Alvin (brother) will lend me his cap I will send it up to Lucy. Tell her to cut the pattern and send it back by the first safe opportunity by some one coming directly here so as to prevent the possibitlity of its getting lost-she can make it of gray, black, or blue, ask her to cut it a little longer, and the crown smaller, for the more it droops the prettier it looks, and if she can get no other vizor to cut the one off the gray cap I left-but think that Mr. Blackley would sell enough patent leather for that-two thin pieces put together and bound around the edges like the one on the gray cap is very pretty. I'll pay all expenses, get things right. I am in no hurry she may take her time-I will send her acouple of buttons to put on it-if she will notice there is a little whale bone in the back of the cap sent-to keep it in the right position-the cloth for the "Rifles" uniforms makes very pretty caps-had better get Blackley to make the vizor. Lend my cap over to show him how it should be done....I have not yet decided about my uniform but will let you know in a day or two...."

It sounds as though he is describing a kepi.

BROTHERS IN GRAY-The Civil War Letters of the Pierson Family ed. by Thomas W. Cutrer & t. Michael Parrish La. State Univ. Press 1997 Ninth Louisiana

Pg. 49 Rueben Allen Pierson to William H. Pierson camp Bienville Va. Sept. 18th, 1861 "... If you have an opportunity send me my overcoat as such an article will be quite comfortable in the cold climate of Va. Mark everything that you send with my name so that I will be sure to get my own things...'

CONFEDERATE CAPTAIN UJANIRTIS ALLEN'S LETTERS TO HIS WIFE ed. By Kandall Allen and Keith S. Bohannon La. State Univ. Press 1998

Pg. 42 Camp Tatnall near Fairfax C.H. Sep 18th 1861 "...Susie my dear, I would like for you to send me several coarse towels when you get a good chance....'

Camp Toombs Va. Sep 22nd 1861 "...My dear your hart would bleed if you could see the misery and suffering that our poor soldiers are doomed to undergo. I may probably write your society (a ladies aid society) a few lines. If I felt,myself equal to the task I should certainly do it. Some active measures must be taken soon; for I think we will have frost tomorrow morning. I wrote to you to send me about four good blankets. I do not know that you have received my letter, and mention it again. Suggest that you line one or two of them. I wrote to Mrs. Boykin about them also. I do not know that I will want those legans. I like the idea of having a tick with a hole in the middle so that I could fill it with straw, and take it out when we were passing about. Uncle Wisdom has written to Cousin Robert to bring one…Let me tell you what to send me. several pairs of drawers, a good silk handkerchief or two. I would not ask for socks but I see you have them already knit. I have five pair; two thick ones. I think I have enough shirts with the exception of overshirts. If I had a good flannel one it would answer a good purpose. If you send me any more clothes than I need I will give to the boys who have no one to provide for them….I would like the best in the world to have a good oil cloth or indea ruber blanket; but do not think you can get one….Poor whiskey sells at two dollars a quart here. At this price I don't think that our company will ever become very intemperate unless we make a rise of some of the "rhino" soon. This suggest to me the idea that our men want clothes more than money…"

Captain Ujaniritis is concentrating on supply from home, doesn't even mention government supply.

The 25th North Carolina Troops in the Civil War by Carroll C. Jones McFarland & Co. 2009

Sept. 18, 1861 "Arriving in Raleigh, the regiment disembarked and pitched camp for a couple of days while waiting to be issued uniforms. Prior to their arrival, there had been some confusion between the state and Confederate governments over which entity was to supply the soldiers clothing. With the realization that winter was fast approaching, The North Carolina Legislture directed Governor Adjutant General James Martin to provide uniforms and shoes for all of North Carolia's troops. Soon every textile mill in the Tarheel State was producing cloth to be turned into winter clothing for the soldiers. A historian later wrote the following tribute to the state officials and to the women of the Confederacy for their valiant efforts to clothe the soldiers during that first winter: 'The unpleasant truth must be stated that the Government did not realize what was ahead of it, and lacked energy to supply the troops from the beginning…Everything that could be made available in the State for clothing the troops was purchased, and the factories cheerfully furnished every yard of cloth they could. Major Deereux and his assistants were quite busy collecting and Captain Garrott equally so in manufacturing. As fast as the articles were received every effort was made by all the officers of the department to furnish the troops with clothing before the severe weather of winter set in. With the large and valuable help given by the ladies of the State, who firnished blankets, quilts and carpets to be cut up into the size of small quilts and lined, and many other articles, the troops of North Carolina were clothed during the first winter of the war in such manner as to prevent much suffering.'…In the brief stopover, the mountain boys received brand new uniforms, which very likely had been manufactured there in Raleigh…"

This source doesn't say how much of these supplies were uniform, other than the 25th North Carolina troops.

THE BROTHERS WAR ed by Annette Tapert Vintage Books, 1988

Pg. 23 "John Holloway served as a private with Company G. 1st Georgia Volunteer Infantry. His letter home was written after seeing action at the Battle of Cheat Mountain, West Virginia, on September 11-13, 1861 Camp Bartow, September 19, 1861 "...We slept on the ground for four nights with only one blanket apiece, and what was the worst thing that to me was that in going up the mountains I lost one of my shoes in the mud and it was so dark that I could not find it and then of course I had to carry one until I came back to camp. You must wonder at soldiers having to do without shoes and blankets sometimes. I believe men can stand almost anything after they get used to it. The hardest part is getting used to it..."

That last sentence-Truer words were never spoken.

DEFEND THE VALLEY Margarette Barton Colt Crown Pub. 1994

Pg. 97 Letter of Frank B. Jones to Susan C. Jones-Camp near Fiarfax C.H. 19th Sept. 1861 "...The weather is getting cool or rather the nights & I would like to have two good warm blankets or a large, thick comfort the one I took with me is an excellent one, I lay down on half of it and cover myself with the other half but it is not enough now..."

By making inquiry at Mr. Boyds or Mr. Williams or Sister Fannies you could hear of a wagon which would bring me down the things I write for, they had best be put in a box, Mr. Phillup Meade comes down once a week in a wagon & he would bring me anything, if you could send it down by him, is my great coat a nice warm one, I charged Denny about making it warm and putting a large cape on it..."

HISTORY OF THE FOURTH REGIMENT SOUTH CAROLINA VOLUNTEERS FROM THE COMMENCEMENT OF THE WAR UNTIL LEE'S SURRENDER J.W. Reid Shannon &Co. Printers & Stationers Morningside Bookshop 1975

Pg. 49 Saturday Evening, 5O'Clock, September 21st (1861) "...This morning, having nothing to do, I went off about one mile from town, into the woods, to patch up my breeches, remaining, awhile in my shirt tail. During the operation, if a dog had seen me and not laughed, he would have undoubtedly switched his tail or boo-hooed and run backwards, with his tail touching his chin. I had left all my clothes at camp, only what I had on, and they had got torn pretty bad right-right where Momma used to slap me. While I was tailoring away at my pants, a gun was fired, a few yards off.

I took long stitches, jerked on my britches, jumped over ditches, went through the switches, and formed a line of march and made for camp. You may ask what kind of a line I formed. Answer: a bee line…"

DEFEND THE VALLEY Margarette Barton Colt Crown Pub. 1994

Pg. 99 Letter of Frank B. Jones to Ann C.R. Jones (mother) Camp near Fairfax C.H. 21st Sept. 1861 "The Surgeons advised wearing flannel, I came off from home with my one flannel shirt expecting to get my trunk soon, but we moved so hurriedly from Winchester that I did not & could not have carried it with me, soon after the battleI took my flannel off as I had no change, the life I led sleeping out in the open air & such constant exposure without flannel was too much for my sysem, as soon as my trunk came I put my flannel on, and in two or three days I was a new man, & have never been sick since. Tell Sue I have my great coat, it is very nice one & it will do for me to cover at night as well as to wear during the day. I sleep on a stretcher & my servant builds me a fire & spreads my blanket on my lowly couch every night…Well it is getting late & I am beginning to think whether I am going to sleep warm or cold to night, my great coat will help the cause, good night!"

THE MEN-49TH REGIMENT VIRGINIA VOLUNTEERS

Requisition by Capt. H.N.B. Wood for New Market Volunteers, Co. C, Sept. 21, 61
12 Wall Tents with Flies
65 Knap Sackks
64 Waist Belts
90 Haver Sacks
68 Canteens and Wraps
(no record of completion)

LETTERS FROM LEE'S ARMY by Susan Leigh Blackford and Charles Minor Blackford pub by Scribner & Sons1947

Pg. 43 Sept. 21, 1861 Falls Church, Va. "We are still on the same duty and there is nothing much to write about but the exploits of Jack Alexander. He has been up to his old tricks again; utterly disregarding all rules of military life, relying on his wit and good fellowship to see him through. Up to now his reliance has not been in vain but at last has reached its limit. He was sent up to Leesburg with two companies for a short time on some special duty, and finding it a very charming place to be stationed, determined to stay there. Col. Radford ordered him to join the regiment near Fairfax Courthouse but he failed to obey the order. It was repeated several times with the like result. At last Col. Radford reported him to Beauregard and the peremptory order was sent. Even that he did not obey but reported alone in a style which would have made you think the Prince of Wales was on a visit. He was dressed in an elegant suit of black velvet, with ruffled shirt and fancy-topped boots in a handsome carriage drawn by two handsome black stallions. His arrival created some amusement among his friends, but had no effect on headquarters where General Beauregard declined to see him but sent word that if he did not report with his company to his regiment within forty-eight hours he would be under arrest…"

Now, that's quite a uniform!

A SOUTHERN SOLDIER'S LETTERS HOME The Civil War Letters of Samuel Burney Cobb's Georgia Legion, Army of Northern Va. Ed. By Nat Turner Mercer Univ. Press, Macon Ga.2002

Pg.15 Camp Wash.Yorktown Va. Sept. 23rd, 1861 My Dearest Wife, "…Last night I stood guard in the rain which gave me a cold. It was an awful night. Tents by the score were overturned and nothing could be found to protect the soldiers from the rain. The wind was very high. I had on an India rubber overcoat, which I obtained from Mr. Hiram Harris, which kept me dry. My leggings too were very valuable… Baldwin's Negro does the cooking, brings water washes dishes & waits on his master, and I could not ask him to wash my clothes. I will not have much to do except for hickory shirts, drawers & socks. Col. Cobb is particular about keeping everything clean about the camps.…Mr. Fitzpatrick goes to obtain a winter uniform. Ifyou can get mine from the tailor do so and have it lined with brown seams. …"

This quote gives you an idea of the consideration shown to the "servants" with the Con federate Army.

Pg. 19 Sept. 26, 1861 Yorktown, Va. My Dearest Wife, "As I am on general guard duty to day at Yorktown I provided myself with a sheet of paper to write to you while off duty. I am on duty 24 hours, but am relieved so I stand guard but 8 hrs out of 24. It is now 9AM and at 9AM tomorrow I am discharged and return to the campground which is 2 miles from this place. I will have to stay here tonight, so I brought my India rubber shawl & blanket. I have on 3 shirts, a vest and coat…"

Pg. 21 Sept. 27th, 1861 Camp Washington, 2 miles from Yorktown Dearest Wife, "…It is said in camp that we will leave here in a short while. I rather think that it is true, for it is certain we are not stationed for winter. I am ready for the uncertain future I hope; let come what will. I am prudent, at least I try to be so. When we leave here I will be troubled about my clothing. I cannot carry on my back all that I brought in my trunk. If we cannot hire a wagon I will be compelled to give some of it away or throw it away. I wish I had left some of it at home…"

U.S. ARMY HERITAGE AND EDUCATION CENTER

Sept. 23, 1861 unknown soldier First Virginia Cavalry Regiment Camp Terry, Va My Dearest Ma: "…received the large bundle sent by Bill Hill. I feel greatly obliged to you for making the coat and pants and for sending the cakes. The coat fits me very well-I have not tried on the pants yet…"

PRIVATIONS OF A PRIVATE-Campaigning With The First Tennessee, C.S.A. and Life Thereafter by Marcus B. Toney pub. by Univ Alabama Press 2005

Pg 9 Sept. 1861 (After the Rich Mountain Campaign) "…stopped a few days at Staunton (Va) where we met many of General Garnett's soldiers, and they were in a bad plight, many of them without shoes and with stone bruises on their heels. In a few days we were on the train for Millboro, where we disembarked after some eight hours' ride. Our destination was Cheat Mountain, some eighty miles from the railroad.

This was our first march fully equipped. Besides our gun, knapsack, haversack, and cartridge box, nearly all our boys had on one side a six-shooter Colt's revolver buckled around them, and on the other side was a large Damascus blade (made at a blacksmith's shop). This too had a scabbard and belt…."

Pg. 16 Sept,1861(marching around Greenbriar, Va. in the mountains) "…When we reached the camp at Valley Mountain, we were in a very bad plight, very hungrey, and many of us barefoot. I was not quite barefoot, as I had one foot shod, the other bare…"

Trouble with shoes again

JAMES MADISON UNIV. ARCHIVES

Spt. 24th, 1861 Letter of John Merrick Camp Blair Fairfax Station (Va) Dear Brother: "…I received the two pair of drawers that were sent by Decker. I would have been glad to have received my pants also. I told John Merrick of several articles that I wished from home, one of them was a blanket of some description for these cold nights makes one think of a good warm bed…"

DIARY OF A CONFEDERATE SHARPSHOOTER-The Life of James Conrad Peters pub by Pictorial Histories Pub Co. 1997

Pg. 19 Sept. 25, 1861 "...It was probably during this time that James received the items that he listed in his diary. With no other explanationhe listed these in his diary:

1 cap 1 pair pants
2 shirts 1 coat
1 overcoat 2 pair drawers
1 saddle blanket
1 haversack 1 nose bag
1 pair boots 1 pair spurs
1 cartridge box & cap box & belt
1 curry comb & brush
1 canteen 1 circingle
1 bridle & martingale
1 tin cup 1 plate
1 shot gun

Much of this equipment was necessary for the handling of a cavalry horse. The martingale was part of the strapping that passed under the horse's neck, between his forelegsand was attached to its belly strap. The circingle (or surcingle) was the belt or band that passed around the body of the horse and helped secure the saddle. We might assume that since a saddle was not on the list of items he received, that James Conrad provided his own saddle with his horse. It is also interesting that the weaponwhich was issued to him was a shotgun. It was a popular theory at the beginning of the war that the cavalry would be doing close-in fighting or conducting charges against infantry or gun emplacements, and therefore the shotgun would be a logical choice in place of a rifle or musket."

"DEAR MOTHER: DON'T GRIEVE ABOUT ME. IF I GET KILLED, I'LL ONLY BE DEAD." Ed. by Mills Lane The Beehive Press 1977

Pg. 69 Tomilson Fort to his Mother Centreville, Virginia September 26, 1861 My Dear Mother: (pickets talking across the lines) "...Nothing makes the Yankees more angry then to to refer to Bull Run. They call us "ragamuffins" and often "the ragged rebels." Our regiment is dressed in a comparatively new uniform and therefore looks better than most of the regiments who go on picket. One of the Yankees called, Where did you steal those fine clothes?" One of our men replied, From the dead Yankees at Bull Run!"

Already being called "ragged rebels," so this is not a post-war term.

CIVIL WAR STORIES-Letters-Memoires-Anecdotes Union and Confederate by Walbrook D. Swank pub by Burd Street Prees 1996

Pg. 51 Letters of Private John Jasper Culpeper CSA Sept 26, 1861 Manassas, Va. Dear Father and Mother, Sisters and Brothers, "I want you to send a good long bed blanket and one of those blankets to wear with a hole in the middle to put over my head and let it be thick and warm for it is nearly as cold now at night as it is there in the dead of winter. Send me two pairs of drawers, one good shirt, a pair of buckskin gloves, and one or two pairs of socks and a nice silk handkerchief and some good bread and some money and one thick pair of pants and send my hat, I forgot it and left it at cousin Mary's...I want one pair of suspenders..."

Supply from home folks

RECOLLECTIONS AND LETTERS OF GENERAL ROBERT E. LEE by His Son, Capt. Robert E. Lee pub b y Garden City Pub Co. 1926

Pg. 49 Sept. 26, 1861 Camp on Sewell's Mountain (Va. now W.Va.) Letter to Mrs. Lee: "...It is raining heavily. The men are all exposed on the mountain, with the enemy opposite to us. We are without tents, and for two nights I have lain buttoned up in my overcoat. To-day my tent came up and I am in it. Yet I fear I shall not sleep for thinking of the poor men. I wrote about socks for myself. I have no doubt the yarn ones you mention will be very acceptable to the men here or elsewhere.If you can send them here, I will distribute them to the most needy..."

Is it any wonder why we love this man?

"DEAR MOTHER: DON'T GRIEVE ABOUT ME. IF I GET KILLED, I'LL ONLY BE DEAD." Ed. by Mills Lane The Beehive Press 1977

Pg 69 A.J. Reese to his Aunt Lewisburg, Virginia September 27, 1861 (after marching for two days) "...My feet were sore. I bought me a new pair of shoes at Lynchburg and put them on new, and they hurt my feet.

Aunt, do not send me anything of any weight (unless) I send for it, for I have more than I can carry. I left most of my things back in Jackson River in Leiutenant McDonald's trunk that is my heaviest things. If I had not, I could not have carried my load at all. I love to receive anything from home, but I would hate to throw anything away. A coat and my pant(s) are all I want or all I need at present...."

Is he referring to his uniform jacket or an overcoat?

THE CIVIL WAR LETTERS OF GENERAL FRANK "BULL" PAXTON A Lieutenant of Lee &Jackson ed. by John Gallatan Paxton Hill Jr. College Press 1978

Pg. 21 Camp near Fairfax C. H. Sept. 28 1861 "...Jim Holly came this evening and tells me he has the pair of pants which you sent me, and that Waltz will bring some more things for me. You need not get the overcoat; my coat for the present answers a very good purpose, and if I find hereafter that I need an overcoat, I will send to Richmond for it..."

THE MITTELDORFER LETTERS

Yorktown, Sept.29 "...Ma I wish you would send me my other shirt as it is very cold down hear now, and them socks you gave me was all moth eating and one pair are all wone out already...(same letter)

Dear Brother David, You must not think hard of me by not sending you them oysters which promised to send you for when I left Gloucester we had to leave all at once and I did not have time to Pack my Knapsack and now we are hear with nothing but our blankets and tents and we don't get nothing to eat but fat meat and bread for Dinner Coffee for Supper..."

War History of the Old First Virginia Regiment, Army of Northern Virginia by William Ellis Jones Book & Job Printer 1884

Pg. 14 Sept. 30 1861 "During our stay at Fairfax Courthouse the city of Richmond furnished the whole regiment with new uniforms, otherwise nothing of much interest occurred, to mention, except constant picket, guard duty and drilling..."

THE MITTELDORFER LETTERS

Gloucester Point, Oct.16th "...Pa if you can get any more of that Red binding like you got for my pants I had made at Mr. Mills I wish you would get it and send it down for I can get 10 cents a yard for it down hear. Send the piece I left at home...."

The Thirty-Seventh North Carolia Troops- Tar Heels in the Army of Northrn Virginia by Michael C. Hardy McFarland & Co. 2003

Pg 20 Oct. 1861 "The companies had been given tents for sleeping quarters, but soldiers still wore their clothes from home and carried their hunting rifles and shotguns. When the individual companies offered their services to the state, they were accepted provided that they could arm themselves. While the men expected to receive uniforms from the state, they were oftimes slow in arriving. Private Tugman wrote home again commenting on the lack of attire: "I want you to make me a pair of pants and a shirt (.) if we could get our uniforms this winter I would not need them."

Still dressed in civilian clothing and carrying civilian arms.

THE JOURNAL OF WOMEN'S CIVIL WAR HISTORY-Accounts of the Sacrifice, Achievement & Servive of American Women 1861-1865 ed. Eileen Conklin Thomas Pub. 2001

Pg. 62 "…One especially interesting presentation, held in October, 1861, featured Miss Lavina Williams, lately of the New Orleans Tigers. Miss Williams served as a French Vivandiere with this unit and was an active participant in the Battle of Manassas. During her exhibition she demonstrated the style and the duties of the brave Vivandieres as well as the "remarkable use of the knife peculiar to the Zouaves" and shared other comments on their mode of fighting…"

I'd have loved to have seen that performance. Early Vaudeville?

16th TENNESSEE VOLUNTEER INFANTRY REGIMENT :Clothing, Arms and Equipment (website)

In Oct. 1861 Joseph Carey, an artilleryman, wrote "we received a uniform this morning from the citizens of Panola County and also a goodly number of blankets and underclothes…."

Amember of John H. Anderson's Brigade wrote "Most of the boys are now strutting around with their "Tennessee Clothes" on…" Another said "At last we are once more comfortably clothed. Although we do not make a very uniform appearance, some having light and grey, and others dark colored clothing…"

Multiform from the folks at home, but at least they were dressed and supplied for winter.

FOOTPRINTS OF A REGIMENT-A Recollection of the 1st Georgia Regulars 1861-1865 by W.H.Andrews, 1st Sergeant Co. M pub. by Longstreet Press 1992

Pg 24 Oct. 1861 "The army is building strong fortifications around Centreville. The boys don't relish a pick or shovel much but have to knuckle down to it. We also have plenty of room for battalion drill, and Col. Magill certainly knows how to put the boys through. On dress parade the regiment maked a fine appearance, and (it) seems to be quite a treat for the soldiers camped around us to watch the regiment go through with the maneuvers. The boys have to turn out for parade in apple pie order, shoes blackened, brasses brightened, and white gloves on. The Regulars can go through the maneuvers on dress parade to perfection…"

Still blackened shoes and white gloves?

"The Tigers are a hard set, said to be the wharf rats form New Orleans. They have the Zouave, or bloomer, uniform, red pants extending full to the knee, where it is gathered to a band at the knee, the lower part of the leg being enclosed in leggings. Their jackets are of bright blue, their caps are in the shape of a sugarloaf and hang down by the side of the head. Around their waist is a belt in which there is a large knife. Altogether they are a hard-looking set, and if all accounts are true, they don't belie their looks…"

WEEP NOT FOR ME, DEAR MOTHER (Letters of Eli Pinson Landers from Gwinnett Co. Ga. The Flint Hill Grays. Eli was 19 years old when he enlisted in Aug. 1861) ed. by Elizabeth Whitley Roberson Pelican Pub. Co. 1996

Pg. 34 Letter to Eli Landers from his mother, Oct. 1861 "…I would a sent you an oilcloth but Jim and Uncle Ely went and got theirs before I knew it and they said when you stand guard Arch and Lige would lend you theirs and I was scarce of money and had to pay cash for your shoes…" Eli began writing home almost as soon as he reached Richmond (1861) He mainly asked for flannel drawers and woolen caps. In September he asked for a long frock-tailed coat that would come to his knees to protect him when it was raining. Later in October he began asking for flannel shirts, buckskin gloves, shoes, and blankets.…Eli's mother answered his request for clothing with a letter in October: "We could not get your pants ready and as for flannel their ain't none to be had about here. We will send your pants when we do your shoes or boots too and I want to know which you had rather have, boots or shoes."

WEEP NOT FOR ME, DEAR MOTHER (letters of Eli Pinson Landers from Gwinnett Co. Ga. The Flint Hill Grays. Eli was 19 years old when he enlisted in Aug. 1861) ed. by Elizabeth Whitley Roberson Pelican Pub. Co. 1996

Pg. 43 (near Richmond) October 1861 My Dear old Mother "…You wanted to know if I needed any shoes. I don't need them now but soon will and they cost 6 or 7 dollars here. If you can I want you to send me a good pair of homemade ones.…"

I WROTE YOU WORD-The Poingnant Letters of Private Holt, the Chalotte Grays, 56th Virginia Infantry Regiment Gannett's Brigade, Pickett's Division, Longstreet's Corps, A.N.V. by John Lee Holt ed by James A. Mumper pub by H.E. HGoward Inc. 1991

Pg.21 Richmond Oct. 3d 1861 My dearest Ellen, "...We have come pretty much to the conclusion not to have any new uniform this winter as we think the one we have will last us through the winter so you may dispense with making mine & if I need it hereafter I will try to get one some way. I would be very glad for you to make me some yarn drawers just single wove yarn cloth will be nearly equal to flannel You can cut them by some of my old drawers if you can make them if you have mixed any wool it wont make any difference as I would as soon they were gray as not & if you have more than enough you may make me a fatigue shirt of it..."

Pg.26 New Fair Ground, Richmond Va. Oct. 24th, 1861 "....About my drawers I want you to get them done as soon as you can conveniently But you need not think I will become impatient as I know you have a very bad chance to get along with it & write me word about what time you think you can finish them so I can inform you how to send them to me It doesn't make any difference about the fatigue shirt at all as I only thought you might have the wool to spare & could very easily make it with my drawers I don't know that I shall need one at all as the ones weve got may last us all the winter & if they don't I reckon we can get some some way ...."

Pg. 27 Richmond, Va. Oct 29th 1861 "...you wrote me about some calico in your last I have made some inquiries down in town about it. I can get it at 25* per yard but for nothing less If you will inform me in your next how much you want I will get it for you & send it to you by the first opportunity. Our company have drawn new uniforms which will only cost us $7.50 apiece ready made which I think very cheap as they are very good ones made of heavy woolen goods much better than the first we got I want to send my old ones home by the first chance I get & I think they will do very well for Henry's winter clothes as I have not soiled them much the coat especially is almost as good as new & I think it wont like (lack) of fitting him as it is a good deal too small for me if you think the pants will do you can alter them to fit him I wrote you word some time ago that I thought I had socks enough for the winter & I think I have but you may knit another pair of gloves as you have the opportunity if you can as I think I shall need them before winter is out & they are indispensable to the comfort of a soldier in cold weather...."

U.S. ARMY HERITAGE AND EDUCATION CENTER

Oct. 4, 1861 Pvt M.H. Emeney 14th Virginia Volunteer Infantry Camp Curtis, Land's End Va. Dear Johnny: "...The other night our tent fell over in a tremendous rain and caught me under it and nearly smothered me and wet me to the skin. I had to cut a hole in the tent to get out and my shoes floated off in the stream that covered the whole campground and I was walking about all night in my stockings in water a foot deep..."

Ah, the joys of a soldier's life!

DEAR SISTER-CIVIL WAR LETTERS TO A SISTER IN ALABAMA Frank Anderson Chappell pub. by Branch Springs Pub. 2002 (Third Alabama Regiment)

Pg. 44 Norfolk Va. Oct. 7 1861 My Dear Sister "…I acknowledge the receipt of a very good pair of socks and bed tick of which I am very glad. I have socks enough now to last me nearly a year…"

U.S. ARMY HERITAGE AND EDUCATION CENTER

Oct. 8, 1861 C.M. Amoss, Co. C, Cobb's Legion of Georgia Volunteers My Dear Georgia: "…you need not send me any other clothing than 2 linen shirts if you have them and the other shirt you are making for me. I would like to have a new overcoat but will wait and see what kind I want. I think I will buy it in Richmonmd with the new suit I will be obliged to get when I'm promoted…"

CONFEDERATE CAPTAIN UJANIRTIS ALLEN'S LETTERS TO HIS WIFE ed. By Kandall Allen and Keith S. Bohannon La. State Univ. Press 1998

Pg. 53 Camp Toombs Va. Oct 9th 1861 "…I am very well pleased with that cloth. Exchange for a coat of it by all means, though do not cut it untill I tell you. You have no chance to make a fit…"

A SOUTHERN SOLDIER'S LETTERS HOME The Civil War Letters of Samuel Burney Cobb's Georgia Legion, Army of Northern Va. Ed. By Nat Turner Mercer Univ. Press, Macon Ga.2002

Pg. 31 Oct. 9th, 1961 Camp Washington, Yorktown, Va. Dearest Wife, "…If you have it and this reaches you in time, send me a small pillow; knapsacks are hard, but my head is getting so hard I can stand it…"

Pg. 37 Camp Marion, Yorktown Va. Oct. 18, 1861Dearest Wife, "…Last night it rained very hard, but I passed the night very pleasantly, as I did not get wet and slept as soundly as a dollar. I have cover enough now. I do not sleep cold. Our mess has not less than 12 or 15 blankets, which with our coats, India rubbers, & (?) answers our purpose very well. When our house is finished I wish two articles sent by the first opportunity; 1st, a good blanket; 2nd, a small pillow. I do not need anything else and if I had more they would be in the way. I will keep the trunk and late in the winter season or early in spring I will send home my overcoat & blankets, at least one of them…."

"DEAR MOTHER: DON'T GRIEVE ABOUT ME. IF I GET KILLED, I'LL ONLY BE DEAD." Ed. by Mills Lane The Beehive Press 1977

Pg. 76 Benjamin Moody to his Family Richmond Virginia October 9, 1861 Dear Wife and Children: "…I want you to send me some clothes if you have got them ready when Whitley comes back-a pair of drawers and if you can get me a pair of shoes, I want you to send them to me, as shoes has got very high here and these will not do me at all this winter. And send my pegging awl and shoe hammer, and I can but leather and half-sole my shoes. And tell Bob to make me a pair of heels and nails and send them to me, if he has time…"

This soldier is taking the shoe matter in hand.

HISTORY OF THE FOURTH REGIMENT SOUTH CAROLINA VOLUNTEERS FROM THE COMMENCEMENT OF THE WAR UNTIL LEE'S SURRENDER J.W. Reid Shannon &Co. Printers & Stationers Morningside Bookshop 1975

Pg. 53 Army of the Potomac, Germantown Va. Thursday, October 10th, 1861 "…I drew some coffee for the company this morning and sent it to them. Don't laugh at me when I tell you what I sent it in. I took the legs of an old pair of drawers of mine (perfectly clean), and put the coffee in one leg and the sugar in the other. Rather a queer kind of saddlebag was it not? I also sent the boys potatoes, in bags as black as the ace of spades, or clubs either; but we have got so that we don't want anything better than a gourd or a turtle shell to eat out of. Please send me a turtle shell or two, as I am needing a tray very bad. If you can do so I will take it as a great favor of you …"

Eating out of a turtle shell? Asking for one to be sent from home? This is the first I've ever heard of such things.

DEAR IRVIE, DEAR LUCY-The Civil War Letters of Capt. Irving A. Buck, General Cleburne's AAG & Family pub by Buck Pub. Co. 2002

Oct. 10, 1861 Head Quarters Dear Lucy, "The cap and uniform came, the former is a perfect beauty, and it is the prettiest that I have ever seen, and I have had numerous offers to "trade." Benton received one from Lynchburg last night, but it is not as pretty as mine, and you may accept my thanks for it. The uniform fits very well and reflects great credit upon Nell and yourself. A. has bought a set of Va. buttons for it. I have engaged a set for my uniform when I have it made. I paid a big price for them, but they are of the finest quality fine guilt. I will try to come up in a week or two to have my uniform cut, and get some bedding as the nights are getting airish."

WELCOME THE HOUR OF CONFLICT-William Cowan McClellan & the 9th Alabama ed by John C. Carter pub by Univ of Al. Press 2007

Pg. 88 Oct 10th, 1861 ShoalFord Ala. Thos. J. McClellan to William McClellan Dear Will, "I was in Huntsville yesterday for the purpose of starting your cloths to you. They consist in two under shirts two blouses one blue cotton shirt two pairs of gloves one large home made blanket one pair of dark striped jeans pants, the blanket is dyed purple, a pocket handkerchief, one bottle cordial and one of home made wine and two large looking pipes a present from poor old Hartwell, and I have been thus particular so that you may know what to look for upon their arrival, the box in which your things are packed is rather too frail I fear to carry them safely being the one in which the caster was brought fromk the North, perhaps you remember it..."

Pg. 89 Oct 11th, 1861 Athens (Ga) Matilda McClellan to William McClellan My Dear Brother, "...Mother is going to send you twelve pair of yarn socks and six pair of linsey drawersin the box of uniforms to be distributed by Capt. Hobbs among the men and for fear your box will not arrive you had better speak for a surplus of each, if they get there before your box..."

Pg. 97 Oct. 31st, 1861 Centreville, Va. William McClellan to Robert McClellan Dear Brother, "...I have not received my cloths from Venable yet I am needing Them Very much. We are looking for him every day. When we retreated a week or so ago our Baggage was all sent to the Junction. I lost all of my shirts save the one I had on. We have had ice here a half of an inch thick, several Big White frosts..."

HANDLEY LIBRARY ARCHIVES, WINCHESTER, VA Diary of John Hites, 33rd Va., Stonewall Brigade

Pg 19 Oct. 11 1861 (inspection by the top brass) "The Brigade behaved remarkably well and was complemented by General Smith for the soldier-like appearance of the men. General Johnston was dressed with fine gray cloth coat, standing collar with stars on either side, gray cap and blue pants, rode a bay horse. General Beauregard's dress was blue throughout; rode a sorrel horse. General Smith wore citizen's clothes, rode a fine bay..."

Pg. 25 Oct. 18th, 1861 "...A great many troops around Centreville. Thirty barrels of flour, $600 dollars worth of shoes left behind by one of the US Regiments in their hasty retreat..."

MY DEAR EMMA-The War letters of Col. James K. Edmonson 1861-8165 ed.by Charles w. Turner PhD McClure Press 1978

Pg. 56 Camp near Fairfax C.H. October 12, 1861 "...So you have bought some cloth and intend to make your husband a suit of clothing out of it. Well, I can't say that I object to that for I know that I will need it when the weather gets cold. But how are you going to have it made? You have not got my measurements. Do you intend to make the coat a drape coat? If you do, I wish you would have the shoulder straps of a captain put on it (oblong square with two bars)-let it be of plain material, not to cost much. If you have enough cloth, I would like to have a double breasted military vest, but if you have not enough do not go to the trouble and expense of getting more for I can get along without it..."

By "drape coat" I guess he means a sack coat and not a cape.

VOICES FROM COMPANY D Diaries by the Greensboro Guards, Fifth Alabama infantry Regiment, Army of Northern Virginia ed. by G.Ward Hubbs Univ. of Ga. Press 2003

Diarists: JHC John Henry Cowin
SP Samuel Pickens
JP James Pickens
JST John S. Tucker
VET Veteran from Co. D, 5th Alabama Regiment
HB Henry Beck

Pg. 61 Oct. 13, 1861 Manassas JHC "...Wrote a letter to Aunt Ann in regard to having a couple of over coats made for Brother and my self, as it appears that if we do not provide for ourselves, nobody else will. None of us have any winter clothing yet and but little prospects of getting any....Three men left...Father for clothing for the company. He will first go to Richmond and if unable to procure the goods there, do not know where he will go..."

Pg 65 JHC "...Sent Steve down to the Junction after Father, who got here about twelve o'clock. He is in fine health and has arranged every thing satisfactorily concerning the uniform..."

U.S. ARMY HERITAGE AND EDUCATION CENTER

Oct. 13, 1861 Lt Stanley S. Callendish Co. G, 4th South Carolina Volunteer Infantry Germantown, Va. My Dear Wife: "...I have written to you that I have received all the clothing you sent...I have everything I need now except the boots-and will not need them badly for a month. I will probably buy a new uniform in Richmond as my old one is quite holy-I have had 2 pair of uniform pants but need a good dress suit…"

JAMES MADISON UNIV. ARCHIVES

Oct. 13th, 1861 Letter of Enoch V. Kaufman Page Volunteers of 10th Regiment of Virginia Volunteers Fredericksburg, Page County, Va. Dear Uncle: "…Ma is marking at yours and his boots she has got me a pair done they are about knee high. They have got all your cloths done and I expect (?) will start back in a week or two. He is fattened up very considerable since he has been at home…"

Oct. 23rd, 1861 Massanutten Page County, Va. Dear Brother: "…John H. Neubalken says he is going down next week if he goes they will send all your clothes along and you can put your old ones in above those you don't want and send them back and have them done over again if they are worth it. Goods of all kinds are very scarce and high the stores are very empty scarcely anything in them. I think some of the Luray merchants have gone to Richmond to try to bring some goods…"

VOICES FROM COMPANY D Diaries by the Greensboro Guards, Fifth Alabama infantry Regiment, Army of Northern Virginia ed. by G.Ward Hubbs Univ. of Ga. Press 2003

Diarists: JHC John Henry Cowin
SP Samuel Pickens
JP James Pickens
JST John S. Tucker
VET Veteran from Co. D, 5th Alabama Regiment
HB Henry Beck

Pg. 61 Oct. 14, 1861 Manassas JHC "Father has an unlimited furlough to go in search of cloth for a uniform for the Compny. Do not know when he will start. The boxes sent from Greensboro arrived this morning. More socks than anything else. Mother sent twenty-six pairs and three pairs of gloves…"

Pg. 61 Oct. 15, 1861 Manassas JHC "…Lieutenant Dedman and Christian, Mr. Hutchinson and Father left this morning at for o'clock. The three former for home, Father for clothing for the company. He will first go to Richmond and if unable to procure the goods there, do not know where he will go…."

THE CONFEDERACY IS ON HER WAY UP THE SPOUT Letters to South Carolina 1861-1865 ed. by J. Roderick Heller III and Carolynn Ayres Heller Univ. of Georgia Press 1992

Pg. 28 Camp Winder Richmond Oct. 14, 1861 Dear Brother and Sister "we are giting a good sply of winter clothing a greate deal sent us from gorgia…" Milton Barrett 18 regt. Ga. V co. A in the care of captain JBO Neal

Here's an early account of the clothing the State of Georgia sent to the troops-see the letters of Oct. 19th.

LEE& JACKSON'S BLOODY TWELTH-Letters of Irby Goodwin Scott First Lieutenant Co. G Putnam Light Infantry Twelth Ga. Vol. Inf. Ed. by Johnnie Perry Pearson Univ. Tn. Press 2010

Pg. 37 Camp Bartow Pochahontas Co. Va. Oct. 15th, 1861 Dear Father, "…There was an order that our regiment should box up all the extra clothing we had and let them be sent back as far as Montery (Monterey). So we packed up our trunk full and sent it to Montery. I cannot get them and shall have to wait another opportunity. Mr. Morton wished me to send back Wat's cloths but they too are in Montery and I cannot get them…"

HISTORY OF THE FOURTH REGIMENT SOUTH CAROLINA VOLUNTEERS FROM THE COMMENCEMENT OF THE WAR UNTIL LEE'S SURRENDER J.W. Reid Shannon &Co. Printers & Stationers Morningside Bookshop 1975

Pg. 56 Camp near Bull Run Prince William Co. Va. October 19th, 1861 "…Some time ago we sent some of our blankets to Manassas Junction for safe keeping; had been trying for some time to get leave to go after my blankets; but could not get leave; so yesterday four others and myself got leave to flank the guard which was at the bridge and go after our blankets; so we went up the creek about one mile, pulled off our shoes and socks and waded across. Jack McKeen, who is an Irishman, pulled on his B.B. pants. The water was over knee deep, and cold as Greenland, but we got across and went on our way rejoicing. It was about five miles. We got our blankets and some other little things that we needed and started back. By this time it was raining, but through rain and mud we made our way back to Bull Run, and behold! It had risen about two feet. We did not pull off anything this time, but just took it dry so (or wet so, I should have said). I came on and put on dry clothes, and felt pretty well, considering…"

I have no idea what he means by "B.B." pants.

FAR, FAR FROM HOME- The Wartime Letters of Dick and Tally Simpson, 3rd South Carolina Volunteers ed by Guy R. Everson & Edward W. Simpson pub by Oxford Univ Press 1994

Pg. 79 Oct. 19th '61 Richard Simpson to Caroline Miller Near Union Mills (Va) Dear Aunt "I would have no objection in the world, if I needed anything, to ask you for it, for I know you well enough that you would not hesitate one moment. But Uncle John has sent our clothes and shoes from Laurens, and Ma has sent some and intends sending more underclothes. So you see there is nothing I could ask you for..."

Pg. 81 Oct 25th '61 Richard Simpson to Anna Simpson Near Centreville, Va. Dear Sister Anna, "...I never slept as cold in my life. I had three blankets and an overcoat, but I was awake from twelve o'clock so cold I could not sleep. I don't know what I will do this winter. Tell Ma I would like it very much if she would send us some heavy underclothes."

THE AMERICAN CIVIL WAR LETTERS AND DIARIES

Letter from Joseph E. Brown to Judah P. Benjamin October, 19, 1861

Sir,

Expecting that Georgia will, as far as may be in her power,endeavor to clothe her troops who are in the Confederate service, in conformity with the act of Congress (No. 256 of the third sesson, Provisional Congress, held at Richmond, p. 50) I address you this note, respectfully asking your construction of said act on certain points. First, where a state shall clothe her own troops, will the clothing be required in uniforms, or will any substantial woolen clothing do? As you are aware, it is now difficult to supply clothing in uniforms. Second, how is the money value of clothing to be acscertained and agreed upon, and what evidence will be required of its delivery by the State? Third, will it be paid for to the state furnishing it on delivery to the commanding officer of a company or regiment, or must the clothing be delivered to each member of such company or regiment? Should the latter be required, it will be difficult, if not inpracticable, to effect the delivery, as some members of a given company may be away from the main body on picket or other special duty. Your response to these inquiries will oblige me much.

I have the honor to be,
Your obedient servant,
Joseph E. Brown

Letter from Judah P. Benjamin to Joseph E. Brown, Oct. 25, 1861

Confederate States of America,
War Department
Richmond, October 25, 1861
Governor Joseph E. Brown
Millidgeville, Ga.

Sir, I have the honor to acknowledge receipt of your Excellency's letter of October 19, and to reply. First, it is not required that clothing furnished by States shall be uniform in order to be accepted. Second, Commutation is allowed for clothing furnished at the rate of $25 for six months, payable to the captains of companies (or commanding officers) upon vouchers rendered to the Quarter-Master general's department that their men are furnished with clothing according to regulation for time specified. I enclose to Your Excellency a copy of the regulation in regard to the clothing of volunteers, and also a copy of a circular letter recently printed in the fourteenth section of which the subject of commutation of clothing is embraced.

I have the honor to be sir, your obedient servant,

J.P. Benjamin
Acting Secretary of War

Here are the official letters regarding supplying the Georgia troops for the winter. As can beseen, both officials regarded uniformity unimportant as long as the troops were clad warmly.

A SOUTHERN SOLDIER'S LETTERS HOME The Civil War Letters of Samuel Burney Cobb's Georgia Legion, Army of Northern Va. Ed. By Nat Turner Mercer Univ. Press, Macon Ga.2002

Pg. 40 Oct. 20, 1861 Camp Marion Yorktown, Va. Dearest Wife," I will provide you a bird's eye view of our tent. As you come in there are six trunks piled up on the right; on the left there is a basket of potatoes and a pile of dity shoes and dirty clothes. A stob is also driven in the ground with short pags onj it to hang up canteens. In the back of the tent there is a gun rack with 5 guns on it. Our blankets are out drying. A rope above our heads runs from the front of the tent to the back and on it are our clothes, cartridge boxes, etc. Our knapsacks are lying down at the head of the tent for pillows. I am seated on a camp stove and am writing on a trunk which rests on another camp stove. I tell you we have a mery time of it occaisionally."

Pg. 42 same camp Oct. 23, 1861 Dearest Wife "...I wish you would tell Pa to have me another pair of shoes made at Ray's. These I have are good ones yet, but sometimes they get wet and I want a dry pair to put on. He can send them by one of the Baldwins if it not to late.

I want them made of the best leather-strong and stout with eyelets in the shoe string holes. Have me a pair or two of extra strings sent on with the shoes…."

Pg. 45 Oct. 27th, 1861 same camp Dearest Wife, "…Yesterday I went and bathed in the creek. The water was very cold, but I felt a delightful glow all over my skin after I came out and dressed Lucious (slave) washes my clothes for me very well in deed and he is quite serviceable in doing many little jobs for me…"

Pg. 47 30 Oct. 1861 About 1 mile from Camp Marion Dearest Wife, "I got off guard again to day. I did not wear my uniform, but borrowed one, had no cap, but borrowed one; had no blacking but greased them so they shined, so the adjutant chose me as the only one excused…"

JAMES MADISON UNIVERSITY ARCHIVES

Oct. 20th, 1861 Letter of 1st Lt. Reuben A. Scott Co. B, 10th Regiment Virginia Infantry Strasburg Va. Dear Mollie: "…I wish I had some good news to tell you but I have none unless it is that we are expecting our Pay some time the last of this month and will be very thankfully received by many of us though I cant say we have suffered any yet for want of money=may be that some of the men suffers those cool nights for want of something to keep the(m) warm some of the men are getting smartly ragged and I am fearful if they don't get a new supply soon we will be pronounced ragged militia…I wrote yesterday the militia with their flint lock muskets can do execution equal to the volunteers with their improved arms I don't wish to hear any volunteer burlesque the militia or I will insult them sure…"

This soldier describes the prevailing raggedness in the 10th Regiment Va. Inf., also, he defends the militia. This is the only soldier I came across that actually defends them.

WRITING & FIGHTING FROM THE ARMY OF NORTHERN VIRGINIA ed. by William B. Styple Belle Grove Pub. 2003

Pg, 71 Sixth Alabama Inf. Union Mills, Va. Oct. 26, 1861 "…The wearing apparel of many of the guard who brought the prisoners from Leesburg to Manassas was in rather a seedy condition, and after their arrival at the latter place one of our troops approached a very finely dressed Federal officer, and smiling, asked him if he did not feel cheap to be brought there a prisoner by those ragged rebels. The officer replied, "you may laugh now, but our men will laugh next week." (alluding to the approach of McClellan's overwhelming forces.) The Confederate rejoined, "I shall laugh at you anyhow now, and take the chances of getting whipped next week."

CONFEDERATE LETTERS AND DIARIES 1861-1865 Walbrook D. Swank-Col. U.S.A.F. Ret. Papercraft printing and design Co. Charlottesville, Va. 1988

Pg. 69 Letters with Regard to Charles Thomas Shelton Private Co. H. 28th Va. Inf. Botetourt (Va.) Artillery Battery and Anderson's Artillery Battery Maney's Tenn. Brigade

Camp at Centreville, Oct.26th, 1861?"…I am very much obliged for the bundle of clothes but would certainly gotten them then. Fortunately I have managed to sew up the pants of my old ones with a piece of some other old breeches but not in a very beautiful way….Uncle Wm. Has been quite sick and is still very unwell and he had about three weeks ago to send his baggage to Manassas so has no change of clothes. I carried him a suit of mine & thus am in a predicament but hope he will be able to get his washed before we have to move & then I will get mine again….' Charles

GRANDFATHER'S JOURNAL (Franklin Lafayette Riley) Company B Sixteenth Mississippi Infantry Volunteers Harris' Brigade Mahone's Division Hill's Cops, A.N.V. May 27, 1861-July 15, 1865 Austin C. Dobbins Morningside 1988

Pg. 47 Saturday-Sunday, Oct. 26-27, 1861 Camp one mile west of Centreville "…In cold, rainy weather picket duty is unpleasant. Fortunately, on the 14th, I managed to buy an oilcloth, which makes life easier. I also have a canteen marked U.S. (U.S. stands for United South, C.S.A. stands for Can't Stand Abe.) An oilcloth is an indispensible item of equipment. It serves as protective clothing. It provides warmth, becomes a covering for rifle-pits on picket, and (in camp) keeps blankets from getting wet from the ground. In other words, it makes bad weather tolerable…"

This is the first time I have come across the Confederate definitions of the initials "U.S." & "C.S.A.". As a re-enactor, I have found my oilcloth to be superior protection from the elements than the rubber poncho issued to me by the U.S. Army in 1982.

16th TENNESSEE VOLUNTEER INFANTRY REGIMENT: Clothing, Arms and Equipment (website)

On the 27 Oct. 1861 "The boys got shirts, shoes, pantaloons, coats and overcoats, some of which latter garments survived the war."

This source doesn't mention where the clothing came from, whether it was the home folks, the State of TN., or the government in Richmond or what color it was.

WRITING & FIGHTING FROM THE ARMY OF NORTHERN VIRGINIA ed. by William B. Styple Belle Grove Pub. 2003

Pg71 Nineteenth Georgia Vols. Camp Pryor, near Manassas, Va. Oct. 27, 1861 "...There was a striking contrast between the dress of captives and captors, and their appearance brought vividly to our minds the days of the first revolution, when our forefathers, in rustic, tattered suits, led captive the sleek, well-fed British soldier, arrayed in gay uniforms. Then, as now, the tax-gathering invading tyrant prided himself upon his good looks, good fare, and elegant clothing, and counted considerably on the potency of these for the victory he came to win over the sons of freedom; and now, as then, captivity, defeat and disgrace is their just reward. These Yankees had heavy cloth and cassimere uniforms, and many of them heavy army overcoats-everything, in fact, necessary to their comfort- while their victorious escort were clothed in coarse homespun, with wool hats on their heads. It was a striking illustration of that great truth that fine clothes do not make men honest, moral, wise or great; if it were so, these Yankees would never had been found in arms against us..."

A very true statement regarding clothes not making men honest.

MILITARY COLLECTOR AND HISTORIAN-Journal of the Company of Militey Historians Vol.XLI fall, 1989 Enlisted Uniforms of the Maryland confederate Infantry: A Case Study, Part 1 by Ross M. Kimmel

Pg 103 Oct. 28 1861 "The Marylanders remained in the Fairfax region until October, reforming picket duty and getting involved in minor skirmishing with the enemy. Judging from the diary of Pvt. George West, Co. C, this service was fairly arduous and probably had a telling effect on the unit's clothing and equipment, although West reported on 28 October, "All of us received new cloths to day, which pleased us very much; as some were very much in need."...New efforts were made to secure clothing and equipment, both to outfit recruits and replace worn out or lost goods. Appeals were published in Southern newspapers for donations of money and clothing for the Marylanders. Bradley T. Johnson reported, "clothing and blankets thus collected supplied the regiment to some extent during the remainder of the time it was in service." Socks and gloves were especially appreciated. Whether or not the clothing thus collected was military or civilian in style is not stated, though Johnson indicated that, as a result, the men were "well uniformed."

LEE& JACKSON'S BLOODY TWELTH-Letters of Irby Good-win Scott First Lieutenant Co. G Putnam Light Infantry Twelth Ga. Vol. Inf. Ed. by Johnnie Perry Pearson Univ. Tn. Press 2010

Pg. 41 Camp Bartow Pochahotas Co. Va. Oct. 29th, 1861 Dear Father, "...We are paid for two monthes and a half which will amount to about twenty seven dollars. Mine will be about twenty five as I drew a pair of shoes from the government…Mother wrote to know whether I had enough bed cloths. I have enough for the present. If we move I have as many as I can carry. I can draw blankets here from the government but they are not very good and cost five dollars and a half a pair. I shall wait till we get in winter quarters before I get anything of the kind. I will let you know if I need anything of the kind…"

The first mention of shoddy government goods.

AS RECORDED IN THE POCKET DIARIES OF PRIVATE ROBERT A. MOORE, Co. G, 17th Miss. Regt. Confederate guards, Holy Springs, Mississippi ed. by James w. Silver McCowat-Mercer Press 1959

Pg. 74 Wednesday, Oct. 30, 1861 camp near Leesburg "…A few of the boys received their clothes from Manassas today. They are so proud of their new clothes as a negro is of his regular suits. I tell them I do not think they will fight as well in them as they would in their old clothes…"

THE PAINFUL NEWS I HAVE TO WRITE-Letters and Diaries of Four Hite Brothers of Page County in the Service of the Confederacy Army of Northern Virginia Series Stonewall Brigade ed.by Harlan R. Jessup Butternut & Blue 1998

Pg. 37 Daniel Hite (father) to John Luray Va. Oct 31st 1861 "…your uncle Stage thinks you had better taken the over coat of Burners. He did not think he could get cloth to furnish you one this side of Christmus…we have got nearly all of yours cloths ready and are awaiting youre order…"

A SCYTH OF FIRE-A Civil War Story of the 8th Georgia Infantry Regiment by Warren Wilkinson & Steven E. Woodworth pub by Harpe Collin pub 2002

Pg. 115 End of Oct., 1861 "The cold winds finally came, and the men began to feel keenly their lack of adequate clothing for the season. They had not left home equipped for a winter in Virginia, and what they had taken with them had suffered a great deal from eight months' hard service. By the end of October, the crisp autumn nights had prompted the Atlanta Grays, Company E, to appeal to the people of Atlanta to provide them with new unifrims. "The coat should be a heavy frock, with military cape attached," read their notice in the Atlanta Daily Intelligencer, "out of any kind of material, so that it is warm."

Once again, the soldiers are not interested in uniformity as long as they are supplied with warm clothing.

LEE'S TIGERS-The La. Inf. In the Army of Northern Va. by Terry L. Jones Univ. of La. Press

Pg. 22 Nov. 1861 "…The 9th Louisiana's Sergeant Edmond Stevens described a typical morning to a friend: About one hour before the break of day you are interrupted by a loud beating of a bass drum which they call revile. You at once rise & at double quick time drag on your old dust wallowed coat, & as for your pants it (is) contrary to the rules of camp to take them off during the hours of rest. You then lay an old wool hat on your head which you have picked up in the road while traveling up on some wild march & it having refused to be owned by some laboring Negro. You then lay your feet into a pair of shoe soles without any upper leather being attached to them. You start with said clothing around you with the speed of some wild flying fowl to the parade ground to answer your name at Roll call. You then proceed to kindle you a fire with a few sticks of wood which was hauld (to) you (a) number of miles, & that is nearly impossible with me because there is not the first splinter if lightwood here…"

A detailed description of this soldier's ragged uniform.

SHENANDOAH 1862 by Peter Cozzins pub by Univ. of North Carolins Press 2008

Pg. 40 November, 1861 in the Shenandoah Valley- "Ashby's troopers were armed largely with what they brought from home or could scrouge, and they were poorly uniformed, even by Southern standards. Said a Union prisoner of Ashby's cavalry, on studying his captors: "They ain't rigged out like Uncle Sam's men. I can assure you that they are clothed in all sorts, gray homespun overcoats, pants of all colors and grades; some have straw hats and caps, and a great many are in citizen's clothes; in fact, they look pretty shabby."

Pg. 237 "On April 26, (1862) acting upon a tip from a Unionist refugee, a task force composed of two companies of Federal infantry and the Washington and Ringold cavalry companies-120 men in all- captured between 50 and 65 of Ashby's men near the village of Columbia Furnace. The Virginians were holed up in two churches, trying to escape the rain and cold, when the Yankees fell upon them just after midnight. Their captors admired their appearance, if not their diligence. The commander of the Federal detachment thought that : "These cavalrymen were well mounted and armed generally with sabers, Colt revolvers, together with some kind of rifle or gun for longer range shooting or carbine service. Among them were a few colt revolving rifles, two Sharp's rifles one or two Enfield rifles, but the prevailing arm was the double barreled shotgun, mostly fine guns, many of them English make, all loaded with buck and ball when we captured them. They were well uniformed in gray, and were native Virginians, about the best-looking Rebel soldiers that we came in contact with."

A BOY OF OLD SHANANDOAH by Robert Hugh Martin ed. by Carolyn Martin Rutherford McClian Printing Co. 1977

Pg. 12 "Now to those distant recollections. I had noticed that while the Confederates wore drab uniforms the color of dust, the Yankees wore blue and appeared better dressed…"

FAR, FAR FROM HOME-The Wartime Letters of Dick and Tally Simpson, 3rd South Carolina Volunteers ed by Guy R. Everson & Edwasrd W. Simpson pub by Oxford Univ Press 1994

Pg. 84 Nov 1, 1861 Tally Simpson to Mary Simpson Centreville, Va. Dear Sister, "Buddie returned from the 4th with not one single article of clothing for Cousin Jim, Buddie, or myself. All the others of the company have received what they wanted as far as I know, such as woolen socks, scarfs, under shirts, woolen shirts, drawers, &cc, but what have we got from home? I leave the question for home folks to answer.…But this is a fact-you have not sent to me what is made up at home-one article-my overcoat!"

Pg. 89 Nov 10th 1861 Tally Simpson to Mary Simpson In camp Near Centreville Dear Siater, "When I was on the battle-ground the other day, we picked up an old hound. He looked like he would tree, so we brought him to camp. We had the good fortune to catch several squirrels and two very fine opossums, and expected to catch many more since they were so abundant, but Col. Williams put a stop to it by saying that the first private he caught hunting he would put him in the guard house, and the first officer under arrest. So hunting is at an end. Oh, how I wish I were home and had as many possums as I could eat…"

Pg. 92 Nov 21, '61 Tally simpson to Mary Simpson In camp Near Centreville,Va. Dear Ma, "Howdy to all the negros. When it is convenient, have sent to us some good winter boots…"

DEAR IRVIE, DEAR LUCY-The Civil War Letters of Capt. Irving A. Buck, General Cleburne's AAG & Family

Pg. 42 Nov. 2, 1861 Head Quarters 1st Corps A of P near Centreville, Va. Dear Lou, "… Speaking of this the first good opportunity you have I would like you to send us both more bed clothing as we begin to need them. I also want a paper of large tacks…I left in my trunk a vest that buttons up high, and is faced with black ribbed silk which is considerable worn, but the vest is good. I wish if you can get anything that you would put a new facing on it. And I have a pair of pants of the same material which if bound at the bottom will do very well for the office. I had thought of giving them away. I have a set of small brass buttons for the vest. I wished these things fixed in case I should come up, for if I do, my stay will be very short…"

"DEAR MOTHER: DON'T GRIEVE ABOUT ME. IF I GET KILLED, I'LL ONLY BE DEAD." Ed. by Mills Lane The Beehive Press 1977

Pg. 81 Theodore Montfort to his Children Meadow Bluff, Virginia November 3, 1861 My Dear Children, David Molley and Tebo: "...Tell your mother to send me, with my other things I have written home for, several pair of good new woolen socks. Can't Molley knit me a pair? How glad I would be to have a pair knit by her..."

WELCOME THE HOUR OF CONFLICT-William Cowan McClellan & the 9th Alabama ed by John C. Carter pub by Univ Al. Press 2007

Pg. 98 Nov. 3rd, 1861 Centreville, Va. on Cub Run William McClellan to Martha McClellan Dear Mother, "I have just received my Box, I am under many obligations to you for the many valuable things you have sent me. The socks came just in Time as I had Worn out the last pair I had, The shirts also came just in time as I had lost the last ones some days ago when they were sent to the Junction to keep the Yankees from getting them, But some of our own men were kind enough to steal them for me. My green shirts are very much admired by the boys. I am wearing now the jeans pants. I left home with brown jeans you recollect, I am very proud of the home made Blanket it is just the sort of one I needed, the Cordial and wine was also very good. I need nothing now to complete my Winter clothing, Save a good pair of heavy boots, to wade the snow and mud in, I am told the snow is frequently 2 feet deep here. Tell Bob to see Britle in Athens and get him to make me a pair of No.9 long legs. Mr. Brittle will know What sort to make. You can send them by someone passing, this is Sunday I have nothing to do but sun my cloths, comb my head..."

REBEL BROTHERS-The Civil War Letters of the Truehearts (from Galveston, Texas) ed. by Edward B. Williams Texas A&M Univ. Press 1995

Camp near Winchester, Va. Army of the "Valley District" under command of General T.J. Jackson Thurs, 5 November 1861 "...The ground has been frozen for some days past, and it is quite cold. I have only one pair of single blankets, but manage to keep warm by sleeping with my great coat all on. I don't know what I shall do when we have snow and ice in real good earnest. Hope to be able to get another pair ere long. I have had some difficulty in getting winter clothes. The tailor in Charlottsville sent me a suit, a few days since, but it proved to be too smaal for me; so I had to sell it at a loss of $3.00; and buy another suit at $18.00 Clothes of all kinds are very dear here. A suit (pants and jacket) of the coarsest heavy negro cloth, such as our uniforms are made (at a) cost (of) $21.00 if made by a tailor. I succeeded in getting one for $18.00 by having it cut only by a tailor, and made by a seamstress...."

THE PAINFUL NEWS I HAVE TO WRITE-Letters and Diaries of Four Hite Brothers of Page County in the Service of the Confederacy Army of Northern Virginia Series Stonewall Brigade ed.by Harlan R. Jessup Butternut & Blue 1998

Pg. 42 John Hite to father Nov 6th/61 Camp near Centreville "...I have about $35.00 but my overcoat cost $13.00; made ten or twelve dollars on apples, enough to pay for my overcoat..."

LEE& JACKSON'S BLOODY TWELTH-Letters of Irby Good-win Scott First Lieutenant Co. G Putnam Light Infantry Twelth Ga. Vol. Inf. Ed. by Johnnie Perry Pearson Univ. Tn. Press 2010

Pg. 42 Nov. 6th, 1861 Camp Bartow Pochahontas Co. Va. Dear ones at Home, "...I enjoy good health get plenty to eat have good warm cloths to wear....I have tried on my coat and it fits fine my pants I have not tried yet but know they are all right. Nick has not returned yet. Lieut. Marshall saw him in Staunton and said that he was improving very fast. They offered him a discharge but he would not accept of it. He ought to have accepted it and went home through the winter and then if he wished he could return to the army. His cloths and such things as will keep. I will box up with the rest of the boys cloths who are off sick and they will be in the care of Capt. Davis. Such things as will not keep I do not know whether Capt. Davis intends sending them off now or keep them until we go back. It is a bad chance to send them from here. He will not get them I think in a short time.... I have plenty of cloths and bed cloths for the present. I am looking for the other box every day...P.S. ...I also got my bed tick, Pillow, some medicine, my leggings and some other things which I have not time to mention..."

Pg. 45 Nov. 12, 1861 Camp Bartow Pocohantas [Pocohantas] Co. Va. Dear father,"...The Colonel is very much taken by our new suits and wants apair of pants like them if he can find a pair that will suit..."

MY DEAR EMMA-The War letters of Col. James K. Edmonson 1861-8165 ed.by Charles w. Turner PhD McClure Press 1978

Pg. 66 Camp Centerville, Nov. 7, 1861 My dear Wife "...I wish you would try to get for me one of these late style military caps. They cannot be gotten in Staunton, I know that they can be in Richmond. They are gray and the top hangs in front. Don't put yourself to any trouble however for it is just a notion that I have taken that I would like to have one. I can do very well without it..."

It sounds as though this soldier is describing a kepi.

AS RECORDED IN THE POCHET DIARIES OF PRIVATE ROBERT A. MOORE, Co. G, 17th Miss. Regt. Confederate guards, Holy Springs, Mississippi ed. by James w. Silver McCowat-Mercer Press 1959

Pg. 76 Thursday, Nov. 7th, 1861 camp on Goose Creek, in the Valley,Va."…Several wagons came in this evening from Manassas loaded with winter clothing for our Reg. All who received anything at all, received more than they could carry. I received nothing at all as there are several boxes for our Co. behind…"

A SOUTHERN SOLDIER'S LETTERS HOME The Civil War Letters of Samuel Burney Cobb's Georgia Legion, Army of Northern Va. Ed. By Nat Turner Mercer Univ. Press, Macon Ga.2002

Pg. 55 same camp, Nov. 7th 1861Ever Dear Wife "…you spoke of sending me another pair of leggings. Really, dear kind wife, I do not want them. I never use them unless on a march or standing guard. They are right new. So do not send me any leggings, Dearest, until these wear out. You asked me to write if I should need anything. I will certainly do that. I need nothing in the way of clothing. If you can send me anything in the way of substantial eating it will be very acceptable.…"

Pg. 58 Nov. 15, 1861 Dearest Wife, "I have just received my shoes and a letter from Ma & Pa each…"

Pg. 64 Nov. 19th, 1861 Big Bethel, Va. Dearest Wife, "…P.S. Say to your mother that I have a need for woolen drawers now. She can send me a couple of pairs as the winters here are very severe before they are over…"

Pg. 66 Nov. 21st, 1861 Camp Marion, near Yorktown, Va. Dearest Wife, "My shoes do very well. I have them on now. Some boxes for the Company have been received, but are not opened. I presume they are the boxes of comforts Bro. John sent…"

I WROTE YOU WORD-The Poignant Letters of Private Holt-John Lee Holt ed by James A. Mumper pub by H.E. Howard Inc. 1991

Pg 31 New Fair Ground, Richmond, Va Nov. 8, 1861 My Dearly Beloved Wife, "…After I had commenced my letter yesterday we received a box containing our clothes I got my 2 pair of drawers & a pair of gaiters & like them first rate The gaiters are the very thing I wanted & thank you with all my heart for them I should have written you word to have made me some But I knew you had so much to do that I thought of buying them if I really needed them But I am truly glad you made them as they are much better ones than I could have bought without paying a very extravagant price for them & the drawers are also all that I could wish them to be & Oh how it makes my heart swell with emotion to think I have one at home that is looking so much after my comfort and happiness…"

Pg. 36 New Fair Ground Richmond, Va Nov. 22d 1861 My Dearest Ellen, "…I will send my things by Mr. Berkley My old uniform coat & pants & my my cotton drawers & I also send in the pockets all my old letters as I do not want to destroy them & did not want any unnecessary luggage in my knapsack …"

JAMES MADISON UNIV. ARCHIVES

Nov. 8th, 1861 Letter of Enoch V. Kauffman Camp near Center Ville (Va) Dear Uncle: "… tell John that I have use for that comfort and took the liberty to keep it here and the soap also…"

"P.S. When on my way down I found my boots were too small for me and trade them off and upon hearing that John had gone home sick I told ma that I would take his boots and write to him to have a pair made and I would pay for them which I hope will make no difference to him. If he prefers it will send him the amount or pay him when he gets back…"

AS RECORDED IN THE POCHET DIARIES OF PRIVATE ROBERT A. MOORE, Co. G, 17th Miss. Regt. Confederate guards, Holy Springs, Mississippi ed. by James w. Silver McCowat-Mercer Press 1959

Pg. 77 Sunday, Nov. 10th, 1861 north-Mt. Pleasant, Marshall Co., camp on Goose Creek "…Another box of clothing was brought in camp from the junction. My clothes were in the box…"

Pg.77 Monday, Nov. 11th, 1861 camp on Goose Creek "…Our Reg. is being bountifully supplied with winter clothing, also with blankets…"

MY DEAR EMMA-The War letters of Col. James K. Edmonson 1861-8165 ed.by Charles w. Turner PhD McClure Press 1978

Pg. 67 Winchester, Nov. 11 1861 My dear Wife "…This morning I walked to the city for the purpose of buying me a pair of those heavy soled long legged boots and a pair of gauntlet gloves and other little articles. I succeeded in getting the gauntlets but not the boots.…"

DEAR SISTER-Civil War Letters to a Sister in Alabama by Frank Anderson pub by Chappell Springs Pub. 2002

Pg. 21 "On November 12,(1861) the companies then in camp received their first issue of uniforms. "We have received over coats and dress pants of the finest kind," one private wrote. Another private echoed the same thoughts: "I drawed a fine overcoat worth fifteen dollars and a dress coat worth ten dollars and a fine pair of pants and a haversack..." The soldiers were issued six-button gray sack coats, with sewn-down black epaulettes, as specified by the 1861 North Carolina uniform regulations from the adjutant general. Company K's letter book, in which issued items were documented, shows that each man in the company received one great coat, one sack coat, two pairs of pants, two pairs of drawers, one pair of shoes, one blanket, one knapsack, one haversack, one cap box, one belt, one cartridge box with strap, one gun sling, one gun, thirty cartridges, forty percussion caps, one canteen with strap, one bayonet with scabbard, and one pair of socks. The next day, November 13, there were more requisitions, and more needed supplies were received: one desk, two split bottom chairs, one fair bank sael, four tents for hospital with a fly, one wall tent for the assistant surgeon, one field officer's tent, four wall tents,two flies for tents, and two field officer tents with flies..."

A bountiful supply from the State.

BROTHERS IN GRAY-The Civil War Letters of the Pierson Family ed. by Thomas W. Cutrer & t. Michael Parrish La. State Univ. Press 1997 Ninth Louisiana

Pg. 62 Rueben Allen Pierson to Wm. H. Pierson Camp Fla. Va. Nov. 12th, 61 "...my clothes are the very thing for this climate and they came to hand in good time..."

MY DEAR EMMA-The War letters of Col. James K. Edmonson 1861-8165 ed.by Charles w. Turner PhD McClure Press 1978

Pg. 68 Camp Near Winchester (Va.) Nov. 13 1861 My dear Wife "...I want a pair of heavy boots, I cannot get them in Winchester, but I think it likely I can get them in Newtown..."

Good Luck

WAR DIARIES: The 1861 Kanawha Valley Campaign by David L. Phillips and Rebecca L. Hill, Cief Reseatcher Gauleu Mount Press 1990

Pg. 272 Retreat from Cotton Hill Nov13th, 1861 Isaac Smith "...A number of the regiments had no transportation and were obliged to burn nearly everything they had. We were in the rear with the 36th and saw piles of tents, with broken cooking utensila and articles of every description blazing away as all had to be consumed and destroyed. As we marched along that night we could see where flour had been thrown away, tents and along the line of march blankets, overcoats, and etc. even were destroyed and many of our poor ragged fellows got hold of some good things thus thown away...."

This is an immense loss, as most of the blankets and clothing counldn't be replaced.

VOICES FROM COMPANY D Diaries by the Greensboro Guards, Fifth Alabama infantry Regiment, Army of Northern Virginia ed. by G.Ward Hubbs Univ. of Ga. Press 2003

Diarists: JHC John Henry Cowin
SP Samuel Pickens
JP James Pickens
JST John S. Tucker
VET Veteran from Co. D, 5th Alabama Regiment
HB Henry Beck

Pg. 74 Nov. 13, 1861 Manassas JHC "...Do not know when we will get our blankets and clothing now..."

THE JOURNAL OF WOMEN'S CIVIL WAR HISTORY-Accounts of the Sacrifice, Achievement & Servive of American Women 1861-1865 ed. Eileen Conklin Thomas Pub. 2001

Pg. 62 "...The most pressing need was for blankets, with each of the twelve companies in need of at least six dozen. John S. Hard, Captain of Company F, wrote to the Ladies of Graniteville on November 14, 1861 that he had "been informed that you are willing to contribute a sufficient number of blankets to prevent the men who are unable to supply themselves from suffering during the winter which has already begun, I beg permission to inform those who are so disposed that any contribution sent to Mr. B.C. Hard, Graniteville will be most acceptable." Quartermaster Lovelace wrote to suggest that the only acceptable answer to the question of what soldier's need would be: "First blankets, Second, blankets, and Third, more blankets." He went on to say, "Send us blankets and coverlets that will enable us to sleep warm and comfortable at night and we can then stand the rigors of winter by day and Yankeedom combined." The societies of Liberty Hill, Bethany, and Mt. Vernon received the enthusiastic thanks of Captain B.M. Talbert for the "liberal supply of winter clothing." These societies were not the only ones working for the soldiers. Two "spirited" young ladies, Miss Tilly Smith and Miss Betty Watson, forwarded the following items to Col. Bacon's regiment in September: 10 blankets, 10 pairs of drawers, 3 cotton shirts, 6 flannel shirts, 9 towels and handkerchiefs, 11 pairs of socks, 1 pair wool socks, 3 tin wash-pans, 1 comfort, and 2 bed ticks. These patriots, too young to be admitted to the aid societies, nevertheless worked on their own to supply the soldier's needs. Throughout the region women and children were busy weaving cloth and knitting for the soldiers…"

These clothes were probably mostly civilian, as they were made by the folks at home.

WAR DIARIES: The 1861 Kanawha Valley Campaign by David L. Phillips and Rebecca L. Hill, Cief Reseatcher Gauleu Mount Press 1990

Pg. 276 Nov. 15, 1861 Isaac Smith on the further retreat: "On this march we saw the true character of our retreat. The road and road side was strewn with articles of every description-tents, boxes, guns, clothes, provisions, knapsacks, broken harness, cooking utensils, dishes. Waggons were left fast in the mud with their loads untouched-at one place twelve wagons were left, most of them turned upside down, and at the same time a number of horses had drowned in the mud, that is had sunk beyond hope of extrication and had been shot. At some places mudholes were filled with tents to make passage for the wagons. All this was a perfect harvest for the 22nd. Being in front of the regiment we noticed this was only a fragment following up, and halted for the stragglers to catch up, waited a long time and they did not appear-went back and found the fellows resting behind. The rascals claimed to be tired down as a reason for their halt, and no wonder, for when I started them out again I found about every other man loaded down with flour, frying pans, buskets, mess kettles, and such things. I found myself, eleven good percussion guns, and gave them to the men, but made them carry their flintlocks also…"

Why? I'd have left those flintlocks in a ditch. It must have been hard to discard items you know you would need and couldn't replace.

A BOY OF OLD SHANANDOAH by Robert Hugh Martin ed. by Carolyn Martin Rutherford McClian Printing Co. 1977

Pg. 56 Camp Kernstown Nov. 16, 1861 Letter from Dr. Albion Martin to his wife: "I do not know as I shall need the shirts. I have only worn the calico once, sent it out to wash last week, but it has not returned yet and may never. I put on the calico you sent me and I presume it is the first, real clean shirt I have had on for three monthes or four. I may need another if we stay in Winchester this winter. I can afford to wear a white shirt sometimes…"

MY DEAR EMMA-The War letters of Col. James K. Edmonson 1861-8165 ed.by Charles W. Turner PhD McClure Press 1978

Pg. 69 Camp Near Winchester(Va.) Nov. 17 1861 My dear Wife "…I am in a quandary, whether to have me a pair of boots made or a pair of shoes and a pair of Buckskin gaiters to wear with them. I can get the gaiters I presume made in Winchester. I will send you enclosed measure for a pair of good, heavy scotch bottomed shoes made in gaiter or half boot fashion to come up above the ankle. If they are not the best quality I do not want them. Do you think you can have them made to suit me? If you do, then just go right along and have them made for I will need something of the kind shortly-in the meantime I will try and have me a pair of gaiters made of Buckskin for them….I got your letter containing cravat, for which I am very much obliged to you but I have no shirts and collars to wear with it. Don't you know that I sent all my linen home long ago and I don't think that it will look very well around a calico concern…"

It makes me wonder why a cravat would even be sent to a soldier, even an officer.

HISTORY OF THE FOURTH REGIMENT SOUTH CAROLINA VOLUNTEERS FROM THE COMMENCEMENT OF THE WAR UNTIL LEE'S SURRENDER J.W. Reid Shannon &Co. Printers & Stationers Morningside Bookshop 1975

Pg. 57 Army of Northern Va. Centreville, Fairfax County, Va. Nov. 18th, 1861 "…A stormy wind is blowing, and colder day I never saw, or want to see. It is a bad time in camp; every man is wrapped up in a blankets and handkerchiefs (or shirt tails), tied around their jaws and ears. And this is only the beginning of winter….

Yesterday, while no one was in the tent, a coal of fire blew into our baggage and burnt a hole in the narrative of my broadcloth coat. It also burnt holes in several other garments unnecessary to mention…"

Thus adding to this soldier's ragged appearance.

OCCUPIED WINCHESTER 1861-1865 Garland R. Quarles Winchester Va. 1976

Pg. 31 Kate Sperry visiting Pedleton's Battery near the town spring in Winchester, Va Nov. 19 1861

"we then examined a tent to discover how heated without a stove-and its done in this manner, as near as I can recollect: a ditch two feet wide and two or one and a halfdeep is dug, beginning in or near the center of the tent-said ditch being covered with earth and stones, ans a hole left at each end-the hole in the inside being covered with large stones on the top, somewhat resembling a fireplace. The hole on the out side is walled round with earth, a hole being left in the center for the smoke to draw through, and a fire is built under the stones inside, and the draught from the door of the tent draws the smoke back through the little mound and the tent is redered quite comfortable-considering." (Speery-Nov. 19 1861)

This is ingenious. I intend to try it once I get a chance, though I hope I don't end up burning down the tent.

REBEL BROTHERS-The Civil War Letters of the Truehearts ed. bt Edward B. Williams Texas A&M Press 1995

Camp Near Winchester, Va. Army of the "Valley District" Nov. 20 1861 Dear Minny "... The land is very rolling and here and there may be seen ledges of rock jutting out of the well-sod soil. These ledges of rock serve a very good purpose for hiding our mess fires behind; and for sitting on while eating, etc. We have succeeded in getting a supply of wheat straw for beds, which adds much to our comfort. The ground has been frozen for some days past, and it is quite cold.I have only one pair of single blankets, but manage to keep warm by sleeping with my great coat all on. I don't know what I shall do when we have snow and ice in real good earnest. I hope to be able to get another pair (blankets) ere long. I have had some difficulty in getting winter clothes. The tailor at Charlottsville sent me a suit, a few days since, but it proved too small for me; so I had to sell it at a loss of $3.00 and buy another suit at $18.00. Clothes of all kinds are very dear here. A suit (pants and jacket) of the coarsest heavy negro cloth, such as our uniforms are made (at a) cost (of) $21.00 if made by a tailor. I succeeded in getting one at $18.00 by having it cut only by a tailor, and made by a seamstress. I am very well pleased with what I have seen of this vicinity..."

16th TENNESSEE VOLUNTEER INFANTRY REGIMENT: Clothing, Arms and Equipment (website)

Even with this Regiment were poorly supplied by the Government and while in West Virginia, late 1861, "Captains of individual companies were ordered to acertain their wants of their respective commands, and report a list of same, to be sent by a detailed officer to our homes in Tennessee to solicit supplies." ...The 20 Nov. 1861 these items from home arrived"...Two or three car-loads of these stores" they included "blankets, quilts, coats and almost anything to wear you could think of...Also, while in (West) Virginia, "...day after day we marched over muddy roads and snow covered mountains...almost without clothing." A member of Samuel R. Anderson's Brigade at the time wrote, "Most of the boys are strutting around with their "Tennessee Clothes" on, while another comented, :at lest we are once more comfortably clothed. Although we do not make a very uniform appearance, some having light and gray, and others dark clolored clothing." Jas. Morris Skelton, 11th Tennessee Infantry, "Fix up my overcoat in as small bundle as possible...ans send it to me...tell Ma to send me a pair of linsey drawers...tell Lon to send me a pair of thick gloves..."

Once again, supply from the home folks, but the account doesn't say whether these clothes were uniform or civilian.

THE CRY IS WAR, WAR, WAR The Civil War Correspondence of Lts. Burwell Thomas Cotton and George Job Huntley, 34th Regiment North Carolina troops by Michael W. Taylor Morningside 1994

Pg.37 George Huntley Raleigh, N.C. Nov. 22nd, 1861 "…I want you to have me a linsey shirt made and send it by Mr. Jones. You can get some coat lining at Phillip Davises that will answer, or you can get some thin linsey woolen cloth it will do very well. Don't make it out of jean for it will be too thick…"

LEE& JACKSON'S BLOODY TWELTH-Letters of Irby Good-win Scott First Lieutenant Co. G Putnam Light Infantry Twelth Ga. Vol. Inf. Ed. by Johnnie Perry Pearson Univ. Tn. Press 2010

Pg. 45 Camp Bartow Pochahontas Co. Va. Nov. 25th, 1861 Dear father, "…The Colonel is very much taken with our new suits and wants a pair of pants like them if he can get a pair that will suit…The society sent us enough cloths for twice. We have boxed up what we did (not) need and it will be sent back either to Montery (Moterey) or Staunton. …"

Good luck getting those clothes back.

THE CIVIL WAR: THE SOUTH ed by Thomas Streissguth pub by Greenhaven Press 2001

Pg. 115 Nov. 26, 1861Rueben Allen Pierson Ninth Louisiana Infantry Camp Florida, Va. Dear Father: "…The weather is very cold. We had a light snow a few nights back which is still lying on the ground in some places. I have an abundance of clothes to last me till spring, and intend to take every precaution to make myself healthy…"

CHARLOTTE'S BOYS

Pg. 78 Herman A. Crane to Charlotte Branch Richmond Nov. 27th 1861 My Dear Mrs. Branch"…(P.S.) I have bought a camp stove an oven and some other necessary articles for the comfort of Horace and his mess which I think will be found very valuable to them and contribute very much to their comfort. They can cook in their tent with this stove in bad weather-it is made of boiler iron very portable, not liable to brake or get out of order, and when moving can pack up most of their cooking utensils in it and take it up by the handle…"

I wonder how far they carried it? It must be somewhat heavy, I'd like to know this stove's fate.

WRITING & FIGHTING THE CONFEDERATE WAR The Letters of Peter Wellington Alexander ed by William B. Styple Belle Grove Pub. Co. 2002

Pg. 55 Catching Prisoners Army of the Potomac Centreville, November 29, 1861 Refering to extremely rainy weather "Such is the weather. And yet an order was sent out last evening from headquarters requiring an immediate inspection to be made of all baggage in the army-with a view, it is whispered, to its reduction. A return is ordered to be made of all personal baggage above one suit of outer and two of under clothing, and one blanket where there is an overcoat, and two blankets where there is no overcoat. There is but little straw to be had, the tents in many instances are old and dilapidated, and they are too small and crowded to keep fires in them. Where there are but two or three to a tent, the men manage to have a little fire by digging a small hole in the ground and filling it with live coals. The blankets are small and the supply scant; but such as they are, if the men are to be stripped of them, much suffering and sickness will be the certain consequence. They would sooner give up half their rations than their blankets; yet if an emergency should arise, they would cheerfully burn them to save them from the enemy."

Already the stripping down to absolute necessities.

U.S. ARMY HERITAGE AND EDUCATION CENTER

Nov. 29, 1861 Pvt. George W. Maddox 18th Georgia Regiment Co G Three miles form Dumfries Va. Dear Pa: "…Woolen clothing is out of reason and I would like for you to have me a coat and pair of pants and vest made and sent to me with those coats belonging to the Confederacy. Shields has my measure, tell him to cut the coat a little larger than the measure, say about 2 inches around (?). Have Georgia buttons on coat and vest and send me the reciept of this whole and I will pay it. Have the coat padded. I guess you can have it done (for) 28 or 30 dollars. I have never bought any clothing except an overcoat and am getting needy. Let me hear form you soon in relation to the clothing as I will have to make other arrangements if you can't get them…"

CIVIL WAR LETTERS OF CAPTAIN A.B. MULLIGAN, Co B, Fifth South Carolina Cavalry-Butler's Division, Hampton's Corps 1861-1865 by Olin Fulmer Hutchinson, Jr. pub by The Reprint Co. 1992

Pg. 2 Charleston, Nov. 29, 1861 My Dear Mother and Sisters, "It is very warm here & if I get the office I speak of I shall want down my thinner clothing.

You can buy all the jean and linsey you can get at $1 to $1.25 for jeans & 50c for linsey. It pays a good profit here."

A SOUTHERN SOLDIER'S LETTERS HOME The Civil War Letters of Samuel Burney Cobb's Georgia Legion, Army of Northern Va. Ed. By Nat Turner Mercer Univ. Press, Macon' Ga.2002

Pg. 71 same camp Nov. 30 1861 "...The box of shirts that Mrs. Shaw sent us was distributed to the most needy. I did not apply for one as there were many here more needy than myself..."

Makes you wonder how ragged these men were.

16th TENNESSEE VOLUNTEER INFANTRY REGIMENT: Clothing, Arms and Equipment (website)

Lucy Virginia French from McMinnville, wrote in her diary for 30 Nov. 1862: "We made shirts and pants for them (9th Texas) and I took up my carpets and made blankets for them..."

THE STONEWALL BRIGADE James I. Robertson Jr. La. State Univ. Press 1961

Pg. 170 winter 1861-62 "...Urgent appeals were sent home for food and clothing; many in the Stonewall Brigade even volunteered to spend their leaves collecting provisions for their comrades. The Valley folk responded to the calls with patriotic sacrifices. In one week Rockbridge County con tribute 175 blankets, 75 pairs of socks, 50 pairs of shoes, leather for an additional 50 pairs, and no less than $750 dollars in cash..."

Where did these prople get the leather for 50 pairs of shoes plus leather for 50 more pair? The must have used up all the leather in the Valley.

SOLDIER OF SOUTHWESTERN VA. The Civil War Letters of Capt. John Peston Sheffy ed. By James I. Robertyson Jr. La. State Univ. Press 2004

Pg. 93 Winter-near Raliegh Courthouse (Va.) 1861-62 "They went under the guidance of the Woods Rangers or as we call them here, Bush-Wackers, of whom there is quite a number with us dressed in bark-dyed apparel with their long rifles and deer-skin pouches. Well may the Yankees fear them for they rarely draw a bead and pull a trigger without bringing a pigeon...."

THE STONE WALL The Story of a Confederate Soldier by Brad Smiley Zebra Communications, Woodstock, Ga. 1998

Pg. 67 march to Centreville, winter, 1861 "…I could hear the crunching, crispy sounds of fresh-fallen snow beneath my bare feet…"

I cannot imagine suffering through this. What can't be avoided must be endured.

VOICES FROM COMPANY D Diaries by the Greensboro Guards, fifth Alabama Infantry Regiment, Army of Northern Virginia ed. By G. Ward Hubbs Univ. of Georgia Press 2003

Pg. 61 JHC "…Three men left -"…Father for clothing for the Company. He will first go to Richmond and if unable to procure the goods there, do not know where he will go…"

VOICES FROM COMPANY D Diaries by the Greensboro Guards, fifth Alabama Infantry Regiment, Army of Northern Virginia ed. By G. Ward Hubbs Univ. of Georgia Press 2003

Pg. 65 JHC "…Sent Seve down to the Junction after Father, who got here about twelve o'clock. He is in fine health and has arranged every thing satisfactorily concerning the uniform…"

UNIFORMS OF THE CIVIL WAR Lord, Wise, A.S. Barnes & Co. 1970

Pg. 20 "…A greater part of the clothing donated for all armies under the Appeal was described as "the handiwork of the fair country woman." Walnut dyed brown, black, or grey cloth, checked shirts, wool or cotton homespun jeans of the "bush" variety was commonly seen in the ranks…

The winter of 1861-62 and the contributions of the Great Appeal, would see the continued development of the Confederate un-uniform appearance, part civilian, part military, we have come to recognize as their trademark. A mixture of brown and grey jeans clothes, multi-colored blankets, hats or caps, whatever could be made into uniforms was shipped out to the Confederate camps…"

We've already read of this. The people made and donated anything to cover the soldiers without regard to color, material and cut. As I have stated before, there was a lot more civilian clothing in the ranks of the Confederate Army.

THE HASKELL DIARIESby John Haskell pub by G. P. Putnam's Sons 1960

Pg. 16 winter at Centreville, Va. "The division commander, who would probably have put next to Hood, was A.P. Hill, who that winter was colonel of the 13th Virginia. Hill was a very pleasant, attractive man, quite good-looking and rather dandified in his dress, which was always a blue, blouse shirt of broadcloth, with very conspicuous insignia of his rank and a treble row of large gold buttons…"

RED CLAY TO RICHMOND by John J. Fox pub by Angle Valley Press 2006

Pg. 14 Dec 2 1861 "The weapons issued to the 35th Georgia created another problem. Some of the barrels on the altered muskets exploded when fired, creating injury…"

Pg. 15 Dec 19 1861 "…All ten captains, obviously unhappy with their colonel's response, breached military protocol on December 19 when they sent a letter that outlined the quartermaster's deficiencies to Confederate Secretary of War Judah P. Benjamin. They claimed that the quartermaster had not filed a bond with the confederate War Office in Richmond. The lack of this bond prevented the men from receiving any pay. "Many of the soldiers are barefoot without overcoats. The soldiers through his neglect are without money and clothes. The want of these things in this climate proves fatal to many."…Lieutenant Colonel Gustavoius A. Bull revealed the state of readiness in the 35th Georgia from his blunt inspection report of December 31, 1861. In Company D he remarked: "Discipline-Firm; Instruction-Good; Military Appearance-Fair; Arms-Altered Muskets; Accoutrements-Wanting;Clothes- Worn."

A good deal has been written regarding the high casualties from sickness in the Confederate Army. Here could be one of the causes-lack of adequate clothing.

Pg. 18 "Moody became a waggoneer on December21. He left for Richmond the following day to get a wagon and team of horses. A week later he returned. He soon reported that the job did not suit him since the wagons never stopped rolling. He never had time to eat and in twenty-five days of driving through snow, sleet and rain he had ruined most of his clothes. The monthly pay he recieved of $18.50 was better than the $11 per month he had received as an infantry private, but Moody argued that the extra twenty-five cents per day was not worth it. He claimed this is why most of the white wagoneers quit."

BROTHERS IN GRAY-The Civil War Letters of the Pierson Family ed. by Thomas W. Cutrer & t. Michael Parrish La. State Univ. Press 1997 Ninth Louisiana

Pg. 67 Rueben Allen Pierson to Wm. H. Pierson Camp Florida, Va. Dec. 3rd, 1861 Dear Father "…You wrote me to state in my next letter whether I had received my bundle of goods or not. I have received them all and also the $25.00 sent by Mr. Candler. I have as many clothing as could do me any service through winter. I have splendid overcoat which cost me in a trading way ($5.75) five dollars and six bits. I have as much money as I want and will have more than I started with when we draw…"

THE CRY IS WAR, WAR, WAR The Civil War Correspondence of Lts. Burwell Thomas Cotton and George Job Huntley, 34th Regiment north Carolina troops by Michael W. Taylor Morningside 1994

Pg. 41 Dec 3, 1861 "…I also want you send my woolen jeans coat and my shirt that I wrote for either by Mr. Dickerson or Wm. Jones, for that coat is as good here as the one I have and I want to send this one home at the first opportunity I have…."

WEBSITE-confederateuniforms.org

The Richmond (Va) Daily Dispatch December 6, 1861 "…the camp of the Issaquah Artillery, from Louisiana. This was really a fine looking, well uniformed set of men. Their uniforms, like all their artillery, was of light gray with red trimmings, their caps having a wide, red band…"

DEAR IRVIE, DEAR LUCY-The Civil War letters of Capt. Irving A. Buck, General Clebjurne's AAG & Family

Pg. 42, Dec. 6 1861 Head Quarters 1st Corps A of P Dear Lucy, '…I will send out clothes and the basket up by the first opportunity…Ask Father to send my boots down by the first safe opportunity…"

Pg. 43, Dec. 12 1861 same Camp Dear Lucie, "I have just received the carpet bag and clothes. They came o.k. except the catsup froze last night and caused the cork to come out, but did no further harm than to soil the flannel jacket which I will send up to have washed again….You need not cut up about the matter for I have a trunk full of clean clothes but it's a little too cold to change so often…I received the socks…"

Pg. 44, Dec. 21 1861 same camp Dear Lucie, "… I have been thinking that it would be a good idea to have two or three shirts made of brown cotton with linen bosums to wear this winter, as bleach muslin will be scarce herafter. Ask Ma what she thinks of it…'

Pg. 45 Dec. 27, 1861 same Camp Dear Lucy, "Many thanks for the cravats, which were very nice…I send my shoes up to be mended. Ask Father please to have them repaired as soon as possible. My boots have ripped, and I am nearly on the ground. Alvin's also in want of boots…"

"DEAR MARTHA..." The Confederate War Letters Of A South Carolina Soldier Alexander Faulkner Fewell compiled and edited by Robert Harley Mackintosh, Jr. The R.L. Bryan Co. 1976

17th South Caroline Inf. Company E
Pg. 10 Columbia S.C. Dec. 7th 1861 Mrs. M.A. Fewell Dear Wife "...I am in Columbia today looking up a uniform for Our Company but Cannot Succeed in getting One. I Can get the Cloth but Cannot find trimmings...."

Seriously? He can get the cloth but not the trimmings? This man has no idea how bad its gonna get. In a year or so, he'll be extremely thankful to get the cloth, never mind the trimmings.

THE CIVIL WAR INFANTRYMAN-In Camp, on the March, and in Battle by Gregory A. Coco pub by Thomas Publications

Dec. 8, 1861 "...A 1st Georgia non-commissioned officer, Sergeant Walter Clark, remarked on an unusual style of cloth not often utilized in Confederate clothing. On December 8, 1861 in Winchester, Virginia, a supply of blankets had arrived for the company from citizens of Augusta.

"One of the contributers had no blankets and in lieu of them donated a handsome crumb-cloth, which, like Joseph's coat of many colors, red and green being the prevailing tints. In the distribution this fell to Elmore Dunbar, the wag of the company. Not needing it as a blanket, he took it to a tailor in Winchester, had it transformed into a full suit, cap, coat, and pants, and donning it had an innumerable company of gamins, white and black, following in his wake all over town..."

Now this is a swell uniform! I'd loved to have actually seen it.

LETTERS FROM LEE'S ARMY Compiled by Susan Leigh Blackford Annotated by her husband, Charles Minor Blackford, Charles Scribner's & Sons 1947

Company B of the Second Virginia Cavalry- Charles Blackford was first lieutenant, later captain.
Pg. 62 December 8th, 1861 Leesburg Va. "I am now writing with my new coat on. It is very comfortable and fits admirably. It is much more agreeable than the short jacket which allowed the wind too many liberties. The cap also fits well, and the visor is a great help as it will protect my neck and ears from the biting blast which so often seems so bitter I must be frozen."

I agree with this man regarding the extra wind protection a long coat provides vs. a short jacket.

THE CONFEDERATE VETERAN VOL. XIX 1911

Pg. 221 May 1911 Extracts From A Letter By Lieut. E.P.Miller In camp Near Leesburg December 9 1861 Dear Sister Carrie, "I have a pair of Yankee shoes and a coat. But for these shoes I would be barefooted."

CIVIL WAR LETTERS OF CAPTAIN A.B. MULLIGAN,Co. B, Fifth South Carolina Cavalry-Butler's Division-Hampton's Corps 1861-1865 by Olin Fulmer Hutchinson, Jr. pub by The Reprint Co. 1992

Pg. 4 Charleston, Dec. 9th, 1861 My Dear Mother and Sisters, "I am careful to leave off the wool socks. They are intensely too heavy for this climate. I want you to pack my large trunk & send it to me by express as soon as you can. Send my dark suit, coat pants, & vest for winter. Also my marino socks & cotton flannel draws. Also my gray winter coat…(Dec. 10th)"…I want my large heavy old boots put in the trunk also…"

Both the suit and coat referred to were probably civilian.

HANDLEY LIBRARY ARCHIVES

James A. Miller Collection correspondence C.W. era misc. New Market, Va.
Winchester, Dec. 10th, 1861 (Abram Miller C.W. Letters Dear Julia, "…wish you would have my other pants made. Make them by the last pattern, the jeans pants that I have been wearing are beginning to wear out. I will have to darn them if I don't want them to get past darning…"

"THE BLOODY THIRTY FIRST"

Reflections on the 31st Regiment of Virginia Volunteers at Allegheny Mountain by Jason C. Spellman (Dec. 13 1861) "John Robson of Company H. describes the Confederate forces at Allegheny Mountain as equipped with "a scanty supply of blankets and rations." (Robson 20) In a December 9th letter to his wife, Henry H. Dedrick asks, "Dear Lissa I wrote you to send me some pants the first chance you get and the rest of them that I wrote for as I am nearly out of pants…" "In January 1862, Secnd Lieutenant James B. Galvin of Company I. wrote the Lutheran Sabbath School Association to thank the institution for providing them with fifty pairs of drawers. He writes, "The boys were very much in need of the kind considerations of the benevolent of Augusta County. The Lewis Rangers will long remember the kind esteem and gift..."(Roy Bird Cook Collection)

"While the author does recommend overalls, thick, water-proof boots, red flannel shirts, knit shirts, etc..." (for re-enactors of the 31st Va.)

HAM CHAMBERLAYNE-VIRGINIAN Letters and Papers of an Artillery Officer in the War for Independence 1861-1865 with introduction, notes and index by his son C.G.Chamberlayne Richmond, Va. Press of the Dietz Printing Co. Publishers 1932

Pg. 53 J.H. Chamberlayne to L.P. Chamberlayne Camp near Staunton Dec. 15th, 1861 My dear Sister "...Mother said something of a pair of warm gloves & you of a helmet, both will be welcome...."

A helmet? Some kind of winter hat? (like a ski cap, maybe?)

CONFEDERATE LETTERS AND DIARIES Walbrook D. Swank Papercaft Printing and Design Inc. 1992

Pg. 138 Letters of Private James O. Chisolm Captain Wiley G. Coleman's Co. Virginia Heavy Artillery F.W. Smith's Battery (Third Richmond Howitzers) Reserve Artillery Second Corps, Army of Northern Virginia Centreville (Va.) Dec. 15th 1861 Dear Sister "...I want you to make me a pair of good thick pants and send by the first opportunity. I have not got my boots yet but I have not needed them yet. I can do very well without them. I have a new pair of shoes I have never had on which will last me a month or so I reckon..."

Pg. 95 Letters Pertaining to John Taylor Anderson, Private, Co. C, 13th Virginia Infantry Dec 15th, 1861 Camp Hill (Va) Dear Sister Sallie, "...Hope we may get back to roads & the railroad where we can get anything from home we want during the winter, when we go into winter quarters I expect to send home more bad clothing if I find I need them my comfort(er) answers a very good purpose..."

HANDLEY LIBRARY ARCHIVES-

James A. Miller Collection correspondence C.W. era misc. New Market, Va.
Winchester Dec. 15th, 1861 Dear Julia, "...I have come to the conclusion to get you to make me a pair of the pants, off of the price that I send you. It is a very high price but I suppose I can't do any better..."

I WROTE YOU WORD-The Poignant Letters of Private Holt by John Lee Holt ed by James A. mumper pub by H.E.Howard 1991

Pg 44 College Hill Abingdon Virginia Dec. 15th, 1861 My Dearly Beloved Wife, '…Andrew Mason got here to us Saturday morning about day He brought my gloves for which I feel truly thankful to you I think I shall now have gloves enough to last me as I hav'nt soiled the others much yet But I reckon as you get the chance If you had you better knit me another pair of socks or two as I may need them & perhaps I can have some way of getting them after awhile…"

IN THE SHADOW OF THE ENEMY The Civil War Journal of Ida Powell Dulany ed. by Mary L. Mackall, Stevan F. Meserve, Anne Mackall Sasscer Univ. Tn. Press 2009

Pg. 44 "Hal's letter to Ida, December 17, 1861 Camp Letcher "…Send me down as soon as possible a wagon load of things. Lt. Plaster and myself have opened a Mess, I have just left Mr. Bolling and son and nephew. I should have had my letter ready for today's mail, as it is I shall have to put off sending it until tomorrow. In opening a mess we will have to supply ourselves again with plates etc…I shall enclose you an order for them to Mr. Thomblin who will send them to you and you can send them down by the wagon. I wish you would send me a list of the things you send down, and see that the things sent (including) a half dozen of each. I forgot to say cups & saucers, in other words a full compliment. (In addition to the cutlery, plates and cups, Hal also ordered "2 small shallow dishes, 2 small deep dishes, 1 tin coffee pot, 1 tea kettle.")

Wow, here is an extraordinary order for mess equipment. It makes one wonder how long it lasted once the army began to move again.

A LIFE FOR THE CONFEDERACY-As Recorded in the Pocket Diaries of Pvt. Robert A. Moore Co. G, 17th Mississippi Regiment Confederate Guards Holly Springs, Miss. ed. by James W. Silver McCowat-Mercer Press Inc. 1959

Pg. 88 Dec. 19th, 1861 camp near Leesburg "…Received our uniforms this morning…"

No mention as to color, cut, or who supplied them, also see the quote below.

THE CONFEDERATE VETERAN VO. XXVI 1918

Pg. 64 Letters FromThe Front by Thomas Caffey from Alabama "Camp at Mosely's Chuch, Near Norfolk, December 19, 1861 Dear Irene "You may tell ma I have four pairs of woolen socks; but if she sees proper, she can send more by John Pierce. I have clothes enough, I think, to last me till I come home, provided the Yankees do not take them from me. Our company now has new uniforms, which cost twenty-eight dollars apiece,; and as each man had his uniform to pay for, it made a sad hole in our commutation money...."

HANDLEY LIBRARY ARCHIVES-The Memoirs of the 49th Virginia Volunteers C.S.A.

Pg 226
Special requisition, for Capt. Crowder's Co., Dec. 1861
70 Blankets
70 Overcoats
& 2 boxes.

For Capt. Wm. H. Crowder's company of Va. Volunteers now encamped at Ariington's Depot, Nelson Co. Virginia, & is yet unattached, the muster roll numbers 80 men. Sined: John G. lobban, Lt, comdg.
(endorsed)
Received at Richmond the 20th day of Dec. 1861 of Capt. I.B. McClellan, Quartermaster, in full ot the above requisition:
Seventy overcoats & seventy pairs Carpet Blankets & 2 Boxes.

Signed: Jno G. Lobban, Lt Comdg.

DEAR SISTER-CIVIL WAR LETTERS TO A SISTER IN ALABAMA Frank Anderson Chappell pub. by Branch Springs Pub. 2002 (Third Alabama Regiment)

Pg. 56 Camp at Mosebey's Church near Norfolk Va. Dec. 22 1861 dear Sister "...Sister, do not think of doing anything for me for I need nothing. I have plenty of clothes and blankets. I could spare you one now..."

Finally, a fortunate, well-dressed soldier.

HANDLEY LIBRARY ARCHIVES-

James A. Miller Collection correspondence C.W. era misc. New Market, Va.
Winchestyer Dec. 22nd, 1861 Dear Julia, "...You wished to know if I want my dark pants. I don't want them at present. I inquired about those shoes several times but found them not done. I think it is useless to depend upon Meifs, Julia any longer...I just finished darning my socks, I tell you I done it up brown..."

RICHMOND VOLUNTEERS 1861-1865 by Louis H. mandarin & Lee A. Wallace pub. by Richmond Civil War Centennial Committee Westover Press 1969

Pg. 242 Jackson Guard "...The organization of the Jackson Guard was begun by Capt. Hiram B. Dickinson about May 27 1861....On Dec. 24 1861 "records indicate on that date-in Richmond-the Jackson Guard was issued overcoats, articles which would have doubtless been much appreciated earlier while they were in the western part of the state..."

I was informed by an armchair professor that the government, whether state or central, NEVER issued overcoats throughout the war. I wish there was a more detailed description of them and who issued them.

CONFEDERATE LETTERS AND DIARIES Walbrook D. Swank Papercaft Printing and Design Inc. 1992

Pg. 96 Camp Hill Va. Dec. 24th 1861 Dear Sister, "...I wish you would nit me a cap to sleep in, get Jimmie to give you some yarn and nit it in the shape of those nets cousin Pattie was nitting when I was there only have it thicker something like a comfort and send it in my Christmas box...."

HISTORY OF THE FOURTH REGIMENT SOUTH CAROLINA VOLUNTEERS FROM THE COMMENCEMENT OF THE WAR UNTIL LEE'S SURRENDER J.W. Reid Shannon &Co. Printers & Stationers Morningside Bookshop 1975

Pg. 63 Centreville, Va., Dec. 24 1861 "...In your letter you say my dog Bear has not forgotten me. I will bet you a jewsharp to a fiddlestring that if you don't mind him when I come home he will bite me, thinking I am an orangotang, and the very first words you will say will be, "Jesse, do pray shave before you-before long." My whiskers come down to-well, they come away down yonder, and I can put my moustaches over my ears. Am I not a paragon of beauty?..."

I envy him his moustaches

A SOUTHERN SOLDIER'S LETTERS HOME The Civil War Letters of Samuel Burney Cobb's Georgia Legion, Army of Northern Va. Ed. By Nat Turner Mercer Univ. Press, Macon Ga.2002

Pg. 86 same camp Dec.25 1861 "...I am very well pleased with my pants; it is a good article and is just the material and color I desired...."

SHENANDOAH 1862 by Peter Cozzins pub by Univ of North Carolina Pree 2008

Pg. 66 Dec. 26, 1862 Winchester Va. John Worsham of the 21st Virginia describes Stonewall Jackson: "We saw standing in the crowd on the sidewalk a man with full dark whiskers and hair, dressed in uniform, wearing a long dark blue overcoat with a large cape, his coat reaching to his boots, which were worn outside of his pants in regular military style,and on them were bright spurs. His head was covered by a faded gray cap pulled down so far over his face that between the cap and whiskers one could see very little of it. That man was Stonewall Jackson."

WAR DIARIES: The 1861 Kanawha Valley Campaign by David L. Phillips and Rebecca L. Hill, Cief Reseatcher Gauleu Mount Press 1990

Pg. 386 Dec. 26 1861 General Floyd's address to the men after the campaign"...On all occassions, under all circumstances, your patriotism and courage have never faltered nor forsaken you. With inadequate transportation, often illy clad, and with less than a full allowance of provisions, no private has ever uttered a complaint to this general..."

HANDLEY LIBRARY ARCHIVES-

James A. Miller Collection correspondence C.W. era misc. New Market, Va.
Winchester, Dec. 27th, 1861 Dear Julia "...I take this opportunity of writing you a few lines, I am sorry to inform you of the fact that Paul (slave) lost my pants and oil cloth, and I wish you to have me another pair of the same sort of goods made and send them by the first opportunity..."

THE THIRTY-SEVENTH NORTH CAROLINA TROOPS-Tar Heels in the A.N.V. by Micael C. Hardy pub by McFarland & Co. 2003

Pg. 27 "...On December 31, 1861, the regiment turned in its form 51, showing the equipment received in the prior year. They had received 157 caps-most men probably still wore their civilian or slouch hats from home, 621 private's coats, 630 pairs of trousers, 76 shirts, 126 pairs of drawers, 64 pairs of gloves, 770 overcoats, 166 knapsacks, 826 knapsack straps, 34 wall tents, 111 wall tent flies, and two iron pots, along with other items such as chairs and a desk. Obviously, most still wore their shirts and drawers from home. Some men may not have worn drawers at all, if they were not accustomed to doing so in civilian life. Officers did not receive clothing from the depots. They were responsible for the purchase of their own clothing and often had tailors or family at home custom make their uniforms..."

LETTERS AND PAPERS OF AN ARTILLERY OFFICER A.N.V. IN THE WAR FOR SOUTHERN INDEPENDENCE 1861-1865 Capt. John Hampden Chamberlain-Virginian Dietz Printing Co. Pub. 1932

Pg. 59 Camp near Winchester Va. Dec. 31st 1861 My dear Mother "…Thanks for the helmet; I will wear it, not indeed while standing guard, for that I never have to do, but, not less comfortably, when sleeping…"

OK, so in this case a helmet is some sort of winter or sleeping cap.

FOUR YEARS UNDER MARSE ROBERT by Robert Stiles pub by Pelican Pub. Co. 1998

Pg. 70 Ft. Johnson, winter 1861-62 "A militia company from a neighboring county was ordered to the fort. Due to increased jealousy with the artillerymen and the thought they were there to be sacrificed, one night the author was awakened with the word that the militia were formed up and leaving the fort. He had his men to block the only exit and addressed them (the militia) when "While I was speaking I noticed immediately in front of me, standing on an irregular line of officers, a remarkable and grotesque figure. He was an old, gaunt man dressed in an old Continental uniform or something very like it. I recall the cocked hat, blue, buff-faced coat of that cut, fa'top boots, and a drawn sword in his hand about the length and model of a scythe blade."

Middle South

INTRODUCTION

In the middle states, nonuniformity was more pronounced. Units were either spectacularly equipped or dressed in civilian clothes with civilian weapons, or somewhere in between. Everywhere the people were rushing to produce uniforms for the troops, from any cloth they could obtain, and here butternut was more common than gray. From these eyewitness accounts, it seems that the soldiers in the middle south wore mostly civilian clothes or "uniforms" made by the homefolks

History Series XVIII John McGlone series ed. Southern Heritage Press 1997

Pg. 4 mustering in 11th Mississippi Inf. "We Wilkins boys did look natty. Mr. Harrison Johnston, a tailor from Colombus, made our uniforms from some heavy cotton serge. Our belts, straps, packs, cartridge boxes and tin canteens were sent here from the central commissary in Atlanta. Our black "Jeff Davis" hats came from the militia supply depot in Jackson and we turned up the left brim and pinned it up with a big brass star that we got from the Brooksville general store. The star matched the big white star on our bonnie blue company flag. Our 1855 model 58 caliber U.S. percussion rifles with Maynard tape primers came from the arms depot in Jackson. We wore brogan work shoes that Daddy bought from Uncle Doc's general store in town."

I wonder how that tape primer held up under field conditions.

FROM THE FLAME OF BATTLE TO THE FIERY CROSS-The 3rd Tennessee Infantry by James Van Eldik pub by Yucca Tree Press 2001

Pg. 33 Mustering in: "It would be doing violence to the feelings of a gallant company of soldiers not to make special mention of the noble part taken by the ladies of Mount Pleasant in providing a neat and comfortable outfit of clothing, etc.

Among older citizens too [were those] who were conspicuous for their liberality in donating means to uniform and equp the company, and provide for the support of such as would leave their families in a destitute condition."

WEBSITE-confederateuniforms.org

Jan 22, 1861 The Daily Dispatch "Capture of the New Orleans Barracks by a company of State troops... The troops had received their undress uniform, under-clothing and shoes yesterday, but had no caps as yet; and when drawn up in a line, there was motley array of silk hats, slouched tiles and glazed caps, all of which will soon be replaced by graceful Zouave cap, of navy blue cloth. The undress uniform is a dark blue jacket coming down to the hip, single-breasted, with five pelican buttons, and dark blue pants, with a stripe of yellow cord..."

New Orleans Bee, "Departure of Volunteer Companies for Fort Pickens...the Louisiana Guards...The company leaving were dressed in a fatigue uniform of blue flannel, Zouave style, and appeared admiringly calculated for a soldier's duty..."

THE CONFEDERATE VETERAN VOL.XXXIII 1925

Pg. 183 The Story of the Nankeen Shirt "The following story is reproduced in the "Enterprise" of Mansfield, La., from the account written by a lady of Natchitoches just after the war, and its basis is historical fact. It is hardly necessary to explain to "Veteran" readers that "nankeen" is a variety of cotton grown in the South during the war, of which the lint is a dark brown or copper color and does not fade. It fact, the more it is washed the brighter the color becomes.

It was used extensively for clothing by our people during the war, and nankeen clothes may be said to have been a standard article of raiment in the South."

Going to Meet The Yankees- A History of the "Bloody Sixth" Mississippi Infantry, C.S.A. by H. Grady Howell, Jr. Cickasaw Bayou Press Miss.

Pg. 7 Shiloh, Rankin City, Feb.16, 1861 Letter of requisition to the States Quartermaster General William Barkesdale: "Dear Sir we have formed a volunteer company at the above place in Beat No. (4) & stiled ourselves the Rankin Grays& we have bin informed that your honor would furnish us with Clothfor our uniforms on our aplication to your honor so if it meets your approbation & it is inconformity with your costom to do so will you please drop me a few lines at Brandon & when we get fully Augornized I will inform you honor & you will froward us the cloth. By the order of the Capt. N.J.J. Thornton, Ellis M. Myers, Treas. Of the R.N. Grays"

The material eventually arrived as did several gross of military buttons and rank insignia. Artillery buttons were sent by mistake on May 8th, but this error was soon corrected and infantry buttons reached the company by May 18th."

UNIFORMS OF THE CIVIL WAR by Robin Smith & Ron Field Lyons Press 2001

Pg. 254 KENTUCKY "...In his recollections of service as an officer in the 4th Kentucky Cavalry, George D. Musgrove remarked that as a rule he was '...fond of gray attire, his style being regulation cavalry boots, a red sash, a large black felt hat, of the slouch variety, with the brim of one side turned upand pinned to the side of the crown with a silver crescent or star, the whole surmounted by a huge, black ostrich plume.'

As the 2nd Kentucky Cavalry, commanded by John Hunt Morgan, set out from Knoxville in 1862 on its first major raid, they were described as lacking 'general uniforms', although some were in 'new regulation gray, others in butternut jeans'.

UNIFORMS OF THE CIVIL WAR by Robin Smith & Ron Field Lyons Press 2001

Pg. 241 "... John Johnston recalled receiving 'a gray flannel shirt, gray pants with a dark stripe down each leg and gray coats', when he enlisted in The Danes, Co. K., 6th Tennessee Infantry. The Jackson Grays, of the same regiment, wore a gray coat with black collar, and gray cap with company letter G on its dark band..."

UNIFORMS OF THE CIVIL WAR Lord, Wise, A.S. Barnes & Co. 1970

Pg. 64 "Regular C.S. units were often left alone if captured in Federal garments during a major campaign or battle. One Confederate remarked: "Nearly all the equipments of the

Army of Northern Virginia were articles captured from the Yankees. Most of the blankets were marked "U.S.", and also the rubber balnkets or cloths. The very clothing the men wore was mostly captured, as we were allowed to wear their pants, underclothing and overcoats. As for myslf, I purchased only one pair of shoes and one jacket after 1861."

UNIFORMS OF THE CIVIL WAR by Robin Smith & Ron Field Lyons Press 2001

Pg 188 Georgia "…Fort Pulaski was occupied by the 1st regiment Georgia Volunteers, a volunteer militia unit commanded by Colonel Alexander R. Lawton, on 3 January 1861. The Augusta Independent Volunteer Battalion seized the Augusta Arsenal 20 days latert. The companies involved in these actions wore a variety of distinctive fatigue uniforms. The republican Blues, Co. C, 1st Regiment, wore dark blue shell jackets trimmed with white cord on collar, shoulder straps, and pointed cuffs; sky-blue pants with broad white seam stripes; and dark blue forage caps. The Irish Volunteerts, Co. E, wore 'service hats, jackets, dark pantaloons and waist belts.' Within the Augusta Battalion, the Clinch Rifles donned their 'dark green cloth shell jackets, possibly with yellow lace trim around collar and on cuffs; black pants, and green model 1856 caps with stiffening removed. The Richmond Hussars wore an army blue shirt trimmed with yellow, a black Hardee hat with black feather plumes, and sky-blue pants with broad seam stripes….according to contemporary newspaper reports during 1861, many infantry companies either adopted or changed to gray unforms trimmed with black, whilst most officers wore blue. A typical account is held within the memoirs of captain james C. Nesbet who commanded the Silver Grays, Co. H, 21st Georgia infantry: 'The uniforms of gray, made to order, had to be shipped by E. Winship, Macon, Georgia, for which I paid…the men, uniformed in gray, presented a good appearance. The lieutenants were uniformed in home-made blue jeans. My uniform was of regular U.S. Army blue, tailor made, a present (with my sword and belt) from my sister…On the 10th of that month (April 1861) Governor Brown requisitioned his state for 3000 military companies and required them all to have a plain service uniform and 'change of underclothing'. After numerous enquiries regarding the type of service uniform needed, he announced on 28 May that the volunteers should have a coat or jacket; two pairs of trousers; one forage or fatrigue cap; two flannel shirts, preferably gray or blue (not red as they presented 'an excellent mark for the enemy'); and one light, black necktie. In response, a wide variety of uniforms were adopted. Those reported being worn by companies passing through Augusta by the 'Daily Chronicle and sentinel' during this period are quite typical, e.g. Burke Guards (Co. A, 3rd Georgia) 'Their uniform is dark gray trimmed with green; officers with coats, privates with jackets, slouched hats; Brown rifles (Co. G, 3rd Georgia)-'gray with red trimmings'; Dawson Grays (Co. C, 3rd Georgia)-"Georgia gray trimmed with black'; Home Guard (Co. D, 3rd Georgia)-'Georgia gray'; Governor's Guards (Co.E, 3rd Georgia)-'a red jacket, blue-black pants, with white stripe, and German fatigue cap'; Wilkinson Rifles (Co. F, 3rd Georgia)-'Georgia kersey, buff colored; Southern Rifles (Co. A, 4th Georgia)-'Georgia gray trimmed with black velvet';

LeGrange Light Guard (Co. B, 4th Georgia)-'"Rosswell gray" (cloth with a dark bluish-gray cast-ed.)jackets and pants trimmed with black. Georgia buttons' Twiggs Volunteers (Co.C, 4th Georgia)-'a durable cassimere, manufactured at the Eagle Factory, Columbus; the pants with dark stripe. A portion of the company wear red shirts with both cloth and glazed caps': Baldwin Blues (Co. H, 4th Georgia)-'a dark blue, very neat and serviceable'.

The 'flannel shirts' also varied greatly, prompting Governor Brown's instructions. A letter from 'Camp Oglethorpe' near Macon, dated 5 April, 1861, describes troops wearing: 'red shirts, blue shirts, gray shirts, and shirts without order and indescribable to an unpractised eye…' Those worn by the Clinch Rifles encamped at the same place the following month included polka dots and patterned bib fronts.

The Zouave fashion was represented in Georgia by a boy's company commanded by Captain Speillers called the Young Zouaves, formed in Augusta in 1860, who wore 'bright blue jackets and fiery red trousers'. About 30 members of the Macon Volunteers, led by Captain R.A. Smith, wore a version of the Zouave uniform. The Macon Telegraph reported: 'a group of gentlemen surrounding a figure, who, from his fantastic dress…was either a Japanese, a Chinese, a Sioux Indian, or one of the latest importation from Africa. We drew near, and discovered the fantastic figure to be that of our fellow-citizen, Mr. D.B.W., Orderly of the Volunteers, and was dressed in the uniform of the Macon Volunteer Zouaves. This uniform is made of bright cloth, and in a strange fashion, and presents a picturesque and graceful appearance.'

The 'Sicilian'-style stocking cap, complete with tassels and Havelock, was also popular amongst Georgia troops early in the war. The Thompsoin Guards, Co. F, 10th Georgia Infantry, wore 'cap covers…parti-colored or plaid, long and pointed, and so arranged that they may be thrown back on the neck or over the visor'.

UNIFORMS OF THE CIVIL WAR by Robin Smith & Ron Field Lyons Press 2001

Pg. 168 Mississippi "…Numerous Mississippi companies volunteered for Confederate service in uniforms which owed nothing to the regulations of 1861. The Mississippi Rifles, Co. A, 10th Mississippi Infantry, wore a dress uniform described in 1860 as being 'of dark green cloth, Hungarian hats, ostrich plumes'. The collar, worsted epaulettes and cuff tabs on their single-breasted frock coats were red, as were their trouser stripes. Their 'Hardee'-style dress hat bore a red ostrich plume and was pinned up on the right by a regulation U.S. eagle; on the front was a Mounted Rifles-bugle, placed horizontally, over large metal letters MR. During February 1861, this company acquired a fatigue uniform consisting of a seven-button grey coat with dark facings on collar, pointed cuffs and shoulder straps, plain grey pants and a grey cap with dark band. The Van Dorn Reserves, of Aberdeen, were mustered into service as Co. I, 11th Mississippi Infantry, in a uniform of 'red jeans'. The Prarie Guards, Co. E, of the same regiment, originally wore a dress uniform consisting of grey frock coat with dark-colored plastron front and epaulettes, grey pants with broad seam stripes, and black Hardee hat with ostrich plume and brim looped up on the left. A member of this company later informed his parents that he had sold his 'red jeans pants for four dollars,' possibly indicating that more than one company of this regiment was thus clad for war service.

Mississippi regiments in Virginia were very poorly supplied. According to the diary of Roberty A. Moore, a member of the Confedertae Guards, camped near Leesburg, Virginia, during August 1861, the 17th Mississippi infantry purchased 'for the reg(inment) goods for a uniform' which was taken 'back to the homes of the different companies' to be made up. Received by the end of October, these uniforms consisted of gray 10-button shell jackets with a single small button on either side of a black-trimmed collar. Cuffs were decorated with black cord forming a distinctive single loop. The front and bottom jacket edges were also trimmed with black cord. Some jackets had a single pocket on the right breast. Pants were also gray with 2-inch wide seam stripes.

As 1861 drew to a close, the lack of clothing began to effect the Mississippi troops closer to home. The 1st and 3rd Mississippi were described as 'the poorest clad, shod, and armed body I ever saw,' by Brigadier-General Floyd tilghman, commanding Camp Alcorn in Kentucky on 2 November of that year...."

UNIFORMS OF THE CIVIL WAR by Robin Smith & Ron Field Lyons Press 2001

Pg. 182 Alabama "...Not all Alabamian companies adopted these prescribed uniforms. One officer informed the Governor that his company had bought uniforms which he feared might 'differ from the state uniform'. He went on to explain that it was 'like the Dutchman's Wife: not much for pretty, but hell for strong.'

Pg. 184 Alabama "...Some of the newly-formed companies also adopted very individual, locally made garb. A reporter in Montgomery noted that many Alabama volunteers wore:'... old flannel bags, closed and drawn to a point at one end, with tassel dependent. This style of fatigue head-dress was introduced by one of the Mobile Companies, and in an incredibally short space of time the fever for posseing them spresd from rank to rank, and company to company, until nearly everyone now is supplied...."

Pg. 238 Tennessee "...Harris Zouave Cadets or Memphis Zouaves ...(June 1860) were reported to be wearing the "Zouave fatigue" dress consisting of flowing pants with a scqarlet stripe, blue roundabout, bound with the same color and plain blue cap." During a "Succession Demonstration," which took place by torchlight on the night of 8 Febuary1861, they paraded "dressed in their gorgeous scarlet costumes"...The Highland Guard, raised among the "Scotch" citizens, who were to be dressed in "the picuresque uniform of the highlands of Scotland, plaid kilt and trews."

GOING TO MEET THE YANKEES-A History of the "Bloody Sixth' Mississippi infantry, C.S.A. by H. Grady Howell, JR. Chickasaw Bayou Press

Pg. 7 "…In early February of 1861 the "Rankin Guards" was reorganized under the personal direction of Dr. Thornton and renamed the "Rankin Greys." Captain Thornton once again assumed command but his staff changed almost entirely.…Even the company's uniforms were changed, for on February 16th the "Greys" painfully spelled out the following letter of requisition to the State's Quartermaster General William Barksdale:

"Shiloh Rankin City Feb. 16, 1861

Dear Sir we have formed a volunteer company at the above place in beat No.(4) & stiled ourselves the Rankin Grays & we have been informed that your honor would furnish us with Cloth for our uniforms on our applicatin to your honor so if it meets your approbation & it is inconformity with your custom to do so you will please drop me a few lines at Brandon& when we get fully agonized I will inform you honor & you will forward us the cloth

By the order of the Capt. N.J.J. Thornton
Ellis M. Myers Treas. Of the R N Greys"

The material eventually arrived as did several gross of military buttons and rank insignia. Artillery buttons were sent by mistake on May 8th, but this error was soon corrected and infantry buttons reached the company by May 18th.…"

THE CONFEDERATE VETERAN VOL. XVII 1909

Pg. 460 Sept. 1909 Spring 1861-"…The 11th Georgia Volunteers were mustered into service on Peachtree Street in Atlanta Ga., and were there drilled for service. Among these was a company dressed in uniforms of yellow jeans…"

Yellow? What shade? Butternut can be described as yellow, but as the writer was probably familiar with that color, these must have been a brighter yellow.

THE CONFEDERATE VETERAN VOL. XXV 1917

Pg. 121 March, 1917 In The Year 1861 compiled by John C. Stiles Vol. IV "Official Records" "Supplies Wanted-A Confederate colonel said that his men needed only rifles, clothes, greatcoats, knapsacks, haversacks, canteens, and indeed everything except a willingness to fight. The last clause describes Tennessee's part in the war to a nicety."

The colonel describes the condition (destitution) of his men very well.

MOUNTANEERS IN GRAY John D. Fowler Univ. of N.C. Press 2004

Pg 35 April 1861 East Tennessee- companies forming for Confederate service. "...the ladies of Hawkins county made the uniforms worn by William Miller and Daniel Phipps when they left a distraught Charlotte and marched off to face their new lives as soldiers. Patriotic citizens donated the light gray uniforms worn by the Hamilton Grays, and Edward Marsh, a wealthy Chattanooga businessman, gave the Marsh Blues their uniforms, equipment, and name..."

A MISSISSIPPI REBEL IN THE ARMY OF NORTHERN VIRGINIA-Memiors of Pvt. David Holt ed by Thomas D. cockerell & Michael B. Ballara La. State Univ. Press 1995

April 1861
Pg. 64 (War clouds Gather 1856-1861) Wilkinson Co., Miss. "the maternal authority took precedence over the military, and the swimming hole took precedence over all else in the summer. Since every cadet had shotgun, not even a jaybird was safe within a half mile of camp. We skinned the various varities of birds,and, after the were fried in bacon grease, all tasted alike.

"The distinctive feature of the cadet's uniform, which was made of brown factory jeans and donated by Judge (J.M.?) McGehee, who had a factory near town, was a broad band of turkey red calico down the outside seam of our trousers and bands of the same red material around the cuffs on our jackets. Most of us wore felt hats with the brim turned up on the right side. We were always in uniform except on Sundays when we went to church...."

Pg. 65 The Masonic Hall and Lodge rooms were given to the ladies without charge every day of the week excepting Sundays. Every woman and girl who was big enough to work congregated here to make clothes for the soldiers. This was continued until late in the war when Judge McGehee's factory was burned by the Yanks.

This factory made unbleached cotton cloth in two grades; one four ounces and the other eight ounces to the yard. The heavy quality was used for jeans out of which coats and trousers were made. The ladies dyed all the cloth with sweet-gum bark, which gave it a blueish-grey tint. The outer garments were lined with the eight ounce cotton cloth. The underwear was made from the four ounce cloth. In this manner the soldier was clad all in one color. After he had been at the front long enough to become the host of many inhabitants, they too, partook of the same color scheme. Rightly, they were called, "greybacks." A good lesson was learnt in the effectiveness of color protection, as our bluish-grey was almost invisible to the enemy, particularly when lying down. The two town tailors cut, without pay, every soldier's garments to fit..."

MIDSHIPMAN IN GRAY-Selections From Recollections Of A Rebel Reefer by James Morris Morgan ed by R. Thomas Campbell pub by Burd Street Press 1917

Pg. 33 April 1861 Baton Rouge, La. "…The military ideas of these soldiers were very crude-very few, if any of them knew the manual of arms, and they insisted on calling their colonels and captains, "Billy," "Tommy," and "John." As for the uniforms(?) they would have put to shame an opera-bouffe army. I remember particularly the "Delta Rifles" of Baton Rouge whose dress was much admired by the ladies, but which greatly tickled my risibles. It was composed of some green gauze-like-looking fabric, the tunic of which, like the sleeves, was trimmed with long fringe which reached below their knees, and these men expected to go to Virginia and possibly spend the winter amidst its snows."

Fringe on the sleeves? Doesn't that sound somewhat awkward? I bet it looked nice, though not very military.

DRUMS OF WAR Hosted by Rootsweb

April 1861 "The uniform of the 23rd (Miss. Inf) was not the grey usually associated with the Confederate soldier, but brown. During the early part of the war and to an even greater extent in its later stages, each soldier provided his own uniform; and in areas far from large towns, such as Tippah county, it was much easier to dye homespun jeans to a butternut or brown shade with walnut hulls and copperas than it was to obtain a good grey color in any way. That the use of brown uniforms in the western armies is evidenced by the number of references in northern to the excellent, if unintentional, camouflage provded by butternut coloring…"

A good over-all statement regarding butternut.

Foreigners In The Confederacy by Ell Lonn Univ. N.C. press 1968

Pg. 110 April 1861 "…The ambitious project of a Garibaldi Legion to be composed exclusively of Italians must have fallen far short of realization, as only one company seems to have completed its organization. As was usual in those early days of glowing hopes, the uniform was a matter of prime importance. If the Italians ever did parade in the uniform prescribed for this legion, they must have presented a striking appearance. It was to be much like that worn by Garibaldi's soldiers; a high-peaked black felt hat, boasting a moderate-sized brim turned up on the left side, with a small buch of green, black and white feathers; around the crown a green silk cord terminating behind in a tassel, with gilt buttons in front; a round jacket of red woolen cloth; bottle green pantaloons, cut wide and reaching below the knee, held in place by gaiters or leggings of the same material buttoned on the outside; and a black belt and cartridge box to complete the costume."

Pg. 112 The French Legion ..."Thus it added to the streets of New Orleans one more gay uniform, for the French Legion donned that of the French Army-red pantaloons and a horizon-blue coat. The charm of the unusual appealed as always to the small boy, so that the tradition of the French colors passed into boyhood slang in this southern city and lived long after the war. The cry "The Red Legs are coming," became a boys warning to run."

DARK AND BLOODY GROUND Thomas Ayres Taylor Trade Pub. 2001

1861 the War craze in New Orleans
Pg. 38 "...There was a company made up of Greek immigrants bedecked in native uniforms, another composed of German Gymnasts, and yet another of professional gamblers. Firemen formed a company and policemen another. The military frenzy extended beyond New Orleans. At Keatchie in Desoto Parish, Scotsmen formed a miliotia company called The Highlanders. Their uniforms featured plaid kilts...."

THREE MONTHES IN THE CONFEDERATE ARMY Henry Holze pub. by Univ. Al. Press 1952

Pg.1 "The twenty third of April, 1861, is a day long to be remembered in the local traditions of the city of Mobile....It was now a holiday parade, such as had often enlivened the stretsof the peaceful city. The showy uniforms in which,in happier times, harmless citizens delighted to play at soldiering, had been left behind, and the officers and men were clad in a stout, serviceable gray, specially selected for a rough campaign..."

PORTRAITS OF CONFLICT-A Photographic History of Louisiana in the Civil war by Carl Maneyhon & Bobby Roberts Univ. of Arkansas Press 1990

Pg. 33 "Another of the early units called into service to be sent to Pensacola was Colonel Coppen's Zouaves. These troops...formed in the spring of 1861 and modeled themselves after the popular French Zouaves. They were dressed in uniforms of baggy scarlet trousers, blue shirts, and heavilty braided blue jackets. This picturesque uniform was completed with a fez, instead of the kepi or slouch hats worn by most troops. The commands were initially given in French..."

Pg. 55 "One of the most colorful Confederate infantry units that served in the Virginia peninsula was the 1st Battalion, Louisiana Zouaves. In March, 1861, the units' future commander Gaston Coppens obtained personal permission from President Jefferson Davis to raise the Battalion. Coppens modeled his unit on the "Zouave d' Afrique," infantry formations that had been raised by the French from tribesmen in Algeria. The Louisiana Battalion had an international flavor, as Irish, German, Swiss, Poles, and especially the French Creoles joined its ranks. Coppens copied the French units' garish uniforms, outfitting the enlisted men with loose dark blue jackets and close-fitting vasts of the same color. A three foot long "sky-blue merino" secured the baggy scarlet trousers, which were complemented with leather leggings, white gaiters, and black shoes. Their caps were made of close-fitting soft flannel with blue tassels that hung behind them…"

UNIFORMS OF THE CIVIL WAR Lord, Wise, A.S. Barnes & Co. 1970

Pg. 23 "One soldier from the regulars wrote: Pensacola Florida April 6 1861 "Our company have at last received our uniforms. It consists of heavy brogans, sufficiency of underclothing, grey homespun pants and a yarn blouse, made like a butcher's gown, (many a brass button!) and a glazed cap, giving us a very unique appearance…"

THE HISTORY OF THE CONFEDERACY 1832-1865 Clifford Dowdey Barnes and Noble Books 1955

Pg, 102 "…The University Greys, from the state university and its town of Oxfords, Mississippi became Co. A of the 11th Mississippi on April 12, 1861. They were sent to the Shenandoah Valley "…in their fine-looking frock-coated uniforms, with black felt hats looped on three sides and topped with pompoms, and plumes for the the lieutenants and nineteen-year old Captain Lowery…"

REMINISCENCES OF A PRIVATE William E. Bevins of the First Arkansas Inf. C.S.A. Univ. Ark. Press 1992

Pg. 14 May, 1861 "I was put on guard inside the Fair Grounds. It rained all night. I had on new pump-soled boots, and being by mistake, left on duty, these tight boots caused me considerable pain.(Footnote #14-The reference to "pump-soled" boots implies thin-soled and rather insubstantial footgear.)

THE CIVIL WAR MEMOIR OF PHILIP DANGERFIELD STEPHENSON, D.D. ed. By Nathaniel Chears Hughes, Jr. UCA Press 1995

Pg. 18 May 1861 "I was about the last recruit for the regiment, at least for a season. When they fitted me out in soldier clothes, it was rare work. All the uniform hats, shoes, etc., had been picked over and only odds and ends were left. Lieutenant Bartlett roared as I tried on one thing after another. I finally emerged-and was a sight! I had on a long frock coat of coarse brown cloth, butternut color, very tight, buttoned up to the chin on my long, rail-like body. My pants, of the same stuff, were a mile too big, baggy as sacks, legs rolled up at the bottom. Our uniforms were mostly the same dirt color, the coats having brass buttons and black cuffs and collars. My hat, a common light colored wool, was passible as to fit, but my shoes, coarse brogans, were a No.9 and a No.8! I laughed it off and was proud of being in uniform."

Kinda catch-as-catch can regarding the uniforms here.

MY DIARY NORTH AND SOUTH William Howard Russell T.O.H.P. Burnham 1863

Pg. 602 May 1861 Mobile Al. Fort Morgan "...Inside the work was crammed with men, some of whom slept in the casements- others in tents in the parade ground and enceinte of the Fort. They were Alabama Volunteers, and as sturdy a lot of fellows as ever shouldered a musket; dressed in homespun coarse grey suits, with blue and yellow worsted facings and stripes-to European eyes not very respectful to their officers, but very obedient, I am told, and very peremptorily ordered about, as I heard..."

WILD RIDERS OF THE FIRST KENTUCKY CAVALRY-A History of the Regiment in the Great War of Rebellion 1861-1865 by Sergeant E. Tarrant pub by Gennison Pub Co. 1997

Pg. 50 May 1861 "...After returning from this expedition, companies A,B.and C were were armed withy the Army Sharpe rifles with saber bayonets, one of the most effective arms in the service, and specially adapted to the dragoon or heavy Cavalry service. The other companies were afterward armed with the musket, a very inefficient arm, and particularly inconvenient for Cavalry. The men were compelled to retain these for a long time, much to their displeasure. Clothing was issued to the men, but only one or two garments at a time. We first drew pants and shirts, and two months after entering the service overcoats were issued to us. It was after four months' hard service before we drew full suits and were armed with the navy pistol..."

I don't know what this writer means by "Sharpe rifles with saber bayonet" as these didn't exist. As far as I know, the saber bayonet was only made for the Mississippi rifle. Also, another refrerence to overcoats issued to the troops.

WEBSITE-confederateuniforms.org Daily Advocate (Baton Rouge, La)

May 2,1861 Creole Guards-"...The Creole's are a fine body of men, numbering about 80. They were dressed in blue flannel trimmed with yellow, presenting quite a fine display..."

May 14, 1861 "…The following is a complete list of the various articles made up by the ladies : Pelican Rifles-18 shirts, 16 pairs drawers, 73 pairs pants, 73 coats, Total,429. National Guards-131 pairs drawers, 180 shirts, 60 pair pants, 60 coats,Total,431. Delta Rifles-130 pieces on hand: 175 canteen covers, Total 305. Making all together 1211 pieces…'

TITHES OF BLOOD by Billy Ellis Southern Heritage Press Murfreesburo, TN. 1997

Pg. 14 May 11, 1861 "…The newly elected officers tried out their new authority by squaring up the mass of men and equipment. While we were thus occupied, another company marched into the staging area. The men were all done up in the finest outfits with grey frock coats with red frogging, trousers with red stripes up the side and black felt hats pinned up on three sides with horse-hair cockades.

To top it all off, the men had red-lined capes! If that ain't enough the company was followed by a large group of support personnel. "Who in thunder is you all?" inquired one of our men. "The University Greys" came the proud reply. "What University?" "University of Mississippi" they boasted.

We prarie boys had never seen a man wearing a cape before. Some of the "Greys" seemed a bit over-educated and most of these planter aristocrats also had their little darkey man-servants with them. After we had all shared the privations of war, however, we all became brothers…"

Pg.17 "… One of the Confederacies wealthiest companies was probably the Van Dorn Reserves of Aberdeen. Each man was furnished with a tailored uniform, a Colt revolving rifle, and a purse of gold. The company also carried a war chest containing several thousand dollars…'

YELLOW JACKETS BATTALION by Arthur W. Bergeron Jr.

Pg. 51 The 10th Louisiana Infantry battalion, nicknamed the "Yellow Jackets" In a letter written after the war a former officer of the battalion explained. It received the name of the Yellow Jackets Battalion as most of the men were dressed with home-made cottonade suits."

Butternut described as yellow.

THE THIRD MISSISSIPPI REGIMENT-C.S.A. by Dale Greenwell

Pg. 14 May 18, 1861 "…Mr. Elmer, or I should say Lieutenant Elmer wuz mounted on a brown horse, just as strong lookin' and as brave as the gray one. The other officers diden' have mounts but wuz dressed just as handsome. All the other men wore the same colors but it wuz an odd bunch to look at. There wuz all sizes, different hats of different colors, black shoes, brown boots, red bandanas, orange handkerchiefs, white scarves, and other wraps around their throats. But all in all they looked like a rough bunch of men ready for a good fight. It wuz right then I knew that I belonged in that outfit..."

THE COMPANY OF MILITARY HISTORIANS-A Survey of Confederate Central Government QuartermasterIssue Jackets by Leslie D. Jenson

Pg. 4 "Capt. John M. Galt AQM in New Orleans, to let contracts for 5,000 uniforms for regular army recruits. These uniforms were to consist of a blue flannel shirt to be worn as a blouse, steel grey woolen trousers, red or white flannel shirts, plus drawers, socks, bootees, blankets and leather stocks. Caps were added later...

On 31 May he was told to have suits of gray made up as fast as possible, and to let Myers (the Quartermaster General) know how fast clothing could be furnished. Galt's reply that he could furnish 1500 suits per week resulted in an order for 5,000 gray jackets and pants... "or any color you can get..." On 4 June Galt was asked if he could supply 50,000 men from the resources of the city and the next day he was told to have "...clothing of every description, jackets, pants shoes, drawers shirts, flannels, socks..." made up as quickly as possible and sent to Richmond. At the same time he was told to stop the manufacture of the recruit clothing as the recruiting service was being discontinued. Once again, he was told to keep up the manufacture of the 1500 suits per week, although they were now to include "jackets" instead of the "tunics" Prescribed in the regulations...On 5 June he (Myers) had told Galt: "...the mean description of cloth that the volunteers have been provided with is almost entirely worn out, and in a few weeks they will be destitute of most of the articles of clothing. The law requires volunteers to furnish themselves but as they cannot do so in the field, we must look after their comfort in this respect..."

Pg. 5 Explaning the Commutation System: "...A letter to Capt. J.A. Johnson at Norfolk (Va.) explaned the new system: "...if the Captains of Companies can make an arrangement to obtain clothing to be paid out of the $21 due for the next six months, after the commutation has been paid for the first six months, it would be better than to issue Government clothing to the volunteers. If that cannot be done, such articles of clothing as are absolutely necessary may be issued to the Captains of Companies for their men, with the instruction that the value of the Clothing is to be charged and deducted from the $21 allowed for the next six months..."

GRANDFATHER'S JOURNAL (Franklin Lafayette Riley) Company B Sixteenth Mississippi Infantry Volunteers Harris' Brigade Mahone's Division Hill's Cops, A.N.V. May 27, 1861-July 15, 1865 Austin C. Dobbins Morningside 1988

Pg. 10 Friday, May 31, 1861, Camp Clark (near Corinth, Miss.) "We are not very well equipped, however. We have brought our own weapons: flintlocks, shotguns, carbines,

Mississippi rifles, Yagers, and Kentuckys. Our uniforms also are of different types and materials. Jackets are single-and double breasted. Trousers are of varying shades of gray and blue (some are even checked). Fortunately, regulations do not require standard uniforms. Eventually, says Captain Funchess, we will all be furnished the same kinds of muskets and uniforms."

Started off in multiform, and what a logistical n ightmare for the ordinance officer trying to get ammunition to match all those different weapons!

CANNONEERS IN GRAY The Field Artillery of the Army of Tennessee by Larry J. Daniel pub by Univ. of Alabama Press1984

Pg. 4 Summer 1861 Captain Arthur M. Rutledge's battery from Nashville "...Their attire varied considerately. Some wore a solid gray uniform, including pants decorated with a red stripe denoting artillery; others, a solid dark coat and pants; still others, a combination of dark coat and gray pants. Hats and caps were also nondescript, but the crossed-cannon insignia of the artillery were affixed to most of them..."

Website-CONFEDERATE CAVALRYMAN: Mud Camp Ford, Marrowbone Creek, Kettle Creek, and Turkey-neck Ford The Riviting Story of James Edwards Evans: 1st/3rd KY Cavalry, CSA, Morgan's raider Camp Douglas Prisoner of War 2008 http://evans family treelimb.blogspot.com/2008/12/mud-camp-ford-marrowbone-kettle-creek.html

Pg. 4 Summer 1861 "Legends which state that Morgan's men lived off the land, pillaging any food and supplies they might need, appear to be largely true. These were not perfectly groomed cavalrymen in freshly ironed grey uniforms with plumed hats and highly polished boots. This was a motley crew. Lacking uniforms issued by the Confederacy, some wore homemade uniforms while others were seen wearing whatever clothing they had happened to be wearing when they enlisted. Boots were also in short supply. There are stories of shops along the path of the raid being looted of every shoe. A few of Morgan's men being seen riding barefoot. Many of the men wore large, noisy spurs and their hats pinned up on one side with a crescent or a star. Pinning up their hat on the side of their dominant hand allowed the men to wield their sword or Bowie knife without Knosking or slicing off the brim of their hat. Even the horses were there own, either brought from home or purchased with their own money. Confounding as it may be to comprehend, the Confederate Army did not supply its cavalrymen with horses. The Confederacy was simply too short of funds to do so. Lack of funds also extended to lack of weaponery. The men carried whatever weapons they owned or could get their hands upon. Not all the men had been furnished with Confederate issued guns. Some carried their own hunting rifles. Confederate sabres were often abandoned in favor of Bowie knives, which were far easier to wield. Supplies such as blankets and camp gear were insufficient for the number of men. Lucky men carried a woolen blanket provided by a loving wife or mother. Furthermore, this ragged group was completely cut off from Confederate supply."

Eyewitness-The Civil war As We Lived It—The American Iliad by Otto Eisenschiml & Ralph Newman pub by The Universal Library 1947

Pg. 42 June 1861 Camp Randolph, Chickasaw Bluffs, Miss. William Howard Russel, a London newspaperman ".We returned to the steamer and proceded onward to another landing, protected by a battery, where we were received by a guard dressed in uniform, who turned out with some appearance of soldierly smartness. The general told me the corps was composed of gentlemen planters and farmers. They had all clad themselves, and came from the best families in the state of Tennessee."

WEBSITE-16TH Tennessee Volunteer Infantry Regiment: Clothing, Arms and Equipment

Pg.1 June 6, 1861 Savannah Republican, Georgia "The coat is to be a short tunic of cadet gray cloth, double-breasted, with two rows of buttons down the breast, two inches apart at the waist, and widening towards the shoulders.-The pantaloons are to be made of sky-blue cloth, full in the legs. The buttons to be of plain gilt, convex form, three-quarters of an inch in diameter…trimmings blue for infantry…(they) will bear only the number of the regiment."

LETTERS TO SECRETARY CHASE FROM THE SOUTH, 1861 American Historical Association, 1899

Pg. 47 Letter from T.D. Winter June 10, 1861 "…Some of the troops were comfortably equipped, while many had no military clothing, their arms were mostly what was taken from the Baton Rouge and Little Rock Arsenals, and were the old flint locks altered to percussion…The best appearing and best drilled Regiments as far as I have seen are the Mississippi Regt. But None of them have the stamina or soldierly bearing that marks the companies that I have seen Since my return North…My opinion is that our soldiers have the advantage of them in discipline strength and better officers…"

OK, Yankee, we'll see.

GRANDFATHER'S JOURNAL (Franklin Lafayette Riley) Company B Sixteenth Mississippi Infantry Volunteers Harris' Brigade Mahone's Division Hill's Cops, A.N.V. May 27, 1861-July 15, 1865 Austin C. Dobbins Morningside 1988

Pg. 19 Wedesday, June 26, 1861 Camp Clark "Wrote letters to Papa and Balsorah, to Papa, thanking him for the package of food as well as underclothes and socks…"

THE CONFEDERATE SOLDIER by LeGrand J. Wilson pub. by Memphis State Univ. press 1973

Pg. 21 "I shall never forget the 9th day of July, 1861. My company (the First Mississippi Regiment) was ordered to meet at Wall Hill, a village in the western part of Marshall County, Miss. to start for Iuka, Miss…My young wife insisted that I shood take her nice sole leather trunk (a wedding present),and she packed it with all my best clothes, a fine pair of shoes, embroidered pair of slippers, comb, brush, toilet articles and shaving apparatus. They would not allow me to make any suggestions or have anything to do in the premises. My old Nurse Rose rolled up a lounge feather bed blankets, pillows, etc., and I really had more baggage than the entire company possessed six monthes later on….We reached Iuka about 5P.M. In the meantime we had a regular July rain and thunderstorm, which did not add much to our comfort, but we had to learn to be soldiers, and we stood it like little men. It was amusing to see the men sheltering themselves. They were afraid to take advantage of a tree on account of the lightning, hence bushes were in demand. A few of the boys had unbrellas, and each was out in an open space and had half a dozen occupants…"

Unmbrellas? Really? I wonder how long those lasted.

GRANDFATHER'S JOURNAL (Franklin Lafayette Riley) Company B Sixteenth Mississippi Infantry Volunteers Harris' Brigade Mahone's Division Hill's Cops, A.N.V. May 27, 1861-July 15, 1865 Austin C. Dobbins Morningside 1988

Pg. 24 Friday, July 12, 1861, Camp Clark "…Package of shoes arrived from Papa. The shoes are stiff but I'll get used to them in time. I appreciate them very much…"

SOUTHERN INVINCIBILITY Wiley Sword St. Martin's Oress 1999

Pg. 49 4th Alabama Capt. Nat Dawson July 14 1861 "…On July 14 Nat Dawson confided how he was becoming "exceedingly lazy" about his army career. "My spare time is spent in studying tactics, and reading (news) papers." Only the purchase of natty new uniforms for the company-grey pants with a black stripe, close-fitting grey flannel jackets with a black collar and wristbands, and grey caps with linen havelocks-seemed to briefly replenish the unit's sagging esprit de corps..."

GRANDFATHER'S JOURNAL (Franklin Lafayette Riley) Company B Sixteenth Mississippi Infantry Volunteers Harris' Brigade Mahone's Division Hill's Cops, A.N.V. May 27, 1861-July 15, 1865 Austin C. Dobbins Morningside 1988

Pg. 25 Tuesday, July 16, 1861 Camp Clark "...we are going to Richmond. Actually, we are not ready to leave. To equip even 1000 men is a tremendous task. We still lack knapsacks, cooking equipment, blankets, tents and clothing. When we receive our knapsacks, they say, we will be ready to leave..."

LAW'S ALABAMA BRIGADE IN THE WAR BETWEEN THE UNION AND THE CONFEDERACY by J. Gary Laine & Morris M. Penny White Mane Pub. Co. 1996

Pg. 20 15th Alabama Infantry July 27, 1861 "The group sported new homemade grey uniforms with red trim."

Red trim for infantry? So much for uniform regulations

THROUGH SOME EVENTFUL YEARS-Diary of Susan Bradford Eppes Press of the J.W. Burke Co. 1926

Pg. 157 July 28th, 1861 "...Colonel Robert Howard Gamble is organizing "Gamble's Artillery" and Charley Hopkins has enlisted in that company and so have many others from Tallahasse. Aunt Sue brought a beautiful piece of French opera flannel and asked me to make Charley two shirts. I am a little doubtful as to my ability but if I find it too difficult I can get my Lulu to finish them for me; she sews so neatly and she makes all my clothes, under Mother's direction. These shirts are blue and are to have real silver buttons, which Aunt Sue has had made at the jewelers. She says silver will not tarnish nas common metal buttons might do. Mr. Pratorius is making Charley's uniform. I suppose I will learn all the different uniforms after awhile. The infantry is grey, trimmed with blue, the buttons are of brass and the officers have gold lace on their sleeves, a chevron they call the design on the sleeves; a captain has three gold bars on his collar; the privates do not have any gold lace. Charley is in an artillery company and they wear a little red, but the uniform is grey, too. Cousin William Bradford is in a cavalry unit and his grey uniform is trimmed with con-color. They all look fine to me and I grow more patriotic all the time but sister Meg says that is because I am not married..."

THE CONFEDERATE SOLDIER by Le Grand J. Wilson pub. by Memphis State Univ. Press 1973

Pg 30-31 "We were in camp during July and August…During the fifth week letters from home brought the pleasant intelligence that the good people held a mass meeting at Wald Hill for the benefit of the Alcorn Rifles, and readily made up a purse of $2,000 to purchase uniforms for the company. This indeed, was pleasant news, good news for the boys. It showed that the dear ones at home were "thinking" about us, and studying our welfare. It was a pleasant reminder, and had more effect in dispelling the blues than all the games. They knew that the State of Mississippi nor our dear little Confederacy had Quartermaster's supplies for her soldiers; and as we expected to be ordered north into Kentucky, by the time the goods could be purchased and made up, cold weather would be coming on, and we would really be in need of heavier clothing. God bless these home folks.

We were requested at to send home our measures as a committee of ladies and merchants had gone to Memphis to purchase the goods. Luckily, we found a tailor in the regiment, and had him detailed to measure the men, which was accomplished, and the measures sent home.

Some one must be sent back for these uniforms and Quartermaster's stores. Who would be the lucky man? That was thiry-nine years ago (old comrade) and I don't know how the question was decided, but I do know that the writer received the appointment, and as the boys boarded the east-bound train for Bowling Green, Kentucky, I started west for home, the happiest man in the regiment, and reached Holly Springs at 9 o'clock that night. Securing a buggy and driver, I was soon on my way to the old homestead, eighteen miles west….Next morning we rode over to Brock's Chapel…Now it was changed into a military workshop to manufacture clothing for Confederate soldiers. Six sewing machines occupied the altar. Two tables were erected upon the pews for the tailor who had volunteered to cut the clothing, and assist the ladies in making it up. The whole audience of twenty-five or more mothers, wives and daughters were busy at work….I was astonished at the amount of work accomplished, and the quantity of clothing the good people had prepared foe "the boys," as they loved to call them.

As I was present and assisted in packing, I remember something of the quantity: 102 suits complete, gray uniforms, 400 shirts, 200 pair of drawers, 500 pairs home knit woolen socks, besides a host of extra articles for soldiers I might find in need, and last a box of nicely rolled bandages and soft clothes for the surgeons."

16TH TENNESSEE INFANTRY VOLUNTEER REGIMENT : Clothing, Arms and Equipment (website)

Memphis Daily Avalanche August 1861 asked the wives, mothers and daughters to make each man "…Two pairs of pants in heavy brown or gray mixed jeans, …One roundabout, or army jacket, of the same material…One heavy vest of jeans, linsey, or kersey. One overshirt of woolen or mixed goods, One or two pairs of drawers...Two pair of heavy woolen socks. One good blanket...An overcoat, or loose sack coat, or hunting shirt with belt."

Notice that brown is the first mentioned color. Also, I wonder how they expected the average person to manufacture all those clothes.

"DEAR MOTHER; DON'T GRIEVEABOUT ME. IF I GET KILLED I'LL ONLY BE DEAD." ed by Mills Lane pub by The beehive Press 1977

Pg. 42 August 1, 1861 A.F. Boyd to his Father-from Big Shanty, Georgia; Dear Father; "... We are well. We are now preparing to go to Virginia. We will leave some time next week. As Mr. McAfee has a furlough to go home, I will send for some things by him. I want you to send me a pair of suspenders and two shirts. Have them made of good strong cloth, out of something that won't show dirt. I want them to wiat (wear?) over my other shirts. The other boys are getting them. Now is the time to get them, for when we get to Virginia thet will not be easily gotten. I will thank you if you will speed this thing. Mr. McAfee will show you what kind of material to get..."

The Pinkerton Decective Agency's Reports to General McClellan

Report of T. Webster on trip to Memphis & Knoxville, Aug. 7, 1861 Wed., July 31st, 1861 "...At Iuka Camp 1500 not armed, all uniformed."

Aug. 2nd, 1861, "...Camp Sneed is about a mile from Knoxville. There is 600 men, not armed, all uniformed."

THE CONFEDERATE VETERAN VOL. XIX 1911

Pg. 370 August 1911 Raymond, Miss. In War Times-Reminiscences by One Who Was A Child at the Time by Estelle Trichel Oltrogge "I was only six years old when the war began...

One of the first things the ladies of Raymond did was to organize a sewing society for the benefit of the soldiers. The Episcopal chuch (St. Mark's) was the place of meeting and the Misses Peyton, Dabney, Nelson, Gray, Belcher, Alston, Mrs. Gibbs, and my mother were prominent in the movement. From time to time boxes of clothing were sent to the soldiers. Our church bells were given to be made into cannon."

Websight 16th Tennessee Volunteer Infantry Regiment

In August 1861, the Military and Financial Board placed a notice in the Fayetteville (TN) Observer appealing to "the wives, mothers and daughters, of Tennessee to manufacture woolen goods and stockings for those who are defending their homes" also to "prepare goods for one suit of clothing and knit two pairs of stockings. If this shall be done, every soldier will be amply clothed & provided against the suffering of a winter campaign." Two weeks later in the Memphis Daily Avalanche they were asked to make for each man "Two pairs of pants of heavy brown or gray mixed jeans...One roundabout, or army jacket, of the same material...One heavy vest of jeans, linsey or kersey. One overshirt, of some woolen or mixed goods. One or two pairs of drawers...Two pair of heavy woolen socks. One good blanket... An overcoat, or loose sack coat or hunting shirt with belt." Daniel Rouse,7th Tennessee, 14 August 1861 wrote "our clothes are beginning to give out and the worst of it is we cannot get any more."

Extreeme example of supply from home folks, the equipment these troops were issued must've been mostly home-made or civilian cut.

REBEL SONS OF ERIN Ed Glasen Guild Press of IN 1993
September 1861

Tenth Tennessee-"...Fancy uniforms, bought personally by McGavock, arrived in September. The new look gave the lads the appearance of Tennessee Zouaves. The jacket and pants were Confederate grey with scarlet trim, and best of all, the insides of the jackets as well as the shirts, were bright scarlet. The commissioned officers also crimson and gold trimming on their jacket sleeves. The enlisted men took good care of the jackets for a while; but Fort Henry was still hot in the fall. Soon the area was swarming with ditch diggers in bright red shirts which stood out for miles around..."

REMINISCENCES OF A SOLDIER OF THE ORPHAN BRIGADE Lt. L.D. Young Paris Ky

Pg. 12 "...The 6th of September (1861) found me in this town (Paris, Ky), where I began preparations for the life of a soldier, by substituting my "pumps" for "Brogans," which I knew would be more suitable, really indespensible for a soldier on the march over rough and rugged roads. I sent back home my pumps and horse, the latter afterward confiscated and appropriated by the Yanks. Now I am sure my Brogans presented a striking and ludicrous contrast to my "clawhammer blue broadcloth and gold buttons, and to which I shall have occasion to refer to again. But I was going to war and why should I care for comment or criticism? That night found me in Lousville, a shy, cringing guest of the Old Lousville Hotel, my Brogans giving me more concern than anything else, being in such striking contrast to my clawhammer broadcloth and gold buttons...Federal officers, aides and orderlies, who were stopping there; that humbug Kentucky "neutrality" no longer being observed. I was now almost ready to call on the Lord to save me. But my fears were intensified when a gentleman of middle age, whom I had noticed eying me closely, walked across the room, putting a hand on my shoulder and asked me to a corner of the room. "Angels and ministers of grace defend me"-in the hands of a detective. I'm gone now! Noticing my look of fear and trepidation, he said, "compose yourself young man, I am your friend-the shoes you wear (Oh, the tell-tale shoes! Why didn't I keep my pumps) lead me to believe you meditate joining the army and if I'm mistaken you are aiming to go South to join the Confederates." I was now halting between two opinions; was he aiming to have me commit myself, or was he really a friend? But proceeding, he said, "It is but natural that you should suspect me, but I am you friend nevertheless, and am here to advise and assist young men like you in getting through the lines (a somewhat calmer feeling came over me now) and you will have to be very cautious, for I fear your Brogans are a tell-tale-(Ihad already realized that). "You see," said he, "excitement is running high and almost everybody is under suspicion, myself with others." I ventured to ask his name, which he readily gave me as Captain Coffee of Tennessee, to me a very singular name.

Feeling sure of his man and continuing, he said, "The train that leaves here this morning will likely be the last for the state line (and sure enough it was) and you will find excitement running high at the station; they have guards to examine all passengers and their baggage, and when you reach the station go straight to the ticket office, secure your ticket and go to the rear of the train. Go in and take the first vacant seat and for Heaven's sake, if possible, hide your Brogans, for I fear they may tell on you." I had by this time become thoroughly convinced that he was really my friend and decided to take his advice....Quickly procuring my ticket and entering the car, I secured the rear seat and with fear and trembling attempted to hide my Brogans by setting my satchel on them. (We had no suitcases then.) ...The train guards or inspectors-fully armed- were busy examining passengers and their baggage. My heart almost leaped from my bosom as they came down the aisle. But just before they reached the rear of the car the bell rang and the train started. The guards rushed for the door, leaving me and one or two others unquestioned and unmolested...."

UNIFORMS OF THE CIVIL WAR by Robin Smith & Ron Field Lyons Press 2001

Pg.235 "...observed by a correspondent of the Register of Rock Island, Illinois, on 11 September 1861:"... The uniform of the Confedrate army (of the West) is multiform. They are not uniformes at all, generally speaking, it is impossible to distinguish a colonel froma private. The only mark of distinction about them, except for their arms, is a piece of flannel stitched to the left shoulder. I was told that white flannel was the distinguishing mark of the troops, yellow that of Arkansas, red that of Louisiana, and so on. Of couse this only applies to the Southwest."

OK, so much for uniformity.

BROKENBURN-The Journal of Kate Stone 1861-1865 ed. By John Q. Anderson La. State Univ. Press Baton Rouge

Pg. 53 Sept. 16 1861 Kate and her brother "went to Omega (La.) this afternoon to buy flannel. Could get only red for Brother's underclothes and did not get enough of that. Will have to finish the set with yellow…"

A CIVIL WAR DIARY OF A UNION WOMAN IN THE SOUTH ed by George Washing ton cable pub by The Devon Press 1893

Sptember 25, 1861 New Orleans "When I opened the door of Mrs. F's room…the rattle of two sewing-machines and a blaze of color met me…

"Ah, G., you are just in time to help us; these are coats for Jeff Thompson's men. All the cloth in the city is exhausted; these flannel-lined oil-cloth table-covers are all we could obtain to make overcoats for Thompson's poor boys. They will be very warm and serviceable."

"Serviceable, yes! The Federal army will fly when they see those coats! I only wish I could be with the regiment when these are shared around." Yet I helped make them.

Seriously, I wonder if any soldiers will ever wear thease remarkable coats-the most bewitching combination of brilliant, intense reds, greens, yellows and blues in big floweres meandering over as vivid grounds, and as no table-cover was large enough to make a coat, the sleeves of each were of a different color and pattern. However, the coats were duly finished. Then we set to work on gray pantaloons, and I have just carried a bundle to an ardent young lady who wishes to assist…"

I'd loved to have seen those coats, and I would have worn one rather than being without an overcoat. But, seriously, can you picture someone wearing one? So much for an imposing, martial image.

DIARY OF A CONFEDERATE SOLDIER John S. Jackman of the Orphan Brigade ed. by William C. Davis Univ. S.C. Press 1990

Pg. 13 Sept. 26th, 1861 (getting ready to leave for the Rebel army) "…W.S. said to me, "Let us go to Bloomfield to-night, and join the party going through to Dixie!" or something to that effect. I had scarcely thought of such a thing before, but in an instant my mind was made up, and I answered, "All right." I immediately returned home and put on a heavy suit of cloths, and tried to slip off from the folks, but they divined my purpose. I told them I would only be gone a few days-…Taking with me but a traveling shawl, I mounted and joined W.S. at his home…"

Another reference to a shawl as men's appaeral.

Pg. 17 Sept. 29th 1861 "…We waded a deep creek without breaking ranks-it would not have been soldierly to have done otherwise-and my boots drew to my feet so, when in the sun, that I could not walk…"

DIARY OF A CONFEDERATE SOLDIER John S. Jackman of the Orphan Brigade ed by William C. Davis S.C. Univ Press 1990

Pg. 18 Oct. 1st 1861 "…We commenced camp life- learning how to cook, pitch tents, drill etc. etc. I could not walk about much, my feet were so sore. Afterwards all the nails came off my toes. Saw my brother Joe and several old aqaintances of the 2d. I had expected to see the soldiers better clad than I found them-they were very ragged and dirty…"

Pg. 19 Rowlett's Station, Ky. Oct 2d. 1861 "…Just before daylight, my time came to go on vidette, and I had not been on post long before I heard many hooves clattering on the pike, advancing with the rattling of sabres, and loud talk. My hair at first went on end, but soon the horsemen were close up, and I could see through the grey light of morning, their still greyer uniforms. They were scouts returning to camp…"

THE CONFEDERATE VETERAN VOL. 1

Oct. 1893 Pg. 308 A Queer Order: "I remember the first battle order I ever heard. It was at Fort Donelson, in the fall of 1863 (Ed.-this remeberance had to have been in the fall of 1861, due to the fact that Fort Donelson was surrenderedon Feb. 16, 1862).

There were only about half a dozen companies there, drilling and fortifying. The senior Captain was Tom Beaumont, of Clarksville, with whom I was messing.

In those days we had not given up all home habits; we wore white shirts and underclothes, had washing done, kept measureably clean, and every night went to bed in our tents, undressing and retiring "like folks."

One day it was rumored that the gunboats were in the river blow us, and coming up. About midnight, we were all sleeping soundly, the long roll began to beat in the company stationed on the riverbank. At once there was a stir in camp; officers were calling the men to fall in; there was hurrying to and fro. Captain Beaumont was always when on duty in faultless dress and now he did not neglect his toilet. Quickly he put on his uniform, buckled on his sword, and stepped out of his tent to take command of his company.

But the men had not been as thoughtful as he. They sprang up and grasped their muskets, and formed line in front of their tents, but every man of them had forgotten to put on his trousers, and they stood there, in the starlight, in their night-clothes like "sheeted ghosts," trembling with cold and excitement. As the captain and I stepped out, and his eye glanced along the line, his sense of propriety got the better of his military ardor, and he shouted out his first command, "Confound your fool souls, go and put on your breeches!" In a moment the whole stuation dawned on the men, and with shouts of laughter they prepared for battle by donning that needful article of apparel. But it was a false alarm, and they soon took off their breeches and went to sleep."

A Keystone Rebel-The Civil War Diary Of Joseph Garey, Hudsen's Battery Mississippi Volunteers ed by David A. Welker pub by Thomas Pub 1996

Pg. 33 Oct. 6th 1861 Camp Beauregard, Ky. "We received a uniform this morning from the citizens of Panola Co. & also a goodly number of blankets and underclothes from the same kind donators…"

Supply from home folks.

REMINISCENCES OF A PRIVATE William E. Bevins of the First Arkansas Inf. C.S.A. Univ. Ark. Press 1992

Pg. 99 Retreat from Perryville "…October 9th(1862) we marched fifteen miles and passed Harrodsburg…Here George Thomas and I each bought three yards of undyed jeans to make ourselves some trousers when we got back south…"

THE CIVIL WAR LETTERS OF CAPTAIN ELLIOT H. FLETCHER OF MILL BAYOU, MISSISSIPPI COUNTY, ARK. July to Dec. 1861 Pulaski County Historical Society, 1963

Letter from Elliot H. Fletcher Jr. to Elliot H. Fletcher, Sr. Oct. 20, 1861 "…There is a considerable amount of clothing coming from Ark. And other sources for Hardee's Brigade-I will endeavor to get all I can-…The Ark. Troops are poorly clad and badly equipped but are far better soldiers than any here-…"

REMINISCENCES OF A PRIVATE William E. Bevins of the First Arkansas Inf. C.S.A. Univ. Ark. Press 1992

Pg. 107 "October 24th,(1862) camped about six miles from Knoxville. Here we were given time to wash and dry our clothes. On this raid we had only one suit and to get it clean meant to strip, wash, let the clothes dry on or hang them on bushes to dry, while we waited… George Thomas and I brought out our white jeans which we had bought in camp Dick Robinson, and had carried all these miles. We got some copperas from a kind old rebel lady, took walnut hulls and dyed our cloth. It was a good job, too…"

UNIFORMS OF THE CIVIL WAR Lord, Wise, A.S. Barnes & Co. 1970

Pg. 27 October 30, 1861 Columbus, Ky. Confederate troops under General Leonidas Polk by a correspondent of the New York Herald: "...The troops were so rough, ill-clad and un-uniformed did they appear, that there seems a great room for improvement. About half the soldiers I saw there were uniformed, while the balance had an Army cap, coat, pants with a stripe or military mark of some kind, and the rest simply some ordinary (civilian) costume..."

UNIFORMS OF THE CIVIL WAR Lord, Wise, A.S. Barnes & Co. 1970

Pg.17 Hancock, Enoch 3rd Tennessee Infantry A.C. No. 1528 9-19 Tennessee State Archives, Special Collection. Enoch Hancock was a private in the 3rd Tennessee Infantry, camped near Bowling Green, Ky. in Nov. 1861 in a letter home, wrote: "I have drawn one of the heavy army overcoats and will have no use for the other one, (sent from home). Captain Clarke made a requisition, and wants the whole company uniformed alike..."

A CIVIL WAR DIARY OF A UNION WOMAN IN THE SOUTH ed by George Washington Cable pub by The De Vinne Press 2005

Pg. 191 Nov. 26, 1861 "The lingering summer is passing into those mistry autum days I love so well, when there is gold and fire above and around us. But the glory of the natural and the gloom of the moral world agree now well together. This morning Mrs. F came to my room in dire distress. "You see," she said, "cold weather is coming on fast, and our poor fellows are lying out at night with nothing to cover them. There is a wail for blankets, but there is not as blanket in town. I have gathered up all the spare bed-clothing and now want every available rug or table-cover in the house. Can't I have yours,G? We must make these small sacrifices of comfort and elegance, you know, to secure independence and freedom."

"very well," I said, denuding the table. "This may do for a drummer boy."

UNIFORMS OF THE CIVIL WAR Lord, Wise, A.S. Barnes & Co. 1970

Pg.29 Columbus Ky. December 1861 the Freeport Weekly Press concerning Confederate reinforcements: "...Since the Battle of Belmont, (November 7 1861) Columbus has been largely reinforced. The Arkansas and Tennessee troops looked tolerably well clothed, but by no means uniformed. The new regiments from Louisiana (13th Infantry), and Mississippi (3rd Infantry) were nothing more than mobs. They had no equipments of any kind, and most of them wore blue blankets with holes cut out for their arms, and girded around their waists with rope..."

Not even multiform. Sartorial chaos.

THE JOURNAL OF JULIA LeGRAND Everrett Wadley co 1911

Pg. 35 December 1st, 1861 New Orleans "Just completed another bundle of clothes for poor Claude, which we hope will reach him before Christmas, the other having failed to reach him. Mrs. Brtown (Mrs. Shepherd) went with me to Lyon's to choose his coats and gloves. We have roasted some coffee and made some cake, which we have stuffed in his pillow. I wonder how long the poor boy's head will lie peacefully on the latter. We have cut up our flannel double-gowns to make him shirts, as everything is so dreadfully high these blockade times. I have longed for money that I might send him many things to gladden both, his heart and those of his comrades, in their darksome little log huts at Manchac...."

A Keystone Rebel-The Civil War diary Of Jesepg Garey, Hudsen's Battery Mississippi Volunteers ed by David a. Welker pub by Thomas Pub. 1996

Pg. 46 Dec. 2nd, 1861 "...Our camp reminds us to day of the picture painted by historians of the Valley of Forge during that dark period of the revolution with the exception of our being better clothedthan they were for we have no barefooted or naked soldier; but otherwise it presents the same dismal aspect..."

SOJOURNS OF A PATRIOT The Field and Prison Papers of An Unreconsrtucted Confederate edited with commentary by Richard Bender Abell & Fay Adamson Gecik Southern heritage Press 1998

Letters of Pvt. Augustus Pitt Adamson
Pg. 17 Camp Bailey, Campbell County. Georgia Dec 5th, 1861 Dear Sister, "...I should like to have a light bed quilt, for we will not draw blankets..."

FROM THAT TERRIBLE FIELD-CIVIL WAR LETTERS OF JAMES M. WILLIAMSON, TWENTY-FIRST ALABAMA VOLUNTEER INFANTRY by John Kent Folmer pub by Univ Al Press 1981

Pg. 10 Dec. 12th, 1861 Fort Gaines (near Mobile, Al.) Dear Lizzie, "...We've had another cold storm from the north, dust and smoke have filled my tent for twenty-four hours, and my eyes are sore as a consequence and face and clothes as dirty as they well can be, we were to have been inspected this morning by one of the high officials, but on account of the rough seas, I suppose, he did not come and instead of the inspection our colonel put us through a very severe drill; it was hard on account of the wind which blew so fiercely, drifting the sand in our faces while it penetrated with cold our thin blue uniform, the knapsacks on our backs cap-sheaved our misery…"

Pg. 13 Dec. 24th, 1861 Fort Gaines Dear Lizzie, "…I like private life very well; have just been through my first tour of picket duty and had a jolly good time of it: for want of something better to write about, I will tell you its story-Saterday morning at 71/2 o'clock we started for the last post of the picket-King one other man from the infantry and myself-each carried his arms and equipments complete- a blanket with two ends tied to-gether thrown like a scarf over the right shoulder; a haversack filled with eatables, and a canteen full of water, an oil-cloth covering, and water proof leggings tied to the blanket made a heavy load, under which we marched to the post of the advanced picket…"

SOJOURNS OF A PATRIOT The Field and Prison Papers of An Unreconsrtucted Confederate edited with commentary by Richard Bender Abell & Fay Adamson Gecik Southern heritage Press 1998 letters of Pvt. Augustus Pitt Adamson

Pg. 20 Camp Griswoldville, Jones County, Georgia Dec. 16th, 1861 Dear Father, "…I need nothing at present but will want a pair of shoes before very long and they cannot be got here…"

LIFE IN DIXIE DURING THE WAR by Mary A.H. Gay Charles P. Byrd Pub. 1897

Pg. 42 "A patriotic co-operation between the citizens of Decatur and Atlanta (Georgia) soon sprang up, and in that, as in all things else, a social and friendly interchange of thought and feeling and deed existed; and we were never so pleased as when aiding each other in the preparation of clothing and edibles for "our soldiers," or in some way contributing to their comfort,

Many of us who had never learned to sew became expert handlers of the needle, and vied with each other in producing well-made garments; and I became a veritable knitting machine. Becides the discharge of many duties incident to the times and tending to useful results, I knitted a sock a day, long and large, and not coarse, many days in succession. At the midnight hour the weird clock of knitting needles chasing each other round and round in the formation of these useful garments for the nether limbs of "our boys," was no unusual sound, and tears and orizons blended with woof and warp and melancholy sighs. For at that dark hour, when other sounds were shutr out, we dared to listen with bated breath to "the still, small voice" that whispered in no unmistakeable language suggestions which would have been rebuked in the glare of the noonday sun.

No mother nor sister nor wife nor aunt of a Confederate soldier, need be told what were the depressive suggestions of the "still, small voice" on divers occasions.

When the knitting of a dozen pairs of socks was completed, they were washed, ironed and neatly folded by one of our faithful negro women, and I then resumed the work of preparing them for their destination. Each pair formed a distinct package. Usually a pretty necktie, a pair of gloves, a handkerchief and letter, deposited in one of the socks, enlarged the package. When all was ready, a card bearing the name of the giver, and a request to "inquire within," was tacked on to each package… And then these twelve packages were formed into a bundle, and addressed to an officer in command of some company chosen to be the recipient of the contents."

Trans Mississippi

INTRODUCTION

Sartorial chaos is the term that comes to mind when reading of the uniforms in the Trans-Mississippi Department. The men were clad in a confusing mixture of militia uniforms, civilian clothing, federal uniforms (or parts thereof) captured when the federal forts were taken, Indian clothing and homemade uniforms. Due to the complexity of colors and styles, and the prevalence of blue, the Confederate troops often usen strips of cloth tied around their arms to designate them from the enemy. The lack of adequate clothing was much more acute here, and the desperate appeals were made to the homefolks for any article of clothing they could spare.

UNIFORMS OF THE CIVIL WAR by Robin Smith & Ron Field Lyons Press 2001

TEXAS Pg. 211 1861 William D. Cater, member of The Lone Star Defenders, Co. C, 3rd Texas cavalry, recalled that his uniform consisted of: 'Black coats, with vests to match, brown (Huntsville made) jeans pants, black hats and black boots made of calfskin tanned leather. It looked well enough but was very hot to wearin the summer; however, we wore them when ready to start. Nothing was said about the color of the shirt or cravat. Mine…was white and the neckwear was a black silk string tie. This, of course, was soon a thing of the past …

The 8th Texas Cavalry, also known as Terry's Texas Rangers, wore a great variety of dress during initial monthes of service. En route east with the first battalion of the reiment, R.C. Hilliard observed of their appearance in a letter home from New Iberia, dated 19 September, 1861: Some in Red, some in Blue-Brow(sic), Green, yellow-some in broad sombreros, some in caps, some without either, as daring a set as ever marched to battle.' After reaching New Orleans, the Daily Picayune of 30 September described the Tom Lubbock Rangers, Co.K, as being: '…all atheletic men and dress(ed) fantastically in hunting shirts of different materials, with large boots worn on the outside, coming over the knee, with Mexican spurs attached.

Some wore fancy Mexican pants trimmed down the side with little brass buttons (cochos), and silk sashes around their waists. Others had the Confederate flag, worked in different colored leathers to represent it, on the legs of their boots.' Captain John G. Walker, commander of the above company, was further described as wearing a buckskin hunting shirt that hugged his large form, 'immense boots, large Mexican spurs, sombrero, and a 'beautifully worked' Mexican blanket across his shoulders. By late February, 1862, the clothing of this company was described as being 'shabby, ragged and dirty', the only element of uniformity being a red star on their hats and caps. Later in the war, the 8th Texas Cavalry attempted to introduce a hint of uniformity in their clothing by the addition of red trimmings to jackets, shirts and trousers…"

Red trimmings for cavalry. I guess they were making due with what they had.

UNIFORMS OF THE CIVIL WAR by Robin Smith & Ron Field Lyons Press 2001

Pg. 214 "…According to a memoir written by Private O.T. Hanks, The Texas Invincables, Co. K, 1st Texas Infantry, left home in the uniforms of 'good gray woolen goods cut and fitted by W.A. McClanahan and his helpers, and trimmed with blue collars and cuffs'. The Invincibles' accouterments were similiarly of local manufacture. One member recalled that their 'cartridge boxes were made of leather by our home saddlers and harness workmen,' while another confirmed that he and a local saddler had 'made each of the boys a leather built pistol and knife scabbard and cap box'….

UNIFORMS OF THE CIVIL WAR by Robin Smith & Ron Field Lyons Press 2001

Pg. 216 "…Evidence suggests that one, if not more of the companies comprising the 4th Texas originally wore dark blue U.S. Army sack coats, and possibly also trousers of the same provenence. Although the Sandy Point Mounted Rifles, also known as the Henderson guards, enlisted in civilian dress, each man was issued a 'blue sack coat, very full, almost in the shape of a gown', together with blue trousers, a pair of shoes, two pairs of socks, and two shirts, whilst at Camp Van Dorn near Houston. It would seem reasonable to assume that these were large size coats taken over by the state with the capture of Federal military property. Similiarly, members of the Grimes County Grays, Co. G, and the Porter Guards, Co.H, were photographed wearing sack coats of dark color…"

MILITARY COLLECTOR & HISTORIAN-vol XLVIII,No.4 Winter 1996

Confederate Clothing of the Houston Quartermaster Depot by Frederick R. Adolphus Chief Quartermaster of the District of Texas was Captain Edward C. Wharton.

"Wharton contemplated making talmas in lieu of great coats. Again, this plan was never fulfilled due to a shortage of materials. His pattern, however, called for three yards of double width cadet gray cloth, or 61/4 yards of other single width woolen goods, with 8 buttons each. It was to be sewn with flax thread. The talma was cut similar to an overcoat. Wharton did issues a few talmas, bu these were the India-rubber models from Union stocks captured in San Antonio in 1861. He leaves no records of having made any of his own.

Stable frocks, also called fatigue frocks, were made in limited quantities. This article called for 51/2 yards of heavy, unbleached single width cotton goods. It required six white bone buttons and was sewn with flax thread. The stable frock was cut much like an overcoat.

Wharton made a small stock of overalls as well, which required three yards of heavy, unbleached single-width cotton goods and five white bone buttons. It was sewn with flax thread. Overalls were essentially large trousers that could be fit overt the wearer's regular trousers."

This source doesn't say to whom these overalls were issued. Probably engineer troops, if there were any, or to any "servants" engaged in construction work.

CADET GRAY & BUTTERNUT BROWN Thomas M. Arlikas Thomas Pub 2006

"Private S.A. Hale of the 7th Arkansas Infantry described how he was uniformed at one point in the war: "A broad brimmed flop hat, a good pair of Federal infantry shoes, some home made yarn socks, a pair of trousers too large in girth, and excxeedingly short of leg, a shirt made out of piano cover of flax or hemp, with large red figures or cornucopias, and the body color like the old womam's china…"

Now here's a shirt made of a piano cover. I wonder how common this was?

UNIFORMS OF THE CIVIL WAR by Robin Smith & Ron Field Lyons Press 2001

Pg. 234 Arkansas "…The Eldorado Sentinels,Co. A., were 'well-uniformed' in neat gray caps and frock coats, with black cap band, collar and cuffs.…The Camden Knights, Co. C., wore dark blue caps, pants and hunting shirts, the latter cut in varying styles, either plain or with light blue trim.…The Jacksonport Guards, Co.G., adopted light gray caps and trousers, with black cap bands and seam stripes. Their dark gray blouses had the company initials JG appliquéd on either side of the breast in black cloth capitol letters. …The City Guard, Co. H., 6th Arkansas Infantry, from Camden, enlisted in 'gray roundabout and pants trimmed with red' and 'glazed caps'.…The Ouchita Grays, Co. K., wore 'gray roundabouts and pants trimmed with green', with glazed caps.…"

UNIFORMS OF THE CIVIL WAR by Robin Smith & Ron Field Lyons Press 2001

Pg. 251 MISSOURI "...the 2nd Missouri Regiment, a pro-slavery unit organized in the city (St. Louis) during February 1861, adopted as a regimental uniform a dark gray zouave jacket and full pants, trimmed with blackcord; gray shirt; and gray cap with black top...The Emmet Guard wore blue tail coats faced with buff; and sky-blue pants with buff seam stripes. The Washington Blues had a similar coat with light blue facings, and dark blue pants with light blue stripes...."

BROTHERS IN GRAY-The Civil War Letters of the Pierson Family ed. by Thomas W. Cutrer & t. Michael Parrish La. State Univ. Press 1997 Ninth Louisiana

Pg. 81 David Pierson to William Pierson? Boston Mountains Ark. Feb. 22 1861 (1862) "... Half the men here have lost all their clothes. My trunk & things are safe, but I have not seen them for several days, the trains being ahead..."

CIVIL WAR STORIES Letters-Memoirs-Anecdotes Union and Confederate by Walbrook D. Swank pub by Burd Street Press 1996

Pg. 74 Sping 1861 "A Picturesque Army" General Price and his army have been described as follows:

"As few people have an idea of the character of the man, I give you a hasty pen-and-ink sketch, as he appeared to me during a brief interview. He is over six feet in height, with a frame to match, full but not portly, and straight as an Indian. His carriage is marked with dignitry, grace and gentleness, and every motion bespeaks the attitude and prescence of the well-bred gentleman. He has a large Websterian head, covered with growth of thick white hair, a high, broad, intellectual forehead, florid face, no beard, and a mouth among whose latent smiles you never fail to discoveer the iron will that surmounts all obstacles.

The army of General Price is made up of extremes. It is a heterogeneous mixture of all human compounds, and represents in its various elements every condition of Western life. There are the old and the young, the rich and poor, high and low, the grave and the gay, the planter and the laborer, farmer and clerk, hunter and boatman, merchant and woodsman-men, too who have come from every State, and been bronzed in every latitude, from the mountains of the Northwest to the Pampas of Mexico.

Every man has come from his homestead fitted with the best and strongest which loving mothers, wives and sisters could put upon him. And the spectacle presented as they are drawn up in line, whether for marching or inspection, necessarily forms an arabesque pattern of the most parti-colored crowd of people upon which human eyes have ever rested. Some are in black, full citizen's dress, with beaver hats and frock coats; some in homespun drab; some in gray, blue and streaked; some in nothing but red shirts pants, and big top-boots;

Some attempt a display with the old-fashioned militia uniforms of their forefathers; some have banners floating from thier "outer walls" in the rear; some would pass for our friend the Georgia Major, who used to wear nothing but his shirt-collar and a pair of spurs."

Some are in rags,
Some in bags,
And some in velvet gowns"

Well said.

WEBSITE-CONFEDERATE UNIFORMS & EQUIPMENT-Texas—Early Civil War Uniforms

San Antonio Express [San Antonio, Tx] March 25, 1861 "we are pleased to announce that the Quitman Rifles, under the command of Capt. W.L. Hill, are now organized. The uniform adopted by the company is a cadet jeans, trimmed with green…"

RAGS AND HOPE: The Recollections of Val C. Giles, Four Years With Hood's Brigade 4th Texas Inf. By Val C. Giles N.Y. 1967

Pg.23 April 1861 "We were a motley looking set" wrote a Texan. "In my company were about four different shades of grey, but the trimmings were all black braid. As far as pride went, we were all generals."

Website Missouri State Guard Historical Information

"The Guardsmen were loosely organized at best and brought whatever arms they had at home, if any. These were generally hunting rifles and shotguns. They had no uniforms and wore their everyday clothes, old Mexican war/Indian war/Federal uniforms, etc."

REMINISCENCES OF A PRIVATE-William E. Bevins of the 1st Arkansas Infantry, C.S.A. pub by Univ. Arkansas Press 1992

Pg. 7 Spring 1861 "When the war cry sounded, Capt. A.C.Pickett, a fine lawyer and a Mexican War veteran, made up our company and called it the "Jackson Guards." This company to the number of one hundred and twenty was formed of the best boys in the county. Sons of plantation-owners, lawyers, doctors, druggists, merchants-the whole Soutrh rose as one man, to defend its rights. The young men, many of us barely twenty years of age, knew nothing of war. We thought we could take our trunks and dress suits. We besieged Capt. Pickett and nearly drove him to distractionwith questions as to how many suits we should take. He nearly paralyzed us by telling us to leave behind all fancy clothes, and to take only one suit, a woolen top shirt, and two suits of underwear."

This tendancy for "oversupply" was everywhere in the South at the start of the war.

Website-WITT EDWARDS CSA UNIFORMS-

Spring 1861 The Blue and the Grey or Butternuts and Blue or Blue on Blue? "Colonel Demorse of the 29th Texas had this to say about uniforms in 1862, I had heard a great deal about Georgia cloth manufacture and Columbus has two mills, but none of the products that I could find or hear of were half as good as our homemade jeans."

1. "We have never drawn any clothing, shoes, salt or anything else from the Quartermaster department. What little clothing the men had they had collected for themselves."
2. "Aside from a few well worn butternut colored uniforms belonging to some veterans of Company "E" all the men looked stangely alike-mud colored or grey home spun jeans; red and white checked or brown wool shirts muddy brogans, wide low porkpie hats or an occasional Stetson."
3. "Of the five thousand one thousand are without arms many have not clothing, without shoes and what any one in their right senses would say was in a deplorable conditionlooking like Siberian exiles than soldiers." I have been in an almost nude condition."
4. "The regiment has not received any clothing for three months, and only a very small supply since November, so that a large part of the men are in a destitute condition. The destitution of clothing is very great, and much suffering and sickness prevails on account of it Camp on Beech Creek, November, 8, 1863" Brig. Gen. D.H. Cooper.
5. "The men were in very destitute condition as to clothing, and (owing to your change of the line of operations from the North Fork road to the Fort Smith road) temporarily out of flour." Hdqrs. Fagan's division, Waverly, Mo. October 19, 1864

    1.Newspaper ad" Wanted: jeans, linseys, white domestics, cottonades, yarn socks. For clothing for the soldiers. I will pay liberal prices for the above mentioned articles in any quantities, delivered at Washington (Arkansas) Geo. Taylor Capt. + A.Q.M. C.S.A.

    2."Cotton cards for sale. Cards for sale at Government clothing rooms. Linsey, jeans and socks taken in exchange at fair prices. Apply to Maj. J.D. Thomas Q.M. C.S.A.

> 3."All clothing designed by the citizens of Hempstead for Capt. Williamson's company, the "Southern Defenders," are requested to be delivered at the store of D. & V. Block by the 10th of November. The clothing needed for each member is on e coat, two pairs of pants, two pairs of socks, two pairs of drawers. It is to be hoped that the citizens of Old Hempstead will respond to the call, as the members of this company are sadly in need of the above articles. Geo. M. Williamson 2nd Lieut."

"Our poor Osages are almost necked for want of clothing."

"I wrote you sometime since for some clothing. If you have not sent them please forward them immediately."

"Pa, I wish you would send an overcoat oil cloth."

"I don't know whether you ever got my letter or not so I will emmiminate again first and formost I want a heavy comfort lined quilt or blanket or something equally as warm. Aheavy suit of clothes, jeans pants lined, pair of double boots, army overcoat with cape. Heavy woolen shirt onne heavy cotton shirt, and anything else you may think I need."

"I shall go back so as to get some clothes for you but there is no chance to get only to spin them but Charlotte and I can do it in two or three weeks."

"Mrs. Cline came in today to see me and has offered to help me about dyeing my cloth and help me to get it sown I will soon have some jeans for you and Perry and Claude."

"I would yet mention that the people cannot tell us from rebels is simply for this reason: as many of the bushwacking rebs as can get the Federal uniform wear them, if they kill one of our men or take one prisoner they strip them of all their clothing."

"A detachment of this division just arrived from Park Hill, Cherokee Nation, reports that seven of our Indians (3rd Indian Home Guard) known as Pins, were killed at that place a few days ago by a party of rebels wearing the federal uniform. This is not the only instance during the past yeart of small detachments of our troops having been entrapped by the enemy who were dressed in the federal uniform."

Maj. Gen. Taylor wrote Gen. Kirby Smith: "The Clothing Bureau is liberal in promise and utterly barren in performance. A radical change is imperatively required. The troops in the field are withour pay, insufficiently supplied with food, and almost destitute of shoes and clothing". Hdqrs. Trans-mississippi Department Shreveport, May 26 1864

MILUM by June Turney Young (geanealogical website)

Spring 1861 "George Washington Young served in the Confederate Army in the 2nd Missouri Cavalry under Joseph C. Shelby. He wasn't truthful about his age in order to be accepted on his fourteenth birthday and the Civil War was ended on his seventeenth birthday. He fought in the Battle of Pea Ridge and his family still has his Civil War overalls, boots and razor."

PEA RIDGE & PRARIE GROVE by William Baxter pub by Univ of Ark. Press 2000

Pg 17 Spring 1861 "...The ladies, too, caught the war sprit; uniforms, sashes and banners grew under their active hands; and when the fever was almost at its height, in marched the "Hempstead Rifles," from the Southern portion of the State. Most of them were fine-looking fellows, some of them men of wealth, position and influence; some of them in former years students of Arkansas College. Their march had been a long one, their drill was perfect, their step and look that of veterans, their arms and uniforms all that could be desired; their number, though small, seemed large to people unaccustomed to military spectacles; and when with drums beating and banners flying they marched into into the College grounds, and their tents rose as by magic through that hitherto peaceful enclosure, the enthusiasim of the people knew no bounds. A most liberal hospitality was manifested by the citizens; the ladies serenaded their defenders, and the soldiers in gallant style responded with "Advance the Flag of Dixie!" In imagination, Southern independence was achieved, and attentions were lavished upon the soldiers as if victory had already crowned their efforts. Then came the Third Louisiana Infantry, armed with the famous Mississippi rifle, admirable in drill and discipline, perfect in uniforms and accouterments, by far the best regiments in the South-West. These, however, with those before mentioned, were the only Southern troops that I ever saw in anything like a regular uniform, although on several occasions I saw the armies of Price, M'Culloch and Hindman...The Provost Marshal...came to her house and demanded her blankets and carpets for the use of the Confederate army..."

A SEMBLANCE OF A WEAPON Arms& equipment - Frontier Guard Discussion Board

Pg 9 April 1861 "Such a variety of weapons provided no end of frustration for those ordered to provide ammunition. Quartermaster Harding found how difficult it was providing ammuition to a company armed indifferently with weapons, no two of which were the same caliber. Some bullets were made in molds purchased by Harding before the war, and buckshot was crudely cast in bullet molds made from green oak logs. The supply of gunpowder was limited. It was not only used for ammunition but occasionlally as a substitute for salt...What ammunition there was for these weapons was often carried in cloth bags, powder horns, and trouser pockets for want of a proper cartridge box. Private Richard Hubbell carried bullets in one vest pocket, powder in another, and percussion caps in a third. One State Guardsman said his company was given a cloth bag filled with buckshot, and told to pour a handful in before firing. John Bell said those with cartridges carried them in their pockets, and those with shotguns carried powder in horns and shot in shot pouches. Without proper cartridge boxes, an army might become unarmed if their powder became wet…"

Pg. 13 "…Listed among the noted absecences of equipment is a lack of a common uniform. Keely's company, a pre-war St. Louis militia group that joined Parson's 6th Division,had dark blue frock coats and forage caps, and white buff leather. The Calloway Guards, of Burbridge's Infantry Regiment, were said to have been the only uniformed company at Carthadge, which Joseph Mudd said were grey in color.

For the most part, the men of the guard seemed to have worn clothes from home, which reflected their occupation and standing. When clothes wore out new clothing was produced. Henry Cheavens spent his time before Wilson's creek sewing shirts and pants. Cloth was plentiful, but the finished products were not.

Any commonality at all was due to color. Butternut, produced fromdyes in walnut hulls was an economical way to color homespun cloth. Butternut has been described as a rather tired looking brown, often with yelowish tones. The Guard was decribed by a Federal soldier at Carthedge as having no uniforms, being entirly clad in the

homespun butternut jeans worn by every Missouri farmer in those days. It was so common that the Guard has been referred to as the "Butternut Boys."

Probably the most unusual description of guardsmen comes from a period newspaper: "Here went one fellow in a shirt of brilliant green, on his side an immense cavalry sabre, in his belt two navy revolvers and a Bowie knife, and slung from his shoulder a Sharp's rifle. Right by his side was another, upon whose hip dangled a light medical sword, in his hand a double-barreled shotgun, in his boot an immense scythe.... Generally the soldiers were armed with shotguns and squirrel rifles. Some had the old flintlock muskets, a few had Minnie guns or sharp's or Maynard rifles, while all, to the poorest, had horses."

There was apparently no way to distinguish men of the different branches of service, except,the men assigned to the provost guard in the training camps on Cowskin Prarie were noted by Peter Lane as wearing red ribbons around their shoulders as a token oftheir office.

The absence of proper uniforms was not limited to the avervage private. Most officers lacked any indication of position or rank. Hans Adamson, in his book "Rebellion in Missouri" states that officers used pieces of colored cloth, sewn to their shoulders, as insignia. James Mudd, a very observant slodier in Clark's 3dr Division, noted that he saw only two uniformed Guard officers before Wilson's Creek. His regimental commander, Col. John B. Clark, Jr. wore a soldier's grey jacket and black military hat. The division commander, John B. Clark, was finely dressed in a black broadcloth frock coat and black slouch hat…"

Absolute sartorial chaos

Website FIRST MISSOURI BATTALION

April 1861 "…Again these men came straight off the farm, or were out of the city with little of no military experience. As such they arrive ready to enlist in the guard dressed in what they wore from day to day as Missouri citizens and civilians, (including civilian overalls made from cotton or wool jean)…At Cowskin Prarie in July 1861 many of the men in the Missouri State Guard had alrady gone through some of their clothes and were given bolts of cloth and patterns to make their own. It is thought that around 30% of the men had some uniformity on a company level even if it was motley and not regular army issue uniforms…"

ONE OF CLEBURNE'S COMMAND ed. By Norman D. Brown Univ. of Austin Press 1980

April 1861 A Regiment of Texas Lancers"…Lances for the regiment were being manufactured at Chapel Hill. Each man was required to furnish himself with the best horse he could procure, two suits of winter clothing, blankets, "a bowie knife and the best fire-arms he can obatain; if possible a double-barreled shotgun and six-shooter…"this will be the only Regiment of Lancers in the service, and Lancers are the most formidablecavalry in the world. We have chosen this arm at the earnest solicitation of Gen. (David) Twiggs. The lance simply takes the place of the sword in a change,and is much the most terrible weapon…"

Notice that this "fearsome weapon" never caught on

Pg.8 Oct. 1861 "We are put to some trouble about getting our clothes washed-sometimes we may have our clothes out and an order come to march and then we have to walk two or three miles to get out clothes-and then have to take them before they are dry…"

website UNIFORMS OF THE 3RD TEXAS CAVALRY Randy McDonald 2007

"…It is safe to say that there is no official uniform of the 3rd Texas Cavalry and that the entire regiment never all wore the same uniform. In fact, most of the time, the regiment probably wore a mixture of both civilian and military style clothing in a variety of colors, styles, and materials…We know, for example, that the well-to-do Company A from the Marshall area, all rode out of town wearing nice looking grey uniforms with black trim. The men in Company B did not have uniforms per se, but did make an effort to all purchase brown pants, black boots, and black hats. Few details are known about the clothing of the other companies but it is recorded that on some occasions the men had to tie strips of colored cloth on their arms so they could distinguish between units…"

April 1861 to December 1862 "…Almost all clothing during this period was supplied by local citizens and Ladies Aid societies who collected clothing and sewed a few uniforms as the Confererate Government was unavable to adequately supply uniforms. My estimate is that during this period, at least 75% of the regiment would be seen wearing nothing but civilian clothing including civilian vests, sack coats, and frock coats. The remaining 25% would be wearing a mixture of civilian and homespun style uniform parts...Any uniforms would have been mostly in the "common" or commutation style and made from loose-wooven wool-jean or jean cloth type of material rather than pure wool and often would have included wooden buttons. Grey would have been the favored color but more and more brown and butternut wool-jean would have appeared as the war drug on..."

WINTER OF 1862-1863

"By the Winter of 1862 the clothing of the third had become well-worn and they were noted as being "barefooted and naked."

Website "A Semblance of a Weapon" Arms & Equipment of the (Missouri) Frontier Guard

Spring 1861 "despite the apparent absence of equipment, some lucky units seemed very well supplied indeed. Richard Hubbell, of Captain Reeve's company, Steen's Cavalry regiment, was issued a tent, tin plate and cup, knife, fork, and spoon, presumably had a horse to carry it all. Listed among the noted absences of equipment is a lack of common uniform.

Major General Sterling Price, commander of the entire State Guard, did not apparently dress the part. Three soldiers from Missouri, Arkansas, and Louisiana all described Price as wearing a suit of linen clothes, not over clean, with a saber, and riding an old-looking gray horse. One man mistook him for just another old Missouri farmer. Fortunately, General Price did not need a fancy uniform to inspire his men..."

WEBSITE -confederateuniforms.org

April 5, 1861 Des Ark, Arkansas The costitutional Union-The Des Ark Rangers, "The uniform adopted by the rangers is a red flannel shirt, with deep blue breast and back, blue cuffs and black velvet collar with three rows of brass buttons in front; black pants with red stripes up the sides, U.S. Cavalry fatigue cap, with ostrich plume, with colt's Navy repeatersand U.S. Dragoon Sabers."

FOURTEEN HUNDRED AND 91 DAYS IN THE CON-FEDERATE ARMY A Journal Kept by W.W. Heartsill of Camp Life; Day by Day of the W.P. Lane Rangers From April 19, 1861 To May 20, 1865 ed. by Bell Irvin Wiley Broadfoot Pub. Co. Wilmington, N.C. 1987

Pg. 5 April 20, 1861 "…And now begins our first lessons in military service. We have no transportation, and upon every horse may be seen, either a coffee pot, frying pan, tin cup, or some article of camp equipage. Every man is supplied with cooked rations to last several days; and as to clothing and blankets, an old Texas Ranger would think us a Caravan, crossing the desert, with a tremendous stock of merchandise; than a regularly organized company going out Indian hunting in the far west. Now let your humble servent make a list of articles of board pet; (Who by the way is as pretty an animal as is in the Company; a jet black, with long wavy mane and tail; and as fat, and as plump as a Guinea pig,) Here's a maifest of Pet's cargo; myself, saddle, bridle, saddle blanket, curry comb, horse brush, coffee pot, tin cup, 20lbs. Ham, 200 biscuit, 5lbs. Ground coffee, 5lbs. Sugar, one large pound cake (presented me by Mrs. C.E.Talley) 6shirts, 6prs socks, 3prs drawers, 2prs pants, 2 jackets, 1pr heavy mud boots, one Colt's revolver, one small dirk, four blankets, sixty feet of rope with twelve inch iron pin attached; with all of these, and diverse and sundry little mementoes from friends. And when I tell you I am not an exception; you can imagine how we are packed up…"

Rebels Valiant-Second Arkansas Mounted Rifles (dismounted) Wesley Thurman Leeper Pioneer Press 1964

Pg 10 May 1861 Although a soldier in the Confederate Army for almost 3 ½ years, John Wesley Leeper never actually owned a Confederate uniform. Most of the time he wore "Yankee clothing taken from prisoners or deceased members of the enemy army."

"In the battle of Carthage the Confederates had no uniforms. The officers could be distinguished from the enlisted men only by bits of red flannel, or a piece of cotton cloth stitched on the arm or shoulder, on a homespun jacket or a broadcloth coat! Naturally, the bright clothes worn by the officers made them easy targets for the Federals, some of whom could actually hit what they aimed at!"

THE CONFEDERATE VETERAN VOL. XIX 1911

Pg. 287 May 1911 Fun In Camp by Clarence Key Spring 1861 "When the 2nd Texas were camped on Skull Creek, near San Antonio Texas…

"Some fellows from another regiment stopped at our campfire and entered into conversation with us. Somehow the question of graybacks came up, and our first sergeant began to speak, and suddenly stopped, saying "Wait a moment; I will not tell this story without witnesses." He looked around and called two men whom he saw, and when they came, he resumed the story. "One of our fellows," he said, "had a pair of buckskin trousers, and the graybacks in them were so numerous that they almost drove him crazy. One day when camped at noon he took advantage of the hot New Mexican sunshine and laid off his trousers. A few moments later he looked for his trousers, and the graybacks had dragged them into the shade of a wagon. Is that not so?" he asked his witnesses. "Yes," they said; "it is true, for we saw it."

Hey, I believe it

THE THIRD TEXAS CAVALRY IN THE CIVIL WAR by Doudlas Hale pub by Univ. of OK Press 1993

Pg. 30 June 1861 "…A public subscription in prosporous Harrison County collected enough money to equip each of the men in Company K with a smart new uniform in cadet gray, but most of the regiment were not so lucky. The troopers of company B had to purchase their own uniforms, and in doing so strove for style over function. The chose black coats, vests, hats and boots, and acquired a quantity of heavy brown jeans from the Texas prison shops sufficient to put them all in breeches. They looked fine on parade, but their uniforms were stifling hot under the June sun…"

CIVIL WAR ON THE WESTERN BORDER by Jay Monaghan Bonanza Books

Pg. 156 June 1861 Battle of Carthage In midmorning Jackson's column met Price's Missourians and, behind them, a regiment of neatly uniformed Louisianans-Louis Hebert's pelican Rifles-and also a battalion of Texas boys, eighteen to twenty years old, in frontier dress. At the rear of the column came a new brigade of "butternut" volunteers from Arkansas commanded by N. Bartlett Pearce.…Governor Jackson's civilian veterans of the Carthage Battle lined the road to admire the Confederates' neat grey uniforms, the resplendent Louisiana officer's gold braid, gold buttons, and stars. Real soldiers, sure enough! Military-minded Missouri boys wanted such uniforms for themselves.…"

WEBSITE-ARMS AND EQUIPMENT OF THE CIVIL WAR- Early Civil War Uniforms

June, 1861 South Arkansas-Southern Arkansas Community College "In some regiments each company had a different uniform. For instance, when the Sixth Arkansas Infantry was organized in June 1861, all ten companies wore different uniforms. Company A, the "Capitol Guards," wore gray nine button shell jackets with red trim, duck trousers, and gray forage caps. Company H, the "City Guards," from Camden, wore gray shell jackets, pants trimmed in red and glazed Mexican-era caps. Company K, the "Ouchita Grays," wore gray shell jackets and pants trimmed in green with gazed caps…"

Can you imagine watching these units on parade?

CONFEDERATE CAVALRY WEST OF THE RIVER by Stephen B. Oates Univ. of Texas Press, Austin 1961.

Pg. 57 June1861 "The "uniforms" of the cavalry were, as the circumstances of their procurement might suggest, as promiscuous in color and assortment as they were insecure in fabrication. Footwear was of all shapes and types-moccasins, high-cut boots, short-top boots and low quarter shoes called "pumps". Socks, usually cotton or wool, were of all colors. The typical trousers were either grey woolen "Kentucky jeans" or woolen plaid jeans....The usual shirt, called the "grey back" was made of cotton, long-sleeved, with a high collar. The men often enlisted in their "Sunday" shirts. Coats were both single and double-breasted and varied widely in color and design. The hat which "topped off" the soldiers attire was likely to be a wide-brimmed felt, colored brown or jet-black, or a grey cap, shaped like a French kepi. Sometimes bright colored handkerchiefs were worn when hats were not available..."

Pg. 56 "Probably the largest source of clothing was the innumerable women's organizations that began to be formed concurrently with the raising of the first regiments. In Marshall, Texas, four committees were set up on July 1, 1861, to collect blankets, socks, shoes, hats, and miscellaneous items to be sent to the Lane Rangers, then on their way to duty on the Texas frontier. Clothing for McIntosh's, Carroll's, and Churchhill's Arkansas cavalry regiments came from the citizens of northwestern Arkansas, who donated not only every piece of material they had that could be converted into clothing, but also blankets, curtains, and carpets for bedding. The cavalry companies raised at Fort Smith, and even some that rendezvoused there, were supplied with uniforms made by the women living in the community.

In other communities Ladies' Aid Societies were organized to make uniforms and collect necessary items that might add to the comfort of the troopers. By November, 1861, the Ladies' Aid Society of the Lancaster vicinity had collected and sent to B.W.Stone's Texas Cavalry Regiment coats, jeans, flannel and linsey shirts, winter drawers, winter vests, boots, shoes, woolen mittens, bed comforters, blankets, and other items, valued at $1,676.50.

Volunteers provided much of their own attire, receiving an allowance for it when they were mustered-in. Fearing that they would be inadequately supplied, the men who joined the Lane Rangers at Marshall, Texas, April, 1861, brought with them an incredible array of clothing and miscellaneous items..."

ADOLPHUS 1996

Pg. 173 Summer 1861 Captain Wharton described the manufacture of the Houston Depot jackets as follows: "...Single breasted with seven buttons made of 1 ¾ yards of double width coarse cadet grey cloth, basted with spool cotton and sewn with flax thread... Bleached domestic sleeve lining taking ¾ yard and unbleached domestic for the body lining and pockets...(being) heavy weave cotton material from the penitentiary mill..."

CIVIL WAR ON THE WESTERN BORDER by Jay Monaghan Bonanza Books

Pg. 153 summer 1861 battle of Carthage Governor Claib Jackson "…Jackson's army had no uniforms. Officers could be distinguished from the men only by bits of red flannel or a piece of cotton cloth stitched on the arm or shoulder of a homespun jacket or broadcloth frock coat…."

Website-CONFEDERATE UNIFORMS & EQUIPAGE-Texas Early Civil War Uniforms

"The ranchero, {Corpus Christi, TX} June 8, 1861 "The artillery company of this city has adopted a very neat uniform, viz: red jacket with yellow trimmings, white pants with red stripe…"

Now that would've been an attractive uniform

LETTERS TO SECRETARY CHASE FROM THE SOUTH 1861-Letter from T.D. Winter to Salmon Portland Chase

June 10, 1861 "Some of the troops which left were comfortably equipped, while many had no military clothing, their arms were mostly what was taken from the Baton Rouge and Little Rock Arsenals, and were the old flint locks alterd to percussion."

WILSON'S CREEK William Garrett Piston & Richard W. Hatchard III Univ. N.C. Press 2000

Pg. 116 July,1861 at Cowskin Prairie "Clothing was issued, including undershirts, drawers, flannel coats, vests, cotton shirts, and calico shirts. These were presumably civilian rather than military items. The supply of ready-made clothing was clearly inadequate, as large quantities of bulk cloth were distributed, together with clothing patterns. In his diary Cheavens noted, "Cloth was given, and most all went to work making clothes." Cheavens made himself a pair of pants while others in his company made shirts. His diary entry gives no description of the results, but if everyone used the same color of cloth it would have given his company a common appearance. Cotton trim, which was also issued, was probably used to decorate shirts and pants in a military fashion. Such endeavers may have raised the proportion of the State Guard wearing some matching items, though not necessarily complete uniforms, to nearly 30 percent. The variety of cloth used-jeans calico, toweling, twills, bed ticking, hickory shirting, blue and brown drill cloth, osnaburg, striped cotton cloth, Lindsey, cottonade, satinet and cassimere-worked against standardizatiion. As the average soldier probably had little experience with needle and thread, the results must have been wonders to behold. When one considers the combination of such camp-engendered sartorial efforts, the variety of prewar militia uniforms, unifroms made hastily by home folk at the outbreak of the war, and the ordinary civilian clothing that so many of the men wore, the Missourians gatherd at Cowskin Prairie presented and appearancs unique in the annals of the Civil War…"

Can you imagine having the soldiers cutting out and sewing their own uniforms?

Pg. 143 Battle of Wilson's Creek-McCulloch's men, "To avoid confusion, each man in his Confederate units, and possibly those in the Arkansas State Troops as well, tied a band of white cloth around his left arm (many members of the Missouri State Guard already "wore a red badge on their shoulder" for identification)."

Anexcellent idea

WEBSITE-confederateuniforms.org

July 3rd, 1861 Ultimathule, Arkansas The Sevier County Star Co., "the company uniformed with a light blue suit…"

Website-The Texas Heritage Museum—Hill College

1st Texas Infantry, Co. I July 17th 1861 "…After encamping at Crockett and down on Hickory Creek for some time, the organization was declared complete and we were ready for the fray. It was soon found that we were not full-fledged soldiers without a uniform. So our good peoples, then as now, equal to every emergency, purchased quite a lot of Huntsville jeans and every man was measured and fitted in a neat uniform of the most approved style.…It may be interesting to say something of this, our first day's march. It will be remembered that our uniform was made of all wool, Huntsville jeans, originally white, but now dyed black. Time, the 17th day of July. Our Captain insisted upon a strict observance of military rules; consequently, we were tightly buttoned up in a close-fitting suit of all wool cloth with the thermometer at 101 in the shade. It will be easily seen that it did not require much exertion to get up a profuse perspiration; this reality assimilated with the dye which was not well set in the cloth and by the time we had gone two or three miles, we were the blackest, smuttiest, white soldiers in the Confederate army…"

I wonder how long that color remained in the men's skin.

WILSON'S CREEK William Garrett Piston & Richard W. Hatchard III Univ. N.C. Press 2000

Pg. 243 Aug 1861 Battle of Wilson's Creek Missouri State Guards, "...Organized as the First, Second and Fifth Infantry...the brigade included companies that wore blue uniforms and others that wore gray. Their combined ranks numbered over one thousand men. As the confusion was great and all Civil War units tended to have at least a few skulkers, it is unlikely that 100 percent of them exited their camps and reached the battle line in time for the first Southern push up Bloody Hill. But enough of them did so to cause the Federal commander the gravest possible concern...

The Elwood Guards and Phoenix Guards returned safely to the regiment, but the Leavenworth Light Infantry experienced one of the strangest incidents of the battle. Having become separated from the others, they failed to hear Lyon's recall. After the momentum of their original charge petered out, Clayton dressed the company's ranks and continued marching south in search of the enemy. When a unit wearing gray uniforms approached perpendicular to his left flank, he assumed that it was Sigel's men breaking through the Southerner's rear. Actually, it was Clarkson's Fifth Missouri, apparently sent by Weightman to counterattack. Clarkson, in turn, took it for Granted that the blue-coated Kansans were fellow members of the Missouri State guard. When he asked Clayton the direction of the enemy, the Federal captain pointed southwest. The two opposing units then formed a single line and blithely marched off in that direction. They had not gone far before Clayton noticed that each of the gray-clad men wore a red flannel badge on his left shoulder, a distinction not used by any of the Union troops. Far from panicking, Clayton showed remarkable presence of mind. After voicing a loud complaint that his ranks were being pressed too closely, he ordered his men to march to the right oblique until a gap of thirty yards developed between the two forces. This action aroused the suspicion of Clarkson's adjutant, Captain Michael W. Buster. Riding up, he ordered the Kansans to halt and identify themselves. Clayton brought his men to a stop but he then yanked Buster off his horse and placed a revolver to his chest, shouting, "Now sir, god damn you, order your men not to fire on us, or you are a dead man." The adjutant fully matched Clayton in bravery and coolness. Turning he saw that Clarkson was wheeling the Fifth Missouri to face the Kansans, having obviously realized their true identity. "There, sir, is my colonel," Buster calmly replied, at which point the Missourians opened fire. Amazingly, Buster was unharmed by this close-ranged volley. He suffered only a slight wound when Clayton shot him at point-blank range and a second one from the bayonet of Sergeant Patrick Brannon, who lunged at him. The Federals were intent only on escape. Clayton yelled for his men to "run for their lives," and they did just that, rejoining the rest of the regiment in disorder..."

CIVIL WAR ON THE WESTERN BORDER by Jay Monaghan Bonanza Books

Pg. 172 Battle of Wilson's Creek, August 9, 1861 "…for the Missouri horde in coarse cotton shirts and yellow "jean pantaloons" were veterans, and like the Kansans on the other side, they looked forward to settling old scores in this fight…"

Once again this "yellow" was probably light butternut

DEE BROWN'S CIVIL WAR ANTHOLOGY by Dee Brown pub by Clear Light pub. 1998

Pg. 11 August 9, 1861 Wilson's Creek "McCulloch and McIntosh, who were in uniform, mounted to ride back to their troops. Price, in a suit of rough linen, was buttoning hie suspenders as he ran for his horse. "A stout, farmer-looking old gentleman," one of the soldiers there described him. In his haste, Price forgot his hat, but later in the morning someone gave him a black plug hat to shield his head from the August sun. An Arkansas artilleryman said that throughout the battle that tall black headpiece "ranged over the field like an orriflame to the Missourians."

Meanwhile, the first troops ordered into battle were tying pieces of white cloth around their left arm to distinguish them from the enemy. (Lack of distinguishable uniforms caused more confusion at Wilson's Creek than in any other Civil War battle). Many men on both sides had no uniforms; others wore state militia uniforms of varying colors, including blues and grays on both sides. Most of the 3rd Louisiana companies wore new blueish-gray uniforms, while the 1st Iowa Volunteers on the Union side wore uniforms of a similar shade of gray… Hebert immediately started off his columns, and many of the infantrymen marched off without their coats, tying strips of white canvas over their shirtsleeves…"

REBELS VALIANT-SECOND ARKANSAS MOUNTED RIFLES (DISMOUNTED) Wesley Thurman Leeper Pioneer Press 1964

Pg. 58 Wilson's Creek, August 9 1861 "…Gen. McCulloch was doubtless a very conspicuous target. Gifted towards wearing flashy uniforms, opinions differ as to what he was wearing this particular day, but it is generally believed that he was wearing a black velvet coat, with patent-leather, high-top boots, and a broad-brimmed planters, or Texas-type hat. One did not have to be a genius to realize that he was not the drummer boy! It was said that McCulloch never wore a regular uniform, and considered a sword to be "a useless and heavy ornament."

WILSON'S CREEK William Garrett Piston & Richard W. Hatchard III Univ. N.C. Press 2000

Pg. 16 Aug.10, 1861 "...The Hempstead Rifles, an old militia unit commanded by John R. Gratiot, were the first to arrive at Camp Walker. Passing through Fayetteville en route, they received a flag from the local citizens. Reverend William Baxter, president of Arkansas College in Fayetteville, noted of the Hempstead Rifles that "their drill was perfect, their step and look that of veterans, their arms and uniforms all that could be desired." From Nashville in the same county came Joseph L. Neal's Davis Blues, sporting frock coats with eight rows of fancy trim and twenty-four buttons across the chest. In Van Buren, on the northern bank of the Arkansas River not far from Fort Smith, Captain H. Thomas Brown led the Frontier Guards, who represented "the flower of Van Buren chivalry." The local paper boasted that these men, "the very elite of the city-'gentlemen all," were they best drilled in the state. They were certainly among the better dressed. Raised back in January, they wore dark blue coats and sky blue pants that had been manufactured in Philidelphia. At the extreme of sartorial spendor, however, were the Centerpoint Rifles, under Captain John Arnold, a local physician. Thanks to the hard work of the ladies of Centerpoint, they wore matching red shirts called hickory, adorned with five red stripes across the chest. Their blue trousers also had red stripes down the ouside of each leg....Woodruff 's Totten Light Battery wore gray jean uniforms trimmed in red, compliments of the ladies of Little Rock. These apparently replaced a prewar uniform of unknown type. The women of Little Rock sewed uniforms not only for eight companies raised locally, but for several other units stationed there as well. Such community-level support was as important for volunteers in Arkansas as it had been for those in Louisiana...At Fort Smith there was a prewar unit, the nearly all-Germen Belle Pointe Guards. For dress parade they wore fancy frock coats with heavy gold epaulets and tall plumed shakos bearing the brass letters "BPG."..."

WILSON'S CREEK William Garrett Piston & Richard W. Hatchard III Univ. N.C. Press 2000

Pg. 21 Aug.10,1861 "...The Texas Hunters, Capt. Thomas W. Winston, due to the ladies of Harrison County, wore cadet gray uniforms and bore an elaborate silk banner, one side of which was emblazoned with the words "Texas Hunters" above a painted hunting scene; the other side was a version of the Confederate national flag. With Colt's revolving rifles, that were probably the best armed unit in the state at that time..."

WILSON'S CREEK William Garrett Piston & Richard W. Hatchard III Univ. N.C. Press 2000

Pg. 82 Aug 10,1861 Missouri State Guard Units "...Distinctive uniforms, another another important community tie, were also largely absent. When prewar units like the Independence Grays or the Washington Blues of St. Louis joined the state guard, they retained their old militia uniforms. But if few of the newly raised companies had matching outfits it was certainly not from community indifference. In a short space of time the women of Warsaw managed to clothe two State Guard companies and sew them a flag. One company wore blue, the other gray, the colors having yet to take on any political significance. Although a full uniform was doubtless planned, one volunteer company frm Bolivar had only matching pants-brown jeans with red calico stripes down the outside seams. Several companies designating themselves "Rangers" were quite fancifully uniformed. Those from Plattin wore red caps and shirts with gray pants, while the men of Moniteau sported gray shirts, gray pants, and water repellant oil-cloth caps. DeKalb County sent its mounted company to war in gray hunting shirts and caps, and black trousers with yellow stripes, to mark their cavalry service. The LaGrange Guards also had gray caps and shirts, but trimmed in blue, and their pants were white with black stripes. But for style none could beat the Polk County Rangers, who adopted a uniform of baggy red Zouave trousers and short gray jackets. Nevertheless, probably no more than 15 percent of the State Guard wore uniforms made by their home folk at the onset of the war..."

Pg. 87 "Colonel Joseph M. Kelly's Washington Blues-After 1858 the unit wore dark blue frock coats and sky blue trousers and carried the model 1855 Springfield rifle. White waist belts and cartridge box slings, and tall shakos for dress parade, they made a natty appearance..."

Pg. 97 "McRae's Battalion, Arkansas Volunteers-Surviving records, which are not complete, reveal that its companies were a mixed lot. Levels of training ranged from "good" to "insufficient" and discipline from "fair" to "indifferent," varying from percussion muskets to "Common hunting guns of the country." Some men had cartridge boxes, waist belts, canteens and blankets, while others had none. Two thirds of the men were issued matching pants and blouses, apparently gray, but shoes were desperately needed..."

It seems shoes were needed everywhere in the South.

WILSON'S CREEK William Garrett Piston & Richard W. Hatchard III Univ. N.C. Press 2000

Pg. 255 Aug 10,1861 early in the battle, "...As neither army wore a standard color or style of uniform and Sigel's men expected with Lyon's forces at some point, many also thought that the gray-clad Louisianans were members of the first Iowa, which possessed several companies wearing gray...." the confusion was terrible, but "...Sigel did not remain mystified for long, but even after realizing that the men shooting at him were Southerners, there was little he could do to save the situation. Some Federal soldiers returned fire, but others refused, continuing to believe that they faced friends...."

WILSON'S CREEK William Garrett Piston & Richard W. Hatchard III Univ. N.C. Press 2000

Pg. 11, Aug 10, 1861 "...By now the Third (regiment) was reasonably well equipped with tents, blankets, knapsacks, and canteens. Each of the regiment's separately raised companies wore uniforms manufactured by the folks in their hometowns. The cut and quality must have differed substantially, but apparently all of their uniforms were gray. Watson's company, now comanded by Captain John P. Vigilini, as Tunnard had been elected major, wore large brass belt buckles emblazoned with a Louisiana pelican...."

SIBLEY'S NEW MEXICO CAMPAIGN by Martin Hardwick Hall Univ. of Texas Press

Pg. 38 fall 1861 "...The soldier's "uniforms" particularly those of the enlisted men, were of a nondescript nature. Most wore only the civilian clothes they had brought with them. With winter weather approaching, Sibley and his regimental officers addressed pleas to the citizens of Texas to contribute warm clothing and blankets for the brigades needy. In San Antonio the Ladies' Southern Aid Society was instrumental in collecting a large amount of blankets, comforters, quilts, flannel shirts, socks, drawers, and other items, as well as some cash. Several planters from the area donated one to two bales of cotton, from which the sales proceeds were used to purchase needed goods. The quartermaster apparently issued some equipment, for a member of the Fifth Regiment related that he was given a full military uniform, whish included a haversack, pants, drawers, pantaloon boots, and a broadcloth coat with brass buttons. It is quite probable that these were goods which the State of Texas had acquired from the Federal quartermaster depots when General Twiggs surrendered the department...."

THE THIRD TEXAS CAVALRY IN THE CIVIL WAR by Doudlas Hale Univ. of Ok. Press 1993

Pg. 61 Aug. 10, 1861 Battle of Wilson's Creek "...Frequent cases of mistaken identity that plagued the Union commanders. Since some units on both sides were clad in various shades of gray, it was extremely difficult to distinguish friend from foe on the battlefield, and the outnumbered Yankees missed several opportunities for success..."

REBELS VALIANT-SECOND ARKANSAS MOUNTED RIFLES (DISMOUNTED) Wesley Thurman Leeper Pioneer Press 1964

Pg. 57 August, 1861 "…To add to their troubles, insects of various kinds were running them wild. Some of the soldiers washed the insects from their bodies by riding naked in the rain. Veterans said that whiskey poured down a man's back, and also down his throat, discouraged the pests!"

Its worth a try.

WESTWARD THE TEXANS-The civil War journal of Private William Randolph Howell ed by Jerry D. Thompson pub by Texas Western Press, Univ of Texas 1990

Pg. 63 Sibley Brigade August 17, 1861 "I spent the day very pleasantly. Attend singing school perhaps for the last time in Plantersville. Have the yellow stripes put on my uniform. Take a last fairwell oif several friends. Visit Miss Molly and she has the kindness to put the initials of my name on my blankets…."

Oct. 22 1861 "…Only "weevil eater" crackers for a day or two past…"

Nov 12, 1861 "…Have hawk for breakfast…"

Dec. 15 1861 "…Boys trading with sutler. Boys a great many of them "get tight" and get a new suit of clothes most of them…"

No description as to color or cut

ALL AFIRE TO FIGHT-The Untold tale of the Civil War's Ninth Texas Cavalry by Martha L. Crabb pub by Avon Books 2000

Pg. 4 August 20, 1861 Fort Worth, Texas "…Captain Quayle sat his splendid horse with pride and assurance, his lithe frame erect, his brown eyes missed nothing. His troopers were mounted on an assortment of fine horses, Indian ponies, and Texas mustangs, even a few mules. The men wore a semi-uniform of jean fabric in varying shades of blue. Broad-brimmed Texas hats shaded their eyes. Each man was armed with a long gun and a six-shooter or two…"

Pg. 7 "Another band of Tarrant County men arrived early in September…Titus County's A.W. Sparks, who was determined to "pull his freight" in this war, had left college to enlist. He described the recruit's equipment:

"There were rifles, flint and steel, but most were full-stock percussion machines that had been used for killing bear, deer, and other wild animals. Double-barrel shotguns were the favorite. A few pistols were in the command, and were in great demand by the officers. Each soldier carried a huge knife, usually made from an old mill file, shaped by the blacksmith and ground according to the fancy of the owner."

Another veteran remembered that "some of the knives were three feet long and heavy enough to cleave the skull of a mailed knight, through helmet and all." The horses were affair average of Texas mustangs, but a few had strains of noted blood. Clothing was light, unsuited for hard service, but most of the new cavalrymen wore tall boots made of Texas tanned leather. A large flap on the front of the boots protected the rider's knees. Blankets were often pieces of carpet taken from floors."

Website-Trans-Mississippi Confederate Uniforms-Part 2

Pg. 1 "journal entries of Pvt. Randolph Howell, Co. C, 5th Texas Cavalry, "May 2 1861—Ma agrees to make my "soldiers" shirts on the morrow
May 3, 1861 I superintend the making of said soldier's shirts."

Website-Trans-Mississippi Confederate Uniforms-Part 2

Pg. 5 3rd Louisiana Infantry—"in Sptember, 1861 they received one of their states first commutation issues. Sgt. William Watson. A Scot serving with the third, recorded that he encountered a newly resplendent member of his company: "But I see you have got a new rig-where did you get that?" said I referring to anew suit of clothes I saw he had got on. "Oh," said he "you don't know about that yet. A whole wagon of things has come from Baton Rouge to us with new clothes, shoes, stockings, and shirts"…The nature of this new uniform was described by Orderly Sgt. W.H. Tunnard "This clothing was manufactured in the State Penitentiary and was of a substantial material known as jeans, being a grayish-blue color, with the exception of Company K, which had dark brown. The outfit…infused a new feeling and spirit amongst the men."

THE SECOND TEXAS INFANTRY-from Shiloh to Vicksburg by Joseph E. Chance Eaken Press, Austin Tx. 1940

2nd Inf. Regt. Sept.1861 Lt. Col. Rodgers and Capt. John Creed More (promoted to Col. In Provisional Confederate Army Pg.15 forming the 2nd Texas Inf. Regt."…He immediately set out to find uniforms for his men when none were to be had. Finally, in desperation, Moore clothed his rag-tag regiment in Federal uniforms captured from Yankee troops in Texas at the time of succession. These same captured troops also furnished rifles and muskets to fill out the armament needs of the regiment…."

HORSE SWEAT AND POWDER SMOKE-The First Texas Cavalry in the Civil War Sterling S. McGowan Texas A&M Univ. Press 1999

Pg. 92 "Early in the war, the Confederate government admitted that it could not properly supply the army, and obtainiong proper clothing and uniforms persisted as an obstacle difficult to overcome. The task of providing uniforms and clothing to the military fell to the in dividual states. Anything made of cloth-tents, blankets, and wagon sheets, for example-had to be supplied at the state level. Governor Clark directed thet all coth manufactured by the state penitentiary be utilized only for military purposes. As Texas controlled no other manufacturing resources to provide uniforms for his troops, the burden of clothing newly formed regiments fell upon private citizens. In March, 1861, for instance, Capt. Sidney G. Davidson wrote to his wife, asking dfor a pair of pants, one whits shirt, and two pairs of cotton socks, because his quartermaster had no clothing to to his men. Initially some local companies outfitted themselves with a variety of uniforms, but shortages of material prevented most soldier from donning regulation attire. In September, 1861, the 1st Mounted Rifles received a large issue of uniforms, but the 779 uniforms allocated failed to clothe the 1,009 members of the regiment. The definitive yellow gilt braid and brass buttons of fancy cavalry uniforms were seldom seen on Texas horsemen. Sometimes officers acquired uniforms trimmed with braid, but the common soldier seldom had fancy, yellow-striped cavalry pants.

Troops in the 1st Texas Cavalry wore a miscellany of mixed uniforme and civilian clothing. Typical attire included cotton, wool, and sometimes linen pants. The men usually donned shirts of the same material. Flannel shirts were also popular and appeared as part of army clothing issues. Invoice of clothing revealed a multiplicity of of colors in both shirts and pants: blue, red, black, brownchecked, undyed, and hickory all were issued. Materials varied, too, with cotton linen and flannel being most prevalent. Quartermasters also distributed cotton and woolen drawers and stockings when they were available. Cavalrymen preferred the tough, homespun "butternut" clothing over the grey flannel material produced at the penitentiary at Huntsville. The "butternut" material outlasted the flannel,especially in jacketys and pants. Riding through trees and brush quickly ripped the soft flannel cloth to shreds. Write wrote that, late in the war the men had "scant clothing"; "as for me my wife spun and wove the most part of my clothes and sent them to me."

The army issued hats and shoes, but widespread shortages left the choice of both up to the individual. Issued hats came in many types and colors, but most Texans wore a wide-brimmed hat of fur felt or cloth. Colors varied from black to brown and light grey. Virtually no one in the 1st Texas Cavalry complied with General Orders No. 4 from the Confederate War Department, which defined the type of forage cap authorized for wear by Confederate soldiers. Texans distained the little round "French style Kepi" with yellow sides and crown denoting the cavalry branch. Kepis, even with a "duck or linen Havelock apron falling behind to protect ears and neck," failed to shield the wearer from the intese Texas sun or a cold driving rain; therefore, Texans opted for more familiar and functional wide-brimmed hats. Shoes and "bootees" were distributed infrequently, so troopers donned all types of footwear. Tall and short boots, shoes of all kinds, and moccasins protected the cavalryman's feet.

By 1863 the regiment was uniform only in its nonconformity. The Texas cavalrymen were adorned with what they normally had worn or used prior to joining the army. Freemantle described a group of Texas cavalrymen as dressed in "flannel shirts, very ancient trousers, jackboots with enormous spurs and black felt hats ornamented with the "Lone Star of Texas." Upon meeting two of Joseph Taylor's men, he remarked that "these Rangers wear the most enormous spurs I ever saw." He also commented that most Texas horsemen "looked rough and dirty." Every Texan freemantle met "carried a six-shooter."

Tents, blankets, and cold-weather clothing never reached the regiment in sufficient quantities to prevent misery during inclement weather. As early as September, 1861, McCulloch, as departmental commander, wrote to Maj. Edward Burleson that enough Sibley tents for the 1st Mounted rifles were not available, for "everything in San Antonio is exhausted and we still have an army to be supplied from the department." Tentage remained a luxury during the entire war. Troops employed carpets and curtains partially to compensate for the shortage of blankets. Texas citizens collected winter coats, vests, heavy drawers, and blankets and shipped them to Texas soldiers in the field...."

U. S. ARMY HERITAGE AND EDUCATION CENTER

Sept. 16, 1861 Letter to "the Daily Express" newspaper on the 3rd Arkansas Infantry Regiment: "...Vanbarr-there is little doing now except among the women; reached into the sock movement with prodigious energy. "Sock" is a figuration which expresses every type of clothing a soldier can wear..."

Brothers in Gray

Pg. 54 David Pearson to William H. Pearson Camp Jackson, Ark., Oct. 17th/61 (To Mnt. Lebanon, La) Dear Fahter, The wagon has arrived and we sick ones have had a slight peep into our immense and valuable stocks of goods & good things. The boxes and bales of clothing, blankets & shoes &c. I would not open as I had them to store here not knowing that it would be safe to send them on to the Company now & preferring to have all together when the goods were given out. But my own little private box suffered from the blows of a hatchet as soon as it arrived. My surprise at finding so much as I proceeded to take out, my over joy at finding myself the owner of so much, and the thought of receiving them from home and other influences operating upon my mind all at once made me nervous for hours. I should not be surprised if I danced & cut up a great many capers over the contents of that little box. But I soon quieted down with a "Drink" in my throat & a segar in my mouth satisfied that a cold winter had no terrors for me. Tell Aunt Nan that the "jeans pants" came in a good time as the last pair I had were well nigh worn out. The socks, too, were much appreciated as my toes were beginning to push through my old ones. I am now stepping about with a new pair of boots and socks also. As for shirts, I was pretty well supplied, but they will be no particular trouble to me. The overcoat you sent me I did not need as I accidentally made a purchase of one sometime ago & a very good one too. I sent yours back as I have but little chance of carrying it & the boys are all well supplied with clothing. Blankets, neck ties &c. all thankfully received..."

Large supply from homefolks

FOURTEEN HUNDRED AND 91 DAYS IN THE CON-FEDERATE ARMY A Journal Kept by W.W. Heartsill or Camp Life; Day by Day of the W. P. Lane Rangers From April 19, 1861 To May 20, 1865 ed. by Bell Irvin Wiley Broadfoot Pub. Co. Wilmington, N.C. 1987

Pg. 45 Oct. 21st, 1861 "...M.J. Harris, G.W. Jarrott, and L.R. Witt, are sent to San Antonio to mett Wagons loaded with clothing from Harrison County. Oh how pleasant it is to know that we are remembered by kind friends at home; the good Ladies of Harrison County have loaded two wagons with ready-made clothing shoes and a few hats, all for the Rangers, dear kind friends this will never be forgotten by grateful hearts...."

ALL AFIRE TO FIGHT-The Untold Story of the Civil War's Ninth Texas Cavalry by Martha L. Crabb pub by Avon Books 2000

Pg. 17 November 1861 "When Sim's ten companies, about seven hundred men, reached Boggy Depot, (Indian Territory) the regiment formed as best they knew how and strung out on the road. The ragged column of new soldiers displayed all the colors of the rainbow, gaudy shawls and handkerchiefs, Indian trade goods purchased at the post...."

Pg. 23 "Early Friday morning, November 15, (1861) shrill bugle notes exploded into the darkness. The Texans pulled on their boots and hurried to the picket lines to feed the horses, then breakfasted on rations cooked the day before. When the bugler sounded Boots and Saddles, each man saddled his horse and strapped on forty loads of shot and powder, his arms, a peck of shelled corn for his horse, blankets, canteen, a tin cup, and his half-cooked or burned rations. Each man wore a blue-and-red string tied around his left arm. The string was the Confederate's badge, to be worn by both Indians and Texans. The strings had been passed out earlier with firm instruction to wear them and to let no Indian or white man pass without one. The Federal Indians, the Texans were told, would wear corn shucks in their headdresses or plaited in their hair."

CIVIL WAR IN THE INDIAN TERRITORY by Steve Cottrell Pelican Pub. 1998

Pg. 22 1861 "...By November 15, Colonel Cooper was ready to ride from Fort Gibson with a mounted force of 1,400 men. His motley little army included six companies of the 1st Chocktaw and Chickasaw Mounted Rifles, the 1st Creek Cavalry Regiment, the 1st Seminole Cavalry Battalion, and 500 troopers of the 9th Texas Cavalry who had been assigned to support the Indians. Cooper's Native-American troops were well-supplied with shotguns and rifles they had brought from home along with their own ponies. Most wore civilian clothing of wool and cotton with trade blankets for warmth. A few wore buckskins, and some even painted their faces for war. Nearly all wore their hair in the traditional, shoulder-length fashion..."

LONE STAR & DOUBLE EAGLE- Civil War Letters of a German-Texas Family Menetta Altgelt Goyne Texas Christian univ. Press 1982

Pg. 22 Mouth of the (St.) Bernard (River) 10 November, 1861 Rudolf to Family "...The coast here between the Brazos anf Lavaca bay is guarded by cavalry. There is a station every five miles which patrols constantly. We came across three such stations on the way from the Brazos to here. The soldiers here, in contrast to the troops in Galveston, make a very pleasant on me. These seem to be farmers. They don't wear uniforms and they bear their own weapons, whereas those in Galveston are almost all dock workers (mostly Irishmen) and quite a dissolute gang that can be kept in check only by means of great strictness..."

Pg. 23 Caney Rifles Camp 13 November 1861 Rudolf to family "...In addition there is still a lack of cooking utensils, but there was no dissatisfaction anyway because it is evident the captain is doing what he can to procur everything and hasn't any more than all the rest. We do have to wear uniforms. We have dark grey jackets and pants of the same material and caps of light grey flannel with a black stripe. The officers wear exactly the same clothing and are distinguished only by stripes on their shoulders, the captain three, the first lieutenant two, and the second lieutenant one..."

CONFEDERATE CAVALRY WEST OF THE RIVER Stephen B. Oates Univ. Texas Press 1961

Pg. 58 "Winter demands for additional clothing and blankets forced the quartermaster for General Ben McCulloch's army, encamped at Van Buren, Arkansas, to appeal for contributions from the citizens and merchants of Arkansas. A receiver assigned to each town was to package the articles donated and send them to Fort Smith. Contributions being slow, the quartermaster soon appointed two agents to purchase clothing and blankets,the costs to be deducted from the soldier's pay. The quartermaster also requested contributions form

Texas. In Dallas and contigous counties, citizens working in collaboration filled three wagons with clothes, transmitting them to Greer's Third Texas Cavalry of McCulloch's army.

Late in 1861 Rip Ford's Second Texas Cavalry was deplorably short of clothing. Since being stationed on the Texas frontier, it had received no contributions from the people of the state. Captain H.A. Hamner, commander of one of the frontier forts, lamented that his troopers were "near literally naked, and without shoes and socks." To remedy this, the ladies of Jackson County set about collecting clothes and blankets to be sent to the regiment.

In January, 1862, Sibley's army in New Mexico was "thinly clad, and almost destitute of blankets." Sibley later complained that his had fought through the entire campaign without a dollar of help from the quartermaster department. Upon returning to Texas, however, the men received large contributions of clothing from the Ladie's Southern Aid Society of San Antonio.

Shortages of warm clothing for calrymen became still more acute during the exceptionally cold winter of 1862. The men of Shelby's Iron Brigade, encamped for the winter at Camp Marmaduke, Arkansas, were in great need of blankets, overcoats, shoes and socks. Shelby complained to Marmaduke that "we have never drawn any clothing, shoes, salt, or anything else" from the quaretermaster department. What little clothing the men had they had collected for themselves. Many pof the Texas and Arkansas cavalry regiments were in the same condition. Unit commanders sent special agents to home counties to request contributions."

CIVIL WAR IN THE SOUTHWEST-Recollections of the Sibley Brigade ed by Jerry Thompson pub by Texas A&M Univ. 2001

Pg. 19 Dec. 24, 1861 El Paso, Tx "…Joe Boggs of the 7th Regiment, Rube Purcell of the 4th, Tom Slack of the 5th, and Fred Tremb;le of the 2nd, told me that they took a shirt the other day and boiled it for two hours and all the good it done was to make the eggs depsited in the shirt hatch out, but I think this was a joke they were rigging off on a greenhorn. Our shoes are all worn out and many of the men are completely barefooted. A few are bareheaded.We are on half-rations and have been for twenty daysand yet the men are all in fine spirits…"

Pg. 23 "The boys are utilizing all the hides of the beeves that are killed and all the horses that die in making sandals for themselves or shoes for their horses…"

Here we read about not only utilizing green beef hides for the men, but also for the horses.

Greyhounds of the Trans-Mississippi by Richard Lowe LA. State Univ. Press 2004

Pg. 13 The 17th Texas Infantry, part of Walker's Texas Division. "The ranks and files of the new companies gradually began to take on some regularity and precision in the dusty drill fields, but the appearance of the men was decidedly variegated. Some wore homespun shirts and rough work jeans under floppy felt hats; others enjoyed store-bought clothes; a few preened in uniforms made by mothers and sisters. Even a year later Private Blessington noted the lack of uniformity in dress among his comrades: Then as to costume,it is utterly impossible to paint the variety our division presented. Here would be a fellow dressed in homespun pants,with the knees out of them; on his head might be stuck the remnants of a straw hat, while a faded Texas Penetentiary cloth jacket would perhaps complete his outfit. His neighbor, very likely, was arrayed in breeches made out of some cast-off blanket, with a dyed shirt as black as the ace of spades, and no hat at all. Then would come a man with awoolen hat made like a pyramid, sitting jauntily upon his head, while, to introduce his style of hat, he had it covered over with assorted buttons; and, to top the climax, had a red tassel sewn on top. Notwithstanding his gaudy hat, a part of a shirt, and occasional fragments only of what had once been a pair of military pantaloons, made up the rest of his attire…"

Once again, absolute sartorial chaos

1862

EAST

General

A History of The Southern Confederacy by Clement Eaton pub by The MacMillan Pub. Co. 1954

Pg. 84 spring 1862 "The observant Northern reporter was much impressed with contrast in appearance and manner between officers and privates in the Confederate Army. The privates wore homespun suits of gray or butternut; some were wrapped in blankets of rag carpet, some had shoes of rough, untanned hide, others were in Federal blouses, and a few sported beaver hats. They were brown, brawny and wiry, "intese, fierce, and animal.' Their officers, on the other hand, were "young, atheletic fellows, dressed in rich gray cassimere, trimmed with black, and wearing soft black hats adorned with black ostrich feathers. Their spurs were strapped to elegantly fitting boots, and they lokked as far above the needy, seedy privates as lords above their vassels." They appeared to be strongely animated by state pride.

Pg. 91 "Confederate soldiers, if they comformed to army regulations, wore a gray double-breasted coat which extended halfway between the thighs and the knees, and trousers of sky-blue. Actually, they wore a variety of uniforms, including homespun shirts, dyed a yellowish or butternut hue with walnut hulls and copperas, and often captured Federal blue uniforms. Instead of the army regulation cadet cap or kepi they frewquently wore a wide-brim slouch hat. A toothbrush was carried in the buttonhole....

Probably the most serious deficiency in the Confederate armies was the lack of shoes, which forced many of the men to go barefoot, even in winter. Their were times when numerous barefoot soldiers in both Lee's army and the Army of Tennessee would try to protect their feet from sharp stones and frozen ground by tying burlap cloth around them. Yet it must be noted that some Confederates were accustomed to going barefoot during the summer months; and would at times remove their heavy army shoes to walk more comfortably. Although the Confederate Government imported 550,000 pairs of boots and shoes from Europe, the supply did not meet the demand. Indeed, Lee may have suffered a check at Antietam because of the tremendous amount of straggling in his army, which undoubtedly was caused, in part, by lack of shoes.

The frequent lack of soap and of changes of clothing took away some of the glammer of a soldier's life. Alexander Donelson Coffee, an officer in Zollicoffer's army in East Tennessee, described a C onfederate regiment as follows: They were the hardest roughest looking set you ever saw, and I don't think there could have been a clean shirt in the reg. for a month." The manuscript journal of the Shaker community at Pleasant Hill, Kentucky, describes the soldiers of Humphrey Marshall's Confederate Brigade passing through their settlement as "ragged, greasy, and dirty and some barefoot, and looked more like the bipeds of pandemonium than beings of this earth…they surrounded our wells like the locusts of Egypt and struggled with each other for the water as if perishing with thirst, and they thronged our doors and kitchen windows begging for bread like hungry wolves…they tore the loaves and pies into fragments and devoured tem. Some even threatened to shoot others if they did not divide with them.… Notwithstanding such a motely crew, they abstained from any violence or depredations and appeared exceedingly grateful." Duing Longstreet's retreat from Suffolk, Virginia, Clifford Lanier, (brother of Sydney) wrote to his father: "We are all well but very dirty-expect to bathe in the Nottaway River this evening tell Ma." Unwashed soldiers in closed railroad and passenger or box cars gave off a very annoying oder. Confederate Foot soldiers did their own washing, and soap was often a luxery. Thus gray lice-"graybacks"-became the baine of both armies."

THE HISTORY OF THE CONFEDERACY 1832-1865 Clifford Dowdey Barnes and Noble Books 1955

Pg. 175 1862 "…In Jackson's "foot cavalry," the beautiful uniforms of the first militia and volunteer companies were faded and patched, if not gone altogether. New uniforms were largely homespun, in an off-grey brownish color, and there was a sprinkling of Union blue and civilian garments. Hats were whatever covered the uncut and frequently un combed hair.

Gone were the handsome, compartmented leather knapsacks containing stiff collars, whits gloves, and cested linen stationary. A canvas haversack swung from a cord across the right shoulder, containing the barest necessities and-for the more elegant-a knife, fork, and spoon, a razor and small mirror. Many men neglected to shave on the marches, many did not yet have to, and older men let their greybeards grow.

Whatever the men abandoned, each held on to his tin cup-which served as both utensil and a dish, and was tied outside his haversack-and to his canteen, which usually swung in the middle of his back from strings looped over his head.

A blanket roll swung from the shoulder opposite the haversack cord, crossing the body from left shoulder to right hip. At noon in the Valley the burden became so intolerable that recruits threw them away. The men experienced in the hot Valley days and cold nightr s endured the torment. No tents were carried in the skimpy wagon train and men slept in pairs, on one blanket and covered by another. As the field-trophy business prospered, men began to cover their blankets with a fine Federal issue of India-rubber sheets, two of which together made a cozy tent for rainy nights...."

LIFE IN THE CONFEEDERATE ARMY: Being Personal experiences of a Private Soldier in the Confederate Army: and Some Experiences and Sketches of Southern Life. By Arthur P. Ford and Marion Johnstone Ford the Neale Pub. Co. 1905

Pg.12 "At this period of the war the Confederate Government allowed each soldier a certain sum yearly for his uniform, and each company decided for itself what its own uniform should be. In consequence, "uniform" was really an inappropriate term to apply to the dress of various organizations. At first our company was uniformed in grey woolen frock coats, and trousers of the same material, with blue caps; next we had grey cotton coats and trousers with grey cloth hats; then very dark brown coats with blue trousers furnished by the government, and grey felt hats; and finally the grey round jacket, also furnished by the government, which assumed to provide also the hats, shoes, and underclothing. The shoes, when we could get them, were heavy English brogans, very hard on our feet, but durable. It was in the summer of 1862 that we received our first allowance for uniforms, and our quartermaster applied to a tailor in Charleston to furnish them, but there was considerable delay in getting them, and the tailor wrote that goods were then scarce on account of the moonlight nights, but that in about a fortnight, when the moon waned, they would be in greater supply, and the uniforms could be furnished at $2 more per man than the government allowed. So in due time we all supplemented the government's allowance and got new uniforms of very inferior, half cotton grey stuff, which served us for the rest of the year. Afterwards the government tried to furnish the men gratuitously with the best it could, and we did the best we could with what we got".

These first quotes are excellent overall descriptions of Rebel soldiers of 1862

THE WOMEN OF THE SOUTH IN WAR TIMES compiled by Matthew Page Andrews pub by The Norman Remington Co. 1923

Pgt. 26 "Supplies of clothing of all kinds rapidly diminished as the war continued. Neatly trimmed thorns were often used in place of pins, and it was discovered that persimmon seeds made excellent buttons when thoroughly dried and pierced with the necessary holes for needle and thread, which, in their turn, became alarmingly scarce so that the loss of a sewing needle became a household calamity. Buttons were also made out of gourds, cut into moulds and covered with cloth of any color or kind. Corn shucks, palmetto, and many kinds of grasses were woven into hats and bonnets. Every variety of dye was homemade. When the dyes failed to hold their respective colors, the articles were "redipped" again and again. When hat trimmings were worn "too long a time," the hats were reshaped and dyed another color.

All girls and women learned to card and spin and knit, if not previously aquainted with these arts. Every woven stocking was of especial value. When the feet were entirely worn out, the upper part was carefully unraveled and the thread first twisted on the spinning wheel and then knitted into new stockings or into gloves or mitts. All woven wearing apparel was treated in the same way. Leather became very scarce and the providing of shoes a big problem. Women learned, in time, to make their own uppers and all of their bed room and house slippers. Soles for outdoor use proved to be the greatest difficulty. Sometimes they were made of wood, and, again-well, there were times when there were no shoes available!"

A good description of the shortages of that the home folks were forced to deal with.

Pg. 426 "In the narrative of Mrs. Hadley, reference has been made to the possession and use of a sewing machine. Comparatively few of the Southern women had this great aid to the making of clothes. Mrs. John D. Weeden of Huntsville, Alabama, writes of the experience of her mother, Mrs. Robert M. Patton of Florence: "we kept a number of garments to make at home. I was just through college, and I made, together with my mother and a serving woman she had employed, uniforms, underwear, and several overcoats, so heavy that we had to work on them while lying on a table. Every stitch was done with our fingers. We had no machine until 1869, when my father bought me one."

UNIFORMS OF THE CONFEDERACY A.C.W.S. Ltd. U.K.

On the Road to Malvern Hill, July1, 1862

"…We have a report of what they looked like several months into the campaign. Col. Wolsley, a visiting English officer and veteran of campaigns in Burma, India, The Crimea,and China accepted Lee's invitation to attend a large scale military review and inspection. As thousands of Confederate troops marched past, the British officer cast a critical eye on the lines of marching troops. He observed that some units were, to a man, outfitted in short jackets, caps, and trousers of grey clioth, while others presented a "harlequin appearance" being dressed in every conceivable of kind coat, both as regards to color and cut." But despite their untidy appearance and shabby garb, the Col. did not fail to notice a sure sign that these Rebels were serious soldiers. Their rifles were clean, well cared for and ready for use. Above all, it was the proud being of the Confederates-"an unmistakeable look of unconscious strength"-that won Wosley's undying respect. "Never had he seen an army," he said, "that looked more like work."

This is a description from the spring-early summer 1862. It seems that, according to Wolsley, there was a combination of uniform to multiform.

THEY WHO FOUGHT HERE Bell Irvin Wiley & Hirst D. Millhollen The Macmillan Co. N.Y. 1959

Pg. 79 "Overcoats were rarely issued by Confederate authorities after the first year of the war. Many Southerners "captured" greatcoats from the Federals, but most of them got along without these heavy garments. Blankets were frequently unobtainable, and in the latter half of the war were almost as scarce as overcoats. Fitzgerald Ross, an Englishman who accompanied Lee's army on the Gettysburg campaign, reported that many soldiers carried blankets made of carpeting and that during inclement weather these vari-hued coverlets were turned into overcoats by cutting holes in the middle for the head and draping them over the shoulders."

CONFEDERATE LETTERS AND DIARIES 1861-1865 Walbrook D. Swank-Col. U.S.A.F. Ret. Papercraft printing and design Co. Charlottesville, Va. 1988

Pg. 19 (no date) My dear Aunt Elizabeth, "…Oh! I was going to say that I had got my new overcoat. It is a large, coarse affair & I find no difficulty in putting it on over my old one which I do when it is very cold…."

TWO ENGLISH VISITORS DESCRIBE THE CONFEDERATE ARMY

A. "The Personnel of the Army is Very Varied" 1861or '62 "The appearance which a regiment presents on parade is remarkable to the eye of a European. Many are composed of companies who have uniforms of different colors; but in these cases there is always some distinctive badge by which their particular corps can be easily told. This defect, consequent to the companies being raised in different neighborhoods, is being quickly remedied, and we saw numerous regiments which had lately arrived, whose dress was all that the Horse Guards could desire…."

"…The Washington artillery, comprising many batteries is composed of the best blood of New Orleans. The gunners, dressed in light-blue uniforms, are all men of independent means…" "From the same city comes a very different, unit called the New Orleans "Zouaves," dressed in blue caps, blue braided jackets, and trousers striped with light gray and red. These men look like pirates- bearded, fierce-looking fellows…As they marched past the General with a long swinging step, singing a wild martial air, we thought they were as formidable a body of men as we should care to see…'

"From the reports we had heard in the North, we expected to find ragged and half-clad regiments; instead of which we failed, during many rides through the various camps, to see one man who was not clad in serviceable attire. It was expected that winter clothing would be served out before the 1st of November, and that dress would become more uniform….

But the point to which the chief attention of officers is directed is the arms. Besides the Enfield rifle, most of the privates in the army carry at least one revolver and a bowie-knife; these are invariably kept bright and in good condition; and the early training which all southerners undergo in shooting squirrels as soon as they are able to handle a gun, gives them a facility in using their weapons and a correctness of aim that renders their fire unusually formidable."-Anonymous, "A Month with the Rebels"

B. "The High Standard of Intelligence" 1861-62 "The Confederate soldier at first sight certainly presented a somewhat uncouth and even sorry appearance: about his person any kind of coat, or more commonly nothing beyond shirt and pantaloons; on his head, as the case may be, a cap, a straw hat, a slouch hat, or no hat at all. A closer scrutiny, however, showed that essentials were well provided. Besides his musket and cartridge-box, every man had a canteen, most men a blanket and a haversack. A more suitable equipment for summer service in Virginia could hardly have been devised.

What gives peculiar interest to the Confederate soldier's dress is the individual history which attaches to each separate article. From the blanket he sleeps on to the cartridge he shoots with, almost everything has been appropriated from the enemy at one time or another. This rifle was exchanged for the old flint-lock on the field of Manassas; that canteen was taken at Shiloh; the grey mare yonder, with the M'Clellan's saddle, was captured in the cavalry charge at Williamsburg; these boots were taken out of the Yankee stores at Winchester. The Negro who is following with the saucepan and the extra blanket, being wiser than his master, has consulted comfort rather than prejudice, and prevailed upon himself to wear a Yankee uniform, in consideration that the former proprietor was a full colonel....

Entire Batteries pass down the road, with "U.S." in prominent white letters on the caissons. It is no exaggeration to say that a great part of the Confederate army has been equipped at the expense of the United States. Flint-locks ands fowling pieces have been exchanged for good, Minie rifles. There was, however, so great a want of small arms, that a considerable part of the army was still equipped with smooth-bore of home manufacture, loaded with a ball and three buckshot..."

A somewhat confusing description of the Confederate soldiers, but it reinforces the idea of multiform in style of dress.

LETTERS OF WILLIAM F. WAGNER, CONFEDERATE SOLDIERed. By Joe M. Hatley and Linda B. Huffman pub, by Broadfoot's Bookmark 1983

Pg. 9 Salisbury Roan City N.C. 1862 ..."Dear Wife I will send some Money with Lemiel Dear Wife I want you to try and make them sherts and send them if you can but if you cant I will try and make out with what I got"...

THE REBEL BOAST by Manly Wade Wellman pub. By Henry Holt & Co. N.Y. 1956

Pg81 1862 "Passed by the medical examiners, the two newcomers drew their uniforms. There had been no such wealth of equipment at Camp Ellis or at Yorktown. Supply clerks gave each of them a dress uniform, a suit of fatigues, an overcoat, two shirts, two pairs of drawers, and two pairs of shoes..."

Here is a mention of a dress uniform. Issuing these did'nt last long.

Pg57 1862 Yorktown "George Wills, the impeccable of dress, deplored the appearance of the Louisianans. "They are the worst looking men you ever saw in your life," he scribbled a description for the home folks, "they all had on leggings wore red pants, with about three times as much cloth in them as necessary, and a long red bag for a cap, they are burnt black as mulattoes." Briefer and kinder was the impression of a Virginia cannoneer: "A Louisiana arrived about one hour after the fight was over. They are a fine looking set of fellows."

Apparently the appearance of the Louisians Zouaves attracted much attention. There are many descriptions of them.

MORGAN COUNTY DURING THE CIVIL WAR AND "STONEWALL" JACKSON'S BATH CAMPAIGN JANUARY 1862 Morgan county Historical and Genealogical Society 2006

Pg. 12 "They made a fine showing marching in close order through the streets of Winchester the next day on their way to their camp at Baker's farm on the Romney road. That day they got their first glimpse of Jackson standing on the sidewalk on a corner of the street. One Richmond soldier from the 21st Va. Wrote "As we filed to the left at one of the cross streets, we saw standing in the crowd on the sidewalk a man with full dark whiskers and hair...and wearing a long blue overcoat with a large cape. His coat reached to his boots, which were worn outside of his pants in regular military style....his head was covered by a faded grey cap pulled down so far over his face that between cap and whiskers was very little to see. Yet as we passed we caught a glimpse of a pair of dark flashing eyes from beneath the brim of his cap. That man was Stonewall Jackson."

A nondescript appearance for a genious.

A SOUTHERN SOLDIER'S LETTERS HOME The Civil War Letters of Samuel Burney Cobb's Georgia Legion, Army of Northern Va. Ed. By Nat Turner Mercer Univ. Press, Macon Ga.2002

Pg. 16 Jan. 1862 "...Mr. Fitzpatrick goes to procure a winter uniform. If you can get mine from the tailor's do so and have it lined with brown seams. I wish you could buy me a bottle of brandy and send it by him..."

HAM CHAMBERLAYNE-VIRGINIAN Letters and Papers of an Artillery Officer in the War for Independence 1861-1865 with introduction, notes and index by his Son C.G.Chamberlayne Richmond, Va. Press of the Dietz Printing Co. Publishers 1932

Pg. 151 J.H.Chamberlayne to M.B. Chamberlayne Hd. Qrs. Arty. Corps, Camp near Bowling Green Jan. 1st, 1863 My dear Mother, "...Now set your mind at ease about the uniform; it is all I could wish and indeed gave me quite a childish pleasure. Everybody says it is handsome & fits perfectly...."

Lt. Chamberlayne is praising the home-made uniform his mother made for him

Letter head missing Jan 1 1862 "...You said I must send you my old socks I have none but will do me a great deal of service yet they have some hole in the toes & heels which I can mend & make them last me a good while yet & I am afraid to send them for fear I cant get them again when I want them I am in hopes I can make what I have last me all the winter so if you cant get wool enough if you will knit me some of cotton they will do very well for the summer but I would prefer woolen ones if I could get them ..."

Sending home the old socks to either be repaired or unraveled and the yarn reused.

U.S. ARMY HERITAGE & EDUCATION CENTER Letters of James Griffin

Jan 2nd 1862 My Darling Leila "...My Darling you have never said anything about receiving my trunk which I sent by John Nicholson. I presume however you must have received it. In it I sent all my thin socks home. I wish you to (send) some of these back to me, as I wish to wear them next to my feet, and the woolen ones over them-I am sure my feet will keep much warmer, as the wool socks cause my feet to perspire and then when I am exposed to the cold, my feet get very cold. Please send my boot hooks also...I have gone through so much of this winter without an overcoat. And what is more remarkable, I haven't suffered for the want of one-I borrowed one the other night when I went out in the sleet-and I think once or twice before with those exceptions I have worn none this winter. I ordered one immediately after mine was burned from Charleston, and it has just come-I have come to the conclusion that they are humbugs anyhow...I am also obliged to you for the clothing you sent. I didn't need anything except the towels and hankerchiefs. I have lost some that I had. The shirts you sent are very pretty. I will wear them after the cold weather is gone. I wear nothing now but the calicoe. The comfort is very fine but so far we have had plenty of cover, it will however be no drudge unless we have to retreat from the Yanks. In that case it might be in the way. The major and I now have quite an extensive wardrobe. If the Yanks were to take our camp they would make money out of us. The Major received, a box from home a few days ago and in it came our overcoats at last-now that the winter is nearly over. But they are stunners I tell you, made of English cloth, Confederate gray-but such a piece how much to you suppose— Seventy dollars in cash and then two dollars and a half, freight-So much for the fire. Do my Darling give my love to Minnie and tell her I am greatly obliged to her for the next cap-but see here, it looks to me like a babies bonnet. Hasn't she made some mistake, or does she suppose I have a baby out here to wear it..."

Unfortunately, there is no further description of this "babies bonnet." I wonder if this English cloth, which he describes as Confederate gray, is the same color as the English cloth that was imported in such quantities in 1863-64?

A SOUTHERN SOLDIERS LETTERS HOME-The Civil War Letters of Smauel Burney Army Cobb's Legion, Army of Northern Virginia

Pg. 94 Camp Marion, (Va) Jan. 2 1862 Dearest Wife, "...I am glad to hear that your mother has given me material for a suit. It will add much to the value of the suit to know that my dear wife fashioned it with her own hands. Take your time and do not sew so that your headache will come on you again. If you have not cut it out, make my coat sufficiently large as I have grown stouter since I left. Take care of it for me, and when I come home I will put it on and wear it all about..."

Reliance on the home-folks for resupply of clothing. This continues throughout the war, as we shall see.

FAR,FAR FROM HOME-The Wartime Letters of of Dick and Tally Simpson, 3rd South Carolina Volunteers by Guy R. Everson & Edward W. Simpson Jr. pub. by Oxford Univ. Press 1994

Pg. 103 Jan. 3rd, 1862 Letter No. 45 TNS to Anna Tallulah Simpson Camp near Centreville Dear Sister, "Ma asks whether I wish some of Sloan's men to bring my things. I have no objection for I will need them badly before Buddie and Cousin Jim return, especially the boots as I am nearly out of shoes. Send me a looking glass. I don't get a chance to see myself more than once a week. I wish one in earnest and hope you will send it..."

THE CONFEDERATE VETERAN VOL. VI

March, 1898 Pg. 117 Early Experiences in Camp by J.B. Polley Jan. 3, 1862 Winter Quarters of Fourth Texas, near Dumfries, Va. Charming Nellie-"the weather has been terribly cold and rainy for the last three weeks. I have suffered from it perhaps more than anybody else in the company; for, to please Brahan's fastidious taste as to soldierly appearance and to keep even with him, I weakly yielded before we left Richmond to his suggestion that we should buy caps, and foolishly gave the splendid hat I brought from Texas to a darky. The top of the cap tilts to the front at an angle of foty-five degrees, and thus carries water over a visor just big enough to catch hold of with thumb and forefinger down on the point of my nose, and the back of it follows the slope of the occiput, and conveys every drop of rain or flake of snow that falls down my spinal column. Brahan, orderly sergeant; I, humble private. He stays in camp, while I stand guard, do fatigue duty, and otherwise expose myself. And thus, you see, although I have kept even with him as far as presenting a soldierly appearance goes, he does not near keep even with me in the way of discomfort..."

Ed.-I wore a gray kepi everyday for 11 years, no matter what the weather. Private Polley gives an exceelent description of the qualities of the kepi, though he doesn't tell how hot the darn thing is during summer weather. I fully understand why the slouch hat was preferred.

THREE YEARS IN THE CONFEDERATE HORSE ARTILLERY by George M. Neese- a Gunner in Chew's battery, Stuart's Horse Artillery, A.N.V. Morning\side Bookshop Dayton, Ohio 1983

Pg. 15 1862 Jan. 5 "This afternoon I went through a small Yankee camp which they had left in double-quick time last night, on this side of the river, a little below Hancock. The Sibley tents are still standing, and their former occupants bequeathed us their camp-kettles, bed-ticks, and even some of their clothing...."

Resupply from the Yankees.

SHENANDOAH 1862 by Peter Cozzins pub by Univ. North Carolina Press 2008

Pg. 75 Jan. 5, 1862 Jackson's Bath (Va.) Campaign reported a Virginia trooper, '...We crept along, freezing as we crept, pretty nearly all day...." Reported privates Lany Blackford "... We were furnished, in common with the rest of the army, with a battle badge, viz., a piece of white cotton tied around the right arm, receiving as an additional inducement for the wearing of it that orders had been issued that in the event of battle our men must shoot every man without one..."

These "battle badges" were more common than I realized before I began this research. In a multi form army it is a common-sense solution.

JAMES MADISON UNIVERSITY ARCHIVES

Probably between Jan 5th& 13th 1862 Letter of 1st Lt. Reuben A. Scott Co. B, 10th Regiment Virginia Infantry Mollie: "…I just heard Billy wheeler say what would be the use of his getting married as he could cook wash & mend his breeches that is what he is doing now (mending his breeches) we can do pretty well while living in the woods like beasts but when we get into a house we will find it better to have a lady to manage if if nothing more (I like to have forgot & nurse the baby)…"

HANDLEY LIBRARY ARCHIVES

James A. Miller Collection correspondence C.W. era misc. New Market, Va.

Romney Canpaign Morgan Co. Jan. 6th, 1862 Dear Julia, "…I ate my supper out of my haversack, and walked to the creek and took a wash and came back to our tent which we fixed to sleep in by spreading my comfort on the ground to lay on and Top Coffman, Col. Tallinger Siebert and myself slept in one of these small tents we covered with my blanket and Top's bed clothes we sleep tolerable well considering that we had no day light, we got up next morning about 6 o'clock a great many of the men didn't strike their tents and just laid on the ground and covered with their bed clothes…"

I wonder how well these men slept. I have slept rolled up in two wool blankets while being covered with three inches of snow. I didn't know about the snow until I awoke the next morning. Once out of the blankets, I was cold.

HANDLEY LIBRARY ARCHIVES-Hugh O. Pierce Papers Co F. 51st Virginia Militia

Pg. 12 Romney Campaign "The cold became intense. I had a new pair of boots and a new overcoat, and realizing the necessity of taking care of them, I lay down on the pile of reserve wood, assured myself that my soles would not be burnt, and pulling my cape over my head, I managed to snatch some sleep between shivers. What we ate I cannot remember but one thing certain we had no bedclothes that night. I saw one man lying so close to our fire that one shoulder of his coat and half his cap were burnt without his knowing it. Some one roused him before he was entirely cremated. The next morning at least one half of the men had the back of their coats and pants scorched, and scorched linsey does not make a handsome uniform....(later) I was given a patent-leather knapsack, two new woolen undershirts and other articles."

Consider how tired a man must be to sleep while his clothes are burning.

THREE YEARS IN THE CONFEDERATE HORSE ARTILLERY by George M. Neese- a Gunner in Chew's battery, Stuart's Horse Artillery, A.N.V. Morning\side Bookshop Dayton, Ohio 1983

Pg.17 Jan. 6 ...."This morning before daylight some of our boys went down to the Hancock depot on the Baltimore and Ohio Railroad, which is on the Virginia side of the Potomac, and captured some splendid army shoes, jackets, and coats, all new and of good quality. They went in the dark, for the good reason that there were Yankee sharpshooters on the other side of the river ready to plant bullets in any Rebel that would be despicable enough to dare to touch any of Uncle Sam's goods."

GEORGIA BOYS WITH STONEWALL JACKSON by Aurelia Austin Univ. of Georgia Press 1967

Pg 22-23 Camp Centersville, Virginia January the 6, 1862 "...Father...Johnny Sprewel sent my boots to mee by Samuel Fields Whoo brought shooes for the Yellow Dogs. I paid for the boots myself. Thay cost me $8. Thay are Double sole, Water proof. I could have got $15 for them before i ever saw them. If you pleas, write to John that I have got the boots and paid fields 8 Dollars for them. Thay just fit me & I am Well pleased with them...Giv my best respects and wishes to Aunt Matilda & Elizor Gober for the socks..."

WELCOME THE HOUR OF CONFLICT-William Cowam McClellan & the 9th Alabama ed by John C. Carter pub by Univ Al. Press 2007

Pg. 124 Jan 8, 1862 Cedar Grove (Va) winter quarters William McClellan to Thos.J. McClellan Dear Father, '...Did you send my boots by Smiths. Uniforms. They have not arrived yet[,] boots or uniforms I may get them in a day or so..."

LEE & JACKSON'S BLOODY TWELTH-Letters of Irby Goodwin Scott First Lieutenant Co. G Putnam Light Infantry Twelth Ga. Vol. Inf. Ed. by Johnnie Perry Pearson Univ. Tn. Press 2010

Pg. 54 Camp Aleghany (Alleghany) Jan. 9th, 1862 Dear Father, "...I let Jacob Filer have his new shoes as he needed them. Let me know what they cost and he will pay for them. I also let him have his comfort and some of his little things. The rest of his cloths are nearly all worn out.…I have plenty of cloths for the present. I find it best for a soldier not to have much clothing for he will be certain to loose some every time he moves and besides they are a great deal of trouble to him…If you have a good chance you may send me a good hat if there is not a good opportunity you need not trouble yourself as my old one will do for a while yet…"

It seems as though hats were in as short supply as shoes-well, almost.

MY DEAR EMMA-The War letters of Col. James K. Edmonson 1861-8165 ed.by Charles w. Turner PhD McClure Press 1978

Pg. 76 Camp at Unger's Store (Va.) Jan. 10 1862 My dear Wife "…When My Company left Winchester Camp I took my new shoes with me, but wore my old ones and when I got to Hainsville thinking that we were only going to dam no. 5 and then return and my new shoes being somewhat in my way I sent them back and since that my feet have been on the ground; fortunately for me yesterday I bought a second hand pair of boots, which I think will take me through…"

It seems as though shoes were always a problem.

"DEAR MOTHER: DON'T GRIEVE ABOUT ME. IF I GET KILLED, I'LL ONLY BE DEAD." Ed. by Mills Lane The Beehive Press 1977

Pg. 93 Lavender Ray to his Brother Morgan County, Virginia January 12, 1862 (the Romney Campaign, capturing a Yankee camp near Handcock, Md.) "…Some of the soldiers got a great many things, such as fine blue overcoats, new jackets, pants, knapsacks, haversacks, plates, minie' rifles, cups shoes, &c. We had a good deal of fun reading love letters and looking at Yankee books, letters, &c., ambrotypes, &c.…"

HANDLEY LIBRARY ARCHIVES

James A. Miller Collection correspondence C.W. era misc. New Market, Va.

"…we start for Romney this morning, Camp above Hanging Rock, Jan. 12th, 1862 Dear Julia, "…If you have an opportunity I wish you would send me my wool shirts…I am writing in our tent with our bed clothes spread we generally go to bed right early, I at first slept with my hat on but lately I have been sleeping with my red handkerchief twice around my head…I have long straw for the ground and spread my bed clothes on it and will attempt first to write you, can't imagine how snugly we sleep…"

THREE YEARS IN THE CONFEDERATE HORSE ARTILLERY George M. Neese Morningside Bookshop 1983

Pg. 19 January 14 1862 Romney Campaign "...That little old faded cap that General Jackson wears may shelter a brain that is filled with skelitons of strategic maneuvers, war maps, and battlefield plans, but if he thinks we are India-rubber and can keep on courting Death with impunity, by marching in the snow with wet feet all day, and then be snowed under at night, he will find that by the time the robins sing again half of his command will be in the hospital or answering roll call in some other clime.

This morning when I got up I crawled from under four inches of snow on my blanket, and this was the third time we were snowed under in the last two weeks. We marched in the snow all day, and this evening I stood barefooted in the snow, on a little plank however, wringing the water not only out of my socks, but shoes too. My shoes are Confed. and the leather is only half tanned. I wrung them out this evening like an old heavy dish rag, and now they look like dog feed. Looking at my dog-feed shoes sitting by the campfire is what causes the pessimistic reflections to troop through my brain...."

Imagine enduring these conditions for two-three weeks, constantly, with no relief in sight.

OCCUPIED WINCHESTER 1861-1865 Garland R. Quarles Winchester Va. 1976

Pg. 31 The R.Y. Conrad house, Loudon Street, used by Jackson's command as a hospital after the Bath Campaign Kate Sperry observes on Jan. 16, 1862

"There are about 3,000 here now on the sick list. Oh my! There goes a love of a chap with a horse blanket and his head stuck through a hole in the middle of the blanket, which being originally white but now faded and worn, has gay flowers and pictures of wagons drawn by jet-black steeds all over it-you can almost see the dust these refractory animals make in rolling along, the pictures are so lifelike. Think I'll fall in love with that fellow." (Sperry-Jan. 16, 1862)

How's that for a fierce, military appearance? I'll bet the soldier was quite fond of this blanket-probably brought from home.

JAMES MADISON UNIVERSITY ARCHIVES

Letters of Reuben & Mary Scott-Reuben A. Scott 1st Lt. Co. B, 10th Regiment Virginia Infantry
Jan. 17th, 1862 Port Republic, Va. Dear Reuben: "...Your pants are at your Papa's, and will be sent to you by the frist opportunity..."

Jan. 21st, 1862 Port Republic, Va. Dear Reuben: "...Have you got your pants yet? If so, how do they fit you? I left them at your Papa's, for them to send to you..."

THE ILLUSTRATED LONDON NEWS vol.40 no. 1127,

p. 62 January 18 1862
ILLUSTRATION OF THE WAR IN AMERICA
THE ADVANCED POST OF GENERAL
BLENKER'S DIVISION SURPRISED
BY CONFEDERATE CAVALRY

Our Special Artist of the Federal camp, visiting the advanced posts on the 12th ult., came upon General Blenker's pickets at Auandale (Annandale), Va (sic), about ten miles from Washington. Whilst he was in the neighborhood a dash was made at them by a squadron of Confederate cavalry-fine, rough-looking fellows, dressed in nondescript uniforms, red shirts, grey tunics; some with boots, and some without; armed with sabres and revolvers. Many of them were very powerfully built..."

Another eyewitness to the multiform nature of Rebel uniforms.

YANKEE IN GRAY-The Civil War Memiors of Henry E. Henderson The Press of Western reserve univ. 1962

Pg. 92 Jan. 19th 1862 "Camp Carendelet" (2 Miles east of Manassas) Jan. 19th '62 Dear father, "...The box of clothing Mr. Dowe kindly brought to me while yet at Gordonsville, and, though I was alredy pretty well supplied, many of the articles I found quite useful for myself, and all will be needed by some of my fellow-soldiers. The nice woolen socks and the jeans coat were particularly serviceable, as well as the mittens and comforter..."

This is one of the few references to mittens. I would think that mittens or gloves would be essential.

MY DEAR EMMA-The War Letters of Col. James K. Edmonson 1861-8165 ed.by Charles w. Turner PhD pub by McClure Press 1978

Pg. 79 Romney, Jan. 20 1862 My dear Wife '...The last 18 miles that I marched in my boots, I broke down and have since sold them and managed to get me a pair of new shoes..."

THE CIVIL WAR LETTERS OF GENERAL FRANK "BULL" PAXTON- A Lieutenant of Lee & Jackson ed by John Gallitin Paxton Hill Jr. pub by Cooege Press 1978

Pg. 98 Jan. 23, 1862 Jackson's Romney campaign Bull Paxton wrote to his wife, "…I don' t think you would know me if you could see me now, I think I am dirtier than I ever was before, and may be lousy besides. I have not changed my clothes for two weeks, and my pants have a hole in each leg nearly big enough for a dog to creep through. I have been promising myself the luxury of soap and water all over and a change of clothes today, but the wind blows so hard and cold I really think should feeze in the operation. I am afraid the dirt is sticking in, as I am somewhat afflicted with the baby's complaint-a pain under the apron.I am not much afraid of it, however, as I succeeded in getting down a good diner, which with me is generally a sign of pretty far health …"

Obviously a rash due to ground in dirt and lack of washing. Just imagine the misery of the Romney campaign, Paxton was an Officer!

LETTERS FROM THE STONEWALL BRIGADE Ted Barcay, Liberty Hall Volunteers by Charles W. Turner Rockbridge Pub. Co. 1992

Pg. 46 Jan. 25, 1862 after the winter marches to Romney, W.Va. Dear Sister "…I will give Ma a history of my clothes.

Firstly, I am getting rather bad off for a coat as this one is burnt and worn out together, but am in no hurry for one, if she thinks proper I can get one made here (Winchester, Va.) or she can have one made and sent to me. One pair of my pants are burnt a little at the foot, but I wear my pants in boots every day and put on my new pants on Sundays, so I can do very well in that line.

As for shirts, when at Romney I got so dirty not having changed for three weeks as my baggage was left in Winchester, I bought a change of underclothes, shirt, drawers, and stockings, so I am pretty well off except the coat.

My boots needed a half sole so I got a shoemaker to put one on this morning I see they are burnt a little at the side, but I will have a patch put on that so I can get along very well.

Ah! I forgot my hat. Well, you can tell cousin John (Barclay) I say he cheated me in that as I wore it out in less than three weeks, but I got myself a very good cap which does very well.

But you can send me a blanket or something of that kind. I don't know either, as we are going into a house, whether or not I will need one but I can write you. You think, I reckon, this is about enough in the clothes lines, so I will stop…"

LEE& JACKSON'S BLOODY TWELTH-Letters of Irby Goodwin Scott First Lieutenant Co. G Putnam Light Infantry Twelth Ga. Vol. Inf. Ed. by Johnnie Perry Pearson Univ. Tn. Press 2010

Pg. 58 Camp Alleghany Pochohontas Co. Va. Jan. 25th, 1862 Dear Father, "…I need a hat whch cannot get here which I wish you to send me the first chance. I was glad to hear of the boots you are having made for me. My shoes are wearing out very fast having to walk so much on the frozen ground. My over coat looks fine. The last suit of cloths you sent us are not much account. Are beginning to wear out. If you have the chance send me a good pair of pants…"

HANDLEY LIBRARY ARCHIVES-James A. Miller Collection correspondence C.W. era misc. New Market, Va.

Martinsburg, Jan. 26th, 1862 Dear Julia, "…found your letter here also the shirts and the picket cap which will answer a very great purpose. I only (?) that I hadt it when we are out in the mountains. I am very much pleased with it and that you were so kind as to make it and send it to me. I prise it very highly, I slept in it last night…"

Picket cap? I guess some kind of winter cap, probably a knitted cap.

GRANDFATHER'S JOURNAL (Franklin Lafayette Riley) Company B Sixteenth Mississippi Infantry Volunteers Harris' Brigade Mahone's Division Hill's Cops, A.N.V. May 27, 1861-July 15, 1865 Austin C. Dobbins Morningside 1988

Pg. 64 Monday-Tuesday, Jan. 27-28, 1862 Camp near Manassas "Rain and sleet. Letter from Bal (his fiance') who as usual sends me a quotation for me to ponder. Subject: Cockroaches, vermin which are "easily destroyed" she writes, by "cutting up green cucumbers at night and placing them where roaches commit depredations. What is cut off from the cucumber in preparing them for the table answers the purpose very well, and three applications will destroy all the roaches in the house. Remove the peelings in the morning and renew them at night." Cucumbers in January?"

Here's a folk remedy for you, if we had cockroaches I'd give this a try.

HANDLEY LIBRARY ARCHIVES

James A. Miller Collection correspondence C.W. era misc. New Market, Va.

Martinsburg, Jan. 31st, 1862 Dear Julia, I wish you woud send by the first opportunity a pair of socks as the ones that I have are getting rather shody. When you write I wish you would send me the length of (Harper's?) as I think perhaps I can get him a pair here which will do for him when those wear out which he has, send the exact length and I can make allowances…"

Mount Up!-ATrue Story Based on the Reminiscences of Major E.A.H. McDonald of the Confederate Cavalry Harcourt, Brace 7 World Inc. 1967

Pg. 34 Jan-Feb. 1862 "The smartly uniformed Federals at least looked like soldiers. The Confederates wore what they had and what they pleased. In their army the only firm regulation as to dress was that they must not wear the uniform of the enemy. Even that prohibition had to be relaxed as time went on…"

Maj. McDonald here mentions multiform through-out the war

REBEL PRIVATE FRONT AND REAR-Memoirs of a Confederate Soldier (Texas Brigade A.N.V.) by William A. Fletcher pub by Dutton Books 1995

Pg. 12 Jan-Feb 1862 "When I was discharged from the hospital I reported to command near Dumfries (Va). The Federals and Confederates were camped on opposite sides of the Potomac River. We moved camp in the early part of '62-the men were well equipped with clothing and bedding and nearly all started with an overload, and the roadside during the first days march was strewn for miles with clothing, blankets, etc., which was done to lighten the men's carrying weight.

Pg. 19 "…The color of the Confederate uniform had the advantage over the Federal in not showing them (lice) when on the out side of the clothing…"

He doesn't mention whether this is gray or butternut in not showing lice, though I would imagine its gray.

LEAVES FROM THE DIARY OF A YOUNG CONFEDERATE-Randolph H. McKim, late 1st Leiutenant & ADC 3rd Brigade, Johnson's division, ANV Longmans, Green & Co. 1911

Pg. 57 Winter Quarters, 1861-1862 Feb. 1862 "…One day word came to our quarters that two ladies desired to see my cousin, W. Duncan McKim, and myself at Fairfax Station. This was exciting news, but I found Duncan very reluctant to obey the summons. In civilized life he had been very exquisite in dress and manners, and he shrank from appearing in the presence of ladies, surrounded as they would be by well-dressed and well-mounted staff officers, in his rough private's garb. He seemed particularly sensitive about wearing a roundabout jacket instead of a coat before them. However, he yielded to my persuations, and we prepared to go to the station, brushing and polishing up to the best of our ability. I think we succeeded in finding or borrowing each, a white collar for the occasion!…"

Pg. 93 Stonewall jackson's Valley Campaign-referring to the sight of Gen. Jackson-"...This popularity was the more remarkable when it is remembered that he was very stern, very silent, very reserved, and by no means an ideal leader in appearance. His figure was bad, his riding was ungraceful (he rode, as I remember him, with short stirrups and with one shoulder higher than the other), and his uniform usually rusty, with scarce anything to mark him out as a general..."

THE CONFEDERATE VETERAN VOL VI

Sept. 1898 Pg. 421 Feb. 1862 Fitz Lee in the Army of Northern Virginia by Frank A. Bond "At this time, John S. Mosby (afterwards the famous guerilla chief) was adjutant of our regiment (Maryland Company in the First Regiment of Virginia cavalry). There could not have been a greater contrast between two men as there was between Lee and Mosby. Lee was the precise and punctilious soldier, with a great regard for all the etiquette of the profession. Mosby was absolutely careless of all this, and seemed to take a pride in violating every rule that it was safe to do. For instance, he used a civilian's saddle and bridle, and his uniform was trimmed in red instead of buff. It was said that when he was promoted from private to adjutant and went to Richmond to equip himself he found a ready-made uniform for a lieutenant of artillery that fitted, and, being cheap, he bought it. When at dress parade he paced down the line on a small sorrel horse, with his citizen's equipments and his artillery uniform, it was gall and wormwood to our lieutenant Colonel; but our colonel, William E. Jones, was great friend of Mosby's, and it was thought rather enjoyed Col. Lee's chagrin."

LETTERS FROM THE STONEWALL BRIGADE Ted Barcay, Liberty Hall Volunteers by Charles W. Turner Rockbridge Pub. Co. 1992

Pg. 48 Feb. 1, 1862 (Winchester) Dear Sister "...In regard to my wardrobe. I was congradulating myself that I was so well off, but you seem to think it is rather dilapidated. The only thing I need is a coat. I will have the boots footed here and will do very well...P.S. Try and get me a gray coat if you can. Anything rather than brown or blue, a light gray if possible..."

LEE& JACKSON'S BLOODY TWELTH-Letters of Irby Good-win Scott First Lieutenant Co. G Putnam Light Infantry Twelth Ga. Vol. Inf. Ed. by Johnnie Perry Pearson Univ. Tn. Press 2010

Pg. 59 Camp Allghany, Feb. 2nd, 1862 Dear Father, "...Do not send me more cloths until I write for them except what I wrote you for. A hat, pair of pants, and those boots you had made for me..."

SOJOURNS OF A PATRIOT The Field and Prison Papers of An Unreconstructed Confederate edited with commentaey by Richard Bender Abell & Fay Adamson Gecik Southern heritage Press 1998 letters of Pvt. Augustus Pitt Adamson

Pg, 33 Camp Bartow, Chatham County, Georgia Feb. 2nd, 1862 Miss A.A. Adamson Dear Sister, "...we drawed our knapsacks, haversacks, cartridge boxes and cap boxes the other day..."

HANDLEY LIBRARY ARCHIVES

Stanley Russell Co. H, 13th Virginia Regiment Feb. 4, 1862 Dear papa "...I wish you would write soon and send me five or six dollars. I need money in a great many ways here to buy Candles, molasses Butter and a great many other things. We draw nothing but flour & meat I get neither sugar or coffee.... Tell Ma I need no more clothing at present, I have not worn my coat since I came here..."

Does he mean overcoat or jacket? I would imagine he is referring to an overcoat.

HANDLEY LIBRARY ARCHIVES

James A. Miller Collection correspondence C.W. era misc. New Market, Va.

Winchester, Feb. 4th, 1862 Dear Julia, I will write you a few lines to send by Mr. T. Reid he is down and expects to return this evening. I also send by him two pair of pants and one of my old shirts also your apron which you left at Betsy's..."

LETTERS FROM THE STONEWALL BRIGADE Ted Barcay, Liberty Hall Volunteers by Charles W. Turner Rockbridge Pub. Co. 1992

Pg. 51 Feb. 5 1862 Dear Sister "...Either shoes or boots will do me but you need not have them very heavy as I do not expect to tramp soon but expect to go into the courting business and to succeed I must have some dikes...."

Dikes refers to more fancy, lightweight shoes as opposed to a heavy shoe such as a brogan.

A CONFEDERATE CHRONICAL-The life of a Civil War Survi-vor by Pamela Chase Hain Univ. of Missouri Press 2005

Pg. 54 "February 6, 1862. Wragg's regiment in winter quarters at Camp Sam Jones, Centreville (Va.).

"My Dear Papa,I wish, Papa, that if you can get any cheap grey cloth that you would have me a pair of pants made and send them on with Capt.B. when he returns which will be in about 30 days. Do send me a pair of high shoes or boots, no. 6, never mind how heavy or common they are."

Pg. 55 "...According to Cuningham, one sick Confederate soldier exclaimed when seeing a healthy-looking Yankee, "You look like you wuz such a happy man! You got on sich a nice uniform, you got sich nice boots on, you ridin' sich a nice hoss, an' you look like your bowels wuz so regular."

DEAR SISTER-CIVIL WAR LETTERS TO A SISTER IN ALABAMA Frank Anderson Chappell pub. by Branch Springs Pub. 2002 (Third Alabama Regiment)

Pg. 61 Camp at Mosebey's Church Feb. 7 1862 Dear Sister "...You recollect I was speaking of going on board the Merrimac several weeks ago. I was at that time rejected. About three weeks ago one of the officers of the same came to see if we were still in the notion to go. We all rejected him that, but McAlewit, he is now in the naval service, and I thought I was clear of it the (undeciferable) but yesterday orders came to the Col. To send in all that had sent in their names, myself and 11 others of the S.R. to be sent to the navy yard this morning with all our clothes..." Except for the intervention of his Col., Battle would have ended up in the navy. It was at this time they changed over to artillery...."

This statement by Frank Anderson would indicate, I believe, that the crewmwn on board the "C.S.S. Virginia" were dressed in their army infantry uniforms, due to the comment regarding being sent to the Naval Yard with all their clothes. According to the website: CW Navy and Marine Forum- the author states he believes they were given blue naval uniforms. Anderson's letter is a month before the Virginia went out and played hell at Hampton Roads, I would suggest the naval officers had more on their mind then issuing scarce uniforms to the crewmen.

CHORLOTTE'S BOYS-Civil War Letters of the Branch Family of Savannah ed. by Mauriel Phillips Joslyn Rochbridge Pub. Co. 1996

Pg. 91 Sgt. Hamilton Branch to Charlotte Branch On Picket Feb. 8/62 My Dear Mother "... Mother I wish you would return my thanks to Mr. Butler for the shoes. They are splendid. A little too large but do first rate. Also, return my thanks to Miss Fannie Tarver for the pulse warmers she sent me..."

Pulse warmers? Is that some kind of a wristband?

A SOUTHERN SOLDIERS LETTERS HOME-The Civil war Letters of Samuel Burney Cobb's Legion, Army of Northern Virginia ed by Nat Turner Mercer pub by Mercer Univ. Press 2002

PG. 117 Camp Marion Feb. 9th, 1862 My Dear One, "Last night I had a good wash and put on my nightshirt, which reminded me of home so much. I do not wear my white shirts, only when the others are not clean. The weather has been so rainy and bad that Lucious (slave) did not wash for me last week." *Nightshirt? Really?*

Pg. 120 Camp Cobb's Legion, Feb. 10th 1862 "…I send by George my overcoat & those two flannel shirts I bought a few days ago…"

LETTERS AND PAPERS OF AN ARTILLERY OFFICER A.N.V. IN THE WAR FOR SOUTHERN INDEPENDENCE 1861-1865 Capt. John Hampden Chamberlain-Virginian Dietz Printing Co. Pub. 1932

Pg. 63 Camp near Winchester Va. Feb. 15th, 1862 My Dear Mother "…I reached Winchester safely on Thursday morning & write now only to let you know that I found V. Mann &c. well & am as comfortable as I could expect to be in camp, not only in general, but also in particular, in the matter of shoes, clothing &c…"

HISTORY OF THE FOURTH REGIMENT SOUTH CAROLINA VOLUNTEERS FROM THE COMMENCEMENT OF THE WAR UNTIL LEE'S SURRENDER J.W. Reid Shannon &Co. Printers & Stationers Morningside Bookshop 1975

Pg. 69 Centreville, Va. Feb. 16, 1862 "…I hope I can soon come home, but when I do I will be nearly in the condition in which I came into this world, so far as pants go, but I will try to keep them patched up until then. It is known here that I keep a large needle. Someone is constantly wanting to borrow it. When I ask the question, "What do you want with it the answer invariably is, "To sew up my breeches." Of course, I always let them have it, well knowing what a spectacle I would present had I no needle… The weather is the coldest I have ever seen. I have on a flannel shirt, a cotton ditto, my uniform coat, my broadcloth coat, my overcoat, and all my old breeches and I am trembling as I write, but hope my nose won't drop again. I will stop writing and try to warm…"

Pants would wear out the soonest, the men in his company seem to have quite a job repairing their pants.

Website learnnc.org The Battle of Roanoke Island Conduct of the Ninth New Jersey Volunteers.

Correspondence of the Newark Advertiser. Camp Burnside, Roanoke Island Feb. 18, 1862 "...As to uniforms, they had none, but were dressed in all kinds of suits and had all kinds of arms; a great uniformity existed, however, as to Bowie knives-every man carried one, varying in length friom six inches to two feet. Maj. Wilson, of the New Jersey Ninth, has a bowie, taken from a rebel, two feet in length-a fearful weapon and one that no civilized person should carry into battle. Our men use them wherewith to cut their wood for cooking..."

Here's a Yankee reference to multiform. These were probably garrison troops to have held on to their Bowie kn ives for so long, most of these were either discarded or sent home after the first march.

HAM CHAMBERLAYNE-VIRGINIAN Letters and Papers of an Artillery Officer in the War for Independence 1861-1865 with introduction, notes and index by his son C.G.Chamberlayne Richmond, Va. Press of the Dietz Printing Co. Publishers 1932

Pg. 66 J.H. Chamberlayne to M.B. Chamberlayne Camp near Winchester, Feb. 23d 1862 My dear Mother "...Would that I could by any means induce you to look a little more on the side that's next the sun, beginning with even so small a matter as my socks shoes and drawers. Be it known unto you, most anxious of Mothers, that my handtrunk holds drawers of the best and that "my lower extremities" in elegant phrase, are clothed in stout cowskin, defying wind and weather, and that your son is still reckoned an able bodied soldier with neither wet feet cough nor shiver..."

Cowskin drawers? I'd have loved to have seen those, but they could not have been worn in the summer, he would have sweated to death.

HANDLEY LIBRARY ARCHIVES

James A. Miller Collection correspondence C.W. era misc. New Market, Va.

Martinsburg, Feb. 24th, 1862 Dear Julia, I have an idea of buying a coat for summer wear as I saw the goods that would make a very nice one the other day. I will get it and send it to Winchester and if I have a chance will send it to Nellie..."

U. S. ARMY HERITAGE AND EDUCATION CENTER

Feb. 24, 1862 Henry S. Figures 4th Alabama Volunteer Regiment "Camp Alabama" Dumfries, Va. My Dear Ma: "...I am going to send some of my clothes home by him (Mr. Duryee) for

I have too many to carry on my back if we'd go. I will send two undershirts (not the ones you sent me) one pair of drawers, four or five pair of socks and two white handkerchiefs..."

I have no idea what he means by "undershirt." He's not sending much home.

"DEAR MOTHER: DON'T GRIEVE ABOUT ME. IF I GET KILLED, I'LL ONLY BE DEAD." Ed. by Mills Lane The Beehive Press 1977

Pg.101 John Wood to his father Chatham county, Georgia February 25, 1862 Dear father: "...You just ought to see the Savanah Militia at work, especially those wealthy speculators who would (have) been a commissioned officer but could not be persuaded to be a private with their broadcloth coats, silk cravats, fine starched linen shirts, calfskin boots on, half knee deep in mud and water, spade in hand, throwing sand mud like a piney wood salamander, much to the amusement of our Newton (County) boys. The boys plague them sometimes, I think too much, by calling them "militia!" When the volunteers see them walking about, they are sure to holler out, "Left, left, left!" ..."I drew $32 yesterday. Had to pay Colonel Henderson $8.60 for my uniform coat. It is the dearest coat to be scarce goods that I have ever come across before..."

If he thinks the price for his jacket is dear now, wait 'till next year.

RICHMOND VOLUNTEERS 1861-1865 by Louis H. mandarin & Lee A. Wallace pub. by Richmond Civil War Centennial Committee Westover Press 1969

Pg. 37 Crenshaw Battery "...The Crenshaw Battery, a company of light artillery, was organized in March 1862...The Battery was named for William G. Crenshaw, its first captain, who outfitted the company with "handsome uniforms," overcoats and shoes; and who advanced the necessary funds to the Confederate Government for the purchase of horses and guns..."

GEORGIA BOYS WITH STONEWALL JACKSON by Aurelia Austin Univ. of Georgia Press 1967

Pg. 29 Retreat from Centreville, spring 1862 J.T. Thompson Camp near Orange Court House Corng. County, Va. March the 26trh, 1862 "...Wee had to burn up nearly all of our cloathes, and bagage...There was more blankets throan away on the march than horse teem could pull, and cloathes of the very best kinde..."

It has always mystified me about the waste of equipment, especially clothes and blankets on this retreat. Gen. Johnson had all the time in the world to organize it, so why was there so much wastage? The railroad was right there in Manassas, the gear could've been tagged and shipped to Richmond and stored.

DETAILED MINUTIAE OF SOLDIER LIFE IN THE A.N.V. Carlton McCarty So. Historical Society Papers, Richmond, Va. Vol2

Spring 1862 Pg 14 Rev. J. William Jones D.D. sec. So. Hx. So. "Orders to move! Where? When? What for?-are the eager questions of the men as they begin their preparations to march. Generally nobody can answer, and the journey is commenced in utter ignorance of where it is to end. But shrewd guesses are made, and scraps of information will be picked up on the way. The main thought must be to "get ready to move." The orderly sergeant is shouting "fall in," and there is no time to lose. The probability is that before you get your blanket rolled up, find your frying pan, haversack, axe,&, and "fall in," the roll-call will be over and some "extra duty" provided.

No wonder there is bustle in the camp. Rapid decisions are to be made between the various conveniences accumulated, for some must be left. One fellow picks up the skillet, holds it awhile, mentally determining how much it weighs, and what will be the weight of it after carrying it five miles, and reluctantly, with a half ashamed, sly look, drops it and takes his place it ranks. Another having added to his store of blankets too freely, now has to decide which of the two or three he will leave. The old water bucket looks large and heavy, but one stout-hearted, strong-armed man has taken it affectionately to his care.

This is the time to say farewell to the bread-tray, farewell to the little piles of clean straw laid between two logs, where it was so easy to sleep; farewell to those little piles of wood, cut with so much labor; farewell to the girls of the neighborhood; farewell to the spring, farewell to "our tree" and:our fire,' goodbye to the fellows who are not going, and a general goodbye to the very hills and valleys.

Soldiers commonly threw away the most valuable articles they possessed. Blankets, overcoats, shoes, bread and meat, - all gave way to the necessities of the march; and what one man threw away would frequently be the very article another wanted and would immediately pick up. So there was not much lost after all."

OK, This makes sense, but I imagine a great deal of gear was discarded.

WEBSITE—confederateunforms.org

The Richmond (Va) Daily dispatch March 4, 1862 "$50 bounty. Crescent Zouaves Battalion. Wanted-Recruits to fill up the battalion of Crescent Zouaves, under the command of Major

W. Holstered.A bounty of fifty dollars will be paid each recruit upon enlistment. A neat uniform of gray cloth, Zouave style, will be furnished."

A CONFEDERATE CHRONICLE

Pg. 56 March 4, 1862 Thomas Wragg, sick with dysentery, writes from the Second Georgia Hospital in Richmond My Dear Papa, "I write these few lines to let you know that I am sick in the 2d. Geo. Hospital and ask you to send me on some money as I have not got a change of clothes I being oblige to leave everything behind at Manassas. My own suit is all in rags and I have not a cent to buy any others…"

If his suit was "all in rags," I imagine the uniforms of his comrades would be no better.

A SOUTHERN SOLDIER'S LETTERS HOME The Civil War Letters of Samuel Burney Cobb's Georgia Legion, Army of Northern Va. Ed. By Nat Turner Mercer Univ. Press, Macon Ga.2002

Pg. 130 Camp Marion Yorktown, Va. March 5, 1862 "…Everything is topsy turvey. I never saw more baggage in my life; the wagons have been busy for the past five days hauling our things to Winn's Mill. I succeeded in getting all my plunder there, but when we leave for Suffolk I expect to lose some of my articles as I have more baggage than is allowed a soldier. I shall put my best clothes in my knapsack & carry them on my back. The balance of my things I will leave to the mercy of any who may take them…."

CHARLOTTE'S BOYS-Civil War Letters of the Branch Family of Savannah ed by Mauriel Phillips Joslyn pub by Rochbridge Pub Co. 1996

Pg. 100 Sgt. Hamilton Branch to Charlotte Branch On the Road 2 ½ miles from Camp Sam Jones Winter Quarters 8th Regt. Geo. Vols. March 8.62 My Dear Dear Mother, "We left camp this morning at 7oclock and marched to this place. It was pretty huge. We had to carry our knapsacks with everything we had in the world, mine had 4 blankets, a tick and a change of underclothes and an oilcloth…."

Pg. 107 Sgt. Hamilton Branch to Charlotte Branch Camp near Orange C.H. (Va.) April 5th/62 My Dear Mother, "I want a pair of pants but here that Col. Lamar is agoing to get uniforms for the regiment from the Government and one pair will be as much as I care to carry this summer. My valise which was at Manassas was burnt up and all of my clothes that were in it, but I have two changes which is as much as I wan't to tote. I intend to send off two of my blankets off as soon as it gets a little warmer…."

Wow, this soldier was over-equipped, too bad he didn't think to send some of those clothes home sooner. Notice the mention of a valise but no mention of a knapsack.

Pg.110 Sgt. Hamilton Branch to Charlotte Branch Bivouac near Orange (April) 10/62 "There was a trunk arrived in camp this morning marked W.D.Coombs. One of the boys thought it was his and opened it but seeing my name on the pants and books thought that they were mine so turned the trunk over to me. A jar of syrup had broken and spilt all over the things and a jar of preserves also. The drawers and shirt and stockings came just in time and the pants are worth their weight in gold. I am now all right in the clothes line...."

"Pants are worth their weight in gold," an eloquent statement of the clothing situation.

A SOUTHERN SOLDIER'S LETTERS HOME The Civil War Letters of Samuel Burney Cobb's Georgia Legion, Army of Northern Va. Ed. By Nat Turner Mercer Univ. Press, Macon Ga.2002

Pg. 132 Suffolk Va. March 10 1862 "...The 17 mile march from Winn's Mill to the place we took the river was decidedly tiresome-it was 17 miles and I think my knapsack weighed 30 lbs. which I carried on my back all the way...In moving any quantity of luggage, clothing cooking utensils, all were lost. I saw many good clothes burned. Our camp has only 7 tents with them; we are very much crowded..."

Once again, where were the officers? I guess I don't understand the situation at the time.

U.S. ARMY HERITAGE & EDUCATION CENTER Letters of James Griffin Hampton Legion

March 12, 1862 Head Qrs of the Legion Camp near Fredericksburg, Va My Darling Wife "...We then got off. Had our wagons too heavily loaded for the roads and had to leave many things besides. All of which were destroyed to prevent the enemy from getting them. We traveled over the worst roads that I ever saw or hope to see again. Such whooping, halooing, whipping and cutting and stalling in spite of all. Then into the mud the men had to go to push out. We worked hard all day, and until after night and made about twelve miles. We bivouacked in a pine thicket. Here we met the other regiments and next morning all traveled the same road. It was a sight to see the line-just think we had about twenty-five hundred infantry-fourteen guns each drawn by six horses, the same number of caissons each drawn by four horses-and about one hundred wagons all stretched along the road and then the Cavalry besides. The head of the line was several miles in front of the rear. And the roads which were bad enough at first after all this train had passed over them was perfectly awful to look at. We couldn't possibly haul the baggage, and had to detroy it all along the road. We saved for the men, scarcely anything but their blankets and a few cooking utensils, and some of the officer's trunks. I saved my trunk but lost my tent and my nice mess chest which Dr. Muse made for me. I hated it, but it had to go. I had them burned and had to burn every tent that the men had. And what is worst they lost nearly all of their baggage. We will get more tents for the men tomorrow. They are now camping out of doors but fortunately the weather is beautiful....Some one stole Maj. Conner's new seventy dollar overcoat whilst we were on the march-pretty hard luck...We four made up our minds to stand it with the men. The Doctors had half a dozen stretchers along (these are pieces of canvas about six feet long and two and a half wide they are used to carry the sick and wounded men on.) We got these and with three of them made a pretty good shelter over us and spread the other three on the ground to lie on. This was our bed covering and all. We went to bed wrapped in our overcoats until one of the servants came up with a few blankets. We covered up with these and slept pretty well-next morning we had breakfast with a light bill of fare and set out early..."

OK, maybe this explains why so much gear had to be discarded.

LETTERS WRITTEN DURING THE CIVIL WAR 1861-1865 Charles Fessenden Morse Privately Pub. 1898

Pg.43 March 15, 1862 Winchester "...While we were in town, a skirmish took place on the Strasburg road four or five miles from town, resulting in our capturing between twenty and thirty prisoners (Rebels-ed.); we saw them marched into town, some in uniform, some not...."

RECOLLECTIONS AND LETTERS OF GENERAL ROBERT E. LEE by His Son, Capt. Robert E. Lee pub by Garden city pub Co. 1926

Pg. 68 March 15, 1862 Richmond, Va. My Dear Mary: '...On returning to my quarters after 11 P.M. Custis informed me that Robert had arrived and had made up his mind to go into the army. He stayed at the Spottswood, and this morning I went with him to get his overcoat, blankets, etc. There is great difficulty in procuring what is good. They all have to be made...".

LEE & JACKSON'S BLOODY TWELTH-Letters of Irby Goodwin Scott First Lieutenant Co. G Putnam Light Infantry Twelth Ga. Vol. Inf. Ed. by Johnnie Perry Pearson Univ. Tn. Press 2010

Pg. 62 Camp Alleghany, March 16th, 1862 Dear Father, "…We all have plenty to eat and to wear, and are generally in fine spirits. I recieved a nice pair of pants, gloves and also a ball of thread by Milton Little which I was very glad to get…"

PARKER'S VIRGINIA BATTERY Robert K. Krick Va. Book Co. 1975

Pg. 14 March 18, 1862 at Camp Lee "…A first order of business for Captain Parker was providing the clothing and equipment necessary to uniform his men. To that end he authored a special requisition the first Tuesday morning in camp, calling for delivery of 109 overcoats, and the same number of caps, blankets, shirts and pairs of shoes. As a gesture toward maintenance of personal hygene, the requisition asked for 218 pairs of socks and a like number of drawers. As a final frill, the order called for one drum and one fife. It is apparent that Captain Parker had 109 bodies to clothe. The twenty-six militiamen probably retained their prior uniform with changes of insignia whenever that might be managed in the rush of other business. Presumably Parker himself and perhaps one or two of his officers would be providing their own uniform. The requisition is a firm indication that about 135 men were on hand to begin training at Camp Lee plus or minus a man or two…"

No mention of whether this requisition produced any results. I cannot imagine the Confederate government issuing overcoats to the troops in March.

THE CRY IS WAR, WAR, WAR The Civil War Correspondence of Lts. Burwell Thomas Cotton and George Job Huntley, 34th Regiment north Carolina troops by Michael W. Taylor Morningside 1994

Pg. 68 Marion County, Hamilton, N.C. March 20, 1862 "…You spoke of summer clothing-I cannot tell you whether I will want any from home or not. If we draw any, I shan't want any but if the government don't find us some I shall want a shirt or two and some drawers and maybe a pair of pants.…"

JAMES MADISON UNIVERSITY ARCHIVES

March 21st, 1862 Letters of 1st Lt. Reuben A. Scott Co. B, 10th Regiment Virginia Infantry Dear Mollie: "…Mollie we had orders with the rest to Pack up and send off our baggage and send it off which leaves me in a rather bad situation I want to change my clothes but they are three miles up the road and I am here without them but I look for our baggage back here soon…"

HISTORY OF THE FOURTH REGIMENT SOUTH CAROLINA VOLUNTEERS FROM THE COMMENCEMENT OF THE WAR UNTIL LEE'S SURRENDER by J.W. Reid pub by Shannon &Co. Printers & Stationers Morningside Bookshop 1975

Pg. 71 Camp Taylor, Orange County, Va. March 23d, 1862 "…Although this trip was gratifying to me it was attended with a good many hardships, such as hard marching, heavy baggage, and for the last two or three days came through enough mud to daub every negro cabin in the Confederacy. We carried our knapsacks, with our clothing and blankets in them, our haversacks our provisions and canteens of water, cartridge boxes of ammunition, our bayonet belts with bayonets in them and our muskets on our shoulders-a pretty good load…."

These soldiers seem to have hauled their gear for the enitr march.

LIFE AND LETTERS OF WILDER DWIGHT: Leuit.-Col. Second Mass. Inf Vols. Boston, Mass. 1891

Pg. 349 Letter From Wilder Dwight, March 25, 1862 At Harper's Ferry "…Our men shot up at them and took them in the head and breast. The woods are torn and shivered by musketry and cannon. Thirty men in Confederate homespun, shot in the head, lie in this wood…"

A SOUTHERN SOLDIER'S LETTERS HOME The Civil War Letters of Samuel Burney, Cobb's Georgia Legion, Army of Northern Virginia. Ed. By Nat Turner Mercer Univ. Press, Macon Ga.2002

Pg. 141 March 20th, 1862 Camp Hunter Suffolk, Va. My Dearest Wife "This is a damp night, & rather cold. We may be roused up before morning to take the cars; if so, I am all right as I have reduced my effects so that my knapsack will hold all my things, & that is packed and under my head when I sleep. I still have the pillow you sent me."

Pg. 142 Goldsboro N.C. March 26th 1862 My Dearest Wife "… left from Suffolk on 17 March, arrived 24th march "…I have lost nothing in all our moves that I consider very valuable. I lost my black hat and my comfort is on the way. I have but one pair of pants-those that you sent me-the others I could not carry to the James River when we first moved, and I gave them to Lucious. Don't send me a single thing in the way of clothing. I have several changes of underclothing, and my pants are of such excellent material they will do till I come home. My shoes are a little worn, but they are good enough till I come home. In coming here I put on two pairs of socks, two shirts, one vest & two coats; used Annie's comfort & Ma's black merino scarf. The result is that I kept warm & caught no cold while nine tenths of the Company have colds & are complaining more or less. I mention all these little things, my Dearest Wife, for you wrote I must tell you all. Grandma's gloves have been of untold benefit to me. Many times they have kept my fingers from aching, and I have often, when I put them on, thought of the kind good heart that gave them. They are a little worn...."

LEE'S TAR HEELS, The Pettigrew-Kirkland-McRae Brigade by Earl J. Hess pub by Univ. North Carolina, 2002

Pg. 17 March 26, 1862After the Battle of New Bern, N.C. The 29th, North Carolina Infantry "...but his most pressing problem was to resupply the regiment. A flood of donations from well-wishers from all over the state came to Kingston; in fact, so much clothing arrived that Vance informed the newspapers on March 26 that no more was needed. He also made certain that the men expressed their gratitude to all by printing in the "Raleigh North Carolina Standard the names of each donor and the articles they contributed. Company officers filed requisitions to obtain equipment that was not available on the home front. Canteen straps, shoes, jackets, trousers, haversacks, knapsacks and caps eventually were drawn from Confederate military stores to complete the regiment's refit..."

I wonder how many of the clothes and blankets donated were civilian? I consider this more proof that there was more civilian clothing in the Confederate Army than has been admitted.

LEE& JACKSON'S BLOODY TWELTH-Letters of Irby Goodwin Scott First Lieutenant Co. G Putnam Light Infantry Twelth Ga. Vol. Inf. Ed. by Johnnie Perry Pearson Univ. Tn. Press 2010

Pg. 63 Camp Alleghany March 27th, 1862 Dear Father, "...I shall send off all my cloths which I cannot carry in my knapsack...It is said that we will draw next time for 4 months and our cloths. I understand that the Society in Eatoton expects us to pay each ten dollars for the last suit of cloths sent us. If they furnished them I am willing to pay the ten dollars when we receive pay for them. I know it takes no little to cloth all the soldiers from Putnam..."

RECOLECTIONS OF A Md. CONFEDERATE SOLDIER AND STAFF OFFICER UNDER JOHNSON, JACKSON AND LEE by McHenry Howard Press of Morningside Bookshop 1975

Pg.75 Sun. Mar. 30, 1862-Richmond-"I had bought a plain grey coat, without sign of rank, to replace my soldier's jacket."

LETTERS FROM THE STONEWALL BRIGADE Ted Barcay, Liberty Hall Volunteers by Charles W. Turner Rockbridge Pub. Co. 1992

Pg. March 30, 1862 from Mt. Jackson Dear Sister "…I had to buy a complete fitout in underclothes as I left all of mine in Winchester in the wash. We have not been paid off yet and cannot tell when we will…"

MILITARY COLLECTOR AND HISTORIAN-Journal of the Company of Military Historians-Enlisted Uniforms of the Maryland Confederate Infantry: A Casr Study, Part 1 by Ross M. Kimmel Vol. XLI Fall, 1989

"…In late March, (1862) McHenry Howard and William Duncan received commissions as staff officers, to General Charles A. Winder and Isaac R. Trimble respectively. They left the 1st Maryland and went to Richmond, where they had trouble engaging hotel accomidations because, "our jackets and other clothinfg were shabby." Also, a surviving muster roll of Captain Charles Ederlin's Company (Co.B, erroneously identified on the roll as Co.C), dated 30 April, 1862 …reports the men's clothing as "poor and insufficient." …Pvt. John Gill's account of the Battle of Front Royal (23 May 1862). While pursuing fleeing Yankees, Gill saw one fall dead wearing a "long pair of cavalry boots." He relieved the dead man of the boots and wore them himself for many monthes afterward…"

Of course he relieved the Yankee of his boots, he's a Rebel soldier, ain't he?

DEAR IRVIE, DEAR LUCY-Civil War Letters of Capt. Irving A. Buck, General Cleburne's AAG & Family pub. by Buck Pub. Co. 2002

Pg. 62 March 30, 1862 Bel Aire, Front Royal, Va. My Dear Brothers, (referring to the Yankee occupation of Front Royal) "…I do not know how the change of affairs has affected the servants here-I can detect lttle if any change in them. But I believe as a general thing the love of freedom is strong within them that they would risk almost anything to obtain it. I do believe though that they are a little afraid of their "deliverers." You never heard such cruelties as they've perpetrated in Winchester-they ordered two or three of Mr. E. Bowens servants to do some very hard service in which they demurred whereupon they were shot and bayoneted. They worked them and beat them as no Southern gentleman would dream of doing, and are afraid to leave them at liberty at night lest they should run away, so they lock them in the jail. Some have escaped and returned to their masters and bring awful accounts of their treatment…" Lucy Buck

Yeah, the Union Army wasn't the "good guys" history would have us believe, their atrocities towards "contrabands" far overshadowed the unproven, alledged, "massacre" at Fort Pillow.

Pg. 26 "…The captain's repeated requisition s for clothing had also born fruit. His only additional clothing and supply needs were expressed in a requisition dated the morning the battery marched forth on its first campaign: two pairs of shoes, six caps, six pants, thiry pairs of socks and one Fly Tent—"Needed for destitute men of my company—the Tent need for myself."…"

CIVIL WAR LETTERS OF CAPTAIN A.B. MULLIGAN, Co. B, Fifth South Carolina Cavalry-Butler's Division-Hampton's Corps 1861-1865 by Olin Fulmer Hutchinson pub by The Reprint Co. 1992

Pg. 20 Charleston March 31st, 1862 My Dear Mother, "I am in want of summer shirts, pants, socks &c. Our uniform is gray cloth & sky blue pants trimmed with buff for the officers. We have not yet selected the uniforms for the company. (Capt. Muligan was forming his own company at this time)…"

THE PERSONAL RECOLLECTIONS AND EXPERIENCES IN THE CONFEDERATE ARMY by James Dinkins 1897

Pg. 54 April 1862 fourteen-year-old James Dinkins excerpt taken from "William Blake, a warm friend of the Little Confederate (James), was detailed by Colonel Griffin as courier for the regiment. He was called "Billy Blake," and was a pet of the entire regiment. He was exceedingly handsome, and up to this time managed to keep himself well dressed. He and the Little Confederate were about the same age. They were very successful foragers, and generally knew what was going on. By some means, Billy got hold of a box of paper collars, the first they had ever heard of. He divided them with his friend, and they agreed when one was soiled it should be given to Uncle Freeman (a slave) to wash. They each gave Uncle Freeman some soiled clothes and two paper collars, requesting him to have them ready that afternoon. Soon Uncle Freeman had the things in a kettle boiling. When he was ready to take them out, which he proceeded to do with a stick, he could not find the collars. He knew he had put them in the kettle together with other things, and could not account for their absence. The two boys were sitting at the root of a large tree, watching and listening to Uncle Freeman. He said, "Hi, here! What dun come of dem nice white collars?" He raked the bottom of the kettle again and again, but found no collars. He then emptied the water and found a few feragments of paper. He said, "My God, dis is mighty curious. I put dem collars in that kettle sure, and I been standing here all the time." The boys heard him talking, so Billy said to him, "Uncle Freeman, hurry up! Bud and I want to go." Uncle Freeman walked over to the boys with a few scraps of paper in his hand. He said, "Mars Billy, did you give me any white collars to wash?" "Yes," said Billy. "We gave you two, and we would like to have them right away. We are going to town." Uncle Freeman was greatly troubled. He could not explain the loss, so Billy told him he must pay for them, and that each one was worth a dollar. Billy collected two dollars from him, and arranged with another friend, Jim Finly, to tell Uncle Freeman they were made of paper, and, of course, could not be washed. Well, now, maybe Uncle Freeman did'nt rear and charge! It was a long time before Billy Blake could get any more clothes washed by Uncle Freeman. He talked about it fior several weeks, saying, "Nobody but a Yankee would er made collars out of paper to 'cieve folks. "Of course, the two dollars were returned to Uncle Freeman many times over..."

Apparently the soldiers still wore standing collars (when available). for formal wear. Victorian clothing Obsession

HISTORY OF THE FOURTH REGIMENT SOUTH CAROLINA VOLUNTEERS FROM THE COMMENCEMENT OF THE WAR UNTIL LEE'S SURRENDER J.W. Reid Shannon &Co. Printers & Stationers Morningside Bookshop 1975

Pg. 74 Camp Taylor Orange County,Va. April 1862 "...We have just been furnished with eighty rounds of cartridges to the man. That looks a bit squalish don't it? But I have become used to it. I presume there have been ten thousand rounds of cartridges thrown away since we left Centreville because we did not like to carry them. We would say they got wet. These just served may also get wet.

I'd never heard of Confederate soldiers discarding ammo this way. I guess it happens in every war.

Now let us talk about something that is nearer my heart or nearer my back. I was engages in patching those dad rotted old breeches again the other day. I could not get a patch that was precisely the same color as the pants, but so near the same thing you would hardly notice the difference, the pants being black and the patch piece of an old white blanket. All will be one color long before this reaches you. I have two old pairs which I patch and wear, wash and tear time about. They will soon be gone forever, but I am perfectly satisfied that they will go in peace, for there is no doubt of their hol(e)iness. I have one good pair of pants left, but am trying to save them to come home in, for if you were to see me in my old ones you might mistake me for a zebra, leopard, or something else equally outrageous..."

Camp near Richmond Va. June 1862 (After the seven days battles) "...Among other things I got, and by the way, not before I needed it, was a hat, new to me, but somewhat frazzled by its original owner. It fit me to a fraction..."

PARKER'S VIRGINIA BATTERY Robert K. Krick Va. Book Co. 1975

Pg19 Later spring, April, 1862 "…The 109 overcoats and other supplies ordered on March 18 had still not been seen one month later. Parker dashed off a new requisition for 119 jackets and 119 pants, with the comment that the men had been mustered in but never supplied. The shoes and drawers and blankets were not mentioned this time…"

Pg. 26 "…The captain's repeated requisitions for clothing had also born fruit. His only additional clothing and supply needs were expressed in a requisition dated the morning the battery marched forth on its first campaign: two pairs of shoes, six caps, six pants, thirty pairs of socks, and one Fly Tent-"Needed for destitute men of my company-The tent need for myself…"

BERRY BENSON'S CIVIL WAR BOOK, Memoirs of a Confederate Scout and Sharpshooter Ed. By Susan Williams Benson Univ. Ga. Press 1992

Pg. 2 Spring, 1862 Morris Island-"…A one-gun battery was about to be built not far above Cummings Point to be commanded by Col. Tom Lamar of Edgefield District and I was one of eight taken from the Regiment to man it. And npow we worked hard, often night as well as by day, shoveling sand and rolling with barrow up plank inclines, and many a time we were wet through by rain, not being allowed to stop. Once having no dry garment to sleep in, I took a cotton sack, and cutting a hole in the bottom for my head and a hole in each side for my arms, I had a sleevless shirt. Taking another sack, I cut two holes in the bottom, thrust my legs through, and tying the mouth of the sack about my waist, I had a pair of drawers…"

Ingenious…

THE CONFEDERATE VETERAN VOLLXX OCT. 1912

Pg.459 April 1862 "Simple Story of a Soldier-II by Samuel Hankins, 3rd Mississippi Infantry "The first year of the war (1861) was a picnic compared to the three remaining years. We had good tents in which to quarter, plenty of clothing, with little marching and fighting to do; also we had plenty of rations and there was an excess of rice. I became so tired of rice that that I have had no appetite for it since.

It was not until April, 1862, that the war began in earnest. It seemed that the commanders of both armies at that time came to the conclusion that maintaining armies was very expensive and that the issues must be forced.

We were stationed of the heights south of the Rhappahannock River, near Fredericksburg, Va., when orders were read to us on dress parade one evening to cook three day's rations, strike tents next morning by daylight, and be ready to move by sunrise. There was an unusually busy time in camp. At that period of the war every soldier had either a trunk or valise in connection with his knapsack, and every company had its tent, cooking utensils and baggage wagons. In order to lighten my load I took from my knapsack and placed in my trunk everything except one change of underwear, one towel, a cake of soap, a comb, and a little book on how to cook fancy dishes-a thing that the Lord knows I had no need for. I also had two heavy blakets, a rug, a knapsack, three day's rations, a hearvy gun, and a cartridge box containing forty rounds of ammunition-a good load for a bronco. I placed my trunk in one of the baggage wagons. When all was in readiness, the bugle sounded for us to fall in line. There was a heavy cloud, and just as our orderly sergeant finished calling the roll the cloud seemed to split wide open, and such a downpour of water I had never seen. Almost drowned, and notwithstanding that the deluge continued, we moved off. When we reached the lowlands, a distance of about one mile, we found all the small streams overflowing, and those not bridged had to be forded. Frequent heavy showers continued, and we were drenched.

After some three miles' march, my rug weighed about fifty pounds, so I decided to drop it. A few hundred yards further on, I abandoned one of my blankets and a little later my knapsack. I knew I had plenty of clothing in my trunk, so I felt easy. Here let me state, however, that when I threw away my knapsack I lost the last change of underwear, the last towel, the last cake of soap, and my comb. My garments remained on me until they wore off, except for some sunshiney days when on the bank of some stream they were taken off and washed. What became of the wagon with my trunk I have not found out up to the present time. Fifty years have come and gone since I began looking for it. I was not alone. What became of the thousands of blankets and clothing thrown away that day?"

A very good question. Did they just vanish, were they burned, stored or were they stolen?

A TRUE HISTORY OF COMPANY I, 49TH REGIMENT NORTH CAROLINA TROOPS by W.A. Day printed at the Enterprise Job Office, 1893

Pg. 11 April 1st, 1862 Raliegh, N.C. "…After the organization we drew out gray uniforms, blankets, knapsacks, haversacks, and canteens. We were then full-fledged Confederate Soldiers…"

THE JOURNAL OF CHARLES R. CHEWNING, Co. E, 9 Virginia Cavalry C.S.A. Researched and Edited by Richard B. Armstrong Cedar Creek Va. Archives

Pg. 1 ".Boulevare (Va.) April 2 1862 "…This morning we were sworn in as soldiers in the Ninth Cavalry, Company E, a great day for all of us. Our spirits are high and we all look grand in our new gray uniforms. I was given a fine gray wool coat and pants with two white cotton shirts. I am glad Captain Crutchfield told me to bring Pa's old rifle seein' as there are none of those fine muskets we have heard about for us...."

THE CRY IS WAR, WAR, WAR The Civil War Correspondence of Lts. Burwell Thomas Cotton and George Job Huntley, 34th Regiment North Carolina Troops by Michael W. Taylor pub by Morningside Press 1994

Pg. 70 Wayne County Camp near Goldsboro, N.C. April 3 1862 "...Tell Pap that I want some more Black Powder the first good chance he has to send them and I also want you to send me one good coarse pair of socks as soon as you can and you may take good care of the sheep and your wool for jeans britches is selling here at eleven dollars a pair, that is five dollars and a half apiece or for one pair. I can tell you something now about my summer clothing. I shall want one good coarse shirt, and one pair of summer britches and one pair of drawers...."

The "black powder" mentioned in this letter is not gunpowder, but a medicine.

THE CONFEDERATE VETERAN VOL. VI

April 1898 Pg. 151 Polley to Nellie-Humerous Incidents by J.B.Polley April 5, 1862 Camp near Fredericksburg Va. Charming Nellie-"There is a member of my company whom I shall dub Jack, lest, by revealing his identity, the tale I relate should cling to him longer and closer than that of his overcoat. Looking more to his own comfort and and sense of the fitness of things than to uniformity of dress and the consequent soldierly appearance for which my friend Brahan is such a stickler, Jack disdainfully rejected the munificent offer of the Confederate States Government to furnish him a gray and strickly military overcoat for $5 on a credit, and expended $25 on the purchase of one of a quality and fashion to commend itself to the most fastidious aristocrat. The first night out from Dumfries the weather was so intensely cold that he decided not to remove any of his garments, and so, wrapping himself in couple of blankets, he laid down very close to a huge log fire, where, lulled by the genial warmth, he soon fell soundly asleep, and began to snore at his liveliest and merriest gait. About midnight, Bob Murray's acutely sensitive olfactory nerves were offended by the scent of burning cloth. He had only to look once to discover that the fire had burned lower and lower, Jack had edged his back nearer and nearer to it, and that at last a stray coal had lighted a flame that was playing sad havoc with his blanket and coat. Aroused by Bob's shouts, Jack did some rapid hustling around, but alas! Too late to preserve the anatomy, the pristine symmetrical "tout ensemble," of the cherished garment and prevent its transformation from an elegant frock into a nondescript, altogether too open in the back to be comfortable, with two pointed tales hanging in front, instead of in the rear-in short, in two sections, whose only bond of union was the velvet collar. Next morning the crestfallen owner sought to repair the damage by sewing the burnt edges together, but that heroic remedy, while reducing the tails to one, and that pointing in the right direction, rendered it impossible to button up the front, and kept him so busy during the day answering questions that when night came he was too hoarse to talk…"

Poetic justice?

SOJURNS OF A PATRIOT The Field and Prison Papers of An Unreconstructed Confederate ed by Richard Bender Abell & Fay Adamson Gecik pub bySouthern Heritage Press Murfreesboro, TN 1998

Pg. 42 Camp Bartow, 30th Regt. Ga. Vols. April 6th, 1862 "…The next time you get a chance you can, if you wish, send me a pair of pants, some kind of summer goods, as jeans is too warm for this country and I am afraid we will have to stay here all the time.…"

CIVIL WAR LETTERS OF CAPTAIN A.B. MULIGAN, Co. B. Fifth South Carolina Cavalry-Butler's Division.Hampton's Corps 1861-1865 by Olin Fulmer Hutchinson pub by The Reprint Co. 1992

Pg. 21 Camp Gist April 6th 1862 My Dear Mother & Sisters, "I do not stand in need of anything in the eating line but do stand in need of shirts,&c. If you can get some good check, good apron check, fast colored calico or graham of small check & not too thick please to make me about five shirts. Collar same size as my dress shirts & a plain band so I can wear a white collar."

I hadn't heard that Confederate officers normally wore collars, though it being a Victorian period fashion, I suppose it was more commonplace than I thought.

RED CLAY TO RICHMOND by John J. Fox pub by Angle Valley Pres 2006

Pg. 35 "The soldiers of the 35th Georgia marched northward with the rest of Pettigrew's Brigade early on April 7.(1862) The rain poured down as they crossed the Rappahanock River and slogged through the mud. Five miserable miles later the column halted. The men received orders to pitch tents. Twenty-four-year-old Lieutenant William C. Goggans, of Company A, wrote: "We continued our march through the day though owing to the inclemency of the weather we made but little progress. [A]rrived in four miles of the expected enemy when we taken up camp lying up on the cold and frozen woods With but few tents, and the bad clothes…"

Pg. 38 late April 1862 “”[T]imes is hard hear at this time. [W]e have nothing but bread and meete (meat) to eat. [T]hair is so many men hear thay cant hall (haul) evry thing wee need. [We have got no tents hear to doo us eny good. [T]hay sent them off from hear. [W]hen wee left ashland wee left all all wee had but 2 suits of under cloes (clothes) and 1 pair of pants and 1 blanket so as to make our lod (load) as lite as possible.” Hiram Hammond reported that some of the men did have small open-ended tent flies for protection.”

CONFEDERATE LETTERS AND DIARIES ed by Walbrook D. Swank pub by Papercaft Printing and Design Inc. 1992

Pg. 19 Letters of James Malcom Hart Private Crenshaw's Artillery Battery (Virginia) Pegram's Battalion, Hill's Army Corps, Army of Northern Virginia Camp Lee Apr. 10th, 1862 My dear Aunt Elizabeth “…I was going to say I got my new overcoat. It is a large coarse affair & I find no difficulty putting it on over my old one which I do when it is very cold.”

Pg. 18 Camp Lee Apr. 10th, 1862 My dear Mother, “…I wish you to get Ned McCloud to make me a pair of high quarter shoes to march in. I cannot wear these that are furnished by the government. Mr. Johnson can bring them when he comes back….”

“DEAR MARTHA…” The Confederate War Letters Of A South Carolina Soldier Alexander Faulkner Fewell compiled and edited by Robert Harley Mackintosh, Jr. pub by The R.L. Bryan Co. 1976 17th South Caroline Inf. Company E

Pg.51 April 10th 1862 Ebenezerville So.Ca. Mr. A.F. Fewell Dear Brother “…You wanted a pair of shoes for you and Elias Neely. I had heard so before you had written to me and saw Brown and told him to make them such as E.T. Avery's and he said he would do so. I sent up for them yesterday but (he) had not made them but will this or next week. The price is $5.00 a pair….”

An absolute bargain compared to what the price for shoes would be later in the war.

U.S. ARMY ARCHIVES AND EDUCATION CENTER

April 11th, 1862 Henry I. 4th Alabama Infantry Regiment Merriport (Va.) My Dear Wife: “…Our work since December has been making clothing for prisoners (Confederates taken prisoner), the first were some of those captured from Marshall by Garfield and sent to the barracks here in a most destitute condition. Some had been hiding in the woods for weeks. One had after the battle lain in the river all night to escape being taken and the rest was made prisoner: those the few Southern ladies here supplied suits, commencing with the hat and ending with shoes. Many here have friends others aquantences among the prisoners, several ladies and gentlemen visited the camps from Covington and Newport, can you not aid in supplying their wants anything from a ¼ (?) will help, suppose you were to get up and pack a box of half-worn vests, shoes, coats and pants and send (to) Camp Douglas near Chicago, let some friends take them and see their given as intended; all that have been sent have been new ; but a letter yesterday was received asking for a change of clothing for 9 soldiers who had none and that old or new would be acceptable…"

At that point, anything to wear

LEE& JACKSON'S BLOODY TWELTH-Letters of Irby Good-win Scott First Lieutenant Co. G Putnam Light Infantry Twelth Ga. Vol. Inf. Ed. by Johnnie Perry Pearson Univ. Tn. Press 2010

Pg. 70 Camp Johnson, Augusta Co. Va. April 11th, 1862 Dear Father, "…You wished to know whether I needed any cloths or not and let you know. It is now to late for you to get this letter before Jim Pike leaves. I am not much in need of anything. I will need about three shirts for summer (I mean cotton shirts). I have plenty of socks (woolen) but they will not be good for summer. So you can send me 3 pr. of thick cotton socks. I have plenty of drawers. I should like to have a good pr. of shoes for summer wear, not too heavy and would prefer them made in Madison if convenient. I want them with broad bottoms and heels. I also want two rows of large headed tacks in the heels to prevent the rocks from wearing them off too soon. I have worn my boots ever since I got them besides marching in them and they are now pretty good. It does not take long to wear out shoes in this country…"

Remember that last statement, shoe supply was always a problem

Pg. 71 April 18, 1862 Camp Shenandoah, Augusta Co. Va. Dear Father "…Gen. Johnston has issued an order that no more transportation will be furnished to carry clothes or edibles more than is allowed in the army regulations. Everything we from home hereafter we will have to hire transportation, and if we have more clothing on hand than we can carry on our backs it is that much lost. I have found from experience that two good suits of clothing is as much as a soldier can well take care of. All that is necessary is a change. I have a good many things in Staunton which I have never had any use for. I intend if I should get the chance to send these home. I was glad to hear that Lieunt. Reid was bringing us tents. We will not be so badly crowded and they are much better than the government tents…"

WEBSITE-CONFEDERATE UNIFORMS.ORG The Richmond (Va) Daily Dispatch

The Richmond (Va) Daily Dispatch, April 12, 1862 "The Tensas Cavalry. It's origin, Tensas Parish, Louisiana. The uniform, of which we had two suits, a dress and a fatigue, The dress was of blue cloth, trimmed in yellow. The fatigue was of gray and of coarser material. Cavalry boots reaching to the knee. A gray hat, with a black ostrich feather. Each man's measure was taken and the uniform and boots were made in New Orleans. Each man's uniform cost him $48.00…"

Another mention of a dress uniform. I wonder what became of them? Check out the price, an expensive uniform for the times.

"DEAR MARTHA…" The Confederate War Letters Of A South Carolina Soldier Alexander Faulkner Fewell compiled and edited by Robert Harley Mackintosh, Jr. The R.L. Bryan Co. 1976 17th South Carolina Inf. Company E

Pg. 58 Ebenezerville April 15 1862 "…Dear Alice. "…I want to go and get something to make you a coat and vest. I have maid anough money one way and another to by your cloths. I cut out seven pairs or pants last Monday and made them all against Saturday night and cut out seven more pair yesterday. I am maken your pants…"

WELCOME THE HOUR OF CONFLICT-William Cowan McClellan & the 9th Alabama ed by John C. Carter pub by Univ Al. Press 2007

Pg. 158 April 15, 1862 Lebanon Church (Va) William McClellan to Thos J. McClellan Dear Father, "…Lt. Floyd and my self came back to our old camp this morn ing to get sum clean cloths, tell Mother those shirts and socks came just at the right time. I have just washed and put on one of them…"

JAMES MADISON UNIVERSITY ARCHIVES

April 17, 1862 Letters of 1st Lt. Reuben A. Scott Co.B, 10th Regiment Virginia Infantry Harrisonburg, Va. Dear Papa (Mr. Amos Scott): "…Papa our mess wants a baker and would be much obliged to you to send us one a skillet or an oven wiil do send us lid if you can get it for us and send me a bill of what it cost and I will get you the Pay (.) Mr. Whitin(?) is coming down in a few days he will bring it for us if you can see him before he starts…"

Now, how long do you think they toted those items in the upcoming campaigns?

"DEAR MARTHA…" The Confederate War Letters Of A South Carolina Soldier Alexander Faulkner Fewell compiled and edited by Robert Harley Mackintosh, Jr. The R.L. Bryan Co. 1976

17th South Carolina Inf. Company E
Pg. 60 Ebenezerville April 18 (1862) "…Dear Alice. I got you a coat with a little wool in it. A dark gray for 7 dollars. Youir Father thinks that it will suit you bad. I think that it is full short in the skirt. If it don't soot they will take it back. I got some dark goods to make you a hunting shirt. If you want it maid write if I will make it like you told me or will I make a shirt out of it. I paid for all that I got but the Coat. I am sorry that John Galden diddent let me now that he was going dow(n). I could have sent youir summer Cos (clothes) dow(n) and box with something good to eat…"

CONFEDERATE LETTERS AND DIARIES 1861-1865 ed by Walbrook D. Swank-Col. U.S.A.F. Ret. pub by Papercraft Printing and Design Co. Charlottesville, Va. 1988

Pg. 21 Creshaw's Battery, Camp Lee April 18th, 1862 "(My dear Uncle)

Mr. Thomason a member of our Company goes up tomorrow. I propose to send up by him my uniform overcoat for Mother to make some improvements in. I wish the cape taken off and the underside lined with oil cloth, and then button holes worked at even distances around the collar so that the cape may be taken off and turned over, so as to have the oil cloth either above or below. If the button holes are not all the same distance apart they will not hit right when the cape is turned. Mr. Thomason returns Tuesday & will bring back the coat with him…."

SOJURNS OF A PATRIOT The Field and Prison Papers of an Unreconstructed Confederate ed by Richard Bender Abell & Fay Adamson Gucik pub by Southern Heritage Press 1998

Pg. 79 April 19 1862 Camp Floyd, Abington, Va Letter from Private John Lee Holt, "My dearly Beloved Wife; "…Meredith has got a furlough and is going home tomorrow…I want you to send me my cotton drawers by Meredith when he comes back& I will try & send my woolen ones home by the first opportunity if Pa comes out here as he speaks of I can send them by him & I want to send some other things also The drawers are all I want you to send me as I have as many clothes as I want of every sort…"

I wonder if he got those woolen drawers back next winter. At least he is completely equipped for clothes at this time.

"DEAR MOTHER: DON'T GRIEVE ABOUT ME. IF I GET KILLED, I'LL ONLY BE DEAD." ed. by Mills Lane pub by The Beehive Press 1977

Pg. 116 A.J. Reese to his Aunt Beufort, South Carolina April 20, 1862 Dear Aunt: "…I would like for you to make me two cotton shirts, striped ones if you have the cloth, and send them to me the first chance you get and keep account of all the clothes you send me and I will make it straight, I hope, before long…"

HANDLEY LIBRARY ARCHIVES- Diary of William J. Thomas 2nd Maryland Battalion

Pg. 30 April 24 1862 "Raining, commenced with snow. Made a bunk with blanket and india rubber but did not trench it, hence, though the rain did not reach me, the water from above running down the slope did. I fell asleep and awoke to feel the water running in a stream from my head to my heels. Geo. pretty much the same. I lay as long as possible on the right side, but finding one side wet and one side dry was not comfortable, also being tired of lying on the same side I turned and soon the same operation commenced on that side. A continual stream kept running through my clothes until morning, when I was called for guard. I then wrung out my drawers and put on my pants, feeling anything but comfortable. Made a different bunk and ditched it."

FAR, FAR FROM HOME-The Wartime Letters of Dick and Tally Simpson, 3rd South Carolina Volunteers by Guy R. Everson & Edward W. Simpson pub. by Oxford Univ. Press 1994

Pg. 117 April 24th, 1862 Letter No. 50 TNS to Mary Simpson Cutis' Farm on the Pennensula, Va. Dear Sister, "We are still living in the open air without tents, but with little houses made of blankets, we make out very well. I am doing remarkably well with the small amount of clothing I have on hand. I am fearful about keeping myself shod. My boots are giving way, and there are no propects for another pair…"

Once again shoe shortage.

"DEAR MOTHER: DON'T GRIEVE ABOUT ME. IF I GET KILLED, I'LL ONLY BE DEAD." Ed. by Mills Lane The Beehive Press 1977

Pg. 117 Benjamin Moody to his Wife Yorktown, Virginia April 25, 1862 Dear Wife: "… We have got no tents here to do us any good. They send them off from here. When we left Ashland, we left all we had but two suits of underclothes and one pair of pants and one blanket, so as to make our load as light as possible…"

CONFEDERATE CAPTAIN UJANIRTIS ALLEN'S LETTERS TO HIS WIFE ed. By Kandall Allen and Keith S. Bohannon La. State Univ. Press 1998

Pg.90 Camp on the Rappadan River Apr 25th 1862 "…Send my hair Greece and anything else that you can conveniently. … You need not make me many if any shirts untill I write for them, because I can do without for a while yet and might not be able to take care of them. I have a change of clothing in my carpet sack with the wagons and I hear that they are ordered somewhere from Gordonsville. I hear that our baggage is being sent away from there too. A thousand wash-women could not keep this regement clean, situated as we have been. Half of the time we draw hard bread (crackers) and are compelled to broil our meat on a stick, using our pants shoes and coattails for handkerchiefs towels dishrags etc. It is quite common to see a person wipe his knife on his boot and commence eating...." *Hair grease? Is this soldier that vain? Here is the introductory quotes on Confederate Army life*

Pg. 105 "...My clothes got wet at Winchester and have not been dry since, taking all the rains and I could not have a chance to dry them. They are almost rotten, my papers all ruined. To give you an idea, some ground peas that I had had sprouts two inches long...."

THE CRY IS WAR, WAR, WAR The Civil War Correspondence of Lts. Burwell Thomas Cotton and George Job Huntley, 34th Regiment north Carolina troops by Michael W. Taylor Morningside 1994

Pg. 75 Caroline Co., Va. April 27th 1862 "...I wrote home for some summer clothing before I left Goldsboro. If you have the chance you may send me one cotton shirt, but don't send no more till I write for it..."

A SOUTHERN SOLDIERS LETTERS HOME-The Civil War Letters of Samuel Burney, Cobb's Legion, Army of Northern Virginia ed by Nat Turner pub by Mercer Univ. Press 2002

Pg. 158 April 27, 1862 Army of the Penninsula Camp Georgia Legion My Dearest Wife, "... It rained all day but held up at night. We built good fires & kept as dry as we could. I had on three flannel shirts & a blanket over my shoulders which kept me dry. My feet got wet as my shoes are bad. I dried them several times..."

DAILY LIFE IN CIVIL WAR AMERICA ed by Dorthy Denneen Volo & James M. Volo

Pg. 170 "...Confederate soldiers acquired so much Federal equipment that it was difficult to discriminate between friend and foe simply by uniform. "A Rebel Captain and some of his men were clothed in our uniform," wrote a frustrated federal officer, "a growing practice, so reprehensible that it should be met with condign (well-deserved) punishment, as the deception engendered is always apt to cost lives and disasters." In winter, large contingents of Southern troops were seen sporting sky blue Federal trousers and greatcoats. Federal commanders insisted that Southern troops captured wearing federal equipment be treated as spies. The south countered that such items were legitimate objects of capture under the rules of war, to be used at the pleasure of the captors, leaving a dispute that was never resolved.

A resident of Winchester, Viginia, Cornelia McDonald, decribed the uniform of a fallen Southern gallant with the rank of major in 1862. "He was dressed in a beautiful new un iform, grey and buff; a splendid red silk scarf was around his waist." …"A Federal writer described the clothing of a fallen foe in 1864: "His feet, wrapped in rags, had coarse shoes upon them, so worn and full of holes that they were only held together by many pieces of thick twine. Ragged trousers, a jacket, and a shirt of…'tow cloth', a straw hat which had lost a large portion of both crown and brim…"

DIARIES.WRITINGS AND STORIES OF GEORGE D. BUSWELL

Co. H 33rd regiment Virginia Infantry Stonewall Brigade privately pub. Camp Winder April 27th 1862 letter to brother "Since I wrote home last, the transportation from the army has been increased by order of Gen. Lee. Company officers are allowed 50 lbs each, we will be allowed 150 lbs. so we have concluded to have our mess chest brought back. If Eli Frazier does not get it down, Perry will try to get it to us when he comes. I will also have my pants, that I had sent away in the trunk, brought back. I think I can keep two pairs with me at least for awhile. If you have an opportunity, you may get the rest of my clothes home…"

THE CONFEDERATE VETERAN VOL. XXXVII 1929

Pg. 131 April 1929 Experiences at Seven Pines by D.B. Easley 18th Virginia May 1862 "… and a ball struck me on the round bone which projects outside on the right knee and stopped about an inch above the ankle. It felt as if something heavy had fallen on it. I looked and saw a small hole in the only new uniform I got during the war…"

A MARYLAND BOY IN LEE'S ARMY by George Wilson Booth Univ. of Nebraska Press 2000

Pg. 35 May 1862 Valley Campaign "…Among the strange things that had fallen into our hands were a number of sets of armor, metal breastplates and thigh protectors, which were found on the prisoners or in the baggage of their camps. We amused ourselves by setting up these armor plates and firing at them at short range to test their power of resistance. At fair range they would turn a revolver ball very well, and a rifle or musket ball if from any considerable distance, but at close range they were vulnerable to the latter. It has been denied that these doughty warriors wore these appliances, but I can testify to their existence and use, and, moreover, Colonel Johnson succeeded in sending one to the rear and it is in his possession at the present writing…"

A first-hand account of the use of body armor.

THE CONFEDERATE REGULAR ARMY by Richard P. Weinert Jr. pub by White Mane Pub Co. 1991

Pg. 87 May 1862 The Maryland Confederate Regulars, Company C, "…There seems to have always been a shortage of adequate clothing for the company. The small arms carried by the men were mixed lot, some being ancient smoothbore muskets altered to percussion with a few new Model 1851 Springfield muskets…"

ROCKBRIDGE ARTILLERYThe Story of a Cannoneer Under Stonewall Jackson by Edward Moore Neale Pub. Co. 1907

Pg. 79 May 1862 immediately after the Valley Campaign, camp somewhere around Strasburg, Va. "…To give an idea of the ready access we had to the enemy's stores, I had been the possessor of nine gum-blankets within the past three weeks, and no such article as a gum-blanket was ever manufactured in the South. Any soldier carrying a Confederate canteen was at once recognized as a new recruit, as it required but a short time to secure one of superior quality from a dead foeman on a battlefield…"

The Rebs started relying on supply from the Yankees

HANDLEY LIBRARY ARCHIVES-Diary of William J. Thomas, 2nd Maryland Battalion

Pg. 31 May 1 1862 "…Our "flies" were brought up. Hereafter we expect to use these instead of tents, being more comfortable in summer and more easily transported…"

THE CONFEDERATE LETTERS OF BENJAMIN H. FREEMAN Compiled & Edited by Stuart T. Wright pub by Exposition Press 1974

Pg. 11 May 4 1862 Camp Mangum near Raleigh, NC Dear Mother: "I this morning packed up my clothes while I got the chance (to) send them home. I sent two shirts one pair of draws (drawers) one coat one pair of Pants Give them to Pa to wear…"

LEE& JACKSON'S BLOODY TWELTH-Letters of Irby Good-win Scott First Lieutenant Co. G Putnam Light Infantry Twelth Ga. Vol. Inf. ed. by Johnnie Perry Pearson pub by Univ. Tn. Press 2010

Pg. 75 Camp Vally Mills, West View, Augusta Co. Va. May 4th, 1862 Dear Father, "...You can send clothing for the government has as much as it can do to supply those in the army who cannot get the things from home..."

A very true statement.

THE CRY IS WAR, WAR, WAR The Civil War Correspondence of Lts. Burwell Thomas Cotton and George Job Huntley, 34th Regiment North Carolina Troops by Michael W. Taylor pub by Morningside Press 1994

Pg. 78 same camp, May 4th, 1862 "...Some time ago I wrote home for more clothing, but I have written several letters that you never got, I don't expect. I will tell you what I want now. You may send me one shirt and one pair drawers and pair socks and some Black Powders. That's all I want now. I may want some pants some time this summer, but I don't know what time. I will let you know..."

RED CLAY TO RICHMOND by John J. Fox pub by Angle Valley Press 2006

Pg. 39 May 5th 1862 "...A courier arrived later with orders for the 35th Georgia to hussle back to the fighting at Williamsburg. Raindrops pelted their backs as the firing grew louder, but less frequent. When they reached the battlefield, the fighting had ceased. Bodies of soldiers from both sides littered the ground. The soaking rain made their uniforms indistinguishable...(Private Moody)"...The miseries of being absent from our families and fathers and mothers and sickness and exposure to rain, mud and dust, cold and heat, lying and rolling on the ground in the dirt without a change of clothes, sleeping without blankets, suffering under hard and rigid officers, suffering scornings from commanding bearings, driven from pillar to post by commanders that don't understand their business..." *Ah, the joys of army life!*

Pg. 41 "Martha Moody closed her sad letter by saying that she would send some clothes to her husband and she urged him to check the pants pocket because she would put a piece of her new dress there."

I WROTE YOU WORD-The Poignant Letters of Private John Holt-John Lee Holt 1829-1863 ed. by James A. Mumper printed by H.E. Howard 1991

Pg. 80 Camp Fulton Richmond Va. May 6th, 1862 My dearest wife, "...I received the drawers you sent by Pa & send by him my flannel drawers & some other clothes that I have no need of now & I expect I shall have to send some more home yet as they say we will draw new uniforms again before we leave here..."

ONE OF CLEBURNE'S COMMAND-The Civil war Remini-scences & Diary of Captain Samuel T. Foster, Granbury's Texas brigade, C.S.A. Univ. of Texas Press, 1980

Pg. 41 at Richmond May 6 1862 "...I got me a good suit of Confederate gray uniform coat and pants, cap, sword & belt and some underclothes socks shoes &c& ..."

He doesn't say whether this was government issue or from home folks.

VOICES FROM COMPANY D Diaries by the Greensboro Guards, Fifth Alabama infantry Regiment, Army of Northern Virginia ed. by G.Ward Hubbs Univ. of Ga. Press 2003

Pg. 85 May 6, 1862 retreat from Wiliamsburg Va. JST "...Commenced retreating again this morning at 2 O'clk A.M. the troops nearly all broken down from fatigue, hunger, & want of sleep. The road for 5 miles was strewn with Blankets, Over coats, Clothing, Knap Sacks, Cooking Utensils, Sick Men &c. &c...."

ONE OF CLEBURNE'S COMMAND-The Civil War Remini-scences & Diary of Captain Samuel T. Foster, Granbury's Texas brigade, C.S.A. pub by Univ. of Texas Press, 1980

Pg. 40 Penensula Campaign, May 6, 1862 "...I stop to see my brother here I find my brother Hale Foster-he is bare footed, carrying a frying pan and a blanket.

Taken all together they are the hardest lot of men I ever met-If this is soldiering, then it is certain we have not seen any yet-These men have no baggage wagons-Carry all their baggage and cooking utensils on their backs, and are not burdened at that-Bare footed men were plenty-some were bare headed-some had pieces of clothing on. Some had a piece of meat sticking on his Bayonett. Some had his frying pan stuck in his gun barrel-as a convienent way to carry it..."

This is the description of the Rebels for the next three years.

A CAPTAIN'S WAR LETTERS AND DIARIES of William H.S. Burgwyn 1861-1865 ed. By Herbert M. Schiller White pub by Mane Pub Co. Inc. 1994

Pg. 3 Headquarters 48th Regiment N. C. Troops Camp Near Goldsboro May 6th 1862

"...I hope this will reach you before you start to Richmond as I wish you would get me some things there. A saddle, bit, and bridle and an oil cloth suit. All, I don't think, will amount to over fifty-five dollars. The saddle, thirty; bit, five; can make out without the bridle; and oil cloth suit, twenty."

I doubt this soldier got any of these things on his list. I'd love to see an oilcloth suit. If they were available, there would be more references to them in the letters.

THEY CALLED HIM STONEWALL by Burke Davis pub by The Fairfax Press 1954

Pg. 17 May 8, 1862 Valley Campaign "...They were lean and becoming leaner and would carry no superflorious weight, for whatever reason. They slept in twos, each furnishing a blanket and an oilcloth, which they carried in rolls over their shoulders. Their bed, warm in any weather, consisted of an oilcloth on the ground and one on top, with two blankets in between..."

They had no overcoats, for they had long since unworthy of the effort of carrying them through good weather; they wore short grey jackets, many of them torn off raggedly at the hips. Beneath, they wore white cotton garments, for in there the lice were easier to control; and when the underclothes were taken off, it was forever. Washing seldom helped, since Jackson, with his swift movements, gave them little chance to propare hot water.

No soldiers ever marched in lighter order, for there was seldom anything in the thin blanket but a few berries, persimmons, or an apple in season, and perhaps a bit of soap. They were ragged, vermin-infested, thin, pestered by the itch-but durable and of a fierce, unbreakable morale. No one knew how, but they gained in confidence each week...."

Say what you will, they were virtually unstoppable.

THE YOUNG LIONS-Confederate Cadets at War by James Lee Conrad pub by Stackpole Books 1997

Pg. 58 May 8, 1862 "The (VMI) cadets parted with Jackson's army at Lebanon Springs on May 16, and marched twenty miles to Saunton, losing about half their number along the way because of lack of shoes..."

THREE YEARS IN THE HORSE ARTILLERY by George M. Neese pub by Morningside Bookshop 1983

Pg. 59 May 10, 1862 Shenandoah Valley Campaign chasing Bank's army toward Winchester-"…After Jackson's infantry came up and passed to the front, and while our battery was awaiting orders, a few of us got permission from the proper authority to go on a twenty minute pilfering raid among the debris and spoils scattered all along the road of Bank's routed army.

The first prize we struck was a wagon standing in a wheat field, loaded with large square boxes full of military clothing. The first box we opened was full of dark blue frock coats with brass eagle military buttons.

I got four coats, but they were too blue for a Rebel to wear on the field, and too bulky knapsacks strewn over the field and road. However, most of them had already pessed through the raking process thoroughly applied by Confed. snatchers. After a real ragged Rebel rifles a knapsack I would not give a cancelled postage stamp for what he leaves…."

Oh, yeah, they're learning!

LEE'S TIGERS-The La. Inf. In the Army of Northern Va. by Terry L. Jones Univ. of La. Press

Pg. 77 Valley Campaign, May 10, 1862 chasing Bank's army down the Valley (Middletown, Va.) "…While gathering up prisoners, the Louisianians let out whoops of laughter when they found a number of apparently inexperienced troopers strapped to their saddles. Other Tigers were surprised to find some of the Yankees wearing antiquated breastplates, including some Federal dead with neat, round bullet holes drilled through the armor…"

Seriously, cavalrymen strapped to their saddles? I'd have laughed myself silly. This quote also illustrates one of the reasons the body armor was discarded.

HADLEY LIBRARY ARCHIVES-Personal Recollections by Henry V. Niemeyer, 9th Virginia Infantry, Co. I the "Old Dominion Guards"

May 10, 1862 Peninnsula Campaign "…Our knapsacks, with clothes, bibles, and many precioius articles, began to feel so heavy on the tired man, that we took them off and laid them under a tree, expecting to return and get them. But we were doomed to disappointment, and there was seldom a time after that when I could boast of an extra pair of socks or shirt. I have often stopped long enough to wash my thin cotton shirt in a ditch, wring it out as dry as I could, put it on, and let it dry the best way possible…"

Right there he should have realized that to set a knapsack down was to lose it and its contents.

A SOUTHERN SOLDIERS LETTERS HOME-The Civil War Letters of Samuel Burney, Cobb's Legion, Army of Northern Viginia ed by Nat Turner pub by Mercer Univ. Press 2002

Pg. 164 May 13, 1862 Baltimore Cross Roads, Camp Georgia Legion, Dearest Wife, "You have no idea what value we esteem a few little things. A tin cup-you have no idea of its value. We beat up coffee in it, make coffee in it-by the by, good coffee too. A canteen is of the greatest value. I gave two dollars for one a day or so ago. A negro lost mine in going after water. My haversack too is of great value, but my pocketknife, you remember the one I swapped with Billy for a two bladed one-I would not take ten dollars for it. A spoonful of salt, sugar, pepper, etc., is carefully husbanded for we never know when our commissary department will be replenished. We have one frying pan and one oven in our company. I am this morning barbequing some beef, having nothing to cook it in. We have as our sauce, pepper, salt, wild onions & water."

Salt, pepper, etc., were carried in twists of paper or cloth.

Pg. 166 May 18th, 1862 Camp Georgia Legion, Richmond, Va. My Dearest One,"...Send me by Captain Knight or any reliable person firat passing two summer shirts, two or three pairs of socks, my hat and several pairs of drawers. Two pair will do..."

Pg. 171 May 28th, 1862 [Morris' Farm] Camp Georgia Legion Near Richmond Va. My Dearest Wife, "...Yesterday I got a tub and went in the shade on the hillside and had a good bath all over. I mounted clean clothes, and had my shoes blacked (for occasional decency's sake) lit my pipe, sat down in a chair and read hymns from a Methodist book..."

He won't be getting his shoes blacked for very long.

Website civilwarhome.com Civil War letter of LeRoy McAfee,

49th NCT Co.K Godsboro, S.C. May 14th, 1862 My Dear Sister, "...Tell Annsi to come right on and bring two pillows a blanket, and comfort. I have lost my camp chest. It was impossible for me to get it on at Charlitte & I left it in the agents care & he sent it but I have never received it. All items clothes & bed clothes are in it. I hope I get it yet..."

Good luck, LeRoy.

HANDLEY LIBRARY ARCHIVES-Diary of William Randolph Smith Co. F, 17th Virginia Infantry pub by Manassas Chapter, United Daughters of the Confederacy 1986

Pg. 11 May 15, 1862 (marching from the Valley to near Richmond), "...Many of our shoes gave out on this march and our boys had to take it barefoot. I traveled two days barefoot but now we are near the city and I hope we will be able to procure shoes, etc., which the men stand so much in need of..."

Once again, good luck, soldier.

LETTERS FROM THE STONEWALL BRIGADE Ted Barcay, Liberty Hall Volunteers by Charles W. Turner pub by Rockbridge Pub. Co. 1992

Pg. 67 May 16, 1862 camp at Mt. Solon Dear Sister "...I do not care how soon I get to Staunton as I have had this suit of clothes on for over three weeks. I found my knapsack again, one of the regiment had taken care of it for me, but the clothes had been wet so long they were of no account. The stockings I will send home as they are very good except some holes in the feet..."

About those stockings, he must mean good to unravel for the yarn.

FOUR YEARS IN THE CONFEDERATE ARTILLERY-The Diary of Pvt. Henry Robinson Berkely ed. by William H. Runge pub by Univ. N.C. Press 1961

May 19 1861 Pg. 5 "...I went up to Beaver Damn Depot and got my uniform..."

That's the entire entry, no statement as to whether it was issued by the government, sent from home, or retieved from storage.

DEFEND THE VALLEY by Margarette Barton Colt pub by Crown Pub. 1994

Pg. 162 MEMOIR OF ROBERT T. BARTON May-June 1862 Valley Campaign Robert is forced to hide in a pond to avoid capture "As soon as the firing ceased I crawled out of the water as wet as a rat and as weak as a kitten. I took off my grey artillery jacket which was covered in mud. Beneath it was a blue flannel shirt and that too, and my pants, were disfigured with mud. I was absolutely dazed and confused, but presently seeing a line of infantry resting in the field in the direction of where the enemy had been, and which had a Virginia flag over it, I went towards it, expecting to find out something about the whereabouts of my command. When very close to the infantry, I was called off by the dreadful entreaties of a wounded man for water and help, As I turned to go to him I was ordered in a very peremptory tone by one of the infantry officers to come to him. I refused, in a tone equally asperemptory, and went on to the wounded man. When I reached him I found him fatally wounded. Both arms broken and the ball had gone through both lungs from side to side. I gave him some water and he begged me to lift him up. This I did, but he died in my arms. I was occupied some minutes in this when I became aware of shells passing over my head and exploding around me. I did not know whether they came from friend or foe, but no matter what the source they were equally dangerous to me. I sought shelter from them in a kind of ravine or track which ran across the field, and this I pursued for some distance. Finally I emerged from it just in time to confront some infantry which I found to be part of the 5th regiment, Stonewall brigade, under the command of Major Williams of Augusta Co. Va. He was as much surprised to see me as I was to see him and in response to my enquiry, said he was going to dislodge some Yankee infantry in the field just ahead. I told him he was greately mistaken and begged him not to fire into them as they were our troops, for I had passed by them, spoken with them, and seen them bearing the Virginia flag. At this Major Williams, leaving his command behind a vine grown fence, went forward by himself but soon returned and laughing at me for my mistake, told me I had been in the hands of a Yankee West Va. Regiment. At that time they claimed to be the only true Virginians and they carried the Virginia flag. My wet and muddy condition and my blue undershirt deceived them as to colors…

"…I toiled along through the fields and rough roads through bivouacs of troops and hospitals of wounded men. My shoes were worn out and my feet were almost on the ground, so when I came to a Yankee with a good pair of shoes on and whom I supposed to be dead, I started to pull off his shoes. But he turned over and groaned so that I desisted. Thinking he would die slowly I sat down by a tree to wait until I could get the shoes. I went to sleep and when, after some time, I woke, I found my Yankee dead, but someone has gotten the shoes…"

Sorry, but I'd have taken them right away-where do you think he's going? That yanke certainly won't need them in Hell!

CADET GRAY & BUTTERNUT BROWN by Thomas M. Arlikas pub by Thomas Pub 2006

"back east in Virginia, Branch's North Carolina Brigade, after the Battle of Hanover Courthouse in May 1862, presented an un-uniform appearance "Some were wrapped in blankets of rag carpet, others wore shoes of untanned hide. Others were without shoes or jackets, and their heads were bound with handkerchiefs. Some in red shirts, some in stiff beaver hats, some were attired in shreds and patches of cloth, and a few wore the soiled garments of the civilian gentleman. The mass adhered to homespun suits of grey or butternut, and the coarse blue kersey common to slaves. In places I caught glimpses of red zouave breeches or leggings, blue federal caps, Federal buttons, and Federal blouses…"

Multifirm apparently is the norm here.

RECOLLECTIONS FROM 1861-1865 by John H. Lewis ex-Leiutenant in Huger's & R.H. Anderson's & Pickett's Division, Army of Northern Virginia pub. by Peak & Co. 1895

Pg. 33 May, 1862 "…It amuses me today to look back and see ourselves with our new clothes and hear the soldiers of Manassas and Williamsburg, who were lying on the roadside, and as we passed (as I thought insulting us) by telling us to come out of those clothes, and insinuating that we would be somewhat spattered by the morning; and it was so. We did not have to wait until morning. By night we were as dirty or nearly so as the boys who had insulted us, and began to look like old soldiers…."

REMINISCENCES OF A REBEL by Rev. Wayland Dunaway pub by Neale Pub. 1913

May 1862 47th& 40th Virginia Regiments Co. L mentions their "neat gray suits."

FOOTPRINTS OF A REGIMENT—A Recollection of the 1st Georgia Regulars 1861-1865 W.H. Andrews 1st Sgt. Co. M pub. by Longstreet Press 1992

Pg. 36 May,1862 Pennensula Campaign "A horseman came dashing up the road at full speed. In arriving at our regiment he asked for our surgeon, Dr. Cherry. The Dr. being pointed out to him, he leaped from his horse, handed the bridle reins to a soldier, walked up to the doctor, and asked hom to perform a surgical operation on him. He had been shot through the arm just below the elbow while resting his arm on his gun. The surgeon called four men to assist him. He stretched the poor fellow on his back and almost in the twinkling of an eye, had it off. He rose from the ground, thanked the surgeon, vaulted into the saddle, and away he went as though nothing had happened. He was what I call game. After defeating the enemy at West Point, (we) continued the retreat to Richmond…'

This unknown soldier had more grit than 100 modern people. I actually wonder if he survived. I guess so, a man like that's too tough to die easily.

Pg. 44 Garnett's Farm, May 1862 "While we were halted, I was keeping a sharp lookout to the front. I saw as I supposed, a yankee not far in advance making his retreat. I placed my gun to my shoulder, took deliberate aim, and pressed the trigger. Just as I was in the act of shooting, the yankee stooped down to pass under a limb, and who should it be but Lt. Fred B. Palmer, who had a yankee overcoat on his arm that he had picked up in the enemy camps. The cold chills crept up my spine after I found out my mistake…"

One of the dangers of utilizing captured uniforms. We'll hear more about this as the war progesses.

Michael W. Taylor Morningside 1994

Pg. 81 Spotsylvania Co. Va. May 20th, 1862 "…I want you to write whether you ever got the money and the clothes that I sent home by Tolliver Hughes. I have wrote several times to know about them. I got the socks and the powders that Wm. Martin brought. I wrote home for a pair of drawers and a shirt and in addition to them you may send one pair of summer britches. Don't send any more than I write for. Just send me one pair of drawers, one shirt, one pair pants. I sent a pair of shoes home by Scot Hill when I was at Goldsboro. Write whether you got them or not. Tell Tincy she had better save all the wool she has in place of knitting socks to give away. You well know the worth of woolen cloth next winter. Bryants Old Koot is coming home and I am going to send my carpet sack and my woolen jacket by him to Ben Washburns…."

Here's a man whose careful with his clothing.

MIDSHIPMAN IN GRAY- Selections fromRecollections of a Rebel Reefer by James Morris Morgan Burd Street Press 1917

Pg. 67 May 20, 1862 "Passing through the lobby one morning (Spotswood Hotel, Rich. Va.) I met an old acquaintance, a Louisiana Zouave, dressed in red Turkish trousers with a short blue jacket elaborately trimmed with yellow braid-of course he too had an arm in a sling…"

A SOUTHERN SOLDIER'S LETTERS HOME The Civil War Letters of Samuel Burney Cobb's Georgia Legion, Army of Northern Va. Ed. By Nat Turner Mercer pub by Univ. Press, Macon Ga.2002

Pg. 167 Camp Georgia Legion, Near Richmond Va. May 21st, 1862 "…Pa wrote me that he would send me a pair of pants. I do hope that this may reach you in time to prevent it. I know not when we may be ordered off somewhere and I would be compelled to sell or throw them away. The retreat tought me not to have a rag more than necessary. I saw numbers of coats, pants, & drawers, & blankets cast aside on the retreat to lighten the soldier's load. I disposed of my nightshirt, which I am sorry I ever bought. I hope I may have a chance of sending my winter shirts home. I have some things in Mr. Fitz's trunk if it ever reaches

Madison. You can get them and can form some idea of dirty clothes. One of those shirts your mother dyed for me is in it. I must tell you that I threw my pillow away soon after passing Williamsburg, but not till it got wet. That pillow has been a great comfort to me. If you have time I wish you would make me a very large haversack of material stout in body & dark in color to send by Mr. Porter. I have one, but it is small and of little account The one I had when I left home was out to be washed when I left Goldsboro, which with the other articles I never got. Make it strong and let it have two pockets like my first one...."

SAD EARTH, SWEET HEAVEN- The Diary of Lucy Rebecca Buck During The War Between The States pub. By Buck Pub. Co. Birmingham, Al. 1992.

Pg 83 May 23, 1862 "The N.O. Tigers played a most amusing prank on the Yankees today. It seems that in their hasty flight yesterday they left arms, ammunition and clothing, tents, wagons and a large amount of commissary stores in our possession. The Tigers doffed their uniforms and donned the Yankee blue- then they got on the cars and steamed off to Markham where the news of the fall of Front Royal had not arrived and the Federal troops of course took them to be some of their own men, and coming out of quarters at the invitation of the Tigers a number of them concluded to "take a ride up the road a little ways." The hospitable Rebels not only extended the ride to Front Royal but also gave them lodging and board there au gratis."

Those yankee soldiers must have felt so supid to be tricked by the Tigers

FAR,FAR FROM HOME-The Wartime Letters of Dick and Tally Simpson, 3rd South Carolina Volunteers by Guy R. Everson & Edward W. Simpson Jr. pub. by Oxford Univ. Press 1994

Pg. 126 May 23rd, 1862 TNS to MS Richmond, Va. Dear Sister "I am in much need of clothing, in fact almost shoeless and hatless. I suppose by this time Ma has received my letter in which I reported my condition with reference to clothes. My boots are still living, but in the last gasp of death, but we will draw from the Government the regular English army shoe this evening or tomorrow. My hat is on my head and that is all; whether it does much good or not I can't say. The worst part of it is there is no prospect for another. However I have made requisition for one. I wish you and Ma would make me up three summer overshirts and two pair of cotton drawers. If you can possibly get hold of some cotton undershirts, send me a couple. I would like to have a couple of prs of socks, blue like the ones I left at home this last time. I think you knit them. If you have an opportunity, send me some of your homemade envelopes..."

SHENANDOAH 1862 by Peter Cozzins pub by Univ. of North Carolina Press 2008

Pg. 298 May 23, 1862 Advancing on Front Royal, Va. Campbell Brown described the Louisiana Tigers "I shall never forget [their] style. [Wheat] was riding full gallup, yelling at the top of his voice-his big sergeant major running at top speed just after him, calling to the men to come on, and they strung out according to their speed or stomach for the fight, all running-all yelling-all looking like fight. Their peculiar Zouave dress, light-striped baggy pants, bronzed and desparate faces, and wild excitement made up a glorious picture." Behind Wheat's rowdy band, atop Dickey's Ridge, the remainder of Taylor's Louisiana Brigade stood in reserve, its disciplined ranks and "perfectly uniformed' men the envy of the army. "each man was wearing white gaiters and leggings, said an admiring Georgian, "while the blue-gray uniforms of the officers were brilliant with gold lace, their rakish slouch hats adorned with tassels and plumes."

THE COMANCHES, White's Battalion, Virginia Cavalry Laurel Brigade by Frank M Myers pub by Continental Books 1956

Pg. 50 May 23 1862 Front Royal Va. "...after capturing Kenly's 1st Maryland...for the men deemed themselves discharged from further attendance upon him (Gen. Ewell), and pitched in for plunder, every man doing his best to equip himself for service, they being as yet mostly armed with double-barrel guns only, and riding citizen saddles brought with them from home. Many of them succeeded in securing sabres and pistols, and nearly all possessed themselves of gum cloths, canteens and other articles of great value to soldiers..."

If you've ever read of the Valley Campaign, this was one of the problems after chasing the Yankkes out of Front Royal and down the valley Pike-the cavalry stopped for plunder, allowing a slew of Yankees, wagons, etc. to escape.

Pg. 53 Pursuit of the enemy after the Battle of Winchester, Va. "...Here White's company, which had been scattered in squads, scouting and fighting, and acting as escort and body-guards for the different Generals, re-united about sunset, and nearly every man was completely armed and equipped with sabres, revolvers, and everything necessary to fit them for service, including Yankee bridles and halters, and many saddles bearing the letters U.S., which letters also embellished the shoulders of many of their horses and all their blankets.

Next morning Gen. Ewell gave them a box containing twenty new carbines of the "Merrill" pattern, which he directed should always be carried by the scouting details..."

Dear Irvie, Dear Lucy-Civil War Letters of Capt. Irving A. Buck, General Cleburne's AAG & Family pub. by Buck Pub. Co. 2002

Pg. 72 May 24, 1862 Bel Aire, Front Royal Va. Lucy Buck; My Precious Brothers, (referring to the Rebel march up the Valley after the Valley Campaign) "...When the main body of the army came in we all went over to the street opposite Mr Petty's and saw them come in. Poor Fellows! So dusty and worn they looked, some barefooted, many of them ragged and nearly all ravenous, but far from dispirited, for it was one incessant cheer from one end of the line to the other, whenever the regimental battle flag was borne by we could salute it and it seemed to delite them greatly. They would wave aloft their bread, pickles, meat, pies or whatever edibles they had in their hands and cheer themselves, Jeff Davis, the C.S. and the ladies. One poor little fellow as he passed by turned to us and remarked with a sin-comic expression, "Ah, ladies, I am too tired to holler now!"..." Lucy Buck

DEFEND THE VALLEY by Margarette Barton Colt pub by Crown Pub. 1994

Pg. 154 Memoir of Robert T. Barton 1862 "...I recall that when I got back in Winchester on May 25 I found that my mother and sister had made me a handsome new artillery uniform and in some way had gotten me a new felt hat. I put them on and went a photographer's (then called a daguerrean gallery) and had my picture taken. It is this that I intend to have enlarged and will keep for my boy so that when he grows up he may see his father as a soldier boy of nineteen years..."

SHENANDOAH 1862 by Peter Cozzins pub by Univ. of North Carolina Press 2008

Pg. 355 May 25, 1862 Battle of Winchester "Scattered over the ground in front of the 5th Connacticut were scores of dead and wounded North Carolinians, most quiet, all looking, quipped a Yankee officer, "like bags of shit in a grain field."

Pg. 371 May 25, 1862 charging through Winchester, Va. "...The filthy aspect of the army went unnoticed in the general thanksgiving. One pretty girl was heard to exclaim, "Oh, you brave, noble ragged, dirty darlings you! I am so glad to see you."

Pg. 367 May 26, 1862 Chasing the Yankees down the Valley-"...The inveterate scrounger Lt. McHenry Howard at least got something from the beaten foe: "In passing over where the Federal line had been I observed a fine officer's greatcoat-the long detatchable cape with red flannel-lying on the ground with a little dog on it. I dismounted, routed the dog, and secured it..."

A SOLDIERS RECOLLECTIONS- Leaves From the Diary of a Confedrate by Randolph H. McKim pub by Zenger Pub Co. 1910

Pg. 106 May 25, 1862 fighting around Bolivar Heights Harper's Ferry (Va) "...There was some fighting-chiefly a duel of artillery-but the only man I remember seeing injured was an artilleryman who was shot in the thigh by a rifle ball at a distance of approximately 900 yards. That was looked upon as a remarkable achievement at that period in the history of the war. How different it is today! I also recall that the wound was a horrible one-the flesh was dreadfully torn and lacerated. The enemy had resorted to the reprehensible practice of using explosive bullets..."

Here's the first account of either army using exploding bullets. There is all the information I could find (first hand accounts) a little farther.

LETTERS FROM THE STONEWALL BRIGADE Ted Barcay, Liberty Hall Volunteers by Charles W. Turner Rockbridge Pub. Co. 1992

Pg. 72 May 27, 1862 after capturing Bank's wagon train Dear Sister "...Our army was rigged out in full suits of Yankee clothes yesterday, but as several had been taken up for Yankees by our cavalry, Gen. Jackson ordered the clothes to be given up, so again we see the old Confederate gray, while yesterday everything was Yankee blue..."

This was a very common-sense order and probably resulted in saving many Rebel soldier's lives. I have from an old account (I'm trying to discover the source) that these jackets were sent up the valley and re-dyed with walnut hulls. This usually resulted in a dark brown or black color, but usable to the Confederate Army.

THE CONFEDERATE VETERAN VOL XXVI 1918

Pg. 65 Letters FromThe Front by Thomas Caffey from Alabama -Drewry's Bluff, Four Miles South of Richmond, Dear Mary May 27. 1862 "...When Norfolk was evacuated I lost all my clothing and blankets; and as we had a heavy frost last night, I felt the loss very sensibly. I hope to be able to replace them soon..."

GRANDFATHER'S JOURNAL (Franklin Lafayette Riley) Company B Sixteenth A.N.V. May 27, 1861-July 15, 1865 ed by Austin C. Dobbins pub by Morningside Press 1988

Pg. 81 Wednesday-Friday, May 28-30, 1862 Winchester-Charlestown-Harper's Ferry "On Sun. we pursued the enemy 6-8 miles north of Winchester. Here, in the deserted enemy camps, we replenished our supplies, obtaining new trousers, shirts, and jackets. Even our officers are wearing motley. The clothes will have to be dyed-or given to our commissary, for strict orders have been issued for us not to wear Yankee uniforms..."

I believe this only applied to the Yankee jackets, as many troops in Jackson's Army were wearing blue pants.

LETTERS FROM A SURGEON IN THE CIVIL WAR John Gardner Perry pub by Little, Brown, & Co. 1906

Pg. 236 May 28th, 1862 On one of the beds here lies, fast asleep, a Confederate surgeon,-a thoroughbred South Carolinian, who never, before the war, passed his state lines. He was captured with a number of others in the last engagement before Richmond, and as most of these men were wounded, he was detailed to care for them. Dressed entirely in Alabam\a homespun-which is the ugliest snuff-colored stuff imaginable,-a broad-brimmed planter's hat covering his head and stained with mud and blood from head to foot, the appearance of this officer when he first arrived was strange enough; but his face was bright and intelligent..."

LETTTERS TO AMANDA-The Civil War Letters of Marion Hill Fitzpatrick Army of Northern Virginia ed. by Jeffery C. Lowe and Sam Hodges pub by Mercer Univ. Press 1998

Pg. 9 May 30th, 1862 31/2 miles north of Richmond (Letter no. 4) Dear Amanda "...We marched from Ashland here, and got here yesterday evening nearly worn out. I have lost the most of my things. I now have but one pair of pants, one blanket, 2 pr. drawers, 2 shirts. I could not carry them. It was very hot a part of the time and a great many have lost all...I want you to send me a pair pf britches if you can but nothing else until we get stationed..."

Pg. 10 June 1st, 1862 same camp, Dear Amanda "...I wrote you about losing my clothes and wrote you to send me a pair of britches, but I did not want you to trouble about it now. If I had them I could not carry them and travel like we have to. When we get settled again, you can send them if there is a chance there will be some arrangements made to get clothes after awhile. I expect that half the Regiment (45th Georgia, Co. K, "Ray Guards") is in the same fix I am and some a great deal worse, but still there is no grumbling..."

The Army of Northern Virginia won't get "settled" until the middle of Dec., after the battle of Fredericksburg.

WRITING & FIGHTING FROM THE ARMY OF NORTHERN VIRGINIA ed. by William B. Styple pub by Belle Grove Pub. 2003

Pg. 104 Columbus Gaurds-Comp. G, 2nd Ga. Inf. Camp on Jno. Edmund's Farm, near Richmond, Va. May 31, 1862 "…I presume it is needless to "bore you" with an account of our march to Richmond, suffice it to say that it was one of the hardest jobs I ever undertook. Very few thought of carrying their knapsacks or clothes, all of those being thrown away. Being in the pioneer squad I managed to get them through, it being the privilege of the pioneers to have their baggage hauled…."

It must have driven the supply officers crazy-in both armies- due to the discarding of clothing, blankets, etc., while on the march, the men needed resupply after every march. This was not as much of a concern in the Confederate Army, as there was very little to issue, plus the men learned early on to carry only what was absolutely necessary.

THE CONFEDERATE VETERAN VOL. 3

Sept. 1895 Pg. 270 spring 1862 Witticisms of Soldiers by Capt. James Dinkins "After the Army of Northern Virginia had fallen back from the Peninsula to Richmond in the spring of 1862, Ben F. Muse, a member of Company C, Eighteenth Mississippi. "…He had never been accustomed to hardships and until he went into the army never wanted for anything. But on this occasion, his clothes consisted of a pair of old ragged pants, a greasy old flannel shirt and one "gallus." …"

UNIFORMS OF THE CIVIL WAR Lord, Wise, A.S. Barnes & Co. 1970

Pg. 43 Battle of White Oaks Swamp, June 1862 the soldiers of A.P.Hill's Corp were described: "…in a Medley of garments, which could hardly be called a uniform, though grey and butternut were prevailing. Some of them had a strip of carpeting for a blanket, but the raggedness of their outfit was no discredit to soldiers who fought as bravely as they did…"

Here again, first-hand accounts of Rebel's rag-gedness.

BATTLEFIELDS OF THE SOUTH AN ENGLISH COMBATANT Collector's Library of the Civil War Time Life Books

Pg. 307 June 1862 "If by accident any European were to visit our lines, what a poor opinion he might form of the true merit of our soldiers! Accustomed to see fine bodies of men, splendidly drilled, and tastefully uniformed, he would be inclined to look upon us as parcel of ragged, ill-fed, slovenly-looking, mud-colored militia, unfit for service, and doomed to discomfiture at the first volley from an enemy…"

Yeah, they might not be fancy, but they sure can play Hell with the Yankees!

THE PERSONAL MEMOIRS OF JOHNATHAN THOMAS SCHARF OF THE FIRST MARYLAND ARTILLERY ed by Tom Kelly pub by Butternut and Blue 1992

Pg. 16 June 1862 The Pennensula Campaign, near West Point, Va. "…After a terrible amoint of suffering and privation we got there and crossed (the Chickahominy River). A great many of our wounded men up to this time died, and one man hung himself by his drawers near a spring on the road. This was the most terrible march on record and the men suffered most for they were issued on one occasion hard corn to roast. This was the march that made our men feel what war was, as it was the most they had ever endured…"

It must have been terrible for a man to have hung himself.

Pg. 23 June 1862 pursuit of the enemy, Pennensula Campaign "…We moved about and crossed the stream and viewed the Yankee entrenchments. They were completely black with the blue-coated rascals. Some of them was filled. We passed further up the road and we came across piles of knapsacks 30 feet high for the enemy had taken them off when going into the fight and would not stop in their flight to get them. We went through them like a dose of salts, getting everything we wanted. We did nort stop to unbuckle them but just cut (them) with our knives. We cut them open and took what we wanted and left the balance for stragglers, as they got now to be plentiful. We now advanced and slept near the battlefield of Cold Harbor. On the march we got all kind of plunder as the enemy now was in full retreat…"

Resupply from the Yankees.

Pg. 24 June 1862, pursuit of the enemy, Pennensula Campaign "…General Pender rode up to the battery and wished to know if we had any muskets. If we had any, he wanted us to go with him and kill or capture a Yankee Sharpshooter on this side of the creek, who had fired on him several times. We told him we had one or two, and we went with him. We was also joined by some soldiers on our way hither. One of the soldiers was killed by a sharpshooter, but we managed to wind up the other one that had shot at the general. We went to his body and he was getted up splendidly with most everything and we took all he had, for he hed now entered the other world. We stripped him of his overcoat, etc…"

HISTORY OF THE FOURTH REGIMENT SOUTH CAROLINA VOLUNTEERS FROM THE COMMENCEMENT OF THE WAR UNTIL LEE'S SURRENDER by J.W. Reid pub by Shannon &Co. Printers & Stationers Morningside Bookshop 1975

Pg. 80 June 1862 Seven Days Battles May 1862 Fort Richmond "…I lost all my clothing and blankets…"

FRONT RANK-Written for the N.C. Centennial Commission by Glenn Tucker Heritage Printers N.C. 1962

Pg. 21June 1862 "…After Seven Pines John Augustus Young, as Lt. Col. Before Seven Pines, Young, in critical health was sent home to procure uniforms. His illness disqualified him from further field duty. Vance set him to work making uniform cloth and he manufactured it at top energy in his plants until the end of the war. He never forgot the old fourth. At his own expense he provided every member with a brand new uniform and cap…."

You gotta love a guy like that!

OUR WOMEN IN THE WAR-A Series of Papers Written by Southern Ladies-S.C. News & Courier 1884-1885 Arranged by Miss Hattie Kilmore 1998 Old Confederate ways by Miss Claudine Rhett, Charlestown, S.C.

Pg. 278 Peninsula Campaign, June, 1862 "…Some days subsequent to this adventure I was quietly reading at my window, while in the yard below a poor man named Bonneville was sawing wood for Mrs. Smith. Too lame and sickly to be of use in the Confederate army, he remained at home with his family in a little farm house so near our lines and so buried in the woods that it had not yet been discovered by the Yankees. On this occasion he wore a blue overcoat, and lest this should expose him to being mistaken by the picket for a Federal soldier, he had bound around his hat the well known white band which served in our army as a Confederate badge when gray uniforms had given place to many colored rags and tatters…."

I had never before I began thie research, heard of a white band being a universal badge of Confederates, but there is more than one reference to this.

BATTLEFIELDS OF THE SOUTH AN ENGLISH COMBATANT Collector's Library of the Civil War Time Life Books

Pg. 177-178 Peninsula Campaign June, 1862 I could not but smile at the indifference of a tall, hard-fisted Texan, who was cautiously "hunting up a pair of boots and pants." He was warned not to show his head above the parapet, for the Yankee sharpshooters, armed with rifles of a long range, with telescopic "sights," were "thick as blackberries" in the woods to the front, and were excellent shots. "Darn the blue-skins any how; who's scared of the blue bellies? (that is Eastern men) Let all the Yankees go to -, for all I care. Let 'em shoot and be d-d! I'm bound to have a pair of boots any how!" And so saying, he passed over the parapet, down its face, and returned with the body of an enemy, which he had fished out of the water. He first pulled off the boots, which proved to be an excellent pair; then proceeding to rifle the pockets, he found sixty dollars in gold. He was much astonished and delighted at these discoveries; but when he examined the haversack and found it well stored with capital rations, including a canteen full of fine rye whiskey, he was electrified with sudden joy, dropped boots, haversack, money upon the ground, and half-emptied the canteen at a draught. Setting down the can, he smacked his lips, and thus soliloquized: "Well! Poor devil, he's gone, like a mighty big site of them; but he was a gentleman, and deserved better luck. If he'd been a Massachusetts Yankee, I wouldn't a cared a darn! But these fellows are the right kind. They come along with good boots and pants, lots to eat, money in their pockets, and are no mean judges of whiskey. These are the kind of fellows I like to fight!"

Now this is aggressively resupplying oneself from the Yankees.

SHENANDOAH 1862 by Peter Cozzins pub by Uiv. Of North Carolina Press 2008

Pg. 424 June 2 1862 Valley Campaign "…More good news came that afternoon, when Fremont wrote from Woodstock of the hundreds of Rebel stragglers encountered along the road and nearby fields and forests, adding that "clothing, blankets, muskets, and sabers are also upon the road…"

Pg. 426 June 2, 1862 "The Valley army made camp between Rude's Hill and New Market. It had rained intermittently thoughout the day. "To march at times we have to lock arms to steady each other or fall into the mud." A Mississippi rifleman told his mother. "The road was shoe-mouth deep in mud," recalled Capt. William C. Oates of the 15th Alabama. "My feet were blistered all over, on top as well as the bottom…" *That is special misery. Try to imagine that!*

Pg. 498 June 10, 1862 after the Battle of Port republic- "…Remembered an officer of the 13th Virginia: We encamped on the side of the mountain where it was so steep we had to pile rocks and build a wall to keep from rolling down when asleep, and to add to our discomfort the inevitable rain began to fall, and the men were wet to the skin…The army had passed through terrible scenes and looked rough and dirty, as well as ragged." *More misery!*

A SOUTHERN SOLDIERS LETTERS HOME-The Civil War Letters of Samuel Burney, Cobb's Legion, Army of Northern Virginia ed by Nat Turner Pub by Mercer Univ. Press 2002

Pg. 176 June 7, 1862 [Mrs. Christian's Farm] Camp Georgia Legion Near Richmond Va. My Dearest Wife, "After I closed my letter yesterday the Captain arrived, bringing me the letter you sent and all the articles. These two shirts were greatly admired; by none more than your husband. My pants are beautiful indeed, and fit me finely. The drawers suit my notions exactly. The socks are the prettiest things I ever saw; though you forgot the size of my foot. Everything pleases me much indeed for my delight & pride is heightened when I consider my dearest wife made them. The next time send me something to eat. Even a small package. You might send me another pair of socks."

Pg. 179 June 11th, 1862 [Mrs. Christian's Farm] Camp Georgia Legion Near Richmond Va. My Dearest Wife," I am delighted with my new clothes; everything looked so nice. I am proud of my wife. I suppose Pa is having a new pair of shoes made. Did you get my overcoat? I sent it in Alf Atkinson's trunk, but neither he or I know whether it has gotten home. I had several pieces of clothing in Mr. Fitz's trunk, but I do not remember them."

LEE& JACKSON'S BLOODY TWELTH-Letters of Irby Godwin Scott- First Lieutenant Co. G Putnam Light Artillery,. Twelth Georgia Volunteer Infantry by Johnnie Perry Pearson pub by Texas Univ Press 2010

Pg. 78 June 12th 1862 Camp Near Port Republic, Augusta Co.Va Loved ones at Home,"… Homer Paschal says tell his father to send him a hat & a pair of shoes by the first one coming on to the company…"

Pg. 83 19 June 1862 Camped near Charlottesville, Va. Dear Father; "…I do not want you to try to send me any more (clothing) for I can't get them. They are also liable to be stolen. I can make out with what the government gives us, there is not much chance in getting any clothing from home. I lost my knapsack that was left in Stanton (Va.) with all my clothes except what I had on. I got some more from the boys and with what Henry Thomas brought I have plentry…"

I hope he made out OK depending on the government to supply him.

THE CIVIL WAR: THE SOUTH ed. by Thomas Streissguth pub by Greenhaven Press Inc. 2001

Pg. 87 Ride Around McClellan by John Esten Cooke June15, 1862 "…Everywhere were seen the traces of flight-for the alarm of "hornets in the hive" was given. Wagons had turned over, and were abandoned-from others the excellent army stores had been hastily thrown. This writer got a fine red blanket, and an excellent pair of cavalry pantaloons, for which he still owes the United States…"

Good lord, man, don't say anything, they might still want you to pay for them!

BATTLEFIELDS OF THE SOUTH AN ENGLISH COMBATANT Collector's Library of the Civil War Time Life Books

Pg. 303 June 16, 1862 Stuart's ride around McClellan- the return of the troopers. "The appearance of our gallant troopers was certainly very unprepossessing. The men were dusty, dirty, and looked more like negroes than whites. Their horses could scarcely move, for in addition to the long gallop, their riders had overweighted them by loading their saddle-bows with strings of shoes, bundles of blankets, and new weapons of various kinds: not infrequently the horse and entire outfit were Federal property."

What did he expect?

LONE STAR CONFEDERATE-A Gallant and Good Soldier of the 5th Texas Infantry ed by Groege Skoch & Mark W. Perkins pub by Texas A&M Univ Press 2003

Pg. 93 June 27, 1862 Gaines Mill, Va. Robert Campbell of the Bayou City Guards, Co. A "In crossing the creek I got one foot bogged, and left my shoe, making the charge with one bare foot. Lieut. Clute made the charge with us unhurt. He had a large gray overcoat strapped on his back. A few seconds before he was killed, he laughingly turned to the boys, saying: "Boys, I have got a ball in my coat"-a ball having gone into his coat and stopped there. I turned my head from him, and in less than ten seconds he was dead, a piece of shell having passed through him…The Yanks whipped and the fight over, I was sent back three or four miles as a guard over prisoners, where we were relieved by Virginians. I went till morning without a shoe, when I got one-a few days before I had marched barefooted…"

THE COMANCHES, WHITE'S BATTALION VIRGINIA CAVALRY LAUREL BRIGADE by Frank M. Myers pub by Continental Books 1956

Pg. 80 June 28, 1862 Pennensula Campaign "…Here White's men got into a snap with some of the Pennsylvania Bucktail riflemen, but the Captain led them in a charge, in which they captured a whole set of German-silver wind instruments for a band, and several prisoners, killing and wounding some of the "Bucktails." They also got a splendid suit of armor belonging to a Colonel, over which they had a great deal of amusement, but in their experiments with the breastplate they learned that it was bullet-proof against Colt's army revolvers and all the guns they could find, with one exception, and that was the Maynard rifle, which tore a hole in it large enough for a hens egg to pass through…"

At what range? This was a formidable piece of armor, for I have fired through two inches of oak board at twenty paces with an army Colt…

THE CONFEDERATE VETERAN VOL II

Sept. 1894 June 30, 1862 Frazier's Farm Thrilling War Experiences by N.B. Hogan Company I Eleventh Alabama Infantry "…Company I was called the "Yellow Dogs" on account of their uniforms being made of copperas-colored goods, and no better fighters ever went on the field…."

You tell 'em, Johnny!

A HISTORY OF THE 2nd SOUTH CAROLINA INFANTRY : 1861-1865 by Mac Wyckoff pub. by Sergeant Kirkland's Museum & History Society Inc. 1994

Pg. 32 June 30, `1862 after Savage Station Confederate surgeons assisting Yankee doctors who had stayed behind with the wounded "…Even more graphic is this description reported by Gregory De Fontaine: "I beheld another sight, which few men, thank god, have ever witnessed. In the middle of the yard something was lying upon the ground. At first glance I supposed it to be a roll of dirty blankets, but observing that it had motion, walked up to it. "Don't look there," said one of the Yankee nurses, "or you will see what will follow you to your dying day." Just at that moment the blanket was turned down by the object beneath-you could hardly call it a human being-and a faint voice ejaculated, "Water!" I could hardly believe my senses. There lay a man with the right side of his face, including the eye, nose, right ear, and the entire right lobe of the brain shot away, and a deep cavity in their place, in which you might have inserted two large fists. Maggots, mosquitoes, ticks, flies and vermin of every description filling the gaping hole by the millions. They were crawling through his hair, in his mouth, over his face, and some had entered and were eating out the half closed eye on the opposite side. The man had been wounded…and for nearly three weeks had lingered in the condition I have described-a mass of corruption, suffering the torments of the damned and yet unable to die…"

I think I would have shot this poor man, I would not have been able to leave him like that. There is no further informantion as to who he was or how much linger he lived.

SEVEN MONTHES IN THE REBEL STATES DURING THE NORTH AMERICAN WAR 1863 by Captain Justus Scheibert Confederate Centenial Studies #9, Confederate Publishing Co. Inc. 1958

Summer 1862"The army, which was recruited by universal conscription extending from the sixteenth to the forty-fifth year, made a very strange impression in its outward appearance, since nothing in the way of uniformity was to be seen, for everyone wore whatever he could get, or whatever his wife wove for him at home…"

More proof of multiform

CAMPAIGNS OF A NON-COMBATANT and his Romaunt Abroad During the War by Geo. Alfred Townsend pub. by Blelock & Co. 1866

PG. 70 summer 1862, Penninsula Campaign "…The fine works of Yorktown are monuments to negro labor, for they were the hewers and the diggers. Every slave-owner in Eastern Virginia was obliged to send one half of his male servants between the ages of sixteen and fifty to the Confederate camps, and they were organized into gangs and set to work. In some cases they were put into military service and made excellent sharpshooters. The last gun discharged from the town was said to have been fired by a negro…"

Here's another account of African-Americans in active Confederate military service

STONEWALL IN THE VALLEY by Robert G. Tanner pub by Stackpole books 1996

"Southern uniforms, or lack of them, also amused Coloman. The army had grown shabby as a year of war had tattered the bright attire of the previous Spring. Comfort rather than style was now the criteria for apparel. Civilian clothes abounded. Stiff boots had given away to brogues with wide, thick bottoms and flat heels. The towering busbies and shakoes that adorned the ranks-and blew off in a strong wind-during the early days had been replaced with slouch caps. Dick Waldrop of the 21st Va. Ambled along in a pair of pants at least six sizes too big and with legs the size of salt sacks; he loved them, for they afforded plenty of stretching room." 1862 summer

Multiform-including many civilian clothes abounds.

THE WOMEN OF THE SOUTH IN WAR TIME Compiled by Matthew Page Andrews pub by The Norman Remington Co., Balt. Md. 1923

Summer 1862 Pg. 26 "…Supplies of clothing of all kinds rapidly diminished as the war continued. Neatly trimmed thorns were often used in place of pins, and it was discovered that persimmon seeds made excellent buttons when toughly dried and pierced with the necessary holes for needle and thread, which, in their turn, became alarmingly scarce, so that 'the loss of a sewing needle became a household calamity.' Buttons were also made out of gourds, cut into molds and covered with cloth of any color or kind. Corn shucks, palmetto, and many kinds of grasses were woven into hats and bonnets. Every variety of dye was homemade. When the dyes failed to hold their respective colors, the articles were "redipped" again and again. When hat trimmings were worn "too long a time," the hats were reshaped and dyed another color.

All girls and women learned to card and spin and knit, if not previously acquainted with these arts. Every woven stocking was of especial value. When the feet were entirely worn out, the upper part was carefully unraveled and the thread first twisted on the spinning wheel and then knitted into new stockings or into gloves or mitts. All woven wearing apparel was treated in the same way...."

THE WOMEN OF THE SOUTH IN WAR TIME Compiled by Matthew Page Andrews pub by The Norman Remington Co., Balt. Md. 1923

Summer 1862 Pg.426 "...In the narrative of Mrs. Hadley, reference has been made to the possession and use of a sewing machine. Comparatively few of the Southern women had this great aid to the making of clothes. Mrs. John D. Weedon of Huntsville, Al., writes of the experience of her mother, Mrs. Robert M. Patton of Florence: "We kept a number of garments to make at home. I was just through college, and I made, together with my mother and a serving woman she had employed, uniforms, underwear, and several overcoats, so heavy that we had to work on them while lying on a table. Every stitch was done with our fingers. We had no machines until 1869, when my father bought me one..."

We can't give enough praise to those brave, determined ladies.

HISTORY OF HAMPSHIRE, W.VA. H.U. Maxwell and H.L. Swisher pub by McClain Printing Co. Parsons W.Va. 1972

Summer 1862 Pg. 606 Adventures of Boney Loy-Among the well-known members of Company I was William B. Loy, nicknamed "Boney," who lived through many dangers and lived to see peace restored. He returned to Hampshire and proved by his life that the bravest in war are the best citizens in peace. He was of small stature, but of iron constitution, capable of enduring excessive fatigue; taking part in the hardest marches, the severest battles, and always at his post. In the battle above mentioned (Front Royal), he had a long, hard time of it. When the fight was over he wrapped himself in a new rubber blanket and lay down among the dead and dying, and was soon asleep. During the night some stragglers who were robbing the dead, found him, and supposing g him dead also, rolled him over, pulled his blanket out, and began to fold it up. But Loy awoke and soon convinced the thief that he had tackled a very lively corpse. The straggler turned away, remarking, "take your old blanket; I thought you were dead." Loy wrapped the blanket bout him and again lay down to sleep. When he awoke in the morning he found that his gun and boots had been stolen. Unarmed and barefooted he started out to forage, and soon found a rusty gun, which he took; but he was not so fortunate in procuring coverings for his feet, which were so small that he was hard to fit. But, finally he found a yankee with boots about the right size, and he proceeded to pull them off. He received a kick in the stomach from the yankee whom he had supposed dead, and the rebuke, "What are you about! Can't you let a man die in peace? Can't you wait till he is dead before you rob him!" As Mr. Loy had no intentions of robbing a wounded soldier, he let go the boot with many apologies and moved off. He found no other boots of the proper size and returned to camp barefooted. It was not long after that Bank's commissary stores were captured by the rebels, and Boney Loy had the pick of several hundred cases of yankee boots, and succeeded in finding a pair that fit him exactly…"

GEORGIA BOYS WITH STONEWALL JACKSON by Aurelia Austin pub by Univ. of Georgia Press 1967

Pg. 40 "we ar station in 16 miles of Richmond" J.T. Thompson Summer 1862 "Tell mother to make mee 2 coton shirts, 2 par of drawers, 2 or 3 par socks. I hate to bother her, but everything is so no count and high hears thet I don't want them…I would prefere my shirts striped and my drawers purple, and you can do as you pleas about the socks…"

Purple drawers? Really? That's a new one on me.

LIFE AND CAMPAIGNS OF LIEUT.-GEN. THOMAS J. JACKSON by Prof. R.L. Dabney, D.D. pub by Sprinkle Pub. 1866

Pg. 389 Summer 1862, after the capture of Winchester, Va. "…Winchester had been the great resort of Federal sutlers, who had impudently occupied many of the finest shops upon its streets, and exposed their wares for sale in them. The headlong confusion of Bank's retreat left them neither means nor time to remove their wealth. All was given up to the soldiers, who speedily emptied their shelves. It was a strange sight to see the rough fellows, who the day before had lacked the ration of beef, and hard bread, regaling themselves with confectionary, sardines, and tropical fruits. Their spoils, however, were about to produce a serious evil. The stores of clothing captured by the men in these shops, and in the baggage of the fugitives, were so enormous, that in a day the army seemed to be almost metamorphosed. The Confederate gray was rapidly changing into the Yankee blue. Had this license been permitted, the purposes of discipline would have been disappointed, and the dangers of battle multiplied. General Jackson speedily suppressed it by this adroit and simple measure.

He issued an order that every person in Federal uniform should be arrested, and assumed to be a prisoner of war going at large improperly, until he himself presented adequate evidence of the contrary. The men of the Provost-Marshal had not acted upon this order many hours before the army became gray again as rapidly as it had been becoming blue. The men either deposited their gay spoils in the bottom of their knapsacks, or sent them by the baggage trains which were carrying the captured stores to the rear, and donned their well-worn uniforms again…It has been related how the soldiers themselves were permitted to dispose of the contents of the sutler's stores. A large part of the army was thus equipped with clothing, boots and shoes, blankets, oil-cloth coverings, and hats. …"

DIARY OF A LINE OFFICER Augustus Cleveland Brown Privately Pub. 1906

Summer 1862 Pg. 53 Pine Grove or Harris Farm, Ewell's Corps "…I particulary noticed among the rebel dead a handsome boy of perhaps eighteen years, who, though clad in the dirty butter-colored uniform of a private, showed every indication of gentle birth and refined home surroundings…"

HISTORY OF THE SOUTHERN CONFEDERACY by Clement Eaton Free Press Paperback Macmillan Pub. 1954

Pg.30 "In the summer of 1862 the northern journalist George Alfred Townsend interviewed some Confederates from North Carolina captured in the peninsula campaign. "The privates wore homespun suits of grey or butternut; some were wrapped in blankets of rag carpet, some had shoes of rough, untanned hide, others were in federal blouses, and a few sported beaver hats."

A Southern Soldier's Letters Home-The Civil War Letters of Samuel Birney Army of Northern Va. ed by Nat Turner,pub by Mercer Univ. Press, 2002

Pg.16 Summer 1862 "…Baldwin's Negro does the cooking, brings water, washes dishes, & waits on his master and I could not ask him to wash my clothes. I will not have much to do except for hickory shirts, drawers and socks. Col. Cobb is particular about keeping everything clean about the camps…." *An example of the civility shown to the "servants" with the army.*

"Mr. Fitzpatrick goes to procure a winter uniform. If you can get mine from the tailor do so and have it lined with brown seams…."

THE STORY OF A CONFEDERATE BOY IN THE CIVIL WAR-David E. Johnson of the 7th Va. Infantry Regiment Commonwealth Press Inc. Radford Va. 1914 1982ed.

Summer 1862 Pg.135 "A musket, cartridge box with forty rounds of cartridges, cloth haversack, blanket and canteen made up the Confederate soldier's equipment. No man was allowed a change of clothing, nor could he have carried it. A grey cap, jacket, trousers and colored shirt-calico mostly-made up a private's wardrobe. When a clean shirt became necessary, we took off the soiled one, went to the water, usually without soap, gave it a little rubbing, and if the sun was shining, hung the shirt on a bush to dry, while the wearer sought the shade to give the shirt a chance. The method of carrying our few assets was to roll them in a blanket, tying each end of the roll, which was then swung over the shoulder. At night this blanket was unrolled and wrapped around its owner, who found a place on the ground with his cartridge box for a pillow. We cooked but little, having usually little to cook. The frying pan was in use, if we had one."

THE PERSONAL RECOLLECTIONS AND EXPERIENCES IN THE CONFEDERATE ARMY by James Dinkins 1897

Pg. 58 July 1, 1862 after the Seven Days Battles-"…Several thousand federal soldiers lay dead and wounded on the field and in the adjacent woods. Our Little Confederate had lost his shoes in the mud of the Chickahominy bottom the day before, and asked a friend (Fort Sanders) to accompany him among the dead, and see if they could find a pair to fit. They examined several pairs, and finally Sanders said, "Here is a good pair of boots, but they are so wet I can not pull them off." He told the Little Confederate, "Hold on to one arm while I pull at the boot." And while thus engaged the Yankee's leg came off. A shell had nearly torn it off before, but we had not observed it. When Saunders fell backward with the leg, the Little Confederate said, "I do not want any shoes," and starting away, passed a man he supposed to be dead, who had a splendid haversack which the little fellow fancied he wanted. He thought it would be no harm to take the haversack, and stooped down to do so. As he pulled at it, the Yankee opened his eyes and asked for water, saying, "There is a spoon in my haversack." The Little Confederate took the spoon and gave him water from a pool near by. The man died after drinking the third spoonful. The Little Confederate did not disturb the haversack, but he kept the spoon, and has it yet… ."

SOUTHERN INVINCIBILTY by Wiley Sword pub by St. Martin's Press 1999

Pg.162 July 2, 1862 night after Malvern Hill- Henry King Burgwyn Jr., officer in the 24th North Caorolina Infantry "To add to their misery, a cold front moved in, and a heavy rainstorm pelted the soldiers unmercifully. "I had on a Yankee overcoat and my body coat (uniform), together with an oil cloth coat, (and yet) I was still shivering," admitted the combat-shaken Burgwyn....Having gone for about two weeks without taking off any part of his clothing, Henry Burgwyn reflected that he was truly "an object for curiosity." Powdered clay from the dusty roads and a "coating of filth" layered his body, and he was famished beyond belief. "Dry crackers, middling pork, and swamp water" had been his entire fare for the two week's campaign. Finally, "cold, wet, and badly used up," Harry Burgwn admitted, "I only hope I will never be "pushed to the wall so tightly."

SOUTHERN INVINCIBILITY Wiley Sword St. Martin's Press 1999

Pg. 118 spring 1862 "One refined Louisiana soldier who hailed from an urbane New Orleans district thought the troops of Sidney Johnson's Kentucky army "unprincipled and very degraded men and officers." Rough-and-tumble in mannerisms, and ragged in dress, they were regarded as yahoos-a poor class of uneducated backwoods ruffians who constantly cussed, drank, and chewed tobacco. Even their officers seemed to be not distinguished, upper-class gentlemen, but a tougher sort who dominated by the force of their malevolent nature..."

SOUTHERN INVINCIBILITY by Wiley Sword pub by St. Martin's Press 1999

Pg. 134 August 29, 1862 At Second Manassas "During the same action, a Georgia colonel had joked with his men, "Boys, we have come back to our old stomping ground (First Manassas). If any of you kill a Yankee, put on his shoes quick, and if you get into a sutler's store, eat all the cheese and crackers you can possibly hold."

Pg. 151 Aug 29, 1862, 2nd Manassas "An officer stood amazed in 1862 as some of Jackson's hatless men ransacked Manassas Junction's captured sutler's tants and found "women's hats and tied them on with the long red ribbons and trimmings attached." Though their appearance was "ludicrous," thought the officer, he watched as they "sang songs of merriment and danced aroung their camp fire at two o'clock that night, eating lobster salad and drinking Rhine wine." Such men, concluded the officer, "could never be whipped upon any fair field...no matter what odds were against them. To kill them was the only way to conquer them."

If only the Rebel food supply could've been more ample, clothing too.

CIVIL WAR MEMOIRS OF TWO REBEL SISTERS Mollie Hansford, 7 miles north of Winchester & Victoria Hansford Kanawha Valley-Coalsmouth-now St. Albans, W.Va. ed. by William D. Wintz Pictorial History Pub. Co. 1989

Pg. 34 Mollie to Victoria regarding Union army taking the slaves during Bank's retreat down the Valley "...Most of our servants went to Baltimore where hundreds died of exposure during the first winter. They had been used to wearing thick linsey dresses, yarn stockings and heavy shoes. When they began wearing calico dresses, cotton stockings and thin shoes in all kinds of winter weather, many of them got sick…

It was perfectly surprising how well the Negroes did all during the war, even after Lincoln's proclamation. We lived so near the border they could have done a great deal of mischief if they had a notion. They seemed happy since they were not compelled to work. They were fed by the army and they drew rations just as the soldiers but only when the Yankees had control of the area. Some, however, were too proud to take anything. Hundreds of others never left their homes until their "white folks" had to send them off when they became too poor to keep them."

I never knew of but one Negro to spy on the "white folks" and report to the Yankees. He afterwards killed himself by jumping into a well in his master's front yard…"

ROCKBRIDGE ARTILLERY The Story of a Cannoneer Under Stonewall Jackson by Edward Moore pub by Neale Pub Co. 1907

Pg. 70 Antietam Campaign Sept 1862 "…Instead of the well-equipped bodies of soldiery to which they (the Maryland citizens) had been accustomed, they now beheld the ragged, barefooted Confederates, who appeared at their very worst…"

This was probably the main reason so few Marylanders joined the Confederate ranks.

SUMMER 1862 VMI MS# 390

P.B.McKay 1862 from Baldwin Miss. Dear Mary "…it is reported that our tents were burned up too if they are then most our clothes are burned up. I put my jeans coat and pants one shirt one pr. drawers one blanket in the tent and wrapped them up in it. We will soon find out the truth of the matter and I will let you know if I need any thing. It is too warm for jeans cotton suits me better. I have a uniform coat that is very well for the present…"

THE CONFEDERATE VETERAN VOL. XXV 1917

Pg. 414 Sept. 1917 In The Year 1862 compiled by John C. Stiles from "Official Records" "Barefooted Men-Colonel Benning, C.S.A., reports that his regiment carried three hundred and thirty-five men into the second Manassas fight; and of these, one-third were shoeless, without a piece of leather on their feet. Captain Waddell also reports over one hundred men in the same fight who were barefooted, "and many of whom left bloody footprints among the thorns and briers through which they rushed with Spartan courage upon the serried ranks of the foe." However, after this battle they got enough Yankee shoes to go around."

JOHN DOOLEY CONFEDERATE SOLDIER-His War Journal ed. by Joseph T. Durkin S.J. Professor of Am. History Georgetown Univ. pub by Georgetown Univ. Press 1945

early June 1862 "My wardrobe consisted of a change of clothing wrapped in a blanket, and my weapon, for I had but one, was a tolerably respectful Springfield musket."

DIARY OF A YOUNG OFFICER SERVING WITH THE ARMIES OF THE UNITED STATES DURING THE WAR OF THE REBELLION Josiah Marshall Favill June 1862

June 1862 Pg. 109 "...In less than half an hour, the little party returned, bring in three villainous looking fellows, wearing immense bowie knives, slouched hats, and butternut clothes. We first took away their knives, and then asked them all the questions we could think of. They belonged to a brigade of Texans that had just arrived fron Richmond, and were entirely unconscious of our proximity..."

REBEL WAR CLERK'S DIARY May 10, 1862

June 1862 Pg. 318 "Detachments of Federal troops are now marching into the city every few hours, guarded (mostly) by South Carolinians, dressed in homespun, died yellow, with the bark of the butternut tree. Yesterday evening at 7 o'clock, a body of 2000 arrived, being marched by the way of Brooke Pike, near to my residence. Only 200 butternuts had them in charge, and a less number would have sufficed, for they were extremely weary..."

Pg. 423 Quartermaster at Charlotte, N.C. "...He also desire the removal of the "foreign Legion" there, paroled prisoners taken from the enemy and enlisting in our service. They are commiting robberies, etc. I saw Gen. Lee at the department again this morning. He seems vigorous, his face quite red, and very cheerful. He was in grey uniform, with a blue cloth cape over his sholdiers..."

A HISTORY OF THE 2nd SOUTH CAROLINA INFANTRY: 1861-1865 by Mac Wyckoff pub. by Sergeant Kirkland's Museum & History Society Inc. 1994

Pg. 23 June 1862- Pennensula Campaign Thomas Reeder wrote, "the romance of camp life is pretty well played out." What the men wore "could scarcely be called clothes..."

LEAVES FROM THE DIARY OF AN ARMY SURGEON John Bradburn, 1863

Pg. 312 Diary of Thomeas T. Ellis June 1862 "…I have just had an interview with Professor Lowe, the aeronaut, who witnessed the battle of Friday from his balloon. He describes the evolutions of battalions, the charges of the cavalry and infantry, the flashing of the artillery, and the carnage of the fight, as truly grand. He says the rebels also sent up a balloon, and he and the occupant of the rebel balloon for some time viewed each other through their telescopes. The distance was too great to permit him to distinguish one division from another, but he could plainly dicern the blue uniform of the Union troops from the butternut and many colored clothing of the rebels…"

OK, Here we have Prof. Lowe's own testimony to the multiform clothing of the Rebels! See below

THE CIVIL WAR INFANTRYMAN, In Camp, on the March, and in Battle by Gregory A. Coco pub by Thomas Publications, Gettysburg, Pa

June 1862 Pg. 35 "It was not unusual, though, in the early months of the war, to see Southern soldiers in civilian clothes. Several accounts from the Seven Day's Battles of 1862 report Confederates fighting entirely in non-military attire. Perry Mayo verified this fact in a May 1862 letter to his father. "A great many deserters come in to our lines every day. They are a hard looking set. They are not dressed in any particular uniform and most of them are dressed in citizen's clothes." New York private Simon Hulbert said practically the same thing on May 11, recalling, "we could tell a rebel when we came across them for they have no uniforms, only citizens clothing."

In letters home to his wife, Amanda White, Sergeant Marion H. Fitzpatrick, 45th Georgia, kept one of the best records of the types and changes, requisitions and issues of both civilian and government clothing he received between 1862 and 1865. According to his inventory, it is clear he was well supplied during most of his military service. Only occasionally did he want for necessary items; usually it was shoes. On November 7, 1862 he sent news to Amanda that:…"our wages are raised to $15.00 dollars a month and we are to be clothed by the government and not draw any more computation money.…If that is the case, I will get no credit from anything you send me and it will be best to draw altogether from the government except socks.…We can draw clothing here much cheaper than can be bought in Ga. Some of the boys have already drawn good clothing at reasonable prices.…"

The sergeant, from necessity, became quite handy with needle and thread. On December15, 1862 Fitzpatrick told his spouse that he wore both pair of his britches, and had done so for two months. The outside pair became rather "holy" but he managed to mend them nicely. His only problem was that "…we have nothing to patch with…One of our company burned a hole In one of his shirts and throw it away or rather gave it to any of us…to patch with. It was a pretty good checked shirt-I took the back off and hemmed it with long stitches-washed it and made a first rate hankerchief. I have saved enough to patch my coat pocket and the hole that was burned in my coat…which task I expect to perform now pretty soon."

WITH THE OLD CONFEDS-Actual Experiences of a Captain in the Line by Samuel D. Buck-Co. H 13 Va. Inf. Pub by H.E. Houck & Co. 1925

Pg. 39 June 1862 right after the Valley Campaign "…The army had passed through terrible scenes and looked rough and dirty, as well as ragged. Jackson, himself, was not an exception to the rule. Our persuers having ceased to persue, we sought glory upon another field…"

HISTORY OF THE BEDFORD LIGHT ARTILLERY by Rev. Joseph A. Graves pub by Press of the Bedford Democrat 1903

Pg. 78 June 1962 Pennensula "…From this point on the mill pond, I was ordered to Dam No.1 with my gun and placed in the fortification at that place. It was at this position that Jim Bondurant, Joe Brosious and I slept in a mud hole under the limber chest of the gun, and kept the water from running in our ears by the use of bags that were being used to make the fortification. There was a night attack; the rain came down in torrents; the trenches were filled with infantry; sleeping room was scarce; so we got in the hole filled with water, soon warmed it with our bodies, and then had a soft comfortable bed to sleep in. The next morning, we dipped the water out of our bed, dried our clothes in the sun, and felt no ill effects…"

I cannot imagine sleeping in a water-filled hole. These are tough men.

LEAVES FROM THE DIARY OF A YOUNG CONFEDERATE-Randolph H. McKim, late 1st Leuitenant & A.D.C. 3rd Brigade, Johnson's Division, A.N.V. pub by Longman's, Green 7 Co.1911

Pg. 92 A description of Gen. "Stonewall" Jackson, June, 1862 "…All the while the soldiers of the army adored him. His appearance at any part of the line always and instantly roused the greates enthusiasium, and wild shouts rent the air as long as he was in sight. On these occasions he would put spurs to his horse and gallop out of sight as soon as possible. This popularity was the more remarkable when it is remembered that he was very strern, very silent, very reserved, and by no means an ideal leader in appearance. His figure was bad, his riding was ungraceful (he rode, as I remember him, with short stirrups and with one shoulder higher than the other.), and his uniform usually rusty, with scarce anything to mark him out as a general…"

This man shouldn't criticize his betters.

THE STONE WALL The Story of a Confederate Soldier by Brad Smiley pub by Zebra Communications, Woodstock, Ga. 1998

Pg.115 Seven Days Battles, June 1862-visiting his brother "…Sam was outside his tent deep in conversation with his sergeant as I approached. He wore a slouch-hat with a battered brim and a weathered gray jacket over frayed jeans…(pg.116)…" you should have seen us. Colonel Smith ordered us to tear our undergarments into pieces and tie strips around our arms, so we we could recognize each other." "did it work?" "yeah, many of our boys were wearing pants and jackets from dead Yanks, we might have shot each other, if we hadn't done that…"

White strips as identification badges again.

THE CONFEDERATE VETERAN PRIVATE SOLDIER LIFE-Humorous Features

Pg. 224June 1862 days battles-Malvern Hill "…When night came and all was quiet, Claibe Freeman thought it was a good time to get him self a better pair of shoes by slipping them from a dead man nearby. As he attempted to take them from the "corpse" it told him to "hold on there!" Claibe said he was sorry, but he had mistaken him for a dead Yankee. The man said he was not a dead Yankee, and if Claibe tried that again he would find him to be one of the liveliest Rebels he ever met…." *Whoops!*

CONFEDERATE LETTERS AND DIARIES ed by Walbrook D. Swank pub by Papercaft Printing and Design Inc. 1992

Pg.118 Letter pf Private Jimmie L. Lewis Co. D. 2nd Mississippi Infantry Third Brigade Whiting's Division Army of Northern Viirginia June 1st Camp on Blackwater (River Va.) Miss Sallie F. Anderson "…I reckon you are tired of reading my description of the skirmish. I will only be getting me two good Yankee haversacks and three canteens and a bedroll of blankets india rubber cloth and came back to camp…"

DEAR SISTER-CIVIL WAR LETTERS TO A SISTER IN ALABAMA Frank Anderson Chappell pub. by Branch Springs Pub. 2002 (Third Alabama Regiment)

Pg. 97 Camp near Richmond June 4 1862 Dear Father "…Pa, I am fairing very bad but I hope there is better times coming. I had lost everything I had, my blankets and all, but got one yankey blanket. I am getting so I can sleep anywhere. I waked up Tuesday night with water half way up my side…"

More misery.

HANDLEY LIBRARY ARCHIVES-Diary of William Randolph Smith Co. F, 17th Viginia Infantry pub by Manassas Chapter United Daughters of the Confederacy 1986

Pg. 14 Peninsula Capaign June 5, 1862 "…Lights are seen glancing to and fro across the field of strife, some upon hospitable thoughts intent, but the greater portion in search of booty.All that is valuable is stored away and the balance trampled underfoot. The dead that strew the ground are examined; if a foe, his pockets are unceremoniously rifled; ifa friend, he is passed by with a sigh…"

KEEP ALL MY LETTERS The Civil War Letters of Richard Henry Brooks, 51st Ga. Inf. ed. by Katherine Holland pub by Mercer Univ. Press, Macon, Ga. 2003

Pg. 25 Camp Evans near Rantowls SC June 7th, 1862 "…Wife I do not want you to pay Floyds any thing for my boots for they have come to pieces a ready. I will have them mended and pay for it out of what I was to pay for the making of them and I will pay him the remainder…"

HISTORY OF THE FOURTH REGIMENT SOUTH CAROLINA VOLUNTEERS FROM THE COMMENCEMENT OF THE WAR UNTIL LEE'S SURRENDER by J.W. Reid pub by Shannon &Co. Printers & Stationers Morningside Bookshop 1975

Pg. 92 "…Among other things, I got, and by the way, not before I needed it, was a new hat, new for me, bit somewhat frazzeled by its original owner. It fit me to a fraction…'

Pg. 93 Camp near Richmond, Va. June 7, 1862 "…We are near Seven Pines Battlefield, about three miles from Richmond. It has been raining ever since our coming, and we had to take it as it came, having no other clothing except that on our backs. Bird Phillips brought our blankets in a wagon from the old camp…"

DEAR AMANDA-The Civil War Letters of Marion Hill Fitzpatrick, Army of Northern Virginia ed. by Jeffery C. Lowe and Sam Hodges pub by Mercer Univ. Press 1998

Pg. 11 June 9th, 1862, 2 miles northeast of Richmond (Letter no. 6) during the Pennensula Battles Dear Amanda, "…Rass Hicks is dead and Jack McCrary started yesterday to carry him home. If he does not leave to come back before you get this, send me one shirt and a plain pair of britches if you get the chance. The reason I want a shirt is that I saved the two checkered shirts and they are wearing out already. I saved them because they were the coolest and lightest and it was very warm when we were on the retreat. Do not have a long tail to the shirt, it make it warmer in marching…"

WEEP NOT FOR ME, DEAR MOTHER by Elizabeth Whitley Roberson pub. by Pelican Pub. Co. 1996

16th Georgia Regiment of Infantry Pvt. Eli Landers (age 19)
Pg. 151 Camp near Richmond June 10th 1862 My Dear Mother and Sisters "…Momma I have drew me a pair of pants and I have got 2 coats and I think I can make out without any from home without there was some certain way to get them…"

A SOUTHERN SOLDIER'S LETTERS HOME The Civil War Letters of Samuel Burney Cobb's Georgia Legion, Army of Northern Va. Ed. By Nat Turner pub by Mercer Univ. Press, Macon Ga.2002

Pg. 179 June 11, 1862 [Mrs. Christian's Farm] Camp Georgia Legion Near Richmond, Va. My Dearest Wife "…I am delighted with my new clothes; everything looked so nice. I am proud of my wife. I suppose Pa is having a new pair of shoes made. Did you get my overcoat? I sent it in Alf Atkinson's trunk, but niether he or I know whether it has gotten home. I had several pieces of clothing in Mr. Fitz's trunk, but do not remember them…."

Pg. 180 June17th, 1862 [Camp Comfort] Camp Georgia Legion near Richmond, Va. My Dearest One, "Last Sunday (it was then Tuesday) I received a letter from Pa, which was very acceptable indeed. He said nothing of having my shoes made. See, my Dear One, that I get a pair by the first one coming on. I mean by this, tell Pa for he will attend to it. I guess he had not received my letter stating that I had to sell those Mr. Porter brought because they were too small…"

CONFEDERATE LETTERS AND DIARIES ed by Walbrook D. Swank pub by Papercaft Printing and Design Inc. 1992

Pg. 102 Sallie F. Anderson Gordonsville Orange Co. Va. Augusta Co. June 12th, 1862 Dearest Sallie, "…our Reg. last Sunday near the Union church about halfway between Harrisonburg and Port Republic….I lost my knapsack and every rag of clothes I had. I borrowed a dirty shirt to day and washed it and put it on. It is the only clean one I have had for four weeks. I wrote to Carter to get me some hose. I wish you would get someone to see Sam Atkins & get those shirts from him if he has not sent them and send me as many pairs of socks as you can.

I prefer your socks if you can get them out to me some way please be in a hurry so Andrew will have chance to get to me before we move off again...."

LEE& JACKSON'S BLOODY TWELTH-Letters of Irby Goodwin Scott First Lieutenant Co. G Putnam Light Infantry Twelth Ga. Vol. Inf. ed. by Johnnie Perry Pearson pub by Univ. Tn. Press 2010

Pg. 78 Camp Near Port Republic, Augusta Co. Va. June 12th, 1862 Loved ones at home. "... Homer Paschal says tell his father to send him a hat &a pair of shoes by the first one coming on to the company..."

THE JOURNAL OF CHARLES R. CHEWNING, Co. E, 9 Virginia Cavalry C.S.A. Researched and Edited by Richard B. Armstrong Cedar Creek Va. Archives

Pg. 1 Old Chuch June 13, 1862 "...We made our first great charge here today. We formed up in the wood and charged across a large field. You should have seen them Federals run for home and mother. After the fight I took a fine pistol off a dead officer. He had a belt with a lot of small leather boxes full of caps and bullets and even one with a small powder flask. From a dead horse I got a nice blanket and saddlebags, now I can throw away my old ripped quilt and sleep warm these chill nights..."

VMI Archives MS# 474 Wade Thomas Camp near Port Republic June 14th, 1862

Dear Son, "...Johnson has just come into our shelter says to tell you to send him that Ghingham shirt & pr of drawers& other clothes. I have some twill cotton in my trunk, make me a pair of drawers. Also make up my other pair of pants. There is a small piece of flannel in the trunk ...send this by some reliable person..."

VOICES FROM COMPANY D Diaries by the Greensboro Guards, Fifth Alabama Infantry Regiment, Army of Northern Virginia ed. by G.Ward Hubbs pub by Univ. of Ga. Press 2003

Pg. 92 June 14, 1862 JST Peninsula "...Got a lot of Tents today & are now getting pretty well fixed up..."

WAR DIARY AND LETTERS OF STEPHEN MINOT WELD 1861-1865 pub by Riverside Press 1912

Pg. 428 Letter from Stephen Minot Weld to Stephen Minot Weld June15, 1862 Hall's Mill, near Richmond "...I saw cavalry proceeding at a rapid rate towards Old Chuch, coming from the road to Hanover. At first I thought it was alright, as the pickets had told me that our scouting parties had gone out in that direction. I thought, though, that their uniform looked rather light and so told my driver to stop while I crept up nearer them. I went into some woods on the right of the road and crept along the fence till I came within 50 or 60 feet of the rascals, and could plainly see that they were Sucesh. At first, indeed, I could hardly believe that they were rebels, but thought they must be some regiment of our cavalry dressed in grey, but I remembered that we had none dressed that way. I could see and distinguish the officers by a broad gold strips which they had on the pants and caps. The men were dessed in all kinds of clothes. Some had grey clothes, some the bluish grey, some white shirts, some red, and in fact almost all the colors of the rainbow were there. The coverings for their heads were of all sorts. Some had caps and others slouched hats, etc...."

THE JOURNAL OF CHARLES R. CHEWNING Co. E 9th Va. Cav. Researched and Edited by Richard B. Armstrong Spotsylvania, Va.

Richmond June 16, 1862 "...We are finally back very tired sore and hungry. We fought the Federals at three places and thrashed them soundly each time. We came back with full bags of good eats and a lot of badly needed equipment. Some of our boys found a Federal supply post and brought off all they could carry..."

RED CLAY TO RICHMOND by John J. Fox pub by Angle Valley Press 2006

Pg. 57 June 16, 1862 "Moody reported on June 16 the prevalence of illness in Company E, including Captain Evan R. Whitly. He reported only ten soldiers fit for duty and four of them displayed signs of sickness too. That same morning, stretcher-bearers carried five men from the company to the hospital. To make matters worse, Moody had worn out his clothes. "I am giting most naked for close (clothes)." He had not changed his pants or shirt since the regiment left Ashland on April 16. This is a period of sixty days! Most of the men had no other clothing to wear, The quartermaster had previously gathered all the soldier's extra clothing and personal items and he'd shipped them to Richmond for safekeeping. Moody discovered that washing his filthy clothes without soap in the nearby creek proved futile. His sense of humor showed when he wrote his wife, "want you to change clothes and think of me." He further fretted about not being paid since the end of February. This left little money in his pocket and even less to send home..."

These soldiers keep their sense of humor in situations that I cannot imagine enduring cheerfully.

THE JOURNAL OF CHARLES R. CHEWNING Co. E 9th Va. Cav. Researched and Edited by Richard B. Armstrong Spotsylvania, Va.

Decai Farm June 17, 1862 "…We rested all day and sorted out our share of the booty, we are now ready for anything the Federals care to throw at us. I have a new pair of high boots, they are a little big but my old shoes had more holes than not…"

LEE& JACKSON'S BLOODY TWELTH-Letters of Irby Goodwin Scott First Lieutenant Co. G Putnam Light Infantry Twelth Ga. Vol. Inf. ed. by Johnnie Perry Pearson pub by Univ. Tn. Press 2010

Pg. 84 Camp near Charlottesville June 19th, 1862 Dear Father "…I do not want you to try and send me any more for I can't get them. They are also liable to be stolen. I can make out with what the government gives us, There is not much chance to get any clothing from home. I lost my knapsack that was left in Staunton with all my cloths except what I had on. I got some more from the boys and with what Henry Thomas bought I have plenty…"

POW VOICES FROM CEMETARY HILL-The Civil War Diary, Reports and Letters of Colonel William Henry Asbury Speer (1861-1865) ed. by Allen Paul Speer pub by The Overmountain Press 1997

Pg. 74 Diary entry June 19, 1862 "today I received a uniform set of clothes from C.C. Hardie & some other clothing, all of which will make me quite comfortable. I am under obligation to him and my Masonic friends as long as I live." He was a prisoner on Governor's Island

WRITING & FIGHTING FROM THE ARMY OF NORTHERN VIRGINIA ed. by William B. Styple pub by Belle Grove Pub. 2003

Pg. 109 Letter From The V.A.S.P. Camp near the Chickahominy, June 21, 1862 "…To-day is the "General Review and Inspection." We are but poorly prepared for such an imposing event. Our guns and our side arms are in good order, and will pass a creditable inspection; but our uniforms! There is not a hundred men in the brigade who have hats or caps alike; the greatest variety imaginable, of every style, shape, quantity and description, that can be found in or out of the most exclusive "hatteries" of the world, may be seen in our brigade upon this auspicious "Review Day." There is scarcely less variety in the matter of coats, pants &c. This is owing, in great measure, to the constant and laborious duties to which General Tomb's Brigade has been subjected for the last three or four months. But, what matter all this? If we do not make a great show upon the review, and carry off the palm as the best looking brigade in the service, we can shoot as fast, yell as loud, and charge the Yankees with as much impetuosity as the finest dressed troops in the Confederate army. I am not certain but that our in-different uniforms will make us fight harder, for it won't make much difference if we do get them soiled, bloody or torn…"

Multiform

KEEP ALL MY LETTERS The Civil War Letters of Richard Henry Brooks, 51st Ga. Inf. ed. by Katherine Holland pub by Mercer Univ. Press, Macon, Ga. 2003

Pg. 28 Charleston SC June the 23rd, 1862 "…I want you to send me by the first one that passes one more shirt. I would Like to have it pretty near Like the home made one that I brought with me for my hickory one is nearly worn out, it has got holes in it now an I am not a very good hand to patch. Tomorrow is my wash day I can wash very well. …"

DEAR SISTER-CIVIL WAR LETTERS TO A SISTER IN ALABAMA Frank Anderson Chappell pub. by Branch Springs Pub. 2002 (Third Alabama Regiment)

Pg. 106 Near Richmond Va. June 25-62 My Dear Mother "…Four companies up here employed one Mr. Williams to bring us things from home. I expect he will be at the Springs by the time this letter gets there. If so, I nor Lewis don't need any clothing at present. We are moving so often if we had much we would lose them. There is one thing I would like to have and that is a hat. But I fear they are not to be had in your country for they are not to be had here…"

A TRUE HISTORY OF COMPANY I, 49TH REGIMENT NORTH CAROLINA TROOPS by W.A.Day printed at the Enterprise Job Office 1893

Pg. 17 June 25th, 1862 Richmond "…It rained a shower while we were there and it was quite amusing to see the Militia on dress parade with umbrellas over them. The officers gave their commands in a loud tone of voice, and the men handled their guns like they were afraid of them. We also witnessed a parade of colored men, all bright mulattoes. They handled their guns well and made a splendid appearance. Their main duty was guarding about the city…"

African-American (Mulattoes) acting as guard about the city of Richmond? I've never read anything of this before. It would've been a blast watching the militia drill in the rain with umbrellas.

LIFE AND LETTERS OF ALEXANDER HAYS, BREVET COLONEL UNITED STATES ARMY, BRIGADIER GENERAL AND BREVET MAJOR GENERAL UNITED STATES VOLUNTEERS Pittsbourg Pa. Privately Pub. 1919

Pg 234 June 26 1862 Camp "Fair Oaks" Va. "…Day before yesterday I received to hold "the iron clad 63rd" ready to take the lead in an advance towards Richmond at 8 o'clock A.M.… Steady as veterans they moved forward, and when we had passed our own pickets about 100 yards, we came across the enemy. Steadily and regularly we drove them before us for a mile and a quarter, until we were opposed by the 4th Georgia. The Georgians were dressed in a fancy French Zouave uniform,. Which caused our men to hesitate, and it was reported to me and asked what will we do? I told them to give it to them anyhow, they have no business to be there. Then our boys pitched in again, and in 15 minutes the Georgians were on the road to Richmond. The rout was complete. The quality, elegance, and taste of all their equipment bore evidence that they were all scions of the first families among the Georgian chivalry.…"

"DEAR MOTHER: DON'T GRIEVE ABOUT ME. IF I GET KILLED, I'LL ONLY BE DEAD." ed. by Mills Lane pub by The Beehive Press 1977

Pg.141 John Wood to his Father Richmond, Virginia June 26, 1862 Dear Father: "…My load that I carried while marching to Richmond to the line of battle was two blankets, gun, cartridge box, bowie knife, knapsack, two shirts, two pair of drawers, two pair of gloves, four pair of socks, three books, all my writing accouterments, two pair of pants, I sold my canteen for 50 and one book for 25 and my mess box for 50 (and) lock for 50. I left my can of peaches, knife and fork in our mess box with some things that we were compelled to have…"

HANDLEY LIBRARY ARCHIVES, WINCHESTER, VA. Janes Bradfiels Diary, Co. H. 17th Virginia Infantry

Pg. 5 26th June, 1862 Seven Days Battles- "…Gen. A.P. Hill has been driving the Yankees all afternoon he captured Mechanicsville we lay down after midnight to get a little sleep we had not more than got to sleep when there was a great cry raised and there was a large ditch on each side of the road and about half the Brigade jumped in them it turned out to be two horses who had gotten away from some officer the next morning the boys were muddy as hogs and the ditches full of blankets and clothes and shoes the boys thought the yankee cavalry were right on them…"

BATTLEFIELDS OF THE SOUTH AN ENGLISH COMBATANT Collector's Library of the Civil War Time Life Books

Pg.333 June 27,1862 Pennensula Campaign prior to the battle at Gaines Mill "Lee sat in the south portico absorbed in thought. He was neatly dressed in in a dark blue uniform, buttoned to the throat....Longstreet sat in an old garden-chair, at the foot of the steps, under shady trees, busily engaged in disposing of a lunch of sandwiches. With his feet thrown against a tree he presented a true type of the hardy campaigner; his once grey uniform had changed to brown, and many a button was missing; his riding boots were dusty and worn, but his pistols and saber had a bright polish by his side, while his charger stood near, anxiously looking at him, as if expecting a morsel of bread and meat."

Maxy Gregg- "His uniform looked the worse for wear; even the three stars upon his throat being dingy and ragged, while his common black felt hat would not bring half a dollar at any place in times of peace."

OUTLINES FROM THE OUTPOST by John Esten Cooke ed by Richard Harwell Lakeside Press R.R. Doelly & Sons Co. Chicago Ill. 1961

Pg.50 "It was on the battlefield of Cold Harbor, June 27, 1862:- so much had he thought and fought and suffered-and so often triumphed-before I ever saw him!

I looked at him instantly with singular interest-such as I have felt in few human beings- and with much curiosity.

The appearance of the famous General Stonewall was not imposing. He wore that old sun-embrowned uniform once gray, which his men are so familiar with, and which has now become historic. To call it sun-embrowned is scarcely to describe, however, the extant of its discoloration. It was positively scorched by sun-and that dingy hue, the product of sun and rain, and contact with the ground which is so unmistakable. A soldier from Franklin street, in his fine, new braided uniform, would have scarcely deigned to glance at the wearer of such a coat, and would have elbowed its possessor from the pavement with extreme disdain;-but the men of the old Stonewall Brigade, loved that coat; and admired it, and its owner, more than all the holiday uniforms and holiday warriors in the world. The cap of the general matched the coat-if anything was still more faded. The sun had turned it quite yellow indeed, and it tilted over the wearer's forehead, so far as to make it necessary for him to raise his chin, in looking at you. He rode in his peculiar forward-leaning fashion, his old raw-boned sorrel, gaunt and grim-but like his master, careless of balls and tranquil in the loudest hurly burly of battle.

Moving about slowly and sucking a lemon, (Yankee spoil, no doubt) the celebrated General Stonewall looked as little like a general as possible. There was nothing of the "pride, pomp and circumstance of glorious war" about him, as my outline sketch established. He had the air rather of a spectator than an actor-and certainly no one would have taken him for the idolized leader of a veteran army, then engaged in the battle to decide the fate of the Confederate Capital. His dispositions had been made-his corps had closed like an iron arm around the enemy-and having led them into action, marching at their head, on foot, like a simple captain, he now appeared to await the result with entire calmness, almost with an air of indifference, trusting to a higher Power-to that Lord of hosts who had given him victory so often."

Is it any wonder that we are in awe of him?

BATTLEFIELDS OF THE SOUTH AN ENGLISH COMBATANT Collector's Library of the Civil War Time Life Books

Pg.344 June 27, 1862 After the battle at Gaines Mill "As soon as the camps had fallen into our hands, and the enemy had retreated, our men laid violent hands on whatever food or clothing they discovered. They were so thoughtless in this resect that I saw many of them attired in suits of Yankee clothing, so that it was oftentimes difficult to distinguish between them and our prisoners. I could not blame the poor fellows for securing clothing of some kind; the greater number of them were ragged and dirty, and wearing-apparel could not be obtained at any price in Richmond. It was grotesque to see a tall, well-developed Southerner attired in clothes much too small, but the men themselves were delighted with the change, and strutted about with gold-corded shoulder-straps and striped pantaloons, often not sufficiently long enough to cover the ankle. I forbore making unpleasant remarks about the danger of wearing such clothes: several of our men were shot in consequence; venturing beyond the lines, they were mistaken for enemies, and before explanations could be offered, were laid lifeless."

HORRORS OF THE BATTLEFIELD by J. Wood Davidson

Pg. 48 7 days battles June 28 1862 Cold Harbor "…they calculated for our rising and allowed too much, a few inches too much, and that few inches saved a hundred lives. Above us flashed and popped the explosive balls wherever they hit a tree or skull or bone! These infernal balls explode whenever they hit any hard surface; hence the rarely inflict a slight wound-it is miss or death…"

Here is the section of information on the use of explosive bullets.

HADLEY LIBRARY ARCHIVES-Diary of William J. Thomas 2nd Maryland Battalion

Pg.76 "I saw today, for the first time, an explosive musket-ball, or musket shell. I have ofted heard them explode near me; and insisted upon it, until lately, when never having seen one and never having met one who had seen them, I began to think my ears had deceived me. But now there is no doubt. The ball contains a hollow cone, of hard metal, filled with explosive matter."

THE CONFEDERATE VETERAN VOL. VII

Jan. 1899 Pg. 27 Explosive Bullets by Judge Henry H. Cook "In the "Century Magazine" for December, 1885, is an article purporting to have been written by Gen. U.S. Grant, called "The Siege of Vicksburg." On page 758 this language is used: "The enemy used in their defense explosive musket balls, thinking no doubt that bursting over our men in the trenches they would do some execution. I do not remember a single case where a man was injured by a piece of one of these shells. When they were hit, and the ball exploded, the wound was terrible. In these cases a solid ball would have hit just as well. Their use is barbarous, because they produced increased suffering without any corresponding advantage to those using them."

I have diligently sought, but have not found a Confederate soldier who ever saw an "explosive musket ball." I write this in order to draw attention to this question of "explosive musket balls."

After Bushrod Johnson's Brigade fell back from Dr. Friend's house to a shorter line around Drewry's Bluff, I am sure that Gen. Butler's Sharpshooters, stationed in tobacco barns in our front, used explosive musket balls. I heard at least twenty bullets explode over my company the day before the battle of Drewry's Bluff. I saw one man with four wounds in his face, and he told me that a musket ball exploded near his face. I saw another man with two wounds in his face and two wounds in his right hand, and he stated that a bullet had exploded in front of him.

Many Confederate soldiers have stated to me that there never was such a thing as an explosive musket ball,that the tin or zinc wipers would often fly off of the ball and separate into three or four pieces and create the impression that the ball had exploded.

It is contended by many well-informed persons that no explosive bullet was manufactured until after 1863."

THE CONFEDERATE VETERAN VOL. VII

April 1899 Pg. 156 Explosive and poisoned bullets by Rev. Horace Edwin Hayden, who served in the First Virginia and then in the first Missouri Cavalry, C.S.A. writes from Wilkes-Barr, Pa.:

I note Judge Cook's article on explosive bullets on page 27, Jan, Veteran. I am surprised that the article that I inclose has not been seen by the judge or the Veteran. I wrote it after much correspondence and research, and it was published in the Southern Historical Society Papers in 1880. Many of the facts are taken "verbatim" from the official papers on file in the United Srates War Department. I was refused a copy of that paper, but was allowed to read it and re-read it, with the assurance I could commit it to memory, and use it, which I did with all dispatch. I searched the United States in its preparation.

The following remarkable statement occurs as a note to the account of the battle of Gettysburg, page 78, volume III of "The Pictorial History of the Civil War in the United States of America," by Benson J. Losing, L.L.D.:

"Many, mostly young men were maimed in every conceivable way, by every kind of weapon and missile, the most fiendish of which was an explosive and a poisoned bullet, represented in an engraving a little more than half the size of the originals, procured from the battlefield by the writer. These were sent by the Confederates. Whether any were ever used by the Nationals, the writer is not informed. One was made to explode in the body of a man, and the other to leave a deadly poison in him, whether the bullet lodged in or passed through him. It was illustrated. When the bullet struck, the momentum would cause the copper in the outer disk to flatten, and allow the point of the stem to strike and explode the fulminating powder, when the bullet would be rent into fragments which would lacerate the victum.

"In figure B the bullet proper was hollowed, into which was inserted another, also hollow, containing poison. The latter, being loose, would slip out and remain in the victum's body or limbs with its freight of poison if the bullet proper should pass through. Among the Confederate wounded at the College were boys of tender age and men who had been forced into the ranks against their will."

It is difficult for those who live at the South to realize how extensively such insinuating slanders as the above against the Confederates are credited at the North, even among reading people.

It is with entire confidence in the facts presented in this paper that I deny this author's statement.

I most emphatically deny that the Confederate States ever authorized the use of explosive or poisoned musket or rifle balls, and I assert they the United States did purchase, authorize, issue, and use explosive rifle or musket balls during the late civil war, and that they were thus officially used in the battle of Gettysburg.

It happened in 1864, the day after the negro troops made their desparate and drunken charge on the Confederate lines to the left of Chaffin's Farm and were so signally repulsed, that the writer, who was located in the trenches a mile still further to the left, picked up in the field outside the trenches assailed by the negroes some of the cartridges these poor black victims had dropped, containing the very "explosive" ball described in the above quotation and charged to the Confederates. I have preserved one of these balls ever since. It lies before me as I write. It has a zinc, and not a copper, disc. It never contained any fulminating powder. The construction of the ball led me to make investigations to ascertain its purpose. At first I thought it might be made to leave in the body of the person struck by it three pieces of metal instead of one, to irritate and possibly destroy life. But this theory appeared to me so "fiendish" that I was unwilling to accept it, and became convinced, after more careful examination, that the purpose of the ball was to increase the momentum, by forcing in the cap and expandingthe disk so as to fill up the grooves of the rifle. The correctness of this view is proven herein.

In the first place, alongside the charge made by the author of the "Pictorial History of thr Civil War" against the Confederates of having used explosive and poisoned balls has been made before and often repeated since, it has never been supported by one grain of proof. How did this author ascertain that the balls he picked up on the battlefield of Gettysburg were sent by the Confederates? How did he learn that one was an explosive and the other a poisoned projectile? Did he test the explosive power of the one and the poisonous character of the other? He gives no evidence of having done so, and advances no proof of his assertions. It is a very remarkable fact that no case was ever reported in Northern hospitals, or by Northern surgeons, of Union soldiers being wounded by such barbarous missiles as these from the Confederates.

I have very carefully examined those valuble quarto volumes issued by the The United States Medical Department and entitled "The Medical and Surgical History of the Rebellion," and as yet have failed to find any case of wound or death reported as having occurred by an explosive or poisoned musket ball, excepting that on page 91 of Volume II, of said work there is a table of four thousand and two cases of gunshot wounds to the scalp, two of which occurred by explosive musket balls. To which army these two belonged does not appear.

A letter addressed to the Surgeon General of the United States by the writer on this subject has elicited the reply that the Medical Department is without any information as to wounds by such missiles. I do not find such projectiles noticed as preserved in the museum of the Surgeon General's Department, where rifle projectiles taken from wounds are usually deposited.

In the second place the manufacture, purchase, issue, or use of such projectiles for firearms by the Confederate States is positively denied by the Confederate authorities, as the following correspondence will show:

Beauvior, Miss. June 28, 1879

My Dear Sir: I reply to your inquiries as to ther use of explosive or poisoned balls by the troops of the Confederates States, I state as posively as one may in such a case that the charge has no foundation in truth. Our government certainly did not manufacture or import such balls, and, if any were captured from the enemy they could probably only be used in the captured arms for which they were suited. I heard occasionally that the enemy did use explosive balls, and others prepared so as to leave a copper ring in the wound, but it was always spoken of as an atrocity beneath knighthood and abhorrent to civilization. The slander is only one of many instances in which our enemy has committed or attepted crimes of which our people and their government were incapable, and then magnify the guilt by accusing us of the offense they had committed…

Believe me, ever faithfully yours, Jefferson Davis

Gen. Josiah Gorgas, the Chief of Ordinance of the Confederate States-after the war with the University of Alabama-writes under date of July 11, 1879, that "to his knowledge the Confederate States never authorized or used explosive or poisoned rifle balls." In this statement also Gen. I.M. St. John and Gen. John Ellicott, both of the Ordinance Bureau, Confederate States Army entirely concur.

The Adjutant General of the United States also writes me under the date of August 22, 1879, as to the Confederate Archives now in the possession of the national government, as follows: In reply to yours of the 18 August, I have the honor to inform you that the Confederate States records in the possession of this department furnish no evidence that poisoned or explosive musket balls were used by the army of the Confederate States.

A brief examination of the United States Patent Office Reports for 1862-63, and the Ordinance Reports for 1863-64, will show that the "explosive and poisoned balls" which the author of the "Pictorial History of the Civil War" so gratuitously charges upon the Confederates were patented by the United States Patent Office at Washington, and were purchased, issued, and used by the United States Government, and, what is still more remarkable, that neither of the aforesaid projectiles were in any sense explosive or poisoned.

In repelling and refuting the charge against the Confederates of having used explosive musket or rifle projectiles, I charge the United States Government with not only patenting, but purchasing and using, especially at the battle of Gettysburg, an explosive musket shell; nor do I trust my imagination, but I present the facts, which are as follows:

In April, 1862, the Commissioner of Publc Buildings at Washington brought to the attention of the Assistant secretary of War-then Mr. John Tucker-the explosive musket shell invented by Mr. Samuel Gardiner Jr. The Assistant Secretary at once referred the matter to Gen. James W. Ripley, who was then Chief of the Ordinance Bureau at Washington. What action was taken will appear when it is stated that in May, 1862, the Chiel of Ordinance at West Point Military Academy made a report to the government of a trial of the Gardiner musket shell. In May, 1862 Mr. Gardiner offered to sell some of his explosive musket shells to the government at a stipulated price. His application was referred to Gen. Ripley with the following endorsement:

"Will Gen. Ripley consider whether this explosive shell will be a valuable missile in battle? A. Lincoln"

In June, 1862, Brig. Gen. Rufus King at Fredericksburg made a requisition for some of the Gardiner musket shells. On referring this application to the Chief of Ordinance, Gen. Ripley, that old army officer, whose sense of right must have been shocked at this instance of barbarism, a second time recorded his disapproval, replying that "it was not advisable to furnish any such missiles to the troops ar present in service."

In September, 1862, the Chief of Ordinance of the Eleventh Corps, United States Army, recommended the shell to the assistant Secretary of War, who ordered 10,000 rounds to be purchased-made into cartridges. Of this number 200 were issued to Mr. Gardiner for trial by the Eleventh Corps. In October, 1862, the Chief of Ordinance of the eleventh Corps, then in reserve near Fairfax C.H., sent in a requisition, indorsed by the general commanding the corps, for 20,000 Gardiner musket shells and cartridges. The Assistant Secretary of War referred the matter to the Chief of Ordinance, Gen. Ripley, who for the third time recorded his disapproval of such issue. Nevertheless the Assistant Secretary of War ordered the issue to be made to the Eleventh Corps of the remaining 9,800 shells and catridges, which order was obeyed.

In November, 1862, Mr. Gardiner offered to sell to the United States his explosive musket shell and cartridge at $35 per thousand, calber 58. The Assistant Secretaryof war at once ordered 100,000 of which 75,- were caliber 58 for infantry, and 25,000 caliber 54 for cavalry service.

In June, 1863, the Second New Hampshire Volunteers made a requisition for 35,000 of these shells, and by order of the Assistant secretary of war they received 24,000. Of this number 10,060 were abandoned in Virginia and 13,940 distributed to the regiment. The report of this regiment, made subsequently, shows that in the third quarter of 1863-that is, from July 1 to October 1-about 4,000 of these shells were ised in trials and target firing, and about 10,000 were used in action. The Second New Hampshire Regiment was in the battle of Gettysburg, and 49 of its members lie buried in the cemetery there.

The above statement shows that the Assistant Secretary of War, against what might be regarded as the protest of the Chief of Ordinance purchased 110,000 of the Gardiner explosive musket shells, and issued to the troops in actual service 35,000 leaving 75,000 on hand at the close of the war.

In 1866 the Russian government issued a circular calling a convention of the nations for the purpose of declaring against the use of explosive projectiles in war. To this circular the then Chief of Ordinance of the United States, Gen. A.B. Dyer, made the following reply, which I have but little doubt expresses the sentiment which actuated Gen. Riplet in his disapproval of the purchase and issue of the Gardiner musket shell:

Ordinance Office, War Department
Washington, August 10, 1868

To Hon. J.M. Schofield, Secretary of War.

"Sir: I have read the communication from the Russian Minister in relation to the abolishment of the use of explosive projectiles in military warfare, with the attention and care it well deserves.

"I concur heartily in the sentiments therein expressed, and I trust that our government will respond unhesitatingly to the proposition in behalf of humanity and civilization. The use in warfare of explosive balls so sensitive as to ignite and burst on striking a substance as soft and yielding as animal flesh (of men or horses) I consider barbarous and no more to be tolerated bu civilized nations than the universally reprobated practice of using poisoned missiles or of poisoning food or drink to be left in the way of an enemy. Such a practice is inexcusable among above the grade of ignorant savages. Neither do I regard the use in war of such explosive balls as of any public advantage, but rather the reverse, for it will have the effect of killing outright, rather than wounding, and it is known that the care of wounded men much more embarrasses the future operations of the enemy than the loss of the same number killed, who require no futher attention which may delay or impede them.

A.B.Dyer

Brevet Major General, Chief of Ordinance

I have recorded enough to show the recklessness and falsity of the charge against the Confederates of using such missiles in small arms and the public is hererby specifically "informed whether the Nationals ever used them."

In the Patent Office Report for 1863-64 will be found the following account of the Gardiner musket shell:

"No. 40,468. Samuel Gardiner of New York, N.Y.-Improvement in Hollow Projectiles. Patent dated Nov. 3, 1863.

"The shell to form the central chamber is attached to a mandrel, and the metal forced into a mold around it.

"Claim: Constructing shells for firearms by forcing the metal into a mold around an internal shell supported on a mandrel."

I have a box of these shells in my possession. They are open for examination by any person who may desire to see them.

This summer the distinguished officer who commanded the One Hundred and Forty-Third Regiment of Pennsylvania Volunteers, United States Army, at the battle of Gettysburg informed me that during the last day of the battle, he and his men frequently heard above their heads, amid the whistling of the Minnie balls from the Confederate side, sharp, explosive soundes like the snapping of musket caps. He mentioned the matter to an ordinance officer at the time. The officer replied that what he heard was explosive rifle balls, which the Confederates had captured from the Union troops, who had lately received them from the Ordinance Department.

It is earnestly hoped that the facts presented in this paper will forever set at rest the malicious slander so often repeated against the Confederates, by many who are so willing to believe anything against them, of having autrhorized the use in military warfare of such atrocious and barbarous missiles as "explosive and poisoned" musket or rifle balls."

This is the first-hand information I found regarding explosive bullets. One would think it would be such a bother to manufacture them as to not be worth the effort.

LEE & JACKSON'S BLOODY TWELTH-Letters of Irby Good-win Scott First Lieutenant Co. G Putnam Light Infantry Twelth Ga. Vol. Inf. Ed. by Johnnie Perry Pearson Univ. Tn. Press 2010

Pg. 92 Camp 7 miles from Gordonsville, Va. June 28th, 1862 Dear Mother, "…My coat is nearly worn out, but I thought I would try and make it do until fall. I have plenty of drawers & shirts also socks to last me until fall. I received by Henry Marshall my hat, which was very acceptable. I had the day before cut out the crown of my old one and sewn it back in. Also patched up in many places. The one you sent is a great deal better than any that can be bought here. I tried in Richmond but could not find anything but straw hats which I would not buy.…You can send me a coat by Jake Filer when he comes on. If you get this letter in time to make it like the last one a frock coat. I will need some socks, pants, drawers& an overcoat this winter, but do not try and send them until I need them for I might lose them. There will be some chance in the fall. I have plenty of blankets for the present. It would be difficult to get them from home. I suppose there will be some arrangements made to supply us this winter. We have plenty scattered about if we could ever (get) them. I will also need a pair of over shirts. I live in the hopes of coming home myself in time to get what I need for the winter but I cannot tell when I can come home it depends entirely upon circumstances. I want to come home more now than I have since I have been in the service. You can also send me a pair of shoes by Jake if he is willing to bring them…"

FOOTPRINTS OF A REGIMENT A Recollection of the 1st Georgia Regulars by W.H. Andrews Longstreet Press Atlanta Ga. 1992

1862 Pg. 43-44 Pennensula Campaign June 29 1862 Battle of the Peach Orchard …"While we were halted, I was keeping a sharp lookout to the front. I saw as I supposed, a Yankee not far in advance making his retreat. I placed my gun to my shouldert, took deliberate aim, and pressed the trigger. Just as I was in the act of shooting, the Yankee stooped down to pass under a limb, and who should it be but Lt. Fred B. Palmer, who had a Yankee overcoat on his arm that he had picked up in the enemy camps. …"

FOUR YEARS IN THE CONFEDERATE HORSE ARTILLERY-The Diary of Private Henry Robinson Berkelely ed. by William H. Runge Va. Hist. Society by the Univ. N.Ca. Press 1961

Pg. 20 June 30 (1862) Monday "…We found our company in a field below Cold Harbor. The Yankee dead were quite thick just about this place, while a great many blankets, overcoats, tents, wagons, muskets and plunder of all kinds lay scattered over the field in great quantities. …The bridge across the Chickahominy having been rebuilt, our brigade passed over and we followed it. We went over the battlefield of yesterday evening, where knapsacks, haversacks, oilcloths, blankets and plunder of every description lay thick. It seems to me there were enough blankets and tents to supply 100,000 men. I secured two oilcloths and a beautiful red blanket, but I did not care to load myself down with plunder, knowing that the chances were that we would soon go into a fight…"

VOICES OF THE Civil War BY Richard Wheeler Meridian Books 1976

Pg. 148 June 30, 1862 Battle of Frayser's Farm In a union artillerists words "Our sergeant shouted to the boys as the Rebs came yelling like mad upon us, "Don't run from them!"

I thought to myself, "I ain't going to git from no such ragged fellows as they be."

CONFEDERATE CAPTAIN UJANIRTIS ALLEN'S LETTERS TO HIS WIFE ed. By Kandall Allen and Keith S. Bohannon La. State Univ. Press 1998

Pg.132 Near Sumerset Va. July 1862 "…I wrote to you about shoes because we can not always get them for love or money. I paid ten dollars for a rough brogue in Richmond. We may have a better chance in a month or two. I will need a pair of boots for winter. I do not know if I shall have Hollie to make them or not. I shall want the regular army boot. I do not know what we will do for blankets this winter. You must tell those that have friends in the company that the poor boys can not do well without blankets this winter. I have only two. You must send me yours when I want them. I frequently live in a very primitive manner. If the weather is dry pick out a soft and if wet a hard place on the ground pull my cap over my face put my head on a root or chunk and go to sleep…."

THE CIVIL WAR INFANTRYMAN, In Camp, on the March, and in Battle by Gregory A. Coco pub by Thomas publications, Gettysburg, Pa

Pg40 Still another Virginian, John Casler, 33rd Virginia, in July 1862, wore a federal issue coat. He once became a little careless, as he later remembered: "One morning, as it was a little rainy, I put on a blue blouse, and that evening was on the skirmish line. As we were going through a piece of woods I thought I had better pull off my blue blouse, as I might be taken for the enemy by some "Johnnie Reb" and popped over. So I took it off and hung it on a bush…" John Green captured a fine overcoat in Tennessee in 1862 which belonged to Colonel A.B. Moore of the 104th Illinois. In November, 1863, near Mine Run, Virginia, Leiutenant Galwey, 8th Ohio, saw one of his men, "…during our advance (run) amongst a lot of Confederates, thinking them, with their blue overcoats, his own men. He learned his mistake …(and) broke away and joined us."

Pg77 "Physically, the (Rebels) looked about equal to the generality of our own troops, and there were fewer boys among them. There dress was a wretched mixture of all cuts and colors.

There was not the slightest attempt at uniformity in this respect. Every man seemed to have put on whatever he could get hold of, without regard to shape or color. I noticed a pretty large sprinkling of blue pants among them…Their shoes, as a general thing were poor; some of the men were entirely barefooted. Their equipments were light as compared with those of our men. They consisted of a thin woolen blanket, coiled up and slung from the shoulder, in the form of a sash, a haversack slung from the opposite shoulder, and a cartridge-box. The whole cannot weigh more than twelve or fourteen pounds…The marching of the men was irregular and careless; their arms were rusty and ill-kept. Their whole appearance was greatly inferior to that of our soldiers."

OK, Say that after a battle, Yank.

I WROTE YOU WORD-The Poignant Letters of Private John Holt-John Lee Holt 1829-1863 ed. by James A. Mumper printed by H.E. Howard 1991

Pg. 100 July 1862 My dearest wife, "…You wrote to know if I would want any clothes between now & the winter & would be glad to have some shirts. Somewhat like Cousin Lydia made for Tom sometime ago homespun colored cotton shirts have them colored a kind of checked color I reckon my flannel drawers will last me another winter as for yarn clothes I reckon I can get them furnished to me cheaper than you can afford to make them I shall want some more socks for the winter I reckon I shall have enough to last me till the winter 2 shirts & 3 or 4 pairs of socks will be enough If you have the wool I would not care (mind) if you would have my shirts partly yarn as the would answer the place of flannel…Tell Nick he must make haste & comeback Tell him we put his knapsack with the baggage but it was taken off at Richmond & we found it & brought it on here but we had to march 3 or 4 miles last night & could not carry it so we took out all his clothes but one old pair of pants & his old boots & put them in our knapsacks So he had better try to get him another knapsack I let Chas Brightwell have my old one I reckon he could get that if he will see him or maybe he could get one of some of Uncle Dicks boys as they all had knapsacks…"

DEAR AMANDA-The Civil War Letters of Marion Hill Fitzpatrick ed. by Jeffery C. Lowe and Sam Hill Mercer Univ. Press 1998

Pg. 18 July 1st, 1862, Near Richmond, Va.(Letter No. 9) Dear Amanda "…I just have to write on scraps of paper, one piece I picked up in a Yankee camp. I lost my overcoat and blanket. I got another blanket but lost it in the fight last night. I picked up another before I stopped and slept on it last night. I have it yet…"

Pg. 19 July 23rd, 1862 Near Richmond, Va. (Letter no. 10) Dear Amanda,"…Well, Coot, I have been writng a good deal about clothes, but I have now come to one shirt and one pr.

drawers, having lost my knapsack, which I explained in Mother's letter. A few days ago they sent around for all that wanted clothes to make a requisition. I put down for 1 shirt and pr. drawers, not knowing what you would send me by Mcrary, but after I received what you sent and received a letter form Alex stating that he could not get my shirts off, I enlarged my requisition considerably, but it was too late to get it in, but if I get the first requisition I can make out very well and will also try to buy some if I get the chance..."

FOOTPRINTS OF A REGIMENT A Recollection of the 1st Georgia Regulars by W.H. Andrews pub by Longstreet Press Atlanta Ga. 1992

Pg. 49July 1, 1862 before the Battle of Malvern Hill ..."From what I saw of Gen. Jackson, he is a very ordinary looking man of medium size, his uniform badly soiled as though it had seen hard service. He wore a cap pulled down nearly to his nose and was riding a poor rawboned horse that did not look much like a charger, unless it would be on hay or clover. He certainly made a poor figure on a horseback, with his stirrup leather six inches too short putting his knees nearly level with the horse's back, and his heels turned out with his toes sticking behind his horse's foreshoulder. A sorry description of our most famous general, but a correct one...."

FROM HUNTSVILLE TO APPOMATTOX R.T. Cole's History of the $th Regiment, Alabama Volunteer Infantry, C.S.A., Army of Northen Virginia ed by Frank L. Byrnes pub by Univ of Tenn. 1996

Pg. 249 July 1 1862 Battle of Malvern Hill Footnote #17 "A modern author has described the Union position as thus; "Across his whole front Porter had placed his infantry in three tiers on the hillside, behind hastily built lines of logs and loose earth packed in knapsacks..."

Using knapsacks as sand bags? Ingenious but rather expensive.

A SOUTHERN SOLDIER'S LETTERS HOME The Civil War Letters of Samuel Burney Cobb's Georgia Legion, Army of Northern Va. Ed. By Nat Turner Mercer pub by Univ. Press, Macon Ga.2002

Pg. 190 July 3rd, 1862 Camp Georgia Legion near Richmond, Va. Dearest one, "I have a fine rubber taken from the Yankee camp. Our boys have supplied themselves with many Yankee things: sugar, coffee, clothing, everything..."

Pg. 191 same camp July 5th, 1862 (Saturday) "We entered the Yankee camps last Sunday morning, and, at the risk of being tedious, I will mention some of the thousand things I saw. To wit: cooking untensils of every sort, soap, candles, ambrotypes, pipes, paper, envelopes, newspapers, crackers beef, sugar, coffee, syrup,knapsacks by the thousands, haversacks, canteens, coats, pants, boots, shoes, hats, combs, brushes, Indea rubbers (I got a fine one), guns, cartridge boxes, sick Yankees by the thousands, tents, axes, saws, hammers, wagons, salt, a prepared vegetable matter put up in square cakes for making soup, cots, camp stools, Yankee letters, blankets-I could not tell half I did see... Yesterday I had a good wash & put on my clean clothing. The shirts you sent me fade, but that does not hurt the excellent material. I think they are the prettiest shirts seen in the war. My overcoat I expect is lost. It never went to Ga- they would not take it in the cars...."

SOJOURNS OF A PATRIOT The Field and Prison Papers of An Unreconsrtu8cted Confederate edited with Commentary by Richard Bender Abell & Fay Adamson Gecik pub by Southern Heritage Press 1998 letters of Pvt. Augustus Pitt Adamson

Pg. 77 Camp Hardee 30th Regiment, Georgia Vols. July 4th, 1862 Dear Sister, "...I would be glad if Ma would send me a quilt or blanket before long, I want nothing heavy. I am not particularly needing it at present but will in a month or so....If she sends a quilt, let it be a thin one because I have enough things to carry now..."

KEEP ALL MY LETTERS The Civil War Letters of Richard Henry Brooks, 51st Ga. Inf. ed. by Katherine Holland pub by Mercer Univ. Press, Macon, Ga. 2003

Pg. 31 James Island near Charleston July the 8th, 1862 "...Wife you wanted to know if I wanted any more pants. I do not want any more hear yet I have as many as I want to toat now but you can make me a pair of yarn pants and keep them until I send to you for them. I was very glad to get the shirt you sent to me by George it suits me very well. I want you to send me 2 pair of yarn socks for the heel an to (toe) of both pair I have here is worn through an I will send them home when I can and Let you work on them...."

"DEAR MARTHA..." The Confederate War Letters of A South Carolina Soldier Alexander Faulkner Fewell compiled and edited by Robert Harley Mackintosh, Jr. pub byThe R.L. Bryan Co. 1976 17th South Carolina Inf. Company E

Pg. 79 Laurel hill Va. 5 Miles from Richmond 10th July 62 Dear brother "...Our Regt. Still in advance after a mile or more again encountered the rascals trying to defend their camp of which there was many. But here they succeeded in destroying a large amount of Stores-hundreds of wagons guns and every conceivable article but off from here we drove them like sheep. Just at their camps our Regt. Supplied with shoes (new) and here I got my sword and could have fitted myself out in as fine (a) suit of clothes as you ever saw but no time for swaping horses..."

REBEL PRIVATE FRONT AND REAR Memoirs of a Confederate Soldier by William A. Fletcher pub by Dutton Books 1995

Pg. 42 July 10, 1862 in camp near Richmond "Our nearness to the city gave us a good deal of peddlers daily, both from country and city, and as there was no "pure food" law in force we bought about everything that was offered, without question, if it suited our taste or fancy. Sausage was one of our favorite dishes, and as the vendors were on hand in considerable numbers early in the morning, we had sausage on the bill of fare when desired. So one morning, while our mess was eating, I found what I supposed a cat's claw and all stopped eating at once and an examination was hurriedly made of the uneaten portion, and a cat's tooth was discovered. A report of the find was soon circulated and it was said that there were other finds of a similar character. Sausage was sold by weight and the more bone, the heavier. This was practicing "all things are fair in war." Some of the boys tried to vomit, but the cat kept on its downward course, so there was a slump in the sausage market; and as far as that camp was concerned, no argument could reinstate sausage and it was soon not wanted, there fore, not an article offered."

If the "sausage" tasted good, I don't think I wouldv'e minded it being cat.

THE STONE WALL The Story of a Confederate Soldier by Brad Smiley pub by Zebra Communications, Woodstock, Ga. 1998

Pg. 149 July 10, 1862 camp near Richmond "...Mama, you must make me a pair of pants and send me as soon as you can, for mine is nearly worn out, and I have not got a cent of money, not even to pay postage..."

Apparentely, this soldier and the soldiers who wrote the requests in letters written in the months beforehand are having trouble getting uniforms from the government.

LETTERS FROM LEE'S ARMY Compiled by Susan Leigh Blackford Annotated by her Husband, Charles Minor Blackford, pub by Charles Scribner's & Sons 1947

Company B of the Second Virginia Cavalry- Charles Blackford was first lieutenant, later captain.

Pg. 86 July 13th, 1862 camp about three miles from Richmond."...Lee was elegantly dressed in full uniform, sword and sash, spotless boots, beautiful spurs and by far the most magnificent man I ever saw. The highest type of the Cavalier class to which by blood and rearing he belongs. Jackson, on the other hand, was a typical Roundhead. He was poorly dressed, that is, he looked so though his clothes were made of good material. His cap was very indifferent and pulled down over one eye, much stained by weather and without insignia. His coat was closely buttoned to his chin and had upon the collar the stars and wreath of a general. His shoulders were stooped and one shoulder was lower than the other, and his coat showed signs of much exposure to the weather."

WRITING & FIGHTING FROM THE ARMY OF NORTHERN VIRGINIA ed. by William B. Styple pub by Belle Grove Pub. 2003

Pg. 110 Letter From V.A.S.P. Camp near Richmond, Va. July 14, 1862 "…During the campaign (the Seven Days Battles) there was of course no chance to get changes of clothes. We were scarcely recognizable by our best friends by reason of the dust, tattered garments, and almost bootless feet. I venture the assertion many of us would have taken our image in a looking glass for some other person-perhaps an Arab-from the long, uncombed hair and shaggy beards.…My feet rebelled against the "powers that be" and burst their prison bonds,; my long worn fatigue suit showed signs of giving way; and the broiling sun threatened to crisp my little glazed cap into the size and shape of a tin dipper, leaving my brain to fry in the merciless heat of the sun…"

Apparently, these men, officers included, were quite ragged.

THE CRY IS WAR, WAR, WAR The Civil War Correspondence of Lts. Burwell Thomas Cotton and George Job Huntley, 34th Regiment North Carolina troops by Michael W. Taylor pub by Morningside Press 1994

Pg. 92 Camp near Richmond Va., July 16th, 1862 "…I am going to send my overcoat home by David Murro

Pg. 92 same camp, July 19th 1862 "…I han't got my clothes yet. I heard that Wm. Martin sent them to Richmond by the express company. I han't had the chance to send to Richmond to see about them yet, and I am afraid I won't get there at all, though they may be at Richmond now. I will know in a day or two. I will write to you as quick as I get them.…"

FAR, FAR FROM HOME-The Wartime Letters of Dick and Tally Simpson, 3rd South Carolina Volunteers by Guy R. Everson 7 Edward W. Simpson Jr. pub. by Oxford Univ. Press 1994

Pg. 138 July 18, 1862 TNS to ATS Camp Jackson, Va. Dear Sister "Our regt. has been uniformed (in) gray woolen cloth and roundabout coats.…"

Apparentely government supply.

WAR HISTORY OF THE OLD FIRST VIRGINIA REGIMENT, ARMY of NORTHERN VIRGINIA by Charles T. Loehr pub. by Wm. Ellis Jones Book & Job Printer 1884

Pg. 26 "...On the 20th, crossed the Rapidan at Raccoon Ford. On the 21st, (July 1862) we were halted and held in reserve in the woods on the left of the road, about one-half mile south of Kelly's Ford. At that point, quite a brisk engagement was fought, cavalry and artillery being principally engaged. The enemy's shelling created a panic among the negro cooks, who, as they came running past our brigade, received the usual salutations, "Going all the way to-night uncle? Anybody been troubling you? Hold on, you got plenty time; you are going the wrong way, you will get lost,"&. Most of them, however, had no time for talking, but one old fellow, less scared, or more tired, however, exclaimed: "I tell you marsters, dem dar shells keep on singing 'whar you nigger?' Whar you nigger?' I tell you, when I herd dat, I got, I did."

This might be the reaction of any body of men under shell-fire for the first time.

GRANDFATHER'S JOURNAL (Franklin Lafayette Riley) Company B Sixteenth Mississippi Infantry Volunteers Harris' Brigade Mahone's Division Hill's Cops, A.N.V. May 27, 1861-July 15, 1865 Austin C. Dobbins pub by Morningside Press 1988

Pg. 93 Monday-Wednesday, July 21-23, 1862 Camp near Richmond "We now have replacements for the equipment we lost at Centreville and when we were with Jackson. It feels strange to part company with friends. My shirt, which was originally Union issue, I don't mind discarding, but my jacket in of an age when it should be respected, not cast aside. And my trousers, although ragged, have served honorably through the windstorms of the valley and the snows of the hills, the mud of the swamps and the dust of the plains. They are ragged but they have been loyal companions. Yet they must be discarded...Clean-shaven and in new clothes I look fairly respectable..."

Governmentr supply? This soldier's sarcasm is quite eloquent.

THE CRY IS WAR, WAR, WAR The Civil War Correspondence of Lts. Burwell Thomas Cotton and George Job Huntley, 34th Regiment north Carolina troops by Michael W. Taylor Morningside 1994

Pg. 92 same camp, July 24th, 1862 "...I got my clothes yesterday evening. The honey had run out and stained my clothes a good deal but I don't think they are hurt. It will wash out. I am well pleased with my clothes except the britches. They are entirely too large...."

HANDLEY LIBRARY ARCHIVES, WINCHESTER, VA Wartime Diary of Joseph Franklin Kaufman Co. I 10th Virginia volunteer Infantry

Pg 25 July 25 1862 "Nothing of interest today. I had my shoes half soled today, cost 25 cents, washed my shirt. Drew molassas today."

JAMES MADISON UNIVERSITY ARCHIVES

28th July, 1862 Letters of 1st Lt. Rueben A. Scott 10th Regiment Virginia Infantry Camp Fresatti Va. Dear Mollie: "…Mollie last Saturday morning we were called up before day and hurriedly served up 2 day Rations and expected to have a fight and marched about five miles through the heat then stopped about 3 or 4 hour & got orders to come back to the same camp during the time 2 very hard rains fell upon us we kept dry with our Yankee oil cloths, those captured oil and Gum cloths are the greatest invention of the day to keep us dry when it rains, and lay them on the wet ground to sleep on they keep the dampness from us. No soldier ought to be with out one-& if the war continues a year longer and old Abe give each one of those three hundred mens he has called for one a piece and we get in many Battles with them and have the luck we formerly have all our army will have one a piece nearly all Gen. Jacksons Army has one now…"

I think he means 300,000 men called up for Union service.

WASH.& LEE UNIV. Archives, Lexington, Va. Letters of Bethel J. Davidson Camp near Guienie's Station

Camp near Gordonsville July 31st, 1862 Dear Mother "…I received the socks which you sent by Ron Rordan while we were near Richmond, and am much obliged to you for them.

Tell Pa to have my shoes made as soon as possible, for not being able to get any mending done, I will soon be barefooted

WEBSITE-CONFEDERATE NON-UNIFORMITY

August, 1862 the sacking of Manassas Junction by Jackson's men"…Nor was the outer man neglected. From piles of new clothing the Southerners arrayed themselves in the blue uniforms of the Federals." Note that this was August 1862, barely 18 months after the war's beginning. Already the Southerners, badly in need of clothing, were happy to get U.S. uniform parts."

After the Capture of Harper's Ferry, Sept. 1862 "…As James Robertson writes, "Hundreds of Hill's men eagerly donned pieces of new blue uniforms… During their short stay in Harper's Ferry, they made good use of their time. Blue uniforms whole or in any combination thereof, became the order of the day."

The Fighting for Chatanooga, Time-Life "Longstreet's troops were traveling light. Hood commented that the men were destitute of almost everything except pride, spirit, and 40 rounds each. They did have something rare in the Confederacy: new uniforms. Curiously the new clothes were blue, and except for the tight cut, resembled the standard Union uniform."

When the War passed This way, by Conrad and Ted Alexander "here's the way one Rebel cavalry unit appeared to local residents as they entered Pensylvania during the Gettysburg Campaign. "These lean, lank, dark-tanned men, clothed in a host of different uniforms, were the antithesis of everything known about corrct military attire. A few wore the standard Confederate grey, but most were dressed in coarse-textured homespun, tattered and torn, but so grimy that one had to guess the original color. The men's pants of all shades-black, brown, grey and blue- were generally tucked into high cavalry boots or roughly cobbled brown shoes."

DEAR AMANDA-The Civil War Letters of Marion Hill Fitzpatrick ed. by Jeffery C. Lowe and Sam Hodges pub by Mercer Univ. Press 1998

Pg. 21 Aug. 1st, 1862 Near Richmond, Va. (Letter no. 11) Dear Amanda "I wrote Alex about getting my shirts. I am so proud of them I can hardly see straight. Everybody admires them and wants them. I am well fixed in the clothing line now, two shirts and two pr. drawers is as much as I want at a time. I am having my undershirt washed today for the first time in five weeks, only dabbed out in cold water and no soap once. I have on both the shirts you sent me now. I will put on my undershirt as soon as it gets dry. Fortunately I carried two pr. of socks with me on the tramp, but they need darning. I doubt whether you would know me or not hardly if you were to see me now. My old hat has about ten holes in it which I have sowed up with wire thred. I also let down the top and sowed it in with white thread, and have not shaved since I left Macon. But all this I bear cheerfully, if I can be of any service to my country. I want no blanket or overcoat till cold weather for I would be almost certain to lose them if I had them…"

Pg. 23 August 10th, 1862 A.P.Hill's division Hospital Near Richmond, Va. Dear Amanda, "I wrote to Alex to send me a hat, but I have bought one from the executer of one of our Comp. that died recently. So he need not send it. It is a very good hat. I bought it at auction and paid $3.50. I also bought a pair of socks so ypou need send me only one pr…"

CONFEDERATE CAPTAIN UJANIRTIS ALLEN'S LETTERS TO HIS WIFE ed. by Kandall Allen and Keith S. Bohannon pub by La. State Univ. Press 1998

Pg 136 same camp August 4th 1862 "…The people will not believe how the "bloody 21st" fought. By the way, did I tell you how we came by that name? It was given by Major Wheat's Battlion. When we first came into service everybody was afraid of these fellows. While we were in winter quarters our boys found out that one tiger could not whip more than one common man and turned in to whipping them whenever they became troublesome. They actually made them afraid to pass by our regiment. And they gave us that name…I only have one pair of socks. All the others are gone the way of everything in this regiment, lost and stoled. Did I tell you about loosing some clothes I bought in Richmond. I found two fellows wearing my shirts and requested them to wash and bring them up as they were taken through mistake…"

HANDLEY LIBRARY ARCHIVES

James A. Miller Collection correspondence C.W. era misc. New Market, Va.

Camp near Liberty Mills August 4th, 1862 Dear Julia, You said you wrote several times about what you must do with my coat. I wrote to you when I was in Charlottesville if you had an opportunity to send it to me, but as I am now in the field I would of prefered if you had kept it as I have a very poor opportunity to take any extra baggage with me. You said that you intended to send to Mr. Baisely for goods for me a coat and pants. I wish if you have a chance you would also send to him for enough for an overcoat…"

WEEP NOT FOR ME, DEAR MOTHER (Letters of Eli Pinson Landers from Gwinnett Co. Ga. The Flint Hill Grays. Eli was 19 years old when he enlisted in Aug. 1861) ed. by Elizabeth Whitley Roberson pub by Pelican Pub. Co. 1996

Pg. 158 Camp near Richmond Va. Aug. 4th, 1862 Dear Mother "…Liz,(sister) Pink wants you to send him a good pair of No.9 shoes by the first one that passes. Ma I want you to send me a pair of No.9s too if you please for I am nearly barefooted and shoes is so hi here…."

LEE& JACKSON'S BLOODY TWELTH-Letters of Irby Goodwin Scott First Lieutenant Co. G Putnam Light Infantry Twelth Ga. Vol. Inf. Ed. by Johnnie Perry Pearson pub by Univ. Tn. Press 2010

Pg. 93 Camp 7 miles from Gordonsville Va. August 5th, 1862 Dear Father, "…If you see Jake Filer before he leaves home say to him that J.D. Johnson & Abner Zachry wishes him to bring them a hat. They say if any one can find them Jake can. Some of the boys are getting bad off for hats. I think a great deal of my hat that you sent me. The sizes of Johnsons & Zachrys hats are 7 ¼ & 7…Abner says to tell Mrs. Boswell to send him two cotton shirts and two pair of drawers some cotton socks, a coat, a handkerchief, &c. You may send me a pair of pants. If you cannot get my things by Jake you can send them by Leut. Marshall…"

Pg. 95 Aug. 13th, 1862 (same camp) Dear Father,"…Send me the cloths (clothes) I wrote for by the first opportunity…"

"DEAR MOTHER: DON'T GRIEVE ABOUT ME. IF I GET KILLED, I'LL ONLY BE DEAD." ed. by Mills Lane pub by The Beehive Press 1977

Pg. 179 Henry Graves to his Aunt Petersburg Virginia August 7, 1862 Dear Aunt Hattie: "…(PS) My pants are wearing out and wish you would please make me a new pair and send me, if possible from the same material or at least send me a patch or two, or I will have to patch dark pants with a light piece…"

LEE'S TIGERS-The La. Inf. In the Army of Northern Va. by Terry L. Jones pub by Univ. of La. Press

PG. 113 August 9, 1862 Cedar Run, near Slaughter Mountain

"…The Tigers seemed more intent on securing the field for booty than winning the battle. Father Gache of the 10th Louisiana saw numerous members of Starke's brigade robbing Yankee dead and wounded. He wrote a friend, "These wretched men (and their number was greater than you might suppose) were not concerned with bringing help to the wounded, but in emptying their pockets and stealing their clothes.…There were some who went so far as to strip a dead man of every last piece of clothing to leave his body lying naked in the dust. I came upon two of these ghouls kneeling on either side of a corpse they had just despoiled fighting about who should keep the poor man's canteen…"

Pg. 118 Looting the Federal Depot at Manassas "…Here you would see a crowd enters a car with the their old Confederate grays and in a few moments come out dressed in yankee uniforms; some as cavalry; some as infantry; some as artillerists; others dressed in the splendid uniforms of Federal officers…"

This illustrates the desperation of thr men for clothing.

LETTERS OF WILLIAM WAGNER, CONFEDERATE SOL-DIER ed. by Joe M. Hatley and Linda B. Huffman pub, by Broadfoot's Bookmark 1983

Pg. 10 Salisbury N.C. August 10 1862 …"and then cloath must be send for as soone as poseable for I poot my in I had on to day and one shirt and 2 chackits and some more things that I couldn't take with me we will get our uniformes when we git to Raley."

LETTERS FROM LEE'S ARMY by Susan Leigh Blackford and Charles Minor Balckford pub by Scribner's Pub 1947

Pg. 100 Aug. 11, 1862 Battlefield of Major's Gate (Slaughter's Mountain) "…I saw what I had seen before; men pinning strips of paper with their names, company, and regiments to their coats so they could be identified if killed…"

There are several accounts of soldiers doing this in both armies.

CONFEDERATE CAPTAIN UJANIRTIS ALLEN'S LETTERS TO HIS WIFE ed. by Kandall Allen and Keith S. Bohannon pub by La. State Univ. Press 1998

Pg. 142 CampNear Sumerset, Va. August 13th 1862 Dear Susie "… You advise me to put on leather strap when I go into battle. I have no doubt but that strap prevented a very serious wound. But our idea is to get rid of straps and blankets on account of excessive heat….I have a Yankee sword, canteen and haversack. I swaped canteens with a prisoner. Their things are of much better quality than ours and our soldiers are quite eager to get them. The truth is all of them have them…."

I'm not sure what Capt. Ujanirtis means by a leather strap.

Pg. 145 same camp August 15th, 1862 Dear Susie "…I think that cotton comforts or quilts would answer as good purpose considering circumstances as blankets for the negroes. The question is will your cow hair blankets pay for your trouble. I may be compelled to call on you for one myself. I intend to gather up as many as I can before winter comes…."

HAM CHAMBERLAYNE-VIRGINIAN Letters and Papers of an Artillery Officer in the War for Independence 1861-1865 with introduction, notes and index by his son C.G.Chamberlayne Richmond, Va. pub by Press of the Dietz Printing Co. Publishers 1932

Pg. 92 J.H. Chamberlayne to M.B. Chamberlayne Camp at Todsburg, (6miles N.E. from Gordonsville, 3 miles from Orange C.H. August 14th, 1862 My dear Mother "…Please don't attempt to send by John (slave) more than a pair of cotton socks, a couple of handkerchiefs & a silk undershirt for me…."

HANDLEY LIBRARY ARCHIVES

James A. Miller Collection correspondence C.W. era misc. New Market, Va.

Camp near Liberty Mills August 14th, 1862 Dear Julia, I wish you to get the goods for my coat, pants and overcoat. I must have them and if you can't do any better I think I think it would pay better to send to Bederick for the goods, if you can I wish you would as soon as possible as it will soon be getting cool and then I will need them…"

"DEAR MOTHER: DON'T GRIEVE ABOUT ME. IF I GET KILLED, I'LL ONLY BE DEAD." ed. by Mills Lane pub by The Beehive Press 1977

Pg. 180 Jack Felder to his Sister Richmond, Virginia August 14, 1862 Dear Sister: "…You will please tell Ma to send me a shirt and two pairs of socks by Dick.…PS You can say to Pa I lost my bootes. I loaned them to ( ) as my feet were blistered so badly I could not wear anything, and while he had them in his possession he was killed and some scounderel stole them off his feet. I have a tolerable good pair now, but they won't last long…."

LETTERS FROM LEE'S ARMY Compiled by Susan Leigh Blackford Annotated by Her Husband, Charles Minor Blackford, pub by Charles Scribner's & Sons 1947
Company B of the Second Virginia Cavalry- Charles Blackford was first lieutenant, later captain.

Pg. 109 August 17th 1862 "At Michell's Station we captured a small picket under a very intelligent sergeant. After getting all the information in my reach I came back with our prisoners. The sergeant was communicative and I took him to the General's tent, thinking he might give some valuable information. When we got there the staff was standing around the tent, holding their horse and the General's sorrel was just in front, ready for himto mount. My prisoner took his stand at the sorrel's rump to await with the rest of us the General's advent. He at once commenced, I supposed in nervous agitation, to stroke the sorrel's rump with his right hand and to pass his left hand through the tail, pulling out each time a number of hairs. This he did so often that his hand was quite full of them and one of the staff, with some asperity, just as the General came up to the horse's head, ordered him to stop, which he did and at once commenced cramming the hair into his pocket. General Jackson saw what he was doing and, to my infinite relief, said in a mild voice, "My friend, why are you tearing the hair out of my horse's tail?" The prisoner took off his hat most respectfully and with a bright smile said, "Ah, General, each one of these hairs is worth a dollar in New York." Was there ever a more delicate compliment to a man's reputation? The General was both amused and pleased at the tribute, by an enemy, to his fame. He was confused by our presence and actually blushed. He merely directed me to send the prisoner to the rear and did not question him any further. I did so, but he carried his trophies with him."

That is a great, but justified, tribute to the General.

CONFEDERATE CAPTAIN UJANIRTIS ALLEN'S LETTERS TO HIS WIFE ed. by Kandall Allen and Keith S. Bohannon pub by La. State Univ. Press 1998

Pg. 151 Lynchburg, Va. Aug. 18th, 1862 "…My dear, it is no use talking. I must rely on you for such clothing as I may need. I can not buy a good shirt here for less than ten dollars, socks one dollar. I do not want anything of the kind just now. I regret that Boykin did not carry my old suit home. I can buy a tolerable pair of shoes here for twelve dollars. I can get such things (shoes) from the quartermaster if I can do no better...."

A CONFEDERATE SURGEON'S LETTERS TO HIS WIFE Spencer Glascow Welch, Surgeon Thirteenth South Carolina Volunteers, McGowans Brigade pub by Neale Pub. Co. 1911

Pg. 20 Orange Co. Va. August 18, 1862 "A wounded soldier who has been in Jackson's army for a long time told me his men had but one suit of clothes each, and whenever a suit became very dirty the man would pull it off and wash it and then wait until it dried. I believe this to be a fact, because when I see Jackson's old troop on the march none have any load to carry except a blanket, and many do not even have a blanket; but they always appear to be in fine spirits and as healthy and clean as any of our men."

A CONFEDERATE SURGEON'S LETTERS TO HIS WIFE ed by Spencer, Welch & Glascow pub by The Neale Pub Co., 1911

Sept. 24 1862 Charlestown, Jefferson County, W.Va. "I have not written to you in three or four weeks, because there has been no mail between us and Richmond. I have seen sights since then, I assure you. If I should tell you what our army has endured recently you could hardly believe it. Thousands of the men now have almost no clothes and no sign of a blanket nor any prospect of getting one. Thousands have had no shoes at all, and their feet are now entirely bare. Most of our marches were on graveled turnpike roads, which were very severe on the barefooted men and cut up their feet horribly. When the poor fellows could get rags they would tie them around their feet for protection. I have seen men rob the dead of their shoes and clothing, but I cannot blame a man for doing a thing which is almost necessary in order to preserve his own life..."

THE STILLWELL LETTERS-A GEORGIAN IN LONG-STREET'S CORPS ARMY OF NORTHERN VIRGINIA ed. Ronald H. Morely pub by Mercer Univ. Press 2002

Pg. 28 Richmond Virginia, Aug. 18, 1862 Dear Molly "...Get lining for my coat, get strong coarse grade, put plenty of pockets in it. Tell Pa to try and get me an overcoat of coarse goods before winter if he can. I was cold last night standing guard but that is nothing for we will have some very hot weather here yet. I will want one more shirt this winter but will let you know when. ..."

This was something I was bewildered by when I became a re-enactor. None of the clothes had adequate, or any pockets. I agree with this soldier - the more pockets the better.

VMI Archives MS# 222

James Henry Reid VMI Aug. 18th, 1862 Dear Pa "…I was on guard about 2 O'Clock last night & had nothing but my white cloths on. I very near froze. I would write for my thick winter coat but Gen. Smith read a letter yesterday from Charleston saying the cloth has run the blockade & arrived safely. It will be here in a few days so I will try to stand it as my order for jacket pants & overcoat is 3rd on the list & Mr. Vanderslice will soon make it. Gen. Smith says he has $30,000 worth of cloth, about 15,000 yards or more because it did not cost more than $2 per yard in Europe. Don't forget my buttons send them by Read also $10 for matting chair &c. Send my other blanket as soon as you can but do not pay a big price for one I would Rather wait awhile…"

P.S. It takes 6 yards single width of cloth to make me a uniform please also send 4yards double width of Flannagans cloth to make me an overcoat. I want Brown's cloth for my uniform & Flannagans for my overcoat. 6 yards single & 4 yards double width be sure to put it up so it will not look like cloth as anything of that kind is stolen directly…"

This illustrates the difficulty faced by cadets at V.M.I. in getting clothing.

"DEAR MOTHER: DON'T GRIEVE ABOUT ME. IF I GET KILLED, I'LL ONLY BE DEAD." ed. by Mills Lane pub by The Beehive Press 1977

Pg. 182 Shepard Pryor to his Wife Rapidan River, Virginia August 18, 1862 My Dear Penelope: "…Dear, I wrote you some time ago that I wanted you to send me a pair (of) shoes. You will please getr Harris ti make me a nice heavy pair of shoes and send them by the first safe opportunity you have. I will need them before I can get them. Number eight. And send me by Uncle Spencer's a hat, 71/8. My hat will be worn out by the time he comes, if I should live…"

A CAPTAIN'S WAR LETTERS & DIARIES OF WILLIAM H.S. BURGWYN 1861-1865 ed. by Herbert M. Schiller White pub by Mane Pub Co. Inc. 1994

Pg. 12 Thirty-Fifth Regiment N.C. Troops Camp Near Richmond August 22nd 1862

"…I think it would be better if you sent me some three or four dollars by Harry for I would not be able to get any about Gordonsville. Don't forget the drawers. Better send cotton flannel to him. Please also send me another blue flannel shirt like the one I have. We are not allowed to take much baggage and those things are the best to take that will not show dirt and will keep you warm at night. I don't think I can afford to let Harry have his blankets again. The weather has been unusually cold and I will need them all in winter can't he bring me some?..."

THE SOUTH REPORTS THE CIVIL WAR by J. Cutler Andrews pub by Univ. of Pittsburgh Press 1985.

Pg. 199 August 25, 1862-reporter for the Charleston Courier reporting on the Army of N. Va. marching towards the Battle of Second Bull Run: "I look around me and see men barefooted and ragged, bearing their muskets and a single blanket each, yet all inspired by the hope of another battle. I have seen some too, who were hungry-stragglers who would come up to the camp fire, tell a pitiful story of sickness or fatigues, and then ask for a bit of bread and meat. ...Speaking of the bare feet, I suppose that at least forty thousand pairs of shoes are required to-day to supply the wants of the army. Every battle contributes to human comfort in this respect, but it is not every man who is fortunate enough to "foot" himself upon the field. It has become a trite remark among the troops, that "all a Yankee is now worth is his shoes;" and it is said, but I do not know how truly, that some of our regiments have become so expert in securing these coveted articles, that they can make a change and strip every dead Yankee's feet they pass without coming to a halt."

Another account of Ragged Rebels, also showing the critical shoe shortage at this time.

FRENCH HARDING- Civil War Memoirs ed. by Victor L. Thacker pub by McClain Printing Co. Inc., Parsons W.Va. 2001

Pg. 65 Aug. 25th 1862 marching in Campaign of 2nd Manassas "...many of our men made this march entirely barefooted, and many others practically so..."

CONFEDERATE CAPTAIN UJANIRTIS ALLEN'S LETTERS TO HIS WIFE ed. by Kandall Allen and Keith S. Bohannon pub by La. State Univ. Press 1998

Pg. 155 Lynchburg Va. Aug. 26th 1862 "...Lynchburg is the same. On the street are the same raged soldiers (I saw one just now with the seat of his pants patched with a piece of black oilcloth eightenn inches in diameter)...By the by, are the people thinking of doing anything for the company this winter. I hope the boys will take care and send all the money home they can. They cant get clothing for it here; I think the government intends to clothe the soldiers hereafter. I hope it will. When I speak of the people assisting the company I do not mean gratuitously by any means. But the soldiers friend can procure clothing for them at much less cost than he can..."

This quote shows lack of reliance in government supply, earnestly requesting the home folks to outfit the men for winter.

LETTTERS OF WILLIAM F. WAGNER, CONFEDERATE SOLDIER ed. by Joe M. Hatley and Linda B. Huffman pub, by Broadfoot's Bookmark 1983

Pg. 11 County Va Camp Cambell Proctors Creek Chesterfield August 26 1862 ..."Dear Wife I would be verry glad for some person to come from Catawba so I could send home some of my cloath I have too many things to carry if we should go a long march we drawed some cloathing we drawed wamises (an outer jacket made of rough, long wearing fabric, Webster's New World Dictionary of the English Language College Edition pg. 1644) and pants and draws and shirts and caps each of us a soot (suit or uniform) all but shoes and sock and I would be very glad if some person would come so I could send some of my things..."

Government supply.

Pg. 13 August 31th, 1862 Newton Catawba City NC "...Dear Husband you said you would be glad if the would some Boddy come out their from Catawba to send some of your clothing home Dear Husband I would bee wery glad if the would some Boddy goo out..."

ROCKBRIDGE ARTILLERYThe Story of a Cannoneer Under Stonewall Jackson by Edward Moore pub by Neale Pub. Co. 1907

Pg. 79 August 26, 1862, just after sacking the Yankee's depot at Manassas Junction "...Here we spent the remainder of the day, but not being allowed to plunder the cars did not have the satisfaction of replacing our worn-out garments with the new ones in sight. We were very willing to don the blue uniforms, but General Jackson thought otherwise..."

Pg. 111 "Moving through a body of woods, toward the firing line we soon began meeting and passing the stream of wounded men making their wy to the rear. And here our attention was again called to a singular and unaccountable fact, which was noticed and remarked repeatedly throughout the war. It was that in one battle the large majority of the less serious wounds received were in the same portion of the body. In this case, fully three-fourths of the men we met were wounded in the left hand; in another battle the same proportion were wounded in the right hand; while in another the head was the attractive mark for flying bullets, and so on. I venture the assertion that every old soldier whose attention is called to it will verify the statement..."

I'd never heard of this before, but, since he's the veteran, I believe him.

WAR TALKS OF CONFEDERATE VETERANS by Mr. George S. Bernard Fenn& Owen 1892 The Campaign in Maryland

Pg. 14 Aug. 28, 1862 (the night march before the battle of 2nd Manassas) "…An incident occurred on this night march that I have often recalled: My shoes had begun to give out, and I had to fasten the soles to the upper leathers by making holes through each and tying them together with leather shoe strings passed through these holes, a device which did not serve to prevent gravel and sand from freely entering the shoes to my great discomfort, impeding my marching and compelling me at times to fall behind the line…"

A LETTER FROM CHARLES EDWARD JORDAN TO HIS FAMILY AND FRIENDS Library of the Univ. of Va. 1952

Pg. 20 August 28, 1862 heading toward Maryland "…The writer, with other children and ladies, stood by the roadside filling canteens with water until the supply from the well and cisterns was entirely exhausted. We almost worshipped these hungry, ragged soldiers, so glad were we to see our boys again and to feel that we were again under their protection…"

A very moving quote. Why don't the artists of Civil War prints us this scene?

VMI

Aug. 28 1862 Dear Pa & Ma "…I received my box this morning and enjoyed the contents very much but was disappointed at not finding the small Va. Buttons as I had plenty of large V.M.I. buttons and did not want any large Va. The shirt collars cakes and apples all received safe & sound…"

"P.S. Please send my cloth as soon as possible 61/2 yards Brown's & 4 yards Flannagan's as I wrote you in my last for my uniform and overcoat. 61/2 single width for uniform 4 double width overcoat & small Va. Staff buttons…"

THE PERSONAL MEMOIRS OF JOHNATHAN THOMAS SCHARF OF THE FIRST MARYLAND ARTILLERY ed by Tom Kelly pub by Butternut & Blue 1992

Pg. 47 Aug 30 1862 Battle of Second Manassas "…On the next day we continued the march to Sudley Ford and from thence to the Leesburg Turnpike, three miles from Germantown. Here General A.P. Hill and Jackson completed the work of battle, which I may say began at a distance of 60 miles from this place and last for twenty days. Here we remained until the next evening, the object being to cut off the enemy's trains and harass his rear, but their good speed enable them to save the greatest portion. Yet the line was strewed with abandoned guns, caissons, wagons, ambulances, commissary and quartermaster stores and ordinance of every kind and small arms of every pattern, knapsacks, cartridge boxes, canteens, haversacks, blankets, overcoats blankets tin cups and frying pans at almost every step and along in their splendid race from Groveton to the Stone Bridge and for miles beyond..."

What a chance for the collector! Where's my time machine?

THE PERSONAL MEMOIRS OF JOHNATHAN THOMAS SCHARF of the First Maryland Artillery ed by Tom Kell pub by Butternut & Blue 1992

Pg. 58 Dec 15, 1862, 1862 after Battle of Fredericksburg "...One poor Yankee had crawled into a ditch to get some water and he fell into it with his head down into the mud. He could not get up and he died in that position. He had been scratching the bank all around him and you could see the points of his fingers in the mud four inches deep and the ends of his fingers were worn off. It made me sick to see him. I passed along a little farther and saw 47 dead Yankees, nicely dressed, lying in a row. One of them had a fine pair of low quarter sewed shoes, and I relieved him of them and put them on. I moved along a little farther and saw where the Yankees had been drawn up into lines of battle. Here I looked around and found a new knapsack and clothes and buttons and I bundled up a large lot...

I was dressed in Yankee clothes-blue jacket and pants. I got at Harper's Ferry a red Zouave cap with long tassel, and the Yankee shoes I just got, so I was a complete Yankee in looks, and I was almost as feared of our men as the Yanks..."

HANDLEY LIBRARY ARCHIVES, WINCHESTER, VA James Bradfield Diary Co. H 17th Virginia Infantry

Pg. 9 Aug. 29th, 1862 Campaign of Second Manassas "...then into Haymarket, go by and see Mr. Gordon and he treated me very kindly and also gave me a pair of shoes ..."

WAR TALKS OF CONFEDERATE VETERANS by Mr. George S. Bernard Fenn& Owen 1892 The Campaign in Maryland

Pg 20 Aug. 29, 1862 (day after the battle of 2nd Manassas) "...The next morning it was my purpose to provide myself with a pair of shoes from some dead federal soldier, but upon inquiring I soon discovered that I ought to have set about this at a much earlier hour, as there had been during the night and early morning a very general removing of shoes, not only from the federal dead, but also from many of the dead Confederates. So I abandoned all hope of getting a pair until, on my way with a party of my regiment to the wagons to the place of rendouvous, we came to a dead Confedertae lying near the roadway, on whose feet were a pair of good shoes. Noticing this, one of our party, pointing to the dead man, said to me, "There is a pair of shoes that will fit you.' I went to this poor fellows feet, untied one of his shoes and began to pull it off. This was, of course, not easy work, and whilst engaged at it I suddenly fully relized what I was doing-taking a dead man's shoes, and these the shoes of a dead Confederate! I at once stopped and swore I would go bare-footed before I would do an act which was so repugnant to my feelings. My comrades rather ridiculed my squeamishness, but I felt better at having let the dead Confederate retain his shoes. My feet might suffer, but my conscience would not...

Soon after the reassembling of our command and its taking its position on the battlefield in bivouac, I was quietly resting near the line of stacked guns when Nat Osburn of the 12th, a personal friend, having heard of my being it want of a pair shoes, came with apair of neat looking boots and kindly tendered me their use. How Nat came by them I do not know, nor have I ever enquired. Gentleman then, as gentleman he has always been, I am satisfied that he did not himself take them from the body of a dead man. He would have shrunk, as I did, from any such act. Nevertheless, I have no doubt but that those boots were taken from the rigid feet of some poor fellow, Federal or Confederate, who had yielded his life upon that field.

I accepted the tender of the boots, thanking Nat for his kindness, and asked him what I should do with them when I should get another pair of shoes. "You can return them to me." was his reply.

In a little while I had cast away my old shoes and donned the boots, and many were the congrdulations I received in my good fortune in securing them. The next morning the order to march came. I stepped off bravely with my new boots, and for the first half mile felt no inconvienence from them. But we soon came to some hill-sides, and then I began to find that the boots were as unyielding as if made of cast-iron, and soon became convinced that to wear them would be more painful than to march bare-footed. I accordingly doffed the boots, and struck out with my naked feet. I would have thrown the boots away, but they were not mine-I had promised their owner to return them when I ceased to use them. Besides this, I was not without hope that I might yet break them. So, tying them together with a string, I swung them from the end of my blanket-roll, and, occasionally changing their position, attached them to the end of my rifle, and thus made my way mile after mile over the turnpikes almost all the way from Manassas to the Monocacy junction near Frederick, Maryland. At night, however, the weather being cool, I had to wear the boots to keep my feet warm, and when we forded the Potomac at Edward's Ford I wore them as a protection against the sharp-edged pieces of stone I feared my bare feet might encounter at the bottom of the river. Walking over such obstructions on the turnpikes was bad enough-doing the same thing with the obstructions under water might be worse..."

THE CONFEDERATE VETERAN VOL. XXX 1922

Pg. 61 "Second Manassas, Fifty-Eight Years Afterwards by John N. Ware "Maybe You Have Never Heard of the Railroad Cut" August 29, 1862 "For nine hours this murder had gone on and here in the little woods, on one side of the cut, lie four thousand men in blue, and on the other two thousand in all sorts of uniforms, from sunbleached gray rags to those fine Federal uniforms acquired the day before by the simple process of laying on of hands. A grim irony that they serve at once as shrouds."

FROM CORSICANA TO APPOMATTOX by John Spencer pub by The Texas Press 1984

Pg. 40 August 30, 1862, 2nd day at 2nd Manassas Fourth Texas "...The remainder of the Union army is finally driven from the battlefield, and would later retire into the defenses of Washington. In the meantime, the men from Texas, who already have the nickname "ragged Texans" because of the tattered condition of their clothing, begin relieving the dead Federal soldiers clothing, shoes, and socks..."

RECOLLECTIONS AND LETTERS OF GENERAL ROBERT E. LEE by His Son Capt. Robert E. Lee pub by Garden City Pub Co. 1926

Pg. Aug. 30, 1862 after battle of Second Manassas -Letter from Robert (son) "...My appearance was even less prepossessing than when I had met my father at Cold Harbor, for I had been marching night and day for four days, with no opportunity wash myself or my clothes; my face and hands were blackened with powder-sweat, and the few garments I had on were ragged and stained with the red soil of that section..."

RED CLAY TO RICHMOND by John J. Fox pub by Angle Valley Press 2006

Pg. 109 Aug 30 1862 on the battlefield at Second Manassas "...First Sergeant Draughton S. Haynes of the 49th Georgia recorded his impressions of the Manassas Battlefield. He passed through on foot three days after the battle as he searched for Thomas' Brigade. Haynes had missed the fight as he recovered from illness in Richmond. "I passed through the battlefield of Manassas and found dead and wounded Yankees by the hundred, it was the most horrible sight I beheld. There was not a Yankee left with a pair of shoes on and a few had every rag of clothes taken off. Many of our men are barefooted therefore I could not condemn them for taking shoes off the dead. Many of the Yakees bodies had turned perfectly black, and to pass them would almost make a person vomit..."

In other words, better get them Yankee shoes/clothes soon, or they'll be no good.

HAM CHAMBERLAYNE-VIRGINIAN Letters and Papers of an Artillery Officer in the War for Independence 1861-1865 with introduction, notes and index by his son C.G.Chamberlayne Richmond, Va. pub by Press of the Dietz Printing Co. Publishers 1932

Pg. 101 Dear Mother, referring to Battle of 2nd Manassas August 30,1862 "…Starkes La. Brigade, & the 2nd Brigade of Jackson's 1st Div., the ammunition partly giving out, fought with the stones from the ground; this I know to be a fact. Lewis Randolph, it is said, was seen to kill one man with a stone…"

I have heard both re-enactors and arm-chair professors tell me that the stone-throwwing incident at Secound Manassas was a legend. Well, gentlemen, here's a fisrt-hand acoount of it.

RAW PORK AND HARDTACK Civil War Memoir From Manassas to Appomattox ed. by Walord D. Swank, Colonel, UASF, Ret. Civil War heritage Series, vol X pub by Burd Street Press 1996

Three brothers, Robert Catlett Cave, Rueben Lindsey Cave, Lindsey Wallace Cave
Pg. 35 At 2nd Manassas Aug 30, 1862 "…A very large man, Jim Ferris of the 5th Texas found himself in a dilapidated state of dress as Second manassas ended. His pants were too short and his ankles were lacerated and bleeding. Deciding that the estate of a dead Yankee might provide him a pair of leggings, he foraged over the field of the dead, searching for a corpse of appropriate size and wondering if there really were ghosts. Finding a body of suitable size, he began to remove the leggings. Suddenly the "corpse" sat up and exclaimed, "Great God alive man! Don't rob me before I'm dead, if you please!" The horrified Ferris sprang about 20 feet at one bound before recovering himself and apologizing. He gave the wounded man his canteen before leaving. Rather than risk waking another "corpse" he decided to do without leggings and just return to camp. On the way he came across another large man lying full length on the ground and wearing leggings. Ferris put his hand on the man's shoulder, gave it a shake, and asked, "Say, mister, are you dead or alive?" Receiving no response Ferris was soon the proud posseeor of a magnificent pair of linen leggings…"

RICHMOND VOLUNTEERS 1861-1865 by Louis H. Mandarin & Lee A. Wallace pub. by Richmond Civil War Centennial Committee Westover Press 1969

Pg. 133 August 30, 1862 Henrico Mounted Guard Company A "…At the end of August 1862 the company was reported as being well clothed, accoutered with cartridge boxes and cap pouches, and armed with 104 sabres and 20 shotguns…"

TOO AFRAID TO CRY-MARYLAND Civilians in the Antietam Campaign Katyleen A. Ernst pub by Stackpole Books 1999

August 30 1862 Pg. 38 "…The men shivering on the bank (of the Potomac River) were not an impressive lot. Most had long since shucked their knapsacks, marching hard with light blanket rolls and grimy haversacks and, here and there, a bedraggled toothbrush stuffd into a buttonhole. "We are a miserable looking sight," Franklin Riley of the 16th Mississippi admitted in his diary. "We are dirty, unshaven, tired; our clothes are smelly: toes gap from our shoes…We have not made a very favorable inpression on Maryland. Observing his comrades, Edgar Warfield of the 17th Virginia wondered if every Maryland cornfield had been robbed of its scarecrows. The few civilians who ventured to the river to watch the crossing agreed-and yet knowing that the army that had so often bullied the robust Yankees was composed of such gaunt scarecrows demanded at least grudging respect. "They were the dirtiest, lousiest filthiest, piratical-looking cut-throat men I ever saw," wrote one young man who watched them. "A most ragged, leanand hungry set of wolves. Yet there was a dash about them that the Northern men lacked…"

THE CONFEDERATE VETERAN VOL. VII

Jan. 1899 Pg. 15 August, 30 1862 Battle of Second Manassas "Richard H. Evans, of Cleveland, Ohio reports "…At that battle Gen. Stonewall Jackson ran out of shot and shell, and fired bars of railroad iron at us; and I want to say to you that when those ugly things came flying through the air with a rotary velocity and a double whiz of a whirlwind the feeling was very uncomfortable in that immediate vincinity. Wonderful fighters those Southerners. We captured thousands of them that early in the conflict with their shoes worn off, the blood from their feet bespattered on the rough road, and with only parched corn in their haversacks. It was an honor to fight such dauntless men…"

I'd never before heard of Jackson's artillerists using railroad iron at Second Manassas, What an effect that would've had!

THE CONFEDERATE VETERAN VOL. VII 1899

Pg. 354 August 31 1899 Full of Years and Honors by Mrs. T.A Robertson regarding Col. Cadwallader Jones of the Twelth South Carolina Infantry on the march, August 1862, to Antietam-"...Beneath that historic old gray coat there was as big a heart as ever led an army to victory (he was referring to Stonewall Jackson). On the same march our army I'd love a better description/picuthe asked me it there was anything of value in the depot. I said there was not, and remarked that I had been looking through the building for shoes for my men who were nearly barefooted. "How many?" he said. I answered that there were about a dozen or more. "I have just captured a box of shoes," he said, "and will send you some to-night." About ten-o'clock they arrived, and were speedily distributed. I slipped my feet into a pair of them with extreme satisfaction, and the men all hurrahed for Jackson..."

Once again, is there any doubt that we love this man?

BEST LITTLE IRONIES, ODDITIES & MYSTERIES OF THE CIVIL WAR by C.Brian Kelly pub by Cumberland House 2000

Pg.205 "...it happened on the heels of his victory at Second Manassas (Bull Run)—on a rainy day, August 31, 1862. Dressed in his "rubber suit" of overalls and a poncho," an incident occurred where Gen. Lee sprained both wrists, and broke a bone in one of them..."

I would love to have a better description or picture of this rain suit.

WRITING & FIGHTING FROM THE ARMY OF NORTHERN VIRGINIA ed. by William B. Styple Belle Grove Pub. 2003

Pg. 143 August 31, 1862 "Not A Straggler-"...On the morning after the great battle of Manassas Plains, Sergeant --, Co. A 16th Mississippi Regiment, being barefooted, straggled off from his command, traversing the battlefield I n pursuit of a pair of shoes which some frightened Yankee might have thrown away in his fright. After looking for a time in vain, he at last saw a pretty good pair, on the pedal extremities of a dead Yankee. He sat down at the feet of the dead Yankee, pulled off his shoes and put them on his own feet. Admiring the fit, and complimenting himself upon this addition to his searching abilities, he arose, and with knapsack on his back, and gun in hand, was about starting to overtake his regiment, when he observed coming towards him a small squadron of cavalry, all of whom, as it was drizzling rain, were wrapped in their large rubber oilcloths overcoats. It will be remembered that cavalry are frequently assigned to the duty of picking up the stragglers, and hence there is not good feeling between the infantry and the cavalry. As they approached Sergeant--, the foremost one asked:

"What are you doing here sir, away from your command?"

"That's none of your business," answered the Sergeant.

"You are a straggler, sir and deserve the severest punishment."

"It's a lie, sir, I am not a straggler-I only left a few minutes ago, to hunt me a pair of shoes. I went all through the fight yesterday, and that's more than you can say-for where were you yesterday when Gen. Stuart wanted you cavalry to charge the Yankees after we put 'em running? You were lying back in the pine thickets and couldn't be found; but today, when there is no danger, you can come out and charge other men with straggling."

The cavalry man, instead of getting mad, seemed to enjoy this raking over from the plucky little Sergeant, and as he rode on, laughed heartily at it. As the squadron was filing nearly past the Sergeant, one of them remarked: "do you know who you are talking to?"

"Yes-to a cowardly Virginia cavalryman."

"No sir-that's General Lee."

"What?"

"And his staff."

"Thunderation!" With this exclamation, the Sergeant pulled off his hat, and readjusted it over his eyes, struck a double quick on the straightest line for his regiment..."

I wonder how long it took for this man to get over this incident.

FOOTPRINTS OF A REGIMENT-A Recollection of the 1st Georgia Regulars 1861-1865 W.H. Andrews 1st Sgt, Co. M pub. by Longstreet Press 1992

Pg. 68 Aug.31, 1862 Day after the Battle of 2nd Manassas "...Horiible sights to look upon, with their clothing burnt off and their flesh to a blackened crisp. Saw the dead in all conceivable positions. Some on their knees still grasping their guns, others died eating, with their hands and mouths full of crackers, how sickening. Did not think I could ever eat another cracker. Most of them had been robbed by someone. Some had nothing on but their underclothing. If they had on any pants the pockets had been turned. Strange that it should be so, but it is nevertheless. You can't find a (dead) man on the battlefield that has not been robbed. I can't stand the idea of handling a dead man. At the same time, I am not afraid of ghosts..."

EYEWITNESS-THE CIVIL WAR AS WE LIVED IT Eyewitness-The American Iliad by Otto Eisenschiml & Ralph Newman pub by The Universal Library 1947

Pg. 212 Late Aug, 1862, starting the Antietam Campaign "the drum beat the long role for us, the 17th Va., and the men fell into line. The troops were all in light marching order; a blanket or oilcloth, a single shirt, a pair of drawers and a pair of socks rolled tightly therin was swung on the right shoulder while the haversack hung on the left. These, with a catridge box suspended from the belt, and a musket carried at will, made up Johnny Rebs entire equipment. There were not two men clothed alike in the entire regiment, brigade or division; some had caps, some wore hats of every imaginable shape and in every stage of dilapidation, varied by the different shades of hair which protruded through the holes and stuck out like quills upon a porcupine; the jackets were also of different shades, ranging from light gray with gilt buttons, to black with wooden ones; the pant were for the most part that nondescript hue that time and all weathers give to ruins; some of the men wore boots, but many were barefooted; all were dusty and dirty...Our rations were doled out in sparing quantities; three crackers per man and a half pound of fat pork was the daily allowance..."

I wonder if those black jackets could've been some of the Yankee jackets captured in the Valley Campaign, dyed with walnut hulls, and issued. That is only enough rations for one square meal, I'd think.

FROM HUNTSVILLE TO APPOMATTOX R.T.Coles History of the of 4th Regiment, Alabama Volunteer Infantry, C.S.A. Army of Northern Virginia ed by Frank L. Byrne pub by Univ of Tenn. 1996

Pg 58 Late August 1862 "The regiment on its march from Gordonsville and before reaching the Rappahannock were sadly in need of shoes. Lieutenant Colonel McLemore ordered me to call on General Hood and get some relief if possible. I found him during the march at the head of our little division. He ordered me to go back tro Louisa Courthouse, where detail from the division, a member of C Co. being one of the number, were making shoes. At the same time, he gave me an order on the Quartermaster for a wagon, with orders to bring back all the shoes made. Arriving at the shoe factory, I found only a scant supply on hand and waited a day longer, hurrying up the men to furnish as many as possible..."

I'll bet there still was not enough.

Website The American Civil War Article No.1 The Wearing of Federal Uniforms by the Army of Northern VA,

August 1862 to April 1865 "The first soldier of the 55th Va.to mention purloining and using an item of Federal uniform was Pvt. William Rouzie of Co. F. On September 8 1862, he wrote to his sister, "we took Manassas (on August 27th 1862) and got just what we wanted. I got pants (i.e. sky blue kersey trousers), a nice oil cloth and various other things." *This shows poor research, because, as we've seen, the Rebs were not shy about reporting the utilizing of captured (by whatever means) Federal clothing and gear.*

"Union General G.H. Gordon who fought the Confederates at both 2nd Manassas and Sharpsburg: "From piles of new clothing the southerners arrayed themselves in the blue uniforms of the Federals."

"During the night of December 13th, the hundreds of dead Union soldiers in front of the Confederate position at Fredericksburg were stripped of their clothing leaving most of them naked by morning. The rebels took this clothing in order to use it."

"Pvt. Samuel H. Darnell of Archer's brigade of Hill's division remembered escaping from the Federals after his unit was overrun at Fredericksburg on December 13th 1862, by the following means: "I had on a Yankey coat and another coat over it. I got the Yankey coat at Harpasfirry. I throwed my top coat open so they could see the under coat so them seeing I had on one of there coats they never ordered me to throw down my gun(.) Thet fullowed our men some distance about a quarter of a mile. I went on with them as far as they went my way…"

"in the new year of 1864, Frank M. Mixson of Jenkin's brigade of Longstreet's corps took part in a skirmish with some federal troops in East Tennessee. He recalled: "The enemy fell back as we advanced. We had not gone more than a couple of hundred yards before we ran over some dead Yankees. Here was my opportunity, and I embraced it. The first one I got to I stopped, pulled off his pants, shoes and stockings, got right into them, there and then. The shoes were new and fit perfectly; the stockings were good wool and came up to my knees, and the pants were all right, except a little too long, but I rolled them up about as they are worn these days (ca.1900?) and they too were a fit. I felt grand."

"By the fall of 1864 the Confederate supply situation was again deteriorating. When the 55th Va.'s brigade moved forward to renew the attack at Pegram's Farm on September 30th, it passed large numbers of Federal prisoners coming the other way and many of these men were stripped of their clothing; so many in fact that when the Confedertae brigade went into action it was momentarily mistaken by Federal officers for one of their own units…"

"In January 1865, Allen Redwood, then serving in the 1st Marylnd Cavalry Battalion, paid a visit to his old comrades in Co. C, 55th Va., then stationed at Chaffin's Bluff on the Richmond lines. He described their apparel thus: "A few old uniform jackets, once grey but now stained by dust and faded by sun and rain to a dingy yellow, still hold out against the vicissitudes of war, but the garb is uniform no longer: garments of civic cut and color prevail, interspersed with others, the dye of which proclaims them the spoil of the battle-field, stripped, under the prompting of hard necessity, from those who would never again need them…"

FOOTPRINTS OF A REGIMENT-A Recollection of the 1st Georgia Regulars 1861-1865 by W.H. Andrews, 1st Sergeant, Co. M, pub by Longstreet Press 1992

Pg. 78 Sept. 1862 "Lee's Army is greatly reduced, but what men he has is fighting men, as everyone so inclined has had the opportunity to fall out. Barefooted men are not compelled tro keep up or go in battle, thousands being in that condition. I have seen numbers of poor soldiers who could have been tracked by their blood, trying to march over the rough turnpike roads, where a horse could not travel without being shod...."

Pg. 82 Sept. 18, 1862 day after Antietam "Next morning early, resumed the search and found the brigade not far from where we threw our knapsacks when we went into action. Everything I had was gone. Overcoat, blankets, clothing. And all. Right there and then I swore by Jeff Davis, Abe Lincoln, and all of the rest of them, that I would never drop my knapsack again. If I got where I could not carry it, I would lie down with it..."

An excellent idea. Clothing was already too hard to replace to lose it in this manner.

TOO AFRAID TO CRY-MARYLAND Civilians in the Antietam Campaign by Katyleen A. Ernst pub by Stackpole Press1999

Pg. 58 Sept. 1862 "...Her refined population (Maryland's) could only see as the result of long soldiering, rags and filth, and barefooted soldiers...and so the sentiment of "My Maryland" evaporated in poetry and paper..."

Pg. 75 "When asked why they were so dirty and ragged, a wag called, "Our mommas always taught us to put on our worst clothes when we go to kill hogs." Another bystander wanted to know why the men were barefoot. "We wore out our shoes running after the Yankees," came the reply."

Pg. 81 Funkstown Angela Davis, a union sympathiser, observed: "Poor forlorn looking set of men, who certainly had seen hard service, as they were tired, dirty and ragged; and had no uniforms whatever. Their coats were made of almost anything- their hats looked worse than those worn by the darkies; many were barefooted, some with their toes sticking out of their shoes, and others in their stocking feet; their blankets were of every kind and description, consisting of drugget, rugs, bed clothes, in fact everything they could get, put up in a long roll and tied at the ends which with their cooking utensils, were slung over their shoulders. Poor, brave, uncomplaining men."

Pg. 83 Hagerstown "...Soon residents of Hagerstown witnessed the bewildering spectacle of bedraggled men sporting beaverskin top hats, sucking lemons, puffing cigars....Men lucky enough to get new shirts or trousers often donned them in the steets, leaving their filthy rags in the gutters..."

Now these are Ragged rebels!

WAR TALKS OF CONFEDERATE VETERANS by Mr. George S. Bernard Fenn& Owen 1892 The Campaign in Maryland

(Pg. 22) Sept. 1862 "So, with boots dangling alternately from blanket-roll and rifle, I made the best time I could with bare feet, taking the public roads along which our brigade was moving, and scoring about nine miles before I reached the command in bivouac just north of Monacacy Junction and near Frederick city.

I was not the only bare-footed man on this tramp by many hundred, and by this connection a strong paragraph from a vigorous Southern writer descirptive of the trials and tribulations of many of our army on the marches of this campaign may properly here be reproduced. Mr. E.A. Pollard the editor of the Examiner, that historic, fiery war-time Richmond journal, in his work, "The Southern History of the War," written during the war, referring to these marches says:

"The route of the extraordinary marches of our troops presented, for long and weary miles, the touching pictures of the trials of war. Broken down soldiers (not all 'stragglers') lined the road. At night time they might be found asleep in every conceivable attitude of discomfort-on fence rails and in fence corners- some half bent, others almost erect, in ditches and on steep hill-sides, some without blanket or overcoat. Daybreak found them drenched with dew, but strong in purpose; with half rations of bread and meat, ragged and bare-footed, they go cheerfully forward. No nobler spectacle was ever presented in history. These beardless youths and grey-haired men, who thus spent their nights like the beasts of the field, were the best men of the land-of all classes, trades and professions. The spectacle was such as to inspire the prayer that ascended from the sanctuaries of the South-that God might reward the devotion of these men to principle and justice by crowning their labors and sacrifices with that blessing which always bringeth peace."

"There was one thing, however, that cheered us all up, now that we were on the soil of Maryland-the sympathy of the people. "Find people along the road almost unamimously in favor of the South," is the entry made in diary relative to the march on Sunday, September 7th.

My personal experiences on this day, embracing much suffering and great joy incident to relief therefrom, with a history of those boots, which now for a week I had so faithfully clung to in the manner described, are given in the note book in the following paragraphs:

"Thus impeded in my locomotion I was forced to straggle no little, and the day after I slept in the straw stack of the Maryland farmer, I was unable to overtake the brigade until it had gone into camp at the point at which my last entry left it, three miles from Frederick city, where I found it bivouacked in a wheat field-two or three hundred yards from the road- to make my way over the sharp stubble which was agony to my suffering feet. But I had gotten among the boys only a few moments, when my friend Jim Nash desired to know if I would like to have a pair of shoes. My reply and the joy at the delightful prespect of being once more shod may be imagined. Being assured that nothing would be more acceptable than a pair of shoes, Jim seized me in his arms and bore me across the stubble several yards to a tent. Presuming his intentions good, I did not object to the forceable abduction, and found myself at the tent of Capt. Sam Stevens, our quartermaster, who delivered to me a handsome pair which fit exactly, and were nice enough (I thought) for a gentleman to wear to a ball-the last pair of a lot he had that day purchased in Frederick city. No one who had not suffered as I had for several days past can appreciate my pleasure at the rescipt of these shoes.

But to the boots. I was no sooner supplied with the shoes, than sundry applications were made for my 'boots,' which I gave to my late fellow-straggler, Billy Pucci…"

VOICES OF THE CIVIL WAR by Richard Wheeler pub by Meridian Books 1990

Pg. 180 Sept. 1862 Antietam Campaign-an unnamed Confederate private tells of his situation when "some thieving reb" made off with his oilcloth:

"I had no blanket…As a makeshift, I begged a newspaper, a copy of the New York World, and lay on that; and, as it kept the moisoned earth from my person, it answered quite well.…I would fold it up with great care every morning. But one night it rained, and there was nothing left of it. Anyway, I have always had a tender feeling for the New York World ever since."

Ingenious. Don't let this Quote getr out, as the army might want to try this bedding on the modern army, imagine how much money it would save!

TRUE TALES OF THE SOUTH AT WAR-How Soldiers Fought and Families Lived, 1861-1865 collected and ed. by Clarence Poe pub by Univ. of N.C. Press 1961

Pg. 23 reminiscences of Berry Benson 1st Regiment S.C. Volunteers (Sharpsburg Campaign, Sept. 1862) "…I cast cast about and found an old broken plowshare in a field on which we baked…

"Have you ever seen a proud man? One who looked proud? I have seen the personification of pride; a man bearing in his face the proudest look I ever saw in mortal man. And he was barefoot. It was in the Valley, after the battle of Sharpsburg, as we were marching along the turnpike, a newfallen snow on the ground, that, happening to cast my eyes over to one side, I saw him, a young man, tall and vigorous, but utterly barefoot in the snow, standing in a fence corner, his gun leaning against his shoulder-and of all the proud faces I have ever seen, his was the proudest. It was a periode that seemed to scorn not only the privations and cold, but the exposure of his sufferings to other eyes, and even the very pity that it called forth…"

More than mortal men.

JOHNNY REB'S WAR: Battlefield and Homefront by David Williams McWhiney Univ. Press 2000

Pg. 13 "...By September (1862), after a summer of almost constant marching, nearly all of Lee's men had worn out their shoes, and the Confederacy found it difficult to supply them with new ones. Most of what shoes the army possessed had been removed from the feet of the dead as they lay rotting on the Manassas Battlefield. John Worsham of Major General Thomas J. "Stonewall" Jackson's "Foot Cavalry" reported that of the hundreds of dead Yankees he saw, not one was wearing a pair of shoes. Nor did the feet of deceased Rebels escape plunder. Private George Bernard remembered in his memoirs that after the battle there was "a very general removing of shoes, not only from Federal dead, but also from many of the dead Confederates."

Though the need for footgear among the Southerners was great, there were those who simply could not bring themselves to plunder a lifeless corpse. Private Bernard counted himself one of this number after a vain attept to overcome his anxiety.

"I went to this poor fellow's feet, untied one of his shoes and began to pull it off. This was, of course, not easy work, and whilst engaged at it I suddenly fully realized what I was doing-taking a dead man's shoes, and these the shoes of a dead Confederate! I at once stopped and swore I would go bare-footed before would do an act which was so repugnant to my feelings."

Pg. 15 Antietam Campaign "Most soldiers counted themselves fortunate even to have a decent shirt and a good pair of pants. One former Confederate remembered in later years that he did not believe there was a single shred of underclothing in the entire army. A Harper's Weekly correspondent wrote of the Rebel garb: "With the exception of the officers, there was little else but homespun among them, light drab-grey or butternut color, the drab predominating; although there were so many varieties of dress, half citizen, half military that they could scarcely be said to have a uniform.

Aside from the lack of adequate clothing, there was also the problem of cleanliness, or rather the absence of it. One Maryland womon wrote of the Southerners, "Oh, they are so dirty! I don't think the Potomac River could wash them clean." The clouds of dust stirred up by the marching columns caked layer upon layer of filth on the already dirty faces. One soldier, commenting on the movementfrom Leesburg to White's Ford, said that the dust was so thick, it was impossible to discern a man three yards distant Another young Rebel proposed "to drill holes through the dirt on some of the boys' faces and blast it off, as water is thought to be inadequate to the task."...

"...The Rebel troops, having been in the field all summer, had deeply tanned skin and were unused to seeing soldiers of light complexion such as those of the Federal garrison. "as we Marched along the street one of our troopers sang out to one of the men on the sidewalk, "I say, Yank, what sort of soap do you fellows use? It has washed all the color out of your faces," at which our side cheered. To this the man retorted, "Damn me, if you don't look like you have never used soap of any sort." Shouts of laughter greeted the reply from our men as well as the Yanks, and our man called back as he rode on, "Bully for you, Yank; you got me that time."

GENERAL LEE'S ARMY-FROM VICTORY TO CALLAPSE by Joseph T. Glattharr pub by Free Press a Div. of Simon and Schuster

Pg. 183 "In September (1862) an artillery captain called his comrades "a set of ragamiffins" and predicted, "If we don't gain a victory soon or capture Harper's Ferry, so as to get possession of Yankee spoils, our whole army will be naked & barefooted." By mid-November, as early signs of winter appeared, soldiers itched for a fight. "The rebels have all taken up an idea that the Yankee army has just been furnished with new Overcoats & Blankets for the winter," Pvt. James P. Williams explained to his aunt, and they want to get a few of them before cold weather sets in." About the same time, a Louisianian told his brother not to send warm clothes. If he could not make out with his currant issue, "I will supply myself with Yankee clothes the next fight I get into." After every battle they had access to Union knapsacks and all they contained. "Heretofore I would never wear Yankee clothes but as "necessity is the mother of invention" I will have to pick up the next Yankee knapsack I come across," he wrote. After the Battle of Fredericksburg, a Virginia private explained why the Yankees were naked: "our men stripped the dead bodies to get clothes to keep them warm."

LETTERS TO AMANDA-The Civil War Letters of Marion Hill Fitzpatrick ed b y Jeffery C. Lowe and Sam Hodges Mercer Univ. Press 1998

Pg. 28 Sept. 27th, 1862 Near Martinsburg, Va. (Letter no. 14) Dear Amanda, "…John Wilder left the things you sent me at Gordonsville and I am glad he done it. Tell Alex that the hat I have got now will last probably till the war ends, as it ie a good homemade wool hat. When we go into winter quarters I will be glad to get the suit of jeans you are preparing fpr me, as this suit is getting thin and thredbare. But I will not grumble if I cannot get them…"

LEE'S ARMY IN CONFEDERATE HISTORY Gary W. Gallagher Univ. of S.C. Press 2001

Pg. 29 The 1862 Maryland Campaign Sept. 1862 "…As the army marched through Maryland, a member of the 15th Georgia In fantry oberserved that "a great many of our soldiers were barefoot." This man "had on a pair of shoes No.5 and the other No.10," but neirther he nor anyone else in the regiment had changed their clothes for the past forty-five days…A man in the 8th Georgia Infantry reported only ten men in his company on September 23. Several of those present lacked shoes, and "8 others are at Winchester with no prospect of getting any."

If ordered to march, the men would "suffer terrible." In late September, a pair of privates in Georgia regiments provided tellingly terse comments. "The Army is in poor condition, half naked and barefooted," said one in the 4th Georgia Infantry. "My own clothes and shoes are in pieces and ther is no chance of getting them replaced." The second man used only eight words to make his point: "Times is hard hear. Provision is scarce hear.

Some soldiers tried to find something hopeful in their raggedness and hunger. Members of the 47th Alabama Infantry, for example, interperted the extreme shortage of shoes and clothing as a sign the war was about to end. "(T)he officer has made out requisition for close for us,: stated James P. Crowder, "tho we have never got any yet and I don't think that we will ever get any. That is the reason we think peace will be made they are not a fixing for winter…"

CONFEDERATE INFANTRYMAN 1861-65 Ian Drury Osprey 1993

Sept. 1862 Pg. 9 "…A union soldier who was captured at Antietam observed that only a single Confederate regiment wore regulation Confederate grey uniforms, describing the rest of his captores as being clothed in "homespun butternut."

VMI

Sept. 1862 "…I asked Gen. Smith this morning about the cloth he said he did not know when he would get cloth so you had better send mine up. He has given some boys furloughs as to go home to provide their winter clothing. He says if I get the gray like you have his will be something like it and I will not want another uniform. Please send it on a Friday so I can go down & get it on Saturday. You know how much to send for uniform & overcoat. The uniform of brown's & the overcoat of Flannagan's. I wrote you some time ago how much it took to make them. I reckon you had better wait till Ma comes back before you send it but be sure to send it on a Friday. Bundle it up good and write me when you send it …"

TRUE TALES OF THE SOUTH AT WAR Collected and Edited by Clarence Poe univ. of N.C. Press 1961
reminiscences of Barry Benson

Sept. 1862Pg. 23 "…My partner, Matt Hitt tells (this story)…In Maryland (Antietam Campaign), two lines of battle fronted each other, partly seen, partly hidden; and the Confederate commander, to get a clearer idea of the force opposing him, called for a volunteer to undertake the dangerous duty of riding down the enemy's front near enough to count the flags as he went. Matt Hitt rode out from the ranks, and received his orders. Mounted on a splendid animal. But with a uniform which consisted of a red flannel shirt, a pair of white cotton drawers (being trouserless), and a broad felt hat with its brim pinned up in front with a horseshoe nail, he rode straight to the front very deliberately, the enemy watching him without firing, not understanding the movement. But getting within a close range, near enough for his purpose, he suddenly wheeled his horse, spurring down the line at a furious gallop, wildly cheered by the enemy the whole way, and not being fired upon once! That was gallentry on both sides!"

BATTLE OF ANTIETAM: Two Great American Armies Engage in Combar>>HistoryNet

Sept. 1862"Another interesting but inconclusive observation of Confederate uniforms was made by Union surgeon James I. Dunn in a letter to his wife after Antietam. He wrote, "All this stuff about their extreme destitution is all bash....I have yet to find a rebel even meanly clad or shod. They are as well shod as our own men. They are dressed in grey...."

"Two weeks after the battle, Lee's army regrouped around the lower Shenandoah Valley village of Bunker Hill. One soldier from the 4th North Carolina wrote home: "pa, I want you to have me a pair of boots made. Those shoes you made for me ripped all to pieces. Our regiment used everything we had. I have no blanket nor any clothes but what I got. I have got the suit on that you sent me. They came in a good time. I like them very well. If I had a pair of shoes I would be the best clothed man in the regiment..."

Who was Dr. Dunn looking at? All the other descriptions we have of the Army of Northern Virginia at this time decribes them as extremely ragged.

LANDSCAPE TURNED RED- The Battle of Antietam by Stephen W. Sears pub by Ticknor and Fields/Houghton Mifflin Co. 1983

Sept. 1862 Pg 97, the march through Hagerstown, Md. "The local merchants were quickly sold out of shoes, clothing, and food. In a dry-goods store Owen (William Owen of the Washington Artillery) and his comrades discovered a large stock of old-fashioned bell-crowned beaver hats, "just the style our fathers wore," and took a shine to them. In an army noted for the diversity of its headgear, the men of the Washington Artillery could make the proud claim that their tall beavers were unique."

"the 400 pairs of shoes purchased there brought the total so far found in Maryland to less than 1,700 pairs, far too few "to cover the bare feet of the army."

EYEWITNESS THE CIVIL WAR AS WE LIVED IT-The American Iliad by Otto Eisenschiml & Ralph Newman pub by The universal Library 1947

Pg. 243 Sept. 1, 1862 battlefield of Second Manassas "...A Federal Surgeon, Dr. Horace H. Thomas, who received permission from the Confederates to help the wounded of Pope's army-"The next morning, September 1, we set out, with a flag of truce. The medical director divided us civilians into squads of eight, with two stretchers to each ambulance; and we enjtered upon the mournful task of gathering up our poor wounded fellows from the wide battlefield. The dead were unburied and presented a study of ghastly interest. I saw hardly a decent pair of pantaloons, a blouse, or a pair of shoes on a dead man. If any of these articles of clothing were too shabby to be worth stealing and were left on the body, the pockets were invariably turned inside out..."

Well, what did he expect?

DEAR AMANDA-The Civil war Letters of Marion Hill Fitzpatrick ed. by Jeffery C. Lowe and Sam Hodges pub by Mercer Univ. Press 1998

Pg. 25 Sptember 2nd, 1862 Near Fairfax Courthouse, Va. (Letter no. 13) Dear Amanda "... We got to manassas the day after it was captured....I got me a good yankee zinc canteen which fortunately was nearly filled with water..."

A MEMOIR OF CAPTAIN C. SETON FLEMING OF THE SECOND FLORIDA INFANTRY C.S.A. by Francis P. Fleming pub by Times-Union Pub House 1881

Pg. 48 Sept. 2, 1862 Alexandria Road, Va. My Dear Mother:(regarding Battle of Second Manassas) "...to see men go up to a dead Yankee, cut his haversack off, and his canteen also, and if his shoes were good to haul them off ; it looked as though men had forgotton they were human beings; but we were out of provisions, and many of our men were barefooted. I made my supper on hard bread taken off dead Yankees, and was glad to get it..."

According to my ethics prof., this is known as "the barbarization of warfare."

MANASSAS TO APPOMATTOX The Civil War Memoirs of Pvt. Edgar Warfield 17th Virginia Infantry pub by EPM Pub Inc

Pg. 108-109 Sept 4,1862 Antietam Campaign "...Then an order came for all the barefooted men to remain behind and report in Winchester....None of us had any underclothing. My costume consisted of a pair of ragged trousers, a stained, dirty jacket, and an old hat, the brim pinned up with a thorn. A begrimed blanket over my shoulder, a greased, smeared cotton haversack full of apples and corn, a cartridge box full, and a musket completed my outfit. I was barefooted and had stone bruises on each foot.

Some of my comrades were a little better dressed, some were worse. I was the average. But there was not one there who would not have been 'run in' by the police had he appeared on the streets of any populous city, and fined next day for undue exposure…

Yet these grimy, sweaty, lean, ragged men were the flower of Lee's army. These tattered, starving, unkempt fellows were the pride of their sections. These were the men-

'Whose ancestors followed Smith along the sands

And Raleigh around the seas'

Bearing out this testimony are the official records and letters from high officers, including those of General Robert E. Lee. On November 14, 1862, a communication to the War Department, for information of the Secretary, said that "General Lee desires to state that in Pickett's division alone there are 2,071 barefooted." In the same month Longstreet's corps reported 6,648 men without any covering for their feet. But fortunately for them it was not the dead of winter.

Two months later, however, there was plenty of winter, with much snoe and cold, and the same conditions prevailed. Writing to his Congressman in January, 1863, a Louisiana soldier told how, out of 1,500 men reported for duty, 400 were totally without covering of any kind for their feet, the Fifth Regiment could not drill for want of shoes, and the Eighth Regiment would soon be unable to do so for the same reason.Even when shoes should be supplied the men would be unable to wear them for a long while, such was the condition of their feet. A large number of men were without a single blanket, and some had not a particle of underclothing, while overcoats were objects of curiosity. He said further that the troops had no tents and were almost totally unprovided with cooking utensils for the petty rations they received.

General Lee, writing to his wife in October, 1863, said that thousands were barefooted, thousands more had only fragments of shoes, all were without overcoats, blankets, or warm clothing. Later on, in writing to the Secretary of War, he said that only fifteen in one regiment had shoes and that bacon was issued only once in several days. On one occasion he said that the troops were in line of battle three days, exposed to the severities of the winter, without a particle of meat. In January, 1864, he wrote to the Quartermaster general in Richmond that a brigade that had recently gone on picket had been compelled to leave several hundred men in camp because they could not bear the exposure of duty, having no shoes or blankets.

Speaking for myself, I recall that while passing through Frederick City, Maryland, with my command I noticed two men standing on the sidewalk calling attention of some ladies to my condition.

I was not entirely shoeless, for I had the soles of my shoes held to the uppers by pieces of bandages, which I had to renew quite often. But I was good and ragged all right! My hat I had found at a farmhouse in Virginia. It was part of a straw that had been painted or varnished black, and half of the rim was missing. It took the place of a good brown felt hat that I had up tp within a few days of our entering on Maryland soil and that I lost one night when, tired and footsore, I was allowed by the driver of one of the wagons of our regiment to get in and ride. Crawling out just before daybreak I found that my hat was missing. It had evidently fallen out during the night.

Referring to the condition of our army at this time, when we entered the enemy's territory, a Union clergyman who was in Frederick City at the time wrote to governor Curtin, of Pennsylvania, that he saw all of Lee's army that passed through that city on September 10 on its way to Sharpsburg, and that "they were ragged and shoeless, but full of fight."

Later on in the war a northern writer had this to say with respect to the impressions made upon him by Lee's troops when they pushed into Maryland.

"The Confederate army, as they marched through out country presented a solid front. They came in close marching order, the different brigades, divisions, and corps all within supporting distance of each other. Their dress consisted of nearly every imaginable color and style, the butternut predominating. Some had blue blouses with they had doubtless stripped from the Union dead. Hats, or the skeletons of what had been hats, surmounted their poorly covered heads.

Many were ragged and shoeless, affording unmistakable evidence that their wardrobe sadly needed to be replenished. They were, however, all well armed and under perfect discipline. They seemed to move as one vast machine. Laughing, talking, singing, and cheering were not indulged in, and straggling was scarcely seen...."

Ragged Rebels

WEBSITE-EMMITSBURG AREA HISTORICAL SOCIETY-The Confederate Soldier during the 1862 Maryland Campaign by John Miller

Spt. 4-7 1862 "...As the Confederate army forded the Potomac River on September 4th-7th, they began marching towards Frederick, Maryland. William Judkins of the 22nd Georgia described the march from the Potomac River to Frederick, Maryland: "We marched through several towns in Maryland and through fine farms and stopped at Frederick City, Md, on the Monocacy river, remained one day and washed our clothes in the river and put them on wet. We were trying to drown some of the lice of which we had plenty. We had not washed our clothes in about a month, and the bugs were getting unbearable...

Confederate soldier David E. Johnston wrote about his uniform during the Maryland Campaign. "A musket, cartridge box with forty rounds of cartridges, cloth haversack, blanket and canteen made up the Confederate soldier's equipment. No man was allowed a change of clothing, nor could he have carried it. A gray cap, jacket, trousers and colored shirt-calico mostly-made up a private's wardrobe. When a clean shirt became necessary, we took off the soiled one, went to the water, usually without soap, gave it a little rubbing, and, if the sun were shining, hung the shirt on a bush to dry, while the wearer sought the shade to give the shirt a chance. The method of carrying our few assets was to roll them in a blanket, tying each end of the roll, which was then swung over the shoulder. At night this blanket was unrolled and wrapped aroung its owner, who found a place on the ground with his cartridge box for a pillow. We cooked but little, having usually little to cook. The frying pan was in use, if we had one…

Jacob Engelbrecht, a civilian, wrote that "Many (Confederate soldiers) were barefooted and some had one shoe & one barefoot-they really looked "ragged and tough." The first 8 or 10 thousand got a tolerable good supply of clothing and shoes and boots but the stores and shops were soon sold out …

Shotwell, a Confederate soldier in the 8th Virginia Infantry was shoeless and could not keep up with Longstreet's wing as it marched to Hagerstown.In Funkstown, a civilian offered his boots to the soldier but they were four sizes too big. The soldier gave them back realizing that the oversized boots would make his feet blister and bleed even more…

Jed Hotchkiss, Stonewall jackson's famous mapmaker, recalled the condition of those Confederate soldiers. "… are as dirty as the ground itself and nearly the same color. The enemy looked at them in amazement…"

HANDLEY LIBRARY ARCHIVES, WINCHESTER, VA JOURNAL OF LT WILLIAM CARTER 3rd Virginia Cavalry transcribed by Wil Burk, 2009

Sept 5th, 1862 "Mounted, and marched towards Leesburg…We then marched towards Poolesville in Montgomery County and dashed the place, capturing some thirty-four prisoners and several horses & killed several. Part of the 3rd & 5th Regiments were engaged. The men supplied themselves here with boots, gloves & hats at very low prices, the merchant taking Confederate money without any hesitation…"

Eyewitness The Civil War As We Lived It-The American Iliad by Otto Eisenshciml & Ralph Newman pub by The Universal Library

Pg. 247 William M. Owen, an officer in the Washington Artillery "On the 12th(Sept) we reached Hagerstown (Md.)—We did some shopping in Hagerstown, devoting ourselves chiefly to the dry goods line, and bought waterproof cloth and some drew patterns to present to our lady friends in Richmond, where they were in great need of such things. One merchant had upon his top shelves about one hudred old-fashioned, bell-crowed beaver hats, just the style our fathers wore. The store was soon relieved of the stock of beavers, and the streets were thronged with men with the new hats. They wore them on the march, and went into the next battle with this most peculiar headgear for warriors…"

THE ANTIETAM CAMPAIGN Ed. By Gary W. Gallagher pub by Univ. of N.C. Press 1999

Sept. 1862 Pg. 108 "Lt. George L.P. Wren of the 8th Louisiana Infantry noticed that at second Manassas he "did not see a man but that had been stripped of his shoes…(They) being a very scarce article, there was a great demand for them." Newspaper correspondent Felix G. De Fountaine cocurred, noting with a bit of exaggeration that some Southern regiments could "charge and strip every dead Yankee's feet they pass without coming to a halt."

Pg. 114 "Hill's men also took the opportunity at Harper's Ferry to cast off their ragged garments in exchange for Federal uniforms. Capt. Andrew Wardlaw wrote his wife that throughout the Federal camps "the whole ground…was pretty well covered in places with old clothes which our soldiers had thrown off, substituting new ones." So many men in James J. Archer's brigade donned captured clothing that one member claimed that "but for their tattered Battle flags (they) might have ben taken for a brand new Brigade from Boston."

Longsteet's veterans received a warm welcome in Hagerstown. Virginian Alexander Hunter remembered that "not only were the men and women outspoken in their sympathy for the Southern cause, but they threw open their hospital doors and filled their houses with soldiers, feeding the hungry, and clothing the naked as well as their limited means allowed."

Pg.115 "The 400 pairs of shoes found in Hagerstown combined with the 250 pairs found in Williamsport and those obtained in Frederick were scarcely sufficient, Lee acknowledged, to cover the bare feet of his men."

Pg. 121 "A South Carolinian described the men as "sunburnt, gaunt, ragged, (and) scarcely at all shod." Surgeon Spencer G. Welch wrote his wife that "thousands of our men now have almost no clothes and no sign of a blanket nor any prospect of getting one either. Thousands have no shoes at all." Lt. William L. Cage of the 21st Mississippi related that his command was "without tents, rather poorly clad, and blankets very scarce." Col. Edward T.H. Warren noted that the men in his 10th Virginia Infantry were "ragged, dirty, and full of lice" and that 175 of them were without shoes. Warren remembered how his "heart used to bleed as I would read the account of the sufferings of the patriot army at Valley Forge, and little did I think that the time would come when I would command men in a like destitute condition."

"The "emaciated, limping, ragged filthy mass" of Lee's army blamed their woes in part on the shortcomings of logistical officers. Situations like that encountered by Col. Stephen D. Lee. Who "failed in several attempts" to obtain desperately needed shoes and blankets from the chief quartermaster, undoubtedly caused anger and frustration. A soldier who identified himself as "Barefoot" in a letter to the Macon "Daily Telegraph" suggested that only "willfull negligence" could have resulted in more than one third of the men in the army being without shoes. Maj. Franklin Gaillard of the 2nd South Carolina Infantry told his wife that the army's problems with straggling could not be avoided "unless the Government has it in its power to put its Quartermaster, Commissary, and Medical Department in better condition."

Pg. 122 "In an article titled "Gross Mismanagement," a contributer to the Mobile Tribune alledged that government officials had failed to forward donated clothing to soldiers. "There was a letter received by a soldier, "a writer to the Columbia Guardian noted, "stating that he was suffering greatly-barefoot and almost naked-but he did not want any more sent until there is provision made to take them safely from Richmond to camp, as there is clothing and shoes there now if he can get them.'

Pg. 123 "…A member of the 17th Mississippi Infantry wrote from Virginia that "in the forced marches recently made, all the clothing and many of the blankets were lost." "Something must be done," he demanded, "either by the government or the people at home." A "poor country girl" wrote the editor of the Columbus Daily Sun, reminding women that "God has given you the work to do, it is a sacred duty, and it matters not if no relation or dear friend appeals to you for help, all are brothers, friends, in the common cause." A contributer to the Montgomery Daily Mail claimed that "the only thing that can be done is to set to work, and endeavor to atone for the reisness of the Government."

So, was there clothing/shoes available but not shipped to the soldiers or were there just no supplies available?

LANDSCAPE TURNED RED The Battle of Antietam by Stephen W. Sears 1983 tickner & Fields New Haven and New York

Sept. 20 1862 After the battle of Antietam, a Penn. Soldier was assigned to a burial detail "After the Union men were all gathered up and buried then we commenced gathering up the Rebs… Many of the Rebel dead were lying about stiff and stark in their dirty white uniforms. Cartridge boxes, cartridges, broken bayonets, and knapsacks, cooking utensils and clothing strewed the ground, much of the latter having been taken from the merchants of Frederick City, and other towns through which the Rebels had passed. We seen among the Rebels boys of sixteen and fifteen and old grey headed men. There was not to the best of my knowledge in all that was buried two dressed alike."

Notice the mention of the use of drab-colored clothing, "their dirty white uniforms."

A MISSISSIPPI REBEL IN THE ARMY OF NORTHERN VIRGINIA-The Civil War Memoirs of Private David Holt ed. by Thomas D. Cockrell & Michael B. Ballard pub by La. State Univ. Press 1995

Sept. 15, 1862 after Antietam "…Bill West was a curiosity. He wore a skull cap with a patent leather visor. A bullet from the right clipped off the visor on one side, and one from the left clipped it off on the other. Only a little triangular piece of the visor was left. A bullet had split the cap open on top of his head from front to back and had cut his hair down to the scalp, giving him a very wide part in the wrong place…"

That's a close call

THE SOUTH REPORTS THE CIVIL WAR by J. Cutler Andrews Univ. of Pittsburgh Press 1985.

Pg 202-203 A reporter for the Mobile Daily Advertiser and Register, Sept. 1, 1862 regarding the Battle of 2nd Manassas "Many of them (the soldiers) are also barefooted. I have seen scores of them today marching over the flinty turnpike with torn and blistered feet. They bear all these hardships without murmuring;…As for tents, they have not known what it was to sleep under one since last spring…"

WRITING & FIGHTING THE CONFEDERATE WAR The Letters of Peter Wellington Alexander ed by William B. Styple pub by Belle Grove Pub. Co. 2002

Pg 96 Further from the Late Battles In Front of Fairfax C.H. September 1, 1862 March to Maryland-"It is now (midnight) raining, and has been for several hours. The army has not had a mouthful of bread for four days, and no food of any kind, except a little green corn picked up on the roadside, for thirty-six hours. The provision trains are coming up, but many of the troops will have to go another day without anything to eat. Many of them are also barefooted. I have seen scores of them to-day marching over the flinty turnpike with torn and blistered feet. They bear all of these hardships without murmering, since every step they take brings them that much nearer to bleeding Maryland. As for tents, they have not known what it was to sleep under one since spring."

The population of Maryland was not worthy of such sacrifice.

THE FIELD DIARY OF A CONFEDERATE SOLDIER WHILE SERVING WITH THE ARMY OF NORTHERN VIRGINIA by Draughton Stith Haynes pub by Ashantilly Press 1963

Pg. 14 September 2nd (1862) "…I passed through the battlefield of Manassas and found dead and wounded Yankees by the hundred, it was the most horrible sight I ever beheld. There was not a Yankee left with a pair of shoes on a few had every rag of clothes taken off. Many of our men were barefooted therefore I would not comdemn them for taking shoes off the dead. Many of the Yankee bodies had turned perfectly black, and to pass them would almost make a persom vomit…"

A CONFEDERATE SURGEON'S LETTERS TO HIS WIFE Spencer Glascow Welch, Surgeon Thirteenth S. Ca. Vols., McGowans Brigade Neale Pub. Co. 1911 Continental Book Co. Marietta Ga. 1954

Pg27 Ox Hill, Va. Sept. 3, 1862 Early Sunday morning (31st) we started away, and I passed by where Goggan's body lay. Near him lay the body of Captain Smith of Spartanburg. Both were greatly swollen and had been robbed of their trousers and shoes by our own soldiers, who were ragged and barefooted, and did it from necessity.

SWORDS AND ROSES-The Foot Soldier by Joseph Hergescheimer & Alfred A. Knopf 1929

Pg. 316 Sept 4. 1862-advance into Md. "The Second Brigade, General Jackson's Corps, with John Worsham,crossed the Potomac at White's Ford,. John was detailed to the Federal Hospital to make a careful list of its inmates; he disposed of his gun and ammunition and bore his other baggage with him. He had now, in place of the original elaborate and imported affair, an oilskin haversack, a tin cup, a rubber cloth and blanket, a pair of jeans drawers and one pair of wool socks.The socks and drawers were put in the blanket, the blanket was rolled in the rubber cloth, the ends were drawn together and fastened with a short strap and it was pulled over his head and swung from a shoulder. John Worsham had become a soldier…"

LEAVES FROM THE DIARY OF AN ARMY SURGEON John Bradburn, 1863

Sept.4 1862 "…A body of rebels have also crossed the Potomac at Noland's Ford, and marched on Buckeystown, five miles from Point of Rocks. They are sadly in want of clothing and shoes, a greater part of their cavalry and infantry being barefooted.…The rebels assisted with the burial of our dead last night, whom they stripped of their clothing, except their pantaloons. Our men say that the rebels were so hungry, they rushed for the haversacks of our killed and wounded…" After Battle of Antietam"…The death of many was so instantaneous that their arms were in position of firing their pieces, while others still retained the bitten cartridge in their hands. They appeared to be mostly young men, many of them mere boys. The difference between the clothing of the Union and the rebel dead was very marked. The Union troops were all well clad, while the rebels were in rags; in many instances without any pretence at uniform. Their garments were of all colors and styles. Their firearms, however, were all good, and they used them well.…"

ROCKBRIDGE ARTILLERY- The Story of a Cannoneer Under Stonewall Jackson by Edward Moore pub by Neale Pub. Co. 1907

Pg. 131 Sept. 5, 1862 Frederick, Md. "As previously mentioned, our extra baggage-and extra meant all save that worn on our backs-had been left weeks before near the banks of the

Rapidan, so that our apparel was now in sad plight. Dandrige had lost his little cadet-cap while on a night march and supplied its place from the head of a dead Federal at Manassas, his hair still protruding freely, and burnt as "brown as a Pretzel bun." The style of my hat was on the other extreme. It had been made to order by a substantial hatter in Lexington, enlisted, and served through the war on one head or another. It was a tall, drab-colored fur of conical shape, with several rows of holes punched around the crown for ventiliation. I still wore the lead-colored knit jacket given me by "Buck" Ranson during the Banks Campaign. This garment was adorned with a blue stripe near the edges, buttoned close at the throat, and came down well over the hips, fitting in the manner of a shirt. My trousers, issued by the Confederate Quartermaster Department, were fashioned in North Carolina of a reddish-brown or brick-dust color, part wool and part cotton, elaborate in dimensions about the hips and seat, but tapering and small at the feet, in imitation, in shape and color, of those worn by Billy Wilson's Zouaves at first Manassas. This is an accurate description of our apparel. Among our fellow-soldiers it attracted no especial attention as there were many others equally as striking. Very naturally, we were at first eyed with suspicion by the people we met and when we inquired for a place to get refreshments were directed "down yonder"; in fact anywhere else than where we were.

We soon found a nice little family grocery store; that is, one kept by a family, including among others two very comely young women. Here we found O'Rourke, an Irishman of our company, who had a talent for nosing out good things-both solids and liquids. We were served with a good repast of native wine, bread butter, etc.; and, in case we should not have leisure for milder beverages, had a canteen filled with whiskey.

While enjoying our agreeable cheer, a man about thirty years of age came in, he said, to make our acquaintance. He was quite a sharp-looking fellow, with small, keen black eyes, a "glib" tongue and told us that he was an out-and-out rebel, proud to meet us and ready to oblige. Steve forthwith proposed, as evidence of his goodwill, an exchange of headgear. He dilated eloquently on the historical value of his own cap, and, while it did not entirely suit him, exposed as he was to the weather, pleasant associations as a souvenir; and, moreover, the hat the stranger wore was most suitable for a soldier and would do good service to the cause. At lengh the exchange was made and Steve having donned the nice black hat, we took our leave. We had scarcely walked a square when our attention was attracted by the sound of rapid footsteps approaching from the rear, and, turning we saw our new and interesting acquaintance coming at a run. As he passed us, with a high bound he seized the hat from Dandridge's head, threw the cap on the pavement, and disappeared like a flsh around the corner..."

Pg. 140Later-after the Antietam Campaign-"As some time would be consumed in handling the prisoners and the transfer of arms and stores, I set out in the afternoon for Charlestown, ands, as usual, went to my friends the Ransons. After a refreshing bath I donned a clean white shirt and a pair of light-checked trousers, and was ready to discuss the events of the campaign with General Lindsay Walker, who was also a guest of the house…"

Pg. 160 in winter quarters- "The infantry of the Stonewall Brigade was in camp seven miles from us, toward the railroad. Having ridden there one morning for our mail, I met two men in one of their winter-quarter streets. One of them, wearing a citizen's overcoat, attracted my attention. Then, noticing the scars on his face, I recognicised my former messmate, Wash. Stuart, on his return to the battery for the first time since his fearful wound at Winchester the preceeding May…"

DIARY OF LEWIS H. STEINER A.D.F. Randolph 1862

Sat. Sept.6, 1862, Frederick Md.
Pg.8 "…At ten o'clock Jackson's advance force, consisting of some five thousand men, marched up Market Street and encamped north of the town. They had but little music, what there was gave us "My Maryland and Dixie in excrable style. Each regiment had a square red flag, with a cross, made of diagonal blue stripes extending from opposite corners: on these blue stripes were placed thirteen white stars. A dirtier, filthier, more unsavory set of human beings never "strolled" through a town-marching it could not be called without doing violence to the word. The distinctions of rank were recognized on the coat collars of officers, but all were alike dirty and repulsive. Their arms were rusty and in an unsolderly condition. Their uniforms, or rather multiform, corresponded only in a slight predominance of grey over butternut, and in the prevalence of filth. Faces looked as if they had not been acquainted with water for weeks: hair, shaggy and unkempt, seemed entirely a stranger to the operations of brush or comb. A motlier group was never herded together. But "these" were the chivalry-the deliverers of Maryland from Lincoln's oppressive yoke.…Our stores were soon thronged with crowds. The shoes stores were most patronized, as many of their men were shoeless and stockingless. The only money most of them had was Confederate scrip, or shinplasters issued by banks, corporations, individuals, etc. -all of equal value. To use the expression of an old citizen "the notes depreciated the paper on which they were printed." The crowded conditions of the stores enabled some of the chivalry to "take" what they wanted, (confiscate is the technical expression) without going through the formality of even handing over Confederate rags in exchange.…"

Mr. Steiner sounds rather pompous, doesn't he? I wonder what he'd have written if the Rebels treated Maryland as the Yankees treated the rest of the South?

THE CIVIL WAR READER RICHARD B. HARWELL pub. By Smithmark Pub. 1957

Pg. 161 Report Frederick L. Olnstead, Frederick Md. Sat. September 6, 1862 "...About nine o'clock two seedy-looking individuals Market Street as fast as their jaded animals could carry them. Their dress was a dirty,faded gray,their arms rusty and seemingly uncared for, their general appearance raffish or vagabondish...At ten o'clock Jackson's advance force, consisting of some five thousand men, marched up Market Street and encamped north of town...A dirtier, filthier, more unsavory set of human beings never strolled through a towm-marching it could not be called without doing violence to the word. The distinctions of rank were recognized on the coat collar of officers, but all were alike dirty and repulsive. Their arms were rusty and in an unsoldierly condition. Their uniforms, or rather multiforms, corresponded only in a slight predominance of gray over butternut and in the prevalence of filth. Faces looked as if they had not been aquainted with water for weeks; hair, shaggy and unkempt, seemed entire stranger to the operation of brush or comb. A motlier group was never herded together....(Pg. 166) How the rebels manage to get along no one can tell. They are badly clad. Many of them without shoes. Uncleanliness and vermin are universal. The odor of clothes worn for monthes, saturated with perspiration and dirt, is intense and all-pervading. They look stout and sturdy, able to endure fatigue and anxious to fight in the cause they have exposed...(Pg. 169) Wednesday, September 10 "...The most liberal calculations could not give them more than 64,000 men. Over 3,000 negroes must be included in this number. These were clad in all kinds of uniforms, not only in cast-off or captured United States uniforms, but in coats with Southern buttons, State buttons etc. These were shabby, but not shabbier or seedier than those worn by white men in the rebel ranks. Most of the negroes had arms, rifles, muskets, sabres, bowie-knives, dirks, etc. They were supplied, in many instances, with knapsacks, haversacks, canteens etc., and were manifestly an integral portion of the Southern Confederacy Army....(Pg. 170) "...The men were mostly without knapsacks; some few carried blankets, and a tooth-brush was occaisionally seen pendant from the button-hole of a private soldier, whose reminiscences of home-life were not entirely eradicated..."

Were these "servants" dressed in the cast off uniforms of the Rebs or were they fighting soldiers? More research needs be done on this subject.

A GLORIOUS ARMY- Robert E. Lee's Triumph 1862-1863 by Jeffery D. Wert pub. by Simon & Schuster 2011

Pg.111 Sept. 7, 1862 "....The men are poorly provided with clothes. And in thousands of instancesare destitute of shoes..."We were in wretched plight," recalled a South Carolinian. "The men were simply exhausted; diarrhea and dysentery were rampant. Estimates put the number of sick and wounded who would have to be left behind as high as 5,000. Thousands of stragglers had left the ranks during the previous weks. Many were barefoot, with pieces of clothing serving as uniforms. When a Marylander saw them, he described them as "these bundles of rags, these cough-racked, diseased and starved men." Another Marylander, a young boy, watching them pass, said the Rebels "were the dirtiest men I ever saw, a most ragged, lean and hungry set of wolves."…"

WRITING & FIGHTING FROM THE ARMY OF NORTHERN VIRGINIA ed. by William B. Styple Belle Grove Pub. 2003

PG. 146 Letter From V.A.S.P. Near Frederick Md. Sept 7, 1862 (en route to Antietam) "… Here I witnessed a novel sight. Preparatory to wading the stream (at this ford four hundred yards wide and two and a half feet deep,) the army, officers and all, bared their legs and waded over! While every variety, color and style of coat could be seen, there was perfect uniformity in the lower dress! At a distance it was an amusing sight. (I would advise my lady friends to shut their eyes while they read this paragraph!)…Crossing those streams yesterday made our feet extremely sore, in consequence of which, many very many gave out. I suffered the keenest agonies from my swollen and blistered feet; but my pride kept me from falling out. I did not want to set my boys such a bad example…"

A TRUE HISTORY OF COMPANY I, 49TH REIGIMENT NORTH CAROLINA TROOPS by W.A.Day printed at the Enterprise Job Office 1893

Pg. 27 Sept. 7, 1862 "…We had nothing to do but to stand guard. One man in Company I, drew the shoulder blade of a beef for his ration, roasted and ate the meat, then kneaded his dough and baked his bread on the bone…"

Ingenious

HANDLEY LIBRARY ARCHIVES

James A. Miller Collection correspondence C.W. era misc. New Market, Va.

Sept. 7th, 1862 Dear Julia, If you have not made my over coat yet you need not make it until you hear from me. Perhaps I will be able to get one here I have sent to town for one and if I get one I won't need the one that you are making just keep it until you hear from me. We captured some clothing from the Yankees at Frederick…I think you had better had my coat, vest & pants made and keep them until we get settled. I want the buttons off that coat that I left at home put on this coat have them cleaned, black cuffs and collar, and a star on each side of the (?). Perhaps C. Spritzer can make the stars, use black cloth or if the goods are very fine they sometimes use black velvet. If you have not the over coat just leave it for the moment, and if it is made, keep it until you hear from me…"

LETTERS AND PAPERS OF AN ARTILLERY OFFICER A.N.V. IN THE WAR FOR SOUTHERN INDEPENDENCE 1861-1865 Capt. John Hampden Chamberlain-Virginian Dietz Printing Co. Pub. 1932

Pg. 104 Monocacy Junction, B&O R.R. 3 miles from Frederick City, same County, Md. September 8th, 1862 My dear Sister "…Now, it appears that our commanders have at last considered some rest necessary for the troops. It is certainly necessary, "if compatible with the public interest." A dirtier, more ragged exhausted set would be hard to find, the world over. To one who sees and knows the condition and privations of this army, their endurance and great deeds especially within the last month makes food for the extremest wonder. Upon the private soldier needless pity is often thrown away, but in this case too much admiration is hard to give them;…Clothing, hats, shoes, ammunition were successively wanting; but they charged with the shout and the steel and the day was theirs…"

These were tough men.

HANDLEY LIBRARY ARCHIVES, WINCHESTER, VA Letters of Henry Jennings Co. A 5th Regiment Viginia Volunteers Jackson's Brigade

Sept. 8th, 1862 Camp near Frederick City, Md. Dear Uncle,"…When I was in the city I bought a pair of boots for 6 dollars that would have cost 25 dollars in Richmond my clothes were very dirty and got clean ones here we left out knapsacks at Culpeper…"

I wonder if they ever saw those knapsacks again.

WEBSITE-55TH va.org/article 00001

Pg.1 Sept. 8, 1862 Pvt. William Rouzie, Co. F, 55th Va. he wrote to his sister: "…we took manassas [on August 27, 1862] and got just what we wanted. I got pants [i.e. sky blue kersey trousers], a nice oil cloth and various other things…" Union General G. H. Gordon who fought the Confederates at both 2nd Manassas and Sharpsburg: "From piles of new clothing the Southerners arrayed themselves in the blue uniforms of the Federals." Although Gordon implies the Confederates were taking coats as well as trousers at Manassas, it is perhaps signifigant that none of the Confederate accounts admit to doing so. Underwear and trousers wear out quickest and, initially, it was these the Rebels were interested in…" *& shoes, hats, socks & shirts.*

GRANDFATHER'S JOURNAL (Franklin Lafayette Riley) Company B Sixteenth Mississippi Infantry Volunteers Harris' Brigade Mahone's Division Hill's Cops, A.N.V. May 27, 1861-July 15, 1865 ed by Austin C. Dobbins pub by Morningside Press 1988

Pg. 103 Tuesday-Wednesday, Sept. 9-10, 1862 Camp near Middletown "…Passing through Frederick City, singing and with our band playing "The Girl I Left Behind Me", we frightened the onlookers with a loud Yell. We are a miserable looking sight. We are dirty, unshaven, tired; our clothes are smelly; toes gap from our shoes. Gen. Jackson, who wears homespun and an old slouch hat, looks just as bad…"

DIARY OF LEWIS H. STEINER A.D.F. Randolph 1862

Pg. 19 Sept. 10 "…The most liberal calculations could not give them more than 64,000 men. Over 3,000 negroes must be included in this number. These were clad in all kinds of uniforms, not only in cast-off or capture United States uniforms, but in coats with Southern buttons, State buttons, etc. These were shabby, but not shabbier or seedier than those worn by white men in the rebel ranks. Most of the negroes had arms, rifles, muskets, sabres, bowie-knives, dirks, etc. They were supplied, in many instances, with knapsacks, haversacks, canteens, etc., and were manifestly an integral portion of the Southern Confederacy Army. They were seen riding on horses and mules, driving wagons, riding on caissons, in ambulances, with the staff of generals, and promiscuously mixed up in the rebel horde. The fact was patent, and rather interesting when considered in connection with the horror the rebels express at the suggestion of black soldiers being employed for the National defense.…The movement to Frederick proved to be a failure. Their friends were anxious to get rid of them and of the penetrating ammoncial smell they brought with them…"

Has anyone done research on this and can tell us what precentage of the soldiers were African Americans? Why are there no accounts of them falling out through lack of shoes?

LEE'S LIEUTENANTS by Douglas Southhall Freeman Charles Pub by Schribner's & Sons volII

Pg. 200 At the capture of Harper's Ferry 1862 before Antietam "A newspaper correspondent got an even more unfavorable picture of Jackson "He was dressed in the coarsest kind of homespun, seedy and dirty at that, wore an old hat which any northern beggar would consider an insult to have offered him, and in general appearance was in no respect to be distinguished from the mongrel, bare-footed crew who followed his fortunes. I had heard much of the decayed appearance of the Rebel soldiers but such a looking crowd! Ireland in her worst straits could present no parallel, and yet they glory in their shame…"

Shame? You dirty Yankee dog, you shouldn't misspeak regarding your betters, yes, I said Betters!

THE CONFEDERATE VETERAN VOL. XXVI 1918

Pg. 259 June 1918 In The Years Of War by John C. Stiles compiled from "Official Records" Series III,Vol.II 1862-63 "Ragged Rebels-Governor Curtin, Of Pennsylvania, wrote McClellan on Sept. 10 (1862) saying: I have a letter from a clergyman in which he states that one of his elders traveled seven miles through the Rebel camps and found near Frederick not less than 120,000 men. The Rebels appeared to believe their whole army in Maryland would exceed 200,000 Their soldiers are running over the country, hunting something to eat, are ragged and filthy, but full of fight." He spoke a parable when he said they were "full of fight," and they were that way all the way through."

Yes, full of fight, but it would have been nice to have the 200,000 men accredited to them.

A SOUTHERN SOLDIERS LETTERS HOME-The Civil War Letters of Samuel Burney Cobb's Legion, Army of Northern Virginia ed by Nat Turnewr pub by Mercer Univ. Press 2002

Pg. 206 Sept. 12th, 1862 Winchester, Va. My Dearest Wife, "I left the valise with the shoes in Richmond with Charlie Baldwin. Tell Mrs. Fritz that I have carried Mr. Fritz's pants all the way so far and I hope to get them to him. I have delivered none of the letters to the boys because I have not got to them. I met some eight or ten sick ones going back to Rapidan & gave them theirs and they were very glad to get them."

WRITING & FIGHTING FROM THE ARMY OF NORTHERN VIRGINIA ed. by William B. Styple pub by Belle Grove Pub. 2003

Pg. 158 Private Letter, re: South Mountain, Sept.14, 1862 "...I had on a pair of old boots which were bursted to pieces. A rock got into the toe of one of them and hurt me so badly I had to stop to get it out..."

RECOLLECTIONS FROM 1861-1865 by John H. Lewis ex-Leiutenant in Huger's & R.H. Anderson's & Pickett's Division, Army of Northern Virginia pub. by Peak & Co. 1895

Pg. 55 Sept. 17th, 1862 "...The men of our army were as a general rule true as steel; but there were exceptions, as in the case that I shall relate. When crossing the Potomac, going to the field, one of the men, who was accustomed to being in the rear when a fight was in progress, and at the same time have a plauseable excuse for it, was on this occasion, as he said, nearly caught. He had crossed the canal, and to save his shoes, had taken them off. He had no idea of a fight at this point; but while washing his feet, preparatory to putting on his shoes, a gun in front gave notice of something wrong going on. He listened intently for further evidence of the situation, and hearing several guns in quick succession he deliberately threw his shoes into the canal, with the expression (alluding to the shoes), that you came very near getting me in trouble this time, and retired to the rear, giving as a excuse no shoes. To the reverse of this I have seen on the line of battle barefooted, with their feet bleeding, facing death in all forms of horror, and pleading no excuse to escape from what they felt to be their duty. There is no place better than a field of battle to test the higher qualities and nobility of man…"

I wonder how that first man could live with himself.

The Confederate Veteran-September-October 1992 Drab-The forgotten Confederate Color by Fred Adolphus

Pg. 38- Drab- The color of undyed wool Sept. 17, 1862 "Alfred R. ward, famous for his drawings for Harper's weekly, had this to say of the Viginia "Black Horse Cavalry" while he was detained behind Confederate lines: he noted that among the enlisted troopers, "… there was little else but homespun among them, light drab-gray or butternut color, the drab predominating…" and "Light jackets and trousers with black facings, and slouched hats, appeared to be …the court costume of the regiment."

THE CONFEDERATE VETERAN VOL. XXIX 1921

Pg. 133 April 1921 Sharpsburg by John N. Ware Sept 17, 1862 "…Strange-looking men they are, burned almost black, lean and long of face and frame, unbelievably dusty and dirty, clad, if you can call it clad, in fantastic rags, and shod, when they are shod at all, in absurd shoes, some with toes gone, others with soles tied on with strings or green withes (strips of green, pliable wood) …."

FROM HUNTSVILLE TO APPOMATTOX R.T. Coles History of 4th Regiment, Alabama Volunteer Infantry, C.S.A. Army of Northern Virginia ed b y Frank L. Bryne pub by Univ of Tenn Press 1996

Pg. 73 Sept 18, 1862 Letter form R.T. Coles to his Mother (Retreat from Antietam) "…Have endured many hardships, been hungry a great many times, had not changed my clothes for several weeks, as our baggage wagon was not with us after we left Richmond. Crossing a small creek in Maryland, General Hood was sitting on his horse on the bank of it to make us hurry across and blocking the column in our rear, one of the boys asked him when our wagons would be up that we were all so lousy and dirty as the dickens; General Hood said, "Step out, step out, and cross over, so am I." All the boys in hearing presented him with a lusty cheer- misery loves company, you know. The rest of the boys whose parents are not in the Yankee lines have been very kind to us. There is a company in the regiment from Tuskegee. Their good people sent us a large box of clothing before we left Richmond. Our former Adjutant, Joe Hardie, of whom I have so oiften written, whom I superseded, left us at Yorktown last May; has written me several kind letters. His mother, through him, sends a message to me to call on her for anything I need in the way of blankets, clothes, and so forth..."

THE CONFEDERACY IS ON HER WAY UP THE SPOUT Letters to South Carolina 1861-1865 ed. by J. Roderick Heller III and Carolynn Ayres Heller pub by Univ. of Georgia Press 1992

Sept. 17, 1862 Pg. 77 Antietam "A correspondent for the New York Herald reported the Texas Brigade's actions in Miller's cornfield as follows: "That those ragged, filthy, wretched, sick, hungry and in all ways miserable men...should prove such heroes in the fight, is past explanation. Men never fought better. There was one regiment...that stood up before the fire of two or three of our long range batteries and two regiments of infantry and though the air was focal with the whistle of bullets and the scream of shells there they stood and delivered their fire in perfect order..."

I'll say it again, more than mortal men.

THE HISTORY OF A BRIGADE OF SOUTH CAROLINIANS-KNOWN AS GREGGS by J.F.J. Caldwell pub by King & Baird1866

Pg.86 fall 1862 "It is difficult to describe the condition of the troops at this time, so great and various was their wretchedness. They were sunburnt, gaunt, ragged, scarcely at all shod, spectres and caricatures of their former selves. Since the beginning of August, they had been almost constantly on the march, they had been scorched by the sultriest sun of the year, they had been drenched with rain and the heavy dews peculiar to this latitude, they had lost much night rest, they had worn out their clothing and shoes, and received nothing but what they could pick up on the battlefield, they had thrown away their knapsacks and blankets, in order to travel light, they had fed on half-cooked dough, often raw bacon as well as raw beef, had devoured green corn and green apples, they had contracted diarrhea and disentery of the most malignant type, and, lastly, they were covered with vermin. They now stood, an emaciated, limping, ragged, filthy mass, whom no stranger to their valiant exploits could have believed capable of anything the least worthy.

Orders were published for instant and thorough ablution, and the men were marched,by squads and companies, to the Opequon. Clothing, or the sweaty, crawling rags we dignified with that appelation, was likewise looked after. But it availed little. Great numbers had to be sent to hospital, and those who remained were fretted half out of their lives with purging and lousing..."

THE HISTORY OF A BRIGADE OF SOUTH CAROLINIANS FIRST KNOWN AS "GREGGS AND SUBSEQUENTLY AS McGOWAN'S BRIGADE by J.F.J. Caldwell-lately an officer of Co. B 1st Regiment South Carolia Volunteers pub by Morningside Press 1866

Pg. 77 Sept. 17 1862 Antietam "...This was an exciting field to view. Far along in front of the Confederate army, on our left, we could see the blue lines of the Federals, moving to the attack over the smooth, round hills, marching in perfect order with banners flying and guns and bayonets glittering in the sun. Never, even in the regular armies of France and Austria, have I witnessed such accurate marching. And their appearance was greatly improved by their well-kept, loose blue uniform, which gave them a massive look, entirely unlike the tight, light-colored and variegated garb of the Confederates..."

TOO AFRAID TO CRY-MARYLAND Civilians in the Antietam Campaign by Katyleen A. Ernst pub by Stackpole Books1999

Pg. 160 Sept. 18, 1862 day after the Battle (Antietam), James Snyder returned to his home in town "...Inside he found "little heaps of dusty rags"-the discarded, filthy Confederate uniforms shucked by the soldiers who had exchanged them for the Snyder's boys clothes. James was astonished to find one of the offenders lying in bed, stark naked. Irate, James demanded, "What are you in bed in that condition for?" The soldier looked up at him almost pleadingly. "Young man," he replied, "I am here because I'm sick, and I didn't want to spoil the clean bed with my dirty clothes, so I took them off."

Well, at least he's considerate.

THE AMERICAN CIVIL WAR: AN ENGLISH VIEW The Writings of Field Marshal Viscount Wosely pub by Stackpole Books 2002

Pg. 29 Sept. 20 1862 After theBattle of Antietam, traveling down the Shenandoah Valley to visit at Gen. Lee's camp "...Every day during our journey to Wichester we passed batches of convalescents...It was extremely painful to see such numbers of weakley men struggling slowly home, many of them without boots or shoes, and all indifferently clad; but posts were established every seventeen miles along the road, containing commissariat supplies, for provisioning them....It was amusing to see "U.S." marked upon every wagon and almost all ambulance-carts which we passed. The North have not only clothed and equipped the millions of men whom they boast of having had at various times enrolled, but the also have similiarly supplied the Southern armies. Into whatever camp you go, you are sure to see tents, carts horses, and guns all marked with the "U.S." Officers have declared to me, that they have seen whole regiments go into action with smooth-bore muskets and without greatcoats, and known them in the evening to be well provided with everything-having changed their old muskets for rifles! The Northern troops have been so liberally supplied with all, and I may say, more than a soldier wants in the field, that they do not value their knapsacks or blankets and in actions invariably throw them away before they "skedaddle"; knowing that if they succeed by their swiftness in living to "fight another day," their Government will provide them with a new kit, rifle, and all. About two hundred Northern prisoners passed us during our journey, and it was curious to observe the difference between their costume and that of their escort; the prisoners being well clothed in the regular frock coat and light blue trousers, whilst their mounted guard wore every variety of attire-jackets or coats, it seemed to matter little to them; and, indeed, many rode along in their shirt-sleeves, as gay and happy as if they were decked with gold and the richest trappings..."

I have never heard of these provisioning posts, set up every 17 miles up the Valley, but he paints an accurate picture of the near reliance the Rebs had for Union supplies.

Pg. 37-38 "...It is now a very common thing to see men of large property serving as privates in the ranks, whilst the captains are in social positions their inferiors, being perhaps merely the sons of small farmers in the neighborhood of their own plantations. Many of these richly landed proprietors have been shoeless for weeks at a time; and a friend of mine who had seen Jacksons corps on the march informed me that a number of them had been pointed out to him marching contentedly along with some old tattered flannel shirt and a pair of Yankee uniform trousers for their only clothing, whilst their bare feet bled at almost every step they took..."

Pg. 38-39 "...The infantry accouterments are the same as those used in the Federal army; indeed I saw very few that had not been taken from the Northerners. Their cartridge-boxes resemble those which our sergeants used to wear, being nearly square, very thin, and only holding forty rounds. The interior arrangement of these boxes is far from convenient; for, having expended the twenty rounds in the upper division of the tin case, which fits closely inside, it has to be withdrawn altogether, and turned with the other side uppermost, to admit of your getting at the twenty rounds in the second compartment. To be obliged to do this in action would be troublesome; for I have tried the experiment, and found, even when at my ease, that itr was often difficult to extract the tin case, owing to the leather outside having shrunk from moisture. The belts are supposed to be black. I have no doubt that they were so when taken from their former owners, but blacking is such a scarce commodity in the Confederate States, that it is only at some few hotels even in Richmond you can have your shoes polished in the morning, and then not without paying extra for the luxury. In the division that I saw inspected, there was not a barefooted man on parade, those without shoes having remained in camp. Large supplies of shoes and boots reached Winchester during my stay there, and were immediately distributed amongst the men. Several thousand pairs of long boots, made in England, and of a similar pattern to those served out to our infantry in the Crimea, had alse been issued to the army since its return from Maryland... Several regiments were to a man clothed in the national uniform of gray cloth, whilst others presented a harlequin appearance, being dressed in every conceivable variety of coat, both as regards color and cut. Gray wideawake hats, looped up on one side, and having a small black feather, are the most general head-dress; But many wear the Yankee black hat or casquette of cloth. That which is most unmilitary in their general appearance, is the long hair worn alike by officers and men. They not only allow their locks to hang down the backs of their coats, but many pass them behind their ears as women do. Some, doubtless, are anxious of imitating the cavaliers of Charles I's time in dress and appearance, as I noticed many, particularly the mounted officers, copy their style as portrayed in Vandyke's pictures in every particular, the color of their clothing alone excepted. As the regiments marched past me, I remarked that, however slovenly the dress of the men of any particular company might be, their rifles were invariably in good serviceable order...."

Resupply by the government was not very ample or timely. The next two month's letters by the soldiers invariably mention raggedness nakedness and requests for clothing.

I had heard that the metal bin in the cartridge boxes was removed, and the cartridges dumped in. Most of the re-enactore I know also do this with theirblanks.

CONFEDERATE CAPTAIN UJANIRTIS ALLEN'S LETTERS TO HIS WIFE ed. by Kandall Allen and Keith S. Bohannon pub by La. State Univ. Press 1998

Pg. 163 Near Martinsburg Va. Sept. 21st, 1862 (after Sharpsburg) "...Ol F and Wm Cooley arrived on the nineteenth (19). They brought me the drawers and socks and more than all the ambrotype and you dear long letter...Have Bogart & Forbes cut my coat by the measure he took last winter. That was a little too small. I can get buttons for it. One pair of pants will be enough. I will accept the boots, recollect the legs large made of thick leather come to the knee. Sole remarkably thick,heels low. I want them for winter I have my shirts yet. I think I have enough shirts...."

LETTERS OF WILLIAM F. WAGNER, CONFEDERATE SOLDIER ed. by Joe M. Hatley and Linda B. Huffman pub, by Broadfoot's Bookmark 1983

Pg. 14 Charles Sitty Court House Va. September th 21st 1862…Dear Wife I send some of my Cloath back to the ole camp I send one pair of pants and one pair of drawers and one pair of socks the socks I send in a mistake the waggon that took them was a bout to leave before I knowed they was going to send cloah and I raped(wrapped) them in be fore I knowed it and still got too much to carry I aught to left some more I augh to leave my over coat yet or throw it away"…

KEEP ALL MY LETTERS The Civil War Letters of Richard Henry Brooks, 51st Ga. Infantry ed. by Katherine Holland pub by Mercer Univ. Press, Macon, Ga. 2003

Pg. 43 Furgerson Hospital Lynchburg Va. Sept.21th 1862 "…My Dear you wanted to know if I wanted a coat. Wife I need a coat very bad my old Brown one is nearly gone. I have Stitched it about so that I have kept it together yet an I can patch it some yet. I do not want you to try to send me a coat for I would never get it and it would be a final loss…"

RED CLAY TO RICHMOND by John J. Fox pub by Angle Valley Press 2006

Pg. 123 Sept. 22, 1862 "A South Carolinian described the condition of the men in the Light Division. "They were sunburnt, gaunt, ragged, scarcely at all shod, specters and caricatures of their former selves." He continued, "They now stood, an emaciated, limping, ragged, filthy mass, whom no stranger to their valiant exploits could have been believed capable of anything the least worthy."

The large quantity of captured supplies from Harper's Ferry helped Lee's army during this rebuilding period. These stores probably benefited Thomas' soldiers most because the Georgians hed remained behind at the captured town. They had time to pick and choose what they wanted. Goggans exhibited pride in his loot. "I am somewhat better situated for traveling than I have been in former times. Our mess has a horse and a little wagon which we carry along with us to hall our plunder in & I have me a very fine Yankee overcoat, hat and pants. A navy pistol and sword all setting up know (now)…"

THE STILLWELL LETTERS-A GEORGIAN IN LONG-STREET'S CORPS ARMY OF NORTHERN VIRGINIA ed. by Ronald H. Morely pub by Mercer Univ. Press 2002

Pg. 54 Sept. 22, 1862 "…Molly, I was never bothered as bad to know what to do in my life about my clothes. I will need then this winter but if we keep marching like we have been doing for some time I can't get them nor I could not carry them with me. So I reckon you had better hold for the present unless we get stationed somewhere. You may send my coat anyhow if you can but nothing else unless it is the pair of drawers and they are bad to keep clean of lice unless they can be boiled every week but send them along if you have a good chance with my coat. If I need the rest or get where I can take care of them I will try and let you know some way or other if I can...."(next morning)

"...Molly, I had like to forgot, if you send any of my clothes, try to send, if they can be had easy, me a pair of shoes no.7. I did want boots but as I have not drawn my money I can't pay for them and I don't want you to spend what little you have...."

GEORGIA BOYS WITH STONEWALL JACKSON by Aurelia Austin pub by Univ. of Georgia Press 1967

Pg. 46 September 22, 1862 from Winchester, Virginia Jeff Thompson "Dear Parents...If you Get this letter soon I wish you would take my cloath(e)s down to Monroe. Lieutenant Arnold is at home. If you Get to see him send mee 1 pair pants, 2 shirts, 2 par drawers, 2 or 3 par socks, 1 par shooes. Don't bother to send nothing else...I need cloths wors than anything else..."

LETTERS AND PAPERS OF AN ARTILLERY OFFICER A.N.V. IN THE WAR FOR SOUTHERN INDEPENDENCE 1861-1865 Capt. John Hampden Chamberlain-Virginian pub by Dietz Printing Co. Pub. 1932

Pg. 111 Hd. Qrs. Light Divn. Spt.22 1862 Camp Branch, 3 miles from Martins burg, Berkely Co. Va.

My dear Sister "...As for clothes, I am rather out at the elbows in the matter of shirts and boots, but can come by some one way or another. When in Maryland I was entirely too busy, one of the days too being Sunday, to try to make any purchases, & the stores were mostly closed. Else I should have obtained many things for all of you..."

A CAPTAIN'S WAR LETTERS AND DIARIES OF WILLIAM H.S. BURGWYN 1861-1865 ed. by Herbert M. Schiller White pub by Mane Pub Co. Inc. 1994

Pg. 22 Thirty-fith Regiment N.C. Troops Camp Near Martinsburg, Va. September 23rd, 1862 "....I have no more time to write more as I have written Mother and have got to write her some more as our quartermaster goes to Raleigh today to get clothing, guns, etc., etc., for the men."

"DEAR MOTHER: DON'T GRIEVE ABOUT ME. IF I GET KILLED, I'LL ONLY BE DEAD." ed. by Mills Lane pub by The Beehive Press 1977

Pg.189 D.B. Garden to Mrs. William McWorter General Hospital, Prince Edward County, Virginia September 24, 1862 Dear Madam: "God in his providence has seen fit to lay the hand of affliction heavily upon you. He who you so much loved is no more. You husband into this ward as a patient on July 11th suffering from chonic diarrhea which continued (not withstanding every possible attention both in the way of nursing and the administration of medicine) to pray upon his system until he became completely overcome of all strength and died on the evening of September 22nd, a little past midnight....

Appended we have a list of articles left by him which, according to the military laws, have been handed over to the quartermaster of this place, Captain Marye. I made an effort to send them on by a gentleman who will pass Athens, Georgia in a few days, but the Quartermaster said he did not have it in his power to grant my request and that the effects of soldiers who die here at the hospital had to be delivered over to him and that they were kept here subject to the orders of his nearest relative and if not called for at all then they were sold. I presume it is your desire to get his knapsack and content s home. An order from you will enable any one to get the knapsack from the quartermaster. A true copy of his effects: one portmanteau (?) and $5 in money, one knapsack, one haversack, one hairbrush, three shirts, two pair drawers, one blanket, one pair socks, one canteen, one pair boots, one hat, one pair gloves, one guardcap, two comfort(ers), one package letters, two needlecases, one daguerreotype, one testament, one hymn book, two toothbrushes, one knife, and one Masonic certificate. His knapsack has his name, company and regiment and list of effects posted on it. He is buried at the hospital buring ground near the place with head piece over his grave to designate his remains. The head piece also has his name in full and company and regiment to which he belongs. Respectfully yours..."

He was one well supplied Rebel soldier.

A SOUTHERN SOLDIER'S LETTERS HOME The Civil War Letters of Samuel Burney Cobb's Georgia Legion, Army of Northern Va. ed. by Nat Turner pub by Mercer Univ. Press, Macon Ga.2002

Pg 213 camp Near Martinsburg, Va. Sept. 24th, 1862 "... If you ever have a chance send me one or two cotton shirts, several pairs of woolen socks, a thick pair of drawers, a pair of pants & my overcoat. The shirts I left with Geo. Pierce I will hardly ever see again as he himself is absent and the shirts probably lost. My shoes are good yet, but I guess you better send them if you get a chance, as it may be some time before I get ones from Ray. I left an order with him to have me a pair made....Send me also that flannel vest...."

A CONFEDERATE SURGEON'S LETTERS TO HIS WIFE Spencer Glascow Welch, Surgeon Thirteenth South Carolina Volunteers, McGowans Brigade pub by Neale Pub. Co. 1911

Pg31 Charlestown, Jefferson Co. W. Va. September 24, 1862 I have not written to you in three or four weeks, because there has been no mail between us and Richmond. I have seen sights since then, I assure you. If I should tell you what our army has endured recently you could hardly believe it. Thousands of the men now have almost no clothes and no sign of a blanket nor any prospects of getting one, either. Thousands have had no shoes at all, and their feet are now entirely bare. Most of our marches were on graveled turnpike roads, which were very severe on the barefooted men and cut up their feet horribly. When the poor fellows could get rags they would tie them around their feet for protection. I have seen the men rob the dead of their shoes and clothing, but I cannot blame a man for doing a thing which is almost necessary to preserve his own life. I passed Groggan's body two days after he was killed at Manassas, and there the poor fellow lay, robbed like all the others (Do not say anything about this, for his family might hear of it.)

…"My brother was well when I last saw him. He and I have three flannel shirts between us, and I have some other very good clothes. I have but one pair of socks, and they are nearly worn out. I had a good pair, but some one stole them."

WELCOME THE HOUR OF CONFLICT-William Cowan McClellan & the 9th Alabama ed by John C. Carter pub by Univ Al. Press 2007

Pg. 181 Spt. 24 1862 Winchester, Va. William McClellan to Bobert McClellan Dear Bob, "…The enemy are reinforcing rapidly our army is almost broken down barefooted and ragged but they will fight as long as there is a pea in the dish.…Tell Mother to make a suit of cloths as soon as possible. I am needing them very bad 2 shirts, 2 pairs of drawers, jacket & Pants. No undershirts[;] Body Lice are too bad This is all I need. Some body Will have the kindness to Bring cloths to the poor boys of Limestone especially Mr. Phillips…"

FAR, FAR FROM HOME-The Wartime Letters of Dick and Tally Simpson, 3rd South Carolia Volunteers by Guy R. Everson & Edward W. Simpson Jr. pub. by Oxford Univ. Press 1994

Pg. 151 Sept. 24, 1862 TNS to ATS Camp Near Martinsburg, Va. Dear Sister, "Well, to my clothing. I want two or three pair of woolen socks, a strong pair of boots, a couple of shirts woolen, and a couple pair of woolen drawers, scarf, two hand kerchiefs, pair of woolen gloves, sleeping cap. I am without a blanket and oil cloth, they having been stolen from me the day of the fight after we had unslung knapsacks to enter the fight. Where are the blankets Mrs. Latta sent me? Send one of them I will draw one in a few days. You can make me an overcoat such a one as Buddies would recommend, but don't send it till I write for it as I may not be able to carry it. I shall not want any leggings if I get my boots. I am afraid my wants will tax you all too much..."

WEEP NOT FOR ME, DEAR MOTHER (Letters of Eli Pinson Landers from Gwinnett Co. Ga. The Flint Hill Grays. Eli was 19 years old when he enlisted in Aug. 1861) ed. by Elizabeth Whitley Roberson pub by Pelican Pub. Co. 1996

Pg. 88 from Martinsburg, Va. September 25, 1862 re: Antietam Campaign My Dear Respected Mother "...We lost all of our knapsacks and blankets. We have to lie round the fire of night...You wanted to know if I needed any clothes. If you can get them I would be glad of a suit of jeans for we are run around so much we can't keep nothing only what we have on our backs and one good suit would last me nearly all winter...."

WAR HISTORY OF THE OLD FIRST VIRGINIA REGIMENT, ARMY of NORTHERN VIRGINIA by Charles T. Loehr pub. by Wm. Ellis Jones Book & Job Printer 1884

Pg. 27 Sept. 1862 (near Martinsburg, Va.) "...Most of our men were shoeless and deficient in clothing, and rest was much needed.

On the 27th we marched to within three miles on Winchester (Va.), and camped at the Washington Spring for a month.

Here ended the campaign. The troops were often without rations; they were deficient in clothing, especially in shoes. Walking barefooted over the rocky roads was more than most of us were used to. It was a painful sight to see the bloody and blistered feet as the men moved wearily along, but however much they suffered, they managed to keep up..."

These were some tough men.

THE CIVIL WAR LETTERS OF GENERAL FRANK "BULL" PAXTON- A Leiutenant of Lee & Jackson ed. by John Gallatin pub by Hill College Press 1978

Pg. 20 Camp near Fairfax, C.H. Va. Sept 28, 1862 "...Jim Holly came this evening and tells me he has the pair of pants you sent me, and that Waltz will bring some more things for me. You need not get the overcoat; my coat for the present answers a very good purpose,. And if I find hereafter that I need an overcoat, I will send to Richmond for it ..."

HANDLEY LIBRARY ARCHIVES

James A. Miller Collection correspondence C.W. era misc. New Market, Va.

HdQrtrs 28th Va. Regt. Sept. 28th, 1862 Dear Julia, "...The last (letter) contained samples of the goods which you purchased for my clothes. I think it will suit very well...You wish to know about my overcoat I suppose you better send it if you have a good opportunity you had better have the vest made as I will need it as soon as the weather gets cold. I would prefer one that would button up to the neck but that wiil do. pants which I have are getting to have holes in them, and my boots are nearly gone...I saw W. Book the other day I told him to have me a pair of boots made but as there was a pair made for me in Winchester I will not need them..."

A SOUTHERN SOLDIER'S LETTERS HOME The Civil War Letters of Samuel Burney Cobb's Georgia Legion, Army of Northern Va. ed. by Nat Turner pub by Mercer Univ. Press, Macon Ga.2002

Pg216 Camp Georgia Legion, Near Winchester Va., Sept 30th, 1862 "...We must go somewhere to winter. I shall need some winter clothing. Get me some nice jeans and have me a suit made. My measure is in town at Jordan's tailor shop. Put me a side pocket in my coat, both inside & out. You can put those eagle buttons on my coat. Besides the suit will you please prepare me the following articles to be sent on by the first chance: a good warm vest, that Marseilles shirt, two pairs of drawers, two or three pairs of socks, the shoes I ordered to be made at Ray's, those buff handkerchiefs...."

WAR HISTORY OF THE OLD FIRST VIRGINIA REGIMENT, ARMY of NORTHERN VIRGINIA by Charles T. Loehr pub. by Wm. Ellis Jones Book & Job Printer 1884

Pg. 14 Sept. 30 "...During our stay at Fairfax Courthouse the city of Richmond furnished the whole regiment with new uniforms..."

DEAR IRVIE, DEAR LUCY-Civil War Letters of Capt. Irving A. Buck, General Cleburne's AAG & Family pub. by Buck Pub. Co. 2002

Pg. 99 Sept. 30,1862 Bel Aire, Front Royal, Va.(Lucy Buck) My Own Dear Brothers, (referring to return from Antietam) "...I never before appreceated the trials of a soldier's life, but during the last three weeks thousands of disabled and wounded have passed through town, nearly all of them poorly clad, and most of them weak, sick, and almost starved. It was pitiable to see how eagerly they begged for a little bread and milk-Always offering to pay for what they got when they had the money, though of course no one feels like taking anything from one so worn and battered in our country's service..."

SILK FLAGS AND COLD STEEL The Civil War in North Carolina: The Piedmont by William R. Trotter pub by John F. Blair, Pub.

Pg. 85 fall 1862 "...When a shortage of winter clothing loomed at the front, Vance appealed directly to the populace. Thousands of blankets, rugs, and overcoats were donated to the cause from all parts of the state..."

Here is the "Appeal" for clothing of any sort for the second year.

THE STONE WALL The Story of a Confederate Soldier by Brad Smiley pub by Zebra Communications, Woodstock, Ga. 1998

Pg. 175 Fall 1862, home on wounded furlough, his mother said"...Althea made you a pair of jeans, and Papa got you some brogans. Those clothes you're wearing can go straight to the trash. They're not even fit to be mended..."

Keep in mind he probably didn't look any worse than most of his comrades.

SILK FLAGS AND COLD STEEL The Civil War in North Carolina: The Piedmont by William R. Trotter pub by John F. Blair, Pub.

Pg. 86 Fall 1862 "...Vance established new plants, encouraged cottage-industry output by women and children, permitted his purchasing agents to offer attractive prices for suitable goods, and strove mightily-and mainly through the force of public proclamation and patriotic appeal-to keep the profit-hungry mills from gorging themselves beyond reason....To do all this, however, Vance had to fight a major paper-battle with the Confederate Bureaucracy. His main enemy was Abraham C. Meyers, a South Carolinian whom Jefferson Davis had appointed head of the Quartermaster Department. Their first clash concerned leather goods. With so many Confederate soldiers going barefoot, Vance argued, why not explore the possibility of making harnesses out of heavy-gauge cotton cloth and diverting all the tanneries' output to the manufacture of shoes?..."

That actually sounds like a good idea. They did something similar in the Trans-Mississippi.

DEFEND THE VALLEY Margarette Barton Colt Crown Pub. 1994

Pg. 186 Letter Of David W. Barton To Balley W. Barton With Postscript Of Fannie L. Barton-Winchester, fall 1862 "...I fear Genl. Smith will be disappointed in his cloth the army having impressed it as Mr. Gaver was making it. Gaver has no doubt written to the General explaining all. Mr. Russell gave one big promise to get the wool & I hope has attended to it…"

Pg. 191 "I hope General Smith's vigorous and perserveering efforts to secure the cloth will prove successful. He appealed to General Lee and his sergeant told me yesterday he expected to take back with him a load of cloth. My factory men are under military rule and cannot sell any exept to old customers…"

I can understand the army impressing all the cloth, it was needed so badly. The cadets could, I would think, make due with older, mended uniforms until the war was over.

LETTERS OF A NEW MARKET CADET Beverly Stanard ed. by John G. Barrett & Robert K. Tyrner Jr. pub by Univ. N.C. Press 1961

Pg. 2 fall 1862 "…Phil Hiden is trying to get a furlough to go down to Charlettsville to see his brother James Married. If he succeeds, he will come on to Orange, so that will be a good opportunity to send my box. Says he will bring it. I also want my pants that (dark brown) Bob gave me, sent. Repair them if they need it, before you send them …"

THE ANTIETAM CAMPAIGN Ed. By Gary W. Gallagher pub by Univ. of N.C. Press 1999

Pg. 124 Fall 1862 "North Caroline Governor Zebulon B.Vance proclaimed that his state would be unable to clothe and shoe its soldiers "without again appealing to that overflowing fountain of generous charity-the private contributions of our people." Vance declared that if every farmer tanning hides would spare one pair of shoes and every mother knit one strong pair of cotton or woolen socks, the army would be "abundantly supplied." Blankets were also in great need, and the governor urged their donation as well as carpet substitutes. If owners did not feel able to donate items, Vance assured them that "a liberal price will be paid for everything."

"Some white Southerners believed that the logistical crisis facing the Confederate armies in the fall of 1862 also called for sacrifices from the slave population. As one contributer to the Memphis "Appeal" argued "(T)here is no negro in the South who is not better off…than some of the best soldiers and first gentlemen in all the land." A planter in middle Georgia argued that slave owners "can well afford to let their negroes go barefooted for one season" in order to send shoes to the army. In a letter to the Montgomery Weekly Advertiser, "Lowndes" said that planters should give up a portion of their "negro cloth" and instruct their wives to dye it grey for army uniforms. Shoes, he continued, should only be given to slave men doing outdoor work. Slave women and girls could remain barefoot indoors spinning and weaving."

Here is the "Appeal" in more detail.

Pg. 127 fall 1862 "A soldier writing to the Columbia Daily Southern Guardian agreed, noting that although several thousand shoes had been distributed within his army corps by mid-October, there remained double that number of barefoot men."

"The Confederate Quartermaster Department's issuing of clothing to the army came in haphazard fashion, the garments often varing widely in quality. Sometimes the allotments were pathetically small; Colonel Warren of the 10th Virginia Infantry wrote that there were "not more than ½ doz. Pair of socks being sent to the regiment for distribution at one tIme." While some soldiers received garments from relief associations or families and friends, others, like Pvt. Eli P. Landers waited to draw government clothing since the revocation of the commutation system by the Confederate Congress to date from October 8, 1862. Landers told his mother that although soldiers paid a high price for government clothing, "it would be better to pay…for them here than to send some to me and I not get them."

Seems like there is slim pickin's clothing/shoe wise, no wonder the soldiers are writing home for clothes/shoes.

FROM CORSICANA TO APPOMATTOX by John Spencer pub by The Texas Press 1984

Pg. 47 In camp at Winchester, Va fall 1862 after the battle at Antietam. "…The Texans have been in constant movement since Eltham's Landing back in May, and they are glad to rest for awhile. Many of the men are now without shoes, and all of their uniforms are in rags. But with good rations and some new uniforms, they begin to look soldierly again…"

LETTERS AND PAPERS OF AN ARTILLERY OFFICER A.N.V. IN THE WAR FOR SOUTHERN INDEPENDENCE 1861-1865 Capt. John Hampden Chamberlain-Virginian pub by Dietz Printing Co. Pub. 1932

Pg. 116 fall 1862 "…I wrote to Dr. Bagby a hurried note, asking him to get from William Ferguson a suit of clothes or the cloth. Mother will furnish the money & I will remit to her when I draw. I cannot and will not stand the tailor's prices…"

STONEWALL by Byron Farwell pub by W.W. Norton and Co. N.Y. London

Pg. 421 A citizen of Hagerstown in Md., witnessing the passage of Confederate troops during the 1862 Md. Invasion wrote: "I have never seen a mass of such filthy, strong-smelling men. Three of them in a room would make it unbearable, and when marching in column along the street the smell was most offensive... They are the roughest set of creatures I ever saw... and the scratching they kept up gave warrant of vermin in abundance."

A unionist in Frederick wrote to a friend: I wish, my dear Minnie, you could have witnessed the transit of the Rebel army through our streets.... I could scarcely believe my eyes; was this body of men moving so smoothly along, with no order, their guns carried in every fashion, no two dressed alike, their officers hardly distinguishable from the privates-were these, I asked in amazement, were these dirty, lank, ugly specimens of humanity, with shocks of hair sticking through holes in their hats, and thick dust on their dirty faces, the men that had coped and countered successfully, and driven back again and again our splendid legions with their fine discipline....?

And then, too, I wish you could see how they behaved-a crowd of schoolboys on a holiday don't seem happier. They are on the broad grin all the time. Oh! They are so dirty!

They were very polite, I must confess...Many of them were bare-footed. Indeed, I felt sorry for the poor, misguided wretches, for some were limping along so painfully, trying to keep up with their comrades."

Pg. 296 The valley campaign after the capture of Bank's supply wagons. "Many of his (Jackson's) ragged troops had acquired Union uniforms to replace their worn-out clothes. Although Jackson himself often wore old parts of his old blue VMI uniforms, he warned the troops now that anyone caught in a Federal uniform would be treated as a prisoner of war, and he instructed Major Dabney to issue orders compelling them to give up all loot, reminding them that "all captured property belongs to the Government, and for individuals to appropriate it is theft."

MILITARY COLLECTOR AND HISTORIAN-Journal of the Company of Military Historians Vol. XLI Fall, 1989 Enlisted Uniforms of the Maryland Confederate Infantry: A Case Study, Part 1 by Ross M. Kimmel

Pg. 105 "...A Yankee who had been captured at Antietam (in which battle the 2nd Maryland did not participate) saw the unit at Winchester(Va). He was impressed; "each company, as it passed, gave us the military salute of shoulder arms." He went on to comment:

They were noticeable at that early stage of the war, as the only organization we saw that wore the Confederate regulation gray, all other [Confederate] troops having assumed a sort of revised regulation uniform of homespun butternut..."

WEBSITE BLUE AND GRAY MARCHING

Pg. 2 Oct. 1862 "…a recently paroled Union officer who had been captured after Antietam told the New York Times, "The Rebel troops are rapidly receiving their new uniforms, consisting of dark gray woolen jackets and light blue pants, etc…"

Finally, here is mention of government supply.

DEAR IRVIE, DEAR LUCY-Civil War letters of Capt. Irving A. Buck, General Cleburne's AAG & Family pub by Buck Pub Co. 2002

Pg. 100 Oct. 1862 Bel Aire, My Dear Alvin, (brother) "…the ink is so bad I can hardly make a mark. Would you and Irvie wear fine yarn socks? If so we will try and knit some we cannot get the cotton…" Lucy Buck

Pg. 106 Oct. 1862 Bel Aire My Dear Alvin, "…I wrote to you by Mr. _ and sent you some clothes which I hope you will get before this reaches you …" Elizabeth Ashby Buck (mother)

A GLORIOUS ARMY-ROBERT E. LEE'S TRIUMPH 1862-1863 by Jeffery D. Wert pub by Simon & Schuster 2011

Pg. 149 Oct. 1862 "In ragged uniforms and barefoot, the "skeleton regiments and brigades" of the Confederacy needed time for healing.

The wagon trains of supplies hauled critically needed shoes, undergarments, pants, coats and blankets. The men's letters and diaries at this time described their destitute condition: "Our army is almost without clothes"; "(We) are nearly naked and barefooted"; "We are a dirty, ragged set." At first the clothing items arrived "by degrees," but by mid-October the wagons brought 9,000 garments a week. The demand outstripped the supllies, however. One regiment dubbed their bivouac site "Barefooted Camp." Longstreet ordered beef hides sewn into shoes, which the men called "Longstreet's Moccasins." By November and the approach of cold weather many men still lacked shoes. Despite the shortages, the troops were, claimed one of them, "in very good spirits."…"

Resuppying the necessary clothing and shoes seems like an uphill battle.

THE SOUTH REPORTS THE CIVIL WAR by J. Cutler Andrews pub by Univ. of Pittsburgh Press 1985.

Pg. 217 A reporter for the Savannah Republican and the Mobile Register, Alexander, stated after the Antietem Campaign "The men must have clothing and shoes this winter. They must have something to cover themselves while sleeping, and to protect themselves from the driving sleet and from storms when on duty. This must be done, though our friends at home should have to wear cotton and sit by the fire. The army in Virginia stands guard this day, and will stand guard this winter over every hearthstone in the South. The ragged sentinel, who may pace his weary rounds this winter on the bleak spurs of the Blue Ridge, or along the frozen valley of the Shanendoah and the Rappahanock, will also be your sentinel, my friend at home... He suffers and toils and fights for you, too, brave-hearted women of the South. Will you not clothe his nakedness then? Will you not put shoes and stockings on his feet? Is it not enough that he has written down his patriotism in crimson characters along the battle-road from the Rappahanock to the Potomac, and must his bleeding feet also impress their mark of fidelity upon the snows of the coming winter? I know what our answer will be. God has spoken through the women of the South, and they are his holy oracles in this day of trial and tribulation..."

Flowery speech, but his point is well made.

THE COLONELS DIARY: JOURNALS KEPT BEFORE AND DURING THE CIVIL WAR BY THE LATE COLONEL OSCAR L. JACKSON, SOMETIME COMANDER OF THE 63RD REGIMENT O.V.I. David P. Jackson Privately Pub. 1922

Pg. 72 Oct. 1862 "...It seems to me that the fire of my company had cut down the head of the column that struck us as deep back as my company was long. As the smoke cleared away, there was apparently ten yards square of a mass of stuggling bodies and butternut clothes. Their column appeared to reel like a rope shaken at the end..."

LEE'S TAR HEELS -The Pettigrew-Kirkland-McRae Brigade by Earl J. Hess pub by Univ. of North Carolina Press 2002

Late Oct. 1862 stationed in N.C., "Adequately clothing them was another problem. Lt. R.R. Crawford was sent to Raleigh to round up supplies. All the clothing due the brigade, except overcoats, was on its way by late October, along with 300 pairs of shoes for each regiment. Crawford suggested to Pettigrew contract directly with private manufacturers for more shoes, as they would be of much better quality than those issued by the government..."

These men are not even with the main armies and still cannot get adequate clothing and shoes.

WEEP NOT FOR ME, DEAR MOTHER (Letters of Eli Pinson Landers from Gwinnett Co. Ga. The Flint Hill Grays. Eli was 19 years old when he enlisted in Aug. 1861) ed. by Elizabeth Whitley Roberson pub by Pelican Pub. Co. 1996

Pg. 89 Eli to his mother, Oct. 1862 "…If you get a good chance to send me any clothes I will pay the man who brings them for his trouble. If you don't have a good opportunity I will try to make out without them though I am like a terrapan. All I have got is on my back and that is dirty and common but I am as well fixed as most of the boys. I lost my blanket in the fight of the 17th and lay out on the ground till the other day when I bought me a blanket and a small tent which cost me $5.00…"

A SCYTHE OF FIRE-THE CIVIL WAR STORY OF THE EIGHTH GEORGIA INFANTRY REGIMENT by Warren Wilkinson & Steven E. Woodworth pub by William Morrow Pub. 2002

Pg. 190 Oct. 1862 "…Dwinnell had to admit that in many ways, "the sight of the 'old Eighth' is now saddening." Aside from the regiment's scant numbers, its ranks presented a distinctly ragged appearance. The soldiers' clothes were "much the worse for wear," wrote Dwinnell, poor ghosts of the finery they had worn to Richmond seventeen months before. The men were also in desperate need of new shoes. "We are getting a little clothing and a few pairs of shoes," Dwinnell noted in early October," one pair of shoes to a company at a time, and perhaps one suit of clothes." At this rate, he added, it would be a very long time before the army was sufficiently clad or shod…"

This rate of supply would be funny if it weren't so serious. Were supplies so scarce as to cause this trickle?

CIVIL WAR MEMOIRS OF TWO REBEL SISTERS ed.by William D. Wintz Pictorial History Pub. Co. 1989 Victoria Hansford-Kanawha Valley, Western Va., Coalsmouth, now St. Albans, W.Va.

Pg. 40 Oct. 1862 "The Yankees were always interrogating the Negroes. Most of them were true and steadfast, but a few would let out little things that could get us in trouble. However, our colored people never in any way caused the Yanks to bother us, as long as they were with us.

Now and then "Peter Slick" or "Claw Hammer" would stage a raid in our neighborhood against the Yankees. They were two partisan ranger leaders who often made their appearances in the most unexpected places, remaining only an hour or two at any one place.

Some of the ladies would give them a small bag of salt which they could hang on their saddles when they appeared in their neighborhood-they always needed salt. Sometimes we would give them shirts, socks, and other clothing when we got the chance. Oh, I remember toward the end of the war when the South became so poor. Our dear soldiers were fighting for us almost ragged and always hungry. We did all we possibly could for them and we all hoped on and they fought on…"

Footnote: "the night raiders that Victoria wrote about were part of the Confederate resistence forces that operated behind the Union lines during the latter part of the war.

Captain Peter M. Carpenter, alias "Peter Slock," lived in Coalsmouth. He commanded an unattached company of local insurgents who operated mainly between Kanawha and Big Sandy Rivers. In 1864 the company was accepted into confederate service as part of Swan's Battalion Virginia Cavalry.

"Claw Hammer was the by-name of Colonel Vincent A. Witcher, commander of the 34th, Battalion Virginia Cavalry. He had established a reputation as a daring "behind the lines raider."

There needs to be more research dsone on these two Kanawha Valley partisans.

FOOTPRINTS OF A REGIMENT A Recollection of the 1st Georgia Regulars by W.H. Andrews pub by Longstreet Press Atlanta Ga. 1992

Pg. 91 After Antietam, Oct. 1862 around Luray, Va. "...At the same time numbers of them were barefooted and almost destitute of clothing, the rags on their backs being all they have, having lost their baggage in Maryland. It seems strange that the government can't furnish shoes to its soldiers when that need them so badly..."

The only answer I can give is that the Government Quartermaster Department was badly overwhelmed by the demand.

"DEAR MOTHER: DON'T GRIEVE ABOUT ME. IF I GET KILLED, I'LL ONLY BE DEAD." ed. by Mills Lane pub by The Beehive Press 1977

Pg. 193 Edgar Richardson to his Mother Goosetown Virginia October 1, 1862 Dear Mother: reteat from Antietam "...I have not read a letter from home since we left Hanover Junction, the letter that Hope brought me. And I thought I was going to have a fine time over the nice things you sent me, but I was disappointed, for the trunk was lost and I have not heard of it since. I never was so sorry of anything in my life. You also wrote that you sent me two shirts in a box expressed to John Hughes. It is in Richmond, and we have never had any chance to get it. I have made out tolerable well without them, as I had two. But I think if I don't get them soon I will be pretty ragged.

We draw a uniform, blanket, shirts, drawers, socks, shoes, hat in a few days, and I will feel like a new man when I get them. Mother, you wrote me a good while ago that you had started a hat to me. I wish the next letter you write you would let me know who you sent it by, as I have never heard anything from it..."

I wonder if, when, and how much uniform resupply he was able to draw.

THE STILLWELL LETTERS-A GEORGIAN IN LONG-STREET'S CORPS ARMY OF NORTHERN VIRGINIA ed. by Ronald H. Morely pub by Mercer Univ. Press 2002

Pg. 60 Camp near Winchester W(estern) Va. Oct. 1, 1862 (after Antietam) My Dear Molly "…I think we will remain here or hereabout until we get all of our sick and wounded off and then go back in the direction of Richmond. My reasons are our army is almost without clothes. Many of them barefooted and none of them have more than one suit hardly and this country is already eat out of everything almost that an army wants. We can't get provision nor clothing, and taking all things together (with) the coldness of the climate of the country, I don't think it would be best to stay here this winter…."

LETTERS OF WILLIAM F. WAGNER, CONFEDERATE SOLDIERed. By Joe M. Hatley and Linda B. Huffman pub, by Broadfoot's Bookmark 1983

Pg. 16 Camp Salisbury Oct. the 3rd 1862…"Dear Wife I wrote in that letter last Sunday a bout sending me a wollin shirt and a pair of gloves if you have any wool to spare send me the gloves any how If I don't git a shirt it don't make much difference If I cant send some of my cloath home I cant carritt them no how I got too much to take"…

SOJOURNS OF A PATRIOT The Field and Prison Papers of An Unreconsrtu8cted Confederate edited with commentary by Richard Bender Abell & Fay Adamson Gecik Southern heritage Press 1998 letters of Pvt. Augustus Pitt Adamson

Pg. 89 Camp 30th Ga. Vols. Oct. 3rd, 1862 Dear Sister, "…I got the coat that Ma sent by T.A. Ward; it fits me well…"

HAM CHAMBERLAYNE-VIRGINIAN Letters and Papers of an Artillery Officer in the War for Independence 1861-1865 with introduction, notes and index by his son C.G.Chamberlayne Richmond, Va. pub by Press of the Dietz Printing Co. Publishers 1932

Pg. 115 J.H. Chamberlayne to L.P. Chamberlayne Camp at Bunker Hill, 12 mile from Winchester Oct. 3rd, 1862 "…I wrote to Dr. Bagby a hurried note, asking him to get from William Ferguson a suit of clothes or the cloth. Mother will furnish the money & I will remit to her when I draw. I cannot and will not stand the tailor's prices…"

THE CONFEDERATE VETERAN VOL. IV 1896

July 1896 Pg. 220 Letter from J.B. Polly to "Charming Nellie" Oct. 3, 1862 Second Manassas-"…the anecdote I have just told you is a darker shadow than usual; so let me lighten it by another: Jim Ferris, of the Fifth Texas, found himself at Second Manassas in a dilapidated condition externally. The legs of his pants lacked several inches of the proper length, and in the absence of a pair of socks his ankles were lacerated and bleeding. While running wild with his regiment when it "slipped the bridle" on the 30th, it occurred to him that he might readily supply deficiencies in his wardrobe by administrering on the estate of a dead Yankee. A pair of leggings to button around the calves of his legs would answer the purpose admirably.

Being a very large man himself, only the body of a large man could be depended upon to supply Jim's need; and in the search for such a one he wandered to and fro over the silent field of the deaduntil, awed by his surroundings, cold chills began to run down his back at the least noise; and he expected every minute to encounter a ghost. Finally he found a corpse of apparently suitable size, and hastily turning back from its legsthe oilcloth which covered it from head to foot, began with no gentle hand to unbutton aleggin. At the first jerk the supposed deadest of all the many dead flung the oilcloth from his head, and, rising to a sitting posture, exclaimed: "Great God alive, man! Don't rob me before I am dead, if you please!" In horrified amazement, Jim sprang twenty feet at one bound; but, knowing no ghost could speak so sensibly, natural politeness prompted an instant apology. "Indeed Mr. Yankee," said he, in the most gentle and whinig tone that he could assume, "I hadn't the least idea you were alive, or I never would have been guilty of the discourtesy of distresseing you. Please pardon me and let me know what I can do to make amends for my rudeness." "I would like to have a drink of water," Said the revived corpse. "Take my canteen sir," rejoined Jim, instantly offering it, "and please oblige me by keeping it; I can easily get another."

After this experience, Jim decided that, rather than risk waking another corpse, he would do without leggings; but on his way to camp he came across a stalwart form lying at full length upon the ground, and at the very first glance saw that here could be obtained the needed leggings. No mistake must be made, though; and so, laying his hand on the shoulder of the Yankee, he gave it a shake and asked, "Say, mister, are you dead or alive?" There was no response and next morning Jim Ferris strutted about the camp in a magnificent pair of linen leggins."

CONFEDERATE CAPT. UJANERTUS ALLENM'S LETTERS TO HIS WIFE ed. by Randall Allen & Keith S. Bohannon pub by La. State Univ. Press 1998 "Campaining With "Old Stonewall"

Pg. 170 Near Bunker Hill, Va. October 4th, 1862 Dear Susie, "…My fatigue (jacket) had become quite soiled and the gilt bars corroded, and the other day while passing a sentinel he says "halt! Halt!! Thare you fellow." Surprised, I asked what was the matter. "go back over this line, go back sir. Nobody is allowed to pass but commissioned officers." I bawled out rather angrily, "Well, ain't I a commissioned officer?" he scrutinized me closely from head to foot and said apologetically, "You may be, but you don't look much like one." This was a crusher to me and the next minute found me hunting the wagons and my trunk.

You spoke in your letter about Boykin or someone else coming to bring clothes for the boys. They should not come until we get somewhat stationary, and get transportation for them to the regiment..."

Pg. 172 Near Bunker Hill, Va. October 13th, 1862 My Dear Susie "...Thare is another phrase that some mischevious fellows use when they hear a shot or shell; "Hide out chidren, your dad is coming home drunk...."

The last few days have been rather chilly here. We are in a poor fix for winter. Quite a quantity of clothing has been sent to this brigade, but it is not very warm. Our regiment has had a suit of Columbus jeans put up but it has not arrived yet. What the boys get from home will not be a burden to them....We have a fine time doing nothing but eat bread and beef. We can make a Georgia cook ashamed of herself cooking beef. This is a fact; our boys excel in this. A soldier can live tolerably well and make himself comfortable where a civilian would starve and die. He is at home, with his canteen and haversack well stored. If night overtakes him he stops makes a cup of coffee and broils a bit of bacon, or perhaps he has an apple, a few beans, a young pumpkin or roastinear; stews them in his cup and with the aid of a little pepper and salt stored away as carefully as if it were gold; makes a good repast for a hungry man; rolls up in his blanket lord of all he serveys sleeps soundly and dreams of home. Did you ever see a picture called the soldier's dream? I have seen it somewhere, possibly in an old magazine. The artist had certainly seen life in camps and had a wife and baby..."

Pg. 178 October 30th, 1862 My Dear Susie "...We have just drawn a new suit of clothes for the men or for those that are present. I regret that so few of the company (about 30) are here. How do the friends of the company intend to send clothing to the boys. They must not send anything at the present for we are moving so much that the boye would be compelled to throw away what they did not wear. The Quartermaster will furnish transportation for all things sent to the boys if any one should come along. The "Georgia Relief and Hospital Association" is a good medium through which to send clothing to the soldiers. You spoke of sending me a coat. Don't be too hasty about it at present. One thing we can not get; shoes. Many of the men are barefooted...."

Still not enough shoes.

LETTERS AND PAPERS OF AN ARTILLERY OFFICER A.N.V. IN THE WAR FOR SOUTHERN INDEPENDENCE 1861-1865 Capt. John Hampden Chamberlain-Virginian pub by Dietz Printing Co. Pub. 1932

Pg. 119 Camp at Bunker Hill Va. Oct. 4 1862 Dear Sister "…I wrote you a note the other day about getting me some cloth for a uniform; I hope 'tis not too much trouble…"

THE CIVIL WAR LETTERS OF GENERAL FRANK "BULL" PAXTON A Lieutenant of Lee & Jackson ed. by John Gallatan Paxton Hill Jr. pub by College Press 1978

Pg. 57 Bunker Hill, Va. October 5, 1862 "…I fear our troops are to suffer much from want of clothing, and that our supplies will prove greatly inadequate for our wants…"

It surely seems so.

GEORGIA BOYS WITH STONEWALL JACKSON by Aurelia Austin pub by Univ. of Georgia Press 1967

Pg. 55 James Thompson, Camp near Winchester, Va. October the 5th, 1862 "You wanted to know if I was under "Stone Wall" or not. I am. He is a sorry looking chance. He is a little old drid (dried) up looking man (who) puts mee more in the mind of Arter Leetch in his life time than anybody else, only he is an older man…You said you was afraid that I was bare footed on some of thes long marches. I have got good shoes. I Got them from Lieut. Burson the day before wee left Richmond. He had an extry pair he let mee have or I should have been bare footed. Thir is plenty of lawyers and Doctors heare bare footed and nearly necked that used to ware broad cloth…"

A SOUTHERN SOLDIERS LETTERS HOME-The Civil War Letters of Samuel Burney, Cobb's Legion, Army of Northern Virginia ed by Nat Turner pub by Mercer Univ. Press, 2002

Pg. 220 Oct. 5th, 1862 [Camp Tom] Camp Ga. Legion Near Wichester, Va. My Dearest Wife, "…There is no use for money here much- the country is about eaten out. The boys are all out of money; some are half-naked, many are without shoes & they look pretty bad…. Tell Pa to send me a suit of clothing, two pairs of warm drawers, two shirts (cotton), several pair socks (woolen), my shoes, a towel or two, & some soap. Get some gold lace and sew one little strip of it on my coat collar, right under my ear or where my ear will be when the coat is on. Mrs. Frits will show you where to put it. Pa & Ma will assist you in fixing up these articles for me, and Pa will get them off for me."

VMI

Oct. 5 1862 Dear Ma "…I recd. The cloth safely. Also Skates cap cover & apples for which I am very much obliged. Gen. Smith told me yesterday morning that he thought he could get cloth in 2 or 3 weeks but he would not have enough to give the cadets overcoats only jackets & pants. If so I will keep the fine and only use the coarse for an overcoat & if he gives me jacket & pants I will send the other back. You say in your letter you send both cap covers, I recd. only one. Please send the other for this one does not suit the cap & I can easily see it.

Pa says in his letter "as to your freezing on post at night it seems to me the woolen clothes you carried ought to protect you." I never brought any woolen clothes with me. The only woolen thing I brought was my cloth coat and that I put in the arsenal soon after I came here & there were about 75 trunks on top of mine but I went in yesterday & got some boys to help me & got my coat out. White, one of my roommates has bought a very good overcoat which I can wear at night, it keeps me quite comfortable. I think I can get along as far as clothes are concerned…"

HADLEY LIBRARY ARCHIVES

James A. Miller Collection correspondence C.W. era misc. New Market, Va.

Oct. 7th, 1862 Dear Julia, I received all the things that you sent in good order. The pants fit very well, and the coat and over coat and vest is rather too full breasted but will do very well. I am very much pleased with the suit,

And all who have seen it say that is very nice, it is most too nice to wear in camp. I have not worn it yet. I have been waiting for it to rain so as to settle the dust, we are almost suffocated with the dust, it has been very dry in this county. You anticipated my wants better than I myself, I never thought about a cravat until you wrote and then I looked at mine and it beginning to wear, my watch guard is getting rather flimsy and won't last much longer. The stars on my coat collar please me very well. I was very glad that you sent me the drawers, as I only had two pairs on hand now I have four so I can change oftener when we are moving, the socks will come in very well as what I have on hand are getting rather much worn, I used the last of the thread for darning socks which you put in my housewife this morning. The sheets are very good I tried to get several in Frederick city but could not succeed.

I still have my two towels which I brought from home, I will keep the one that you sent me until I need it. The soap is also very fine I will use it to wash my clothes with. I got several pounds of (?) soap in Maryland. I received the boots also they are very good and I am very well pleased with them, my old ones were nearly gone they will do for dry weather a while yet…I had just one pair of pants on hand when I received the pair from you, and that had a hole in the seat which needed patching. I will try and patch it before long. I had gotten rather hard looking with my old suit, but when I get my new ones on I will then turn over a new leaf…"

Frank Miller was a Dr. with the army, an officer, and still had to struggle for clothes.

THE SOUTH REPORTS THE CIVIL WAR by J. Cutler Andrews pub by Univ. of Pittsburgh Press 1985.

Pg218 In Oct. 8, 1862, Alexander told of seeing Rhodes Alabama Brigade pass through Richmond on August 19, 1862 "…it was there that I saw for the first time a barefooted Confederate soldier."

Where the hell had this man been for the last year?

THE CONFEDERATE LETTERS OF BENJAMIN H. FREE-MAN Compiled & Edited by Stuart T. Wright pub by Exposition Press 1974

Pg. 13 Oct. 18 1862 Camp French (Va) Dear Farther: "…Captain Lawrence says he could not bring Those…things you sent. I shall draw (some) in a few days I expect. If I do not I will (write) to you for them and you can send them by some one. I am sorry he did not bring them. Ma I would have been glad to get that Ginger to cure my Belly…"

HAM CHAMBERLAYNE-VIRGINIAN Letters and Papers of an Artillery Officer in the War for Independence 1861-1865 with introduction, notes and index by his son C.G.Chamberlayne Richmond, Va. pub by Press of the Dietz Printing Co. Publishers 1932

Pg. 122 J.H. Chamberlayne to M.B. Chamberlyne October 9th, 1862 "…I earnestly hope that you have not bought me a uniform suit from the tailors; I tell you I cannot afford it. All I will need at all is the jacket, shirts, socks, & tobacco. Upon any good opportunity I would be glad for you to get from Wm. Bentley material for the coat and pr. of pants. For a long time to come I will be sufficiently served by the pr. of pants I now wear. They do not at all need mending as you seem to suppose…"

LETTERS AND PAPERS OF AN ARTILLERY OFFICER A.N.V. IN THE WAR FOR SOUTHERN INDEPENDENCE 1861-1865 Capt. John Hampden Chamberlain-Virginian pub by Dietz Printing Co. Pub. 1932

Pg. 120 Hd. Qrs. Art. Corps Camp near Bunker Hill Va. Oct. 9 1862 My dear Mother "… About the clothes; please do not distress yourself, I got a good hat at Frederick City, will get a pair of boots in a day or two, they have been ordered & promised me. I need principally socks and a couple of outside flannel shirts. About a coat I am not at all anxious, don't be in hurry about it. The Jacket I think will fit me as it is, merely have a pair of bars put on each side of the collar, and an edging of gold braid to the cord on the sleeve (so). The jacket is exactly what I want. Please have two pockets inserted in it. 3 Pr. socks, 2 flannel shirts, jacket, and tobacco is all I want and there is no urgent need of them. My coat is somewhat soiled and worn, but, I assure you my that (hat?) and my outfit generally do very well. That old hat, indeed, had grown rather seedy before I gave it up, but it has been more than a month since I left it off…Don't be anxious about my clothes; and don't send the things up but by someone who will come direct to this division…"

LETTERS OF WILLIAM F. WAGNER CONFEDERATE SOLDIER ed. by Joe M. Hatley and Linda B. Huffman pub, by Broadfoot's Bookmark 1983

Pg. 18 Camp near Richmond Va. Oct. 10th 1862 "You can send that gallen jug I had at Salisbury and some little things to Eat if you can Dear Wife a bout that shirt you stated that you would make and send it as soon as you could git the cloath Dear Wife I can informe you not to make it unless I can send some of my cloath home for I got too much to carry If I could send a pair of pants and drawers home don't make the shirt unless them cloath comes home"…"

HANDLEY LIBRARY ARCHIVES-Letters of John H. Stone, 1st Lt. Co.B, Maryland Infantry

Pg. 11 Oct. 10, 1862 "for several days we have had much rain which causes much annoyance in the way of wet clothes. Many of the men are destitute of blankets and tents. Consequently, they are much exposed in inclement weather. I expect to go to Richmond in a few days to provide such things as we need. Provisions are scarce around Winchester. Yesterday a lady presented us with a fine lot of sweet meats, and it is needless to say we enjoyed them.

General Longstreet's Corps has just passed through Winchester in a drenching rain storm. Poor fellows they are to be pittied [sic], wet to the skin and no change of clothes, but such is the fortuned of a soldier. Man that is born of woman and enlists in Jackson's army, has but few days to live, short rations and much hardtack, sleeps but little and marches many miles."

The extreeme joys of a soldier's life.

HAM CHAMBERLAYNE-VIRGINIAN Letters and Papers of an Artillery Officer in the War for Independence 1861-1865 with introduction, notes and index by his son C.G.Chamberlayne Richmond, Va. pub by Press of the Dietz Printing Co. Publishers 1932

Pg. 124 October 11, 1862 J.H.Chamberlayne to M.B. Chamberlayne "…I repeat, for goodness' sake don't but me a suit from the tailor's, wait as long as you please till the Qr. Mr.

gets cloth; then material for a uniform coat& overcoat & pr. of pants I would be glad to get; meanwhile I shall do well with the jacket, socks, shirts and tobacco. And for them I am in no hurry….My present outfit does very well; I shall get boots in a few days, and a hat I have, a good & pretty one…"

FIERY DAWN Civil War Battle at Monroe's Crossroads North Carolina Sharon Kane and Richard Keeton http://www.nps.gov/seac/fierydawn.ch1b.html

1862 "Before dawn, October 11, the Confederate cavalry assembled in down town Chambersburg., then ransacked the Union Army depot for overcoats, pants, hats, underwear, woolen socks, rifles, sabers, and pistols, as much as they could carry. Ajounalist reported, "The whole town was converted into one vast dressing room. On every hotel porch, at every corner, on the greater portion of the street doorsteps, might be seen Rebel cavalry donning Yankee uniforms, and throwing their own worn out and faded garments into the street." …"Heavy fog concealed the Confederates' movements in the early hours of their ride. Many wore the stolen clothes of their foes, including Union blue overcoats…." Sunday, Oct. 12,1862 "Many of the troopers still wore Union overcoats, which served dual purposes of staving off the morning chill and providing disguise…"

One of the good uses of captured blue uniforms.

WRITING & FIGHTING THE CONFEDERATE WAR The Letters of Peter Wellington Alexander ed by William B. Styple pub by Belle Grove Pub. Co. 2002

Pg.111 What the Government has done and is doing for the Sick, Wounded, and Destitute Soldiers Winchester, Va. October 12, 1862 "Nearly two weeks after the Battle of Sherpsburg, two young gentlemen, of irreproachable moustaches, were introduced into my room at a hotel in this place by the landlady, who informed me that they would be my room-mates for the present. It appeared from their conversation that they had just arrived from Richmond-that they had been acting in the capacity of assistant surgeons there for nearly a year, and that they had been dispatched to Winchester to assist in taking care of the wounded in the battle of Sharpsburg. Two questions of much magnitude occupied their attentions for half an hour or more-to wit: 1st, whether they should report to the surgeon in person or by note; 2nd, whether, in the event they reported in person, they should "dress up" or go as they were. They finally decided to dress first, and then send up their report in writing. The consideration which brought them to this conclusion arose from the fact that they were without paper, and the idea of going into the street to purchase a supply in their present plight, could not be entertained for a moment. Nearly two hours were devoted to their toilet. After washing and scrubbing ever so long, their hair and moustaches had to be carefully cleaned and oiled, their uniforms, covered all over with gold lace, neatly dusted, and their boots duly polished. One of them put on a ruffled calico shirt with a large diamond pin and immense gold studs, a pair of white linen pantaloons, and a handsome black cloth coat made up in the extreme military style. He first thought he would wear a pair of gaiter shoes, but on consulting "Jim" (his companion) it was finally agreed that boots would become the set of his pants better. So he put on the boots. Having finished their elaborate toilets and started out of the room, the following laconic dialogue ensued:

Boots-"I say, Jim, don't you think we had better take a drop before going out?"
Jim-"Yes, I do think we had. I feel rather shaky after last night's affair.".

"…you are ready to enquire, of what use can such dainty gentry in a dirty hospital filled with stern sufferer-men with broken bones and gastly wounds, whose bodies are covered with filthy rags and alive with vermin-with nothing to lie upon but a little straw, and the air they breathe poisoned by exhalations from the festering wounds and feverish bodies around them…"

Seriously, I wonder, along with the writer, whether these two were a help or a hazard? How long do you suppose they lasted at that hospital?

CLASH OF SABRES-BLUE AND GRAY Col. Walbrook D. Swank, USAF Ret. Avonelle Asso. Ltd 1981—Thomas S. Davis Henrico Light Dragoons- 1st Regiment of Va. Vols.

Pg. 50 Oct. 12th, 1862 Chambersburg Raid "…on the12th the men arrived at Hagerstown… The men were busy mending the threadbare rags that they wore for clothing…"

Pg. 70 after the Chambersburg Raid, "…The rigors of the campaign had taken its toll among the troops. The men were in dire need of shoes and clothing and nearly half of the cavalry was ineffective because of lack of horseshoes…"

LETTERS OF WILLIAM F. WAGNER, CONFEDERATE SOLDIER ed. By Joe M. Hatley and Linda B. Huffman pub, by Broadfoot's Bookmark 1983

Pg. 20 Camp near Richmond Va. Oct. 13th 1862 …"Dear Wife I had stated in my last letter that you shouldn't make that shirt intil I would send some of my cloath home Dear Wife I took a notion I wouldn't send any home it is gitting cole now and I can ware two pair at once and Lemiel would take a pair if I would sell them and I don't know when we draw a gain just make the shirt and send it if you can Dear Wife"…

VOICES FROM COMPANY D Diaries by the Greensboro Guards, Fifth Alabama Infantry Regiment, Army of Northern Virginia ed. By G. Ward Hubbs pub by Univ. of Georgia Press 2003

Pg.113 October 13, 1862 SP "...Jamie & I went to Greensboro & made arrangements with Mr. Harry Johnson for leather from his private tan-yard to make into shoes, for our Negroes. We let him have a Spinning Jenny valued at $225.00 & he is to pay for it in leather. Sole leather is at $1.00 per lb., and Sides at an average of $5.00. It will not be enough but it is all we can get. Mr. J. says he has been offered $4.00 per lb. for it..."

HANDLEY LIBRARY ARCHIVES-James A. Miller Collection correspondence C.W. era misc. New Market, Va.

25th Va. Regt. Camp near Bunker Hill Oct. 14th, 1862 Dear Julia, "...I wish if you have a chance you would send me my woolen drawers and socks, and also that woolen comfort that I had last winter....I have been wearing my new suit. I am very well pleased with it, There are quite a number of our men shoeless, and some of them are rather ragged..."

ARMY LIFE IN VIRGINIA Free Press Association 1895

Pg.198 Letter from George Grenville Benedict Twelfth Vermont Regiment Oct 14, 1862 "...Our Chaplan returned to us today after an absence of four days, having been under rebel rule at Chambersburg in the meanwhile. He left us at Baltimore to accompany a Vt. Lady on her way to her brother, an officer of the Third Vt, who was lying at the point of death at Hagerstown; and was returning by way of Chambersburg when the rebels occupied the town. He thinks there were about 1500 of them. They were well mounted, and well clothed as far as their captured U.S. clothing went- the men under strict discipline and perfect controlof the officers, who, conducted themselves for the most part in a very gentlemanly way..."

WEEP NOT FOR ME, DEAR MOTHER (Letters of Eli Pinson Landers from Gwinnett Co. Ga. The Flint Hill Grays. Eli was 19 years old when he enlisted in Aug. 1861) ed. by Elizabeth Whitley Roberson pub by Pelican Pub. Co. 1996

Pg. 151 Camp near Winchester, Va., Oct. 17th, 1862 My Dear Mother "...Mamma I have drew me a pair of pants and have got 2 coats and I think I can make out without any from home without there was some certain way to get them...."

THE CONFEDERATE LETTERS OF BENJAMIN H. FREEMAN Compiled& Edited by Stuart T. Wright pub by Exposition Press 1974

Pg. 16 Oct 18, 1862 Camp French Dear Mother: "...I got my Ginger (,) thred at last and cloths and I was glad to get those apples and Bread and Chickens it is good it makes me think about home..."

WRITING & FIGHTING THE CONFEDERATE WAR The Letters of Peter Wellington Alexander ed by William B. Styple pub by Belle Grove Pub. Co. 2002

Pg.113 HELP NEEDED AT ONCE! LET NO ONE WAIT! Richmond Va. October 18, 1862 "I am glad to learn that my appeal in behalf of the army has been received with so much favor throughout the Confederacy. It has been a coal of fire even upon the back of the Government, which has already begun to send forward supplies of clothing and shoes. Thirty wagons loaded with winter supplies reached Winchester the day before I left, and I met others "en route" for the same destination. I called at the Clothing Bureau in this city this morning, for the purpose of improving my own wardrobe, which is none the better for the Maryland campaign, but was told that there was not a yard of officer's cloth in the whole establishment, the supply having been exhausted some time since. There was a considerable stock on hand of coarse strong cloth, which is being made up for the troops as rapidly as possible. An officer connected with the Bureau informed me that 33,000 garments had been sent up to Gen. Lee's army within the last twenty days, and that clothing for the army was being made up at the rate of 9,000 garments per week. The Government has fifty-eight tailors in its employ, whose business is to cut out the garments, and two thousand seven hundred women who make them up. The scraps of woolen cloth left by the cutters are sent to the Penetentiary, where they are converted into quilts, &c, for use of the army, whilst those of the cotton fabrics are disposed of to the paper manufacturers.

Allowing three garments to a man-coat, pants and shirt-the 33.000 pieces sent up to the army will furnish an outfit for 11,000 soldiers. This will afford very great relief as far as it goes, yet it will fall far short of the necessities of the army. Estimating the clothing manufactured at all the government in the country at 20,000 garments per week, and the number of troops in the field at 850,000 men, it will require more than a year at this rate to furnish each man with one suit of clothes. I do not include in this estimate blankets, shoes, socks. And gloves, which are absolutely indespensible in a climate like this.

I have no means of knowing how many complete suits of clothing the government will be able to provide; but estimating them at 100,000 including a blanket, pair of shoes, two pairs of socks, and one pair of gloves, there will still be left 250,000 men, who must perish unless they are supplied by the people at home. If we suppose the Government to be able to furnish winter outfits to 200,000 men, there will yet be 150,000 men who must look to the open hearts and willing fingers at home. The government, however, will not be in a condition to supply so many of the troops with blankets, shoes, socks, or gloves. Indeed, I am not aware that any provision has been made to secure a supply of either of these indespensible articles. Possibly some action was taken by Congress to have the shoemakers in the army detailed temporarily for the purpose of making shoes; but the shoes are needed now. This step, to have had any benefit, should have been taken monthes ago. It is too late now to procure supplies of leather, thread and pegs; and even if we had an abundant supply of each, it would be monthes before a sufficient number of shoes could be manufactured to meet the present wants of the army.

These facts will enable the people of the country to appreciate the magnitude of the labor before them. All my figures are merely rough estimates, especially in regard to the number of men in the field; but they are sufficiently accurate for the purpose for which they are offered. Whilst the country will be amazed that no more effort has been made by those in authority to provide the army with suitable clothing, it will readily perceive the necessity of the most prompt and energetic measures on the part of the people, if they would meet the srortcomings of the Government. If every man, woman, and child in the South were to exert themselves to the utmost in this good work, still there would be many a brave fellow in the field who would suffer all the pains of a rigorous winter, if not death, before the much needed relief could be received.

A statement appeared in one of the Richmond papers yesterday, based upon the report of "a passenger in the cars," to the effect that the condition of the troops was excellent, and that all they needed to render them entirely comfortable was a supply of blankets. Such statements as this may be gratifying to the public, but they are a cruelty to the army. I know, as every other observing man who has been with the army knows, that the condition of a vast number of our troops is deplorable. A few regiments and companies may have an adequate supply of clothing and shoes, but a large majority are in no condition to encounter the rigors of the approaching winter. Why, there are men in the hospitals of Winchester who are as naked as babes just born, and I saw here in the heart of Richmond this morning a poor emaciated soldier, who was hardly able to drag his bare feet along the cold pavement! In the army I know there are thousands of as true men as ever fired a musket, who have neither shoes or stockings, nor more than one suit of clothes, and that a summer suit, and dirty and ragged at that."

A good overall picture of conditions, eventhough his figures were not exact, It seems the government was trying but it was like swimming up Niagra Falls, the demand constantly outstripped the supply.

VMI

Oct. 18 1862 Dear Pa "…I have had my uniform made which makes me feel quite comfortable. Gen. Smith expected to get some cloth from near Winchester but Gen. Lee preferred it for his army and Gen. Smith will have to do without it. I don't know what the Rats will do…

P.S. Please send me my old cadet pants old gray ones some Friday. Ma knows which ones…"

THE STILLWELL LETTERS-A GEORGIAN IN LONG-STREET'S CORPS ARMY OF NORTHERN VIRGINIA ed. Ronald H. Morely pub by Mercer Univ. Press 2002

Pg. 69 same camp Oct. 19th 1862 "…If Mr. Evans comes back you can send my with him or anyone else you think will bring them. Sore, I will need them before long though I am not suffering for them. I could draw clothes from the government but I had rather have them…"

THE OLD DIMINION RIFLES

Camp Near Sheppardstown, Oct. 19th, 1962 My Dear Father, "…I am just off of a scout in Pennsylvania. The people were very much frightened as you will see from the papers The second day after we got into Pennsylvania we obtained a paper (Baltimore Sun) which said if McClellan did not annihilate Gen. J.E.B. and his whole command, it would be a disgrace upon the Federal army. Nearly every man had on a blue overcoat & they thought us Yankees. The whole scout where we did not stop we stole 1200 horses…." Your Affect. Son, Sidney S. Stringer Cols 1st Va. Cav. Winchester Va…."

LIFE AND LETTERS OF THOMAS J. JACKSON (STONEWALL JACKSON) by Mary Anna Jackson pub by Harper & Brothers, 1891

Letter from Thomas Johnathan Jackson to Mary Anna Morrisom Jackson Oct. 20, 1862

"…Do not send me any more handkerchiefs, socks, or gloves as I trust I have enough to last until peace. You think you can remember the names of all the ladies who make presents to me, but you haven't heard near all of them. An old lady in Tennessee, of about eighty years, sent me a pair of socks. A few days since a friend in Winchester presented me with a beautiful bridle and martingale for a general officer, according to the Army Regulations. Mr. Porter, of Jefferson, sent me a roll of grey cloth for a suit of clothes, and friends are continually sending things to contribute to my comfort. I mention this merely to show you how much kindness has been shown me, and to give you renewed cause for gratitude…"

Yes, General, we'd all do what ever we could for you.

LETTERS AND PAPERS OF AN ARTILLERY OFFICER A.N.V. IN THE WAR FOR SOUTHERN INDEPENDENCE 1861-1865 Capt. John Hampden Chamberlain-Virginian pub by Dietz Printing Co. Pub. 1932

Pg. 129 J.H. Chamberlayne to M.B. Chamberlayne Camp of Light Division, Oct. 20th, 1862 My Dear Mother, "…The cold keeping off so long will enable us to clothe the men, A thing of which they were in great need and which too little is being done & will finally be done much more completely than the alarmists think. For the clothes, I thank you. Your arrangements are good. Pray send me by Tom the jacket, shirts, pants, socks, and over or great coat, made up. The tailor here may be sick, may be killed, may desert or have a round dozen of accidents happen to him. Pray let the cape be full long, as also the skirt. Thank Dr. B. for me. I will need no uniform coat till I come to Richmond, & for all I see, that may be a year or six months. By Col. W. you might send the tobacco and also a blanket; not a bought one, but one from a bed, one of yours. The nights up here begin to be frosty as well as kindly. I need but one, so that be a warm white one. Please send 4 pr. cotton socks, 2 pr. woolen. My socks are nearly gone....

Today somebody kicked up a red fox, an old big fellow, in the grass, just as we got into camp near the infantry. You see there were some 11000or 12000 men camped around somewhat in a circle. The country was open, grass short, the men as eager as so many shouting school children; we had a glorious chase; the fox doubled & twisted, ran here & there, the men stumbled & fell about & yelled & pelted after him. All his doublings and turnings served but to increase has pursuers, so his thousand shifts led him but to his death. Some (one) among the lousy crew, more fortunate than his fellows, caught him amidst such a hurly-burly as you never saw. Verily, an army is such a monstrous sight that the very brute beasts stand aghast at it and their instinct fails at this unlooked for circumstance. Squirrels hares & partridges fall an easy prey & here an "old red" succumbed..."

Eating a fox? I wonder what they taste like.

DEAR SISTER-CIVIL WAR LETTERS TO A SISTER IN ALABAMA Frank Anderson Chappell pub. by Branch Springs Pub. 2002 (Third Alabama Regiment)

Pg. 120 Camp near Bunker Hill Va. Oct. 22 1862 Dear Sister "...My last letter to you was rather discouraging to you. I am glad now that I can write now under better circumstances. I told of so many being barefooted. We are getting shoes and clothes and blankets now. I told you that Lewis was almost out of pants and shoes. He has new ones now. We are to get overcoats this week which we are beginning to need very much for the mountain frost don't feel very good..."

Now, finally supplies of clothing and shoes are coming. I wonder if those overcoats of which he speaks were ever received.

CHARLOTTE'S BOYS-The Civil War Letters of The Branch Family of Savannah ed by Mauriel Phillip Joslyn pub by Rockbridge Pub. Co. 1996

Pg. 134 Sgt. Sanford Branch to Charlotte branch Richmond Oct. 24 (1862) Dear Mother, "...Shellman leaves for Savannah this evening to get cloths for the regiment. I hope he will be able to procure them, we want them bad enough..."

A CAPTAIN'S WAR LETTERS AND DIARIES OF WILLIAM H.S. BURGWYN 1861-1865 ed. by Herbert M. Schiller pub by White Mane Pub Co. Inc. 1994

Pg. 27 Thirty-fifth Regiment N.C. Troops Camp 4 miles north of Winchester October 21st, 1862 Writing to his mother requesting her to send clothing.

"A jacket and pants made of the thickest and warmest and most lasting cloth. I would prefer a grey ink kind but the color is of no importance. The jacket made double breasted and the pants long and full wide in the legs. Keith the tailor has my measure and he can cut them out and if necessary make them. Two flannel undershirts. Three thick colored flannel shirts. Three cotton flannel drawers. The (three?) pair of cotton socks. Half dozen handkerchiefs. Comb and brush; fine tooth comb. Tooth brush. Two cravats. A Beauregard sentinel cap made of worsted like Katie makes them to keep my head and ears warm. A good pair of warm gloves with long cuffs. Three towels. Three cakes of soap. Pen and ink (I will supply the paper and envelopes) and about five thickness of blankets about as wide and long as those you fixed for me before and fixed in the same manner. Sewing materials. You see I ask for a complete outfit for I lost everything I had with me at Sharpsburg and my trunk and things I sent back to Warrenton are of no more use to me than if I did not have them but as soon as I can find any way to get up with them I will send them to you at Raleigh.

You can send the clothes by this Mr. Barclift if he will take them which you can find out by getting Father to ask him or if he will not or cannot take them a man from my company, William G. Morris, whom I have this day detailed to go to Mecklenburg County, N.C., to get clothes for the company, will on his return take charge of them...."

Goodness, was this soldier completely naked?

CIVIL WAR REGIMENTS-A Journal of the American Civil War, Treasures from the Archives: Select Holdings from the Museum of the Confederacy

Pg. 112 Oct. 22, 1862, Washington Artillery, Somewhere in Va. "...We are sumptuouely fed and comfortably clothed, notwithstanding reports in the Northern Journals to the contrary..."

This is no wonder, they were a very elite (wealthy) unit

KEEP ALL MY LETTERS The Civil War Letters of Richard Henry Brooks, 51st Ga. Inf. Ed. By Katherine Holland pub by Mercer Univ. Press, Macon, Ga. 2003

Pg. 51 same place, Oct.23rd, 1862 "...if you make me a coat keep until I send for it or I can get to come home put a pocket in each Breast on the inside..."

HANDLEY LIBRARY ARCHIVES

James A. Miller Collection correspondence C.W. era misc. New Market, Va.

Camp near Bunker Hill Oct. 24th, 1862 Dear Julia, "…I wish you to send to me that woolen (concerna?) to wear over the head in cold weather as it may get cold any day…I just sent my clothes out to have them washed. I told the boy to boil them well so as to kill all the vermin that may be about them…"

HAM CHAMBERLAYNE-VIRGINIAN Letters and Papers of an Artillery Officer in the War for Independence 1861-1865 with introduction, notes and index by his son C.G.Chamberlayne Richmond, Va. pub by Press of the Dietz Printing Co. Publishers 1932

Pg. 132 J.H. Chamberlayne to M.B. Chamberlayne Camp against Bunker Hill, Oct. 24th, 1862 My dear Mother, I repeat that all your arrangements in the clothing line are good and that I would prefer the great coat to be made up in Rd (the homeplace)-and would like it to be full long in the skirt & cape, which latter is better when separate and made to button on to the coat collar.…I need pressingly only one article, socks; pray send both cotton and yarn…"

FAR, FAR FROM HOME-The Wartime Letters of Dick And Tally Simpson, 3rd South Carolina Volunteers by Guy R. Everson & Edward W. Simpson Jr. pub. by Oxford Univ. Press1994

Pg. 157 Oct. 25, 1862 Camp Near Winchester, Tally N. Simpson to Anna T. Simpson "… Nevertheless, since negros draw rations, now it will not be so hard to support three or four to a mess. Rations are distributed to 8 exclusive of the officer's servants, and as there are only six at present in our company, all are entitled to draw.

Have you made my over coat, and if so, what kind is it? When you do send Lewis (a servant), he should be well clothed. Besides, he should have a thick blanket and an overcoat. I have heard nothing of the bundle you sent to Laurens to be conveyed to me. What was in it?…"

This is the frist I've heard of servants drawing rations. I wonder how long that continued?

LETTERS FROM LEE'S ARMY Compiled by Susan Leigh Blackford Annotated by her husband, Charles Minor Blackford, Charles pub by Scribner's & Sons 1947

Company B of the Second Virginia Cavalry- Charles Blackford was first lieutenant, later captain.

Pg. 130 Bunker Hill, Oct. 26th, 1862 tearing up the Baltimore & Ohio railroad near Harper's Ferry "…My picket was stationed at the house of a section forman, whose young and pretty wife was a great rebel. Her husband, whatever his sympathies, was in the employ of the railroad company and had thought it best to remain inside the Federal lines. She was quite a refined person for one of her position and more educated than might be expected. She was kind to us and delighted above all things in hearing of Lee, Jackson, and Stuart, for whom she had the most romantic fascination.

It happened that on the second day there General Jackson and one or two of his staff rode out to inspect the enemy's position from our post. He stood and gazed from his horse through his glass long at the enemy's position, during which time our pretty hostess found out who it was and seemed almost overcome with the double emotion of awe and admiration. She watched him earnestly, and just as she thought he was through and might go off, ran into the house and brought out her baby, quite a handsome boy of about eighteen monthes and handing it up to the General asked him to bless it for her. He seemed no more surprised with this strange request than Queen Elizabeth at being asked to touch for the "Kings Evil." He turned to her with great earnestness and, with a pleasant expression on his stern face, took the child in his arms, held it to his breast, closed his eyes and seemed to be, and I doubt not was occupied for a minute or two with prayer, during which we took off our hats and the young mother leaned her head over the horse's shoulder as if uniting in the prayer. The scene was very solemn and unusual.… Around-about the soldiers in their worn and patched clothing, in a circle at a respectful distance, while his staff officers stood a little off to one side. Then Jackson, the warrior-saint of another era, with the child in his arms, head bowed until his graying beard touched the fresh young hair of the child, pressed close to the shabby coat that had been so well aquainted with death…."

Oh, yes, this brings tears to my eyes every time I read it. Is it any wonder we hold him in such awe?

THE CAMPAIGN FROM TEXAS TO MARYLAND WITH THE BATTLE OF FREDERICKSBURG-Rev. Nicholas A. Davis, Chaplain 4th Texas Regiment, CSA Printed at the Office of the Pesbyterian Committee of Publications of the Confederate States 1863

Pg. 96 Oct. 26th A VISIT TO THE CAMP-(Winchester) On the 26th inst., learning that the army had moved back to within six miles of the town, I went out and had the pleasure of seeing those of my old regiment, that were left, after marching several hundred miles, and passing through the fire of six days, in battle. The men looked worn and tired. Their clothes were ragged and many of their feet were bare; and in their coats, pants and hats could be seen many marks of the bullet. They had many times performed long marches, and fought hard battles without rations..."

CONFEDERATE LETTERS AND DIARIES ed by Walbrook D. Swank pub by Papercaft Printing and Design Inc. 1992

Pg. 34 Letters with regard to CharlesThomas Shelton Private, Co. H 28th Virginia Infantry Botetourt (Virginia) Artillery Battery and Anderson's Artillery Batterry Maney's Tennessee Brigade Camp at Centreville Oct. 26th, 1862 Dear ones at the home of my childhood, I am very much obliged for the bundle of cloths but fear that I will never see them. I am sorry that I did not have them sent to me by express. I would certainly have gotten them then. Fortunately I have managed to sew up the pants of my old ones with a piece of some other old breeches but not in a very beautiful way. If I am so unfortunate as to lose those you sent I will soon be like Jim Banks....Uncle Wm. Has been quite sick and is still very unwell and he had about three weeks ago to send his baggage to Manassas so has no change of clothes. I carried him a suit of mine & am thus in a predicament but I hope he will be able to get his washed before we have to move & then I will get mine again...."

Apparentely there were a number of people looting the trunks during shipping. There are many accounts of this happening.

VMI

Oct. 26 1862 "...You may sell my jacket and overcoat if you want to but don't you think my overcoat will make me a good coat or vest when cloth gate scarce, but you can do just as you please. It is in the largest box at the office with my gun. My winter coat vest & pants will fit me a year hence do not sell them....I have an opportunity of buying a first rate pair of high top shoes made something like the gaiters Pa got in Washington (which were the best shoes I ever had) for $15. Mr. White the father of one of my roommates who has a store uptown had them before the war and offers them to me as a special favor (they do not fit his son). They are the finest calf-skin double soles worth $25 or $30 in Richmond or Lynchburg. I will need them this winter as my English shoes have proved a failure and have worn out already. If Pa thinks I had better take them he can send me a check or if he thinks not I will not get them. It is certainly a bargain & I am sure I will need them.

Gen. Smith has succeeded in getting cloth so I will have 2 uniforms. I have done without an overcoat & if I get a cadet overcoat I will send my cloth back home...."

FIFTH VIRGINIA INFANTRY Va. Regimental History Series by Lee A. Wallace Jr. 1988

Pg. 42 Oct. 28 1862 camp near Millwood, Va. James McCutchan writes "…It was getting cold, and some of the men, he wrote, had no blankets and not even an overcoat, "How do you like that way of doing? You all at home don't know what all we have to go through & yet we are more lively here than you all are at home…"

THE STILLWELL LETTERS-A GEORGIAN IN LONG-STREET'S CORPS ARMY OF NORTHERN VIRGINIA ed. Ronald H. Morely pub by Mercer Univ. Press 2002

Pg. 70 Camp near Winchester N.W. Virginia October, 28, 1862 My Dear Molly "…I need a heavy coat worse than anything else and a pair of gloves….I also drew a pair of shoes from the government at five dollars and swapped them off for a pair of English shoes of the best kind of lined and bound double soled shoes that sell for twelve or fifteen dollars in Richmond and gave one dollar to boot…"

Lucky swap.

RED CLAY TO RICHMOND by John J. Fox pub by Angle Valley Press 2006

Pg. 125 Oct. 28, 1862 "William Goggans sent his father a list of items he needed to help ward off the cold weather:

1. Close bodied coat made in uniform stile. 2. Pair of jeans pants lined. [B]e careful not to have them made too large.4 shirts, 2 nice and 2 plain. 2 pair of Drawers. 3 or 4 pair of socks. One pair of heavy home made boots as the winter is severe. [T]hese things will be of great benefit to me. [A]lso a head cover to sleep in. [M]y pants & coat I want to be made of Gray cloth or one pair of the pants Gray and the other Brown. [A]lso a good heavy vest. [Y]ou may think it strange of me for sending for so much but I an tyred of being unclothed. I had forgot to say a cover led (coverlet) to sleep under & some potatoes, chestnuts and some (of) that good Brandy that my lips are watering for. I hardly thing [think] that I should get to come Home During the Winter. I send you the best Over Coat the Yankees ever wore. I do not mean they have worn this but this is my prize of Harper's Ferry. [I]t is fine and I want you to ware it and think of your boys at Harper's Ferry and other Battles. I hope it may suit you. [I]t is worth $75.00 hear but I give it to you to remind you of your boy…"

Another soldier who needs everything. I'll bet he had another Yankee overcoat for himself, I cannot think of sending one off at the end of October.

GEN. LEE'S ARMY

Pg.215 To provide shoes for the men, Lee took several steps. In November 1862, he withdrew all shoemakers from the ranks-271 of them-and placed them at work making shoes. Officers also encouraged men to convert rawhides from butchered cattle into usable foot coverings. D.H. Hill pushed the alternative so strongly that his men referred to him as "Rawhide Bill."

Another step in the right direction as pertains to shoes.

FRENCH HARDING Civil War Memoirs ed. by Victor L. Thacker pub by McClain Printing Co. Inc., Parsons W.Va. 2001

Pg. 116 Nov. 1862 Mine Run Campaign "…Our men were then only half fed, clothed and shod, but they were, as always, ready and anxious to again meet and measure strength with the enemy…"

TWO MONTHES IN THE CONFEDERATE STATES- An Englishman's Travels Through The South by W.C. Corsan pub by La. State Univ Press 1996

Pg. 102 Nov. 1862 "We met them (Jackson's Corps) all along the railway between Hanover Junction and Staunton, in great numbers-at Louisa Court- House, Gordonsville, Chalottesville, &c., : a hardy, active-looking set of men, evidently used to rough lodging and fare, but full of enthusiasum and anxiety for a fight. I noticed comparatively few young men among them. They looked like troops that had served in several campaigns, and knew their duty. Of course they were clad, shod, and armed just like all the other confederate troops I ever saw: no attempt at uniform, either in hats, clothes, or anything else; but the same dingy homespun dress, nondescript caps, strong shoes, unshaven, unwashed, uncombed heads and faces, and the same bright rifles and bayonets I had seen all through the South."

Pg. 104 ""…It seemed General Jackson himself never halted at any of the towns through which he passed, but, with his staff, pushed through at a smart trot, dressed in a long military cloak, trousers stuffed into his jackboots, his head adorned with a general's hat and feathers, and riding a magnificent horse-good humoredly acknowledging the cheers, blessings, and good wishes of the poor frightened people he met, by all of whom he was regarded as little less than an unconquerable deliverer…I was told there was not a man in his army without shoes and blankets, and that the whole of the force had an ample supply of tents and stores…"

Maybe not everyone was so well supplied, according to the letters wev'e seen. Also, Stonewall dressed in a general's hat? I've never read of that.

THE COMANCHES White's Battalion, Virginia Caavlry Laurel Brigade by Frank M. Myers pub by Continental Book Co. 1956

Pg. 128 Nov. 1862 "…The next day the raiding in the enemy's rear was resumed, and several wagons and prisoners brought in; and about dark the Major learned that a Yankee train had deposited a quantity of tents and baggage in an old house at Neersville. So putting his people in line again, he started for them, and about midnight took quiet possession of exacty the supplies needed by the command for winter quarters, all of which were safely brought away…

The total number of prisoners made in the whole series of operations was about one thousand, and fully two hundred wagons were destroyed and brought out together, besides an immense amount of stores and arms destroyed by the Yankees themselves, to keep them from falling into the hands of White's men…"

FOOTPRINTS OF A REGIMENT A Recollection of the 1st Georgia Regulars by W.H. Andrews pub by Longstreet Press Atlanta Ga. 1992

Pg. 93 Nov. 1862 near Orange and Culpepper Court House. "…Our soldier boys are still without shoes. Gen. Lee has issued an order giving the green cow hides to the soldiers to make moccasins out of by turning the hair side in next to the foot. Have seen several soldiers with them on. Don't imagine they feel much like shoes, but they are better than going barefooted." …"It has been several monthes since the troops were paid off and our clothes are almost as scant as our shoes. Nothing unusual to see Yankee clothing in our camps, which was stripped off the dead on the battlefield. Saw Sgt. Alex Clemency of Company G wearing an officer's cap with a slot of his brains sticking to it. Sgt. Bridges of Company M wears a frock coat with a ball hole in the waist of it, and the tails covered in blood where the fellow was shot in the back. Don't think the boys wear them from choice, but from necessity…"

That sounds like dire necessity.

Pg. 95 late Nov.1862 "…Gen. Lee has issued an order putting all barefooted men on duty. No one excused on account of not having shoes. Three days after the order was issued you could not find a barefooted man in camps. Don't know where the shoes come from, but my honest belief is that many were carrying them in their knapsacks instead of wearing them on their feet. What is it some men won't do to keep out of battle. I don't mean to say that all had shoes thatr were barefooted, for no doubt many good soldiers were without them and could not get them. Besides, being paid off enabled them to buy them...."

How many, do you suppose, were just hiding their shoes? I'll bet not many, it would be miserable walking around in the cold barefooted, just to get out of pulling duty.

THE CIVIL WAR INFANTRYMAN, In Camp, on the March, and in Battle by Gregory A. Coco pub by Thomas Publications, Gettysburg, Pa

Pg 80 Union prisoner of war Simon Hulbert described, in November 1862 that the Southerners"...do not go in for making a great show (of) Blacking Boots, belts, scouring brass (and) burnishing guns to make them look bright. But if the gun is only clean on the inside so that it will go off, it does not make any difference how rusty it is outside...

The men are generally tall, slim & wirery (sic) fellows, quick as cats, real American people...They are mum as dead men as far as talking is concerned in the ranks. Every one knows what he has to do."

Pg 80 Private Lewis Bisswll of Connecticut had a chance to look over 1700 Confederate prisoners captured in the Shenandoah Valley (no date given). He called them the "flower of their army," and "smart healthy men," who "are very quick, walk like horses. Our men do not pretend to keep up with them." He described their uniforms as "light grey. The coat comes to the waist. They wear slouch hats. Caps are seldom worn. What few are seen are U.S."

As early as May 1862, Lieutenant Galwey called the look of his command, like that of "a pack of thieving vagabonds-no crowns in our hats, no soles to our shoes, no seats to our pantaloons."

This tells of the respect the Yankees had for the Rebs, regardless of their raggedness.

SOLDIERS BLUE AND GRAY by James I. Robertson Jr. pub by Univ of S.C. Press 1988

Pg. 77 Nov 1862 "...a private in the 57th North Carolina informed his brother that he had "only one shirt & one pair of draws & when I wash them I hafta put on my coat..."

CONFEDERATE CAPT. UJANERTUS ALLEN'S LETTERS TO HIS WIFE by Randall Allen & Keith S. Bohannon pub by La. State Univ Press 1998

Pg. 179 Camp Near Berryville Va. Nov. 1st, 1862 My Dear Susie "...All that are here have drawn an entire suit of clothes and look so neat and trim that you would not suspect us of being the Ragged Rebel Roadways Reedy Relief set that we were a few days ago. Now if the men could get shoes they would do very well for the present. I think it will at least be Christmas before we are stationary. I think I can do very well until that time, with the exception of shoes...."

The Captain's men must've received resupply from the government. Shoes remain a problem, however. How do you all like that nickname?

Pg. 181 Camp on Shanendoah River Va. Nov. 7th, 1862 My Dear Susie "...You ask me relative to clothing. Most of your enquiries are answered in previous letters. I have a comfort. (My dear, it is snowing now.) A good pair of gloves would be acceptable. If I can get a hat some blankets and shoes and boots I can do quite as well as last winter. I understand all the bed clothing sent to the rear last spring is destroyed. This being the case I have no blankets at all. I have a rubber cloth and two overcoats. I have good shoes now but was barefooted a few days ago. I anticipate quite a treat by way of something to eat and drink when our clothes are sent to us..."

He's now talking about receiving clothes from home, as explained by his stating he anticipates getting something to eat & drink when the clothing arrives.

Pg. 182 Camp on Shanendoah Nov. 9th, 1862 My Dear Susie "...The ladies cotton dresses reminds me of a substitute for shoes we are beginning to adopt in the army; moccasins made of raw hide. We have the hides and any one can soon make a pair. I think it would be a good idea for the farmers to adopt them...I can't say that I need anything more than you propose to send me, and could do without the pants and vest for some time and if I was shure of coming home I would rather you would not send them. By the by send me some handkerchiefs-cotton, silk, osnaburg or bagging. I am using my last which is nothing more than the skirt of an ancient shirt...."

VMI

Nov.1,1862 Dear Pa "...Gen Smith's cloth was expected today. I will then have two uniforms. I will take care of the one made out of his cloth and wear my own every day because his will be much prettier. He will not let me have an overcoat because the cloth will hardly furnish all with uniforms. I cannot take an overcoat & no uniform because all are obliged to have uniforms alike to wear on dress parade &c., so I will be obliged to use my cloth. Besides an overcoat out of my cloth will not cost near as much as one out of his...."

Nov. 1862 "…P.S. Ask Ma to look and see if I left my buckskin gloves with her (or) if I brought them with me they have disappeared in some way although I am more careful of my clothes than anyone in the barracks. If you have them please send them to me.…What did the cloth you bought from Flannigan cost you?"

Nov. the 2nd 1862 My Darling Mother "…The cloth has come for our uniforms at last and I hope we will get them soon. Sister spoke of my wearing the jacket that Aunt Sarah gave me. The reason was that it was so narrow across the breast that I got reported for not holding my shoulders back and I quit wearing it. The jacket and overcoat you sent me has been quite a treat to me as it has been very cold since you sent the jacket…"

A SCYTHE OF FIRE-THE CIVIL WAR STORY OF THE EIGHTH GEORGIA INFANTRY REGIMENT by Warren Wilkinson & Steven E. Woodworth William pub by Morrow Pub. 2002

Pg. 194 Nov. 3rd, 1862 "…A great many of them were barefoot by this time, so their corps commander suggested a way for them to improvise shoes. On November 3 he had orders read out to the troops at the regimental dress parades warning that henceforth no man would be excused from ranks for lack of shoes. Instead, he was to procure a piece of fresh beef hide at the slaughter pens where animals were butchered to feed the army. Then he should cut the rawhide to size, and, as one Texan put it, "whang the moccasins on with rawhide thongs." That is, he should sew the hide around his feet, putting the hairy side inward, next to the foot, to serve in place on a sock, and thus make for himself a comfortable piece of footwear. At least, that was the theory. Advance contemplation of the obvious practical difficulties lead some regiments to receive the reading of the order with shouts of laughter. The Eighth Georgia's Tom Gilham seemed to find it a fairly acceptable sort of footwear, aside from the fact that when a man finally decided to take his "shoes" off, he had to cut them off and then make a new pair the next time. Other Confederates were apparently less adept at sewing cowhide and looked as if they had each foot stuck in a twenty pound ham,

Somehow, between mending the clothes they had, getting some of their old ones shipped to them out of storage in Richmond, and drawing a few more from the quartermaster, they managed to get by without severe suffering…"

THE CAMPAIGN FROM TEXAS TO MARYLAND WITH FREDERICKSBURG-Rev. Nicholas A. Davis, Chaplain with the 4th Texas Regiment CSA Printed at the Office of the Presbyterian comitte of Publications of the Confederate States 1863

Pg. 130 Nov. 4th, 1862

To The Editor of the Whig—Richmond, Nov. 4th.

I have just arrived from Fredericksburg; the prpospacts are good for a fight, but our men are not all shod. On yesterday evening an order was read on dress parade to the effect that, being barefooted would not excuse a man from duty. Those who were without shoes, were ordered to make moccasins of raw hide, and stand in their places; and we felt that Texans will come as near discarging their duty as any who will meet the next struggle; but I ask the good people of Richmond and surrounding country, if they will stand by and see them go into the fight without shoes. We are too far from home to look to our friends there for help-We acknowledge the kindness shown us last winter, and many of the recipients have poured out their life's blood on the soil of Virginia.

We are from the far South, and the cold is severe to us. It will require at least one hundred pairs of shoes, and five hundred pairs of socks to complete one suit for our men. Those who are disposed to contribute, will please send forward their mite to the depot of the Young Men's Christian Association, or the depot of the 4th Texas Regiment, on 15th Street, between Main and Cary, over Ratcliff's, and it will be forwarded immediately.

N.A.Davis,
Chaplain 4th Texas

In answer to this appeal, we received from Miss Virginia Dibrell, (collected from various contributions) $268.25; Miss Matties M. Nicholas and Mrs. Garland Haines (proceeds of a concert at the Buckingham Female Institute), $175.05; from the Ladies Soldier's Aid Society, New Market, Nelson County, a box filled with clothing; Mrs. Wm G. Paine, seventy-eight pairs socks; Mr. Wm Bell, Chairman of the Purchasing Comittee of the Citizens of Richmond, one hundred pairs of shoes; Young Men's Christian Association, thirty rugs, one hundred forty-six pairs of drawers, one hundred and nine shirts, ninety-four pairs of gloves, and four hundred and ten pairs of socks, besides a number of smaller sums and packages, which have warmed both the feet and hearts of our men; who feel it is unnecessary to attept to express their gratitude for these unexpected favors. But, by the way of acquitting the claims of the young ladies, the boys are willing to promise to take them home with them, and work for them as long as they live.

In return for the liberality extended to our men, the Brigade, after the Battle of Fredericksburg, contributed near $6000 to the sufferers of this unfortunate city-Hood's minstrels giving about $400 of that amount."

That is a heart-warming response from the citizens, and, from the troops regarding the citizens of Fredericksburg.

CONFEDERATE CENTENNIAL STUDIES #26 LAWLEY COVERS THE CONFEDERACY by William Stanley Hoole pub by Confederate Pub Co. 1964

Richmond, Oct. 8, appeared in the London Times Nov. 4, 1862 (Francis Lawley was a reporter for the London Times) "...Many a man who until the commencement of this war [was used to every luxury], has for months been marching under a musket, without one single change of rainment, feeding often on green maize and raw pork, lying at night on the bare earth with but a single blanket between him and the canopy of heaven…"

FOUR YEARS IN THE CONFEDERATE ARTILLERY-The Diary of Pvt. Henry Robinson Berkely ed. by William H. Runge pub by Univ. N.C. Press 1961

Pg. 34 Nov. 5 1862 "…I tried hard to get Sgt. Cunningham to take this old farmer's advice (marching back to Culpeper C.H. at night) and told him a good many of us had no overcoats, but he insisted on trying it…"

DEAR IRVIE, DEAR LUCY-Civil War Letters of Capt. Irving A. Buck, General Cleburne's AAG & Family pub. by Buck Pub. Co. 2002

Pg. 110 Nov. 6, 1862 Head Quarters Department of South Carolina and Georgia Charleston, South Carolina Dear Ma, "The shirts fit admirably-please accept our thanks for them-but Ma you should not have sent the money, we really did not need it and it was painful for us to think that perhaps, you had deprived yourself and the children for us-, we are now well supplied with clothing. A (Alvin) and myself are going to buy a suit of blue army cloth, jacket pants and vest, from the Quarter master's office, which will cost us $25.00-at any other place they would charge us at least $100.00…"

By "blue army cloth," does he mean the bluish-gray English cloth that was starting to come in?

DEAR AMANDA-The Civil War Letters of Marion Hill Fitzpatrick, Army of Northern Virginia ed. by Jeffery C. Lowe and Sam Hodges pub by Mercer Univ. Press 1998

Pg. 30 Nov. 7th, 1862 Camp near Berryville, Va. (Letter no. 15) Dear Amanda ""I am looking everyday now for my clothes. I wrote Lou to tell you not to send a vest but I do not know whether you got the letter in time or not. The reason I did not write for bedclothes is that I feared you would have none to spare and also feared if I got them before we quit moving so much, I would lose them, and another thing, our wages are raised to $15.00 a month, and we are to be clothed by the government and not draw any more computation money. At least that is the opinion of many. If that is the case, I will get no credit for anything you send me and it will be best to draw altogether from the government except socks. I wrote Lou in my last letter to her for you to send me an overcoat, but I now countermand the order, for I suppose I can draw, if not I can make out very well without it. We can draw clothing here much cheaper than they can be bought in Ga. Some of the boys have already drawn good clothing at reasonable prices and excellent blankets at $4.00…"

Unfortunately that's not going to last.

A SOUTHERN SOLDIER'S LETTERS HOME The Civil War Letters of Samuel Burney Cobb's Georgia Legion, Army of Northern Va. Ed. By Nat Turner pub by Mercer Univ. Press, Macon Ga.2002

Pg. 224 Camp Georgia Legion, Near Culpeper Va., Nov.8th, 1862 "…I tell you some of the boys are in pitiful condition; some with no blankets, no shoes, ragged coats and pant. I feel sorry for them but cannot help them, as there are no supplies of shoes or clothing in this country…."

Apparentely the shortage of blankets, clothing and shoes was by no means over. See the letters below.

BROTHERS IN GRAY-The Civil War Letters of the Pierson Family ed. by Thomas W. Cutrer & T. Michael Parrish pub by La. State Univ. Press 1997 Ninth Louisiana

Pg. 132 Ruebin Allen Pierson to Mary Catherine Pierson In Camp near Rockbridge, 12 miles east of Winchester (Va.) Nov. 8th, 1862 Dear Sister "…We are not well supplied with blankets and clothing yet. Some of the boys have not a single blanket and are very much in need of one as we had a fine snow yesterday. A few of the boys are stark barefooted and many others will be in the same condition in a short time if we do not get a supply of shoes. I heard this morning that a large lot of tents, blankets, clothing & shoes were on the road between here and Staunton, intended to supply the wants of Jackson(')s corps of the army; if this be true we will soon be supplied with all the necessities of a winter's campaign…"

LETTERS OF WILLIAM F. WAGNER, CONFEDERATE SOL-DIER ed. by Joe M. Hatley and Linda B. Huffman pub by Broadfoot's Bookmark 1983

Pg.24 Camp near Richmond Va. Nov. 9th 1862 …"it is gitting verry cole it snowed last nite and we have no tents but I don't Believe we stay here long no how I think we will take up winter quarters before long I don't know how I could carry that comfort I wrote for unless we was stationed once but if you can send it just send it I will try to carit some how…"

THE CIVIL WAR LETTERS OF GENERAL FRANK "BULL" PAXTON A Lieutenant of Lee & Jackson ed. by John Gallatan Paxton Hill Jr. pub by College Press 1978

Pg. 62 Camp near Port Royal (Va.) Nov. 9 1862 "…The day before yesterday we had a snow, and the weather is now quite cold. Winter seems to have set in, and it finds us sadly prepared for it. A large number of our soldiers are entirely barefooted, and very many without blankets, living in the open air, without tents and with a very small supply of axes to cut wood for fires, there is much suffering..."

FOUR YEARS IN THE CONFEDERATE ARTILLERY

Pg. 34 November 10, (1862) We remained at Culpeper until (the) 19th of November, and during this time Uncle Landon and Mrs. Winston came up to see us, bringing us clothes, shoes, blankets and home eatings..."

VMI

Nov. the 10th 1862 Dear Brother "...I wrote to Papa some time ago about some shoes and he never wrote me a word about them & Gen. Smith says he cannot and will not furnish us shoes and I am nearly barefooted and if Ma has not sent me the box please send me a pair in it...."

WELCOME THE HOUR OF CONFLICT-William Cowan McClellan & the 9th Alabama ed by John C. Carter pub by Univ Al. Press

Pg. 185 Nov. 10th, 1862 Culpeper Court House William McClellan to His Sister Dear Sister, "...Al Martin arrived last night bringing my Pants & gloves they were just in time as I had put the last patch on my old ones they would have. Tell Mother I am very thankful to her for them. I am barefooted but hope I will get some shoes before long...Fletcher has my cloths in Richmond..."

Pg. 186 Nov. 14th/62 Culpeper Court house William McClellan to Thos. J. McClellan Dear Father, "I have received 4 letters and all of the clothes sent me except those sent by Fielding, he has not arrived yet. My uniform is admired and prized by every body, I cannot express my thanks to my good old Mother for them. They fit me splendidly. I have been offered 10 dollars for my co. Davis gloves. I need nothing now save boots or shoes. I am completely barefooted. We have been expecting to draw shoes for some time but failed so far..."

Pg. 188 Nov 18th/62 Culpeper Court house William McClellan to Matilda McClellan Dear Sister, "All of my things except those Mr. Fielding has have come to hand, I read your letters over and over again each time with interest. I cannot express my thanks to you all for the things you sent me, my cloths fit me first rate it is decidedly the finest suit in the Regt. all I need now is Shoes and the Shirts Fielding has for me, I think I will draw shoes in a day or two, I went down to the 4th Ala a day or too ago for my cloths they are carried 7 miles below us...I have just received a letter from John Fletcher informing me of the clothes he sent me by Scruggs, which I have received..."

HAM CHAMBERLAYNE-VIRGINIAN Letters and Papers of an Artillery Officer in the War for Independence 1861-1865 with introduction, notes and index by his son C.G.Chamberlayne Richmond, Va. pub by Press of the Dietz Printing Co. Publishers 1932

Pg. 137 J.H. Chamberlayne to M.B. Chamberlayne Camp 5 miles from Winchester, on the Berryville road, Nov. 11th, 1862 My dear Mother, "…All the things were as I could have wished them, being comfortable, fit, & comely, the jacket particularly with its trimmings is much admired. With my new outfit I cut as jaunty a figure as an ungainly person could expect.

Do not worry yourself about the overcoat, I can well wait for it, my blood runs thick quick & warm. For the size, why I am about 1 size smaller than Hart, and anyone can tell what is meant by a long military cape. Col. W. brought me also the blanket which completes my bed gear…'

LAW'S ALABAMA BRIGADE IN THE WAR BETWEEN THE UNION AND THE CONFEDERACY by J. Gary Laine & Morris M. Penny pub by White Mane Pub. Co. 1996

Pg. 37 Nov. 12, 1862 "The 47th and 48th Alabama took up the line of march for Fredericksburg on Nov. 14. Many men left the camp barefoot as a cold rain fell, causing the roads to turn into mud and icy slush as the temperature dropped. Later that afternoon a frigid wind blew from the north adding to the men's misery. Sheffield went to brigades headquartersand confronted Colonel E.T.H. Warren, brigade commander. An irate Sheffield issued Warren an ultimatum: "Colonal, I have many men in my regiment barefooted. I don't have the ambulances to haul them, and before I will see them march over frozen ground without shoes, I will build winter quarters here and remain until spring. Therefore, if you wish us to remainwith your brigade you must send transportation for my barefooted men." Warren immediately made wagons available to transport Sheffield's barefoot men."

This was a very humane officer.

A CAPTAIN'S WAR LETTERS AND DIARIES OF WILLIAM H.S. BURGWYN 1861-1865 ed. by Herbert M. Schiller pub by White Mane Pub Co. Inc. 1994

Pg.32 Camp Near Madison C.H. November 12th 1862. "I still "Thank God" keep in the best of health, and am only in great need of clothing which I expect to get every day."

HANDLEY LIBRARY ARCHIVES

James A. Miller Collection correspondence C.W. era misc. New Market, Va.

Camp near Front Royal November 12th, 1862 Dear Julia, "…I slept out last night and the night before with nothing but my saddle blanket and a small comfort which was under my saddle, but last night I slept on a few rails before a fire. The night before I slept on the ground, had my over coat along it answers a very good purpose. I cover my head up with the cape and by that means keep my head and neck warm…"

AS RECORDED IN THE POCKET DIARIES OF PRIVATE ROBERT A. MOORE, Co. G, 17th Miss. Regt. Confederate Guards, Holy Springs, Mississippi ed. by James w. Silver pub by McCowat-Mercer Press 1959

Pg. 116 Thursday, Nov. 13th, 1862, bivouacked near Culpeper C.H. "…Have learned this evening that clothing and shoes cannot be gotten from the government. The army stands in great need, of shoes in particular…"

OK, what do you do in a situation like that? It would take days for someone from the regiment returning to Mississippi and then longer for the clothes to be made up. That is a rather final note-"clothing and Shoes cannot be gotten from the government." (Sounds as though that "ragged Rebel" wasn't such a myth after all.)

LETTERS FROM LEE'S ARMY by Susan Leigh Blackford and Charles Minor Blackford pub by Scribner's Pub. 1947

Pg. 138 Nov. 13, 1862 Linden Station (near Fredericksburg) Va 2nd Virginia Cavalry. "…Longsteet's army is much better clothed than Jackson's…"

THE CONFEDERATE VETERAN VOL. XXVI 1918

Pg. 259 June 1918 In The Years Of War compiled by John C. Stiles from "Official Records" Series III,Vol. II 1862-63 "Barefooted Men-On Nov. 14 (1862) in General Longstreet's Corps alone there were 6,648 men without any leather covering for their feet. But, fortunately, not in the dead of winter."

Several letters have spoken of snow already in this area. How severe does the weather have to be to be termed "winter?"

PARKER'S VIRGINIA BATTERY by Robert K. Krick pub by Va. Book Co. 1975

Pg. 75-76 Nov 14, 1862 "...Another shortage which cropped up to bedevil the men of the battery at this time was the lack of footwear. On November 14 (1862) it was reported that twenty percent of the men in the battalion were barefooted, or about sixteen men in each battery. The time would come when the battalion would consider itself well shod if only one man in five was without shoes.

Other clothing was also in short supply. Overcoats and blankets were apparently so difficult to get through regular channels during this rather cold fall that Captain Parker was driven to a most unusual expedient. He wrote to the Council of the City of Richmond, asking that the battery's hometown provide him with thirty blankets and twenty overcoats for the use of his company. There is no evidence available to indicate whether his petition was successful. The Council received the communication at its November 24, 1862, meeting and referred it on motion to the Committee on Arms.... William Parker remarked that camp life gave "some hint of what would happen if the fair sex should suddenly take wings and fly away." The wash-tub was all but extinct, and the members of the battery had "dirty shoes, as well as dirty shirts, dirty hands and dirty faces, dish-rags incredibly and universally dirty..."

Website-The Confederate

Pg. 1 "Abraham Lincoln once asked (General) Winfield Scott the question: Why is it you were once able to take the City of Mexico in three monthes with five thousand men, and we have been unable to take Richmond with one hundred thousand men?

"I will tell you," said General Scott, "The men who took us into the City of Mexico are the same men who are keeping us out of Richmond"

Confederat Veteran Magazine, September 1913, Pg. 471,

Pg. 2 Extract from the "Charleston Mercury" of Feb. 5, 1863 regarding the army after the Antietam Campaign. "We find in the London Times another long letter from Mr. Lawley, its correspondent in the South:

Culpeper Court House, Va. Nov. 14, 1862 "Meanwhile in the shelter of the dense woods about Culpeper, in wonderful spirits, with physique greatly improved since the bloody day at Sharpsburg, are clustered the tatter-demalion regiments of the South. It is a strange thing to look at these men, so ragged, slovenly, sleeveless, without a superfluous ounce of flesh upon their bones, with wild, matted hair, in mendicants rags, and to think when the battle flag goes to the front, how they can and do fight..."

I cannot add anything more to this quote, Mr. Lawley has said it all.

A SOUTHERN SOLDIER'S LETTERS HOME The Civil War Letters of Samuel Burney Cobb's Georgia Legion, Army of Northern Va. ed. by Nat Turner pub by Mercer Univ. Press, Macon Ga.2002

Pg. 225 same camp, Nov. 16th, 1862 "…I have been busy distributing clothing & shoes to the Company. We drew 5 pairs of shoes for our Company which relieves that number of men. There are others barefooted that will have to wait on the slow operations of the Quarter Master Department for shoes. If our people in tend to supply our Company with clothing they had best do so at once, else they will be suppressing (?). Now today we drew eight pair pants, 11 pairs drawers, 15 shirts, six coats, five pair shoes &c. True this does not supply the Company, but it will do so if we continue to draw every day or so, or week or so even. The Government prices for articles of clothing are very exorbitant, and the boys are almost literally compelled to purchase at any price for actual need of clothing…"

What a nightmare for the soldiers!

VMI

Nov. the 16th 1862 Dear Ma The preacher wants the people here to cut up their carpets to make blankets for the soldiers. They are going to give the carpets in the aisle of the churches here to them. Ma I want you to buy one of Aunt Lee's linsey dresses most suitable to line my overcoat with as we can get nothing thicker than osnaburg to line them with and we have to give the biggest kind of price for it. Send me a piece of homemade soap to wash my feet with…"

A CAPTAIN'S WAR LETTERS AND DIARIES OF WILLIAM H.S. BURGWYN 1861-1865 ed. by Herbert M. Schiller pub by White Mane Pub Co. Inc. 1994

Pg. 34 Camp Near Madison C.H. November 17th, 1862 "You can imagine how gratified I was to receive the blankets as a present from Uncle Tom to be distributed amongst my men. It shows he has a great feeling for me well knowing how highly the men would appreciate such generosity and as soon as I receive the blankets you are going to send me I intend to give them out but till then I will need them myself and they are the very sort of blankets my men are now thoroughly supplied with blanket and clothing the man who I detailed to go home and get them has returned and they have as much as they can carry."

They couldn't wait on the government and got re-uniformed from the home folks.

JAMES MADISON UNIVERSITY ARCHIVES

17th Nov. 1862 Letters of 1st Lt. Reuben A. Scott Co. B, 10th Regiment Virginia Infantry Camp 4 miles below Winchester Dear Mollie: "…Mollie we have plenty of meat and Bread to eat last saturday we had a large Pork pot pie I think it was good as I ever eat yestoday we had a fine turkey & to day we had beef hash not much danger of starving yet awhile so long as we get plenty of beef & Bread as for clothing the army has tolerable good clothes some few have no shoes and other have not got their over coats from home and places they sent them last spring some look very dirty but it is their own fault they have had ample time during last week to wash their clothes…"

23rd Nov. 1862 Letters of 1st Lt. Reuben A. Scott Co. B, 10th Regiment Virginia Infantry Camp Near Mt. Jackson, Va. Dear Mollie: "…as to clothing we are not suffering some have not got their over coats yet you must not believe every thing you hear about the army suffering for clothes and something (to) eat we have plenty of that but have to suffer otherwise such as exposure to bad weather…I Recd yours (letter) but had nothing of importance to write at that time you said that you forgot to give me any soap and forgot to give me my comb & Brush it was my fault more than yours I might have thought of it myself as to the Brush I don't want it but would like to have my comb & a little soap is very acceptable at any time to keep ourselves clean we cant get any soap at any Price though we have not suffered for any yet as some of the mess receive a little from home every few days as for making me a cap I can do very well without any but my head gets right cold at night…"

27th Nov. 1862 Letters of 1st Lt. Reuben A. Scott Co. B, 10th Regiment Virginia Infantry Camp Near Liberty Mills orange County (Va.) Dear Mollie: "…Mollie we have plenty of beef & Bread to eat and have flour a head there is a few men bare footed some I expect threw away their shoes to have an excuse to keep from marching…"

This is one Regiment that's doing OK.

WRITING & FIGHTING FROM THE ARMY OF NORTHERN VIRGINIA ed. by William B. Styple pub by Belle Grove Pub. 2003

Pg. 162 Letter From Tout Le Monde-Rapidan River Nov. 18, 1862 "…The troops are becoming better clad, and every day, as fast as they are received, shoes is issued to the most needy. The army never was in better fighting condition nor in better health. …"

What army is this guy seeing?

UNDER THE STARS AND BARS-A History of the Surrey Light Artillery pub by Press of Morningside Bookshop 1975

Pg. 65 Nov. 20, 1862 Battery 16, on the James River, near Richmond "…A brisk and biting wind is coming down across the James that finds its way readily through the faded and thin uniforms of the men. In the absence of overcoats, the men go about wrapped in their blankets, which are thus made to do double service-a cover by night, a protection by day. Even a piece of an old tent, anything that can be utilized, serves to keep out some of the cold…"

Using anything they have to keep warm.

BROTHERS IN GRAY-The Civil War Letters of the Pierson Family ed. by Thomas W. Cutrer & T. Michael Parrish pub by La. State Univ. Press 1997 Ninth Louisiana

Pg 134 Ruebin Allen Pierson to Joseph Pierson in Camp (near Winchester, Va.) Nov. 20th, 1862 "…I hear that Mr. Wells is coming to bring us all some shoes & I am very glad for several of the boys are now barefooted and it is nearly am impossibility to get them at any price here. I gave eleven dollars per pair for course brogans and could have sold them for fifteen since. Such are the extortionary rates now asked & every day they grow worse…."

This would've been great news, here is another Regiment rellying on the home folks.

CAPTAIN GREENLEE DAVIDSON, C.S.A. Diary and Letters 1851-1863 ed. by Charles W. Turner pub. by McClure Press 1975

Pg. 58 Artillery Corps Light Division Camp Lee 4 miles east of Winchester (Va.) Nov. 21st, 1862 "…The snow soon covered the earth and the barefooted and thinly clad men of my Company looked as if they were almost ready to perish.

I am glad to say, however, that I soon received a partial supply of shoes and winter clothing so that my men are now quite comfortable…I am really suffering for a new uniform, a new pair of boots and good warm socks. Don't forget a comfort to wrap around my neck…"

Apparentely not all the men are "quite comfortable," he writes of suffering from a lack of everything.

THE SOUTH REPORTS THE CIVIL WAR by J. Cutler Andrews pub by Univ. of Pittsburgh Press 1985.

Pg219 "In the Memphis Appeal of Nov. 21, 1862, its Richmond correspondent contended that the sight of Confederate soldiers marching barefooted through the slush of the city during a snowstorm on Nov. 7 had had more effect than Alexander's letters in bringing home to the citizens of Richmond the shoeless and blanketless condition of the army."

Can you imagine marching, for any length of time, barefooted through slush?

REMINISCENCES OF CONFEDERATE SERVICE by Francis W. Dawson ed. by Bell Irwen Wiley pub by La. State Univ. Press 1980

Pg. 55 Nov. 1862 "Dawson had obtained a commission in the C.S. Navy, but redsigned it order to take a lieutenant's position with the Purcell battery. He had "provided himself with the gray uniform of the Confederate Navy." But now…"There was joy indeed at Oakland when the news of my promotion was received there; and the young ladies set themselves to work at once to contrive ways and means whereby my gray navy coat could be converted into the tunic of an Artillery officer. The most troublesome part of it all, we found, was to get the Austrian knot on the right arm, the "curleycue" as we called it, into the right shape. It is so long since, and these things are so soon forgotten, that it may not be out of place to mention here that my new uniform was a gray tunic with scarlet cuffs and scarlet collar; an Austrian knot of gold braid on each arm; two bars of gold lace, denoting the rank, on each side of the standing collar; gray trousers with broad red stripes; a scarlet kepi, trimmed with gold braid, and commonly known, by the way, as the "woodpecker cap." …"

Pg.190- In a letter to his mother from Petersburg, Va. Nov. 22, 1862 he writes "It might interest you to form some idea of your Confederate son's present appearance, and I will endeaver to give you some idea. My coat is a blue grey, with scarlet cuffs and collars, embroidered with a filigree of gold lace from the wrist to above the elbow, and two gold bars on the collar to denote my rank, buttons of course in profusion. The pantaloons are of the same texture as the coat, with a broad red stripe at the seams. My cap is the shape of the French Kepi (Albert will describe it to you) the top and sides scarlet and the band black; the whole embroidered with lace in the same style as the coat sleeve."

RED CLAY TO RICHMOND by John J. Fox pub by Angle valley Press 2006

Pg. 133 "The Light Division marched through Winchester (Va) at 2:30 A.M. on November 22. A Winchester woman who witnessed the move described the sorry scene, "They were very destitute, many without shoes, and all without overcoats or gloves, although the weather is freezing. Their poor hands looked so red and cold holding their muskets in the biting wind." …"…climbed the western slope of the Blue Ridge Mountains at Fisher's gap. The troops somehow held up under the strain of the elements. Snow and sleet made the mountain crossing difficult and dangerous. Many soldiers left bloody footprints as the sharp rocks and ice pierced their rag-wrapped feet. The men plunged their chapped hands deep into pockets or under armpits as the relentless wind tore at their clothing…"

I cannot imagine marching & camping out equipped like this. I'd have froze.

"DEAR MOTHER: DON'T GRIEVE ABOUT ME. IF I GET KILLED, I'LL ONLY BE DEAD." ed. by Mills Lane pub by The Beehive Press 1977

Pg. 195 Thomas McCollum to his Wife Fredericksburg, Virginia November 25, 1862 Dear Margaret: "…The weather is pretty cold at nights and we had snow about the 1st of November, and we are barefooted and nearly naked. We have to make shoes out of raw cowhide. Shoes (are) very hard to get where we are and very dear. Common dollar shoes (cost) $15.00 and can't get them at that. So you must not think hard of me for not seding you any money…"

SOJOURNS OF A PATRIOT The Field and Prison Papers of An Unreconsrtu8cted Confederate edited with commentary by Richard Bender Abell & Fay Adamson Gecik pub by Southern Heritage Press 1998 letters of Pvt. Augustus Pitt Adamson

Pg. 110 Nov. 26th, 1862 Dear Father, "…Tell Ma to send me a pair of pants when Will comes back. She will know which to send, for she wanted me to bring them when I was at home…"

CONFEDERATE CENTENNIAL STUDIES #26 LAWLETY COVERS THE CONFEDERACY by William Stanley Hoole pub by Confederate Pub Co. 1964

Pg. 36 Nov. 26 1862 (Times, Jan. 1, 1863 "…As for the fighting men, Lawley observed, they were in wonderful spirits, although many were "ragged, slovenly, sleeveless, without a superfluous ounce of flesh upon their bones, with wild matted hair, in mendicant's rags, [but] when the battle flag goes to the front, how they can and do fight!" Said Lee to Lawley, "there is only one attitude in which I never should be ashamed of your seeing my men, and that is when they are fighting…"

A SOUTHERN SOLDIER'S LETTERS HOME The Civil War Letters of Samuel Burney Cobb's Georgia Legion, Army of Northern Va. ed. by Nat Turner pub by Mercer Univ. Press, Macon Ga.2002

Pg. 228 Camp Georgia Legion, Near Fredericksburg, Va, Nov. 27th, 1862 "…We are still drawing clothing from the Government. Last night we drew 5 blankets & 5 pair shoes-still we have some men barefooted, & this weather is very cold…."

Drawing clothing from the government? This isn't even a trickle!

FORGET-ME-NOTS OF THE CIVIL WAR: A ROMANCE by Laura Elizabeth pub by Press of A.R. Fleming Printing Co. 1909

Nov. 27, 1862 "…There are hundreds of them (soldiers) barefooted and ice on the gound all day. General Hill issued an order yesterday requiring all the barefooted men to make sandals of raw hides with the hair on the inside. It answers the purpose very well. It's a wonder the idea had not been thought of sooner, before the men suffered so much. Gorman says that Pat Sims will be here to-day with the things for the Regiment. I hope he will be, for I need my boots very badly, also my pants. I shall draw a pair of pants from the Regimental clothing, also a pair of shoes. I bought me a Yankee overcoat, a very comfortable one, for $12.50, a better coat than our men draw at more money…"

According to this soldier, pants and shoes were available to draw at this time. Then why are there so many barefoot men? Why the need for the raw hide shoes?

AS RECORDED IN THE POCKET DIARIES OF PRIVATE ROBERT A. MOORE, Co. G, 17th Miss. Regt. Confederate guards, Holy Springs, Mississippi ed. by James w. Silver pub by McCowat-Mercer Press 1959

Pg. 118 Thursday, Nov. 27th, 1862, camp near Fredericksburg "…Orders from Gen. Longstreet to make rawhide shoes when others cannot be procured…"

CHARLOTTE'S BOYS-The Civil War Letters of the Branch Family of Savannah ed by Mauriel Phillip Joslyn pub by Rockbridge Pub. Co. 1996

Pg. 137 Sgt. Sanford Branch to Charlotte Branch Camp near Fredericksburg Nov. 27th 1862 Dear Mother, "…We left Orange CH on last Wednesday and marched 3 days in the rain, a distance of 52 miles. I had just bought a new pair of shoes and walking in the water blistered my feet awful. By the second day I had to go barefooted. It was very cold and I suffered very much. On the 3rd day I cut my shoes so that I could wear them…If you have an opportunity to sent me a Blanket please do as it is quite cool…"

What a heartbreaker- he finally got new shoes and ended up having to cut the sides so he could wear them.

AS RECORDED IN THE POCKET DIARIES OF PRIVATE ROBERT A. MOORE, Co. G, 17th Miss. Regt. Confederate guards, Holy Springs, Mississippi ed. by James w. Silver pub by McCowat-Mercer Press 1959

Pg 118 Saturday, Nov. 29th, 1862camp near Fredericksburg "…Soldiers badly clad for winter…"

TRUE TALES OF THE SOUTH AT WAR Collected and Edited by Clarence Poe pub by Univ. of N.C. Press 1961

Reminiscences of Barry Benson
Pg. 28 Fredericksburg Barry Benson winter, 1862 The men in camp would call anyone in clean clothes "Hospital Rat!" "…the wearing of clean clothes without holes in them was evidence which, though it might be merely circumstantial, was to them strong enough to warant the attack…"

PARKER'S VIRGINIA BATTERY by Robert K. Krick pub by Va. Book Co. 1975

Pg. 97 Winter 1862 "…Lieutenant Brown suffered from the high cost of living when he began to outfit himself for his wedding trip. In late December he was obliged to pay $63.50 for three handkerchiefs and one pair of boots. One of the artillerists encamped at Carmel Church turned the situation to his advantage by setting himself up in business selling clothes made for the purpose by his wife. He was getting $5 for a pair of Drawers, $16 for a pair of shoes, $25 for pants and $10 for a vest. Not too many monthes later the men would look back on even these unaccustomed high prices as bargains…"

A SCYTHE OF FIRE-THE CIVIL WAR STORY OF THE EIGHTH GEORGIA INFANTRY REGIMENT by Warren Wilkinson & Steven E. Woodworth pub by William Morrow Pub. 2002

Pg. 196 winter 1862 marching towards Fredericksburg "…for Sanford Branch, marching in the ranks of Co. B, that this was little consolation (the sandy soil). He had gotten a new pair of shoes-real shoes these, not sewed on cowhide-just before the regiment had started the march, and the long miles of walking in new shoes that were thoroughly wet had blistered his feet terribly on the first day. Now, for the second day's march, he decided to walk barefoot and carry his shoes. That too proved unsatisfactory, for the temperature was not much above freezing, and walking barefoot all day in the chilly rain and mud was a painful proposition. When for the third consecutive morning the regiment prepared to take to the road, Branch finally broke down and cut slits in the sides of his new shoes in order to ease their tightness and make them wearable on his blistered feet…"

VOICES OF THE CIVIL WAR by Richard Wheeler pub by Meridian books 1990

Pg. 208 Dec., 1862 an unnamed Union picket decribes the Rebel pickets across the Rappahanock River:

"It was quite cold, and many of the rebel pickets wore [captured] Federal overcoats, and when not on duty occupied holes excavated in the banks opposite us."

RECOLLECTIONS OF A CONFEDERATE STAFF OFFICER by G. Moxley Sorrel pub by Bantam Books 1992

Pg. 105 Dec. 1862 "The march to Fredericksburg in bad weather and almost bottomless roads had caused great suffering to the men and some losses among the animals. It was then that Longstreet told his men of an expedient that as an old soldier he had often resorted to. "Rake" he sent word to the men, "the coals and ashes from your cooking fires and sleep on that ground; it will be dry and warm." And so it proved. Also, there being many barefooted men, "take the rawhides of the beef cattle, killed for food, cut roughly for a moccasin-like covering for the feet, and there you are with something to walk in." But this did not go. The footwear had nothing like soles of stiffening, and in the mudand icy slush of the Virginia roads the moist, fresh skins slipped about as if on ice. The wearers, constantly up or down, finally kicked them aside and took the road as best they could, barefooted or wrapped with rags or straw. Richmond did its best to supply, but there was always trouble for want of shoes. Great quantities were run it from England by blockade, but they were worthless, shoddy things that might be done for in a days use. I once wore a pair of them, and in a single day of wet and mud the cheats came to pieces and developed paper and odds of leather things, where should be good, strong, well-tanned cow skin."

OK, the raw hide moccasins aren't working on the march, and now the English shoes, after being brought all the way from Great Britain, wouldn't even last a day's march. This situation would cause anyone to cuss.

THE CONFEDERATE VETERAN VOL. XVI 1908

Pg. 636 Dec. 1908
Reminiscences Of Fredericksburg by Sam R. Burroughs "About one-fourth of General Lee's army was shoeless, and had been since prior to the Sharpsburg campaign. While encamped at Culpeper C.H. and before moving into position at Fredericksburg green beef hides were issued, out of which moccasins were made. These came to us in patterns, regardless of the size of feet they were intended to cover, with instructions to stitch them up with the hairy side in, in order that the hair might serve the function of the absent sock. However, the first few

mile's march through rain and deep mud disposed of this uncanny footwear. Near the first of December, 1862, the ladies of Richmond sent Hood's texas Brigade a box of shoes, which when prorated gave the company of which I was a member, (Co. G, 1st Texas Regiment) two pairs. There being eleven men in our company without shoes, the writer included, the orderly sergeant, James Kennedy, prepared as many straws, and the boys lined up and pulled. The result showed that Marshell Hamby and Tom Main were the lucky ones."

THE CONFEDERATE SOLDIER by LeGrand J. Wilson pub. by Memphis State Univ. Press 1973

Pg. 99 Dec. 1862 "…We were tired of Richmond, tired of guard duty, tired of camp. We wanted to see active service, wanted to be numbered with the veterans. At 1 o'clock we were ordered into line. Every man and officer was in his new uniform, and guns and accoutrements as bright as silver dollars…."

TRUE TALES OF THE SOUTH AT WAR-How Soldiers Fought and families Lived 1861-1865 Collected & ed. by Clarence Poe pub. by Univ. N.C. Press 1961

Pg.28 Dec. 1862 Reminiscences of Berry Benson, 1st South Carolina Volunteers (A clean white shirt made Benson suspect at Fredericksburg) "…I remember very well on going through the camps before reaching my own, being hailed with continuous cries of "Hospital Rat! Hospital Rat!" About hospitals, just as they do about hotels and such places, rats always collected in numbers, big ones, and got fat of stealing and waste, of course, and as there were some men who shirked the camp and the campaignand, under pretense of being sick, spent a large portion of their time at hospitals, the good soldiers cocieved a natural hearty dislike and contempt for these, and applied to them the epithet of Hospital Rat as implying their having made the hospital a permanent abode. But as soldiers are not very discriminating in their judgements, or rather, the temptation to fling a stone is too exciting, they sedom stopped to inquire the passerby really deserved the name or not; the wearing of clean clothes without holes in them was evidence which, although it might be merely circumstantial, was to them strong enough to warrant the attack. Private or officer, he could not escape the shelling, and many's the man who, having arrived close to his camp early in the evening, has hung around in the woods till dusk, before venturing to run the guantelet. "Hospital Rat! Hospital Rat." The stereotyped reply to which was, by those courageous enough to face it: "You go to hell!" which only thickened the abuse. I remember walking once through a strange camp at Fredericksburg, having on a clean white shirt, albeit of coarse cotton, bosom and all, but its whiteness made it a target, and I was hailed with "clean shirt! clean shirt! come out of that shirt!" The face of the aforesaid iron dog would grow red under such a volley…"

SOJOURNS OF A PATRIOT The Field and Prison Papers of An Unreconstructed Confederate edited with commentaey by Richard Bender Abell & Fay Adamson Gecik pub by Southern heritage Press 1998

Letters of Pvt. Augustus Pitt Adamson
Pg. 111 Camp Young, Near Savannah, Georgia Dec. 1st, 1862 Dear Sister, "…The pants I told Will I wanted are the black pair that Ma wanted me to bring when I was home. Ma can send me a shirt before long, if convienent to do so,but I am not needing it much…"

LETTERS OF WILLIAM F. WAGNER, CONFEDERATE SOLDIER ed. by Joe M. Hatley and Linda B. Huffman pub, by Broadfoot's Bookmark 1983

Pg.25 Near Federicksburg Va Dec. 1st 1862…"Dear Wife you stated in your letter that you send some of my things in that made up box Dear Wife I am afraid I will never get to see them at all if you onley wouldn't to send them with them things and wated til some boddy would a come out hear of course you ditent know so I cant Blame you for it for they tole you it would go safe I need the socks and would be verry glad to git my shirt and gloves I may git them some time but it is verry dout fool wheather I Ever git them or not of course I reckon they are at Richmond but we are out hear and cant git them and they may sell them out at Richmond and we may never git them or hear from them any more…"

MEMOIRS OF LIFE IN & OUT OF THE ARMY IN VA. DURING THE WAR BETWEEN THE STATES. By Capt. Charles Blackford, "The Wise Troop" Vol.1

Pg. 235 Dec. 2d 1862, Camp near Spottsylvania Court House "We are very uncomfortable here in the wintry air and on the frozen ground. We have nothing but the most meager supply of army rations, no tents, no cooking utensils, and only such blankets as each man carries on his person. I am writing now in the open air, of course, as we have nothing to enclose it, by the side of a fire, the fickle smoke from which blows first one way and then another, but always in my eyes, which must account for the straggling writing. I am so cold I can scarcely keep my pen in my hand or my paper on my knee. It is getting colder every minute and the wind is blowing very hard."…

FAR, FAR FROM HOME-The Wartime Letters of Dick and Tally Simpson, 3rd South Carolina Volunteers by Guy R. Everson & Edward W. Simpson Jr. pub. by Oxford Univ. Press 1994

Pg. 162 Dec. 2nd, 1862 In Camp Near Fredericksburg Tally N. Simpsom to Mary Simpson

My Dear Sister, "The box from Laurens has come, and I am glad to say that my bundle of clothing and the nice little box of peach leather are now in my passion. Is it worth while to thank you in long and affectionate terms?"

THE CONFEDERATE VETERAN VOL. XXVI 1918

Pg. 359 In The Years Of War compiled by John C. Stiles from "Official Records" Series III, Vol. II 1862-63- Barefooted and Clothingless Men- Gen. Lee reported that on Dec. 2, 1862, there were three thousand men in his army absolutely barefooted, while there were a great many shoes in Richmond in the hands of extortioners who wanted fifteen dollars a pair for them. The Adjutant General of Hay's Louisiana brigade reported that "among fifteen hundred men reported for duty there are four hundred without covering of any kind for their feet. There are a large number who have no blankets; some without a particle of underclothing, having neither shirts, drawers, nor socks, while overcoats, from their rarety, are subjects of curiosity." What a difference between their condition and that of the soldiers of today!"

I would have taken some soldiers and seized those shoes from the speculators, arresting them at the same time.

FAR,FAR FROM HOME-The Wartime Letters of Dick & Tally Simpson, 3rd South Carolina Volunteers by Guy R, Everson & Edward W. Simpson, Jr. pub by Oxford Univ. Press 1994

Pg. 164 Dec. 3rd, 1862 Tally N. Simpson to Mary Simpson NOTICE-Owing to the fact that winter, cold disagreeable winter, is now on hand, and that all privates in the army are oftimes exposed to its severity, both in camp and on picket, it is therefore earnestly solicited by one T.N. Simpson-Priv, Co.A, 3rd S.C. Regt.-that a nice comfortable sack coat be made for him by the inmates of Mt. Jolly, "Opossum Corner," Anderson District, South Carolina. He would like it made of thick, substantiakl cloth, lined from collar to tail, and to fit similar to RW Simpson's over coat, and sent on the very first opportunity. As he has nothing but a short jacket without an overcoat for this severe weather, he needs the above mentioned article very badly indeed. Prompt attention to this matter will ever be remembered with the most profound gratitude…"

Pg. 170 Dec. 25th, 1862 Camp near Fred'burg, Tally N. Simpson to Anna T. Simpson My Dear Sister, "…I have received the bundle of clothes sent to Columbia. The bundle contained one shirt, one scarf, and two pairs of socks…I am a thousand times obliged…"

JAMES MADISON UNIVERSITY ARCHIVES

3RD Dec. 1862 Letters of 1st t. Reuben A. Scott Co. B, 10th Regiment Virginia Infantry Camp Near Guinia Station (Va.) Dear Mollie: "…Mollie I wrote to you to send me a pair of Gloves since I wrote to you I got a mate to the one I brought from home and will not need any more for some time I need nothing at present unless you see a chance to send me a piece of soap-we got up this morning and washed our clothes and put on clean under clothes so we feel much better this evening you would have laughed to see me washing this morning you may be sure I done it well…"

7th Dec. 1862 Letters of 1st Lt. Reuben A. Scott Co. B, 10th Regiment Virginia Infantry Camp Near Guinia Station Caroline County (Va.) Dear Mollie: "…The weather has been very cold last Friday it commenced raining about 11 o'clock A.M. and rained until 4 o'clock P.M. when it turned to snow & sleet the snow got one & half inches deep it ceased about 9 o'clock at night when it got excessively cold the snow it still lying on the ground we have not got any tents yet not do I think we will very soon there has been no move toward getting any tents for us to make a shelter out of our oil cloths by putting up two forks and a pole on them with poles laid one and on the ground and the other end on the pole that is on the forks making a kind of shed with one side open we make a big log fire in front which prevents us from freezing…"

28th Dec. 1862 Letters of 1st Lt. Reuben A. Scott Co. B, 10th Regiment Virginia Infantry Camp Near Rapohannock Academy Dear Mollie: "…Mollie I wish you would send me a pair of my old pant so I may get them by the 20th or 25th of Jna'y I will need them by that time if I don't see a chance to get a pair from the Yankees but guess we wont get a chance at them this winter & I hope we may never get into another fight…"

A TRUE HISTORY OF COMPANY I, 49TH REGIMENT NORTH CAROLINA TROOPS by W.A. Day printed at the Enterprise Job Office 1893

Pg. 32 "…On December the 3rd it snowed about four inches deep and the weather was very cold; but we were very well clothed and had good blankets, though some of the men had worn out shoes. Wesley Benfield of Company I went into the battle barefooted, in the snow. Afterward he made moccasins out of raw cow hide…"

BRIGHT & GLOOMY DAYS-The Civil War Correspondence of Capt Charles Frederick Bahnson,A Moravian Confederate ed by Sarah Bahnson Chapman pub by Univ. TN. Press 2003

Pg. 38 Camp near Drewry's Bluff, Dec. 4, 1862

Memorandom
A blanket or quilt. 12 or 15 panes of glass 8X10. A piece of chalk. Some Neats Foot Oil. A Wash Pan that Julious Mickey promised to let me have. Two buckets that Mr. Ackerman promised to make. Some sole leather to make a pair of deck soles for my boots, & some for my shoes. A couple of pegging awls, & some pegs. 2 doz. Red clay pipes, & some reed stems. Some pieces of red flannel to mend my drawers & shirts. A pillow case....Lieut. Swan said he would bring a box for me, & I would be very glad if you would send me the above articles to-gether with some apples & whatever eatables you may see fit to send..."

What is this soldier going to do with 12 or 15 panes of glass?

VOICES FROM COMPANY D Diaries by the Greensboro Guards, Fifth Alabama Infantry Regiment, Army of Northern Virginia ed. by G. Ward Hubbs pub by Univ. of Georgia Press 2003

Pg.122 Dec. 4 1862 SP "...I recd. No letters but a nice lined blank.(blanket) & havelock Mama sent (...) Capt. And have many I can carry..."

THE CIVIL WAR LETTERS OF GENERAL FRANK "BULL" PAXTON A Lieutenant of Lee & Jackson ed. by John Gallatan Paxton Hill Jr. pub by College Press 1978

P g. 65 Spottsylvania C. H. December 4, 1862 "...Our soldiers are not clothed or fed now as they used to be. We are short of everything. I hope this winter that much may be supplied, and next spring we may be able to begin the campaign in fine condition.

We have bright, clear weather now, but it is the season when we may expect it not to last. Soon we shall have snow, bad roads, cold weather and the usual attendants of the season. I wish now we had the order to prepare for it and build such cheap huts as would shelter. Now very few of them have tents and many are thinly clad; some are barefooted and few without blankets. I wish that I had the power to supply their wants, but I can do but little..."

VOICES FROM CEMETARY HILL-The Civil War Diary, Reports and Letters of Colonel William Henry Asbury Speer (1861-1865) ed. by Allen Paul Speer pub by The Overmountain Press 1997

Pg. 85 (Letter) Camp of the 28th N.C. Regt. 6 miles from Fredericksburg on the R.R. Dec. 4, 1862 "...Our men have stood the march very well. They are as tough as hounds & as fat as bears but ragged. They are drawing plenty of pants, drawers, coats & shoes today, but they can't get any socks. All the people who can send their friends a (pair) ought to do so. Blankets are very scarce..."

These soldiers are drawing clothing and shoes at this time, obviously from the government quartermaster

DEAR AMANDA-The Civil War Letters of Marion Hill Fitzpatrick ed. by Jeffery C. Lowe and Sam Hodges pub by Mercer Univ. Press 1998

Pg. 33 Dec. 4th, 1862 Near Guiness Station, Va. (Letterno. 17) Dear Amanda "…I am well, but about worn out marching and about to get barefooted and naked too…We had some pretty rough weather on the march, but considering the time of year we were greatly blessed. I suffered more with sore feet than anything else. I threw away my old socks and took it without any and done much better than with the old holey things. I bought a pair and wore the two last days and got on very well. I paid a dollar for them. They had been worn some and I nearly finished them just in two days.

My feet are nearly well now. My shoes are nearly worn out. I would wear any thing the way we had to march and the kinds of roads we had to go over. A great many are entirely barefooted. My coat caught on fire on night while I was asleep and nearly burnt out one of the pockets and burnt a considerable hole besides. I learn that Capt. Browne is in Richmond with our clothes. I would be happy to get mine just at this time, but it is all for the best that he did not get to us before we started on this march. They say we will draw shoes soon and I will get a pair then. The things you sent by John Wilder are in Gordonville yet. I may get them after awhile…."

He says that Capt. Brone is in Richmond with their clothes, it's a good bet he's bringing them from home.

RED CLAY TO RICHMOND by John J. Fox pub by Angle Valley Press 2006

Pg. 134 Dec.4 1862 "…They finally arrived in Fredericksburg on December 3 after marching 140 miles in twelve days. The weather in Fredericksburg failed to improve. Four inches of snow covered their sleeping bodies on the night of December4. Sergeant John Morgan's shoes, during the long march, either completely disintegrated or fell into tatters because he wrote his wife on December 8; My feet are on the ground and I don't know when I will get any more [shoes]. I am tolerably supplied with clothes. I have now drawers only what I have on at this time and I have been wearing them six month. [T]hey are covered with lice. [T] hey nearly eat me up…"

Pg. 144 "Private James Plummer, Company F, suffered wounds at the battle of Fredericksburg. He died in a hospital two days later without seeing the suit and boots sent from home. Members of his company opened his package and distributed the clothing. Captain McElvany mentioned in a letter to his own family that Plummer's new boots fit hisfeet very well. The officer also listed a number of clothing items that he needed. These items included shirts, socks, drawers and a hat. He wanted a new overcoat and a drop coat too. He hoped that his father would visit soon and bring some supplies from Gwinnett County for the men of Company F. This company numbered about fifty men fit for duty as another Christmas away from home approached.

Sergeant James Kimbrough returned from Georgia at the end of December 1862 or early January 1863. He brought a large amount of supplies that included shoes, blankets, and assorted clothing…"

I wonder if by "drop coat" he means asack coat or something similar.

LETTERS FROM LEE'S ARMY by Susan Leigh Blackford and Charles Minor Blackford pub by Scribner's Pub 1947

Pg 140 Dec. 5, 1862 Capt. Blackford of the Second Virginia Cavalry to his wife Susan At Camp, neat Spotsylvania Courthouse (Va) "…My coat is giving signs of dissolution which warns me I must be making arraingements for another: so have one made for me out of the cloth I sent you by Callahan. I do not want yellow cuffs or collar, but have it braided with gold lace, bars on the collar and knots on the sleeve, of the regulation style. Let the buttons be of the handsomest staff variety you can get. I burned a hole in my coat yesterday, and am in daily dread my pantaloons will not stand much longer the strain of this cruel war. To be breechless in this weather in the face of the enemy will not do…"

AS RECORDED IN THE POCHET DIARIES OF PRIVATE ROBERT A. MOORE, Co. G, 17th Miss. Regt. Confederate Guards, Holy Springs, Mississippi ed. by James w. Silver pub by McCowat-Mercer Press 1959

Pg. 120 Saturday, Dec. 6th, 1862 camp near Fredericksburg "…One man from each camp is to go home for clothing if Gen. Lee's consent can be obtained…"

THE CIVIL WAR LETTERS OF GENERAL FRANK "BULL" PAXTON A Lieutenant of Lee & Jackson ed. by John Gallatan Paxton Hill Jr. pub by College Press 1978

Pg. 66 Camp near Guiney's Depot (Va.) Dec. 7 1862 "…We have a quiet Sunday to-day. Everything in camp stopped except the axes, which run all night and all day, Sunday included. With the soldier it is, "Keep the axes going or freeze." They are the substitute for tents, blankets, shoes, and everything once regarded as necessary for comfort. The misfortune is that even the axes are scarce; the army is short of everything. It seems strange, but, thanks to god for changing their natures, they bear in patience now what once they would have regarded as beyond human endurance…"

MEMOIRS OF LIFE IN & OUT OF THE ARMY IN VA. DURING THE WAR BETWEEN THE STATES. By Capt. Charles Blackford, "The Wise Troop" Vol.1

Pg. 236 Same camp-December 7, 1862 "…It is true I have the advantage of some few in the activity of my mind in inventing schemes to hide my nakedness should my garments give way before my new suit arrives. I have neither patch, pin, or paste to mend a rent. Possibly they may hold out, or yet again a Yankee bullet or sabre may render me indifferent to such casualties…My hand is almost frozen. I am writng on the bottom of an inverted stewpan. I warm it by the fire and then throw an oil-cloth over it, an am only thus able to keep my hand from freezing…"

BROTHERS IN GRAY-The Civil War Letters of the Pierson Family ed. by Thomas W. Cutrer & T. Michael Parrish pub by La. State Univ. Press 1997 Ninth Louisiana

Pg. 135 Ruebin Allen Pierson to William H. Pierson In Camp near Fredericksburg, Va. Decr. 9th, 1862 Dear Father "…Some of the boys are still without shoes and consequently have kept themselves about the fire. Most of them have good clothes and none of them are without a good blanket. We have been looking for Wells to bring us on a lot of shoes for some time but he has not arrived up to this time. A lot of shoes would be quite a treat to us now…"

WEEP NOT FOR ME, DEAR MOTHER by Elizabeth Whitley Roberson pub. by Pelican Pub. Co. 1996

16th Georgia Regiment of Infantry Pvt. Eli Landers (age 19)
Pg. 152 Camp near Fredericksburg Dec. 10th 1862 Dear Mother "…Mr. G.W. Shamblee came in yesterday evening. We was all very glad to see him. He brought everything through safe. I was glad to get my overcoat for I was needing it very bad. It is worth $50.00 to me for we need everything we can get to keep us warm for the weather is very cold here now…."

LETTERS TO AMANDA-The Civil War Letters of Marion Hill Fitzpatrick ed by Jeffery C. Lowe and Sam Hodges pub by Mercer Univ Press 1998

Pg. 39 Dec. 15th, 1862 Near Fredericksburg, Va. (Letter no. 19) Dear Amanda "…I wrote to mother on the 10th inst. And told her all about my clothes &c. If I had not got my shoes overcoat and blanket I would have faired but middling by this time. As to old Browne's coming with our clothes I have about given that out. I get along pretty well now. I wear both pairs of my britches and have been wearing them for nearly two months. The out side pair got nearly impossible but I worked on them late the other day and they do finely now. The great misfortune here the most of the time is we have nothing to patch with. I have been without a handkerchief for some time till yesterday evening. One of the company burnt a hole in one of his shirts and throwed it away or rather gave it to any of us here (there being a few of the sick and wounded here) to patch with. It was a pretty good checked shirt. I took The back off and hemmed it with loud stitches washed it and made a first rate handkerchief. I have saved enough to patch my coat pocket and the hole that was burnt in my coat that I wrote you about, which task I expect to perform now pretty soon...."

Pg. 42 Dec. 29th, 1862 General Hospital No. 20 Richmond, Va. (Letter no. 21) (Marion was wounded in the side, he didn't say which, but not seriously it seems) Dear Amanda, "They have hospital underclothes, that is, shirt and drawers for us to wear all the time we stay here, so I had to pull off my shirts and drawers the first night I got here and it will be a very rare occurrence if I ever see them again, but when I leave I will get either them or others in their stead. The first shirt and drawers I got hold of was worse than get out but I did not keep them long before I made a negroe get me a good sett. They are the most singular made shirts I ever rewad of. The tail is as long almost as I can remember and are split up very little ways on the sides. They have no collar but a button that buttons in the bosom, and no wristbands or buttons at the ends of the sleeves..."

GRANDFATHER'S JOURNAL (Franklin Lafayette Riley) Company B Sixteenth Mississippi Infantry Volunteers Harris' Brigade Mahone's Division Hill's Cops, A.N.V. May 27, 1861-July 15, 1865 by Austin C. Dobbins pub by Morningside Press 1988

Pg. 110 Thursday-Friday, Dec.4-5, 1862 Meridian (Mississippi) He went on furlough to get married to Bal "...I would have liked to stay, but what has to be has to be. I am returning outfitted with new clothes- shoes, trousers, shirt and jacket-and letters and packages for Co. B..."

Website civilwarhome.com Civil War letters of William (Billy) A. Elliot Ltter #4

December the 9 1862 Franklin Depot Virginia Dear Father "...I got your letter you sent with Mr. Brown in due time. I got my shirt & drawers you sent with him...I want you to send me some plain thread and a good big needle in the box..."

CONFEDERATE CAPT. UJANERTUS ALLEN'S LETTERS TO HIS WIFE by Randall Allen & Keith S. Bohannon pub by La. State Univ. Press 1998

PG. 192 Near Port Royal Va. Dec. 10th, 1862 My Dear Susie "...This remarkable cold weather reminds me very forcibly that I would like to have my coat...My dear I almost believe that cotton is warmer for socks than wool. Do not trouble yourself about wool... Lawton's Brigade of Georgians in our division have no tents at all. Neither do they trouble themselves to fix up bunks of brush or do anything else but grumble and wish themselves back at Savannah. We have only three fly tents (tents half closed at the ends like this;/) to the company…P.S. I would be glad if you could send me a pair of boots and also a pair of shoes. I am thinking of having all my shoes made at home, and try and take care of them…."

Pg. 206 near Fredericksburg "…2nd P.S. The fact is we can get nothing here. It would take a thousand (?) to set me in good running order. Cant go to Richmond or anywhere else unless the regiment goes. If those clothes don't come soon I will be bareheaded, barefooted and bare backed. That is the fact…"

A HISTORY OF THE 2nd SOUTH CAROLINA INFANTRY : 1861-1865 by Mac Wyckoff pub. by Sergeant Kirkland's Museum & History Society Inc. 1994

Pg. 62 Dec. 10, 1862 after the Battle of Fredericks burg "…The South Carolinians did not feel guilty about helping themselves to abandoned Federal supplies. Robert Strand picked up a canteen, oil cloth, two plates, gunstrap, knapsack, haversack and as many crackers as he could carry…"

WEEP NOT FOR ME, DEAR MOTHER Letters of Eli Pinson Landers from Gwinnett Co. Ga. The Flint Hill Grays. Eli was 19 years old when he enlisted in Aug. 1861) ed. by Elizabeth Whitley Roberson pub by Pelican Pub. Co. 1996

Pg. 152 Camp near Fredericksburg Va. Dec. 10th, 1862 Dear Mother "…I have been looking for Mr. Shamblee for some time. I told the boys when he come he would bring me my overcoat with some potatoes in it and when I unfolded it I found my words true. I said I would not take 5 dollars for them. I roasted them last night. Mamma I am at a loss to know what is best to do about clothes. I have got as much as I need all but pants. I have no pants worth anything and if I don't get to draw some before long I will be without any and the Quartermaster says we will not draw anymore clothing money. What we draw from now on will come out of our wages so I will just say to you if you can when E.M. comes back to send me one pair of pants. That is all that I need as for a waistcoat I have got a short coat that will do for that. I don't know whether there will be anymore clothing come in to draw or not…."

Eli is uncertain whether there will be any more clothes to draw from the quartermaster.

THE BROTHERS WAR-CIVIL WAR LETTERS TO THEIR LOVED ONES FROM BLUE & GRAY by Annette Tapert pub by Times Books

Pg. 112 Horatio Newhall sergeant 44th Mass. Vol. Inf. Co. C—coast of N. C. Dec. 11-22 1862 "…I never saw such a mean looking set as the prisoners were. They had all kinds of uniforms. Mostly their uniforms were of a dirty gray homespun…"

DEAR SISTER-CIVIL WAR LETTERS TO A SISTER IN ALABAMA Frank Anderson Chappell pub. by Branch Springs Pub. 2002 (Third Alabama Regiment)

Pg. 123 Camp at Rappahannock Academy Near Port Royal Va. Dec 12th 62 Dear Sister "…It is with much pleasure that I can today with pen and ink (for it has been with a pencil for a long time) write to you with new shoes and clothing on. Yesterday just in time to save me from raw hide slippers our goods came. You never seen anyone run into new clothes any faster than I did. We had just received orders to be ready to march at a moments warning and hence my hurry. My clothes fit very well. So did Lewis', all but his pants. They are about a yard too long. From their length I suppose you and Ma think that he has grown considerably, but you are mistaken.

I am a little uneasy about John. I can't hear from him and it's the same at home. By the by, I also received some clothes for him. I having as much as I could manage, what must I do with his? I thought it best to sell them. I sold the shirt and pants. I shall try to lug with the drawers and socks, though I have a load of my own, though I am getting to be a fairly good pack horse. Yesterday I bought me a good overcoat.…I am more thankful for my clothing, so I will close…"

Supply from home folks.

BROTHERS IN GRAY-The Civil War letters of the Pierson Family ed by Thomas M. Cutrer & T. Michael Parrish pub by La. State Univ Press 1997

Pg 138 Ruebin Allen Pierson to David Pierson In Camp near Fredericksburg, Va. Dec. 12th, 1862 Dear Brother "…Some of the boys are still barefooted and others have no good clothes but I hope we will soon be supplied as we are camped near the railroad and only a few hours(') run from the (illegible)…."

THE CONFEDERATE VETERAN VOL. XXVI 1918

Pg. 108 March, 1918 Letters From The Front- Thomas Caffey to his family in Alabama Frederickburg, December 12, 1862 Dear Ma: "The clothing you sent me came to hand this morning, and I assure you that nothing could have been more acceptable to me. My only fear is that I will be unable to carry what I have, but I will try to do so at all events.

The overcoat is either not meant for me or I am too little for it, I don't know which; but I am pleased with it, and it will prove a good protection to me this cold weather...The shoes you sent fit me well..."

VMI Letter #5

December 13, 1862 Franklin Depot, Va. Dear Father, "...I want you to send me a good woolen pair of pants and a good piece of hard soap and some thread and a couple of needles..."

EYEWITNESS- THE CIVIL WAR AS WE LIVED IT-The American Iliad by Otto Eisnshciml & Ralph Newman pub by The Universal Library 1947

Dec. 13, 1862 A description of Jackson & Stuarts forces at Fredericksburg..."Off in the distance were Jackson's ragged infantry, and Stuart's battered cavalry, with their soiled hats and yellow butternut suits..."

WEBSITE-55TH va.org/article 00001

Pg. 2 "During the night of December 13th, the hundreds of dead Union soldiers in front of the Confederate position at Fredericksburg were stripped of their clothing leaving most of them naked by morning. The rebels took this clothing in order to use it..."

FOUR YEARS ON THE FIRING LINE by James Cooper Nisbet-Captain Company C, 21st Georgia Regiment McCoat-Mercer Press 1963

Pg. 127 Dec. 14,1862Fredericksburg, the night after the battle- "...that night our men were lying on the slope of the deep cut expecting an attack at any time. I was walking the railroad track behind mt company, trying to keep from freezing. I heard a groan, then another. I asked: "Who's that?"

The man said, "Its Fred Oyler, Cpatain; Its mighty hard to stay here in the frozen mud without shoes, and no fire. My old shoes came off in the fight, and I am barefooted."

I said: "Why didn't you go back on the battlefield and pick up a pair, when I told the sergeant to allow a certain number to go at a time?"

He said, "I hate to."

I said: "We can't have fires; the enemy will open on us with a hundred cannon and interfere with our work of removing the wounded."

I ordered him to go back and secure a pair of shoes or boots for his freezing feet, and an overcoat or anything he could find to protect himself from the cold. Very reluctantly the man obeyed the order. I had dismissed the occurrence when I heard some one roll down into the cut, crying and groaning: "O Lordy! O Lordy! O Lordy!"

"Who's that?" I exclaimed. "Stop that noise!"

Oyler had materialized again. "I told you, Captain, I didn't want to go back yonder!"

"What happened to you, Oyler?" Iasked.

Shuddering, he replied: "I went over yonder and was trying to get me a pair of boots. And when I got one half off a man's foot-the fellow came to life! And grabbed me! Oh, he did, Captain! He's pulled out nearly all of my hair!"

The boys all around us were laughing. I answered my good private-he was a fine soldier, if he did have ghost-nerves: "Now, see here Oyler, that's a queer story! You've got to show me. Come ahead!" We went back to the spot he had evacuated so suddenly, passing over the ground where Archer's men had driven a Union brigade back into the railroad cut and over which we, too, had fought. Our ambulances were slipping along very quietly, taking up the Yankee wounded. Hazardous work, this! The Yankee pickets were firing in the direction of every sound that indicated a Reb. Many dead lay upon the field.

Dimly enough the moon was shining, through thaty sleety November Drizzle. My man stood looking about him in the uncertain light for some time. At length he muttered: "There's the feller!"

There he was, wrapped in a blanket, sitting up in the moon-light, surrounded by dead men. He had overheard us and exclaimed: "Wonder what damn rascal that was, that tried to steal my new boots?"

"Who is that?" I demanded.

"Is that you, Captain Nisbet?" promptly came back the enquiry. "this is Jim Beckham."

"What are you doing out here, Beckham? Every man was ordered to return to the cut as soon as he had supplied his needs."

"Yes, sir; and now that you've caught me, I'm going to tell you all about it, Captain. I came out here and got an overcoat, blanket, oil-cloth and a good pair of boots; and then as it was so muddy in the crowded cut, I thought I'd lie down here and sleep some-I was that tired and tuckered out. I expected to run and jump in the cut, if the firing commenced. Well, I was dreaming about Sally and the children at home when I felt something tugging at my boot. I peeped over my blanket and saw a fellow stooping over, hard at work. Had my boot nearly off!I raised up and seized his hair. I'll tell you, he gave the most unearthly shriek I ever heard and fell backward, leaving his hair in my hands, as he ran."

"Here he is!" I said, pointing to Oyler. "And now that you have disobeyed orders, you take Oyler and get him a pair of boots, overcoat, blanket, and anything else he wants and bring him back to the cut."

Beckham said as he jumped up: "Yes. Captain, I'll get him what he wants, and keep the spooks off'n him too." Which he did...."

GENERAL LEE'S ARMY-FROM VICTORY TO COLLAPSE by Joseph T. Glatthar pub by Free Press a div. of Simon and Schuster

Pg. 175 Dec. 14, 1862 after the Battle of Fredericksburg "There was no room for civility. After the Federals withdrew, Confederate soldiers descended like locusts to pick clean what the Yankees left behind. "As the boys say," crowed a Mississippi orivate, "Burnside is old Lee's quartermaster." A North Carolina officer commented that "our men went to work robbing the dead without ceremony." while a member of Early's staff explained to his grandmother, "They were stripped to the skin by our Soldiers who have long since lost all delicacy on the subject." A Confederate artillerist penciled in his diary, All the Yank dead had been stripped of every rag of their clothing and looked like hogs that had been cleaned." In some instances, Confederates dug up buried Yankee dead to get their clothes."

OK, reader, what would you have done in a similar situation? All the previous letters state the men had few clothes, no shoes, blankets overcoats, tents to keep them warm. These actions seem necessary for survival.

WAR HISTORY OF THE OLD FIRST VIRGINIA REGIMENT, ARMY of NORTHERN VIRGINIA by Charles T. Loehr pub. by Wm. Ellis Jones Book & Job Printer 1884

Pg. 32 Dec.14, 1862 day after the Fredericksburg Battle "…Some of our men, however, did get some shoes from the dead, which was excusable, as we were badly shod…"

GENERAL LEE'S ARMY-FROM VICTORY TO COLLAPSE by Joseph T. Glatthar pub by Free Press a div. of Simon and Schuster

Pg.174 Dec. 14, 1862 Private James H. Hoyt-"On the battlefield of Fredericksburg in Dec. 1862, he gazed upon hundreds of lifeless, naked Yankee bodies. Rebel troops had swooped down after the fighting and stripped them of everything, emptying their pockets, swiping their shoes, confiscating their pants, shirts, and coats, and removing everything of any possible value. Nearby, six of his comrades hovered over a dying Yankee, waiting for him to expire before they plundered him as well.

VOICES FROM COMPANY D Diaries by the Greensboro Guards, fifth Alabama Infantry Regiment, Army of Northern Virginia ed. By G. Ward Hubbs Univ. of Georgia Press 2003

Pg. 126 Dec. 15, 1862 SP after Fredericksburg "…found that the Yanx had gone & so silently that our skir. Knew nothing of it. The most of the skir. Had gone forwd. plunderg.

& soon men could be seen coming in every direct. Over the field picking up things-I found our Lieut. In charge was not strict and no use being there & I put out too. Got me a nice new Minnie Musk. Made at Bridesburg U.S. 1862 - Threw away the old smooth bore I had. Got a hatchet and a butcher knife wh. Gave to John for cookg.-a little bot. ink-2 books & grape Gil got in woods.- tried to get oil cloth but found no good one & a good new Yankee canteen...."

THE CONFEDERATE VETERAN VOL.1

Oct. 1893 Pg.370 Dec.15, 1862 Sacrifice of Federals at Fredericksburg by Murat Halstead, northern journalist "I saw the cloud of battle over Franklin's flanking movement far down the river, where alone there was a rational hope of doing any thing. But the pillar of cloud did not advance, and the rumbling of many guns was not continued. There was a temporary success there, and 200 or 300 North Carolina troops were taken prisoners. It was pathetic to see their home-made outfits, their knapsacks of worn carpets-carpets used as blankets and coverlets and patchwork quilts that had seen some service, the butternut jackets and ragged hats. I had seen North Carolinians before, for my father's people were of them. I saw in the poor prisoners many things that reminded me of "our folks" in the old times. Those North Carolina boys were lank, yellow, weather-beaten, rough-haired, with bony limbs, and wore ragged jackets. They had plenty of teeth and eyes, and many of them would be called "jays" or "greenhorns," but they were terrible soldiers, with the hardihood of wild animals, tireless on the march as wolves, and glad to get an ear of corn for a ration, while a hunk of shoat was a luxury, and a chew of tobacco dissipation."

VOICES OF THE CIVIL WAR by Richard Wheeler pub by Meridian Books 1990

Pg. 220 Dec. 15, 1862 after the battle of Fredericksburg, northerner Regis de Trobriands reports: The dead were hideous-black, swollen, covered with clotted blood, riddled with balls, torn by shells. The rebels, poorly clothed, had left then neither shoes, nor trousers, nor overcoats..."

FOOTPRINTS OF A REGIMENT A Recollection of the 1st Georgia Regulars by W.H. Andrews Longstreet Press Atlanta Ga. 1992

Pg. 100 Dec. 15, after the Battle of Fredericksburg, winter, 1862-63 "...I drew a piece of carpet in lieu of a blanket, not having anything in that line since the Battle of Sarpsburg, and had it not been for the kindness of Pvt. Jordan J. McMullen of Company M, would have suffered from the severe cold weather. He has a homemade blanket, overcoat, and oil cloth which he allowed me to share with him. We would stretch the oil cloth over some sticks, make us a bed of leaves or straw, and cover with the overcoat and blanket. How was that on frozen ground and ice on the creek two feet through. While nothing to compare with a feather bed, we would sleep warm...."

REBEL PRIVATE FRONT AND REAR-Memoirs of a Confederate Soldier by William A. Fletcher-Texas Brigade pub by Dutton Books, 1995

Pg. 65 Dec. 15, 1862 after the Battle of Fredericksburg": "...In the morning we were sent to the front to relieve the battle line that I had passed through during the night and nearly all the dead Yankees who were in sight were naked....when we had taken our place as relief, we were not confined to line and all who wished were sight-seeing a short distance to the front as the dead bodies were nearly all naked and lying on their backs. There was exposed to view a surprisingly large number of them who were so diseased, one would think: "Why weren't you fellows all in the hospital; or, were you run into our protected front to put an end to your miserable condition," and the idea that struck me was: "What will the Yanks be fighting us with next, and was not the ending better for them."

Pg. 67 "...I saw that our part of the line had stripped the dead the most. The unacquainted would think that this work was done by the line soldier, but was not, only in cases of actual necessity. It was largely done near Richmond and by those who made a business of it, as the clothing, when washed, was good stock in second hand stores and its benefit was that it supplied the wanting soldier and poor citizen at a low price. I heard of no effort to stop the practice, and there was no harm in stripping the dead, when the party stripped was a party to blockading our ports, which created the urgent necessity..."

FOUR YEARS IN THE CONFEDERATE ARTILLERY-The Diary of Pvt. Henry Robinson Berkely ed. by William H. Runge Univ. N.C. Press 1961

Pg. 39 Dec.15, 1862 (after the Battle of Fredericksburg) "...Robert B. Winston and I went over the battlefield. We went to the extreme eastern end of the line and followed it up to Fredericksburg. We got some plunder; most of it had already been carried away. I got about a dozen pairs of good drawers and an oilcloth...All of the Yankee dead had been stripped of every rag of their clothing and looked like hogs which had been cleaned...."

BROTHERS IN GRAY-The Civil War Letters of the Pierson Family ed. by Thomas W. Cutrer & t. Michael Parrish La. State Univ. Press 1997 Ninth Louisiana

Pg 136 N.M. Middlebrooks to David Pierson Camp near Troy, Miss. Dec. 16th, 1862 Dear Friend "...Beldon told me you wanted to know what the boys most needed. Well, I think they most need Blankets, Socks, & yarn Pants, Shoes, &c. If you can, get me two pair of stout woolen pants and a couple of overshirts..."

A CAPTAIN'S WAR LETTERS AND DIARIES OF WILLIAM H.S. BURGWYN 1861-1865 ed. By Herbert M. Schiller White Mane Pub Co. Inc. 1994

Pg.42 Tuesday, December 16th 1862 "Sent some of my men on the battlefield to get themselves overcoats, blankets, and after finding the enemy had evacuated the town and they got themselves more than a supply. I obtained an overcoat which I very much needed..."

LETTERS FROM LEE'S ARMY Compiled by Susan Leigh Blackford Annotated by her husband, Charles Minor Blackford, Charles Scribner's & Sons 1947

Company B of the Second Virginia Cavalry- Charles Blackford was first lieutenant, later captain.

Pg. 143 Fredericksburg Dec. 17th 1862 "...I have had no change of clothing for a long time and don't know when I will..."

A CAPTAIN'S WAR LETTERS AND DIARIES OF WILLIAM H.S. BURGWYN 1861-1865 ed. By Herbert M. Schiller White Mane Pub Co. Inc. 1994

Pg. 43 About old camp four miles south of Fredericksburg December17th, 1862 "...Just before being relieved finding the enemy's pickets not firing at me or showing themselves I conjectured they had retreated (which they had) and gave permission to some of my men to visit the field of battle and supply themselves with overcoats and things which they needed and consequently they obtained from dead Yankees as many overcoats, shoes, and boots, and haversacks, and enough provisions to restore three or four regiments. I have now an overcoat an (sic) taken from a dead Yankee also a fine pair of boots and a cap. Some of my men found watches on the Yankees."

CIVIL WAR LETTERS OF 2ND LIEUT. JOHN D. DAMRON

49th N.C.T. Co. K Fredericksburg, Va. Dec. 17th 1862 Dear Father "...I have not received the clothing mother sent me. The boxes were sent here from Richmond the day we were ordered to the battlefield & we could not get them. Some were sent back & some are scattered everywhere. We will probably never see them..."

WRITING & FIGHTING THE CONFEDERATE WAR The Letters of Peter Wellington Alexander ed by William B. Styple Belle Grove Pub. Co. 2002

Pg. 125 The Late Battle-Further Particulars Heights of Fredericksburg, Va. December 17, 1862 "...A few hundred men are still without shoes and proper clothing. These are permitted to remain at the campfires and take care of the baggage. How long shall the state of things continue? The condition of the great body of the troops, however, is much improved, thanks to the timely action of the people at home; but it might be redered yet more comfortable. There should be no relaxation, therefore, in the patriotic work of furnishing supplies; for clothing and shoes soon wear out in a rugged campaign like this. Very few men have gloves, or more than one pair of socks…"

DEAR SISTER-CIVIL WAR LETTERS TO A SISTER IN ALABAMA Frank Anderson Chappell pub. by Branch Springs Pub. 2002 (Third Alabama Regiment)

Pg. 125 Camp near Fredericksburg, Va. Dec. 17th 62 Dear Sister "…(about the battle) Our regiment captured a brass band and all the men. We got many good blankets and other valuables. Would you suppose a man could take clothes off a dead man, oh well, we do. Overcoats and shoes ain't nowhere if the yank has not been dead over two days…"

U. S. ARMY HERITAGE AND EDUCATION CENTER

Dec. 17, 1862 Samuel Wilson 55th North Carolina Infantry Regiment Dear Sis and Mom: "…Thom told him he had been appointed quartermaster and was sent back on business, I suppose to get clothing…"

THE BROTHERS WAR-CIVIL WAR LETTERS TO THEIR LOVED ONES FROM BLUE & GRAY Annette Tapert Times Books 1988

Pg. 102 Dec. 18, A.D. 1862 Near Fredericksburg, Va. Dearly Beloved Parents "…I now once more have or take the opportunity of writng a few lines to let you know how affairs are here. I am somewhat unwell at present. I was taken with a chill then a pain on my side night before last, but now I feel right better this morning. I think it was just a bad cold, which I have taken because I have nothing but old pieces of shoe on my feet. My toes are naked, and my clothing are getting ragged.

I have not got my box of clothing yet, and I don't know whether I ever will get them or not because the boxes are very often robbed at the depots. I wrote to you to bring me a box of clothing as soon as you possibly can, and come with them yourself so that you can be certain I will get them because I need them very much.

There has been a very hard battle fought here at Fredericksburg Saturday. Our regiment was in the heart of the fight. I did not go into the battle because I am so near barefooted the colonel gave orders that all the barefooted men should stay at the camp. I can tell you I was glad then that my shoes did not come, because I would rather lose a hundred dollars than to go in a battle…Your affectionate son, C.A.Hege …"

LETTERS OF WILLIAM F. WAGNER CONFEDERATE SOLDIER ed. By Joe M. Hatley and Linda B. Huffman pub, by Broadfoot's Bookmark 1983

Pg. 26 Camp near Fredesburg Va. Dec.18th 1862…"Dear Wife we are at our ole camp a gain where we was before the fite but I don't know how long we stay hear Dear Wife I haint got them things you send don't send any more without you are shoore some boddy will come tous"

HANDLEY LIBRARY ARCHIVES-James A. Miller Collection correspondence C.W. era misc. New Market, Va.

Camp near Port Royal Dec. 18th, 1862 Dear Julia, "…I wish you would hurry up those pants that you are making. Have a black stripe put down the legs fix it so that it can be taken off I should get out of the service, those that those that you sent me by (Cp?) have worn out in the seat and those you had made for me are getting thredbare along the legs where the saddle makes them. And if you can get Failer's to make me a hat I wish you would do so…"

THE CRY IS WAR, WAR, WAR The Civil War Correspondence of Lts. Burwell Thomas Cotton and George Job Huntley, 34th Regiment north Carolina troops by Michael W. Taylor Morningside 1994

Pg.112 The Letters of Burwell Thomas Cotton Co. K,34th Regt. N.C. Troops Pg. 129 Camp Near Fredericksburg Dec. 18th, 1862 "…If Pa comes to see me you need not send my yarn drawers as I prefer cotton here in camp. I will need some pants and socks. I will need my overcoat. I would be glad to have a pair of shoes with iron on the heel. Shoes are very hard to get here. …"

HANDLEY LIBRARY ARCHIVES, WINCHESTER, VA. Letters of Michael Freeze Pvt. Co. C 23rd North Carolina Infantry

Transcribers note: This letter is undated-To Dovey AC Freeze (wife) "…if you send close with Deaton send one pare of pants too pare of socks and glovs if you hav got them I beleav that is all that I need at this time and I cant cary most when I need when we march the talk is gin that a brigade will go to North Carolin but don't know how true…"

Near Fredericks Burrow Dec the 19 1862 Dovey A Freeze dear Wife…"you said that you had made me som close and I would nead som of them very bad if I had them. I nead socks if I hand them for my cooton socks are nearly don and my shooes ara bit don I wrote aleter some time ago for brother Jacob to get BC Parker to make me apair of shooes and sand them if he could and some socks if he sands the shooes I want you to sand me too pare of socks and one pare of pants it mite be that I wouldn't nead them but sand them if you get achanc but sand the socks any how if you can …"

SOJURNS OF A PATRIOT The Field and Prison Papers of An Unreconstructed Confederate ed by Richard Bender Abell & Fay Adamson Gecik Southern Heritage Press Murfreesboro, TN 1998

Letters of Pvt. Augustis Pitt Adamson
Pg.121 Camp Young, S.C. Dec. 19th, 1862 Mr. Adamson dear Friend about the breakup of the camp "…I will try to send the balance of Pitt's things tomorrow if I can. You will find Pitt's things at the bottom of the box and I will send Will's cane bed and a par of socks. And also I will send H.L. Hamilton's close in the same box…"

Pg.120 Camp near Fredericksburg Va. Dec. 20th 1862 "….I write this time more particularly about my clothes (it was bitter cold at Fredericksburg, with snow on the ground.) We have been looking for Pa to come out here for some time & he has not come yet & Adelias letter did not say anything about his coming if he don't intend to come any time shortly I want you to mark all my clothes & put them in a bundle & mark the bundle to me & send them immediately to Mccajah Clarks or Bob Cronins store as Capt Clark and Lieut Cronin have sent home by some of their folks to come out here & bring all the things wanting by the company They will be boxed up & some one will come with them it is important that every bundle should be well marked so it can be told whose they are I want you to send my overcoat to me shirts drawers & boots I reckon I shall have socks enough if my boots are large enough to wear them I would not care (mind) if I had a pair of oversocks & I wish I had written you word to have me a pair of pants as it seems a hard matter to draw any here but I reckon I can get a pair after a while …Send my clothes as soon as you can as I need them this cold weather…"

LETTERS FROM LEE'S ARMY Compiled by Susan Leigh Blackford Annotated by her husband, Charles Minor Blackford, Charles Scribner's & Sons 1947 Company B of the Second Virginia Cavalry- Charles Blackford was first lieutenant, later captain.

Pg. 152 from Mrs. Blackford Dec. 20th, 1862 "…I have gotten the clothes for which you wrote from Page Co and they are awaiting your orders.

VMI

Dec. the 20th 1862 My own Dear Mother "…I want you to send me a couple of pair of white gloves as we are not allowed to wear any but white ones and I could not keep one pair clean and tis so cold to hold a cold steel gun in your hand at night. I wrote a note in one of Aunt

Sarah's letters to you to get me some linsey to line my overcoat with as we can get nothing but cotton cloth. I have gotten my jacket & pans which are very comfortable…I have not gotten my shoes on account of the river being frozen up…"

I Wrote You Word-The poignant Letters of Private John Holt-John Lee Holt 1829-1863 ed. by James A. Mumper printed by H.E.Howard 1991

Pg. 120 Camp Near Fredericksburg, Va. Dec. 20th, 1862 My Dearly beloved wife "…I write this time more particularly about my clothes (it was bitter cold at Fredericksburg, with snow on the ground) We have been looking for Pa to come out here for some time & he has not come yet & Adelias letter did not say anything about his coming if he don't intend to come any time shortly I want you to mark all my clothes & put them in a bundle & mark the bundle to me & send them immediately to McCajah Clarks or to Bob Cronins store as Capt. Clark & Lieut. Cronin have sent home for some of their folks to come out here & bring all the things wanting by the company They will be boxed up & some one will come with them it is important that every bundle should be well marked so that it ccan be told whose they are I want you to send my overcoat to me shirts drawers & boots I reckon I shall have socks enough if my boots are large enough to wear them I would not care (mind) if I had a pair of oversocks & I also wish I had written you word to have me a pair of pants as it seems a hard matter to draw any here but I reckon I can get a pair after a while…"

THE CONFEDERATE VETERAN VOL. IV 1896

Sept. 1896 Pg. 305 Incidents At Fredericksburg-Camp Near Fredericksburg, Va. Dec. 20, 1862 J.B. Polly to "Charming Nellie" "…Only two regiments of our division were engaged in any undertaking which might be called a battle. These were the Fify-seventh and Fifty-fourth North Carolina Regiments, composed of conscripts-young men under twenty or old men-all dressed in homespun, and presenting to the fastidious eyes of us veterans a very unsoldierly appearance. But we judged hastily: ordered to charge a body of the enemy, they did it not only with most surprising recklessness, but kept on charging without intermission or let up, until, to save them from certain capture, Gen. Hood recalled them peremptorily…"

THE CONFEDERATE VETERAN VOL. XVI 1908

Pg. 164 April 1908 Private Soldier Life- Humerous Features by James Reese (of the Edney Grays) Dec.20, 1862 after the Battle of Fredericksburg "The enemy recrossed the river and gave up the fight at that point. Burnside was relieved of the command. Two days later we moved back to our old camp for some days. General Ransom's Brigade was ordered back to Richmond. While we were passing through Richmond the General had us to double-quick to keep us out of mischief. There were crowds of well-dressed free negros who had come out to look at the ragged "Rebs." Occasionally the troops would make an awkward maneuver, the darkies would get mixed in with the rank, and were almost run over. Often they would come out bareheaded. A few days afterwards many dirty Rebs were seen wearing good hats that they claimed to have captured in some previous skirmish..."

"...Our next move was to North East River. Here some of the boys got a possum, and it was so thin that Jasper Williams proposed to throw in a piece of bacon for a share of the possum. Still, it was too thin to be good; and if the Confederacy had not been in narrow straits for supplies, we would never have eaten that possum..."

GRANDFATHER'S JOURNAL (Franklin Lafayette Riley) Company B Sixteenth Mississippi Infantry Volunteers Harris' Brigade Mahone's Division Hill's Cops, A.N.V. May 27, 1861-July 15, 1865 Austin C. Dobbins Morningside 1988

Pg. 113 Sunday, Dec. 21, 1862 Camp near Fredericksburg "Cloudy. Looks like snow. Fortunately the Yankees have supplied us with tent flies and warm clothing. Mon. evening, after the battle, the fields were blue. Tues. morning, after the Yankees withdrew, the fields were white..."

HAM CHAMBERLAYNE-VIRGINIAN Letters and Papers of an Artillery Officer in the War for Independence 1861-1865 with introduction, notes and index by his son C.G.Chamberlayne Richmond, Va. Press of the Dietz Printing Co. Publishers 1932

Pg. 145 J.H.Chamberlayne to M.B. Chamberlayne Camp near Moss Neck, Dec. 22nd, 1862 My dear Mother, "...Pray do not hurry about the cloth. I purposely fail to send the buttons. Wait for the English..."

SOJOURNS OF A PATRIOT The Field and Prison Papers of An Unreconsrtu8cted Confederate edited with commentaey by Richard Bender Abell & Fay Adamson Gecik Southern heritage Press 1998 letters of Pvt. Augustus Pitt Adamson

Pg. 123 Camp Clingman near Wilmington, New Hanover county, North Carolina Dec. 22nd, 1862 Dear Sister, J.T. Sanders is still at Savannah. He said he would send home what things I left there. We drawed a new uniform the day before we left there but it was a sorry article. I had no use for mine, nor never expect to have. I told Jess to send them all home.

Please tell Ma I have as many bed quilts as I can carry. Some of the company have already drawed blankets. The rest will draw soon, I think. The shoes I got when I was at home proved to be not much account. The Quartermaster says we will draw shoes also. If not, I want Pa to have me a good pair made, let them cost what they may, I want a good pair,..."

FREDERICKSBURG! FREDERICKSBURG! George C. Rable Univ. N.C. Press 2002

Pg. 277 "To make matters worse, scavengers had often stripped the bodies-rather like cleaning a hog or skinning a squirrel, depending on the preferred metaphor. A fortunate Confederate might find a new rifle or a full haversack uncontamminared by the owner's blood. There was a raft of scarce items: a good overcoat, a warm blanket, or a sturdy pair of shoes that fit. An Alabama officer saw two barefoot soldiers standing over a Yankee who had received a mortal wound, waiting for him to die so they could grab his shoes. One impatient fellow tried to pull a shoe off a supposedly dead Federal who suddenly stirred. "Beg Pardon Sir," the Rebel said, "I thought you had gone above.

Such courtesy hardly characterized prevailing attitudes or practices. Some contemporary accounts describe a field of white-clad corpses, but others talk of bodies stripped naked. The ultimatwe humiliation for the Yankees-to be laid bare before their enimies-reflected the desparate shortages in Lee's army, as did bodies dug up for their clothing. Other indignities, such as cutting off a finger to steal a ring, reflected only barbarity. Just as Federals had lost their moral compass in sacking Fredericksburg, so Confederates now foraged among the dead with an alarcrity they would have once found shocking.

That barefoot men would steal shoes was self-justifying, and most Confederate accounts stressed sheer necessity.... The wretched bluecoats, according to one Confederate artillerist, had "burned houses and drove old men, women and mothers with infants at the breast, and little children into a December night to die of cold and hunger."

During the burial truces, the Federals discovered how their dead had been stripped. Some shied away from mentioning in letters home that even men's underwear had been pilfered. But more often than not the bluecoats described what they saw in tones of moral outrage. Stories spread that unscrupulous villains had pulled the coats off the wounded. Although he admitted the poorly clad Rebels needed clothes, a member of the Irish Brigade denounced their "barbarity." Raging over such diabolical acts, a Maine recruit decided thar slavery had "destroyed much of the finer sensibilities of the Southern people."

Not for a minute would Cofederates concede the moral high ground. How could these Yankee hipocrates object to a ragged soldier grabbing an overcoat when they neglected and abused their own dead? "They would pitch them in like dogs," claimed one Georgian who had witnessed the federal burial details. This was especially shocking because anonymous death terrified soldiers.

Pg. 532 notes to pages 277-78 #26 MC. An artillery private tried to grab a pair of boots but desisted when he tugged on one boot and much of the man's leg came with it (the dead man had received a mortal wound right above the knee) See Walters "Norfolk Blues" 49 One unlucky Rebel donned a Yankee overcoat and was mistakenly shot dead by a Confederate sharpshooter. For enterprising lads, it was worth taking a chance because even a bloody and soiled coat might fetch $40 in camp. See W.R.M. Slaughter to his sister, January 4, 1863,

Slaughter Letters, VHS; L. Calhoun Cooper to his mother, December 18, 1863 Cooper Letters, Kennesaw Mountain National Battlefield Park.

Pg. 532 notes to pages 277-78 #36 "federals foraging for food also took shoes, coats, and blankets from dead comrades. When the enemy stripped the dead, of course that became an outrage, but both attitudes and practices showed how inured some men had grown to corpses on battlefields.See Robert Goldthwaite carter, "Four Brothers in Blue," 197-98: "Annals of War," 265, Lord; "history of the Ninth New Hampshire," 230.

Pg. 533 notes to pages 279-80 #38 A Richmond editor duly noted how careless the Federals had been with their dead but gently suggested that if Confederates really needed to strip the bodies, they should at least leave the underwear. See Richmond Daily Enquirer, December 22, 1862.

LETTERS AND PAPERS OF AN ARTILLERY OFFICER A.N.V. IN THE WAR FOR SOUTHERN INDEPENDENCE 1861-1865 Capt. John Hampden Chamberlain-Virginian Dietz Printing Co. Pub. 1932

Pg. 146 Dec. 23rd, 1862 My dear Sister "…I spent a couple of hours with Virginius to day Mother's note says she has the uniform made up; it makes no difference either way, I am glad she is rid of the trouble. I hope she will not send it up. I do not want it at all now, and will send John down, some time within a month, he can then bring it up and bring me a trunk…"

TRUE TALES OF THE SOUTH AT WAR Collected and Edited by Clarence Poe univ. of N.C. Press 1961

Reminiscences of Barry Benson

Pg. 82 Colonel L.L. Polk's Wartime Letters Camp French, Dec. 24 1862 "…I intend to send you money every time I can. Adjudant Jordon says he will take my boots at $35. He may have them if he will and as soon as I get it I will send the money to you to use; for I can draw a pair of shoes soon and… (they) will do for me…"

LETTERS OF WILLIAM F. WAGNER, CONFEDERATE SOLDIERed. By Joe M. Hatley and Linda B. Huffman pub, by Broadfoot's Bookmark 1983

Pg.29 Camp near Fredericksburg Va Dec th 24th 1862…"Dear I am sorry that you had to knit 2 pairs of socks and gloves before I got one pair for I reckon you neadit the wool your self for you and the children "…

CHARLOTTE'S BOYS-The Civil War Letters of the Branch Family of Savannah ed by Mauriel Phillips Joslyn pub by Rockbridge Pub Co. 1996

Pg. 141 Sgt. Sanford Branch to Charlotte Branch Camp near Fredericksburg Dec. 25 (1862) Dear Mother, "...Rev. Mr. (David) Porter & Mr. Alcott of Sav. Hqts. Georgia Hospital & R. Assoc. are here.Thay gave me a fine pr. of pants, I having sent all my cloths to Richmond and burnt the pair I had on..."

THE CONFEDERATE VETERAN VOL.3

April 1895 Pg. 101 "about X-mas, '62" Mrs. Belle Lee Parkins, Landsdowne Virginia-In a subscription letter Mrs. Parkins states: "I had found out where a blockade speculator had stored a wagon load of boots, shoes, hats, gloves, etc., and, seeing these soldiers with their feet sticking out of their ragged boots, I told them. When they passed our house returning, each had something new to show me, and gave me hearty cheers."

RELUCTANT REBEL The Secret Diary of Robert Patrick 1861-1865 ed. By F. Jay Taylor La State Univ. Press 1959

Pg. 71 Dec. 28th, 1862 "The sugar and molsses is of such an inferior quality that we can scarcely use it, and as for clothing, I have never received anything from the Government yet because the Government had nothing to give me. I have received, instead of the clothing due me in within the last two years, the sum of $50.00 which would not buy me two pairs of boots to-day for they have been selling for the last twelve months at $40.00 a pair. I am not complaining of these things, but merely mention it to show that these are times not only to try men's souls, but it also tries their purses."

FOOTPRINTS OF A REGIMENT-A Recollection of the First Georgia Regulars 1861-1865 W.H. Andrews, 1st Sgt. Co. M Longstreet Press 1992

Pg. 102 Dec. 29, 1862 The home of Chief Justice Marshall, Richmond, Va. "By some means (I reckon Capt. Hill must have told him I was in the yard), he insisted on my going in the house. I begged to be excused, but he would not receive any excuse. So I had to go in. He carried Capt. Hill and myself into the parlor where thwere was five young ladies. Capt. Hill was aquainted with them, and after telling them howdy, turned and introduced them to me separately. How small and cheap I felt with my dirty anf ragged uniform. My pants were burst out in the rear from my knees down, besides being soiled every other way, To make matters worse, there was a large mirror on each side of the room and at the end, all sitting on the floor and must have been at least nine feetr high, besides a large, fine glass on the mantel piece. I could not look in any direction without seeing myself, and I certainly looked as bad as I felt…"

Pg.103 winter 1862-63 The regulars went into quarters at camp Lee, near Richmond, Sgt. Andrews and Capt. Hill went into town to visit the Captain's aquantice, Chief Justice Marshall. "…He carried Capt. Hill and myself into the parlor where there was five young ladies. Capt. Hill was aquainted with them, and after telling them howdy turned and introduced them to me separately. How small and cheap I felt with my dirty and ragged uniform. My pants were burst out in the rear from my knees down, besides being soiled every other way. To make matters worse, there was a large mirror on each side of the room and one at the end, all sitting on the floor and must have been at least nine feet high, besides a large, fine glass on the mantle piece. I could not look in any direction without seeing myself, and I certainly looked as bad as I felt…."

RECOLLECTIONS FROM 1861-1865 by John H. Lewis ex-Leiutenant in Huger's & R.H. Anderson's & Pickett's Division, Army of Northern Virginia pub. by Peak & Co. 1895 (1983)

Pg. 56 winter 1862-63 "…Here at Bunker Hill we rested for some time from marches and battles. Cold weather was approaching, and many of the men were poorly clad and numbers were without shoes; but we were getting used to that…"

Middle South

General

THE CONFEDERATE VETERAN VOL. XXV 1917

Pg. 222 May 1917 In The years 1861-62 compiled by John C. Stiles "Blue Uniforms in the C.S.A.- Colonel Mouton, of the 18th Louisiana, said of the Shiloh fight:" Anxious to intercept the enemy, I rushed on at a double-quick; but, unfortunately, our troops on the right mistook us for the enemy, owing, I presume, to the blue uniforms of a large number of my men, and opened fire on us with cannon and musket s." Colonel Trabue, C.S.A., said "I was likewise delayed and embarrassed by some Louisiana troops who were dressed in blue like the enemy." General Duke, in his admirable book, Morgan's Cavalry," states that these Louisianians, getting tired of being assailed alike by friend and foe, retaliated by returning the fire of any body of men that shot at them, saying, "We fire at anybody what fires at us."

Good policy

HANDLEY LIBRARY ARCHIVES-Civil War Diary & Letterts of William Tull 5th& 9th Louisiana Infantry

Early in 1862 "Perhaps some of the younger members of your chapter would like to know whar our wives and mothers and sisters were doing all these trying days. Why, they were working in the field, rain or shine, cold or hot, sick or well, looking after stock, going to mill and looking after all other outdoor business. At night they were carding and spinning till a late hour making all their own and their children's clothing. In many instances they made and sent to the boys at the front trousers, shirts, underwear, socks and gloves, and sometimes shoes made of leather tanned at home in vats dug out of large logs in the woods. One can well imagine how an affectionate husband, son, or sweetheart would appreciate such gifts as these, and again you can easily divine the tender fondness with which such tasks were performed though it were wrought out in tears and sacrifices."

"I would like before closing this chapter to say a word concerning the "Homespun dress the Southern ladies wore", but here language fails me. Do you think that our girls were not proudin those days of home spun dresses? Let me disabuse your minds even of the intimation of any such idea. There never was in the world or any state of society a prouder set of women than were our Southern girls who wore the homespun. Those homespun dresses were not common goods. They were made at a priceless cost. After all, they were really beautiful. The girls vied with each other to excel in an effort to have their dresses show as many different colors and to resemble as nearly as possible the finest goods ever seen in the market. To see them art church or at some dress occasion donned in their homespun was a sight to be produced only in such chivaloric days. Everyone seemed to feel herself a Queen, and in this (sentiment) she was entirely correct."

THE CIVIL WAR MEMOIR OF PHILIP DANGERFIELD STEPHENSON, D.D. ed. By Nathaniel Chears Hughes, Jr. UCA Press 1995

Pg.93 1862? Murfreesboro Tenn. "The only house I entered in Murfreesboro was a large old mansion on the north side of the street, somebody's headquarters. A typical character starts out of the darkness of the past as I think of that house, and I can see him now coming down the stairs in the middle hall, clanking his saber on every step. A Texas Ranger,one of Wharton's men. Six feet or so, in grey jacket and pants with buff trimmings, a great slouch hat over a long, lean, blue eyed face, with a heavy yellow mustache, and long yellow hair down over the shoulders, a buckskin belt with an army revolver on each side, great cavalry boots above the knees-there's your Texas Ranger. No swagger; quiet enough; but- dangerous as everybody knows."

THE CONFEDERATE VETERAN VOL. XXV 1917

Pg. 163 April 1917 In The Years 1861-62 compiled by John C. Stiles Vol. VII, "Official Records" "Invisability of Confederate Uniforms- A Union Colonel reported that in the Donelson fight "the deadened leaves of the oak shrubs were almost identical in color with the brown jeans uniform of the enemy and rendered it almost impossible to distinguish their line until a fire revealed it." Our army is to-day experimenting with a mixture of brown and gray for a national uniform, and it is well within the bounds of reality that the Confederate color will be adopted."

Proof that-in the middle South theatre of the war, butternut was already being extehsively used.

THE JOURNAL OF JULIA LeGRAND Everrett Wadley co 1911

Pg. 37 Jan. 1862 "everybody sending blankets to our soldiers. We have sent all of ours except two thin ones. Mrs. Chilton and I go to the Ladie's Sewing Society and bring home bundles of work to do for the soldiers…"

Pg. 182 "…Katy Wilkinson has sent us some more work, as we have often pressed her to do. We have sewed belts on pieces of dark cloth, doubled, which are to be worn on the girl's persons as skirts, and after crossing the lines, to be worn on the back of some Confederate soldier…"

These ladies are ingenious as well as determined to help their soldier boys.

MOUNT UP-A True Story Based on the Reminiscences of Major E.A.H. McDonald of the Confederate Cavalry Harcourt Brace & World Inc. 1967

Pg. 35 Jan. 1862 "…The smartly uniformed Federals at least looked like soldiers. The Confederates wore what they had and what they pleased. In their army the only firm regulation as to dress was that they must not wear the uniform of the enemy. Even that prohibition had to be relaxed as time went on…"

THE SOUTH'S FINEST-The First Missouri Confederate Brigade From Pea Ridge to Vicksburg by Phillip Thomas Tucker White Mane Pub. Co. 1993

Pg. 103 Jan. 1862 "…During that January in Mississippi, the Missourians finally received genuine Confederate uniforms for the more than a year and a half after leaving home and more than a year in Confederate service! In one proud Rebel's words: "There was a suit of uniform issued to every man in the Briggade. Grey pants, grey jackets, & grey caps. The collars and cuffs of the jackets were trimed with light blue. The men feel very proud of them being the first uniforms that they have recieved."..."

The Civil War Reminincences of Major Silas Grisamore C.S.A. ed by Arthur W. Bergeron Jr. La. Univ. Press 1993

Pg. 16 New Orleans Daily Delta, Jan. 11, 1862 (18th Louisiana) "...The line had a fine, substantial appearance, though many of the men were rather roughly appareled compared with our neat and showy city troops. They looked, however, as if got up more for effectiveness than display. After being reviewed in line, the brigade marched by companies, in review, and evinced, for such new troops, a high state of efficiency and drill..."

FROM THAT TERRIBLE FIELD-CIVIL WAR LETTERS OF JAMES M. WILLIAMS TWENTY-FIRST ALABAMA VOLUNTEER INFANTRY ed by john Kent Folmer pub by Univ Al Press 1981

Pg. 25 Jan 12th, 1862 Fort Gaines, (near Mobile, Al) Dear Lizzie, "...the advanced post of the picket we "gathered shells" again, and as we did not "throw them one by one away" I send my collection to you in the carpet sack-There are some dirty clothes which you will, be so good as to have washed and send to me-send me all the flannel underclothes I have-that is if there are any at home; also send that gray "Georgia" suit-it is warm and will be a change of costume for me occasionally-I am tired of looking blue and bob-tailed gray by turns!-that Base ball shirt you may keep; it has shrunken until its originally skimpy proportions will no longer button over me, and if I do wear it again I will be in danger of catching a nickname that would out-do Judas-"Cutty Sark"-I don't know if you've ever read [Robert Burn's poem] "Tam O'Shanter"? "Cutty sark being interpereted signifies "short shift"...

Pg. 31 Jan 23D 1861 Fort Gaines Dear Lizzie, "...The gloves fit well, and will be a great comfort to me if I should be on guard such a night as this..."

UNIFORMS OF THE CIVIL WAR Lord, Wise, A.S. Barnes & Co. 1970

Pg. 32 "...The troops that fought under Confederate Brigadier General Felix R. Zollicoffer at Mill Springs (Jan.18, 1862) were "well clothed in jeans, but they were without overcoats. Their discarded knapsacks contained two or three days rations. They were supplied with blankets of army regulation, white and black striped which were still bailed when captured..." Attempting to escape from Island No.10, the Confederates were cut off near Tiptonville, five to seven thousand men surrendering. "As to uniforms: "They had no uniforms but were dressed as they left home, generally in homespun colored butternut jeans. Their blankets of every kind and color, quilts, table clothes and carpeting were the material most were made…"

"According to one Illinois soldier, only a single Confederate regiment was in uniform at Island No.10, the 1st Alabama. They were wearing single breasted frocks of a dark blue jean material. These frocks were made for the 1st Alabama by the Ladies Aid Society as donations in answer to their appeal for new clothing."

According to this, the Rebels wore mostly multiform or no uniform at all.

YANKEE IN GRAY-The Civil war Memoirs of henry E. Handerson The Press of Western Reserve Univ. 1962

Pg. 92 "camp Carondelet," (La.) Jan.19th, 1862 Dear father; "…The box of clothing, Mr. Dowe kindly brought to me while yet at Gordonsville,and, though I was already pretty well supplied, many of the articles I found quite useful for myself, and all will be needed by some of my fellow-soldiers. The nice woolen socks and the jeans coat were particularly serviceable, as well as the mittens and comforter…"

DEAR IRVIE, DEAR LUCY-Civil War letters of Capt. Irving A. Buck, General Cleburne's AAG & Family pub. by Buck Pub. Co. 2002

Pg. 51 Transfer to the Western Army-Head Quarters 1st Corps A ofP Jan. 25, 1862 Dear Lucie, (sister) "You will please get mine and Alvin's (brother) clothes in perfect repair, every stitch that we have, both summer and winter-and pack them in my trunk that they will be ready at any moment-so that if needed no delay will be experienced…I will try to exchange my heavy shawl for one finer and lighter-to have a couple of shirts made, as I do not know about our washing …If I should send a shawl home to make shirts, please sew the pockets on the outside this: (draws picture) and trim with some kind of binding…I send my vest and Alvin's pants to have mended…"

PINKERTON SPY'S REPORT,

Headquarters of the Army Jan 31st 1862 "…A Lieutenant at Knoxville stated that they were not half armed but well dressed…At Nashville are 2 Regts. Of Infantry…all comfortably but coarsely dressed… "3rd Aug. 1862…"Camp Sneed is about a mile from Knoxville. There is 600 men, not armed, all uniformed…."

It's a shame this spy's report didn't include the color of the uniforms.

THE GREYJACKETS Anonymous Jones Bros. & Co. 1867

Pg.141 "In the the month of Febuary, 1862, when the United States troops occupied Jacksonville, Florida, some Confederate soldiers were captutred. A motley crew they were, whose picturesque varirty of raggedness bore here and there some indications of aim at military style, but nothing of what could be called "uniform." …"

Multiform prevails everywhere.

Pg. 191 Brigadier-General Roger A. Pryor at Manassas, 1862 (2nd Manassas) was captured and also escaped due to the fact that, when he met some Yankee troops, "His uniform being covered by a Mexican "poncho," they did not observe that he was not one of their own men; nor was there any mark visible upon his person to indicate he was an officer. …"

MILITARY COLLECTOR AND HISTORIAN-Journal of the Company of Military Historians Vol. XLI#4 Winter, 1989 Captured Clothing at Fort McHenry, 1862 by Thomas Arliskas

Pg 203 Feb6, 1862 "When Fort McHenry was captured on the Tennessee River on February 6, 1862, the retreating Confederates left behind enough clothing to clothe what one Union soldier estimated as "a thousand men a lifetime." Another account of the captured clothing follows:

In the way of clothing, if the southern Army suffer for the want of it, I cannot imagine what would satisfy them. It was evident no attept was paid to uniformity, the disderatum, being doubtless to cover nakedness. Coats, pants, and vests were found of every known material, though what be called walnut-bark dyed jeans greatly predominated. Most of the pants were ornamented by a broad black stripe down the outer seam, sometimes of velvet, but mostly of cloth or serge. Shirts and drawers, like the outside garments were all of home manufacture, and of the coarsest description. I saw only a few pairs of boots. Hats and caps were diversified, yet they had a uniform cap, gray with a black band…"

THE CONFEDERATE SOLDIER by LeGrand J. Wilson pub. by Memphis State Univ. Press 1973

Pg. 57 The author has escaped from Fort Donelson and needs to shed his Confederate uniform in order to get through Yankee lines"…I could hardly content myself to eat my supper before dressing up in my new suit, and as that suit of "old clothes" enabled me to make my escape, I think it is entitled to a full description, if it is possible, for me to describe them. The pants were of a dark gray cloth usually known as "salt and pepper" but had been worn until the pepper was barely discernable. They had been worn by someone whose weight must have approached 200 pounds andas I am a small man weighing 140 I could hardly hope for a fit, and when I drew them on I was astonished at the length of the former owner.

By shortening the suspenders and using my pocket knife at the other end a very respectable fit was at last affected. I found them very roomy for cold weather, and well ventilated besides. The vest was yellow, a dingy yellow, resembling the cloth that comes around a canvassed ham. The coat was originally of checked goods, but the checks were hardle discernable, from long service. The lining was dilapidated, and the sleeves had air-holes at the elbow.

The owner was doubtless a small man for in it I found a tight fit. The cap was a daisy. It was made of the tanned skin of the American coon with the "narrative" left in its proper place, and was a perfect fit....(later) "Wait a few moments," said the lady, as she left the room. In a short time she returned, and put around my shoulders a heavy, warm, black Talma or cloak, then wrapping a beautiful yellow nubia (a light, knitted woolen head scarf for women- Dictionary.com) around my ears and head..."

FROM THAT TERRIBLE FIELD-CIVIL WAR LETTERS OF JAMES M. WILLIAMS ed by John Kent Folmer pub by Univ Al Press 1981

Pg. 35 Feb. 14th, 1862 Fort Gaines Dear Lizzie,"...I am glad that you sent the shoes. I was beginning to feel the want of them; they were waiting dry for me when I came in soaking wet from the picket through the rain-I say that I was soaking wet; it was only my feet that were in that condition, my body being cased in oil cloth from head to foot; I never go on picket without carrying my oil cloth cloak-capcover & cape, and leggings-so that no matter how hard it rains I only have my face and feet wet..."

UNIFORMS OF THE CIVIL WAR Lord, Wise, A.S. Barnes & Co. 1970

Pg. 29 Descriptions of prisnoners taken at Fort Donelson February 16 1862

"...The uniforms of the prisoners are just no uniforms at all, lacking all the characteristics of infantry, cavalry, or artillery costume, it being wholly un-uniform in color, cut, fashion, and manufacture.

Some have coats of a butternut color cut in a regular saque style, and others fashioned like those of our soldiers as jackets or frocks. Their pants are as diversified in color. Many have no overcoats at all, and supply their places with horse blankets, hearth rugs, coffee sacks, etc, Their knapsacks consist of bags (carpet sacks) of all colors and sizes, comparing well with their coats and hats. The same remarks apply to their canteens and other accouterments, no half dozen of which seem to be made by the same manufactury..."

"...Some were clothed warmly, while others were very ragged, but such a thing as uniformity in dress was impossible to find, as there were two dressed alike. Butternut colored breeches with a broad black stripe down the sides seemed to be the favorite running gear for the legs, while old blankets, patchwork quilts, a few coats and considerable cheap cotton carpet made up the remainder of the wearing apparel. The carpet coats were made by putting a puckering string in the edge of a piece of carpet and gathering it around the neck. With the exception of Col Davidson of Mississippi, their officers could not be distinguished form the privates…"

"…There is no two of them a size, nor the same dress, nor the same color. Hats of every fashion worn for the last twenty years, pants of every hue of butternut brown. Coats of every fashion, as well as no fashion at all. Many had blankets over their shoulders, and they too of many colors. Some had pieces of carpet, others half worn horse covers, some had "old king cotton" shawls…"

"…The said uniforms of all shades of colors, grey, brindle, and butternut, the last predominating. Hats band caps of all shades, forms, and quality, and boots and shoes ditto. Even the six Rebel surgeons…are not better dressed, though some of them have made an attempt of distinction by shoulder straps and gold on their sleeves…"

"…In the way of clothing…it was evident that no attempt was paid to uniformity. Coats, pants, and vests, were found of every known material, walnut bark dyed jeans greatly predominated. Most of the pants were ornamented by a broad black stripe down the outer seam, sometimes of velvet, but mostly of cloth or serge. Shirts and drawers are all of home manufacture, and of the coarsest description. I have a package of a half-dozen shirts made of a fabric many degrees coarser than canvas duck. Hats and caps were diversified, yet they had a uniform cap-grey with a black band…"

"…Some of the Rebels had wrapped themselves in in old patched bed quilts, which they had brought with them when they mustered into the Army. Others had covered themselves with white cotton blankets. Still others wore bright backing, evidentally furnished by some merchant. One had wrapped himself in a faded piece of threadbare carpet…"

"…(On uniforms), brown predominated, but (some) were clad in grey-all shades, sheep, iron, blue and dirty grey. Most Confedertaes were in citizen clothes, their own military insignia being black stripes on their pants. Many officers had the regular grey uniform, while others the army blue, the only difference being a great profusion of gold lac.

For protection against the chilling wind, ht soldiers used a comglomeration of overcoats, blankets, quilts, buffalo robes, and pieces of carpeting of all colors and figures. Each of the Rebels had a pack slung over their shoulder…"

A thorough description of the chaotic multiform conditions of these Confederate troops.

UNIFORMS OF THE CIVIL WAR Lord, Wise, A.S. Barnes & Co. 1970

Pg. 42 A special correspondent for the Boston Journal reported from the evacuated Confederate camps at Yorktown in the spring of 1862 "…The equipments and clothing of the rebel dead were of the most miserable kind. No attempt of uniformity of dress could be seen. Here and there an officer had a flannel stripe sewn to his trousers…the men were dressed in common linsey butternut and cotton suits of the commonest and coarsest materials. They had few knapsacks, being suppied with a schoolboy's sachel, sometimes of flimsy leather, but more commonly of cotton osnaburg, with here and there a rope to sling over their shoulders…"

THE CIVIL WAR LETTERS OF JOSHUA K. CALLOWAY ed. By Judith Lee Hallock Univ. Ga. Press 1997

Pg. 12 Corinth, spring 1862 "…I could have picked up any number of blankets and quilts, but my own was all I wanted to carry. A great many of our men threw away their blankets…."

THE SOUTH'S FINEST-The First Missouri Confederate Brigade From Pea Ridge to Vicksburg by Phillip Thomas Tucker White Mane Pub. Co. 1993

Pg.11Spring 1862 "For instance, colorful dress was worn by such soldiers as William and Thomas Duvall. Both brothers in Col. Rive's regiment wore sturdy pull-over hunting shirts or "battle shirts" which were also adopted by Missouri guerillas. These durable garments had been lovingly sewn by mothers, wives and grandmothers for "their boys." Just like any country private, General Price donned a homespun "war-coat" in battle…"

Pg.18 "From a Memphis warehouse the troops of Colonels Rice and Burbridge at Cove Creek were given an odd-looking uniform of jean material. These new Confederates were not at all flattered their first uniforms, for these garments were the typical clothing of slaves on the cotton plantations of the deep south. The jean material consisted of an undyed wool, white in color and with wooden buttons. But worst of all, these unorthodox Confederate uniforms still reeked of the odor of sheep. Looking like anything but "the South's Finest," the Missouri boys, nevertheless, could not have been issued a more durable uniform. Other Rebels later laughed and bleated like sheep in poking fun at Col. Little's veterans clothed in white. Fortunately for the ridiculed members of the Missouri Brigade, these uniforms later turned a dirty brown from wear and the elements. This unusual "Confederate" uniform actually enhanced morale and camaraderie, giving Col. Little's troops a distinctive look, which strengthened unit identity and pride and seemingly early signified the Missourian's role as crack troops in this war."

One of the first accounts of "drab" color being issued.

1. The clothing of the troops was distinctive in its lack of uniformity. "Here you see the well dressed gentleman with nothing to mark the soldier but the cartridge box,

body belt and shotgun. There is a group of Mississippi boatmen in their slouched hats, cowhide boots, coming up to the knee."

SHILOH THE BATTLE THAT CHANGED THE CIVIL WAR. Pp93-94 by Larry J. Daniel pub by Simon & Shuster 1997.

Spring 1862 "The army that assembled at Corinth was thoroughly western in origin, the overwhelming majority coming from Tennessee, Kentucky, Alabama, Mississippi, Arkansas and Louisiana. A sprinkling of troops hailed from Texas and Florida, and Georgia furnished a battery and an infantry company, the latter attached to the 38th Tennessee. Though the army contained relatively few foreigners, some ethnic outfits came from the larger cities. The 2nd Tennessee of Memphis claimed the sobriquet of the "Irish Regiment." The 21st Alabama, largely from Mobile, had a company of French and another of Spaniards. The 20th Louisiana comprised six companies of Irish and four of Germans. The most colorful outfit was the Avengo Zouaves- six companies of the 13th Louisiana from New Orleans. One soldier thought them to be "a hard-looking set composed of Irish, Dutch, Negroes, Spaniards, Mexicans and Italians with few or no Americans." Their bright red caps, baggy trousers of the same color, and blue shirts with gold braid that glistened in the sun set them apart in the army.

The uniforms worn by most of the men were nondescript. "Some wore uniforms, some half uniforms, some no uniforms at all," observed a Louisianian. Artilleryman Richard Pugh from New Orleans found that the troops were not as poorly clothed as he had expected and all seemed to have good shoes. Many of the men wore a cotton uniform with a butternut hue called "Kentucky Jeans." Several of the Gulf Coast outfits, such as the Washington Artillery and Crescent Regiment, donned dark blue coats and trousers. Just prior to the battle, the 2nd Texas received undyed cotton uniforms, prompting one ungrateful member to comment:" Do these generals expect us to be killed, and want us to wear our shrouds?"

DIARY OF A CONFEDERATE SOLDIER John S. Jackman of the Orphan Brigade ed. by William C. Davis Univ. S.C. Press 1990

Pg. 25 March, 1862 near Murfeesboro "...Here we received a lot of overcoats, hats and gloves-a present to the regiment, from the merchants of New Orleans.

The day after our company wagon was sent to the city for clothing; but before it got back in the evening, the regiment had moved. I was left to help load in our baggage. We had to tumble the boxes off into the road, to make room for our camp equipage. After we were loaded, I took an axe, bursted some of the boxes, and heaped clothing on top of our load as long as it would stay-the balance was burned. We marched about 10 miles and bivouacked..."

BROKENBURN-The Journal of Kate Stone 1861-1865 ed. By John Q. Anderson La. State Univ. Press Baton Rouge

Pg.99 Mar 6 1962 At the lodge, Kate noticed "a perfect love in blue uniform and brass buttons galore.…He is one of the escaped heroes of Fort Donaldson."

FROM THAT TERRIBLE FIELD-CIVIL WAR LETTERS OF JAMES M. WILLIAMS, TWENTY-FIRST Alabama Volunteer INFANTRYed by John Kent Folmer pub by Univ Al Press 1981

Pg. 51 March 30th, 1862 Corinth, Miss. Dear Lizzie,"…I suppose that as old Provost the tailor is a slow coach my uniform will be still in his hands when you get this-get Mr. Tailor to hurry him up- I am afraid that the army may move from here before it comes, and I will have difficulty in getting it, or maybe lose the package altogether-I have forgotten to tell you to send my watch which I need now very much-and a quire of paper and a buch of envelopes-a bottle of ink would enable me to write more legible letters sometimes…"

FROM THAT TERRIBLE FIELD-CIVIL WAR LETTERS OF JAMES M. WILLIAMSON, TWENTY-FIRST ALABAMA VOLUNTEER INFANTRY ed by John Kent Folmer pub by Univ Al Press 1981

Pg. 53 April 2 1862 Corinth, Miss. Dear Lizzie, "…if it is not too late leave out my shawl and my gray coat I will get along with my big blanket (which can be strapped on the outside of the valise) and my uniform coat and fatigue jacket-as the cold weather is over this will be sufficient-…I expect to leave even that behind when we come to make forced marches, so that the smaller the package the longer it will follow me…"

DIARY OF A CONFEDERATE SOLDIER John S. Jackman of the Orphan Brigade ed. by William C. Davis Univ. S.C. Press 1990

Pg. 31 April 6, 1862 Moving up to take part in the battle of Shiloh "…I met a fellow dressed in a suit of "butter-nut" jeans, who was limping, but I don't believe was scratched. He asked me, in that whining way; "has you'ns been in the fight yet?" I thought he meant some general, and asked my "brown" interrogator what troops General Youens commanded. He seemed astounded, and at last made me understand him, I told him "no" and went on. I afterwards got quite familiar with the "youens" and "weens'" vernacular of "Brown Jeans." (Note: Jean was a common material in homemade uniforms for the Western soldiers, and, as throughout the Confederacy, attepts to color the cloth gray with ersatz dyes most often resulted in a butternut color. Jackman's reference to "Brown Jeans" probably also betrays a middle-class Kentuckians slight distain for the unsophisticated and ill-educated boys from Alabama, Mississippi, and Tennessee.)

U.S. ARMY HERITAGE AND EDUCATION CENTER Diary of Rufus W. Daniel Co C, Arkansas Infantry Regiment

April 6th, 1862 Shiloh "…Went down to the Yankee camp late in the evening with some more of our boys. Got me a Yankee cap and haversack. There was a great many things in their camps, such as shoes, clothing, blankets & C&C. Some of our boys, as soon as we charged on their camps and drove them out fell back behind to plunder and pick up everything they could find. Such men are not worthy of the name of soldier…"

CIVIL WAR IN SONG & STORY by Frank Moore pub by P.F. Collier 1865

Pg. 39 by a Union officer "Many of our regiments were paid off just previously to the battle, and our dead comrades were robbed of hundreds of thousands of dollars. The rebels were surprised and abashed at the supreme wealth of our army. They attired themselves in our uniforms, and rifled from officer's trunks tens of thousands of dollars worth of fine clothing, toilet articles, and interesting souvenirs of every man's trunk. They made themselves stupid and drunk on our fine victuals and wines. They seem to have gone mad with the lust of plunder."

VOICES OF THE CIVIL WAR by Richard Wheeler pub by Meridian Books 1990

Pg. 103 April 6, 1862 Battle of Shiloh John A. Cockerill, a sixteen-year-old Union regimental musician reported: "…a motley crowd of Confederate prisoners,: marching to the rear under guard. Another observer, he says, asked what company the prisoners belonged to: A proud young chap in gray threw his head back and replied, "Company Q of the Southern Invincibles-and be damned to you!"

"The underbrush had been literally mowed off by the bullets, and great trees had been shattered by the terrible artillery fire…All the bodies had been stripped of their valuables, and scarcely a pair of boots or shoes could be found upon the feet of the dead. In most instances, pockets had been cut open, and one of the pathetic sights I remember was a poor Confederate lying on his back, while by his side was a heap of ginger cakes and sausage which had tumbled out of the trouser pocket cut by some infamous thief. The unfortunate man… had been killed before he had an opportunity to enjoy his bountiful store…"

The Rebs have already started to obtain clothing, etc. from the dead Ynakees.

Further on, I passed…the corpse of a beautiful boy in gray who lay with his blond curls scattered about his face and his hands folded peacefully across his breast. He was clad in a bright and clean uniform. Well garnished with gold, which seemed to tell the story of a loving mother a sisters who had sent their household pet to the scene of war. His neat little hat lying beside him bore the number of a Georgia regiment….He was about my age…At the sight of the poor boys corpse, I burst into a regular boo-hoo and started on…"

THE SOUTH'S FINEST-The First Missouri Confederate Brigade From Pea Ridge to Vicksburg by Phillip Thomas Tucker White Mane Pub. Co. 1993

Pg.45 April 7 1862 Transferring East of the Mississippi "…For days, the Missouri soldiers rode the transports like curious spectators in homespun uniforms, consisting of butternut, militia uniforms, civilian clothes and undyed wool of dirty white…"

U. S. ARMY HERITAGE AND EDUCATION CENTER

April 11, 1862 Newport, Ky. Mrs. Thornton regarding defense of Fort Donelson My Dear Will: "… I could tell you of young men, Gentlemen who stood 3 days and nights in water to their knees working at the guns of same whose shoes and stockings froze to the ground… They had not prepared for such an attack by land, had they have been reinforced by fresh troops how different the results to the whole Mississippi Valley; many here have friends, others acquantences among the prisoners, several ladies and gentlemen have visited the camp from Covington and Newport can you not aid in supplying their wants anything from a (?) will help suppose you were to get up and pack a box with half-worn vests, shoes, coats, and pants and sent to Camp Douglas near Chicago. Let some friend take them and see them given as intended. All we have sent have been new but a letter on Sunday was received asking for a change of clothing for 9 soldiers who had none and that old or new would be acceptable…" (regarding supplying P.O.W.s)

Any clothing for the men at this time.

THE CONFEDERATE VETERAN VOL. XXV 1917

Pg. 464 Oct. 1917 In The Years Of war compiled by John C. Stiles from "Official records" 1862 "Seven Hundred Suits of Clothes Lost-On April 15, 1862, Gen. M. Jeff Thompson wrote Colonel Broadwell: "I have had several persons in hot pursuit of the seven hundred suits of clothes which you purchased for my command, but none of them have yet been able to overtake you or the clothing. My men are really suffering, and their ragged appearance, now that they are Confederate troops, is disgraceful to those who should provide for them. I do not mean you, but myself and quartermaster. So, please hurry them up, and if blankets can be procured, for God's sake let us have them." This general was a very plain-speaking man, but he knew what he wanted."

FROM THAT TERRIBLE FIELD-CIVIL WAR -LETTERS OF JAMES M. WILLIAMS ed by John Kent Folmer pub by Univ Al Press 1981

Pg. 56 April 17, 1862 Monterey [Tenn] My Dear Lizzie, "What a strange exciting life this is!—and how soon custom has made it easy-a year ago I was a clerk writing in my books and weel fed, clean-peaceful man-now I live out of doors, sometimes without a tent to shelter me from the weather, a dingy suit of clothes that have not been off longer than to take a bath for a week-my fare is fat bacon and heavy bread-my life is dangerous-yet I sleep well at night as I used to do: and am happy too..."

Pg. 59 April 20, /62 Corinth, Miss. Dear Lizzie, "...Lieunt. Cothran has a letter from home saying that "his uniform will be done this week, and sent on along with Lieut. Williams' "that leads me to suppose that mine will be here to-morrow or next day. Since the battle I have regretted that I ever ordered a blue uniform-it is just like that of the enemy and it is feared that in the confusion of battle somew of our officers were killed by men of our own side-I wiil never go into battle with my blue coat on that account but will wear my old gray jacket-I wish I could have a gray officer's fatigue jacket made- but I suppose the material is not to be had now..."

PG. 63 April 23D /62 Head Quarters 21st Regt. Ala Vol. Corinth,Miss Dear Lizzy, "...I have the use of Leiunt. Cluis' sword, and I go on parade in my old gray suit, as independent as General Jackson-As to the article of shoes, I furnished myself with a pair of Lincoln's army shoes out of one of his store-tents on the battle field; and get along with them very well for the present-They are big and coarse, but good. And "Death to blacking"-so when the uniform comes I will dress up as gay as anybody and in the mean time I will take a pride in being a good soldier in citizen's clothes!..."

Pg. 64 April 24 /62 Head Quarters 21st Ala Regt. Vol. Corinth Miss My Dear Lizzy,"...I have been looking at Lieut. Cothran's coat and admire its appearance, very much, as well as its price-Now if you have not already got my jacket under way, do not have it made; but go to Provost and order a coat similar to the one he made for Lieut. Cothran, and send it to me as soon as you get itdone-It is a kind of [rusty gray and?] looks neat; it is light and suitable for summer, and very cheap; costing I believe, only $16-it will do for every day, and battle wear; if I had known, I never would have ordered the blue one; still it is handsome, and I fancy I look quite military in it. I will bring it out on dress parade this evening-the blue pants are much admired and will do for an occasional grand dress display-The black stripe one the gray ones is right—As to the hat which I left behind and sent for this morningsend it as soon as you canfix it up- I have nothing of that kind fit to wear-and I think it will be quite handsome-I don't want any gold band on it- am sick of them-turn it up on one side and fasten with a gold star; or, better still, a silken loop and tassel. (black of course)- get me a full black feather if you can find it in yown-(I think that Conning has some)-trimit to suit your own taste, but to please me have as little gold as possible-none is best-

John Pippen says he is going to present me with his sash as he captured a better one on the field-so I lack but little-First, a tolerably neat pair of shoes, (I have a coarse pair for very rough service) that are a little narrower than they are long-if they have not been sent try to find me a pair of 6s that will answer the purpose-Second, my sword-Here I am a distinguished man and without a sword of my own!...

Put me up a couple of pairs of socks. If you have no woolen let them be cotton-I lost several pairs and am rather short-Iam also short a heavy single blue blanket, and a Yankee canteen covered with reddish gray cloth and a cut on one side, I have an idea that they may have gone to town along with Dixon or Werthman; you might mention it to Dixon if he is not too ill of his wound; and if they are with his things have them sent to me-Do not say anything to him about it unless he is cheerful and strongas it might worry him-The blanket and canteen I picked up on th e battle field brought them home, and put them into Capt. Jewetts tent-Werthman and Dixon were soon laid in it wounded and it may have gone off wirth their bedding as I missed it directly after they were sent away. When I inquired for the canteen one of our boys said that he had filled such a one with water and put it on one of their cots-I don't care so much for the canteen as for the blanket, but have use for both..."

Pg. 65 April 25 1862 Head Quarerters 21st Ala Regt. My Dear Lizzy, "...Military movements again look serious; and we may have active times again right suddenly, I will observe what you say about appearing upon the field in the fatal blue uniform; I have no desire to be killed by my own friendsin mistake though many of our officers wear the blue coats all the time..."

Website-Tennessee Volunteer Infantry Regiment: Clothing, Arms and Equipment

Pg. 2 "On the 19 April 1861 while at Corinth Micheal Manzy "brought a cap and shirt."

In a General Review of the Army of Tennessee, June 1862 "All of our brigade went out to be reviewed by Mager General Poke and by Brigadier Donlson...We was inspected guns canteens, knapsacks, clothing and all some us had was what we had on."

6 June 1862 "I have at this time one shirt, one pair of pants, one coat, no blanket. You nsee I don't have much trouble in caring my clothing."

22 July 1862 "At 0200 all up we drawed a few cloth six pair of pants to the company a few shoes a few drawers. I got one pair of pants, needed a shirt very much but they was none for me."

Inadequate government issue

RICHMOND DAILY DISPATCH

April 24, 1862 claimed that three fifths of the Confederate Army at Corinth were wearing Yankee hats and coats after overrunning the Union camps on the first day at Shiloh. Confederate commanders issued frequent orders for such captured jackets to be dyed grey, threatening to confiscate any that were not…"

THE CONFEDERATE VETERAN VOL 1

Sept. 1893 Pg. 267 Reminiscent Paragraphs by W.A.C. "Company B, of the Forty-third Mississippi Infantry, had a veritable camel, belonging to Lieut. W.H.H- and the use he was put to was to carry the baggage of the officer's mess. The horses of the command were afraid of the camel, and the driver was instructed to stop just outside the camp when it halted. But in a forced march toward Iuka, Miss., the command had halted just after dark, and the camel and driver got in the line of march, before he knew it. The result was that a horse made a break with a fence rail attached to his halter, and running through the camp, he stampeded men and animals in every direction. Many men took trees or any other protection, and the panic spread through much of the brigade, and many men and animals were badly hurt, and one or two horses, I think, were killed. The camel was in the siege of Vicksburg, and was killed there by a Minnie-ball from the enemy. But none of the Forty-Third have forgotten the stampede near luka. Miss.,just before the battle of Corinth."

A camel? Really? I'll bet he was eaten after he was killed in Vicksburg.

THIS INFERNAL WAR-The Civil War Letters of of Sgt. Edwin H. Fay ed. by Irwin Bell Wiley with the assistance of Lucy E. Fay 1958

Pg. 44 Army of Tennessee Feby (April) 26 1862 My own dear wife "…I have wrapped up my two shirts (blue ones), a pair of pants, three prs. socks in my leggings an am to carry them on my horse. My blankets and oil cloth I shall wrap around them. We drew these little valises to put behind our saddles and they will not hold but a pair of my pants and a pair of socks. I have strapped it to my valise and sent it in the cars.

Send me if you can a yard of oil cloth. My buggy boot would be the very thing, if you would cut it out…"

Here begins Sgt. Fay's Letters. He seems to perseverate on his clothing.

THE CIVIL WAR LETTERS OF JOSHUA K. CALLOWAY ed. By Judith Lee Hallock Univ. Ga. Press 1997

Pg. 30 Corith to Tupelo "…I wish you to send by the first one passing, one shirt, one pair of socks…"

CONFEDERATE VETERAN Nov-Oct. 1992 Drab-The forgotten Confederate Color by Fred Adolphus

May 1862 Corith, Miss. 2nd Texas infantry "Prior to the Battle of Shiloh, Colonel John C.Moore, the regimental commander, requisitioned "properly colored" uniforms from New Orleans as his men were wearing Union Blue clothing and he did not want his soldiers to be mistaken for Yankees. The requested uniforms, made from unbleached Huntsville factory cloth, arrived in Corinth before the march to Shiloh, and a member of the regiment reported that, "When the packages were opened, we found the so-called as white as washed wool could make them. I shall never forget the men's consternation and many exclamations not quoted in the Bible, such as "well, I'll be D-!" "Don't these things beat h- l" "Do the generals expect us to be killed, and want us to wear our shrouds?" Joseph E. Chance describes the issue of his clothing in the regimental history of the 2nd Texas as well. "the new uniforms waiting in Corinth to greet the regiment on their arrival there were unconventional, to say the least. Bundles of white wool uniformes had been sent with no designation as to size. The uniforms were issued and a comical scene ensued. Soon the company grounds were full of men strutting up and down, some with trousers dragging under their heels, while those of others scarcely reached the tops of their socks; some with jackets so tight they resembled stuffed toads, while others had ample room to carry three day's rations in their bosoms. The exhibition closed with a swapping scene that reminded one of a horse-trading day in a Georgia couty town." The Yankees, however, did not take such a light-hearted view at seeing these uniforms. The viciousness of the Texan's attack at Shiloh caused one federal prisoner to remember the regiment as : "them hell-cats that went into battle dressed in their grave-clothes."

It would look quite strange to see these troops on the march dressed in those uniforms. Apparently the Yankees were also impressed with these troops.

WILLIAM WATSON'S RECOLLECTIONS OF LIFE IN THE ARMY OF TENNESSEE 1887

Pg.381 May 1862 "…Summer clothing arrived to be distributed…this did not come from the army bureau, through the quartermaster's department, but from the homes and families of the men themselves. This consignment was greatly augmented by "ladies associations" which had now become a powerful factor in the administration of the war... Nothing seemed too good for them to sacrifice. Beautiful silk dresses (and other materials) had been cut up to make tunics for the soldiers."

More resupply from the home folks.

FROM THAT TERRIBLE FIELD-CIVIL WAR LETTERS OF JAMES M. WILLIAMSON Twenty-First Alabama Volunteer Infantry ed by John Kent Folmer pub by Univ Al Press 1981

Pg. 72 May 3 1862 Corinth, Miss. Dear Lizzie, "...I had finished my letter yesterday when Campell brought yours of 29th& 30th. I only opened it to barely acknowledge the receipt of them and the very acceptable accompaniements of sword-socks and hat- As I told you the hat is very much admired by everybody-the design is new-and the "fixings" are simple and exquisitally tasteful-every body says- I am delighted beyond all my expectations-I cant see a feather in the whole army so gracefully set in, and pinned-like "nights sable curtain"-with a "star." Indeed I am almost ashamed to cap my phiz with suych a piece of work!-my wife cant be exelled for taste every body agrees now-The great beauty of the thing itself is enhanced by the facy there is not another like it in the whole army-(there will be soon I'll venture)-Maybe you think that I make too much of a trifle? It cant be-I love you and every work of your hands that reminds me of you-though it is only a pincussion-So if I write of the hat all day, it will not be silly or childish!-The socks are good and comfortable-and made by my wife; the sword is handsome, and enables me to return the one I had borrowed from Lieut. Cluis-When I get my gray coat I intend to sell the blue one and be done with everything that looks the least bit Yankee-ish..."

CIVIL WAR LETTERS TO THEIR LOVED ONES FROM BLUE & GRAY Annette Tapert Times Books 1988

Pg. 49 Edwin Fay Minden Rangers Corinth Miss. May 5, 1862 "...Our baggage we had sent from G'd Junction was gone forward and may be for all I know in the hands of the enemy, so I am short of clothing having sent most of it to relieve my horse from the weight (later) I believe I have told you all about my probably losing my clothing in the car in my valise. One of my overshirts, one Marseilles, and 3 prs. of socks. My needles and thread...."

THE BROTHERS WAR ed by Annette Tapert Vintage Books, 1988

Pg. 50 Edwin Fay, Minden Rangers Corinth Miss. May 5th 1862 "...I believe I have told you all about my probably losing my clothing in the car in my valise. One of my overshirts, one

Marseilles, and 3prs. of socks. My needle and thread. …I have not changed my clothing in two weeks but intend this evening to try and put on some clean clothes if I can find a place to wash in.The water around here is only the sweepings of 10,000 camps distilled and would sicken a carrion crow. I drink as little as possible. Oh dirt, dirt, I have eaten more than my bushel already and if I ever get back I assure you that I must have things clean in future as an atonement…"

Its a wonder, with the lack of sanitation, that the causualties due to sickness were not more.

THE CIVIL WAR REMINISCENCES IF MAJOR SILAS T. GRISAMORE, C.S.A. ed by Arthur W. Bergerson Jr. La. Univ. Press 1993

Pg. 47 Corinth, Miss. May 7, 1862 (18th Louisiana) "our company received a new out fit of hats, pants and jackets which were run out of New Oleans previous to its capture…"

THE CIVIL WAR LETTERS OF JOSHUA K. CALLOWAY ed. By Judith Lee Hallock Univ. Ga. Press 1997

Pg 12. Corinth May 10 1862 Dear D. (wife) "I am plum strait this evening. I have just got back from the creek where I took a good wash and put on a borrowed shirt; but it is the first clean shirt I have had on since I left home. I also pulled off my green shirt for the first time since I left. It is worn out. Send me any other shirts by the first chance. I believe I wrote to you to send the boots I left at Manderson('s) shop."

WRITING & FIGHTING THE CONFEDERATE WAR-The letters of Peter Wellington Alexander ed. By William B. Styple Bell Grove Pub. Co.2002

Corinth, Miss. May 12, 1862Pg. 84 "…The more one sees of the hardy Western men who have followed Van Dorn and Price across the Mississippi, the more he is impressed with their martial bearing. It is seldom you find one in anything approaching a uniform. They wear all sorts of garments, cut in all sorts of fashions, with a belt around their waist, a slouched hat stuck upon their heads, and their pants in their boots. Yet there is something in their step and manly forms, and in their frank,devil-may-care look, that cannot fail to arrest the attention of one who does not judge by outside appearances alone…."

Multiform

THE CIVIL WAR LETTERS OF JOSHUA K. CALLOWAY ed. By Judith Lee Hallock Univ. Ga. Press 1997

Pg 14. Corinth Miss. May 13, 1862 Mrs. Dulcina Callaway: "…I wrote to you to send me my boots from Manderson('s) shop. I prefer those because they are lighter than those I got at Oakgrove (Chilton County, Alabama). However, if the weather stays as dry as it is at present my shoes will do me some time yet, but when it is rainy the mud is from shoe mouth to half leg deep.

You ask me if I need my shirts. I do need one very much. I don't care, however, about my undershirt now. I have not had on my yellow one since I left Mobile. I wore it all the time I was there, especially when I was strolling about over town, I saw none as pretty as mine. I heard of a great many women and children speak of its beauty there.

We have all our bed ticks filled with leaves and at night we make our beds & spread our blankets and sleep comfortably…"

ALL AFIRE TO FIGHT-The Untold Story of the Ninth Texas Cavalry by Martha L. Crabb pub by Avon Books 2000

Pg. 101 May 15, 1862 camp near Mooreville, Miss. after retreat from Corinth-the unit has been dismounted and serving as infantry-"Dress parades were not always dressy. Sul Ross wrote his wife that the men were "almost in a state of nudity" and that a third of his regiment appeared at review barefoot. Another group of Ross's men, whose pants had been "expended in the public service," drilled in their underdrawers."

How do soldiers, clad (or unclad) to that extent manage to carry on?

THE RAGGED REBEL, A Common soldier in the W.H. Parsons' Texas Cavalry 1861-1865 by B.P. Gallaway, Univ of Texas Press, Austin 1988

May 17 1862 veterans of a skirmish at Searcy Lane LA reported "a mysterious wild boy, too young for military service, who had tried to enlist in Roger's squadron. When this was denied him, he tagged along on foot and was present when Roger's boys pounced on the federal patrol. During the battle that followed, the tattered urchin crawled among the wounded federals and cut their throats with a large bowie knife, killing "all the wounded [Yankees] he could find". When Roger and his rangers withdrew, the apparently kill-crazed boy was left standing in the road, splashed with the blood of his helpless victims"

Was this boy Charlie Mansons great-great grandfather?

BROKENBURN-The Journal of Kate Stone 1861-1865 ed. By John Q. Anderson La. State Univ. Press Baton Rouge

Pg. 110 May 22 1862 She notices the changes in people. "A year ago a gentleman never thought of carrying a bundle, even a small one, through the streets. Broadcloth was "de rigueur." Ceremony and fashion ruled the land. Presto-change. Now the highest in rank may be seen doing any kind of work that their hands find to do. The men have become "hewers of wood and drawers of water" and pack bundles of all sorts and sizes. It may be a pile of blankets, a stack of buckets, or a dozen bundles. One gentleman I saw walking down the street in Jackson, and a splendid-looking fellow he was, had a piece of fish in one hand, a cavalry saddle on his back, bridle, blankets, newspapers, and a small parcel in the other hand; and over his shoulder swung an immense pair of cavalry boots. And nobody thought he looked odd. Their willingness to fetch and carry is only limited by their strength. All the soldiers one sees when traveling are loaded down with canteen, knapsack, haversack, and blankets. Broadcloth is worn only by the drones and fireside braves. Dyed linsey is now the fashionable material for coats and pants. Vests are done away with, colored flannel, merino, or silk overshirts taking the place. A gentleman thinks nothing of calling on a half a dozen young ladies dressed in home-dyed Negro cloth and blue checked shirt. If there is a button or stripe to show that he is one of his country's defenders, he is sure of warmest welcome. Another stops to talk with a bevy of ladies. He is laden down with a package of socks and tin plates that he is carrying out to camp, and he shifts the bundles from side to side as he grows interested and his arms get tired. In proportion as we have been a race of haughty, indolent, and waited-on people, so now we are ready to do away with all forms and work and wait on ourselves."

THE CIVIL WAR LETTERS OF JOSHUA K. CALLOWAY ed. by Judith Lee Hallock Univ. Ga. Press 1997

Pg. 18 Camp near Corinth, Miss. May the 24th, 1862 Mrs. D. Calloway, "…You speak of clothing. I should like to have one shirt and one pair of socks. I have lost one pair, but my Yankee socks replaced them, so I still have two pair; but one is worn out at the toe. Whem you send them be sure to put my initials on each piece…"

DEAR MOTHER: DON'T GRIEVE ABOUT ME. IF I GET KILLED, I'LL ONLY BE DEAD." Ed. by Mills Lane The Beehive Press 1977

Pg. 126 Lavender Ray to his Mother Chattanooga, Tennessee May 26, 1862 Dear Mother: prisoner exchange at Huntsvile, Ala., talking with Yankee troops "…They expressed a wish that our government would uniform their soldiers so they could tell them from citizens, saying the citizens often fired at the train, and, when caught, would escape being hung by saying they were soldiers, and our soldiers often escaped being captured by pretending to be a citizen. I told them that was exactly why we did not uniform them, so as to give each a chance to fight and each to escape…."

THIS INFERNAL WAR Edwin Hedge Fay/Bell Irvin Wiley Univ. of Texas Press 1958

Pg. 64 May 27 1862 Near Van Dorn's Headquarters My Own Dear One "...you ask me about my clothing and tell me to take care of my heavy jeans pants. I have worn them all the time and I find them very comfortable tho I suffer some from cold when on picket even then. As regards wearing my woolen shirts, I have only one and it is torn clear across the back having commenced under the arms. The gores were not large enough. I am afraid to sew it up for it will tear again. I have worn it every day since leaving Vicksburg. I hope I may get my valise again and get the other one. If I have to stay this winter you can make me some shirts out of such plain as my brown pants are made of. Several have them...I do not want more than ¾ yd. of oil cloth and there should be strings or straps or buttons and strings sewn on it so as to fasten the ends together when I roll my clothes in it. I shall have a pair of pants, 3 shirts, 2 drawers, 4 prs. socks to roll in it and that is all. I was going to send back 50 dollars of my money but yesterday I bought a Double Barrel Gun from Mr. Henry who caries this, paid 30 dollars, so shall not send any till we draw I don't know when...You ask about cottade pants? If we don't have a great deal hotter weather than we have had then my heavy jeans pants will last me this campaign but if you have a good opportunity you may send me a pair tho blue is a very bad color unless it is very light blue. I shoot at blue clothes myself..."

NORTH-SOUTH ALLIANCE David Pierson

Memphis Daily Appeal, (Memphis, TN.) May 30 1862 P.1 c.5 Gen. Sterling Price and the Missouri Army (From the Correspondence of the Charleston Courier.) Corinth, May 7- "...Every man has come from his homestead fitted with the best and strongest that loving mothers, wives, and sisters could put upon him. And the spectacle presented as they are drawn up in line, whether for marching or inspection, necessarily forms and arabesque pattern of the most patri-colored crowd of people upon which human eye has ever rested. Some are in black-full citizens dress with beaver hats and frock coats; some in homespun drab; some in grey, blue and streaked; some in nothing but red shirts, pants, and big top boots; some attempt a display with old fashioned militia uniforms of their forefathers; some have banners floating from their "outer walls" in the rear; some would pass for our friend, the Georgia Major, who used to wear nothing but a shirt collar and a pair of spurs.

"Some are in rags, some in bags, and some in velvet gowns!"

Another example of extreme multiform.

THE CIVIL WAR LETTERS OF JOSHUA K. CALLOWAY ed. by Judith Lee Hallock Pub. by Univ. Ga. Press 1997

Pg. 29 Camp near Baldwin, Miss. June 1862 Mrs. Dulcina Calloway "Our sleeping is not so good. We have only 4 tents in the company. My mess has one of them. Our house hold furniture consists of 1 trunk, 1 gun, 4 knapsacks, 1 Sword & a bedstead. Yousee a representation of the bedstead at the top of this page (there was no illustrationin the book-ed.), with us asleep on it. It consists of 4 forks driven in the ground, about a foot high, with poles laid in them similar to the head & foot of a bedstead proper. Then we lay 5 poles length ways, leaving a space of about 18 inches between each couple. Then we skin hickory saplings & stretch the bark across these poles, about six inches apart, as you can see the fine marks in th episture. This bark gives way where it is tied, in drying, and swahs, some pieces more than others. We spread half our blankets on this rack for a bed & cover with the balance. It is like lying on a fodder rack between 2 logs 18 inches apart. Knapsacks for pillows. Most of the company sleep on scaffolds made of poles altogether, under a large brush arbor we have our street. My mess has a brush arbor in front of our tent, which answers the double perpose of portico and a dining room; our kitchen is out of doors; our smoke house, dairy, &c is under the bed. We keep house on a grand scale!I tell you we have a gay time!...I wish you would send by the first one passing, one shirt and one pair of socks, and believe me Your Faithful & Loving—Josh Calloway..."

LIFE IN THE CONFEDERATE ARMY-Being the Observations and Experiences of an Alien in the South During the Amewrican Civil War by William Watson pub. by Scribner & Welford 1888

Pg. 381 Tupelo, Miss.June, 1862 "...We had no tents, but we had got accustomed to do without them. We made large huts or bowers of green branches, which kept off the sun by day and the dew by night. The weather was now beautiful with very little rain. The sick began to recover and the men got their clothes washed and mended, and to add to their comfort, a large quantity of summer clothing arrived to be distributed among them. This did not come from the army bureau, through the quartermaster's department, but from the homes and families of the men themselves. This consignment was greatly augmented by "ladies associations," which had now become a powerful factor in the administration of the war, and, thanks to the action of General Butler in New Orleans, the zeal now displayed by them was almost incredible. Nothing seemed too good for them to sacrifice. Beautiful silk dresses had been cut up and made into tunics for the soldiers. Beautiful shawls and plaids had been cut up and sewed together and bound to form blankets or wrappers and seemingly everything which could be applied to the use of the soldiers was turned to account.

Our regiment being from Louisiana came in for a fair share of these articles; and on the following Sunday morning, when the regiment turned out for parade inspection, they certainly presented a clean and neat though somewhat fantastic, appearance; and the pretty pictures, as they called them, on some of their beautifully flowered tunics was the subject of a good deal of merriment. I could not help contrasting the difference in the men's appearance with the dirty, smoke-begrimed ragged wretches that they were on the retreat after Pea Ridge.…The inspector, who was arrayed in a brilliant captain's uniform, shining buttons and gold lace in profusion, which completely out-did our boys with the pretty pictures on their tunics…"

Supply from home folks who are using whatever cloth they have to supply the troops.

THE CIVIL WAR LETTERS OF JOSHUA K. CALLOWAY ed. by Judith Lee Hallock Univ. Ga. Press 1997

Pg. 24 June 1862 Camp near Baldwin, Miss. Mrs. D. Calloway "…We marched all night Thursday night and all day Friday and rested Friday night. My load consisted of my knapsack, with 1 Pair pants my fancy shirt, one pair socks, 1pair drawers 1 pound box, 40 rounds of cartridges&c.,&c.,…"

I wonder what he means by "fancy shirt."

THE CONFEDERATE VETERAN August 1900

Pg. 351 "The Dog That "Was Eat." "H.D.Foote, (Company G, First Mississippi Cavalry)' Columbus, Miss. writes: "Seeing Comrade Christian's mention of Comrade Page's report in the February Veteran reminds me very forcibly of the dog incident. Well do I remember the time and circumstances. The dog-a fine, large, fat, black setter-followed the coal wagon into camp, but did not return with it. It was, I think, more a thrust at Capt. Sponable that caused the dog to be killed, although it was most assuredly eaten.…One day the dog was missing; the next day the ad. appeared on the bulletin board, with the little epitaph as printed. While this was being read, the dog's meat and bones were boiling in the big kettle, and it made a fine dish of stew. The next day the pit cleaner found the head and hide of the dog.…"

These hungry men took matters into their own hands.

FROM THIS TERRIBLE FIELD-CIVIL WAR LETTERS OF JAMES M. WILLIAMS, Twenty-First Alabama Volunteer Infantry ed by John Kent Folmer pub by Univ Al. Press 1981

Pg. 84 June 5 [1862] Bivouac in the woods 7miles from Balwin Station Dear Lizzy,"…A trick was played me here that I would not have believed anywhite man capable of-while we were making our bed on the floor I heard a soldier say to his companions that he had no blanket and would have to sleep on the floor just as he was-When the lady offered us a bed

I went to him and told him that I would lend him my shawl for his cover that night-when I got up the next morning the villain had gone, and carried my shawl off with him-but I do not wish you to send it just yet. I have as much as I wish to carry at present-when we once more settle down a littleI will send for it."

THIS INFERNAL WAR Edwin Hedge Fay/Bell Irvin Wiley Univ. of Texas Press 1958

Pg. 73 Priceville June 10th, 1862 My Own Dearest "…I must tell you that when I came back to camp I pulled off my clothes and wrapped up in my blankets and had them washed. I never had been so dirty before and the branch was so muddy that Rich could not get my clothes clean tho he got off some of the dirt. Just imagine to yourself my dear, your husband riding for ten days in dust so thick that part of the time he could not see the horse before him, and sweating all the time, and you can form some idea of how dirty I did look. You never saw a negro half so dirty before. The rest had no advantage over me tho in it. My last baggage had gone to Okoloa and though we went through there, yet many of my clothes were dirty and I could not change, having only 2 pr. drawers and two shirts. My Iuka baggage I hope to get again, as 3 men from our Co. and 3 from fuller's started today. It is within the present Yankee Line but they hope to pop in and get a wagon and bring it out. I hope so for I shall get my other overshirt and soap &c., &c. I hope to get my valise also for I have nothing to carry my clothes in but my leggings tho I wrote you for a piece of oil cloth, which I hope you will send. My socks too are most up there. I may get them and I may not, but I am better off than most of the boys…I want you also to make a wallet out of a seamless bag or some strong goods. Sew up the ends and cut a hole through the center through both sides so it will fit over my saddle behind. I can carry my haversack in it. I also want a hat. Mine is about worn out sleeping in it and sitting on it. A soft hat 7 ½ size, but be sure Nat can bring it before you buy it, as it may be he cannot bring it conveniently. I believe this comprises my list of wants for the present…I have looked over your letters and I find nothing except about the shirts. Don't make them of slazy stuff. You had a great deal better get some of the heaviest Lowells or even such stripes as you made the negroes dresses of just before I left home. I have seen such in camp and they look very well. Something strong is necessary for clothes get very dirty in camp and it takes a great deal of water to get them clean…"

Lowells is a heavy-duty cotton cloth used to make flour sacks. It seems this soldier is having problems getting his clothing from storage.

Website- Units Stationed at Tupelo (Miss), Just Prevoius to Corinth James M.

Williams, 21st Alabama infantry, June 11, 1862 Camp near Tupelo, Miss. "…Our army has come down to the principles of Price and Van Dorn-when we move all baggage is dispensed with so I mean to pack a knapsack and send my valise home or throw it away-Don't send my shawl, it is too heavy to carry and I have determined instead to carry an oil cloth which when it rains and I have no tent I can stretch to small trees or stakes for a shelter-Badger will carry another and the two together will make quite a good little tent…"

June 26 Same camp-"…a new uniform for the entire regiment has arrived in town (Tupelo). I have not seen it. It is doubtless some home-made cotton stuff, but in this rough service that is just what we want…'

June 30 Same camp-"…and I have been off the whole afternoon seeing my men fitted to a new coarse uniform which has been obtained for the regiment …"

He doesn't mention the color, but states the uniform is made of cotton cloth.

THIS INFERNAL WAR Edwin Hedge Fay/Bell Irvin Wiley Univ. of Texas Press 1958

Pg. 95 Near Headquarters of the Army of the West Camp Priceville near Tupelo 18 June 1862 My Own Dearest "…I shall need some drawers, and when you make them be sure and put some pockets in them like, but larger than watch pockets. I mean in the same place.…I bought an India rubber oil cloth to put under my bed, of one of the Yankee prisoners and gave him a dollar and a half for it. It has a hole through so I can wear it as a poncho. I am pretty well provided with clothing for the present. My drawers are ripping in the seams but I am going to sew up the rents-I need another pair however, as I have only a change of clothing and it is not always convenient to wash…My suspenders sweat through and get dirty and I want some I can have washed. Get some one to knit them for me. If I could get another cravat I would like it but do not need it at present…"

A cravat? With all the troubles this soldier has been having just to keep fully clad, here he is wanting a cravat.

DARK AND BLOODY GROUND Thomas Ayres Taylor Trade Pub. 2001

Pg. 117 Vienna, La. June 25 1862 forming new regiments at Monroe, La. Colonel Henry Gray was a proficient drillmaster. "The colonel had a total distain for personal display. He wore civilian clothes, as did most of his men although he had a uniform, it was devoid of braid or insignia indicating his rank…"

Rebel soldiers in mostly civilian clothes.

THIS INFERNAL WAR Edwin Hedge Fay/Bell Irvin Wiley Univ. of Texas Press 1958

Pg. 102 In Camp (Priceville)June 27 1862 My Own Dear One "...I am very thankful for the socks you sent me for in the hard ride we made trotting my horse wore out a new pair for me entire. I find the bought socks last much better than the knit ones, at least those Miss Mosely knit. They are knitted too loosely and give way at once. I wrote you I had my valise but my clothing is still down in Okolona most of it. I hope I shall get it back before long....I have looked at the socks and they are so nice-I do thank you and prize them highly for they are the product of your own hands-O my dear I do hope you will when in health learn to spin and weave and do such things as that-It is an honor I think for a woman to clothe her husband by her own handiwork but no more..."

NORTH-SOUTH ALLIANCE David Pierson

Joshua K. Calloway 28th Al. Inf. June 28 1862 Tupelo, Miss. "...Captain Hopkins and Lieut. Mims are at home and will probably bring my things. Mr. Hargrove will perhaps come before they do and if he does, he will bring them. Don't hesitate to ask anybody to do it, and if you do send them don't send that coarse shirt, I'll never get rid of the one I've got, and if you can send me a pair of summer pants. When I start again I shall throw away my old brown ones..."

THIS INFERNAL WAR Edwin Hedge Fay/Bell Irvin Wiley Univ. of Texas Press 1958

Pg. 110 Camp 4 miles from Priceville (July 2, 1862) Dearest "...Being orderly too, insures the transportation of my valise since I keep the Co. books in it. Jos. Hamilton made me the present of a striped shirt- I have sent to Okolona for my drawers and things there, so I am pretty well supplied with clothing at present. I don't know what I shall do when I get out-If we get on the west side of the River, you can send me some. John LeSueur says after the 16th of July he will bring on clothing & things to the Co. wherever it is...I have a pretty good pair of suspenders now given me by Capt. Wimberly which will do for the present..."

U. S. ARMY HERITAGE AND EDUCATION CENTER

July 3, 1862 Capt. A.W, Bell 39th North Carolina Infantry Chasleston, TN My Dear Wife: "...I sent my winter clothes by E(?) and the boys..."

THE CIVIL WAR LETTERS OF JOSHUA K. CALLOWAY ed. by Judith Lee Hallock Univ. Ga. Press 1997

Pg. 41 Camp near Saltillo, Miss. July 13, 1862 Mrs. Dulcina Calloway, "...Capt Hopkins did not bring me any clothes, he says he told one of the boys he would bring them but he don't remember whether they carried them over to him or not. You don't say in your letter whether you sent them by him or not. If, however, you sent that coarse shirt I shall not complain if they are lost. I should like to have a lighter one of some kind, white linen bosomed shirts are very common, though colored ones are more so. I am not particular about pants. Anything for coolness. And while you are sending be sure to send a handkerchief or two…"

BROTHERS IN GRAY-The Civil War Letters of the Pierson Family ed. by Thomas W. Cutrer & t. Michael Parrish La. State Univ. Press 1997 Ninth Louisiana

Pg 105 David Pierson to Catherine Pierson Camp near Tupelo, Miss. July 19th, 1862 Dear Sister "…Sunday is a sort of holiday among soldiers as well as "Negroes," and today of course I put on my Sunday clothes. I feel like I was "dressed up," but if you could see me you would be surprised at what I call "dressed up." A shirt and pair of pants washed on half rations of soap and that had not felt a smoothing Iron in months with shoes without blacking constitute the "dress part," for the coat has to be worn all the while. But clean clothes make a soldier feel so gay that little is thought of ironing and polishing…"

Even though Pvt. Pierson's dress clothes leave something to be desired, at least "dressing up" puts him in a cheerful mood.

Website-Units That Fought At Corinth

6th Mississippi Infantry July 20, 1962 Milldale,
Miss. "The sixth Regiment received a huge clothing requisition on July 20 to replace the crumbling garments worn by many of the men. This issueance amount to 66 hickory shirts, 24 flannel shirts, 114 homespun shirts, 37 cotton shirts, 452 pairs of cottonade pants(of which 42 were dyed blue), 270 pairs of drawers, 500 pairs of shoes, 104 pairs of socks, 13 uniform coats, 2 caps, 78 hats, and 69 blankets…"

This issue, probably from the government, hopefully went a long way to fully suppying these soldiers.

LETTERS OF A CONFEDERATE SURGEON 1861-65 The Hurley Co. 1960

Pg.270 Letter from Julious Newport Bragg to Anna Josephine Goddard Bragg July 31, 1862 "…The poor son of toil, whose horny hands bear testimony that his wife, and little ones derive their support from "the sweat of his brow" dons his brown homespun, the work of his wife, and at the call of his country, though in his ignorance he knows not what the war is for, he bide perhaps his final adieu to his wife and children, leaving them to the shallow charities of a cold world, and prayerfully asking God's blessing upon them, and for the bravery to do battle against the enemy…"

NORTH-SOUTH ALLIANCE David Pierson

George Ashbury Bruton 19th La. Inf. July 31 1862 Camp near Tupelo Miss.

"…We are not allowed to have but one blanket and 2 suits of clothes. I have got 2 shirts & 2 prs of pants and one pr. Of socks & the heels of them is worn out and what I have got is more than I want on a march…" August 9 1862 same camp "…you stated in your letter that you wish to know how my clothes are holding out. I have plenty of everything but socks. I am out of socks. We drawed clothing the other day we got good lincy pants for $4.25 a pair and good hickrey shirts for $1.25 and drawers for $1.00 per pair. I drawed pants drawers and shoes. I have got the same old hat that I wore off form home and it is a good old hat yet. So I have plenty of clothing everthing but socks…"

Pvt. Burton is able to draw almost everything from the quartermaster at this time.

SARAH MORGAN-The Civil War Diary of A Southern Woman A Touchstone Book 1991

Pg. 195 book1 Aug. 1862 "…Miriam must have asked the name of some of the officers; for just then she called to me "He says that is Mr. Read!" I looked at the foot of the levee, and saw two walking together. I hardly recognized the gentleman I wwas introduced to on the McRae, in the one that now stood below me in rough sailor pants, a pair of boots, and a very thin and slazy lisle undershirt. That was all he had on, except an old straw hat…"

1862 "There was one handsome Kentuckian, whose name I soon found to be Talbot, who looked charmingly picturesque in his coarse cotonade (sic) pants, white shirt, straw hat, black hair, beard and eyes, with rosy cheeks…"

NORTH SOUTH ALLIANCE: Uniforms:Uniforms of the Confederacy: Louisiana & Missouri Uniforms http://www.nsalliance.org/uniforms/louisiana/html

Pg. 2 "Below is the quaretermaster report of goods in the charge of Maj. J.H. McMahon Q.M. for Meridian MS on Aug. 25, 1862, 5weeks prior to the battle of Corinth

Number	Articles & Remarks
199	Army Caps 19 damaged
18	Hats (Black wool)
300	Jackets (Assorted)
2011	Army Overcoats (with Capes)

210	Army Overcoats (without Capes)
1647	Coats and Five Overcoats (Assorted) Citizens {style}
16	Coats, but Trimmed and remade {Militery}
254	Linen and Cotton Summer Pants
532	Pairs of Pants (Assorted)
40	Pairs of Pants Unmade
1984	Shirts (Assorted)
5043	Pairs of drawers
937	Pairs of socks
262	Pairs of Cotton socks Light
274	Pairs of Boots (Assorted)
400	Pairs of Shoes(Assorted)
7	Oil Cloth Knapsacks
69	Oil Cloth Cloaks
6	Pairs of Oil Cloth Overalls
114	Oil Cloth Cap Covers
35	Oil Cloth Havelocks
297	Blankets (Assorted) Mostly Carpet
106	Haversacks

It seems that a good deal of the clothing on this list, especially overcoats, were altered civilan clothing and the blankets mostly carpet.

DIARY OF A CONFEDERATE SOLDIER John S. Jackman of the Orphan Brigade ed. by William C. Davis Univ. S.C. Press 1990

Pg. 52 Aug. 6, 1862 Jackson Miss. "…After day light about 60 from the reg't. able to go, went to the railroad, but could not immediately get a train, so we came back to camp, about noon, and I drew new uniforms, and other clothing. The first we had drawn for a long time…"

NORTH-SOUTH ALLIANCE David Pierson

W.H.A. Cox 18th Al. Inf. August 10 1862 Camp Bulah, Al. (9 days after leaving Tupelo)"… We are pleasantly situated but it is so mighty hot here. I have been assigned to duty as second

Lieutenant of the Company but have not got my commission yet. Col. Holtzclaw requires all of the officers to uniform themselves. I have bought mine, which cost me $115.00 for coat, pants, and hat, about 5 times what they ought to have cost but we all have to get them. The uniform is grey Casmir. Swords but little better than mine, that is a little larger, sells for $50.00 I shall not buy one.I also have a sash which I picked up on the Shiloh Battlefield. My sword and sash will save me at least $80.00 this time. Every thing is very high, that is such as soldiers want, a fine good pair of shoes sells for $20.00, boots $35, hats from $8 to $20 and everything else in proportion…"

THIS INFERNAL WAR Edwin Hedge Fay/Bell Irvin Wiley Univ. of Texas Press 1958

Pg. 136 Camp Louisiana August 13th, 1862 My Own Darling "…We are cut down to one wagon and no tents at all, all baggage that cannot be carried on horseback is to sent off or burned. My valise will have to go tho I will have to throw away some of my clothing. I have been wearing my plain cloth breeches all this hot weather. They are not much account now but not torn at all. I had a watch pocket put into them and also into my green breeches. A widow Lady (grass) put them in for me…My clothing is quite good. If you have not sent the pants you better not do it I reckon as I have no way of carrying any more clothing than I have. If we get out I can supply myself at the QrMasters department. Everything I have lasts well. I told you of buying some clothes at the sale. Jim Leavey's drawers and undershirt. I am wearing the socks you sent me dearest and they fit me fine. I have never seen but one better pair, and they were double heels and toes too and looked as if they would last forever…"

This soldier is carrying a valise, I guess instead of a knapsack, I'll bet his "plain cloth breeches" are undyed- drab colored. He also mentions having "green breeches." I wonder if his faith in getting resupplied from the quartermaster was well-placed.

FROM THAT TERRIBLE FIELD-CIVIL WAR LETTERS OF JAMES M. WILLIAMS, Twenty-First Alabama Volunteer Infantry ed by John Kent Folmer pub by Univ Al Press 1981

Pg. 102 August 19 1862-Fort Morgan Mobile. Al.Dear Lizzy, "…I wish you would make me a pair of pants of that blue blanket which I left at home-make them full in the leg, and large at the foot. With a black or dark blue cloth strip on the seam so_ wide that is an inch and a quarter-if you can't get the material for the stripe put in a white cord, but I much prefer the stripe as it is according to regulation. If you think that the blanket is very much better, a sample of which I enclose I will send it to you-still I would rather use the other one which is already cut.-Capt. Dorgan has a pair of blanket pants and they do very well for every day service and really look well, though they are rough…Goodbye. write by every boat: send down the pair of shoes I sent to you from Tupelo…"

Note the request for pants made from a blanket, and blue colored too.

Pg. 103 Aug. 25 1862 Fort Morgan Dear Lizzy,"…Your letter came by the Saturday boat, and with it the shoes, which I wanted for one of the men who was badly afflicted with bare feet…"

Pg. 105 Aug. 27 1862 Fort Morgan dear Lizzy,"…A party has just been made up to draw the seine to-night after dark, and of course I'm one-we will appear in a fancy costume of shirt and drawers…10 o'clock P.M.- have had a glorious time fishing caught fish enough for the whole regiment-just got back-

Send me an old pair of pants to wear in the water and a pair of old shoes and hat if you can find 'em-be particular about the old shoes for I never go in the water without fearing for my feet: what with cat-fish-and "stinger-ees" and oyster-shells on the banks my feet are in danger…"

SARAH MORGAN-The Civil War Diary of A Southern Woman A Touchstone Book 1991

Pg. 271 Aug. 19 1862 "…three soldiers came in to ask for molasses. I was alone downstairs, and the nervous trepidation with which I received the dirty, coarsely clad stangers who however looked as though they might be gentlemen…"

You could never tell gentlemen in the Rebel army by their dress.

Website 16th Tennessee Volunteer Infantry Regiment:Clothing Arms and Equipment

Pg. 2 7 August Michael Manzy "brought a hat, a shirt, a pair of drawers, sock, suspendersand a handkerchief."

19 August 1862 "The men were awakened at three a.m. and drew some pants, shoes and drawers, "no shirts."

THIS INFERNAL WAR Edwin Hedge Fay/Bell Irvin Wiley Univ. of Texas Press 1958

Pg. 144 Camp Louisiana August 21st, 1862 My Darling "…First and foremost I want a pair of boots made at Ditmer's by that crooked legged "Dutchman" Fred. I want him to make them especially for me. He knows me and will make them right. I want them made large in the Leg and a regular cavalry Boot. Ditmer must not charge too much for them, though I want the best he can possibly make for this winter. My old boots are tolerably good yet, and my shoes too, but I don't know when I can get another pair, so I'll send now for fear…"

NORTH-SOUTH ALLIANCE David Pierson

Sam Love, 8th Texas Cavalry August 25 1862 Tupelo, Miss. "…Tea I want you and mother to make and send me several shirts 3 or 4 spcks one or two pr. Drawers & …C…and I want you to tell others to do the same for it is going to be impossible for us to get Such things here but worse than all do I want Father to Send me a Pr. Of Boots for it is impossible for us to get them even now. Capt. Ross got back from Mobile day before-yesterday. He bought a pr. Of shoes (just such as I have bought for $5 and $6) and had to give $18.00 for them So that a good pr. Of Boots at the same ratio would cost $35 to $40, and the most common brogans are Selling from $8to $10 the reason of the high prices is the scarsity of leather and the great demand there are thousands in the army that are barefooted and cannot get Shoes and the reason that I write to you is because the demand is not so great at home and I will need a pr. Of Boots this winter if I Should not get a furlough for it is likely we will have a good deal of scouting to do if we Should be so fortunate as to get our horses which is very probblr. When speaking of myself I have not included John (brother?)but he will need as much as me. I hope the citizens will do what they can to get clothing for their friends and relations in the army. The people here are willing to do all they canbut they have got so many in the field that they cannot do much for the Texians. So we will have to depend upon the citizens of Texas…"

An appeal for clothing directly to the home folks, with no confidence in the government supplying them.

ONE OF CLEBURNE'S COMMAND ed. By Norman D. Brown Univ. of Austin Press 1980

Pg. 8 Pvt. Fowler, Co. H Fall 1862 "…We are are put to some trouble about getting our clothes washed-sometimes we may have our clothes out and an order come to march and then we have to walk two or more miles to get our clothes-and then have to take them before they are dry…

A CONFEDERATE GIRL'S DIARY Sarah Fowler Morgan Dawson Mifflin & Co. 1913

Pg. 234 Sept. 1862 "…And what a sad sight the Fourth Louisiana was, that was then parading! Men that had fought at Shiloh and Baton Rouge were barefooted. Rags was their only uniform, for very few possessed a complete suit, and those wore all varieties and colors and cuts. Hats could be seen of every style and shape, from the first ever invented down to the last one purchased evidently some time since. Yet he who had no shoes looked as happy as he who had, and he who had a cap had something to toss up, that's all…"

Here we see extremely ragged, multiform Rebels.

THE CIVIL WAR LETTERS OF JOSHUA K. CALLOWAY ed. By Judith Lee Hallock Univ. Ga. Press 1997

Pg. 55 In Camp at Smith's Cross roads, Ray co. Tenn. 35 miles north of Chattanooga September 1st, 1862

"In regards to the clothes you speak of, you must judge what I need. I have two good pair of pants-the pr. That Mrs. Palmore gave me & a pair that I got from Jeff Davis, uniform pants-two good coats. I have the two shirts-two pair of drawers that I brought from home-of course they are worn out, except the old brown coarse one, and I am tired of it. I gave $1.50 for an old one two weeks ago and tore it up last night for gun rags for Company K. The socks that I brought from home are gone long since. I have one pair, however, that was given to me at Tupelo, Miss. But I have worn them constantly for 3 weeks without washing, and they are pretty well worn out. You see that I need a shirt or two and one or two pairs of drawers, two pair of socks. And I want you to send my boots. I sold those I had because they were too small. I got ten dollars for them. My shoes are worn out nearly…"

THIS INFERNAL WAR Edwin Hedge Fay/Bell Irvin Wiley Univ. of Texas Press 1958

Pg.151 La Grange Tenn. Camp on Wolf River Sept. 5th, 1862 My Own Dear One "…I lost one of my blue linen shirts and the pair of drawers I b'ot of Jim Leary's estate and a pair of socks together with my gun on the battlefield. I wish I had another shirt and an undershirt of Lowell's if no net ones can be had, also a pair of drawers. I found a pair of saddlebags on the field full of clothing but not such as I will wear, and this half quire of paper which has proved very acceptable, also a pocket inkstand. If you make me shirts, make them fuller in front so they won't gape open when buttoned…"

I do not know what he means by a net shirt.

FROM THAT TERRIBLE FIELD-CIVIL WAR LETTERS OF JAMES M. WILLIAMS, Twenty-First Alabama Volunteer Infantry ed by John Kent Folmer pub by Univ Al Press

Pg. 106 Sept 6 1862 Fort Morgan, Mobile Al Dear Lizzy, "…Buy me some white gloves if you can find them-if you cant get white get buff-and if neither, any color that you can find-…Send down my old worsted sash for Cothran…"

THE CIVIL WAR DIARY OF SARAH MORGAN

Sarah Morgan Dawson (describing clothes for the 30th La. Inf. Sept. 14 1862 Linwood Plantation, La. "…I have been so busy making Lieutenant Bourge's shirt…It is dark purple merino. The bosom I tucked with pleats a quarter of an inch deep, all the way up to the collar, and stitched a narrow crimson silk braid up the center to hold it in its place. Around the collar, cuffs, pockets, and band down the front, the red cord runs, forming a charming contrast to the dark foundation. I devoted the sole article the Yankees let fall from my two workboxes-a bunch of soutache-to the work. Large white pearl buttons completed the description, and my shirt is really as quiet, subdued, and pretty a one as I ever saw. I should first hear the opinion of the owner, though. If he does not agree with the others, I shall say he has no taste…"

My goodness, this poor Leuitenant! I hope he kept a poker-face and thanked the lady for going to so much trouble.

UNIFORMS OF THE CIVIL WAR Lord, Wise, A.S. Barnes & Co. 1970

Pg. 39 "…Offical report of General Patrick R. Cleburne: As we ascended the hill, we were fired into by our own artillery in the rear…I can only account for this blunder from the fact that most of our men had on blue Federal pants." The blue kersey trousers Cleburne refers to were taken from captured Union supplies at Richmond, Kentucky, on September 17, 1862.

BROKENBURN-The Journal of Kate Stone 1861-1865 ed. By John Q. Anderson La. State Univ. Press Baton Rouge

Pg. 54 Sept. 18 "We are hard at work until sundown on Brother's flannels. As it will be so cold (he was stationed in Va.) and he suffers so even here in the winter-he is so sensitive to the cold-we are making the shirts and drawers double, red on one side and yellow on the other. They look funny to me but are real warm. I wonder if he will like them. May 12, 1862 (pg.106) We will commence on some clothes for My Brother tomorrow. He certainly did laugh over the gay red and yellow flannel suits we sent him in the fall. He did not wear them at all but gave them to Uncle Bo who sported around in them to the delight of the whole camp where they were a great joke."

Red and yellow flannel suits? (Probably union suits.) I guess anything for warmth, but I'd hate to be spotted wearing those.

THE CIVIL WAR REMINISCENCES OF MAJOR SILAS T. GRISAMOREed by Arthur W.Bergerson Pub. by La. Univ. Press 1993

Pg. 82 Silas T. Grisamore, 18th La. Inf. Sept.18 1862 Pollard, Ala. "...Whilst at Pollard I obtained a lot of clothing, consisting of jackets, pants, shirts, and kepis.

The pants and shirts ahd been made by the kind-hearted ladies of Alabama, who were thinking of their absent mountaineer husbands and lovers and were consequently much too large fpr our little Creole troops; the jackets, however, had been made by some tailors on contract and were of a good size for 10-year-old boys; the kepis were made of the same material with leather visors that would either stand straight up in front or turn square down over the eyes. They were all made of a species of grey cotton cloth and had they been made of a proper size they would have been of much service to the men...

There was a little devilish Frenchman in on of the St. James companies named Macon. One day after drill, when the men had all gone to their tents or were dozing in the shade of the trees, this Macon put on one of the biggest pair of pants he could find and by rolling up a yard of each leg succeeded in getting his feet clear, then he put on a shirt that reached to his knees and a jacket that would not button by six inches and extending barely halfway to his waist; then he put on a small kepi with the visor down behind, and thus equipped, he issued out of his tent and with both arms extending into the air ran all around the camps yelling at every jump, "See what Alabama has done, see what Alabama has done." Whist the sleepy boys, being thus summerarily aroused from their dreams, raised a whoop the like of which never was heard in those woods before...Pollard was also remarkable for the manufacture of a article facetiously called "Beer."

Over persuaded by the eloquence of one of my friends, I once invested five cents in a mug in that article and drank-part of it. I studied over it awhile and came to the conclusion it was composed of dish water, soap suds, old buttermilk, rotton potatoes, mixed together in a gopher hole, dipped out with an old shoe, and strained through a saddle blanket..."

Pollard's larking about with this "dress uniform" on might have been a result of this villainous "beer."

BLOODY BANNERS AND BAREFOOT BOYS-A History of the 27th Regiment Alabama Infantry, C.S.A. The Civil war Memoirs and Diary Entries of J.P. Cannon M.D. Compiled and Edited by Noel Crowson and John Brogden 1997

Pg. 130 prisoners, taken at Fort Donaldson returning -Jackson Miss. "...On the 24th of September"...After drawing clothing, blankets and guns, the regiment moved to Holly Springs..."

Apparently supply from the government.

SARAH MORGAN-The Civil War Diary of A Southern Woman A Touchstone Book 1991

Pg. 273 book 3 Sept. 24 1862 "Yesterday the General saluted us with "Young ladies, if you will ride in a "Confederate carriage," you may go to dress parade this evening." Now, in present phraseology, "Confederate" means anything that is rough, unfinished, unfashionable or poor. You hear of Confederate dresses, which means last year's. Confederate bridle means a rope halter. Confederate silver, a tin cup or spoon. Confederate flour is cornmeal, etc. In this case, the Confederate carriage was a Jersey wagon with four seats, a top of hichory slats covered with leather, and the whole drawn by mules. We accepted gladly, partly for the ride and sight, partly tro show we were not ashamed of a very comfortable conveyance; so with Mrs. Bridger as chaperon off we went in grand style..."

THIS INFERNAL WAR Edwin Hedge Fay/Bell Irvin Wiley Univ. of Texas Press 1958

Pg. 160 Baldwin Miss. Sept. 25th, 1862 My Darling One "...but we have heard from them and they will all be in in the morning. I hope so for Rich is with them and all my baggage. I have nothing with me except the clothing I have on, my uniform pants and brown coat and my shawl, blue linen shirt, undershirt & drawers. I told you I believe that I lost drawers shirts and socks on the battlefield at Denmark, I got a pair of drawers (drilling) good stuff at the Quartermaster for 1.00, quite as cheap as you could make them at home. I am glad indeed to get them for I need three pairs. I lost the pair I b'ot of John Leary's Est. as before mentioned. The two pairs you made me I have got yet tho one is ripped a little but I intend to mend them the first time I get a chance..."

This soldier is always losing his clothing. His wife must be getting tired of contiuously having to supply him.

THIS INFERNAL WAR Edwin Hedge Fay/Bell Irvin Wiley Univ. of Texas Press 1958

Pg. 163 Tupelo Miss. Spt.26th 1862 My Own Dear Sarah "...As regards undershirts I have found a most excellent one, and now have two that will do me. As for the gray Jeans, I am wearing my uniform pants now and my green ones are almost as good as new. Jones has my measure for Coat & pants somewhere on his books. He can cut the coat and pants too, if you desire to make them. As for woolen socks I shall not need them. The Boots and Testament are all I need at present..."

CONFEDERATE VETERAN

Conferate Veteran September-October 1992 Pg. 38 DRAB The Forgotten Confederate Color by Fred Adolphus "...They have done quite a bit of research on what shades of grey were used and the frequency with which butternut appeared in the Southern ranks, but little attention has been given to another color that was widespread in Confederate armies. That color is drab-the color of undyed wool...Alfred R. Waud, famous for his drawings for Harper's Weekly, had this to say of the Virginia "Black Horse Cavalry" while he was detained behind Confederate lines: he noted that among the enlisted troopers,"...there was little else but homespun among the, light drab grey or butternut color, the drab predominating..." and slouched hats appeared to be ...the court costume of the regiment." Waud's sketch appeared in September 27, 1862, edition of Harper's Weekly indicating an early war usage of this color in Virginia....Joseph E. Chance describes the issue of this clothing in his regimental history of the 2nd Texas as well." The new uniforms waiting in Corinth to greet the regiment on their arrival were unconventional, to say the least. Bundles of white wool uniforms had been sent with no designation as to size. The uniforms were issued and a comical scene ensued. Soon the company grounds were full of men strutting up and down, some with trousers dragging under their heels, while those of others scarcely reached the tops of their socks; some with jackets so tight they resembled stuffed toads, while others had ample room to carry three days rations in their booms. The exhibition closed with a swapping scene that reminded one of a horse-trading day in a Georgia couty town....Company B of the 18th Texas cavalry, upon its formation as the "Morgan Rangers" of Bastrop, was lucky enough to have uniforms made for its members. Captain Hiram S. Morgan spent his own money to outfit the troops in grey double-breasted coats and grey trousers with yellow cavalry stripes on the legs. The fabric used for these uniforms was a yellowish-gray, Huntsville penitentiary jeans. These uniforms were issued in early 1862 ...In the summer of 1862 Walker's Texas Infantry Division received extensive issues of cotton clothing. Allotments of 8,000 yards of osnaburg to each regiment were sewn into tents, knapsacks, haversacks, and clothing, by the women of Smith County. The troops spent the summer in cooler cotton fabrics rather than traditional woolens. As most cottons left the factory as "gray goods" it is a safe bet that these uniforms were undyed...."

We'll see many examples of drab clothing issued.

WESTERNERS IN GRAY-The Men and missions of the Elite Fifth Missouri Infantry Regiment by Phillip Thomas Tucker pub by McFarland & Co. 1953

Pg. 65 Sept. 28, 1862 linking up with Van Dorn's First Missouri Confederate Infantry in northeast Mississippi "...Lieutenant Joseph Boyce, First Missouri, described the meeting: "[The men] quietly awaited the arrival of [McCowan's] heroes of Wilson's Creek, Lexington, etc., 'Here they come, boys!' and we rushed to the road to welcome them. Many old friends met who had parted at Camp Jackson, and our pleasure was great, indeed, to meet so many friends and former comrades. They presented a very soldierly appearance, marching and moving like veterans. They were well armed but indifferently uniformed."…"

Another mention of the Rebs being poorly clad.

TWO MONTHES IN THE CONFEDERATE STATES-An Englishman's Travels Through the South by W.C. Corson ed. by Benjamin H. Trask La. State Un iv. Press 1996

Pg. 28 Oct. 1862 "…attached to the Army of the Southern Mississippi, encamped at Camp Moore, some thirty miles from the Ponchiatoula.…Their dress, arms, and accouterments were the same as those of all the military I ever saw in the Confederacy, so that our description here will suffice for all.

They wore suits (that is, a jacket and trousers) of "homespun" cotton, either gray or dingy brown; a woolen shirt; rough strong shoes; and a sort of "billy-cock" hat, all of course much the worse for wear. They each had a splendid rifle and bayonet, in beautiful order, and cartridge box etc. of strong plain leather; but no sword, revolver or bowie-knife. This, with a blanket rolled up and strapped to their shoulders, completed their equipment. Of course they were strangers, evidently, to razor, comb, brush, or even soap, I fear; but they spoke good English, in a quiet, determined manner, and not through their noses. They were small, lithe men; not much of them, but all game. I could very well see why President Lincoln had not "subjugated the South," if the South were made up of such men as these; and, in the long run, I found that was actually the fact…"

A good description by a British subject, also a true measure of the men. It'll take quite a bit to "subjugate" these soldiers.

Footnote #14- "…At the beginning of the war, Confederates wore a wide variety of uniforms or homemade clothing. As the years advanced, "butternut" became very common- "uniforms colored a yellowish brown by dye made of copperas and walnut hulls" (Faust, ed.,HTIE-CW,101) James I Robertson Jr., Soldiers in Blue and Gray (Columbia S.C., 1988) 16. For the rebels "every shape and form of hat was in evidence from the snappy French-inspired kepi to huge broad-brimmed coverings that resembled inverted coal scuttles" (Robertson, Soldiers in Blue and Gray17) a "billy-cock" was a round, low-crowned felt hat worn by men and occasionally young women. It may also refer to wearing the hat cocked like a bully (OED II,196).

Pg. 42 Camp Moore, Southern Mississippi "…The men are a fine sturdy set of fellows; quite unlike the wiry, cadaverous type with which the "Southerner" is usually associated. They were of course destitute of any regular uniform, dressed as a rule in homespun of all colors, and looked as if they had slept in the woods for six months. Their arms were in good order, and all I saw had Northern or British rifles. The men seemed healthy and contented; were waited on, hand and foot, by troops of negroes who seemed to look upon themselves as part of the army, and did any task eagerly; and, if well handled, in such a country, I am satisfied there was plenty of mischief in them (the soldiers-not the slaves-ed.)

This same witness describing rough, multiform-dressed men.

CONFEDERATE VETERAN Vol. XXX #5 Nash. TN. 1922 Peter Pelham Poulan, Ga.

Pg. 171 "Early in October 1862, the First Alabama Regiment, Partison Rangers Lavergne, TN. "Our Regiment had nothing but homemade uniforms. Most of us had citizen's clothes, no brand on our horses, equipment or anything else. We had to furnish our own horses and saddles and all equipment."

Website 16th Tennessee Volunteer Infantry Regiment: Clothing, Arms and Equipment

Pg. 2 18 October 1862 when camped near Barbersville on the Cumberland Riverthey drew "coats."

28 October 1862 troop details were sent home to gather winter clothing. "our friends being regarded as much more reliable source from whom we might draw than the general government, it being rather poorly supplied.'

Lucy Virginia French from McMinnville, wrote in her diary for 30th Nov. 1862 "We made shirts and pants for them (the 9th Texas) and I took up my carpets and made blankets for them."

This shows to what extent the civilians would go to clothe their soldiers.

STONES RIVER-Bloody Winter in Tennessee by James Lee McDonough pub. by Univ. TN. Press 1980

Pg. 31 Oct. 1862 "…John Gold of the Twenty-Fourth Tennessee Infantry, also related that he thought he would starve on the trek back from Perryville. Still Another soldier reported that "the retreat from Perryville was one of fearful suffering." More than two hundred men in his brigade were barefooted…"

Once again, destitute of shoes.

TWO MONTHES IN THE CONFEDERATE STATES-An Englishman's Travels Through the South by W.C. Corson ed. by Benjamin H. Trask La. State Un iv. Press 1996

Pg. 64 "...I was told, for instance, of a very large lot of strong army shoes being sold by a house to the Confederate Government at fifteen or sixteen dollars per pair, which could have been sold outside easily at twenty to thirty dollars per pair. These shoes, it was said, went to Bragg's army in Kentucky, and really enabled his men to accomplish the long and rapid marches which characterized that arduous though indecisive campaign. I saw instances of similar liberality in smaller matters fifty times with my own eyes while in the Confederacy; and there can be no doubt that what with the open-handed patriotism of the merchants and manufacturers, the unwillingness of officers and men to draw a fraction of pay if they can avoid it, and the freedom of Government purchases and transactions from the rapacity of contractors and all kinds of swindling go-betweens, the war is not costing the Confederate Government five dollars where it is costing the Federal Government twenty at least..."

If only this were entirely true.

Pg. 69 Florence, South Carolina, soldiers returning to the Army of Northern Virginia from furlough "...The men told fearful tales of what they had suffered for want of shoes, blankets, medicines, and tents, in the snow, frost, and sleet, of the winter campaign of 1861-62 in Virginia and North Carolina; and when we met the first snow at Goldsboro, the wish was universal. That either the winter was over or the war at an end..."

TWO MONTHES IN THE CONFEDERATE STATES-An Englishman's Travels Through the South by W.C. Corson ed. by Benjamin H. Trask La. State Un iv. Press 1996

Pg. 125 chapt. "Impressions of an English Businessman" "...Secondly, the pressure for clothing, boots, arms, ammunition &c. in the South, will not cause the Rebellion to collapse. Setting aside the enormous quantities of goods which run the blockade, I may say that many large merchants and capitalists assure me that, in another six or twelve months, the Confederate States would be able, not only to feed but clothe and arm her whole population.

Before leaving Richmond, I saw samples, for instance, of very neatly made shoes-the upper leather tacked to thin wooden soles, the leather so well tanned, and the shoes so neatly made, that they looked like a superior leather shoe. The contractor offered to supply very large quantities, and to increase monthly. Of course, machines were used, and negro labor chiefly employed in making them. These shoes, which would outwear at least two pair of the ugly brown-paper abominations with which New England formerly supplied the South, were offered at about a third of the price of the imported shoe, and a large reduction in price promised. There is no doubt that for negroes these shoes will come into extensive future use, and for the troops will be now both cheap and serviceable.

At the time the probable want of shoes promised to be one of the greatest sufferings inflicted on the South by non-intercourse with the north and the blockade. In the spring of 1862, this necessity was at its height. Wherever I went printed cards were even yet nailed on the inside of bedroom doors at the hotels, on which were some such words as, "If you put your boots outside your door they will be stolen;" showing plainly that necessity had at one time driven the regular guests to strange shifts.

I was also shown a very serviceable hat of Southern manufacture, made of wool and cotton, and at about one-fifth the price of the imported hats and caps. The manufacturer said he could make then either light and porous, or thick and heavy, so as to suit both summer and winter wear. Several mills had also commenced, in North and South Carolina, weaving very neat materials for women's and children's dresses. They also were composed of cotton and wool; the patterns were checks and stripes chiefly, and of course the colors were few and simply arranges. There is no doubt, however, about these cloths coming into extensive use, and gradually bringing the price of clothing within limits again…"

It seems, as we shall see, that the soldiers did not agree with this witness regarding the desirability of those wooden-soled shoes.

Pg. 127 footnote #3 "…Drill is "a coarse twilled linen or cotton fabric used for summer clothing" (OED,IV< 1052).

ALL AFIRE TO FIGHT-The Untold Tale of the Civil War's Ninth Texas Cavalry by Martha L. Crabb pub by Avon Books 2000

Pg. 117 Oct. 3, 1862 Battle of Corinth, Miss. "…The valiant Colonel Rogers, determined to make a grade or a grave that day, lay dead on the ramparts of (Battery) Robinette, his body armor pierced by seven bullets…"

According to this witness, the Col. was still wearing body armor at this date, not that it did him any good.

HADLEY LIBRARY ARCHIVES-Diaries and Letters of William Tull 5th& 9th Louisiana Infantry

Oct. 3, 1862 Battle of Corinth, Miss. "…It was here that my faithful lieutenant who had guided me up to this time received a grape-shot centrally in his forhead which scattered his brains all over my face and breast. Some of his noble brains also struck the breech of another comrade's gun and stuck there. This fellow let them remain there as a souvenir of the battle and they adhered till dry and became as hard as wood…"

THE BLOODY CRUCIBLE OF COURAGE Brent Nosworthy Carroll &Graf Pub. 2003

Pg. 14 Oct. 4 1862 Corinth Miss. Union 1st Brigade awaiting the Confederate assault: Capt. Jackson gave the following pep talk to his men: "Boys, I guess we are going to have a fight. I have two things I want you to remember today. One is, we own all the ground behind us. The enemy may go over us but all the rebels yonder can't drive company H back. The other is, if the butternuts come close enough remember you have good bayonets on our rifles and use them…"

I included this quote due to the Capt. Jackson's reference to the Rebs as "butternuts."

THE CIVIL WAR: THE SOUTH ed. by Thomas Streissguth Greenhaven Press Inc. 2001

Pg. 124 Battle of Perryville Ky Oct. 8, 1862 "…Bragg says: "We captured, wounded and killed not less than 25,000 of the enemy, took over thirty cannon, 17,000 small arms, 2,000,000 cartridges for the same, destroyed over a hundred wagons and brought out of Kenticky more than a hundred more with mules and harness complete, replaced our horses by a fine mount and lived two monthes on rations captured from th enemy, and secured material to clothe the army…"

THIS INFERNAL WAR Edwin Hedge Fay/Bell Irvin Wiley Univ. of Texas Press 1958

Pg. 171 Camp near Salem, Miss. Oct. 18th 1862 My Own dear Wife "…Well night before last john Lesueur came in and the boxes and trunks from Minden. I got all my things and got on the clothing, all of it except pants, undershirts and socks. They fit very well but are full large as I weigh now only 170 lbs. I have the striped shirt next my skin and the debage over it. The drawers are soft and nice and I am very thankful for them though I stood in no need of them as my valise is already full of clothing. I have worn my overshirts but very little since I left home and had plenty of clothes. My pants are all good except the plain cloth and I shall now give them away. My uniform pants are good and I have worn them a great deal. My green ones will do good service yet, so I am well supplied. I had rather have had handkerchiefs for I loaned my red one to Linn and he lost it tho' I have two very good ones yet. My boots fitted me very well and I was glad to get them but why did Ditmer charge me $25.00 while Cpt. Webb's and Linn's only cost $22.00. I want your father to let Mr. Ditmer pay three dollars more per hundred for flour than anyone else. Please say to Mr. Wimberly that "I am very well thank you" (on the bottom of my boots he wrote "How Dye Do")..."

Finally this soldier is fully equipped.

BLOODY BANNERS AND BAREFOOT BOYS-A History of the 24th Regiment Alabama Infantry C.S.A.

The Civil War Memoirs and Diary Enties of J.P. Cannon, M.D. compiled and edited by Noel Crowson and John Brogden Pg. 17 The 24th Alabama was mustered into service of the Confederate States in Florence, Alabama, on December 24th, 1861...Oct. 20 1862 "... our division locating near Shelbyville on the bank of the Duck River. While there, some of us enjoyed a vsit from friends from home, who supplied us with much needed clothing and shoes. These items along with a limited number of tents having been issued, we were pretty well equipped for winter weather..."

Once again, the necessity of being re-supplied by the home folks.

UNIFORMS OF THE CIVIL WAR Lord, Wise, A.S. Barnes & Co. 1970

Pg. 41 A Confederate Lieutenant in the 12th Alabama Infantry in a letter home to his wife: Camp near Knoxville October 24 1862 "...It is a sad parcel of soldiers here, who are now naked and barefooted. We have had a snow. The ground is covered about t en inches. The unkindest cut of all is that we had to throw away our knapsacks and all out clothes at Spart, Tennessee, on the 5ht of September, and cosequenly we are now naked, barefooted, dirty, filthy and lousy..." On Oct. 31st he wrote again: "...Captain McFord starts here tomorrow after clothes for the Company, and this letter must address that subject. I want my overcoat, my boots, 2 pairs of drawers, 2 shirts, and as many socks as you have, 2 pairs of pants, a comforter, and a night cap. There was a small amount of clothing issued to the regiment this morning. I got a pair of drawers, and 1 shirt of good stout domestic, and 1 pair of socks. I shall want a uniform suit. Get enough jeans from Mrs. Walters or someone else to make them. Lieutenant Mims will tell how to cut it..."

Guidelines: Confederate Clothing Issue [Archive]-Authentic Campaigner Website & Forums VMI88

Here are some excerpts from an unpublished manuscript based on the remembrances of two soldiers in the 33rd Alabama Infantry, Army of Tennessee (Oct. 24, 1862) "Arriving at Knoxville about October 24th, we had (issued)...a suit of clothes each, woolen gray jeans, jacket lined with white cotton sheeting, with four C.S.A. brass buttons, a pair of unlined gray jeans pants, white cotton sheeting shirt and drawers and white cotton machine knit sleazy socks and a pair of rough tan brogans, hand made wooden pegged shoes. Some drew gray hats…Most,or all of us had been using finger knit woolen socks which were sent to us from home."

Government supply

November 1862 "[Triune Tennessee] We were not entirely dressed in gray uniforms, many occasionally received boxes of provisions and clothing, shoes or boots and homemade lamb's wool or beaver or coon skin fur hats from folks, and it was quite common to see soldiers wearing home woven gray blue brown or black woolen jeans pants or overcoats, gray or black hats and a majority of us wore wool socks sent us from home, while others wore the entire regulation gray uniform including gray caps."

U.S. ARMY HERITAGE AND EDUCATION CENTER Diary of Rufus W. Daniel Co. C, Arkansas Infantry Regiment

Oct. 26, 1862 "Rested all day for the first time in nearly 2 months after making a long and tiresome march of 500 miles. Snowed all day and very cold and a good many of our boys are barefooted and nearly naked for clothes."

Oct. 28ht, 1862 "Nothing new, drew some clothing for the reg't.'

Oct. 29th, 1862 "Drew more clothes, I drew a coat for guard."

BLOODY BANNERS & BAREFOOT BOYS-A HISTORY OF THE 22ND REGIMENT ALABAMA INFANTRY C.S.A. The Civil War Memoir and Diary Enteries of J. P. Cannon Md compiled & ed by Noel Crowson & John V. Brogden pub by Burd St. Press 1997

Pg. 17 Oct. 26 1862 "…We had waded every stream from Chattanooga to near Louisville and from there back to Knoxville. Our clothing, well-worn from the start, was now in rags and tatters, shoes were worn out and many were entirely bare-footed, so when we awoke on the morning of the 26th, and found four inches of snow on the ground and a cold wind blowing from the North, we felt that our lot had been cast in hard times…our division locating near Shelbyville (Tn) on the bank of the Duck River. While there, some of us enjoyed a visit from friends from home, who supplied us with much needed clothing and shoes. These items along with a limited number of tents having been issued, we were pretty well equipped for winter weather…"

Supply from the home folks.

LETTERS OF ARCHIE LIVINGSTON, 1ST SGT. 3RD FLORIDA INFANTRY,

CO.G "Madison Grey Eagles" Knoxville 27th Oct. 1862 "...Yesterday a snow storm commenced & lasted until this morning which found many, many soldiers entirely unprepared for the occasion. Numbers were without shoes & blankets and only clothed by a shirt & pr pants of thin material and even unprotected by a tent or tent (fly?)....Please get our woolens ready so as soon as we learn of our destination you can send on. Levy needs 2 pr winter heavy pants-I am shoeless& so is Levy because we could not get those at Chattanooga. There is a rumor that we are to draw (?) articles soon, if so we can manage. You had better get each of us a pair ready & send when we advise you to forward our woolens which will be done very soon after our (?) are uniformed & then we will want them right off..."

THE CIVIL WAR LETTERS OF JOSHUA K. CALLOWAY ed. By Judith Lee Hallock Univ. Ga. Press 1997

Pg. 62 Camp Near Knoxville, Tenn. Oct. 27th, 1862 "Mrs. D. Callaway: My dear wife, As Mr. Brown is going to start home in the morning I will write you a short letter; though it is so cold & so late I can not write much. We have had a big snow. The ground is covered about ten inches. It began Saturday and covered the groung with 3 inches & yesterday it was very cold and a little before night it began again & this morning it was about ten inches deep, but the sun has been shining all day and it thawed rapidly; but it is very cold to a parcel of soldiers who are nearly naked and barefooted....

The "unkindest cut of all" was that we had to throw away our knapsacks & all our clothes at Sparta, Tennessee, on the 5th of September, and consequently we are now naked, bare footed, dirty, filthy, and lousy (with body lice only) beyond description. We have never been paid off yet. My little old blanket has long since failed & but for the kindness of my messmates who let me sleep with them, I should long since have "gone under." (It all feels) really that we are "naked, poor, despised, forsaken."

This illustrates an example as to why the soldiers were chronically short of clothing. I'll bet they never saw those knalsacks again.

Pg. 63 Camp Near Knoxville, Tenn. Oct. 29th, 1862 "Mrs. Dulcina Callaway: My Dear wife, Capt. H.M. Ford starts home tomorrow after clothes for the Company and this letter must be devoted to that subject...I wish you in the first place to take my old Carpet Sack & if you can't get a key to fit it send it anyhow...

I want my overcoat, my boots, 2 pair of drawers, 2 shirts (such as you can parade), as many socks as you have on hand, one or two pair of pants & a comforter or a night cap; it is very disagreeable to sleep bareheaded. I have ruined two or three hats sleeping in them. I shall want a uniform suit if one of the boys will go up to Mr. Palmore's he can probably get enough of jeans from Mrs. Watters or someone else to make them. I know my dear that it is imposing on you to send to you for so many things, but I can do no better. If you can get the cloth you will not have time ti make them to send them by Ford, but you can make them at your leisure and send them by the first one who passes, Indeed you might do better to send all the things by Lieut. Mims who will go after clothes for Capt. Hopkins Company. I hope I shall be able to get a furlough after a while, but can not do without the clothes till then if I can possibly get them before…"

UNIFORMS OF THE CIVIL WAR Lord, Wise, A.S. Barnes & Co. 1970

Pg.41 "An artilleryman from Cheatham's Corp recorded in his diary on October 29, 1862: "Captain Stanford, W.B. May, Charles Roberts, and William Brooks detailed to go home after clothing. Hurrah for me-I was able to draw an overcoat this evening. Well boys, I am wiiling to divide it on these cold nights when on duty."

This overcoat he was issued was probably of civilian make, donated to the army

THE CIVIL WAR LETTERS OF JOSHUA K. CALLOWAY ed. By Judith Lee Hallock Univ. Ga. Press 1997

Pg. 64 Camp Near Knowville, Tenn. Oct. 31st, 1862 Mrs. D. Callaway: "Lieut. Mims starts home tomorrow….He will bring all my clothes. Then for fear you have not got my other letter I will tell you what I want & how to send it.

Being an officer, (Leiutenant) I am entitled to a certain amount of baggage to be hauled, hence I want my Carpet Sack and if you can't get a key to lock it you must tie it up. I want my overcoat, my boots, two pair of pants, 2 pair Drawers, 2 shirts, such as you have, 2 or 3 pair of socks, my old sheep skin vest, if it is worth sending; some gloves; a comfort to wear around my neck and a woolen net cap to sleep in, if you have such a thing. Now if you can get the jeans to make my uniform and send it I should be very glad. Leiut. Mims will tell you how to make them, i.e. how to cut them, and if you can't get them ready to send by Mims make them and send them by the the next one who passes. I suppose I have called for enough to fill the Carpet Sack. If you have anything else that you think I would like to have send it, especially a Bible or hymn book, or both, and if the Carpet Sack will not hold all tie some on outside, and if the Carpet Sack is too bad to bring you can probably buy one at Hawley's at a reasonable price if you can spare the money, but if the old one will hold things till they get to me I can get a knapsack…. There was a small lot of clothing issued to the Regiment this morning. I got one pair of drawers & 1 shirt, of good stout domestic, and 1 pair of socks…"

Website Trans Mississippi Confederate Uniforms

Part 3 Nov. 1862, Coldwater, Miss. Waul's Texas Legion-"The diarist Phillip Amsler (Co. E. 2nd Btn.) noted on Oct. 13th that "we received our arms consisting mostly of old firelock muskets converted to percussion, with bayonets. Also cartridge boxes, bayonet scabbard and belt, (these) being new and in good order with forty rounds of ammunition(Hasskarl & Hasskarl 1985:8) On Nov. 9 he wrote that "we received a good uniform last week consisting of good blue cloth pants, a gray woolen jacket well lined, and a gray cap. Quite a comfortable suit. We can also draw shirts and drawers if we want any."(Hasskarl & Hasskarl 1985:12)

Another example of blue pants being issued by the quartermaster.

THE CIVIL WAR INFANTRYMAN, In Camp, on the March, and in Battle by Gregory A. Coco Thomas publications, Gettysburg, Pa

Pg 35 Nov 1862A Florida sergeant named Washington Ives who was stationed in Chattanooga, Tennessee in late 1862 described his newest wardrobe to a sister, along with prices: "Our boys are drawing shoes and drawers the pair of kersey pants for $2.62 (and) 1 coat of the same material as Mr. Burtchaetts suit for $5,25…" Sergeant Ives would have been surprised to learn that less than three years later in late April 1865, a set of underwear cost, according to Col. Alfred Belo, 55th North Carolina, "…twelve hundred dollars in Confederate money," which normally would have been "some two dollars and fifty cents a suit."

ONE OF CLEBURNE'S COMMAND ed. By Norman D. Brown Univ. of Austin Press 1980

Nov 1862 "…There has so far been no clothing issued to the troops here-and they beginto get scarce when on the first of Nov/62 we step into a new suit apiece-all around-jacket pants and cap.-The men all look so different-You can't tell one from another unless you see his face…"

No Pardons to Ask, No Apologies to Make, The Journal of William Henry King, Gray's 28 Louisiana Infantry Regiment Univ. Tenn. Press 2006

Pg. 63 Nov. 1st, 1862 camp near Tallula, La. "Our measures were taken today to cut our uniforms…"

THE CONFEDERATE VETERAN Jan. 1900

Pg. 73 "Reminiscences From Missouri by John M. Berry Nov 8, 1862 "After the battle of Perryvillewe took up our march, via Camp Dick Robinson, where a large supply of army stores were captured and destroyed. Thence, through the bushwacking, wild-cat mountains we reached Knoxville, Tenn. about the 4th of November, almost destitute of clothing and shoes. We had hardly anything to eat except parched corn. After a few day's rest, with better food and clothing, the spirit of the army returned, and we were again ready for duty."

LETTERS OF ARCHIE LIVINGSTON, 1ST SGT. 3RD FLORIDA INFANTRY,

Fair Ground Hospl No2, Atlanta Ga. Nov.24 63 Archie's brother Tede

"...A boy belonging to a member of Co. A in our Regt. Promised me on yesterday to take a box for Archie but I have not seen anything of him since. He left the Regt. some two or three days since, and brot a letter from Archie with (army?) socks, Drawers, Flannel &c from Archie for our deposit, until he needs them. He says that his suit of jeans fits exactly and is admired, by all in the Regt....I wish if you have not sent my clothes-you would send those that you have as soon as possible for there is no telling when I may go. My shoes are too large for me, but I will make them do, but the next ones I have made in the size smaller. These are 7 when I could wear a five but a small 6 is the size. If it will not delay my bundle any-& you could do it without much inconvienence, send me a pr. For there are plenty of men that will take these from me...."

UNIFORMS OF THE CIVIL WAR Lord, Wise, A.S. Barnes & Co. 1970

Pg. 63 "The plight of wounded Federal soldiers after the battle (Stones River, Dec. 1862) brought out feelings of disgust and anger in the Union ranks over their poor treatment while in the hands of the Rebels. "It is a burning shame that the enemy will pillage the dead and wounded on the field. Our men were stripped and laft exposed to the terrible rains that fell during the three days of the fight."

It seems to become a habit among the Rebs to pillage the dead, though I don't think those stripped dead soldiers minded the rain.

A CONFEDERATE GIRL'S DIARY Sarah Fowler Morgan Dawson Mifflin & Co. 1913

Pg 30 Dec. 1862 "...Before me stood my pattern of nearness in a rough uniform of brown homespun. A dark flannel shirt replaced the snowy cambric one, and there was neither cravat nor collar to mark the boundary line between his dark face and the still darker material. And the dear little boots! O ye gods and little fishes! They were clumsy and mud-spattered!..."

WESTERNERS IN GRAY-The Men and Missions of the Elite Fifth Missouri Infantry Regiment by Phillip Thomas Tucker pub by McFarland & Co. 1953

Pg. 95 Dec. 1862 "Clothing shortages grew acute as December winds howled and the weather became colder. As throughout the conflict, shoes were in short suppy for the exiles stranded on the east side of the Mississippi. Many Missouri boys stood barefoot during roll call on frosty mornings…one of the Fifth Missourians favorite anecdotes described a popular Confederate general inquiring during a review of an Arkansan, "Where is your cap box, sir?" The private then loudly asked Joseph E. Johnson, "What do I want with cap box with this damned old Flint Lock musket?"

STONES RIVER-BLOODY WINTER INTENNESSE by James Lee McDonough pub by Univ. TN Press 1980

Pg. 51 Dec. 1862 "…One of the soldiers in the Twenty-Eighth Tennessee Infantry, named Spencer Tally, was from nearby Lebanon Tennessee. Ariving at home, he was pleasantly surprised to find that his mother had made him and his brother "a goodly supply of heavy jeansand woolsocks that reached well near the knees. Many of our neighbors had clothing ready for their sons and we had a full load of good clothing and other things to bring back to the boys in camp.' W.E. Yeatman, Second Tennessee Infantry, risking capture by the Union army, slipped westr into Nashville to see his father and mother. In addition to the good food and clothing that he received, Yeatman said, "I remember that my mother decorated my felt hat with a lot of her old black Ostrich plumes, and the boys thought I was a general when I rejoined them." The feathers however, proved to make a good target and Yeatman quickly realized he could not wear then in battle…"

NO PARDONS TO ASK, NO APOLOGIES TO MAKE- The Journal of William Henry King, Gray's 28th

Louisiana Infantry Regiment ed. by Gary D. Joiner, Marilyn S. Joinerand Clifton D. Cardin Univ. of Tenn. Press 2006

Pg. 71 camp near Tallula, La. Dec'r 5th, 1862 "…W.H. Pinkard of our Comp. came in on the early stage to-day, & reports Mitchell of our Comp. & others, in charge of our uniforms and clothing, somewhere between here & Arcadia. We are waiting for them, & it is now probable we will be off soon…Dec'r 7th, To-day I look for an opportunity to start for Vienna, but find none. Mitchell has not yet arrived. Should he not reach here before I leave, & by some chance I miss him on the road, I would be likely to miss some valuble articles of clothing… Dec'r 8th, Mitchell gets the wagons in this morning before day. We open the boxes, take out our clothing…"

THIS INFERNAL WAR Edwin Hedge Fay/Bell Irvin Wiley Univ. of Texas Press 1958

Pg. 181 Camp 3 Miles East of Grenada Dec. 9th 1862 My Own Loved One "...My old coat is the only one I have. If you could get some jeans and that old man could cut and make me a coat, you might perhaps find some opportunity of sending it to me though I can get along very well without it I reckon for some time yet. It has been very cold for the last few days and the ground is hard frozen every night but I have slept warm in the open air and have not suffered from cold except my feet. I borrowed a pair of woolen socks but cannot see any difference. I can wear them if I had them but it makes no matter. I wish you would learn to knit me some undershirts of cotton. Try and do so if you can..."

BROTHERS IN GRAY

N.M. Middlebrooks to David Pierson Camp near Troy, Miss., Dec. 16th, 1862 Capt. David Pierson, Mt. Lebanon, La. Dear Friend, "...Belden told me you wanted to know what the boys most needed. Well, I think they most need Blankets, Socks, and yarn Pants, Shoes,&c. If you can, get me two pair of stout woolen pants and a couple of overshirts..."

ALL AFIRE TO FIGHT-The Untold Story of the Civil War's Ninth Texas Cavalry by Martha L. Crabb pub by Avon Books 2000

Pg 135 Holly Springs Miss. raid Dec. 20 1862 "McCulloch's Missourians broke into the sutler's store and "commenced an indiscriminate pillage." Griffith appealed to the men to gety about their of burning; but soon Tennesseeans, Mississippians, and Texans vied in the work of pillage, the Texans always keeping a sharp lookout for their commanders. The ragged, half-starved men gloried in their loot. They found "plentiful" cigars and kept three thousand puffing.

The cavalrymen's appearance was completely transformed. They donned new pants and overcoats, plumed hats, and glistening cavalry boots. They broke open boxes of new Remington and Colt revolversand carried off two to six each. They gobbled the sutler's canned peaches and oysters, candy and cheese, and stuffed their saddlebage with bacon, pork, hardtack and coffee. A Third Texas private found $20,000 in new, crisp U.S. greenbacks, which he traded for five dollars in silver coins."

Pg. 140 Dec. 21, 1862 "From Wolf Creek, Van Dorn led his men north into Tennessee. The raiders rode at breakneck speed, stopping only to cut telegraph wires, burn stockades and tear up the railroads. They ripped up cross ties, set them afire, then heated the rails until they were hot enough to twist around trees. Christmas Eve they captured a Federal regiment's winter quarters and hauled off knapsacks, canteens, blankets, overcoats, shirts, fifty pairs of socks, nine days rations, and the colonel's horse, overcoat, and dress coat..."

A godsend in blankets and overcoats.

THE CONFEDERATE VETERAN VOL. XIII 1905

Pg. 264 Dec. 28, 1862 letter from Mrs. Cole Ripley Miss. "…You will have heard before reading this how Van Dorn with three or four thousand cavalry, dashed into Holly Springs (Miss.) about a week ago, capturing eighteen hundred Yankees. He burned up three million dollars worth of arms, stores, clothing, blankets etc., after supplying his men with boots, blankets, blue coats and pants, and fine arms. We heard the explosion of the magazine here, shaking the houses, and rattling the windows, over forty miles off…"

DIARY OF A CONFEDERATE SOLDIER John S. Jackman of the Orphan Brigade ed. by William C. Davis Univ. S.C. Press 1990

Pg. 67 Dec. 29, 1862 near Nashville "…We immediately fell in and advanced, in line of battle, over a rocky ravine and through an old field, where the weeds were up to our shoulders, and so thick we could hardly march. The evening was warm, and I had a heavy overcoat on, which with tugging through the weeds, caused me to nearly suufocate. I pulled it off at once, with the intention of abandoning it, but again picked it up, and buckled it under my belt. Well I did so, for afterwards, it came in good place…"

UNIFORMS OF THE CIVIL WAR Lord, Wise, A.S. Barnes & Co. 1970

Pg.63 "…Army of Tennessee just before Stones River, December 31, 1862 by a soldier in the 33rd Alabama Infantry: "We were not entireily dressed in grey uniforms; many occaisionally received boxes of provisions and clothing, shoes or boots, and homemade combed wool or beaver or coon skin fur hats from folks back home, and it was quite common to see soldiers wearing home woven grey, blue, brown, or black woolen jeans pants or overcoats, grey or black homemade hats, and a majority of us wool socks sent us from home, while others wore entirely regulation gray uniform including gray cap."

A good description of the prevailing multiform.

THE CIVIL WAR INFANTRYMAN-In Camp, on the March and in Battle by Gregory A. Coco pub by Thomas Pub

Pg. 36 "Regarding uniform prices, which varied widely in Confederate service, Lieutenant Charles Denoon, 41st Virginia, voiced that government shoes sold for eight to ten dollars, and the short waisted jackets, called "round abouts" or conversions, ran 12 to $14 dollars. According to the young officer it took a soldier four month's wages to buy a suit of clothes. Another Virginian, John L. Holt, calculated in August 1861 that his uniform would cost $33.00, and he expected to receive "round about coats" as they took less cloth in construction than frock coats. He requested from home an overcoat and apair of "oversocks," and he wanted the wool for his overcoat to be mixed "about ¾ black to ¼ white (which) will make it about the proper color…" he asked his wife Ellen to make for him "some yarn drawers just single wove yarn cloth (which) will be nearly equal to flannel." Holt then informed Ellen that he could get calico for 25 cents per yard, and that the company had just drawn a new uniform at $7.50 apiece, which were "good ones made of heavy woolen goods."

Trans Mississippi

General

ONE OF CLEBURNE'S COMMAND-The Civil war Remini-scences & Diary of Captain Samuel T. Foster, Granbury's Texas brigade, C.S.A. Univ. of Texas Press, 1980

"…Lances for the regiment were being manufactured at Chappell Hill. Each man was required to furnish himself with the best horse he could procure, two suits of winter clothing, blankets, a "bowie knife and the best fire-arms he could obtain, if possible a double-barrelled shotgun, and a six-shooter."" We call upon our friends, and the friends of Southern independence throughout the State, to assist our men in arming and equipping themselves," the officers stated. "this will be the only Regiment of Lancers in the service, and Lancers are the most formidable cavalry in the world. We have chosen this arm at the earnest solicitation of General (David) Twiggs. The lance simply takes the place of the sword in a charge, and is much the most terrible weapon…"

I have it from anecdotal evidence that a Confederate cavalry unit made a charge with lances at Shiloh. Its not surprising that there is little or no mention of using such an out-dated weapon.

CONFEDERATE VETERAN Sept.-Oct. 1992 Drab: The forgotten Confederate Color by Fred Adolphus

Pg. 38 "In the Trans-Mississippi region drab clothing is much in evidence as having been used. Company B of the 18th Texas Cavalry, upon its formation as the "Morgan Rangers" of Bastrop, was lucky enough to have uniforms made for its members. Captain Hiram S. Morgan spent his own money to outfit in gray double-breasted coats and gray trousers with yellow cavalry stripes on the legs. The fabric used for these uniforms was a yellowish- gray Huntsville penitentiary jeans. These uniforms were issued in early 1862 …"

It seems that almost all the cloth in the Trans-Mississippi Dept. was manufacture at the Huntsville penitentiary.

MILITARY COLLECTOR AND HISTORIAN-Journal of the Company of Military Historians Vo. XLI #4 Winter 1989 Descriptions of Rebel Prisoners in Missoiri by Thomas Arliskas

Pg 171 "The following from a letter written by a soldier in the 15th Illionois, who at that time were in camp at Rolla, Missouri, was published in the January, 1862 edition of the Woodstock Sentinel (Woodstock Ill.). The letter states the Confederates were captured near Black Water creek in Missouri:

Arriving just after they got in on Saturday night, the sight was a novel one to see, used as I have been to seeing soldiers in uniform. That specimen of rebeldom was arrayed in the inevitablte butternut color, homespun pants, covered with "coats of many colors" shapes and patterns, not a few having overcoats like ours, which must have been stolen. Evidence of the plunder of Lexington [Missouri] was to be seen on all hands, many of the tents they had were made of bed ticking, or common factory cloth.

Men were seen within the ring carrying pieces of bedticking, just as they came from the store, while blankets of white, red, and blue, pure or mixed, stalked throught the crowd upon the shoulders of the burly prisoners.

The number was said to be thirteen hundred men…with a large number of nondescript arms, principally shot guns …with loads of quilts, coverlids and blankets."

The continuance of multiform in the Trans- Mississippi.

THE CONFEDERATE VETERAN VOL. XXV 1917

Pg. 82 Jan. 1917 "Official Records" Vol. III State Troops-A Missourian wrote the Secretary of War of the Confederate States: "The State troops are all wiiling to be transferred to the Confederate service, and not a dissent would have been made if the transfer had been made by order without referring to the men. They had been in the army for five months and had never received any pay or clothing; and when it was left to their individual choice, being naked and barefooted, trhe natural impulse to each individual was: "I must go home." And they went…"

THIS BAND OF HEROES-Granbury's Texas Brigade, C.S.A. by James McCaffery pub by Texas A&M Univ. 1996

Pg. 5 Jan. 1862 Camp McCulloch, Nuner's Mott, four miles from Victoria, Texas "The fact that this motley array of citizen-soldiers could be molded into anything resembling a military machine was a credit to the officers entrusted with this assignment. Difficulties abounded. Firstof all, the men had to be uniformly equipped with clothing and weapons. Each company had arrived in camp with it members either garbed in some distinctive type of militia uniform or simply wearing whatever clothes they had happened to put on when they went to enlist. Company G from Travis County, for instance, looked very military in their uniforms of salt-and-pepper gray, trimmed in green. The good ladies of Austin had formed a Needle Battalion to make uniforms and they saw to it that their boys were properly clothed. The men of Company A, sported blue flannel frock coats and jeans trousers, all trimmed in red. Sometime during the regiment's stay at Camp McCulloch the entire unit received uniforms made of cloth manufactured at the State Penetentiary at Huntsville. They were not gray, as Hollywood would have us believe was the only color for Confederate uniforms, but were a light brown color often referred to as "butternut."

Pg. 18 Companies destined for Darnell's regiment arrived in Dallas throughout January and February 1862. The recommended equipment for each man included a double-barrelled shotgun, a revolver, and a large knife. Most of the men rode in to town in civilian garb and carrying all sorts of firearms. One noteworthy exception to this generally unmilitary appearance was provided by Captain Hiram S. Morgan's company from Bastrop, Texas. Morgan spent a good deal of his own money equipping his men, "The Morgan Rangers." They were outfitted in gray double-breasted coats and gray trousers with yellow cavalry stripes on the legs. The fabric used for these uniforms was also a product of the state penetentairy at Huntsville."

UNIFORMS OF THE CIVIL WAR by Robin Smith & Ron Field Lyons Press 2001

Pg.217 A Dallas Herald article reported that Co. B, 18th Texas Cavalry, was dressed in a 'yellowish-gray tunic coat and pantaloons made of Penetentiary Jeans, with two rows of brass buttons on the front of the coat and a yellow stripe down the side of the pantaloons', when they arrived in the city on 22 January, 1862....

Colonel John C. Moore of the 2nd Texas Infantry (also known as the 2nd Texas Sharpshooters) was noted for caring for the welfare of his troops. As a last resort he also took advantage of captured federal clothing, and issued his 'rag-tag regiment' with dark blue U.S. Army sack coats like those worn within Hood's Brigade in Virginia. The 2nd Texas laterrecieved uniforms of undyed wool a few days before leaving Corinth for Shiloh in March, 1862. After the battle, a Federal prisoner is reputed to have inquired: "Who were them hell cats that went intp battle dressed in their graveclothes?...The 16th Texas Infantry was described as being clad in 'wool, and straw hats, homespun pants and faded penitentiary jackets' in 1863..."

WEBSITE-MILITARYHISTORYONLINE.com Confederate Invasion of Arizona

Pg1 Jan. 8 1862 "…The third part was to send Captain Sherod Hunter, Company A, Baylor's Regiment westward to Tucson, to establish his headquarters there…Hunter's command were attired in civilian clothing, which they had when they enlisted in the Confederate Army. His men did not have uniforms of any description, no gray clothing at all. Also his men were armed with a wide variety of weapons, from shotguns to military muskets, percussion and flintlock, a variety of Colt Army and Navy revolvers, and also included single shot pistols…"

BROTHERS IN GRAY

Pg.81Feby 22 1861 (1862) Boston Mountains, Ark. David Pierson to William Pierson?

"…Half the men here have lost all their clothes. My trunk & things are safe, but I have not seen them for several days, the trains being ahead…"

REBELS ON THE RIO GRANDE-The Civil War Journal of A.B. Peticlas ed. by Don E. Alberts pub. by Univ. of N.M. Press 1984

Pg. 51 22 Feb. 1862 after the Battle of Valverde"…We got about 130 stand of small arms, 6 pieces of artillery, and a considerable quantity of ammunition, several six-shooters, and a considerable number of cast off overcoats. (J.T.) Williams found a silver watch and overcoat, and I picked up a blanket in place of the one I had thrown off…."

REBELS ON THE RIO GRANDE-The Civil War Journal of A.B. Peticlas ed. by Don E. Alberts pub. by Univ. of N.M. Press 1984

Pg. 52 23 Feb. 1862 We passed through a small Mexican village…We got some $3000 worth of goods out of a store belonging to a captain who had been in the fight. These things were confiscated; also some work oxen and a large flock of sheep. The wearing apparel was divided out to the different regiments and companies, and we had a dinner and breakfast of mutton…"

CIVIL WAR IN THE SOUTHWEST-Recollections of the Sibley Briagde ed by Jerry Thompson pub by Texas A&M Univ. 2001

Pg. 74 Feb. 24th 1862 after the Battle at Valverde, on the march for Socorro "The weather was very cold and most of us were afoot, and many were barefooted and a few bareheaded…."

And this army continued to advance.

THE CONFEDERATE REGULAR ARMY by Richard P. Weinert, Jr. pub b y White Mane Pub Co. 1991

Pg. 33 Feb. 24, 1862 Co. A, C.S. Cavalry "...Ingraham reached San Antonio from Richmond on February 24 and succeeded Bradley in command of the company. The company had moved from San Antonio Barracks to a camp six miles out of town on the Salado River. Ingraham found the company in good shape and well armed with Sharps carbines and sabres. The only thing that worried him was their uniforms. These were in good condition, but unfortunately were blue and he was afraid the men would be mistaken for Yankees the first time they went into battle..."

ALL AFIRE TO FIGHT-The Untold Tale of the Civil War's Ninth Texas Cavalry by Martha L. Crabb pub by Avon Books 2000

Pg.48 Cantonment Slidell near Fort Smith Ark... "Colonel Sims returned from Texas in the middle of February (1862)....Sims and others coming from home brought clothing and recruits, food and mail. The boisterous greeting was for coats and cakes, news and friends, as well as the colonel..."

Pg.65 March 1, 1862 Horsehead Creek "...Another group of recruits and furtloughed men reported, bringing "clothing &c from home."

Pg 65 "Major-General Van Dorn and his escort rode into the Confederate camp at Strickler's Station Monday, March 3. A forty-gun salute, the proper number for a major general, echoed through the snow-covered mountains. The handsome, flamboyant major general reined his splendid black mare to a stop in front of McCulloch's spartan headquarters. Resplendent in a gold-embroidered blue coat and dark blue pants tucked into his blackened cavalry boots, Van Dorn shook hands with his old friend, Ben McCulloch. The Texan wore his usual civilian clothes-he fought three wars without ever wearing a uniform. Van Dorn wore all the flash and glitter allowed, which included four Hungarian loops of gold braid extending from the elbow to the cuff of his tunic, a wreath containing three gold-embroidered stars on each side of his collar, and two one-inch gold stripes decorating the outer seam of his pants."

REBELS VALIENT-SECOND ARKANSAS MOUNTED RIFLES (DISMOUNTED) Wesley Thurman Leeper Pioneer Press 1964

Pg. 59 Retreating from Elkhorn Tavern- spring 1862 "...The men eventually made their way to Van Buren in small groups. Their clothing was in rags, and their shoes worn out, but they could, at least, find food at the Confederate Commissary in Van Buren!"

THE FIRST MISSOURI CONFEDERATE BRIGADE, by Ephraim McD. Anderson Times printing Co. St. Louis Mo. 1972

Pg.159 Early in 1862 (before March) "Our force was also augmented by the arrival of Gen. Albert Pike and his Indian Brigade, which came trotting by our camp on their little Indian ponies, yelling forth their wild whoop, as was the custom of their tribes when going on the "war path." Their faces were painted, and their long straight hair, tied in a queue, hung down behind; their dress was chiefly in the Indian costume-buckskin hunting shirts, dyed of almost every color, leggings and moccasins of the same material, with little bells, rattles, ear-rings, and similar paraphernalia. Many of them were bare-headed, and about half carried only bows and arrows, tomahawks, and war clubs, presenting altogether an appearance wild and savage. They were mostly Cherokees..."

REBELS VALIENT-SECOND ARKANSAS MOUNTED RIFLES (DISMOUNTED) Wesley Thurman Leeper Pioneer Press 1964

Pg. 58 "Gen. McCulloch was doubtless a very conspicuous target. Gifted towards wearing flashy uniforms, opinions differ as to what he was wearing this particular dy, but it is generally believed that he was wearing a black velvet coat, with patent-leather, high-top boots, and a broad brim planters or Texas-type hat..."

Pg. 59 Retreat from Elkhorn Tavern "...The time was early March (1862) in the Ozark Mountains and the men had no tents, no overcoats, their shoes were worn out, and they had practically nothing to protect them from the very cold, and at times, sleety weather.

The story persists to this day that some of the more frivolous tried to warm themselves by singing "In The Good Old Summer Time...."

THE FIRST MISSOURI CONFEDERATE BRIGADE, by Ephraim McD. Anderson Times printing Co. St. Louis Mo. 1972

Pg. 161. Chapter XLII (Before March 1862) camp in the Boston mtns "Our regiment was uniformed here; the cloth was of rough and coarse texture, and the cutting and style would have produced a sensation in fashionable circles: the stuff was white, never having been colored, with the exception of a small quantity of dirt and a goodly supply of grease- the wool had not been purified by any application of water since it was taken from the back of the sheep. In pulling off and putting on the clothes, the olfactories were constantly exercised with a strong odor of that animal.

Our brigade was the only body of troops that had these uniforms issued to them, and we were often greeted with a chorus of b-a-a-s, and the salutation, "I say, mister, do you ones belong to Mr. Price's company?" This last had been picked up in the country by a squad of the boys, who had been asked the question by a venerable Arkansas dame, and it had become a very common saying in camp. Our clothes, however, were strong and serviceable, if we did look and feel somewhat "sheepish" in them.

At the same time, we drew knapsacks, an essential part of the soldier's equipment, which had not been previously supplied."

"Drab" colored clothing issued to the Missourians.

REBELS VALIENT-SECOND ARKANSAS MOUNTED RIFLES (DISMOUNTED) Wesley Thurman Leeper Pioneer Press 1964

Pg. 59 Retreating from Elkhorn Tavern- spring 1862 "…The men eventually made their way to Van Buren in small groups. Their clothing was in rags, and their shoes worn out, but they could, at least, find food at the Confederate Commissary in Van Buren!"

REBELS VALIENT-SECOND ARKANSAS MOUNTED RIFLES (DISMOUNTED) Wesley Thurman Leeper Pioneer Press 1964

Pg. 109 Battle at Richmnd Ky Spring 1862 "…Some Confederates donned the clothing of Federal soldiers, whose dead bodies they had stripped. The garments were turned inside out. One Confederate remarked, "I'm Yankee within, and Reb without!"

These Confederate soldiers were poorly clad, and were, no doubt, thinking of the winter ahead of them…"

THE THIRD TEXAS CAVALRY IN THE CIVIL WAR by Doudlas Hale Univ. of Ok. Press 1993

Pg. 104 spring 1862 Corinth Miss. Brig. Gen. Joeseph L. Hogg became brigade commander "…With characteristic insolence the vetrans of the Third cavalry delighted in ragging the greenhorns, officers or not. In his Prince Albert coat, stiff-collared white shirt, and tall silk hat, Hogg was the most conspicuous of the newcomers and inspired the most good-natured ridicule from the men…The boys called General Hogg "Professor" or Parson" to his face and made fun of his hat, The general seems to have endured it all with good humor…"

THE CONFEDERATE VETERAN VOL. XIX 1911

Pg. 19 Jan. 1911 Amusing Incidents Of Service by Clarence Key spring 1862 "Sims had been enjoying a furlough in San Antinio, and arrived at camp two days after his time was up. He professed much contrition and promised the captain that thereafter he was going to be a "good soldier." He always had plenty of money in his pocket-I never saw a gambler flat broke. We were soon to get four month's pay. When pay day came, we all dressed in our best for muster. Impatiently the company waited for Sim. The captain sent a peremptory message, and presently Sim came with colassal self-assurance. He was ridiculously gotton up: dressed in a black frock coat (Prince Albert), black satin waistcoat, black doeskin trousers, and patent leather Oxford tie shoes, boiled starched shirt, standing collar, balck satin cravat, and a diamond stick pin. He was armed with a brand-new Enfield rifle, a new Colt forty-five, a new, shinig cartridge box and belt. He came out smiling blandly and not in the least abashed at finding that we had been left behind by the regiment because of his delay. When he took his place in the ranks, the captain called to him sharply: "Simpson!"

"Sir?" said he.

"What do you mean by coming on parade in those ridiculous duds, sir?"

Sim looked hiself over with a very self-satisfied glance and said, "I was told to put on the best I had for muster, Cap'n and I did so."

"Didn't you get a grey cloth doublet and hat the other day like the other men?"

"Why yes," said Sim, smiling amicably. "Yes Cap'n Edwards, I got one all right, thank you sir."

"Very well then, go and put them on at once."

"Yes, Cap'n," said Sim; "I'll do it with pleasure. Certainly, Cap'n Edwards, I'll do it with pleasure."

He changed his clothes and we joined the regiment on the parade ground."

Pg. 20 "…Now it is not an easy thing to carry a five-gallon demijohn safely on a pack mule. I had an abomination, given to me by a considerate and kind friend in Havana, an India rubber air pillow. As I could not possibly use it to sleep on, I suggested that we carry the whiskey in the pillow. With much difficulty we coaxed the liquor into the pillow and set out. On the first day we took our ration of whiskey all right, but on the next day the odor of the stuff was fierce. The sulpher had gotten into the spirit…"

This is the only description I have read of an "India rubber air pillow.

PANORAMA OF LIFE IN THE SOUTH-A Treasury of Confederate heritage. Ed. By Walbrook D. Swank Burd Street Pess 2003

Pg. 395 March 1862 just before the battle of Pea Ridge, Gen. Ben McCulloch and staff near Fort Smith, Ark. "…when a stranger rode up and inquired the way to Gen. Stone's quarters. The stranger was a perfect specimen of the genus "butternut." He was dressed in bilious looking jeans, with a homemade hat and coarse boots, and wore his hair and beard very long. He was mounted on a good horse, and carried on his shoulder a long, old-fashioned rifle. …"

LONE STAR & DOUBLE EAGLE- Civil War Letters of a German-Texas Family Menetta Altgelt Goyne Texas Christian univ. Press 1982

Pg. 44 Camp Winston no date (probably 2 march 1862) Rudolf to Family "…There are two stores, a sutler and the Commissary. But they have hardly anything anymore. The smallest shoes that they had was size 9. We bought a pair of boots for $10, a pair of shoes for $3.50, two hickory shirts, rather poor quality, at $1.25 apiece; two pairs of cotton socks at 75* a pair; and two silk handkerchiefs at $1.00 apiece. Really poor quality cotton ones would have cost 75* apiece, and the silk ones seemed to be not exactally bad…"

THE CONFEDERATE CHEROKEES Jonn Drew's Regiment of Mounted Rifles by W. Craig Gaines La. State Univ. Press 1989

Pg. 80 March 6 1862 the night before the Battle of Pea Ridge "…About midnight Drew's regiment marched to its assigned positions with the remainder of Pike's brigade. A member of Price's division in the 1st Missuori Brigade later wrote of the Indians movements: "They came trotting gaily into camp yelling forth a wild war whoop that startled the army out of all its propriety. Their faces were painted for they were "on the war path," their long black hair qued in clubs, hung down their backs, buckskin shirts, leggings, moccasins adorned with little bells and rattles, together with bright colored turkey feathers fastened on their heads completed unique uniforms not strictly cut according to military regulations. Armed only with tomahawk, and war clubs, and presented an appearance somewhat savage, but they were mostly Cherokees, cool and cautious in danger, active and sinewy in person, fine specimens of "the noble red man."…"

APPENDIX-PG 481-"Anderson's description of the clothing, weapons and appearance of the Chorkee Mounted Rifles is overdrawn and completely inaccurate. The enlisted men were dressed in linsey-woolsey, while the officers, many of whom were slave owners, were attired in uniforms. The men carried shotguns and hunting rifles. Many of them, like their white counterparts, had Bowie knives stuck in their belts."

Yeah, but its so much more fun to believe the frist description!

SOUTHERN CONFEDERACY APR. 24 1862; William Stevenson, THIRTEEN MONTHES IN THE REBEL ARMY, pp. 36-37; Folmar ed. TERRIBLE FIELD, PP88; Ella Lonn, FOREIGNERS IN THE CONFEDERACY, pp496-502; John McGrtath, "IN A LOUISIANA REGIMENT," pp 103-4, 113, 116.

Lyman to wife, March 15 1862, Joseph Lyman Letters, YU; Cincinnati Commercial, April 15, 1862; John C. Moore, "Shiloh Issues Again" pp316-17; Barnes F. Lathrop, "A Confederate

Artilleryman at Shiloh" pp378n. Following the battle, a Northern journalist noted that most of the Confederates wore homespun or butternut. Chicago Times, April 24, 1862.

WESTWARD THE TEXANS-The Civil War journal of William Randolph Howell ed by Jerry D. Thompson pub by Texas Western Press, Univ of Texas 1990

Pg. 95 Albuquerque N.M. Sibly's Brigade March 17, 1862 "Lieutenant Clough in town drawing clothing for our company."

March 20, 1862 "…I am left to bury John Naile. I get a nice black suit for the occasion and a nice coffin is furnished and with the Brass Band to escort his remains out of town, we bury him in the sand hills near Albuquerque…"

CIVIL WAR IN THE SOUTHWEST-Recollections of the Sibley Brigade ed by Jerry Thompson pub by Texas A&M Univ. 2001

Pg. 85 March 27th, 1862 Glorietta Pass "While we were fighting in the canyon, the enemy sent a detachment of 300 men around in our rear and burnt up every wagon and all the provisions and bedding and clothing we had…"

REBELS ON THE RIO GRANDE-The Civil War Journal of A.B. Peticlas ed. by Don E. Alberts pub. by Univ. of N.M. Press 1984

Pg. 91 (after the Battle of Glorietta Pass, Sante Fe N.M.) 2 April, 1862 "…Still lying up refitting. Drew a blanket apiece…"

Pg. 94 4April, 1862 "…Still lying in quarters. Clothes are being gotten together and distributed to the companies who lost everything in the battle…"

Pg.97 8 April 1862 "…About 12M we left town, but not in order by any means, as the order was to leave scattering. About 2 hours after we started we all got together on the valley road to Alberquerque and in spite of new shoes and long rest we marched rapidly, but towards night the wagon guard got very strong, and I was one of them as my feet were sore indeed…"

CIVIL WAR IN THE SOUTHWEST-Recollections of the Sibley Brigade by Jerry Thompson epub by Texas A&M Univ 2001

Pg. 100 April 5th, 1862 Santa Fe N.M. The wife of Federal General Canby is assisting the wounded of both sides "…Colonel Scurrey met her at the door and told her about the burning of our train, clothing and bedding, the suffering of the boys, and the freezing of the wounded…directly she said "Colonel, these men must not suffer anymore. There are a large number of government blankets where you would never find them, but I will tell you where they are," and she disclosed the hiding place. We got them and in this way we were supplied with two blankets to every three men..."

Pg. 106 April 14, 1862 Battle of Peralta "About 11 o'clock a cheer from Coopwood down on our extreme right announced that something had occurred. Looking down in that direction we beheld the gallant Scurrey coming at the double-quick with the 4th and 5th to our assistance....Thet had waded the river about waist deep to get to us and their clothes were actually frozen upon them. I mean their rags since we had no clothes..."

Pg. 123 April 18th, 1862 retreat from Peralta "We camped on this creek (Rio Grande) the night of the 18th, and would have got a very good night's rest if it had not been for Davidson. He had not had a blanket since the battle of Glorietta and by some means he did not find Phil Clough to "spice with him," so he built a fire and laid down by it. About 12 o'clock he commenced hollering "Fire! Fire! Fire!" In fact he hollered fire until he got everybody in the regiment roused up and Wes Seymour asked him what in the h-l was the matter when he said, "I'll be d-d if I haven't burnt up the whole gable end of my breeches!" And if the seat be the "gable end," it was certainly gone. However, the boys killed three antelope the next day and he got one of the hides, and to use his own expression, "welded another gable end" to his pants and we suppose that he went to see his sweetheart in those pants when he got to San Antonio ..."

WESTWARD THE TEXANS-The Civil War Journal of William Randolph Howell ed by Jerry D. Thompson pub by Texas Western Press, Univ. of Texas 1990

Pg. 100 April 17, 1862 (Retrteat from Glorietta) "...We camp at a branch opposite LaJoya. The Yankees camp too. We get supper and orders to burn up all our clothes but what we could "put on our backs' and to take 7 days rations only..."

LONE STAR & DOUBLE EAGLE- Civil War Letters of a German-Texas Family Menetta Altgelt Goyne Texas Christian univ. Press 1982

Pg. 55 New Braunfels 19 April 1862 Rudolf from Father "...Johann has a saber, all of them are getting pointed hats like the Tyroleans, trousers packs, blankets, etc. I have bought an old carbine for you, one that loads from the back, for which you will have to make yourself a new shaft though, if you want it..."

I don't know what this writer means by a "new shaft" for a breech-loading rifle.

CONFEDERATE VETERAN Sept.-Oct. 1992 Drab: The forgooten Confederate Color by Fred Adolphus

Pg. 39 "In the summer of 1862, Walker's Texas Infantry Division received extensive issues of cotton clothing. Allotments of 8.000 yards of osnaburgs to each regiment were sewn into tents, knapsacks, haversacks and clothing, by the women of Smith County. These troops spent the summer in cooler cotton fabrics rather than traditional woolens. As most cottons left the factory as "gray goods," it is a safe bet that these uniforms were undyed…"

CIVIL WAR IN THE SOUTHWEST-Recollections of the Sibley Brigade by Jerry Thompson pub by Texas A&M Univ 2001

Pg. 128 May, 1862 at San Antonio"…In this way we continued to make the long stretches between water until at last we reached San Antonio, where we all were given a good suit of clothes, each furnished with a square meal…"

REBELS ON THE RIO GRANDE-The Civil War Journal of A.B. Peticlas ed. by Don E. Alberts pub. by Univ. of N.M. Press 1984

Pg. 128 11 (Franklin, Texas) May 1862 "…Lying in camp eating scant rations and wishing for a change of clothes. News comes from below that the long-looked-for-train bringing up the clothing etc., sent us from Victoria is near at hand. Ship up from Ft. Quitman brings this news. We wait impatiently. Most of us are wearing the same suit we started from Santé Fe in …"

Pg. 129 14 May 1862 "…Received today the clothing, and the boxes were opened, numerous packages were directed to individuals and a quantity of clothing sent to the company…. Lura Case sent me a great roll of linen bandages; Lucy Davies a pair socks and a comfort. Mrs. Davies a large bed quilt, most welcome of all. M.D. (Mary Dunbar) 2 pair socks and a comfort, besides a comfortable little note in the interior. M.G. (Marion Goodwin) sent me a substantial pair of socks…Mrs. Shirkey sent me 2 pair socks; good substantial articles. Besides these things I drew of the company donations 1 blanket, 1 pair pants, 1 heavy shirt and 2 pair socks, so I am now well supplied in socks at least I gave Lytle a pair of socks as I did not need all I had…"

Supply from the home folks.

THE THIRD TEXAS CAVALRY IN THE CIVIL WAR by Doudlas Hale Univ. of Ok. Press 1993

Pg. 30 "…A public subscription in prosperous Harrison County collected enough money to equip each of the men in Company K with a smart new uniform in cadet grey, but most of the regiment were not so lucky. The troopers of Company B had to purchse their own uniforms, and in so doing strove for style over functuon. They chose black coats, vests, hats and boots, and aquired a quantity of heavy brown jeans from the Texas prison shops sufficient to put them all in breeches. They looked fine on parade, but their uniforms were stifling hot under the June sun…."

FIELDS OF BLOOD The Prarie Grove Campaign by William L. Shea Univ. N. Ca. Press 2009

Pg. 52 Fall 1862 Brashears, Ark. Gen Hindman informed his superior, Gen. Holmes "For the present I am very anxious to avoid a general engagement, I have not ammunition enough for two hours of fighting, am barely able to subsist the troops when stationary, and would find it very difficult when moving, and there are so many of the men without shoes that it will be a distressing thing to march them any distance."

http://www.lazyjacks.org.uk/tranmis1.htm

Pg. 2 Codwater, Miss. Fall 1862 John K. Earns surgeon, 41st Tennesse Inf. (Smith 1994) "I returned from Holly Springs about sunset, and when I got to the regt., I found the boys all in Uniform which they had drawn. Their pants were all sky blue; their coats grey round about, with cuffs and collars trimmed in blue. Grey caps for all. This will add much to their appearance in the field…"

http://www.lazyjacks.org.uk/trammis1.htm

-Jan. 1864Pg. 4 Blessington (1875: 115) wrote of the dress of Walker's Division after the Red River Campaign: "It is impossible to point out the variety our division presented. Here would be a fellow dressed in homespun pants, with the knees out of them; on his head might be stuck the remnant of a straw hat, while a faded penitentiary cloth jacket would perhaps complete his out fit. His neighbor very likely was arrayed in breeches made of some castoff blanket, with a dyed shirt as black as the ace of spades and no hat at all…" Another Greyhound remarked that most of the division's clothes left in storage before the Red River Campaign were either stolen or had rotted (Johnnson 1998:71)

JO SHELBY'S IRON BRIGADE by Deryl P. Sellmeyer pub by Pelican Pub. Co. 2002

Pg 38 Aug. 1962 Camp Kearney, six miles from Newtonia, Missouri "…The brigade lacked much of material things. True, the men had horses, many of them good, but the Confederate

Government had firnished little. Self-sufficient, Sheby's men provided their own arms, horses, accouterments, and cooking untensils. Most were poorly clad and without uniforms, but they expected little. They were Southern patriots. They had chosen to fight for their state, their country, and their honor…"

GRAY GHOSTS OF THE CONFEDERACY Guerrilla Warfare ion the West Richard S. Brownlee La. State Univ. Press 1858

Pg.104 Oct. 1862 "…The Shawneetown raid was made primarily to obtain clothing, an item the guerrillas were chronically short of. As Confederate uniforms were not available to Quantrill and his men in 1862, even had it suited their purpose to wear them, they developed a dress peculiar to themselves which became known up and down the border. Its distinguishing item was a "guerrilla shirt." This shirt, patterned after the hunting coat of the Western plainsmen, was cut low in front, the slit narrowing to a point above the belt and ending in a rosette. The garment had four big pockets, two in the breast, and ranged in color from brilliant red to homespun butternut. They were made by the mothers, wives and sweethearts of the guerrillas, and many were elaborately decorated with colored needlework. With their brilliant shirts, wide-brimmed slouch hats of the plains, and mounted on the finest horses in western Missouri Quantrill's boys made a colorful appearance…"

KIRBY SMITH'S CONFEDERACY

PG.59 "In October,1862, Shelby advised Marmaduke that his brigade included "a great many men without a blanket, overcoat, shoes or socks…We have never drawn ant clothing, shoes, salt, or anything else. …As the "chill winter" of 1862-63 set in, newspaper columns were sprinkled with urgent appeals from many regiments for coats, trousers, footwear, hats, overcoats and blankets. From Pine Bluff, for instance, a trooper of the thirty-first Texas Cavalry wrote to describe the "hard, heavy, severe suffering" of his comrades and to ask whether "our kind friends, our countrymen, the good people of texas, {would} help aid and assist us with clothing for the winter? One pair of good yarn socks, may prevent a soldier's feet from being frozen.…How would your hearts rejoice to know that you had saved one poor soldier from the pangs of the crip{p}led." The Nineteenth Texas Cavalry even placed newspaper advertisements to solicit the donation of firearms!…Under the circumstances, the troops' frequent resort to illegal impressments and plunder was not surprising. Some even went so far as to loot government warehouses! Nor was it surprising that, when all else failed, disgusted soldiers preferred desertion to destitution.

The soldier who quit often found conditions at home little better than those in the army.… Ladies made do with "Confederate dresses," the remains of their prewar wardrobes; table settings at the most fashionable homes were made of tin, not silver; rope halters had long since replaced leather bridles…"

Pg.64 The Arkansas leather industry consisted of a number of very small piecework tanneries clustered in the vicinity of Washington and Camden. These tanneries pressed cattle hides procured from local stockmen or from the military commissariat, and the cobblers and saddlers- most of whom were soldiers detailed from the army- converted the leather into boots, shoes, cartridge boxes, and horse equipments. When the tanneries were unable to obtain cattle hides, the shoe- and harness- makers fashioned brogans ans animal trappings from the skins of wild deer, squirrels, and raccoons.

GRAY GHOSTS OF THE CONFEDERACY Guerrilla Warfare ion the West Richard S. Brownlee La. State Univ. Press 1858

Pg.129 Oct. 9, 1862 Baxter Springs, Kansas massacre "...Gen. James G. Blunt, Union commander of the District of the Frontier, was approaching from Fort Scott to Fort Gibson. "Blunt was guarded by a hundred men from the Third Wisconsin and fourteenth Kansas Cavalry. He had with him in his wagon his band. Quantrill and 250 of his men formed a lion e of battle across the path of the approaching train. As many of the guerillas were dressed completely or partially in Union uniforms, General Blunt decided that they were an honor guard from Fort Baxter sent out to meet him. He had his cavalry escort dress its ranks, and trotted on toward Quantrill at a leisurely pace. When Blunt's men were sixty yards away, the guerrillas fired a volley into them and launched a screaming charge. The Union cavalry fled in wild disorder...."

http://www.lazyjacks.org.uk/tranmis1.htm

Waul's Texas Legion Phillipm Amsler (Co. E, 2nd Btn.) noted on October 13th, 1862 that "we received our arms consisting mostly of old firelock muskets converted to percussion, with bayonets. Also cartridge boxes, bayonet scabbard and belt, (thse) being new and in good order with forty rounds of ammunition"(Hasskarl and Hasskarl 1985:8) On November 9th he wrote that "we received a good uniform last week consisting of good blue cloth pants, a grey woolen jacket well lined, and a grey cap. Quite a comfortable suit. We can also draw shirts and drawers if we want any." (ibid)

TRANS-MISSISSIPPI CONFEDERATE UNIFORMS Part 3

Nov 1862-June 1865 K.C. Mac Donald "...Camp Cold Water near Holly Springs, Mississippi Oct.26 1862 John K. Earns, surgeon, 41st Tennessee Infantry (Smith 1994) "...I returned from Holly Springs about sunset, and when I got to the Regt., I found the boys all in uniform which they had drawn. Their pants were all sky blue; their coats grey round about, with cuffs and collars trimmed with blue. Grey caps for all. This will add much to their appearance in the field..."

Rudolf Coreth 36th Texas (dismounted), 16 Nov. 1863 Houston "… We received our winter cloths: pants, jackets, hats, and blankets. The trousers and jackets are of grey woolen cloth. Everything is pretty good. The order came that each man is to get two complete suits and, in order to complete these, another requisition for clothes was made, but they haven't arrived yet…"

They will have to be satisfied with the first issue; I doubt the second requisition ever arrived.

CONFEDERATE RAGE, YANKEE WRATH by George S. Burkhadt pub by Southern Illinois Univ. Press 2007

Pg. 45 Oct. 29, 1862 "Island Mound, Missouri 1st Kansas Colored troops met a sronger enemy force…Lieutenant Elkanah Huddleston (their commader) reported, "Of the loss of the enemy but little is known as they held the field long ehough to get off their dead and wounded and also to strip our dead and carry off the clothes."…"

FIELDS OF BLOOD The Prarie Grove Campaign by William L. Shea Univ. N. Ca. Press 2009

Pg. 80 Early Nov. 1862 Gen. Hindman urged Gen. Holmes to send to Fort Smith "shoes, uniforms, blankets, tents, and camp equipment…supplied with new arms "The shiny Enfields contrasted strongly with the tattered garments worn by many of Hindman's troops. No soldiers in the Confederacy were more woebegone in appearance than those camped along the Arkansas River in the fall of 1862. "They are the ragedist lot of men I ever saw, a great many of them barefooted and bareheaded and almost naked," wrote a Missouri officer. "When men grumble here it is chiefly about clothing and surely they have a right to grumble, and I most vigorously grumble with them," declared a threadbare Lieutenant Nathaniel Taylor, a Texas cavalryman. "Our clothes are nearly all worn out and we look more like a great army of beggars than anything else.…The relatives of the boys had better do the best they can for them."

"The Rebels called on relatives, friends, and patriotic citizens to send warm clothing, or any clothing at all, as temperatures drifted downward. It was still early in the war, and appeals of this sort were successful more often than not. Before the year was out Col. Guess published a letter in several newspapers thanking the "ladies of Texas" for the "promptness and liberality with which they have furnished us with good warm clothing."

Ragged Rebels

LONE STAR & DOUBLE EAGLE- Civil War Letters of a German-Texas Family Menetta Altgelt Goyne Texas Christian univ. Press 1982

Pg. 71 Sisterdale, November 1862 Rudolf to Family "...(Johann) to ride to to comfort tomorrow and buy himself a hat. (Cristoph) Flach (a Kapp son-in-law), who was here the other day, told him that he still has a soldier's hat that is too small for him and Johann wants to but it if it fits him. If Munzenberger should have gotten our winter clothes, I would like to request that you use the parts that do not belong to the uniform, and my two coats that are at your place, if you can use them, for I shall probably have enough with my leather clothes..."

THE RAGGED REBEL, A Common soldier in the W.H. Parsons' Texas Cavalry 1861-1865 by B.P. Gallaway, Univ of Texas Press, Austin 1988

Nov. 20, 1862 Dave Nance loaded his mule (which he part-owned with a mess mate), and left to rejoin his unit. "He was dressed in the ordinary costume of a Trans-Mississippi soldier of the day- an old felt hat, boots and jeans and a jacket made from undyed cotton which had turned brown. A knapsack containing buckshot hung from one shoulder and a powder flask hung from the other. Having borrowed a young, spirited saddle mare from Quill (his father) and an old double-barreled shotgun from uncle Otwa, Dave prepared to return to war.

KIRBY SMITH'S CONFEDERACY

Pg. 67 ...From first to last, home manufacture-highly inefficient but indispensible- remained the Trans-Mississippi Confederacy's primary source of clothing, shoes and related items. Throughout the Department, thousands of women and young girls spun thread, wove cloth, knitted socks and scarves, fashioned hats, stitched shoes, hemmed blankets, rolled bandages, sewed together haversacks, and made cartridge boxes and harness straps....Sometimes, when wagons were available, the ladies of a given district were able to supply an entire company of neighborhood soldiers, but more often individual families were content to outfit themselves and their own military kin. On November 6, 1862, Thomas Farrow sent his absent son "1 cotton shirt, 2 pair socks, 2 pair linsey pants, 1 pair of drawers, one westcoat, 4 twists of tobacco, comfort." Eight days later another father mailed "2 pairs pants 2 overshirts 2 pair drawers one pair shoes 4 pair socks" to his soldier son. Soldiers neglected by their folks back home were often obliged to beg clothing from their comrades. An infantryman informed his sister that a messmate named Grace "is all most naked his Breeches is in strings all he has got fit to ware is a over shirt Joe gave him a par of drars & shirt I gave him a par of breeches all I have except what I have on,"

Extensive supply from the home folks.

FIELDS OF BLOOD The Prarie Grove Campaign by William L. Shea Univ. N. Ca. Press 2009

Pg. 186 "The undergrowth was so thick that in our advance we did not see the rebels until we were almost right on to them," recalled one Indiana soldier. Another Hoosier noticed that the Confederates "could hardly be distinguished from the leaves; their butternut clothing being exactly the same color."

THIS BAND OF HEROES-Granbury's Texas Brigade, C.S.A. by James M.McCaffery pub by Texas A&M Univ. 1996

Pg. 25 Dec. 1862 Camp Hope, near Austin, Arkansas "The men heard many rumors while at Camp Hope. The most persistent of these was that they would be ordered into Missouri for the winter. They were told to obtain warm clothing from home because the government could not provide it for them Letters home at this time read like shopping lists: "If it is convenient, send me a Double-breasted jeans vest and one or two Pr. pants and a shirt or two" :I want one good thick pair of breeches [,] an overshirt, both of wool or part wool and a couple of pairs of drawers, soft wool if you can get it, a vest, a couple of homespun cotton shirts...three or four pairs of socks, a pair of homemade suspenders and a soldier's cloak or overcoat." "I want you to make us some overshirts; make mine greens (jeans) and dy[e] them purple or brown..." "I would like to have a heavy jeans, well-lined overcoat, also a linsey or cotton overshirt, one pair of pants, and a pair of slips and socks."

BROKENBURN-The Journal of Kate Stone 1861-1865 ed. By John Q. Anderson La. State Univ. Press Baton Rouge

Pg. 308 "[Tyler Texas] Dec. 4 Mrs. Carson has been in a perfect rush since getting good clothes for Joe. ...He is nearly handsome now in a new suit of Confederate grey."

FIELDS OF BLOOD The Prarie Grove Campaign by William L. Shea Univ. N. Ca. Press 2009

Pg. 140 Dec. 7, 1862 Cav. Fight at muddy Bottoms "One of the Rebels brandished the national colors of the seventh Missouri Cavalry. "By this time the pursuing enemy were upon us, bearing our standard and wearing out blue overcoats," declared a loyal Arkan sas officer...." With so many combatants dressed in blue, the struggle was intense and chaotic. "We had a hand to hand fight that lasted about ten minutes," recalled a Confederate officer.

"It was a hot and exiting battle. We were all mixed up, every fellow for himself, all dressed pretty much alike, except the hats were mostly of different style."

What a nightmare for the participants of this skirmish!

FIELDS OF BLOOD The Prarie Grove Campaign by William L. Shea Univ. N. Ca. Press 2009

Pg. 148 morning Dec. 7th, 1862 "As the Confederat infantry neared Prarie Grove, "They also passed several corpses. All had been stripped of their uniforms and equipment, and several had been trampled into the mud by horses. It was a sobering sight for men unaccustomed to the detritus of battle."

1863

EAST

VMI MS# 361

Kent Langhorne-2nd Va. Cav. Dear Aunt "...Tell Pa I want my gray jacket & order me a pair of shoes as I have drilled so much since I have been here that they are nearly worn out and Gen. Smith says that it is impossible for him to furnish shoes and the reason I write for my jacket is that there is about 100 boys to get their uniforms before me and my coat will not be decent to wear to church..."

MILITARY COLLECTOR AND HISTORIAN-Journal of the Company of Military Historians Vol. XLI Fall 1989 Enlisted uniforms of the Maryland Confederate Infantry: A Case Study, Part 1 by Ross M. Kimmel

Pg. 106 2nd Maryland-"...They started the campaign around New years 1863 in excellent condition. The diary of S.Z. Ammen reported:

The men are in fine condition, well-equipped and clothed. In addition to good uniforms most of them have overcoats, and the necessary outfit of blankets and rubber cloths...for pillows they use their caps and shoes, and it may be-if the enemy is not near- their odorous socks..."

These Rebs are well equipped, they even have overcoats.

"...By April, a woman who saw them in Winchester (Va) remarked, "Such a parody of a dress parade! The men looked cold and thin in their lean ranks..."

This gives a good idea of the life of those uniforms, they were well equipped in January, but by April their uniforms were apparentely worn out.

LIFE IN THE CONFEDERATE ARMY:Being Personal Experiences of a Private Soldier in the Confederate Army: and Some Experiences and Sketches of Southern Life by Arthur P. Ford and Marion Johnstone Ford pub by The Neale Pub. Co. 1905

Pg. 78 Marion Ford: "The years of the war sped on, and brought privations and sorrows which each year seemed to intensify. Our home was no longer the bright place it used to be, for we had lost many friends, and self-denial was the order of the day. We were very busy, too, and that helped to keep us cheerful.

There were new accomplishments to aquire. We learned, and taught our maids, to card and spin the home-grown wool, and when that did not suffice for the extraordinary demand we had supernumerary mattresses ripped up; the ticking was considered to make handsome frocks for the servants, and the woolwhen dyed and woven made excellent homespun suits for ourselves, that were not to be despised for durability and warmth. There was quite a rivalry as to who could make the prettiest dyes for our dresses, but aftyert a time black was most worn. Then we had our old light kid gloves to ink pover carefully, so that we might not go barehanded to church. We thought the gloves a great success when we first dyed them, but when we came to wear them, the ink never seemed to dry, and would soak through and dye our hands most uncomfortably. Our greatest achievement after all, I think, was the pile of socks we knitted by the lightwood blaze at night.Our old-fashioned butler always placed a candle-a tallow one, or still worse, a home-made myrtle wax one- upon the table, but we considered it an extravagance to light it unless there was something urgent to read. I am surprised now that we did not mind the heat of the blaze more in summer, but I do not remember our thinking of it. There was one great spasm of patriotism when every worsted curtain in the house was cut into soldier's shirts. Some of these were in brilliant colors and patterns, and I cannot but think might have served as targets for bullets. We even undressed the piano and converted its cover into a blanket for a soldier. We were chagrined afterwards to hear form some of our friends who had done the same thing, that the latest advice from the fields was that the soldiers found the garments, so improvised, very unsatisfactory and begged the ladies not to sacrifice their belongings so recklessly."

Do you really think the soldiers were that picky?

HAM CHAMBERLAYNE-VIRGINIAN Letters and Papers of an Artillery Officer in the War for Independence 1861-1865 with introduction, notes and index by his son C.G.Chamberlayne Richmond, Va. pub by Press of the Dietz Printing Co. Publishers 1932

Pg. 152 J.H. Chamberlayne to L.P. Chamberlayne (Jan. 1863) My dear Sister, "...Capt. Crenshaw goes down tomorrow and I have waited today to send this by him. He is a trusty gentleman and my very good friend. Speaking to him of an overcoat, he kindly proposed to give me one....I would be glad if you would then have have the cape taken off & put on with buttons and button holes so as to be moveable at pleasure. You might then dispense of the coth. I don't want a dress uniform coat. I can wait indefinitely for it. In fact don't want it, at any time, for any purpose, nor pants.

Don't send the overcoat by any chance passenger,only by some one of whom you are perfectly sure, otherwise let it wait indefinitely. With that I am completely set up in clothes..."

Here's an officer who doesn't want a dress uniform, plus he wants his sister to be extremely careful when sending that overcoat.

FROM THE RAPIDAN TO RICHMOND by William Meade Dane D.D. Private 1st Co. Ricmond Howitzers pub by Owens pub. Co. 1987

Pg. 35 Jan. 1863 Sketch of Winter Camp Life "Leading up to an account of this, I may mention some circumstances in the way of the boys in camp. Living the hard life, we were-one would suppose that fashion was not in all our thoughts; but even then, we felt the call of fashion and followed it in such lines as were open to us. The instinct to "do as the other fellow does" is implanted in humans by nature; this blind impulse explains many things that otherwise were inexplicable. With the ladies it makes many of them wear hats and dresses that make them look like hoboes and guys, and shoes that make them walk about as gracefully as a cow in a blanket, instead of looking, and moving like The young graceful gazelles—that nature meant, and men want them to look like. Taste and grace and modesty go for nothing-when fashion calls.

Well-the blind impulse that affects the ladies so-moved us in regard to the patches put on the seats of out pants. This was the only particular in which we could depart from the monotony of our quiet, gray uniform-which consisted of a jacket, and pants and did not lend itself to much variety; but fashion found a way.

There must always be a leader of fashion. We had one-"The glass of fashion and the mould of form" in our gang was Ben Lambert. He could look like a tombstone, but was full of fun, and inventive genius.

Our uniform was a short jacket coming down only to the waist, hence a hole in the seat of the pants was conspicuous, and was regarded as not suited to the dignity and soldierly appearance of a Howitzer. For one to go around with such a hole showing-any longer than he could help it-was considered a want of respect to his comrades. Public opinion demanded that these holes be stopped up as soon as possible. Sitting about on rough surfaces-as stumps, logs, rocks, and the ground-made many breaks in the integrity of pants, and caused need of frequent repairs, for ours was not as those of the ancient Hebrews to whom Moses said, "Thy raiment waxed not old upon thee"-ours waxed very old, before we could get another pair, and were easily rubbed through. The more sedate men were content with a plain, unpretentious patch, but this did not satisfy the youngsters, whose aesthetic souls yearned for "they knew not what," until Ben Lambert showed them. One morning he appeared at roll call with a large patch in the shape of a heart transfixed with an arrow, done out of red flannel. This at once won the admiration and envy of the soldiers. They now saw what they wished, in the way of a patch, and proceeded to get it. Each one set his ingenuity to work to devise something unique. Soon the results began to appear. Upon the seats of one, and another, and another, were displayed figures of birds, beasts and men-a spread eagle, a cow, a horse, a cannon. One artist depicted a "Cupid" with his bow, and just across on the other hip a heart pierced with an arrow from Cupid's bow-all wrought out of red flannel and sewn on as patches to cover the holes in the pants, and, at the same time, present a pleasing appearance. By and by these increased in number, and when the company was fallen in for roll call the line, seen from the rear, presented a very gay and festive effect.

One morning, a General, who happened to be in camp-the gallant soldier, and merry Irishman, General Pat Finnegan, was standing, with our Captain, in front of the line, hearing the roll call.

That done, the Orderly Sergeant gave the order, "Bout face!" The rear of the line was thus turned toward General Finnegan. When that art gallery-in red flannel-was suddenly displayed to his delighted eyes the General nearly laughed himself into a fit.

"Oh boys," he cryed out, "don't ever turn your backs upon the enemy. Sure they'll get ye-red makes a divil of a good target. But I wouldn't have missed this for the world."

The effect, as seen from the rear, was impressive. It could have been seen a mile off-bright red patches on dull gray cloth. Anyhow it was better than the holes and it made a ruddy glow in camp. Also it gave the men much to amuse them.

Ben set the fashion in one other particular-viz., in hair cuts. He would come to roll call with his hair cut in some peculiar way, and stand in rank perfectly solmn. Ranks broken, the boys would gather eagerly about him, and he would announce the name of that "cut." They would, as soon as they could, get their hair cut in the same style."

I would have loved to have seen that assembly. I know you all have read about this in "The Life of Johnny REb." But here is the original quote.

SEVEN MONTHS IN THE REBEL STATES DURING THE NORTH AMERICAN WAR 1863 by Captain Justice Schiebert Confederate Pub. Co. Inc. 1956 Confederate Centennial Series #9

Pg. 36 "The army, which was recruited by universal conscription extending from the sixteenth to the forty-fifth year, made a very strange impression in its outward appearance, since nothing in the way of uniformity was to be seen, for everyone wore whatever he could get, or whatever his wife wove for him at home."

Even this late in the war, according to witnesses, multiform still prevailed.

WEEP NOT FOR ME, DEAR MOTHER (letters of Eli Pinson Landers from Gwinnett Co. Ga. The Flint Hill Grays. Eli was 19 years old when he enlisted in Aug. 1861) ed. by Elizabeth Whitley Roberson pub by Pelican Pub. Co. 1996

Pg. 163 Portion of a letter "…If you can I want you to send me a wool hat and some thread and needles and a case to put them in for I have lost mine…Mammy you need not send me any clothing for we have drawed a suit of clothes but if I send my money home in time you had better get your winter shoes before they get so high and if you can have me a good firm pair of strong shoes made for me for they are from 8 to 10 dollars a pair here…I want to know if you ever got my overcoat and wool shirt or not. I sent them in Capt Reeder's trunk…"

Eli was able to draw "a suit of clothes" probably from the government quartermaster.

LETTERS OF A NEW MARKET CADET Beverly Stanard, ed. by John G. Barnett & Robert R. Turner pub by Univ. N.C. Press 1961

Pg. 2 My dear Sister "…Phil Hiden is trying to get a furlough to go down to Charlottesville to see his brother James Married…If he succeeds, he will come onto Orange, so that he wil be a good opportunity to send my box. Says he will bring it. I also want my pants that (dark brown) Bob gave me, sent. Repair them if they need it, before you send them…"

CONFEDERATE ECHOES A Soldier's Personal Story of Life in the Confederate Army From the Mississippi to the Carolinas by Albert Theodore Goodloe-First Lieutenant Company D Thirty-Fifth Regiment Alabama Volunteer Infantry C.S.A. pub by Zenger Pub. Co. 1897, 1983

Pg. 170 Camp near Hamilton's Crossing Va. My dear mother "…The coat & vest suit me exactly-many thanks for them & paper & soap-I needed them…"

HISTORY OF KERSHAW'S BRIGADE by Augustus Dickert pub by Broadfoot Pub. Co. 1899

Pg.490-493 "In this imperfect history of the times of which I write, I cannot resist at this place a deserved tribute to the noble women of the South, more especially of South Carolina. It was with difficulty that the soldiers going to the army from their homes after the expiration of their furloughs, or going to their homes when wounded or sick, procured a night's lodging in Richmond, for it must be remembered that that city was already crowded with civilians, officers of the department, surgeons of the hospitals, and officials of every kind. The hotels and private residences were always full. Scarcely a private house of any pretensions whatever, that did not have some sick or wounded soldier partaking of the hospitalities of the citizens, who could better care for the patient than could be had in the hospitals. Then, again, the entire army had to pass through the city either going to or from home, and the railroad facilities and the crowded conditions of both freight and passenger cars redered it almost obligatory on the soldiers to remain in the city overnight. And it must be remembered, too that the homes of hundreds and thousands of soldiers from Tennessee, Maryland, Kentucky, Mississippi, and all from the Trans-Mississippi were in the hands of the enemy, and the soldiers were forbidden the pleasure of returning home, unless clandestinely. In that case they ran the risk of being shot by some bush-whacker or "stay outs," who avoided the conscript officer on one side and recruiting officer on the other. In these border states there was a perpetual feud between these bushwhackers and the soldiers. It was almost invariably the case that where these "lay outs" or "hide outs" congregated, they sympathized with the North, otherwise they would be in the ranks of the Confederacy. Then, again, Richmond had been changed in a day from the capitol of a commonwealth to the capitol of a nation. So it was always crowded and little or no accomidations for the private soldier, and even if he could get quarters at a hotel his depleted purse was in such condition that he could not afford the expense. Nor was he willing to give a month's wages for a night's lodging. A night's lodging cost five dollars for supper, five for breakfast, and five for a bed, and if the soldiers were in any way bibulously inclined and wished an "eye opener" in the morning or a "night cap" at supper time, that was five dollars additional for each drink. Under such circumstances the ladies of South Carolina, by private contributions alone, rented the old "Exchange Hotel" and furnished it fron their own means or private resources. They kept also a store room where they kept socks for the soldiers, knit by the hands of the young ladies of the state; blankets, shirts,and underclothing, from the cloth spun, woven, and made up by the ladies at home and shipped to Richmond to Colonel McMaster and a staff of the purest and best women of the land. Only such work as washing and scrubbing was done by negro servants, all other was done by the ladies themselves. Too much praise cannot be given to Colonel McMaster for his indefatigueable exertions, his tireless rounds of duty, to make the soldiers comfortable. The ladies were never too tired, night or day, to go to the aid of the hungry and broken down soldiers. Hundreds and thousands were fed and lodged without money and without price. Car loads of the little comforts and necessities were shared out to the passing soldiers whenever their wants required it. Never a day or night passed without soldiers being entertained or clothing distributed. One night only was as long as a soldier was allowed to enjoy their hospitality, unless in cases of emergency. The officers of the army, when able, were required to pay a nominal sum for lodging. Better beds and convienences were furnished them, but if they wewre willing to take private's "fare" they paid private's "fee," which was gratuitous. As a general rule, however, the officers kept apart from the men, for the officer who pushed himself in the private's quarters was looked upon as penurious and mean. It was only in times of the greatest necessity that a Southern officer wished to appear thus. If the Southern soldier was poor, he was always proud. This hotel was called the "South Carolina Soldiers' Home," and most of the other states inside the lines had similar institutions. In every home throughout the whole South could be heard the old "hand spinning wheel" humming away until far into the night, as the dainty damsel danced backwards and forwards, keeping step to music of her own voice and the hum of the wheel. The old women sat in the corners and carded away with the hand-card, making great heaps of rolls, to be laid carefully and evenly on the floor or the wheel. Great chunks of pine, called "lite'wood," were regularly thrown into the great fireplace until the whole scene was lit up as by an incandescent lamp. What happiness, what bliss, and how light the toil, when it was known that the goods woven were to warm and comfort young "massa" in the army. The ladies of the "big house" were not idle while these scenes of activity were going on at the "quarter." Broaches were reeled into "hanks" of "six cuts" each, to be "sized," :warped," and made ready for the loom. Then the little "treadle wheel" that turned with a pedal made baskets of spools for the "filling." By an ingenious method, known only to the regularly initiated Southern housewife, the thread was put upon the loom, and then the music of the weaver's beam went merrily along with its monotonous "bang, "bang," as yard after yard of beautiful jeans, linsey, or homespuns of every kind were turned out to clothe the soldier boys, whose government was without the means or opportunity to furnish them. Does it look possible, at this late day that almost the entire Southern army was clothed by cloth carded, spun, and woven by hand, and mostly by the white ladies of the South?"

This is the first I've read of the "Exchange Hotel" and its services. These ladies performed an extremely valuable service to the soldiers. Regarding that last sentence, what do you think was the percentage of clothes/uniforms for the Confederate Army that were made by home folks?

RAGS AND HOPE-The Recollections of Val C. Giles, Four years with Hood's Brigade, Fourth Texas Infantry,23 N.Y. 1963

Pg. 147 1863 A South Carolina veteran gave his wife a report on the state of his trousers. "They will soon be gone forever, but I am perfectly satisfied that they will go in peace, for there is no doubt of their hol(e)iness…if you were to see me in (them) you might mistake me for a zebra, leopard, or something else equally outrageous." Tennessee's James Anthony declared "Our uniforms were uniform in one respect only. We were uniformly ragged! We had rags of all sizes…Rags of all colors textures and makes; Rags of bright colors and gloomy ones."

These soldiers emphasized their raggedness proudly.

CRACKER CAVALIERS by John Randolph Poole pub by Mercer Univ. Press 2000

Pg. 11 "The 2nd Georgia trooper carried his rifle or shotgun not in a saddle boot, but slung over his backon a leather strap, usually barrel down. By 1863, most carried a handgun or two, more likely stuck in a belt than carried in a holster. On his belt the cavalryman hoped to have a cartridge box and a pouch for percussion caps. Some of the men were never issued these items, however, and many others lost to wear and incessant soakings with rainwater. Replacements were hard to come by, and many of thre troopers had to carry their ammunition in pockets, haversacks, and saddlebags. Their the ammunition would mingle with a tin mess kit, two spare horseshoes, a few nails, and a small hammer, along with spare socks, shirts, and underwear. A wooden or metal canteen and perhaps a pair of field glasses would hang from the saddle.

Cavalry or infantry, southerners in the Western Theatre usually wore brimmed hats rather than kepis. A photograph of Pvt. Williiam Harrison Morrow of F company shows him wearing a kepi and with a Navy Colt in his belt. However, Pvt. Morrow later served in the Georgia Militia, and the grey uniform and other accouterments shown in the photograph may be from that service.

In winter, the trooper hoped to augment his shirt, shell jacket and wool trousers wth a heavy coat. Many "suffered greately" for lack of jackets, pants, overcoats, shoes and blankets. Replacements for worn out gauntlets and riding boots were also often unavailable. Records show that clothing was issued to at least some of the men in the 2nd Georgia in March and June of 1864, Henry Strickland's 1864 wedding day photograph shows himin a simple grey tunic, but that garment may have been made by his mother or sisters especially for the occaision. Most of the men depended on their families to send them homemade clothing...."

Remember that last sentence, it proved true for most of the Rebel soldiers in every region.

THE ARMY OF NORTHERN VIRGINIA-LEE'S ARMY IN THE CIVIL WAR 1861-1865 by Phillip Katcher pub by Brown Ref. Group 2003

Pg. 68 "...One recruit wrote home in 1863 after receiving all the accourterments could provide him: I was issued two haversacks today, miserably weak and sleavy, made of thin cotton cloth. "Otherwise, he was given only a gun, ammunition, and carried a change of underwear and soap and a towel he brought from home. In the opening weeks of the war, by comparison, the first volunteers arrived in their pre-war parade uniforms, often claw-hammer tail coats and leather shakos that were to prove impractical in the field. Other volunteers simply arrived in civilian clothing. Although the Confederate Government quickly adopted an official uniform, of blue flannel shirt, grey flannel trousers, and a cap, it was unable to get manufacturers to produce enough to supply more than its small regular forces around New Orleans…"

Fifth Virginia Infantry Virginia Regimental History Series by Lee A. Wallace Jr. 1998

Pg. 45 "In January 1863 a generous contribution of clothing for the 5th Virginia was sent by the Ladies Cap Association of Staunton, through Eliza Kinney, and the Soldier's Aid Society of Greenville, through Mrs. M.J. Tate…"

Supply from home folks.

A spacious log church with an altar at the intersection of two wings was completed on the first of February, 1863. Services and prayer meetings were frequent, and were attended by Jackson and Paxton, who wrote, "I was much pleased by the appearance of my men. They looked clean and comfortably dressed, and were attentive to the sermon."

WEEP NOT FOR ME, DEAR MOTHER by Elizabeth Whitley Roberson pub. by Pelican Pub. Co. 1996 16th Georgia Regiment of Infantry Pvt. Eli Landers (age 19)

Pg. 96 Winter (Jan) 1863 "…I have nothing new to write this morning but I thought that I would tell you that we had received that box of jeans and clothes that was started when I was at home (about a month ago). It come to the company on the 12th (Jan). Some of the clothing was very badly damaged and almost rotten, but none of the individual things was injured. I drawed me another coat out of the box but I have to pay $7.50 for it to make those equal that don't get one. But I had rather pay that for such coats than to draw the government clothes. I sold them leggings for two dollars…"

Eli states he'd rather pay for a coat made by the home folks than to draw the government clothes. Was the reason the poor quality of the government issue clothing?

LIBRARY OF VA. Robert Isbell Box # 41457

Camp near Culpeper Court house Jan. 1863

Dear Anna In my last letter I stated that I had lost all of my clothing in the fight we had on the Rappahannock River. I have since made a (?) in under clothing to last me some time. I did not mind losing the clothing I had brought from home with me but I had laid out all the baggage I had in clothing. Some of it I had got very cheap, it was my intention to have sent them to my wife (?) but it so happened that I had them with me the day of the fight and lost them all with my horse. I am very much in need of a pair of pants at this time as the pants I have on have holes in the seat. I have no money to buy anything as we have not been paid off as many days. Coats are cheaper in Culpepper than they were in Lynchburg…This regiment a scout up towards Leesburg in a few days, if it does I will have to borrow a horse to go with it, as it will be a very good chance to get some cheap clothing…"

This soldier doesn't even mention the possibility of drawing clothing from the quartermaster.

THE HISTORY OF A BRIGADE OF SOUTH CAROLINIANS-KNOWN AS GREGGS by J.F.J. Caldwell pub by King & Baird1866

Pg. 105 January 1863 Clothing was issued now, according to the system, which dated from October, 1862…Most of the men rubbed out a jacket in two or three monthes-a pair of pantaloons in one. It was coarse, stiff and flimsy. Sometimes even cotton pants were offered us in mid winter. Scarcely a particle of flannel was to be had. The cut was worst of all. Anybody could put on the clothing, but scarcely any object in nature, except a flour barrel, could find a fit. Shoes were scarce, blankets curiousities, overcoats a positive phenomenon…"

Remember this quote, it explains why the soldiers were usually so ragged, especially when they had to rely on the government for these "coarse, stiff and flimsy" uniforms.

THE STILLWELL LETTERS-A GEORGIAN IN LONG-STREET'S CORPS ARMY OF NORTHERN VIRGINIA ed. Ronald H. Morely pub by Mercer Univ. Press 2002

Pg. 94 Camp Fredericksburg Jan. 1 A.D. 1863 (Molly) "…My pants are smartly worn, more especially the seat but I have patched so I think they will do me until I get my new clothes. It was a mistake about any clothes coming some time ago as I wrote to you but I think I will get them the last of this week…I have good shoes yet, my socks will do tolerably well. I have darned them with saddle thread. I will have a set of metal buttons to put on my coat when I get it. I am going to get Smith to cover my hat and I am going to quilt it myself…."

Ingenuity in the face of adversity. He doesn't mention whether the clothing he's expecting is coming from home or drawn from the governemt.

VMI MS# 190

Pg. 120 William R.M. Slaughter, 2nd Lieutenant Co. L, 6th Alabama Vol. Inf. Camp near Grace Church Va. Jan. 4, 1863 (re: Fredericksburg) "...It was then that a most melancholy accident happened. I.M. Iverson from Lowndes Co., and of the Third Ala. Reg., was among the skirmishers, but Iverson advancing found a splendid Yankee overcoat, which he put on. He was a very brave boy and as the line continued to advance, he got some distance ahead. One of the Southern Rifle Company, seeing him advance, and mistaking him for a Yankee, shot him, the ball penetrating his heart and killing him instantly...

Seriously he was a veteran soldier, he should have considered this. If he wanted to wear it, turn it inside out

I walked over to where the Yankee lines of battle had been. There lay their dead in great heaps unburied. They had been stripped of all their outer garments, and especially of their shoes, by our men. The grass upon that portion of the field where many of them had fallen had been set on fire by the explosion of shells. Their hair, whiskers, eyebrows and lashes had been burned, and their faces and hands had been partially roasted..."

JAMES MADISON UNIVERSITY ARCHIVES

Jan. 4 1863 Letters of 1st Lt. Reuben A. Scott, Co. B, 10th Regiment Virginia Infantry, Camp Skinker's Bend, (Va) Dear Mollie; "...Mollie I have plenty of clothing at present I will need a pair of pants in Feb. or the first of March and perhaps a pair of socks but the one I brought from home is good yet got no holes in them my boots need half soling and leather is so hard to get I don't know how I will do to get them mended but I wiil find some way..."

So far, so good for Lt. Reuben.

HANDLEY LIBRARY ARCHIVES

James A. Miller Collection correspondence C.W. era misc. New Market, Va.

Hdqrtrs, 25th Va. Regt. Jan. 4th, 1863 Dear Julia, "...Tell Larpes that he must make himself a rope or string bridle to ride his colt with as leather is too high. I can't afford to but him a leather bridle, and he must cobble himself a saddle out of some of my old clothes or your sheep skin..."

SOJOURNS OF A PATRIOT The Field and Prison Papers of An Unreconsrtu8cted Confederate edited with commentary by Richard Bender Abell & Fay Adamson Gecik pub by Southern Heritage Press 1998 letters of Pvt. Augustus Pitt Adamson

Pg. 124 Camp Young, near Savannah, Ga. Jan. 4th, 1863 Dear Sister, "…We drawed blankets while in North Carolina. I need nothing, without it is a shirt…."

A Captains War Letters and Diaries of William H.S. Burgwyn 1861-1865 ed. by Herbert M. Schiller pub by White Mane Pub Co. Inc. 1994

Pg. 56 Near Kenansville January 5th, 1863 The Capt. Sent his servant, Pompey home briefly …He is to start for Raleigh Monday and remain there Tuesday and return to me Wednesday. I sent by him both coats you let me have because when I get the other one I would not be able to easily carry them and I would not have any use for them.

If you can easily do it please put two more pockets in it on each side at right angles to the two you have put in so that when my arms are at full length they will be in there; make them pretty deep.

Harry has given me his blue Lexington (V.M.I. cadet) coat. Please put two horizontal bars of gold cord on each side of the collar as you did on the jacket to designate my rank."…

LETTERS TO AMANDA-The civil War Letters of Marion Hill Fitzpatrick Army ofNorthern Virginia ed by Jeffery C. Lowe and Sam Hodges pub by Mercer Univ. Press, 1998

Pg 49 Jan. 5th,1863 General Hospital No. 20, Richmond, Va. (Letter No. 23) Dear Amanda, "I have just been fixing up to start to my Reg., and I tell you my heart throbs with joy at the idea of again being with my comrades in arms and getting to wear my new suit of clothes…I did not get my old clothes back, but I come out pretty well at least better than I expected. I got two pretty good white cotton shirts. One of them is a shade too small and the other a shade too large but they do finely. I got a very good pair of white cotton drawers, but they are a little too short in the legs and I had to sew up one of the legs the first thing I done, it being ripped nearly all the way. Upon the whole they will do finely as I am not quite so particular as I once was, and I hardly think it necessary for you to comply with the request t I made in my last letter about sending me shirts, in fact I had rather you would not send them till I see how things are going to work and I write for them…"

The shirts & drawers were hospital issue, I have not read of a soldier who was in the hospital and had his old uniform returned to him. Maybe they were too ragged and lousy and were discarded.

Pg. 51 Jan. 8th/63 Camp Near Guiness Station, Va.(Letter No. 24) Dear Amanda, "...I found my clothes all straight, I put them on right away and felt like a new man. They fit me exactly; and it is given up by all that it is the prettiest suit there is in the Company. My shirts are just the idea and the comfort cannot be beaten, my gloves are also fine, but I had a good pair already. I was offered a dollar for my old pair, but thinking they were worth more I laid them away in my knapsack for harder times. I was truly sorry you sent the coverlead (probably a coverlet or quilt), as I had two good blankets. I sold it for $10.50. I hated the worst in the world to do it but I could not carry it and rather than run the risk of losing it, I sold it. We may stay here a good while, but it is very uncertain. Tip Hammock and I sleep together now. Tip had a good coverlead and blanket, and we sleep very comfortably. We have one tent and some flys..."

THE PAINFUL NEWS I HAVE TO WRITE-Letters and Diaries of Four Hite Brothers of Page County in the Service of the Confederacy Army of Northern Virginia Series Stonewall Brigade ed.by Harlan R. Jessup pub by Butternut & Blue 1998

Pg. 121 John Hite to father Jan 7th 1863 Camp Winder Caroline Co. Va. "...The boots I had made were too tight in the instep, sold them, and bought another pair; would be glad if you could send me leather to have them halfsoled, as they will need it in several weeks...."

CONFEDERATE CAPTAIN UJANIRTIS ALLEN'S LETTERS TO HIS WIFE ed. by Kandall Allen and Keith S. Bohannon pub by La. State Univ. Press 1998

Pg. 206 "2nd P.S. The fact we can get nothing here. It would take a thousand(?) to set me in good running order. Cant go to Richmond or anywhere else unless the regiment goes. If those clothes don't come soon I will be bare headed, bare footed, and bare backed. That is the fact..."

Another example of a ragged officer.

Pg.206 Port Royal Va. Jan. 7th 1863 writing about the Battle of Fredericksburg-"...Our men will give a wounded yankee the last drop of water they have if none of our wounded are about and then strip his dead comrade. Take their shoes, caps, haversacks, canteens and especially their money...."

THE STILLWELL LETTERS-A GEORGIAN IN LONG-STREET'S CORPS ARMY OF NORTHERN VIRGINIA ed. by Ronald H. Morely pub by Mercer Univ. Press 2002

Pg. 98 same camp Jan. 8th 1863 "...I have bought me a new jeans vest for three dollars and a half and sold my old one for two and a half so you see I am all right....Give my thanks to

Uncle for his present of shoes and to all their kindness of helping you. My clothes fit like a bug's shirt, everything just right..."

"DEAR MOTHER: DON'T GRIEVE ABOUT ME. IF I GET KILLED, I'LL ONLY BE DEAD." Ed. by Mills Lane pub by The Beehive Press 1977

Pg. 211 Edward Davenport to his Mother Chester Station Viginia January 8, 1863 My Dear Mother: "...My boots are most too large, though I can wear them very well. I was offered $30 for them as soon as I got them..."

A MEMOIR OF CAPTAIN C. SETON FLEMING of the Second Florida Infantry, C.S.A. by Francis P. Fleming pub by Union-Times Pub. House 1881

Pg. 120 Jan. 9 1863 Camp near Fredericksburg, Va. My Dear Aunt Tilly; "...Many thanks to your kind offer to procure clothing for me. I am just now, as well supplied as a soldier in the field should be. If at any time, I should need anything of the kindI shall be glad to avail myself of your kindness. I must also thank you for the jacket that you sent me. I have not yet recieved it, but have no doubt that Mrs. Reid will send it to me at her earliest opportunity, as I learn that it is in Richmond..."

JAMES MADISON UNIV. ARCHIVES

Jan. 29, 1863 Letter of Enoch V. Kaufman Camp Skinkers Rock (Va) Dear Uncle: "...Tell ASng (Aunt?) that I have got an overcoat at last I drew one the other day from the Quarter Master it cost me $18.00 it is very low according to the way everything that is selling here..."

The overcoat he writes about was probably a civilian one as the government manufactured few, if any overcoats.

LETTERS FROM LEE'S ARMY Compiled by Susan Leigh Blackford Annotated by her Husband, Charles Minor Blackford, Charles pub by Scribner's & Sons 1947

Company B of the Second Virginia Cavalry- Charles Blackford was first lieutenant, later captain.

Pg. 159 Jan. 10th, 1863 "...Try to get me two or three gallons of chestnuts, I want to make coffee out of them..."

HANDLEY LIBRARY ARCHIVES

James A. Miller Collection correspondence C.W. era misc. New Market, Va.

HdQrtrs 25th Va. Regt. Jan. 10th, 63 Dear Julia "...You said you had cut me a pair of pants. I wish you would send them to me by the first opportunity. I wish you would have me a hat made and send it to me as soon as possible as I will soon be out of mine..."

CONFEDERATE CAPTAIN UJANIRTIS ALLEN'S LETTERS TO HIS WIFE ed. by Kandall Allen and Keith S. Bohannon pub by La. State Univ. Press 1998

Pg. 207 Camp near Port Royal Va. Jan.11th 1863 (Dear boykin) "...Capt Hood starts tomorrow to Georgia to procure shoes for the regiment....I have, or rather will, give him your name and also that of John G. Goss knowing that you would give him all the assistance possible to furnish shoes to the barefooted of the company and regiment. The Government will pay six dollars per pair for shoes for the soldiers provided they are furnished under the supervision of the inferior court or other civil authority of a county. I would be glad if you could have several hundred or fifty or even a dozen pair provided so that the captain would get them. Don't let it be said that old Troup is a laggard in providing for her barefooted soldiers....Capt Hood will bring any shoes or clothing that any person may wish to send to any member of the company...Please give publicity to this last, and tell the people I say the men are barefooted and want shoes. And they must have them. The boys send their money home to them and will be satisfied if they can only get shoes socks and hats. They can get a limited supply of other things from "Jeff Davis". We can not get shoes!!..."

Shoes again needed, desparate request for supply from home folks.

Pg. 209 Camp near Port Royal Va. Jan. 12th 1863 (wife) "...Many thanks for your kind letter, the handkerchief and also for the boots, though it would have been equally as well for my feet and much better for my temper if I had never seen the boots. They are too small entirely for camps besides they are worthless. Certainly Holle is a very base man. They are not the style that I wrote for. Shall I trouble you again for another pair? If Matthews had leather he could make such as I want. He sent John such a pair as I would like to have only that the legs are not near large enough and three or four inches too short. ..."

What a great deal of trouble for a pair of boots.

A SOUTHERN SOLDIER'S LETTERS HOME-The Civil War Letters of Samuel Burney Cobb's Georgia Legion, Army of Northern Virginia.pub by Mercer Univ. Press 2002

Pg. 234 Jan. 12, 1863 Camp Georgia Legion near Fredericksburg, Va. My Dearest Wife, "... Tell Carter & Bob that I have a pair of shoes for them, some boy's shoes that some softhead sent to the army for men to wear..."

This soldier is sending these too small shoes home for his sons, as they were too small for any soldier.

WELCOME THE HOUR OF CONFLICT-William Cowan McClellan & the 9th Alabama by John C. Carter pub by Univ Al. Press 2007

Pg. 206 Jan 12th, 1863 Fredericksburg Va Headquarters Provost Guard Anderson Division Dear Father, "…[F.J. "Ted"] Batts has arrived with my clothing and Boots the Boots I am afraid are too small, I can get them on but they are too tight in the in step. I exchanged with Lt. Gilbert for a while but his are too small also, I expect I will have to sell them if I do I will send the money home and get a pair a little larger probably I can get shoes for the present, tell Mother I have got as many clothes as I want, if we had to march I would have to throw away some of them, I am very sorry I cant ware those nice new Shirts she sent me if I was to put one on in less than two days I would have a pint of Body Lice on me, I am wareing the linsey drawers sent me, I am wareing the vest Batts Brought me, with this suit on I will not suffer much. There is not a man in the army officer or Private that does not have from a Battalion to a Brigade of Body Lice on him, I could soon get most of them but there is always some filthy man in the camps that perpetuates the race. When they first got on me they pestered me almost to death but now I cannot sleep sound unless I have a few on me…"

It says something when a man has body lice for so long they don't bother him anymore.

WEEP NOT FOR ME, DEAR MOTHER (letters of Eli Pinson Landers from Gwinnett Co. Ga. The Flint Hill Grays. Eli was 19 years old when he enlisted in Aug. 1861) ed. by Elizabeth Whitley Roberson pub by Pelican Pub. Co. 1996

Pg. 96 Fredericksburg, Va. Jan. 14th, 1863 Dear Mother "…I have nothing new to write this morning but I thought that I would tell you that we had received that box of jeans and clothes that started when I was home. It come to the Co on the 12th. Some of the clothing was very badly damaged and almost rotten, but none of the individual things was injured. I drawed me another coat out of the box but I have to pay $7.50 for it to make those equal that don't get one. But I had rather pay that for such coats than to draw the government clothes. I sold them leggings for two dollars…."

THE STILLWELL LETTERS-A GEORGIAN IN LONG-STREET'S CORPS ARMY OF NORTHERN VIRGINIA ed. by Ronald H. Morely pub by Mercer Univ. Press 2002

Pg 98 Headquarters Second Brigade, First Division, Army of the Potomac, January 15 1863 My Dear Molly "…My health dearest, is good and when I am dressed in my fine suit I look well. My clothes fit so nice and they are so warm and comfortable, all just right except my drawers, they were most too small. I suppose you did not think I had fattened so much I am ready for old winter and snow…"

DEAR IRVIE, DEAR LUCY- The Civil War letters of Capt. Irving A. Buck, General Cleburne's AAG & Family pub by Buck Pub. Co. 2002

Pg. 126 Jan. 15, 1863 Head Quarters, Dept. of South Carolina & Florida My Dear Lu, "… Have just received a note from Irving, ordering uniforms for his brother officers…" Your Affectionate Brother, Alvin

LETTERS FROM LEE'S ARMY Compiled by Susan Leigh Blackford Annotated by her Husband, Charles Minor Blackford, pub by Charles Scribner's & Sons 1947

Company B of the Second Virginia Cavalry- Charles Blackford was first lieutenant, later captain.

Pg. 159 Jan. 16th, 1863 "…Our army has never been in such condition as to health, spirit, arms and clothing as at present. There are no barefooted men and the style of their arms has been greatly improved by the acquisitions of the battle of Fredericksburg…."

This quote matches the one for the 2nd Maryland. Apparentely the army was in top shape in the first monthes of 1863.

CONFEDERATE CAPTAIN UJANIRTIS ALLEN'S LETTERS TO HIS WIFE ed. by Kandall Allen and Keith S. Bohannon pub by La. State Univ. Press 1998

Pg.210 same camp Jan.17th 1863 "…We have just received a small lot of shoes through the blockade. They are the English shoe and surpass anything of the kind I ever saw in my life…. Most of the men are vaccinated …"

SOJOURNS OF A PATRIOT The Field and Prison Papers of An Unreconsrtucted Confederate edited with commentary by Richard Bender Abell & Fay Adamson Gecik pub by Southern heritage Press 1998 letters of Pvt. Augustus Pitt Adamson

Pg. 129 Camp near Wilmington, N.C. Jan. 18th, 1863 Dear Father, "…I got the shirt you sent me…"

CHARLOTTE'S BOYS-Civil War letters of the Branch Family of Savannah ed, by Mauriel Phillips Joslyn pub by Rockbridge Pub. Co. 1996

Pg. 145 2lt. Sanford Branch to Charlotte Branch (undated, probably around Jan, 20 1863) camp near Fredericksburg Dear Mother "Your lettr & package per (Hollie) Cole came to hand yesterday and both were very acceptable. I asure you I had on my last pr. socks and a handkerchief is something although much needed I have not seen for a long time...

Fred left camp this morning for the Officer's hospital, Richmond. He is trying to get a furlough and I think he will succeed. Don't mention this to anybody. If he gets to Savannah and a uniform can be made for a living price I should like to have one made. Please write Hammie (his brother) to enquire what one can be made for and let me know and I will try and send the money..."

A TRUE HISTORY OF COMPANY I, 49TH REGIMENT NORTH CAROLINA TROOPS by W.A. Day printed at the Enterprise Job Office 1893

Pg. 39 Jan 21 1863 traveling from Va. to Wilmington, N.C. "...We built what is known as Collier's houses. They were made by placing a fork in the ground and laying a pole one end in the fork and the other on the ground, then leaning cord-wood sticks against the pole and covering the whole with leaves and dirt. They made very good shelters...(at Wilmington) We drilled every day among the stumps in our drill ground. We drew new uniforms, which we needed badly..."

Another quote of being supplied with new uniforms. These were probably issued by the state of North Carolina.

CIVIL WAR LETTERS OF WILLIAM (BILLY) A. ELLIOT

Magnolia Dauplin County, N.C. Jan. 23, 1863 Dear father, "I am sory to inform you we have to deliver up our tents this morning, and then we will have to lie out like hogs...Robert Ewing is going to get a box from home. You had better put my pants in..."

Jan. 27 same camp Dear Father "...Send my pants with Powel Auten and I want two Pare of socks for some rascal stole one pare of them I had here..."

Soldiers are still requesting clothing from home, especially socks.

Camp near Kinston North Carolina April 30 1863 Dear Mother "...Father I have sent my old clothes all home but just what I need. The capt. Had a box made and put all our cloths in it. It was sent in the care of Cruse. My cloths and Powel Auten and James Stowes and Thomas Prim is all in a bag together..."

Its a great idea, sending excess clothing home until it was needed. I wonder if these soldiers ever saw these clothes again.

THE CONFEDERATE VETERAN VOL. XXVI 19818

Pg. 157 April, 1918 Letters From The Front-Thomas Caffey to his family in Alabama- In Winter Quarters by his own Fire, January 24, 1863 Dear Mary: "You asked if I am in need of pants. If you could see me, you would not ask that question, as I am nearer out of "kivering" than I ever was before in my life. I wrote Ma my wishes, however."

HANDLEY LIBRARY ARCHIVES

James A. Miller Collection correspondence C.W. era misc. New Market, Va.

Camp near Buckner's Neck Jan. 25th, 1863 Dear Julia I had a chimney put to my tent day beore yesterday it does very well and if it should get cold will soon repay for the trouble of building, it is built of wood and the cracks filled up with mud and after it was built I drove some stakes on the inside about six inches from the sides and filled mud in between so as to keep the wood from burning, it is built on the order of the chimneys that the Irish generally build to their shanties, the sticks which were driven in an now burnt out and the mud has gotten hard. It throws out heat very well, and altogether is a good job…"

Ingenuity in the face of adversity.

MANASSAS TO APPOMATTOX The Civil War Memoirs of Pvt. Edgar Warfield 17th Virginia Infantry pub by EPM Pub Inc

Pg. 117 "…On January 27, 1863 we were ordered out in a drenching cold rain which continued all day. The troops marched about fifteen miles over miserable roads and finally went into bivouac in a pine forest near Salem Church. During the night the storm continued, changing into a snowstorm. The winds howled about us. Many trees were torn up by the roots, endangering the lives of the men. We were without tents or shelter other than that which we made for ourselves with blankets or boughs of trees, and we were compelled to lie down to rest drenched to the skin. Snow fell to a depth of eight inches. The suffering at this time among the troops was something fearful, so destitute were they of shoes, clothing and tents…."

What misery! And more so as the men were in ragged uniforms with no winter clothes.

LETTERS OF WILLIAM F. WAGNER, CONFEDERATE SOLDIER- Letters ed. by Joe M. Hatley and Linda B. Huffman pub, by Broadfoot's Bookmark 1983

Pg. 33 Near Port Royal Va Jan th 27th 1863 "Dear Wife I must say to you that haint got our boxis yet and I don't know when we will git them yet I don't know wheather Herman has landed yet or not they had talked of going to day for them but we got orders las nite to be Reddy at a minits notice so the colnel wouldn't let them go on the a count of that we are a bout 12 miles from the station Rabb has come some 3 days ago but his Boxis is at the station yet some time I am afraid we want git them at all but I hope we will ...."

I doubt these men received their boxes. Anything left at the station for that long was bound to be plundered.

Dear you had stated in your last letter a bout some cloathing I can say to you I still have cloathing enough yet my over coat I a bout wore out but I think I can draw one before long..."

What kind of duty was this soldier performing where he wore out an overcoat?

Pg 34 Camp near Port Royal Va Jan the 28th 1863 "...Dear I can say to you I Received that neadle and thread you send me Dear I can say to you that we haint got our Boxis yet and I don't know when we will git them we cant git no waggon to go for the the offesers don't care a fig for it I heard this morning the Boxis had landed if we onley had them now for it is unsertin how long we can stay at one plase til we have to leave we had orders the other nite to be Reddy at a minits Notice and so it is hard telling how long we git to stay at one place..."

Transportation must have been in a sorry state already as rthe officers wouldn't send a wagon to pick up the men's uniforms, and this in the middle of winter.

THE CONFEDERACY IS ON HER WAY UP THE SPOUT Letters to South Carolina 1861-1865 ed. by J. Roderick Heller III and Carolynn Ayres Heller pub by Univ. of Georgia Press 1992

Pg. 83 Headquarters camp near Fredericksburg,Va. Jan. 28th, 1863 after the battle Dear brother and Sister "...I gest I will git them things you sent me. You will except my thanks for the gloves, and Socks is the very thing I nead...." Milton Barrett

HANDLEY LIBRARY ARCHIVES, WINCHESTER, VA James Bradfield Diary 17th Virginia Infantry

Pg. 13 Guineas Station Va. Jany 28th, 1863 "Snowing very hard all day and have no shelter but a blanket it is also very cold at night still snowing hard."

Where are the winter quarters for the 17th Virginia?

HANDLEY LIBRARY ARCHIVES, WINCHESTER, VA Letters of Henry Jennings 5th Regiment, Virginia Volunteers Co. A Jacksons Brigade

Jan 28th/63 Winder City, Caroline County, Va. Dear Aunt,"…I am getting very bad of for socks as for the rest of the clothes that I left home with they are good yet if I can get my boot half-soled they will last me till April if nothing happens if you have a chance I wish you would send me some socks and a pair of good hip boots and a calico shirt or two if you can…"

Hip boots? How would he march in those?

WRITING & FIGHTING FROM THE ARMY OF NORTHERN VIRGINIA ed. by William B. Styple pub by Belle Grove Pub. 2003

Pg. 181 Lawton's Brigade Near Port Royal, Va. Jan. 31, 1863 "…Whilst this army, generally speaking, is in excellent condition, it is my duty to inform the friends of Gen. Lawton's Ga. Brigade, composed of the 13th, 26th, 31st, 38th, 60th,and 61st Ga. Regiments, that many of the men in this brigade are entirely barefooted, and many more are without socks, which are a necessary for a soldier's comfort in such a climate as this. In the 60th Ga. Regiment 150 men did not participate in the Battle of Fredericksburg, because they were without shoes; and this was to some extent the case with several other regiments. Some of the men in this brigade have been supplied since, but still, many are without any kind of a shoe…"

Despite what Capt. Blackford wrote on the 16th Jan., obviously not every unit was well equipped.

THE MISSISSIPPI BRIGADE OF BRIG. GEN. JOSEPH R. DAVIS by T.P. Williams pub by Morningside Books 1999

Pg. 65 Feb. 1863 Goldsborough, N.C. letter from Capt. Thomas G. Clark, of Company F, 42nd Mississippi "…We receive the clothes that you sent us which came at a very good time…"

These soldiers were supplied by the home folks.

THE HISTORY OF A BRIGADE OF SOUTH CAROLINIANS-KNOWN AS GREGG'S by J.F.J. Caldwell pub by King & Baird 1866

Pg. 168 Feb 1863 "…Good rations were issued us generally. There was rather too much cornmeal and far too little bacon, (Beef was a thing of the past now) but still we did not starve. Clothing was not plentiful, nor blankets, nor shoes, and those we received were inferior. Large numbers of boxes of provisions were sent us by our friends at home, which contributed much to the comfort of the troops. I must not omit, in this connection, the ladie's associations in different parts of South Carolina, who forwarded considerable supplies of clothing to us, at great trouble and even greater expense to themselves…"

The home folks obviously continued to send a considerable quantity of uniforms; there is more mention of this than being supplied by the government.

FIFTH VIRGINIA INFANTRY Va. Regimental History Series by Lee A. Wallace Jr. 1988

Pg. 44 Feb. 1863 Major Elisha Franklin Paxton who wrote "I was very much pleased by the appearance of my men. They looked clean and comfortably dressed, and were attentive to the sermon."….

THE HEART OF A SOLDIER : AS REVEALED IN THE INTIMATE LETTERS OF GENERAL GEORGE PICKETT Letter from George Edward Pickett to Lasalle Corbell Picket pub. by Seth Moyle Inc. 1913

Pg.215 Feb. 1863 "…Why, my darling, during these continuous ten days march, the ground snowy and sleety, the feet of many of these soldiers covered only with improvised moccasins of raw beef hide, and hundreds of them without shoes or blankets or overcoats, they have not uttered one word of complaint, nor one murmuring tone, but cheerily singing or telling stories.…You would hardly recognize these ragged, barefoot soldiers as the trim, tidy boys of two years ago in their handsome grey uniforms, with shining equipment and full haversacks and knapsacks…"

Another eyewitness description of ragged, shoeless Rebs. The army was obviously not all well-supplied, especially in shoes. See below

VOICES OF THE CIVIL WAR by Richard Wheeler pub by Meridian books 1976

Pg. 250 Feb. 1863 "At present, says southern General Fitzhugh Lee:

General Lee was surrounded by embarrassments...The troops were scantily clothed, rations for men and animals meager. The shelters were poor, and through them broke the snows, rains and winds...."

STEPHEN ELLIOT WELCH OF THE HAMPTON LEGION ed by John Michael Priest pub by Burd Street Press 1994

Pg. 17 Feb. 1st, 1863 Legion's camp near Fredericksburg My Dear Parents, "At last your oldest boy is an officer in the Army...If you have a chance to send anything please send me my "Hardee" and "School of the Guides." Should no other opportunity offer (itself) send the "guides" book by mail. I'll send to Richmond for a copy of the "Army Regulations." If Father (Smuel B. Welch) sees a chance I wish he'd inquire (about) the price of (a) Confederate coat and sword. The latter can be purchased in Richmond for $28.00 at the Ordinance Office. The coat out here costs about $75.00or $100.00 a heavy sum certainly, but (it) can't be helped. The coat I shall use for dress & my jacket will answer for all marching or rough purposes. The sash which I left (at) home will come in very well, though such things are rarely used in the Army nowadays, so mine may rest at home, a trophy of Manassas...Please enquire the price of a black felt hat which I should have, or else an infantry oficer's cap..."

Lt. Welch is requesting officer manuals, learnig to be an officer while on the job and before the army begins to move in the spring.

HANDLEY LIBRARY ARCHIVES

James A. Miller Collection correspondence C.W. era misc. New Market, Va.

HdQrtrs Med. Depart. 25th Va. Regt. Febu. 1st, 1863 Dear Julia, "...I have already been repaid for building my chimney it answered a very good purpose the day of the snow...We have had a good deal of rain lately and the roads are getting very bad, though you can still see the horses going through the mud but if it still gets deeper after while you can't see nothing but heads, sticking out of the mud. *Now, that's mud!*

If you have an opportunity to send down to Mr. Barley I wish you would send him some of that Va. Money to buy me some goods for a coat and pants such as you bought me, and if you have a chance to send him word you can tell him to keep the coat there unless I can send him an order for it.

My coat is getting right smartly worn so I wish you would try and get me goods for another...."

UNDER THE STARS AND BARS-A History of the Surrey Light Artillery, Recollections of a Private Soldier in the War Between the States by Benjamin Washington Jones pub by Morningside Bookshop 1975

Pg. 74 Feb. 6, 1863 "Rations are not as varied and plentiful with us as once they were. We do not get meat every day now, and the little that we do get seems to have shrunken to twelve ounces to the pound by the time it has reached us. It is seldom that we get bacon, and first-class beef does not come our way. And so, to help out the shortage of meat, finding that several large, sleek rats had taken up their abode in the feed-house, and were making too free with the corn, one of the men conceived the idea of utilizing them to his own account. He captured some of them, and, after dressing them nicely, fried them to a crisp and inviting brown, using plenty of black pepper, to disguise any oddish flavor the venison might possess. He declared that the meat was as good and sweet as any chicken he ever ate. But I suspect it had been a long time since he had tasted chicken."

At this point I don't see the squeamishness of this soldier for rat. I'll bet he has eaten squirrel when at home.

HANDLEY LIBRARY ARCHIVES

James A. Miller Collection correspondence C.W. era misc. New Market, Va.
Med. Dept. 25th Va. Regt. Feb. 9th, 1863 Dear Julia "…I am going to send to Richmond for goods for to have me a coat and pants made as by the time I get them and send them home to have them made I will need them…"

HANDLEY LIBRARY ARCHIVES-Papers of Colonel William Barkendale Tabb 59th Virginia Infantry Regiment

Pg. 18

Hd. Qrs Diascund Bridge
February 9th, 1863

Lieut. F.S. Ballard
Comdg. Co. A. 32nd Batt. Va. Cav.
Sir,

I have been informed that the men in your company are offering for sale the saddles, &c, captured on the 7th inst. I apprise you that you may take measures to stop them. In Capt. Hamelet's consolidated report, 13 horses saddles and bridles are accounted for as in the possession of Co. A. Having acknowledged the correctness of the report, you are responsible for the property. I respectfully advise you to ascertain the names of the men to whom the horses &c were distributed, and get their receipts, giving them to understand that all property belongs to the government, and if lost or disposed of, will be replaced from the pay of the soldiers to whom it was issued. If any of your men have more than one set of equipments, take from them whatever is not necessary, and give it to the men most in need. If, after such an apportionment, anything is left, turn it over to the Quarter Master.

Respectfully, Your obdt. Servant
W.B. Tabb Col. Comdg

Hd. AQrs. Diascund Bridge
February 9th, 1863

Brg. Genl Henry a. Wise
Comding & C
General,

"All the horses, arms, &c, captured, and are now needed to equip my cavalry; numbers of them are without arms or horses. I respectfully ask leave to distribute what I took and get the captain's receipts for what is issued to their respective companies, as government property..."

"My Quarter Master, Capt. Shrewsbury, complains that he has written to Maj. Cleary for shoes, of which my men are greatly in need; but can get no answer from him..."

Squabbling over spoils of war, trying to equip everyone. No answer as to whether the reqeast for shoes was filled or when.

HANDLEY LIBRARY ARCHIVES-Diary of John H. Stone 1st Lt. Co B Maryland Infantry

Pg. 22 Feb 10, 1863 "yesterday we had our usual snow storm. Late in the day it turned to rain and hail. Having nothing much to do I concluded to change my coat from sack to frock. In two days I completed the job. Now I have a coat and cape which I can remove at pleasure."

Footnote-"The slow days of winter were a time for Stone to improve his clothing. After making a pair of trousers and clothes chest, he remodeled his coat. A sack coat was a loose fitting garment that fell straight from the shoulders with no waist seam. It was a popular civilian germent, very similar to the modern sports coat, although slightly longer. To make his into a frock coat was quite a task. A frock coat had a tight-fitting tunic Which was joined at the waist with a loose skirt extending below mid-thigh. The detachable cape was not typical of officer's frock coats, unless he is speaking about his outer coat. It should be remembered that officers were allowed a wide latitude in dress since they were not issued clothing Although there were dress regulations to follow, most officers tended to suit themselves with whatever garments taste and budget permitted." Frederick P. Todd, American Military Equipage, 1865-1872 (3 vols. Providence: Company of Military Historians 1974 I Pg. 57

SOLDIER'S LETTERS FROM CAMP, BATTLE-FIELD, AND PRISON John E. Whipple pub by Bunce & Huntington 1865

Pg. 242 Feb.11, 1863 North Carolina "…Here are found large tracts of pine, from which our lean, lank, sallow butternut-dressed Southern brethren obtain their pitch, tar, and turpentine…"

A Yankee describing the Rebs as "butternuts."

A Captains War Letters and Diaries of William H.S. Burgwyn 1861-1865 ed. by Herbert M. Schiller pub by White Mane Pub Co. Inc. 1994

Pg. 60 Near Kenansville N.C. February 12th, 1863 "…I also find myself very unpleasantly situated in going to these parties since the first I went to I went in my jacket and the (illegible). I had to borrow a suit. I think I shall write Father and ask him to give me his uniform suit and have it made to fit me."

THE CONFEDERATE VETERAN VOL. XXVI 1918

Pg. 198 May 1918 Letters From The Front-Thomas Caffey to his family in Alabama- Round Oaks Chuch, Caroline County, Va. February 16, 1863 Dear Mary: "If this letter reaches home before Jule leaves, you can send my jacket by him and the pants by Hopper. I bought some that will do for a while. I was compelled to have 'em, as I had a "flag of truce" hanging from a prominent part of my old 'uns. I need no shirts, but if Ma has sent any I hope they will not be white, as they show dirt too much. A fellow sometimes don't get the chance to change his rags more than once per month, and when such is the case the lice get so numerous that they tote a fellow clean away…"

No mention as to whether the jacket he requests is civilian or military, the pants were probably civilian.

FROM CORSICANA TO APPOMATTOX by John Spencer The Texas Press 1984

Pg. 51 Feb. 17, 1863 "…Marching into Richmond the next day, the men who are near being barefooted stain the snow with blood as they march…"

Feb. 23, 1863 "That same night, they camp about four miles south of Richmond and a few days later move two or three miles farther to Falling Creek. Here they remain for several days, visiting Richmond on passes, and retrieving some of their personal and private property that they had stored in the "Texas Warehouse." This is a building rented by the officers of the Texas Brigade for storage of their property while they campaign."

THE HAT RAIDS

"At Falling Creek, the quartermaster issues new clothing and shoes, and except for hats, they are again reasonably well equipped. But hats, like shoes, are scarce in the Confederate army, and every man has to equip himself with whatever he can get. And to do this, the Texans hit upon a scheme to get them off the heads of unsuspecting passengers on the trains that chug across a high bridge at the creek. As the train slows for the bridge, the Texans, hidden in the trees and thickets near the track, start yelling and shouting loud enough to arouse the curiosity of the male passengers on the train. When they put their heads out the windows to see what the commotion is, a big broom made out of a brush sweeps their hats to the ground where the graycoats from Texas grab them and strike out for camp.

This method of hat procurement is successful for a while, but eventually the hats of some Confederate Congressmen and high ranking army officers and their staff are brushed off, and before long a guard is posted at the railroad bridge to prevent the Texans from getting any more hats by this method."

I gotta admit this was an ingenious way to get hats!

SOJOURNS OF A PATRIOT The Field and Prison Papers of An Unreconsrtucted Confederate edited with commentary by Richard Bender Abell & Fay Adamson Gecik pub by Southern Heritage Press 1998 letters of Pvt. Augustus Pitt Adamson

Pg. 138 Camp Young, Near Savannah, Ga. Feb. 23rd. 1863 Dear Sister, I sent a pair of pants by Mr. McKown…"

THE PROMISED LAND-Being a Glimpse of Anti-Bellum Georgia, Taken from the "Farm Journal" of Thomas McGuire, Atlanta, Ga. 1949

Pg. 29 Feb. 23, 1863 "Fixing up a bundle for James H.C. which is 4lbs butter in 2 bottles, 33/4 lbs of sausage, 1 small bag sage,& pepper, 1 small ball sewing thread, 1 hat, 2 pr. of cotton socks, 1 pr. wool socks, ½ quire paper, 1 package envelopes, sewed up in a bundle and marked "J.H.C. McGuire, Co. C Cobb's Legion Georgia Volunteers, Fredericksburg, Va. c/o Mr. Pendley…"

I'll bet this soldier was happy to receive this bundle!

THE CRY IS WAR, WAR, WAR The Civil War Correspondence of Lts. Burwell Thomas Cotton and George Job Huntley, 34th Regiment North Carolina troops by Michael W. Taylor pub by Morningside Bookshop 1994

Pg. 131 same camp Feb. 25th 1863 "...Sergt. Norman McLeod returned to the Regt. I am very sorry you did not get the chance to send my pants by him as I need them very bad. ..."

AS RECORDED IN THE POCKET DIARIES OF PRIVATE ROBERT A. MOORE, Co. G, 17th Miss. Regt. Confederate Guards, Holy Springs, Mississippi ed. by James W. Silver pub by McCowat-Mercer Press 1959

Pg.? Friday, Feb. 27th, 1863 on Provost Guard in Fredericksburg "...Mr. (John B.) Roberts reached here from Miss. With clothing for our Co..."

Another company supplied by home folks.

R.E.LEE Voll III Douglas Southall Freeman Charles Schribner's Sons 1935

Pg. 242 March 1863"...While he was on the Rappahanock, a soldier called at Lee's tent with his wife. Lee invited the couple in and soon learned all about them by friendly questions. "She was from Abbeville district, S.C." he enthusiastically wrote Mrs. Lee that night. "Said she had not seen her husband for more than two years, and, as he had written to her for clothes, she herself thought she would bring them on. It was the first time she had travelled by railroad but she got along very well by herself. She brought an entire suit of her own manufacture for her husband. Spun the yarn and made the clothes herself..."

Would any other General have invited the couple in and spoke with them? Is it any wonder we love him so?

WELCOME THE HOUR OF CONFLICT—William Cowan McClellan & the 9th Alabama ed by John C. Carter pub.by Univ Al Press 2007

Pg. 216 March 1, 1863 Fredericksburg, Va Headquarters Anderson's Division William McClellan to Thos. J. McClellan, Dear Father "...I have received all my Cloaths. I Swapped boots with Gilbert and got a pair to suit me. I have plenty of cloathe to last me sometime needing nothing..."

Suplied by home folks.

LETTERS FROM LEE'S ARMY by Susan Leigh Blackford and Capt. Charles Minor Blackford pub by Scribner's Pub 1947

Pg. 170-171 March 1 1863 from Mrs. Blackford to Capt. Blackford, Lynchburg, Va. "...I am much interested in having my servant's clothes woven and I am also having some homespun dresses made for my self and Nannie (daughter). I do not suppose I shall get the cloth you engaged for me last summer in Loudon (County, Va.). Mrs. Minor (mother) brought Nannie a nice new calico when she came over, which was a grand present. It costs $2.50 a yard. If the war lasts much longer I do not see what people will do. The poor will not be able to get even rags to cover them…"

DIARIES, LETTERS AND RECOLLECTION OF THE WAR BETWEEN THE STATES Vol III Winchester, Frederick Co. Historical Society Papers 1955

Pg. 95 Letter of Mager William Steel-the Valley Brass Bandin Jackson's Old Division, 2nd Brigade, 48th Regiment, Virginia Volunteers Corbin's Neck, March 1, 1863 Dear Sister Lomie: "…I would like to have a heavy shirt of colored goods and two pair of socks. I believe that is all I want…"

LETTERS TO AMANDA-The Civil War Letters of Marion Hill Fitzpatrick, Army of Northern Virginia ed by Jeffery C. Lowe and Sam Hodges pub by Mercer Univ. Press 1998

Pg. 55 March 5th, 1863 Camp Near Guinea's Station, Va. (Letter No. 26) Dear Amanda, "…I have got another good Enfield rifle and excellent equipments, which I am very proud of. I have washed once since I got back, I got my clothes clean with but little trouble because I had soap. I do not mind washing atall now. One of my overshirts have commenced wearing out already. I patched it good the other day. I can patch fine now. I drawed a pair of pants yesterday. They were sent here by a Relief Society and did not cost me anything. They had no buttons and but one pocket, and no buckle on the strops (probably suspenders) and the strops would not meet behind. I have been working on them of late. I put on buttons and fixed the strops behind and put on a buckle, and started to put in another pocket, but I am about to stall on that. I got a pocket from an old pair I found lying out of doors…"

Pg. 57 March 8th, 1863 Camp Gregg Near Guinea's Station, Va.(Letter No. 27) Dear Amanda,"…I wrote you in my last about my pants, I have them fixed up finely. I have liked to have stalled on the pocketbut kept working on it till I got it all right. They are coarse but they are just the idea to wallow in in camps, and I got them in a good time, for my others were wearing off thin rapidly. I am all right in the clothes line now…"

Ingenuity in the face of adversity.

CHARLOTTE'S BOYS-Civil War Letters of the Branch Family of Savannah ed by Mauriel Phillips Joslyn pub by Rochbridge Pub Co. 1996

Pg. 150 2lt. Sanford Branch to Charlotte Barnch March 5, 63 Camp 8th Geo. Vols. Dear Mother, "I was disappointed in getting cloth from the Quartermaster but cloth enough for 3 suits to a Regt. were given to this Brigade. The officers of this Regt. drew for this cloth and I of course lost. I know not how to thank you for your kind proposals to give me a uniform for my birthday present....'

This is an absolute pittance of cloth.

KEEP ALL MY LETTERS The Civil War Letters of Richard Henry Brooks, 51st Ga. Inf. ed. by Katherine Holland pub by Mercer Univ. Press, Macon, Ga. 2003

Pg. 69 Camp near Fredericksburg Va. March the 6th, 1863 "...Pool brought me one pair of Socks an one cap, one pair gloves, an Pepper an Sage, one pipe an stems an one newspaper an neck tie all of which I was very glad to Receive..."

I can imagine him being glad to receive everything but the neck tie. Where is he going to wear that?

A CIVIL WAR MARRIAGE IN VIRGINIA: Reminiscences and Letters Letter from Green Barry Samuels to Kathleen Boone Samuels pub by Carr pub. Co. 1956

Pg. 267 March 7, 1863 "...I did not send to Richmond for a new uniform as Cousin Abe supposed. My uniform is pretty good yet and will answer some months yet. Uniforms are very expensive costing $200.00. I will buy this spring a couple of grey blankets and have them made into a uniform, it will be much cheaper. As I am soon to be a man of family I must learn economy...."

A good idea, there are more references to making uniform pieces from blankets.

HANDLEY LIBRARY ARCHIVES

James A. Miller Collection correspondence C.W. era misc. New Market, Va.
Hdqrtrs Med. Dept. 24th Va. Regt. March 8th, 1863 Dear Julia "...I got lining for a coat, could not get any small Va. Buttons for a vest nor could I get any goods for to stripe pants with I will send you the goods that I bought by the first opportunity..."

THE CIVIL WAR LETTERS OF GENERAL FRANK "BULL" PAXTON A Lieutenant of Lee & Jackson ed. by John Gallatan Paxton Hill Jr. pub by College Press 1978

Pg. 76 Camp Winder (Va.) March 8 1863 "…My men are comfortably fixed here, and when we move the huts must be left behind, and, besides this, most of the blankets sent off, as we have no wagons to haul them. My men, I fear, when we move will have to get along with such clothing and blankets as they can carry. Many of our horses have died this winter for want of forage, and those that remain are much reduced in flesh and strength …"

CIVIL WAR MARRIAGE IN VIRGINIA REMINISCENCES AND LETTERS pub by Carr Pub. Co. 1956

Pg.166 March 9, 1863 "…I will send my measure to Harrisonburg and get you to have the uniform made for me, where you will be able to get the lining &c. I cannot tell. You might take it from one of my old coats which could be replaced after the war…."

THE CONFEDERACY IS ON HER WAY UP THE SPOUT Letters to South Carolina 1861-1865 ed. by J. Roderick Heller III and Carolynn Ayres Heller pub by Univ. of Georgia Press 1992

Pg. 92 same camp March 11, 1863 Dear Brother and Sister (Milton Barrett missed the preson bringing his box from home) "…Jinkins brigade has left hear. It is in camp near Petersburg so I will not see JB King. But the socks and gloves will not be lost for if I don't git them some other poor fellow wil that needs them perhaps more than I…"

This man was extremely generous. I hope he received his colthes.

RECOLLECTIONS OF AN OLD DOMINION DRAGOON The Civil War Experiences of Sgt. Robert S. Hudgins II Company B, 3rd Viginia Cavalry ed. by Garland C. Hudgins and Richard B. Klees pub by Publisher's Press, Inc. 1993

Pg. 63 Kelly's Ford March 17, 1863 "…We saw a great deal of Stuart while stationed at Culpeper, his striking figure easily visible with his plumed hat and his flowing cape lined with yellow. Our uniforms, by comparison, were becoming faded and worn, but we made the most of what we had and were deeply thankful for even that. We were no longer a brigade of "dandies" as in '61, but could now be considered soldiers in every sense of the word…."

Even Stuart's troopers were becoming ragged.

THE PAINFUL NEWS I HAVE TO WRITE-Letters and Diaries of Four Hite Brothers of Page County in the Service of the Confederacy Army of Northern Virginia Series Stonewall Brigade ed.by Harlan R. Jessup pub by Butternut & Blue 1998

Pg. 135 Isaac Hite to father Camp Lee March 21st 1863 "…I got my clothing that I left in Richmond last Spring, that is my jacket and sham, my pants he let a black boy wear them out that lived with them last year. I told him it was all right, as they were of small force…"

This soldier received the clothing he had stored, probably with a citizen, all except his pants. According to "Webster's 3rd Inernational Dic-tionary," a sham is a decorative piece of cloth that is made to simulate an article of personal or household linen and is used in place of it or over it. Maybe a shawl?

THIS BAND OF HEROES-Granbury's Texas Brigade, C.S.A. by James M. McCaffery pub by Texas A&M Univ. Press 1996

Pg 58 March 23rd 1863 City Point, Va. P.O.W.s from Arkansas Post exchanged."…The next day they were free! Some of the officers were admitted to hospitals in Petersburg. Others went to Richmond, where they drew a year's back pay in brand new Confederate currency. The printing presses had just started rolling out the fifty million dollars per month authorized under an act dated March 23, 1863. The first important purchases made with this money were for new uniforms and boots. The newly clad Texans drew scant notice in the busy Richmond streets, for the city was alive with richly caparisoned officers, many of whom did their best to avoid combat…"

HANDLEY LIBRARY ARCHIVES

James A. Miller Collection correspondence C.W. era misc. New Market, Va.
Med. Dept. 28th Va. Regt. March 23rd, 1863 I still sleep very comfortably under my blankets yet they have not gotten too warm yet, as soon as warm weather I will send all those that I do not need home, as it will be very difficult whether we will be able to haul just such things as we can't get along without, if we have to move the men will have to take just what they can carry on their backs and leave the remainder here…"

HANDLEY LIBRARY ARCHIVES-WINCHESTER, VA Letters of Michael Freeze Pvt. Co. C 23rd North Carolina Infantry

March the 23 1863 Dear Wife," I got them close that you had sent to me but I have more close than I can cary on a march and winter close don't sell wellin camp now I wiil sell or send some of them if I can…"

THE CONFEDERATE VETERAN VOL. XXVI 1918

Pg. 199 May 1918 Letters From The Front- Thomas Caffey to his family in Alabama Camp Santee, Caroline County, Va. March 24, 1863 Dear Mary: "I had a bully dinner to-day. What do you suppose was the bill of fare? It consisted of rice, bacon, biscuit, and a huge pie made of sparrows. David Smith, an enterprising genious belonging to our mess, made traps while we were on picket and caught enough of the tiny creatures to give all hands a good bait. I tell you they were good; and as we are not accustomed to the sight of fresh meat, the little critters were highly appreciated…"

I'd never heard of eating sparrows.

A SOUTHERN SOLDIER'S LETTERS HOME The Civil War Letters of Samuel Burney Cobb's Georgia Legion, Army of Northern Va. ed. by Nat Turner pub by Mercer Univ. Press, Macon Ga.2002

Pg, 240 same camp March 27th, 1863 "…I bought yesterday from our worthy Quartermaster, Capt. Crane, 2 yds. of army grey cloth, which is sufficient to make me a coat. It was $7.00 per yard. It is in great demand by the officers of the Army on account of its cheapness, and had it not been for the fact that Crane & I are good friends I would not have had it. I will either send it to a gentleman in Richmond for safe keeping or to you if I find a safe chance. I would prefer to send it to you. I will keep it until I need a coat and then have it made up. Thet charge over 100 dollars in Richmond to make a coat and furnish the trimmings. I shall not have mine made there…"

A TRUE HISTORY OF COMPANY I, 49TH REGIMENT NORTH CAROLINA TROOPS by W.A. Day printed at the Enterprise Job Office 1893

Pg. 40 March 27 1863 Goldsboro, N.C. "…We went into camp in the woods below the city, near the old field where Colonel Ramsuer used to drill us. We drew shoes there with wooden bottoms, also cloth shoes…"

This is the first mention of being issued these shoes. Unfortunately the writer doesn't mention the soldier's opinions of them.

WELCOME THE HOUR OF CONFLICT-William Cowan McClellan & the 9th Alabama ed by John C. Carter pub by Univ Al Press 2007

Pg. 223 March 28, 1863 Head Gen. Anderson's Division First Army Corps William McClellan to Matila McClellan- Matila, "…You must say Mrs. Bibb is hard at work making money, dressed out in homespun....In your letter you speak of cloaths, all I need at present is a pair of Pants, two cotton shirts, two pair cotton drawers. Pants I need worse than anything else. I bought an overcoat from Featherston for 45 dollars it is a very warm coat. I never had a coat in Richmond as Fielding told you..."

CAPTAIN GREENLEE DAVIDSON, C.S.A. Diary and Letters 1851-1863 ed. by Charles W. Turner pub. by McClure Press 1975

Pg. 70 Camp Maury (Va.) March 29 1863 Dr. Tyler (John) "...I am very obligated to you for the handsome pair of slippers you sent me, they came at the right time, as I was just out of a pair..."

Slippers? Really?

THE CONFEDERATE VETERAN VOL. XVI 1908

Pg. 165 April 1908 Private Soldier Life-Humerous Incidents by James Reese (of the Edney Grays) Spring 1863 Plymouth N.C. "The battle began about five o'clock in the morning, and at three in the afternoon the flag on the last fort went down. As soon as we got into town we began to hunt for something to eat. Cheese, crackers, bacon, canned goods, and everything else that could be eaten were devoured by the hungry Rebs. Those Grays who were living or not too badly wounded got one square meal. After the inner man was satisfied, we began to hunt for something to wear. Quite a number went in for fine footwear. Although a paper collar and a fine shoe would hardly harmonize with a dingy, faded gray uniform, yet such combination became quite common....

...When we moved again, it was by way of Kinston to Newburn. It was a long, sandy march of five days, and the boys that wore fine boots (captured at Plymouth) got tener-footed as the thin bottoms caused blisters. Stark Simms said pride was great sin, and he was bound to acknowledge the corn. John B. Edney offered three dollars for a peck of dried beans to "founder" his boots with, as he had found that that was the best thing he had ever tried to cure a tight (fit)..."

A VIRGINIA GIRL IN THE CIVIL WAR by Myrta Lockett Avary pub by D. Appleton and Co. 1903

Pg. 95 spring 1863 "...There was no return to Baltimore by flag of truce; the only way to get there was to run the blockade, a most dangerous and doubtful undertaking at this period of the war....My heart was set on seeing mother. To be left alone now by both Millicent and Dan would drive me crazy; for Millicent to run the blockade alone would serve me as ill.

Besides, I wanted some things for myself, some pins and needles and nice shoes and pocket handkerchiefs and a new hat and a new cloak, and I wanted a new uniform for Dan. Dan had had no new uniform since his first promotion, a long time ago. He was an officer of high rank, and he was still wearing his old private's uniform. He had traveled through rain and snow and mud, and had slept on the ground and fought battles in it. Though I had many times cleaned that uniform, darned it, patched it, turned it, scoured it, done everything that was possible to rejuvenate it, my shabby-looking soldier was a continual reproach to me. When Dan would come and see me I used to make him wrap up in a sheet or blanket while I worked away on his clothes with a needle and thread, soap and water and smoothing irons. I was ready to run the blockade for a new uniform for Dan if nothing else, but to tell him I was going to run the blockade-there was the rub! Evening came and Dan with it, and the telling had to be done somehow.

"Dan," I began, patting the various patches on his shabby knee, "I want you to have a new uniform."

"Wish me a harp and a crown, Nell! One's about as easy as the other. You'll have to take it out in wanting, my girl."

"I expect I could buy Confederate cloth in Baltimore."

"Maybe-if you were there."

"Dan, I think I'll slip across the border and buy you a Confederate uniform, gold lace and all, from a Yankee tradesman, and then slip back here with it, and behold you in all the glory of it. Wouldn't that be nice, Dan?"

"Rather!"

Dan refuses to permit Nell to "run the blockade" for some time, but finally gives in to her pleas. She and Millicent made it to Baltimore, where she was told it would be impossible to come right out and purchase a Confederate uniform. She met a union officer, Captain Locke who agreed to help her. "...It was Captain Locke who helped me out. He told me where I could buy it, and offered to get for me himself, but he was taking so many risks on his own account that I was determined he should take none on mine. He directed me to a tailoring establishment on the corner of Charles and St. Paul's Streets. The head of this establishment sympathized with the South and had supplied many Southern uniforms, and his store had a convienent double entrance, one on St. Paul's and one on Charles Street. One morning I went in at the Charles Street entrance. I had chosen an early hour, and I found no one in but the tailor.

"I want to but a Confederate uniform," I said. "Captain Locke referred me-"(there was a delay of two days, as the shop was being watched.)

"I have to be very careul lately," he apologized for waving me off the previous day. "These Yankees suspect me and are always on the lookout. Now we will get the uniform in a hurry. I have several pieces of fine Confederate cloth just in that I will show you. Is your husband a Private?"

"Oh, no-o!" I exclaimed indignantly.

"I thought not," he said suavely. "What is his rank?"

"He is a captain of cavalry now. That is- he was when I left home. But I haven't heard from him since. He may be major or colonel by now. Can't you fix up a uniform that would do for him if he is a captain or a colonel or a major when I get back, or-that would do for a general?"

"Certainly, certainly, madam,very wise of you to think of that."

He showed me several pieces of very fine and beautiful cloth in Confederate grey, and I made my selection.

"The question is, how are you to get it across the line. In what way will you carry it?"

"Ah, that I don't know. Captain Locke advised me to consult you."

The tailor, who seemed to have a liberal experience in such matters, considered for a moment.

"Are their any other ladies going with you?"

:my mother."

"It is easy then. I will cut this cloth into lengths that will be alright for the tailor who makes the uniform. You and and your mother can make it into two Balmoral skirts (A bamoral was a petticoat, a woolen underskirt worn under a long dress looped up for walking. Ed.). That's the way to get your cloth home. Now for the buttons and gold lace. Will you travel in the wrap you have on?"

"In one like it; I shall pack this in my trunk. The inspectors will not be so likely to condemn this if they find it in a trunk as they would be to condemn a new one. So I will get a new cloak South; mother will wear another.

"I see." He was impressed with the scheme and made a mental note of it. "Send me your cloaks and I will fix the buttons alright."

Cloaks of the period were log, sacque-like affairs, double-breasted and with two rows of buttons. The tailor changed the buttons on our cloaks for Confederate brass buttons covered with with wadding, and then with cloth like the wrap. The gold lace was to be folded flat and smooth. Mother was to rip the lining from the bottom of her satchel, lay the lace on the bottom, and carefully paste the lining back. We wanted to take Dan some flannel shirts, and again fashion favored us. Ladies wore wide plaid scarfs passed around their necks and falling in long ends in front. We got seven yards of fine soft flannel in a stylish plaid and cut it in two lengths. Mother, being quite tall, could wear a longer scarf than myself, so,between us, we managed to carry around our necks two good shirts for Dan. (After considerable trouble, Nell returns to Culpeper)"...I sent word to Dan by them (the soldiers) that I was there.

He came- the raggedest, most widowed-looking officer! But weren't we happy!

"Oh, Dan!" I cried, after the first rapture of greeting, "I got it so it would do for a captain or a major or a colonel or a general. Didn't I do right?"

"What are you talking about Nell? Got what?"

He looked as if he feared recent adventures had unsettled my intellect.

"Your uniform, Dan," I answered, but my countenance fell.

"My uniform?"

Just like a man! He had forgotten the principal thing-next to seeing mother, of course-that I had gone to Baltimore for.

"Your uniform, Dan. I've got it on. Here it is," and lifted my skirt and showed him my Balmoral. "Isn't it a beautiful cloth? And I have kept it just as nice-not a fleck of mud on it. And here are the buttons on my cloak, and I have the gold lace in mother's satchel, and-

"Nell, dear, I haven't time to talk about uniforms now. You will sleep here to-night. Next morning I will try to get a room for you at Mr. Bradford's…"

What a Gutsy lady! Nell was 19 when she performed this feat-she would have ended up in Fort McHenry prison if she had been caught.

Pg. 241 review at Brandy Station, spring, 1863 "…How well I remember Stuart as he looked that day! He wore a fine new uniform, brilliant with gold lace, buff gauntlets reaching to his elbows, and a canary-colored silk sash with tasseled ends. His hat, a soft broad-brimmed felt, was caught up at the side with a gold star and carried a sweeping plume; his high, patent-leather cavalry boots were trimmed with gold. He wore spurs of solid gold, the gift of some Maryland ladies-he was very proud of those spurs-and his horse was coal-black and gloosy as silk. And how happy he was-how full of faith in the Confederacy and himself!…"

Pg. 342 Talking with a mule driver-"…But what Oi've got agin a mule is that they don't know an honest Amerikin in grey clothes-or mixed rags it is now-from a nasty, thavin' Yankee…"
Stupid mule

THE STONE WALL The Story of a Confederate Soldier by Brad Smiley pub by Zebra Communications, Woodstock, Ga. 1998

Pg. 212 Spring 1863 returning to his unit "…Mama had made me another cinnamon-hued uniform. Mrs. Mays stopped by and asked me to carry a package, containing a pair of pants, a shirt, and some fruit, for George I was delighted to do so…"

A cinnamon hued uniform? What had she used to make the dye? I'd liked to have seen it.

A REBEL CAVALRYMAN WITH LEE, STUART AND JACKSON by John O. Pue pub by W.B. Conkey Co. 1899

Pg. 191 The Army on the March; "It is when on the march that the soldier exhibits himself to the greatest advantage. Before he grows fatigued he is full of devilment and animal spirits, and guys everybody who happens to pass by. If there is anything peculiar in the dress or appearance of a person, it is discovered at once, and is loudly commented upon and ridiculed. If the hat is unusually large, the cry is raised at once, and follows the unfortunate wearer until he makes his escape, "Come out of that hat, I see your feet "; or, if boots predominate the cry is, "Come out of those boots, I see your ears flapping." If there was a long-continued chearing, it was Jackson or a rabbit, and "Old Jack," with the exception of General Lee, was the only General who received universal applause.

Singing was a favorite pastime with the soldiers when marching. The popular songs were "Dixie," "Maryland My Maryland" "The Marseillaise Hymn," "Annie Laurie," "The Bonnie Blue Flag," and "Rocked In The Cradle Of The Deep."

When a spring of water, or a pump was reached, the thirsty men crowded and pushed, and sometimes fought to be the first to fill their canteens. I have seen men so thirsty that they drank out of mud-holes. Apples, onions and corn stood little chance of escape when close to the line of march. Sometimes men will "flank out," as they call it, to forage, going two or three miles from the line. When evening approaches, and the men are worn out from fatigue, how close they stick to the ranks, and how quiet the rascals become! When the march continues in the night, and they can hardly put one foot before the other, how they grumble and swear! And let the column halt for just a moment, and they drop in their tracks, and are sound asleep in the twinkling of an eye. Imagine a man marching all day and all night, carrying a musket and forty-eight rounds of cartridges, a haversack containing his rations, together with a knapsack containing his blankets and clothing; the whole outfit weighs from 75 to 125 pounds. How many of us could stand it now? No wonder the poor fellow drops in a fence corner, falls asleep, and joins the army of stragglers on the morrow.

When Jones made his raid through West Virginia, I often saw the whole brigade asleep on horseback, reeling and nodding like so many drunken men, In infantry, men were often known to march on foot in the column, fast asleep.

On a protracted march, the infantry suffered terribly with their feet. The only remedy was frequent bathing in cold water. The most beautiful sight I ever witnessed, and one which suggested the Resurrection Morn, was seeing on two or three occasions, the men rise from their beds, after a heavy snowfall. Before they rose up, the bivouac resembled a vast graveyard, they were asleep in couples throughout the encampment; the snow covering them up, they resembled small mounds.

The bugles of the different regiments sounding the reveillie, and the men, rising from their snow-covered beds, looked as though they were actually rising form their graves and shaking off their winding sheets, but the comments upon the snow and the weather soon dispelled the illusion."

This writer says the weight of gear a Rebel soldier carried to be 75 to 125 pounds. According to every other write, this is a gross exaggeration, the closer approximation being 25 pounds.

CHANCELLORSVILLE 1863-The Souls of the Brave by Ernest B. Furgurson pub by Alfred and Knopf Inc. 1992

April 1863 "...The rangy troops filing by Lee's command post looked nothing like the innocent boys, brave and wide-eyed in their fancy uniforms, who had posed for ambrotypes before heading off to war two years before.

Somewhere back in the Valley, on the Peninsula, on the way to Sharpsburg, they had thrown away knapsacks, overcoats, pistols, daggers, extra underwear, and other nonessentials. Now each man rolled his blanket in his ground cloth and looped it in a horseshoe over a shoulder, tied at the opposite hip. Personal odds and ends, writing paper, precious apples or squares of cornbread, were in his haversack slung over the other shoulder. His wooden canteen, or a tin one taken from the Yankees, hung beside it. A cup might dangle from his belt or by a thong from a blanket roll; here and there a frying pan rattled with its handle stuck into the muzzle of a musket. Most of the time his weapon was carried casually over a shoulder: the .58-caliber Springfield rifle musket and the British made .577 Enfield, the most common weapons of the war, were just under five feet long-over six feet with bayonet fixed-too unwieldy to be carried comfortably at sling arms. They weighed between nine and ten pounds complete. Cartridges, a dozen to the pound, were more often crammed into pockets than in ammunition boxes where they were hard to pinch out in the hurry of battle. For many infantrymen, the broad-brimmed slouch hat had succeeded the stiff-billed forage cap. Polished boots were a remote memory; the troops who wore shapeless brogans thought themselves lucky as they set out around the flank of the Union army..."

The Union Army is about to receive some rough handling by these Rebs.

THE CONFEDERATE VETERAN VOL. XXI 1913

Pg. 113 March, 1913 Simple Story of A Soldier by Samuel Hankins April 1863 Suffolk, Va. "A few days after completing our quarters a member of our company who was wounded and had been at home on furlough returned. He brought with him a full suit of good woolen clothing, also underwear and a pair of homemade shoes and socks my dear mother had made for me. Everything except the shoes had been made with her own hands...."

THE CONFEDERATE VETERAN VOL. XXVII

Pg. 144 April 1919 In The Years of War compiled by John C. Stiles from "Official Records" Series III Vol. II 1863-64 "Confederate Balloon in Charleston Harbor- I have always thought that when the balloon made of ladies' silk dresses, called the "Lady Davis," I believe, was lost near Richmond the aeronautical branch of our service died with it; but not so, for on July

21 Major Brooks, U.S.A. reported: "This morning the enemy made a reconnaissance from a balloon over Fort Johnson." And General Beauregard also mentions one."

General Beauregard was always one interested in new inventions of war. Remember, he was the one that had the Hunley shipped from Mobile Bay to Charleston. I'd like to know more about this Charleston balloon, as I thought th Lady Davis was the only one.

HANDLEY LIBRARY ARCHIVES-Diary of John H. Stone 1st Lt. Co B, Maryland Infantry

Pg 27 April 1, 1863 New Market, Va. My Dear Sister, "...Cloths are out of sight, cap $10, coat $125.00, pants $50, vest $20, boots $50, shoes $15-30, woolen shirts $20, Maryland buttons $1, drawers $5, blankets $30 each, ...These are the prices asked and received in the Valley of Virginia..."

LETTERS OF WILLIAM F. WAGNER, CONFEDERATE SOL-DIER ed. by Joe M. Hatley and Linda B. Huffman pub by Broadfoot's Bookmark 1983

Pg 44 Camp Near Fredericksburg Va April the 4th 1863 ..."Dear Wife I send my comfert and wolin shirt and neckless and gloves and one little hat for Elfonso (his son) and a cap you can work over if you want aney of the litle Boys to ware it if not you can throw it a way Dear I must say to you that you would better wash that shirt rite good for I Expect it had somr anumails in it the neckless I never wore it two days in all..."

By neckless I suppose he means a scarf.

LEE& JACKSON'S BLOODY TWELTH-Letters of Irby Goodwin Scott First Lieutenant Co. G Putnam Light Infantry Twelth Ga. Vol. Inf. ed. by Johnnie Perry Pearson pub by Univ. Tn. Press 2010

Pg. 104 12th Ga. Regt. Camp near Fredericksburg, Va. April 5 1863 Dear Father,"...On fast day myself and several officers of my Reg. went over to see the battle field near Fredericksburg. I went to the place where our boys charged them in the railroad. You can see now hundreds of old shoes. Shoes that belonged to our men. They leaving them and swaping them with the dead Yankees, knapsacks, canteens, &c. which were destroyed...As to clothing I have plenty for the present. As much as I can take care of when we leave here on a march. You can have me a coat and pants ready and I will write you when I need them. Bud had better not bring much clothing with him if he comes for he will have to carry them on his back. If you see a good chance you may have me a suit made of Confederate grey cloth (uniform) if the war lasts cloths will be higher. Also keep a lookout for a hat for me…"

P.S. April 6 63 "…I shall need some summer cloths. I would like for you to try and have me a uniform Leit made of grey cloth. I do not want the finest. Send it by Bud if you can get it ready…"

HANDLEY LIBRARY ARCHIVES

James A. Miller Collection correspondence C.W. era misc. New Market, Va.
HdQrtrs Med. Dept. 28th Va. Regt. Camp near Buckner's Neck April 8th, 1863 Dear Julia "…You wrote about drawers I think you had better get goods enough and make me 2 pairs and also get cotton for 3 or 4 shirts but don't make them up yet as cotton will still get higher than it is at present…"

THE CONFEDERATE VETERAN VOL. XXVI 1918

Pg. 199 May 1918 Letters From The Front-Thomas Caffey to his family in Alabama—Camp Santee, Caroline County, Va. April 9, 1863 Dear Mary:"…If you had sent me a pair of cotton drawers, I would have been much obliged. The only ones I have now are the woolen ones Ma sent me last winter. If the war lasts ten years, I hope she will never send me woolen goods again unless she can make outside shirts of them…"

ARMY LIFE IN VIRGINIA:Letters From the Twelth Vermont Regiment and Personal Experiences of Volunteer service in the War for the Union, 1862-1863 bY George Grenville Benedict pub by Free Press Association 1895

Pg. 128 April 9, 1863 (Referring to Confederate deserters) "Three of them came in today, one of them a pretty intelegent young man of twenty-five, the other two bright-eyed and good-loking boys of 17, all members of the 5th Virginia Cavalry. They were clothed in the coarse cotton and butternut colored jackets and trousers which commonly form the uniform of a rebel soldier when he has one; and tell the often repeated story of scanty rations, hard treatment and poor pay. The twelve dollars a month which they are paid barely cover the cost of their clothes, at the rates at which they are charged for them, so that trhe rebel soldier in fact works for his food and clothing and not over much of either …"

Notice the colors mentioned, also this soldier states these were the common colors of the Rebal uniform "when he has one."

GRANDFATHER'S JOURNAL (Franklin Lafayette Riley) Company B Sixteenth Mississippi Infantry Volunteers Harris' Brigade Mahone's Division Hill's Cops, A.N.V. May 27, 1861-July 15, 1865 by Austin C. Dobbins pub by Morningside Press 1988

Pg. 133 Friday-Saturday, April 10-11, 1863 Near U.S. Ford "Orders issued by the Union army threaten that any Confederate soldier who wears Union clothing or equipment may be charged and shot as a spy if he is taken within Union lines. Guess I better not be taken. I'm not a spy, but some of my equipment is Federal issue. In fact, this is true of most of us. Although inclined to be cantankerous, the Federal Quartermaster has furnished us with supplies for a long time. No, we can't allow him to be ungracious. It would hurt his character (which is bad enough already). For his own good, we must continue to accept his generousity..."

It goes to show how frustrated the Yankees were at The Rebs capturing and using all that good ol' U.S. Army equipment.

THE PAINFUL NEWS I HAVE TO WRITE-Letters and Diaries of Four Hite Brothers of Page County in the Service of the Confederacy Army of Northern Virginia Series Stonewall Brigade ed.by Harlan R. Jessup pub by Butternut & Blue 1998

Pg. 137 John Hite to parents Camp Winder Apr. 12th 1863 "...I would be glad if you could send David & I a few Pieces of soap as we don't draw but very little, that smells like carn; (some say it was made of mule(s) when they die), also my cotton pocket handkerchief, & my two check shirts as these are nearly worn out..."

VOICES FROM COMPANY D Diaries by the Greensboro Guards, Fifth Alabama Infantry Regiment, Army of Northern Virginia ed. by G. Ward Hubbs pub by Univ. of Georgia Press 2003

Pg. 156 April 13 1863 SP "...It was diffic. To get any one to bring a box that Mama couldn't send anything to eat, but only some clothing & pr. Boots for Biscoe, a nice pr. Gloves for me..."

HANDLEY LIBRARY ARCHIVES-WINCHESTER, VA Letters of Michael Freeze Pvt. Co. C 23rd North Carolina Infantry

Fredericks April the 13 1863 Dear wife,"...I don't want you to send me any cloth at all for I have more cloth than I can take off I will let you know in time when I need cloth the wether is vary cold hare yet for the time of year..."

Camp Near Fredericksburg Aprile the 26 1863 Dear darling, "…you no in time when I nead clothes atall I will let you know in time when I nead clothes the next letter you sand me I want you to send me some of your yellow paper if you have it this you sent me is so hard…"

WELCOME THE HOUR OF CONFLICT-William McClellan &The 9th Alabama ed by John C. Carter Pub by Univ Al Press 2007

Pg. 224 April 13th 1863 Camp Near Fredericksburg Va. William McClellan to Matilda McClellan Dear Sister, "…Tell Mother all I need very bad at this time is a pair of Pants. I have had these I have on patched 3 times, old Mrs. Mills says they wont bare any more…"

Sounds like those new clothes from January are starting to wear out. That would fit near the estimated time-1 month for pants.

Pg. 225 April 22 1863 Dear Sister, "…My health very good, my cloaths good save Pants. They have been patched three times now show a little too much of my person. Body Lice are very plentiful now, I pulled off a shirt last night and threw it down, this morning I saw it moving first one way, then another. I thought at first it was a rat under it, but upon inspection found it was the lice moving about hunting a poor Soldier…"

Throw that shirt into the fire!

CIVIL WAR LETTERS OF CAPTAIN A.B. MULLIGAN, Co. B, Fifth South Carolina Cavalry-Butler's Division-Hampton's Corps 1861-1865 by Olin Fulmer Hutchinson,Jr. pub by The Reprint Co. 1992

Pg.75 13 April 1863 In Camp below Green Pond,(S.C.) My Dear Mother & Sisters, "I am compelled to have summer shirts and I want my brown linen coat made into shirts. Do make at least two shirts & send them by Simon. Make them to lap over a little in the breast & to wear with my gold buttons & studs all over. Send my lined coat or duster. Do get help & make the studs so as to send Simon as soon as possible…"

14 April same camp My Dear Sister Julia, "…I wrote yesterday in addition to the articles mentioned in yesterday's letter. I want my mosquito nets. The small one to put over my head & the other for my cot …"

"I only want the two summer vests made last, one white & one buff with standing collars. If you can pick out two or three of my linen borax shirts that will do to wear & am not apt to send them…"

A duster is not a frequently mentioned Civil War garment.

LETTERS OF A NEW MARKET CADET Beverly Stanard ed. by John G. Barrett & roberty K. Tyrner Jr. Univ. N.C. Press 1961

Pg. 6 Virginia Military Institute April the 14th, 1863 My darling Mother, "...Well Mother Gen. Smith has at last gotten cloth, and as I had never had a suit my name was put down for one. I can have my jacket made at last so now have or will have two suits which will do me until July...I wrote you about making me collars did you ever get the letter. My cap must be black..."

Pg. 7 Footnote #1 "Cloth for cadet uniforms was extremely difficult to aquire since the output of the mills was allocated tro the armies in the field. When some material was finally secured in the fall of 1862, Gen. Smith issued the following order: "A full supply of winter clothing having been supplied by the institution for the use of the cadets, the articles thus supplied will constitute the uniform of the cadets until further orders. Cadets who have old clothing previously supplied as uniform, or who have been authorized to wear as a temporary substitute the supplies brought with them, will still be allowed to wear them on all undress or fatigue duty; but no departure from the prescribed uniform will be permitted inj the making or wearing of any other clothes." General Orders No. 95 Dec. 6, 1862 V.M.I. Order Book, 1862. This order was repeated in March of the next year when it was brought to the Superintendant's attention that several cadets had violated these instructions by "having clothes made in Lexington since Dec. 6, 1862, of goods not uniform..." These cadets were reported "for positive and willful diobediance of orders." General Orders No. 18, March 31, 1863 V.M.I. Order Book. 1863"

Picky, picky, picky

LEE& JACKSON'S BLOODY TWELTH-Letters of Irby Goodwin Scott First Lieutenant Co. G Putnam Light Infantry Twelth Ga. Vol. Inf. ed. by Johnnie Perry Pearson pub by Univ. Tn. Press 2010

Pg 107 Camped near Fredericksburg, Va. April 14th, 1863 Dear Mother, "...Mother I want a suit of cloths which I have written to you about before. I do not want them to fine you can get them either in Atlanta or Macon also the trimmings. I would like for the coat to be cut like Abner's double breasted do not have the collar too wide or too long. I want them for summer and fall wear. I see from the signs my coat will soon wear out. Put a black stripe of velvet or something of the kind on the leg of my pants though I don't care much about it...."

MY DEAR EMMA-The War letters of Col. James K. Edmonson 1861-8165 ed.by Charles w. Turner PhD pub by McClure Press 1978

Pg. 122 Head Quarters 27th-Va. Infty. April 15, 1863 My dear darling Wife "...Our baggage is being cut down to almost nothing. No officer is allowed a trunk or box to carry his clothing. I have cut my baggage down to what I can carry in a knapsack and have sent my trunk with its contents to you. Thomas and Lewis have some clothing in it ..."

Remember in an earlier quote the writer states that many of the horses had perished last winter? This is probably why the baggage is being reduced.

LETTERS AND PAPERS OF AN ARTILLERY OFFICER A.N.V. IN THE WAR FOR SOUTHERN INDEPENDENCE 1861-1865 Capt. John Hampden Chamberlain-Virginian pub by Dietz Printing Co. Pub. 1932

Pg. 168 Camp Maury Va. April 16th, 1863 My dear Mother "...We are constantly expecting a move, and with more reason every day. Whatever opportunity you may have, do not send me up the undress coat and vest. The transportation furnished will be so small that I do not intend to try and carry my trunk or anything beyond an extra pair of pants and two suits of underclothing, all in the hand trunk, and my greatcoat. My trunk I shall either send to you shortly or leave it at Mr. Woolfolk's, to be carried down at his best opportunity..."

Carrying his greatcoat-he does not mention carrying any blankets-the greatcoat would do to replace them.

CONFEDERATE CAPTAIN UJANIRTIS ALLEN'S LETTERS TO HIS WIFE ed. by Kandall Allen and Keith S. Bohannon pub by La. State Univ. Press 1998

Pg. 226 Camp near Hamiltons Crossing April 17th 1863 "...I may send some things that I brought with me. I will send four flannel (nett) suits, 2pr. nett drawers, 1 pr double do., 1 overshirt, 1 common cotton shirt, 1 pr thin socks a bundle of collars and that gold lace. Let Mrs. Fears have half of it to trim a coat for Ol.Send her word the first chance that you can get it. I also send a little knife, fork, and spoon captured at Fredericksburg to Bobbie. I think they will suit him to eat with very nice. You see how they are put together. The knife is inserted in the handle of the spoon and the fork over the blade of the knife and holds it together. I will also send a jacket that I have no use for..."

Capt. Ujanirtis is unloading all his excess baggage before the spring campaign. See below

Pg. 228 Camp Near Hamilton's Crossing Va. April 20, 1863 My Dear Susie, "...Possibly you will not get the package that I sent you. It contains only some collars and a pair of sleaves. Make the express company responsible. I shall send more clothing home than I expected. I think the chance is good for us to lose all of our clothing except what we wear. The government can neither furnish transportation or knapsacks…"

THE STILLWELL LETTERS-A GEORGIAN IN LONG-STREET'S CORPS ARMY OF NORTHERN VIRGINIA ed by Ronald H. Morely pub by Mercer Univ. Press 2002

Pg 140 Fredericksburg, Saturday the (April) 18th, 1863 Dear Molly, I have as many clothes as I can take care of except pants. I need one or two pair, otherwise I am well supplied…."

A SOUTHERN SOLDIER'S LETTERS HOME The Civil War Letters of Samuel Burney Cobb's Georgia Legion, Army of Northern Va. ed. by Nat Turner pub by Mercer Univ. Press, Macon Ga.2002

Pg.245 same camp, April 19th, 1863 "…You may make me a pair of pants of some substantial stuff. I will send for them when I need them. My pants are wearing out a little…."

FAR, FAR FROM HOME-The Wartime letters of Dick and Tally Simpson,3rd South Carolina Volunteers ed by Guy R. Everson & Edward W. Simpson Jr. pub.by Oxford Univ. Press 1994

Pg. 214 April 20 1863 Camp near Fredericksburg (Letter 87) Tally Simpson to Caroline Miller, Dear Aunt,"…My purpose in writng you is to inform you that James leaves for home tomorrow morning. He carries Harry's and my winter clothing. Mine you can let our folks have at any time. You can easily distinguish the different articles. Harry sends home one blanket, I, three…"

CONFEDERATE ECHOES A Soldier's Personal Story of Life in the Confederate Army From the Mississippi to the Carolinas by Albert Theodore Goodloe-First Lieutenant Company D Thirty-Fifth Regiment Alabama Volunteer Infantry C.S.A. pub by Zenger Pub. Co. 1897

Pg. 169 Camp Maury, Va. April 23rd, 1863 My dear Mother "…On further reflection, I wish you would send up the undress coat and vest at the first opportunity that seems entirely safe; some one may be going down who can bring it…"

FLORA AND FAUNA OF THE CIVIL WAR-An Environmental Reference Guide by Kelby Ouchley pub.by La. Univ. Press 2010

Pg. 192 Lieutenant Sidney Carter, 14th South Carolina Volunteers, in a letter to his wife from near Berryville, Virginia, on April 23, 1863: "I must tell you of a groundhog that I saw last Sunday dug from his hole and given to me. I ate his meat and on Monday, dressed his skin to make shoe strings. I will enclose you a pair and a pair for Father."

DIARIES.WRITINGS AND STORIES OF GEORGE D. BUSWELL Co. H 33rd Regt. Va. Inf. Stonewall Brigade

Pg. 5 April 27 1863 "…I wrote a letter to Papa by Jack Johnson, also sent my knapsack, boots & 3 pairs of socks by him. I sent my ambrotype by Hamilton Keyser, I suppose he has sent it home by this time. I had it taken at Guiney's Station, it cost $8.00…Since I wrote last, the transportation for the army has been increased by order of General Lee. Company officers are allowed 50 lbs. each, we will be allowed 150lbs. so we have concluded to have our mess-chest brought back. If Eli Frazier did not get it down, Perry will try to get it to us when he comes. I will also have my pants,that I sent away in the trunk, brought back. I think I can keep two pairs with me at least for awhile. If you have an opportunity, you may get the rest of my clothes home…."

Pg. 10 after battle of Chancelerlorsville "Yesterday we marched from chancellors to this (camp). Though the distance was not so great, it was a very hard march with some of us. The roads were very slippery. You may imagine we felt very rough when we got here, for tomorrow would have been two weeks since we changed clothes, and we had been wading through and laying in the mud and water for 9 days. I did not have my shoes or any of my clothing, except hat and overcoat, off for 8 days and nights, didn't have my overcoat off for 3 days…."

SOJOURNS OF A PATRIOT The Field and Prison Papers of An Unreconsrtucted Confederate edited with commentary by Richard Bender Abell & Fay Adamson Gecik pub by Southern heritage Press 1998 letters of Pvt. Augustus Pitt Adamson

Pg. 150 Camp near Pocotaligo Beaufort Dist. S.C. April 27, 1863 Dear Sister, "…I want you to send me those pants and that grammer which was sent home when you have a sure chance. I am not needing the pants at the present time but you can send them when you have a chance…"

THE STILLWELL LETTERS-A GEORGIAN IN LONG-STREET'S CORPS ARMY OF NORTHERN VIRGINIA ed. Ronald H. Morely pub by Mercer Univ. Press 2002

Pg. 148 Fredericksburg, Va. April 28 A.D. 1863 Dear, in regard to my summer clothes I will shall not need money. I have just sold a pair of drawers tonight for two dollars that I drew from Mare Jeff at sixty cents. I have three pairs left. I have four shirts, three pairs of socks and the thumb stalls that Aunt Ann (Stilwell) sent me. I don't need anything now except one or two pairs of pants and a hat. Still, if you don't get a chance to send them I can make out very well. Soldiers don't wear out anything hardly but pants. Sitting so much on the ground soon wears out the seat. I don't want any woolen clothes this summer. You can tell Uncle that I can draw pants that will suit better for summer than woolen and can get them cheaper than they can be made at home and I will need them (the woolens) worse next winter. My coats are both good yet...."

THE CIVIL WAR MEMOIRS OF CAPTAIN JAMES J. SEYMOUR- Remeniscences of a Louisiana Tiger by Terry L. Jones pub by La. State Univ. Press 1991

Pg. 49 April 29, 1863 watching the movement of the Union Army: "...On this occasion Gen. Jackson was clad in a spare new uniform and his unusually spruce appearance excited much attention and remark among his admiring "foot cavalry," as the soldiers of the 2nd Corps were called. Previously, in camp,on the march & in battle, the General had worn an old, rusty, sunburnt gray coat and a faded blue cap of a peculiar pattern, the top of which fell forward over his eyes. Alas! A few days afterwards this new uniform served as his burial dress..."

CIVIL WAR LETTERS OF WILLIAM (BILLY) A. ELLIOT

April 30 1863 Camp Near Kinston, N.C. "...Father I have sent my old cloths all home but just what I need. The Capt. Had a box made and put all our cloths in it. It was sent in the care of Cruse. My cloths and Powel Auten and James Stowes and Thomas Prim is all in bag together. The bag is Mr. Prims..."

Hanover Junction Va. May 25th 1863 Dear Brother (G.R. Elliote) "...Tell Mother I want her to send me some white cotton thread the first chance..."

LETTERS TO AMANDA-The Civil War Letters of Marion Hill Fitzpatrick ed by Jeffery C. Lowe and Sam Hodges pub. by Mercer Univ. Press 1998

Pg. 67 Apr. 30th, 1863 The battlefield of Fredericksburg, Va. (Letter No. 33) Dear Amanda, "...I left my knapsack at the camp with the sick. The orders were to bring everything with us but I could not toat mine. I brought my blankets, a shirt, pair of drawers and a pair of socks besides what I have on. The boys we left said they would take care of it if they could and if they could do no better would leave it at a private house..."

Once again, I wonder if he ever saw that knapsack again.

THE CONFEDERATE VETERAN VOL. 1897

Pg. 119 March, 1897 "A Mr. Wheeler, of New York state, claims to have the bullet that killed Stonewall Jackson. The story is that the surgeons who amputated Jackson's arm impatiently threw the bullet against the wall, and that Officer Wheeler, of his saff, picked it up. The owner died some time ago, and the cousin mentioned as having the bullet found it with the history recently in going through the old clothes of the deceased."

Where is that bullet now? It should be in Lexington at VMI, or in the Museum of the Confederacy.

CONFEDERATE CENTENNIAL STUDIES #21 A Visit to the Confederate States of America in 1863-Memior Addressed to His Majesty Napoleon III by Charles Geraud pub by Confederate Pub. Co. Inc 1962

Pg 76 May, 1863 observing Lee's army "Thus I was able, with my own eyes, to evaluate the excellent conditions in which these two army corps operated. If, viewed as a whole, their uniforms left something to be desired, it was nonetheless adequate as regards details..."

Pg. 88 "one evening at Adjutant-General Samuel Cooper's I heard the governor of North Carolina say that, during the numerous excurtions on the soil of his State, the enemy had carried off whole families of Negroes by main force and that, in several instances, the kidnappers having been surrounded by local troops as they were about to re-embark, the Negroes seized the opportunity to escape and return to their master's homes. When this happened, the Yankees would vent their rage on the pickaninnies, grabbing them from their mother's arms and throwing them into the water. On other occasions they have resorted to mass drowning of Negroes, when the latter resisted kidnapping.

The Yankees excercised the same cruelty towards the whites. On a ship transporting prisoners, most of whom were ill with smallpox contacted in the filthy, disease-ridden pens used to house them, they "amused" themselves with tying healthy men to sick men, in pairs, so as to spread the sickness by this kind of contact. Then, when the disease grew serious, the sick were tossed overboard into the sea, and the operation ended with shouts of "hurrah."

These are the activities of the "holy" Union Army.

DIARY OF A SOUTHERN REFUGEE DURING THE WAR by Judith White Brockenbrough McGuire pub by J.W. Randolph & English 1889

Pg. 360 May1863 "...I remember so well when, during our stay in Winchester, the first summer of the war, while General Johnston's army was stationed near there, how he, and so many others, would comwe in to see us, with their yet unfaded suits of grey- already sunburnt and soldier-like, but bright and cheerful. Alas! Alas! How many now fill the graves of heroes-their young lives crushed out by the unscrupulous hand of an invading foe!"

HANDLEY LIBRARY ARCHIVES-James A. Miller Collection correspondence C.W. era misc. New Market, Va.

HdQrtrs Med. Depart. 28th Reg. Va. Inf. Buchkannon May 1st, 1863 "…I also want to buy several calf skins so I can have boots and shoes this winter for you and myself…"

GRANDFATHER'S JOURNAL (Franklin Lafayette Riley) Company B Sixteenth Mississippi Infantry Volunteers Harris' Brigade Mahone's Division Hill's Corps, A.N.V. May 27, 1861-July 15, 1865 ed by Austin C. Dobbins pub by Morningside Press 1988

Pg. 137 Sunday, May 3, 1863 Near Catherine's Furnace (Battle of Chancellorsville) "General lee, who was watching, commended our actions. One of our men, who had been wounded in the hand, spoke to Lee. "By God General", he said, "the Yankees have done me up, but we have given them h---." Lee replied "well, you are a brave soldier, but you must not swear." Then dismounting, he wrapped his white linen handkerchief around the man's hand, made a sling with a red silk one, and told him to go to the hospital to get his wound dressed. No wonder we love the General…"

I can truely endorse that last sentence, we love you, General Lee!

ARMY LIFE IN VIRGINININIA:Letters From the Twelth Vermont Regiment and Personal Experiences of Volunteer Service in the War for the Union. 1862-1863 by George Grenville Benedict pub by Free Press Association 1895

Pg. 145 May 4, 1863 attack by Mosby's men "…They accounted for their surprise by averring that the front rank of rebels were clothed in U.S. uniform, and thet supposed them to be a friendly force…"

VOICES FROM COMPANY D Diaries by the Greensboro Guards, Fifth Alabama Infantry Regiment, Army of Northern Virginia ed. by G. Ward Hubbs pub by Univ. of Georgia Press 2003

Pg. 162 May 5 1863 Battle at Chancellorsville "…All the boys have trophys fr. Bat. Field & well supplied with oil cloths, blankets, canteens & haversacks &c…"

This makes sense, the Yankees were so surprised they wouldn't have had any thought for this gear.

FAR, FAR FROM HOME-The Wartime Letters of Dick and Tally Simpson, 3rd South Carolina Volunteers ed by Guy R.Everson & Edward W. Simpson pub by Oxford Univ. Press 1994

Pg. 226 May 7, 1863 camp near Fredericksburg (Letter 91) Tally Simpson to Richard Simpson Dear Pa, "Such a time I have never seen before. I am as dirty as a hog. I have lost all my clothes and have none to put on till these are washed. My shoes are out, and my feet are so sore that I can scarecely walk. We have no tents, and the weather is as cold and rainy as any in wintertime. I must say this much-we have been well fed. I have not suffered in that respect a single moment. Genl Lee says his infantry can never be whipped..."

This last statement is very near true.

LEE& JACKSON'S BLOODY TWELTH-Letters of Irby Goodwin Scott First Lieutenant Co. G Putnam Light Infantry Twelth Ga. Vol. Inf. ed. by Johnnie Perry Pearson pub by Univ. Tn. Press 2010

Pg. 110 Camp near Fredericksburg, May 8th, 1863 Dear Father Battlefield at Chancerlorsville "...I never saw as much plunder in any fight as the Yanks threw away coats, blankets, oilcloths, caps, canteens, Havre sacks &c. of which our boys supplied themselves bountifully. A man could have got almost anything he wanted...While we were here it rained a day and night part of the time in torrents but having supplied ourselves with small Yankee tents, we managed to keep pretty dry...I like the sample you sent of my shirt. I am afraid it is most to fine for me to ruin here in the war..."

HANDLEY LIBRARY ARCHIVES

James A. Miller Collection correspondence C.W. era misc. New Market, Va.

Med. Depart. 28th Va. Reg. May 8th, 1863 Dear Julia, "...I slept dry with my oil clothes thru next day thru the 7th we came about 21/2 miles it assisted (?) all day and I took my oil clothes off and put them on my saddle and got off to walk down a steep hill and they either fell off or some one stole them off I just went about 18 yards I missed them in a very few minutes but they were gone. The wagon with our things got as far as Beverly but in all probability the things are mostly lost, I generally layed on one of the oil clothes and covered with the other but now I have nothing but my over coat left. I am now sleeping in the ambulance with Capt. Marnitt he has plenty of bed clothing ..."

Where does all this gear end up?

WELCOME THE HOUR OF CONFLICT-William Cowan McClellan &The 9th Alabama ed by John C. Carter pub by Univ Al Press 2007

Pg. 226 May 8th 1863 Fredericksburg, Va. William McClellan to his Sister- Dear Sister, "...Send me some cloaths by Lt. Gilbert when he comes, Pants, Jacket, two shirts, two drawers..."

Pg. 234 May 1863 same camp Dear Sister "...Send my cloaths by the first man passing. I need them now when I go to see Miss Maria..."

Asking for his sister to re-uniform him. I guess he can't draw from the government.

True Tales of the South at War-How Soldiers Fought and Families Lived 1861-1865 Collected and ed by Clarence Poe pub. by Univ. of N.C. Press 1961

Pg. 83 Col. L.L. Plk's Wartime Letters "May 9, 1863-Wednesday we started to Cove Creek. That evening and night it rained-no, it poured down. I had nothing but my overcoat, neither did the Captain. We stayed in an old field. I lay down wet in the water and slept.... I can wear out a good pair of socks in two days. If I had some boots I could do much better..."

"DEAR MOTHER: DON'T GRIEVE ABOUT ME. IF I GET KILLED, I'LL ONLY BE DEAD." ed. by Mills Lane pub by The Beehive Press 1977

Pg. 235 William Stillwell to his Wife Fredericksburg Virginia May 10, 1863 "...Tore my shoes all to pieces and had to pick up some old shoes by the roadside. I suffered very much. Nobody can tell, only the poor soldiers, what it is to march all day and night in bad weather. I never draw but a days ration of meat in nine days, but I had plenty, captured my ration from the Yankees, meat, sugar, coffee, crackers, salt, peper, even the paper on which I write is captured, I got about $50 or $75 worth, that it would cost me that to buy it. Now I've got some paper and envelopes to last me a long time. I got me needles, thread, pins, hair brush, comb, portfolio to keep my papers in, good canteen, two of the best blankets worth $10 apiece. Also I captured books, hymn and testament by the wholesale, so I made the trip very profitable, if I did suffer...."

I think I'd have been more interested in the captured edibles.

PARKER'S VIRGINIA BATTERY

Pg. 115 May 10 1863 after the battle of Chancerlorsville; "…The temporal rewards gleaned from the battlefield by Parker and his men were probably just as much appreciated as the indelible military rewards. Most of the men had not had much food since they left Carmel Church; now they were suddenly thrust into an immense Federal camp. Parker wrote: "Our boys supplied themselves with hard bread (of which each Yankee had eight day's rations) and coffee, and as much clothing, tobacco, sugar oilcloths etc., as they could possibly carry." The clothes were almost as much in demand as the food. Some of the men came across a huge mound of brand new knapsacks which contained fine garments, many of them never before worn. A number of the cannoneeers carried their new clothes in the most practical fashion-on their bodies. The rag-tag company was transformed in a few moments into an unfamiliar state of sartorial splender. Among the other loot was a cache of seventy rubber ponchos which Capt. Parker appropriated for the battery. A stray enemy horse was corralled to carry these to the rear. Many an artillerist was kept dry during the next two years by means of this Chancellorsville plunder…"

Pg. 134 The bountiful supply of fine clothes captured near the Chancerlorsville house had put half of the battery into the best attire they had worn in monthes, but Brown's section had not shared in the bonanza and were pretty ragged. Colonel Alexander evaluated the condition of the clothing in Parker's Battery as "jaded" at the end of May…"

You would think they wouldv'e divided the spoils more equitably.

A REBEL WAR CLERK'S DIARY at the Confederate States Capitol Vol.1 Diary of John Beauchamp Jones pub by Lippincott & Co. 1866

Pg. 310 May 10 1863 "…Detachments of Federal troops are now marching into the city every few hours, guarded (mostly) by South Carolinians, dressed in homespun, dyed yellow with the bark of the butternut tree. Yesterday evening at 7 o'clock a body of 2,000 arrived being marched in by the way of the Brooke Pike, near to my residence. Only 200 butternuts had them in charge, and a less number would have sufficed, for they were extremely weary…"

UNIFORMS OF THE CIVIL WAR by Lord, Wise pub by A.S. Barnes & Co. 1970

Pg. 55 May 10 1863 Chancellorsville (Va.) "a wounded Yankee soldier observed the soldiers of Ramseur's Brigade consisting of the 2nd, 4th, 14th and 30th North Carolina Regiments: "…advanced to where (he and other) wounded men were lying. They made a soldierly appearance, though not a handsome appearance, as no two uniforms were exactly alike in style or color or material. The officers were much better dressed than the men: they had light gray uniforms, well fitted. They looked well armed and equipped, and as far as I could observe, were under rigid discipline…"

It seems that some units at least continue their multiform style of dress.

THE STONEWALL BRIGADE by James I. Robertson Jr. pub by La. State Univ. Press 1961

May 10, 1863 Stonewall Jackson dies. Pg. 246 "Yet the final muster for the Stonewall Brigade actually came in July, 1891, when an impressive statue of Jackson was dedicated over Old Jack's grave in Lexington. A handful of gray-haired veterans, stoop shouldered and slow of foot, gathered with thirty thousand to pay final tribute to the general. The soldiers were dressed in faded and tattered gray uniforms, and white whiskers covered most of their faces, but their devotion remained ever as strong. On the night before the ceremony a chill came in the air. The survivors of the Stonewall Brigade had been the center of attention throughout the day, and sympathetic townspeople were anxious that they should have warm and suitable accommodations for the night. But a diligent search of homes, hotel and dining room did not yield a soldier.

Frantically, program chairmen and local citizens combed the entire city; near midnight the Stonewall Brigade was found. There in the moonlight the old men sat huddled in blankets and overcoats around Jackson's statue in the cemetery. The citizens urged the men to get up from the damp ground and partake of the hospitality already arranged for them. No one stirred until one man finally arose. Speaking for the others, he said simply, "Thank ye, sirs, we've slept around him many a night on the battlefield, and we want to bivoac once more with Old Jack." And bivoac they did…"

Yes, this account definitely brings tears to my eyes.

THE STILLWELL LETTERS- A GEORGIAN IN LONGSTEET'S CORPS, ARMY OF NORTHERN VIRGINIA ed by Ronald H. Morely pub by Mercer Univ. Press 2002

PG. 156 May 10 1863 Same old Camp, My Dear Molly;"…After nine days hard marching and fighting in rain and mud, bombshells and blood we have driven the enemy in confusion back across the river and to my surprise have returned back to our old camp in good health though very tired and nearly broked down. I was in mud often knee-deep. Tore my shoes all to pieces and had to pick up some old shoes by the roadside…"

Pg. 166 May 29 1863 Camp near Fredericksburg, Viginia My Dear Molly; "…Molly, I felt so bad when I wrote last that I forgot to write about my clothing though I have wrote to you about it but you had not received my letter when you wrote last. I am afraid that you have already sent them and if you have, I will be very sorry as I have as many clothes now as I can take care of. I have drawn a full suit of uniform. The whole regiment had to take them, having no other pants all winter except my jeans that were worn out and I thought it best to take two pair of pants and did so, therefore I don't want anything but socks, if you have any chance sent two or three pairs of light socks. Light ones will last me as long and be more comfortable in summer. The socks is all I need dear unless I could get a hat and I suppose that's very hard to do right now…"

Now that the army is on the move, too much clothing would definitely be a burden, or would have to be gottren rid of, either sold, stored or discarded.

LEE & JACKSON'S BLOODY TWELTH-Letters of Irby Goodwin Scott First Lieutenant Co. G Putnam Light Infantry Twelth Ga. Vol. Inf. ed. by Johnnie Perry Pearson pub by Univ. Tn. Press 2010

Pg. 113 12th Ga. Regt. May 12th, 1863 Near Fredericksburg Va. Dear Mother, "…I have never heard a word from my box. We heard they were in Richmond and have tried to get them here but have failed. I have given up all idea of ever seeing them. Capt. Reid sent up an application for a few days leave of absence to go to Richmond but I don't think it will be granted…"

THE CONFEDERATE LETTER OF BENJAMIN H. FREEMAN Compiles & Edited by Stuart T. Wright pub by Exposition Press 1974

Pg. 19 May 13, 1862 Stonewall Jackson's funeral service in Richmond. Private Benjamin H. Freeman Co. K, 44th North Carolina was part of the guard of honor: "Dear Father and Mother, "…Our regiment had to hold an escort…over General Jackson's corpse. His coffin was wrap[p]ed in the flag of the Confederacy with fine [w]reaths of flowers and vines…all along it. I never saw as many Ladies and Children in my life. I thought I had see[n] a great man[y]….The Capitol Square was full of men and women [gazing] upon our Regiment. General Elgin said it was the finest Regiment he ever saw. We was dressed in our new uniform Dress. It looked very nice…"

I really wish Pvt. Freeman had described this "new uniform Dress."

Pg. 67 Footnote #2 "After the first half-year of the war, there was no uniform dress for the Confederate army. Most soldiers wore shirts of homespun and mismatched pants of wool. Underclothing was never scarce, although according to the letters of many it was "scarcely" changed. And in general, due to the "jealous exertions" of North Carolina Governor Zeboulon B. Vance, his troops fared better than those of other states…"

VOICES FROM COMPANY D Diaries by the Greensboro Guards, Fifth Alabama infantry Regiment, Army of Northern Virginia ed. by G.Ward Hubbs pub by Univ. of Ga. Press 2003

Pg 167 May 16, 1863 SP "…Threw away undershirt and put on a nice overshirt had taken out of D. Barnums trunk at Mrs. Barnes-cotton drawers & socks instead of woolen pulled & pr. cass (cassimere?) pants also David's. Then had hair shampood & trimmed & boots blacked & felt 1000 pr. ct. better…."

No doubt.

LETTERS TO AMANDA-The Civil War Letters of Marion Hill Fitzpatrick, Army of Northern Virginia ed by Jeffery C. Lowe and Sam Hodges pub. by Mercer Univ. Press 1998

Pg. 70 May 16th, 1863 Camp Naer Guiness Statuion,Va. (Letter No.35) dear Amanda,"…It rained a god deal the evening we got down there, and at night faired off cold. I was on post that night…We both had overcoats and a blanket, and stood it pretty well…"

"Several of the sick we left here have come back to us from Richmond among them Tom Rickerson. Tom is quite feeble yet but is improving. When he left here he took two pair of my pants out of my knapsack and saved them for me. I gave him one pair and took the new pair you sent me. I was proud to get them sure as I was certain they were lost. My knapsack soap,&c. is lost for good. I have plenty of clothes again in fact more than I can carry on a march. I wrote Lou about getting an overcoat and bed quilt. We are well fixed up in the sleeping line now. Drew, Webb and myself have a Yankee tent just large enough for us three to sleep under. We put up a few logs and covered them with the tent and have quite snug little place. Each of us have an oilcloth and then my old quilt is just the idea to sleep on. I have one good blanket that I expect to keep, the one I carried home with me. Doc gave me an oilcloth, it is light and is the very thing to keep my blanket dry on a march…I got me another canteen in the fight (Chancelorsville) which I do not believe I told you about. It is just like my old one only it is not mashed up and it was full or nearly full of coolwater when I picked it up, which was a great help at the time…"

HANDLEY LIBRARY ARCHIVES, WINCHESTER, VA James W. Beeler Diary Cutshaw's Battery and Carpenter's Battery

Pg 8 May 17th1863 "in camp drawed clothing."

Once again, no description of these uniforms as to color, cut, etc.

VOICES FROM COMPANY D Diaries by the Greensboro Guards, Fifth Alabama Infantry Regiment, Army of Northern Virginia ed. by G. Ward Hubbs pub by Univ. of Georgia Press 2003

Pg. 169 May 20 1863 SP returning to Richmond after being exchanged "…I had my clothes washed- pants & Jacket too, & got a coat out of David's trunk. John took my old letters, woolen under clothes &c. to put my valise at Mrs. Colquits'…"

THE CRY IS WAR, WAR, WAR The Civil War Correspondence of Lts. Burwell Thomas Cotton and George Job Huntley, 34th Regiment North Carolina Troops by Michael W. Taylor pub by Morningside Press 1994

Pg. 109 Camp Gregg near Guiny Station, Va. May 20th /63 "…I want you to get Dobbins to make me just as nice a pair of calf skin shoes as he can and send them to me just as soon as you can, No. 8 and high heels and nice every way. You have an idea what sort will suite me, Tins. I want you to send me two pairs of drawers. Two nice striped shirts with pockets on the outside of both of them, a good pocket handkerchief-I want them tomorrow on review, so fly round, if you please. I want them all soon. I want nice shoes and them large enough, No. 8. I don't want the shoes blunt. I want one pair of socks….I want nice shirts, Tins, for I am a Lieutenant now…"

It doesn't sound as if the shoes he's describibg would last long on a march, but I suppose he knows best. Notice, once again, the requeast for pockets.

GRANDFATHER'S JOURNAL (Franklin Lafayette Riley) Company B Sixteenth Mississippi Infantry Volunteers Harris' Brigade Mahone's Division Hill's Cops, A.N.V. May 27, 1861-July 15, 1865 ed by Austin C. Dobbins pub by Morningside Press 1988

Pg. 142 Monday-Tuesday, May 25-26, 1863 Camp near Fredericksburg "we are told that General Hooker requested General Lee to stop our men from fishing (seining) in the river. No doubt Hooker thinks the fish are Yankee and objects to their being caught by Southerners. Or perhaps he sympathizes with the fish. No, actually he objects to the "communication" fishing brings between his troops and ours. Apparently he has some secrets (such as what he is going to do next?) that he wants to keep from us…"

Excellent sarcasm, Pvt. Riley!

HANDLEY LIBRARY ARCHIVES

James A. Miller Collection correspondence C.W. era misc. New Market, Va.
Buffalo Gap Agusta Co. May 26th, 1863 Dear Julia, One of our boys played a nice trick on an old union man in Braxton. He had a pair of yankee pants on which he had captured at Beverly before he got to the house he found out what he was and that he had been feeding the yanks and when our men came in said he had nothing and would not give them anything, this fellow told the old man he was a yankee captain and that he wanted to go to (?) to inform the yanks that they could whip and drive our men out of the country and he was bearing dispatches, that he had thrown his coat away and put on a Rebels to prevent being taken by our men. The old fellow wanted him to stay and have supper cooked for him but this fellow told him he must be in a hurry that if he delayed he might possibly be taken and the lady of the house filled his haversack with bread, and then he wanted a horse to ride to which the old fellow consented told him he would take 2 if necessary, and he went to look at the horses and found one too old to make the trip so he consented to take one and gave the old fellow an order on the yankee Quarter Master for the hire and the worth of the horse in case he should get crippled or captured and signed his name as Captain of the yankee army and started and got through the mountains on his horse it had no shoes and its feet got sore and he left it with a friend at the Warm Spring, so he made a horse by the operation, we were all surprised at the boy as no one thought him so cunning...."

This illustrates the lack of intellect you need to be a Yankee sympathizer. I wonder if the Yankee quartermaster ever paid that man for the horse? Probably not, as the Yanks stole so many the quartermaster couldn't keep up.

RED CLAY TO GEORGIA by John J. Fox pub by Angle Valley Press 2006

Pg. 174 May 26, 1863 Private James Garrett "...He again reported that he had all the summer clothes he needed, but he advised them to get some wool to make him some clothes for the following winter..."

LETTERS FROM THE STONEWALL BRIGADE Ted Barcay, Liberty Hall Volunteers by Charles W. Turner pub by Rockbridge Pub. Co. 1992

Pg. 83 May 26, 1863 after the battle of Chancerlorsville Co. 14th Va. Alexander Telford Barclay Dear Sister "...As you have been asking a good many questions about my clothes, I will set you at rest on that point. I have worn out a suit that I left home with, pants, coat, and socks, but as I was getting tolerably ragged, the brigade secured a supply of English clothes. So as I was one of the needy ones, I am rigged in a splendid suit of blue, costing only eighteen dollars for the suit, and I bought socks; my shirts are in a very good condition yet and as I have to play the turtle here (carry my earthly effects on my back), I do not wish to tote more.

I had my boots mended and they will do for some time yet, but you may send my others down as soon as possible, but do not hurry and take any kind of article, I wish my boots to be soft and not too heavy, as heavy boots are apt to blister the feet in warm weather...."

There must not have been many suits of English clothes, as they were only issued to the most needy.

A TEXAN IN SEARCH OF A FIGHT by John Camden West pub by Press of J.S. Hill & Co. 1901

Pg. 163 May 30 1863 "...You need not make or send anything to me as I am unable to march with it, and will have to throw it away. Mother gave me a nice pair of pants; they were cut out and made for $1.50..."

Quite a bargan at this stage of the war.

THE CRY IS WAR, WAR, WAR The Civil War Correspondence of Lts. Burwell Thomas Cotton and George Job Huntley, 34th Regiment North Carolina Troops by Michael W. Taylor pub by Morningside Press 1994

Pg. 110 same camp May the 31/63 "...I want some clothing just as soon as you can get it to me. I want a real nice striped or checked pair of pants if you han't started nary pair and if you have started arry pair you need not mind about sending any more. I want two striped or checked pair of shirts, a pair of drawers and a pair of socks. I want two pants, one pair of socks. I want one pair of real nice calfskin shoes, I want Dobbins to make them high heels and nice every way, narrow bottoms with the toes rather round. No. 8 will do. You know what sort will suite me. I need the shoes very bad. I am nearly barefooted. ...If I can get the shoes soon it will save me from paying out a good deal of money. 1 pair pants, 2 shirts, 2 pair of drawers, a pair of socks, one pair of shoes. Remember, I am a Lieutenant...."

Wow, he wants quite a wardrobe; striped or checked pants and shirts?

HANDLEY LIBRARY ARCHIVES-The Memoirs of the 49th Regiment Virginia Volunteers C.S.A.

Pg 227
Reciepts:

Received at Camp on the 31st of May 1863, of Capt. I.T. Bingham, AQM Smith's Brigade, the following articles of QM stores:

(7952) Seventy nine hundred & fifty Two pounds Corn
(290) Two hundred & ninety pounds Hay
(156) One hundred & fifty six pair Pants @ $1.25
(49) Forty nine Jackets @ $12
(100) Ten Caps @ $1.75
(96) Ninety six pairs Socks @ $1.00
(83) Eighty three Shirts @ $1.50
(10) Halter Chains (2) Pairs Hames

(Signed) R.Irvin Reid
2 Lieut & Actg Rgt QrM
49thVa Inf

GEN. LEE'S ARMY

Over the next year, shoe shortages periodically plagued the army. Soldiers continued to produce their own, or the officers contracted for the men. For some reason, the government kept purchasing shoes, either made at home or abroad, that were too small for the men. Had the shoes been too large, ay least soldiers could have wrapped their feet and still used them. In one batch, Lee's army received 10,000 pairs, of which it sent back 3,024 as unfit. They were poorly made, too small, or too low. If footwear did not extend above the ankle, mud sucked them off their feet.

By midsummer 1863, clothing shortages once again reached epidemic proportions. "I am getting nearly naked," a soldier revealed to his folks at home. Another, the son of a Confederate senator, described himself to his sister, bottom to top. "My boots were utterly worn out, my pantaloons were all one big hole as the Irishmen would say; my coat was like a beggar's and my hat was actually falling to pieces." One regimental commander thought the army needed 30,000 pairs of shoes and estimated half his men were barefoot or almost so. By the late fall, troops still had no tents, no overcoats, and no blankets. With evident admiration for the toughness of his comrades, Sgt. Hill Fitzpatrick stated "They build a fire and lie down on the ground before it and sleep when it is cold enough to freeze a man well wrapped up." The Confederacy employed 3,000 women to manufacture clothing; it was not nearly enough. Soldiers wore out shoes and garments quicker than the laborers could produce them.

A Virginia private and prewar carpenter stated "I have Rather bin in hopes tha ware going to Fight attall that it wood come off for I want Some overcoats and Blankets if our men Whip them I wood Stand a good chance to get some," he explained to his wife..."

This is a continuing story-the soldiers wearing out clothing faster than it could be replaced.

THE CONFEDERATE VETERAN VOL. XVI 1908

Pg. 339 July 1908 Thirteenth Virginia Infantry-Humor by Alexander Hunter June 1863 "(An episode of the war from a private's notebook)

For a limited time no regiment in the army had more glorious enjoyment than the 13th Virginia Infantry. Fully, they deserved it, for it had been their first opportunity during the war of falling into a soft place. They were in the van of Ewell's Corps when he advanced, and had taken a distinguished part in driving Milroy out of Wincester (Va.) in June, 1863, and capturing his entire stores.

Such an abundance of plunder they had never seen before, and each man in the regiment was arrayed in style; among other things, linen, underwear, shining patent leather boots, and black slouch hats to cap the climax. There were creature comforts and almost forgotten delicacies too numerous to mention and went far to swelling the full tide of that earthly content which rolled in upon each man's soul and reflected itself in every linement of his face."

In these accounts of Rebs capturing and eating vast amounts of unusual delecacies, there is no mention of it causing the men to be sick, or have diarrhea. Had their systems hardened until they could eat any thing, or was diarrhea a usual state of affairs?

A MISSISSIPPI REBEL IN THE ARMY OF NORTHERN VIRGINIA- The Civil War Memoirs of Private David Holt ed by Thomas D. Cocknell & Michael B. Billard pub by La. State Univ. Press 1995

Pg. 190 June 1863 near Berryville, Va. on the road to Gettysburg "...My rabbit's fur hat, which I had brought from my dad's home to Bedford County, had been showing the wear of time and the tear of hard usage for a distressing period. And now, at the most pressing time, the crown gave out. It had long passed the frazzling stage and simply ceased to wear. Have you ever noticed how unmercifully Nature comes down when it catches you in a tight place? The sun, that I always admired and felt friendly to, took advantage of my plight, and tried to burn a hole in the top of my head.

I secured permission to stop at a nearby cottage and see if I could get the hat mended. A real pleasant young lady answered my rap at the front door and, when I had made known my wants, invited (me) in. She studied the matter for a few minutes and said, "The only piece of cloth that I have will be just the thing, if you don't mind the color." I said I could stand any color, they all suited my complexion.

She brought out a piece of woolen goods, baby blue in color. She did a jam-bone job of sewing, and also marked me with a glaring, unmistakeable mark, that got me into several scraps, but it kept out the sun, and I was happy. After Company K and the regiment, and the Twelth Mississippi, which was next to us, finished guying me about the hat and became used to it, I had a period of peace and comfort in my old hat...

At Berryville, I was presented a muffler and a pair of woolen gloves (sent) by the little girl whom I had kissed at the depot when I left home They (had been) intended for a Christmas present, six monthes before. Freight was slow in those days. Some way I lost the precious things before winter came again.

At Chambersburg (Pa.) we stopped to rest. The whole company was lying down on the sidewalk except Bill Phipps, who stood in the middle of the street. The front door of a palatial residence opposite him opened, and a man stepped out onto the porch. He was a large man, about the size of Bill, finely dressed, and had an air of defiant impudence that was offensive to the lasrt degree. He looked like a Durham bull showing off his disdain for weaker things.

Bill caught his eye and vociferated, "Come out of that hat. And don't say you ain't in there, for I see your legs sticking out from under it."

The man swelled up, visibly, threw back his houlders, and said, "I'll come out of it when you are man enough to make me."

"Oh," replied Bill, "Is that your game?" Then he quickly loaded his gun, and putting a cap on the tube, cocked it, covered the man and saying, "Will you once? Will you twice? Will you three...?"

The man quickly threw the hat on the pavement, saying," There, take it. The Lord knows you need it, and a lot more clothes besides, you ragged rebel."

Bill did not lower his gun, but said "Come out of that coat."

"I won't pull off my coat for any man, except to fight him." Replied the man.

"you can take your choice of pulling it off alive or have me pull it off you when you are dead." replied Bill. "one, two three-"and off came the coat alongside the hat.

"Come out of them breeches," Bill continued.

"I demand the protection of an officer!" exclaimed the man, "I appeal to the captain or commanding officer of this company to save me from the disgrace of disrobing on the street." But no officer seemed to be there. At least none moved.

"I don't care a pckled damn about you being naked on the street," said Bill, "I want them Breeches."

Then the man modified his manner and said "Soldier, I have faced that loaded gun long enough. You win, and if you come inside, I will give you a complete outfit of clothes."

Bill, receiving a nod from his officer, went inside the house. He left his old rags inside. Soon the door opened wide and a nicely dressed young woman came to the door with Bill's old duds. She was holding them with a pair of tongs as far from herself as she could, holding back her skirts with the other hand. But Bill did not care. He had a fine civilian suit.

The natives seemed kind but curious. They had a notion that we were a lot of ignorant savages, particularly we from Mississippi. Their surprise was great when they found us courteous and gentlemanly. Princes disguised in rags..."

OK, what color was that civilian suit? Warriors dressed in rags, more likely.

SOLDIERS BLUE AND GREY by James I. Robertson Jr. pub by Univ. S.C. Press 1988

Pg. 77 "...A year Later (summer 1863) a private in the 57th North Carolina informed his brother that he had "onley one shirt & one pair of draws & when I wash them I hafta put on my coat..."

LIFE IN THE CONFEDERATE ARMY: BEING PERSONAL EXPERIENCES OF AS PRIVATE SOLDIER IN THE CON-FEDRATE ARMY by Arthur P. Ford and Marion Johnstone Ford pub by Neale Pub. Co. 1905

Pg. 23 June 1863 James island, S.C. -"...The quartermaster's department was as badly crippled as the commissarie's and we could get no new shoes, and several of our men were actually barefooted in consequence; but it being summer, and on a sandy coast, there was nort as much suffering as might have been otherwise..."

These were garrison troops and didn't need shoes as badly as the fighting troops.

A MISSISSIPPI REBEL IN THE ARMY OF NORTHERN VIRGINIA—The Civil War Memoirs of Private David Holt Ed. by Thomas D. Cocknell & Michael B. Billard pub by La. State Univ. Press 1995

Pg. 202 June1863 en route to Gettysburg, Pa. "Here's your mule," was a great expression at that time. Chris had hollered it out many times that night. After the fence episode, we scattered out across a field and down a hill. Chris yelled "Here's your mule," and he was there, sure enough, and dead at that. Chris stumbled over the feet and fell over the dead body of the mule. Fortunately he had his blanket around him. Some of the boys rescued him, but he left his blanket with the mule. He became very sick but kept up and was with us when daylight came.

We halted by a small steam that was swollen and muddy, and waded in and washed the mud off our clothes. Chris was in the water, washing off, when the surgeon of the regiment came riding along.

"Doc, I have plan that will make you and me a whole lot of money," said Chris.

Doc put on an expression of interest, but did not say a word. He feared a "sell."

Chris continued, "Say Doc, I am a live mummy. I am Ramses the Third. I have absolutely thrown up all my internal viscera and would have thrown up my toenails, but they are non-detachable. I have not a drop of blood in my body, and I am living on the memory of what I was when I ruled Egypt. Now I propose that you sell me to a dime museum."

But about that time the deal fell through, as we were ordered in and continue the march. We all felt sorry for Chris. His emptiness was excessive, but he kept his place in the ranks.

We went over South Mountain, and, while in the mountains, one of the men noticed a tree of mountain birch. He said the bark was sweet and tasted like wintergreen. He stepped out of ranks and brought back a sample. Soon every man in the company was chewing bark. We had to get it as near to being a powder as possible in order to eat it. That was all the food we had for the fourth and fifth of July. There were very few blackberries along that road.... We lacked rations and some of us lacked shoes, but there was no grumbling...

After awhile the surgeon came up and proposed that I should ride for the purpose of seeing what a fine traveler his horse was, So I mounted and took the gun across my lap. I soon rode beyond the wagons and came to the troops. The Second Midssissippi had halted to rest and lay on the side of the road.

When I came along, a fellow jumped and grabbed the bridle of the horse, waved his cap, and let out a mighty yell. He said, "France has recognized the Confederacy and has sent her most noted general over as a testimony of her good will. We are honored by a visit from his highness. Let us give him a royal welcome. Attention regiment! Open ranks! Present Arms! Where is the music?"

The music came, a fife, a tenor drum, and a brass drum. He called for a guard of honor, and about ten men responded. Then the procession started between the open ranks. The (musicians) played "The Girl I Left Behind Me," and the regiment presented arms. I took off my hat and bowed left and right. Comments were freely made on my appearance, and the fellow had a ready answer for each one.

"What is that blue patch on the topof his hat?"

"Why that is a decoration he won at the Battle of Balaclava."

"Look at the fringe on the bottom of his breeches. What does that stand for?"

"Why, you fool, they don't stand, they hang. Only generals of high rank are allowed to wear them kind."

"That looks almost like a gun he has across his lap."

"No, that's no gun. That's his official batton."

:What's them kind of shoes he wears?"

"Why they are the new kind of French skintights. Only princes are able to but that kind of a shoe.They are waterproof."

"The general must be a powerful fighter. He smells like a wolf. I can smell him from here."

"Why, that's French Eau De Cologne you smell. It was made expressly for the general."

I tried to keep up a bold front, but I was badly hacked, especially by the horse laugh I got from the colonel, W.W. Stone. When we reached the head of the regiment, they turned me loose with a rousing cheer by the whole regiment…"

THE HASKELL MEMOIRS-The Personal Narritive of a Confederate Officer ed by Gilbert E. Govan and James W. Livinggood pub by G.P. Putnam's Sons 1960

Pg. 48 en route to Gettysburg June 1863 "A few days after this battle, (Chancerlorsville), we started into Pennsylvania. Our army had daily orders to do no damage, and no troops could have passed through the country of their best friends with less harm. I heard of but one act of violence, the murder and robbery of an old man, and the first news we got of it was the sight of the two murderers, hanging by the roadside, having been executed by General Lee's orders."

CONFEDERATE CENTENNIAL STUDIES # 26 Lawley Covers the Confederacy by William Stanley Hoole pub by Confederate Pub. Co. 1964

Pg. 57 June 1863 Francis Lawley was a reporter for the London Times "…A traveler would wonder at the endless files of footmen and horsemen, accompanied but troops of negro camp followers, the men still ragged and unkempt but hardly one without good substantial shoes; the mules and horses for the most part sleek and fat, the army altogether in infinitely better shape than I ever saw it before…"

Despite having ragged uniforms, the men were all shod, according to Mr. Lawley.

WEEP NOT FOR ME, DEAR MOTHER by Elizabeth Whitley Roberson pub. by Pelican Pub. Co. 1996 16th Georgia Regiment of Infantry Pvt. Eli Landers (age 19)

Pg. 161 June 1863 Portion of a letter written somewhere in Pennsylvania on the way to Gettysburg. "…I sent a set of uniform buttons by George Walker to go on my coat. It was 16 big ones and 6 little ones…. 16th Georgia Regiment of Infantry Pvt. Eli Landers (age 19)

Pg. 163 Portion of a Letter."…Mammy you need not send me any clothing for we have drawed a suit of clothes but if I send my money home in time you had better get your winter shoes before they get so high and if you can have me a good strong pair of firm shoes made for me for they are from 8 to 10 dollars a pair here….I want to know if you ever got my overcoat and wool shirt or not. I sent them in Capt. Reeder's trunk …"

FROM HUNTSVILLE TO APPOMATTOX R.T. Coles History of 4th Alabama Volunteer Infantry, C.S.A. Army of Northern Virginia ed by Frank D. Stocker pub by Univ of Tenn. Press 1996

Pg. 203 June 1863 Gettysburg Campaign, near Greencastle, Pa. "…A member of Co. K, from Scottsboro, Ala. Going to the spring with his camp kettle for water, reached out into the spring and filled his kettle; but as he was thin from light diet, in drawing the full kettle toward him, he staggered, and his cap, sateuated with the dirt and perspiration of a long service, fell into the water, and disappeared from sight. He returned to the camp capless. Shortly afterwards, Jack Stewart, a tall member of Co. G, six feet six inches high, and the thickness of a fishing pole, went to the same spring with his kettle to procure water. Reaching out the full length of his arm, he drew in his kettle filled with water. Returniong to the bivouac, he put the ration of beef for his mess into the kettle, and left it to boil over a slow fire, while the men, tired out, dropped off to sleep. Next morning at daybreak we were aroused to prepare for the onwaerd march into the land of our enemies. As rapidly as it could be done, the boiled meat was taken from the kettles and fairly divided among each mess. As this process was going on, there was heard a guttural muttering from Jack Stewart expressive of intense, disgust and disappointment. It was "________, boys! Just look here!" All eyes were turned on Jack Stewart. The finger of his left hand were spread out in his right. He held a forked stick, on which was suspended the well-boiled cap of Company K. The broth in the kettle was well-clolred with dirt and perspiration from the cap, and the mass in the kettle was digusting. Poor Jack and his messmates had to go without meat. *How nasty was that hat?*

We were a joyous crowd. Marching rapidly northward, we soon entered Greencastle. Leaning over a fence that enclosed a cottage was a man with two ladies. They appeared to be absorbed looking at us; and while we were looking at them, (a man of) Company K, bareheaded, his shock of hair waving in the sunlight, went rapidly up to where the man and the ladies were standing. Not a word spoke he, not a motion made he, until he was in arms length of the man; and then, without bow or other recognition of their prescence, he simply lifted the man's hat and transferred it to his own head. The last we saw of that man and his companions he was scratching his naked head and the women were laughing at him. We were a merry lot. Entering the one long street of Greencastle, we found the people not at all afraid of us, as might have been expected. John Young, a private of Company I, of Huntsville, Ala., a man so bow-legged that he took in all sides of the street, remembering the wrongs that Huntsville had suffered at the hands of the Yankeees, went up to an old gentleman standing in the presence of some ladies at the foot of a stairway that ascended immediately from the street, and lifted from the gentleman's head a beautiful new felt hat, at the same time carelessly dropping his own well-worn Confederate wool covering. The old gentleman seemed dazed. Rubbing his hands through his thin hair, he realized the situation, and was overheard to say,: "I really believe that soldier has taken my hat."

A HISTORY OF THE 2nd SOUTH CAROLINA INFANTRY : 1861-1865 by Mac Wyckoff pub. by Sergeant Kirkland's Museum & History Society Inc. 1994

Pg. 77 march to Gettysburg June 1863, re: destruction of civilian's property by Confederate soldiers. "…One Pennsylvania Dutch farmer who found tracks of mud on his porch exclaimed, "Mien Gott! I'se heard of de horrors of war before but I never see what dey was till now!…"

THE REBEL BOAST by Manly Wade Wellman pub. By Henry Holt & Co. N.Y. 1956

Pg 111 June 1863Co. from Enfield, N. Carolina on the march towards Gettysburg "Jeb Stuart's 9,000 cavalry troopers were superbly mounted, dashingly led. The infantry, by contrast, seemed ploding, dingy and unshowy; but it was as good as ever, answered drum or bugle. By harshest experience it had learned to travel light. The road to glory, went another of those mordant army aphorisms, is not to be followed with much baggage, and long ago these men had forsaken spare shoes and coats, frying pans, sheath knives, water-proof ground cloths. That summer, Lee's representative infantyman wore only a shabby shirt and pants, a battered but defiant slouch hat, and shoes of he could get them. More than likely he had thrown away his cartridge box and carried his cartridges in his pocket. What food he might posses was crammed in a lumpy haversack. His canteen, looted from a dead Yankee at Manassas or Fredericksburg or Chancellorsville, bumped his lean hip. Slung over his shoulder was a blanket roll. Unshorn, wolfish-eyed, tattered, he seemed all savage except for his bright-burnished musket, deadly at both ends. *I bet these were some scary-looking men.*

Men of the Forty-Third and Daniel's other regiments were, by contrast to their new mates, well equipped with new shoes and uniforms. A few, like the fastidious George Wills, still wore underwear and carried razors."

UNIFORMS OF THE CIVIL WAR by Lord, Wise, pub by A.S. Barnes & Co. 1970

Pg. 55 "A Union soldier of the 146th New York Infantry made note of the appearance of a group of Confederate pickets near Richard's Ford In June 1863: "…They were clad in either butternut or grey clothes and were generally well-dressed as far as comfort was concerned, but they didn't present a very military appearance.

Some wore hats of black, some of grey, and some wore caps which we recognized as having been intended originally for use in the Union Army, but had been passed into the service of the confederacy by right of conquest…"

You betcha, Yank!

The Story Of A Cannoneer Under Stonewall Jackson-The Rockbridge Artillery by Edward Moore pub. by Neale Pub. Co. 1907

Pg. 183 June 1863- On the road to Gettysburg "No one at all familiar with the Rockbridge Artillery will fail to remember Merrick. A lawyer and native of Hagerstown, Maryland, having been educated abroad, he was an accomplished scholar and a fine musician, with a stock of Irish and other songs which he sang admirably. In person he was very slender, over six feet in height, with a long neck,prominent nose and very thin hair and whiskers. Cut off from home and being utterly improvident, he was entirely dependent on quartermaster's goods for his apparel and when clothing was issued his forlorn and ragged appearance hushed every claim by others who might have had precedence. This Confederate clothing, like the rations, was very short, so that Merrick's pantaloons and jacket failed to meet, by several inches, the intervening space showing a very soiled cotton shirt. With the garments mentioned-a gray cap, rusty shoes and socks, and, in winter, half the tail of his overcoat burnt off-his costume is described."

"Our march from Greencastle was through Chambersburg and Shippensburg, and when within eight or ten miles of Carlisle, we passed through one or two hundred Pennsylvania militia in new Federal uniforms, who had just been captured and paroled. Before reaching Carlisle, we very unexpectedly (to us) countermarched, and found the militiamen at the same place, but almost all of them barefooted, their shoes and stockings having been appropriated by the needy rebels. As we first saw them they were greatly crestfallen, but after loosing their footgear all spirit seemed to have gone out of them…"

First, can you imagine sending untried militia against the Army of Northern Virginia? Second, I wouldn't have wanted to explain why they did not only not stop the Rebels, but gave them their shoes.

CONFEDERATE VETERAN VOLUME XXX Oct, 1922—Crossing The Potomac by I.G. Bradwell, Brantly, Alabama

(I include this to show that there were overalls in use in Civil War times. A professor assured me overalls were not invented until 1880-ed.) Gettysburg Campaign, "We marched the next day without interruptions and made our camp near a village. The next morning the Captain sent me and a comrade ahead of the column to fill the canteens with water. We stopped in front of a beautiful residence, with a grassy lawn in front and hailed. An old gentleman, dressed in blue overalls, with a wide straw hat on his head, came out..."

LEE'S LIEUTENANTS by Douglas Southhall Freeman pub by Charles Schribner's & Sons volII

Pg. 36 Gettysburg Campaign, June 1863 "...Many of "Old Alleghany's" men had been barefooted; most of them were road-worn; the prisoners had been well shod. This had suggested an exchange. En route to Carlisle, Johnson had lined up his captured Pennsylvainia militiamen in their new Federal uniforms and had relieved them of their shoes and socks for the benefit of his soldiers. John Casler recalled: "Some of our men thought it was cruel, but Johnson said they were going home and could get other shoes quicker than he could, as he had work for his men to do. "Ed. Moore was amused, rather than shocked. Said he of the prisoners "...they were greately crestfallen...After losing their footgear all spirit seemed to have gone out of them. They lingered, it may be, in anticipation of the greeting when met by wives and little ones at home, after having sallied forth so valiantly in their defense. How embarrassing barefeet would be instead of the expected trophies of war."

The militia are lucky they didn't get into a fight with these fellows, they'd had more to grieve than a few shoes and socks.

BRIGHT & GLOOMY DAYS-The Civil War Correspondence of Capt Charles Frederick Bahnson, A Moravian Confederate ed by Sarah Bahnson Chapman pub by Univ. TN. Press 2003

Pg.64 June 1863 Culpeper Court House (Va.) "...Please send me my suit of clothes by Cyris Chadwick; the extra piece or "reenforcement" on the pantaloons goes on as above; the larger portion behind the inside seam. The coat has seven buttons on a side in front & four behind; the vest has eight. I can get the buttons here, but would be glad if you would have the button holes made at home, they must be an equal distance apart..."

COVERED WITH GLORY The 26th N.C. Infantry At The Battle Of Gettysburg by Rod Gragg pub by HarperCollins

Pg46 Mid June 1863 "Unlike the men of the 26th North Carolina, most of Lee's troops did not have "splendid grey uniforms" of recent issue. Their worn, ragged appearance made them look less than imposing. "Their clothing is serviceable, so also are their boots; but there is the usual utter absence of uniformity as to color and shape of their garments and hats…(grey) of all shades, and brown clothing, with felt hats," noted an observer. "Hundreds had no shoes," a veteran of the march would recall, "(and) thousands were as ragged as could be, some with the bottom of their pants in long frazzles, others with their knees sticking out, others out at their elbows, and their hair sticking though holes in their hats. Some of the men patched their clothing… one man having the seat of his pants patched with bright red, his knee patched with black, another with a piece of grey or brown blanket." Few had knapsacks like the Northern soldiers, but many had blankets rolled and looped over one shoulder and worn across the chest with the ends tied together on one side of the waist. They carried a variety of black leather cap and cartridge boxes-including many that were U.S. issue.

Continued ragged multiform.

Pg47 "Thanks to Governor Vance, their former commander, they were also the best uniformed troops in Lee's army. A few were barefooted, but all had new uniforms. As governor, Vance had established a factory in Raleigh to manufacture uniforms and overcoats for North Carolina's soldiers, and he had encouraged blockade-running to supply Tarheel troops with uniforms, arms and equipment from Great Britain. Ten days before the 26th began its march, (15 June 1863), a shipment of new uniforms from North Carolina had reached the regiment in Virginia. The troops were issued new kepis, trousers, and jackets. The kepis were received without enthusiasm: Like most Southern troops, the men of the 26th preferred common broad-brimmed hats, which offered protective shade. Their trousers varied in color and quality, but they were clean and lice-free. The prize of the lot was an issue of jackets. There were hundreds of them-all alike and all the same variation of Confederate grey. Tramping along with the rest of Lee's army, the troops of the 26th may have groused about having "pantaloons of every color," but the new uniforms gave them a fresh start in ridding themselves of the lice that plagued troops in the field-and now they were surely one of the best-uniformed regiments in the Army of Northern Virginia."

I'm happy for these men, but that isn'rt too hard to accomplish-being the best uniformed men in Lee's army.

MECHANICSBERG PA NEWSPAPER

In June 1863 about General Albert G. Jenkins Cavalry Brigade (a part of Gen. Ewell's Corps) "Some were clad in butternut uniforms, while the majority had no uniforms at all; many, indeed, having nothing but a shirt, pants and hat. A few looked like Pa. farmers. They were armed with all sorts of weapons...The men were, with few exceptions, a stout-looking set of fellows picked men for hard service and would have done some good fighting had they been attacked. They were, as a body, pretty well behaved."

SOUTH GEORGIA REBELS by Alton J. Murray 1976

Pg.? "On the first day of June (1863) we were ordered to cook two days rations, which we did. We left our camp about dark for the Gettysburg Campaign. The first little branch that we came to every man was trying to walk the foot-logs, when General Gordon jumped off his horse and waded the branch back and forth, to show the boys how to wade." (Note: the "boys" were probably trying to keep from ruining new shoes.)

THE ANSON GUARDS by Smith

Pg161 June 1, 1862 "The war was barely eighteen months old when a N. C. soldier wrote of the Army of N. Va. "One fifth of Lee's Army was barefooted, one-half in rags and the whole of them famished. The marvel of it is that any of us were able to carry on."

Amen, brother, I couldn't have said it better myself.

HANDLEY LIBRARY ARCHIVES

James A. Miller Collection correspondence C.W. era misc. New Market, Va.

Buffalo Gap June 2nd, 1863 Dear Julia, "...I also put some dirty woolen clothes. I would have sent them in that condition but was unable to have them washed. I will also leave a roll of my bed clothes with my over coat as I think it best to leave it..."

WRITING & FIGHTING THE CONFEDERATE WAR The Letters of Peter Wellington Alexander ed by William B. Styple pub by Belle Grove Pub. Co. 2002

Pg. 146 Culpeper Courthouse, Va. June 6, 1863 "Your readers will be glad to hear that Gen. Lee's army is in excellent condition and spirits. The health of the men was never so good; and they are well clothed and pretty well shod. Thus far I have seen but two barefooted men, and they may have laid aside their shoes merely for the march. The horses, wagons, and harnesses are also in better condition than they have been for twelve monthes past; whilst our supply of ordinance and ordinance stores is abundant. The people at home, however, should persevere in their patiotic efforts to manufacture all the clothing, leather, and shoes they possibly can; for they will all be needed by or before next December. I am not informed of what the Government is doing to procure supplies for the army; but it may be safely concluded that with all their efforts, they will not be able to obtain sufficient supplies for the men in time for next winter. Let the people never forget that but for their prompt response to the appeal for clothing and shoes last fall, Gen. Lee could not have fought the battle of Fredericksburg in December That was one of the most brilliant and decisive victories of the entire war; and every man and woman, every boy and girl, who gave a pair of shoes, a yard of cloth, or a pair of socks to the brave men who defeated the enemy on the frozen plains of the Rappahanock, helped to win the battle, and is entitled to part of the honor conferred by the victory…"

A great morale-building article, even if its not entirely true as regards the condition of the uniforms of the soldiers, as we have seen.

RECOLLECTIONS OF AN OLD DOMINION DRAGOON, The Civil War Experiences of Sgt. Robert S. Hudgins II Company B, 3rd Virginia Cavalry ed by Garland C. Hudgins and Richard B. Klees pub by Publisher's Press 1993

Pg. 73 June 6 1863 "In the earliest days of June, word went throughout the camp that Gen. Stuart was going to have one of his famous reviews. We spent several days prior to the big event cleaning, polishing and grooming. I got Corral as slick as a peeled onion, and my spurs and accouterments sparked in the sun like a mirror. I had gotten a brand new uniform from home and felt very grand and proud of it, especially as I was now a sergeant, and the uniforms bore stripes…"

Pg. 81 The Gettysburg Campaign June 1863 "…We finally got to Hanover town on the last day of June and proceeded through there to Carlisle, Pa.

It was while on this raid that one of the most humorous incidents of the whole war occurred. "Bang" Phillips, Joe Ham and myself had decided to go on a little foraging expedition as we had very meager rations for several days. We rode up to a farmhouse of one of the Dutch farmers to ask if we could buy something to eat. After a knock on the door a comely woman carrying a baby of about six monthes answered. We asked her very politely if we could buy some food as we hadn't much to eat in recent days. She responded, "I have nothing, and if I did, I'd not give it to you." "Bang" began edging closer to the woman as he asked her again, this time stating it as though she shouldn't let us starve. She again responded, "You dirty Rebels will get nothing from me. I'd like to see the whole murderous lot of you die." Without warning, "Bang" snatched the baby from her arms. She let out a scream and it was obvious that her former bravado was gone. "Bang" threatened her with the possibility, though untrue, that we'd have to eat the baby if we couldn't get something else. He then offered to trade her the baby for some bacon, whereupon she set out ham, fowl, bacon, bread and butter. We had a glorious feast and took the remainder back to camp after paying her (in Confederate money) for all we had taken...".

You've probably heard this story before, but here is the original account.

CONFEDERATE LETTERS AND DIARIES ed by Walbrook D. Swank pub by Papercaft Printing and Design Inc. 1992

Pg. 34 Letters pertaining to John Taylor Anderson Private, Co. C, 13th Virginia Infantry, Gordonsville Grays Smith's Brigade Early's Division Army of Northern Virginia To Gordonsville, Harper's Ferry, June 7th, 1861 Pg. 92 Dear Sister, "...Tell Pa to send the box by the first chance. Sallie don't put yourself to any trouble for my clothes. I reckon that Mr. Parrott will come over that way before he comes back if you have not got the clothes ready you will have other chances to send them..."

THE CONFEDERATE VETERAN VOL. XXVII 1919

Pg. 265 July 1919 In The Years Of War—compiled by John C. Stiles from "Official Records" Series III, Vol. II 1863 June 8, 1863 "Carbines and Saddles Made in Richmond-General Lee on June 8 told the chief of ordinance: My attention was called to the saddles and carbines made in Richmond. I could not examine them myself, but was assured by officers that the former ruined the horses' backs, and the latter were so defective as to be demoralizing to the men." But he mitigated this by saying that he knew thet were doing the best they could, considering the material to work on."

General Lee is entirely too kind, these saddles and carbines were defective from the start. The carbines wouldn't seal properly at the breech (they were breech loaders) and would spit fire in the eyes of the troopers using them. I'd have sooner had a double-barreled shotgun, myself.

CIVIL WAR LETTERS OF DANIEL HAYWOOD GILLEY

Co. F, 16th Virginia Regiment
June the 9,1863 back page "...You wanted to know if I kept any of the clothes that was on the battlefield. I got one shirt and a pair of drawers. I threw away all of my clothes in fight but a shirt or too. I have got what I have on and one shirt and a pair of drawers besides and

that is all. I want you need not be uneasy about me having clothes, I can get plenty of them here…"

HANDLEY LIBRARY ARCHIVES

James A. Miller Collection correspondence C.W. era misc. New Market, Va.

Camp near Culpeper Court House June 9th, 1863 Dear Julia "…I had to start out without anything but my oil cloth…Our wagons did not get up and I had nothing but my oil cloth, I was too cold for me to sleep so I went to a fire and sat up all night perhaps I may have slept a half hour during the night…"

THE CRY IS WAR, WAR, WAR The Civil War Correspondence of Lts. Burwell Thomas Cotton and George Job Huntley, 34th Regiment North Carolina Troops by Michael W. Taylor pub by Morningside Press 1994

Pg.112 In line of battle near Fredericksburg June the 10th/63 "… A few more lines. I wrote three letters a few days back for some clothes. I want the clothes yet, two nice shirts, two pair drawers, one pair pants, one pair socks, one handkerchief-pants striped or checked, shirts same way without it is too much trouble, and one fine pair of calfskin shoes. I want them soom, for I am you know what. Write soon…"

This officer can't get government issue clothes, he asking for them from home.

VOICES FROM COMPANY D Diaries by the Greensboro Guards, Fifth Alabama Infantry Regiment, Army of Northern Virginia ed. by G. Ward Hubbs pub by Univ. of Georgia Press 2003

Pg. `177 June 13, 1863 SP passing through Millwood Va. & capturing a Yankee camp"… Some of the boys also got Lemons, a good many got boots & shoes, also clothing- Drawers, shirts, pants &c. A great many haversacks and canteens were found…"

HANDLEY LIBRARY ARCHIVES-Diary of William J. Thomas 2nd Maryland Battalion

June 13 In the Valley "…Edelen had his shawl. Geo. W. Edelen and I laid down on the ground and covered with this…"

PAPA WAS A BOY IN GRAY-Memories of Confederate Veterans by Their Living Daughters by Mary W. Schaller pub by Thomas Pub 2001

Pg. 66 Meridith Thomas Jenkins of North Carolina Co. H, 54th North Carolina Regiment June 14, 1863 "…On June 14, Meridith and his comrades rejoiced in the spoils of war following the defeat of the Federals at Winchester (Va). Helping themselves to the goods in the Fedral supply wagons, the boys of the 54th North Carolina "washed and put on clean Yankee pants, shirts, and boots…"

FOUR YEARS IN THE CONFEDERATE ARTILLERY

Pg. 47 enroute to Gettysburg June 15 (1863) "…We encountered, in the streets of Winchester, over a hundred abandoned Yankee wagons. I went through a number of these, but saw nothing which I cared to take. I was on the lookout for a pair of new boots, but found none…We went on down the Harper's Ferry Road and encamped about six miles below Winchester. We captured about 3,000 men with all their baggage, wagons, arms, ammunition, commissary andquartermaster's stores. They succeeded in carrying of nearly all their mules and horses. We got, also, all their cannon and a large supply of uniforms and underclothes and blankets. The latter were all new and found in boxes packed just as they had come from the factory…"

This kind of thing could drive a Yankee quarter-master crazy.

HANDLEY LIBRARY ARCHIVES-Diary of William J. Thomas 2nd Maryland Battalion

Pg 35 June 15, 1863 "…I had on a pair of shoes which were about equal to none, most of my right foot was out of the shoe. I was amused at Miss F., who, noticing my bare toe showing, could scarcely refrain from laughing…"

Is this better than no shoes at all?

HANDLEY LIBRARY ARCHIVES

James A. Miller Collection correspondence C.W. era misc. New Market, Va.

Winchester June 16th, 1863 Dear Julia, "…I have the promise of several calf skins so if I get them you can send down for them and have me a pair of boots made. I will also leave my blanket with Martha as I will have enough without it …"

LETTERS OF WILLIAM F. WAGNER, CONFEDERATE SOL-DIER ed. by Joe M. Hatley and Linda B. Huffman pub by Broadfoot's Bookmark 1983

Pg54 Near Winchester Va June th 17th 1863 ..."Dear I never saw as many things at one plase in my life cloathing and Rashins and waggons and sugar and coffey Reddy ground up I got a litle pocket fool of coffey and a new haver sack and a shirt our boys some of them got new suted all over and some got lots of writeing paper"...

BRIGHT & GLOOMY DAYS-The Civil War Correspondence of Capt Charles Frederick Bahnson, A Moravian Confederate ed by Sarah Bahnson Chapman pub by Univ. TN. Press 2003

Pg. 65 June 19th, 1863 getting ready to march to Gettysburg "...We start this morning for Pennsylvania, I think, or at least we move onward, & I know of no other way to go...We pressed a large number of boots & shoes at this place, paying Government price, & I am now up to my knees in leather, for the sum of only $12.00.... Of course we have no chance to send letters home unless we send someone to the rear; our baggage train is now cut down as low as possible; all my baggage now consists of an overcoat, 2 blankets, an extra set of drawers,(I intend to press a shirt when the one I have on gets dirty.) In haste..."

Capt. Bahson seems comfortable with the stripped-down marching order of the army.

THE STILLWELL LETTERS-A GEORGIAN IN LONG-STREET'S CORPS ARMY OF NORTHERN VIRGINIA ed by Ronald H. Morely pub by Mercer Univ. Press 2002

Pg. 176 Camp at Ashby's Gap in the Blue Ridge Mountains N. Va. June 20, 1863 (to Molly) "...I have got all my clothes yet (as I) get them hauled. I haven't worn my new uniform but one Sunday yet, I am saving it for hard times and I know very well he (hard times) will be along this summer for I met him last year up here in the mountains...."

"DEAR MOTHER: DON'T GRIEVE ABOUT ME. IF I GET KILLED, I'LL ONLY BE DEAD." ed. by Mills Lane pub by The Beehive Press 1977

Pg. 245 Theodore Fogle to his Parents Snicker's Gap, Virginia June 21, 1863 March towards Gettysburg "...That night we bivouacked on a high hill and slept in a clover field. Some of the officers had no blanket or covering of any kind. Toward morning the weather grew cold and some of us suffered. I did tolerably well, for before leaving Culpeper I strapped my shawl on my shoulders. I knew the wagons were going another road, and (I) did not wish to spend the night without cover...That afternoon we passed through a little village called Upperville.

You can hardly imagine anything more beautiful than that little village nestled among the mountains. It shows nothing of the desolating effects of war. The houses are clean and neat and the people look happy. Oh, how ashamed I felt passing among such nice people! I was so dirty and shabby, and my face and hands were browned by the sun and weather....(a few days later) Snicker's Gap "...We bivouacked on top of the mountain. Just before night the rain came down in torrents. It seemed as if the windows of heaven were opened. I had no shelter but my shawl that soon became soaking wet. And then my clothes were washed nicely. A shower bath is a very good thing, but when you are compelled to stand in one for two or three hours all pleasure is lost. I slept for a few hours that night with the wet ground for my (mattress) and my shawl for covering. You can imagine how comfortable I was I was some what unwell yesterday but am well again today..."

Pvt. Fogle at least maintains a good attitude, I don't know if I'd be so jovial after having to sleep on the wet ground, soaked to the skin.

The Fremantle Diary-A Journal of the Confederacy pub. by Burford Books 1954

Pg. 180 22 June, 1863 Pender's Division, A.N.V. (near Winchester,Va.) "The soldiers of this division are a remarkably fine body of men, and look quite seasoned and ready for any work. Their clothing is serviceable, so also are their boots; but there is the usual utter absence of uniformity as to color and shape of their garments and hats: gray of all shades, and brown clothing, with felt hats, predominate. The Confederate troops are now entirely armed with excellent rifles, mostly Enfields. When they first turned out they were in the habit of wearing numerous revolvers and Bowie knives. General Lee is said to have mildly remarked: Gentlemen, I think you will find an Enfield rifle, a bayonet, and sixty rounds of ammunition as much as you can convienently carry in the way of arms." They laughed, and thought they knew better; but the six-shooters and Bowie knives gradually disappeared, and now none are to be seen among the infantry..."

Pg. 185 23 June 1863 Talking to two wounded officers "...They gave us an animated account of the spirits and feelings of the army. At no period of the war, they say, have the men been so well equipped, so well clothed, so eager for a fight, or so confident of success-a very different state of affairs from that which characterized the Maryland invasion of last year, when half the army were barefooted stragglers, and many of the remainder unwilling and reluctant to cross the Potomac..."

Pg. 186 25 June, 1863 Marching with M'Laws Division, Longstreet's Corps, crossing the Potomac at Williamsport "...They marched very well, and there was no attempt at straggling; quite a different state of things from Johnston's men in Mississippi. All were well shod and efficiently clothed.

In the rear of each regiment were from twenty to thirty Negro slaves, and a certain number of unarmed men carrying stretchers and wearing in their hats the red badges of the ambulance corps; this is an excellent institution, for it prevents unwounded men falling out on pretense of taking wounded men to the rear. The knapsacks of the men still bear names of the Massachussetts, Vermont, New jersey, or other regiments to which they originally belonged…"

Pg. 191 27 June 1863 (near Greencastle, Pa.), civilians watching the army march by, "Others were pointing and laughing at Hood's ragged Jacks, who were passing at the time. This division, well known for its fighting qualities, is composed of Texans, Alabamians, and Arkansians, and they certainly are a queer lot to look at. They carry less than any other troops; many of them have only got an old piece of carpet or rug as baggage; many have discarded their shoes in the mud; all are ragged and dirty, but full of good humor and confidence in themselves and in their general, Hood…"

Once again the Maryland & Pennsylvania civilian population is presented with the specyacle of those ragged victorious Rebels.

GRANDFATHER'S JOURNAL (Franklin Lafayette Riley) Company B Sixteenth Mississippi Infantry Volunteers Harris' Brigade Mahone's Division Hill's Cops, A.N.V. May 27, 1861-July 15, 1865 ed by Austin C. Dobbins pub by Morningside Press 1988

Pg. 147 June 24, 1863, Petersburg, Maryland marching towards Gettysburg-"So far- except for some rails, a few overly friendly chickens, and some hats which we have long-armed from citizens in the towns-we have obeyed General Lee's order to the letter."

DIARIES, WRITINGS AND STORIES OF GEORGE D. BUSWELL, Co. H 33rd Regiment, Virginia Infantry, Stonewall Brigade

Pg. 16 June 24, 1863 Camp Near Chambersburg, Franklin County, Pa. From Stonewall Book: "…The troops filed through Hagerstown and were subjected there to loud jeers from the citizenery. One woman, leaning precariously from her upstairs window taunted the Rebels for their shabby uniforms…"

HANDLEY LIBRARY ARCHIVES

James A. Miller Collection correspondence C.W. era misc. New Market, Va.

June 25th, 1863 Camp near Chambersburg, Pa. Dear Julia, "…Calico is selling for 50 cents I must try and get enough for several shirts. I did not succeed in getting any thing at Winchester every thing was captured and turned over to the Quarter Master who always take enough for themselves if any one else gets nothing..."

I think this complaint regarding the quartermaster is prevalent in every war, in every army, so its probably true.

RECOLLECTIONS OF A CONFEDERATE STAFF OFFICER by G. Moxley Sorrel pub by Bantam Books 1992

Pg. 145 June 25, 1863 marching through Chambersburg, Pa. "We "perswaded" the principle shopkeepers to keep open, and they displayed some of their wares, doubtless old or unsaleable stuff that they could not hide. Everything was strickly paid for in our national currency-Confederate bills!

I did get something, however. Our good commissary, Maj. Moses, managed to secure (by payment, of course) a bolt of excellent velveteen, wearing quite as well as courderoy. Indeed, he got some of the latter also, and sent the plunder to our headquarters, where the stuff went around sufficiently to give me a coat and trousers, which did good service, I think, till the end of things. He also managed to get a few felt hats, and deserved more, for he was grumbling furiously at the ill success of his important requisition for cash, stores, and army supplies; also for the sound rating and liberal abuse he had taken from the irate females in furious rage at his work."

Lee's Army acted with commendable restraint during the Gettysburg Campain. If the Rebel had taken on a "scorched earth" policy in Pennsylvania, it might have drawn troops from the Vicksburg front.

THE CIVIL WAR READER RICHARD B. HARWELL pub by Smithmark Pub. 1994 (originally 1957)

Pg. 228 Gettysburg "Diary of a woman resident June 26 (1863) The lst regiment stacked arms, on both sides of the street in front of our door, and remained for an hour. They were a miserable-looking set. They wore all kinds of hats and caps, even to heavy fur ones, and some were barefooted...." (Pg. 231) "...Will our army be whipped? Some said there was no danger of that yet, and pointed to Confederate prisoners who began to be sent through our streets to the rear. Such a dirty, filthy set, no one ever saw. They were dressed in all kinds of clothes, of all kinds and no kinds of cuts. Some were barefooted and a few wounded...."

Consider this: the officials and Mr. Freemantle all say the army was well-equipped and well-shod. The soldiers and civilians all mention the ragged appearance of the army.

FAR, FAR FROM HOME-The Wartime Letters of Dick and Tally Simpson, 3rd South Carolina Volunteers ed by Guy R. Everson & Edward W. Simpson Jr. pub by Oxford Univ Press 1994

Pg. 248 26 June, 1863 Williamsport, Md. (on the march towards Gettysburg) (Letter 103) Tally Simpson to Mary Simpson Dear Sister, "Up in the mountains the nights are extremely cold and as many as three blankets feel comfortable. So you can imagine how we fared on picket with wet clothes, and not a spark of fire. The worst of it all was, thinking we were going into a fight, we left our blankets and had nothing but oil and tent cloths to cover us. Tom Mormon McAbee, one of our company, and myself lay upon an oil cloth and covered as best we could, which was bad enough, and you better believe we had a rough time of it…"

MILITARY COLLECTOR AND HISTORIAN-Journal of the Company of Military Historians Vol.XLI Fall, 1989 Enilisted Uniform of the Maryland Confedrate Infantry: A Case Study, Part 1 by Ross M. Kimmel

Pg. 106 June 26, 1863 "…In June, after helping drive Milroy out of Winchester, the men had the opportunity to don captured yankee clothing. The recollections of a unit veteran are worth recording:

One thing of importance I recall in connection with Milroy's flight was the matter of shoes and socks and a change of underclothing. A lot of supplies were left behind when Milroy took to the Mountains and we boys of the second Maryland all got a couple of changes of underclothing, socks and shirts…

He went on to indicate that, while troops of other units put on yankee blue, the 2nd Maryland was "not so reduced as others, and had a sort of aversion to putting on blue jackets or pants.

Indeed, the Marylanders did seem able to keep up appearances better than other rebel units. Sgt. James W. Thomas, Co. A, recounted this incident on the road to Gettysburg in an 1894 transcription of his wartime diary:

On this days March (26 June 1863) an old man walked along talking to us. He said, "They have been telling us you Rabs were a ragged set, but you seem to have pretty good clothes; and that you were badly armed (or words to that effect), but you have good guns, and what's funny to me, all of them have U.S. on them."

Our regiment was better clothed than most and all our guns had been captured on battle fields…"

GRANDFATHER'S JOURNAL (Franklin Lafayette Riley) Company B Sixteenth Mississippi Infantry Volunteers Harris' Brigade Mahone's Division Hill's Cops, A.N.V. May 27, 1861-July 15, 1865 ed by Austin C. Dobbins pub by Morningside Press 1988

Pg.147 Sunday-Tuesday, June 28-30, 1863 Chambersburg "…Morale is high. However, our shoes are wearing out. Many are barefoot….In Chambersburg only a few windows opened for Confederate flags to be thrust out and waved. As we passed, the ladies made fun of our appearance. "Bejabbers," responded one of our men. "We always put on our dirty clothes when we go hog killing." The response was rough-but it was deserved. The women here are so insolent and ugly. Apparently this is the place they get the comic pictures they put in the almanacs."

Pvt. Riley is not favorably impressed with the Yankee women.

A SOLDIER'S RECOLLECTIONS-Leaves From the Diary of a Confederate by Randolph H. McKim pub by Zenger pub. Co. 1983

Randolph McKim was in the First Maryland Confederate Infantry, Army of Northern Virginia Pg. 166 June 28th. "On Sunday, the 28th, we were still marching northward toward Harrisonburg, and were now within less than a day's march of Carlisle. My notes mention that the men were much broken down, many of them having to march barefooted."

Here we see again a first-hand account of the army having many barefooted soldiers.

VOICES OF THE CIVIL WAR by Richard Wheeler pub by Meridian Books 1976

Pg. 288 Gettysburg Campaign, June 28, 1863 General Gordon marched his brigade into York,(Pa.): "…The church bells were ringing and the streets were filled with well-dressed people. The appearance of these churchgoing men, women and children…strangely contrasted with that of my marching soldiers. Begrimed as we were, from head to foot, with the impalpable gray powder which rose in dense columns from the macadamized pikes and settled in sheets upon men, horses and wagons, it is no wonder that many of York's inhabitants were terror-stricked as they looked upon us…"

LEE'S LIEUTENANTS Douglas Southhall Freeman Charles Schribner's & Sons volII

Pg. 32 vol II Gettysburg Campaign 28th June 1863 "…Gordon entered York. As his men hurried through the town en route to Columbia Bridge, they were so dust covered and wild in appearance that they scared the women…"

No wonder. These men had a dirty, savage appearance.

FIGHTING FOR THE CONFEDERACY-The Personal Records of General Porter Alexander ed by Gary W. Gallagher pub by Univ. of North Carolina Press 1989

Pg. 229 Gettysburg Campaign, June 30th,1863 Marching from Chambersburg, Pa."…about noon,. Seeing a house with a pump in the front porch, I rode up to see if we could get a drink.The Dutch owner was in the porch when I came up & was in a state of abject despair. The infantry ahead of us had not only made a path along the edge of his wheatfield, but in trying to pump their canteens full of water at his well had pumped the well dry & [left] it very wet & very muddy. I could see deep trouble in his face as I came up & in the meekest manner possible asked if I could get a drink of water. He almost shouted, "No! Dere ain't no water! De well is done pump dry! And just look at dis porch vere dey been! And see dere vere dey trampled down dat wheat! Mine Gott! Mine Gott! Ise heard of de horrors of war before but I never see what dey was till now!" That sounds like a made up anecdote, but it is verbatim & literatum as I saw & heard it myself."

This farmer wouldv'e had a stroke if he'd lived in the South and the Yankee army had passed through. They'd have probably burned his house and out buildings down, slaughtered or stole all his stock, and robbed the inhabitants.

HISTORY OF HAMPSHIRE, WEST VIRGINIA by H.U.Maxwell and H.L. Swisher pub by McClain Printing Co. 1972

Pg. 626 "THE APRON FLAG"- A battle flag carried by Company D has become famous in song and story. It was a child's apron, and it is still preserved as one of the most cherished momentoes of the war. Its history is briefly told. Lee's splendid and all but invinceable army, with which he had crossed the Potomac and invaded Pennsylvania, had met the northern hosts on the hills of Gettysburg, and, after one of the most desparate battles in the history of the world had been defeated and was slowly retreating southward to the Potomac. The army was yet powerful, but it had met disaster, and the soldiers realized that they were no longer led by the star of victory. Among the regiments that had passed through the storm of battle was the Eleventh Virginia Cavalry. It was making its way through a hostile country and among unfriendly people. The news of the battle had gone over the land, and the people along the lines of retreat looked with scorn and hatred upon the weary soldiers as they made their way south. There was no firendly word or sympathetic look among all the citizens of the country through which they passed. Thus, with feelings of dejection and discouragement, the Confederates marched through the streets of Hagerstown, Maryland, and out by a stone mill. Here the eyes caught sight of the first token of fiendship they had seen among the inhabitants in days. A little girl stood on a porch near near the mill watching the soldiers pass. She wore a small Confederate flag for an apron. The discovery was greeted by rousing cheers by the weary soldiers, who little expected to find a friend in that place, and several of them went up to the child and asked her for pieces of the apron as souvenirs. She cheerfully took the apron off and gave it to them. Charles Watkins, of Hampshire County, fastened it to a stick, and said he would use it for a battle flag and defend it with his life.

He little knew how soon he would be called upon to redeem this pledge. Scarcely had they passed beyond the town when Union troops opened fire on them from the front. The battle began at once, and was fiercely fought for a few minutes, when the Federals fell back and the Confederates continued their retreat. But Charles Watkins, who was a youth of nineteen, marched no further. He had been cut down in the midst of a furious charge. The apron flag lay beneath his body and was stained with his life blood. The flag was preserved, and was often exhibited at Confederate reunions throughout the South."

I'd like to see this apron flag.

THE CONFEDERATE VETERAN VOL. XXVII 1919

Pg. 225 June 1919 In The Years Of War-Compiled by John C. Stiles From "Official Records" Series III, Vol. II 1863 "Barefooted Men-General Rhodes, C.S.A. says in his Gettysburg report: "In concluding this report I beg leave to call attention to the heroes of it: the men who day by day sacrificed self on the alter of freedom; those barefoot North Carolinians, Georgians, and Alabamians, who, with bloody and swollen feet, kept to their ranks day after day for weeks. When the division reached Darksville, nearly half of the men and many officers were barefooted, and fully one-fourth had been since we crossed the Blue Ridge. These poor fellows had kept up with the column and in ranks during the most rapid march of the war, over the worst of roads for footmen-the turnpike. These are the heroes of the campaign." This division must have consisted of men from the three States mentioned, as the whole army was in the same fix."

Notice the subject of this account; barefooted Rebels. I cannot imagine enduring what these men endured.

THE CONFEDERATE VETERAN VOL. XIII 1905

Pg. 209 "A Barefooted Boy Dead At Gettysburg" by Capt. John H, Leathers, Louisville

The war between North and South furnishes us, on both sides of that terrible conflict, thousands of examples of courage and bravery unexcelled in the history of the world. The heroes of that war were not confined to held high positions. There were heroes whose names have never been mentioned and who in thousands of instances fill unknown graves; but they were none the less heroes.

The incident I am about to relate is a true one, and furnishe\s an illustration of courage and daring unsurpassed in any war. During the fall and spring of 1861 and 1862, when Stonewall Jackson's army was in camp at Winchester, both armies had pbeen busy after the battle of Bull Run in recruiting and preparing for the conflict which both sides knew would be a long and bloody one. The North was aroused and amazed at the defeat at the battle of Bull Run. Thus the men of the North and millions of money were brought into requisition to stamp out the rebellion. The South, on the other hand, rose to a man, and we might add to a woman, in defense of their homes and what they believed to be their rights. The flower of the youth of the Shenandoah Valley flocked to Stonewall Jackson. "The common people" also came with the same patriotic impulse to join his forces, and among these many sturdy sons of the mountains of Virginia.

Among them was a young mountaineer by the name of Jo Ersom. Jo was a boy of about nineteen years of age, about "six foot" tall, as straight as an arrow, with big black eyes, dark complexion, and long, straight black hair, looking half Indian. He was dressed as a mountaineer and barefooted. He had never worn shoes except in the roughtest winter weather. From his appearance, the boys, who were aways ready to give every one a nickname that seemed to suit, dubbed him "Killoola," and he went by that name all through the war.

At first he was imposed upon by the other soldiers who had been in the war long enough to learn a thing or two, and he was made the "hewer of wood and the drawer of water" for the entire company, which he bore without a murmer. He drilled along with the company, and soon filled his place as a member in the ranks. In the battle of Kernstown, four miles above Winchester, in a terrific little fight between Jackson and Shields, Jo received his first baptism of fire, and he behaved so splendidly that he at once earned the confidence and respect and affection of the entire command. From that day on he was known as a brave soldier.

It is known to those who are familiar with the history of the war that after the defeat of Hooker at Chancellorsville Lee immediately prepared for the invasion of Pennsylvania, and sixty days after the battle of Chancellorsville the great struggle at Gettysburg took place.

Before starting out on the campaign Gen. Lee endeavored to provide his army with the best arms and equipments he could obtain, and as far as possible with new clothing. Many of these new things he managed to get through the blockade from England, and among other things thus brought through was a splendid lot of English army shoes, which were distributed through the army to those who most needed them. Jo,who rarely ever wore shoes at all because his feet did not suit shoes, drew a pair of these English army shoes, of which he was very proud. He could wear them only a little while at a time, but he would not sell them for love or money; and on the march from Virginia to Gettysburg he would wear them until his feet commenced to hurt, then he would take them off and go barefooted, carrying his shoes on his gun, and then put them on again, and so on until the army reached Gettysburg.

It is known to those familiar with the history of the war that in both the first and second day's fight at Gettysburg the Confederate army drove everything before them. It was on the first day's fight that poor Jo lost his life. Jackson's corps, then commanded by Gen. Ewell, advanced upon the enemy, who had entrenched themselves on the crest of a long and rocky hill. Jo was in the ranks of his company, and started in this charge with his shoes on. After the line advanced through a wheat field some quarter of a mile or more, he began to lag behind, and, finding that, with the quickening pace of the men who were then about ready to charge, he could not keep pace with them, he stopped, took off his shoes, tied them together with the leather shoe strings and threw them across his left arm, and hurried forward over the rough and stoney ground barefooted to regain his place in the ranks. As the enemy's skirmish line was broken, the order was given for the Confederates to charge the breastworks of the Federals on the crest of the hill some four hundred yards distant. The charge was made with the terrific yell of the Confederates and met with galling fire of the Federals, who were waiting for the charge; and when the smoke of the battle cleared away, the Confederates occupied the position the Federals had been driven from. Among the dead lying on the very top of these earthworks was poor Jo Ersom, barefooted, and his shoes lying across his left arm. This poor, untutored mountain boy had given all he had to give to his country-his young life's blood."

I wonder how many "Jo Ersom's" there were in the Civil War.

THE HASKELL MEMOIRS—The Pesonal Narritive of a Confederate Officer by John Haskell ed by Gilbert E. Govan and James M. Livingood pub by G.P. Putnam's Sons 1983

Pg. 54 "The battle of Gettysburg (July1-3) will, no doubt, rank as the turning point of the war though perhaps it may better be called the braking-point of the South's resources. For months our men had been on rations such as no troops ever campaigned on or did a tithe of the work ours were called on to do. Corn meal and damaged bacon were the staples, often so damaged that to live on them insured disease. Medicines, chloroform especially, had got so scarce that small operations as painful as great ones were done without it. Much of that which was used was of such bad quality that it it was used only as a choice of two evils.

Delicacies for the wounded were unheard of. They lived on damaged bacon or lean beef or went hungry. Clothes and shoes were scant and insufficient, except for those which were taken from our friends, the enemy. Overcoats would have been almost unknown but for them, though for that matter we would have fared badly for everything but for their contributions..."

THE CIVIL WAR INFANTRYMAN, In Camp, on the March, and in Battle by Gregory A. Coco pub by Thomas Publications, Gettysburg, Pa

Pg 80 Capt. Harry T. Owen 18th Virginia observed in July 1863: "The veterans faces were tanned by summer's sun and winter's storms and covered by unkempt beards. Boys who had enlisted in their teens appeared with long tangled locks, changed and weather-beaten now, apparently, into men of middle life."

This is a phenomena common to a great deal of young men who became veterans of many battles in many different wars in different times & countries.

VOICES OF THE CIVIL WAR by Richard Wheeler pub by Meridian Books 1976

Pg. 173 July 1 1863 first day's battle at Gettysburg; "…The charge of Gordon's Georgia Brigade of Eary's Division at 3 P.M. gave the coup de grace to the Federal line…The sight of Jackson's veterans once more threatened to close with them in hand to hand combat struck a chill to the hearts of men they had so recently defeated, and who now had to face that long brown line hardly distinguishable from the corn over which it trampled, save for the fringe of steel glittering above it in the July sun, and for a dozen crimson standards which flaunted defiantly the starry cross of the Confederacy…"

A TRUE HISTORY OF COMPANY I, 49TH REGIMENT, NORTH CAROLINA TROOPS by W.A. Day printed at the Enterprise Job Office 1893

Pg. 42 July 2nd, 1863 Twenty miles below Richmond, Va. "…We were ordered to take the caps off of our guns lest an accidental discharge might betray our position. When we moved back in the road one man in Company I was bareheaded which caused a good deal of fun at his expence. He had mistaken the order to uncap his gun and uncapped his head…The black women brought in pies, etc., to sell and one day they brought in some dog meat, which they called shoat. Some of the boys got a dose of it before they found out what it was. They gave the negroes a thrashing which put an end to the dog trade. The 25th Regiment said we carried the dog's head to the doctor's quarters and it barked at the doctor. Whenever we marched by the other regiments they would bark at us…"

I'd like to have the testimony of that doctor, to see not only if the dog's head barked, but how much an how loud it barked.

VOICES OF THE CIVIL WAR by Richard Wheeler pub by Meridian Books 1976

Pg. 319 July 3rd, 1863 moving out at the start of Pickett's charge to support the infantry, Longstreet's artillery chief reports: "But as our supporting guns advanced, we passed many poor, mangled victims [of the Federal artillery fire]…I remember one with the most horrible wound that I ever saw. We were halted for a moment by a fence, and as the men threw it down for the guns to pass, I saw in one of the corners a man sitting down and looking up at me. A solid shot had carried away both jaws and his tongue. I noticed the powder smut from the shot on the white skin around the wound. He sat up and looked at me steadily, and I looked at him until the guns could pass; but nothing, of course, could be done for him."

I wonder how long that poor soldier lived.

CIVIL WAR REGIMENTS- Journal of the American Civil War, Treasures from the Archives: Select Holdings from the Museum of the Confederacy Vol.5 pub. by Regimental Studies Inc.

14th Tennessee Infantry-Historical Sketch by Sgt. R.T. Mockbee Pg. 27 July 3rd, Gettysburg, Picketts Charge "…The Confederate infantry clad in somber homespun with nothing bright about them but their bloodied battle flags and the glittering sheen of cold steel…"

Pg. 30 mid July 1863 "The wearied men glad once more to be on Virginia soil, and for the time free from molestation from Meade and his men, bivuoacked near the river, and found a god nights rest. Shoes were issued to many who had been doing strenuous duty on the march, in the trenches at Hagerstown and at Falling Water with bare and sore feet since leaving Gettysburg."

PAPA WAS A BOY IN GRAY-Memories of Confederate Veterans by Their Living Daughters by Mary W. Schaller pub by Thomas Pub 2001

Pg. 38 July 3, 1863 William John Henry Durham of Georgia "At Bainbridge, Ga he enlisted in Company A, 59th Georgia Infantry on May 3, 1862 … Later that evening, her Father and another man wandered around the battlefield, searching the bodies of the fallen for shoes. Bill was barefoot. They fially found a good-looking pair on a Union soldier.

"But he wasn't dead," Irene continued the story. "the Yankee pleaded, "Please don't take my boots off until I die."

"Daddy's companion retorted, "Well, we can take care of that right now." And he lifted his gun to shoot the man. "But my father grabbed him and said, "you leave him alone. If you shoot him, I'll shoot you." So they left the Yankee alone…"

I think this is misplaced courtesy, but then, I wasn't there.

ARMY LIFE IN VIRGINIA Letter from George Grenville Bennett July 4, 1863 Burlington, VT pub by Free press association 1895

Pg. 193 July 4, 1863 referring to Gen. Barksdale, of Miss. "A party from the 14th (Vermont) was sent to search for him, but he was not found till near morning. I saw the body soon after the life had left it, next morning, and, having seen him on the floor of Congress, recognized it at once. He was dressed in a suit of the light blueish-gray mixture of cotton and wool, worn commonly by the rebel officers, with gold lace upon the coat sleeves and down the seams of the trousers. His vest thrown open disclosed a ball hole through the breast, and his legs were bandaged and bloody from gunshots through both of them. He had fought without the wig which Speaker Grow once knocked off in the Hall of Representatives, and his bald head and broad face, with open unblinking eyes, lay uncovered in the sunshine. There he lay alone, without a comrade to brush the flies from his corpse…"

The death of another brave Southern officer - the bitter end to another Southern man.

A MISSISSIPPI REBEL IN THE ARMY OF NORTHERN VIRGINIA—The Civil War Memoirs of Private David Holt Ed. by Thomas D. Cocknell & Michael B. Billard pub by La. State Univ. Press 1995

Pg. 200 retreat from Gettysburg July 4, 1863 "We never halted at our old line of breastworks but continued on a night march.The rain fell on the road in about the right proportions, and the tramping troops acted as sort of a mud mill, working the mud into the right consistency to make brick. It clung to our feet and to our clothes. When one stepped into a rut, he found it a hard matter to pull out his feet.

My shoes were of Confederate half-tanned leather, the soles being pegged on. They had had a preliminary soaking all day in that skirmish pit, making them well-prepared for the trick that they contemplated playing on me. It was so dark that it was immpossible to pick the way. I stepped into a rut that was nearly knee-deep. I pulled out one foot, and the sole of that shoe came off. Then I pulled out the other, and the sole of that shoe came off also. There I stood, shoed but shoeless, with uppers but no soles on my feet. I walked on and soon the mud packed into the uppers, so that I carried over ten pounds of mud per foot. I reached down in the dark and cut the strings and scattered the uppers, like the last rose of summer, fondly over the road. My socks held out for awhile, the the bottoms wore out while the mud began packing around my legs inside the socks, as if to take a plaster cast of them.

We marched rapidly, and I had no time to adjust things, so I pulled off the socks and threw them away. Now I had my feet on the ground, and they surely found all the jagged stones within reach. I got out of the road and walked along the side, in the grass. I was getting along first rate, when the brigadier general came along and ordered me to get back into the road. I said I was bare-footed and that the stones cut my feet. He stormed out that he was not going to allow a private to talk back to him, and he called the guard with orders to take me in charge and bring me to headquarters at daylight. The general rode on, and the guard grabbed me. I do not know who the sergeant was, but he said, "Are you David Holt?" I said that I was.

"That general is a fool to expect a barefoot man to walk in that road," he said, "Walk where you can…"

Sgt. Holt was having a very bad day.

CIVIL WAR RESOURCES AT THE TENNESSEE STATE LIBRARY AND ARCHIVE

"On July 5th, 1863, Private William M. Moss of Co. D, First Tennessee, was captured with another unarmed companion. He later described his clothing the day he was captured. "I had on a pair of cotton pants, an old shirt, a pair of old shoes without socks, and an old coon skin hat with a tail behind. The other fellow was dressed about like me. The Federals had all gathered around, and were looking at us like a show..."

Is this what the arm-chair historians mean when they say the Rebs were always well clad and shod, the "Ragged Rebel" being a post-war myth?

PARKER'S VIRGINIA BATTERY by Robert K. Krick pub.by Va. Book Co. 1975

Pg. 175 Retreat from Gettysburg, July 6, 1863 (during the torrential rains which harassed the retreat) "...As one of them complained, "wet clothes...were the 'latest agony' in soldier fashions." Captain Parker may have been the only dry artillerist in the whole column. He claimed that he never once got wet during the entire war, thanks to a carefully contrived set of rain gear. This consisted of a captured oilcloth with a head hole in the center, a slouch hat that "turned the rain like a tin roof," and a pair of waterproof cavalry boots extending six inches above his knees. Parker asserted that this attire had enabled him to ride "two days and nights in a driving rain without getting a drop of water on me."

Pg. 176 July 10 1863 Parker expressed "strong criticism of Lee's order protecting private property, declaring that it had occasioned "great discontent among the officers and men." His men were needing shoes, hats, and clothes, but no one would sell these things to him for Confederate money..."

I agree, these items that were in such dire need should have been impressed be the Confederates. Remember, Parker's Batterymen had captured vast amounts of Yankee supplies not two monthes before, at Chancellorsville, but apparentely were already wearing out.

LETTERS TO AMANDA-The Civil War Letters of Marion Hill Fitzpatrick Army of Northern Virginia ed by Jeffery C. Lowe and Sam Hodges pub by Mercer Univ. Press 1998

Pg. 76 July 6th, 1863 Ferguson Hospital, Lynchburg, Va. (Letter No. 38) Dear Amanda, "I have two shirts, two pr. Drawers, two pr. Pants, one blanket, one small oilcloth, and my overcoat with me. I have the last pants you sent me. They gave the boys in our Reg, just before the last march (a) choice to have their tents hauled or a portion of their knapsacks. Of course they all preferred the knapsacks. They carried one knapsack for every five men. I put a pair of pants and some other little tricks in one and sent them on. I think one of my company that is here will get a furlough before long. If he does he will carry my overcoat home for me, or will carry it to Knoxville and you can get it from their. I shall leave it here with him and if he does not get off home he can sell it for something and save the money for me. There was a general waste of things when our Regt. left the camp. I picked up a nice light blanket and brought it here with me, besides the heavy blanket of my own, but knowing I could not carry it on the march, I sold it the other day for $2.00…I have three pairs of socks with me, I have not wore any hospital clothes here. They have our clothes washed for us gratis once a week…"

Pg. 78 July 20th, 1863 General Hospital 2nd Ward, 3rd Dvision Farmville, Va. (Letter No. 40) Dear Amanda, "I have been fixing up for the trip today. I have my blanket, oilcloth, and clothes out sunning. I have just washed my meat bag and the inside of my haversack, and have them out drying. I had a shirt, a pr. of drawers washed last Saturday, so I will have clean clothes to start with. I have three very good pair of socks. I have learned to darn first rate and I find it a great advantage…"

This hospital has first-rate conditions for the men.

THE FREMANTLE DIARY-A Journal of the Confederacy pub by Burford Books 1954

Pg. 225 6 July, 1863 retreat from Gettysburg "I saw a most laughable spectacle this afternoon-a Negro dressed in full Yankee uniform, with a rifle at full cock, leading along a barefooted white man, with whom he had evidently changed clothes. General Longstreet stopped the pair, and asked the black man what it meant. He replied "The two soldiers in charge of this here Yank have got drunk, so for fear he should escape I have took care of him, and brought him through that little town." The consequential manner of the Negro, and the supreme contempt with which he spoke to his prisoner, were most amusing…"

More evidence of African-Americans serving in the Confederate ranks.

Pg. 235 9 July, 1863 "The hills near Hancock (Md.) were white with Yankee tents, and there were, I believe, from 8000 to 10,000 Federals there. I did not think much of the appearance of the Northern troops. They were certainly dressed in proper uniform, but their clothes were badly fitted and they were often round-shouldered, dirty, and slovenly in appearance; in fact, bad imitations of soldiers. Now, the Confederate has no ambition to imitate the regular soldier at all. He looks the genuine Rebel; but in spite of his bare feet, his ragged clothes, his old rug, and toothbrush stuck like a rose in his buttonhole, (This toothbrush in the buttonhole is a very common custom, and has a most quaint effect.), he has a sort of devil-may-care, reckless, self-confident look, which is decidedly taking."

Yeah, and, more often than not, he is chasing that round-shouldered, dirty, Yankee soldier.

FOOTPRINTS OF A REGIMENT A Recollection of the 1st Georgia Regulars by W.H. Andrews pub by Longstreet Press Atlanta Ga. 1992

Pg. 145 Battle of Waterloo on John's Island July 7 1863 "...The Negroes found out that the troops in front of them were the ones they fought at Olustee, Fla., and did not carrry in the fight as much as a pocket knife. As they were pretty well shod, the boys decided to pull off their shoes and bring them back to the line, but they smelled so bad, could do nothing with them. Tried washing them in the branch, but the more they rubbed the worse they smelt and finally had to throw them away. You may know the boys wanted shoes pretty bad to take them off a dead Negroe's feet...."

HANDLEY LIBRARY ARCHIVES

James A. Miller Collection correspondence C.W. era misc. New Market, Va.

July 7th Camp near Littonsville (near Hagerstown)1863 Dear Julia "...When I sent my over coat home I forgot to tell you that visor was in the pocket which I wish you would take care of. I have a sort of a worstia(?) cap that I am now wearing which I got out in the north west... If you can possibly get me goods for a pair of pants I wish you would do it as the ones I have are about giving out....I did not get but one article during my trip it is goods for a dress. I bought it in a dark stair and at the time thought it was black but when I got to see it by a good light it proves to be brown and not much account. I am ashamed almost to send it to you, if you don't want it it may do for coat lining or some other purpose..."

LEE& JACKSON'S BLOODY TWELTH-Letters of Irby Goodwin Scott First Lieutenant Co. G Putnam Light Infantry Twelth Ga. Vol. Inf. ed. by Johnnie Perry Pearson pub by Univ. Tn. Press 2010

Pg. 128 Hagerstown, Md. July 8th, 1863 Dear Father "...Have me a pair of boots made as soon as you can. I have nearly worn out my shoes. Get Neagle of Eatonton to make them No 9s full size, and high in the instep. You have best have Bud some made he will need them after a while boots or shoes either will do him. Send mine by the first opportunity..."

SWORDS AND ROSES by Joseph Hergescheimer pub. by Afred A. knopf 1929

Pg. 319 July 8 1863 Williams port, Md. The retreat from Gettysburg "…The Confederate army was reduced to the extremities of destitution and hunger; hundreds of men, now, were without shoes, there were no recognizable uniforms; the bottoms of pants were in frazzles; knees were bare and elbows stuck out; hair stuck therough the holes in hats; it was a gaunt army of rags and patches…"

An account of Ragged Rebels, see below.

REBEL PRIVATE FRONT AND REAR-Memoirs of a Confederate Soldier by William A. Fletcher pub by Dutton Books 1995

Pg 87 William Fletcher was with the First Texas Approximately July 8, 1863 retreat from Gettysburg "…We broke camp that evening after dark and started marching again. My shoes were old and so were my clothes. My pants were frazzled and split up to the knees, so I cut them off just below the knees, and thought if I looked like I felt, I was a fright. Short sleeves worn to near point of the elbow, no socks or drawers, and knee breeches. It was not long after leaving camp, marching in mud about six inches deep, I lost the sole of one shoe. I jerked off the upper and tried walking a short distance with one bare foot. It looked like at nearly every step there was a rock to jam between toes as my foot slipped down and foreward. I soon pulled off the other one, thinking that I could walk with less danger to both. This was a mistake, so I soon got out off the road and made my way as best I could through woods and fields, keeping near the road. I found that there was quite a lot of straggling, which was ordinarily done on the side of the road. I traveled all night, and by daylight my feet and legs were well bruised and torn by dewberry vines which always caused me to halt and back out…"

Website ACWS Archives Confederates in Blue- "English Army Cloth" in the A.N.V.

Pg1 "This cloth arrived at the warehouses in Richmond on July 9th, 1863. Records show that this shipment consisted of 18 bales totaling 3,336 yards of 1 ½ yard wide blue gray kersey…Various descriptions have come to light one states "it was a variably toned blue gray wool with a dark hue."…The wool was apparently dyed in two colors and then carded together before spinning into yarn…One story written by a Georgian In Hills Corps wrote he had received clothing that was "blue in color but not like Yankee Blue." He complained that his jacket and trousers did not match…A soldier in the 2nd Georgia, Bennings Brigade, Longstreet's Corps wrote, "sometimes the Govt. would get a supply of fine cloth, and we would get uniforms almost to Blue."…Another report by Augustus Dickert Co. H 3rd S.C. Vols stated the uniforms consisted of "a dark blue round jacket closely fitting."

"Even Union troops had trouble distinguishing Longstreet's men from their own. Lt. C. Clark of the 125th Ohio on viewing Kershaw's Brigade at Chickamauga ordered his men to hold their fire, saying, "at a distance they appeared to wear dusty blue." A volley by Kershaw's men ended the confusion..."

VMI MS# 190

Pg. 152 Florence McCarthy chaplain for the 7th Va. Vol. Inf. Williamsport, Md. July 10, 1863 Dear Sister "...I have been marched nearly to death. In coming from Gettysburg here, we marched three days and two nights without stopping except long enough to cook food. Most of the time it rained and the roads were perfectly awful. My socks have given out, I can buy none, steal none, and it is a matter of impossibility to get a piece of clothing washed. I am lousy and dirty and have no hope of changing flannel for weeks to come. Food has been scarcer than ever. We are now enjoying a resting spell, which has already lasted three days... In all these places (Greencastle, Chambersburg, Williamsport) The Confederate authority opened the stores and compelled the merchants to sell their stocks to the soldier at the regular prices and for Confederate money. But the advanced troops, as usual, got all the plunder. All I could buy was a few buttons and a pair of misses' stockings, which I have worn out. I got stuff for a pair of pants in Williamsport for eight dollars. The last suit Mrs. Cook made for me is coming all to flinders. The lining busts every time the wind blows. My pants in particur are believed to be in a blue way..."

A MISSISSIPPI REBEL IN THE ARMY OF NORTHERN VIRGINIA-The Civil War Memoirs of Private David Holt ed by Thomas Cocknell & Michael B.Billard pub by La. State Univ. Press 1995

Pg. 208 Retreat from Gettysburg, July 10 1863 after crossing the Potomac; "...Several days elapsed before I got rested, and, in the mean time, got excused from all duties. I was not sick, but fagged out and seemed to become more conscious of my feet. They swelled up, and I could not bear to put them on the ground. The surgeon had nothing to put on them that would give relief and suggested a tea made of oak bark.

So off I went into the tanning business and made oak-tanned sole leather out of the hide of my feet "in situ." I greased them with a bacon rind after each soaking in the oak "ooze." It was good treatment, and they rapidly recovered. One day I was called up to the officer's quarters and give a pair of shoes and an outfit of clothes. I was deeply thankful but asked no questions and did not know where they came from.Quartermaster supplies were not being issued, so they must have come from a private source.

It took me over a week to teach my feet how to wear shoes. They would act up and complain at once when they felt the confinement, and I would have to pull the shoes off to pacify them. They acted like spoiled, convalescing babies. I had often heard about "breaking in a pair of shoes," but this was breaking in a pair of feet. They were not amenable to persuasion but deaf to argument and as resentful as a peeved pair of twins..."

RAW PORK AND HARDTACK Civil War Memoir From Manassas to Appomattox ed by Walford D. Swank, Colonel, USAF, Ret. Civil War Heritage Series Vol. X pub by Burd Street Press 1996

Pg. 46 July 10 1863 Three brothers, Robert Catlett Cave, Rueben Lindsey Cave, & Lindsey Wallace Cave-return from Gettysburg; "...The long, toilsome marches, the desparate fighting and the manifold hardships of the campaign had told upon them heavily. They were more ragged and unkempt, more worn and haggard, more slow in their movements, and more grave and silent than I had ever before seen them. They did not seem beaten or cowed; they seemed rather to be conscious of adverse fortune and grimly determined to face it bravely. But they looked dog-tired, and, as someone standing near me said, they seemed to be ashamed of coming back to their friends without having accomplished all that was hoped for..."

This was the first, and only major defeat of Lee's Army.

U.S. ARMY HERITAGE AND EDUCATION CENTER

Letters of John C. Fiser July 12 1863 Camp Near Hagerstown, Md. Dear Wife; "...You might send me about ten dollars for I don't know when we will draw & send me two shirts of some kind. I would like to have check or calico if you could get it but I guess you can't if not send me two linen ones, & I don't know but what got to have a pair of pants. I have worn these very much on this march as it has been a very hard trip..."

LETTERS FROM THE STONEWALL BRIGADE Ted Barcay, Liberty Hall Volunteers by Charles W. Turner pub by Rockbridge Pub. Co. 1992

Pg. 92 Hagerstown, Md. July 13, 1863 after the Battle of Gettysburg Dear Sister "...The army is in fine spirits, but dirty, ragged, and barefooted. I have had on my clothes nearly a month. My pants are nearly worn out, so you may make me up two undershirts, two pairs of drawers, three pairs of socks, a pair of pants and a jacket if you think you can make it to fit. If not; I think I can have one made here; do not make the clothes too large, make them up and keep them until we get back to Virginia.

I can make out with what I have until we get across the river, which I think will not be long. The army is in such a bad condition as far as clothes are concerned and our means of transportation are so limited and provisions so far to haul that we are compelled to recross the river...."

Pg. 94 July 14, 1863 camp near Winchester Dear Sister "...But for fear that you may not get my last letter, I will give you a list of my wants-two shirts, two pairs of drawers, pair of pants, three pairs of socks (woolen), boots and jacket, etc.,etc...."

RED CLAY TO RICHMOND by John J. Fox pub by Angls Valley Press 2006

PG. 191 July 14, 1863 "Lee's army arrived back in Virginia in poor physical shape. The long marching and heavy fighting had exacted a heavy toll. Witnesses noted the bad condition of the men in Hill's corps. many of those troops walked barefooted and nearly naked..."

LIFE IN THE CONFEDERATE ARMY: BEING PERSONAL EXPEIENCES OF A PRIVATE SOLDIER IN THE CONFEDERATE ARMY by Arthur P. Ford and Marion Johnstone Ford pub by Neale Pub. Co. 1905

Pg. 53 Retreat from Gettysburg July 16th, 1863 "It was on the march this day that an amusing incident occurred. I had not owned a pair of socks since I left James island a month before, and my shoes were in such tatterd condition that I could keep the uppers and soles together only by tying them with several leather strings, but most of my toes stuck out very conspicuously..."

LEE& JACKSON'S BLOODY TWELTH-Letters of Irby Goodwin Scott First Lieutenant Co. G Putnam Light Infantry Twelth Ga. Vol. Inf. ed. by Johnnie Perry Pearson pub by Univ. Tn. Press 2010

Pg. 130 Camped Near Darkesville, Va. July 16th, 1863 Dear Father, "...I hope soon to have a clean suit of cloths for I am pretty dirty just about this time. I do not think we made any thing by our campaign into Maryland and Pennsylvania. Our army is badly in need of cloths and shoes. A great many are bare footed. Mine are nearly worn out. I shall draw a pair from the government if possible as soon as the wagons come up from Stantoun (Staunton)..."

FAR, FAR FROM HOME-The Wartime Letters of Dick and Tally Simpson, 3rd South Carolina Volunteers ed by Guy R. Everso & Edward W. Simpson Jr. pub. by Oxford Univ. Press 1994

Pg. 255 July 17th/63 Bunker's Hill, Va. Tally Simpson to Mary Simpson (Letter105) (Retreat from Gettysburg) Dear Sister, "The night we left Harestown was the worst I ever saw. The mud was almost knee deep and about as thick as corn meal batter. We waded through it like horses, and such a squashing you never heard. I believe I had over fifteen or twenty pounds of mud clinging to my shoes and pants. Poor Harry stuck to it like a man. His shoes gave out completely, and he was compelled to go barefooted. Marching over these turnpikes nearly ruined his feet. But fortunately yesterday, while coming through Martinsburg, he bought an old pair of shoes. They were too short and he cut the toes off, and it looked funny to see him trudging along in the mud with his toes sticking about an inch or two out of his shoes."

Still, better than no shoes at all.

Pg. 256 July 18th/63 Bunker's Hill, Va. Tally Simpson to Caroline Miller (Letter 106) My Dear Carrie, "…I venture to assert that one third of the men are barefooted or almost destitute of necessary clothing. There is one company in this regt. which has fifteen men entirely without shoes and consequently unfit for duty. This is at least half the company alluded to…"

DIARIES, LETTERS AND RECOLLECTION OF THE WAR BETWEEN THE STATES Vol III Winchester, Frederick Co. Historical Society Papers 1955

Pg. 100 Diary and Recollections of I. Norval Baker-Private, Co. F, 18th Virginia Cavalry, Imboden's Brigade Retreat from Gettysburg July 18, 1863 "…Some of our company saw a fine looking valise laying in the street and asked Lieutenant Siebert if he would let him get it. He got it, it was locked and he struck it with the butt of his gun and it opened. It contained a very fine officer's suit and some underclothes and a testament on top.… Our regiment was about the last to cross the river, we went into camp about a mile or so south of the river with orders to unsaddle our horses. Our horses back's were raw with ulcers, one and two inches deep and full of maggots. The green flies had put up a job on us, our blankets were full of maggots and rotten, our saddles had from a pint to a quart of maggots in them and we had to run them out with hot water and soap and it was monthes before the horses' backs were cured. The people tell us this is the 18th of July, 1863.…Well, we have cleaned the maggots from out saddles, blankets and horses' backs and laid everything out to dry in a beautiful July sun…"

I'm surprised the horses could still function and more surprised that they recovered.

BRIGHT & GLOOMY DAYS

Pg. 71 Camp near Darkesville 6 miles from Martinsburg, Va. July 20 1863 Dear Father, "As to clothing, I am the happy possessor of one shirt, one pair of drawers & several pair socks; condition:-shirt, extremely dirty (publish it not) thickly inhabited by as an industrious a set of inhabitants as ever you saw; drawers, of an improved kind, made (by wearing) in two pieces, so that if desired can be taken off one leg, without removing the other, likewise dirty & containing a large population; socks quite new & very good. So you see what I own. I will write for what clothing I think I can carry with me, but do not send that new suit unless I write for it..."

If this soldier isn't a ragged Rebel, then I don't know who is.

LETTERS FROM THE STONEWALL BRIGADE Ted Barcay, Liberty Hall Volunteers by Charles W. Turner pub by Rockbridge Pub. Co. 1992

Pg. 97 Martinsburg, W.Va. July 20, 1863 Dear Sister "...If it is in the range of human exertion I wish you would send me the clothing; you cannot imagine my condition. I have no seat in my pants, the legs are worn out, have had but one pair of socks, which are worn out completely, my shirt literally rotted off me, but I was so fortunate as to get a white shirt and a pair of drawers, which both are now so lousy that I can scarcecely bear them.

This evening I caught between 50 and 100 on my shirt and drawers. Excuse plain speaking, but it is certainly not an exaggerated state of affairs.

I would not trouble you so often if I could possibly stand it or there was any chance of getting them here. I offered to give fifty dollars today for under clothing but neither love nor money can get them..."

HANDLEY LIBRARY ARCHIVES-Letters of Stanley Russell Co H. 13th Virginia Infantry

July 21, 1863 Wichester, (Va) Dear Papa,'...If we should leave this country, I want Ma to send my winter clothing to Mr. Nathan Coway at Staunton provided we do not get back home until that time and I am still living..."

LEE& JACKSON'S BLOODY TWELTH-Letters of Irby Goodwin Scott First Lieutenant Co. G Putnam Light Infantry Twelth Ga. Vol. Inf. ed. by Johnnie Perry Pearson pub by Univ. Tn. Press 2010

Pg. 131 Camp near Luray, Va. July 26th, 1863 Dear Father, "...Our army needs rest very bad for the men are worn down marching foot bare &c. A great many are barefooted though there has been a great many shoes distributed. I am almost barefoot myself and not much prospect of getting any soon. I can make out a few days longer and then I may get a chance to draw a pair from the government. I wish you to send my boots by the first good opportunity.... Have Bud some made. He can draw some here when he needs them..."

This a rather confusing quote, as the soldier first says to make him and his brother a pair of boots because he doesn't think he can draw any, then, in the last sentence, stating his brother could "draw some here when he needs them."

A TEXAN IN SEARCH OF A FIGHT Press of J.S. Hill & Co. 1901

Pg 163 Letter from John Camden West July 27, 1863 "…and take our position in the open field, where we threw up breastworks and awaited the advance of the enemy. We remained here the entire fourth day of July, and such another fourth I never expect to spend. We had no meat and very little bread for two days. Had not taken off our accouterments duing the time, and the rain poured incessantly, so that the water on the level plain was two or three inches deep. On the following evening we discovered that the enemy were satisfied and were moving off. We were in no condition to follow. We remained on the battlefield until 2 o'clock at night, during which time I snatched a nap or two by lying of three rails, which kept me above water. In the battle I threw away my haversack and contents, except a flannel shirt and a pair of socks, which I tucked under my belt. I lost the socks and have been for several days without any, but have not experienced the inconvienence I expected, except in having my ankles considerably lacerated by briars in marching across the fields. I have had no change of clothing since, and hence have been compelled to throw away my undershirt, which had become a harber for innumerable body lice. Don't blush or be shocked, no true soldier is free from them, and I will scrub well before I come home. I am having my only underwear washed to-day, and owing to a large rent in my pants, would be subject to arrest in any well managed city, for improper exposure of my person in a public place…I have experienced no inconvienence in health for want of clothing. Since I have been here Allen Killingsworth has given me a pair of socks,and while I write this sentence Charly Darby sends me another pair; so I have two pair, and feel flush on socks. I have a good pair of pants in Richmond, and another for winter in Columbia, so don't trouble yourself by thinking of me or my misfortunes, but smile, chat and keep well…"

I think it inhumane to throw away a shirt with a thriving population of body lice. I mean, what are they going to do? I expect they'll starve.

Camp near Culpeper, C.H. July 27th 1863 Dear Brother, "…If I were seated in a comfortable chair instead of having my naked buttocks upon the sand (for my last article of underwear is in the wash and the seat of my pants is in Pennsylvania…"

VOICES FROM COMPANY D Diaries by the Greensboro Guards, Fifth Alabama Infantry Regiment, Army of Northern Virginia ed. by G. Ward Hubbs pub by Univ. of Georgia Press 2003

Pg. 191 July 27 1863 SP retreat from Gettysburg "…The wagons parked to-night from Criglersville- a small shabby village. I (was) really ashamed to be in a white persons house in the plight in which I was-my pants tattered and torn; but soldiers far from home & where they neither know, nor are known by any one, are sort of privileged characters, & expect to be looked upon with a great many allowances…"

AS RECORDED IN THE POCKET DIARIES OF PRIVATE ROBERT A. MOORE, Co. G, 17th Miss. Regt. Confederate Guards, Holy Springs, Mississippi ed. by James w. Silver pub by McCowat-Mercer Press 1959

Pg. 158 Wednesday, July 29th, 1863 camp near Culpeper Ct. House "…The army is improving very fast indeed & will soon be in fine condition again. Is being well supplied with shoes & clothing…"

Its about time!

LEE & JACKSON'S BLOODYTWELTH-Letters of Irby Goodwin Scott First Lieutenant Co. G Putnam Light Infantry Twelth Ga. Vol. Inf. ed. by Johnnie Perry Pearson pub by Univ. Tn. Press 2010

Pg. 135 Camped Near Madison Court House July 30th, 1863 Dear Mother, "…About clothing you wanted to know what I would need. I want Father to have me a pair of shoes made for winter. I can draw a pair of shoes from the Government that will do for the summer, the shoes that I wore from home are nearly worn out. I will need some pants next fall. My coat will last me all winter. My jeans coat at home will do when I need another. I will also need some socks, that is about all I will need…"

His jeans coat is probably a civilian sack coat.

FOUR YEARS IN THE CONFEDERATE ARTILLERY

Pg. 56 July 30 (1863) Mr. Jack Noel got to camp from our homes bringing us home rations and clothing. We had lost all our clothes, when our cook and wagons were captured in Pennsylvania. It was an accident that our knapsacks happened to be in the wagon that night on which the wagons were taken. Capt. Frank Dean, our quartermaster, ever thoughtful of his men, had said to us the rainy night we left Gettysburg, "Boys, the wagon, which brings you your supper tonight, will be emply after you get your supper out of it, and you can put your knapsacks in that wagon. It will help you a little and you have a hard and wet night in front of you and need all the help you can get." We thanked him and threw our knapsacks in the wagon, expecting to get them the next day, but Mr. Yank scooped up that wagon that night and we never saw those knapsacks again. Hence, we welcomed Mr. Noel and his load. Mrs. Winston had sent him..."

Clothing from home, not waiting for the government to resupply them.

MEMOIRS OF LIFE IN & OUT OF THE ARMY IN VA. DURING THE WAR BETWEEN THE STATES. By Capt. Charles Blackford, "The Wise Troop" Vol. 1

Vol.2 Pg. 86 July 30, 1863 "...Kirkpatrick went home this morning to get some clothes. He lost all he had with his wagon in Pennsylvania, and his servant also. Eugene ought to get a leave on the same ground. I would almost sacrifice my scanty wardrobe for the same privilege...."

WEEP NOT FOR ME, DEAR MOTHER by Elizabeth Whitley Roberson pub. by Pelican Pub. Co. 1996 16th Georgia Regiment of Infantry Pvt. Eli Landers (age 19)

Pg. 111 August 1863 "...I've got a very bad cold after washing yesterday. I washed my clothes and had to go without a shirt till it got dry. I wore the skin off my hands rubbing. I washed 2 shirts, 1 pair of drawers and 1 pair of pants. I hung them out to dry and some fellow took one of my shirts off of the bush so I lost the shirt and my labor and had to buy another one..."

REDCOLLECTIONS OF A CONFEDERATE STAFF OFFICER by G. Moxley Sorrel pub by Bantam Books 1992

Pg. 151 August 1863 after the return to Virginia, camping near the Rapidan River, "Supplies of clothing and shoes had come down from Richmond and the ranks looked decidedly better."

An account of government supply, though no description as to color or cut.

THE CONFEDERATE VETERAN VOL. XXXI 1923

Pg. 61 Feb. 1923 The Lone Star Guards by B.L. Aycock "...I returned to my company, encamped near Fredericksburg, in August, but was not well enough to shoulder a musket and Colonel Baine appointed me ordinance sergeant. The company had recently returned from Pennsylvania, having fought at Gettysburg. Here I saw my comrades barefooted after their march into Pennsylvania..."

Website BRISTOE STATION-CS GUIDELINES

The Road to Bristoe Station Aug.1-Oct. 20, 1863, by William D. Henderson : John R. Cooke's Brigade from N.C. "…A few days back, following the arrival of the North Carolina State owned blockade runner Ad-Vance the pride of the state's fleet in the port of Wilmington this excellent and large brigade had received new uniforms made in England. The men were proud of their grey jackets and blue trousers. As the men formed for the advance, anticipating combat, most of the men in Cooke's Brigade took off their fresh uniforms and placed them in their knapsacks. They donned their old tattered clothing for the hard work ahead…"

State of North Carolina supply. Actually, I understand this. I wouldn't have wanted to stain/tear my new uniform. Notice the mention of blue pants issued.

LETTERS FROM THE STONEWALL BRIGADE Ted Barcay, Liberty Hall Volunteers by Charles W. Turner pub by Rockbridge Pub. Co. 1992

Pg. 99 "Camp Stonewall" near Orange Court House August 3, 1863 Dear Sister "…This morning I took off the only suit I have and had them washed, paying $1.00 for the three pieces, and now I feel I am clean, a feeling I have been stranger to for a long time. But this suit is white and soon will become dirty and we seldom have a chance to wash, so I suppose I will be dirty until winter puts an end to marching, as an active campaign seems to be the order of the day…"

By white suit, does he mean the drab-colored (undyed wool) uniforms issued?

Send down my clothes by the first safe opportunity. I saw Mr. Leech yesterday, that would have been a good opportunity if they were ready…."

LETTERS OF THREE LIGHTFOOT BROTHERS 1861-1864 Edmund Coy Burnett, ed. Savannah Ga. Privately Pub. 1942

Pg. 55 Letter from William Edwin Lightfoot to Fransina McGarity Aug. 6 1863 "…Cousin Frank is almost crazy about going to the war. He thinks he will have to go in the course of a week or two. He has been trying to get quartermasters position in the 37th Ala. Regt. But I don't think he will succeed. I spoke of me having a lum(b)er jacket mad(e) when I left home. I have declined the idea of having it made. You may make me a pair of pants I need them very much…I will name the articles that I want I want one sheet one pillow and a couple of towels and a pair of gloves…P.S. Send me the box as soon as possible for I need some of the things very much…"

I imagine a lumber jacket would look much like a sack coat.

THE STILLWELL LETTERS

Headquarters Brigade Camp 20 miles from Fredericksburg, August 6, 1863 Dear Molly, "12 miles from Chancellorsville where the last battle was fought. At Fredericksburg, it is very likely that we will have to fight there again as the enemy is moving that way. Oh, the suffering that our troops has to suffer. Just think of the searching rays of sun of August and men marching with their baggage on their back. I have seen men fall by the roadside fainting almost every day. Marching barefooted, their clothes almost torn off them and (on) half rations…"

So, still not fully uniformed by August 6.

WRITING & FIGHTING THE CONFEDERATE WAR The Letters of Peter Wellington Alexander ed by William B. Styple pub by Belle Grove Pub. Co. 2002

Pg. 146 Orange County, Va. August 7, 1863 "Having in a previous letter spoken of shoes for the men, I need only add now that they should be made of the best leather to be had, and they should be roomy, have wide substantial bottoms, and fit snugly around the ankles. Their clothing should also be roomy. Close-fitting garments not only chafe the wearer on a march, but they soon wear out…."

From what wev'e read, it seems like all garments and shoes soon wear out.

"DEAR MOTHER: DON'T GRIEVE ABOUT ME. IF I GET KILLED, I'LL ONLY BE DEAD." ed. by Mills Lane pub by The Beehive Press 1977

Pg. 259 Edgar Richardson to his Sister Fredericksburg Viginia August 7, 1863 Dear Sister: "…Sister, I don't want my jacket and pants sent to me, as I have drawn some from the government. But I wish the first chance you get you would send me some drawers, shirts, colored if you can get them, and socks…."

Government supply

HANDLEY LIBRARY ARCHIVES

James A. Miller Collection correspondence C.W. era misc. New Market, Va.

Camp at Orange Court House Aug. 7th, 1863 "…I wish you would get me calico or some of that N.C. goods for two shirts and make them for me as my old ones are getting very much worn. I received the new one by Casper, and there is no likelyhood of goods getting any lower for some time to come…I am very glad that you succeeded in getting my clothes made, and will now wait patiently for them…"

THE CRY IS WAR, WAR, WAR The Civil War Correspondence of Lts. Burwell Thomas Cotton and George Job Huntley, 34th Regiment North Carolina Troops by Michael W. Taylor pub by Morningside Press 1994

Pg.151 Near Orange C.H., Va. August 8th, 1863 "…I want you and Sarah to make me two colored shirts as a white shirt gets so dingy in camp. Take some of my money and by some wool to make me a pair of pants. I will need some drawers. Homespun will do for them. I will need them if I live until winter. I must make out with as little as I can while we are marching…"

LEE& JACKSON'S BLOODY TWELTH-Letters of Irby Goodwin Scott First Lieutenant Co. G Putnam Light Infantry Twelth Ga. Vol. Inf. ed. by Johnnie Perry Pearson pub by Univ. Tn. Press 2010

Pg. 136 Orange Court House Va. August 9th, 1863 Dear Father, "…Franklin (a slave) has lost all his clothes except a shirt.He put them on a wagon on the march and when he came to get them they were gone. He picked up a good light coat somewhere and put his new in his knapsack so that was lost too. I guess he will now learn from bad experience that it will not do to trust wagoners or any one else too much. He can get shirts and things here plenty until fall…The company are all well and are now pretty well all shod. I have been unable so far to procure shoes. My old ones do finely in camp. I understand there is some in camp to sell. I will look them up this morning. I expect we will draw money today. I am undetermined as yet whether to draw any this time or not. With what I hve on hand and what is owing to me, I will have between 2 & 3 hundred dollars on hand but there are two monthes commissary bill to pay, a pr. shoes to buy and so on…"

FAR, FAR FROM HOME-The Wartime Letters of Dick and Tally Simpson, 3rd South Carolina Volunteers by Guy R. Everson & Edward W. Simpson pub by Oxford Univ. Press 1994

Pg. 270 Aug. 9th/63 Camp 3rd S.C. Regt. Tally Simpson to Anna Simpson (Letter110) Dear Sister, "…Last winter when I was out of clothes and blankets I had to draw straws for those given to the company by the government, I invariably came out the "little end of the horn."

Pg. 276 Aug. 25/63 Camp 3rd S.C. Regt. Tally Simpson to Caroline Miller (Letter 112) Dear Sister, "…Tell Ma to send me some socks. I have not owned a pair since I was in Maryland. I have not as yet received the shoes Pa sent…"

LEE& JACKSON'S BLOODY TWELTH-Letters of Irby Goodwin Scott First Lieutenant Co. G Putnam Light Infantry Twelth Ga. Vol. Inf. ed. by Johnnie Perry Pearson pub by Univ. Tn. Press 2010

Pg. 138 Orange Court House Va. August 9th, 1863 Dear Father, "…As to what clothing we will need this fall I hardly know. I have never worn my new suit yet. I don't think I shall wear my coat until I can have it altered in the collar. The collar is so long and wide. I can't tell what Dusenberry (Dusenbury) was thinking about. He shall never cut another for me. I shall want some pants, probably a jean coat which I do not want grey. I prefer a very dark brown or some other deep color, a pr. or so of drawers and some other little things. Bud will also need the same…"

This officer is well supplied as to clothing. Notice he wants a jeans coat, not gray, but brown.

"DEAR MOTHER: DON'T GRIEVE ABOUT ME. IF I GET KILLED, I'LL ONLY BE DEAD." ed. by Mills Lane pub by The Beehive Press 1977

Pg. 261 William Sillwell to his wife Fredericksburg Virginia August 13, 1863 My dear affectionate Mollie: "…Mollie, you desired to know whether I wanted my drawers white or colored. Colored is preferred if convenient, but if not it don't make any difference. Don't be uneasy about my socks. I have one pair of woolen stockings and a pair of cotton socks yet. I can make them do some time or during the summer. I can do very well yet, but thought you had better send them when you could, so you may do so…"

VOICES FROM CEMETARY HILL-The Civil War Diary, Reports and Letters of Colonel William Henry Asbury Speer (1861-1865) ed. by Allen Paul Speer pub by The Overmountain Press 1997

Pg 112 Camp near Orange Court House August 14/63 "…Mother, I want you to have me two shirts made if you can. I want them colored so they will not show dirt & I don't care how strong they are. My old calicoes is about to give out. I have had them over a year…"

KEEP ALL MY LETTERS The Civil War Letters of Richard Henry Brooks, 51st Ga. Inf. ed. by Katherine Holland pub by Mercer Univ. Press, Macon, Ga. 2003

Pg. 99 Camp 20 miles from Fredericksburg Va. August 15th, 1863 "...I want you to send me two pair of socks by Pool or someone of this company when they come as socks is very hard to get here an tell them if I am not with the company to sell them an send you the money for they are worth two dollars a pair here..."
coat, pants, drawers, socks and probably one or two shirts..."

LEE& JACKSON'S BLOODY TWELTH-Letters of Irby Goodwin Scott First Lieutenant Co. G Putnam Light Infantry Twelth Ga. Vol. Inf. ed. by Johnnie Perry Pearson pub by Univ. Tn. Press 2010

Pg. 139 Orange C.H. Va. August 15th, 1863 Dear Father, "...At the rates of prices now we who have to buy our rations and clothing will not have much spare money to lay up...I did want to send home enough to pay for my suit of uniform and boots and may do it yet. I am on the lookout for a pistol for you which will cost $40 that is a good one and I won't but any other sort. They are not very plenty here. The most of the boys have sent them home or otherwise disposed of them...I did not think to write about our shirts in my last letter. I have one good one, which I have never worn. Bud will need some, our vests are good. We will want coats, pants, socks, shirts, over shirts, drawers &c. almost a little of everything..."

This clothing request has got to be a bit overwhelming for a family.

GRANDFATHER'S JOURNAL (Franklin Lafayette Riley) Company B Sixteenth Mississippi Infantry Volunteers Harris' Brigade Mahone's Division Hill's Cops, A.N.V. May 27, 1861-July 15, 1865 ed by Austin C. Dobbins pub by Morningside Press1988

Pg. 157 Sunday-Monday, Aug. 15-17, 1863 Camp near Orange Court House "...Only the animals-hogs especially- are difficult to get along with. They sometimes show disrespect for our flag and attack out men while they are on picket. Just yesterday a hog tried to attack us. To protect ourselves we had to give him the bayonet. Then, of course, we couldn't waste the meat...."

It's a shame these men have to watch for these viscious, disloyal hogs. If they are not careful, a soldier could get injured.

LEE& JACKSON'S BLOODY TWELTH-Letters of Irby Goodwin Scott First Lieutenant Co. G Putnam Light Infantry Twelth Ga. Vol. Inf. ed. by Johnnie Perry Pearson pub by Univ. Tn. Press 2010

Pg. 140 Orange Court House Va. August 20th, 1863 Dear Mother, "...The company are all well. I have not been able to get a pair of shoes as yet, though I expect to send to Richmond in a few days by someone. While here in camps my old ones answer every purpose. There are two men in the company who are entirely barefooted. I don't see why the government does not furnish us shoes and clothing. We have received none since we have been in this camp. I succeeded in getting my coat collar fixed by a tailor in the 4th Ga regt. It only cost me one dollar when if I had it done in Richmond it would have cost five or ten...."

BRIGHT & GLOOMY DAYS-The Civil War Correspondence of Capt Charles Frederick Bahnson, A Moravian Confederate ed by Sarah Bahnson pub by Chapman Univ. TN. Press 2003

Pg. 74-75 Camp near Orange C.H. Va. Aug. 20th, 1863 Dear Father, "...I have only time to write you a few lines; please send me some stuff to make shirts & drawers out of if you can. I got some clothing now, enough for present use, Government Goods, not the nicest or best, but much better than the dirty rags I had on. ..."

Another reference to shoddy government goods, see below.

WEEP NOT FOR ME, DEAR MOTHER by Elizabeth Whitley Roberson pub. by Pelican Pub. Co. 1996

16th Georgia Regiment of Infantry the "Flint Hill Grays" Pvt. Eli Landers (age 19)

Pg. 159 Orange Co. Va. Aug. 21st 1863 Dear Mother "...Sam Dyer will get one (a 24-day furlough) one of his co. drawed for it and he got it. He is so proud he can't hardly behave himself. Momma, if he comes I wish you would send me a pair of sox for I hant got nun and I don't like to do without and as you are making me a coat don't think that I am a great big man and make it too large. I am no heavier than I was when I left home. If you could git the pattern that Capt. Cain's coat was cut by, you could exactly fit me for his coat fits me all around but his pattern may be over in Milton where you can't git it. I don't need no clothing at present. I could draw but the government clothes is so sorry and dear I had rather draw the money and send home rather than draw the clothes..."

VOICES FROM COMPANY D Diaries by the Greensboro Guards, Fifth Alabama Infantry Regiment, Army of Northern Virginia ed. by G. Ward Hubbs pub y Univ. of Georgia Press 2003

Pg. 195 August 22 1863 SP "… There was a large lot of clothing distributed to-day. Our Co. got 11 jackets, 18pr. Pants. a no. of shirts and drawers & several prs. Shoes & socks. The clothing was badly needed. I got a jacket & pr. Pants…."

Is that what this soldier calls a large lot of cl.othing?

WELCOME THE HOUR OF CONFLICT-William Cowan McClellan &The 9th Alabama ed by John CV. Carter pub by Univ Al Press 2007

Pg. 245 August 22, 1863 Orange CH William McClellan to Matilda McClellan Dear Sister, "…I drew a very good suit of clothes [next three lines are illedgible]…"

HADLEY LIBRARY ARCHIVES-Letters Stanley H. Russell Co H. 13th Virginia Regiment

August 22, 1863 Camp near Oranger C.H. Dear Sister,'…I want Ma to save me one or two of those U.S. blankets. Tell Papa to have me a pair of Boots made for next winter. I suppose he can get Mr. Davis to make them, boots that are full broad for Eddy will fit me…"

"DEAR MOTHER: DON'T GRIEVE ABOUT ME. IF I GET KILLED, I'LL ONLY BE DEAD." ed. by Mills Lane pub by The Beehive Press 1977

Pg. 263 Jefferson DeVotie to his Parents James Island South Carolia August 23, 1863 Dear Parents: "…Tell Ma to take good care of my uniform and cloth coat and not let moths get to either to destroy them. I have clothing enough for the present, I believe. Take good care that Jewett does not get hold of my fine cloth coat, for if he does I will never hear of it again or if he does allow me to see it again it would be worthless to me or anyone else… I would not take $150 for it, because I could not get another for twice the money. Don't let anyone have it for any purpose whatever…"

LETTERS TO AMANDA-The Civil War Letters of Marion Hill Fitzpatrick, Army of Northern Virginia ed by Jeffery C. Lowe and sam Hodges pub by Mercer Univ. Press 1998

Pg. 81 Aug. 23rd, 1863 Camp Near Orange Court house, Va. (Letter No. 41) Dear Amanda, "…Cout I want you to send me some sewing thread. I have used all that black you gave me and the white ball, which I have a good deal yet, is too coarse for any of the needles I have now. Also a little red pepper, not much, for I shall loose it. Do not send any clothes. I have as many as I can take care of. I patch my clothes and darn my socks regular and they last more than twice as long by it. I also wash them regular now and can wash as clean and nice as anybody. We draw some soap and I bought 50 cts. Worth so I have a good supply, now…"

BRIGHT & GLOOMY DAYS-The Civil War Correspondence of Capt Charles Frederick Bahnson, A Moravian Confederate ed by Sarah Bahnson Chapman Pub by Univ. TN. Press 2003

Pg. 76 same camp Aug. 24th 1863 Dear Father "…I understand that Maj. P. has received a large supply of English cloth of very superior quality & though I do not need it at present, I would like to secure a portion of it before all is purchased & if Mr. Leinbeck is still in his office, he might be able to assist me. I have seen sample of the cloth & it will make one of the handsomest uniforms that I have ever seen. For coats the cloth is grey, more the color of Mr. Fries' cloth, (than the English cloth I have); but only a trifle darker; & for the pants and vest a beautiful dark blue. I think it is more durable than the other English goods that we got in Richmond…."

Quite a statement when you need a government official to assist you in getting cloth for your uniform.

DEAR SISTER-CIVIL WAR LETTERS TO A SISTER IN ALABAMA Frank Anderson Chappell pub. by Branch Springs Pub. 2002 (Third Alabama Regiment)

Camp near Orange Court house Va. Aug 25 1863 Dear Father "…You said in your letter if I was needing any clothing to let you know. I am very well off in that line except shirts and socks. I would like to have a pair of socks as I have not had a pair since last winter and no chance of getting any…"

BRIGHT & GLOOMY DAYS-The Civil War Correspondence of Capt Charles Frederick Bahnson, A Moravian Confederate ed by Sarah Bahnson Chapman pub by Univ. TN. Press 2003

Pg. 78 Orange Court House, Va. August 26th 1863 My Dear Father "…As to that new suit of clothes, just keep it for me, as I will want something decent to wear while with you. Have button holes made in coat & vest, coat-seven in a row in front, vest-eight. The stripes on the collar need not be put on now, if you have not yet sewed them on, if they are on, just let them remain. It would not hurt to line the pants, if any suitable material can be procured, as the summer is passed, & I had them made for that season…."

LEE& JACKSON'S BLOODY TWELTH-Letters of Irby Goodwin Scott First Lieutenant Co. G Putnam Light Infantry Twelth Ga. Vol. Inf. ed. by Johnnie Perry Pearson pub by Univ. Tn. Press 2010

Pg. 142 Orange Court house Va. August 27th, 1863 Dear Father, "…Mother may cut my coat straight breasted, but to make the same alterations in the collar…"

HANDLEY LIBRARY ARCHIVES

James A. Miller Collection correspondence C.W. era misc. New Market, Va.

Camp near Orange Court house Aug. 28th, 1863 Dear Julia, When you get this letter if you can find a pair of old boot legs you can have me a pair footed instead of all new…"

A good example of leather recycling.

LETTERS OF WILLIAM F. WAGNER, CONFEDERATE SOLDIER ed. by Joe M. Hatley and Linda B. Huffman pub, by Broadfoot's Bookmark 1983

Pg 72 Camp Near Orange Court House Va August 28th 1863…"Dear I can say to you that we have some rite cole weather hear for the several last mornings it was nearly cole enough for frost Dear try and send me a coat if you can with some Boddy Dear I want the coat large Enough so I can ware it over my womas (A wamus is a outer jacket made of tough, long-lasting fabric. Webster's New World Dictionary of the American Laguage College Edition-ed.)Dear I think that Brown Coat I have at home would be large Enough if you can make the sleaves wider they always a most too litle and try and send me that wolin shirt a gain some time when it gits Coleder Dear my jacket was stolen at Winchester but you need not send me one til I write for it …"

He wants his civilian overcoat, which would be the only one available to him, unless he could capture a Yankee coat

HANDLEY LIBRARY ARCHIVES, WINCHESTER, VA Letters of henry Jennings Co A 5th Regiment Virginia Volunteers Jackson's Brigade

August the 28th/63 (no heading) "…Aunt I want you to make me two pair flannel drawers and send them to me by October if you can…"

BRIGHT & GLOOMY DAYS-The Civil War Correspondence of Capt Charles Frederick Bahnson, A Moravian Confederate ed by Sarah Bahnson pub by Chapman Univ. TN. Press 2003

Pg. 80 August 31st 1863 Dear Father "…I am glad you succeeded in obtaining some stuff for shirts 7 drawers; I think two of each (shirts & drawers) will be enough for the present, but you can use your own descretion as regards purchasing more at present. At first I was sorry I did not have my new suit with me, but now I am very well pleased with the idea of having a new suit at home to jump into in case I can get off to see you. Please have the button holes made seven on each side of the coat, & eight on the vest. I intend to get some more cloth at Raleigh, & give it over into your hands to save for me till I need it more than I do at present. …"

LEE'S TAR HEELS- The Pettigrew-Kirkland- McRae Brigade by Earl J. Hess pub by Univ of North Carolina 2002

Sept. 1863 "While the the officers worked to refill the ranks, quartermasters tried to find enough clothing "to suppy deficiencies" in their men's outfits. Nearly every company of the 11th and 44th ordered a wide range of goods, from shoes, jackets, pants, underwear, shirts and socks to caps, fly tents, axes and spades. They received enough to outfit about twenty five men. Quarterly returns of property already in the hands of the men indicated that the other regiments in the brigade had no clothing to spare. There were two pairs of underwear and two shirts for each soldier in Co. F, 52nd North Carolina, but only half as many knapsacks and canteens as needed. Company commanders managed to fill most of the glaring holes in the supply picture by October."

WEBSITE-BLUE AND GRAY MARCHING

Sept 1863 In the Texas Brigade, George Todd of the First recalled: 'We drew new uniforms as we passed through Richmond on our way to Atlanta, Ga. These, especially the pants, were almost blue and caused us to be mistaken for the enemy later on the field of Chickamauga…"

LETTERS FROM THE STONEWALL BRIGADE Ted Barcay, Liberty Hall Volunteers by Charles W. Turner pub by Rockbridge Pub. Co. 1992

Pg. 103 Sept. 1, 1863 after the Grand Review Dear Sister "…Today the soldiers determined to have a sham review, so they appointed their Gens. And Cols. From the ugliest men in the brigade (of course I would not come in under that score) fixed themselves up in Shanghai twinings(ed. footnote-A "Shanghai" was a long frock coat or a hat with a black crown and lighter fabric under the brim; a "Shanghai drill" at West Point was a rapid manner of marching; and "Shanghais" described long, slender legs. It has been suggested that "Shanghai twinings" may refer to shanghaied (kidnapped) Yankee uniforms.)- provided themselves with mules and such specimens of horse flesh as you saw last winter and altogether it was quite a complete affair…"

A CONFEDERATE SURGEON'S LETTERS TO HIS WIFE Spencer Glascow Welch, Surgeon Thirteenth S. Ca. Vols., McGowans Brigade pub by Neale Pub. Co. 1911

Pg 76 Camp near Orange Courthouse, Va. Sept. 1, 1863 "I got a new pair of shoes from the Government for six dollars. Billie's shoes are good yet, because I lent him a pair of mine to march in, and he wore them out and saved his own. Marching on these turnpike roads is very hard on shoes, and our army becomes barefooted in a short time."

Yeah, wev'e seen that shoes don't last long, for whatever reason.

THE JOURNAL OF WOMEN'S CIVIL WAR HISTORY-Accounts of the Sacrifice, Achievement and Service of American Women 1861-1865 ed. by Eileen Conklin pub by Thomas Pub. 2001

Pg. 62 Sept. 2, 1863 Quartermaster Lovelace wrote to suggest that the only acceptable answer to the question of what soldiers need would be: "First, blankets, Second, blankets, and Third, More blankets." He went on to say, "Send us blankets and coverlats that will enable us to sleep warm and comfortable at night and we can then stand the rigors of winter by day and Yankeedom combined.' The societies of Liberty Hill, Bethany, and Mount Vernon received the enthusiastic thanks of Captain B.M. Talbert for the "liberal supply of winter clothing." These societies were not the only ones working for the soldiers. Two "spirited" young ladies, Miss Tilly smith and Miss Betty Watson, forwarded the following items to Col. Bacon's regiment in September: 10 blankets, 10 pairs of drawers, 3 cotton shirts, 6 flannel shirts, 9 towels and handkerchiefs, 11 pairs cotton socks, 1 pair wool socks, 3 tin wash-pans, 1 comfort and 2 bed ticks. These patriots, too young to be admitted to the aid societies, nevertheless worked on their own to supply the soldier's needs. Throughout the region women and children were busy weaving cloth and knitting for the soldiers…"

According to this, there was another clothing drive for the winter of 1863

FROM CORSICANA TO APPOMATTOX by John Spencer pub by The Texas Press 1984

Pg. 69 After the retreat from Gettysburg. "…New shoes and uniforms and light duty make Fredericksburg an enjoyable camp for the men from Texas. They bivouac here until September 2, go on to Port Royal, and guard the river crossings until Sptember 7 Then they pack up again for a march to Milford, where they board railroad cars for Richmond…"

LEE& JACKSON'S BLOODYTWELTH-Letters of Irby Goodwin Scott First Lieutenant Co. G Putnam Light Infantry Twelth Ga. Vol. Inf. ed. by Johnnie Perry pub by Pearson Univ. Tn. Press 2010

Pg. 142 Camped near Orange C.H. Va. Sept. 3rd, 1863 Dear Father, "…Mother wanted to know whether I would need another coat or not. I think my coat will last all the winter…"

KEEP ALL MY LETTERS The Civil War Letters of Richard Henry Brooks, 51st Ga. Inf. ed. by Katherine Holland pub by Mercer Univ. Press, Macon, Ga. 2003

Pg. 103 Camp near Walters Hotel Va. Sept. the 6th, 1863 "…My Dear when you send me them socks I want you to send me a pair of spectacle cases for the case that I have got is ruined an I will get my glasses broke if I dont get a new case. Try to by it in town an if you cant find any in town try all the old women in the country. I do not want spectacles. I only want a good mettle case. I have tried in all the towns I have had the chance to and can not find the mettle case…."

This is the only reference I've found of a common soldier wearing glasses.

REBEL BROTHERS-The Civil War Letters of the Truehearts (from Galveston, Texas) ed. by Edward B. Williams pub by Texas A&M Univ. Press 1995

Pg. 171 Near Rixieville on Hazel River, Culpepper Co. Va. 8 September, 1863 Dear Bow, "…I am sitting under a pine tree on the side of a hill, and writing on the brim of my cap. Have drawn some clothes from the Q.M. and can get plenty more. In my short experience have learned to wash my clothes and catch lice very expertly…It is utterly impossible to keep entirely clear of them, camping on the sandy ground with thousands of other men…H.M.T."

A reference to generous government supply.

HANDLEY LIBRARY ARCHIVES

James A. Miller Collection correspondence C.W. era misc. New Market, Va.

Camp near Orange Court House Sept. 8th, 1863 Dear Julia, "…I put on the clothes today they fit first rate and are very much admired by all who have seen them, the vest does very well it will be too warm for several weeks yet, the sleeves of the coat are about ½ inch too long though not eough to go to the trouble of changing, the suit does very well indeed it fit better than I had expected they would before I received them, I was very much in need of them. The shirts are very nice I have not put any of the last ones on yet but I put the one you sent by Casper on this morning. I have the cravat on it is the first that I have had on since last spring, I still have the one you fixed up last spring in my knapsack. The socks I will not wear at present. I have still two good pair of cotton socks on hand, clothing costs a good deal now but they are better than so much money without clothing. It is a fine thing to have a good wife to make things for one when there is no such thing as buying them, if it had not been for you I would have run out of of things long since…Was Fidler paid for the hat and also for the one that he made last spring if not I wish you would pay him for both…I suppose you better keep my flannels on hand for the present also my over coat, as I am not now in need of them nor will be for some time to come, and our transportation is so limited that we can't haul scarecely any thing now…I will send my old coat and a few other things by the first opportunity. I wish you would take care of the buttons as I may want them put on another coat…"

LEE & JACKSON'S BLOODY TWELTH-Letters of Irby Goodwin Scott First Lieutenant Co. G Putnam Light Infantry Twelth Ga. Vol. Inf. ed. by Johnnie Perry pub by Pearson Univ. Tn. Press 2010

Pg. 143 Orange Court House Va. Sept. 10th, 1863 Dear Father, "…Leather is very high higher than I anticipated. If you could get a pair of old boot legs and have them footed it would save a good deal of leather and also expense. I left a pair of old ones at home which I reckon would do very well. I have a splendid pair of shoes and do not want any more at the present. I want a pair of boots for winter. So you need not send me any. I know boots will be very high but I have the money to pay for them and while I am in the war I am going for comfort if it takes all I make. You may have my coat cut straight breasted, but tell mother not to have the collar so wide and long. My uniform pants are a little too long. Say half an inch, as to hats we can make out a while longer. I expect we can get them easier here than you can…Tell mother I will get all the buttons I can which are eagerly sought after by all the soldiers for the coats we get have wooden Buttons. If I cannot get any you need not trouble about them for I can have those on my old coat put on, as I will have no use for that when I get the new one…"

Another request for old boot legs to be re-footed in order to save money. I was unaware of the widespread use of wooden buttuns on uniform jackets.

TRUE TALES OF THE SOUTH AT WAR-How Soldiers Fought and Families Lived 1861-1865 Collected and ed by Clarence Poe pub by Univ. of N.C. Press 1961

Pg. 85 Col. L.L. Polk's Wartime Letters Spt. 10, 1863 "There are seventy-six in my company now and we have three small vessels to cook in. They seldom get cool. There are not a dozen blankets in the company. Many of the men lie on leaves, three or four together, and cover with one blanket. It is hard, but these noble fellows cannot endorse the course of the thoughtless and misguided who think of a cowardly and ruinous submission."

How fortunate to have such soldiers in this army.

LETTERS TO AMANDA-The Civil War Letters of Marion Hill Fitzpatrick, Army of Northern Virginia ed by Jeffery C. Lowe and Sam Hodges pub by Mercer Univ. Press 1998

Pg. 85 Sept. 10th, 1863 Camp Near Orange Courthouse, Va. (Letter No. 43) Dear Amanda, "Well, Cout, like a true and heroic Southern woman, I suppose you are making my clothes anyhow. I shall appreciate them the more when I get them because you worked and made them for me, but really I did not intend to burden you that task, but you say and I know it is so that it is a pleasure to you to fix my clothes for me. I am proud of you and often say and know that I have the best wife in the world. Do not send them to me yet as we may have much marching to do before we go into winter quarters and I do not need them now nohow. You need not make me a coat as the one I have will last me another winter. There is not a crack in it yet except a small hole in the tail which I neatly patched. I will need a vest, make it military style buttoned straight up in front. As to overshirts I believe I had rather you would not make any atall, for I will have to throw them away when we start to march and when I pull them off I catch cold sure so I had rather do without them altogether. I tell you the less a soldier is burdened with the better he can get along. ..."

Pg. 91 Sept. 27th, 1863 Camp Near Orange Court House, Va.(Letter No. 45) Dear Amanda, "...I have thread enough to last me a long time now. I let the boys that have none have it whenever they want any, and I also do a good deal of sewing for them. Some of them cannot patch yet..."

RED CLAY TO GEORGIA by John J. Fox pub by Angle Valley Press 2006

Pg. 199 Sept. 11, 1863 Private Woodson D. Moon, writing to his wife "…He figured he had enough clothes to survive the winter, and urged his family not to send him any more., "for it I have to move, I will have to throw them away." The holes in the bottoms of his shoes created a problem. "The shoes that I have would do to wear in dry weather if they were half-soled. If you have the leather I want you to send me two half-soles and I will put them on myself." He closed this letter with a short poem. "When you see remember me, though seven hundred miles between us be."… "Wagonloads of equipment, food and clothing reached the men over the next several weeks. These items helped to bolster the well-being and morale of the troops…"

OK, here comes the resupply, probably from the governemt.

HANDLEY LIBRARY ARCHIVES

James A. Miller Collection correspondence C.W. era misc. New Market, Va.

Camp near Orange Court House Sept. 13th, 1863 Dear Julia, "…I left my old coat there to send over by the first opportunity if he should go as far as N.M. (New Market) he will take it along. We had a Corps review on last Tuesday it was a splendid affair I suppose there were about 20,000 troops passed in review all the generals were there. My new suit came in just in the right time,…It has been very dry here until this morning. We had quite a hard shower it commenced raining about 3 o'clock and came down the hill in a large stream and filled up the trench around our tent and it came sweeping through in a hurry wetting out bed clothing and making it very muddy. We all got up and put on our clothes and stayed up day. I got my stockings out and having no clean cotton ones I was compelled to put my boots on without stockings…it is rather close for me the confederates (lice) are too hard to keep off if I put on clean clothes one day in less than 48 hours I will have some on me so I am uneasy all the time…"

I don't think I could get used to that amoint of body lice.

CORRESPONDENCE OF JOHNATHAN WORTH Edwards& Broughton 1909

Pg. 656 Letter from Johnathan Worth to David Gaston Worth and N.G. Daniel, September13, 1863 Raleigh "I have no decent clothes for the winter, excepting an overcoat. Can you get cloth and trimmings to make me a coat, pants and vest-good black-and needful trimmings for $300 or less? If so, buy it for me. If you can't get the black, any other color, except light grey, will do. I want good quality-or none…"

Did he not want light gray as it shows dirt too easily?

THE CONFEDERATE LETTER OF BENJAMIN H. FREEMAN Compiled & Edited by Stuart T. Wright pub by Exposition Press 1974

Pg. 28 Sept 19 1863 Camp Near Orange C.H. Dear Father and Mother; "…This morning I (requisitioned?) for a Blanket, Jacket, Over Coat Pants, Socks, Shirt and shoes. I will get them in a few days. I have drawn a new knapsack since I left home…Pa I want you to have my boots fixed up for the winter. I will send for them when I think I (need) them for they was a friend to me last winter…"

I wonder how much of his requisition he received.

U.S. ARMY HERITAGE & EDUCATION CENTER

James T.Binion, Co. F, 10th Georgia Infantry in a letter to his brother, summer 1863 "…I want you to tell sistet to make me some calico shirts and let me no when she get them done and I send for them …"

Camp near Orange Court House Sept. 20, 1863 Dear Sis "…Your last 2 letters with the hat was duly received and highly appreciated. I am sorry the hat was much too small. I soled it to a fellow who had none for $7.00 and will send you the money when we are payed off, which will be in a few days…"

WELCOME THE HOUR OF CONFLICT-William Cowan McClellan & The 9th Alabama ed by John C. Carter pub by Univ Al Press 2007

Pg. 247 Sept 20th, 1863 Rapidan River William McClellan to Matila McClellan Dear Sister,"…I wrote to you some time ago asking if those two negroes came back, if so to send me one if you all could spare him. I could get along a great deal better with a Negro. He could help me along in a great many ways, if I had him he could do me cooking, Washing, bat a balanket occasionally. I have tried time and time again to Wash but cannot. I blister my hands before I get a Shirt Washed…You must send me some cloths by the first opportunity, don't send them unless you are certain they will come through, cloths are too scarce to be lost now…"

Notice the attitude regarding a "servant," he speaks about one as if he were a piece of equipment. He does speak the truth regarding clothing being too precious to lose/have stolen now.

CIVIL WAR LETTERS OF CAPTAIN A.B. MULLIGAN, FIFTH SOUTH CAROLINA CAVALRY-BUTLER'S DIVISION-HAMPTON'S CORPS 1861-1865 by Olin Fulmer Hutchinson pub by The Reprint Co. 1992

Pg. 89 20th Sept. 1863 Kenansville, (NC) My Dear Mother and Sisters,"…I am wanting my winter clothing now---undershirts, wool drawers, socks, blankets, overcoat, &c. Do have them all ready so that you can put them up in a moments notice for I may get some member of Capt. Harlan's Co. to bring them to me as many of his men live in Union and Spartanburg Districts…"

23rd Sept. 1863 "I am needing my blankets as well as my clothing. Frank (slave) is without a blanket and needs one or two badly. If Patsy can get along comfortable without the larger gray blanket I gave her last winter I wish you would have it washed and I will give it to Frank. You can give Patsy the white blanket instead…."

Now this soldier is very considerate regarding his servant's comfort/ well-being.

LETTERS OF WILLIAM F. WAGNER, CONFEDERATE SOLDIER ed. by Joe M. Hatley and Linda B. Huffman pub by Broadfoot's Bookmark 1983

Pg 74 Camp Near Sumers Ford Rapidan River Va Sept 21st 1863 …"Dear Wife I riten a letter the other day and stated what I wanted Dear I will name it a gain Dear I want a pair of shoes and socks if you can send them so you know that I will git them and that coat and wolin shirt Dear I am nearly bare footit and don't know when I can draw yet and if we draw they are nothing but cloath shoes "…"

Another reference to cloth shoes being issued, this soldier obviously doesn't want them.

DEAR IRVIE, DEAR LUCY-The Civil War Letters of Capt. Irving A Buck, General Cleburne's AAG & Family pub by Buck Pub. Co. 2002

Pg. 184 Sept. 22, 1863 Home-Night One Half Nine O'clock Dear Alvin, "I wish we had something nice to send you by Mr. Bowman but until you all lick the blockade at Charleston I am afraid we will not be able to find material for doing work for you again shortly…" Yours Fondly, Lucie

UNIFORMS OF THE CIVIL WAR by Lord, Wise pub by A.S. Barnes & Co. 1970

Pg. 62 Sept.23 1863 Charles Halleck, An English visitor in Richmond, Virginia in a letter to the Burmuda Gazette wrote that the army was receiving new clothing, "Already have the motley hues of the rank and file given place in a great measure to a neat uniform of gray jackets and trousers, trousers of light blue!"

Issue of blue pants again, but I wonder what percentage of the motley hues have been replaced by these gray jackets and blue pants, these British observers are sometimes quite unreliable in their enthusiasm for the Rebal cause.

HANDLEY LIBRARY ARCHIVES-James A. Miller Collection correspondence C.W. era misc. New Market, Va.

On the Plank Road between Fredericksburg and Culpeper Sept. 27th, 1863 Dear Julia, I have two Yankee blankets one saddle blanket and a thin single cotton comfort, Dr. Barns has one good blanket, we have them when the wagon is up but sometimes we are caught without the wagon and only have my oil clothes and saddle blanket which was the case for 3or 4 nights last week…When you send my over coat I wish you would send me that visor or cap that was in the coat pocket. I was unfortunate enough the other day to lose my sleeping cap…"

Hey, don't laugh at a sleeping cap when camping out doors in cool weather, they are quite comfortable.

LEE& JACKSON'S BLOODY TWELTH-Letters of Irby Goodwin Scott First Lieutenant Co. G Putnam Light Infantry Twelth Ga. Vol. Inf. ed. by Johnnie Perry Pearson pub by Univ. Tn. Press 2010

Pg. 145 Morton's Ford Rapidan River Va. Sept. 30th, 1863 Dear Father, "…If you cannot get buttons for my coat I can take those off the coat I have now. I am a great mind to send my old coat home but I dislike to wear my new one every day. Such clothes cost too much…"

THE STONEWALL BRIGADE James I. Robertson Jr. La. State Univ. Press 1961

Pg. 2 fall, 1863 "…On several occasions grateful citizens of the Valley sent money, food and clothing to the soldiers. Private Gaeribaldi expressed his appreciation by writing: "I must tell you now that there was sent here from Staunton a whole lot of clothes, especially for this Brigade, and that we all had (a) chance to anything we want in the way of shoes, drawers, shirts, pants, jackets…This was by far the best clothing for winter we drew for a long time, so that we are all of this Brigade supplied with good warm clothing…"

If only he could say that regarding government clothes.

DIARIES, LETTERS AND RECOLLECTION OF THE WAR BETWEEN THE STATES Vol III Winchester, Frederick Co. Historical Society Papers 1955

Pg. 120 "The weather is now very cold and my winter clothes at my fathers in Frederick County. I am out of money, have not been paid off in October, 1863. Never drew but one suit of government clothes, as my two sisters, Caroline and Anne, have been making my clothes. Father raised the sheep and had the wool cardedin rolls and my two sisters spun the yarn and had it woven and cut and made my clothes in the military style...."

RECOLLECTIONS AND LETTERS OF GENERAL ROBERT E. LEE by his Son, Capt. Robert E. Lee pub by Garden City Pub. 1926

Pg 103 Oct. 1863 Letter to the Quartermaster-General at Richmond after his movement around General Meade's right to Manassas: "...The want of supplies of shoes, clothing and blankets is very great. Nothing but my unwillingness to expose the men to the hardships that would have resulted from moving them into Loudon (County) in their present condition induced me to return to the Rhappahanock. But I was adverse to marching them over the rough roads of that region, at a season too,where frosts were certain and snow probable, unless they were better provided to encounter them without suffering. I should, otherwise have endeavored to detain General Meade near the Potomac, if I could not throw him to the north side..."

Pg. 104 Oct. 1863 "In a letter of the same time to the Honorable James A Seddon, Secretary of War: "...If General Meade is deposed to remain quiet where he is, it was my intention, provided the army could be supplied with clothing, to advance and threaten his position. Nothing prevented my continuing on this front but the destitute condition of the men, thousands of whom are barefooted, a greater number partially shod, and nearly all without overcoats, blankets or warm clothing. I think the sublimest sight was the cheerfulness and alacrity exhibited by this army in the pursuit of the enemy under the trials and privations to which it was exposed..."

The war would have been very different in 1864 if the Confederate Army couldv'e been clothed and fed in the winter of 1863.

JAMES A. GRAHAM (Captain, Company G) "Twenty-Seventh Regiment" in Histories of Several Regiments and Battalions from North Carolina in the Great War, 1861-1865 Voll II, Walter Clarke ed. pub by Nash Bros. 1905

Pg. 444 Bistoe Station, Oct. 1863 "...One incident of this fight I will mention, which shows the coolness of some men under all circumstances. We had jut drawn new clothing-grey jackets and blue pants- and our men, anxious to keep their clothing bright and new, had most of them put on their old clothes during the march and had them on at this fight. As we were falling back up the hill, Private Laughinghouse of Company E., from Pitt county, finding his knapsack too heavy, determined to throw it away, but as he did not wish to lose his new clothes-having his old ones on- he stopped, changed clothes under this heavy fire, and then picking up his blanket and gun, made his way up the hill unhurt..."

Yes, that is coolness under fire.

A REBEL WAR CLERK'S DIARY AT THE CONFEDERATE STATES CAPITOL vol. 2 pub by Lippincott 7 Co. 1866

Pg. 482 Diary of John Beauchamp Jones October 1863 "...Mr. Jepthe Fowlkes of Aberdeen, Miss. Sends a proposition to supply our army with 200,000 suits of clothing 50,000 pairs of shoes, etc., etc.,from the United States, provided he be allowed to give cotton in return. Mr. Randolph made a contract with him last year, of this nature, which our government revoked afterward. We shall see what will be done now..."

I'm sure the northern factories would have been happy to make clothing and shoes for the Rebels in exchange for cotton. Something like this was done for Confederate P.O.W.s (see pow chapter)

FRENCH HARDING Civil War Memoirs ed. by Victor L. Thacker pub by McClain Printing Co. Inc., Parsons W.Va. 2001

Pg. 110 Oct. 1863 "...Thousands of them were but scantily clothed in tattered garments, and almost an equal number were entirely shoeless or practically so..."

Here we are in Oct. and the Rebels are ragged; either once again or still.

THE LIBERTY RIFLES-RESEARCH English Cloth on Cooke's Foot Cavalry:

English Uniforms and the 27th N.C.T. Andrew Turner "...Capt. John Sloan of Company B states: "Governor Vance's faithful ship, the "Advance" had come in heavily laden, and we were proudly and splendidly dressed in some of the grey cloth of its cargo...Men in the 27th also mention being issued English blankets. Private Thompson wrote his sister about the blankets, "I am sorry that mother sent me a blanket because I have drawn one a great deal better than the one she sent an English blanket."

These new articles of clothing were issued to the 27th on October 8 (1863) while encamped near Gordonsville, Va. Writing to his sister on October 9th about the new uniforms Private Charles Watson states: "Our regiment received a uniform yesterday and I sent my old clothes in a box with the other boys…I didn't send anything but a coat and pair (of) pants…"

U. S. ARMY HERITAGE AND EDUCATION CENTER

Oct. 10, 1863 wife of Lt. Col. W. Leroy Brown, 5th Virginia Battalion Local Defense Troops Chantilly, Va. My Dearest Husband "…Don't forget I charge you to send or bring me all your clothes that need to have anything done to them and if you conclude to have your old black great coat dyed (but I think it is hardly worth it) you must not see how it shows in the county for, it would in total cost more than that old coat is worth to have it dyed, $24.00 some time ago for a ladie's dress and of course much more for your coat. I think taking everything into consideration how much higher everything is daily getting that you had better now get the trimmings for your great coat, (the new one) and have it cut and sent to me to have made by Mrs. Callahan, who I tell you knows all about it. I think I would hardly have the new cloth cut up in a cape when your shawl will answer every purpose the cape will…"

What a shrew! I wonder if he has to ask permission to change his clothes! I bet that old black great coat has a special meaning for him, and she is going to discard it as soon as she can. Also, it would be more military to wear a cape rather than a shawl. Poor man.

FROM HUNTSVILLE TO APPOMATTOX R.T. Coles History of 4th Regiment, Alabama Volunter Infantry C.S.A. Army of Northern Virginia ed by Frank D. Stocker pub by Univ of Tenn. Press 1996

Pg. 157 Oct 10, 1863 "During the night of the 10th, General Meade retreated across the Rappahannock and evaded all attepts to bring him to bay. General Meade finally crossed Bull Run and reached the fortification at Centreville. General Lee then gave up the chase and withdrew his army to its former position south of the Rapidan, giving as the reason for withdrawing the following: "Nothing prevented my continuing in his front but the desptitute condition of the men, thousands of whom were barefooted, a greated number partially shod, and nearly all without overcoats, blankets or warm clothing. I think the sublimest sight of the war was the cheerfulness and alacrity exhibited by this army in the pursuit of the enemy under all trials and privations to which it was exposed."

More than mortal men.

V.M.I. Archives MS#367 Triplett

Oct. 11th/63 My Dear Cousin "…I went in the hospital and came out on Saturday in time to see about James' boots. I visited every shoemaker in Lexington and found it impossible to reply with your request, their excuse is that they have too much work on hand or owing to the scarcity of leather they are unable to fill any more orders, I may be able to get them some time hence, but I suppose you want them immediately, if not, write me and I will do my best for you…"

A TEXAN IN SEARCH OF A FIGHT by John Camden West pub by Press of J.S. Hill & Co. 1901

October 13, 1863 "…My thoughts are all the news I have-we seldom get a paper here. We have been in the mud for over a month in an almost continuous rain, and are not allowed to send to Richmond for blankets and over-coats, which many of us have there, because it will not be thought of until the hospitals are filled with pneumonia and pleurisy.

When some sagacious surgeon, who has been in a comfortable tent, with plenty of blankets will suddenly discover that a barefooted man cannot well keep warm under one blanket which has not been thoroughly dry for three weeks. I have been quite blessed, I was barefoot about a week ago, but then the water was too deep for shoes, so it made very little difference…"

Its common sense to get these soldiers their blankets and clothing from storage.

VMI Archives MS# 421

Yarborough Virginia Military Institute. Oct. 15th, 1863 My Dear Parents: "…The comfort is a very nice one, it is just the (?) I wanted…My overcoat is done, it is a very nice one, I had it cut in a little different style from the cadet overcoats, as I was advised to have it cut so by Mr. Vanderdice & Mr. Cruchfield. I like this style better than the cadet style, Mr. V. says it is worth 25 dollars more cut in this style than it is, as the Institute only offers 6 dollars for the making of a coat…"

CIVIL WAR LETTERS OF CAPTAIN A.B. MULLIGAN, Co. B, Fifth South Carolina Cavalry-Butler's Division-Hampton's Corps 1861-1865 by Olin Fulmer Hutchinson pub by The Reprint Co. 1992

Pg. 94 Oct. 18, 1863 Kenansville, N.C. My very Dear Mother, "I learned about an hour ago that Mr. Lynch of my Co had need of a furlough to visit his father's family in Spartanburg. I immediately went to work putting up 88 pounds of bacon which I had bought at $1 per pound to send by him. It is put up in a champaign basket. I also send a fine shotgun and a package containing my blue sash coat and lined sash and my white pants by him."

He doesn't say whether these are the white cotton pants that were issued starting summer 1863 and he was sending them home for the winter, or were they undyed wool?

RED CLAY TO RICHMOND by John J. Fox pub by Angle Valley Press 2006

Pg. 206 Oct. 18, 1863 Private James Garrett "…It is tolerable cool here now. [W]e have had several rite heavy frost hear lately. [W]e are suffering for blankets. [W]e have got plenty of other clothing. [W]e ly on the ground and cover with our blankets. [W]e have no tents only some little Yankee tents though with all this we are well generally…He requested that his family send him a box as soon as possible with a bed quilt, some butter, a bottle of brandy and some socks. Everything else he needed, could be drawn from the government…"

Confidence in government issue.

HANDLEY LIBRARY ARCHIVES

James A. Miller Collection correspondence C.W. era misc. New Market, Va.

Culpeper Court House Oct. 19th, 1863 Dear Julia, Dr. Barns lost one of my blankets on this trip so we are now one blanket less than we were. I wish you would send my boots and blankets as soon as you can as I am very much in need of my boots…"

LIFE AND LETTERS OF ROBERT EDWARD LEE, SOLDIER AND MAN pub by Neale Pub. Co. 1906

Pg. 486 Letter from Robert E. Lee to Mary Ann Randolph Custis Lee Oct., 19 n1863 "…I have returned to the Rappahanock. I did not pursue with the main army beyond Bristoe or Broad Run. Our advance went as far as Bull Run, where the enemy was entrenched, extending his right as far as Chantilly, in the yard of which he was building a redoubt. I could have thrown him further back, but I saw no chance of bringing him to battle, and it would only have served to fatigue our troops by advancing further. If they had been properly provided with clothes I would certainly have endeavored to have thrown them north of the Potomac, but thousands were barefooted, thousands with fragments of shoes, and all without overcoats, blankets, or warm clothing. I could not bear to expose them to certain suffering on an uncertain issue…"

This is one of the reasons we love him so.

LETTERS TO AMANDA-The Civil war Letters of Marion Hill Fitzpatrick ed by Jeffery C. Lowe and Sam Hodges pub by Mercer Univ. Press 1998

Pg. 95 Oct. 20th, 1863 Camp Near Rappahannock River, Va. (Letter No. 47) Dear Amanda "…My shoes are worn out but I will draw some soon I hope. I have the same shoes I wore home…"

Pg. 96 Oct. 29th, 1863 Camp Near Rappahannock River, Va. (Letter No. 48) Dear Amanda, "…You can fix my clothes and send them by some safe chance. John Wilder may be coming before a great while. There is a talk of sending Capt. Brown, our Q.M., home on a detail to bring clothes to us. If he goes that will be the safest chance. I am in no hurry them. Be sure to send me some soap. You could send that by Henry Pope it you could get it to Knoxville but you have nobody to attend to such things now.

I am writing with ink of my own make which nis simply polk berries squeezed out. I want you to put in a little copperain your next letter to put in it. They say it will turn it black and make it more indelible…"

The Army of Northern Virginia is still giving furloughs for men to go home in order to bring back clothing.

LETTERS FROM A SURGEON OF THE CIVIL WAR by John Gardener Perry pub by Little, Brown & Co. 1906

October 22, 1863 "…At this period of the war blue Federal uniforms were frequently taken from the battlefields and worn by Confederate soldiers…"

Where has this man been? His observation is only about two years late.

HANDLEY LIBRARY ARCHIVES-Letters of Stanley H. Russell Co H. 13th Virginia Regiment

Oct. 22,1863 Camp near Brandy Station (Va) Dear Sister,"...I am getting very scarce of clothing have but one pair of drawers and they are nearly worn out, will soon have but one shirt..."

16th TENNESSEE VOLUNTEER INFANTRY REGIMENT :Clothing, Arms and Equipment (website)

23 Oct.63 at Greenbrier Ridge Va. Some Militia "wore a kind of overcoat with a large cape attached. The boys of the 16th Tennessee at this place recieved coats of the kind, which they called "militia,' a name by which this kind of garment was familiarly known during the remainder of the war..."

Does this mean they were issued militia overcoats?

During 1863 some Confederates were seen "wearing overcoats of English frieze, whose material had run the blockade,homespun Negro cloth, dyed with the juice of the butternut or other vegetable tincture."

Any great coat was more likely to be that of an acquired Federal one, especially in the later years of the war when "nearly every overcoat in the army-was one of Uncle Sam's "but often dyed to change the color."

A CIVIL WAR MARIAGE IN VIRGINIA: Reminiscences and Letters by Carrie Ester Spencer pub by Carr Pub. Co. 1956

Pg. 197 October 24, 1863 Letter from Green Berry Samuels to Katheleen Boone Samuels Camp Brandy Station My Dear Wife, "...Try and get some coarse cotton for me for socks,the constant marches have worn my socks entirely out and I am almost barefooted. I am trying to get some leather for a pair of boots but have not succeeded as yet. I will try and get some in Rockingham (County). I have one pair of pants left and they are very dirty and well worn. My hat is a mere nothing as full of holes as a sieve. I had hoped to have supplied all my deficiencies by this time from the Yankees, but unfortunately they gave us no opportunity. I shall try very hard to supply myself before coming home, as I suppose there is nothing to be gotten about F.R. (Front Royal?). I am really ashamed of my appearance and will not come to see you until I can improve my wardrobe. Should you be able to procure any clothes for me in Warren (County) do so. Mr. Ptty might make me a coat like my Confederate Uniform coat; as for the pants I want them a good deal larger in the legs than my gray pants, they were too small for the service. Be sure and have them long enough ...I believe I have two pair of black pants, the one heavier stuff than the other. You might use this pair to cut out by the length is right but make the new pants larger in the legs…"

A HISTORY OF THE SOUTHERN CONFEDERACY Clement Eaton pub, by The MacMillan Co. 1954

Pg. 138-9 "…Robert Keane wrote in his diary, October 25, 1863:" Our troops in Lee's army are barefooted-failure to provide shoes and blankets during all this year conclusive of mismanagementof Q.M.D. Ordinance department is conducted with greatly more energy and so has got control of foreign transportation…" On August 7, 1863 Pres. Davis appointed Brigadier General Alexander R, Lawton to head the Quartermaster dept. "…the quartermaster had the idvidious job of impressing manufactured goods and other articles needed by the army. Furthermore, as Lawton pointed out, the soldiers were notoriously careless and extravagant in throwing away clothing that encumbered them and often sold or bartered their surplus clothing. However, he reported on January 27, 1865, that, contrary to the impression in the country that the army had been poorly supplied, "with the exception of great coats and flannel underwear the army has been fully provided. In substantiation of his contention he listed large amounts of clothing issued in the latter half of 1864, such as 104,199 jackets, 140,578 pants and 167,862 pairs of shoes for Lee's army ans 45,421 jackets, 102,864 pants, and 102,558 pairs of shoes for the Army of Tennessee…"

This issue is answered in the chapter for 1865.

LETTERS FROM THE STONEWALL BRIGADE Ted Barcay, Liberty Hall Volunteers by Charles W. Turner pub by Rockbridge Pub. Co. 1992

Pg. 109 Oct. 26, 1863 camp at Brandy Station Dear Sister "…The day after we got to this place Chapin came down with my overcoat, shirt, and the remnants of my box….My overcoat fits elegantly and I will find it quite pleasant these cold mornings…"

LETTERS OF WILLIAM F. WAGNER, CONFEDERATE SOLDIER ed. by Joe M. Hatley and Linda B. Huffman pub, by Broadfoot's Bookmark 1983

Pg 78 Camp Near Brandys Station Va Oct 26th 1863 …"Dear I can say to you that I haint got no shoes yet onley some old once that I found I kept pooting on ole shoes till I got a tolerably good ole pair onley they Rub my feet some they are ole and hard but better than none they got some shoes this Morneing but not half Enough to supply they men thare are somr bare footit and lots Jest got ole peeses of shoes Dera try and me a pair as soon as you can for it is hard telling when I can draw a pair hear and send me a pair of galises to, if you pleas mine is all I had found 2 pair but they was too old to be any a count and so I need a pair…"

Pvt. Wagner reports on the inadequate issue of shoes "not half Enough."

HANDLEY LIBRARY ARCHIVES-Letters of Stanley H. Russell Co H. 13th Virginia Regiment

Oct. 28, 1863 Camp near Brandy Station (Va) Dear Papa "…I sent to Gordonsville yesterday for my overcoat expect to get it today if it is lost which I think unlikely…I am sorry you took my clothes to Harrisonburg wish you had kept them until you came down. I wish you would write to me with whom you left them I may get someone to bring them down write as soon as you get this I am worse off for under clothes and pants than anything else. There is no agency in Harrisonburg for forwarding articles. The only one is in Richmond. Let me know if you can have me a pair of boots made…"

CADET GRAY & BUTTERNUT BROWN by Thomas M. Arlikas pub by Thomas Pub 2006

"At the Battle of Kelly's Ford in November 1863, members of Hay's Louisiana Brigade shocked their Yankee captors with fine new uniforms: "The prisoners taken here were better clothed than any we had seen before. All were provided with overcoats and jackets of a much better material than our own. They were of English Manufacture, much darker then the United States uniform, and this furnished conclusive evidence of successful blockade running…."

Yes it did, but there isn't any mention of issuing overcoats of English cloth.

LETTERS TO AMANDA-The Civil War Letters of Marion Hill Fitzpatrick, Army of Northern Va. ed by Jeffery C. Lowe and Sam Hodges pub by Mercer Univ. Press 1998

Pg. 99 Nov. 2nd, 1863 Camp Near Rappahanock Station Va. (Letter No. 49) Dear Amanda, "…I throwed away my knapsack or the one that Drew Webb and I had when we started on our last tramp, but I drawed another since we came here. I have no use for a knapsack on a march but they are very useful in camps…

Cout, it is a serious truth that there are men in our Regt. that have been entirely barefooted till a day or two ago, and have but one inferior suit of clothes and not a sign of a blanket, overcoat, or anything atall to lie on or cover with. They build a fire and lie down on the ground before it and sleep, when it is cold enough to freeze a man well wrapped up. But they will now soon be supplied with blankets and clothing. Mose and I have fixed some logs all around and put it full of leaves like a hog bed which we sleep on and cover with our blankets…"

GRANDFATHER'S JOURNAL (Franklin Lafayette Riley) Company B Sixteenth Mississippi Infantry Volunteers Harris' Brigade Mahone's Division Hill's Corps, A.N.V. May 27, 1861-July 15, 1865 ed by Austin C. Dobbins pub by Morningside Press 1988

Pg. 167 Sunday-Tuesday, Nov. 1-3, 1863 Clear/cool. Sun., pay-day, Dress Parade. Wagons brought a number of old blankets and items that had been sent off by the regiment earlier..."

Here's an account of the return of stored clothing and blankets.

THE PAINFUL NEWS I HAVE TO WRITE-Letters and Diaries of Four Hite Brothers of Page County in the Service of the Confederacy Army of Northern Virginia Series Stonewall Brigade ed.by Harlan R. Jessup pub by Butternut & Blue 1998

Pg. 158 Isaac Hite to father (Diana Is the wife of David Hite) Camp near Brandy St. Tuesday Nov 3rd 1863 "...If Diana has made my hat I wish you would send it down by Martin Gander. I shall soon be bareheaded and barefooted. A requisition was again sent in this morning for shoes and clothes, but whether we can get them I do not know as we have been duped so often...."

Uncertaity of government supply.

BRIGHT & GLOOMY DAYS-The Civil War Correspondence of Capt Charles Frederick Bahnson, A Moravian Confederate ed by Sarah Bahnson Chapman pub by Univ. TN. Press 2003

Pg.87 Camp near Kelly's Ford, Va. November 3rd 1863 Dear father"...And Dr. Hunter is at last compelled to lay aside the spotless clothes he so long sported aside of the dirty garments of returned soldiers; he will find the latter style even if uncomfortable very fashionable, & he will find out that even in the lone hours of midnight he will not be left alone, for he will find friends (Confederates) that stick closer than a brother, & they show their friendship by continual attacks on the good nature & patience of the happy possessor...."

CIVIL WAR LETTERS OF DANIEL HAYWOOD GILLEY,

Co. F, 16th Virginia Regiment
November the 5, 1863 Culpeper County "...Dear Father... I want some things from home. I want you to, if got it, to take some wool and have me a hat made if it so you can Size to make it is number six and seven eights 6 7/8. You can have the hat made and keep it till you can get or see somebody that you can send it by, James Scales will come home some time before long and if no chance before he will bring it...I am going to write for box also. I want

two pair of yarn socks and a pair of galloushes sent with the hat if so you can These caps is we get is no count…"

Galloushes? He must mean galliouses, or suspenders.

HANDLEY LIBRARY ARCHIVES-Letters of Stanley H. Russell Co H. 13th Virginia Regiment

Nov 5, 1863 Camp near Culpeper Court House,Dear Ma,"…Captain Harrison is going down the Valley and says he will bring any clothes to the company that are left in care of Dr. Murphy at Woodstock before the first of December at which time he expects to return. But if Papa is coming down you had as well keep any you may have for me until he comes (provided it is between this and Christmas) Tell him to let me know with whom he left my clothes in Harisonburg so that I can send for them when Will Harrison returns. I have not gotten my overcoat yet-intend to go into Gordonsville after it in a day or two. I want you to send me a blanket, I have but one, have not suffered any from cold yet…send me some soap…"

DEAR SISTER-CIVIL WAR LETTERS TO A SISTER IN ALABAMA by Frank Anderson Chappell pub. by Branch Springs Pub. 2002 (Third Alabama Regiment)

Pg. 173 Camp near Brandy Station Va. Nov 7th 1863 Dear Sister "…We have up cabins, well covered and chimneys built. Myself, Lewis and Raif H sleep together. We have three heavy blankets now and one more we can get when ever we need it. I have an overcoat and Lewis has one in Richmond. I reckon he will get it soon. So you see, we are doing fairly well.…I have never seen men in better health and spirits in my life. As a general thing they could not be pleased better than to get after the Yankees. For we all want our coats and blankets and its about the only chance for us to get a full supply. And we don't mind a few hour's fighting to get to rob a dead yank. Did you think you had a brother who would rob the dead? Well you have. I can plunder a dead yankee without any conscience scruples…" Jim

That's the spirit!

HANDLEY LIBRARY ARCHIVES-Civil War Diary 7 Letters of Franklin Gardener Walter, C.S.A. Co A. 39th Virginia Cavalry

Pg. 64 Nov. 7th, 1863 Staunton, Va. Dear Mother, "…As you heard from Dorsey I lost all my clothing that I had with me at Front Royal but as I came up to Staunton very soon afterwards where I had other clothes, I got along very well without them although the loss of those new shirts that I got whilst at home was a great disappointment…"

DEAR IRVIE, DEAR LUCY-The Civil War Letters of Capt. Irving A Buck, General Cleburne's AAG & Family pub by Buck Pub. Co. 2002

Pg. 189 Nov. 8, 1863 Bel Aire, (Front Royal, Va.) Dear Alvin, "...we have made you two merino shirts-thought they would save you washing and be warmer than white. They are not as nice as we could have wished were made in a great hurry. We send you four collars and two pairs of socks. The latter is a present from Cousin E. Richardson and were poor Willie's. They send their love with the request that you will wear them it is a compliment as not many could have gotten them. I wish we could send you a pair of shoes or boots and a nice pair of pants but we did expect George to stay long enogh to have any made and it is almost impossible to get any kind of goods here. Lucy made you a cap that the materials were so indifferent has declined sending it...Mother E.A.B. (Elizabeth Ashby Buck)

FORGET-ME-NOTS OF THE CIVIL WAR: A ROMANCE by Laura Elizabeth pub by Press of A.R. Fleming Printing Co. 1909

Nov. 11, 1863 Camp Near Morton's Ford, Va. "...My Dear Mother: We are once more in our same camp on the Rapidan, which we left just a month ago. We had just begun to be comfortable in our winter quarters on the Rappahannock, when the Yankees run us out. Last Saturday, about ten o'clock, the Yankees attacked our picket line on the river, composed of the Second and Thirtieth N.C. Regiments of our Brigade, driving them back, taking a great many of them prisoners. Col. Cox, of the Second, was badly wounded and afterwards died. The attack was a perfect surprise. We had just drawn a large supply of winter clothing of every kind,. And the men were just trying them on when we were ordered to fall in, which we did in double quick time, making for the river line of battle with our sharpshooters in front. Twas not long before we came on their skirmishers and a brisk fire commenced, which lasted until dark. Our two lines of battle laid within speaking distance until 12 o'clock that night, when we were very quietly withdrawn, half hour afterwards our sharpshooters followed and we took up our line of march till sun rise, when we were drawn up in line of battle, we stayed until two or three o'clock. The Yankees not coming on us, we started on the march again and never stopped till we crossed the Rapidan. We ate our breakfast Saturday morning in our winter quarters and did not draw a single mouthful to eat, or have any rest except when we were in the line of battle (and then we were hard at work throwing up breastworks), until Monday night, ten o'clock. We waded the Rapidan about 9 o'clock the same night. I think it was the hardest time we have ever had, nothing to eat, accompanied with the hardest marching we ever did. All our things were left in our winter quarters, expecting to go back there, but we did not, so we lost a good many things which we left behind. I happened to take my shawl and oil cloth along with me, which I saved. I lost my two blankets, a pair of cotton drawers, pair of socks, which I had just drawn (I did not draw anything else of the new clothing, which I am glad of, for I should have lost them). I also lost my knapsack, tin plate, tincup, etc. I saved my overcoat, with all the things you sent by Condon. That scrape has taught me a lesson. I bet I'll never leave anything else of mine behind. I don't care where we are ordered to.

Try to get Tom Stith to put the following things in with his own baggage: That worsted shirt, flannel shirt, flannel drawers, two pair socks, please send me a comb, coarse one, also a towel...."

Don't give the Yankees too much credit, it was probably accidental that the assault was made during the issuing of clothing. This soldier has learned, if you leave anything, don't expect to see it again.

THE CONFEDERATE VETERAN VOL. XXVI 1918

Pg. 247 June, 1918 Letters From The Front- Thomas Caffey to his family in Alabama Morton's Ford, on Rapidan River, November 12, 1863 Dear Ma: "Hugh hardy arrived in camp yesterday and gave me a letter from Mary. She stated you had sent me some articles of clothing and a knife by him; but as he has not yet said anything to me about them, I infer that he either did not bring them or left them in Richmond an account of difficulty in getting transportation. If the shirts are cotton, I do not need them, as I have as many now of that description as I can carry on a march. If they are woolen overshirts, they will be very acceptable, for the reason that I have no overcoat with me, and the weather is bitter cold. I will not need a jacket and pants before January; and as Mary informs me that Jule Rast will not be on before that time, you can send them by him.

I have a good pair of gloves you knit for me last winter, which will do me for at least one winter more. You need not send me a comforter, as the wool used in knitting it can be put to better use. You have sent me two since I have been in the army, and if I recollect aright I never used either half a dozen times. In the way of blankets; I have only one and a rubber cloth; but my bed participater, Dave Smith, has two heavy ones, and we therefore manage to get along "bully." I have not sent for any of my things I sent to Richmond, but suppose they will be sent for as soon as we get located for the winter. My wardrobe consists of the following articles: Two shirts, two pairs of pants, five pairs of socks, one jacket and one blanket. In addition, when on the march I have the following burden to bear: One cartridge box with sixty rounds of ball cartridges, one bayonet and scabbard, one gun, one haversack with three days' rations, and one canteen. This is about as heavy a load as I wish to "tote," and consequently you need send me nothing before January unless it is something to feed on, which is always acceptable. If Mary failed to send my knife by High, she can do so at the first opportunity, as I am greatly in need of one; also the shirts can be sent if they are of wool."

This soldier is pretty well equipped.

FOUR YEARS IN THE CONFEDERATE ARTILLERY-The Diary of Pvt. Henry Robinson Berkely ed. by William H. Runge pub by Univ. N.C. Press 1961

Pg. 61 Nov. 14 1863 "…We moved back to Mt. Piscah Church (a few miles southeast of Rapidan Station) and went into camp right at the church. We were not permitted to use the church, although we were short on tents and clothing…."

LETTERS OF A NEW MARKET CADET Beverly Stanard, ed. by John G. Barnett & Robert R. Turner pub by Univ. N.C. Press 1961

Pg. 13 V.M.I. November the 15th, 1863 My dear Sister "…Champe tell Mother I have come to the conclusion that I had better get me an overcoat at once for everything is going up daily. Saylor is going to write for the cloth for me and it will cost $10 or $12 per yard and it will take 8 yards then the lining will cost right much. Then I borrowed $20 to pay for a pair of shoes. So I want her to send me $150. I am out of money now, and would not object to having a little to buy pies, cakes, cider, &ct. occasionally. I also want to have a pair of gloves made…"

Ol' Beverly is a right expensive young man, isn't he?

CIVIL WAR LETTERS OF CAPTAIN A.B. MULLIGAN, Co. B, Fifth South Carolina Cavalry-Butler's Division-Hampton's Corps by Olin Fulmer Hutchinson pub by The Reprint Co. 1992

Pg. 95 16th Nov. 1863 Kenansville, N.C.My Very Dear Mother and Sisters, "I want you to send me the measure of all my servant's feet. Send the precise measure of their feet. I have my boy gather up old shoes, enough about camp to make a dozen pair and I will get lasts and make them myself. Send all the measures for Lula, Patsy, and Sue also."

Another example of the consideration shown to the servants.

THE CONFEDERATE VETERAN VOL.XXVI 1918

Pg. 307 July 1918 Letters From The Front -Thomas Caffey to his family in Alabama- Morton's Ford, on Rapidan River November 19, 1863 Dear Mary: In answer to your question in regard to clothing I have to say that at present I am in need of nothing. The pair of pants Ma made me last spring I have not worn since my return to the army; and as they are in a good state of preservation, they will do me for some time to come. My jacket is good and will suffice till spring. Underclothing I am not at present in need of; but if Jule Rast returns by January, he can, if convenient, bring me a dark cotton shirt and one pair of pants. My hat is getting somewhat dilapidated; and if the material can be had, I would be pleased for you to make me one like the one Aunt Lizzie made for Billy when he came home. I don't want a regular Hoosier concern, but a real nice one that will do to wear anywhere. The articles Ma sent by Hugh Hardy were delivered after my letter to her was written, and I want you to express my thanks to her, particularly for the overshirt. The flannel shirt I have but little use for, as I don't ever intend wearing one next to my hide again. If Jule Rast comes on by January, that will be time enough to send me the pants and hat. If I need anything else, you shall know. It might be as well, however, to include a good warm jacket among the above articles…"

THE CONFEDERATE LETTERS OF BENJAMIN H. FREEMAN Compiled & Edited by Stuart T. Wright pub by Exposition Press 1974

Pg. 30 Nov. 24 1863 In Camp near Orange C.H. Dear Father and Mother: "…Thos. B. Jones has come back and he landed here Yesterday evening Monday he never brought me anything at all as I expected I had been looking for him a long time but when he come I was no better off I thought he was going to bring me a box of victuals, I heard from him several times when he was at home and every time he was drunk and I expect you was afraid to send anything by him for fear he would lose it. Write me word how he acted when he was at home he said he came out to see you I thought a heap of Thos. But I can't think much of him now since I have seen how he has done. I was expecting what he had said when he left the Regt. He said he was going to be certain to bring me a box and my boots and just anything I wanted he would bring it Write to me as soon as you get this letter and let me know how it is he never brought those things…"

RED CLAY TO RICHMOND by John J. Fox pub by Angle Valley Press 2006

Pg. 210 Nov. 27, 1863 Private James Garrett "…He also issued directives to his family to send him some clothes. He expressed his disdain for the poor quality of some government manufactured clothing:

I want you to be sure to knit me a pair of gloves. [I]f you cant get wool take cotton. [T] hey are better than none. I don't want you to buy wool to make me any clothes for I can get them cheaper here than you can make them at home. I have got two coats and a vest that will do me this winter. I want you to make me two shirts and two pair of draws by next spring. I can draw them here but they are not half made and will last no time…Ten days later, Garrett asked that his family send a box of provisions. He repeated his pressing need for gloves. "I need them (gloves) bad. [T]hese nights are too cool to stand guard without gloves. I had to stand few hours this morning bare handed…"

When reading of how much clothing was issued and at what time, keep in mind all of these accounts of the shoddiness of the government issued goods.

THE CRY IS WAR, WAR, WAR The Civil War Correspondence of Lts. Burwell Thomas Cotton and George Job Huntley, 34th Regiment north Carolina troops by Michael W. Taylor Morningside 1994

Pg. 162 same camp, Nov. 28th, 1863 letter to his father "…I would be very glad to see you. If you conclude to come bring me a pair of shoes two or three pair of socks two pair of drawers one pair of pants & two shirts which I wrote to Sarah to make some time since…."

HANDLEY LIBRARY ARCHIVES-Memoirs of the 49th Regiment, Virginia Volunteers C.S.A.

Pg. 227 Nov 30, 1863 Confederate States of America

Quarter Master's Department

Received at Somerville Ford this day, of Capt. I.T. Bingham, Quarter Master, C.S.A., the following articles:

92 Ninety two Pairs Shoes
35 Thirty five English Grey Over Coats
219 Two hundred & nineteen English Grey Jackets
242 Two hundred and forty two Pairs Pants
170 One hundred and seventy Pairs Drawers
264 Two hundred and sixty four fair shirts
19 Nineteen Caps
3 Three tent Flies
24 Twenty four Blankets
(added, in different hand)
4 Tent flies
1 One Horse, good
Nov., 30th, 1863 R. Irvin Reid
2 Lieut & Act AQM
49th Va Inftry

Here's another example of overcoats being issued.

THE STONEWALL BRIGADE by James I. Robertson Jr. pub by La. State Univ. Press 1961

Pg. 216 "...winter of 1863-64 was particularly severe to the survivors of the Stonewall Brigade. Most of the men were shoeless, many lacked even socks. Although some comfort could be obtained by huddling together around campfires, pickets found it necessary to wrap clothing around their numb and swollen feet as protection from the cold. In January, Private Garribaldi wrote that he had not had any socks for the past two months and did not expect to get any in the forseeable future. By the first of February one Valley newspaper reported that there were two hundred men in the brigade without shoes or socks. A Waynesboro shoemaker hastily contributed fifty pairs; his wife knitted a similar number of socks, but the situation remained acute..."

Imagine picket duty, in the snow, dressed as poorly as that. The Army of Northern Virginia was particularly ragged this winter, see below.

TRUE TALES OF THE SOUTH AT WAR Collected and Edited by Clarence Poe pub by Univ. of N.C. Press 1961

reminiscences of Barry Benson

Pg. 88 Dr. J. Richard Corbett referring to the 18th N.C. Regt.At Mine Run winter 1863. Trying to obtain a turkey which had been shot between the lines. "...After sundown, George W. Corbett, my great grandfather, planned a lateral approach to the target. Maneuvering slowly along the ground, weaving in and out between the trees and sliding beneath the underbrush, he succeeded in bagging the game-plus a new overcoat and blanket off an equally venturesome, but less successful blue-coater who lay nearby. The pot boiled that night among the North Carolina ranks..."

The Story Of A Cannoneer Under Stonewall Jackson-The Rockbridge Artillery by Edward Moore pub by Neale Pub. Co. 1907

Pg. 214 Winter 1863 "...In this neighborhood (Frederick's Hall, on the Chesapeake and Ohio Railroad, about fifty miles from Richmond) there were quite a number of nice people, whose society and hospitality afforded those of us so inclined much agreeable entertainment. A white paper-collar became no unusual sight, but when two of our members appeared one afternoon adorned with blue cravats a sensation was created..."

I blame the Victorian Era obsession with clothing.

RECOLLECTIONS AND LETTERS OF GENERAL ROBERT E. LEE by his Son, Cpt. Robert E. Lee pub by Garden City Pub Co. 1926

PG. 103 Capt. Lee regarding his Father: "...During the winter (1863) he devoted himself especially to looking after the welfare of his troops, their clothing, shoes and rations, all three which were becoming very scarce..."

At least he tried.

FRENCH HARDING Civil War Memoirs ed. by Victor L. Thacker pub by McClain Printing Co. Inc., Parsons W.Va. 2001

Pg.117 Winter 1863 "...We were too far from home to expect gifts in the shape of clothing from loved ones there; but now, while others with friends less remote, were receiving such presents, it so happened that a box, containing two dozen pairs of hand knit socks, came to me from a patriotic society of ladies residing in and near Lexington, Va. It was accompanied by a letter written by their president-a Mrs. Miller I think-directing me to distribute the socks to the most meritorious men of my company. I failed to distribute them as suggested; and when I wrote thanking her for the present (which I did at once and in the best style of which I was capable), and telling her that my men were all all so meritorious that I found it impossible to distinguish between them, and had, therefore, given the socks to the most needy; she wrote me a beautiful letter commending my action, in reply..."

WAR HISTORY OF THE OLD FIRST VIRGINIA REGIMENT, ARMY of NORTHERN VIRGINIA by Charles T. Loehr pub. by Wm. Ellis Jones Book & Job Printer 1884

Pg. 40 winter 1863 (Dec.) winter quarters-'...While here received overcoats and blankets donated by the City Council of Richmond...."

I wish they would mention, in these accounts, whether the overcoats were military or civilian issue.

BRIGHT & GLOOMY DAYS-The Civil War Correspondence of Capt Charles Frederick Bahnson, A Moravian Confederate ed by Sarah Bahnson Chapman pub by Univ. TN. Press 2003

Pg 94 Dec. 1863 Dear Father "...My tent is getting rather shabby & in rainy weather &c. get rather too wet to be comfortable, even if the wind does blow, or the cold pinch pretty hard, just as they are not wet; but when a combination of all these evils (at least to us,) are effected, you may rest assured, we are far from being comfortable. We have received a lot of fine English and some U.S. blankets, which came at a very good time, as many of the men had no blankets or over-coats at all, & suffered very much from the bad weather..."

GRANDFATHER'S JOURNAL (Franklin Lafayette Riley) Company B Sixteenth Mississippi Infantry Volunteers Harris' Brigade Mahone's Division Hill's Corps, A.N.V. May 27, 1861-July 15, 1865 ed by Austin C. Dobbins pub by Morningside Press1988

Pg. 171 Tuesday-Thursday, Dec. 1-3, 1863 Camp near Liberty Mills "...Wed. night we camped on the plank road 15 miles from the C.H. Thurs. we returned to our old camp. Our men are annoyed. We need blankets and overcoats and we could have (would have) destroyed Meade's army had it remained..."

FLORA AND FAUNA OF THE CIVIL WAR-An Environmental Reference Guide by Kelby Ouchley pub.by La. Univ. Press 2010

Pg. 81 Captain William J. Seymour, 1st Louisiana Brigade, near Rappahannock Station, Virginia, on Dec. 3, 1863: "In our brigade there are two hundred and fifty men who have neither blankets or overcoats. It is a great wonder that these men do not freeze to death these terribly cold nights. Many of them use pine leaves and boughs wherewith to shield them from the cold, while others sit up by the fire all night."

Every night these men have to endure this cold, it would get pretty old after awhile

THE CIVIL WAR MEMOIRS OF CAPTAIN WILLIAM J. SEYMOUR-Reminiscences of a Louisiana Tiger by Terry L. Jones pub by La. State Univ. Press 1991

Pg. 101 "December 3d. (1863) Our Brigade marched back to the Rapidan, resuming our old position at Racoon Ford. The weather is bitter cold and our poor fellows, standing picket on the high, bleak banks of the River, suffer terribly from want of sufficient clothing. In our Brigade there are two hundred and fifty men who have neither blankets or overcoats. It is a great wonder that these men do not freeze to death on these terribly cold nights. Many of them use pine leaves and boughs wherewith to shield them from the cold, while others sit up by the fires all night, and, borrowing blankets from their more fortunate comrades, sleep during the day..."

CONFEDERATE LETTERS AND DIARIES ed by Walbrook D. Swank pub by Papercaft Printing and Design Inc. 1992

Pg. 34 Dec.4th, 1863 around Mechanicsville Va. Reporting a recent skirmish "…Many were the knapsacks, overcoats, canteens, oilcloths, blankets &c we expected to find when the contest was over.… I want two new undershirts as thse I have are much the worse for wear especially about the wristbands and collar.…I sent back my old clothes in the same box that contained my new clothes. The overcoat I sent I bought from Luck for $8. I thought that the cloth in it would be worth that much. When Uncle James gets his coat wet that coat will do to change.…How do you like the blue patches that I put on my breeches? I reckon that you all laughed at it but I think it was done very well for the first patching that I ever did. …"

LETTERS FROM THE STONEWALL BRIGADE Ted Barcay, Liberty Hall Volunteers ed by Charles W. Turner pub by Rockbridge Pub. Co. 1992

Pg. 118 Dec. 5 1863 he is promoted to first lieutenant for an act of gallantry-he saved the regimental colors during the Battle of Mine run. His bunkmate (George Chapin) was killed grabbing the colors just before Ted Barclay got there. "…I was so unfortunate as to lose my knapsack and now am using his (George's) clothes, but I may be able to draw clothes form the Q.M. They ought to furnish me and must. The shirts I got here are white and get dirty very quick, but I have already gotten too much from home and will depend in the future on the Confederacy…"

Good luck

CIVIL WAR LETTERS OF WILLIAM (BILLY) A. ELLIOT

Dec. 9 1962 Franklin Depot Va. Dear Father "…I got your letter you sent with Mr. Brown in due time. I got my shirt & drawers you sent with him.…mother I want you to send me some plain thread and a good big needle in the box…"

LETTERS TO AMANDA-The Civil War Letters of Marion Hill Fitzpatrick, Army of Northern Virginia ed by Jeffery C. Lowe and Sam Hodges pub by Mercer Univ. Press 1998

Pg. 101 Dec. 10th, 1863 Montpelior, Near Orange, Va. (Letter No. 50) Dear Amanda, "…I will draw a right pretty little pile the 1st of Jan. if they pay us our commutation for clothing as they have promised.…We are looking for Brown with our things in a few days. I begin to need shirts and drawers pretty bad but I keep patching the old ones and make them do. I have got the same shirt and drawers that I wore home last winter and they were not new then…"

HANDLEY LIBRARY ARCHIVES

James A. Miller Collection correspondence C.W. era misc. New Market, Va.

Camp near Morton's Ford Dec. 11th, 1863 Dear Julia, "…I have worn the boots one half a day they did very well, though were rather tight, but they will soon get suited to my feet… present I got last week it was a first rate pair of woolen socks they are white ….and the remainder with natural black wool. They are very good.…I have a notion of buying one of those over coats has been worn since they were drawn, it will cost 50 dollars…"

HANDLEY LIBRARY ARCHIVES-Letters of Stanley H. Russell Co H. 13th Virginia Regiment

Dec. 11, 1863 Camp of 13th Infantry Dear Sister, "…Your letter of the 18th of November sent by Eisha White was received two days ago. I was almost as glad to get that as my clothes, though I know the clothes will do me most good…"

Dear ma "I got my clothes two or three days ago and was as proud as a donkey of a new suit. They fit me very well. The pants are full large but I suppose will be small emough when they shrink. I have not gotten my overcoat yet. I expect the man I left it with has sold it. Just my luck. I can get along very well without, since you sent my clothes. I need a blanket now more than a coat. The government is not issueing any and our soldiers are very scarce of them. I have but one, but my bed-fellow (Mic Copehaver) has two and manage to sleep comfortable since we moved in our cabin. My socks came at the right time. I did not have a pair but what was full of holes. Elisha White brought all of my things up to me, it was very kind of him. I shall never forget him for it. He must have had a hard time bringing them all the way from home…"

Dec. 17th, 1863 Dear Papa, "…I have gotten my overcoat from Gordonsville. Ma may not send the cape as I do not care about it…"

VOICES FROM COMPANY D Diaries by the Greensboro Guards, Fifth Alabama Infantry Regiment, Army of Northern Virginia ed. by G. Ward Hubbs pub by Univ. of Georgia Press 2003

Pg. 205 December 12 1863 SP "…Clothing issued to-day. Troops are very well supplied now…."

Government issue?

CIVIL WAR LETTERS OF WILLIAM (BILLY) A. ELLIOT

Dec. 13 same camp Dear father "…I want you to send me a good woole pare of pants and a good piece of hard soap and some thread and a couple of needles…"

CIVIL WAR LETTERS OF DANIEL HAYWOOD GILLEY

Co. F, 16th Virginia Regiment
December the 13, 1863 "…I have one pair and a half of shoes to make and it is about as much as I do. I have made myself a good pair of shoes once more.…I now want you to send me a box of things as soon as you can. I I named some of the things, a hat if you can get one made two pair of socks, one or two pair, galloushes 9galliouses, suspenders?) and a pair of gloves if got any and one shirt, but don't send me a white one if not a colored don't send none and a vest if got it now. I tell you not to wait to get these little things for I want the box as soon as you can get the hat and socks and galloushes if haint got the rest made don't wait and then I want the box filled up with something to eat, some like taters, onions, a piece of ham, some cakes and tell Puss to send me some apples if she has got any and you can fill the box with such things as you think proper…"

This soldier sounds as though he's very hungry. I've always said, its miserable being cold, more miserable being cold and wet, most miserable being cold and wet and hungry (this is from experience).

FOUR YEARS IN THE CONFEDERATE ARTILLERY

Pg. 112 December 14 (1863) in the Valley near Staunton "…Last night, about midnight, it began to rain very hard and continued to rain for two hours. Very fortunately for us, the rain, which first fell, froze and formed on our oilcloths a thick coating of ice, which kept us perfectly warm and dry, not a single drop getting through to us, and we slept as warm and as comfortable as possible…"

THE CRY IS WAR, WAR, WAR The Civil War Correspondence of Lts. Burwell Thomas Cotton and George Job Huntley, 34th Regiment North Carolina Troops by Michael W. Taylor pub by Morningside Press 1994

Pg. 164 Near Orange C.H. Va. Dec.,15th, 1863 letter to sister "…E.M. Reeves brought everything safe he started with I suppose. I am very glad he did not bring me only one shirt as we received the Box the ladies sent us from Zion last winter. There were some very nice check shirts in it so I took one of them for my own use. I have enough clothing to do me awhile if I do not lose them. My pants fit very well. I sent to Raleigh some ago by the

Brigade A.Q.M. after me a new uniform. He has not returned yet. If he gets it I may send it home and have it made. I did not need it much but I had rather have the cloth (than) the Confederate money. *He's right, at this point cloth held more value thjan Cofederate money.*

I have not tried mt drawers on yet but I think they will fit me very well and I hope they will last longer than the war. ..."

Wishful thinking

WASH.& LEE UNIV. Archives, Lexington, Va. Letters of Bethel J. Davidson Camp near Guienie's Station

Gordonsville, Va. Dec. 17, 1863 Dear mother "...If you can find an old pair of boots at home which are fit to be footed, I wish you would send them to me, as I have a calfskin that will suffice a great deal of it ..."

THE CRY IS WAR, WAR, WAR The Civil War Correspondence of Lts. Burwell Thomas Cotton and George Job Huntley, 34th Regiment North Carolina Troops by Michael W. Taylor pub by Morningside Press 1994

Pg.112 The Letters of Burwell Thomas Cotton Co. K,34th Regt. N.C. Troops Pg. 129 Camp Near Fredericksburg Dec. 18th, 1862 "...If Pa comes to see me you need not send my yarn drawers as I prefer cotton here in camp. I will need some pants and socks. I will need my overcoat. I would be glad to have a pair of shoes with iron on the heel. Shoes are very hard to get here. ..."

Shoes are very hard to get anywhere.

LETTERS OF A NEW MARKET CADET Beverly Stanard ed. by John G. Barrett & Robert K. Tyrner Jr. pub by Univ. N.C. Press 1961

Pg.21 V.M.I. Dec. 19th, 1863 My darling Mother, "...Well we were ordered out on last Tuesday very unexpectedly to march directly to Goshen and then wait orders from Gen. Imboden...We were exposed one day and night to the most disagreeable weather I ever saw. Rain fell in perfect torrents, freezing as it would fall. We intended to have gone on from here after a rest of 2 hours, but as there were a good many of boys shoeless and others with sore feet, we concluded to lay over..."

WRITING & FIGHTING THE CONFEDERATE WAR The Letters of Peter Wellington Alexander ed by William B. Styple pub by Belle Grove Pub. Co. 2002

Pg. 146 Thomaston, Ga. December 20, 1863 "I would acknowledgs the receipt, from the editor of the Savannah Republican, the day before I left Dalton, of a box of English russet half boots, and a few blankets and socks, all of which were immediately distributed to barefooted and needy Georgians. The articles were much needed, and were received with many expressions of gratitude. There are several hundred men still left who are without shoes, while the thermometer is down to 12 deg.!..."

LETTERS OF A NEW MARKET CADET Beverly Stanard ed. by John G. Barrett & Robert K. Tyrner Jr. pub by Univ. N.C. Press 1961

Pg. 34 8. "In order to meet the needs of the cadets in the field, General Smith had purchased shoes from whatever source possible and without regard to price or quality." It was his hope, however, that the state would "authorize the purchase and relieve the cadets of the charge." On December 22nd the Superintendant announced that the adjutant General had authorized the accounts of the cadets to be credited with the cost of these shoes and that the Chief of Ordinance had informed him that his requisition upon the Government for 250 pairs of shoes has been approved. The Institute quartermaster, upon receipt of those shoes, was to issue a pair to each officer and cadet to whom shoes had not been issued previously. Also the Secretary of War detailed three shoemakers to the Institute so that in the future the cadets would be properly shod.General Oders No. 92. December 22, 1863 V.M.I. Order Book, 1863"

VOICES FROM COMPANY D Diaries by the Greensboro Guards, Fifth Alabama infantry Regiment, Army of Northern Virginia ed. by G.Ward Hubbs pub by Univ. of Ga. Press 2003

Pg. 207 Dec. 23, 1863 camp on Rapidan River SP "...Drew very good jacket today-dark steel-mixed. Went over to Qr. Master's and got fit-with Bill Sheldon..."

LETTERS OF A NEW MARKET CADET Beverly Stanard, ed. by John G. Barnett & Robert R. Turner pub by Univ. N.C. Press 1961

Pg. 25 V.M.I. Dec. the 23rd, 1863 Dear Mother "...Well dear Mother we reached our journey's end Monday evening and nar'e Yankee did we kill or see after marching us all over this plagued mountainous country, and ruining our feet, we being badly shod...When we left here we thought we were going to Staunton. I took some collars along in case we should, and when I heard this train I could not but help thinking it was coming to take us there and I had made up my mind if we got that near home, I would work my (coins?) so as to go the whole hog…(added in pencil) Mother I send with my coat a pair of pants for Henry. I wore them on the last march. You will observe that they have seen hard times. After mending the seat they will be made a good pair of pants by having them turned…"

No cloth was wasted, "turning" meant taking out the stitches, washing the cloth, turning the outside of the cloth to the inside, then sewing it back together.

WAR STORIES OF WEST VIRGINIA ed. by David L. Phillips Leesburg, Va. 1991

Pg. 241 Near Lewisburg, Va. December 23rd, 1863 Andrew R. Barbee writing to his wife "I rcd. The shirt flannel, buttons, Hkfs, soap, thread, &c. John also nrcd. His package from sister Kate. We needed the clothes. I need drawers worse than anything else-can't get them here. I can't wear flannel drawers- Heavy cotton. Dick Roberts, (dear old fellow) sent me a pair of most excellent heavy double sided high cavalry boots-he also sent boots and shoes to his Bro. They come in well. Wish someone would send John a pr. Of boots-he needs them-such as mine are cost $200 here. Officers cannot live, feed and clothe themselves on Commission…"

An officer would have to have relatives who owned much cloth to make them uniforms, inflation making it impossible for anyone to buy clothing or boots or shoes.

Pg.246 same date-nearly "Dr. if you or Ma can send John a pr. Of heavy double soled boots & a pair of pants do so. Either will cost $100 in Dixie…"

CIVIL WAR REGIMENTS-A Journal of the American Civil War, Treasures from the Archives: Select Holdings from the Museum of the Confederacy Vol.5

Pg. 137 Fred Brode (Washington Artillery) to Josephine Trinchard, undated fragment, ca. Christmas 1863 winter quarters, Petersburg "I wish you could see me now. I am a pretty hard looking case, a regular hard-up Confederate. But, when I go out, I have anything at my service, that my mess have got, in the way of dry goods. I borrow one's Boots, another one's hat, another one's shirt, and necktie and white collar and you see I get along quite well as long as we are stationed here…"

All well and good, but how many of them could go out at a time?

THE CORRESPONDENCE OF JOHNATHAN WORTH, vol.1 pub. by Edwards & Broughton, 1909

Pg. 656 Dec. 25, 1863 Letter from Johnathan Worth to William J. Gates (Regarding the State of N.C.) "The State clothing department was got up under a resolution of Genl. A ratified 20 Sept. 1861 entitled "Resolution to provide Winter Clothing for the troops." The title shows it was intended to be temporary-"winter clothing." It makes no specific appropriation for the purpose-No limit is imposed on the amount which may be drawn for this purpose. Under this brief resolution, manifestly to supply "winter" clothing, which it was evident would soon be indespensible, a gigantic establishment has grown up and is continued supplying summer clothing and winter clothing-At the same time it passed officers got good pay and clothed themselves. It looked to clothing the rank and file. I understand it now supplies all the fine clothing, etc., for the officers, and who knows at what rates? It is said the goods are sold at rates re-embursing the Treasury; but no data are furnished me on which this opinion is based. It drew from this department during the last fiscal yearmore than half a million more than it re-rmbursed-and at the same time had the benefit of importations by the Advance (state-owned blockade runner) bought on credit in Europe. What it had on hand at the beginning of the year I have no means of knowing-nor have I any means of knowing what amount of clothing it may have supplied to certain State troops, raised east of the Chowan River under an act of the 7th July, 1863. I do not know whether they were organized prior to the 30th Sept.-the end of the fiscal year. Since the 30th Sept. last, some $50,000 more has been drawn than has been re-embursed…"

I wonder if they ever straightened this financial matter out.

HANDLEY LIBRARY ARCHIVES-

James A. Miller Collection correspondence C.W. era misc. New Market, Va.

Camp near Piscah Church Dec. 27th, 1863 Dear Julia, I would like to send my old saddle home and a over coat that I bought and several pieces of other clothing if any one comes over tell them to call or let me know and I will send the things to them…I wish you would have Fidlers to make me another hat as this one is getting rather shabby…"

A BOY'S FIRST BATTLE by H.M. Hamill

Pg. 105 new Florida troops sent to Petersburg, winter, 1863-1864 "…We were hurried to the front of the Army of Northern Virgina and given place in Mahone's Division, along with the veteran soldiers of Lee. I can remember how the old soldiers made mock of our green and unsoldierly ways, and dubbed us with nicknames that made us for a time the jest of the army.

I cannot blame them. Falstaff's variegated soldiers would have put us to shame. I remember that, for lack of better guns, some of us were equipped with big-bore Belgium muskets. If there was one decent uniform in my regiment, other than those of the officers, I fail to recall it. Some of us had brought along our neckties and handkerchiefs, and dazzled the eyes of Lee's clay-colored veterans for a season with our nicely laundered white shirts…"

How many of these damned Belgium muskets were there? They seem to turn up everywhere.

Middle South

CONFEDERATE ECHOES A Soldier's Personal Story of Life in the Confederate Army From the Mississippi to the Carolinas by Albert Theodore Goodloe-First Lieutenant Company D Thirty-Fifth Regiment Alabama Volunteer Infantry C.S.A. pub by Zenger Pub. Co. 1897

Pg. 157 "…The habitation, by preference, of the grayback, was the inner seams of the garments next the skin, whether they were drawers or pants, shirts or jackets; for sometimes the veteran of the stars and bars could afford no undergarments, his only wearing apparel being breeches and jacket, wearing them therefore, next to his skin…."

This would be OK in the summer, but I can't imagine it in the winter.

THE LIFE OF JOHNNY REB. By Bell Irvin Wiley pub by La. State Univ. Press 1970

Pg. 346 "…A Louisianian who in 1863 watched a group of 400 Texans ride by his plantation reported that they bore no resemblance to soldiers. "If the Confederacy has no better soldiers than those we are in A bad row for stumps," he said; "they look more like baboons mounted on gotes than anything else."

THE CONFEDERATE REGIMENT HISTORY SERIES-The 5th & 7th Battalions North Carolina Cavalry & the 6th North Carolina Cavalry & 65th North Carolina State Troops by Jeffery C. Weaver 1995

Pg. 12 winter 1863 & through July; East Tennessee-"It does not require a great deal of personal bravery to go into battle when one is confronted by and open foe, but to be constantly expecting to be shot from a thicket or from the top of every hill one passes, is a condition that tries the nerve of the bravest soldier. This is the kind of duty the Fifth

Battalion was called upon to do in the winter 1862-63 and so continued up to July, 1863, and to give some idea of the hardship of such service, I will add that while we had a commissary and Quartermasters department, we seldom had a ration of bacon or saw a sack of flour, a blanket, a pair of shoes, except such as we furnished ourselves. We were often fifty miles from headquarters in a section of country where it was impossible to carry army supplies in any other way than in a haversack and that was not always with the necessities of life. Sometimes we had something to eat and sometimes we did not have anything to eat. Sometimes we had a shelter over us and sometimes our shelter was the blue sky or lowering clouds. Sometimes we slept under a blanket and sometimes the blanket was the driven snow. Many was the time the command went into winter quarters under an oil cloth in the jamb of the fence with a chunk for a pillow, and awoke in the morning to find the earth covered with snow…"

UNIFORMS OF THE CIVIL WAR by Lord, Wise pub by A.S. Barnes & Co. 1970

Pg. 63 Jan. 1863 Hanson's Men, the Kentucky Brigade,as they marched through Murfeesboro in heavy snowstorm were described as "… poorly shod, with poor caps, some with good jackets, many without, and none with overcoats…more than twenty men of the 6th Kentucky Regiment could not accompany their regiment being destitute of shoes…"

Pg. 63 "A private in the 33rd Alabama remembered: "There was a class of men with us who would rob the dead and did so at Murfreesboro, and men who would not entertain the thought of taking shoes off the dead themselves, but were in need of shoes and not knowing when they could get any, would pay from $10.00 to $25.00 for a second pair of brogan shoes to the man who usually said he bought them but they did not fit.

I think all had exchanged their Enfields for Springfields on the battle fields at this time, January,1863…We had also exchanged our cedar canteens on the battlefields or by purchase by men who had more than one cloth covered, black tin, oval shaped Yankee canteen, and those who had not picked up a U.S. blanket, good black hat, or shelter tent could usually buy such cheap if needed of men who had more than one."

The "Middle South" started 1863 as Reagged Rebels.

THE CONFEDERATE VETERAN VOL. XXVI 1918

Pg. 259 June 1918 In The Years Of War complied by John C. stiles from "Official Records" "Particular About A Fit-Captain Govan, of the 2nd Arkansas, C.S.A., states that during the Murfeesboro fight (Dec 31 1862-Jan. 1, 1863) "the body of General Sill, U.S.A. was brought to the hospital. Private Guest, of my regiment, got the General's gloves and said he would have taken his uniform also, but it was too large for him." A Rebel private in a Yankee General's uniform! Wouldn't that jar you?"

I'll bet he'd have looked swell in that!

http://www.authentic Confederate...Wambaugh, White & Co.by Ken Myers

"...In the Savannah Quartermaster reports of late 1862 and early 1863 they say that the men in the river batteries had been issued English wool jackets with metallic buttons. These men were also issued English tweed trousers. They were also being issued English military shoes. In the same report, they wrote that the quartermaster had French military shoes. The ship, the "Fingal," also brought in black English great coats..."

The garrison trops seem to have been well equipped.

DARK AND BLOODY GROUND by Thomas Ayres pub by Taylor Trade Pub. 2001

Pg. 186 After battle at Donaldsonville (La.) "... At Berwick bay, tons of weapons, supplies and ammunition were loaded on carts and wagons and sent north to New Iberia. Many of Mouton's men left Berwick Bay wearing captured Union uniforms. What the rebels could not transport, they dumped in the bay, including the large seige guns from the fort at Brashear City. Among the discarded loot were thousands of stiff, white collars that were standard issue with the uniforms worn by the troops of Bank's 19th Army Corps. Taylor later wrote a letter to Bank, inquiring about these unusual items. "My men have boiled, baked and fried them and still complain that they cannot eat them," he wrote."

What is the deal with these collars? You'd think that any army would have had enough on its mind to have deleted these. Plus, as General Taylor says, they were inedible no matter how you prepared them.

UNIFORMS OF THE CIVIL WAR by Lord, Wise pub by A.S. Barnes & Co. 1970

Pg. 66 "The Confederate soldier is forced to resort to many expedients to obtain clothing," wrote a member of Cavert's Battery, Alabama Light Artillery, Army of Tennessee. "I have been employed this day in coloring a Yankee overcoat, which I brought from the battlefield of Missionary Ridge..."

It would be worth it. Those Yankee overcoats are excellent in cold weather.

Ancestory.com Chambers County Alabama Confederate Uniforms

"...Most of the men from Chambers County, Alabama, would have worn the Columbus Depot Confdederate jacket. It was butternut brown with hand-dyed indigo wool jersey collar and cuffs that were straight across and not pointed like you see in some pictures. The front had 6 to 8 buttons. The buttons would have been from the state of Alabama…an eagle with the letters AVC for Alabama Volunteer Corps. These jackets were made in Columbus, Georgia and was the closest uniform and supply depot to Chambers County. They were worn by men fighting in Miss., Alabama, and the Army of Tennessee. They were worn with a variety of jean type pants. The most common color was a shade of brown, but they also wore gray, navy and sky blue…My guess is that most of the men from Chambers County wore pants made by their mothers or sisters or wives and they would have tried to match the butternut brown in the jacket…so I guess they would have been some shade of brown. Underneath the jacket they would have worn a vest also made at home. The vest would have had pockets for their pocket watches as the Columbus Depot jacket generally did not have pockets. Under the vest a white or tan shirt, also homemade. Many men wore neck scarves of bandana-looking material wrapped initially in the front, brought around the back and then back to the front and tied in a small knot with the two ends forming a bowtie of sorts…"

CONFEDERATE ECHOES A Soldier's Personal Story of Life in the Confederate Army From the Mississippi to the Carolinas by Albert Theodore Goodloe-First Lieutenant Company D Thirty-Fifth Regiment Alabama Volunteer Infantry C.S.A. pub by Zenger Pub. Co. 1897, 1983

Pg. 116 "…Carrying luggage on the march was one of our troubles, there being certain things which it was needful for every soldier to have at hand all the time. The wagon trains went along with the commands to haul our camp equipage, such as tents, when we had any, cooking utensils, axes, etc., but the soldiers, except the commissioned officers, were required to carry their guns and cartridge boxes, and usually their knapsacks of clothing, when they had had any. We all carried our rations in our haversacks, and canteens for water. Our bedding-blankets and oilcloths-when we had any, might be thrown in the wagons, though it was usual for those who had oilcloths to carry them for protection when it rained, and some of the soldiers who had no oilcloths would carry their blankets for this purpose instead of putting them in the wagons. In the early part of the war we had more baggage of one sort and another than we had afterward, and would try to carry more, but as the war advanced we had less and were less inclined to make pack horses of ourselves. Our plunder was lessened by throwing away some things, losses on the marches, and by the general wear and tear of things. Long before the war ended we would do without all that we possibly could, and make our burdens as light as possible; and to this day I have an abhorrence of surplus baggage, often preferring, even in winter, to take the risk of bad weather to being burdened with an overcoat, and will put off as long as possible carrying one on my "rounds" at the approach of winter. A few of the soldiers preferred to have nothing except what clothing they then had on, and took the chances of getting more when this wore out, and when we stopped to camp at night they would either nod around the camp fires or crowd themselves under the blankets of others…"

A good overall description of any Confederate soldier.

WESTERNERS IN GRAY-The Men and Missions of the Fifth Missouri Infantry Regiment by Phillip Thomas Tucker pub by McFarland & Co. 1953

Pg. 101 "…On January 1, (1863) Lieutenant Warren instantly raised morale when he arrived from his Mobile mission. With much fanfare, he distributed 120 pairs of shoes and 100 pairs of wool socks to soldiers in great need, including those who were barefoot…"

CANNONEERS IN GRAY-The Field Artillery of the Army of Tennessee 1861-1865 by Larry J. Daniel poub by Univ of Alabama Press 1984

Pg. 68 Retreat from Murfeesboro, Jan. 3, 1863 "…"My God what suffering," lamented a Mississippi artilleryman, "Wet through-cold and chilly-no slepp for four or five nights, and march through mud and water, some without any shoes, and some sick, and some with fingers and toes frozen…"

THE BROTHERS WAR ed by Annette Tapert pub by Vintage Books, 1988

Pg. 120 William G. Slaughter Second Leuitenant Company L., 6th Alabama Volunteer Infantry Camp Near Grace Church, January 4th, 1863 "…It was then that a most melancholy accident happened. I.M. Iverson, from Lowndes Co., and of the Third Ala. Regt., was among the skirmishers, but Iverson advancing found a splendid Yankee overcoat, which he put on. He was a very brave boy and as the line continued to advance, he got some distance ahead. One of the Southern Rifle Company, seeing him advance, and mistaking him for a Yankee, shot him, the ball penetrating his heart and killing him instantly….

I walked over to where the yankee lines of battle had been. There lay their dead ingreat heaps unburied. They had been stripped of all their outer garments, and especially of their shoes, by our men…"

SOJURNS OF A PATRIOT The Field and Prison Papers of An Unreconstructed Confederate ed by Richard Bender Abell & Fay Adamson pub by Gecik Southern Heritage Press Murfreesboro, TN 1998

Pg. 124 Camp Young, near Savannah, Ga. Jan. 4th,1863 "…We drawed blankets while in North Carolina. I need nothing, without it is a shirt…"

THIS INFERNAL WAR by Edwin Hedge Fay/Bell Irvin Wiley pub by Univ. of Texas Press 1958

Pg. 202 Grenada Miss. Dec. (Jan.) 4/63 My Own Darling Wife "…As far as the woolen socks are concerned I shall not need them but the undershirts I will and if this war closes as I believe it will you can always knit them for me. It will be good work for odd times…."

THE CONFEDERATE VETERAN VOL. IV 1896

Oct. 1896 Campaigning Under Difficulties by Tom Hall, Jan., 6, 1863 Deer Creek Pass in Mississippi "One sunny Sunday I remember well, when private Swazey came hurrying down the levee that we were lying behind watching for a Yankee head to pop up on a big gunboat, and, short of breath, exclaimed: "Say, boys, come go with me quick. There is a bear in that clump of trees; I saw it go in just now." The clump of trees he referred to was surrounded by water, and was the only land visible except the levee that we were on, but the water through which it was necessary to pass to reach it was not over waist deep, and four of us hurriedly went with Swazey. We soon reached the highest island and deployed so we could close in on bruin and be sure not to miss him. Slowly each of us crept into the thicket, and for a time all were sure that poor Swazey was mistaken in his vision, and finally we were about to give up in despair, for by that time we had all hoped to get some kind of fresh meat, bear or no bear. While we were "guying" him on the subject, and at a moment when I was about to rise and resume my way back to my post of duty, my eye caught sight of a very small bear sure enough, then, quicker than a twinkle, my old trusted Enfield sounded the glad tidings to my comrades that bruin was ours. We quickly cut its throat, and in ten minutes had it swinging from a limb, skinning it. The animal was very poor, for, like ourselves, it had nothing to eat for many days. We were not to be bluffed by its condition, however, for as soon as it was skinned and quartered we were on our way back to the line, anticipating what a good time we would soon have eating it. We had no way to cook it, however, and in order to eat it at all, we were compelled to cut in small slices and dry it over the fire. We managed to save a canteen of grease each, even as it was but had an awful job in doing it."

Augmenting rations (or lack of them)

"DEAR MOTHER: DON'T GRIEVE ABOUT ME. IF I GET KILLED, I'LL ONLY BE DEAD." ed by Mills Lane pub by pub by The Beehive Press 1977

Pg. 212 Jan.10 1863 John Johnson to his family near Murfeesboro (TN), regarding the Battle of Murfeesboro "…I have lost everything you sent me excerpt one pair of socks, which I had on, and my comforter, but found more shirts and drawers but no pants. You must send me some pants as soon as you can, for these I have on are getting some ragged. I have my blanket yet and found one on the battlefield..."

U.S. ARMY HERITAGE AND EDUCATION CENTER Letters of Fred Smith, 7th Texas Infantry Regiment

letter #26 Jan. 10, 1863 Port Hudson, La.(In response to the unit's officers going home on furlough to obtain clothing for the men) My Dear parents, "...We are much in need of the things now and if they stay away much longer we won't need them at all and will have to throw them away. If they don't get here soon, I will have to buy, beg, borrow or steal a shirt somewhere. I have not had a shirt for over two weeks, thinking they would be here every day, and am getting very tired of running about in an undershirt, low neck at that.

I have to keep my coat buttoned up all the time. In the old camp I had two shirts and Theodore's was dropping off almost, and I gave him my best one, and the next time mine was washed, the niggers have it all to rags by "bathing" it. So now I am sans shirt and sans hamper in that respect..."

THIS INFERNAL WAR Edwin Hedge Fay/Bell Irvin Wiley Univ. of Texas Press 1958

Pg. 206 Grenada, Miss. Jany 13th, 1863 My Own Dear Wife "...I feel right anxious about you as I hear nothing from you though I did hear through Lt. Carter's letter that you were making me a coat. If the war does not end soon, I shall need it for my old one is most gone though I fix it up when it gets ragged and it does tolerably well. We are going to get a uniform for the Company if nothing happens as the Govt. will allow us nothing for clothing but requires us to draw it from the Quartermaster Dept. which of course contains little or nothing...John Lesueur has bought a woven worsted quilt and that makes us cover enough at present and warmer weather will come with the spring. The cars are coming I must get a paper...If you have an opportunity of sending me you had better send a pair of drawers as those I drew from the Government would not fit anybody in the world. I have worn them once and can do so again on a pinch. My two pair of Lowells do very well and are by no means worn out. Will last me for a long time but for a change I need another pair. You need not feel uneasy about my clothing for if I need anything at any time very badly I will send Rich home after it. I can do it at any time, and if I do not get some letters soon I shall send him home after them..."

Sgt. Fay mentions the shoddy issued goods.

RELUCTANT REBEL The Secret Diary of Robert Patrick 1861-1865 ed. by F. Jay Taylor pub by La State Univ. Press 1959

Pg. 111 Jan. 17th, 1863: Port Hudson, La. "The weather's freezing this morning. The frost looks like young snow and the ground is frozen hard. This is pretty severe weather on the troops that are without tents, and there are a great many that have none and a great many of the men are destitute of shoes and clothing."

THE CIVIL WAR LETTERS OF PVT. P.C.BONNEY pub by Lawenceville Pub. Co. 1963

Pg. 13 Jan. 17 1863 Memphis Tenn. "…I sent my coat by Henry Imhoff I have the vest and the pants have plenty to eat and to ware I drawd a new pants this week I will have Clothes if I don't git nothing Els…"

Here's one soldier who'se well equipped.

"DEAR MOTHER: DON'T GRIEVE ABOUT ME IF I GET KILLED, I'LL ONLY BE DEAD. ed by Mills Lane pub by The Beehive Press 1977

Pg. 219 Jan. 19 1863 A.F. Boyd to his Father, Vicksburg, Mississippi; "…PS tell Mother that the coat she sent me was too long across the shouldes. But I can sell it for a good price, I have plenty of clothing now without it. I would like to have one nice shirt and a pair of drawers. I haven't got but one pair of socks and they are full of holes. I would be glad if you would send me the sword to me by the first one who travels…"

BROTHERS IN GRAY-The Civil War Letters of the Pierson Family ed. by Thomas W. Cutrer & t. Michael Parrish pub by La. State Univ. Press 1997 Ninth Louisiana

Pg 151 David Pierson to William H. Pierson Camp Snyder's Mill, Miss. Jany 20th, 1863 Dear Pa "…We are stll encamped on the Yazoo River about 14 miles from Vicksburg and decidedly in the muddiest place I have ever lived in. We have some few tents, but the majority of the Regiment is living the best they can under trees, board shelters or in the ground. Some ingenious Frenchmen have erected houses out of long cane which is to (be) found in great abundance all over the country. You would be amused as well as astounded to see them. The weather has been very bad-only one fair day in the week, and so cold as to freeze one away from the fire. Three days ago we had a severe snow-storm which, if it had lay on the ground, would have been fully six inches in depth. Jim and I have a tent (not a good one by any means) with a plank floor in which, by the assistance of some cane tops, and fodder (the latter of which I filched from my horse) and a blanket apiece, we manage to keep tolerably comfortable. The mud has been so bad that we have been compelled to agree to a harsh law about it, to wit: That no one shall go inside the tent with his shoes on. So we just stop at the door and pull off before entering so as to keep the floor and our blankets dry & clean.

We will not suffer the same inconvenience for long, for the Gen'l, after long persuasion, has permitted us to send men after our baggage which is on the Rail Road below Grenada. When we get it we will have tents and blankets and clothes enough to keep comfortable..."

This is a very good idea, getting the clothing, blankets and tents in storage. As we saw from the Eastern Theatre, permission wasn't always granted to retrieve stored supplies.

THIS INFERNAL WAR by Edwin Hedge Fay/Bell Irvin Wiley pub by Univ. of Texas Press 1958

Pg. 217 Grenada Miss. Jany 24th, 1863 Own Darling Wife"...Now in this connection tell Cynthia (servant) if she does not begin to show some signs that way when I come home I'll whip her most to death or sell her to the meanest man I can find on Red River. Be sure you tell her so for I am not going to be fooled with by her any longer. I bought her to breed and I know no good reason why she should not do it and she shall or I won't own her long. Don't raise the objection I fear you will but be governed by me in this thing, for as Phoebe says, "niggers will be niggers." You know she is not virtuous and she adds to it now that other thing you regard as sinful. I have no objection to her having a husband but she has got to have chidren. If she was a virtuous negro I would never say a word my dear you know. *This is the most extreme racist statement I've come across from a Southern soldier or civilian.*

We have decided to purchase a Uniform for the Company with the company fund and if the papers go through, Ben Neal will start to Atlanta in a day or two. I shall write to mother to send me some good things by him on his return. I shall have me a very fine coat made, except the chevrons on the sleeves & bars on the collar, a Captain's coat. I need a nice coat and military will be all the go when the war is over. It will cost $80 or $100 but the company voted to have a uniform and I am not going to have a "jacket" and a pair of breeches, would not wear it no how, so am going to have a uniform coat like the officers, tho not one...The quilt or comfort you need not mind about, for the worst part of the winter is over I think and I may not need them. I am glad you have learned how to make shoes. I would give you some lessons if I was with you. I can make almost as nice a pair of ladies shoes as Ditmer could..."

Sgt. Fay wants an officers coat, he was trying, at the time, to get a commission.

U.S. ARMY HERITAGE AND EDUCATION CENTER Letters of Fred Smith, 7th Texas Infantry Regiment

Letter #28 Jan 26, 1863 Port Hudson, La. Dear Father; "...Now that I have got them, I scarcely know what to do with my overshirts, or rather 1 of them. One is as many as I really need, and if we had to march anywhere, I would have to give away one of them, as my knapsack is leaded down now, with not much in it either. The first march we have to take I expect to have to throw away all but my blankets and a pair of socks...(big wardrobe that)... which however is as much or more than Stonewall's troops have, for they only have 1 blanket and often no socks extra. I intend, however, to hold fast to what I have got as long as possible. The shirts are very nice ones indeed...many people here at once admire and envy them, or rather, envy me!

If they have to march, it doesn't seem as though Pvt. Smith would have any trouble either selling or giving away one of those shirts.

WESTERNERS IN GRAY-The Men and Missions of the Elite Fifth Missouri Infantry Regiment by Phillip Thomas Tucker pub by McFarland & Co. 1953

Pg. 108 Jan. 31, 1863 "To the complete surprise of the Fifth Missouri, new Confederate uniforms arrived on the last day of the month. ...Although they had fought for the South since 1861, these were the first Confederate uniforms given to Colonel McCown's veterans. Indeed, the soldiers of the Fifth Missouri had charged Corinth's fortifications wearing parts of union uniforms and gear, carpet clothes, civilian clothes, cotton garments dyed with walnut hulls (for the butternut color), and even slave apparel....Colonel Mccown's Confederates shed tattered clothes for gray uniforms trimmed in blue, which had probably come from North Carolina storehouses. Cartridge boxes, cap pouches, and "C.S." buckles soon adorned the Fifth Missouri Rebels in their new gray uniforms. Soldiers tossed slouch and old militia hats aside for regulation gray kepis trimmed in blue. Fifth Missourians were transformed by the uniforms. Instead of looking like a bunch of farmers and militiamen, they now looked more like the crack Confederate troops that they were. McCown's newly attired Confederates "feel very proud of them, being the first uniforms that they have received." A proud Lieutenant Warren wrote in his diary that each Fifth Missouri Infantryman could now boast of owning "Gray Pants, gray Jackets & gray Caps. The collars and cuffs of the jackets are trimmed with light blue."

This is the only complete issue these men were ever given.

Pg. 117 "For the men of the Fifth Missouri, the balmy days of early spring quickly passed in western Mississippi. Although they had received some Confederate supplies and Warren's Mobile purchases, some of McCown's boys remained ill-shod and even barefoot before the hard fighting of the Vicksburg Campaign. Mischievious Private Music, for instance, became disabled when he accidentally dropped his Enfield rifle on his naked foot during a difficult drill maneuver."

As always, though, the shortage of shoes.

TRAINING, TACTICS AND LEADERSHIP IN THE CONFEDERATE ARMY OF TENNESSEE-SEEDS OF FAILURE by Andrew Haughton pub by Frank Cass 2000

Pg. 140 "...Early in February Johnston outlined the shortfalls which continued to hamper operations: 'We have a few unarmed men in each brigade; about half are without bayonets. Many barefooted; the number of the latter increasing rapidly. Thirteen thousand three hundred pairs shoes are now wanted for infantry and artillery.' This, of course, had repercussions on the morale and conduct of the Southern troops. 'One half of our company has refused to do duty on account of being barefooted', recorded one soldier enlisted in the Twenty-secound Alabama Infantryin mid-January. Three weeks later he found himself unable to participate in a review due to his own lack of footwear. Inded it took some time to make inroads into the serious equipment deficits under which the army labored..."

Remember thet number, 13,300 pairs of shoes needed.

THE JOURNAL OF ELDRESS NANCY: KEPT AT THE SOUTH UNION, KENTUCKY SHAKER COLONY AUGUST 15, 1861-SETEMBER 4, 1864 pub by Partyhnon Press 1963

Pg. 111 Feb. 1863 "...I'm told there were three thousand bushels of grain stored in the Depot, and some hogs heads of tobacco, the switch was smartly burned. These guerillas were all dressed in federal uniform..."

Go to it, men!

THIS INFERNAL WAR by Edwin Hedge Fay/Bell Irvin Wiley pub by Univ. of Texas Press 1958

Pg. 224 Okolona Miss. Feb. 12th, 1863 My Own Dear Wife "...I am sorry, indeed, that Cahill has not got here with my coat. I need it very much as the coat I have is quite ragged but perhaps when I get into Ten.(Tennessee) I can get me one there. I have no idea I shall ever see that coat, but trivial things happen for the best..."

Pg. 226 Same Camp. Feb. 22d/63 My own dear Wife; "...I was glad for I wanted to hear from you again and am in hopes Cahill will come and I will get my coat as my old one is worn completely out. But warm weather is coming on and I will not need a coat then..."

He must mean an overcoat and not a uniform jacket.

CONFEDERATE ECHOES A Soldier's Personal Story of Life in the Confederate Army From the Mississippi to the Carolinas by Albert Theodore Goodloe-First Lieutenant Company D Thirty-Fifth Regiment Alabama Volunteer Infantry C.S.A. pub by Zenger Pub. Co. 1897, 1983

Pg. 123 "…I remember the to have received a pair of "Yankee boots," as we called them, February 15, 1863, which were procured through the lines for me by Uncle Calvin Goodloe, and brought to me by Joe Thompson, a member of our regiment, who had been at home on furlough. I noted in my diary that they came in the nick of time, and that such boots were selling within our lines for $65…"

DON TROIANI'S CIVIL WAR INFANTRY Text by Earl J. Coates, Michael J. McAfee, and Don Troiani pub by Stackpole Books 2002

Pg. 23 Description of the 14th Mississippi Infantry, captured at Fort Donelson Tennessee, Feb. 18, 1863 "…a soldier in Company B of that regiment remarked that his comrades made for a "motley looking set." As he described it, "We had all our cooking utensils with us, camp kettles, skillets, ovens, frying pans, coffee pots, tin pans, tin cups and plates. We had them on our heads, on our backs, swinging from our sides, and in our hands. Some of the boys were bareheaded, some had hats and caps with no brims…we were quite a show!" According to a reporter for the Chicago Tribune who witnessed the arrival of the first group of prisoners:

"Such a thing as uniformity in dress was impossible to find, as there were no two dressed alike. Butternut colored breeches, walnut dyed jeans greatly predominated. Most of the pants were ornamented by a broad black stripe down the outer seam, sometimes of velvet, but mostly of cloth or serge. Shirts and drawers were all of the coarsest description. Hats and caps were diversified, yet they had a uniform cap-gray with b lack band. For protection against the chilling wind, the soldiers used a conglomeration of overcoats, blankets, quilts, buffalo robes, and pieces of carpeting of all colors and figures. The carpet coats are made by putting a puckering string in the edge of a piece of carpeting, and gathering it around the edge. Their officers could not be distinguished from the privates, although some had a regular gray uniformand others the army blue, the only difference a great profusion of gold lace. Many of the soldiers carried bags (carpet sacks) of all colors, and were dressed in butternut jeans and white cotton (osnaburg) overcoats. All appeared to be rough and hard."

Multiform still prevails.

BROTHERS IN GRAY-The Civil War Letters of the Pierson Family ed. by Thomas W. Cutrer & T. Michael Parrish pub by La. State Univ. Press 1997 Ninth Louisiana

Pg 155 David Pierson to William H. Pierson Camp Snyder's Mill, Feb. 18th, 1863 Dear Pa "…A portion of our baggage left behind when we came here came up yesterday and the remainder will be here tonight. One of my trunks, the only one yet arrived, had been broken open and everything worth having taken from it. I lost at least 250 dollars worth of clothing at present prices from it. It was broken open somewhere upon the route. I have no clue as to the wrong-doer, nor do I ever expect to hear from anything in it again. My other trunk & some blankets have not come up. I am in hopes to get them safe, though there is scarcely room to hope from the way our other baggage was treated..."

Here is an account of the fate of much of the stored baggage-what a disappointment for Pvt. Pierson!

Pg 157 David Pierson toMary Catherine Pierson Camp Snyder's Mill, Miss. Feb. 18th/63 "...The baggage arrived and Dave has received both his trunks broken open and the last bit of clothing taken out. I lost all my clothes, I have not a shifting suit. One pr. of pants that I never have had on, 1 pr. shoes that I left in the trunk, so I am without anything. I have but one blanket, and that I brought from home. The shoes that I have are not worth anything for they are nearly worn out, but I will get a pair made by the regimental shoemaker in a few days. As for my clothes, I do not know what to do.

When we went to leave Vau(gh)n's Station on the R.R. we were ordered to put everything in the wagon but 1 blanket to be carried to the Q.M. Department where everything we had was stolen. I have been waiting patiently for the baggage to come up that I might shift the muddy and dingy clothes that I have on, and now imagine my displeasure at not receiving anything for all the good new suit that I left when we marched from Vau(GH)N'S Station to Yazoo City. But it is no use to care for anything in this place. But if you see any opportunity to send me a couple of shirts, I would be glad to get them. You may meet with an opportunity to send them to Henry at Vicksburg and then he can send them to me.

There is no such a thing in the stores over here to be had, and if the Government don't furnish it to me, I shall be compelled to go ill-clad. If there is any chance for us to send Peter across, we will send him and let him and let him get us some things..."

Notice he mentions a regimental shoemaker.

LETTERS OF A CONFEDERATE SURGEON 1861-65 The Hurley Co. 1960

February 20, 1863 "...I went up to headquarters this evening to procure a copy of "Medical Regulations" which the Medical Director had promised me. He was not in, so I entered into a conversation with his Clerk, who inasmuch as I had on Jeans and he had on store clothes, patronized me extensively. This clerk is a fancy little fellow. He is a regular out and out Jew, and his name is Bach. His hair is black and curly and he parts it it behind and combs a little twist of it over each ear, and withal keeps it well oiled. His collar is irreproachable, and he keeps it fastened close to his little black neck, with a diminuative cravat resembling a hat band. An octangular piece of glass set in a little brass boquet ornamented his shirt busom for a breast pin. A chain of the same metal with one end in his left breast pocket, the other secured in his buttonhole by a hook, stood for a watch chain. His pants are on the "peg leg" order, that is to say, they were some two feet in diameter at the knees and four inches at the ankles. His boots were of unexeptional calf with cork heels, and inasmuch as he held the pedal extremities of a calf I suppose it was well enough..."

I'd like to have seen this dandy on a long march.

THE JOURNAL OF JULIA LEGRAND, NEW ORLEANS 1862-1863 pub by Everett Waddey & Co. 1911

Pg. 318 Feb. 21st, 1863 New Orleans, La. "Yesterday the Confederates, clad in the dear gray uniform and ladened with women's gifts, gathered, according to order, upon the levee. The "Laurel Hill," contrary to expectations, came up, but meantime the "Emire Parrish" was appointed to take them beyond the lines The "Laurel Hill" lay close beside her, also the ironclad "Star of the West." These men have been trying for months to get out, but the authorities feared they would join the "Rebel" army. It was not believed when the order to register was given that so many wished to go. A promise was given that at least a thousand should be sent out on the enchange vessel, but when the day came the number was cut down to three hundred. The excluded were furious....Mrs. Norton was down town in the morning but she did not go to the levee. She met a Confederate soldier dressed in the dear gray and presented him with a $5.00 note which she happened to have about her. He took it as a keepsake, shook hands with her, and hoped someday to see her again. She told him that it did her heart good to look at him. The federals with all their gay parade here are solitary and alone in all their drills and marches; nothing shows the tone of the public mind here than this. No little boys ever follow them except a few daring ones sometimes who hurrah for Jeff Davis, "Stonewall" Jackson or Beauregard in their very faces. Sometimes the "Bonny Blue Flag" is sung to them and children have been arrested for this offense..."

The arrests of children shouldn't surprise Miss LeGrand, she should be glad the cowardly Yankee occupation troops didn't execute those children.

Pg. 318 March 1863 "...I am growing each day fonder of our new flag, I did not love it at first-but my heart was thrilled at the accounts of our gallant Southern heroes. I am proud to hear what brave and honorable gentlemen they are, though too often clothed in homespun and too often shoeless..."

THIS INFERNAL WAR by Edwin Hedge Fay/Bell Irvin Wiley pub by Univ. of Texas Press 1958

Pg. 235 in Camp Okolona, Miss. Feb. 27/63 "…I want you to spin and make me a Partridge net by the time I come home. Lou can make that while you spin and weave me a suit of Osnaburgs or jeans…"

Pg. 236 in Camp, Okolona, Miss. Feby 27/63 My Own Dear one "…I am glad you have commenced the undershirts, hope you will finish them so I can have them this summer. I do not need them much at present though the knitted one I have is all coming to pieces. My coat is very heavy so much more than my old one that it seems very oppressive, but I'll get used to it before long I reckon. I am thinking of paying $18.00 for 24 large and 6 small buttons (Confederate) but don't know whether I will do it or not. They are very pretty & will show off my coat very prettily but I don't much care for show…"

HANDLEY LIBRARY ARCHIVES

James A. Miller Collection correspondence C.W. era misc. New Market, Va.
Pg. 39 The 3rd Louisiana Infantry also received white uniforms at this time. Private Willie H. Tunard described the issue as follows, while stationed at Snyder's Mill, Mississippi in mid-March, 1863. "The regiment received a new uniform, which they were ordered to take, much against their expressed wishes. The material was a very coarse white jeans, 'Nolens volens.' The uniforms were issued to the men, few of whom would wear them, unless under compulsion, by some special order. On March 22nd, orders were issued to cook three days rations and be prepared to move ere daylight the succeeding morning. The weather was gloomy and rainy, the roads in a terrible condition. Some of the men suggested the propriety of wearing the new white uniforms on the approaching expedition, which, it was known, would be among the swamps of the Yazoo Valley. The suggestion was almost universally adopted, affording a rare opportunity to give the new clothes a thorough initiation into the mysteries of a soldier's life. Thus the regiment assembled the next morning arrayed as if for a summer's day festival."

That assembly must have looked extraordinary. I'd have been unhappy with this uniform issue, even if it were the only clothing to be had.

Pg. 39 Another Louisiana unit, the 26th Infantry Regiment, had similar misgivings about the white uniforms. Colonel Winchester Hall, the regiment's commander, recorded tat "About this time (March 1863) we received the fruits of the conscript levees in Louisiana. The men, so raised were placed in various Louisiana commands, after receiving a white woolen uniform. The uniform was unlike any other about us and marked these men among the volunteer soldiers, who treated them with a contempt, in many cases undeserved; but so it was the white uniform was known only as an emblem of reproach wherever it appeared.

Soon after these men were in the harness, our regiment received the same kind of uniform; now the QuarterMaster's Department of the 26th was never so plethoric as to supply our mere necessities in this line, and a suit of clothes all around was a rare occasion. The clothing was sorely needed but a howl of indignation rose from the regiment, at the bare suggestion of wearing the badge of a conscript. The indignation was intensified by the fact that none of the conscripts had been put into the ranks of the 26th, and its integrity as a volunteer organization was intact.

Comfort, appearance, everything was forgotten in the thought that henceforth men who had sought the ranks, and men who had been impressed into the service, would be blended by the uniform, into an undistinguishable mass. The indignation seemed so becoming a volunteer, that officers were loath to invoke coercive measures in their power. They appealed to the men, and showed the folly of giving way to a fancy. One company after another, in time, yielded to what appeared to be inevitable, until Company B-staunch old hearts-stood out alone. Captain Bateman, however, never relaxed his efforts to kindly bring them to a sense of duty, until only two in the company stood out. The Captain reported the case to me. I ordered the men to be tied up by the thumbs until they were disposed to obey the orders of their Captain. They soon relented, but I fear not willingly."

These men were sure stubborn!

DON TROIANI'S CIVIL WAR INFANTRY-Text by Earl J. Coates, Michael J. McAfee, and Don Troiani Stackpole Books 2002

Pg. 47 20th Tennessee Infantry "...The recorded personal effects of a private of co. E who died on March 4, 1863 were probably typical of those of this regiment: 1 Knapsack, 2 coverlets, 2 hats, 3 pair drawers, 2 shirts, 1 pair pants, 1 pair boots, 1 pair socks, 1silver watch, 1 pocket book containing $71.00 paper money."

ALL AFIRE TO FIGHT-The Untold Story of the Civil War's Nith texas Cavalry by Martha L. Crabb pub by Avon Books 2000

Pg. 155 March 5, 1863 Thompson's Station, Tenn. "...The Confederates, always destitute for clothes, stripped the enemy dead and took arms, accouterments and clothing from the captured. Later in the evening victorious Confederates marched Coburn, 72 officers-minus their overcoats- and 1,221 prisoners to Columbia..."

RELUCTANT REBEL The Secret Diary of Robert Patrick 1861-1865 ed. by F. Jay Taylor pub by La State Univ. Press 1959

Pg. 100 March 6th, 1863 same camp "As soon as I arrived here, Captain Raphael asked me to exchange over-coats with him, which I did as my coat, although a very fine one, was too large for me and his just fit me. My coat I obtained at the Battle of Shiloh, out of an officer's tent and I gave it to one of our wounded boys to lie on and he brought it on to Corinth. If it had not been for this, I wound have been compelled to leave it on the field as it was out of the question for me to take care of it. Mine is the most valuable coat, but I saw he was anxious to have it so I traded with him."

BROTHERS IN GRAY-The Civil War Letters of the Pierson Family ed. by Thomas W. Cutrer & T. Michael Parrish pub by La. State Univ. Press 1997 Ninth Louisiana

Pg 167 James F. Pierson to Mary Catherine Pierson Camp Snyder's Mill, Miss. March 15th, 1863 "…The country is entirely destitute of anything in the shape of food or clothing. I lost nearly all my clothing when we left Vau(gh)n's Station, but I have got a pretty good supply again. Dave sent to Mobile Bay by our sutler and got a full supply for us next summer…"

Pg 170 David Pierson to William Pierson Camp Snyder's Mill, Miss. March 21st, 1863 "… We get a new uniform in a week for the whole Reg.…"

Government supply?

THIS INFERNAL WAR by Edwin Hedge Fay/Bell Irvin Wiley pub by Univ. of Texas Press 1958

Pg. 243 March 23rd, 1863 in Sister Sarah's Room, Selma, Ala. My Own Dearly Beloved "… Sister Sarah could not get my pants done (I bought some Prattville goods at $2.00 per yard and she is making them for me), I waited a day longer…"

EYE WITNESS TO THE CIVIL WAR AS WE LIVED IT-The Americanm Iliad by Otto Eisenshiml & Ralph Newman pub by The Universal Library 1947

Pg. 678 Spring of 1863; "A Tennesseean, H.V. Redfield…made a comparison between the two (Union & Confederate Armies) after years of intimate observations…" In clothing there was no comparison. The Southern Uniform was supposed to be gray, but the soldiers wore homespun of all colors. Of overcoats they had no regular supply. Blankets were very scarce, ditto woolen shirts and socks. The splendid double-thick overcoat that every Federal soldier had was usually warmer than all the articles of clothing combined that the Sourthern soldier had. I do not think that the Confederate government attempted to issue overcoats to their men. At least I never saw any among them that bore resmblan\ce to uniformity. But it was in cavalry equipment that the Federal soldier stood out preeminently superior. And over all, he had an oilcloth blanket which fitted around the neck, keeping the whole person dry as well as protecting arms and ammunition."

A good observastion, also more support for the image of multiformity.

THE FIRST MISSOURI CONFEDERATE BRIGADE, by Ephraim McD. Anderson pub by by Times Printing Co. St. Louis Mo. 1972

Pg. 482 "By late spring of 1863 most of the men in Lt. Gen. John C. Pemberton's Vicksburg command were clad in undyed wool uniforms, and not the butternut or bluish gray usually associated with Confederate uniforms. Like the men of the 1st Missouri Brigade, soldiers of these units had harsh words for these undyed uniforms..."

THE CIVIL WAR LETTERS OF JOSHUA K. CALLOWAY ed. by Judith Lee Hallock pub by Univ. Ga. Press 1997

Pg. 84 Shelbyville, Tenn. April 1863 "...I am sorry to learn, which (I) have, that Leiut. Sellick lost the Carpet Bag. It was stolen from him. I had two of the best knit shirts in it I ever saw. The two cost me $13. My old sheepskin and several worn out socks were also in it...Corpl. Smith had a pair of pants and a pair of Drawers in it. So that it contained at least $30 worth of clothing. I hope you will send those things (with) Leiut. Mims or someone else though I don't need anything now but some socks and a towel or two and a handkerchief or two. I bought two pair of socks the other day at a dollar a pair-cotton socks..."

Pg. 80 Camp Near Shellbyville, Tennessee April 1863 Mrs. D. Callaway: "P.S. I forgot to tell you how I needed some socks. I went to put on some this morning and could only find one but that was so badly worn out that I could not wear it; & it has a hole in the toe big enough to let out three of the biggest toes I "ve got. So I had to keep on the best ones of my dirty ones. Now I've got both wadded up & stuck between my toes to keep them from pulling back up my leg and leaving my foot sockless. And this worries my toes terribly as well as my patience.

I also need a handkerchief. I've only got my old calico one, and it's the dirtiest thing you ever saw....

P.S. No. 2. A cotton handkerchief here is worth from 3 to 6 dollars and a Silk one is worth from $8 to $12."

THE COLOR GUARD: BEING A CORPOREAL'S NOTES OF MILITARY SERVICE IN THE NINETEENTH ARMY CORPS by James Kendall Hosmer pub by Walker Wise & Co. 1864

Pg. 137 April 1863 country of the Teche La. "...We came to a spot where the negroes say the rebels meant to make a stand,-then thought better of it. We imagined the sallow, haggard hosts waiting in their butternut-coats behind the fences...Soon we were beyond the village, and, after a mile or two, came to a turn in the road where the advance, a little while before, had had a sharp skirmish. Six or seven dead horses lay in the road; one poor fellow, in butternut, lay stetched on the sod,-the morning light, bright and unpitying, on his dead, uncovered face. Five or six more were in a gully close by There had been no time yet to bury them..."

TRUE TALES OF THE SOUTH AT WAR Collected and Edited by Clarence Poe pub by Univ. of N.C. Press 1961

reminiscences of Barry Benson

Pg. 124 April 1863 "...The war exercises our ingenuity. I have just finished an excellent and useful pair of gloves for Mr. E. knit of rabbit fur and wool-equal proportions spun together. They are warmer than wool and not too coarse for horseback...."

I wonder how well they wore in constant use.

THE COLOR GUARD: BEING A CORPOPAL'S NOTES OF MILITARY SERVICE IN THE NINETEENTH ARMY by James Kendall Hosmer Walker Wise & Co. 1864

Pg. 244 April, 1863 "...They were stout, well-fed men,- some in the butternut dress, some in grey. Their clothing looked serviceable, and was in good condition as the clothing of soldiers is likely to be during a hard campaign..."

A SOLDIER'S DIARY: THE STORY OF A VOLUNTEER 1862-1865 by David Lane privately published

Pg. 270 April 1863 David Lane is a Union soldier "...The weather was warm and pleasant now, but the burning heat of a Southern summer in close upon us. A forced march was before us, with no teams to carry our luggage. We could not carry all our winter clothing, therefore hundreds of good blankets and overcoats were thrown away. When we had marched three or four miles many of the men found they still had too much load, and then the work of lightening up began in earnest. For miles the road was strewn with blankets, dress coats, blouses, pants, drawers and shirts. In fact enough clothing was thrown away for Rebels to pick up to supply a whole brigade. No wonder so many Rebel regiments are dressed in our uniforms…"

A good explanation, but why is there not a group detailed to follow along by the ordinance officer to gather these clothes. Not only to re-issue them but to keep those ragged Rebs from picking them up.

BROTHERS IN GRAY-The Civil War Letters of the Pierson Family ed. by Thomas W. Cutrer & T. Michael Parrish pub by La. State Univ. Press 1997 Ninth Louisiana

Pg 172 David Pierson to William Pierson Camp Snyder's Mill, Miss. April 3rd, 1863 Dear Pa "…I very much regret having wrote you anything about our losses as perhaps it has induced you to believe that our suffering has really been more than what it was. It is true I missed my fine blankets and fine clothes, &c., at first, but have so far supplied their place now as almost to forget it. As for Jim, of course he writes home the darkest side of the case to make you appreciate the fact that he is soldiering, but the truth is, he has had plenty of clothes and been very comfortably situated as well as myself, with one or two exceptional times and places. He has just drawn from the Government a full soldier's outfit consisting of a uniform suit, shirt, shoes, socks and cap, and by some cunning of his own had nearly supplied himself before…."

Here's an account of a generous government supply, see below.

SOJURNS OF A PATRIOT The Field and Prison Papers of An Unreconstructed Confederate Richard Bender Abell & Fay Adamson Gecik pub by Southern Heritage Press Murfreesboro, TN 1998

Pg. 145 same camp, April 4th, 1863 "…We have all drawed new uniforms. Also, shirts and drawers, a pair to the man…."

THE CIVIL WAR LETTERS OF JOSHUA K. CALLOWAY ed. by Judith Lee Hallock pub by Univ. Ga. Press 1997

Pg. 82 Shelbyville, Tenn. In Camp, April 7th, 1863 Mrs. J.K. Calaway: "…it I had a hat I'd be fine looking, but this old cap has got to be the ugliest thing I ever saw….

I send home, by Leiut. Sellick,some articles of clothing which I shall not need this summer. Two undershirts, and some old socks so badly worn that I can't wear them. I have not determined yet whether to send my overcoat or not, if I do I will speak of it in a Post Script. I also have a nice blue coverlet that I am at a loss to know what (to) do with. I have a good mind to send it home. I have not yet got the things I sent for. I need them very much, especially the socks "and a hat".

PORTRAITS OF CONFLICT-A Photographic History of Louisiana in the Civil War by Carl Moneyhon & Bobby Roberts pub by Univ. Ark. Press 1990

Pg. 200 April 18, 1863 "The responsibility of supplying Gardner's troops with the accouterments they required fell on his chief quartermaster, Maj. James W. Sprately. It proved to be a trying task, for the Confederacy was chronically short of almost everything. On April 18, 1863, Sprately wrote the Quartermaster Department in Jackson, Mississippi, asking for spades, shovels, axes, picks, tents, kettles, cooking utensils, socks, drawers, shirts, pants, hats, and especially shoes. He asked if he could get a supply of leather to make shoes. "The articles enumerated," he added, "are absolutey required for the welfare and comfort of the troops in my district." In exasperation he pointed out that "requisitions for the amount required of each article have been sent to Jackson, Miss. several times and up to the present has not been filled." The Quartermaster Depot may have been sympathetic with his plight, but, in fact, there was very little that could be spared for Gardner's troops. His men would largely have to make do with what was already at hand and with what they could scrounge locally…"

Sounds like the story of every Confederate unit.

THIS INFERNAL WAR by Bell Irvin Wiley/Lucy E. Fay pub by Univ. of Texas Press1958

Pg. 253 April 20th, 1863 Camp near Spring Hill, Tenn. My own dear Sarah; "…If I get my discharge I shall go back to Okolona after my clothing. I left my valise there and though I cannot bring it on horseback I can fill my saddlebags. I bought or rather swapped a pair with Parson Radcliff yesterday. Gave him $5.00 difference I had the old pair Rich brought soap in when I left home first time. I got a very nice pair, patent leather, and I now can carry all my clothes…"

SOJURNS OF A PATRIOT The Field and Prison Papers of An Unreconstructed Confederate Richard Bender Abell & Fay Adamson Gecik pub by Southern Heritage Press Murfreesboro, TN 1998

Pg. 150 Camp near Pocotaligo Beaufort Dist., S.C. April 27th 1863 "…I want you to send, me those pants and that Grammer that was sent home when you have a sure chance. I am not needing the pants at present time but you can send them when you have a chance…"

VMI MS# 190

J.R. Hurley collection-private, Co.A 39 Alabama Inf. Regt. Shelbyville Tenn.

April 28 1863 Dear Sister "... I wrote home for clothes but we have drawn as many clothes as we want but as for shoes my shoe(s) is almost worn out and I don't expect I can draw any..."

On Picket Shelbyville Tenn. May 21st 1863 "...you all need not make me any clothes for we can draw as many clothes as we want and I have drawn a good pair of shoes...."

Camp Chattanooga July 7 1863 Dear Sisters "...I lost all my clothes but what I had on. I toted my knapsack about halfway and put it in Dick Mitchell's wagon and it broke down and he had to leave it and my things is gone. I want you to send me some nice home clothes. As soon as you can send me a shirt and a pair of drawers and a pair of pants that will do for a while. I kept my socks..."

What is this? First he says he can draw anything he needs, then, after his knapsack is stolen, he's asking for clothing from home. I guess he couldn't draw any more clothing so soon after being supplied. You'd think he wouls have taken better care of his clothes.

THIS INFERNAL WAR Edwin Hedge Fay/Bell Irvin Wiley Univ. of Texas Press 1958

Pg. 267 May 20, 1863 Camp Spring Hill, My own dear, dear, sarah; "...The reception of the coat question has been frequently decided and entered so upon the docket but as an appeal has been taken this Court decides and affirms the Coat is a decided success and reflects much credit upon the sewer. It will be a fine next winter coat. I thought I wrote about Mrs. Sayre putting on three more pockets. Did I not? The soap, Drawers, wool socks &c. came too and were thankfully received and thankfully acknowledged. Rich can wear the socks next winter if I get back to Okolona to get my baggage. I left it all there save a change. Gladly will I receive the cottonade Pants, if I can get them. I can make drawers of them in the winter. I need another pair..."

Pg. 273 May 28, 1863 24 miles N.E. Columbus, Miss."...I am the dirtiest, dustiest mortal you ever saw I reckon. I had the domestic shirt and drawers you made for me stolen 2 ms south of Columbia, Tenn. They were taken out of my saddle bags. No it was the old pair of drawers I bro't form home with me that were stolen. I'll borrow clothes while I have mine washed and then I won't have so much to carry. I hope I'll have a chance to go to Okolona and get my valise....I believe I forgot to reply to your query as to whether I wanted those cottonade pants. Yes, I do, for those Sister Sarah made me are all worn out in from rubbing against my saddle. I am going to try and have them mended..."

FROM THE FLAME OF BATTLE TO THE FIERY CROSS—The 3rd Tennessee Infantry by James van Eldik pub by Yucca Tree Press 2001

Pg. 139 May 1863 Raymond, Miss. "...Nearly one third of the command at this time had no shoes, having worn them out on the march, and in consequence were very footsore. This, together with their want of supplies, which at times were very short, were subjects of pleasantries with the men who consoled themselves with the prospect of a fight every other day to make amends for their privations..."

It seems they don't even consider getting rations or clothing from the government.

LIFE IN DIXIE DURING THE WAR by Mary A.H. Gay Charles P. Byrd pub. 1897

Pg. 63 Atlanta "...Here I found King, our faithful negro man, as busy as a bee, labeling and packing medicine for shipment. I approached him and said:

"King, Thomie has come" (exchanged from Camp Douglas)

"Marse Thomie?"

"Yes'

"Thank God,' he said with fervor.

When I was about to leave the store, he said:

"Miss Mary, just wait a minute, please, and I will get something that I want you to take to Marse Thomie, and tell him I don't want him to be hurt with me for seding it to him. I just send it because I love him-me and him was boys together, you know, and I always thought he ought to 'er took me with him to the war."

"What is it, King?"

"Just a little article I got in trade, Miss Mary," was all the satisfaction he vouchsafed.

When he handed it to me, knowing by the sense of touch that it was a package of dry goods, I took it to Mrs O'Cooer's millinary establishment, and aasked the priviledge of opening it there. Imagine my astonishment and delight, when I beheld a pattern of fine gray cassimere. I felt of it, and held it up between my eyes and the light. There was nothing shoddy about it. It was indeed a piece of fine cassimere, finer and better than anything I could have procured in Atlanta at that time. The circumstances was suggestive of Elijah and the ravens, and I thanked God for the gift so opportune, and lost no time in returning to the drug store, and thanking King, the raven employed by the Lord to clothe one of His little ones. Nor did I lose any time in adding to the package other articles of necessity, flannel and the best Georgia-made homespun I could procure, and was then ready to take the return train to Decatur. Thomie was deeply touched by the opportune gift, and said that King was a great boy, and that he must see him.

After supper I clandestinely left the house, and ran around to Todd McAllister's and begged him to take the job of making the suit. He agreed to cut the coat, vest and pantaloons by measure, and for that purpose went home with me, shears and tape measure in hand. Having finished this important part of the job, he told me he could not make the suit himself, but thought if I would "talk right pretty to the old lady," she would do it. Next morning I lost no time in "talking pretty" to the old ladyand, having secured her promise to undertake the work, it was soon in her hands. With the help of faithful, efficient women, and I suspect her husband too, the job was executed surprisingly soon. In the meantime, the making of flannel garments, and homespun shirts with bosums made of linen pillow-cases, was progressing with remarkable celerity.

When all was finished and Thomie was arrayed in the new suit, which set admirably well-notwithstanding the room allowed for increasing dimensions, which we doubted not under good treatment he would attain-King Solomon, in purple and fine linen, was not looked upon with more admeration, than was he by his loving mother and sisters…"

A good example of true a master/servant relationship. This book is one that Margeret Michel borrowed heavily from to write "Gone with the Wind." I recommend it if you want to know the real, undramatised version.

THREE MONTHES IN THE SOUTHERN STATES: APRIL-JUNE1863 Diary of Sir Arthur Freemantle pub by William Blackwood and Son, 1863

Pg. 320 May 1863 "…Six of us pigged in one very small room, paying a dollar each for this luxury to an old woman, who was most inhospitable and told us "she didn't want to see no soldiers, as the Yanks would come back and burn her house for harboring rebels." I am always taken for a Confederate officer, partly from being in their company, and partly on account of my clothes, which happen to be a grey shooting suit, almost the same color as most of the soldier's coats…" June 22, 1863 (Pender's Div.) "…The soldiers of this division are a remarkably fine body of men, and look quite seasoned and ready for any work. Their clothing is serviceable, so also are their boots, but there is the usual utter absence of uniformity as to color and shape of their garments and hats: grey of all shades, and brown clothing with felt hats, predominate…"

Once again, the land ladie's fear (justified) that the Yankees would burn her out if they thought she was harboring Rebel soldiers. Not surprising, as burning that woman's house was much preferable to going and fighting the Rebels.

LETTER FROM WARREN HAPGOOD FREEMAN TO J.D. FREEMAN pub by H.O. Houghton and Co. 1878

Pg. 74 May 18, 1863 "…Our papers speak about the prisoners we take as looking half-starved, ragged etc. Now I could never see this. Those that I saw, and I should think there were 2,000 of them, were fully equal in looks and condition to the average of our men; that say we can never subdue them, they will fight till there is not a man left. Their grey uniforms give them a kind of dirty appearance, and they nearly all wore felt hats, but some of them had on very neat and handsome uniforms…"

DEAR IRVIE, DEAR LUCY-The Civil War Letters of Capt. Irving A. Buck, General Cleburne's AAG & Family pub by Buck Pub. Co. 2002

Pg. 150 May 19, 1863 Head Quarters, Cleburne's Division, Western Tn. My Dear Lu, "My wardrobe is in very good condition, have more clothes than I am allowed to carry by orders-and our larder is very well supplied, have beef, mutton, fish (sometimes), eggs, coffee, tea occasionally, butter, rolls and strawberries."

WESTERNERS IN GRAY-The Men and Missions of the Elite Missouri Infantry Regiment by Phillip Thomas Tucker pub by McFarland & Co. 1953

Pg. 220 May 19, 1863 Defenses of Vicksburg, after the repulse of a Union assault "…That night McCowan's men scoured the valleys of death in the darkness, taking anything of value. As in Missouri State Guard days, the Fifth Missouri soldiers took shoes, ammunition and blue pants from the dead federals…."

By now I thought it would be second nature to re-supply oneself by stripping the Yankee dead.

THE CONFEDERATE VETERAN VOL. IV 1896

August 1896 Pg. 277 An Arkansas Boy's Escape "I then determined to jump overboard; and about nine o'clock the night of May 23, 1863 I divested myself of all outer clothing, stealthily crept into the wheelhouse, let all hold go, and, with a leap, a plunge, went down behind the wheel into the Mississippi…About noon I left the swamps and struck a settlement ; but as my garb was not presentable, I had to surround every house and plantation. At three o'clock in the afternoon I found myself in the suburbs of New Madrid, Mo.I ran to the first barn I saw, and sent a negro to the house with the request that his master would send me a pair of pants. He soon returned with a pair of Federal cavalry pants, much too long; but I donned the "blue" with much sarisfaction, not being very particular then as to size or color…When it was "good dark," I ventured to a farmhouse and asked the good woman of the house for my supper…When introduced to the husband, he took me to his room and gave me a pair of new boots…My boots were hurting my feet, so I strung and tied them across my shoulders on a stick…The next morning I traded my boots for a coat that had been used as a saddle blanket, and, after taking dinner with a Mr. Franklin (one of the faithful) I exchanged my Yankee cap and pants for an old white hat and a pair of butternut breeches…"

THIS BAND OF HEROES-Granbury's Texas Brigade C.S.A. by James M. McCaffery pub by Texas A&M Univ. 1996

Pg. 62 Tullahoma, Miss. May 25, 1863 "The men of Churchill's brigade (paroled POWs) were issued new gray uniforms and captured tents and camp equipage and the men began to feel like soldiers again…"

LETTERS OF ARCHIE LIVINGSTON, 1ST SGT. 3RD FLORIDA INFANTRY,

Fairground Hospital No.2 Atlanta Geo May 26, 1863Dear Mother; "…John Inglis got here last Sunday and delivered my shirts, pants & coat &c, all of which fit exactly and I am a thousand times obliged to you & my sisters for them. Every body praises them, especially the pants, coat & vest all the boys down at the cars to day would ask me where I got my (harness?) from…"

FROM THAT TERRIBLE FIELD-CIVIL WAR LETTERS OF JAMES M. WILLIAMS, Twenty-First Alabama Volunteer Infantry pub by Univ Al Press

Pg. 113 May 30 1862 Oven Bluff "…My homespun coat will be "done" in a few days all-ready for a pair or two of stars…'

CIVIL WAR SOLDIERS by Reid Mitchell pub by Viking Peguin 1988

Pg. 51 Summer 1863 At Andersonville: "One prisoner bartered a silver pencil to a guard for a Quart of cornmeal and one-half plug of Cavendish tobacco; he then traded with new prisoners at the rate of one chew tobacco for one brass button; when he had twelve he traded with the guard, exchanging the buttons for two more quarts of meal and one full plug of tobacco. The guards made Confederate uniform buttons from the Union ones…"

THE COLOR GUARD: BEING A CORPOREAL'S NOTES OF MILITARY SERVICE IN THE NINTEENTH ARMY CORPS by James Kendall Hosmer pub by Walker Wise & Co. 1864

Pg. 208 June 1863 Port Hudson "...The most you are likely to see will be a hand put up for a moment, with a ramrod, as the charge is pushed home; or a glimpse of butternut as a fellow jumped past some interval in the sand-bags..."

Website-Confederate Cavalryman: Mud Camp Ford, Kettle Creek, and Turkey-Neck Bend

Pg. 4 June, 1863 "legends which state that Morgan's men lived off the land, pillaging any food and supplies they might need, appear to be largely true. These were not perfectly groomed cavalrymen in freshly ironed gray uniforms with plumed hats and highly polished boots. This was a motley crue. Lacking uniforms issued by the Confederacy, some wore homemade uniforms while others were seen wearing wharever clothing they happened to be wearing when they enlisted. Boots were also in short supply. There are stories of shops along the path of the raid being looted of every shoe. A few of Morgan's Men being seen riding barefoot. Many of the men wore large, noisy spurs and their hats pinned up at one side with a crescent or a star. Pinning up the hat on the side of their dominant hand allowed the men to wield their sword or Bowie knife without knocking or slicing off the brim of their hat..."

WALKER'S TEXAS DIVISION, C.S.A. Greyhounds Of The Trans-Mississippi by Richard Lowe pub by La. State Univ Press 2004

Pg. 108 June, 1863 Fighting along the Mississippi River near Vicksburg, Ferderal Admiral Porter staed "They are a half-starved, half-naked set, and are in hopes of captureing some of the transports with clothing and provisions."

"Some of the Texans might have agreed with Porter that they were a tattered bunch that summer. Their weeks in the swamps had certainly done nothing to improve their appearance. Lt. Theophilus Perry of the 28th Cavalry wrote his wife that "some of the men have not changed their suits in four weeks. They remain naked while they wash their clothes. A number of our men have been left at Monroe (La.) on account of being barefooted." Private Farrow of the 19th Infantry grumbled that "our clothing is in an awful condition (,) some is perfectly rotten. My bed clothes are damaged badly. I will throw all of them away when we leave here but my blanket." Private Blessington laughed that "Falstaff's ragged regiment was well uniformed in comparison with our troops. No two were costumed with any attempt at uniformity." Not only were they shabby in rainment, they were scruffy and filthy beyond recognition. "But few of the troops had shaved in weeks, and, as a consequence, there was a large and general assortment of unbrushed black, gray, red and sandy beards, as well as ferocious mustaches and whiskers-enough to rig out an army of West India Buccaneers. A more brigandish set of Anglo-Saxon forces has never been collected. Blessington wrote," So completely disguised were we all, that I doubt whether our anxious mothers would have recognized us…"

Ragged Rebels

THIS INFERNAL WAR Edwin Hedge Fay/Bell Irvin Wiley Univ. of Texas Press 1958

Pg. 276 25 miles from Canton June 1st 1863 "…After stopping last light I went to the Spring and found a tub and dipped up a tub and had a fine bath and if I had only had some clean clothes I would have felt very well but I have no drawers, having been wearing these all the way from Spring Hill. But I'll send up to Okolona and get my baggage if we ever go into camp again for a few days…."

THE FREMANTLE DIARY-A Journal of the Confederacy pub.by Burford Books 1954

Pg. 134 June 4 1863 Cavalry skirmish near Shelbyville, Tn. (Yankees failed to attack) "I heard the soldiers remarking that they "didn't like being done out of their good boots"-one of the principle objects in killing a Yankee being apparently to get hold of his valuable boots."

This trip through the Confederacy was quite learning experience for Sir Fremantle. Here he has just learned a truism of Rebel soldiers regarding the Yankees.

KATE, THE JOURNAL OF A CONFEDERATE NURSE ed by Richard Barksdale Harwell pub by Univ of Louisiana Press 1998

Pg. 109 June 8, 1863 Northern Georgia, near Lookout Mountain "If my attention had not been drawn to the extravagant dress of the speaker, I could not but think, if he had worn a gown to hide it, that it would have been much more in keeping with his priestly office. His uniform was one of the most showy I have ever seen worn by any of our officers since the war; it was of the finest black broadcloth, cut "a la militaire," with the unsual amount of gilt buttons…

I am told he is much beloved in the army, and has been the means of doing a great deal of good. His clothes were presented to him by his brigade, for his kindness to the men; but I do wish he would not wear them, especially at this time, when such clothes are certain to be the subject of remark…"

Fine clothing is out of place now.

U.S. ARMY HERITAGE AND EDUCATION CENTER Letters of Lt. Wm. D. Cole 35th Alabama Infantry Regiment

June 12th, 1863 Wartrace, Tenn. Cornelia, "...In regard to my clothing I don't want but one pair of cotton pants for we (have) not much use here for cotton clothing. I sleep in my blankets every night and I often get so cold before day that I cannot sleep-I never have seen such cold weather in June before...Be sure and send me my shirts and one pair of jeans pants whether you send any thing else or not...I have lost near all of my clothes. I have not shifting clothes (?) at this time. I have not but one pair of pants. I have one domestic shirt and my striped shirt two pair of old socks and no drawers. So you can see that I have lost almost all that I had. We have no tents and when it rains we have to take it just like the dumb brutes and every thing that we have gets wet and it remains so for I have never seen so much rain in the summer season-I have been wet for two weeks at the time, no clothes to change and it raining all the time..."

I don't know why the entire army wasn't sick with pneumonia.

THE CIVIL WAR LETTERS OF JOSHUA K. CALLOWAY ed. By Judith Lee Hallock Univ. Ga. Press 1997

Pg. 96 Shelbyville Tenn. Picket Camp, as usual June 17th, 1863 Mrs. J.K. Callaway "...Mr. Callen brought my bundle of clothes all that you said you sent. I am very much obliged to you. I have got on my shirt and lighter pants now. I like them very much. The darker pants are not as pretty but I think I can do very well till winter. I will send home my overcoat and one pair pants by Mr. Callen..."

BLOODY BANNERS AND BAREFOOT BOYS-A HISTORY OF THE 27TH REGIMENT ALABAMA INFANTRY CSA-The Civil War Memoirs and Diary Entries of J.P. Canon MD compiled and ed by Noel Crowson & John W. Brogden pub by Burd St. Press 1997

Pg. 35 June 17th, 1863 "We had drawn no clothing for quite a long time and, as might be supposed, were a ragged set with the exception of a few of us who were fortunate enough to have some sent from home. On June 17th the Quartermaster informed us he had received a supply and the announcement was received with demonstrations of joy, but after an inventory of his stock was taken, and a division among the companies completed, it was disappointing. A memorandum of Co. C's will give a fair idea of what the regiment got, as the goods were as nearly equally divided as was possible.

Company C had forty men present and its prorata was five pairs of cotton pants, six shirts, one pair of drawers. The pants and shirts were issued to those who needed them most, but it was a hard matter to decide as all were in about the same fix. When it came to the solitary garment, it was suggested to "draw straws" for them. All who were entirely destitute were ordered into line and fourteen responded. One long and thirteen short straws were prepared and the lottery declared open for business. The drawing then proceeded with much merriment, for the spectators, resulting in the capitol prize being won by Dick Terrill…"

A very insignificant issue of clothing.

Pg. 36 "…The next day…pitched camp at Moore's Ferry…

When we left this camp, we marched back in the direction of Canton and, while at camp on the Fulton farm, some friends from North Alabama arrived with a large quantity of clothing and letters. The ladies at home had sewing societies, wove and made clothing, knitted socks, scraped lint etc., and when the opportunity presented, sent us the fruit of their labors. The clothing came at an opportune time as we had sent everything to Vicksburg almost three months before and never expected to see them again…"

The Ladie's Sewing Societies have saved the day agsin!

THIS INFERNAL WAR Edwin Hedge Fay/Bell Irvin Wiley Univ. of Texas Press 1958

Pg. 283 June 20th 1863 "…John Leseueur and Linn Watkins came last night having come from Okolona but did not bring me any of my clothes so I am minus drawers and don't know what I am going to do but I'll get along some way by borrowing as I have done…"

REMINISCENCES OF A PRIVATE William E. Bevins of the First Arkansas Inf. C.S.A. pub by Univ. Ark. Press 1992

Pg. 125 June 1863 Manchester, Tn. "…June 22nd we went there to relieve a Louisiana Regiment. When we arrived they were on dress parade, eleven hundred strong and their drill was simply fine, but they had never smelled powder nor marched at all. They wore nice caps, fine uniforms, white gloves, fine shop-made laced high shoes. They carried fat haversacks and new canteens, fine new fat knapsacks with lots of underclothing and even two pairs of shoes. They laughed at us in our shabby dress, with our dirty haversacks and no knapsacks. We had one suit of underwear wrapped in our blankets and our accouterments were reduced to the lightest weight possible. They said we were too few to meet the enemy, but we told them we would stay with any who came to engage us. We also told them that they couldn't get one week's campaign with such knapsacks. Some of the Boys said, "We will follow in your wake and replenish our wardrobes…"

That last statement I would say, was quite correct.

DARK AND BLOODY GROUND by Thomas Ayres pub by Taylor Trade Pub. 2001

Pg. 179 Brashear City (La.) June 23, 1863 Confederate attack on-"...A Federal soldier remembered his captors as, "the most ragged, dirty-looking set of rascals I had ever seen. The only thing uniform among them was dirt-shirts, pants, skin being all of a fine mud color... (But) on the whole they were a good-natured, jolly set of country boys."..."Some of the Texans had adorned themselves in brand-new uniforms from the Union supply depot."...

Ragged rebels victorious!

BLACK FLAG OVER DIXIE ed. by Gregory J.W. Urwin pub by Southern Illinois Univ. Press 2004

Pg. 22 (June 27, 1863) "...J.P. Blessington a private in the 16th Texas Infantry commented (on the 19th& 12th Texas Cavalry) "As they passed us, I could not but admire their horsemanship; they all appeared to be excellent horsemen, and at a distance their general appearance was decidedly showy and gallant." Although he noticed their uniforms "contained as many colors as the rainbow," the rifles and swords just issued to the command impressed him..."

PORTRAIT OF CONFLICT-A Photographic History of Luoisiana in the Civil War by Carl Moneyhon & Bobby Roberts pub by Univ. Ark. Press 1990

Pg. 242 Port Hudson, La. "On June 29, 1863, the garrison ran out of beef and almost immediately the hungry soldiers began eating mule meat. Linn Tanner, a bugler in Boone's artillery, remembered how comical it was "to see the facial expression" of the men when they first viewed "the platters of hot steak fried in its own grease, or the chunk of boiled mule as it floated in a bucket of stew." Like most soldiers, Tanner himself was a little apprehensive about having his first taste of mule but he was terribly hungry. When Tanner received his portion he cut off a piece and shoved it in his mouth. Tanner managed to keep the meat down but it was a fight. However, by the next morning he had recovered from his "squeamishness and could eat mule without thinking."

Making due with what they had.

THE COLOR GUARD: A CORPORAL'S NOTES OF MILITARY SERVICE IN THER NINTEENTH ARMY by James Kendall Hosmer pub by Walker wise & Co. 1864

July 1863 After the surrender of Port Hudson, La; "...Here they were, the real truculent and unmitigated reb in butternut of every shade, from the dingy gree that clothes trhe unripe nut, to the tawny brown and faded tan which it wears at other stages—butternut mixed with a dull,characterless gray. There was not attempt at uniform, yet something common, in the dress of the whole company, --a faded lookn as if the fabric, whatever its original hue, had felt the sun until all life and brightness had wilted in the web and had been killed out of the dye. Still the clothing was whole; and upon closer inspection, looked strong and serviceable, thoigh very coarse... The officers, sometimes, wore a uniform of gray, the rank being indicated by badges upon the collar. Sometimes there was nothing to distinguish them from the privates. They were brown and dusty, though no more than we, who, like them, had lived in burrows, on our backs and stomachs, for a month. We really thought, that in condition they were ahead of us. The climate and hard marching had sallowed and dug into our cheeks and shaken us on our pins, whereas they were, htough not fat, by no means guant and emaciated. Still they hinted at rats, mule meat, and other hard matters they had been forced of late to come to..."

Cpl. Hosmer gives us a view of the varying shades of butternut, probably from differing stages of ripness and/or other dye material added to the pot.

UNDER BOTH FLAGS- Personal Stories of Sacrifice and Struggle During the Civil War ed by Tim Gott pub by The Lyons Press 1896

July 4, 1863 The surrender at Vicksburg- by a Union Officer- John F. Black "It would be impossible for me to describe their clothing, and more impossible to conjecture how men clothed as they were could fight as they did..."

U.S. ARMY HERITAGE AND EDUCATION CENTER Letter of Abram M. Glazener, 18th Alabama Infantry Regiment, CSA Co.I

July 7th, 1863 Chattanugee Tennisee Dear Wife, "...I left my knapsack for to be carried up on the cars. I have just got it today, have lsot onething (nothing or everything) but my blanket (and) one pair of socks. I have laid on the ground without anything under me for 12 days. I never saw the like in all my life so many men gave out clothes wagons mules horses and everything left strewn along the way I came through with the wagon....I have had to bye my provisions foir some time if you cannot get my shoes conveniently let them alone as I can draw a pair. I need nothing but a hat and blanket..."

Celine-Rembering Louisiana1850-1871 by Celine Fremaux Garcia ed. by Patrick J. Geary pub by Univ. Ga. Press 1987

Pg. 65 Summer, 1863 The War in Baton Rouge "A day came when father brough home several tin models of peculiarly shaped figures not unlike ill-shaped squares, and a lot, a great lot, maybe a cart-load, of brown paper, and several lead pencils. "Children," he announced, "a soldier's children are young soldiers. I want all this paper cut up into pieces, like these tin models. The country needs them." That evening many young men and ladies came and all fell to work marking around the tin models with a pencil, making no waste and cutting with scissors on the mark. We knew later thet were to be made into loaded cartridges for the soldiers. We cut a long time, then we rolled them on little wooden molds, and finally they were filled and became real war implements....(Baton Rouge) Before night there were 5,000 men camped on the Boulevard. By morning there were twice as many and every boat that landed brought in companies. To be sure, they were not equipped and in some cases the uniformity was only in hats or caps or shirt sleeves. One company had jeans pants, common 75 jeans pants over their tailor-made trousers, but all wore a determined look..."

Sounds like a determined population, even the children.

SOJURNS OF A PATRIOT The Field and Prison Papers of An Unreconstructed Confederate by Richard Bender Abell & Fay Adamson Gecik pub by Southern Heritage Press Murfreesboro, TN 1998

Pg. 162 Camp near Morton Rankin Co. Miss. Letters of Ptvt. Augustus Pitt Adamson to Mr. W. F. Adamson Dear Brother; July 20 1863 After fighting around Jackson Miss. "...I could not carry my knapsack but cut it up and made a sack out of the oil cloth to carry my things in ..."

THIS INFERNAL WAR Edwin Hedge Fay/Bell Irvin Wiley Univ. of Texas Press 1958

Pg.294 Acoss rearl River in rear of Jackson, Miss. July 15th, 1863 No heading; "...As far as clothing is concerned Mother has made me some she writes me and if I need I shall send Rich after them..."

Pg. 298 Camp Brandon Miss. July 23rd 1863 My Own, Own Dear Wife "...I sent out some lowells (corn sacks) and am having me a pair of drawers made. I am also going to have me a shirt made of the same. I am not suffering for clothes now, and there is some talk of our going to Okolona. If I do I can get the clothes I left there..."

U.S. ARMY HERITAGE AND EDUCATION CENTER Letters of Lt. William D. Cole 35th Alabama Infantry Regiment

July 28, 1863 Lynne Station near Chatanooga, Tenn. Dear Wife "...I have had my drawers made. I did not make them myself. I found an old lady near where we are camped that cut and made them for me for one dollar. I get them this morning,-so if or when you have a chance to send my clothing to me you must not send me any drawers…"

FOURTEEN HUNDRED AND 91 DAYS IN THE CONFEDERATE ARMY A Journal Kept by W.W. Heartsill or Camp Life; Day by Day of the W. P. Lane Rangers From April 19, 1861 To May 20, 1865 ed. by Bell Irvin Wiley pub by Broadfoot Pub. Co. Wilmington, N.C. 1987

Pg. 140 Hamilton Co. TN. July 30th 1863 "…Raining and we have no tents. Frank Hamlett and I bunk together and between us we have one blanket; this we have stretched over a pole about three feet from the ground; with the sides tied to stakes near the ground which throws it in the shape of a gable roof, then with a few leaves on the ground and nicely ditched all around, this constitutes our DOMICIL and you may count hundreds of the same sort in the Regiment, some however have nice thatched roofs to their huts and are very well fixed up for the bad weather…."

THIS INFERNAL WAR by Bell Irvin Wiley/Lucy E. Fay pub by Univ of Texas Press 1959

Pg. 307 July 30, 1863 No heading; "…Rich is doing very well (sgt fay's servant rich had broken his leg in a fall from a horse) and I hope will be able to get along in a few weeks. I intend sending him to father's after some clothing for me when he gets well enough to travel. I told you I had sent some Lowells to have a pais of drawers made and they do very well. I could not get the shirts made but I am not suffering for clothing now…"

Pg. 310 August 3rd, 1863 My own darling Wife;"…Mother as you will see will make me the clothing I need and I have written her to get me some socks as Rich has lost mine. I went to see him yesterday evening and his leg is growing together finely. The Cars come into Brandon now and just as soon as he is able to travel I intend to send him to Rocky Mount after my clothes…"

Pg. 318 Camp Brandon, Miss. My own dearly Beloved; "…I want a pair of boots but not just yat as mine are not gone and I cannot take care of two pairs…"

RELUCTANT REBEL The Secret Diary of Robert Patrick 1861-1865 ed. by F. Jay Taylor pub by La State Univ. Press 1959

Pg. 123 August 12th, 1863 Enterprise, Miss. "Drew clothing for the regiment to-day. Bought me some cloth to make shirts. Also 2 pr. Silver sleeve buttons. I called at the house of a citizen to see if I could get my shirts made. I found a homely girl and her mother at the house. In answer to my enquiry as to whether they could make my shirts, the old lady said I could get them in a few days, if I would leave the cloth, and give her the measure of the shirts. This I did."

THE PRIVATIONS OF A PRIVATE-Campaigning with the First Tennssee C.S.A. and Life Thereafter by Marcus B. Toney pub by Univ. Alabama Press 2005

Pg. 50 August 15, 1863 Cavalry raid by the Federals on the Chattanooga depot "…As soon as I saw the stampede on the Square I ran into the depot, got some clothing and shoes out of a box there, and went down under the depot (which had open sides) and bivouacked in the dust with hogs and fleas, which were very industrious…"

This private ingeniously re-uniformed himself, as the depot was burned.

CHICAGO TRIBUNE August 19, 1863

"…Camp Douglas, Ohio was selected as a fit prison for enlisted men. On August 17, 1863 the first group of Morgan's Raiders arrived at the prison gates. A good number of Chicago citizens and the press turned out to capture a glimpse of the famous Raiders.

Generally they are far better-looking men than any of the secesh prisoners we have had here before. Those butternut units and shapeless slouch hats, would make an ugly man of anybody. All of the colors of Joseph's coat were represented in their wearing apparel; the butternut was worn by the careless quiet looking individual, who had their horse blankets and tin cups strung across their shoulders. But the keen, blackeyed, out-and out raiders of the devil-dare stripe, had either a suit of black broadcloth, or a portion of our own soldier's blue uniform…"

REMINISCENCES OF A PRIVATE William E. Bevins of the First Arkansas Inf. C.S.A. pub by Univ. Ark. Press 1992

Pg. 128 Thatcher's Ferry, Tn. South of Harrison Polk's Brigade, August 21st 1863 "… Company G received some much-needed clothing before leaving this region, including ten pairs of shoes, eighteen pairs of drawers, eleven pairs of pants, and eleven shirts.Requisition order in Capt. Shoup's file, Service Records, roll 51…"

Another insufficient issue of badly needed clothing.

U.S. ARMY HERITAGE AND EDUCATION CENTER Letters of Lt. William D. Cole 35th Alabama Infantry Regiment

August 28, 1863 Berchwood, Tenn. Dear Wife "…The clothing you sent by Tom is a total loss…I was informed that I had some clothing left for me at a Depot…and as we are expecting to fight here…a man cannot get 40 miles unless he deserts…I lost one pair of pants on our retreat have been wearing the others since. I fear I will be left entirely naked just about cold weather…I hope the skin will thicken so I can bear the cold…"

Good luck, Lt.

THE CONFEDERATE VETERAN VOL1

Oct. 1893 Pg. 308 A Queer Order-"I remember the first battle order I ever heard. It was at Fort Donelson, in the fall of 1863. There were then only about half a dozen companies there, drilling and fortifying. The senior captain was Tom Beaumont, of Clarksville, with whom I was messing.

In those days we had not given up all home habits; we wore white shirts and underclothes, had washing done, kept measurably clean, and every night went to bed in our tents, undressing and retiring "like folks.'

One day it was rumored that the gunboats were in the river below us, and coming up. About midnight, while all were sleeping soundly, the long roll began to beat in the company stationed on the river bank. At once there was a stir in camp; officers were calling the men to fall in; there was hurrying to and fro. Captain Beaumont was always when on duty in faultless dress and now he did not neglect his toilet. Quickly he put on his uniform, buckled on his sword, and stepped out of his tent to take command of his company.

But the men had not been as thoughtful as he. They sprang up and grasped their muskets, and formed line in front of their tents, but every man of them had forgotten to put on his trousers, and they stood there, in the starlight, in their night-clothes like "sheeted ghosts," trembling with cold and excitement. As the captain and I stepped out, and his eye glanced along the line, his sense of propriety got the better of his military ardor, and he shouted out his first command, "Comfound your fool souls, go and put on your breeches!" In a moment the whole situation dawned on the men, and with shouts of laughter they prepared for battle by donning that needful article of apparel. But it was a false alarm, and they soon took off their breeches and went to sleep."

I think this date is mistaken, as Fort Donelson was surrendered in 1862, but this is the date given in the Confederate Veteran

THE CIVIL WAR INFANTRYMAN, In Camp, on the March, and in Battle by Gregory A. Coco pub by Thomas Publications, Gettysburg, Pa

Pg38 Further to the southwest and over in northern Georgia later in September, an eyewitness encountered General James Longstreet's command and remarked that most of his troops had just drawn new uniforms consisting of dark blue shell jackets and light blue trousers. These men, who had come from Lee's army, impressed the Army of Tennesee veterans by the uniformity of their outfits, and the…"superior style of their equipment, in haversacks, canteens, and knapsacks. The contrast between them and General Bragg's motley, ragged troops was striking in the extreme…." Oddly, a federal, William Miller, 75th Indiana, described the dress of Longstreet's men as "uniformed in White Jackets and Blue Collars and cuffs and blue pants," while Chesley A. Mosman, 59th Illinois, said it was "bluish grey" with sky blue pants.

"Butternut" was one of the colors generally associated with Southern infantrymen during the Civil War. Butternut dye was made from the crushed hulls of walnuts (often mixed with copperas) and the pigmentation varied from a dull brownish-tan to musky yellow. A 9th New York soldier, David Thompson, documented this tint of color from his experiences in the Antietam Campaign. He had observed many dead on the field of Sharpsburg who were, "…undersized men mostly, from…North Carolina, with sallow, hatchet faces and clad in "butternut"-a color fluctuating all the way from a deep, coffee brown up to the whitish brown of ordinary dust." A Confederate officer, Robert Stiles, called it a "sickly, jaundiced, butter-nut hue, like the clothes of some backwoods, cracker regiments wore when they first came to Virginia." Corporal James Hosmer of the 52nd Massachusetts peered intently at he Rebel dress he spotted after the surrender of Port Hudson, Louisiana: "Here they were, the real truculent and unmitigated reb, in butternut of every shade, from the dingy green which clothes the unripe nut, to the tawny brown and faded tan which it wears at other stages,-butternut mixed with a dull characterless grey. There was no attempt at uniform, yet something common, in the dress of the whole company,-a faded look, as if the fabric, whatever its original hue, had felt the sun until all life and brightness had wilted in the web and had been killed out of the dye. Still the clothing was whole; and, upon closer inspection, looked strong and serviceable, though very coarse."

One man, Lieutenant William Berryhill of Mississippi, dyed some of his clothes on August 25, 1864, using chestnut bark and copperas to tint his military jacket, one pair of drawers and two shirts. He decided not to dye three other shirts, one linen, one new Irish linen, and a hickory stripe. He ended his letter by telling his wife, Mary, not to laugh at the idea "of my sweating over the dye pot for there is no telling what a man can do until he tries."

Often the butternut color was mistaken for "yellow," as recognized by Private Smith, 54th Ohio, who in the Georgia summer of 1864, recalled "a mingled line of yellow and grey in all the pomp, splendor and circumstance of glorious war." Smith was viewing an infantry battle line 300 yards distant and ready to advance. Another Yankee, Lieutenant Thomas

Galwey, pronounced some benefits associated with the butternut color. In the summer fields surrounding Gettysburg, his men "found that the enemy (skimishers) kept close to the ground so as to afford an uncertain target, owing to his dun clothes, we began, as the boys called, to be scientific in our fire."

DON TROIANI'S CIVIL WAR INFANTRY-Text by Earl J. Coates, Michael J. McAfee, and Don Troiani pub by Stackpole Books 2002

Pg. 58 A soldier in the 2nd Georgia Infantry, Benning's Brigade, Longstreet's corps, wrote "Sometimes the government would get a supply of fine English cloth, and we would get good uniforms, almost to blue." This same soldier was fired upon by his own friends in Tennessee, "So blue (like Yankees) did we appear." Even the federals had trouble distinguishing Longstreet's men from their own. Lt. Charles Clark of the 125th Ohio Volunteer Infantry, awaiting the attack of Kershaw's Brigade, heard the order "Cease fire!…they are McCook (Union) troops!" He noted that Kershaw's Confederates "appeared at a distance to wear blue, dusty blue. We had never seen a Confederate soldier clothed otherwise than in butternut or grey." A volley by the confederates ended the debate, but many a Federal soldier, and Rebel as well, seemed confused by the appearance of Longstreet's men.…Gen Grant described a confusing encounter on an inspection tour of the picket line surrounding Chattanooga:

(T)he most friendly relations seemed to exist between the pickets of the two armies. At one place a tree which had fallen across the steam was used by the soldiers of both armies in drawing water for their camps. General Longstreet's corps was stationed there at the time, and wore the blue of a little different shade from our uniform. Seeing a soldier in blue on the log, I rode up to him, commenced conversing with him, and asked whose Corps he belonged to. He was very polite, touching his hat to me, said he belonged to Longstreet's Corps. I asked him a few questions, but not with a view of gaining any particular information-all of which he answered, and I rode off."

By the spring of 1864"…The quartermaster general of the Confederacy wanted no more light blue pants, stating that "grey makes up better." Perhaps it was better not to be shot at by one's own men.…"

I don't care what this quote states, blue pants were made and issued throughout the War.

BLUE AND GRAY MARCHING

Longstreet's troops had recently been newly uniformed, consisting of a dark blue round jacket, closely fitting, with light blue trousers, which made a line of Confederates resemble that of the enemy, the only difference being the "cut" of the garments-the Federals wearing a loose blouse instead of a tight-fitting jacket. The uniforms of the eastern troops made quite a contrast with the tattered and torn homemade jeans of their Western bretheren.

As some as Longstreet's men began to arrive at the front their appearance made an impact on the soldiers of the \western army. On Spt. 19, an Army of Tennessee artillerist recorded in his diary "Our first impression was partly caused by the color of their uniform, but more by its uniformity, and the superior style of their equipments, in haversacks, canteens and knapsacks. The contrast between them and Gen'l Bragg's motley, ragged troops was striking in the extreme."

The Yankees too, noticed and were confused by the appearance of Longstreet's men. At Chickamauga, the men of the 125th Ohio hesitated to fire on Hood's advancing troops because of their uniforms. A veteran of that regiment wrote, "Those moving battalions did appear to wear blue, and probably they were clothed in blue jeans. They were Longstreet's men, just arrived from Virginia. We had never seen a Confederate clothed otherwise than in butternut or gray.

"…Harker's Ohio Brigade captured a number of men, probably from the Texas Brigade. Wilber F. Hinman of the 65th Ohio wrote of these men, "it was easy to distinguish them from the soldiers of Bragg's army by their clothing. Most of them wore the regular Confederate uniform, while the dress of the western men was a "go-as-you-please" matter, with every imaginable variety of garments and headcovering."…However, John West of the 4th Texas wrote in his diary that in receiving the affections of the citizenery on the ride west, "Rags and dirt seemed to be a recommendation where gilt and brass buttons failed to excite attention." …W.R. Houghton, of the 2nd Georgia, Benning's Brigade, recalled the following in 1912: "…Sometimes the government would get a supply by blockade runners of fine English cloth and we would get good uniforms, almost too blue. I remember the Jenkin's S,C. Brigade clad in these new uniforms, created a sensation when it appeared in Bragg's Army in 1863, so blue did they appear in the distance and some of our scouts lost their lives by mistaken pickets. The writer was fired upon by his own friends more than once whilst trying to enter the picket line…"

CONFEDERATE VETERAN September-October 1992

Pg. 38 DRAB The Forgotten Confederate Color by Fred Adolphus "…They have done quite a bit of research on what shades of grey were used and the frequency with which butternut appeared in the Southern ranks, but little attention has been given to another color that was widespread in Confederate armies. That color is drab-the color of undyed wool…Alfred R. Waud, famous for his drawings for Harper's Weekly, had this to say of the Virginia "Black Horse Cavalry" while he was detained behind Confederate lines: he noted that among the enlisted troopers,"…there was little else but homespun among the, light drab grey or butternut color, the drab predominating…" and slouched hats appeared to be …the court costume of the regiment." Waud's sketch appeared in September 27, 1862, edition of

Harper's Weekly indicating an early war usage of this color in Virginia....Joseph E. Chance describes the issue of this clothing in his regimental history of the 2nd Texas as well. "The new uniforms waiting in Corinth to greet the regiment on their arrival were unconventional, to say the least. Bundles of white wool uniforms had been sent with no designation as to size. The uniforms were issued and a comical scene ensued. Soon the company grounds were full of men strutting up and down, some with trousers dragging under their heels, while those of others scarcely reached the tops of their socks; some with jackets so tight they resembled stuffed toads, while others had ample room to carry three days rations in their booms. The exhibition closed with a swapping scene that reminded one of a horse-trading day in a Georgia couty town....Company B of the 18th Texas cavalry, upon its formation as the "Morgan Rangers" of Bastrop, was lucky enough to have uniforms made for its members. Captain Hiram S. Morgan spent his own money to outfit the troops in grey double-breasted coats and grey trousers with yellow cavalry stripes on the legs. The fabric used for these uniforms was a yellowish-gray, Huntsville penitentiary jeans. These uniforms were issued in early 1862 ...In the summer of 1862 walker's Texas Infantry Division received extensive issues of cotton clothing. Allotments of 8,000 yards of osnaburg to each regiment were sewn into tents, knapsacks, haversacks, and clothing, by the women of Smith County. The troops spent the summer in cooler cotton fabrics rather than traditional woolens. As most cottons left the factory as "gray goods" it is a safe bet that these uniforms were undyed...."

BLOODY BANNERS AND BAREFOOT BOYS-A History of the 27th Regiment Alabama Infantry CSA The Civil War Memoirs & Diary Entries of J.P. Canon MD compiled & ed by Noel Crowson & John V. Brogden pub by Burd St Press 1997

Pg 45 Spt 1863 "We bunked three together in order to economize bedding, stretching one blanket to ward off rain and heavy dew. The writer and his two bunk-mates had been reduced to two blankets, so when we had one stretched over us, it left only one for bed and cover, and we determined to have more if it was to be found in that part of Mississippi. We did not expect to get a blanket, as the Confederacy had already been stripped of everything of that class for the use of soldiers. We thought we might induce some old lady to part with a quilt, which would answer the purpose. Procuring a pass we started on the search and visited several farm houses where we were told they had given up everything to the soldiers and had nothing to spare. However discouraged, we kept going from house to house until we found an old lady who said she had a "coverlid" which she would sell if we could get her price, "Well, how much do you ask for it, Mrs.?" She replied "Forty dollars." We were not burdened with Confederate money and it behooved us to drive as good a bargain as possible, so we concluded to resort to a little "Jewing" and replied "Oh, that is too much, we can't give any such price." To which the Mrs. countered, "I reckon I o'r't to know what its worth, I spun every bit of the thread and wove it all by myself. The 'fillin in that coverlid is all wool, and its worth $40.00 if its worth a cent."

"But just think of it, we only get $11.00 a month and at that price it would take near four monthes to pay for it."

"its not my fault thet don't give you but $11.00 a month.'

"But you've used it 20 years and ought to sell it cheap to soldiers."

"I don't care if I've used it 20 years, I've took good care of it, and if you don't give $40.00, you don't get it."

The parleying continued for quite a while, and when we saw the old lady begin to weaken a little, we presented three new $10 Confederate bills and the temptation was too great. She took the bills and handed us the "coverlid". It was a good one too, almost as large as a small tent fly and it did good service for us all the winter."

THE ROUGH SIDE OF WAR ed. by Gates

Pg. 94In late Sept. 1863 an Illinois infantryman talked with some pickets of a S. Carolina regiment and described them as "a fine, handsome, stout lot of fellows, better dressed than we are, their uniforms being apparently new… The Carolinians uniform is a bluish gray.… with sky blue pants."

Just before Shiloh, a Confederate noted of the army "Some wore uniforms, some half uniforms, some no uniforms at all."

Were these South Carolinians part of Longstreet's troops? They were obviously dressed in uniforms mde of the British cloth.

WEBSITE ADOLPHUS.COM UNIFORMS

"Henry Orr of the Twelth Texas Cavalry in a letter home to his family in Sept. 1863, therein he asked them to send him a jeans frock coat …"or sack of the loose wrapper style, one similar to the one you sent me last fall…"

LAW'S ALABAMA BRIGADE IN THE WAR BETWEEN THE UNION AND THE CONFEDERACY by J. Gary Laine & Morris M. Penny pub by White Mane Pub. Co. 1996

Pg. 142 Sept.1863 Chickamauga Campaign "Law's Alabamians reached Atlanta at daybreak on September 15, where they were issued new clothing, including hats and shoes. In August, Law's men had been issued new clothing while in Virginia, but some of the men were better supplied than others. Sheffield was diligent in his efforts to see that his brigade was as well clothed as any other, and with the uniform issued in Virginia and the resupply in Atlanta, Law's Brigade was now as well dressed as at any time during the war. When they arrived in north Georgia, many of the ill-clad Westerners were prompted to suggest a trade of a "Bragg jacket for a Lee jacket." Coles reported that his fellow soldiers of the west were not only deficient in clothing, but lacking in all equipment, including artillery."

THE CONFEDERATE VETERAN VOL. XII 1904

Pg. 71 Feb. 1904 Reminiscences of Chickamauga by G.W.R. Bell, Sixth Georgia cavalry "…I am satisfied that it was some of Longstreet's Corps, although it was understood at the time that Longstreet's forces had not arrived. But that cold Friday evening before the fight our regiment, the Sixth Georgia Cavalry, crossed the creek at the same time and place. Feeling sorry for one of the almost barefoot number of the "webfoot" troops, I took him up behind me and carried him over. I noticed the difference in the shade of gray in their uniform and that of our Tennessee army. Theirs was a steel gray, such as our officers wore. Now when that brigade came to our relief (for which I shall always feel grateful), I noticed they had on the same colored uniform as the Longstreet men wore."

THIS INFERNAL WAR by Bell Irvin Wiley/ Lucy E, Fay pub by Univ of Texas Press 1958

Pg. 321 Camp near Clinton, Miss. Sept 2nd, 1863 My own darling One; "…I am looking for Rich back next week and I hope he will bring me a lot of clothing as Mother wrote she had it made for me…"

FROM HUNTSVILLE TO APPOMATTOX R.T. Cole's History of the 4th Alabama Volunteer Infantry C.S.A. Army of Northern Virginia ed by Frank D. Stocker pub by Univ of Tenn. Press 1996

Pg. 134 Sept 17, 1863 "…General Lee had, before we left Virginia, caused to be issued to us clothes and shoes.Frequently, Bragg's men proposed to exchangs a "Bragg" jacket a "Lee" jacket and would make a good many comments about General Lee requiring his Brigade and field officers to walk…"

FOURTEEN HUNDRED AND 91 DAYS IN THE CON-FEDERATE ARMY A Journal Kept by W.W. Heartsill or Camp Life; Day by Day of the W. P. Lane Rangers From April 19, 1861 To May 20, 1865 ed. by Bell Irvin Wiley pub by Broadfoot Pub. Co. Wilmington, N.C. 1987

Pg 152 Sept. 18th 1863 "A great many of the men have not even one blanket to protect them from the approaching winter, and now as I am preparing to WRAP up and ROLL down in my old green Army coat to take my rest in pile of leaves which were diligently together before night with "an eye single" to the comforts of the night; now to think, then to dream of coming events; or of loved ones at home."

A green army coat? Could this be a holdover militia coat?

DON TROIANI'S CIVIL WAR INFANTRY-Text by Earl J. Coates, Michael J. McAfee, and Don Troiani pub by Stackpole Books 2002

Pg. 57 "…Descriptions of Longstreet's Corps upon their arrival and during the battle of Chickamauga, September 19-20, 1863, found them to be uniformed differently and in sharp contrast to the Western Army soldiers under General Bragg. One of Bragg's artillerymen took special notice of the Easterner's uniformity of appearance:" Our first impression was partly caused by the color of their uniform (dark blue-grey jackets, light blue pants)…the superior style of their equipments, in haversacks, canteens and knapsacks. The contrast between them and General Bragg's motley, ragged was striking in the extreme!" Bragg's soldiers, lamented one Western officer," never looked worse. Three weeks of maneuvering in the densest dust (during the Tullahoma Campaign) without washing, had conferred the same color upon everything!' Bragg's Westerners were described as generally "greasy, dirty, raggedy, barefooted, and wearing go-as-you-please… with every imaginable variety of garments and head coverings" wearing practically "no uniform at all.' Bragg's soldiers preferred to wear clothing sent home rather than that issued by the Confederate Quartermaster Department.

A member of Kershaw's Brigade of Longstreet's corps remembered his uniform as a "dark blue round jacket, closely fitting, with light blue trousers: (it) closely resembled those worn by the enemy…."

LAW'S ALABAMA BRIGADE IN THE WAR BETWEEN THE UNION AND THE CONFEDERACY by J.Gary Laine & Morris M. Penny pub by White Mane Pub. Co. 1996

Pg. 174 Sept 20 1863 after the Battle of Chickamauga; "…The battlefield was abundantly covered with the spoils of war. For the Alabamians this meant supplies, clothing and blankets. Joab Goodson and his company supplied themselves with blankets and Goodson later wrote home on stationary picked up on the battlefield. Private James Crowder, Company I, 47th Alabama found a splendid blaket he described as "the best I ever saw…"

THE CIVIL WAR READER by Richard B. Harwell pub. by Smithmark Pub. 1957

Pg. 227 Sept. 20, 1863 Captain Fitzgerald Ross, an officer of the Imperial Austrian Army "In Camp Near Chickamauga "…these Western people nothing had been captured but guns and empty wagons, at which there was great disappointment; and many were quite indignant, thinking themselves cheated. "Why, these Yankees are not worth killing," said General-; "they are not a bit better off than ourselves."

UNIFORMS OF THE CIVIL WAR Lord, Wise, A.S. Barnes & Co. 1970

Pg. 70 Setember 21, 1863 After the Battle of Chickamauga, "A soldier in the 15th Texas Infantry inspected the work of the scavengers and found "many (of the dead) had been stripped of all clothing and many whose pockets had been rifled or turned out…"

At this stage of the war, nobody should have been surprised at this.

THIS INFERNAL WAR by Bell Irvin Wiley/Lucy E. Fay pub by Univ of Texas Press 1958

Pg. 333 Sept. 21st, 1863 "…A fleet of 9 steel clad rams from England have passed into Wilmington and are taking on crews.…Six more are to sail from England so the Yankees say for N.Y.,Boston, Phila. to bombard these cities…I am sorry you were disappointed in learning how to make a hat but the one I had cut down when at home is still good and I think will last another year at least.…"

Can you imagine the northern reaction to 15 steel rams in Southern Hands? I dare say it might have ended the War on a more favorable note.

ONE OF CLEBURNE'S COMMAND-The Civil War Remini-scences & Diary of Capt. Samuel T. Foster Granbury's Texas BrigadeC.S.A. pub by Univ. of Texas Press 1980

Pg.? September 21, 1863, just after the Battle of Cickamauga Tn. "Wounded Yanks calling for help. Just here let us make a dot. I have never yet heard a Confederate soldier call for help while wounded and lying on the field. But the Yanks never fail. I have heard then calling all night long, but I was not permitted (nor was it my duty) to go and assist them…We remain in this vicinity for about 9 or 10 days, when the order comes to fall in and off we go-When we are ordered to march off from a camp ground there are no tents to strike-no baggage wagons to load, but every man puts his gun on his shoulder and walks off-In ten minutes after an order to march from our camp, we are on the move…"

Ok, I don't know about the accuracy of this writer's statement regarding Confederate wounded not calling out, but, I wasn't there, and he was, so I'll just go with what he writes.

RECOLLECTIONS OF A CONFEDERATE STAFF OFFICER by G. Moxley Sorrel pub by Bantam Books 1992

Pg. 166 Sept. 23, 1863 Sige of Cattanooga "The personal appearance of Bragg's army was, of course, matter of interest to us of Virginia. The men were a fine-loking lot, strong, lean, long-limbed fighters. The Western tunic was much worn by officers and men. It is an excellent germent, and its use could be extended with much advantage."

REMINISCENCES OF A PRIVATE William E. Bevins of the First Arkansas Inf. C.S.A. Univ. Ark. Press 1992

Pg. 138 "...On September 30, Company G received another requisition of much-needed clothing. The most important item was a collection of 35 pairs of shoes, but the men also welcomed 17 pairs of drawers, 16 shirts, 10 jackets, and 8 pairs of pants..."

ALL AFIRE TO FIGHT-The Untold Tale of the Civil War's Ninth Texas Cavalry by Martha L. Crabb pub by Avon Books 2000

Pg. 183 Sept. 30, 1863 (guard duty in Miss.) "Reuben was not in camp at Mrs. Treadwell's place. He and two other men from Company A were with Capt. Hamilton C. Dial and detachment scouring the countryside for blankets. Winter was coming on, and the men had no tents. The blankets were vital because, with the brigade con stantly on the move, the men would not be able to build winter quarters. Later in the fall, General Lee would make a special request for blankets for his horsemen."

Pg. 187 "Reuben and Capt. Dial's detachment returned on November 6 with a hundred blankets after scouring the countryside for a month..."

PARKER'S VIRGINIA BATTERY by Robert K.Krick pub by Va. Book Co. 1975

Pg. 208 Fall 1863 Knoxville Tn. "...Equipment for the horses was in desparately short supply. During the Knoxville Campaign, the need for horseshoes became so critical that all dead horses were stripped of both shoes and nails. Broken down animals of both armies were killed by the Confederates in order to get the hardware off their feet. The artillerists even went as far as fishing out dead horses floating on the Holston (River) duing the siege of Knoxville.

Supplies for the battery's human contingent were also a cause for concern. Many of thw men were shoeless; when cold weather set in during December, this would lead to much suffering..."

This is one destitute unit.

GRUMBLE-The W.E. Jones Brigade by Dobbie Edward Lambert pub by Lambert Enterprises 1992

Pg. 36 Fall 1863 Brigadier General "Grumble" Jones Cavalry Brigade in in eastern Tennessee; "…The lack of uniforms was a sorry situation and Jones couldn't have done anything about them if he'd wanted to. The men were hopelessly "mixed" in their appearance. Many had no shoes and flop felt hats were the most common headgear.Pants were worn thin and covered with multi-colored patches and those without jackets merely hung blankets over their shoulders. By '64 so much reliance was placed on captured Yankee goods that from a distance the Brigade looked like a Union formation. Some pro-Union civilians even aided them with information without realizing what side they were on.

While the Yankees slept in tents, most of the Jones Brigade slept in the open with only a poncho over them. Of course, many times during the campaign they could sleep in the saddle with their horses following the horse ahead. Jones usually set the example by sleeping outdoors with the men…"

HISTORY OF KERSHAW'S BRIGADE by Augustis Dickert pub by Broadfoot Pub Co. 1899

Pg. 268 fall 1863 Longstreet's arrival in Tennessee; "…Longstreet's troops had recently been newly uniformed, consisting of a dark-blue round jacket, closely fiiting, with light blue trousers, which made a line of Confederates resemble that of the enemy, the only difference being the "cut" of the garments-the federals wearing a loose blouse instead of a tight-fitting jacket. The uniform of the Eastern troops mde quite a contrast with the tattered and torn home-made jeans of their Western bretheren…"

FLORA AND FAUNA OF THE CIVIL WAR-An Environmental Reference Guide by Kelby Ouchley pub.by La. Univ. Press 2010

Pg. 101 Private John M. King of the 92nd Illinois writes in October, 1863 at Harrison's Landing, Tennessee, of the Confederates just across the river: "Their uniforms consisted of broad-brimmed black hats and their clothes had two shades of color. It was all, or nearly all, homemade, butternut and sheep's gray were the colors. The butternut was made from the bark of butternut and walnut trees and was usually cotton goods."

The sheep's gray was probably undyed wool, the butternut cotton.

THE STILLWELL LETTERS-A Georgian in Longstreet's Corps, A.N.V. ed. by Ronald H. Mosely pub by Mercer Univ. Press, 2002

Pg. 216 Headquarters Bryan's Brigade, Army of Tennessee Camp before Chattanooga Oct. 2nd, 1863 "…Molly, I am needing a pair of pants very bad, I want you to send me a pair of pants as soon as you can.…Molly, I want you to send me a towel…"

Pg. 224 Headquarters Brigade Camp near Chattanooga, Tennessee, Nov. 2, 1863 Dear Molly "…If you get any chance to send my pants and shirt, do so and let me know when and by whom you sent them…"

THE CIVIL WAR LETTERS OF JOSHUA K. CALLOWAY ed. by Judith Lee Hallock pub by Univ. Ga. Press 1997

Pg. 154 Oct. 1863 Missionary Ridge (wife) "…As to my clothing, my dear. I think I can do very well if you can furnish me a few pairs of woolen socks. I believe that I told you that I had got a good pair of pants and lost my woolen shirt. I have now lost a pair of Drawers, those you sent me…"

UNIFORMS OF THE CIVIL WAR by Lord, Wise, pub by A.S. Barnes & Co. 1970

Pg. 65 "Co. D of the 61st Georgia on skirmish duty. Sighting a group of Federal soldiers with heavy knapsacks, the Georgians took after them, "As it was getting late in the fall (October 1863), we took after them on a run! We plundered their knapsacks till the rest of the company came up. I got two tent flies, two fine flannel overshirts, a good oilcloth, some stationary, and one of the best blankets I ever saw…"

Now that's aggressive resupply!

A SOLDIERS LETTERS TO CHARMING NELLIE by J.B. Pollet pub by Neale Pub Co. 1908

Oct 1863 on picket line around Chattanooga: "…The palmetto fellows (South Carolinians) are not even permitted to visit us in the daylight, except in disguise-their new uniforms of gray always betraying them wherever they go. One of them was not only very foumd of, but successful at, the game of poker, concluded the other day to risk being shot for the chance of winning the money of the First Texas, and, divesting himself of his coat, slipped over to the Texas pit an hour before daylight, and by sunrise was giving his whole mind over to the noble pastime.

An hour later a keen-sighted Yankee sang out: "say you Texas Johnies! Ain't that fellow playing cards, with his back to the sapling, one of them d—d South Carolina successionsts? Seems to me his breeches are newer than they ought to be..."

From what I've read in the Confederate Veteran, the South Carolinians were hated by the Yankees in this front as they were the "warmongers" who had started tha War.

HADLEY LIBRARY ARCHIVES

James A. Miller Collection correspondence C.W. era misc. New Market, Va.
Pg. 39 "...David C. Edmonds furnishes a rather colorful picture of a Louisiana militia officer in drab, when he relates the description of General John G. Pratt, of Opelousas on Grand Coteau in October, 1863. Edmonds relates that, although Pratt sported a grey beard, "it looked more like porcupine quills than anything human, and to finish off the beauty of his face, it was sprinkled miscellaneously from the chin to his eyebrows with tobacco juice. His military apparel consists of a drab colored coat, with broad cape, pants of one piece but very greasy; a dirty shirt which had once been red, a rough pair of boots and a broad brim straw hat. His pants were worn without suspenders, and very short in the waist, the flaps of the pockets hanging down like the ears of some old dilapidated dog."...Waul'sTexas Legion, stationed at Fort Pemberton on the Tallahatchie River near Greenville, was issued uniforms of undyed wool in February or March 1863 The uniforms were described as being "...a light grayish tan but would soon take on the color of the Mississippi mud."

FOURTEEN HUNDRED AND 91 DAYS IN THE CONFEDERATE ARMY A Journal Kept by W.W. Heartsill or Camp Life; Day by Day of the W. P. Lane Rangers From April 19, 1861 To May 20, 1865 ed. by Bell Irvin Wiley pub by Broadfoot Pub. Co. Wilmington, N.C. 1987

Pg. 166 Oct. 5th 1863 "... and now at 10 o'clock we halt at the Chicamauga, for the purpose of washing up our clothing, and to try, if possible, to get rid of a troublesome little insect (all soldiers know him) called, for short. "BODY LICE." It has been our misfortune to have a scanty supply of clothing, and for the past two months we have scarcely stoped night or day, and the Brigade, as also the entire army, are lo-yes, lousy, we have plenty of LICE, but will soon be rid of them, if there is any virtue in hot water..."

THIS INFERNAL WAR Edwin Hedge Fay/Bell Irvin Wiley Univ. of Texas Press 1958

Pg. 339 In Camp 8 mis. N.W. Clinton Miss. Oct 2d, 1863 My own Darling; "...Capt. Webb bro't 2 pr. socks and an undershirt for which, my own dear Wife, please accept my warmest thanks and my best love..."

Pg. 343 Camp near Brownville Miss. Oct 8th 1863 My Own Dear Wife "...Our boys went out with a flag of truce and I sent five dollars in gold down and bought two oil cloths and would have got a pair of boots if Ben Neal hadn't thought them too small....I am glad you are learning to spin. I learned while I was at Mr. Thigpen's. The shirt and socks by Capt. Webb I got all safe. I was in hopes I should find some little note tucked away in it somewhere, some surprising little love token, but I fear the realities of married life have taken away all the sentimentality you possessed when a girl. Have they done so? I was disappointed but I breathed a prayer to heaven to bless the dear one who was clothing "her own volunteer" by the labor of her hands. I have not tried on my things yet but I know they'll be right...Give my best love to your mother and tell her I want her to have you & Lou weave a nice piece of cotton goods to make me a suit next summer. The coat I want with a band around the waist and a pleated body, infant waist I believe they call it. They are all the fashion among the cavalry for even dress uniform. What can your Father have me a pair of boots made for. Mine are pretty good yet and may last me this winter yet I fear I shall go barefooted by spring if I don't come on that side of the River. I'll make them last me as long as possible. My hat is as good as when I left home tho a little dirty...I also came for the purpose of having my boot patched and foot measured for another pair for which I am to pay $80. You see shoe leather is quite an object in this part of the world, and I don't know what poor soldiers are to do another year if boots get much higher. I had worn the boots you sent me 374 days yesterday and I think they will last perhaps three months longer, tho' when boots have to be patched I think they are about done....Rich brought me from home two shirts of heavy cotton jeans and two pairs of drawers of the same, 3prs. of socks & two yellow check, gingham pocket handkerchiefs. The overshirts you made me are all worn out..."

THE CIVIL WAR LETTERS OF JOSHUA K. CALLOWAY ed by Judith Lee Hallock

Pub by Univ. Ga. Press 1997

Pg. 145 Camp Wagon Train, 28th Ala. Chickamauga Creek Oct. 10th 1863 "...My bed consists of a pile of hay on which I have a buffalo rug, a sheepskin, an oilcloth, a saddle blanket, five coverlets, two good blankets, a good quilt and a big feather pillow. Am I not comfortable? But my comrades are in line of battle among the rocks on the side of Missionary Ridge, with one blanket to the man without tents and eating cold and scant rations...."

THE CONFEDERATE VETERAN VOL. XXVII 1919

Pg. 465 Dec. 1919 In The Years Of War-compiled by John C. Stiles from "Official Records" Series III, Vol. II 1863 "Barefoot and Barelegged Men- On October 10 Gen. Sam Jones wrote to the Quartermaster-General C.S.A.: "I know from personal inspection that clothing, chiefly pants and shoes, is necessary. I have seen large numbers of men marching to meet the enemy without shoes, and many have been excused from certain duties because they could not with decency appear in public." Sans-culotte, but sans repoche"

CONFEDERATE ECHOES A Soldier's Personal Story of Life in the Confederate Army From the Mississippi to the Carolinas by Albert Theodore Goodloe-First Lieutenant Company D Thirty-Fifth Regiment Alabama Volunteer Infantry C.S.A. pub by Zenger Pub. Co. 1897, 1983

Pg. 150 "...While the flesh of the ox was a success (let us admit) as army diet, his hide, untanned at least, was a failure as foot-covering, called at the time "moccasins." This was tested while on the march northward through Georgia on our way to Tennessee. The night of October 11, 1864, we camped just twelve miles northeast of Rome. Just after we had eaten our supper and jerked our beef for the next day, orders came for all the shoe makers to report at army headquarters. The presumption was that they would be sent to the rear to make shoes for the soldiers, many of whom were barefooted and many poorly shod; and never before was it known that the shoemaker's trade was so largely represented in the army. And those that were not shoemakers that night seemed to regret that they had not learned the trade. "Anything for a change" was the idea which sometimes pervaded the ranks; and so shoemaking just then was thought to be much better than marching, with those who professed to be qualified for such work. But late in the night came the shoemakers back to their respective companies in droves, disgusted with themselves and Gen. Hood and with ox hides. Instead of going to the rear to make shoes out of leather, as the order was very naturally interpreted to mean, they were required to make rawhide moccasins that night in camp and report back to their commands for duty at daybreak the next morning. The returned ones vowed, when they learned the real meaning of the order, that they knew nothing about making moccasins, and furthermore they had never before heard of such things. That we enjoyed their discomfiture when they returned from their shoe-making expedition need not be stated.

But some of the shoe makers-how many I could never learn- toughed it out and made moccasins of the hides of the beeves that were slaughtered that day. They were made with the flesh sides out and the hair next to the bare feet of the soldiers who wore them. Before being put on the feet they looked like hideous pouches of some kind, but no man could have conjectured for what purpose they were made. However, there was much bragging on them the next day by those to whom they had been issued. But the next day and night following it rained, rained, rained and alas for the moccasins and the men who wore them Just such shapes as these moccasins assumed, and such positions as they occupied on the feet, as the men went trudging along through the mud and water, can never be told; nor can any imagination, however refined, justly depict them. The pioneer corps were ahead of us putting poles and rails across the numerous little branches which the rain had made, for us to walk over on; and whenever a moccasin-footed soldier would step on one of these poles or rails into the branch the moccasin would instantly conduct him. Ludicrous remarks and ludicrous scenes without number characterized that day's march, which were as cordial to us in our weariness, and long before night the moccasins and their wearers forever parted company…"

These moccasins were widely used as a temporary, semi-sucessful stopgap. You have to admit, they would be better than no shoes at all, despite theyr'e drawbacks.

THE CIVIL WAR LETTERS OF JOSHUA K. CALLOWAY ed. By Judith Lee Hallock pub by Univ. Ga. Press 1997

Pg. 145 same camp Oct. 11th, 1863 (wife) "Well, I have written all that can be of any interest to you unless it be to tell you about my clothing. I have three pairs of Drawers, and three pairs of socks, one pair of the socks are nearly worn out and one pair is new. I have never worn them at all. I have four pairs of pants, two of cotton (those you sent me). My old uniform pants and a pair which I got from the Government the other day of good woolen goods. I have two domestic shirts and the one you made for me. I have lost that woolen shirt that I got from Mrs. Morrow. I need one or two heavy shirts and some yarn socks, and a vest or two. Though I have no way tocarry them. My old Carpet sack will not hold what I have already. That is why I lost my shirt and all my towels. But send them along, I'll do the best I can…"

Good quality government issue.

LETTERS FROM LEE'S ARMY by Susan Leigh Blackford and Charles Minor Blackford pub by Scribner's Press 1947

Pg. 219 Oct. 11, 1863 Longstreet's Headquarters,TN "…The suicidal policy which Bragg has adopted has rendered futile the victory which Longstreet won for him at Chattanooga. If Lee had been in his place with such an army he would now be chasing the shattered Yankee fragments out of Tennessee. This is a fine body of men, (The Army of Tennessee) and with the confidence they would have in Lee they would be irresistible…I wish you would send me a common bed-tick which I could fill with straw when we are in camp and empty when we move. Make it three and a half feet wide with a long slit in it with buttons, through which I can put in straw…"

The Army of Tennessee was always in desparate need of a commander. Why Gen. Bragg was placed in command of any army is more than I can conjecture.

Website Tennessee Volunteer Infantry Regiment :Clothing, Arms and Equipment :Part 1 Clothing

Pg.2 "…In October 1863, near Chattanooga, troops in the Army of Tennessee were being issued 'jackets of kearsy, blue cuffs, pants, worsted, coats are dark and light gray (mostly with blue collar and cuffs) The pants light and dark gray…it is worsted, a cross between cassimere and jeans.'

Washington Ives, of the 4th Fla. Infantry (Columbus Depot uniforms) wrote, Oct. 14th, 1863, 'I drew a tolerable pair of pants on Sunday…the jackets, drawers and shirts were so inferior that I did not take any. You may send me the old jacket of mine…"

21 Oct. 1863 "our regiment is just drawing some excellent clothing. Jackets of grey, blue cuffs,pants, …shoes, caps, shirts, etc.,… a few days later (Oct 31) he described them in more detail …just drawn comfortable winter clothing and blankets. The coats are dark and light grey mostly with blue collars and cuffs. The pants light and dark gray, similar goods to the jackets, it is worsted cross between cassimere and jeans, very warm and durable…"

Nov. 1, 1863 "The pants and jackets are of superior army goods. The caps and underclothing are miserable…Quantities of new English blankets have been issued, a single one is large enough to cover a double bed…"

A generous government issue of mostly good quality goods.

KENTUCKY CAVALIERS IN DIXIE by George Dallas Mosgrove ed by Bell Irvin Wiley pub by Broadfoot Pub. C0. 1987

Pg. 69 Oct. 12 1863 About 11o'clock I was sent out with a message to general Williams and on my way thither, I saw a strange flag and a motley troop of reckless riders-the most dare-devil looking ragamuffins I had ever seen. Many of them were barefooted, but nevertheless, they wore spurs. As far as I could see up the road they were coming at a gallop, one by one, and as each trooper came by the ordinance wagons he would come to a sudden halt and demand some ammunition. Although it was an irregular thing to do, in the abscence of a regulation requisition, James G. Owen, the ordinance sergeant, handed out the catridges, which most of the men put into their pockets, as they had no cartridge boxes..."

WRITING & FIGHTING THE CONFEDERATE WAR The Letters of Peter Wellington Alexander ed by William B. Styple pub by Bell Grove Pub. Co. 2002

Pg. 146 Oct 16 1863 In front of Cattanooga: "The heavy rain adverted to in my last letter continued to pour down in torrents until last night. Chattanooge Valley, lying between Lookout Mountain and Missionary Ridge, is flooded with water. Our lines extend across this valley, which is drained by Chattanooga Creek, now very much swollen, and, as you may imagine, the condition of the men, especially those in the trenches and on picket, is exceedingly uncomfortable. None of them have more than one blanket, and nearly all belonging to Gen. Bragg's original army, are without shelter of any kind. Longstreet's Corps is somewhat better off, his men having provided themselves with Yankee flies, Indea rubbers, &c., at Chancellorsville and other battlefields.

Enquiry at the Quartermaster's Department in Richmond, and personal observation in the armies of Gen. Lee and Gen. Bragg leave no doubt that the greatest want of the troops this winter will be for blankets. It is not probable that there will be an adequate supply of either clothing, shoes or hats, or even provisions, unless we recover East Tennessee, but the chief want, as already stated, will be blankets. Arrangements are made sometimes since to procure supplies of clothing and shoes, and if our adventures are attended by auspicious gales, the army will be able to get through the winter, with such help as the people at home can, and doubtless will, render. Their response to the call made upon them last winter was the sublimest incident of the war, and will be recorded in history as it has already been in "the books" which are kept beyond the sun, and in which all our accounts, whether for good or for evil, are entered with an unerring hand..."

This writer is frankly stating that the government will be unable to supply the soldiers and another appeal to the home folks is required, in order to provide adequate clothing and blankets.

U.S. ARMY HERITAGE AND EDUCATION CENTER Letters of James A. Hall Co. K, 24th Alanama Infantry Regiment

Oct. 18, 1863 Missionary Ridge James A. Hall to his Father "...A uniform coat and pants to be made by G.W. Doron also a pair of fatigue pants, 2 shirts, 3 pairs of drawers, 4 pairs of socks, 1 pair of shoes, also a pair of shoes to be made by Rollison.Wm W. Myrick can assist in getting them made. I will not need both pairs of shoes now. Only send one pair and keep the other until I need them. (a small pocket bible) Please have these things sent on to me as soon as possible as I am very much in need of some of them. I would not wait for them if I could purchase here, but I can't get anything here…"

LETTERS OF ARCHIE LIVINGSTON, 1ST SGT. 3RD FLORIDA INFANTRY,Madison Gray Eagles

Fair Ground Hospl No 2 Atlanta Ga Oct. 25 1863 Dear Sisters Helen &Scotia Theodore writing in regards to Archie "…He sent me a Jacket, and I have a nice soldier suit of grey. Talking about suits, how does my jeans come on. As soon as you get it done send it by first chance, or by express. The Drawers I am not particular about, I can draw them from the Q.M. I need some socks & Hdkfs.…I am out of shoes & cant draw any.…Your (boy?) Theodore Don't forget my shoes…"

FROM HUNTSVILLE TO APPOMATTOX R.T. Coles History of the 4th regiment Alabama Volunteer Infantry, C.S.A. Army of Northern Virginia ed by Frank D. Stocker pub by Univ of Tenn. Press 1996

Pg. 140 Out Campaign in Lookout Valley" Oct 25, 1863 "We secured sufficient supplies for our needs in the valley and were progressing very well in our isolated retreat, shooting mules to our heart's content, and enjoying the s[poet immensely, until we had reduced the Union army to half rations by forcing it to secure supplies by a more much difficult and circuitous mountain road. On the 25th of October we were very much surprised to learn that the rest of the brigade, the 44th, 47th, and 48th Alabama, which had been ordered over to support us, had been ordered back across the mountain to the main army. We were perfectly aware that we were inflicting great damage on the enemy, and that we would not be permitted to remain there much longer without an effort on the part of the enemy to disposses us.

We had brought our Whitworth rifles fron Virginia with us. These were placed down the river on our extreme left to shoot down the front teams, which after being done, the road was entirely blocked. We then proceded in a leisurely manner to use our English rifles. The road was too narrow between the bluff and river for the teams to turn around or escape in any manner, and they were compelled to stand until all were shot down. I saw one of the Whitworth rifles, an English gun, with a globe sight, carrying a large ball, a few of which had run the blockade in the hands of one of our sharpshooters, kill two mules at one shot, the heavy missile passing through their necks."

These Whitworth rifles were amazing, especially in the hands of a experienced sharpshooter.

LETTERS OF ARCHIE LIVINGSTON, 1st Sgt., 3rd Florida Infantry, Co. G, Madison Gray Eagles

Nov. 24 63 My Dear Sisters, "…A boy belonging to a member of Co. A in our Regt promised me on yesterday to take a box for Archie but I have not seen anything of him since. He left the Regt. some two or three days since, and brot a letter from Archie with (army?) socks, Drawers, Flannel, &c. from Archie for oue deposit, until he needs them. He says that his suit of jeans fits exactly and is admired, by all in the Regt. Bill Philips, who is here sick, says Archie is as fat as a Buck and stands camp life better than any one in the company…Twelve months ago we had first come our of KY and our poor Florida boys who were destitute of clothing had felt several sleet and snow storms before this time of year…I wish if you have not sent my clothes-you would send those that you have as soon as possible for there is no telling when I may go. My shoes are too large for me, but I will make them do, but the next ones I have made in the size smaller. These are 7 when I could wear a five but a small 6 is the size. If it will not delay my bundle any-& you could do it without much inconvenience, send me a pr for there are pleanty of men that will take these from me…"

Blog of the 27th North Carolina Infantry Regiment "Plowshares & Bayonets"

Pg. 2 "…CS Quartermaster stores on hand in Savnnah (Ga) as of Oct. 31, 1863

The clothing on hand consists as follows:

Infantry Jacket: A lot (of 1300) made of English cloth, with metallic buttons, a good article and strongly put up; a lot (of 2600) made of Georgia jeans, from the Richmond (Georgia) factory, with wooden buttons, an inferior article compared with the first.

Pantaloons: A lot (of 150) made of English tweed pants, a good article (the artillery in and around Savannah has been provided with these pants for the last six months); a lot (of 800) made of Georgia homespun, manufactured in Savannah, a strong article of light gray but rather thin for winter; a lot (of 6,700) made of Georgia jeans a pretty good article of light gray. Besides the above, the Quartermaster has on hand a lot of 1400 jackets and pants of Georgia homespun which were turned over to him by the state of Georgia and which, as a last resort, may be used for the troops. It is a poor article, however, thin for the season, and almost white.

Drawers and Shirts: (a lot of) 8000 of white cotton. These shirts and drawers were made in Savannah, under the supervision of the Quartermasters, who employ for that purpose the wives and female relations of Ga. Soldiers.

[Miscellaneous] 6000 pairs of cotton socks; 2000 blankets. The QM also has a lot of 18 second handed blankets fit for use and another lot of 36 damaged,rotten blankets, entirely unfit for use. Oil cloth caps at about 175; gray cloth caps (about) 300.

Thread: 10,000 spools. Bone buttons for drawers and shirts 600 great gross; metallic buttons, 700 gross; shirt buttons 400 gross."

Notice approximately half of the clothing on hand is described as "a poor article." Even if all this clothing were to be issued in a mass issue, it would still be inadequate for the army's needs.

THE STILLWELL LETTERS-A GEORGIAN IN LONG-STREET'S CORPS ARMY OF NORTHERN VIRGINIA ed. by Ronald H. Morely pub by Mercer Univ. Press 2002

Pg. 224 Headquarters Brigade Camp near Chattanooga, Tennessee, November 2 1863 (Molly) "...If you get a chance to send my pants and shirt, do so and let me know when and by whom you sent them..."

WALKER'S TEXAS DIVISION C.S.A. Greyhounds OfThe Mississippi by Richard Lowe pub by La. State Univ Press 2004

Pg. 146 Nov 3, 1863 Battle of Bayou Bourbeau,La. The Rebels chased off the Union forces, capturing their supplies. "...defeat also brought discomfort. "Since the Rebels had burned up all our tents and camp equipage, we were left here upon this bleak prarie without blakets tents or food," An Indiana Hoosier complained. Similar protests circulated around Ohio campfires: "It is really laughable to hear some of the boys bemoan the loss of their clothing, saying once in a while, that some dirty rebel is strutting around in his parade suit, or while he is shivering by the fire, some rebel rascal is snug and warm wrapped in stolen blankets."

Seems like poetic justice to me.

FROM COSICANA TO APPOMATTOX by John Spencer pub by The Texas Press

Pg. 82 Nov. 4 1863 "...But the guns of Naverro County don't stay long on Lookout Mountain. Each man draws 10 days rations on about Nov. 4, cooking it all in the ashes of their campfires. After several weeks of rain and mud and marching and fighting, they are glad to be on the move again-even though some of them are barefooted, and many have no blankets, none of them have winter clothing..."

This unit is a fair example of the rest of the army, going into the winter season with completely inadequate clothing and a lack of blankets.

THE STILLWELL LETTERS-A Georgian in Longstreet's Corps, Army of Northern Virginia ed by Ronals H. Morely pub by Mercer Univ. Press 2002

Pg. 228 Camp Sweetwater Tennessee, Nov. 8th& 9th, 1863 Molly, "...Someone stole my knapsack from the guard as we came up, with one shirt, jacket, bundle of needles and pins, (and) thread. I had just bought two or three quires of paper and the same amount of envelopes and stamps, but as good luck would have it, I had given out a pair of drawers and a shirt and socks to be washed, and they are not lost. Consequently I have two drawers, two shirts, two pair of socks, two jeans. I miss the paper and envelopes worse than anything else...I got my pants, shirt and all you sent..."

Pg. 233 Knoxville, Tennessee, November 23, A.D., 1863 My dear Molly,"...I wrote you that I had got my clothes. You said something about having some cloth to make me a vest, if you have you can do so as the one I have is getting smartly worn but if it is not convenient, never mind, I am not needing it bad..."

We see in the first letter that some soldiers are re-supplying themselves through thievery.

THIS INFERNAL WAR by Edwin Hedge Fay/Bell Irvin Wiley pub by Univ. of Texas Press 1958

Pg. 358 Camp near Clinton, Miss. Nov. 13th 1863 My Own Darling Wife "...I understand from Lancaster that there are plenty of Mexican ponchos or blankets for sale in Minden. I want you to but one for me certain and send back by J.D.H.T. or Watkins. They are worth $200 on this side and my shawl is most worn out. I learn they can only be bought from soldiers. If so please get Mr. Wimberly to get it for me...I left 3 five dollar gold pieces with a lady who is going into Vicksburg to buy me a pair of boots, ditto gauntlets..."

Pg. 361 Camp near Clinton, Miss. Nov19/63 My own darling One; "...I do not recollect whether I told you that I had sent some gold into Yankeedom (at Vicksburg) to buy me some boots, gauntelets, & silk Hdkfs..."

AN ENGLISHMAN IN THE CIVIL WAR by Thompson Yates 1971

Pg. 136 Diary entry made at Nashville Nov. 17,1863 "...On the way we passed an open space where were congregated some fifty or sixty in various faded shades of butternut. Dr. L. said they were Confederate Prisoners. Only one of the prisoners hail a uniform, an artilleryman in a buff jacket with red facings; the mass of rebels in the West fight in their common clothes..."

Another witness to the multiform dress of the Army of Tennessee.

LETTERS OF A CONFEDERATE SURGEON 1861-65 pub by The Hurley Co. 1960

November 19, 1863 "...I wrote the foregoing last night. Since which time the windows of heaven were raised and the rain poured in torrents. This morning overcoats are in great demand, and chimneys are raised up, as if by magic, in front of the tents...(Note from Page)-1 "At this period of the war blue Federal uniforms were frequently taken from the battlefields and worn by Confederate soldiers..."

THE STILLWELL LETTERS-A GEORGIAN IN LONG-STREET'S CORPS ARMY OF NORTHERN VIRGINIA ed. by Ronald H. Morely pub by Mercer Univ. Press 2002

Pg. 232 Knoxville, Tennessee November 23, A.D. 1863 (Molly) "...I wrote you that I had got my clothes. You said something about having some cloth to make me a vest, if you have you can do so as the one I have is smartly worn but if it is not convenient, never mind, I am not needing it bad...."

AN ENGLISHMAN IN THE CIVIL WAR by Thompson Yates 1971

Diary entry made during the Battle of Chatanooga Nov. 23, 1863 "...Very soon a batch of 200 Rebel prisoners were brought in, rough and ragged men with no vestige of a uniform, but with good shoes and looking well-fed..."

DIARY OF A CONFEDERATE SOLDIER John S. Jackman of the Orphan Brigade ed. by William C. Davis pub by Univ. S.C. Press 1990

Pg. 97 Nov. 24, 1863 Chickamauga

When we stopped Johnnie G. and I made us a bed of brush, and tried to sleep, having no other covering than our overcoats-we left all our blankets in wagons-but the night was too cold...The next night a cold rain was pelting down, and while the boys were fortifying I tried to get a little sleep by lying down close to a fire. I did sleep a moment but burnt all the back out of my overcoat-or a big hole in it. Afterwards in the campaign, I often heard soldiers say, pointing me out, "Golly! Didn't a shell come near getting that fellow: look at the hole in his coat..."

How tired do you have to be to remain asleep while the back of your overcoat is burned away?

THE CONFEDERATE VETERAN VOL.XXIX 1921

Pg. 345 Sept. 1921 In The Years Of War-complied by John C. Stiles from "Offical Records" series III vol. II 1863-64 Wearing Yankee Uniforms-On November 26 Gen. S.D. Lee ordered: The wearing of Fedeal uniforms having become so common in this command, and it has sometimes caused fatal mistakes, it is hereby ordered that every article of that description be at once dyed." I am not at all surprised that mistakes were made, as at least one-third of the men were totaly or partly uniformed in Yankee clothes."

That's a lot of soldiers in blue uniforms.

AN ENGLISHMAN IN THE CIVIL WAR by Thompson Yates 1971

Diary entry made in the aftermath of the Battle of Chatanooga Nov. 27, 1863 "…I saw three or four dead Rebels, lying as they had fallen. The first gave me quite a shock. I came on him quite suddenly,his butternut clothing being the same color as the leaves he was lying on; his head and feet were bare…the next man lay on his face, holes in his boots…"

HADLEY LIBRARY ARCHIVES, WINCHESTER, VA—James Bradfield Diary Co H 17th Virginia Infantry

Pg 23 Nov. 29th 1863 (en route to Knoxville, Tn) "29th-but having to issue shoes do not get off until 10 oclock we march through Seguinesville and bivouac on Big Creek 3 miles from Rogersville 18 miles today it is very cold and tonight it is freezing hard."

Unfortunately he doesn't state how many shoes he issued.

THIS INFERNAL WAR by Edwin Hedge Fay/Bell Irvin Wiley pub by Univ. of Texas Press 1958

Pg. 370 Camp near Bolton's Depot, S.R.R. Nov. 30th 1863 My Darling Wife "…I shall also send a pair of pants for a pattern to cut me some by to send back by Gassaway or some one. I want them cut just like the ones sent except the pockets to be put right in front, about two inches below the waistband cut right through the cloth in front. Mr. Lloyd was going to cut these so (I send the ones Sister Sarah made) but was afraid I would not like them, since which time I got the Uniform pair and the pockets were as described above and I like them very much. An inch and a half below the waistband will do. I need a pair of pants very much. My uniform pair are too small in the waist to wear with any comfort. If I knew I would come home before long I would not ask you to send me any but it is very uncertain and I do not know where I can get another pair. If I don't send those pants you can make me some anyhow and put in the pockets as described above. The last pair you made me did not fit very well but you know fitting is nothing anyway for everyone says "he's nothing but a soldier." ..."

I agree with Sgt. Fay that pants need pockets.

SOUTHERN INVINCIBILITY by Wiley Sword pub by St. Martin's Press 1999

Pg. 221 winter, 1863-64 Army of Tennessee "One Arkansas soldier who had been barefoot for two monthes complained that the heavy frosts were hurting his feet."

This soldier must have been so used to going without shoes that it took extreme weather for him to complain.

THE CONFEDERATE VETERAN VOL. XIV 1906

Pg. 407 From Missionary Ridge to Dalton by Robert L. Thompson "...On our return from East Tennessee, I took "French leave" and dropped out of ranks late one day for the purpose of foraging. I slept in a feather bed that night at the home of a kind mother of the Confederacy who lived in Northern Georgia. All the men and boys of the household were absent in the army, with only the womenfolks and darkies at home. When I departed from the good ladies house next morning, she gave me a homemade hat and a suit of clothes, and she put into my haversack a piece of uncooked kid that had been slaughtered the evening before..."

THE CONFEDERATE VETERAN VOL. XVI 1908

Pg. 513 Dec. 1863 How "Johnny" Got Some Blankets "The following incident was recently related by a Federal:

"Once we were camped in the mountains of East Tennessee. I didn't know it could be so cold down South till I tried it for myself. One bitter night I was on picket duty away off from camp, down in the edge of some woods and close beside a little creek. I was tramping along through the snow, kicking my feet and beating my hands together, trying to keep warm, when I heard a voicesomewhere off on the other side of the creek calling softly: "Yank! Yank!"

I knew the enemy was in camp not far away, so I raised my gun in an instant; but the voice called again, "Don't shoot, Yank! I'm all alone and don't mean any harm."

"Who are you then, and what do you want?" I asked as quietly as I could.

"I'm a Johnny," said the voice again, "and I want to see if you can't spare me a blanket."

"You are crazy," said I. "I'd be shot if they caught me giving you a blanket."

"There's no need for you to get shot," said Johnny, "and I'm 'bout to freeze picketing out here in the snow. My uniform is nothing bur rags, and I haven't got any overcoat or blanket or anything. Blankets are scarce over in our camp, and its awful cold, Yank."

He said it solemly in that soft voice of his(the Southerners have a soft, easy way of talking), and-well, the upshot of it was that I promised him I would bring a blanket with me when I came back the next night and leave it to him to get it. Next nightwhen I went to saddle up (our picket line was so far from camp that we had to ride) I got half a dozen blakets out of the commissary and put them under my saddle, and was just about to get away with them when the sergeant spied me. "Hello, there!" said He, "what you going to do with all those blankets?"

My heart was in my mouth, but I knew he couln't see how many I really did have, so I answered back cool enough: "You don't suppose its warm out there picketing a night like this, do you?" And with that he turned away. I tell you, I was glad to see his back!

Well, I got safe out to the wood with my blankets, and pretty soon I heard the same voice calling again: "Yank, Yank, have you got that blanket?"

"Yes," I said, "I have six of them, and I came near getting caught, too."

"Glory!" said Johnny. "Glory! Now you jest slip down to the creek and unfold them a little and drop them in one at a time, and I'll do the rest."

I did just as he told me (Ididn't have to get off my beat to do it), and he went a little way down the creek and fished the blankets out as the current brought them along. When he'd got the last one out, he fell down on his knees(I could see him in the dim moonlight), and never heard anybody pray such a prayer as that Southern soldier prayed for me, kneeling there in the snow in his ragged old uniform. I took off my hat and stood still till he was through, and then he faded away into the darkness."

[Let us quit talking about "time healing the wounds" or the bitter spirit of true soldiers. The forgoing illustrates the kindly regard that existed while the soldiers on both sides were suffering each for his principles.-Ed. Veteran]

This was a good man, even if he was a Yankee.

THEY WHO FOUGHT HERE by Bell Irvin Wiley & Hirst D. Millhollen pub by The MacMillan Co. 1959

Pg. 80 "In Dec. 1863, one of Longstreet's men wrote from Knoxville : "Mother, you have heard of barefooted soldiers at Valley Forge…but no men ever marched more willingly than did our barefooted men over the cold, hard frozen ground (here)…it is indeed an awful sight…" On November 11, 1862, one of Longstreet's soldiers wrote: "General Armistad sent me a pair of raw hide shoes the other day and (they) stretch out at the heel so that when I start down a hill the(y) whip me nearly to death they flop up and down they stink very bad and I have to keep a brush in my hand to keep the flies off of them this is the last of the raw hide as some of the boys got hungry last night and broiled them and eat them so farewell raw hide shoes" (*A soldier would have to be mighty hungry to eat rawhide shoes.)*...The soldier-historian of McGowan's brigade of Lee's Army stated: "Clothing was sparsely issued, and what we received was coarse and flimsy. I do not remember the issue of a single overcoat and but a few blankets. Shoes were scarce. More than a soldier left a blood track on the frozen picket line..." Even worse was the plight of Hood's men in Tennessee. A sergeant of the Forty-Sixth Mississippi wrote in his diary on returning from a furlough in Jan. 1865: "I find my regiment-the whole army in fact-in a deplorable condition... The regiment numbers about 150 men about half of whom are barefoot. All are ragged, dirty, and covered with vermin"...One of Hood's brigadiers in his official report of the TennesseeCampaign stated: "During the whole time...(Dec. 20-30, 1864) the weather was excessively severe... (and) for several days the ground was covered with snow. Numbers of the men had made the march without shoes, some had no blankets and all were poorly clad...What they had to endure was borne without complaint"...Confederates resorted to all sorts of expedients to meet these recurring crises. Uncle Sam was the South's best quartermaster, and a common saying in camp was that "all a Yankee is worth is his shoes." Many a ragged Confederate reclothed himself at the expense of a dead foe in the still of the night following a battle; and some in the light of day compelled live prisoners to swap blue finery for butternut rags. Stonewall Jackson, in May 1862, found it necessary to issue a general order threatening with arrest "all persons found wearing articles of the uniform of the United States." After Forrest's raid through western Tennessee in December, 1862, Sergeant Tom Terrill wrote to his mother: "I saw our Cavalry...on their return; they were about six hundred in number and every man had on a complete Yankee suit consisting of hat, coat, pants, jackets and boots." "General Lee repeatedly urged his wife and daughters to knit socks for the men. In the winter of 1863-64, he delivered to the Stonewall Brigade 263 pairs of socks made by his womenfolk and their friends. On one occasion he reported to Mrs. Lee that he had been recently visited by a humble woman who had come to camp bringing her soldier husband a complete uniform spun, woven and tailored by her own hands. The achievement of this woman, who had also clothed herself and her children with her own handiwork, was duplicated many times over by Southern women. The clothing sent by wives and mothers was frequently more comfortable and more durable than that issued by the quartermaster."

PARKER'S VIRGINIA BATTERY by Rort K. Krick pub by Va. Book Co. 1975

Pg. 214 Dec. 1863 "...More than 200 prisoners were taken along the march away from Knoxville. The prisoners were apparently positioned near the artillery battalion in the order of march, which made for a real treat for the canoneers. General Longstreet had given permission for the men to swap shoes with the prisoners-but only swaps were authorized, not out right appropriation. A ragged secessionist wearing the crudest imaginable rawhide moccasins would approach a group of fresh prisoners and carefully inspect their footgear before selecting a victum. The victums of this practice usually took the inequitable exchange in good humor. One of them remarked, "When a man is captured, his shoes are captured too." Those of Parker's men who benefitted from this profitable system of enforced barter were very fortunate. Because the winter ahead was a season of severe shoe shortages in the army…"

What is this writer comparing this season to? From what wev'e seen in this study, every season is one of severe shoe shortage.

THE REGULAR CONFEDERATE ARMY by Richard P. Weinert pub by White Mane Pub Co. 1991

Pg. 107 Dec. 2, 1863 The company under First Lieutenant Charles Armand Brisset at Pollard, Al., "…After its arrival in Mobile, attempts had been made to fill its ranks, but many of the men were of poor quality. Discipline was good, but the company had no muskets since its retreat from Corinth (Miss.). Its accouterments were in very bad order and entirely unfit, the clothing was insufficient, and the men were without blankets…"

In other words, they were no different from the rest of the army.

LETTER FROM ROBERT RANSOM in Andersonville Diary Dec. 3 1863

Pg. 15 Dec. 3, 1863 "…Gen. Dow is still issuing clothing, but the rebels get more than our men do of it. Guards nearly all dressed in Yankee uniforms…"

LIFE AND LETTERS OF ELIZABETH L. COMSTOCK pub by John Winston & Co. 1895

Pg. 511 December 8, 1863 "…There we waited while 100 cavaliers were again sent off. In less than an hour they returned, reporting that the rebels had intercepted the down freight train, pillaged it of 300 horses, war store of 'great value,' provisions, clothing &c, on their way from Murfeesboro to General Rosencran's head-quarters. After robbing it of all they could carry off, they compelled the engineer and men to leave it, and setting it on fire, started it alone at full speed on our track, designing that it should meet our train and destroy it… The rebel raid had come from the fastness of the mountains of Kentucky, 300 in number. They were all dressed in the Northern uniform, which they had pillaged from a former freight train…"

THIS INFERNAL WAR by Edwin Hedge Fay/Bell Irvin Wiley pub by Univ. of Texas Press 1958

Pg. 374 Bolton's Depot, Dec. 8, 1863 My own darling One; "…We went to Mr. Thigpen's and I took my coats out to have the cuffs and collars trimmed with yellow flannel (Cavalry stripes). His Mother did the work and I borrowed an old coat of his and we went to Mr. Patterson's where we stayed all night…"

Pg. 383 in Camp 2 miles West of Brownsville Miss. Dec. 9/63 My Own Darling "…Grandma made me a pair of pants of Factory Kersey so I am at present well provided…I bought two yards of yellow flannel for the company to trim their coats for $20 per yard. Your "Music" is all I bought for myself. I wanted to buy some staff buttons for my coat but could not afford to pay $25 pr. dozen for them…."

A SOUTHERN SOLDIER'S LETTERS HOME The Civil War Letters of Samuel Burney Cobb's Georgia Legion, Army of Northern Va. ed. by Nat Turner pub by Mercer Univ. Press, Macon Ga.2002

Pg. 258 Resaca Georgia Dec.10th, 1863 "…We have had several days of rain. We stretched out a blanket and kept dry while many without blankets stood out in the rain like you have seen frizzly chickens…Our blanket turned the rain very well. I did not get wet but had to lie in a close place…."

With my luck, I'd have been one of those "frizzly chickens." I cannot imagine enduring several days of rain with no shelter

RECOLLECTIONS OF A CONFEDERATE STAFF OFFICER by G.Moxley Sorrel pub by Bantam Books 1992

Pg. 183 Dec. 10, 1863 manuevering around Knoxville, TN. "The men were happy and cheerful, but awfully in want of clothing and shoes. Some of the latter were made by themselves, but this supply could not go far. I recall a movement by General Granger at Dandridge when the Corps turned out to march. It was bitter winter weather, the ground hard and sharp with ice, and not less than 2,000 of our little army were without shoes. Their bleeding feet left marks at every step."

THE REBEL BOAST by Manly Wade Wellman pub. By Henry Holt & Co. N.Y. 1956

Pg.382 "De Fontaine did not mince words in bringing to public attention the miserable plight of Longstreet's men who were faced with the necessity of wintering in the rugged mountains: "There are at this moment (December 11, 1863) from three thousand to thirty-five hundred barefooted men in this army. Some of them are officers high in rank. One whom I know is a Lieutenant Colonel. All of them are fighting men, who, but for this necessity, would be in the front rank in every hour of danger. The weather is so cold that tha icicles around the waterfalls are as thick as a man's body. In twenty minutes after sundown liquid freezes solid. The surface of the ground is as hard as a rock, and at every step the frozen edges of the earth cut into naked feet, until the path of the army may be almost said to have been tracked in blood. To remedy the evil, I have seen these men, accustomed as they were at home to every luxury, strip their coats and blankets from their backs, and tie the rags around their feet; I have seen them take the fresh hides of cattle, reeking with the warm blood, and fashion therefrom rude moccasins to last them for the day's march; and I have seen them beg in piteous terms of passing horsemen for a brief respite to their painful walk, and where this has failed, offer five, ten and twenty dollars for the privilege of riding a few miles on their wearisome journey. I mention these as facts that have come under my own observation, and which should appeal to liberal and sympathizing hearts with all the eloquence of suffering, and call for that speedy relief which the emergency demands."

Wrapping the feet in rags would be, like the moccasins a very temporary solution. I wonder how these men stood it, day after day.

THE DIARY OF A CONFEDERATE SOLDIER-John S. Jackman of the Orphan Brigade ed by William C. Davis pub by Univ. of South Carolina Press 1990

Pg. 100 Dec. 15, 1863 winter quarters at Dalton, Ga. "We have concluded to build a house for the winter, and have been cutting and hauling pine logs for the purpose, to-day. The troops had four pounds of sweet potatoes issued to-day in lieu of bread. "Hard up." "Ike", who has been over to the cavalry camp, says thet are worse off. He says the "spurred" gentry are cutting down old trees, and robbing the woodpeckers of their winter stores of acorns, to the great discomfiture of the red-headed foresters. He says he saw an old woodpecker espostulate in vain with a cavalryman to leave her stores alone."

You know its "hard times" when your'e driven to cut down trees in order to pilfer the woodpecker's acorns.

REMINISCENCES OF A PRIVATE-William E. Bevins of the First Arkansas Infantry C.S.A. pub by Univ. Ark. Press 1992

Pg. 219 Pulaski, Miss. "December 20th 1863 we marched all day on the pike to Pulaski in a cold rain—a rain that froze on the trees. We had to sleep on the wet ground. Many complained about the "ill-provided-for condition" of his division, "many being barefooted and otherwise badly clothed.") We were called the "straggling squad" because we had to march more slowly than the others, and we were between the infantry and the rear cavalry, commanded by Forrest. In his mind a straggler deserved death. When he came up to a poor little squad, he struck one, a lieutenant, who was in charge of the barefoot squad, over the head with his sword and ordered him to go on and keep up with his command. He would listen to no excuse, as if these barefooted men, braving sleet and snow with bleeding feet, were not doing their duty as loyally as any man in the army…"

THE CONFEDERATE VETERAN VOL. IV 1896

April 1896 Pg. 154 Service of Hood's Brigade by J.B. Polly Bean's Station, Tn. Dec. 21, 1863 Charming Nellie-"…For-if because of the curtailment of one leg of my pants, because my toes protrude conspicuously from dilapidated and disreputable shoes, and my cap is stained witrh dirt and grease, my ensemble is scarcely stylish enough to give me a right ot femine society so liberally and lavishly bestowed on the Toms. Dicks, and Harrys who infest the Texas coast-my canteen is bulging with the nicest strained honey, my tobacco-pouch and haversack with the very choicest smoking tobacco; the sweetening being the munificent reward of a moonlight tramp last night over the mountains to Clinch River, the tobacco the product of a raid by Brahan and myself the day before yesterday on a kind-hearted old farmer. My present state is, in short, the naturally inevitable result of a physical satiety, mental and moral plethora, exemption from any duty, writing to you, and a philosophical mind…"

This soldier has maintained a high morale.

UNIFORMS OF THE CIVIL WAR by Lord, Wise, pub by A.S. Barnes & Co. 1970

Pg. 74 "A Texas soldier in Cleburne's Division summed it up this way: "I am more poorly clad at this time (December 24, 1863), than I ever was in any previous period (of the war). Our money is so depreciated that it will not purchase what we want. I have money plenty… but cannot find good articles of clothing for the winter. The troops are rather poorly clad, wanting shoes and socks very much, and the prospect of getting trhem is rather slim."

What depressing picture for these soldiers, at the start of cold weather.

WORD FROM CAMP POLLARD C.S.A. by William H. Davidson pub by Hester Printing 1978

Pg. 127 Private Jas. H. Barrow 59th Ala. Regt. Ala. Conecuh City. Camp Pollard Dec. 28th, 1863 Dear wife, "…I will first notice your enquiry whether you wish me to make and send my pants. I do not. I have plenty of clothing at present. When I am likely to need more I will let you know in good time. I do not wish you to send me my hat until I notify you as I shall not need it for a good while yet unless I shall have my present one stolen, burned or something of the kind. If anything of the kind happens I shall notify you without delay.

I have made three efforts to get your boxes forwarded home but I have been told each time that there was no chances but to express them. This will cost between six and seven dollars each which I have thought very extravagant. The second effort that I made I feared that I might lose my pants as the boxes were at Pollard in a house but exposed to the thief. I opened the one that my pants was in and brought them back to my cabin in camp. They are yet good except the seat is scrubbed out on the rough benches that we are compelled to use if we have any seats at all. You can send me the cloth the first good chance you have and I will patch them myself or hire it done...."

Here is one soldier, anyway, who is comfortably equipped, even if he does have a hole in the seat of his pants.

HISTORY OF KERSHAW'S BIGADE by Augustis Dickert pub by Broadfoot Pub Co. 1899

Pg 316 Dec. 1863 "...Hundreds would gather at the slaughter pens daily and cut from the warm beef hides strips large enough to make moccasins, and thus shod, marched miles upon miles in the blinding snow and sleet. Overcoats and heavy clothing had been left behind in Virginia, and it is a fact too well known to be denied among the soldiers of the South that baggage once left or sent to the rear never came to the front again...with the dead of winter now upon them, the troops had no shelter to protect them from the biting winds of the mountains or the blinding snow storms from overhead save only much-worn blankets and thin tent flies five by six feet square, one to a man..."

Pg.325 Winter at Knoxville, General Longstreet speaks thus of his army: "...With all the plentitude of provisions, and many things which, at the time, seemed luxuries, we were not quite happy. Tattered blankets, garments, shoes (the latter going, some gone) open ways on all sides for piercing winter blasts. There were some hand looms in the country, from which we occasionally picked up a piece of cloth, and here and there we received other comforts-some from kind, some from unwilling hands, which could nevertheless spare them. For shoes, we were forced to resort to raw hides, from beef cattle, as temporary protection from the frozen ground. Then we found soldiers who could tan the hides of our beeves, some who could make shoes, some who could make shoe pegs, some who could make shoe lasts, so that it came about that the hides passed rapidly from the beeves to the feet of the soldiers in the form of comfortable shoes..."

How many were thus constructed? I mean, what percentage of hides were they able to turn into shoes?

PARKER'S VIRGINIA BATTERY by Robert K. Krick pub by Va. Book Co. 1975

Pg. 217 "...The shoe shortage, which has been mentioned before, reached crisisproportions in mid-December and continued so for much of the cold season. Colonel Alexander sadly noted having personally seen "bloody stains on frozen ground, left by the barefooted where our infantry has passed." He ordered Parker and the other battery commanders to enforce the logical policy of taking shoes from the drivers of the artillery teams, who were riding, in favor of the cannoneers who were obliged to march along beside the guns. Even so, there were far from enough shoes to go around. One Mississippi regiment in Longstreet's corps had only thirty-two pairs of shoes for three hundred men present—barely ten percent of the reigiment was shod. Gibson Clark of Parker's battery recalled marching to Morristown through five inches of snow with just one tattered shoe and the other foot bound up in rags. Davy Richardson reported battery members wearing rags for shoes; they had lots of company in their plight. A Mississippi soldier told his diary on December 31, "I have seen them marching on the frozen ground and their feet bleeding at every step." Men blessed with furloughs faced a barefoot trip through more than sixty miles of snow to the railroad at Bristol.

Efforts to turn raw cowhide into foot coverings were predictably futile, because the hide became brutally hard when it dried. Longstreet encouraged the use of these rawhide makeshifts and also made an effort to have cobbler shops established. A more satisfactory solution was realized when numbers of the men acquired furloughs, returned home, and were outfitted with new shoes and clothes. A measure of relief was provided for those who couldn't get home when the railroad to Virginia was reopened and a shipment of three thousand shoes was received from Richmond..."

ALL AFIRE TO FIGHT-The Untold Tale of the Civil War's Ninth Texas Cavalry by Martha L. Crabb pub by Avon Books 2000

Pg. 193 "The night of December 31, (1863), ice an inch and a half thick formed on the ponds along the drowned, rutted road. The men hovered by their fires, their light clothing barely enough to keep them from freezing. Sam Barron wore only a thin homespun gray jean jacket and was without an overcoat. That evening, Sam hung his gloves in front of the fire to dry and they burned to a crisp."

THE CONFEDERATE VETERAN VOL.XXXVII 1929

Pg. 21 Jan. 1929 Arduous and Continous Service by W.C. Brown Capt., Co, F, 23rd Tennessee "...We were compelled to go to East Tennessee for the winter of 1863-1864, where we suffered for clothes and shoes and food. Our feet were tied in rags. We were without tents or wagons to haul our cooking utensils and had to carry everything we used, and we had to take the weather as it came…"

Trans Mississippi

A CREEK WARRIOR FOR THE CONFEDERACY The Auto-biography of Chief G.W.Grayson pub by Univ. of Ok. Press 1988

Pg. 97 Cica 1863 "…Our soldiers were poorly clad and most of the time my company presented a motley appearance. The Confederacy being hard run had very little in the way of clothing to issue to the men of this part of the country, and we were never very presentable. So when we caught a prisoner from the other side, we generally stripped him clean of such of his wearing apparel as we desired, they being always better than our own, and placed upon him instead such of our own old duds as he could wear. Our government had issued to our men certain wool hats which appeared to be manufactured of the plain sheep's wool without any coloring, while the latter seemed not to have seriously concerned himself about the symmetry and poise of any individual hat. They were all apparently on one block and driven together in long stacks, and when one came near a stack of them he could distinctly discern the odor of the raw material. It smelled very like getting inside a pen where a drove of sheep is confined. Now these hats, while not comely of shape and general appearance, had the further disadvantage of losing after a short service even the little shape and and semblance of figure that had been given them by the manufacturers. The entire brim would invairiably flop down, leaving lttle other signs of its former self than a dirty cotton string, while the crown, without any apparent provocation, would push sharply up in the center, converting the whole into the exact figure of a cone. These hats being a dull whitish color were very susceptible to the effects of dust and dirt, and naturally had a dingy appearance at best, which became execrable after a month's wear.

One such hat that had well nigh served its time and collected its full share of dust and discolorations was owned and worn by McAnally. Being a young man of decidedly Indian taste in manner of dress and ornamentation, (he) embellished it in true aboriginal style with one of the plumes of the wing of the falcon, commonly known in the country as the chicken hawk, the shaft of which had been cadefully pared away and rendered so thin, pliant and limber that the least air disturbance gave it to a vibratory or rather tremulous motion highly responsive to the Indian's idea of esthetics. The feather he had securely fastened in the apex of this hat wher it had for considerable time done service doubtless to the admiration of his comrades in war.

Having through his own courage and proclivities for warlike deeds captured a little old, tall, lank and woebegone appearing fellow of the enemy, Mack proceeded to relieve him of such of his clothing as he desired which would fit him. He took also his hat which he considerately replaced with his own typical Confederate hat, feather ornament and all, and when a moment later I met him in another part of the field, I could hardly recognize him as the same, he being now so differently decked out from what he was when he first met the enemy. He explained how he had captured a prisoner with whom he had made some exchanges of clothing, and how he believed he could point him out among the number of those that had been taken.

At a certain point the prisoners taken in the afternoon work were filing by when he pointed out the unfortunate who was the unwilling cause of his being a hero. He was the most miserable, forlorn and wretched appearing and gangling little, old white man anywhere in sight. On his Confederate hat's apex was blithely and bravely trembling to the breeze his Ke-ak-ka-ta-fa (falcon's feather), while he with downcast contenance marched slowly along in evident ignorance in the gaity and life supposed to be typified by the plumed headgear he wore. Of all the supremely ludicrous, ridiculous, laughable object I have ever been up against this was the crowning one. I enjoyed the big laugh at McAnally's prisoner…"

KIRBY SMITH'S CONFEDERACY

The standards of uniform of most regiments fell short of the norms established by army regulations. Footwear, when available, ranged from low-quarter pumps and Indian moccasins to patent leather riding boots; socks came in all colors; trousers were usually gray, blue or plaid jeans; shirts were often gray cotton, but butternut brown, Union blue, and linen white were almost as common; vests, jackets, and greatcoats came in all sorts of single- and double-breasted designs, varied widely in color and pattern, and normally lacked the brass buttons and braid proper to military dress; and headgear included anything from beaver toppers and jet-black felts to Yankee forage caps and calico kerchiefs. In early 1863, most of the men in the Fourteenth Texas Cavalry Battalion were wearing plaid flannel shirts, wool trousers, short jack boots, enormous spurs, and black felt hats ornamented with the Lone Star of their state. Both the Second Texas Infantry and the twenty-sixth Louisiana Infantry received-and wore-undyed white muslin coats. The Third Texas Infantry paraded in a promiscuous collection of blue and gray uniforms, French kepis, "wide awake" hats, and Mexican sombreros. Captain Sam Richardson scowled his way through a photographer's sitting while wearing a high black cowboy hat, a ruffled gray shirt, yellow cavalry gauntlets, a tooled leather belt with a big gilt buckle, a sheathed bowie knife, a carbine sling, two leopard-skin revolver holsters, and leopard skin trousers with spangles down the seam…"

The trans-Mississippi continues with its tradition of multiuform, see below.

WALKER'S TEXAS DIVISION, C.S.A. Greyhounds of the Tans-Mississippi by Richard Lowe pub by La. State Univ. Press 2004

Pg. 13 Joining Up-"...The ranks and files of the new companies gradually to take on some regularity and precision in the dusty drill fields, but the appearance of the men was decidedly variegated. Some wore homespun shirts and rough work jeans under floppy felt hats; others enjoyed store-bought clothes; a few preened in uniforms made by mothers and sisters. Even a year later Private Blessington noted the lack of uniformity in dress among his comrades:" Then as to costume, it is utterly impossible to paint the variety our division presented. Here would be a fellow dressed in homespun pants, with the knees out of them; on his head might be stuck the remnants of a straw hat, while a faded Texas penitentiary cloth jacket would perhaps complete his outfit. His neighbor, very likely, was arrayed in breeches made out of some cast-off blanket, with a dyed shirt as black as the ace of spades, and no hat at all. Then would come a man with a woolen hat made like a pyramid, sitting jauntily on his head, while, to introduce his style of hat, he had it covered over with assorted buttons, and, to top the climax, had a red tassel sewed on top. Notwithstanding his gaudy hat, a part of a shirt, and occasional fragments only of what had once been a pair of military pantaloons, made up the rest of his attire..."

THEIR TATTERED FLAGS-THE EPIC OF THE CONFE-DERACY by Frank E. Vandiver pub by Harper's Magazine Press 1970

Pg. 174 "Where leather could not be had, multiple layers of cotton cloth were stitched together and soaked in linseed oil served instead. When shoes faded from the memories of the Rebel infantry, the Quartermaster General devised the supreme hoax of the war: wooden soled canvas-topped brogans, said to have satisfied everyone but the wearers".

"Clothing had all but vanished from sale and Texans were now a homespun lot." Freemantle's trip into Trans-Mississippi on April 1863..."

MEMOIRS OF THE REBELLION ON THE BORDER by Wiley Britton pub by Univ. of Nebraska Press 1882

Pg. 198 April 1, 1863 1st Kansas Cavalry "...A detachment of this division just arrived from Park Hill, Cherokee Nation, reports that seven of our Indians, known as Pins, were killed at that place a few days ago by a party of Rebels wearing the Federal uniform..."

Pg. 248 May 13, 1863 "…Nothing of interest occurred on the first day of our return march, but the second day, between Pineville and Scott's Mills, we saw eight or ten armed men on horse-back coming towards us, dressed in butter-nut suits, whom we supposed were bush-wackers. As soon as they saw and carefully observed our blue uniforms, they fired a volley at us from their shotguns…"

THE FREMANTLE DIARY-A Journal of the Confederacy pub.by Burford Books 1954

Pg. 9 2nd April, 1863 about nine miles outside Brownsville, Texas "About three miles beyond this we came to Colonel Duff's encampment. He is a fine-looking, handsome Scotchman and received me with much hospitality. His regiment consisted of newly raised volunteers-a fine body of young men, who were drilling in squads. They were dressed in every variety of costume, many of them without coats, but all wore the high black felt hat…"

Pg. 58 3rd May (Sunday) 1863 "…At 1:30 I saw Pyron's regiment embark for Noblett's Bluff to meet Banks. This corps is now dismounted cavatry, and the procession was a droll one. First came eight or ten instruments braying discordantly, then an enormous Confederate flag, followed by about four hundred men moving by fours-dressed in every variety of costume, and armed with every variety of weapon; about sixty had Enfield rifles; the remainder carried shot-guns (fowling pieces), carbines or long rifles of a peculiar and antiquated manufacture. None had swords or bayonets-all had six-shooters and Bowie knives. The men were a fine, determined-looking lot; and I saw among them a short stout boy of of fourteen, who had served through the Arizona campaign…"

I cannot imagine enduring the Airzona campaign at fourteen. This was one tough lad.

THREE MONTHS IN THE SOUTHERN STATES APRIL-JUNE 1863 Diary of Sir Arthur Fremantle pub by William Blackwood & Son 1863

Pg. 16 8 April 1863 Texas-"… Lieutenant-Colonel Buchel is the working man of the corps, as he is a professional soldier. The men were well clothed, though great variety existed in their uniforms. Some companies wore blue, some grey, some had French kepis, others wideawakes and Mexican hats. They were a fine body of men, and really drilled uncommonly well…"

Pg. 69 10 May 1863 "On approaching Monroe, (La.) we passed through the camp of Walker's Division, (8,000 strong). It was on the march from Arkansas to meet Banks. The division had embarked in steamers, and had already started down the Ouachita towards the Red River, when the news arrived of the fall of Alexandria, and of the presence of Federal gunboats in or near the Ouachita itself. This caused the precipitate return and disembarkation of Walker's

Division. The men were well armed with rifles and bayonets, but they were dressed in ragged civilian clothes…"

Pg. 97 May 22 1863 "The men are constantly in the habit of throwing away their knapsacks and blankets on a long march, if not carried for them…"

WALKER'S TEXAS DIVISION, C.S.A. Greyhounds of the Tans-Mississippi by Richard Lowe pub by La. State Univ. Press 2004

Pg. 108 The Dismal Summer of 1863 Miliken's Bend to Lake Providence "…Frustrated at his failure to punish the rebels, Porter could at least insult them: They are a half-starved, half-naked set, and are in hopes of capturing some of the transports with clothing and provisions. …"

"Some of the Texans might have agreed with Porter that they were a tattered bunch that summer. Their weeks in the swamps had certainly done nothing to improve their appearance. Lt. Theophilus Perry of the 28th cavalry wrote his wife that "some of the men have not changed suits in four weeks. They remain naked while they wash their clothes. Anumber of our men have been left at Monroe on account of being barefooted." Private Farrow of the 19th Infantry grumbled that "our clothing is in awful condition(,) some is perfectly rotten. My bed clothes are damaged badly. I will throw all of them away when we leave here but my blanket." Private Bessington laughed that "Falstaff's ragged regiment was well uniformed in comparison with our troops. No two were costumed with any attempt at uniformity." Not only were they shabby in raiment, they were scruffy and filthy beyond reclognition. "But few of the troops had shaved for weeks, and, as a consequence, there was a large and general assortment of unbrushed black, grey, red, and sandy beards, as wellas ferocious mustaches and whiskers-enough to rig out an army of West India buccaneers. A more brigandish set of Anglo-Saxpon forces has never been collected," Blessington wrote. "So completely disguised were we all, that I doubt whether our anxious mothers would have recognized us…."

VAQUEROS IN BLUE AND GRAY by Jerry D. Thompson pub by State House Press 2000

Pg. 72 June 1863 "…a militia company stationed at Boca del Rio (Texas) with orders to guard the mouth of the Rio Grande. In June, 1863, Vidal (Lt.) reported his company "entirely destitute" of camp necessities and asked headquarters in Brownsville for "kettles, iron pots and spades." Five days later, he asked for one Sibley tent complete with pole and tripod. For his men, who were in ragas, Vidal requested hats, shirts, pants, and fifty pairs of shoes…"

THE FREEMANTLE DIARY ed. by Walter Lord

Pg. 7 James Arthur Lyon Freemantle, a British traveler who was in Texas in 1863, described the dress of a Texas cavalry company as consisting simply of flannel shirts, very ancient trousers, Jack boots with huge spurs, ragged black or brown trousers, and black felt hats "ornamented with the Lone Star of Texas."

Pg. 124 Referring to Liddell's Brigade of Arkansas troops, 1st June, 1863 "…The men were good-sized, healthy and well-clothed, but without any attempt at uniformity in color or cut; but nearly all were dressed in either grey or brown coats and felt hats. I was told that even if a regiment was clothed in proper uniform by the Government, it would be parti-colored again within a week, as the soldiers preferred wearing the coarse home-spun jackets and trousers made by their mothers and sisters at home. The Generals very wisely allow them to please themselves in this respect, and insist only that their arms and accouterments being kept in the proper order. Most of the officers were dressed in uniform which is neat and serviceable-a bluish gray frock coat of a color similar to the Austrian yaegers. The infantry wear blue facings, the artillery red, the doctors black, the staff white, and the cavalry yellow, so it is impossible to mistake the branch of service to which an officer belongs-nor is it possible to mistake his rank. A second lieutenant, first lieutenant, and captain, wear respectively one, two and three bars on the collar. A major, lieutenant colonel, and colonel, wear one, two and three stars on the collar …"

THREE MONTHES IN THE SOUTHERN STATES-APRIL TO JUNE, 1863 Diary of Sir Arthur Fremantle pub by William Blackwood & Son 1863

Pg. 301 July, 1863 "…Now, the Confederate has no ambition to imitate the regular soldier at all; he looks the genuine rebel; but in spite of his bare feet, his ragged clothes, his old rug, and toothbrush stuck like a rose in his button-hole, he has a sort of devil-may-care, reckless, self-confident look, which is decidedly taking…"

GRAY GHOSTS OF THE CONFEDERACY Guerrilla Warfare ion the West by Richard S. Brownlee pub by La. State Univ. Press 1858

Pg. 123 August 20, 1863, the raid on Lawrence Kn. "…Haggard and dusty after a two-day ride, the guerrilla chief still presented a handsome appearance. Wearing a black slouch hat with a gold cord, gray pants and cavalry boots, brown, highly decorated guerrilla shirt, and with four revolvers in his belt…"

THE RAGGED REBEL, A Common soldier in the W.H. Parsons' Texas Cavalry 1861-1865 by B.P. Gallaway, pub by Univ of Texas Press, Austin 1988

Fall 1863- Dave could see that Parsons' rangers had become a hard, angry, pitiful-looking lot. They were dejected, impoverished and filthy. Their headgear consisted of everything from battered felts to strips of homespun wrapped around their heads like turbans. Their undyed brown coats and jeans reflected their continuous abuse and contained innumerable rips, makeshift patches, and colonies of grayback lice..."

Not only multiform, but ragged multiform at that.

WEBSITE-Witt Edwards CSA Uniforms

Pg.4 "For many soldiers however, the thought of wearing Federal blue was unsettling so for want of going cold, they would try to "boil the blue out" of the cloth. But as the war continued objections to wearing the blue became less and less and the Southern army of the Trans-Mississippi took on a decidedly blue tint.

"I would yet mention that because the people cannot tell us from the rebels is simply for this reason: as many of the bushwacking rebs as can get the Federal uniform wear them, if they kill one of our men or take one prisoner they strip them of all their clothing."

"we heard the other day of southern men in Federal disguise coming down the Grand River."

Blue uniforms would have been the only available clothing to these men by this time.

(Raiding the Yankee supply trains) "on the morning of July 5th I learned that there was atrain of 10 wagons loaded with U.S.Sutler goods on the way to Jacksport via Silpher Rock and the some 10 or 12 miles from Batesville. I immediately dispatched 50 men to capture them which they succeeded in doing....On July 6 I received information of another similar train of wagons on the same road. They were in like manner captured...These captures put us in possession of a considerable quantity of goods much needed by our army."

Chaplain Goerge Primrose of the 4th Missouri Cavalry wrote:

"I send you the following daring exploit of Capt. J.W.Jacobs of Burbridge's Regiment, who, on last Wednesday evening captured a train of the enemy in ten miles of Little Rock, burning the wagons and bringing off 22 prisoners and 60 mules and harnesses, also a lot of clothing."

In yet another report it is learned:

"the men that were along say that we captured between 300 and 400 wagons loaded with supplies and commissary stores there were only 127 brought out, and the clothing divided among the men, all got a tolerable out fit.'

Col. Williams report:

"A number of prisoners taken in this fight were dressed in our uniform, and in obedience to existing orders from departmental headquarters, and the usages of war, they were executed instanter." *This sounds very extreme, but it was Yankee policy in the Trans-Mississippi due to the fact that they couldn't engage the enemy in force, The guerilla warfare was so widespread.*

"Lt. Graves, C.S.A. with forty enlisted men, bearers of a flag of truce, arrived here on the 20th, escorting prisoners captured by you (General Price). The escort to this flag [of truce] was clothed in our uniform..."

CONFEDERATE CAVALRY WEST OF THE RIVER by Stephen B. Oates pub by Univ. Texas Press 1961

Pg. 60 "Cavalr Cherokee country, an officer in Stand Watie's brigade wrote his wife in September, 1863, that out of 5,000 men, 1,000 were unarmed and without shoes and a change of clothing, and what anyone in their right sense would say was in a deplorable condition. Watie's army, according to the officer, looked "more like Siberian exiles than soldiers...I have been in an almost nude condition." There seems to have been no disposition to blame the Confederate government, for he added that "the Confederacy certainly does not know our condition. Good soldiers but without the means of resistance. We are neither discouraged or whipped and God forbid we ever shall be...I have still got an old grey shirtand pair of pants on but they are thread bear (sic)." Late in October four small wagonloads of provisions and clothing arrived; certainly not enough to bring substantial relief to the men....

"...The usual shirt, called the "grey back," was made of cotton long sleeved, with a high collar. Men often enlisted in their "Sunday" shirts. Coats were both single and double-breasted and varied widely in color and design. The hat which "topped off" the soldier's attire was likely to be a wide-brimmed felt, colored brown or jet black, or a grey cap, shaped like a French kepi. Sometimes bright colored handkerchiefs were worn when hats were not available.

Trimming for cavalry uniforms-yellow gilt or brass buttons and braid or lace- was scarce in the Trans-Mississippi. Occasionally, officers received such accessories from home, but most of the men had to wear their heterogenious garbs without the regulation buttons of yellow-striped cavalry pants.

Lieutenant Cade, Twenty-Eigth Texas Cavalry, wrote home to his wife late in June 1862, explaining the scarcity of uniform trimmings and urging her to purchase and send him buttons, briad, and yellow cloth strips with which to make striped for his trousers." Anderson Texas Surgeon in the C.S.A. Pg. 19, 23

THE CIVIL WAR ON THE LOWER KANSAS-MISSOURI BORDER by Larry F. Wood pub by Hickory Press

Shelby's raid into Missouri, Sept. 1863 "The rebel procession formed a motley cavalcade, with some men dressed in ragged Confederate gray, some wearing drab civilian attire, some sporting confiscated federal uniforms, and nearly all bedecked with flaming sumac plumes in their hats to identify themselves…"

This is a different identifying badge. Maybe they didn't have enough cloth for the white armbands that had been in use.

THE CIVIL WAR ON THE LOWER KANSAS-MISSOURI BORDER by Larry F. Wood pub by Hickory Press

Major Emory S. Foster of the 7th Missouri State Militia Cavalry, for example, complains in an Oct. 8th letter, from Warsaw that "fifty of these whelps go in advance with a Federal flag and Federal clothing"

BRIGADIER GENERAL D.H. COOPER

Camp on Beech Creek, Nov. 18, 1863 "…The regiment has not received any clothing for three months and only a small supply since November, so that a large part of the men are in a destitute condition. The destitution of clothing is very great, and much suffering and sickness prevails on account of it …"

LONE STAR & DOUBLE EAGLE- Civil War Letters of a German-Texas Family Menetta Altgelt Goyne pub by Texas Christian Univ. Press 1982

Pg. 111 Camp at Houston 22 November 1863 Rudolf to Family "…Last week we received our winter clothes: pants, jackets, hats and blankets. The trousers and jackets are of grey woolen cloth (Tuch); everything is pretty good. The order came that each man is to get two complete suits and, in order to complete these, another requisition for clothes was made, but they haven't arrived yet…"

I wonder if they ever got this second requisition, they should have been gled to have recieved one issue.

CONFEDERATE CAVALRY WEST OF THE RIVER by Stephen B. Oates pub by Univ. Texas Press 1961

Pg. 55 winter 1863-1864 "…On that raid we were half-starving, and Shelby and I rode down to the White River to water our horses. A detachment of the troops was doing the same thing just below us. Among them was Dick Gentry. He was a gallant private and a good fellow. Slung across his saddle was a sack, carefully tied and bleeding at one end. Shelby demanded what he had got there.

"Been having my clothes washed," said Gentry.

"You'd better go back to camp," said Shelby, "or your clothes will bleed to death."

Gentry was lodged in the guardhouse on Shelby's order. That night a quarter of fresh pork found its way to Shelby's headquarters. Shelby looked at it and said, "I haven't an idea where this comes from, but go round to the guardhouse, orderly, and tell 'em to turn Gentry loose. No use keeping a man shut up all his life for a little laundry."

No Pardons To Ask, No Apologies to Make-The journal of William Henry King, Gray's 28 La. Inf. Regt. pub by Univ. TN Press 2006

Pg. 131 Dec'r 21st, 1863 "Blankets are being issued to-day, but no man can draw without a descriptive list. When pay or clothing is to be issued, a descriptive list is demanded, but if duty is required, no descriptive list is needed. The pretext is, the pay or articles drawn, must be entered on the descriptive list that the Government may know what the soldiers have received. According to this rule, if a soldier is so unfortunate as to lose his descriptive list-and many of them do lose their descriptive lists-he can never draw anything more. It is all a pretext-a simple-a foolish-excuse to evade doing justice. A soldier who is so unfortunate as to not possess a descriptive list-no matter what accident has befallen him-he may go cold, yea freeze, for want of a blanket but such is no excuse against a detail for duty…"

Red tape abounds, even in the Trans-Mississippi Dept.

1864

EAST

4 YEARS IN THE STONEWALL BRIGADE by John O. Casler pub by Univ. of So. Ca. Press 2005

Pg. 258-259 (1864?) "Where I got Mrs. Swisher to go to Paw Paw Depot (W.Va.)on the Balt.& Ohio R.R., for me, and run the blockade with some grey goods to make me a new suit, also a pair of boots and a lot of calico. I wanted to take the calico out South, as it was a great object at that time. A young lady who could sport a calico dress those times felt rich, as all the wear was homespun. As Bid Leopard used to say, we could board a week in the valley for a yard of calico or a Hagerstown Almanac."

CONFEDERATE CADETS AT WAR by James Lee Conrad pub by Univ. of S.C. Press 1997

Pg. 182 # 23. "The only surviving of a wartime Florida Military Institute cadet uniform belonged to Beard. The uniform, on display in the Museum of the Confederacy in Richmond Virginia, is a butternut-colored shell jacket with Louisiana buttons. It was possibly among the equipment obtained by Superintendent Johnson during a trip to Virginia in early 1864..."

FRANKLIN GARDENER WALKER C.S.A. Civil War diaries and Letters compiled by his eldest son 1936 edited and retyped by his grandson Erle Preston Carter1986 Hadley Library Archives, Winchester, Va.

Pg. 26 39 Battalion Co. A Va. Cavalry

1864 Clothing received from Government
1 pair shoes at Orange C.H.
1 Jacket
2 Shirts
1 pair pants of Capt. Harris
1 pair drawers
1 pair socks
2 shirts of Capt. Hamilton at Petersburg

CONFEDERATE ECHOES A Soldier's Personal Story of Life in the Confederate Army From the Mississippi to the Carolinas by Albert Theodore Goodloe-First Lieutenant Company D Thirty-Fifth Regiment Alabama Volunteer Infantry C.S.A. pub by Zenger Pub. Co. 1897, 1983

Pg. 226 "...Before leaving North Alabama for Georgia (1864) a short leave of absence was granted to these regiments to visit their homes, which were near at hand, and procure a much needed supply of clothing, shoes, etc...."

An example of reliance of home folks for clothing.

THE CIVIL WAR INFANTRYMAN, In Camp, on the March, and in Battle by Gregory A. Coco pub by Thomas Publications, Gettysburg, Pa

Pg 81 Major Robert Stiles, near Petersburg, 1864 "We were shocked at the condition, the complexion, the expression of the men, and of the officers, too, even the field officers; indeed we could scarely realize that the unwashed, uncombed, unfed and almost unclad creatures we saw were officers of rank and reputation in the army."

Even the officers were ragged now.

GEN. LEE'S ARMY

Pg. 355 Jan 1864 Preparing for the spring campaign of 1864 "...Shortages plagued the army, as they had done for years. "Aunt Frank it is enough to make tears come from the eyes of the most hardened soul to see our brave men marching through the mud & snow almost naked & barefooted," a lieutenant in the 3rd Gergia Sharpshooters wrote. Only five or six men in his company had shoes. Two weeks later, in early February, a Virginian estimated that half the men lacked adequate footwear and wondered "if our government cant do better than that I don't know how we will make out much longer." Lee stuggled to get leather or hides to divisions and brigades, where cobblers and handymen among them could make shoes for the command. Twenty-two men in McLaw's old division took a break from traditional soldiering to produce fifteen hundred pairs of shoes and repair hundreds more that winter. Once again, the army took matters into its own hands when the government failed to provide for its men..."

Pg. 383 "...Just as it exhausted men physically and mentally, trench warfare took its toll on resources and basic necessities for the men. Although Lee's soldiers received a disproportionate share of the Confedercy's clothing, it was not nearly enough. Shoes, submergeded in trench water for extended periods of time, broke down much more rapidly than they normally did in the field. Pants, shirts, socks, and drawers wore out under siege conditions, so that the shortages that plagued Lee's army during the first three years worsened. One Louisiana captain,angered over the inadequate shoes and clothingfor his men, argued that military personnel in Richmond should give up their uniforms for the soldiers in the field. "Our men are shoeless, pantless, jacketless, sockless and miserable and resembled Falstaff's army more than any Corps in the Confederacy, while every man in Richmond, or any other city connected with the Army are dressed in the best of all. God grant that our leaders may soon learn that men cannot march and fight when they are half naked and with feet that leave bloody marks wherever they step..."

OK, this quote illustrates the reasons the Rebs were ragged in 1864, despite generous clothing issues. The clothing issued was often shoddy in the first place and usually wore out quickly, as decribed in the previous chapters. In the trenches, the rate of wear was vastly exellerated.

HISTORY OF THE BEDFORD LIGHT ARTILLERY by Rev. Joseph A. Graves pub by Press of the Bedford Demecrat 1903

Pg. 38 "...early in January their term of enlistment being about to expire, they all enlisted to serve as long as the war might continue. To escape the evils resulting from an election of officers for the Cpmpany, and the right to elect them no one denied, it was proposed and ageed to, that a furlough should be granted to the men and they should consent to continue to serve under the same officers. Hence half the men went home at one time, and the other half after the first half returned. In a letter to the author Capt. Smith writes: "The weather was at times very cold, and when the first batch of men started off on furloughthe snow was perhaps a foot deep. Many of the men were shoeless, T.W.Reed in particular. They had to walk all the way to Bristol, about sventy-five miles, for the railroad had not yet been re-opened." In the history of Parker's Battery, Capt. Smith alluding to the same subject says: "I might describe the bare-footed men going home on furlough from East Tennessee. Tom Reid started through the snow with his feet tied up in rags, and when, after a tramp of many miles, he reached the cars at Bristol, they were bare and bleeding. A little girl, standing in a doorway, saw him and burst into tears, and gave him a pair of socks..."

LETTERS AND PAPERS OF AN ARTILLERY OFFICER A.N.V. IN THE WAR FOR SOUTHERN INDEPENDENCE 1861-1865 Capt. John Hampden Chamberlain-Virginian pub by Dietz Printing Co. Pub. 1932

Pg. 244 Hd. Qrs. Arty. 3d Corps 24th, (1864) My dear Mother "...Franky "did up" the collars you made for me & they are beauties..."

CLASH OF SABRES-Blue & Gray by Colonel Walbrook D. Swank U.S.A.F.Ret. pub by Avonelle Asso. L.T.D. 1981

Jan. 1864 Thomas S. Davis-Henrico Light Dragoons 1st Regiment of Virginia Vols. "…The day before New Year's Day, The troopers finally received their looked-for clothing allowance. A delayed Christmas present, they jestingly called it…"

A delayed Christmas miracle would be more apt.

HANDLEY LIBRARY ARCHIVES, WINCHESTER, VA James Bradfield Diary Co. H 17th Virginia Infantry

Pg. 26 Jan. 1st, 1864 "the troops attack the Yankees ar Bachelor's Creek and capture at there camp clothing, Sutlers stores and ambulances & horses, 3 wagons, 2 carts & mules 250 Pri(soners)."

The clothing was badly needed, see below

LETTERS OF THREE LIGHTFOOT BROTHERS 1861-1864 Privately Pub. 1942

Letter from Thomas Reese Lightfoot to Sinai McCormick Cody Jan. 2 1864 "…The weather is bitter cold,and many of the men are bare-footed and very needy of clothing. The government is rather slow in furnishing us, but we keep up hope and bear it as cheerfully as possible. We are now in comfortable quarters, which is better than is allowed some poor fellows. The campaign is closed I guess for the winter; no telling though, the Yankees may come over and trouble us…"

THE CONFEDERACY ed. by Albert D. Kirwan pub by Meridian Books The World Pub. Co. 1959

Pg. 181 Judith McGuire Jan. 3 1864 "My occupation at home just now is as new as that in the office-it is shoemaking. I am busy upon the second pair of gaiter boots. They are made of canvas, presented me by a friend. It was taken from one of our James River vessels, and has been often spread to the breeze under the "Stars and Bars." The vessel was sunk among the obstructions at Drury's (Drewry's) Bluff. The gaiters are cut out by a shoemaker, stitched and bound by the ladies, then soled by a shoemaker, for the moderate sum of fifty dollars. Last year he put soles on a pair for ten dollars. They are then blacked with the material used for blacking guns in the navy. They are very handsome gaiters and bear polishing by blacking and the shoe brush as well as morocco. They are lasting and very cheap when compared with those we buy, which are from $125."

Its about time those naval stores were put to use, although I guess they could have dumped them all as obstructions at Drewry's Bluff.

VOICES FROM COMPANY D Diaries by the Greensboro Guards, Fifth Alabama Infantry Regiment, Army of Northern Virginia ed. by G. Ward Hubbs pub by Univ. of Georgia Press 2003

Pg. 210 January 5 1864 SP "…It took me nearly all day to sew stripes (Corp.) on my new jacket. I made a nice job of it tho'…"

Pg 210 January 9 1864 SP "…Our Brig. Went on picket to Morton's Ford abt. 10 ms. Early this morng. I was excused by Col. Hall last evening, but so many men with bad shoes that (Gen.) Battle ordered all to go not "actually barefooted."…"

As a commander, this would be the only thing you could do to perform your military duty. The shoes were unobtainable at this time.

LETTERS TO AMANDA-The Civil War Letters of Marion Hill Fitzpatrick, Army of Northern Virginia ed by Jeffery C. Lowes & Sam Hodges pub by Mercer Univ. Press 1998

Pg. 109 Jan. 6th, 1864 Montpelior, Va. Near Orange C.H. (Letter No. 52) Dear Amanda, "…Capt Brown came in yesterday evening but did not bring the boxes. He left them in Richmond. He will bring them on to us when we get stationed. …I have a good pair of shoes, a good blanket and a good overcoat and I hope will not suffer much…"

This soldier at least is well equipped.

Pg. 110 Jan. 13th, 1864 Staunton, Va. (Letter No. 53) Dear Amanda, "I do not know when we will get our boxes. I am nearly out of shirts and drawers, but will have to make out somehow. My old ones done pretty well while I was stationed but are about to wear all to pieces since I have been on the march…"

FORGET-ME-NOTS OF THE CIVIL WAR: A ROMANCE by Laura Elizabeth pub by Press of A.R. Fleming Printing Co. 1909

Jan. 10, 1864 "…I am very well supplied with winter clothing of every kind at present. Just drawn a splendid pair of English shoes. The trip down the river cut my others all to pieces. I did want to send a pair of English shoes to brother, but it seems I can't get ahead so that I can do so. …"

BRIGHT & GLOOMY DAYS-The Civil War Correspondence of Capt Charles Frederick Bahnson, A Moravian Confederate ed by Sarah Bahnson Chapman pub by Univ. TN. Press 2003

Pg 104 Camp Daniels Brigade January 15th, 1864 "My Dear Brother, Allow me to congradulate you upon having once more arrived at home after your long and painful captivity; you have no doubt seen very much but it has also taught you a good lesson, and you are now of my opinion, as regards the Yankees. Your letter came to hand this morning, and I hasten to answer it, as you wished to know something about clothing; I saved your knapsack, and have got your jacket and pants; the other clothing has been lost on our tramps. I can get any clothes you may desire, when I draw again (which I think will be soon,) and will reserve for you a jacket, pr. Of pants, overcoat, shoes and blanket; the underclothing is generally so bad that I will not reserve any unless you desire it. Our overcoats have no doubt gone "up to spout," as all the boxes received from the warehouse, where they were deposited, were robbed of all contents of any value. I can procure very good clothing, and I think you had better not have any made at home, as they will cost much more…"

Capt Bahnson seems very confident in being able to draw clothing from the government. I hope he was correct on this.

THE CONFEDERATE VETERAN VOL. XXVI 1918

Pg. 353 August 1918 Letters From The Front-Thomas Caffey's letters to his family in Alabama- Camp Near Orange Courthouse, Va. January 15, 1864 Dear Mary: "Since my last letter I have received two more blankets from Richmond, which make seven Smith and I now have on hand. I need nothing now in the way of clothing save pants and jacket. My shoes are getting into rather dilapidated condition; and as it is impossible to replace them here, I suppose I will, when they "gin out," have to do like hundreds of others in this brigade-go barefooted. I wrote to William at Raleigh to see if a pair could be procured there, but have not yet had a reply to the letter."

It seems that shoes wereso scarce as to be almost mythical at this time.

LETTERS OF A NEW MARKET CADET Beverly Stanard, ed. by John G. Barnett & Robert R. Turner Univ. N.C. Press 1961

Pg. 32 V.M.I. Jan. the 17th, 1864 Dear Mother "…Mother to give you an idea what sort of man Gen. S(mith) is-after our return from our last march, the government sent up 300 pairs of shoes for the cadets as presents- or to pay for our own that we wore out and now Gen.

S(mith) will not let a cadet have a pair if he has gotten shoes from the Institute in the last 6 months, and if a cadet is shipped before he can get them, They fall in Specs hands who furnishes all his darkeys with a good pair. I shall try hard to get mine, tho' don't expect to wear them, they are coarse army shoes worth at the present prices 30 or 40 dollars. I have a pair I bought before I went on the march that will do me, so shall keep mine (if I ever get them) for Henry, unless he is well supplied…"

As we have seen previously, 'Ol Beverly was a somewhat entitled cadet, who considers it VMI's or his familie's duty to keep him well supplied with clothing.

Pg. 34 Footnote #8-"In order to meet the needs of the cadets in the field, General Smith had purchased shoes "from whatever source possible and without regard to price and quality." It was his hope, however, that the State would "authorize the purchase and relieve the cadets of the charge." On December 22 the Superintendant announced that the Adjutant general had authorized the accounts of the cadets to be credited with the cost of these shoes and that the Chief of Ordinance had informed him that his requisition upon the Government for 250 pairs of shoes had been approved. The Institute Quartermaster, upon receipt of those shoes, was to issue a pair to each officer and cadet to whom shoes had not been issued previously. Also the Secretary of War detailed 3 shoemakers tp the Institute so that in the future the cadets would be properly shod." General Orders No. 92 Dec. 22, 1863 V.M.I. Order Book, 1863

DEAR SISTER-CIVIL WAR LETTERS TO A SISTER IN ALABAMA Frank Anderson Chappell pub. by Branch Springs Pub. 2002 (Third Alabama Regiment)

Pg 184 Camp near Orange Court House Va. Jan 22 (1864) Dear sister "…You all are talking of cold weather. You don't know anything about cold. And another thing is you don't know how to stand cold weather as cold as it is here. I very seldom put on a coat and sleep under two blankets. Sleep as warm as I could wish so when I come home you need not trouble yourself with cover on my bed, and you need not trouble yourself about a bed either.…John Mc. Brought me a pair of shoes which came in a nicely time for I was wearing cloth shoes at the time. Lewis is now in need of a pair though he is not quite barefooted…"

This soldier doesn't seem to think much of those cloth shoes.

RECOLLECTIONS AND LETTERS OF GENERAL ROBERT E. LEE by His Son Capt. Robert E. Lee pub by Garden City Pub Co. 1926

Jan, 24, 1864 Letter from Gen. Lee to Mrs. Lee "…I have had to disperse the cavalry as much as possible, to obtain forage for their horses, and it is that which causes me trouble.

Provisions for the men too, are very scarce, and, with very light diet and light clothing, I fear they suffer, but still they are cheerful and uncomplaining…"

Jan. 1864 Letter to the Quartermater-General "General: The want of shoes and blankets for this army continues to cause much suffering and to impair its efficiency. In one regiment I am informed that there are only fifty men with serviceable shoes, and a brigade that recently went on picket was compelled to leave several hundred men in camp, who were unable to bear the exposure of duty, being destitute of shoes and blankets…."

Here Gen. Lee is again complaining about the raggedness of his men.

RED CLAY TO RICHMOND by John J. Fox pub by Angle Valley Press 2006

Pg 226 Jan 25 1864 "Imagine James Garrett's excitement when private John R. Mooty walked into camp from furlough. Mooty held in his hands Garrett's box filled with provisions from home. Garrett wrote:

[H]e brought my things through all right. [M]y pants are two (too) long for me, I traded them to Segt. John B. Hester for two pair of government pants. So I will have pants enough to do me all year. I have got a new pairs of pants now….I have got soap enough to do me a long time to wash my clothes in…"

Pg. 242 Jan 25, 1864 James Garrett "…One essential item he needed again was shoes. "I expect to make Jeff Davis furnish me in Shoes or I wont do duty for him. I get them from the government at ten dollars a pair. [I]f you have got leather you had better save it for next winter for you will sure kneed it…"

I wonder when he got those shoes from Jeff Davis.

THE PAINFUL NEWS I HAVE TO WRITE-Letters and Diaries of Four Hite Brothers of Page County in the Service of the Confederacy Army of Northern Virginia Series Stonewall Brigade ed.by Harlan R. Jessup pub by Butternut & Blue 1998

Pg. 161 Isaac Hite to his sister Ella Head Quarters A.N. Va. Camped near Orange C.H. January 26/64 "…Yesterday there was some clothing issued to the company again, but as mine happened to be tolerably good I could not get any. In order to get any clothing from the government any more, one must lay round in camp most naked for a month or two. We had one fellow that had been wearing nothing but drawers for some time…"

A good first-hand illustration of the clothing shortage.

PERSONAL RECOLLECTIONS AND CIVIL WAR DIARY 1864 pub by Free Press 1908

Pg. 296 Jan. 27, 1864 Lemuel Abijah Abbott—diary "…Two deserters came into our lines this morning; they report Lee's army in a miserable condition-no rations or clothing and the citizens nearly starving. They say that "Sucession is played out." …"

This Yankee will see the untruth of this last statement later this spring.

WEBSITE THE AMERICAN CIVIL WAR

Headquarters Amy of Northern Virginia — Jan. 30, 1864
Brig. General A.R. Lawton
Quartermaster-General, C.S. Army

GENERAL: Ihave sent two Quartermasters over the ridge to purchase leather for the use of this army. The one in the lower valley reports that he has found 2,880 sides, all in the hands of original manufacturers except 220 sides, which are in the hands of speculators. The officer in the upper valley had only visited three tanneries when he wrote, and had only found 400 sides ready for use, but many were in course of preparation. Some of this leather could be bought at Government prices, though it was offered in exchange for rawhides. They asked as high, in some cases, as $10 a pound for upper and $7 for sole.

The chief quartermaster of the army brought me this morning a sample of the shoes recently sent from Richmond. One pair was of Richmond manufacture and another from Columbus, Ga. They were intended to be fair samples of each lot and were selected with that view. Neither could compare with the shoes made in this army. In the Richmond shoe the face of the leather was turned in, that is, the side of the skin next to the animal was turned out, which is contrary to the practice of the best makers and contrary to the arrangement of nature. Without knowing the result of experiment in this matter, I should therefore think it wrong. The leather of the Columbus shoe was not half tanned and the shoe was badly made; the soles of both slight, and would not stand a week's march in mud and water.

Imagine, after being barefoot for some time and finally getting shoes issued to you, and they are of this abysmal quality.

If I could get leather I could set 500 shoemakers to work. The scraps would answer for repairs. I have the workmen and tools. Can you get for me the leather I have referred to above, or authorize the chief quartermaster of the army to do so? I am not in favor of exchanging hides for leather at the rates established by the schedule, viz, 45 cents for the hides and $2.80

for the leather. The old rule in Virginia, and I believe it is still practiced, was to receive one-half of the leather produced by the hides. I do not know whether we could exchange at this rate. The army is in great distress for shoes and clothes. Every inspection report painfully shows it—artillery, cavalry and infantry. The requisitions sent in are unanswered.

I am With Great Respect Your Obedient Servant,

R.E. Lee
General

Why can't this leather be seized by the army for their supply? Who inspects these miserable production facilities, forcing them to turn out a shoe of sufficient quality? Maybe I don't have all the informantion, but something more shouldv'e been done.

THE HISTORY OF A BRIGADE OF SOUTH CAROLINIANS-KNOWN AS GREGGS J.F.J. Caldwell King & Baird1866

Pg. 168 Feb. 1864 "Clothing was not plentiful, nor blankets, nor shoes, and those we received were inferior. Large numbers of boxes of provisions were sent us by our friends at home, which contributed much to the comfort of the troops. I must not omit, in this connection, the ladies' associations in different parts of South Carolina, who forwarded considerable supplies of clothing to us, at great trouble and still greater expense to themselves...."

Once again, it's the Ladies associations to the rescue!

THE CONFEDERATE VETERAN VOL. XV 1907

Pg. 458 Oct. 1907 Florda Girl Gives Her Shoes To A Soldier Feb.1864 "Col. Knox Livingston, in an address at Bentonville S.C., said: When Florida was invaded, troops were rushed forward to reinforce General Finnegan's commad. Upon the arrival of the soldiers at Madison the women would meet them and serve refreshments to the defenders of their homes. Among these soldiers was a mere lad whose bare feet were bleeding from the exposure and fatigue of the long march. One of the young ladies, Miss Lou Taylor, took the shoes from her own feet and made the hero boy put them on, while she walked home in her stockings..."

I know what your'e thinking, this girl deserves a medal-and your'e right.

THROUGH SOME EVENTFUL YEARS-Diary of Susan Bradford Eppes pub by Press of the J.W. Burke Co. 1926

Feb. 1864 Last night Aunt Sue invited the social world of Tallahassee to meet Colonel Capers. He came, attended by fifty or more of his men, the artillery uniform is beautiful and is particularly becoming to Colonel Capers. I am sure he knows it for I notice he keeps one end of has cape thrown back over his shoulder, bringing the red lining next to his face. He wore a vest of fine red broadcloth, buttoned up with round balls of silver for buttons and that added much to the beauty of his uniform…"

Did Col Capers just receive this uniform? It would have been difficult to keep it so pristine in the field.

BRIGHT & GLOOMY DAYS-The Civil War Correspondence of Capt Charles Frederick Bahnson, A Moravian Confederate ed by Sarah Bahnson Chapman pub by Univ. TN. Press 2003

Pg. 109 Feby 9th, 1864 My Dear Father, I send you a bundle home by Lieut. Jas. B. Tucker; who wishes to obtain three of the bundles of Cloth sent to you from Raleigh. The contents of the bundles are as follows:- one uniform coat very well worn and considerably greased, which I hope is not too far gone to be cured in Salem; I suppose Mrs. Boner had better undertake the job, but I will not dictate, but leave it to your own judgment as to the best mode of cleaning it; next you will find a vest which has shared the fate of its fellow sufferer in this cruel war; buttons and lace or braid belonging to the coat; new set of buttons to go on new uniform at home, braid enough to last for some time; piece of cloth given to me by a friend (McQueen, Surg. Ewell's Provost Guard, formerly of the Batt.)…."

LETTERS TO AMANDA-The Civil War Letters of Marion Hill Fitzpatrick, Army of Northern Virginia ed by Jeffery C. Lowe & Sam Hodges pub by Mercer Univ. Press 1998

Pg. 117 Feb. 10th, 1864 Camp near Harisonburg, Va. (Letter No. 56) Dear Amanda, "…I sent you my overcoat by John Wilder. Clean it up and take care of it for me till next winter when you can send it back to me by the first chance. Put some pockets in the front outside sorter slanting before you send it back. I would not send it now but Joe Walker has given me a good large warm cape to wear as long as I want it, so I can make out without my overcoat very well, and it is such a good one I hate to loose it…I also made a dollar today, sewing. I made a haversack for a fellow. It was his own proposition to give me a dollar for it. I have some sewing of my own to do. I want to patch my old pants and wear them while we stay here and save my new ones. I gave away my old shirts and drawers. They were about gone under sure. I am highly pleased with all you sent me. I will sell about half my soap for fear of having too much and it is too much to pack. I can get $3.00 for half of it..."

Pg. 118 Feb. 18th, 1864 Camp Near Harrisonburg,Va. (Letter No. 57) Dear Amanda. "... Unless Col. Simmons brings my shoes I will have to draw a pair the first chance for these have about played out. I sent you a letter and my overcoat by John Wilder which I hope you received safely. We got our other box the day after John left. The potatoes and cakes were rotten. The butter is sound, but tastes pretty rank. I cannot eat any atall of it since I have been sick. I am going to work it over and see if I can't get some of the old smell out of it. The meat Ma sent me kept nice enough. Last winter it wound have been worth a great deal to me, but now we are drawing more veal (and) nice pork than we can eat, so I sold it. I got $2.00 a lb. for it from a citizen. It weighed 9 lbs. Mose and I have flour and pork enough now to last us 10 days. We are going to sell some of it. My peaches kept just nice enough. They make splendid pies without any sweetening. I put on my new pants to have my old pair washed, and burnt them right away. Send me a scrap like them by Tip to patch them with. I got a lady living near here to mend them but the piece she put on is not quite large enough to do well. I had no scissors and wanted it done is why I got her to do it. I also got her to bind my hat which had got to flopping, for all of which she would not have a cent of pay...I miss my overcoat but my cape does me finely. I told John how to explain to you how to fix the pockets and take out the pocket that is in it. I will want a dress coat and vest next winter, but do not want you to put any buttons on the coat, and I will take the buttons off my old coat and put on it...."

Pg. 120 Feb. 24th, 1864 Camp Near Harrisonburg, Va. (Letter No. 58) Dear Amanda, "I have been making a little money recently by sewing, patching pants, coats &C. They come to me and offer high pay to do it. I hate to charge for it but it takes time and thread and to make a little to buy tobacco &c., I accept of the pay. It takes thread like rip and I will have to trouble you for another small ball by the first chance. I have no scissors and there is none in the Company now and I have to use my knife. It is rough work but soldiers think it very nice.I wish I had a pair of scissors. I could soon make enough to pay for them by cutting hair and I intend to buy a pair the first chance..."

Pg. 122 Feb. 28th, 1864 Camp Near Harrisonburg, Va. (Letter No. 59) Dear Amanda, "...I am nearly barefooted and there is no chance to draw shoes if I wanted to draw and I would hate to draw now as Tip if he has good luck will be here with mine in about six days..."

Also, he'd probably draw those shoe abominations mentioned before.

GRANDFATHER'S JOURNAL (Franklin Lafayette Riley) Company B Sixteenth Mississippi Infantry Volunteers Harris' Brigade Mahone's Division Hill's Corps, A.N.V. May 27, 1861-July 15, 1865 Austin C. Dobbins pub by Morningside Press 1988

Pg. 181 Friday-Sunday, Feb. 12-14, 1864 Camp near Liberty Mills "…More important, that is, more important immediately, Sat. I obtained a pair of shoes, which are less difficult to obtain now than in the past. In our brigade we have a number of shoemakers (3 in our regiment) who, if they can obtain tools and leather, should be able to make 220 pairs of shoes a day. This amounts to 1-2 pairs per soldier a year. Leather will be furnished by the government. In the past, much of it came from saddle skirts, cartridge boxes, and other items which had been left unguarded. Some (the owners) called this stealing. Others called it using military equipment effectively…"

I'd rather have a pair of shoes than cartridge box any day.

STONEWALL JACKSON'S FOOT CAVALRY Company A, 13th Virgin's Infantry by Walbrook D. Swank Col. U.S.A.F (Ret) pub by Burd Street Press, 2001

Pg. 8 Feb. 15, 1864 Pvt. George Peyton- camp in the Shenandoah Valley, near Cedar Mountain "…I have a good Yankee overcoat with cape, and did not get cold…"

Feb. 16, 1864 "…My feet were cold, and I have two blankets and two overcoats on the bed. We sleep as close as we can…."

LIBRARY OF VA. Letters of Virginicus Groner Box 41449

Camp C O Lefy (?)

Feb. 16, 1864 dear Linnsi "…The socks I did not need at present as they are only fit for summer, shirts, neckties, collars I have plenty in camp….the gloves I received I suppose are the ones you wrote me about that Burton Lam wanted if they will fit him he can have them, let me know. I have a pr. of gauntlets and they will do for me. I think, however, that the gloves will be too small for him. The comfort that was (?) in my valise he can have if it will do him any good. I do not use it.

Tell Affie that the things all came to hand, never mind about the flannel. I will try and find something that the front of the coat, When I wrote for—yards I did not think it would be more than one half inch wide or cord. If you can fit it about ¾ of yrds wide, ¼ of yrds will be plenty. I don't want any for cuffs or collars but only for a kind of cord to fit around the top of the collar and down each side of the front …"

BRIGHT & GLOOMY DAYS-The Civil War Correspondence of Capt Charles Frederick Bahnson, A Moravian Confederate ed by Sarah Bahnson Chapman pub by Univ. TN. Press 2003

Pg. 109 February 17th 1864 Dear Father "…I am glad to hear you are not suffering or anyways scarce of the necessary's of life, as I hear many families are; I do not know how you are off for Confederate "rags," but if you need any, please let me know, & I will try to let you have some…"

Some of the soldiers would draw clothing and ship it home for their families or servants.

VOICES FROM CEMETARY HILL-The Civil War Diary, Reports and Letters of Colonel William Henry Asbury Speer (1861-1865) ed. by Allen Paul Speer pub by The Overmountain Press 1997

Pg. 121 N. aOr. 28 N.C.T. Feb. 18, 1864 Ever Dear Father "…I can't picture you the suffering that many of our men have gone through with, for the want of clothes, shoes and other comforts that might be furnished them…"

Another eyewitness of the Rebel's raggedness.

DEAR IRVIE, DEAR LUCY-Civil War letters of Capt. Irving A. Buck, General Cleburne's AAG & Family pub by Buck Pub. Co. 2002

Pg. 208 Feb. 18, 1864 Bel Aire (Front Royal) Va. My Dear Alvin, "…Last Friday night Mrs. Lizzie and scholars gave a set of charades for the benefit of the soldiers. We had a great time preparing for it and t'was a success too, beyond our most sanguine hopes. We realized $100 by it and this we intend donating to the purchase of yarn and socks for the poor barefooted "Southern Soldier Boys."

That's the spirit Miss Buck!

LEE'S TAR HEELS- The Pettigrew-Kirkland-McRae brigade by Earl J. Hess pub by Univ of North Carolina Press 2002

Pg 201 Feb 20, 1864 "With Kirkland back in place, a major effort was made to resupply the brigade with all manner of equipment and clothing. Large quantities of caps, shoes, pants, underwear, blankets, and shirts were ordered by special requisition and distributed to the needy men. The quartermaster of the 44th North Carolina also received a number of axes, picks, and the material to make shoes.... The men were well supplied with knapsacks and haversacks, but about 100 of them had no canteens...."

Finally some kind of re-supply effort has succeeded. This supply was probably from the state of North Carolina.

CONFEDERATE RAGE, YANKEE WRATH by George S. Burkhardt pub by Southern Illinois Univ. Press 2007

Pg. 88 Feb. 20, 1864 Battle of Olustee, Fla. "...Shot in the ankle and left behind when federal forces retreated, a 48th New York infantryman watched as Confederates scoured the battlefield they now controlled. He recalled: "I could see the rebels come to our wounded, and take their money, watches, and whatever they found on their persons; while they stripped the dead altogether..."

What in the Hell did he expact? If you don't like it, Yank, go home!

U. S. ARMY HERITAGE AND EDUCATION CENTER

Feb. 20, 1864 O.T. Smith unknown unit Hammach's Landing, Fla. Dear Mother: "...I would like to have my shirts if you have them made as I don't think any of our company will have a chance to come home..."

HANDLEY LIBRARY ARCHIVES, WINCHESTER, VA—James M. Cadwallader Diary 1st Virginia Cavalry

Feb. 25, 1864 "Still in camp, quite pleasant, had a game of ball this morning, dress parade this evening."

Is this soldier referring to Baseball?

NO SOAP,NO PAY, DIARRHEA, DYSENTERY& DSERTION A Composite History of the Lasr 16 Monthes of the Confederacy ed by Jeff Toalson pub by iUniverse Inc.2006

Pg. 49 Feb. 28, 1864 Halifax Co. N.C. Mrs. Catherine Edmonson Plantation Wife "...Busy yesterday cutting out shirts for Mr. E. out of some sheets and valences. Fortunately I have linen for for the bosoms as it is $15. Saw last week in Halifax a piece of gray confederate Uniform cloth, imported, which was held at $175 per yd.!..."

LETTER FROM VIRGINIA-8th Alabama Infantry-Perrin's Brigade, Anderson's Division-Headquarters Cradle of Innocence-Co. H. 8th Alabama Volunteers

Pg. 279 Feb. 29, 1864 near Orange C.H. Va. "…No troops, I am proud to say, have done more than Alabamians have; on every battlefield from Virginia to Tennessee they have been foremost in the charge; but I grieve to say, no troops in this army have suffered more for want of clothing and shoes than those very heroes have. But a short while ago, at a time when this regiment was performing picket duty on the snow-covered hills of the Rapidan, no less than one-third of its members were barefooted. The State of Alabama had plenty of shoes. Its agent was offering them to all, who could buy them. Was it not shameful that, because the poor fellows could not save money enough from their scanty pittance to pay the State for the shoes, they had to go barefooted on the hard Frozen ground? Why can not Alabama supply its trops as well with shoes and clothing as North Carolina and Georgia do? Has it not the same facilities for importing and manufacturing as the other states have? If not, it ought to. I should not have referred to this subject, had not our wants been supplied by the Confederate Government; for, though soldiers, we are still sensitive, and glory in our independence. We have not forgotten that, in December, 1862, the "Register and Advertiser" published a letter from "Scout," describing the sufferings of the eighth Alabama, for want of shoes, on the icy hills of Fredericksburg, but one solitary offer was made by a gentleman signing himself "W." But, look at the contast: A few weeks ago the Third Alabama was presented to the people of Mobile, as being suffering for want of shoes, and behold, in a few days a sum of over seven thousand dollars was raised to alleviate their suffering. Whether the donors of the patriotic gift were really patriots, I shall leave to an impartial judgement."

Something should have been done before this, and leather or made shoes should be asked for, money isn't much good if you can't get the shoes.

DEAR IRVIE, DEAR LUCY-Civil War Letters of Capt Irving A. Buck, General Cleburne's AAG & Family pub by Buck Pub. Co. 2002

Pg. 214 March, 1864 Bel Aire, Va. Dear Irvie, "Grandma, Ma, Lu and I have been and are as busy as bees trying to make a few little articles that may be useful to you such a(s) handkerchiefs, collars, cravats, and gloves to send by Mr. Wells who speaks of starting on the second, wish we could send you some shirts-let us know if you have a sufficiency of cotton socks, we have knitted you some but do not think he would be willing to carry so much.

Lu and I walked all the way to Clover Hill (about 5 miles-ed.) to get the skin to make you gloves on Friday last but were unsuccessful…"

I met and spoke with Lucy Buck's great-great grand niece and she informs me that Lucy never married and, also, she went further than ten miles from her home in Front Royal.

JACKSON'S FOOT CAVALRY-Company A, 13th Virginia Infantry by Walbrook D. Swank, Col. U.S.A.F. (Ret) pub by Burd Street Books 2001

Pg. 13 March 2, 1864 Pvt. George Peyton- camp in the Shenandoah Vally "...My father came to see me and brought me a pair of boots and some bread and butter...I had to lend everyone who went on post my overcoat, and caght an awful cold..."

Pg. 16, March 10 1864 on furlough home "...In the morning I took a good bath and put on a "biled" shirt..."

Pg. 19 March 19, 1864 "...At 11a.m. we had an inspection. We formed a line and an officer went down and you gave him your gun and he glaced at it and gave it back to you. Some of the men said that when he started this morning, he had a white handkerchief that he rubbed on the guns, but it soon got so black that he stopped using it..."

Were there any materials to clean weapons at this time? I would think so.

Pg. 22 March 31, 1863 "...The army has been much better fed and clothed this winter than last..."

What was this soldier's experience last year? According to the letters, winter 1862- '63 onward were times of critical clothing shortages.

LETTERS FROM THE STONEWALL BRIGADE Ted Barcay, Liberty Hall Volunteers ed by Charles W. Turner pub by Rockbridge Pub. Co. 1992

Pg. 129 camp on the Rapidan March 6, 1864 Dear Sister "...On my arrival in camp (from picket) I met (E.A.) Lacy just leaving and found my hat and a letter in the tent. The hat fits very well and seems to be of very good material, so I suppose it will see me through this war if it last as well as the old one...As to clothing, very well supplied. Pants have a little hole in the seat and I expect to draw a pair in a short time; in the meantime, I have them patched. Have had my boots half-soled and so my wardrobe is all right..."

LETTERS TO AMANDA-The Civil War letters of Marion Hill Fitzpatrick, Army of Northern Virginia ed by Jeffery C Lowe & SamHodges pub by Mercer Univ. Press 1998

Pg. 123 March 6th, 1864 Camp Near Orange Courthouse, Va. (Letter No. 60) Dear Amanda, "I am up the spout. I have not a sign of a shoe to my name, and am worn out, but I did not make the march barefooted. Capt. Gibson had two pair of boots. Henry Gibson wore one pair of the two days, and I wore Henry's shoes. The boots nearly ruined his feet and he had to take his shoes and let me have the boots. I wore the boots till we got here, which was three days, and they broke me down and nearly ruined my feet. This morning I have not put them on atall, nor do I expect to any more if I can help it. I put on an old pair of socks over one of my new pair and am taking it shoeless.I am so stiff that I can hardly walk atall but I hope a few days rest will bring me all right again…Tip's time will be out tonight. I shall look eagerly for him to come and bring my shoes…I am wearing my new britches now. I shipped my old ones when we started on the march. My gloves are about worn out. Please send me a pair by Jack Wilder or the first chance…"

Pg. 125 March 11th, 1864 Camp Near Orange Courthouse,Va. (Letter No.61) Dear Amanda, "Tip came day before yesterday and brought you letter of the 3rd. inst., My shoes, socks, and thread and beeswax all safe…My shoes came in a good time sure for I was without a footcovering at the time. They are a little too large but that is a good failing. My socks I really did not need at this time but they are not in the way at the least. My thread I am proud of. I have put up a regular tailor shop, and I am making my expenses at least by it. I bought a pair of scissors the other day with a nice brass chain attached to them for which I paid $10.00. I intend selling the chain for four or five dollars if I can to help pay for the scissors…I rec. a letter from you of Feb. 22nd, the day before Tip came was glad to hear that you had my coat all safe…"

Pg. 130 March 21st, 1864 Camp Near Orange Courthouse, Va. (Letter No 62) Dear Amanda, "…I go over to Montpelior occasionally and get a good dinner which is a great help to me. I also get my clothes washed there. The wash them nice and iron them, which is a great help. I make money enough sewing to pay for the washing and more too, and sewing is easier than washing. I wear gallows now (A pair of suspenders or braces). I find it a great advantage especially on the march. I made me a pair of leggings off my old pants legs which is a considerable preservation to my new pants…"

This soldier is quite ingenious & industrious.

MILITARY COLLECTOR AND HISTORIAN-Journal of the Company of Military Historians Vol XLI #4 Winter, 1989 Enlisted Uniforms of the Maryland Confederate Infantry: A Case Stuy, Part II by Ross M. Kimmel

Pg. 183 March 7, 1864 "…The writer was Pvt. Summorville Solleras, Compay A, and he was addressing his sister "Meme" at his family home in Calvert County,(Southern) Maryland. The date was M arch 7, 1864:

The gentleman who takes this letter is also in the habit of bringing over for particular parties, small bundles of clothing. He has just arrived with a bundle for young Deale, at whose house, he generally stops. Will you not endeaver to send me the following articles, as I really do need them. Two shirts made of light cassimere with a pocket, two silk handkerchiefs, some socks, a cravat, a toothbrush, a comb, and a brown felt hat and if you possibly can, a pr. of stout shoes No. 7. The articles I have mentioned would cost over here about $400. You must sew them up in a bag tightly and securely and send them to Mr. Deale's with my name marked plainly on them. I have mentioned the matter to Deale, I know his sister, write to her explaining the matter and the bundle will be sent over…"

"…He requested it be sent again by his comrade William Thelin, also a private in Company A, who had gone into Maryland and "will bring over for me anything you may have to send." Sollers specifically requested, "if it is there, my old uniform coat…"

Smuggling clothing and hard-to-get items in from Southern Maryland.

THE CONFEDERATE VETERAN VOL. XXVI 1918

Pg. 353 August, 1918 Letters From The Front-Thomas Caffey's letters to his family in Alabama-Camp near Orange Courthouse, Va. March 7, 1864 Dear Mary: "You asked if I received the soap and paper Ma sent. I did some time ago…Ma need not send my cap cover, as the cap has "gone up the spout" long ago. I gave it to an Irishman belonging to our company who went on furlough some three weeks ago…"

THE COMANCHES WHITE'S BATTALION, VIRGINIA CAVALRY LAUREL BRIGADE by Frank M. Myers pub by continental Book Co. 1956

Pg. 252 March 9 1864 "…Came to Gordonville (Va) and camped. Drew some mule meat and hard-tack about four o'clock-first rations since the 7th…"

March 11th "…Still at this sweet-scented little place waiting for something to turn up, which it did, about 4P.M., in the shape of an old, long-legged, razor-backed, slab-sided, black sow, poorer than Pharoh's kine, and the last one left in the county, but we killed and eat her, and the only meat we've had since the mule gave out…"

Apparently he actually did mean mule meat. Confederate soldiers often referred to pickled beef as "mule meat." I'll bet both the mule and that hog's meat was tough, though better than going hungry.

RED CLAY TO RICHMOND by John J. Fox pub by Angle Valley Press 2006

Pg. 243 March 20, 1864 James Garrett in a letter to his mother: "…I drew my self a new coat yesterday. I have got one that will fit Bud. I have it all the winter but it is good yet. I sent my cape home by Bill Formby. I am about to get out of socks. I want you to have me some knit by the time I come home and also some drawers if you have got the cloth. I cant get a pair that will stand me here…"

This is a common complaint, the drawers and socks issued by the government weren't worth drawing.

THE CONFEDERATE VETERAN VOL. XXII 1914

PG. 257 From Petersburg To Appomattox by Thomas P. Devereux "The corps was removed from the Valley to Petersburg just before Christmas, and for some time lay in camp on Swift Creek, a few miles north of Petersburgand on the railroad to Richmond…

Here we remained in comparative quiet until March 27 (1864), with woefully scanty rations, consisting chiefly of corn bread made with unsifted meal about as large as a man's fist and less than half a pint of sorghum. About once a week we had a small slice of meat and once or twice a little rice. I recall one ration of fresh canned beef (some said horse meat), which was issued in January when we were in winter quarters on Swift Creek. I will tell you where the fresh meat came from. When in California in 1868 I met a Basque Frenchman, who had lived for several years in Buenos Aires. He was telling one day of the immense herds of cattle, mules and horses formerly slaughtered at a certain place on the La Plata River for their hides alone, their carcasses being thrown into the river. He went on to say that a firm of Englishmen set up an immense cannery to preserve the meat, and that several cargoes were sent to the Confederacy through the blockade; hence the horse and mule meat."

Ugh. If I was a Rebel soldier and had partaken in this delicacy, its better to have learned the truth years later.

DIARIES, WRITINGS AND STORIES OF GEORGE D. BUSWELL, Co. H, 33rd Virginia Infantry, Stonewall Brigade

March 27 1864 Camp Stonewall Brigade Dear Brother; "…I reckon you think I have my valise by this time, but I have not. I thought today that O had it, but it has now been stolen, so I cannot get paid for it. It was brought to Maj. Brathwart's Quarters yesterday evening, but did not know it until today. I went after it & found it had been stolen. I very much fear I shall not be able to find it and shall not expect it. Therefore, Papa may have another valise made for me. I want my shoes if Papa comes or sends anything to me…

(Authors footnote) Dad Remembered: seeing his heavy caped overcoat hanging in their home when he was a little boy, and of his "Pa" telling him that when it rained really hard, that under that big caped collar of the coat he stayed dry-even when they had to march all day in the rain…"

Yeah, but those caped overcoats certainly do get heavy soaking up the rain.

FRANKLIN GARDENER WALKER C.S.A. Civil War Diaries and Letters compiled by his Eldest Son 1936 edited and retyped by his Grandson Erle Preston Carter 1986 Handley Library Archives, Winchester, Va.

Pg. 40 Camp Scouts, Guides & Couriers Near Orange C.H. Va. March 28, 1864 Dear Mother: "…I received day before yesterday a letter from Billy dated on the 5th of February and at the same time I received the cotton socks which you had sent to me by Mr. Evans and I was very glad to get them as I had been wearing yarn because I had no cotton heavy enough to wear with a pair of large boots which I have. Dorsey gave me two pair of yarn socks while I was in New Market. I am getting along very well at present in the way of clothing, having as much as I will be able to carry with me on the march. When these I have wear out I suppose I will be lucky enough to get some more one way or another…"

LIBRARY OF VA. Joseph Davis Box # 38768

Winter Quarters Near Orange City Virginia
March 29th 1864

Dear Grandmother "…I have clothing plenty. I have drawn a good Blanket, Coat and pair Pants and one pair Socks. I have not drawn any money yet and I recon we will not until the new money comes out. If I get my bounty money and monthly wage all at one time I will have enuff to buy me a dinner just about…."

At least he was able to draw a complete uniform, less shoes.

VOICES FROM COMPANY D Diaries by the Greensboro Guards, Fifth Alabama Infantry Regiment, Army of Northern Virginia ed. by G. Ward Hubbs pub by Univ. of Georgia Press 2003

Pg. 235 March 31 1864 SP "…Jamie brought me a carpet bag full of nice clothes and other things- a pr. Pants & vest of very nice jeans, 2 nice knit shirts (under), socks, & a pr. Gauntlets-a present from Miss Damar, also a large supply of paper and envelopes, lead pencils, stamps, tooth-brush, combs, handerchiefs, and in fact every thing in the world that I need-except a pr. Shoes, & Jamie had a pr. Boots, but left them as they were expecting me at home on furlough…Jamie has a pr. Boots bought in Richmond, for which he gave a pr. New ones (made in Greensboro at $140.00) & $125.00 cash; thus making them cost $265.00!! For a single pr. Boots you could get before the war for $10.-prodigious!!…"

Supply of clothing from home folks, now if they could only get shoes/ boots from home. Nobody could have affored those prices.

FROM CORSICANA TO APPOMATTOX by John Spencer pub by The Texas Press 1984

Pg. 85 spring 1864 return to the A.N.V. "…Now, with the amusement of East Tennessee behind them, new uniforms on their backs, and new shoes on their feet, the Naverro County infantrymen are ready to participate in the impending battle of the wilderness area of Virginia, where the Yankees are again up to their old "capture Richmond" tricks…"

Completely outfitted in new uniforms, what more could you ask for?

FOUR YEARS UNDER MARSE ROBERT by Robert Stiles pub by Pelican Publishing Co. 1998

Pg. 121 Spring, 1864 winter encampment, Army of Northern Virginia," …One beautiful day in the early spring I was seated in our headquarters tent at work on one of the battalion reports, which was my duty as adjutant to make to Artillery Headquarters, when a very striking-looking head intruded itself in the tent door and, in a very nonchalant, familiar tone, the owner of the head asked, "Is Gibbes about?"

We were not very punctilious about such matters in the Confederate service, perhaps not enough so; but the intruder and interlocutor was obviously, I thought, a private soldier and a specially untidy looking one at that-his hat unquestionably a "slouch," his hair long and unkempt, his long overcoat, of whatever original ground color, now by long usage the color of the ground, and ending in a fringe of tatters around the skirt; under it no sign of a coat or of anything save a gray flannel shirt, no badge or insignia of rank anywhere visable, not even an appropriate place for any, and his badly-worn pants turned up around his very small feet shod in very rough shoes...." He was introduced by Major Wade Hampton Gibbes, of South Carolina, as Col. Edward Willis, of the Twelth Georgia..."

The raggedness of the officers at this time is amazing.

REMINISCENCES OF BIG I by Lieutenant William Nathanial Wood Monicello Guard Company "A" 19th Virginia Regiment C.S.A. pub by McCowat-Mercer Press 1959

Pg. 53 spring, 1864 "Among the many home-like legacies left us by the brigade of General Wise was a large cat. This cat looked so fat and slick, that the idea of making a dinner of her was suggested by a Captain of the regiment, who said: "What nice venison she will make." The cat was slaughtered and nicely dressed and put in a camp kettle to cook. All day the cat boiled and at every trial to stick in the fork to acertain when tender, the report was "not done yet." "Lights out" came and still the cat was no tender. Carefully the camp kettle was set aside for the night and next morning the effort to cook the cat was resumed. The mess quietly indulged in a game of "old sledge" and patiently watched the boiling kettle, but the cat still resisted the fork. Finally, late in the evening of the second day's cooking and waiting it was decided, "Lets eat her anyhow." The mess gathered around the table and Captain Charles-undertook to carve. "What's the matter with this knife, Dick?" "Nothing in the world the matter with the knife; it is that darn'd old cat we have been boiling for two days." And it was a correct conclusion; for no knife was found that would cut that "venison" and the dinner was spoiled..."

If I'd have been there, I would have at least tried to have eaten it, after all, it had been boiled for two days, it should have been digestible if not tasty.

REBEL PRIVATE FRONT AND REAR- Memoire of a Confederate Soldier by William A. Fletcher pub by Dutton Books 1995

Pg. 95 Spring 1864, in camp near Petersburg "If I remember right, it was spring time when we were at this camp; and there was more poor beef issued, by odds, than was ever distributed in the same length of time, to my knowledge. The public road ran near and along front of the camp and when the cow brutes were passing on the way to the slaughterpen beyond, it was a common remark that we would draw beef tomorrow as the quartermaster was driving to see what to kill first-that all that could not travel were said to be for next slaughter. This was not a fact, however, but so near the true condition that it would be hard to draw the line, as I would see the herds passing the road and visiting the slaughter pens, from sight, the conclusion I reached was as follows: The beef stock of all ages and sizes was exhausted in that section, and that they were gathering in the milch cows and one would think,"Old lady-your time next, and if your destiny is a flight to the great unknown, what a meeting of the herd of mother, children and great, great-grandchildren; and if death could be reached by desire, that you were certainly not a resourceful brute." In every brute there was depicted the waiting condition of the owner. The once pride of the family was slowly but surely starving to death and the end was near, for there were numbers that one would think when they lay down they would never rise again until skinned and carted away to their last resting place-the soldier's stomach. The most of this meat, when cooked, would turn to jelly and one would think of sweetening. It was not necessary to have a peg to hang it on-throw it against a tree and it would stick. Need not necessarily be a nearby tree, as there was but little danger of it being stolen, as each fellow had enough of the kind. After being thrown against the tree it had the appearance of some hideous picture of a sea monster trying to climb down, as the tendons would stick where they came in contact with the tree and would slowly stretch from the weight of the body whether the entire piece would go to strings, or not. We never made a test, but I have often pulled meat off-if such it could be called-when the meat was from two to four inches below where it first struck. If the reader of this undertakes to make test to prove the correctness of this statement, I would ask him to go for his material where he can get fair samples under like conditions. Here was where it was reported that some men ate the unborn calf if it was spotted. This word "spotted" was to denote one that had the hair on."

Imagine a diet such as this.

IBID May 1964

Spring 1864 Pg. 24 The 23rd Ohio by T. Harry Williams and Stephen E. Ambrose.

Western Va. "One Federal witness described a typical guerilla. "imagine a stolid, vicious-looking countenance, an ungainly figure, and an awkward, if not ungraceful, spinal curve in the dorsal region, acquired by laziness and indifference to maintaining an erect posture; a garb of the coarsest texture of home-spun linen… and so covered with dirt as not to enable one to guess its original color; a dilapidated, rimless hat, or cap of some wild animals skin, covering his head, the hair on which had not been combed for monthes; his feet covered with moccasins, and a rifle by his side, a powder-horn and shot poch slung around his neck, and you have the beau ideal of the West Virginia bushwacker."

I have actually known some West Virginians who would fir this description. Good people, if you got on their good side.

LEE'S LAST CAMPAIGN by Clifford Dowdy pub by Bonanza Books

Pg.30 spring of 1864 "…Stuart's total figure included recruits of sixteen-year-old boys and middle-aged farmers whose land had been overrun and who had nothing left to work. The newcomers came straight from their homes, wearing such assortments of clothes as they could provide or their families provide for them….and forage for oilcloths from dead Yankees or dead compainions. Some wore boots, some shoes. Not even Genghis Kahn's hordes looked less like traditional mounted troops devoted to the orthodox work of screening the infantry and gaining information about the enemy…"

The cavalry, usually known by their neat uniforms, now descend into multiformity.

THREE YEARS IN THE CONFEDERATE HORSE ARTILLERY by George M. Neese pub by Morningside Bookshop 1983

Pg. 255 spring 1864 "…April 21-Took stage this morning at New Market and arrived in Staunton at sunset. When I got on the stage this morning I noticed a man on it wearing a Yankee uniform. He asked me whether I was going to Lee's army; I told him that was my destination. He remarked then that there would be some hard fighting this spring and summer, as their side was making great preperations for an aggressive vigorous, and an active campaign, by filling up their regiments with new recruits, and, if anything, were inceasing the size of their armies. He was in good humor, and I saw that he was no prisoner. I asked him what he was doing here in Dixie, and where he was going. He said that he was very tired of war and that he knew that there would be a great deal of hard marching and hot fighting this year, and the easiest way out of it all would be to desert and come South, which he did; and was now on his way to the south side of the Virginia Cetral Railroad where, he said, Yankee deserters were allowed to roam at will…"

Remember the Federal casualties of the spring campaign of 1864, and you'll see this Yank had an excellent survival plan.

LAW'S ALABAMA BRIGADE IN THE WAR BETWEEN THE UNION AND THE CONFEDERACY by J. Gary Laine & Morris M. Penny pub by White Mane Pub. Co. 1996

Pg. 231 Spring, 1864 return to Va. "The Confederate Quartermaster Corps busied itself during the winter gathering a supply of clothing, the Alabamians receiving new uniforms at Gordonsville. The 47th Alabama's attire was plain, but sufficient. Pants were grey, jackets were either black or grey, and better yet, new Enfield rifles were issued."

Supply from the government.

THE CIVIL WAR SOLDIER- Historical Reader ed. by Michael Barton & Larry M. Logue pub by N.Y. Press 2002

Pg. 113 "A Mississippian wrote his mother in the spring of 1864: "My hat and boots are the admiration of all the boys they all want them two of the boys went out Courting the next day after I got here. I had to loan one my hat and one my overshirt." …"a Virginian who had just returned from furlough with surplus apparel wrote to his wife: "I sold my pants, vest, shoes, & drawers for sixtyone dollars so you see I am flush again…You will have to make me more pants and drawers, if you can raise the material make two pair of pants and four pair of drawers & I will have A pair of pants and two pair of drawers for sale in that way will get mine clear…if you could make up a good supply of pants vests shirts and drawers, I could be detailed out to come after them….do not tell any one what good pairs pants will bring in camp if they knew it they would go to peddling in clothes keep dark whether you make any for sale or not."

In some portions of the army the practice was followed of selling at auction the clothing of men who had died in camp."

A considerable portion of the Rebel clothing deficiency was supplied by the Federals. The cavalry branch of the service, because of its ability to make swift raids into Yankeedom, profited most in this respect. A Mississippian who was not inclined to exaggerate wrote his mother just after Christmas in 1862 that he had recently seen about six thousand cavalrymen pass his post and "every man had a complete Yankee Suit consisting of hats coats pants Jackets and boots."

Infantrymen frequently did well by themselves in the wake of a battle. The writer's great uncle told of a comrade who lost an arm on the night of the battle of Raymond, Mississippi, attempting to appropriate the uniform of one whom he thought to be a dead Yankee. The practice of reshoeing at the expense of dead and live Yankees was so common that the remark became trite among troops, "All a Yankee is worth is his shoes."

If I were foraging for uniform parts or shoes on the battlefield, I'd at least make sure the man was dead. Losing an arm is too high a price to pay for shoes.

WAR HISTORY OF THE OLD FIRST VIRGINIA REGIMENT, ARMY of NORTHERN VIRGINIA by Charles T. Loehr pub. by Wm. Ellis Jones Book & Job Printer 1884

Pg.44 April 1864 Capture of Fort Williams, Plymouth, N.C. "…It was quite amusing to see our men turning their war-bags (as they called the haversacks) inside out, dropping the old corn dodgers and pieces of rancid bacon in the streets, to make room for cakes, preserves, pies and things, and going through the houses so lately occupied by the enemy's officers and families, but now all deserted, breaking the large mirrors to get a piece of looking-glass, pulling the strings out of elegant pianos to hang the cups on, and generally helping themselves to things that were useful or useless to them..."

MILITARY COLLECTOR AND HISTORIAN-Journal of the Company of Military Historians, Vol. XLI Fall 1989 Enlisted Uniforms of the Maryland Confederate Infantry: A Case Study, Part I

Pg 107 "When the Marylanders emerged from winter quarters in April 1864, they were apparently in top condition. The infantry, numbering 325, was attached to the division of John C. Breckenridge, who was reported as "much pleased" to have the Marylanders and "complimented them highly upon their neat and soldierly appearance, thanks to Mrs. Bradley T. Johnson." When other troops of the Army of Northern Virginia saw the Maryland infantry in their "neat and cleanly uniforms," they mistook them for drafted militia and taunted them."

Well uniformed soldiers are such a novelty that the troops taunt them, thinking them new comers and not veterans.

FROM THE RAPIDAN TO RICHMOND William Meade Dame, Private, 1st Company Richmond Howitzers pub by Owens Pub. Co. 1920

Pg. 64 April, 1864 breaking winter camp..."...Soon after we reached the Captain's tent, orders were given to pack up whatever we could not carry on the campaign, and in two hours, a wagon would leave, to take all this stuff to Orange Court House; thence it would be taken to Richmond and kept for us, until next winter.

This was quickly done! The packing was not done in "Saratoga trunks," nor were the things piles of furs and winter luxuries. The "things" consisted of whatever, above absolute necessities, had been accumulated in winter quarters; a fiddle, a chessboard, a set of quoits, an extra blanket or shirt, or pair of shoes, that any favored child of Fortune had been able to get hold of during the winter. Everything like this must go. It did not take long to roll all the "extras" into bundles, strap them up and pitch them into the wagon. And in less than two hours after the order was given the wagon was gone, and the men left in campaign "trim."

This meant that each man had, left, one blanket, one small haversack, one changeof underclothes, a canteen, cup and plate, of tin, a knife and fork, and the clothes in which he stood. When ready to march, the blanket, rolled lengthwise, the ends brought together and strapped, hung from left shoulder across under right arm, the haversack, furnished with towel, soap, comb, knife, and fork in various pockets, a change of underclothes in the main division, and whatever rations we happened to have, in the other-hung on the left hip; the canteen, cup and plate, tied together, hung on the right; toothbrush, "at will," stuck in two button holes of jacket, or in haversack; tobacco bag hung to a breast button, pipe in pocket. In this rig,-into which a fellow could get in just two minutes from a state of rest,-the Confederate soldier considered himself all right, and ready for anything; in this he marched, and in this he fought. Like the terrapin-"all he had he carried on his back"-this all weighed about seven or eight pounds..."

GRANDFATHER'S JOURNAL (Franklin Lafayette Riley) Company B Sixteenth Mississippi Infantry Volunteers Harris' Brigade Mahone's Division Hill's Cops, A.N.V. May 27, 1861-July 15, 1865 ed by Austin C. Dobbins pub by Morningside Press 1988

Pg. 187 Sunday-Tuesday, April 3-5, (Hail) 1864 Camp near Liberty Mills "...And long ago we learned to live without baggage. Unnecessary: overcoats, boots, cartridge boxes, canteens, bayonets. It doesn't pay to carry clean clothes. They are better picked up on the field from the enemy. Shoes are more comfortable than boots. Cups and cartridges can be carried in our pockets. A tin cup is more serviceable than a canteen,&c. Add 1 man, 1 hat, 1 outfit of clothes, 2 blankets (1 rubber), 1 haversack, 1 bucket or frying pan, 1 rifle, and the picture is complete. Officers are allowed 30 lbs. of baggage. We carry ours on our backs..."

These last two quotes are good over all descriptions of Rebel soldiers at this time.

JACKSON'S FOOT CAVALRY-Company A, 13th Virginia Infantry by Walbrook D. Swank U.S.A.F. (Ret) pub by Burd Street Press 2001

Pg. 23 April 1, 1864 Pvt. George Peyton "...I had on my good Yankee overcoat and did not get wet to the skin. At 1a.m., I was relieved and went back to our poor shebang and lay down on a plank to keep out of the water which was about three inches deep all over the floor of our bedroom. Every time I reached out with my arm or leg, "slosh" it would go in the water. Of course, sleep was out of the question. I had no fire and the night appeared about two weeks long..."

Pg. 28 April 20 1864 "...Wiliam came and brought me a pair of shoes and some grub. I sent my boots home..."

Pg. 29 April 21, 1864 "...I had brigade drill for three hours in the afternoon. I had on a pair of new shoes and they gave me fits. All our shoes are made by men here..."

Pg. 30 April 27, 1864 That night I stretched two oilcloths over some poles and slept under them. Tent gone..."

Notice the quote for April 21: "all our shoes are made by men here."

LETTERS TO AMANDA-The Civil War Letters of Marion Hill Fitzpatrick, Army of Northern Virginia ed by Jeffery C. Lowe & Sam Hodges pub by Mercer Univ Press 1998

Pg. Apr. 3rd, 1864 Camp Near Orange Courthouse, Va. (Letter No 63) Dear Amanda, "You are a witch to guess at my wants sure, for the ham of meat and the $10.00 was the very thing I was needing and I am glad to get them. Also the gloves suspenders patches and thread and tobacco, all of which I rec. safely, and now return my thanks to you for them. You sent more by double of the patching than was necessary, but I will take care of it, and will no doubt find a use for it. My gloves just fit and are just the idea. The suspenders I could have done without as I had a pair that was given to me. The things you sent me are much the best and I treasure them because they came from you...."

Pg. 133 Apr.10th, 1864 Camp Near Orange Courthouse, Va. (Letter No64) Dear Amanda, "There is more clothing and shoes here for the soldiers than I have ever known before. All can draw as much as they need and many I notice have drawn (,) I think (,) more than they need or will need on the march. I have drawn nothing nor do I expect to in a long time yet if I can keep what I have got.

Sounds like a massive issue of clothing by the government.

I fixed my pants the other day. I wish you could see the job. I know you would brag on it I took out the whole piece in front nearly up to the knee and put in a new piece of the patches you sent me, and they are just as good as ever. I would not know what to do without my scissors anyhow. I get just what sewing I can do for the other boys in the Comp. and make expenses by it...".

Pg. 136 Apr. 14th, 1864 Camp Near Orange Court House, Va. (Letter No 65) Dear Amanda, "...You spoke of my suspenders, whether I liked them or not. I like them just well enough. I first wrote or sent word to you to make some cloth ones because I thought wool was so scarce, but I prefer the knit ones because they give way like rubber..."

LETTERS OF A NEW MARKET CADET Beverly Stanard ed. by John G. Barrett & Robert K. Tyrner Jr. pub by Univ. N.C. Press 1961

Pg. 51 V.M.I. April the 8th, 1864 My dear Sister, "...What do you do for milk? It is something we never lay our eyes on here. Our fare is not good by any means, been feeding us off—beef (I don't want to use the word) for some time, and I hardly ever get enough bread to eat. It is a hard matter though to satisfy our appetites, we take so much exercise, drilling &ct and then our meals are so regular-I believe I have really grown a little since last Summer, I know I have fattened, weigh 137 lbs. Tried on some of my summer clothes a few nights ago out of curiousity. You know they were full large for me then. Now my jacket won't meet around me, and my pants require a little sugar or molasses on my shoes to induce them to come down a little..."

Imagine trying to feed a scool full of teen-aged boys that spend their days drilling, exercising Etc.

VOICES FROM COMPANY D Diaries by the Greensboro Guards, Fifth Alabama infantry Regiment, Army of Northern Virginia ed. by G.Ward Hubbs pub by Univ. of Ga. Press 2003

Pg. 239 April, 1864 ANV Va. VET "...The regiment received 100 pairs of socks from "Ladies Aid Society," Lynchburg VA...."

Pg.241 April 10, 1864 ANV Va. JP "...Altho' Sam has no shoes, yet he was detailed for guard this morn'g and went. He could have easily got an excuse, if he had wished; but would not do it...."

Pg. 242 April 11 1864 SP order from Gen. Lee"...that all extra baggage be sent off by the 15th; that Cols. Of Regts. Must inspect their men & see if they are properly provided with clothing-viz. a hat or cap, a coat, 1 pr. Pants, 2 shirts, 2 pr. Drawers, 2pr. Socks & a good pr. Shoes, also a blanket; & that is all the baggage of a soldier must be carried on his person..."

Pg. 244 April 12 1864 SP "...The box of shoes brought on by Tom Cowin reached us this evening & Capt. Williams gave out shoes to those who were in need of them & the balance are to be sent back to Richmond-till they are needed. I drew a pr. Of them. There were 33 prs. In the box for the Co. & 30 prs. For the Brigade...."

Pg. 247 April 18, 1864 ANV Va. HP "...Held a mass meeting of the brigade, of which resolutions of thanks were drafted to thank the people of Ala. For the contribution made up for this brigade...Sam was appointed on a committee of the Brigade, to draft resolutions of thanks to the citizens of Ala., for their liberal donations to this Brigade, of shoes, clothing and other necessities...(VET) Meeting of the Brigade in order to adopt resolutions relative to the clothing, shoes, etc., sent us from Ala. God bless the dear women, they never forget us..."

The Greensboro Guards have been completely resupplied by the home folks.

UNDER THE STARS AND BARS-A History of the Surrey Light Artillery by Lee A. Wallace, Jr. pub by Press of Morningside Bookshop 1975

Pg. 347 Letter Thiry-First Camp Schermerhorn, Va. April 10, 1864 "Page 157, line 3, The Soldiers Home was also known as the Confederate States Barracks, which in April 1863 was placed under the charge of Second Lieutenant Benjamin Bates, company B, 15th Regiment of Virginia Volunteers. Bates, who was promoted to first lieutenant in 1864, continued as commandant for the remainder of the war. On Nov. 17, 1863, Bates informed the Secretary of war that since he had been in charge, he had taken care of an average of 100 men daily, feeding them, and furnishing them transportation to their commands. More tham 3,800 men had bee forwarded to their commands, he wrote. A well uniformed and equipped guard of about 50 men was kept at the Barracks, and in 1864 they appear to have been organized as Co H, First Invalid Battalion. On Oct. 12, 1864 three stoves were received "for the comfort of the troops passing the Barracks to be forwarded to their commands. Bates, on Nov. 29, 1864, requisitioned 2,000 blankets for the use of the returning soldiers. Another requisition by Bates indicates that on Dec. 7, 1863, 4 jackets, 4 pairs of pants,4 caps,4 shirts, and 4 pairs of shoes were received for the use of hired Negroes at the Barracks. The barracks, or Soldier's Home, was located on Franklin Street, Richmond, in April 1863, but its precise location is undetermined..."

It should have been preserved as a historical landmark due to all the good services it rendered for the cause.

DEAR IRVIE, DEAR LUCY-Civil War Letters of Capt. Irving A. Buck, General Cleburne's AAG & Family pub by Buck Pub. Co. 2002

Pg. 219 April 10, 1864 Bel Aire, Front Royal, Va. My Dear Child (Alvin), "...I have succeeded in getting both of you pants but not such as you wanted. Material of almost every kind is impossible to get and so I do not suppose gray cloth could be had in the county unless in the homes of some speculator that I know nothing about but your Uncle Tom happened to have a piece he had made for himself and finding I wanted it he makes you a present of it-and you esteem it a great favor. He could have gotten sixty dollars a yard for it. It is all wool is black but I thought you might exchange it for gray either at some of the shops or with individuals as many citizens would prefer that color. It is the best I could do-but for your Uncle Tom's kindness to us I know not what we should have done during these hard times. He has given us over 100 yards of calico at one time besides many other such favors in fact he is a public benefactor...I wish you would write to your Uncle Tom and thank him for the pants and also for the boots he sent you some time ago. I know he would appreciate it. You can hardly form an idea of the scarcity of almost everything in this neighborhood..."

The black pants would have been acceptable in the army.

Pg. 221 April 19 1864 Home (Bel Aire, Front Royal, Va.) My Dear Alvin, "...Well, we have succeeded in getting you a pair of pants. Uncle Tom sends you a pair of his. Father says he tried everywhere to get the jeans but could hear of but one single piece and that was not dressed and entirely unsuited for the purpose. Uncle Tom is so very kind to us- you don't know how much indebted we are to him and Aunt Bettie...I send you and Cousin Mack each a cravat-poor specimen but the best I could do. Do you want a tobacco bag? There are also three pairs of socks for you...Fondly, Lucie"

RED CLAY TO RICHMOND by John J. Fox pub by Angle Valley Press 2006

Pg. 246 April 14, 1864 James Garrett in a letter to his mother: "...You stated that William Formby had got home safe. I sent my cape by him and he lost it. I would not have taken fifty dollars for it. I have been offered thirty for it. I have got plenty of clothing for the present, except socks. I have got a very nice suit of clothes now so if I do get home I will have a nice suit to wear though I shall not feel disappointed if I don't get to come..."

As the spring campaign was about to open, I doubt this soldier was able to get home at this time.

A TRUE HISTORY OF COMPANY I, 49TH REGIMENT NORTH CAROLINA TROOPS by W.A.Day Printed At The Enterprise Job office 1893

Pg. 48 marching to Plymouth, N.C. "...An old citizen came out and asked us how many pieces of artillery it took to make a cannon. He said he had just had an argument with the old woman about it. He thought it took three pieces and the old woman said it took four and he wanted some of us to tell him which was right. Some told him he was right, and others told him the old woman was right, and the old man left about as wise as he was before..."

Funny, I get a different answer from everyone I ask this question. I guess its one of those military mysteries.

Pg. 55 April 15, 1864 "...Sometime about the middle of April, 1864, the attack on Plymouth (N.C.) was ordered. The 49th regiment was ordered down on the Albermarle Sound and went into camp in a beautiful place near the fishery. The fishery was where the Chowan River enters into the Albermarle Sound. They were fishing for shad with seines a hundred yards long. All the other kinds of fish were hauled out and dumped in piles in the fields. The shad were fat enough to fry themselves like pork. Fish rations were issued instead of bacon.A detail was made from the 49thRegiment to fish…"

I have never seen or caught any shad this fat, but would sure like to.

THE CONFEDERATE VETERAN VOL. XXVI 1918

Pg. 355 Letters From The Front-Thomas Caffey's Letters to his Family Camp 3rd Alabama Regiment, Near Orange Courthouse, Va. April 21, 1864 Dear Mary: "Orders came a few days ago to send all our surplus plunder to the rear so as to have as little encumbrance as possible on the march. My blankets and some articles of clothing I boxed up and forwarded to Major Vandeveer at Alabama Depot, Richmond. I suppose he will take care of them till I need them next winter, provided I am so fortunate as to get off with whole bones in the ensuing campaign. Cushing, of Mongomery, sent me a very good wool hat; and as the one Ma sent me was too warm for summer wear, I sent it back with my other things, thinking it would do in camp next winter…"

Good luck in getting those clothes back next winter.

VOICES FROM COMPANY D Diaries by the Greensboro Guards, Fifth Alabama Infantry Regiment, Army of Northern Virginia ed. by G. Ward Hubbs pub by Univ. of Georgia Press 2003

Pg. 252 April 25 1864 JP "…Sam & I manufactured a very respectable pair of suspenders for himself this even'g, out of an old pair of drawers; he making one & I the other…."

CIVIL WAR LETTERS OF CAPTAIN A.B. MULLIGAN, Co. B, 5th South Carolina Cavalry-Bulter's Division-Hampton's Corps by Olin Fulmer Hutchinson, Jr. pub by The Reprint Co. 1992

Pg. 110 April 25, 1864 Magnolia, N.C. My Very Dear Mother and Sisters, "I am happy to say that I am quite well. I left Richlands two days ago & came here with my company preparatory to starting for Virginia. I saw Col. Jeffords yesterday on my way up & recd. the socks & Eliza's letter which he brought me…"

THE CONFEDERATE LETTERS OF BENJAMIN H. FREEMAN Compiled & Edited by Stuart T. Wright pub by Exposition Press 1974

Pg. 37 April 26, 1864 "Camp Marshall" near Orange C.H. Dear Farther, Mother, Sisters: "…John Huff is gone home. I sent by him my old boot legs. I thought they might be fit to bottom he will bring them to you if he don't he will leave them (at) S.T. Wilders Store for you but he may come to see you…"

FROM HUNTSVILLE TO APPOMATTOX R.T. Coles History of 4th Alabama Volunteer Infantry ed by Frank D. Stocker pub by Univ. of Tenn. Press 1996

Pg. 287 footnote #9 Mongomery (Ala.) Daily Herald Apr. 27, 1864 "A letter in an Alabama newspaper from an unidentified correspondent in the Alabama Brigade described these hardships: "Law's Brigade is positively suffering for clothing, many of the men are about naked, and as a body they are more destitute now than they have been at any previous period of the war. We have received no clothing from the Quartermaster's Department for many, many months, and the only good clothing we have in camp is that brought back by those lately returned from furlough…In conclusion, let me seriously say to the people of Alabama, that the brave boys of Law's Brigade-the heroes of Gettysburg and Cickamauga-have not the wherewithal to shelter them from the cold, nor even to cover their nakedness."

Another appeal for clothing from the home folks.

LEE'S LIEUTENANTS by Douglas Southhall Freeman Charles pub by Schribner's & Sons volII

Pg. 342 The recall of the First Corps, inspection by General Lee, April 29 1864 "…Said one participant, somewhat proudly: "guns were burnished and rubbed up, cartridge boxes and belts polished, and the brass buttons and buckles made to look as bright as new. Our clothes were patched and brushed up, so far as was in our power, boots and shoes greased, the tattered and torn old hats were given here and there 'a lick and a promise,' and on the whole I must say I think we presented not a bad-looking body of soldiers."

Pg. 363 Wilderness Battle "…Close behind Jenkins marched his men who wore uniforms of a grey so deep that they appeard dark blue or almost black in the forrest…."

More English uniforms

Pg. 408 Bloody Angle, Spottsylvania "…One man incredibly ceased fire, examined leisurely a captured knapsack, stripped, put on the clean clothing he found in the case, and then cheerfully resumed his duty as a sharpshooter…"

That's one individual who's cool under fire.

VOICES FROM COMPANY D Diaries by the Greensboro Guards, Fifth Alabama Infantry Regiment, Army of Northern Virginia ed. by G. Ward Hubbs pub by Univ. of Georgia Press 2003

Pg. 256 April 30 1864 JP "…Jack W. & I walked over to the wagon-yard where I got a pair of shoes (No.8) for John, & Jack a pair of pants for himself…"

Website THE BIVOUAC Sharpshooters as Prisoners Gary Yee http://www.bivouacbooks.com/bbv7i1s1.htm Oct. 21 2010

Pg. 2 "…Third North Carolina Assistant Surgeon Thomas Fanning Wood "When the campaign began in 1864 we were in General Ewell's Corps (Jackson's formerly), Ed. Johnson's Div., Steuart's Brigade. Steuart had devised some original badges for his men, of colored cloth, so that at a glance it could be told the Brigade, Regt., Co., of the man, the number of engagements he had been in, whether he was a Sharpshooter or an Ambulence man, etc." However, the adoption of a badge by Steuart's brigade may have been very limited as staff officer McHenry Howard points out: "General Steuart also designed cloth badges (metal was not to be had), to distinguish the men of different regiments a red cross on ground of different colors, or something that way. But the failure to get scraps of cloth from the factories prevented his carrying out this project." When cloth could not be supplied by the quartermaster to implement Steuart's plan, the men resorted to another means as described by the April 28, 1864 letter from Tenth Virginia Sergeant George Miley to his sweetheart, Amelia Baker: "our Brig. Genl. Has an idea that his troops should be marked that they may be distinguished from all others, and requires us to wear a badge on our right arm with a red bar for each battle in which each one has participated. Some or nearly all the boys are receiving theirs from sweethearts. I don't want to be behind and want to wear one made by you. If not asking too much I will transmit the bars when I hear from you and describe if I can, how they are made. "The wearing of patches or markings by the Confederate Army was first used in 1861 and is described by General William L. Cabell: "When the Confederate Army commanded by General Beauregard, and the Federal Army confronted each other at Manassas, it was seen that the Confederate flag and the Stars and Stripes looked at a distance so much alike that it was hard to distinguish one from the other. General Beauregard, thinking that serious mistakes might be made in recognizing our troops, ordered, after the battle of July 18, at Blackburn Ford, that a small red badge should be worn on the left shoulder of our troops, and, as I was chief quartermaster, ordered me to purchase a large quantity of red flannel and distribute it to each regiment. I distributed the red flannel to several regiments, who placed badges on the left shoulders of the men."

This is the first I've ever heard of this.

Pg 2 1864 "…South Carolina's McGowan's Battalion Sharpshooter Sgt. Berry Benson conducted a private reconnaissance and was attempting to return to Confederate Lines when he became fearful of his fate if caught by his own side. "Having no pass, I would be arrested and taken to the camp and punished. Me,a non-commissioned officer and a sharpshooter!" At the Battle of the Wilderness Benson and his fellow sharpshooters resorted to "(B)reaking off twigs of pine, we set the green bunches in our hats to help us to hang together…" Some time during the course of the campaign McGowan's brigade adopted one (a badge). In his sketch of Moses Allen Terrill of Orr's Rifle Regiment (First South Carolina) of Mcgowan's brigade, Sgt. W.T. McGill recalled," The Sharp Shooters were priviledged characters. Thet were distinguished by a badge consisting of a red band running diagonally across the left elbow of the coat sleeve with a red star just above the band. This badge would pass the Sharp Shooter anywhere…"

Pg. 3 "…Private Daniel Chisolm of the 116th Pennsylvania Infantry whose observation of Confederate sharpshooters in Wilcox's Division is noteworthy. "Sunday, April 2nd after Genl. Lee…We took the road and lots of prisoners. The sharpshooters had a red cross on their arms…"

THE PRIVATIONS OF A PRIVATE-Campaigning With the First Tennessee C.S.A. and Life Thereafter by Marcus B. Toney pub by Univ. Alabama Press 2005

Pg. 62 "…By the 1st of May the meat was gone, and many of the soldiers were without shoes. When the meat gave out, we resorted to wild onions, which were plentiful in that section (on the Rapidan River, Va) but hard to dig up. They were about the size of shallots, but very deep rooted, and we had to dig pretty deep with bayonets to get them up. These onions and corn bread without salt did very well toward appeasing the appetite of hungry soldiers."

Pg. 64 "On May I General Lee issued the following order: "Send all extra baggage to the rear"; and on May 3 he issued an order to cook three days rations. The first order was easily complied with. Back to Buckingham County was sent my Baltimore coat. The second order was also easily complied with. Three day's rations were thre pones of corn bread without any sifting and minus salt. We did not have any sifters in General Lee's army; and if we had, we could not have afforded the loss of the bran."

What's a Baltimore coat?

CIVIL WAR LETTERS OF CAPTAIN A.B. MULLIGAN, Co. B, 5th South Carolina Cavalry-Butler's Division-Hampton's Corps by Olin Fulmer Hutchinson, Jr. pub by The Reprint Co. 1992

Pg. 112 May 1st, 1864 Magnolia, N.C. My Very Dear Mother and Sisters, "I Recd. the socks and testament by Lt. Col Jeffords. My winter drawers and shirts both are worn out. I want you to try and get the linsey to make me two pair drawers and two undershirts by July if possible. Let the linsey for the drawers be colored and for the shirts white. My two colored homespun outside shirts are also worn out. I want two new ones if they can be had. Any neat colored check or stripe will do…"

FRANKLIN GARDENER WALKER C.S.A. Civil War Diaries and Letters compiled by his eldest son 1936 edited and retyped by his grandson Erle Preston Carter1986 Handley Library Archives, Winchester, Va.

Pg. 27 May 4th, 1864

Sent by W.B. Harris my shawl, coat, 2 shirts and vest to Mrs. Taliferro's near Orange C.H. Overcoat left with C.l. Channing, Mount Pleasant. On the left of road Sposylvania C.H. to Beaver Dam…"

LEE'S LAST CAMPAIGN-The Story of Lee & His Men Against Grant-1864 by Clifford Dowdey pub by Little, Brown & Co. 1960

Pg. 62 "The Army Was Put Into Motion Today" May 4th, 1864 "…For their role in the coming campaign the soldiers made such a bedraggled appearance that some Northern newspaper correspondents reported Lee's men to be already finished; without any fight left in them, they were ready to give up for a square meal. Some of the captured men and deserters seen in Union lines were in pitiable condition, and the self-confident members of Grant's staff, never having observed the men in units in action, were inclined to take lightly an army composed of emaciated ragamuffins. Veterans of the Army of the Potomac, who had fought against Lee's men, looked beyond the oddiments of patched makeshifts that passed for their "uniforms." As a staff officer of General Meade saw them, "A more sinewy, tawny, formidable-looking set of men could not be…they handled their weapons with terrible effect. Their great characteristic is their stoical manliness; they…look you straight in the face, with as little animosity as if they had never heard a gun."

To those familiar with the appearance of Lee's army, the soldier's costumes gave in mass the impression of being uniforms of a sort by the uniformity of their basic garments and the arrangement of their equipment. In this sense they were less variegated than in the early days of their resplendence, when visored caps, gilt-buttoned frock coats and stripe-legged pants made privates look like European courtiers. Most significant of the change from dandies into Confederate soldiers was the absence of those compartmented leather knapsacks that in the first year contained extra clothing such as white vests, white gloves and dress shirts, for dress parade and parties.

On May 4th, another of the rare May days, the typical Confederate soldier wore a weather-colored slouch hat, its crown dented and the brim, if not too floppy, turned up in front and back. Hair was worn long because that was the style easiest for camp "barbers" to effect on their fellows. The soldier wore a single-breasted jacket-either faded gray or the early days when he furnished his own uniform, of the butternut-colored flimsy of government issue, or a civilian jacket. The buttons in the front bore the seal of his state, not the Confederate seal. The letters CSA were embossed on his belt buckle. He wore a cotton shirt, probably made by his mother or wife, sweetheart or sister. With or without collar attached, he wore no cravat; sometimes a bright pattern of gingham, before it faded, gave him a dash of color about the throat. His pants, rarely matching his jacket, were patched in the seat and frazzled at the cuffless bottoms. His shoes were anything he could find, steal or glean from the dead. They matched those of his fellows in the unpolished discoloration of wear in all weather and in the frayed soles.

Across his body, from his left shoulder to his right hip, he wore a blanket role in an oilcloth, the latter a capture from the United States government issue. From his right shoulder to his left hip, ran a cord attached to a simple canvas haversack. In this he carried a knife, fork and spoon; his comb and razor if he had not stopped shaving; a round mirror in a metal case two inches in diameter; a little needlecase and, at times, a paper package of pins. If still neat about his appearance, he carried a cake of homemade soap and a cloth to serve as a towel. Sometimes a toothbrush went in there, and sometimes in a jacket pocket, where his tobacco was kept.

Any cooked rations that he was issued before a march went into the haversack, if he was not so hungry that he ate it at once. There he cached any oddments of food that he might gather on the march, such as an apple or an ear of corn stolen from a farmer's field, or hardtack gathered from the enemy's dead. In their hunger, men would scrape dried blood off a piece of salvaged hardtack.

Outside the haversack was slung his tin cup, the utensil of all purposes. Pots and pans were carried in the regimental skillet wagon, though some men carried a tin plate that could serve as a saucepan. He might hang his canteen outside his haversack, if the haversack was flat. If it was half full, his canteen swung in the middle of his back from a cord looped over his head. It was a round, tin canteen, holding little more than a pint of water. In the early days, when he got in among enemy wagons, he filled his canteen with molasses in his hunger for sweets. Sometimes attached to his belt he wore a leather cartridge case, either CSA or the fancier USA government issue. More frequently he carried his powder-topped cartridges in his pockets. His bayonet, with an eighteen-inch triangular blade coming to a sharp point, was used more for sticking a farmer's stray pig than the enemy, and its open round hilt, which was made to attach to the rifle, was useful as a candle holder when the blade was stuck in the ground. His bright bayonet was next to his tin cup in general usefulness. This total equipment weighed about seven pounds…."

There is really little more to say regarding a general overview of the Confederate soldier in the spring of 1864.

HANDLEY LIBRARY ARCHIVES-Civil War Letters & Dairy of Franklin Gardener Walter C.S.A. Co A. 39th Virginia Cavalry

Pg. 56 May 4, 1864 "Sent by W.B. Harris my shawl, coat, 2 shirts and vest to Mrs. Taliferro's near Orange C.H. Overcoat left with O.L. Chewning, Mount Pleasant…"

Pvt. Walker is sending off all superfluous clothing for the spring campaign.

ON FIELDS OF FURY by Richard Wheeler pub by Harper/Collins Pub. 1991

Pg. 35 "As I was a shoemaker and had a few tools such as awl, clawhammer, and pocketknife, I was prepared to half-sole the boy's shoes. I made my own pegs and a last. The next thing, and most important, was leather. Sometimes we could get government leather from the quartermaster, but in order to obviate that difficulty I formed a partnership with Sam McFadden, a messmate, of the 14th Louisiana. Sam (would) steal the leather, such as cartridge box lids saddle-skirts and housings from the harness…We would then charge five dollars in "Confed" for the half-soling, and divide, which kept us in spending money.

One night, as we were returning from a visit to our brigade, in passing the tent of the colonel of the 2nd Virginia, we noticed his McClellan saddle hung up on the outside. Sam said this was a good chance to lay in a stock of leather…Consequently we clipped the skirts off and went to our quarters. But, as there were several soldiers in our shanty who did not belong there, we conluded to leave the saddle-skirts on the outside until the coast was clear, knowing full well the colonel would raise a racket in the morning about his saddle being cut. After the crowd had dispersed we went out to bring in our stock, but it was gone. Someone had stolen it from us. We never did hear of those skirts again, and were afraid to inquire for fear the colonel would hear of it and have us punished."

Pg. 122 Battle of the Wilderness, May 6, 1864 "…Union Private Frank Wilkeson was a part of the pursuit (of the Rebels) "I saw many dead Confederates…They were poorly clad. Their blankets were in rolls, hanging diagonally from the left shoulder to the right side, where the ends were tied with strings or a strap. Their canvas haversacks contained plenty of cornmeal and some bacon.I saw no coffee, no sugar, no hard bread in any of the Confederate haversacks I looked into. But there was tobacco in plugs on almost all the dead Confederates. Their arms were not as good as ours. They were poorly shod. The direful poverty of the Confederacy was plainly indicated by its dead soldiers. But they fought! Yes, like men of purely American blood…"

LAW'S ALABAMA BRIGADE IN THE WAR BETWEEN THE UNION AND THE CONFEDERACY by J. Gary Laine & Morris M. Penny pub by White Mane Pub. Co. 1996

Pg. 245 Battle of the Wilderness, May 5, 1864 "Wiedrich's New Yorkers had not experienced this type of warfare before, because a few well-directed volleys were sufficient to send the 15th New York scurrying for cover. Most were dropping their haversacks as they stooped over to avoid fire from the 15th. Billy Jordan, Company B, 15th Alabama, recalled the Wilderness was the "richest battlefield that I ever beheld." That says much about the booty of this battlefield because Law's Brigade had gleamed many winter supplies from the Chickamauga battlefield.

Jordan saw a new blanket lying on the ground and discarded his old one for the Federal issue. Later in the morning he discovered more booty rolled up in the blanket. There was a "fancy laundered shirt" and two new linen tents. Jordan was generous with his spoils of war. The shirt was given to a friend in Co.B. Jordan and his messmate, William Calloway, shared the blanket and the tent for the remainder of the war."

THE CIVIL WAR: THE SOUTH ed by Thomas Streissguth pub by Greenhaven Press 2001

PG. 205 May 6, 1864 Henry E. Handerson staff officer for a La. Battalion "Capture in the Wilderness" "…It must have been about 4P.M. when we reached the depot for prisoners, and I was surprised to find here several hundred luckless individuals like myself, who had fallen early victims to the opening struggle. As later arrivals were drawn up in single file in order to take our names, rank, etc,.a squad of hangers-on about the camps amused themselves by making witty criticisms of our clothing and personal appearance, which I doubt not would have afforded us ready entrance into the famous ragged regiment of the immortal Falstaff…"

THE HASKELL DIARIES-The Personal Memoirs of a Confe-derate Officer by John Haskell ed by Gilbert E. Govan and James W. Livingood pub by G.P. Putnam's Sons 1960

Pg. 65 May 6, 1864 Longstreet's assault in the Wilderness "Longstreet rode near to Jenkin's column. Jenkins was jubilent. He had thoroughly done his work in most brilliant style and knew his promotion to major general was assured. He rode out to meet Longstreet and called to his men to cheer him, which they did with a will. Jenkin's Brigade was one of those who had recently returned from the South, and the men were dressed in new uniforms made of cloth so dark a gray as to be almost black. Mahone's men, some distance off in the thick underbrush, hearing the cheers and seeing this body of dark uniformed men, took them for Yankees and fired a volley. Fortunately they fired high, or there would have been a terrible slaughter. As it was, while they only struck eight or ten mounted men, the effect was horrible, for among the few were Jenkins, shot through the head, and Longstreet, through the neck."

Another Confederate disaster in the Wilderness.

THE PRIVATIONS OF A PRIVATE-Campaigning With the First Tennessee C.S.A. and Life Thereafter by Marcus B. Toney pub by Univ. of Alabama Press 2005

Pg. 68 "...on May 6 (1864) eleven hundred Federals were dead on Palmer's old field. All their haversacks and in many instances their knapsacks, and the pockets of each were turned inside out, showing that their pockets had been picked. Our men threw away their rations of corn bread, as they had three day's rations of hard-tack, besides some bacon and coffee..."

Pg. 73 May 8 (1864) captured at Spottsylvanis Courthouse-"...Many of them (the federal guards) were members of the heavy artillery and had been armed as infantrymen. Each regiment was headed by a fine band.We were in a sorry plight to meet such an array of tinseled regalia. Many of our men were hatless, shoeless, and coatless, and were covered with mud from the trenches. This grand army guyed us all day. As we met one column, a good-natured-looking soldier yelled out: "Hello Johnnies! We are taking you North, and will give you something to eat, put some clothes on your back, and shoes on your feet."

A CONFEDERATE SURGEON'S LETTERS TO HIS WIFE Spencer Glascow Welch, Surgeon Thirteenth S. Ca. Vols., McGowans Brigade pub by Neale Pub. Co. 1911

Pg 95 Wilderness, May 7, 1864 "I picked up an excellent Yankee overcoat on the battlefield, but the cape is off. I will have a sack coat made of it. I also found an India rubber cloth that is big enough for four men to lie on or make a tent of. I have never before seen a battlefield so strewn with overcoats, knapsacks, India rubber cloths and everything else soldiers carry, except at Chancellorsville. The dead Yankees are everywhere. ...Tell Bob that as soon as I draw some of the new issue I will send him the pay for your catskin shoes."

Yes, he wrote "catskin shoes." Maybe it was a joke the two of them shared and he meant calfskin.

LIBRARY OF VA. Journal of Joseph Mcmurman Box # 22076

"May 7th, 1864 Yankee changed their base during the night, Leaving guns, knapsacks &c-in great numbers indicating haste.

Their fortifications were made of blankets and gum cloths filled with earth & men strewn dead were covered up on them."

Notice the desparate building materials of the breastworks.

THE CIVIL WAR INFANTRYMAN-In Camp, on the March, and in Battle by Gregory A. Coco pub by Thomas Publications

May 8, 1864"...Lt. Galwey of Ohio documented this appearance of veteran Southern Soldiers near Spottsylvania Court House, Virginia, in May of 1864 "...(t)hey were all clad in neat gray jackets and pantaloons with entire seats..."

I wonder what units these were.

VOICES OF THE CIVIL WAR by Richard Wheeler pub by Meridian Books 1976

Pg. 390 Private John Cassler-assigned to burial detail "As we started out to bury the dead, there was one of the Federals lying beside the road who had been killed about the first fire, and had lain there nearly three days. I had noticed him the first. I and another soldier started to bury him when the other soldier said, "hold on until I search him."

I said that was no use, as he had been lying there so long he had probably been searched before he got cold. But he kept searching and finally found forty dollars in greenbacks. I then wanted him to divde but he refused to do so. After that I searched every one I helped to bury, but found nothing but a few pocket knives.

We got out of rations during this battle and could not get to our wagons, but the Yankees had four or five days' rations of hard-tack and bacon in their haversacks, and we would get them from the dead. I was so hungry that I have cut the blood of from crackers and eaten them."

FOUR YEARS UNDER MARSE ROBERT by Robert Stiles pub by Pelican Pub. Co. 1998

Pg. 253 10 May, 1864 "One marked feature was that, while fresh troops poured to almost every charge, the same muskets in the hands of the same men met the first attack in the morning and the last at night; and so to was that the men who in the early morning were so full of fight and fun that they leaped upon the breastworks and shouted to the retiring Federals to come a little closer next time, as that did not care to go so far after the clothes and shoes and muskets-were so weary and worn and heavy at night that they could scarcely be roused to meet the charging enemy."

But they carried on, more than mortal men.

FROM HUNTSVILLE TO APPOMMATTOX R.T. Coles History of 4th Alabama Volunteer Infantry C.S.A. Army of Northern Virginia ed by Frank D. Stocker pub by Univ of Tenn. Press 1996

Pg. 221 May 10, 1864 Spottsylvania "...I went over to talk with Colonel Oates. He pointed out to me one of his men who was lying down by a Federal soldier and said: "you see that fellow over there by that wounded Yankee? Well, he has just brought him out of the woods on his back so as to get his boots as soon as he dies."

LEE& JACKSON'S BLOODY TWELTH-Letters of Irby Goodwin Scott First Lieutenant Co. G Putnam Light Infantry Twelth Ga. Vol. Inf. ed. by Johnnie Perry Pearson pub by Univ. Tn. Press 2010

Pg. 166 May 10,1864 Before the Batle of Spottsylvania"...I am needing a pair of pants, but expect get some from the government in a day or two..."

Pg. 167 Epilogue- Irby Scott fell at Spottsylvania-Feb. 15th, 1867 to Mr. Scott (Father), "...I examined the grave & found he had been shot about the right eye the ball coming out back of the head & from appearances his hair seem to be a dark brown he had on a check shirt & I think blue blouse coat he had on brown pants nor shoes that I could discover his grave was North & South. The head South & I think from all appearances a small man or common size. I put some planks around him & covered up the grave well & put a pen around it so that nothing can get to the grave. You can let me know if I have found the right grave or not. If not I will search again. I forgot to state he was buried about 2 feet deep. Very Respectfully Your Friend, James W. Stewart..."

A MISSISSIPPI REBEL IN THE ARMY OF NORTHERN VIRGINIA-The Civil War Memoirs of Pvt. David Holt ed by Thomas D. Cockrell & Michael B. Ballard pub by La. State Univ. Press 1995

Pg. 265 May 10 1864, Spottsylvania; "...We had no way of washing our clothes. When they got dry ehough to brush, we knocked off some of the dirt with a stick. Human gore and

Virginia red clay do not make a pleasant mixture to have on one's clothes, but we had to stand it and not grumble…"

Imagine what these soldiers smelled like when it rained.

NO SOAP, NO PAY, DIARRHEA, DYSENTERY & DESERTION ed by Jeff Toalson pub by iUniverse Inc. 2006

Pg. 115 May 10-12 Near Spottsylvania C.H., Virginia Capt. D.S. Dunlop, McGowan's South Carolina Sharpshooters; "…Our rations were scant and sometimes unsavory…I devoured the hindquarters of a muskrat with vindictive relish. One day during the fight at Spottsylvania…I discovered in a little branch a turtle of the loggerhead variety…I threw him out of the water with my sword, turned him on his back…and popped my saber through his neck and pinned him to the ground…such a stew I had that night…"

OK, I doubt it was a loggerhead turtle, as they are sea turtles, but this was a fortunate find for the Capt.

HANDLEY LIBRARY ARCHIVES, WINCHESTER, VA Diary of James McCown Co. K 5th Va. Volunteer Infantry Stonewall Brigade after Battle of the Wilderness ".

May 11 1864-I went over the field of yesterday and it is an awful sight. The dead and wounded lie thick. The field is covered with the things left by Yankees in their retreat, many of our boys supplied themselves with blankets, boots, paper and envelopes…"

PARKER'S VIRGINIA BATTERY by Robert K. Krick pub by Va. Book Co. 1975

Pg. 249 May 13th, 1864 Battle of Wilderness-"…Captain Parker saw the last of the enemy skirmishers jump from cover and run when the Southern advance approached them. The captain quickly "gave some of my men the hint & they rushed and they rushed forward"—to punish the fleeing enemy? No,.to get "many good spoils." Most of the first corps proceded to indulge in an orgy of looting. An artillerist from the battery adjoining Parker's watched while his comrades crossed the battlefield in search of "watches, rings, money and hats." He claimed that none of the enemy dead were stripped of their clothes, which was quite contrary to the usual custom of the poorly clad Confederates. The reason for this deviation from the norm was probably that the corpses were as much as a week old and were, as Captain Parkwer observed, "very offensive."…"

I guess there are limits.

A TRUE HISTORY OF COMPANY I, 49TH REGIMENT NORTH CAROLINA TROOPS by W.A. Day Printed At The Enterprise Job Office 1893

Pg. 65 May 13th 1864 "We were now nearly surrounded, only one place left to retreat through and that was across a swamp. After the enemy was repulsed we were ordered to fall back at once, carrying off our wounded and leaving our dead on the field. We moved off across the swamp knee-deep in mud. Both of my shoe-strings broke and left my shoes sticking in the mud. I could not think of leaving my shoes, so I got down on my knees and ran my arm down in my tracks and pulled them out and carried them in my hand until the Regiment halted, then sat down and put them on…"

CHARLOTTE'S BOYS-Civil War Letters of the Branch Family of Savannah ed by Muarel Phillips Joslyn pub by Rockbridge Pub. Co. 1996

Pg. 224 1 Lt. Hamilton Branch to Charlotte Branch May 13, 1864 Bivouac Walker's division near Calhoun, Geo. My Very dear Mother "…I was sleeping on and covering with one blanket viz. Sam Douses who was sleeping with me or rather I with him as I have not seen my blanket since we started to march as I put it in Genl. Mercer's wagon and that has not been seen since. The rest of my baggage was put into the officer's wagon also and that has not been seen since, so that I now only carry my sword, sash, haversack and canteen, My cloths are very dirty as we have been marching for the last week on very dusty roads and I have not been able to change my cloths.

Mother, I do not know but that you had better send me some cloths, that is send then to Mrs. (M.E.) Robison. I mean under cloths. You might also send my dark uniform and then if I get where I can wear them I can send to her for them…"

Pg. 235 1 Lt. Hamilton Branch to Charlotte Branch May 29/64 In the trenches near New Hope Church Walker's Division My dear Mother "…Fred Hull has told me he has the bundle for me. The under cloths are much needed as I have not changed mine in three weeks…"

THE BROTHERS WAR ed by Annette Tapert pub by Vintage Books, 1988

Pg. 198 Eugene Blackford,Major Headquarters, 5th Alabama Volunter Infantry,In line of battle near Spottsylvania C.H. Va. May 14, 1864 "…one evening last week, we were lying in reserve behind our front lines, when it gave way, letting the drunken villains in our works. We went forward with ayell, and drove them out at the point of the bayonet, when we came up to one of our batteries which the Yankees had taken for the moment. Some of them were working the guns furiously, firing them upon their own retreating troops. When ordered to stop, they refused, saying they wanted to kill some of the rascals, which we let them do to their hearts' content as we did not understand the working of the guns, and they did...."

I wonder why they were firing on their own troops? I mean, yes, let them continue, theyr'e showing good taste.

THE BATTLE OF NEW MARKET by William C. Davis pub by Doubleday & Co. 1875

May 14, 1864 "...Here was something new to the tired old veterans resting about town, a Company of boys nattily dressed in neat gray uniforms, all carrying the same kind of weapon and marching precisely to the even beat of the drummers. This was an organization and uniformity that Confederate units has not known since 1861. As a result, the corps became an item of some curiousity and derision..."

HANDLEY LIBRARY ARCHIVES

James A. Miller Collection correspondence C.W. era misc. New Market, Va.
Pg. 41 The last reference to drab uniforms is found in the Shanandoah Valley at the Virginia Miltary Institute. A former cadet, John S. Wise, gave an account in 1889 of what the corps wore on May 15, 1864, at the Battle of New Market. The cadets, having worn out their peacetime uniforms in Jackson's Valley Campaign of 1862, were, by this time compelled to use plainer garb and, in Mr. Wise's own words, "we had to resort to coarse sheep's-grey jacket(s) and trousers, with seven buttons and a plain black tape stripe...We were content with a simple forage cap, blue or grey, as we could procure it. The cadet of today disports himself in white cross-belts, shining plates and patent leather accouterments. Then we had a plain leather cartridge-box and a waist belt with a harness buckle... Then, we went into the Battle of New Market with muzzle-loading Belgian rifles clumsy as pickaxes..."

Where are all these Belgium muskets coming from? Already this study has accounted for more than were probably ever produced, let alone run through the blockade.

STONEWALL JACKSON'S FOOT CAVALRY-Company A, 13th Virginia Infantry by Walbrook D. swank Col. U.S.A.F (Ret) pub by Burd Street Press 2001

Pg.47 May 15, 1864 "...Newman only stayed a short time as round shot and shell were coming over all the time and I was afraid he might get hurt. I found out afterwards that he started from home with a lot of clothes, which he lost. Morris Newman found them and carried them back home. The reason he did not give them to Newman, was that he and Newman fell out. Old man Morris wanted to go one way and Newman wanted to go another, so they parted and Newman lost my clothes and Morris found them and would not give them to me. I needed them very much as crawling through the bushes finally tore my pants in two...."

Pg. 53 May 22,1864 "...We got up before sunrise and went to the railroad. We found a cattle stop full of water and pulled off all my clothes and changed from skin for the first time since leaving Sommerville's Ford where I changed on 1 May...We went up the North Anna leaving men as we moved until we reached those posted last night. As our company was not needed, we went on reserve near an old house. We found there a splendid spring of nice, clear, cold water as good as any in Orange Country. I took my dirty clothes and washed them clean in the spring branch. We were very uneasy for fear we would have to move before our clothes dried. Some crows had a nest in the pines and Garnett and some others got the young ones and ate them.I did not try them..."

Now the Rebs are eating baby crows.

U. S. ARMY HERITAGE AND EDUCATION CENTER

May 16, 1864 John H. Kiracafe 18th Virginia Cavalry Regiment Camp near New Market Dear Wife: (regarding the Battle of New Market) "...I captured one prisoner, his horse and all that was on him consisting of #1 saddle, bridle, halter, two wool blankets, new gum cloth and a number of other things..."

Quite a fortunate capture.

JAMES MADISON UNIVERSITY ARCHIVES

Diary of unidentified woman in the Shenanndoah Valley May 16, 1864 "...Have been fixing Hugh to go into service made him a needle case and haversack, he went to Morven this evening after a knapsack Uncle Jerry gave him...The soldiers are gone, one was a very handsome boy apparently not more than seventeen or eighteen, he wore a beautiful red plume in his cap..."

MEADE'S HEADQUARTERS 1863-1865: Letters of Colonel Theodore Lyman from the Wilderness to Appomattox George R. Agassiz ed. pub by Atlantic Monthly Press 1922

Pg. 370 May 20 1864 "...I heard someone say, "Sir, this is General Johnson." I turned around and there was the captured Major-General, walking slowly up. He was a strongly built man of a strong and rather bad face, and was dressed in a double-breasted blue coat, high riding boots and a very bad felt hat…"

CIVIL WAR LETTERS OF CAPTAIN A.B. MULLIGAN,Co. B, 5th South Carolina Cavalry-Butler's Division-Hampton's Corps 1861-1865 by OlinFulmer Hutchinson,Jr. pub by The Reprint Co. 1992

Pg. 120 May 20, 1864 near Richmond, Va. My Very Dear Mother and Sisters, "I wish I had my trunk from home and had a few things from home but I find out the less I have with me here the better. I bought the most convenient little cooking untensil at Richmond that you ever saw. It is a frying pan, a plate so arranged that I can strap it to my saddle and carry it without any inconvenience. I can cook my rice in it too."

Pg. 121 May 29th, 1864 Near Atley's Station 10 miles North of Richmond My Very Dear Mother and Sisters, "…I have ordered Simon my boy to take my trunk, mess chest & cooking utensils &c to either the South Carolina Soldiers Home or the Spotswood Hotel in Richmond & deposit them there for me & to take a recpt for them & he to take my horse & come to me & keep with me in camp. Could you use Simon at home to advantages?"

Simon seems to be very responsible servant.

CIVIL WAR MARRIAGE IN VIRGINIA REMINISCENCES AND LETTERS pub by Carr Pub. Co. 1956

May 25 1864 My Dear Wife … "…Bring my blue pants and all necessary underclothing for me; I brought nothing from the army…" after being wounded, he is somewhere around Harrisonburg, Va.

LETTERS TO AMANDA-The Civil War letters OF Marion Hill Fitzpatrick, Army of Northern Virginia ed by Jeffery C. Lowe & Sam Hodges pub by Mercer Univ. Press 1998

Pg. 148 May 26, 1864 Near Hanover Junction, Va. (Letter No.72) Dear Amanda, "…I shaved yesterday and took off all my whiskers which helped my feelings. If I had the chance to wash the shirt and drawers I have on I would feel much better. I have a clean shirt and pair of drawers along but did not want to put them on unless I could wash these I have on, for they would be too heavy to carry with so much mud on them…My messmate Drew and I have a Yankee tent which we stretch and it does us much good. The boys have got a good many Yankee tricks off the battle fields, some of which are very valuable. I have not found much yet. I got a good blanket and threw away my old one, and a good new haversack in the place of my old one, and a splendid pockette bible, and a small looking glass, and my tent, and a cup, and some buttons. These Yankee tents are very light, and button together so that one man can carry one piece and another man the other piece. Three men can sleep under one of them very well. The one I got is right new and I would not take a pretty for it, especially if I live to go into Camps again…"

Ok, imagine the ethical implications of looting a bible off of a dead enemy.

A MARYLAND BOY IN LEE'S ARMY by George Wilson Booth pub by Univ. of Nebraska Press 2000

Pg. 113 May 26, 1864 Hanover Courthouse Va. Taking prisoners "…They through down their arms, and we found them to be New Jersymen, whose brigade had just moved off, which we also proceded to do in a reverse direction, bringing our prisoners with us. After getting them up the road some distance, Dixie asked if he could go through them. To "go through" in army parliance ment to conduct a searching examination, more particularly devoted to the taking of an accurate inventory of personal effects and belongings. I authorized Dixie to go ahead, and he relieved one of the men of a silver watch, which he asserted was especially valuable to him as the gift of a sister, and appealed to me strongly not to let the little chap despoil him in this way. I explained to him that there was little prospect of his success in holding on to his property, as when we turned him over to the provost guard it was more than likely it would be taken from him, and as Dixie had captured him he was certainly better entitled to the plunder, and refused to interfere. As Dixie turned over the contents of their knapsacks there appeared a pair of army trousers, new and apparently never worn. These took my eye and I offered to purchase, asking the fellow what they were worth. He said they had just been issued to him, and the government price was something like $3. This amount I turned over to him in Confederate currency and in turn took the breeches. He seemed willing to the bargain, but it was really an enforced transaction…"

That Yankee was lucky to get anything at all for those pants, they would have been taken from him farther in the rear.

THE CONFEDERATE LETTERS OF BENJAMIN H. FREEMAN compiled & edited by Stuart T. Wright pub by Exposition Press 1974

Pg. 39 May the 26th? 1864 We are near Chancellorsville In the line of Battle My Dear Farther, Mother, Sisters: "…We are now in line of Battle in a Barn(?) ever since the fourth of May some parts of our army has been fighting ever since the fourth. Ma I should like to be at home to get salid and such like. I am mending a piece of pants…"

LETTERS FROM LEE'S ARMY Compiled by Susan Leigh Blackford Annotated by her Husband, Charles Minor Blackford, Charles pub by Scribner's & Sons 1947 Company B of the Second Virginia Cavalry- Charles Blackford was first Lieutenant, later Captain.

Pg. 249 Near Richmond, May 28th, 1864 "I am in want of a pair of pantaloons; I wish you would tax your ingenuity to get them for me. I want you also, to get that Mr. Seay, who lives in the alley which comes up from Main Street by the Washington Hotel (Lynchburg) to make me a pair of shoes. He has my measure and he can make them out of the pieces of leather you have. The sole leather is at Father's. See that the leather is returned as soon as the shoes get cut, for when that is gone, I do not know where I will get more."

Is there anyone still tanning leather? Or is the demand so great, even with the English shoes running through the blockade that leather is scarce enough to be hoarded as though it were gold?

VOICES FROM COMPANY D Diaries by the Greensboro Guards, Fifth Alabama Infantry Regiment, Army of Northern Virginia ed. by G. Ward Hubbs pub by Univ. of Georgia Press 2003

Pg. 281 May 28 1864 JP in Hospital"...Took a bath to-day-cold-& put on a fresh suit of hosp. clothes-feeling much better after having done so..."

Hospital clothes would be a cotton shirt and pair of drawers.

MEMOIR OF JAMES JOSEPH WILLIAMSON in Mosby's Rangers by Ralph B. Kenyon 1896

Pg. 23 "...Wagons and supplies were destroyed, though of course the men were allowed to appropriate anything before destroying the captured stores....

It has been charged that "Mosby's Men" went in the diguise of Federal soldiers. Such was not the case. They never masqueraded in the uniforms of Federals, except that through force of circumstances men at times wore blue overcoats captured by them from the federal cavalry. This was done because they could get no others. The Confederate Government did not, or could not at all times provide proper clothing, and our soldiers were compelled to wear these to protect themselves from the cold. Rubber blankets were common to both armies and when one was worn it completely hid the uniform...."

A good justification of the use of Yankee uniforms, but this didn't reduce the anger and frustration of the Union commanders and men who were fooled by it.

Pg. 210 1864 after the Berryville Raid "...The bright new captured uniforms of the Federal officers transformed our dusty rebel boys for the time into the holiday soldiers of peaceful days, and the citizens along our route, though well used to raids and the passing of armies through the country, gazed on the scene in mute astonishment, seemingly at a loss whether to stand or run on the approach of the cavalcade..."

THROUGH SOME EVENTFUL YEARS -Diary of Susan Bradford Eppes pub by Press of the J.W. Burke Co. 1926

Pg. 378 June 1864 "...Mrs. Manning, Aunt Robison and I have been busy packing a large box of clothing to be sent tomorrow to the army of Northern Virginia..."

DIARY OF A LINE OFFICER by Augustus Cleveland Brown Privately Pub. 1906

Pg. 66 June 1864 "...A flag of truce was sent out and the body of Col. McMahon, of the 164th N.Y. among others killed on the 3rd, was recovered. His features were not recognizeable, his pockets were rifled and the buttons were cut from his uniform..."

Seriously, at this point in the war, this should have gone without comment.

A CONFEDERATE SURGEON'S LETTERS TO HIS WIFE Spencer Glascow Welch, Surgeon Thirteenth S. Ca. Vols., McGowans Brigade pub by Neale Pub. Co. 1911

Pg 99 Between Chickahominy and Pamunky Rivers, Va. June 1, 1864 "I was glad to know that you have the wool for my suit. I was proud of my old brown suit of last winter, but when I get a Confederate gray, I shall be proud of it, sure enough. I have not drawn any money since last January, but as soon as I do I will replenish your purse. I should like so much to see your catskin shoes."

Again, he spells it "catskin shoes." I know as I've seen it twice now. I hope none of you readers will attempt this, but, if you do, let me know the results.

HAM CHAMBERLAYNE-VIRGINIAN Letters and Papers of an Artillery Officer in the War for Independence 1861-1865 with introduction, notes and index by his Son C.G.Chamberlayne Richmond, Va. pub by Press of the Dietz Printing Co. Publishers 1932

Pg. 225 J.H. Chamberlayne to M.B. Chamberlayne In front of Meadow Bridge 3 miles-near Gardener's & Col. Shelton's June 2nd, 1864 My dear Mother, "...Please ask Mr. Kerr or Col. Broun to save me a haversack, such as one of those made by Ord Dept.-so that I can get it, whenever I get in. You see they are in such demand I wd. have to get apply early in the morning to obtain one, while an Ord. officer could get one with no difficulty. Mine is borrowed & I wish to return it..."

Now even haversacks are getting scarce!

STONEWALL JACKSON'S FOOT CAVALRY-Company A, 13th Virginia Infantry by Walbrook D. Swank Col. U.S.A.F. (Ret) pub by Burd Street Books 2001

Pg. 60 June 3, 1864 Pvt. George Peyton "...While the skillets were getting hot, I pulled off my clothes and took a bath. I changed my clothes and got Deaton (slave) to wash my dirty ones which I had been wearing since 22 May at Hanover Junction..."

June 5, 1864 "...We commenced running back. I ran down the hill through the woods until my foot hung in a snag and I fell headlong down the hill. My gum blanket flew over my head and I never saw it again. It was a brand new one that I had gotten at Spottsylvania Courthouse..."

June 6, 1864 Whenever the enemy moves, Old Jube (Gen. Early) will not be satisfied until he finds out where he has gone, so he keeps us on the run until he finds them. He doesn't know that I have no shoes and but little breeches, torn from pocket to bottom..."

June 8, 1864 word passed along that one man in every 10 would be allowed to go to the creek and wash his clothes. I suppose they thought the other nine could "go so." A large number took advantage of the chance to part company with a good deal of mother earth and also a few insects..."

June 9, 1864 "...Our brigade gave one day's rations to the poor of Richmond, but if rags, barefeet, hunger and no money indicate poverty this army is the poorest set this side of eternity. Today I had to "skew" up both my pants legs which were torn from top to bottom..."

June 11, 1864 "…Last night, since leaving Sommerville's Ford, we did not get orders to be ready to move at 3 a.m. tomorrow. We stayed quiet in camp all day. I put on my clean clothes and washed my soiled ones, but I had no soap. They have not given us any soap for a sometime.I walked up to a house where General Gordon had his headquarters. I got a piece of wire off a wheat fan to put a handle (or bail, rather) on my cup…They gave out one pair of shoes and one pair of pants. My pants were the worst in the company but having sewn them up, the other fellow got the new ones and deserted this evening…" *Bummer!*

June 17, 1864 "…We stopped an hour in Charlettsville (Va). I saw Uncle Lew, my father's youngest brother. I was so dirty and ragged that he did not know who I was…"

This soldier and the rest of Co. A were ragged Rebels. Imagine losing the only new pair of pants issued and the jerk deserts that night! Hanging's too good for him! Imagine being so dirty and ragged your own uncle doesn't recognize you!

MEADE'S HEADQUARTERS 1863-1865: Letters of Colonel Theodore Lyman from the Wilderness to Appomattox George R. Agassiz ed. pub by Atlantic Monthly Press 1922

Pg. 370 June 5 1864 "…On the road stood a couple of Rebel officers, each in his grey overcoat, and, just behind, were grouped some twenty soldiers-the most gipsy-looking fellows imaginable, in their blue-grey jackets and slouched hats; each with his rusty musket and well-filled cartridge box…"

TRUE TALES OF THE SOUTH AT WAR-How Soldiers fought and Families Lived, 1861-1865 Collected and Ed. by Clarence Poe, pub by Univ. N.C. Press1961

Pg. 130 June 5, 1864 Reminiscences of Barry Benson "…Grant has been taught such a severe lesson by Lee and his ragged Rebels that he is the most cautious man to be found…"

Pg. 87 Colonel L.L. Polk's Wartime Letters Gen. Early's raid on Wash. D.C. "June 9, 1864 We have slept on the same ground three nights for the first time since April 14. I have not pulled off my clothes to sleep since that time and over half the time I sleep with my boots on. The pants are threadbare and torn, drawers ditto. I have on the same suit and have worn no other-no change for two monthes. Where I find we will rest for an hour or two, I do without my undershirt until I can wash it out. But there is one thing about it, I find myself the tip of fashion with at least 10,000 Confederates for they are often worse off than myself. For an officer to be ragged and almost barefoot and dirty excites no remark…"

SOUTHERN INVINCIBILITY Wiley Sword St. Martin's Press 1999

Pg. 234 Lt. B.T. Cotton, Army of Northern Virginia June 11 1864 "(I) have not changed clothes but once since the 1st of May…We are all very dirty…but in tolerable good spirits and confident of success whenever Grant sees fit to charge our works…"

V.M.I. MS #282

June 15 1864 Camp at Rosswe's Ferry "…Jane kindly lent me a blanket as I had nothing but a very small one with me and the weather here now is as cold as it is seen in November. I would very much like to have my coat, as I am in my shirt sleeves. Send it to me if you can…"

NO SOAP, NO PAY, DIARREHA, DYSENTERY & DESERTION by Jeff Yoalson oub by iUnivers Inc. 2006

Pg 151 June 16, 1864 Knight's farm, Drury's Bluff, Virginia Pvt. James M. Rawlings, Rockbridge Artillery; "…I…finally succeeded in drawing a pair of shoes nearly 3 inches too long for me…"

FOUR YEARS IN THE CONFEDERATE ARTILLERY-The Diary of Pvt. Henry Robinson Berkely ed. by William H. Runge pub by Univ. N.C. Press 1961

Pg. 83 June 17 1864 We passed through Charlottesville (Va.). I saw Miss Mattie Jones, but did not speak to her, because I was so very ragged and dirty…"

LETTERS OF A NEW MARKET CADET by Beverly Stanard ed by John G. Barrett & Robert K. Turner Pub by Univ. of N.C. Press 1961

Pg. 32 June 17th, 1864 V.M.I. Dear Mother: "…Mother to give you an idea of what sort of man Gen. S(mith) is- after our return from our last march, The Government sent up 300 pairs of shoes for the cadets as presents, or to pay for our own that we wore out and now Gen. S(mith) will not let a cadet have a pair if he has gotten shoes from the Institute within the last 6 months, and if a cadet is shipped before he can get them, they fall into Specs hands who furnishes all his darkeys with a good pair. I shall try hard to get mine, tho' I don't expect to wear them, they are coarse army shoes. Worth at the present prices 30 or 40 dollars. I have a pair I bought before I went on the march that will do me, so I shall keep mine (if I get them) for Henry, unless he is well supplied…"

LEE'S LIEUTENANTS Douglas Southhall Freeman Charles Schribner's & Sons volII

Pg. 537 Petersburg, June 18, 1864 "…Hill's Corps marched through the city to take position on the line. One woman wrote that night in her diary:"…what regiment should come first but our own gallant Twelth Virginia-but oh! So worn with travel and fighting, so dusty and ragged, their faces so thin and drawn by privation that we scarcely knew them."

Pg. 559 June, 1864 Early's advance from the Valley "…Another condition that might impare efficiency was the fact that about half of the infantry, including even company officers, were without shoes. That was no hardship, so far as the weather was involved, but experience in 1862 had demonstrated what injury the stone roads North of the Potomac would do to the feet of unshod men…"

One limiting factor on all three invasions of the north was the unavailability of shoes.

Pg. 553 summer 1864 William "Extra Billy" Smith "…In garb he put comfort above convention. One comrade wrote of him: On a certain hot summer's day that I recall he was seen, a Major General indeed, but wonderfully accoutered! A plaited brown linen jacket, buttoned to trousers of same material, like a boy's; topped off by a large Panama hat of the finest and most beautiful texture, met our eyes, and I must say he looked decidedly comfortable."

Jacket buttoned to trouser? Sounds damn awkward to me.

NO SOAP, NO PAY, DIARRHEA, DYSENTERY & DESERTION ed by Jeff Toalson pub by iUniverse Inc. 2006

Pg. 152 June 19, 1864 Near Dunn's Hill, Petersburg, Virginia Pvt. John Walters, Nofolk Light Artillery; "…I went in town last night under the friendly cover of darkness. I could not face the daylight as my clothes are rather dilapidated and owing to the scarcity of soap not as clean as I should wish them…"

Sounds as though Pvt. Walters could use a new uniform more than soap.

Pg. 152 June 19, 1864 Near Drury's Bluff, Virginia Cpl. Benjamin H, Freeman, Co. K, 44th North Carolina Infantry; '…I washed and put on a clean shirt and draws Today the first time since about the second of May. I threw away the ones I pulled off…I drew on the 17th a pere of draws and a shirt…"

Notice the Corporal threw away the shirt and drawers he "pulled" off. They probably weren't worth washing anyway. (kinda gives a vivid mental picture when he says "pulled off" those clothes after wearing them in the summer for over a month, doesn't it?)

LETTERS FROM LEE'S ARMY Compiled by Susan Leigh Blackford Annotated by her Husband, Charles Minor Blackford, pub by Charles Scribner's & Sons 1947 Company B of the Second Virginia Cavalry- Charles Blackford was first lieutenant, later captain.

Pg. 262 June 21st, 1864 Lynchburg, as Gen. Hunter advances "...General Breckenridge, with some troops, got here on Wednesday night, and we saw them passing out West (now Fifth) Street, it was a most reassuring sight, and never were a lot of bronzed and dirty looking veterans, many of them barefooted, more heartily welcomed..."

Notice all of these recent quotes speak of the Rebels as ragged and shoeless.

LETTERS TO AMANDA-The Civil War Letters of Marion Hill Fitzpatrick, Army of Northern Virginia ed by Jeffery C. Lowe & San Hodges pub by Mercer Univ Press 1998

Pg. 155 June 23, 1864 Jackson Hospital, 3rd Div. Ward (G) (Letter no 76) Dear Amanda, "...I have a shirt and pr of drawers, and my coat and pants washed by the Government since I came here and my clothes are in very good condition now. I have the two shirts and two pr drawers you sent me yet and I shall swing to them late. I have the pants also and only 1 pr. which is all I want. My coat is wearing out, pretty badly. I shall patch it up the first chance I get and try to make it last till the first of next winter when I hope to get a furlough and go home and get my new one. I have three pairs of good socks yet..."

RECOLLECTIONS AND LETTERS OF GENERAL ROBERT E. LEE by His Son Capt. Robert E. Lee pub by Garden City Pub Co.1926

Pg. 132 June 24, 1864 Camp Petersburg "...The ladies of Petersburg have sent a nice set of shirts. They were given to me by Mrs. James R. Branch and her mother, Mrs. Thomas Branch. In fact, they have given me everything, which I fear they cannot spare—vegetables, bread, milk, ice cream. Today one of them sent me a nice peach—the first one I think I have seen for two years..."

Everyone loves you, General Lee!

NO SOAP, NO PAY, DIARRHEA, DYSENTERY& DESERTION A Composite History of the Last 16 Monthes of the Confederacy Jeff Toalson, ed. pub by iUniverse Inc.2006

Pg. 159 June 25, 1864 Near Lexington Va. Dr. Thomas F. Wood 3rd N.C. Inf "… Opportunities for bathing of the most superficial sort were very limited and very few…(few soldiers) had any other clothing than what we had on. A pair of socks had to be taken off, and washed while the owner went barefooted until they dried…many of (the men) went a month without washing…"

THE HISTORY OF A BRIGADE OF SOUTH CAROLINIANS FIRST KNOWN AS "GREGGS AND SUBSEQUENTLY AS McGOWAN'S BRIGADE by J.F.J. Caldwell-lately an officer of Co. B 1st Regiment South Carolina Volunteers pub by Morningside Press 1866

Pg. 213 late June 1864 "…Our health was very bad. The constant exposure to sun and rain, the rancid bacon and half-raw corn bread that were issued us, the filth necessarily accompanying the scarcity of clothing, and the lack of opportunity for bathing or washing our clothes, the vile water of this section of country, &tc…"

Gee, this should be a recruiting poster!

CONFEDERATE VETERAN Nash. Tn. Vol.XX April 1912

Pg. 157 summer 1864 Confederate Grey Uniform Roanoke Va. News "…Towards the last the confederate soldiers wore anything they could get to cover them, whatever they could buy or pick up or capture from the enemy. Probably the clothing in most general use in the ranks was butternut homespun dyed at home with butternut or walnut shells…"

Another good anology by someone who was there.

A PAIR OF BLANKETS War-Time History in Letters to the Young People of the South by William H. Stewart pub by Broadfoot Pub. Co. 1911

Pg 195 Petersburg,Summer 1864 "…We wre shocked at the condition, the complexion, the expression of the men, and of the officers, too, even the field officers; indeed, we could scarcely realize that the unwashed, uncombed, unfed and almost unclad creatures we saw were officers of rank and reputation in the army. It was a great pleasure, too, to note these gallant fellows, looking up and coming out, under the vastly improved conditions which they found themselves.

I cannot allow unchallenged the "unwashed and uncombed" to apply to Mahone's brigade, although we were quite worn to a frazzle and looked forlorn, we certainly washed our faces and combed our hair every day when not actually fighting in line of battle; although our clothes were thin and our stomachs empty, we stood up to the end, and surrendered in closed ranks with loaded rifles at Appomattox.

When time permitted and a stream of water was near, our soldiers would strip their shirts from their backs, wash them and wait for them to dry in the sun to put them on again, as they had no other in the wardrobe; then you may understand that fighting in the trenches down in the earth day and night made their clothes stiff with stains and dirt hard to remove..."

How could these men do any laundry at all in those conditions?

THE CIVIL WAR CATALOG

"...In the summer of 1864, (Petersburg, August) one Confederate soldier likened a walk through camp to a stroll through an ash heap. "Ones mouth would be so full of dust that you do not want your teeth to touch one another." A canoneer wryly remarked that whenever a grasshopper jumped up, it raised such a dust that the Union lookouts reported that the Confederate forces were on the move again.

The dust blew through holes in their worn clothing and caked to the sweat on their bodies. "I have no seat in my pants," lamented a Virginia Rebel soldier, "the legs are worn out completely, my shirt is literally rotted off me." A new issue shirt proved to be so louse-ridden that he could not bear to wear it."

More joys of a soldier's life.

THE STORY OF A CONFEDRATE BOYIN THE CIVIL WAR-David E. Johnson of the 7th Virginia Infantry Regiment pub by Commonwealth Press 1914

Summer, 1864 "A musket, cartridge box with forty rounds of cartridges, cloth haversack, blanket and canteen made up the Confederate soldier's equipment. No man was allowed a change of clothing, nor could he have carried it. A gray cap, jacket, trousers and colored shirt-calico mostly-made up a private's wardrobe. When a clean shirt became necessary, we took off the soiled one, went to the water, usually without soap, gave it a little rubbing, and if the sun was shinning, hung the shirt on a bush to dry, while the wearer sought the shade to give the shirt a chance. The method of carrying our few assets was to roll them in a blanket, tying each end end of the roll, which was then swung over the shoulder. At night this blanket was unrolled and wrapped around its owner, who found a place on the ground with his cartridge box for a pillow. We cooked but little, having usually little to cook. The frying pan was in use, if we had one…"

FRENCH HARDING Civil War Memoirs ed. by Victor L. Thacker pub by McClain Printing Co. Inc., Parsons W.Va. 2001

Pg. 156 Summer 1864 Valley Campaign "…Moving on I discovered, at the place where these men (Yankees) had mounted, a considerable quantity of food and forage, and a number of the finest India rubber blankets I had ever seen…"

An absolute Godsend!

THE GUILFORD GRAYS Co. B 27th North Carolina Regiment by John A. Sloan pub by R.O. Polkinhorn Printer 1883

Pg. 92 summer 1864 "…On these long marches, to prevent straggling, we are frequently halted for a rest, and this opportunity is taken by those who have fallen back to catch up with their commands. Any one passing through the troops at this time, be he officer or private, had to run the gauntlet of the gibes and witticisms of the men. On one occasion, while thus resting, a very tall, lean, lank soldier of the 5th "Georgy Regiment," appeared in the road, dragging along his weary length. His long black tousled hair hung in uncombed ringlets from the holes in his rimless hat; his coat or jacket, a very scant pattern of gray jeans, seemed to be widely at variance with his copperas-colored breeches, as the leather strings attached to them by thorns, to serve as "gallasses," failed to effect a compromise between the two; the pants, from his oft-repeated restings, had been baldly attacked and routed in the rear, and, from long use, had "swunk up" in apparent fright from his sockless pedal extremities, whose coverings of untanned leather were held together by a withe as a shoe-string. In form, and stature, he was modeled strictly after the heron. His avoirdupois gave evidence of unswerving observance of forty days' Lenten season, and that in soul and body he had, and was now, wrestling with that plague incident and concomitant to the experience of every soldier, called the "dia-ree."…"

There, Folks, is the Rebel soldier in 1864!

FIFTH VIRGINIA INFANTRY Va. Regimental History Series by Lee A. Wallace Jr. 1988

Pg. 62 summer 1864 inspection of Terry's brigade, numbering 710 men "…Terry's Brigade was well armed with Enfield rifles, and the greatest deficiencies in the brigade, noted by the inspector, were in bayonet scabbards and shoulder belts for cartridge boxes. Other deficiencies he noted were: 103 coats, 120 trousers, 167 shirts, 179 drawers, 69 pairs of shoes, 3 caps, 33 haversacks, 45 knapsacks, and 20 canteens...."

In other words, deficiencies in everything.

A LETTER FROM CHARLES EDWARD JORDAN TO HIS FAMILY AND FRIENDS Library of the Univ. of Va. 1952

Pg. 31 summer, 1864 Greenwich Va. "...As these various camps were abandoned (Federal camps), many articles of clothing, etc. were left behind, and the women and children made haste to recover anything of use.All kinds of clothing, ponchos, belts, cartridges, etc. The blue uniforms were dyed with walnut shells and made over for the use of the family. The boys eagerly searched the camps for cartridges to use in hunting. The cartridges were of paper at that time, so we emptied the powder, and filled our flasks which were made of cow's horns. The bullets were hammered flat and cut into slugs until we finally invented a way to mold shot by using perforated hot iron bars. Then we had better ammunition..."

These were some ingenious little boys, do you think modern boys would do as well?

The Story Of A Canoneer Under Stonewall Jackson-Rockbridge Artillery by Edward Moore pub by Neale Pub. Co. 1907

Pg. 265 Petersburg, Summer, 1864 "During our stay at Fort Gilmore a company of Reserves from Richmond took the place of the regular infantry. They were venerable-looking old gentlemen- lawyers, businessmen, etc., dressed in citizen's clothes..."

Website-ACWS Archives-Confederates in Blue "English Army Cloith" in the A.N.V.

Pg. 2 "By the summer of 1864 the Richmond Depot was becoming vituallty reliant on this imported English kersey for uniforms, even though some smaller quantities of jeans, cassimere and kersey were still being produced by domestic sources.

By the time of General Grant's arrival at the gates of Petersburg, A.N.V. uniforms were largely made of the blue-gray kersey. In the last half of 1864 up to the war's end, upwards of 75,000 jackets and tens of thousands of pairs of trousers were made of this cloth.

A surviving quartermaster's book records the arrival of 4,400 jackets and trousers on December 29, 1864 as part of the Collie and Tait contract.

As both the Tait jackets and trousers and the Richmond Depot Type III jackets were the final uniforms issued to the Army of Northrn Virginia, both were made of blue-gray kersey, it was probably the only time the A.N.V. ever achieved any kind of uniformity-in color at least."

Yeah, the color of the dirt from the trenches. As mentioned before, these clothes didn't last long in the trenches.

The Young Lions-Confederate Cadets at War by James Lee Conrad pub. by Stackpole Books 1997

Pg.65 Summer 1864 "Cloth was also at a premium, and cadets at V.M.I. were required to furnish their own, much of it homespun, to be made into unifiorms. (Commandant) Smith tried to obtain obtain cloth from the army, but with little success. When some was finally acquired, it was issued only to those who never had a "regulation" uniform. The Citadel (SC) was so starved for cloth that when a Charleston merchant helped to locate a supply, he promptly received the official thanks of the board of visitors. Colonel Garland also had problems clothing his cadets. He was forced to use curtains and sheets to line their jackets and trousers, which had been made with the limited supply of cloth available. To ensure an ample supply of uniform cloth for the university, Garland urged the governor to seize a nearby woolen mill, which was rumored to be the taget of Confederate impressment for the state.

Obtaining shoes for cadets was also a challenge. "General Smith says he cannot and will not furnish us shoes," wrote Cadet Langhorne plaintively to his parents, "and I am nearly barefooted." The colleges procured some footwear by local purchase and through the blockade, or made the shoes themselves. Garland established a cobbler shop at the university, and managed to have an experienced shoemaker detailed from the army to run it. He also bought beef on the hoof so there would be a supply of leather for the shoemaker.

As the year wore on, shortages caused necessary changes to be made in the colleges' heretofore strict uniform regulations. The use of homespun cloth, with its uneven quality and color, changed the uniform cadet gray of the battalions to a hodgepodge of varying shades. When regulation black collar-stocks became hard to obtain, bow ties were substituted. The situation became so bad that Smith was forced to restrict the wear of the practically irreplaceable cadet coatee to only "drill or dress duty."

Pg.68 "Cadets who wished to avoid the practice of foraging and its accompanying risks hunted game in their free time or bartered for food. Uniform items seemed to be a popular medium of exchange with local civilians, and despite the cloth shortage, a V.M.I. cadet reported, "I have seen many a cadet jacket traded off for half a peck of apples; and if a cadet were really hungry, I think he would trade the coat on his back for on apple pie."

Pg. 100 The cadets of G.M.I.(Georgia Military Institute) "…During this time the appearance of the corps changed as resplendent coatees were traded for more plain and practical gray jeans uniforms, and Belgian muskets, canteens, cartridge boxes, and knapsacks were issued. The muskets were huge -69 caliber smooth-bores, and the sixteen-and seventeen-year old soldiers complained loudly about being equipped with such obsolete and inefficient "pumpkin slingers."

Those Belgian muskets again. I know of their inaccuracy, you can barly hit the ground with one, much less a man at any distance. (Say fifty feet, after that no-one knows where the ball goes.)

THE CONFEDERATE VETERAN VOL. IX 1901

Pg. 555 A Wedding Suit In The Sixties by M.L.B. "At the age of sixteen Clifton A. Reid, of this city (Anderson, S.C.) son of the late judge J.P.Reid, volunteered in Co. A, Trenholm's Squadron of cavalry, C.S.A. and served with splendid gallantry until 1864, when he lost his right arm at the battle of Hawe's Shop…While kneeling, and in the act of putting a cartridge into his rifle, a Minnie ball struck his left wrist, making an ugly wound, and then struck the right hand, ranging up through the wrist, shattering the bones of the forearm, requiring its amputation.

The young soldier, thus disabled for further service in the field, came home and at the age of nineteen was married. Seeing this correspondent the other day wearing a suit of homespun jeans, he was moved to describe his wedding suit.He said: "You know it was practically impossible to get anything but homespun in those days, and my old cavalry uniform was ragged, so my mother had woven, by one of the women on the plantation, a beautiful piece of jeans, which she had dyed black. Of this I had made a long-tailed coat and a pair of trousers. I borrowed a white kid glove (poor fellow, he needed only one!) and a white satin vest from Dr. Nardin (himself a distinguished surgeon in the Confederate service), these, with pair of cowhide, homemade boots, constituted my wedding garments."…"

THE CONFEDERATE VETERAN VOL. XII

March, 1899 Sketch of Major Ferguson by Emma Henry Ferguson "In July (1864) about three weeks after the arrival of the writer in England, Maj. Ferguson proposed to send another box to Gen. Lee, and trio of ladies-Mrs. Irvine, the wife of a Scottish manufacturer, and an ardent admirer of Gen. Lee; Lady Florence Eardley, whose mother was a Miss Pope, from Alabama; and Mrs. Ferguson, made up a lavish sum and filled a box with rich and useful articles. It contained a very fine uniform, cavalry boots, gauntlets, and the handsomest Lieutenant General's scarf to be found in London. Also there was cloth to make a uniform for Gen. Longstreet, whose measure he did not have, therefore could not venture upon a makeup.

This box was shipped from Liverpool in August of 1864, and although the blockade had become an almost impossible barrier between the Confederate States and the outside world, the box arrived safely at Wilmington. More remarkable still, the letter to Maj. Ferguson acknowledging its receipt went out safely, and is herewith subjoined:

Petersburg, October 10, 1864

My Dear major: I have delayed thanking you for your letter of July until I could inform you of the safety of the box by Mr. Andrews. I heard of its arrival at Wilmington, but much time elapsed before it reached the careful hands of your brother, Maj. William Ferguson, at Richmond, who kindly distributed the contents.

With my whole heart I thank Lady Eardly, Mrs. Irvine, and Mrs. Ferguson for the useful articles sent me, and beg you to give them my grateful acknowledgements. I know it will give them and you pleasure to learn that Gen. Longstreet has returned to the army, and, though not entirely recovered from his wound, yet I hope sufficiently to resume his duties.

The army appreciates your zealous and self-sacrificing efforts in promoting their comfort, and hail with pleasure the arrival of every cargo you send. May you be able to continue to supply their wants!

I trust your prayers and those of our trans-atlantic friends in our behalf may be heard by our merciful God and answered in his own good time, and may the day not be far distant when you will return to us in peace and happiness!

Very Truly Your Friend and Servant,
R.E.Lee

To Maj. J.B.Ferguson, Confederate States Army

The uniform sent Gen. Lee in the aforesaid box has become historic through two distinct records. The first to chronicle is that he wore it for the first time the day of his surrender to Gen. Grant. An eyewitness of the memorable occasion says: "When the General stepped out of his tent that morning he was dressed in a magnificent new uniform that his staff officers had never before seen, his cavalry boots, gauntelets, and lieutenant general's scarf forming a perfect equipment. He looked as he was, a full-blooded cavalier, a type of high chivalrous manhood, to be remembered by those who beheld him through all time.

When Gen Lee's statue was to be modeled in Paris Mercier, the sculpter, wrote to Richmond, Va. for the uniform he surrendered in to be sent him, so the uniform crossed the Atlantic again, and the equestrian statue on the Lee monument at Viginia's capitol has modeled upon it thefull dress uniform chosen by his friends in England in 1864, a lasting record of devoted adherence to the Confederate cause and personal regard for the mighty chieftain."

The admiration of this man has no limit.

ADVENTURES OF AN ARMY NURSE IN TWO WARS by Mary Phinney, Baroness von Olnhausen pub by Little, Brown & Co. 1903

Pg. 142 July,1864 Plymouth, N.C. "...Our men at Plymouth were all stripped, and in an hour every Rebel was dressed in our uniform..."

C'mon, lady! What do you expect?

UNDER BOTH FLAGS- Personal Stories of Sacrifice and Struggle During the Civil War ed by Tim Goff pub b y The Lyons Press 1896

Pg 205 July 1864 Petersburg-The Battle of the Crater by A.M. Davies, Co. C, 34th Virginia..." Danger became such an hourly occurance, that its presence made it jocular with the soldiers. When a broadside would issue from a Federal battery, and the heavy missiles come hurtiling toward our works, the cry, "more bread," would go up from the nearby soldiers, which meant as soon as night or a flag of truce allowed, the fragments of metal would be exchanged for fresh bread with the junk dealer and baker from Petersburg; and these loaves were indeed a relief from the monotony of hard-tack and coarse corn-meal, called "grits" and often sour...

Fresh meat was a delicacy along the lines, and while horse-flesh was not on the ration list, yet when an officer's horse was shot down between the breastworks, the soldiers of the South, under the cover of the darkness of night, crept over their works and cut fragments of this flesh bringing the same into camp and hugely enjoying it; so much so that a sick soldier in the hospital, hearing of the occurance the next day, sent a message to his messmate to go out the next night and get him a piece, and to cut it from the "breast" and broil it. (These are the words of a poor fellows semi-delirium.)"

I can imagine eating horse, but this is the first time I've heard of the Petersburg junk dealer and baker.

HANDLEY LIBRARY ARCHIVES- Civil War Diaries of William Tull, 5th & 9th Loiusiana Infantry

July 1864 Petersburg "...I was still dressed in my suit of homespun clothes made by my step-mother at home, and the boys soon dubbed me "Copperas Breeched."...To add to all this great loss in men which was generally the same throughout the entire army, we had ceased to look for any clothing, shoes, hats, or other apparel, from out poor Government....The old, ragged battle-scarred column was always at its best when their bleeding feet were stirred by Martial music..."

Ragged Rebels, but still full of spirit!

DAILY LIFE IN CIVIL WAR AMERICA by Dorothy Dennesen Volo & James M. Volo

Pg. 172 July 1864 "…A Confederate haversack found on the field in 1864 contained "a jack-knife, a plug twist of tobacco, a tin cup, and about two quarts of coarsely cracked corn, with perhaps an ounce of salt tied in a rag."…"

RED CLAY TO RICHMOND by John J. Fox pub by Angls Valley Press 2006

Pg. 267 July 1864 "Moore described the stuation on the battlefield when the soldiers of the ambulance corps found Garrett:

[H]e was brought out to the hospital in the night. [T]he men that brought him off the field said they could not find his knapsack.[The clothes he had on hat, shoes and a Yankee tent was all he had with him. Som[e] person stoled the tent. [I]t was some fellow kowdard (coward) that was playing off lying around the hospital Pertending to be sick and nothing the mater (matter) with him. [T]he hat I have got it with mee yet. [T]he Pocket Book and Ambrotype I sent to you By Capt. John M. Mitchell which I hope you have got by this time…"

Confederates pillaging their own dead.

LETTERS TO AMANDA-The Civil War Letters of Marion Hill Fiztpatrick, Army of Northern Vierginia ed by Jeffery C. Lowe & Sam Hodges pub by Mercer Univ. Press 1998

Pg 156 July 3rd, 1864 Line of Battle Near Petersburg, Va. (Letter No 77) Dear Amanda, "…I mended my coat the other day, cut off the sleeves and it does finely now…"

Pg. 162 July 29th, 1864 Skirmish Line Near Petersburg, Va. (Letter No 80) Dear Amanda, "…I hope you were fortunate with you indigo works and will have some pretty cloth…"

STEPHEN ELLIOTT WELCH OF THE HAMPTON LEGION ed by John Michael Priest pub by Burd Street Press 1994

Pg. 40 Bivouac near Malvern Hill, Va. July 3rd, 1864 Well Dear Mother & Annie "Having had a gun, or pistol pointed at me on several occasions by some of our men I procured a pair of nice gray pantaloons & a pair of fine English shoes, so I am well fitted as to clothing.

While out scouting a pair of dark blue trousers with one of our dark gray jackets is apt to make a man think a Yank was in front of him."

Yes, I can see this, why didn't he try the white armband, or didn't he have any white cloth?

VOICES FROM COMPANY D Diaries by the Greensboro Guards, Fifth Alabama Infantry Regiment, Army of Northern Virginia ed. By G. Ward Hubbs pub by Univ. of Georgia Press 2003

Pg. 297 July 4 1864 HB after chasing Yankees out Of Bolivar Hts (Harper's Ferry, W.Va.). "...Our boys found any quantities of eatables & delicacies such as brandy, whisky, candy, ice cream, cakes etc. They all came out next morning with filled haversacks, besides a quantity of shoes and clothing..."

Was Harper's Ferry destined to be a Rebel supply house during this War?

HAM CHAMBERLAYNE-VIRGINIAN Letters and Papers of an Artillery Officer in the War for Independence 1861-1865 with introduction, notes and index by his Son C.G.Chamberlayne Richmond, Va. pub by Press of the Dietz Printing Co. Publishers 1932

Pg. 232 J.H.Chamberlayne to M.B. Chamberlayne Hd. Qrs. Arty 3d Cops July 6th, 1864 My dear Mother, "...If you have time I wd. like a half dozen collars- ¼ of an inch, or more, larger than Harts-slightly rounded at the points & with the band ¼ inch longer than the other part at each end-to be rolling or turned down collars..."

I cannot believe, with the widespread sartorial destitution, this officer wanted collars! And, was picky about them!

FOOTPRINTS OF A REGIMENT-A Recollection of the First Georgia Regulars 1861-1865 W.H. Andrews, 1st Sergeant, Co. M pub by Longstreet Press 1992

Pg. 144 July 8, 1864 Defences around Charleston Harbor,S.C. "...After everything quieted down a lot of the boys went back into the field where our artillery had played havoc with them on the 7th, finding numbers of their dead, but nothing worth depriving them of. The negroes found out that the troops in front of them were the ones they had fought at Olustee, Fla., and did not carry into the fight as much as a pocket knife. As they were pretty well shod, the boys decided to pull off their shoes and brought them back to the line, but they smelled so bad, could do nothing with them. Tried washing them in the branch, but the more they rubbed the worse they smelt and finally had to throw them away. You may know the boys wanted shoes pretty bad to take them off a dead Negroe's feet…"

Good Lord, how bad did these shoes smell?

STONEWALL JACKSON'S FOOT CAVALRY-Company A, 13th Virginia Infantry by Walbrook D. Swank Col. U.S.A.F. (Ret) pub by Burd Street Press 2001

Pg. 79 July 9, 1864 Pvt. George Peyton -Gen. Early's raid on Washington, D.C., Frederick City, Md. "…At the place that we stopped was a big pile of knapsacks, tent flys, etc. These had been issued to some new Maryland regiments and they had gone across the river to join General Lew Wallace who tried to prevent us from crossing. I got two brand new tent flys that could be buttoned together and made into a tent. I need this very much as I had nothing to keep off the rain…They had just been mustered in and had all new things given to them. They left great piles of knapsacks, tents, etc., piled up by the side of the road…"

Once again, a Quartermaster's nightmare, equipping new troops just so they'd abandon everything and the Rebels would get it.

WAR TALKS OF CONFEDERATE VETERANS by Mr. George S Bernard pub by Fenn& Owen 1892

Pg. 119 9th of July 1864 Defense of Petersburg by Col. Fletcher H. Archer "…The companies were then marched out and formed into line, where they were surveyed by their commander. And what a Line it was! In number scarcely sufficient to constitute a company-what with details on account of special service, and for guard duty in the city, there was but a handful of them left. In dress nothing to distinguish them from citizens persuing the ordinary avocations of life. In age many of them with heads silvered o'er with the frosts of advancing years while others could scarcely boast of the down upon the cheek- indicative of the earliest approach to manhood. In arms and accouterments such as an impoverished government could afford them, but by no means adequate to the extingencies of the service in which they were engaged…"

Imagine being so poorly armed and having to face the Yankee Juggernaut.

CIVIL WAR LETTERS OF CAPTAIN A.B. MULLIGAN, Co. B, 5th South Carolina Cavalry-Butler's Division-Hampton's Corps 1861-1865 by Olin Fulmer Hutchinson, Jr. pub by The Reprint Co. 1992

Pg. 133 July 10, 1864 Stoney Creek, Va. My Dear Sister Eliza, "…I am lying under a shelter made of two Yankee blankets pinned together with wooden pins & stretched over a pole placed in two forked stakes with the lower edges of the blanket looped over with stakes driven in the ground about two feet high. My bed is made of a few green leaves with another Yankee blanket wired over them. I place my paper on the ground and lye on my "belly" while I write…As to my sash coat & new pants ordered at home I did write to you that I had no use further here but may order the suit to me soon. You must find an opportunity to send them. You have a good one and the only safe one namely by express…"

CHARLOTTE'S BOYS-Civil war Letters of the Branch Family of Savannah ed. by Mauriel Phillips Joslyn pub by Rockbridge Pub. Co. 1996

Pg. 265 1Lt. Hamilton Branch to Charlotte Branch On the rear guard south bank of the Chattahoocie River July 11 1864 My very dear Mother "I send all my extra clothing to you by William. Do not send me any more until you receive a request for them from me, as I cannot cary them with me, and on a push one suit will do me for a week or two…Mr. Solomon gave me some cloth for handkerchiefs which I am now using…"

GRANDFATHER'S JOURNAL (Franklin Lafayette Riley) Company B Sixteenth Mississippi Infantry Volunteers Harris' Brigade Mahone's Division Hill's Cops, A.N.V. May 27, 1861-July 15, 1865 by Austin C. Dobbins pub by Morningside Press 1988

Pg. 203 Sunday-Tuesday, July 10-12, 1864 Petersburg "…For shelters we build arbors or invert our muskets, sticking the bayonets in the ground and letting the hammers of the guns pinch the corners of a blanket, forming a kind of tent. The covering doesn't do much good, however, It's exhaustingly hot!…"

THE CIVIL WAR DIARY 1862-1865, OF CHARLES H. LYNCH, 18TH CONN. VOL. pub by Case Lockwood & Brainard Co. 1915

Pg. 163 July 11, 1864 Shanandoah Valley "…Our knapsacks, with extra clothing, left here when we began our march up the Valley in May, were taken by the rebs, so we lost our clothing that we expected to find here on our return…"

I find it extremely difficult to feel the least bit sorry for this Yankee unit. Maybe they could take shelter in a farmhouse-Oh! No! they cannot, because they have burnt them all down!

LAWLEY COVERS THE CONFEDERACYBY WILLIAM STANLEY HOLE CONFEDERATE CENTENNIAL STUDIES, CONFEDERATE PUB. CO. 1964

Francis Lawley was a coorespondent with the London Times July 14, 1864 regarding Early's Raid on Washington, D.C. "...The Rebels, many of them barefooted, crossed the Potomac River near Harper's Ferry...At the little town of Martinsburg, on the Potomac, an amount of spoil, such as is conspicuous even in this the most wasteful of wars, was secured by the Confederates. Sutler's stores, sent on in vast masses in anticipation of Richmond's falling before the bovine energy of Grant, and destined to be sold at Richmond when the stars and stripes should float above the capital, passed without exchange of gold, cotton, or tobacco in payment for them into the hands of General Breckinridge. It is reported that numerous patent reaping-machines, which it was the federal purpose to employ in harvesting the rich crops in the Valley of Virginia, were transferred to Confederate hands, and have supplemented the great deficiency of labor under which the inhabitants of the Valley have long labored. There can not be a doubt that the unprecedented haul of horses will furnish fresh teams for General Early's ninety guns, will remount his cavalry, and admit of large supplies being hauled into Virginia..."

This is the first I've ever heard of reaping machines b eing captured by the Rebels, but I bet they were put to good use. I wonder, were they hauled up the Valley before Sheridan's Criminal band burnt the Vally into destitution? Well, if you can't beat the armies on the field, make war against unarmed civilians and destroy everything, it was working for Sherman.

FRANKLIN GARDENER WALKER C.S.A. Civil War Diaries and Letters compiled by his Eldest Son 1936 edited and Retyped by his Grandson Erle Preston Carter 1986 Hadley Library Archives, Winchester, Va.

Pg. 36 Petersburg, Va. July 16, 1864 Dear Brother,"...I will not need the boots for several monthes, but while you are in WinchesterI would be glad if you would get Mr. Harney to cut them out as he has my measure. If you get him to cut them tell him to cut them about one size larger than my measure as boots that fit tightly are a nuisance in the army. I want them so that I can pull them on or off with ease when they are wet. Tell mother I would like to have two or three pairs of home made cotton socks such as she sent me last spring, and a pair of gauntlets made either of cloth or of other material. I do not need these articles at present but will in the fall. Other clothing I can draw from the Government, which is cheaper than getting it from home…"

I hope his confidence in being able to draw from the government was well-placed.

Letter addressed to Mrs. Mararet Walter Winchester, Virginia probably in 1864 "…If you have an opportunity I wish you would send me the two colored cotton shirts which mother said she would make for me. Also tell Billy to save one of those black felt hats for me. The one he had selected for himself about fits me. I do not want it now, but he can keep it for me. If Gen. Banks gets into Winchester he can send it out by you. If you can buy some gray goods, with cap and coat and pants, I will want them after awhile…."

WELCOME THE HOUR OF CONFLICT-Willam Cowan McClellan &The 9th Alabama ed by John C. Carter pub by Univ Al Press 2007

Pg. 260 July 16th, 1864 William Cowan McClellan to Thomas Joyce McClellan Camp Near Petersburg, Va. Dear Father: "…I am needing clothing very bad. If you can send me something now it would come in the nick of time, but do not send clothes unless in care of a reliable person. Boots, Pants, Jackett worn. Need all articles, getting dark have no candle…"

The last couple of sentences sounds like an anology of the Confederacy at this time.

U. S. ARMY HERITAGE AND EDUCATION CENTER

John L. Gwynn 21st Virginia Infantry Regiment Chaffin's Bluff, Va. Dearest Wife: "…I do not want anything but socks and I do not wish you to get anything for me-as the chances are I cannot get them and I need nothing else. If a safe opportunity send socks or send me two pair up to Mr. Sears and he will continue them…"

THE PAINFUL NEWS I HAVE TO WRITE-Letters and Diaries of Four Hite Brothers of Page County in the Service of the Confederacy Army of Northern Virginia Series Stonewall Brigade ed.by Harlan R. Jessup pub by Butternut & Blue 1998

Pg. 163 Isaac Hite to sister Ella Camp Petersburg July 24th 1864 "…Tell Mother I drew a pair of pants a few days ago by hard work, as my old ones still look tolerably well since I patched them…."

PAPA WAS A BOY IN GRAY-Memories of Confederate Veterans by Their Living Daughters by Mary W. Schaller pub by Thomas Pub 2001

Pg. 68 July 26, 1864 Meridith Thomas Jenkins 54th North Carolina Regiment On his way home after being paroled from Elmira, N.Y. "There is one story I remember my father telling," Verna continued, "(Dad) and several of his buddies were on their way home and as they passed through a small town, a woman and a child were selling meat pies. It had been some time since (Dad and his buddies) had eaten so they each bought one.

Dad was still hungry after eating his, so he bought another one. When he was about half through the second pie, the child started crying. The woman asked the child what was wrong.

"I want half the money because you killed my cat too," was the little girl's reply.

Dad said he couldn't finish the rest of his meat pie."

He's being too finicky, especially after just being released from prison, I mean, what's a little more cat meat gonna hurt?

THE CONFEDERATE VETERAN VOL. IX 1901

Pg. 154 April 1901 Story Of Our Great War by the late Mercer Otey Lexington, Va. July 27, 1864 "…Those of us who had only one suit (and the exception was the rule) would have to call to our aid the service of some kind sister or mother or seetheart to rip up the suit and, after beating out the dust thoroughly, reverse the whole garment, which generally passed muster to the satisfaction of everyone…"

This refers to "turning" the material, cutting the seams, beating (or washing) the cloth, them sewing it back together with the outside facing in.

LETTERS AND PAPERS OF AN ARTILLERY OFFICER A.N.V. IN THE WAR FOR SOUTHERN INDEPENDENCE 1861-1865 Capt. John Hampden Chamberlain-Virginian pub by Dietz Printing Co. Pub. 1932

Pg. 245 Hd. Qrs. &c. July 27th, 1864 My dear Sister "…I left with Spence a coat to be turned, the cost to be charged, not paid; bro H. will get it. That & the hat will come together …"

Another coat to be turned.

NO SOAP,NO PAY, DIARRHEA, DYSENTERY& DSERTION Acomposite History of the Lasr 16 Monthes of the Confederacy Jeff toalson, ed. IUniverse Inc.2006

Pg.180 July 30, 1864 Near Atlanta Georgia Lt. Robert M. Gin Co.-I 41st Mississippi Inf. "It is not safe to pull off shoes and go to sleep or one could wake up minus a pair."

CIVIL WAR LETTERS OF CAPTAIN A.B. MULLIGAN, Co. B, 5th South Carolina Cavalry-Butler's Division-Hampton's Corps 1861-1865 by Olin Fulmer Hutchinson, Jr. pub by The Reprint Co. 1992

Pg. 137 July 31st, 1864 Camp of 5th So Ca Cavalry Near Malone's Crossing, Va. My Dearest Mother & Sisters, "...Don't send me anything to eat. Eatables seldom ever reach us in eatable condition in summer. I have frequently seen a ham, bread, cake, &c,&c,&c, all so completely spoiled that it would smell as badly as a Yankee who had been dead for a week. Not more than a fourth of the boxes sent to soldiers ever reaches them & of those they get none are fit to use when they do get it in summer..."

I like the reference to spoiled food smelling as bad as a dead Yankee.

THE HISTORY OF A BRIGADE OF SOUTH CAROLINIANS FIRST KNOWN AS "GREGGS AND SUBSEQUENTLY AS McGOWA'S BRIGADE by J.F.J. Caldwell-lately an officer of Co. B 1st Regiment South Carolia Volunteers pub by Morningside Press 1866

Pg. 221 July-Aug. 1864 "...The contentment of the troops here was a sad commentary on their previous existence. We had no tents, except the scraps of Yankee flies; we were fed on wretched bacon, wormy peas, and corn meal with a small sprinkling of coffee; we lacked shoes and clothing; we were exposed to great heat and kept constantly on some sort of duty; yet we constructed arbors of branches picked blackberries, smoked pipes, (when we had tobacco) and felt very comfortable indeed. We did not envy the City Battalion their fine clothes; we did not envy the heavy artillery their vegetable gardens or their pigpens; we did not even envy the boat hands on the river, who fattened on government bacon; we were perfectly satisfied to be left in the shade for a little while..."

I know the Capitol Fleet was performing a valuable service by their mere presence, but some kind of rotation of service so the army artillery men could rest awhile.

A MARYLAND BOY IN LEE'S ARMY by George Wilson Booth Univ. of Nebraska Press 2000

Pg. 123-124 1864 Early's Raid Summer-(August?) "...From Cockeysville we approached through the Green Spring Valley to within a few miles of Baltimore, which was in a state of great excitement, apprehending capture. A small party under Lieutenant Blackistone, of the 1st Maryland, was sent to the country place of Governor Bradford, near Charles Street Avenue, with orders to burn the house in retaliation for the destruction by Hunter of Governor Letcher's house at Lexington, in the Valley, a few weeks previous. While waiting for this detachment to return we struck the establishment of Painter, the then well-known ice-cream man, about daybreak, and found his wagons loaded with this product, just about starting for the Baltimore market. It was a most ludicrous sight to see the ice-cream dished out to all conceivable receptacles, and the whole brigade engaged in feasting on this, to many, a novel luxury as the column moved along. The men carried it in hats, in rubber blankets, in buckets and old tin cans-in fact, anything that would hold the cream was utilized. No spoons were at hand, but as fingers and hands were made before spoons, the natural and primary organs were brought into play. A number of the men from southwest Virginia were not familiar with this delicious food, but were not slow in becoming acquainted with its enticing properties and expressing themselves as being very much satisfied with the "frozen vittles" as they termed it...."

In my reading I've come across many references of not having utensils such as spoons. Didn't the soldiers carry spoons in their pockets for just such an emergency? When I was in the army everyone carried a spoon in their pocket when in the field.

HISTORY OF THE FOURTH REGIMENT SOUTH CAROLINA VOLUNTEERS FROM THE COMMENCEMENT OF THE WAR UNTIL LEE'S SURRENDER by J.W. Reid Shannon &Co. Printers & Stationers Morningside Bookshop 1975

Pg. 120 summer (August) 1864 Petersburg Va. "...These were dark days for us; half fed, half clothed, some barefoot, our currency worthless..."

THE HASKELL DIARIES-The Personal Memoirs of a Confederate Officer by John Haskell ed by Gilbert E. Govan and James W. Livingood pub by G.P. Putnam's Sons 1960

Pg. 71 August 1864 "At Petersburg both armies fortified their lines and lay opposite each other until the following spring. We did a great deal of fighting, gradually wearing out our half-fed, half-clothed men..."

LAW'S ALABAMA BRIGADE IN THE WAR BETWEEN THE UNION AND THE CONFEDERACY by J. Gary Laine & Morris M. Penny pub by White Mane Pub. Co. 1996

Pg. 299 August 1864 "Many rifles and nearly all military equipment in the possession of the Alabamians came from the federal army. One newapaper correspondent on duty in Virginia believed it would "astonish an outsider to see how great a portion" of the Confederate supplies came from capture. It was said the Coinfederates were so eager to grab anything of value from their enemy that "The Yankees are very shy of placing their best foot foremost when very near the ragged and perishing Rebels." He reported Federal blankets, rubber cloths, knapsacks, rifles, Navy pistols and cooking utensils in plentiful supply in field's Division. The correspondent added, "Many privates sported captured sword belts to their bayonet scabbards and cap pouches."

Little could be done to improve the appearance of the Alabamians whose uniforms resembled rags. According to the report of the brigade assistant imspector general, the Alabama troops were particularly short of shoes and pants with "many men entirely destitute of both."

REBEL BROTHERS-The Civil War Letters of the Truehearts (from Galveston, Texas) ed. by Edward B. Williams pub by Texas A&M Univ. Press 1995

Pg. 203 …Co. Viginia August…1864 "…relative to your boots let me tell you that I think the chances in Rockingham are bad-but that I have at last discovered the place where they can be had and have accordingly left your measure and engaged a fine pair of cavalry boots made of the best material and to be ready by the 14th of this month. Think you may rely on their being ready & as soon thereafter as possible I shall go down after them & either forward or bring them over the ridge…"

I wonder whether he received those boots.

GENERAL LEE'S ARMY

Pg. 383 August 1864 Petersburg,Va. "Just as it exhausted men physically and mentally, trench warfare took its toll on resources and basic necessities for the men. Although Lee's soldiers received a disproportionate share of the Confederacy's clothing, it was not nearly enough. Shoes, submerged in trench water for extended periods of time, broke down much more rapidly than they normally did in the field. Pants, shirts, socks and drawers wore out under siege conditions, so that the shortages that plagued Lee's army during the first three years worsened. One Louisiana captain, angered over the inadequate shoes and clothing for his men, argued that military personnel in Richmond should give up their uniforms for the soldiers in the field. "Our men are Shoeless, pantless, jacketless, sockless and miserableand resembled Falstaff's Army more than any Corps in the Confederacy, while evry man in Richmond, or any other city connected with the Army are dressed in the best of all. God grant that our leaders may soon learn that men cannot march and fight when they are half naked and with feet that leave bloody marks whever they step."

This is a common story regarding armies, with the troops in the field needing uniforms and the office "soldiers" being very well supplied. Although the uniforms that were issued wore out quickly, remember all the references to the shoddy nature of government issue clothing.

THE CIVIL WAR MEMOIRS OF CAPTAIN WILLIAM J. SEYMOUR-Reminiscences of a Louisiana Tiger by Terry L. Jones pub by La. State Univ. Press

Pg. 142 August, 1864 Battle of Winchester "To illustrate the ardent patriotism of the ladies of Winchester, I will here state the remarkable fact that when a number of [Jon Daniel] Imboden's Cavalry rushed pell-mell through the streets of that city, far in advance of all other fugitives from the battle field,a large number of the most respected ladies joined hands and formed a line across the principle street, telling the cowardly Cavalrymen that they should not go any futher unless they ran their horses over their bodies. In this manner a large number of demoralized &fugacious cavalrymen were induced to return to the fight. Mrs. Gordon, wife of the General Commanding our Division, who accompanied her husband through all the arduous marches and perilous scenes of the Valley Campaign, seized the bridle of a recreant cavalryman & leading his horse down Main St. to the edge of town, told him to return to the battle-field or dismount & surrender to her his horse & gun, that she might take his place. It is needless to say that the man returned to his post of duty."

These were some gutsy ladies, especially Mrs. Gordon.

MEADE'S HEADQUARTERS 1863-1865: Letters of Colonel Theodore Lyman from the Wilderness to Appomattox George R. Agassiz ed. pub by Atlantic Monthly Press 1922

Pg. 370 August 1 1864 the Crater aftermath "...Upon the ridge thus formed, and upon the remains of the breastwork, stood crowds of Rebel soldiers in their slouched hats and ghostly grey uniforms. Really they looked like malevolent spirits, towering to an unnatural height aginst the sky..."

TRUE TALES OF THE SOUTH AT WAR-How Soldiers Fought and Families Lived, 1861-1865 Collected and Ed. by Clarence Poe, pub by Univ. N.C. Press1961

"Aug. 2, 1864-We are living very well and have on this whole trip with the exception of a few days. But dirty and ragged! You never saw the like. All laugh and frolic as though it were all right."

LETTERS TO AMANDA-The Civil War Leters of Marion Hill Fitzpatrick, Army of Northern Virginia ed by Jeffery C. Lowe & Sam Hodges pub by Mercer Univ press 1998

Pg. 163 Aug. 5th, 1864 Skirmish Line Near Petersburg, Va. (Letter No 81) Dear Amanda, "…we draw plenty of soap now which is a great help…"

Pg. 171 Aug. 13th, 1864 Skirmish Line Near Petersburg, Va. (Letter No82) Dear Amanda, "…You want me to write you all about my clothes. I shall want a coat like the last one you made for me, but shall need no buttons on it as I have good brass buttons on this coat to put on it. Now I think it would be best for me to draw all my clothes here, especially since thread has got to be such a high price and so hard to get, but if you will insist on making them I shall need one pair of pants, two shirts, and two pr. drawers. I want you to send none of them to me yet, for I hope to get a furlough this winter and carry my old ones home which will do some of you some good and get my new ones if you will make them but I have much rather lighten your labors that much. You spoke of having some of Alex's clothes. Just keep them, till I come home or write for them. The Coat would suit me very well now to wear under this coat, but there is no chance to get it right away, and I shall draw in a few days. So do not try to send it to me. The shirts and drawers that are drawn here are but little account, but the coats and pants are very good and undoubtedly cheaper than can be made at home if the coats were only long tailed. I do not like to wear the shortails alone…"

According to this soldier, the issue clothing, coats and pants, are of good quality.

LEE'S MISERABLES-Life in the Army of Northern Virginia from the Wilderness to Appomattox by J. Tracy Power pub by Univ. N.C. Press 1998

181 August 5, 1864 "…Many of them, already weary of their relative inactivity, also protested that they were being neglected by the Confederate civil and military authorities who could not or would not care for their needs. They complained about long-overdue or inadequate pay, scanty or inferior rations, shortages or poor workmansip in clothing and shoes, and other indignities…Another of Lee's soldiers commented that when his regiment received new issues of clothing and shoes, officers quickly climbed into the wagon "picking out the best

jackets, pants, shirts, shoes, &c, for their own use." The Confederate, who signed himself "A Ragged Private," continued, "There are scores of men in this army who are almost destitute of clothing and would be glad of the commonest articles. But the private soldier is first and formost in one thing only, and that is in battle..."

REBEL BROTHERS-The Civil War Letters of the Truehearts ed. by Edward B. Williams pub by Texas A & M. Univ. Press 1995

Pg. 33 Camp near Winchester Va. Army of the "Valley District" Dear Minny "...I have only one pair of single blankets, but manage to keep warm by sleeping with my great coat all on. I don't know what I shall do when we have snow and ice in realgood earnest. Hope to be able to get another pair ere long. I have had some difficulty in getting winter clothes. The tailor at Charlettesville sent me a suit, a few days since, but it proved too small for me; so I had to sell it at a loss of $3.00; and buy another suit at $18.00. Clothes of all kinds are very dear here. A suit (pants and jacket) of the coarsest heavy negro cloth, such as our uniforms are made (at a) cost (of) $21.00 if made by a tailor. I succeeded in getting one at $18.00 by having it cut out only by a tailor, and made by a seamstress...."

Pg. 109 Defenses around Petersburg, Aug. 7 1864 Dear Henry "...As to the boots, Henry, don't put yourself to any special trouble about them. I have one pair that I obtained from one of the men on tolerable terms; giving my shoes and $21.00 boot; (but have them) made if you can on reasonable terms, and without much trouble. Try to get me some pocket handkerchiefs, neckties, shirt collars, shirts, socks, or the like..."

LETTERS OF JOHN BRATTON TO HIS WIFE Elizabeth Porcher Bratton Privately Pub. 1942

Pg 206 Letter from John Bratton to Bettie Bratton August 7, 1864 Camp near Deep Bottom Dear Bettie"...The Salem grey fades so quickly it is not fit for a coat, besidesI have a coat and got a jacket the other day from the Qr. Mstr. Dept. So you can keep the Salem grey until we are in need of pants. And doubtless Hillard who takes care of nothing will want in a short time. I myself still have plenty of outside clothes, only want undergarments as mine are somewhat dilapidated and what is more, am afraid I cannot wear your homespun. If you cannot get calico, why not send some of the shirts packed away in the wardrobe. They are not doing much service there where they are..."

A CONFEDERATE SURGEON'S LETTERS TO HIS WIFE Spencer Glascow Welch, Surgeon Thirteenth S. Ca. Vols., McGowans Brigade pub by Neale Pub. Co. 1911 Continental Book Co. Marietta Ga. 1954

Pg 104 Near Chaffin's Bluff, on the James River, Va. August 8, 1864 "I received more pay on the 5th, and will send you one or two hundred dollars. I sent Bob the ten dollars for your catskin shoes. I bought an excellent pair of pants from the quartermaster for $12.50. They are made of merino wool. We shall soon have some fine gray cloth issued to the brigade for officer's uniforms. There is not enough for all, so we draw lots for it. If I am lucky enough to get any, I will send it to you."

LETTERS AND PAPERS OF AN ARTILLERY OFFICER A.N.V. IN THE WAR FOR SOUTHERN INDEPENDENCE 1861-1865 Capt. John Hampden Chamberlain-Virginian pub by Dietz Printing Co. Pub. 1932

Pg. 252 In the Trenches-Aug. 10th, 1864 My dear Mother "...Isaiah went to Richmond on Sunday & returned yesterday, bring me cooking utensils, my hat & coat which had been turned &c.-also letters..."

LETTERS FROM LEE'S ARMY by Susan Leigh Blackford and Charles Minor Blackforb pub by Scribner's Pub. 1947

Aug. 10, 1864 Chaffin's Farm, Va. Upon visit to the "Capitol Fleet" "...They do not inspire me with awe, because I can but regard them as machines destined to be blown up if the enemy gets very close. We have not the materials to build such boats. I begrudge the large number of able-bodied men in white pants that cover their decks..."

Capt. Blackford makes a very good point, though if the Capitol Fleet was not there, the Union navy would be shelling Richmond. I do think they couldv'e been more active, so as to tie down more Federal ships, but I don't know the whole situation so I won't make armchair pronouncements. If you want another military example, the German Battleship Tirpitz tied down immense resources of the R.A.F. and Royal Navy during WWII, eventhough it went nowhere.

STEPHEN ELLIOTT WELCH OF THE HAMPTON LEGION ed by John Michael Priest pub by Burd Street Press 1994

Pg. 46 Near Rowland's Mill, Chas. City Co. Va. August 11, 1864 Dear Mother "The next morning, (August 4) I rode near the head of the infantry column-Kersaw's Brigade-and it commenced firing, branching to the left I took a small road leading to the Chas. City (Road) (having soon after daylight gone to the Darbytown Road with six of the scouts) to go to the Legion, hearing it was engaged in a skirmish. Riding carelessly along I thought we should strike the road in rear of our breastworks, but came out 400 yards in front and directly in sight, upon which the 7th (South Carolia) Reg't. opened on us.

I was standing sideways to the works & can't imagine how neither horse or rider was grazed. Not one in the party was touched, neither party was to blame, for but a short time before we rode out, some Yankee cavalry rode up to survey our batteries & were driven off; we came in sight & Duva having on blue trousers & another man a blue coat, they took us to be Yanks and fired…"

August 30th, 1864 In the Trenches, Deep Bottom My Dear Mother, "…The shirt is a very pretty, nice fitting one, & has been much admired by our men…(Ellie) He was looking well healthy & sported a nice black felt hat, & (a) pair of shoes he got from the Yankees. I've got a nice pair of gray pants (which) I drew last week, but they are too long for me…"

HAM CHAMBERLAYNE-VIRGINIAN Letters and Papers of an Artillery Officer in the War for Independence 1861-1865 with introduction, notes and index by his Son C.G.Chamberlayne Richmond, Va. pub by Press of the Dietz Printing Co. Publishers 1932

Pg. 256 J.H. Chamberlayne to M.B. Chamberlayne Trenches-Aug 13th, 1864 My dear Mother, "…Can you get me there the material for two shirts-checked cotton, indigo checks, such as aprons for negro girls used to be made of. The dye must stand & not run-& it ought to be coarse and strong? If so please make me two shirts of it, with collar attached & not too wide & with pockets buttoned…"

KENTUCKY CAVALIERS IN DIXIE-Reminiscences of a Confederate Cavalryman by George Dallas Mosgrove pub by Bison Boooks 1999

Pg. 203 summer 1864, repelling the Salt Raid in S.W. Virginia "…Afterward, while passing over the fields, Sims came upon the body of a dead officer whose head had been [partially torn away] by a cannon ball. The unsympathetic Confederate, with grim humor, took a hand ful of salt from his haversack and threw it into the cavity in the dead officer's head, saying, "There, you came for salt, now take some."

I think that rather generous.

LAW'S ALABAMA BRIGADE IN THE WAR BETWEEN THE UNION AND THE CONFEDERACY by J. Gary Laine & Morris M. Penny pub by White Mane Pub. Co. 1996

Pg. 290 1864 around Petersburg.August 14 a Rebel captured by the 2nd U.S. Sharpshooters: The Confederate was unarmed, which saved his life. The man was described as tall, wearing a grey hat and pants and a blue coat. The tall man in the blue frock coat was 6 foot 2 inch tall Captain John B. Hubbard, Co. K, 48th Alabama, who was given over to the Provost Marshall of the Army of the Potomac on August 16."

HAM CHAMBERLAYNE-VIRGINIAN Letters and Papers of an Artillery Officer in the War for Independence 1861-1865 with introduction, notes and index by his Son C.G.Chamberlayne Richmond, Va. pub by Press of the Dietz Printing Co. Publishers 1932

Pg. 262 Hd. Qrs. Davidson Battery Aug. 19th, 1864 My dear Mother, "...I came out of the trenches yesterday evening, the first time for ten days, for a bath, rest & refreshment..."

NO SOAP, NO PAY, DIARRHEA, DYSENTERY& DESERTION A Composite History of the Last 16 Monthes of the Confederacy Jeff Toalson, ed. pub by IUniverse Inc.2006

Pg. 194 August 20, 1864 Inspection Report- Ramsuer's Division Lee's Army of Northern Va. Near Smithfield, Va. Capt. J.M. Richardson AAG-Inspecting Officer "...The arms are in serviceable condition. Clothing is generally in bad order supplies being much needed by all the brigades. Men barefooted & in tatters are not infrequently seen and in consequence of the want of sufficient clothing present a very soiled appearance...Issues of soap as well as of clothing are very speedily needed..."

Here's an official inspection report stating the men are ragged and shoeless.

MEADE'S HEADQUARTERS 1863-1865: Letters of Colonel Theodore Lyman from the Wilderness to Appomattox George R. Agassiz ed. pub by Atlantic Monthly Press 1922

Pg. 370 August 20 1864 "...In the morning came a couple of hundred Rebel prisoners, taken yesterday. Among them were a number of the Maryland brigade, quite well dressed and superior men, many of them...They had the remains of fancy clothes on, including little kepis, half grey and half sky-blue..."

Here's another reference to blue pants, even though the armchair experts say there were none issued by the government during the war. The Marylanders would have had to have been supplied by the government.

CIVIL WAR LETTERS OF CAPTAIN A.B. MULLIGAN, Co. B, 5th North Carolina Cavalry-Butler's Division-Hampton's Corps 1861-1865 by Olin Fulmer Hutchinson, Jr. pub by The Reprint Co. 1992

Pg. 143 Aug. 21st, 1864 Near White Tavern, Va. My Dearest Mother & Sisters," Do try & have me about ½ dozen pair of wool socks by winter. I want all 3 pair large thick socks for Simon (slave).

I want a nice vest made of the same piece of cloth as my new sash and pants. Make it by my military vest & put the large inside pockets in it-line with wool &c. Don't put buttons on it."

Pg. 144 Aug. 28, 1864 Head Quarters 5th So Ca Cavalry Gravelly Run, Va. My Dearest Mother & Sister, "...If Corpl. Means has delivered the sugar & coffee promptly and calls you on the way back (as he promised me to do) and you have my suit all ready, sock, pants, & vest, I want you to send them to me by him. Put them up in a small box or similiar bundle. I don't expect you to put buttons on the coat & vest. Do at the same time try and send me two colored homespun shirts and two pair cotton drawers. I am much in need of the shirts and drawers..."

CONFEDERATE LETTERS AND DIARIES ed by Walbrook D. Swank Colonel, USAF Retired pub by Papercraft Printing and Design Inc. 1988

Pg. 140 Letters of Private James O. Chisholm Captain Wiley G. Coleman's Company, Virginia Heavy Artillery Aug. 25 1864 Camp Magruder Dear Sister, "...If you have not made my shirts you need not make them. I can get the cloth much cheaper here than you can get in the country. I will have my likeness taken as soon as I get my uniform Which will be in day or two. (He dosen't mention whether he'll be issued a uniform or will receive one from home-ed.)

Here is another reference to having one's likeness taken after he gets a new uniform.

LAW'S ALABAMA BRIGADE IN THE WAR BETWEEN THE UNION AND THE CONFEDERACY by J. Gary Laine & Morris M. Penny pub by White Mane Pub. Co. 1996

Pg. 321 In the Petersburg Trenches, Sept. 1864 "the soldiers were deficient in clothing, shoes, and blankets. In September, Law's Brigade was destitute of shoes and pants. October brought a supply of shoes but by the end of January resupply had rendered the Alabama Brigade only "deficient in pants and jackets." Blankets were never in adequate number during the last winter. Although Field's Division received more clothing in January than any month since the previous July and a large supply of clothing every month since October, it was not enough. On January 31, the quartermaster of the division explained the shortfall by asserting trhe soldiers' arduous duties of "storming works and building fortifications" during the fouth quarter of 1864 made it impossible for supply to keep up with need."

Here is one of the official reports on the raggedness of the men and the reasons behind it.

VIRGINIA REGIMENTAL HISTORICAL SERIES 5th Va. Inf. by Lee A.Wallace Jr. 1988

Pg. 62 Aug. 1864 "Terry's Brigade was well armed with Enfield rifles, and the greatest deficiencies in the brigade, noted by the inspector, were in bayonet scabbards and shoulder belts for cartridge boxes. Other deficiencies he noted were: 103 coats, 120 trousers, 167 shirts, 179 drawers, 69 pairs of shoes, 3 caps, 33 haversacks, 45 knapsacks, and 20 canteens. Most of the command, he reported, had no company and regimental record books, a loss sadly felt by historians today…"

Pg.211 Sept.7,1864 Inspectipon Report-Pickett's Division Lee's Army of Northern Va. Bermuda Hundred, Va. Major Walter Harrison AAG-Inspecting Officer "…Supplies of clothing and shoes have been quite liberal of late and the Division may be said to be in pretty fair condition, in spite of the long list of deficiencies for which requisitions have been made. Arms and accouterments are supplied as fast as the men come in…"

Pg 212 Sept 8, 1864 Inspection Report, Benning's Brigade Lee's Army of Northern Va. Chafin's Farm Va. Capt. H.H. Perry AAG-Inspecting Officer "…The law of Congress providing that officers procure clothing after the men are supplied operates in such manner that the officers are never supplied at all. The issues of clothing are barely sufficient for the necessities of the men and no surplus is ever left for the supplying of officers. At present many are without clothing in this Brigade and the high prices of cloth held by merchants preclude the possibility of any officers buying clothes on their present pay. It was stated some time since that cloth had been issued for the officers of this army but nothing has been heard from it since this information was published to the command. If some more just arrangement is not made before winter season comes in many officers will be very greatly in need of comfortable clothes…"

The official reasons for the officers being ragged. They were actually worse off than the men with the insufficient supply, as they had to wait until all the enlisted men were supplied, and that wasn't happening.

HANDLEY LIBRARY ARCHIVES, WINCHESTER, VA-James M. Cadwallader Diary 1st Virginia Cavalry

Pg. 16 Sept. 9th, 1864 "Very cold today, drawed a blanket, had to lay in bed to keep warm."

TRUE TALES OF THE SOUTH AT WAR-How Soldiers Fought and Families Lived, 1861-1865 Collected and Ed. by Clarence Poe, pub by Univ. N.C. Press1961

"Sept. 11, 1864-"…We get plenty to eat, but are nearly all naked. I expect we have fifty barefoot men in the regiment…"

THE CIVIL WAR LETTERS OF DANIEL HAYWOOD GILLEY-Company F. 16th Virginia Infantry

September 12, 1864 In the Trenches Around Petersburg-Dear Mother,"…You wanted to know how I was faring for clothes. I have got as many clothes now at this time as I want. I can make out very well for clothes…"

Here's one soldier whose well-supplied.

DEAR IRVIE, DEAR LUCY-The Civil War Letters of Capt. Irving A. Buck, General Cleburne's AAG & Family pub by Buck Pub. Co. 2002

Sept, 1864 Home (Bel Aire, (Front Royal, Va.) My Own Dear Irvie, Re: Cousin Mack's Furlough-"…he thought if prompt in his return now there would be more chance of his obtaining a furlough for next December and he is fully resolved to come if he can. This hope makes the parting less bitter yet we already begin to miss him sadly and feel lost without him.

He goes back much more comfortably than he came though. We've repaired his clothes and given him a new outfit from shoes to cravat and tobacco bag. He needed it poor boy…Lucie"

I can't imagine where they got the material, but that's one supportive family.

Pg. 253 Sept. 12, 1864 Petersburg, Va. My Dear Lu, "The weather is very bracing and we are surprised to find it so much cooler here than in the Valley. Fortunately, Van and myself are well fortified with clothing and, if rations don't get short, can winter comfortably…Alvin"

WRITING & FIGHTING THE CONFEDERATE WAR The Letters of Peter Wellington Alexander ed by William B. Styple pub by Belle Grove Pub. Co. 2002

Pg. 146 Richmond, September 15, 1864 "The Examiner states that Major John C. Maynard, Quartermaster of this post, having need of a great number of shoes for the negroes employed in his department, determined last Fall to utilize some of the Yankee skill lying idle in the Libby. He fitted up a shoe shop in the Government stable yard on Navy Hill, and procuring some forty odd shoemakers among the Yankee prisoners at the Libby, who were willing to practice their trade during their captivity, set them to work. These men have made all the shoes and boots required by the Quartermaster's Department in Richmond, and done besides a large amount of work for our army and for citizens. The quality of the work turned out at this establishment is superior to any done in the Confederacy. The prisoners here employed are so delighted with their condition as to be unwilling to be exchanged: they desire nothing better than to live as they are till the end of the war. They are well fed and comfortably lodged and clothed. The report of their happy condition having spread among the prisoners at the Libby and Belle Isle, the artisans of all kinds among them have become anxious to become similarly employed at their respective trades. The guard required for the prisoners thus employed is very small, and the whole experiment has been so successful that Major Maynard has it in contemplation, with the assent of the authorities to enlarge the establishment and increase the numbers of his workmen to one hundred or more…"

By all means, expand this experiment, it's a brilliant idea, the Confederacy needs the services of these prisoners.

STONEWALL JACKSON'S FOOT CAVALRY—Company A, 13th Virginia Infantry by Walbrook D. Swank Col. U.S.A.F. (Ret) pub by Burd Street Press 2001

Pg. 108 Sept. 17, 1864 George Peyton "…We drew some clothes. I got a pair of pants and a pair of drawers which I needed very badly as my pants were nothing but rags. Deaton brought Rube Newman some clothes from home…"

Pg. 118 Sept. 20, 1864 after the Battle of Winchester "...He through away his gun and catridge box and his jacket. All he had on was his shirt, pants, and his knapsack. When we started from Somerville's Ford, Davy Mallory agreed to carry their blankets, and Ben carried the knapsack with the clothes and he was lucky to do it for a bullet had struck the knapsack right in the middle of his back. It went through everything and mad a big bruise on his back. As Davy was captured, Ben threw his clothes away. I will tell you how he did at Fisher's Hill. Ben Jones looked like a picked bird. His pants were frazzeled out up to his knees and he had thrown his gun and cartridge box away. They gave him another gun and cartridge box and on the stampede from Fisher's Hill, he threw that away..."

Throw this man out of the army, he is more of a detriment than a benefit.

Pg. 122 26 Sept. 1864 Shenandoah "...I am almost barefoot and my feet are very sore..."

LETTERS OF ARTHUR R. TINDER TO HIS WIFE, MARGERET TINDER

Brown's Gap, Va. Sept. 27, 1864 Dear Mag, ".I drew a new suit of clothes this morning, and have a plenty just now..."

Maybe supply is starting to improve.Another quote which doesn't state color or cut of the uniforms.

CHISMAN'S BOY COMPANY-A History of the Civil War Service of Co. A, 3rd Battalion, Virginia Mounted Reserves by John L. Heatrwole pub by Mountain & Valley Pub 2000

Pg. 79 Sept. 29 Reserves from the Shenandoah Valley "When the members of the Boy Company arrived they were issued new uniform coats with the large "A" on the buttons denoting artillery service..."

These boys were infantry reserves, but, I guess the only coats available were ones with artillery buttons.

NO SOAP, NO PAY, DIARRHEA, DYSENTERY& DESERTION A Composite History of the Last 16 Monthes of the Confederacy by Jeff Toalson, ed. pub by iUniverse Inc. 2006

Pg. 225 Sept.30 1864 Inspection Report- Pegarm's Brigade Early's Army of the Valley near Waynesboro, Va. Lt. Washington Byron McNemer AAG-Inspecting Officer "Owing to the scarcity of clothing, the active and constant duty this brigade has performed, and the ...

bad condition of their worn and dirty clothing, their "military appearance" and "soldierly bearing" cannot be as favorable as under different circumstances. No soap with which to wash their clothing has been furnished them for several weeks....The practice and privilege generally tolerated throughout the Command, of allowing soldiers to sell, for their own private benefit, property captured on the battlefield, has, I have observed, had a very demoralizing effect upon many of our once bravest and best soldiers. This great desire for plunder, in anticipation of gain, induces many men to swerve from their proper line of duty, leaving their comrades to the duty that they would otherwise have...to do. ...If the men are required to repair their clothing whenever it needed it, the constant demand for new clothing could be greatily diminished. I have seen articles of clothing thrown away and their places supplied by new ones, when really they were not half worn out, but merely came to pieces owing to the indifferent sewing, loss of buttons, and bad thread used in making them. The great scarcity of, and difficulty of obtaining clothing for our armies, should encourage, I think, the greatest economy (by) the men and officers..."

Did this inspector suggest where the men could get needle and thread to repair their clothes? Maybe these thrown away articles cold have been gathered up and seamstresses organized to repair them?

FROM HUNTSVILLE TO APPOMATTOX R.T.Coles History of 4th Alabama C.S.A. Army of Northen Virginia ed by Frank D. Stocker pub by Univ of Tenn. Press 1996

Pg. 185 Petersburg, Va. Sept. 30, 1864 "Before the movement began against Fort Harrisn, the 4th Alabama, still being at Fort Gilmer, J.S. and J. W. Thompson of C company, both good and tried soldiers, were detailed before daylight on the 30th to go over the works on a scouting expedition. During their absence, the regiment had been taken out of the works and ordered the forces which were getting in position to assault and attempt to retake Fort Harrison. When J.S. and J.W. on their return from scouting, approached the works at Fort Gilmer, not finding the regiment in the works, discovered instead of the familiar faces they expected to see, a line apparently dressed out in comfortable blue overcoats, which leveled its guns on them with orders to throw down their arms and come in. They immediately held a hasty consultation. J.W., who had on a new, warm,comfortable jacket, but recently received from the good folks at home, which he prized more highly than all the rest of his worldly possessions, said, "I would, in the event in the event we are compelled to surrender, dislike very much to give up my new jacket." "Yes," said J.S., and I am very much afraid, from the number of dead negroes lying around us here, which we killed yesterday evening, the devils will retaliate." Finding no possible way of escape, they finally threw down their arms and climbed over among their supposed enemy. They rejoiced to find that the regiment had moved and a battalion of the "Richmond Reserves" had been placed on that part of the line. The reserves were a well-organized command under General Ewell, composed of the employees from the different departments in Richmond, and were only called out in cases of emergency. They wore very dark gray suits and were in a position to present a very much better and neater appearance than we "regulars."

Here that white armband indicator would have been helpful, but there might not have cloth available for such. This illustrates what I was saying about the front line troops wearing shabby uniforms while the reserves were well-dressed.

Website 55thva.org/article00001

Pg. 3 By the fall of 1864 the Confederate supply situation was again deteriorating. When the 55th Virginia's Brigade moved forward to renew the attack at Pegram's Farm on Setember 30th, it passed large numbers of Federal prisoners coming the other way and many of these men were stripped of their clothing; so many, if fact, that when the Confederate Brigade went into action it was momentarily mistaken by Federal officers for one of their own units. Supsequent inspection reports for October and November show the 55th still suffering clothing deficiencies."

OK, despite what that inspector said last month about the soldier's greed for plunder to sell, these soldiers wanted the clothing and equipment for themselves.

CIVIL WAR MEMOIRS OF TWO REBELS SISTERS Mollie Hansford, 7 miles north of Winchester (Va) & Vitoria Hansford Kanawha Valley-Coalsmith now St. Albans, W.Va. ed by William D. Wintz pub by Pictorial History Pub Co. 1989

Pg. 53 Victoria; "...After one of the battles in the fall of '64, a young lady of our town was out on the common helping with the wounded. She came across an officer with a new uniform that was unusual then as it was of beautiful blue-gray English cloth. He was lying with his head on a rock and one leg of hie pants had been cut off by a Yank surgeon who had looked at the wound..."

THE HISTORY OF A BRIGADE OF SOUTH CAROLINIANS FIRST KNOWN AS "GREGGS" AND SUBSEQUENTLY AS "McGOWAN'S BRIGADE" by J.F.J. Caldwell- Lately an Officer of Co. B, 1st Regiment South Carolina Volunteers pub by Morningside Press1866

Pg. 255 fall 1864 "...Clothing was sparsely issued and what we received was coarse and flimsy. I do not remember the issue of a single overcoat, and but few blankets. Shoes were scarce, more than once a soldier left a bloody track on the frozen picket line..."

We have a constant trend in the ragged appearance and insufficientcy of supply to the troops.

MEMIOR OF THOMAS ALMOND ASHBY in THE VALLEY CAMPAIGNS by N.Y. pub by Neale Pub. Co. 1914

Pg. 299 Oct. 1864 "…clothing had to be of the plainest character. Many of our men and boys were clothed in the old discarded uniforms of Federals-clothes that had either been left in camps or captured by our soldiers-dyed black with the bark of the tree…."

The dye made from butternut and/or walnut trees turned the blue uniforms black.

PAPA WAS A BOY IN GRAY-Memories of Confederate Veterans by Their Living Daughters by Mary W. Schaller pub by Thomas Pub 2001

Pg. 85 Oct. 1864 Robert Saders Phillips of North Carolina Referring to prison camp guards (Salibery, N.C.)- "…Guard Daniel McRaven wrote that "many of us are nearly barefoot and we get no shoes at any time. I have little to eat…the Colonel (commandant) sent for rations for us and and the prisoners but the train broke down on the track and we could get none. The prisoners were reduced to augmenting their scant rations with acorns that fell into the yard…"

General Lee's Army

Pg. 431 Oct. 1864 Shannandaoh Vally "…AnAlabama Lieutenant noted a week before before the Battle of Third Winchester, "Nearly all my company are barefoot, and most of them are destitute of pants. Such constant marching on rough, rocky roads, and sleeping on the bare ground, will naturally wear out the best shoes and the thickest of pants." He had picked up a worn-out shoe on the march and put it on because it was in better condition than the one that he owned. A North Carolian observed 200 barefoot men in his brigade and a large number without pants. Another officer oversaw a camp with 600 barefoot men at Gordonsville. "God grant that our leaders may soon learn," the Louisiana officer expressed, "That men cannot march and fight when they are half naked, with feet that leave bloody marks whenever they step…"

It is a mystery how they were able to soldier on.

PERSONAL RECOLLECTIONS OF PRIVATE JOHN HENRY CAMMACK: A SOLDIER OF THE CONFEDERACY 1861-1865 pub by Paragon Printing and Pub Co.

Pg. 81 Oct. 1864, escape from the Yankees and attepting to get back to Confederate lines-a family assists them ;" Miss Fox, who is now my wife, made me a pair of pants and father had me a pair of excellent boots made and in other ways my wardrobe was improved and we were well rested and better able for our trip back to "Dixie."

HANDLEY LIBRARY ARCHIVES- The Memoirs of the 49th Viginia Volunteers.

Pg.228 Camp 49th Va. Regt. in Field Oct. 3, 1863

"I certify that the Ordinance stores herein after mentioned were Lost & Expended in the several Battles & Skirmishes in which this Regiment has been engaged from May 5th 1864 to June 30th 1864 & is as correct a Statement as could be made under the circumstances. Viz:

157 Rifles muskets, Cal 57 & 8	43 Screw Drivers
186 Bayonets	2 Cones
157 Cartridge Boxes	2 Spring Vices
157 Cartridge Box Belts	155 Knapsacks
157 Waist Belts	158 Haversacks
186 Bayonet Scabbards	157 Canteens
157 Cap Pouches	100 Gun Slings
49 Wipers	8 Tompions
17 Ball Screws	27730 Rds Ammunition Cal. 57 & 8

(signed) Jno G Lobban
Capt Comdg

It amazes me that the Confederate Army was still issueing/using tompions in 1864. I would have expected them to have been in disuse from early on. I wonder how many of those 8 tompions were accidentally fired down range after being forgotten and left in the muzzle of the rifle?

LETTERS AND PAPERS OF AN ARTILLERY OFFICER A.N.V. IN THE WAR FOR SOUTHERN INDEPENDENCE 1861-1865 Capt. John Hampden Chamberlain-Virginian pubh by Dietz Printing Co. Pub. 1932

Pg. 272 Burleigh (Va.) Oct. 4, 1864 Martha Burwell Chamberlayn to Lucy Parke (Chamberlayn) Bagby Dear Parke "…I am knitting his socks; this house is a bee hive of industry, a loom in one room, a wheel in another. Martha wove the pants her father has on-and made the hat he wears…"

Another example of a supportive family, one of thousands.

THE CONFEDERATE LETTERS OF BENJAMIN H. FREEMAN Compiled & Edited by Stuart T. Wright pub by Exposition Press 1974

Pg. 54 Richmond Va. Winder Hospital Dear Farther: "…On last Friday('s) fight I got this paper envelope a canteen—Shirt Socks Hat Plate Knife Fork Spoons Gloves and all other little things from the Yankees…"

VOICES FROM COMPANY D Diaries by the Greensboro Guards, Fifth Alabama Infantry Regiment, Army of Northern Virginia ed. By G. Ward Hubbs pub by Univ. of Georgia Press 2003

Pg. 316 October 4 1864 HB "…sent brother an overcoat by Cowin's boy Wm.…"

"DEAR MARTHA…" The Confederate War Letters Of A South Carolina Soldier Alexander Faulkner Fewell compiled and edited by Robert Harley Mackintosh, Jr. pub by The R.L. Bryan Co. 1976 17th South Carolina Inf. Company E

Pg. 138 Entrenchments near Petersburg Oct. 4th, 1864 Dear Martha "…I shall send Mr. Steeles oil cloth out by the boys & if Mr. Choate can take it he will-I want you to send it home to J. B. & say to him I am much obliged for the use of it. I yesterday bot me an excellent Rubber one for Twenty Dollars and if I can and money holds out I want to buy one and send it to John William and also a tent cloth. They are small but are large enough to keep one dry…"

The manner in which the Confederate Soldier lived, I would think an oil cloth just as important as shoes, maybe more so.

LETTERS TO AMANDA-The Civil War Letters of Marion Hill Fitzpatrick, Army of Northern Virginia ed by Jeffery C Lowe & Sam Hodges pub by Mercer Univ Press 1998

Pg. 175 Oct4th/64 Near Petersburg, Va. (Letter No 86) Dear Amanda, "…I drawed a Confederate shirt yesterday, the first I have ever drawn My two checked shirts both wore in holes in the back and I took the tail of one and put it in the back of the other, which brought me down to one shirt till I got that one yesterday. I have not had the chance of drawing a Jackette yet but they say some will be issued soon, when I will get one, and a pair of pants too,to wear when it is cold for these are getting thin. I can have my clothes hauled on a march now which will help me along considerably. I and Jim Drew together have used about all the thread you have sent me. Send me about as much more in your next and I think that will do me…"

Pg. 179 Oct 23rd, 1864 45th Ga. Near Petersburg, Va. (Letter No 89) Dear Amanda,"…And I went to get my shoes fixed the another day. I got them half-soled and the eye-seams which had bursted sewed up and they do finely now. The Brigade has one man detailed from each Reg. to mend shoes and it costs us nothing now and is a great help. And yesterday, I and Drew took a general wash on both our shoes and clothes, so with the dodging about that I have to do, with the extra added to it I have been pretty busy….I wrote you about drawing a coat or jackette rather. I drew a pr of pants this week and have a good nice suit now. I wanted to get some pants the color of my coat but could get none to fit. These are a blue color but not like the yankee blue. I have drawed two shirts. They are thin and sleazy but beat no shirts out of all hollow. My drawers you sent me last winter very good yet. Now you just fix up the clothing matter to suit yourself. You know I make it a rule not to meddle with women's affairs but I want you to make me some drawers anyhow, for the government drawers are pretty sorry and soon rip up. In making soldier's clothes all of you recollect that we have some neighbors here called lice and be sure to fell (I believe that is what you call it) all the seams. Or in other words, sew it down tight everywhere so they will have no hiding place. Doc can explain it. You need not make me any shirts or you can make them and cut them up when I get home just as you like any way does me that is the least trouble and most satisfaction to you. If you have the cloth to spare you can make me a vest, if not it makes no difference atall. I begin to need my overcoat like rip now, but I know of no chance to get it…."

He speaks of drawing mismatched clothing, but doesn't make an issue of it. I guess he's glad to draw a new jacket and pants, regardless of color. I wonder if His wife found a way to send that overcoat to him?

THE CRY IS WAR, WAR, WAR The Civil War Correspondence of Lts. Burwell Thomas Cotton and George Job Huntley, 34th Regiment North Carolina Troops by Michael W. Taylor pub by Morningside Press 1994

Pg. 186 Camp 34th Regt. N.C. Troops Oct. 6th/64 letter to a Miss Sallie "…I am very sorry to hear Thos. Haltom has acted so mean trifling, I would think he would give up the cloth as every persons knows he has it He has Thomas cloth and besides that he has a new paire of pants of his and a yarn shirt. Thomas had on the pants I brought from home for him when he was killed and a new pair in his carpet Sack and I don't know whether you received them or not…."

STONEWALL JACKSON'S FOOT CAVALRY by Walbrook D. Swank pub by Burd Street Press 2001

Pg. 126 Oct 8 1864 Shenandoan Valley Pvt George Peyton "…We had an inspection by Lieutenant Kinney. It took me all the morning to clean my gun as the rain had made it mighty rusty…."

Pg. 127 Oct. 10, 1864 "…I went with Lieutenant Stringfellow to the river and washed our clothes. We got a camp kettle to wash in but had no soap. It was a hard job…"

Pg. 130 Oct 19, 1864 Battle of Cedar Creek "…Thus by the stupidity of one man,(Gen. Early) the Conferacy lost the greatest victory gained in the war. It is true, a great many men had left the ranks to plunder. The Yankees had on new clothes and when I went through the camp their dead lay in long rows fully dressed. When I ran through it that evening, all the dead were stark naked…"

Oct. 20, 1864(capture) "…We stayed at Sheridan's headquarters nearly all day. The stragglers commenced coming back and got all around us, cursing and abusing us for stripping their dead. They got so rough that some of our officers appealed to the guard and they then put another line of guards around us and made the stragglers get so far off they could not join us…"

This reinforces what I wrote before, these Yankees are very brave against unarmed prisoners, I wonder where they were during the battle? Now that they have gotten all of the armed Rebels out of the Valley, Its time for them to show their courage by burnig everything in sight.

CIVIL WAR LETTERS OF CAPTAIN A.B. MULLIGAN, Co. B. 5th South Carolina Cavalry- Butler's Division-Hampton's Corps 1861-1865 by Olin Fulmer Hutchinson, Jr. pub by The Reprint Co. 1992

Pg. 156 Oct. 9, 1864 In Camp Near exactally what to write for. If I could only get my coat baggage I would be all right. I shall want the new flannel shirts drawers. My two gray flannel shirts, and if those two fine brown blankets are large enough I would like to have a large over coat made of them like the one Mr. Lockwood made for me last year. Do let Mr. L see them & if he can make one over coat out of them like the one he made last year with my large cape &c get him at it at once & send the coat to me by Sergt. Ructenback. Have it lined with some dark wasted (worsted-ed.) like he made with two large pockets in side of skirts. A pocket on outside breast & one on inside.

Send a pair of extra heavy wool gloves & a fine pair heavy wool socks if you can. I have four (4) heavy Yankee blankets with me and if I get a good chance will get an over coat &c.

I would like to have a good suit for my boy but must clothe him here." *He is referring to his servant.*

Pg. 157 Oct. 11th, 1864 "...I am not in want of the shirt now..."

"DEAR MARTHA..." The Confederate War Letters of a South Carolina Soldier Alexander Faulkner Fewell compiled and edited by Robert Harley Mackintosh, Jr. pub by The R.L. Bryan Co. 1976 17th South Carolina Inf. Company E

Pg. 145 Entrenchments near Petersburg Oct. 11th 1864 Dear father"...no shoes on dirty & ragged yet full of life..."

That's a good overall insight into the Rebels at this time.

"DEAR MARTHA..." The Confederate War Letters of aSouth Carolina Soldier Alexander Faulkner Fewell compiled and edited by Robert Harley Mackintosh, Jr. pub by The R.L. Bryan Co. 1976 17th South Carolina Inf. Company E

Pg. 149 Petersburg Oct. 20th/64 Dear Martha"...Our Company has move about 100 yards to the left on Monday and we lost our old quarters. The Company are now in the hole made by the blow up and are sleeping on hundreds of negroes every night. The place is a bad one indeed. The smell at times is quite unpleasant..."

I can imagine. Especially after it rains, I'd bet.

KENTUCKY CAVALIERS IN DIXIE-Reminiscences of a Confederate Cavalryman by George Dallas Mosgrove pub by Bison Books 1999

Pg. 223 Oct. 21, 1864 After Battle of Cedar Creek "...we halted on a cold, bleak plateau, and scouts were sent forward to ascertain "where we were at...While waitng on the desolate promontory the troops experienced some of the horrible sensations of men freezing to death. Many of the rank and file had neither blankets, nor overcoats, and, besides, they were ravenously hungry…I shiver now when I think of that terrible night-no fires, no blankets, no overcoats; hungry, freezing and lost in close proximity to the enemy…"

You'd really be hard put to be more miserable than these soldiers.

Pg. 228 Nov. 24, 1864 "When we started to rejoin Breckinridge our horses were nearly starved and the men in were in a like condition. Luckily about this time the brigade drew probably four hundred suits of most excellent dark gray clothing, of English manufacture, which had recently run the blockade. The clothing came none too soon, as the troops were suffering greatly from the Spitzbergen weather which had prevailed nearly all the while we were in the Valley…"

Finally, when you least expect it, the Quartermaster comes to the rescue!

LETTER FROM HENRY WARREN HOWE, pub by Couier-Citizen Co. Printers, 1899,

211 Oct. 21, 1864 after the Battle of Cedar Creek "…The Adjudant (of the Thirtieth Mass.) was left on the field until the next morning with all our wounded. He was shot through the back of the neck, and the ball came out through his mouth. The enemy, as they passed, shot him again in the leg, pulled his coat off, and a number of them tried to rob him of his boots. He died in the hospital in Newtown…When we re-occupied our works, we found our wounded and dead stripped of their clothing and robbed.…"

This soldier must be a greenhorn to be shocked at this.

A CONFEDERATE SURGEON'S LETTERS TO HIS WIFE Spencer Glascow Welch, Surgeon Thirteenth S. Ca. Vols., McGowans Brigade pub by Neale Pub. Co. 1911

Pg111 Near Petersburg, Va. October 25 1864 "…Your brother had received his new suit from home. Billie is well and hearty, but he needs a new coat. These Government coats are too thin for exposed duty.…

I have a nice little Yankee axe, which is so light it can be carried in a knapsack, but it just suits a soldier for use in putting up his little shelter tent or for making a fire. All the Yankees have these little axes, and many of our men have supplied themselves with them, as they have with almost everything else the Yankees possess…"

HAM CHAMBERLAYNE-VIRGINIAN Letters and Papers of an Artillery Officer in the War for Independence 1861-1865 with introduction, notes and index by his Son C.G.Chamberlayne Richmond, Va. pub by Press of the Dietz Printing Co. Publishers 1932

Pg. 286 J.H. Chamberlayne to Lucy Parke (Chamberlayne) Bagby Trenches Oct. 26th, 1864 My dear Sister, "…I am in great need of shoes-glad to get a pair as soon as you can…"

CIVIL WAR STORIES Letters-Memoirs-Anecdotes Union and Confederate by Walbrook D. Swank Colonel, USAF, Ret. Pub by Burd Street Pess 1996

Pg. 40 Dr. (Lieutenant Colonel) Thomas L. Boudurant, CSA In Trenches, Chaffin's Farm, Oct. 28, 1864 Dear Alex, "I wish you would ask Mama to let Gabe make me a pair of shoes out of the remnants left. I lost all my clothes except those he made for me. I want them double solid for winter. I like very much the pair he made-they are the size to fit…"

WITH THE OLD CONFEDS-Actual Experiences of a Captain in the Line by Captain Samuel D. Buck, Co. H. 13th Va. Inf. Pub by H.E. Houck & Co. 1925

Pg. 127 Oct 30, 1864 regarding the battle of Cedar Creek, Va. "While we were waiting for orders, Sheridan was moving up from Winchester with fresh corps, that had not fired a gun, and with as many men as we had in our army. Notwithstanding this, we would have whipped them but half of our army was back pillaging the captured wagons, hunting for clothing and shoes, as many were almost naked…"

I know this is one of the reasons the battle was lost, but what are you going to do; the men are only partially clothed and ravenously hungry.

VMI MS# 357

Pg. 14 Baker 18th Va. Cav. Reg. Oct. 30 1864 Shenandoah Valley "…I wanted to lay on my blankets on the floor but the Colonel and his good family would not hear to that and had me to take a bed and my clothing washed, as I had very much soiled clothes on. Had been jarred around so fast the last three months and no time to have them washed or wash them. When we were moving up the back road, the army halted to wait for orders. I went to a little creek to wash my underwear, did so, and when they were half dry the army moved on, so I crept into them and took my place in the ranks. I had but one suit of underclothes with me, I lost the others some time in August when Early fell back…I had an oilcloth with a pocket in it to carry a suit of underclothes in and when it rained we could tie this cloth around our shoulders with strings to keep ourselves dry and in dry weather we carried this rolled up and fastened behind our saddles. I had this oilcloth on for rain it rained awful and so dark I could not see my hand an inch from my eyes when it did not lightening…"

STEPHEN ELLIOTT WELCH of the HAMPTON LEGION ed by John Michael Priest pub by Burg Street Press 1994

Pg. 66 Head Quarters Hampton Legion Williamsburg Road Oct. 30, 1864 My Dear Mother, "…(19th Wisconsin) His whole brigade surrendered I.e. what was left of them. Bratton's & the Texas Brigades took 500 prisoners, 7 flags & a quantitry of rifles, besides innumerable oil clothes, etc. I have a splendid blanket, which I suppose belonged to some negro mother…I haven't had a chance of calling on my friend Miss Walker since Frank's death & in fact have not had the clothes to do so in. Ask Annie if she has a pair of socks please send them to me. I never could think of it when I wrote. I drew two pairs today, but they are worsted & I prefer cotton-perhaps I'd better keep them for father-they are English tho' coarse. I hope our new clothes will come soon. If I get behind the Yankee lines it would be easy to get a whole suit save a jacket…"

This soldier doesn't want a Yankee jacket, probably fears a mistake and being shot by his comrades.

SOUTHERN INVINCIBILITY by Wiley Sword pub by St. Martin's Press 1999

Pg. 240 winter 1864-65 Petersburg "At one point in the siege, Lee complained to Jefferson Davis about the lack of soap, which was more than just a minor irritant: "The great want of cleanliness which is a necessary consequence of these very limited (soap) issues is now producing sickness among the men in the trenches, and must affect their self-respect and morale."

General Lee was right, how could you expect these men to go forever without bathing or washing their clothes?

The 25th North Carolina Troops in the Civil War by Carroll C. Jones pub. by McFarland & Co. Inc. 2009

Pg. 134 Winter 1864-1865 "Bulletts were not the only thing in short supply at Petersburg. There are many testimonies to the fact that Confederate soldiers living in the trenches during that cold winter 1864-1865 were barefooted. On the last day of the year of 1864, General Johnson communicated to army headquareters: "I would call your attention to the fact that there is a number of barefooted men in this command. The inspector-general of the army inspected Ransom's brigade some some ten days or two weeks since, took down the number of barefooted men, and promised the shoes, but they have not been furnished. "The Confederate soldier serving loyally and barefooted at Petersburg during the last winter of the Civil war has certainly not received the acclaim or respect given to General Washington's brave Revolutionary War soldiers who weathered the winter snows at Valley Forge. However, the Rebels living in the saps suffered similar exteme weather conditions and severe deprivations for a cause they believed to be equally righteous..."

Well said.

VMI MS# 357

Pg. 16 Nov. 1864 "...The weather is now very cold and my winter clothes at my father's in Frederick County. I am out of money, have not been paid off since in October, 1863. Never drew but one suit of Government clothes, as my two sisters, Caroline and Ann, have been making my clothes. Father raised the sheep and had the wool carded into roles and my two sisters spun spun the yarn and had it wove and cut and made my clothes in military style... what was left of our company had gone to West Virginia to get their winter clothes and were going with Captain Hill on a raid several hundred miles..."

THE CONFEDERATE VETERAN VOL. XV 1907

Pg. 357 August 1907 Fight At Beverly, W.VA. by Thomas H. Neilson (Co. D, 62d Va. Regt. C.S. Army) early in Nov. 1864 "...Our battalion, (composed of men from different companies and regiments of Gen. John D. Imboden's Brigade, recently ordered to Highland County to recruit our horses, broken down in Early's raid on Washington City and the active campaign in the Shenandoah Valley, lately ended.)

My loved mother had sent me, disguised as a skirt and worn by a Virginia relative through the lines, some gray cloth from Philidelphia, Pa., which I had made into a uniform resembling, as I subsequently learned, those worn by "Jesse Scouts," Federal soldiers..."

RECOLLECTIONS AND LETTERS OF GENERAL ROBERT E. LEE by His Son, Capt. Robert E. Lee pub by Garden City Pub Co. 1926

Pg. 141 Nov. 1864 Petersburg Reminiscence of General Fitz Lee: "...His thoughts ever turned upon the soldiers of his army, the ragged gallant fellows around him-whose pinched cheeks told hunger was their portion, and those shivering forms denoted the absence of proper clothing..."

Nov. 30th, 1864 letter to Mrs. Lee: "...I received yesterday your letter on the 27th and am glad to learn your supply of socks is so large. If two or three hundred would send an equal number, we should have a sufficiency. I will endeavor to have them distributed to the most needy…"

SOUTHERN INVINCIBILITY by Wiley Sword pub by St. Martin's Press 1999

Pg. 238 Nov. 1864 A.N.V. Luther Mills wrote to his brother that "many of the men are entirely destitute of blankets and overcoats, and it was really distressing to see them shivering over a small fire made of green pine wood."

RED CLAY TO RICHMOND by John J. Fox pub by Angle Valley Press 2006

Pg. 288 Nov. 1864 "Some supplies did succeed in reaching the Georgians during the fall of 1864. During this time, the quartermaster received and issued ammunition for .54, .58 and .69 caliber rifles. The supply wagons also brought pants and shirts for the men. In some cases these supplies came a little too late. Many soldiers wrote home requesting clothes, probably for the better fit and color slection. One man even gave directions in a letter to his wife for sewing seams together on pants to prevent hiding places for lice, commonly referred to as "neighbors.' Since shoes supplies were low, twenty-three-year-old Robert A. Jackson, one of three brothers from Company E, became shoemaker in the 35th Georgia. He received his position after he was wounded in the right knee in May 1864 and had trouble walking. The Brigade officially detailed one man from each regiment to repair shoes…"

Pg. 289 Nov.1864 "…Sergeant Marion Hill Fitzpatrick, 45th Georgia, described the type of quarters many Georgians built. "Instead of building huts as formerly, they dug a hole in the ground about six feet deep and ten feet square, put over the top a layer of large logs. On that a layer of boughs and leaves, and cover the whole with dirt which they pile on till it is shaped like a potato hill. They then fix a chimney and are not only very comfortable but protected from the enemy's shells…"

WRITING & FIGHTING FROM THE ARMY OF NORTHERN VIRGINIA

Pg. 300 Sights on a Battlefield 11-2-64 "A friend of mine who has just returned from an engineering tour in the vicinity of Fredericksburg tells me he saw in the Yankee trenches at Spottsylvania C.H. a dead Yankee taking aim with his musket. He had been there for five months. He was sitting bolt upright, with the top of his head blown off, and his gun still capped, was ready to fire. Our ordinance officer, who had been gathering the engines of war dropped on this bloody field, permitted the dead man to retain his musket for the novelty of the spectacle. Owing to the long continued drought, this Yankee, in common with many others who had been left unburied, did not petrify, but dried up like jerked beef. His form was almost perfect, except about the intestines, which had disappeared, and there is no telling how long he would have sat there if the ordinance officer had not pulled his musket out of his hand. The corpse at once sank into a little heap of dust. My friend wrenched off the skull, stuck it on a pole as a monument to mark the spot where this strange spectacle had so long been visible."

The barbarization of war.

"DEAR MARTHA..." The Confederate War Letters of a South Carolina Soldier Alexander Faulkner Fewell compiled and edited by Robert Harley Mackintosh, Jr. pub by The R.L. Bryan Co. 1976 17th South Carolina Inf. Company E

Pg. 157 Entrenchments Petersburg Nov 3rd 1864 dear Martha "...I went out to see Dan on Tuesday & tried on his coat. It fits me better than my own. It is a little longer in the sleeves & skirt than mine but does very well-I have got no oilcloth for John Wm. Yet and as to a knapsack I cant get any but still hope to get him an oilcloth..."

REBEL BROTHERS-The Civil War Letters of the Truehearts ed. by Edward B. Williams pub by Texas A & M. Univ. Press 1995

Pg. 205 Hardy Co. Va. Nov. 8th 64 Dear Chas. "...Am sorry to say that thus far have been unable to procure boots for you Comd has been in Hampshire...Balt. Made Cav'ly boots at $25...but hadn't the needful-can bring you 2 or 3 hndkfs. Will you have white linen or silk? Also have the hat-Can get the gauntlets if I can get the money-Do undershirts. I have two very worn wool undershirts-& made of fine white blanket & the other a white flannel (Yankee obtained on the field at Monocacy) a little worn but good and warm-which I will bring you if you desire-I have two knit ones-got in Md...The leather is...too but can be got only with Yankee money or specie. My only chance is to capture some luckless Yankee who has it. They strip us & we do them..."

LETTERS TO AMANDA-The Civil War Letters of Marion Hill Fitzpatrick, Army of Northern Virginia. ed by Jeffery C. Lowe & Sam Hodges pub by Mercer Uniuv. Press 1998

Pg. 183 Nov. 10th/64 Hd. Qtrs. 45th Ga. Near Petersburg, Va. (Letter No 91) Dear Amanda, "...I wrote to doc three days ago and told him to tell you about my clothes. Since then I have drawn another good pair of drawers from the government and am fixed all right in that line too now. They are the best drawers that we have rec. in a long time. The most of the drawers we get are almost worthless.

Tom Rickerson's furlough has not come back yet but will probably be in a day or two and will write and send by him. I traded for a pair of shoes the other day that I will send to you by him. I think you can wear them though they may be too large for you. I have got to draw the fellow a pair from the government to pay for them. I drew a pair for him the day before yesterday, but they did not suit him, and I kept them for myself..."

THE CONFEDERATE VETERAN VOL. V 1897

Pg. 570 Nov. 1897 Polley Lost A Foot-A Furlough Howard Grove hospital, Richmond, Va. Nov. 10, 1864 Charming Nellie: (J.B. Polley is a cavalryman-his unit not reported) "...he plunged into a tree top, from which he emerged half a minute later minus the tail of his long, light-colored coat..."

No other description, whether light gray, brown etc.

UNDER THE STARS AND BARS-A History of the Surry Light Artillery Lee A. Wallace Jr. pub by Morningside Bookshop 1975

Pg. 223 Camp Henrico, Va. Nov. 15 1864 "...If only the men had warm and comfortable clothing, for to protect them from the inclemency of the winter, and even half as much rations as were furnished us in 1861, we would fare well enough, even royally, so far as creature comforts go. But alas! Both of these highly essential "sinews of war" are conspicuous mostly for their absence. Supplies of every sort are growing scarcer all the time, and we need both warm garments and blankets, and more food. Many of the men have no overcoats, and some no blankets. And the present supply of footgear is discreditable in the extreme..."

STEPHEN ELLIOTT WELCH of the HAMPTON LEGION ed by John Michael Priest pub by Burd Street Press 1994

Pg. 70 Hd. Qrs. Hampton Legion Nov 16, 1864 My Dear Mother "...I am a thousand times obliged for the pantaloons you sent & to Annie for the socks. If the trousers fit me I'll surely keep them as I am still in a pair of borrowed ones & our clothing is still in the Qr. Master's storehouse. I recently went to town to purchase a pair & was treated with indifference by a few upstart clerks that I felt like flogging them. It was rainy weather & after wishing them, very piously, that the Conscript officers might take them & send them to the front, I left..."

By this time only the unfit or invalid men shouldv'e been clerks, the manpower shortage was so great.

REBEL BROTHERS-The Civil War Letters of the Truehearts ed. by Edward B. Williams Texas A & M. Univ. Press 1995

Pg. 131 Camp Sanders near Petersburg November 17th, 1864 Dear Henry, "...Boots, or shoes-particularly a pr. of nice Sunday's-a wool hat, gloves of any kind but more particularly a pr. of buckskin gauntlets. Pocket handkerchiefs-silk or linen (would like to have part of one kind and part of the other and as many as ½ doz.). Neckties-linen for shirt collars, etc. flannel undershirts, knit or sewed as suits you best. Calf skin for footing one or two pair of boots-Cloth gray or other color, for making a cape-and some red flannel or other woolen stuff for lining it. (I am without a Greatcoat, and want it as a substitute therefor). Any one or more or all of the above articles will be acceptable to me; provided you can get them on good terms and can bring or send them across the mountains to me. If they don't come too dear..."

LEE'S MISERABLES by J.Tracy Power pub by Univ. N. C. Press 1998

Pg. 221 17 Nov. 1864 Capt. Zimmerman Davis commanding the 5th S.C. Cavalry wrote to headquarters "...My men are ragged, many have neither overcoats nor blankets, and numbers are obliged to shiver on picket, clad in tattered remnants of jacket and pantaloons..."

Pg. 222 Nov 1864 Pvt. Alfred Newton Proffit wrote his sister that the 18th N.C. had just been issued "...a full suit of clothing some of the prettiest kind, all I lack is my overcoat. If you can send it I would be glad I do not want any blankets if you send any clothing but my coat let it bee a par of socks..."

LEE'S MISERABLES-Life in the Army of Northern Virginia from the Wilderness to Appomattox by J. Tracy Power pub by Univ. N.C. Press 1998

Pg. 221 "...The most common complaints made about the weather were that numerous soldiers had too few overcoats and blankets and too little firewood to keep themselves warm. "Such material as our army is composed of has never before [been] seen," Maj. Giles B. Cook of Lee's staff commented in his diary in late November, after a particularly cold and rainy night. "It is incomprehensible how they can stand so much exposure."

The soldier's ability to withstand that exposure, of course, was to a great extent determined by the quartermaster's success in keeping the army clothed, shod, and supplied with blankets during the winter months. As the production and transportation of goods in the Confederacy were haphazard at best, there was no way to guarantee an equitable distribution of clothing or other items throughout the entire army either in terms of quality or quantity. These disparities were most common, and most striking, in the case of uniforms. Whereas the adjutant of a Virginia brigade in the Fourth Corps remarked in early November, "I fear there will be much suffering as many of the men are badly supplied with blankets, clothing, etc.," a hospital steward in a North Carolina regiment of the Third Corps commented a few days later, "The weather is growing quite cold-our men are all clothed and shod." Several factors contributed to such differences within the army. Some units would be issued good jackets, pants, underwear and hats on a regular basis, whereas others, when they obtained them at all, received inferior items that quickly fell into tatters. Because many soldiers neglected to care for their clothing, often selling, trading, or discarding items, and because they were not held responsible for such conduct by their officers, even those units that had been well supplied suffered chronic shortages. Poor communication between the army and the quartermaster-general's department in Richmond also hampered efforts to keep the Confederates properly clothed.

The great disparity in clothing among Lee's soldiers in aptly illustrated by two letters written during the same week, one by a South Carolina cavalry captain and the other by a North Carolina infantry private. Capt. Zimmerman Davis, commanding the 5th South Carolina Cavalry, wrote headquarters on 17 November, describing the poor conditions in his command. "My men are ragged," Davis wrote, "many have neither overcoats nor blankets, and numbers are obliged to shiver on picket, clad in tattered remnants of Jacket and Pantalons." He requested an essentially complete uniform-consisting of pants, jacket, shirt, and drawers-for more than 200 men in his regiment, which numbered about 375 soldiers. In late December, after Davis's letter worked its way through proper channels up to headquarters and through the same channels back to him, the captain was promised that the uniforms would be issued to his soldiers.Pvt. Alfred Newton Proffit, on the other hand, wrote his sister proudly on 20 November that the 18th North Carolina had just been issued "a full suit of cloathing some of the prettiest kind," stating, "all I lack is my over coat. If you can send it I would bee glad I do not want any blankets if you send any clothing but my coat let it bee a par of sockes." Such varying conditions, even if one conceded in this case that cavalrymen on constant picket duty might be exposed to the elements more often than infantrymen or that the state of North Carolina made extraordinary efforts to ensure that it soldier were properly clothed, were fairly common in the Army of Northern Virginia. For every Confederate who wrote that "we are sadly in need of clothes," there was a fellow soldier who reported," the men are generally worse off for hats than any thing else."

Though it could not be said that Lee's troops were, as a rule, destitute, the comfort of a soldier in one unit could not compensate for the very real need felt by a member of another. An officer in the 26th Virginia, whose regiment was stationed near the Crater, reported in late November that his soldiers were required to spend twelve hours guarding their camp and twelve hours on picket out of every thirty-six hour period. "The effect that one cold night has upon the boys is a little remarkable," Lt. Luther Rice Mills wrote his brother, "They are generally for Peace on any terms towards the close of a cold wet night but after the sun is up and they get warm they are in their usual spirits.' Mills welcomed the recent arrival of shoes and blankets, commenting: "it is to be hoped that our men will do better. We have to carry some men to the hospital for frostbites &c. Some have come off picket crying from cold like children."

The lack of adequate clothing, shoes, and blankets was often cited as a major reason for the increased number of desertions as winter set in and some soldiers went over to the enemy to aquire them. Others depended on their families to send them such articles from home or took what they could from Federal prisoners or deserters. Some men took more unusual steps to supply themselves. On one occasion, according to several deserters from Scale's Brigade of the Third Corps, sharpshooters made a night attack on a Federal picket line for no other reason than "it was expected a sufficient number of overcoats, shoes, and blankets would be captured to pay for the undertaking." Still other Confederates resorted to stealing and robbery to get clothing or other items, either from their fellow soldiers or from civilians near their camps. "There has been a great deal of stealing going on recently & every camp near ours has been robbed at night of provisions clothes boots &c.," one artillery officer wrote in late December. "A robbery of clothes now is quite a serious matter." Though ragged and half-naked Confederates were still the exception rather than the rule in the Army of Northern Virginia, genuine want existed in enough units to induce a considerable number of soldiers to desert or steal to aquire adequate clothing for the winter…"

I disagree that ragged and half naked soldiers were the exeption in Lee's Army. The letters and memoirs we have just read do not support this assertion. What would it take to convince this writer?

CIVIL WAR REGIMENTS-A Journal of the American Civil War, Treasures from the Archives: Select Holdings frm the Museum iof the Confederacy Vol. 5

Pg. 145 Nov. 19th, 1864 Fort Louisiana 4th Co. Battalion W.A. Petersburg, Va. (Washington Artillery) Dear Sister Joe, "…I am pretty well fixed for cold weather as far as clothes is concerned. I have a good Yankee over coat given to me by one of my mess, also a good vest, two new shirts, made for me by the ladies I have mentioned to you Misses Hawkes. They are making me some good woolen socks. They have not charged me for any thing so far. The socks are very nice…"

HANDLEY LIBRARY ARCHIVES, WINCHESTER, VA—James M. Cadwallader Diary 1st Virginia Cavalry

Pg. 18 November 24th 1864 "Had inspection today, moderated some.trade to draw a pair of shoes but couldn't come it."

Pg. 19 November 26th, 1864 "Quite pleasant had inspection this morning, drawed blankets, feel quite well."

HAM CHAMBERLAYNE-VIRGINIAN Letters and Papers of an Artillery Officer in the War for Independence 1861-1865 with introduction, notes and index by his Son C.G.Chamberlayne Richmond, Va. pub by Press of the Dietz Printing Co. Publishers 1932

Pg. 292 J.H. Chamberlayne to M.B. Chamberlayne Camp Walker 4 ½ miles S. of Petersbrg. On Boyden Plank Road Nov. 28th, 1864 My dear Mother, "...I have frequently told you of the shirts r.w. & b.(red, white & blue?-ed.), they are a complete success and most valuable to me. I need no reminder as you may well believe of you or all the dear ones in the great family of Tallahala, if I did, the shirts & socks would be even more precious. Speaking of clothes, Hart was without an overcoat & gave me the great pleasure of accepting the Crenshaw overcoat which you'll remember, while I use the one Archer gave me in Yankee land (When he was a P.O.W.)..."

"DEAR MARTHA..." The Confederate War Letters of a South Carolina Soldier Alexander Faulkner Fewell compiled and edited by Robert Harley Mackintosh, Jr. pub by The R.L. Bryan Co. 1976 17th South Carolina Inf. Company E

Pg. 164 Entrenchments near Petersburg Nov 29-64 Dear Martha (about recieving his box) "...I see two pair of drawers & one pair of socks..."

U. S. ARMY HERITAGE AND EDUCATION CENTER

Nov. 30, 1864 Henry—unknown unit Camp on Charles City Road, Dear Brother Tom: "... the shoes which you sent us by the hands of Captain Mark have come to hand-he having forwarded them per Express, Columbia, S.C. They proved to be a pretty good fit with the exception of being a little long-but this is not a great objection..."

THE YOUNG LIONS-Confederate Cadets at War by Jame Lee Conrad pub.by Stackpole Books 1997

Pg. 118 Nov. 30, 1864 "as the Georgia cadets filed into the Savannah fortifications, the cadets of the South Carolina Military Accademy were trying to turn back a federal advance in South Carolina in support of Sherman's effort to capture Savannah....

The cadets were marched from Pocotaglio throughout the afternoon and evening, and finally halted along the railroad near the Tilifinny. It was a hard, tiring march under trying conditions. "We had come without overcoats and blankets," remembered Arsenal Cadet Sergeant George M. Coffin, "And it was raining, and without breaking ranks we lay down company front on the cornbeds and tried to sleep. I remember putting my plate canteen over my face to keep the rain off."

NO SOAP, NO PAY, DIARRHEA,DYSENTERY & DESERTION ed by Jeff Toalson pub by iUniverse 2006

Nov 30 1864 Major Walter Harrison, Adj. Gen. Office—Inspec Officer Inspection Report, Picketts Division, Howlett Line—Petersburg Va."…2nd to the defficiancies of clothing and shoes. The requisitions have been cut down to the amounts absolutely required at present. A small quantity has just been issued but not nearly sufficient. It is understood that there are large quantities now on hand at the depot at Richmond…A supply of SOAP is especially required…"

Large quantities of clothing at hand? What are the supply officers waiting for? They need to issue this clothing as soon as possible.

GENERAL LEE'S ARMY

Pg. 445 Dec. 1864 "Quartermaster General Alexander Lawson reported that over the last seven monthes, his office had allocated enough supplies for each soldier to have received approximately two pairs of shoes, two shirts, two sets of drawers, two pairs of socks, two pairs of pants, one blanket, and more than one jacket. Yet inspection after inspection uncovered a lack of shoes and clothing in serious, often critical numbers. "The men are suffering for clothing," relayed an inspector in late November, 1864, "many are very ragged and in some instances, strictly speaking, unfit for the field." He considered the delay in delivery of clothing "inexcusable." Late in December, some men in the 9[th]Alabama attended inspection with no pants at all, and fifteen men of the 10th Alabama were barefoot. The same was true in Kershaw's Division. "Some of the men are without pants and others nearly so," an inspector reported.

In mid-March (64),Lawton insisted that "a larger supply of clothing has been issued to the armies in the last three months that in any similar period during the war," yet men in Lee's army still suffered severe shortages. According to an inspector, "Experience has shown that the semi-annual allowance of clothing which would be sufficient to clothe men comfortably in less onerous duty will last scarcely three months in the Trenches, from the greater wear of material in rubbing against the sides of the ditches." During January and February (65), inspectors uniformly determined the condition of clothing as poor. In Robert Ransome's Brigade at the end of January, one in six soldiers had shoes that were irreparable, and others were barefoot. Pickett's Division needed 757 jackets and 1,359 pairs of pants. Rufus Berringer's Cavalry Brigade had "a large number of the men" barefoot. As late as the end of March, soldiers like Private Peter Cross complained, "I can tell you I am naked fur pants you oit (ought) see me then you would see a raged (ragged) man."

The quality of the material tended to be poor. For a long tome, brigades and divisions had manufactured their own shoes, which by all accounts were superior to what the government issued. As an officer commented on the inspection report of Lane's Brigade at the end of 1864, "it has been satisfactorily demonstrated after a Years experience that better shoes can be made in camp than are supplied by the Q.M. Dept." Both Rode's and Early's Divisions ran shoe and tailoring shops for the men, something their commanders never would have established if the clothing and shoe shortage had not reached a grave status. To be sure, the problems at any given moment varied by unit and even by state. In Wilcox's Division at the end of November 1864, the two North Carolina Brigades had received clothing allotments from their state and were "much better supplied" than the other two brigades, from Georgia and South Carolina. At the end of febrtuary 1865, the quartermaster of Georgia had issued clothing to Anderson's Brigade, while the Terxas Brigade, Bratton's Carolinians, and Law's Alabamians endured serious clothing shortages."

THE CIVIL WAR INFANTRYMAN, In Camp, on the March, and in Battle by Gregory A. Coco pub by Thomas publications, Gettysburg, Pa

Pg.37 Although many Rebel troops were so poorly clad, many issues of new and sturdy clothing were received by Southern troops throughout the war. In December 1864 for example, John Green told how the 9th Kentucky quartermaster, had brought out of Savanah suits of "cotton underclothes & grey Jeans Jackets & trousers....for his men. Even a Yank could vouch for the good condition of some Confederates late in the war. Lieutenant Galwey of Ohio documented this appearance of veteran Southern Soldiers near Spottsylvania Court House, Virginia, in May of 1864:..."(t)hey were all clad in neat grey jackets and pantaloons with entire seats...."

PARKER'S VIRGINIA BATTERY by Robert K. Krick pub by Va. Book Co. 1975

Pg. 275 December 1864 "Much of the clothing problem was solved by proximity to Ricmond. The same staff officer noted: "a shoeless rebel in not often seen now."

OK, great! What units is he referring to?

RED CLAY TO RICHMOND by John J. Fox pub by Agle Valley Press 2006

Pg. 290 "On Sunday, December 4, (1864) a special visitor came to the brigade area and broke the monotony of the trench lies. This man came to talk about his inventionthat he believed would win the war for the South. While many men laughed at his idea, he was actually quite farsighted and only slightly ahead of his time. R.O. Davidson talked about hie mechanical bird operated by steam that carried a pilot and a number of shells that could be dropped on fear-stricken Yankees. The Confederate Government had denied his request for aid on the project. Ebbing with confidence, Davidson asked the troops to contribute to his effort. He passed the hat and collected $116 from the Georgians. He planned to make five hundred birds that would be ready for active operations the following Feburary.

An article from the Charleston News and Courer that was reprinted in the Southern Historical Society Papers described a similar visit to McGowan's Brigade during the same period at Petersburg:

One cold, raw day the brigade was called out, withour arms, to hear a speech from scientific personage, who was introduced as 'Professor' blank. The old soldiers crowded around and took their seats on the ground and he unfolded his sceme for the demoralizing and driving away Grant's army. He had just invented an airship. In shape, it was something like a bird. And for that reason he had called it 'Atis Avis', or, 'The Bird of Art', which was the meaning of the two Latin words. The frame was made of hoop-iron and wire. It was covered with white-oak splints. It was to be run by a one-horse-power-engine, and flown by a single brave man. The engine was to be in the body, and to furnish power for keeping the wings in motion. A small door at the shoulder was opened or closed to control the direction of the Bird of Art. A door under the throat was opened when it was desireable to descend and a door on top of the neck when the operator wished to go higher. There was machinery by which the tail could be spread out or closed. In the body of the bird there was a room for a number of shells, and the operator, by touching a spring with his foot, could drop them upon the enemy from a safe distance. The 'Professor' claimed that he had completed one bird and made a test of its speed and how it would work. He had tied it to a flat car, which was coupled to a fast engine. It was then attached to the flatcar with along, strong, rope. The word was given, and the railroad engine started off at top speed. The 'Bird of Art' did the same, and had no trouble keeping up with the iron horse without pulling on the rope. The 'Professor concluded his remarks by saying he needed a little more money to make birds enough to destroy Grant's army,and asked the old soldiers to contribute one dollar each to the cause.any of them did, and the 'professor' moved on and disappeared."

In what was left of the Confederacy at this time, where was he going to have the steam engines built? If he was a con-man the joke was on him as the money he collected was all in Confederate bills.

LEAVES FROM THE DIARY OF A YOUNG CONFEDERATE-Randolph H. McKim, late 1st Leiutenant & ADC 3rd Brigade, Johnson's Division, ANV pub by Longmans, Green & Co. 1911

Pg. 243 The Winter Campaign of 1864-65 "we were now to take an expedition into West Virginia, under command of General Rosser, a dashing and adventurous officer...We started out on Dec. 7th, 1864....We had no wagons, and of course no tents-nothing, in fact but what each trooper carried on his saddle. Each man was supposed to have a small tent-fly rolled up behind him. These were about six feet long and perhaps eighteen inches across,-two of them buttoned together and stretched a small pole cut from the forest and supported by two forked sticks formed a little shelter under which two men could crawl and have some protection from falling weather.

Just at dusk snow began to fall, and it was evidently to be a heavy one. Quickly then these tiny shelter tents began to spring up in the forest. But unfortunately for us, neither Adjutant Griffin not I possessed a tent fly. So we had no resource but to lie down and cover up with what blankets we had and a rubber overall-this as quickly as possible before the ground had become covered with snow. This then, we did, while our comrades standing by the little feeble fires of brushwood, bade us goodbye, saying "We expect to find you buried alive in the morning." This expectation was literally realized, for "Tip" Griffin and I were covered up by a blanket of snow eight inches deep-buried, but still alive…"

Pg. 244 "Another severe experience I recall was this. We crossed one of the mountain brooks not less, I think, than twenty times in a day's march, and the weather was so cold that the water as it splashed upon the horses froze, and their legs and bellies were covered with little icicles. But the forepart of the top of one of my boots was gone, so that my sock was exposed, and it soon became a frozen mass over my foot, so that I was obliged to dismount and walk all day (sometimes to doublequick) to prevent my foot being frozen or frost-bitten…"

ROSANNA BLAKE Confederate Collection, Marshal Univ.

General Orders Head Quarters Army N.Va.
No.70 Dec.7, 1864

In order to prevent the waste of clothing furnished to the army and the suffering caused thereby the Commanding General calls on the Regiment and Company Commanders to see that the men do not dispose of their clothing and shoes, without the cooperation of these officers it is impossible to keep the army supplied. Notwithstanding the liberal issue of shoes in the last few months, the Commanding General is pained to learn that there are many men still without them.

The Commanding officer of each company and Regiment must keep a record of the articles drawn from the Quarter Master by his men, and by frequent in sections keep himself acquainted with the condition of their clothing and shoes, and promptly arrest and bring to punishment those who dispose of them. Division and Brigade Commanders will see that Regimental and Company officers do their duty in the enforcement of this order.

There can be no efficiency where the officers do not constantly look to the comfort of their men, and cause them to take care of their arms and clothing…"

A PAIR OF BLANKETS by William H. Stewart ed. by Benjamin H. Trask pub by Broadfoot Pub. Co. 1911

Pg. 187 Dec. 9 1864 "Our brigade had made a forced march from our camp on the Boydton Plank Road, and were bivouacked in a church grove for the night of the ninth of December, 1864. Major Charles Calpine pooled our blankets and with an oil cloth underneath and one over our blankets, my "Cumberland blankets" with his, made our bed. We slept most delightfully, and were greatly astonished next morning when we peeped out to find our covering rein forced by about two inches of snow…"

LETTERS TO AMANDA-The Civil War Letters of Marion Hill Fitzpatrick, Army of Northern Virginia ed by Jeffery C. Lowe & Sam Hodges pub by Mercer univ Press 1998

Pg. 186 Dec. 8, 1864 Camp 45th Ga. Reg. Near Petersburg, Va. (Letter No 93) Dear Amanda, "Edd Jordon has not come yet. I expect they pressed him in Macon and I feel a little uneasy about my overcoat but I know he will take care of it if he can. I am glad you sent no other clothes but the overcoat as they would only be in my way and I do not need them but would have been proud of the patches if you could have gotten them through to me…."

VOICES FROM COMPANY D Diaries by the Greensboro Guards, Fifth Alabama Infantry Regiment, Army of Northern Virginia ed. by G. Ward Hubbs pub by Univ. of Georgia Press 2003

Pg. 330 December 9 1864 SP "…This has been one of the coldest days of the season-ground hard frozen. Those who drilled complained bitterly. The poor fellows on guard must suffer terribly, for very few are properly clad by this climate and season…"

LIBRARY OF VA. William Hite Box # 29319

Dec. 10, 1864

My Dear Wife "…You can send me my old coat and some pants and socks….You can have the negro shoes made out of the leather up stears (?) and keep that is at the tanyard for the next year…"

GRANDFATHER'S JOURNAL (Franklin Lafayette Riley) Company B Sixteenth Mississippi Infantry Volunteers Harris' Brigade Mahone's Division Hill's Cops, A.N.V. May 27, 1861-July 15, 1865 ed by Austin C. Dobbins pub by Morningside Press1988

Pg. 223 Saturday-Wednesday, Dec. 10-14, 1864 Petersburg "…Marching in freezing weather is no picnic. Bivouacking with sleet falling is no fun either. Few of us are warmly clad. All most of us have are a jacket, cotton shirt, and pants, and one thin blanket…"

How did these soldiers manage to keep from freezing to death?

U. S. ARMY HERITAGE AND EDUCATION CENTER

Dec. 13, 1864 unknown writer 2nd North Carolina Cavalry Berrigen's Brigade Petersburg, Va. "...When John Clapp comes home soon send me a pair of pants or with anybody that is coming out here for I haven't drew anything yet. I could a got a great many blankets when we was on that rode but they was very sleety and wet but I got one oilcloth..."

"DEAR MARTHA..." The Confederate War Letters of a South Carolina Soldier Alexander Faulkner Fewell compiled and edited by Robert Harley Mackintosh, Jr. pub by The R.L. Bryan Co. 1976 17th South Carolina Inf. Company E

Pg. 172 Entrenchments Dec. 14th 64 Dear Martha "...I sent a pair of socks & pants home two jugs and a bundle of clothes and my old canteen strap & tobacco..."

VOICES FROM COMPANY D Diaries by the Greensboro Guards, Fifth Alabama Infantry Regiment, Army of Northern Virginia ed. by G. Ward Hubbs pub by Univ. of Georgia Press 2003

Pg. 333 December 15 1864 SP "...Cp.N. suggestion I put my glove in the heel of my shoe so as to walk without hurting me..."

Pg. 334 December 17 1864 SP traveling through Richmond "...Went to Mrs.'s Barnes and got a blanket-pr. Old shoes to wear, socks & left my new hat in my trunk there & walked about town awhile..."

RECOLLECTIONS AND LETTERS OF GENERAL ROBERT E. LEE by His Son, Capt. Robert E. Lee pub by Garden City Pub Co. 1926

Pg. 1412 Petersburg (Va) Letter to Mrs Lee: "...I received day before yesterday the box with hat, gloves, and socks; also the barrel of apples. You had better have kept the latter, as it would have been more useful to you than to me, and I should have enjoyed its consumption by you and the girls more than by me..."

"DEAR MARTHA..." The Confederate War Letters of a South Carolina Soldier Alexander Faulkner Fewell compiled and edited by Robert Harley Mackintosh, Jr. pub by The R.L. Bryan Co. 1976 17th South Carolina Inf. Company E

Pg. 176 Entrenchments near Petersburg Dec 18th-64 Mrs. M.A. Fewwell Dear Martha "... you write that you have covered me a hat. The one I have is good yet but so abused that you would not know it although I have been careful of it as possible for hats are hard to get in the army and the men are generally worse off for hats than anything else…"

THE CONFEDERATE VETERAN VOLXI Jan. 1898

Pg. 14 Luxuriates in Feasts and Feather Beds by J.B. Polley Dec. 20, 1864 Botetourt Co., Va. "…One of the jokes was on Jim Cosgrove, who helped me off the field the day I was wounded. Cosgrove was found of fun and excitement, plays a practical joke on a comrade whenever he can, and is always making himself heard. One day when rations were slenderestand he hungriest he said to his messmate: "I would eat anything in this world—snails frogs, grasshoppers, dogs, rats: anything but cats. I draw the line at those cussed, sharp-clawed, treacherous creatures."

"I helped eat a cat once," remarked Babe reminiscently and with a far-off look in his hungry eyes, "and it was good too; and I wouldn't object to the leg of one right now."

"But I would," protested Cosgrove. "Just remember that, please; and if you ever have cat for breakfast, dinner or supper, count me among the missing. Why, I'd-I'd eat a buzzard sooner than a cat, any day."

Babe made no reply, but a bright idea struck him; Cosgrove would be on picket that night, and when he came back next day he was sure to be too famished to be inquisitive, and he might be taught that cat was not bad eating, after all his antipathy to it. Lockily for Babe's plans, an old bachelor lived near the camp, whose most cherished possession was a half-grown, fat and sleek pussy, that was in the habit of taking a nightly stroll through the camp. That night Babe lay in wait for it, and the next morning its remains swung from the rafters of its captor's little cabin, and later in the day became the principle ingredient of a "rabbit" pie, so called in difference to Cosgrove. The intended joke would be too good for one man, besides Babe didn't care to be alone with Cosgrove when the truth was revealed to him, and so he invited a friend to dine with them.

"What have you got in the skillet today, old man?" asked Cosgrove when, released from duty, and standing before the messfire, he caught a whiff of savory odors.

"The fattest little cotton-tail rtabbit you ever saw," responded Babe with a childlike smile.

"It smells good anyhow," remarked Cosgrtove approvingly. "Isn't it almost done?"

"Yes, answered his messmate; get off your traps and take a fair start with us."

Soon the three were seated around the skillet, busily consuming its contents.

"Umph!" grunted Cosgrove as he closed his teeth on a juicy morsel; "if this isn't good enough eatin' for Gen. Lee! Where'd you get it Babe?"

"Out of a hollow stump," answered his comrade, with his mouth almost too full for utterance.

The skillet was soon sopped clean enough to bake a cake in. Then, with his feet high up on the jamb of the fireplace, Jim folded his hands across his corporosity and said in his mellowest tone:Lord! Lord! Lord! How good that mess was, and how peaceful I feel! Why Babe, a five year-old child could play with me now and I could be amiable even to a Yankee."

Babe looked at Jim a moment, took his stand in the doorway, and, discovering that retreat was possible, remarked; "I thought you didn't like cat Jim?"

"Cat?" shouted the suddenly surprised gentleman; "cat? Is it cat I've been eatin?"

"Of course it is," said the guest, "and its powerful good eatin' too."

Cosgrove turned pale as a ghost, and endeavored to get rid of the portion of the animal he had appropriated, but in vain. His digestion had not been worked to its limit for a long time, and it clung sucessfully to its prey. Then he got mad, but Babe Metcalf was out of sight and hearing, and the guest could not be held responsible for any deception, and so poor Cosgrove had to stomach both the cat and the joke.

"But," said the Veteran, "you'd better not say 'cat' to him when you meet; he has already thrashed one fellow within an inch of his life for just mewing like a cat."

U. S. ARMY HERITAGE AND EDUCATION CENTER

Dec. 23, 1864 Henry—unknown unit, Fort "Old Pete" on Charles City Road (Va) My Dear Tom (brother) "…As regards clothing, shoes, etc., I am amply supplied having sufficient stock on hand to make me comfortable all winter…

P.S. I wish you would ask Sallie to send me on a darning needle to fix my socks with. I have plenty of yarn and you can enclose it in your next letter to me…"

This soldier sounds as if he's well supplied.

FORGET-ME-NOTS OF THE CIVIL WAR Letter from Walter Lee Laura Elizabeth pub by Press of A.R. Fleming Printing Co. 1909

Pg. 355 December 25, 1864 "…In passing through Raleigh I stayed all night at the "Way-Side-Inn." Next morning in rolling up my blankets I forgot to put my socks in and came off and left them. I never hated anything so bad in my life. Just think, they were the only extra pieces I took along, and then should lose them. If McBride has not left before you receive this please send me another pair…"

NO SOAP, NO PAY, DIARRHEA, DYSENTERY& DSERTION Acomposite History of the Lasr 16 Monthes of the Confederacy Jeff toalson, ed. IUniverse Inc.2006

Pg. 292 Dec.26, 1864 Savanah Georgia Private Johnny Green 1st Kentucky Mounted Inf. "We never had our clothes off and no clean clothes until now. The quartermaster brought clothes out from Savanah to issue to us; they would otherwise have been burned (to avoid falling into Shermans hands)

I got my piece of soap and took a bath in the Savanah River. Lathered well and then soused in good & took a swim. It was pretty cold too. I donned my new clothes…and washed as best I could my old clothes, dried them and put them in my feed sack."

WRITING & FIGHTING FROM THE ARMY OF NORTHERN VIRGINIA ed. by William B. Styple pub by Belle Grove Pub. 2003

Pg. 308 Letter from Bohemia In the Trenches Before Petersburg Dec. 29, 1864 "…It has been cold, wet and snowy weather during the past week. Life in the trenches is by no means, injurious. Our quarters are very much cramped, the ditches are muddy, and the wood issued is base in quality and insufficient in quantity. The men have generally good brick chimneys and manage to keep warm by great economy of fuel. Clothing is greatly needed, and if the Quartermaster of Alabama could manage to send on a supply, he would win the gratitude of many cold, ragged, and shivering men. Socks, pants and jackets are greatly needed. I have seen in the last few days men on guard in the snow and rain with clothing on that was nothing but shreds and patches. It would be useless, however, to send clothing here, and expect the men to pay for it. They have not been paid in six months and not one in ten has any money. Alabama might afford to give clothing to the men who for four years have maintained her honor on a hundred battlefields, and have never yet sustained a defeat. The soldiers knew that the State has clothing, but they fear it will be issued to the "Bomb Proofs," the stragglers and the pets at the post throughout the State. Can you not call attention to this matter?…"

After reading these quotes from the Army of Northern Virginia, how can anyone say they were well equipped and not ragged Rebels?

Middle South

CONFEDERATE ECHOES A Soldier's Personal Story of Life in the Confederate Army From the Mississippi to the Carolinas by Albert Theodore Goodloe-First Lieutenant Company D Thirty-Fifth Regiment Alabama Volunteer Infantry C.S.A. pub by Zenger Pub. Co. 1897, 1983

Pg. 226 "…Before leaving North Alabama for Georgia (1864) a short leave of absence was granted to these regiments to visit their homes, which were near at hand, and procure a much needed supply of clothing, shoes, etc.…"

DAILY LIFE IN CIVIL WAR AMERICA Dorthy Denneen Volo & James M. Volo

Pg.172 "…Most soldiers kept their most personal items in their haversacks or in their pockets, along with two or three days rations, a so-called "housewife" or sewing kit, a tin cup, and any extra ammunition. A Confederate haversack found on the field in 1864 contained "a jack-knife, a plug twist of tobacco, a tin cup, and about two quarts of coarsely cracked corn, with perhaps an ounce of salt tied in a rag…"

RELUCTANT REBEL The Secret Diary of Robert Patrick 1861-1865 ed. By F. Jay Taylor pub by La State Univ. Press 1959

Pg. 151 1864 Pollard Ala. "There is one thing that (Qrtrmaster) Wolfolk does which I do not like, that is, he sells shoes and blankets to the officer's negroes while the poor private who is fighting for the country goes barefooted and without sufficient covering. I think this is a great wrong and Wolfolk ought to be reported for it. A soldier comes in with his toes sticking out of a pair of bottomless shoes, with a thin threadbare tattered blanket across his shoulders, and says "Major can't I get a pair of shoes and a blanket?" "No sir" is the abrupt and uncivil reply. The soldier says no more but leaves the house. A staff officer comes in.

"Good morning Major Wolfolk, how do you do sir?'

"Good morning Captain. I am very well thank you. Come in."

The Captain comes in, takes a seat and directly he draws out a bottle of whiskey.

"Major, suppose we try a little of this. I brought this with me from Mobile and I think it is much better than the rot-gut they have around here."

Wolfolk, who was never known to refuse a drink, helps himself. They talk a while longer and the Captain proposes another drink, and down goes another sockdologer of the "rifle brand." In the meantime a colored gentleman of African descent, makes his appearance, and loiters around the door. Finally, Wolfolk, who is pretty "high up" by this time, sees the darkey and enquires his business. The captain doesn't give the negro time to reply, but says,

"Oh, that's my boy, Major, and I came around to get a pair of blankets and a pair of those English army shoes for him. Can I get them?"

"Certainly, certainly, Captain. Mr. Patrick gives this negro man a pair of blankets and one pair of those best English shoes, and make a memorandum it against the Captain."

This is inexcusable bahaviour and the major shood be cashiered for it.

WEBSITE-55thva.org/article00001

Pg. 3 "in the new year of 1864, Frank M. Mixson of Jenkin's brigade of Longstreet's corps took part in a skirmish with some Federal troops in East Tennessee. He recalled, "The enemy fell back as we advanced. We had not gone more than a couple of hundred yards before we ran over some dead Yankees. Here was my opportunity and I embraced it. The first one I got to I stopped, pulled off his pants, shoes and stockings, got right into them, there and then. The shoes were new and fit perfectly; the stockings were good wool and came up to my knees, and the pants were all right, except a little too long, but I rolled them up about as they are worn these days [ca. 1900?] and they too were a fit. I felt grand."

This quote gives an example of how the Rebs at this stage of the war were always looking for shoes and uniforms from the Yankees when advancing.

THE PRIVATIONS OF A PRIVATE-Campaigning With the First Tennessee C.S.A. by Marcus B. Toney pub by Univ. Alabama Press 2005

Pg. 58 "While in winter quarters at Dalton (Ga.), I received a letter from a relative saying that she would soon get married, and had woven on her loom a nice suit of jeans, and that I must come a week before in order that the tailor could make them…As I had not drawn any clothing from the Confederate States Army for a year, I was entitled to so much money in lieu therof. I think the paymaster payed me ninety-five dollars…"

THE LOYAL, TRUE AND BRAVE ed. By Steven E. Woodworth pub by Scharlarly Resources Inc. 2002

Pg. 162 January 1864 "…Colonel Bolling Hall of the Fifty-Ninth Alabama reported that he had 180 men with no shoes and another 150 who wore only pieces of leather that left the foot half exposed. Yet there is evidence that by spring of 1864 the problem had been largely resolved. On March 7, for example, (Carter L.) Stevenson's division of 6,631 men present listed only 137 as shoeless, down from 2,284 the previous December.

A common Complaint as the army moved towards Atlanta was the lack of creatures you ever saw," confessed a lieutenant, while a canoneer remarked that "I am as dirty as a hog-no clean clothes-all used up." William Stanley admitted to his wife in Alabama: "I have not changed my clothes in nearly five weeks. You may draw an idea what fix my clothes are in." Even on those occasions when there were opportunities to wash, there was little soap…"

BLOODY BANNERS AND BAREFOOT BOYS-A History of the 27th Regiment Alabama Infantry C.S.A.The Civil War Memoirs and Diary Entries of J.P. Cannon, M.D.Compiled and Edited by Noel Crowson and John Brogden 1997

Pg. 50 winter quarters, Canton Miss.

"the first half of January was said to be the coldest weather experienced in that region for years, but we were so well prepared for it with our comfortable houses and plenty of firewood, there was no suffering from cold, although the majority of the regiment was sadly in need of clothing, blankets and shoes. We drew clothing only one time during the winter, three jackets, three shorts, six pair of drawers, two pair of pants, two pair socks to the company. No shoes nor blankets which were needed most of all. Two companies received a consignment from home, which supplied them very well, but taking all into consideration, we had no cause to grumble and sympathy was often expressed for our comrades whose lots were cast in the colder climates of Virginia and Tennessee."

Here we see again the miserably insufficient issue of clothing and the dearth of shoes. Virtually the only clothing and shoes supplied came from the home folks.

LETTERS OF THREE LIGHTFOOT BROTHERS, 1861-1865 ed. by Edmund Cody Burnett Privately Published

Pg. 52 Jan.2, 1864 Letter from Thomas Reese Lightfoot to Sinai McCormick Cody "...The weather is bitter cold and many of the men are bare-footed and very needy of clothing. The government is rather slow in furnishing us, but we keep up hope and bear it as cheerfully as possible. We are now in comfortable quarters, which is better than is allowed some poor fellows. The campaign is closed I guess for the winter, no telling though, the Yankees may come over and trouble us..."

THE CIVIL WAR REMINISCENCES OF MAJOR SILAS T. GRISAMORE, C.S.A. ed by Arthur W. Bergeron Jr. pub by La. State Univ Press 1993

Pg. 134 Jan. 3rd, 1864 Camp Near Calvary Chuch "The ground was frozen hard, many of the men were barefooted, some were without blankets, and others almost destitute of clothing. I remember one morning that one of the men in our company came to me and showed me the only remnant of a blanket that was remaining to him. I think that there were ten holes in it about the size of a man's hand..."

This "blanket" sounds more like a net.

Pg. 138 "our command was so destitute of clothing that it was known as the ragged brigade- only the members of the 28th, whose homes were nearby, had anything like a decent outfit..."

Notice this trend.

Pg. 140 Alexandria, La. Feb. 1864 "...We were fortunate to receive some clothing which was distributed to the most needy..."

ALL AFIRE TO FIGHT-The Untold Story of the Civil War's Ninth Texas Cavalry by Martha L. Crabb pub by Avon Books 2000

Pg. 197 Jan 12, 1864 "Farriers shod horses, but there was little the men could do about their tattered shirts and pants. The army occasionally issued a few garments, but the Texas cavalrymen depended on their families for most of what they wore. The North's blockade had stopped the flow of manufactured goods, including cloth, into Texas, but grandmothers across the state had taught the younger women to weave on looms the grandfathers had built. With sawed lumber scarce, the floor of the Masonic Building in Fort Worth had been carefully removed plank by plank to build looms. But in 1863, another shortage stopped the manufacture of fabric. The women's cotton cards were worn out. The men could not make cards, and there were none to purchase. Texas cavalrymen and their families at home were equally threadbare. A.W. and his messmate were down to one decent pair of pants between them, the other pair being worn badly "at the first and second angles." The man on duty wore the decent breeches. When one messmate relieved the other, the boys exchanged pants at the site."

Its hard to imagine such destitution in an army in contact with the enemy.

LETTERS OF A CONFEDERATE SURGEON 1861-65 pub by The Hurley Co. 1960

January 18,1864 "...Tell Virginia when she cuts my pants to make them a half inch longer in the legs than the pattern..."

NO SOAP, NO PAY, DIARRHEA, DYSENTERY & DESERTION ed by Jeff Toalson pub by iUniverse Inc 2006

Pg. 18 Jan. 19 1864 40 miles above Knoxville Tennessee, 1st Lt. Wm. R. Montgomery, 3rd Battalion Georgia Sharpshooters; "...Marched about twenty miles through the mud and snow...Had to lay out 3 nighrts without any covering except arch of Heaven which you may imagine was by no means pleasant...Aunt Frank it is enough to make tears come from your eyes...to see our brave men marching through the mud & snow almost naked & barefooted. My feet are on the ground...the whole Corps is barefooted & in rags. In my company we have but five or six men with shoes..."

Sounds as though there was a dire need of supplies.

Pg. 24 Late Jan. 1864 Bartholomew Bayou, Louisiana Major Silas T. Grisamoe, AQM Co. G. 18th Louisiana Infantry; "...This was the severest season our troops experienced during their four year's service. On the march to Bartholomew Bayou, the blood from the feet of the men was frequently to be seen upon the frozen ground, owing to the want of proper clothing, the suffering was great…"

LETTERS FROM LEE'S ARMY Compiled by Susan Leigh Blackford Annotated by her Husband, Charles Minor Blackford, Charles Scribner's & Sons 1947 Company B of the Second Virginia Cavalry- Charles Blackford was first Lieutenant, later Captain.

Pg. 234 Longstreet's Headquarters,Jan. 24th, 1864 "An Appeal for Hood's Brigade"(Eastern Tn.) "…They have been campaigning out here on frozen ground, many of them with bare feet, leaving bloody footsteps on the snow and ice. Try to get the ladies in their knitting club to do something for them. Shoes are very scarce. The men get pieces of raw hide from the butchers, and, after wrapping their feet up in old rags, sew the hide around them, making a clumsy ball, which they wear without yanking off until it wears out. I rode behind Robison's Texas brigade a few days ago on a reconnaissance and it was most pitiful to see the poor fellows struggling along, so many of them with this improved shoe and others with none-yet there was not a murmur…The progress, however, was slow; but when ordered into line of battle they were as quick as if shod with the best and as if there was no snow, ice or briars to make their cold feet bleed…"

This is a common description of the ragged and barefoot men. Their morale, however, seems to be good. I cannot imagine engaging the enemy while being forced to live in these conditions.

A SOUTHERN SOLDIER'S LETTERS HOME The Civil War Letters of Samuel Burney Cobb's Georgia Legion, Army of Northern Va. ed. by Nat Turner pub by Mercer Univ. Press, Macon Ga.2002

Pg. 266 Russellville, Tn. Camp Cobb's Ga. Legion, Jan. 26th, 1864 "…I found the Company all on foot; in many cases literally, for some are barefooted…."

HISTORY OF THE BEDFORD LIGHT ARTILLERY 1861-1865 by Rev. Josph A. Graves pub by Press of the Bedford Democrat 1903

Pg. 39 Feb. 1st 1864 East Tennessee "…About this time the men are returning to camp, they have enjoyed their visit home, they were gratified to see the self-denial practiced by their friends and families, to keep them in the field. They come back, with good shoes and clothes, and set about their duties more determined than ever, to do all they can to establish the Confederate Government…"

Another example of resupply from the home folks.

NO SOAP, NO PAY, DIARHHEA, DYSENTERY, & DESERTION ed by Jeff Toalsonpub by iUniverse Inc. 2006

Pg. 36 Undated, probably Feb 1864 Army of Tennessee in NW Georgia Pvt. James A. Holder, 24th Tennessee Infantry; "…Clothing was scarce…when in camp we slept fairly well. Lots of times we had no shoes…did not have much to good eating…acorns and perched corn when we had no better…"

DEAR IRVIE, DEAR LUCY-Civil War Letters of Capt. Irving A. Buck, General Cleburne's AAG & Family pub. by Buck Pub. Co. 2002

Feb.9, 1864 Head Quarters Cleburne's Division, Tunnel Hill, Ga. Lu, Jan. 3, 64 "The only present I received this Christmas was a pair of yarn gloves, from a young lady in Georgia Tell Ma That I am well supplied with clothing, have more than regulations allow me to carry, and enough to last the remainder of the war, the very thing I want is to see you all at home, and I would be happy…"

The Civil War Diaries of Savannah Belle Bright & Charles Alexander Elden of Trenton, Tenn. 1861-1867 Andrew Hays-Completed and Annotated by Robert Dudley Hays pub by Heratage Books 2008

Pg. 28 Feb. 7, 1864 "…At General Wheeler's headquarters I was introduced to a little man, rather stooped, large head, black hair and whiskers, beautiful teeth, dressed in genteel large cavalry boots, gray private's jacket, low felt hat-and this was General Wheeler. He was very polished in manner and quite polite…"

STEPHEN ELLIOTT WELCH of the HAMPTON LEGION ed by John Michael Priest pub by Burd Street Press 1994

Pg. 22 Legions bivouac, near Strawberry Plains (Tenn) Feb. 14, 1864 Dear Mother, "I suppose you've seen in some of my letters that I am in command of the company (Co. H)…I wrote to you about breaking my sword, I believe and also having obtained a pair of yellow brogans, quite gay ornaments for a well furnished parlor, but I am proud of them after trudging barefooted for over two months…"

OK, Two things. Here is a company commander who was barefooted for two monthes. Then, when he got a pair of shoes, they were yellow brogans. Can you imagine yellow shoes with a gray or brown uniform?

NO SOAP, NO PAY, DIARHRREA, DYSENTERY & DESERTION ed by Jeff Toalson pub by iUniverse Inc. 2006

Pg. 39 Feb. 16, 1864 Bayou de Glaze, Louisiana Captain Elijah J. Perry Co. F, 17th Texas Cavalry; "…We have been here on the Mississippi River for about 3 months annoying its free navigation by firing into transports, gunboats, etc., and have done them some considerable damage and a deal of trouble…we have a fine army here in good health, good discipline, well fed, well clad, well armed, well munitioned and confident and woe to the unlucky Feds who provoke us…"

DIARY OF KATE CUMMING in KATE: THE JOURNAL OF A CONFEDERATE NURSE ed. By Richard Barksdale Harwell pub by LA State Univ. Press 1998

Pg. 257 Feb. 26 1864 Mobile, Al."…The city is filled with the veterans of many battles. I have attended several of the parties, and at them the gray jackets were conspicuous. A few were in citizens clothes, but it was because they had lost their uniforms.

The Alabama troops are dressed so fine that we scarcely recognize them. A large steamer, laden with clothes, ran the blockade lately from Limerick, Ireland…."

Feb.27 1864 "…The winter so far has been a very severe one. We have all suffered from the cold, and clothing of all kinds is scarce. We have given nearly everything in the way of bed-clothing to the soldiers, and at night the only way we keep warm is by heaping on us the piano and table covers, and in many instances all kinds of clothing. Many have cut up their carpets for blankets for the soldiers…"

According to Ms. Cummings, the Alabama troops were supplied with uniforms from Ireland. Blankets appear to remain scarce.

THE STILLWELL LETTERS-A GEORGIAN IN LONG-STREET'S CORPS ARMY OF NORTHERN VIRGINIA ed by Ronald H. Morely pub by Mercer Univ. Press 2002

Pg. 242 Greenville, Tennessee February 27th, 1864 (Molly) Referring to his brigade to be mounted as cavalry."…We will not be allowed any baggage except what we can carry on our horses. I am going to cut up my oilcloth and make me a pair of saddlebags to carry one shirt, one pair of drawers, and two pairs of socks. I am afraid I shall have to lose part of my things. Tell James (Speer) not to bring back any clothes with him, if he does he will lose them. He had better come with a horse or (be) prepared to buy one…"

A HISTORY OF THE SECOND TENNESSEE CONFEDERATE CAVALRY by Richard Ramsey Hancock pub by Brandon Print co. 1887

Pg. 338, March, 1864 "...Chalmer's Division, at this time commanded by Colonel McCulloch, was ordered by General Forest to return to Panola. Colonel Duckworth's Regiment, from Richardson's Brigade, and McDonald's Battalion, from McCulloch's Brigade, remained on the Mobile and Ohio Railroad to accompany General Forrest on another expediton into West Tennessee, and, if possible, into Western Kentucky, to which he was incited by several motives:

First-Buford's Kentuckians were in pressing need of clothing and horses; he therefore desired to give that command an opportunity to refit in their own state.

Second-The Tennesseans brought out in December were also, for the most part, in great need of clothing, and had left their homes so suddenly as to make it important that they likewise should be indulgedin a brief visit to that region....companies of Wilson's and four (including the three companies from West Tennessee) of the Second Tennessee, proceeded southward to Trenton, Tennessee. As Wilson's and Russell's men beloged in that vicinity, they were allowed to visit their families and friends, and to procure summer clothing..."

Notice there is no mention of being re-outfitted by the government, but reliance on the home folks instead.

"...Paducah (Miss.) was in possession of the Confederates from a little after 2 until eleven P.M. Buford's men, nevertheless, began to collect in the various stores, warehouses and stables the clothing, supplies and horses, for which the operations had been chiefly undertaken and other parties were set to destroy such public property and war materials as could not be removed, including the quarternmaster's stores, railroad depot with all the rolling stock, and the Marine way with the steamer Decotah, on the stocks for repairs..."

THE CONFEDERATE VETERAN VOL. V 1897

Pg. 267 "Dr. L. Frazee, a private in Company A, Fourth Kentucky, Giltner's Brigade, Morgan's Command, C.S.A., writes of a boy's efforts to become a soldier...in March 1864 at the age of sixteen, I left home to help the Confederate cause...I soldiered fourteen months, and never drew a dollar in pay nor a suit of clothes, nor a horse, gun, or pistol, and but very lttle to eat, and did not surrender until the 18th of May, 1865, at Mt. Sterling, Ky., with nine others..."

DEAR IRVIE, DEAR LUCY-Civil War Letters of Capt. Irving S.Buck, General Cleburne's A.A.G. & Family pub by BuckPub Co. 2002

Pg.217 March 3, 1864 Head Quarters Cleburne's Division, Near Dalton, Ga. My Dear Lucie, "...The trip did the troops more good than a furlough, they are in better fighting trim now than I have ever before seen them. They had jokes of every description on the citizens. Some of them went into the practical and numbers of luckless civilians lost their hats by idle curiosity in getting too near the train..."

NO SOAP, NO PAY, DIARRHEA, DYSENTERY & DESERTION ed by Jeff Toalson pubh b y iUniverse Inc. 2006

Pg. 61 March 5, 1864 Near Dalton, Georgia 1st Sgt, Robert Watson, Co. K 17th Florida Infantry; "…It is just two years today that we have been in the Confederate Army, and it has been two hard years for us for we have had nothing but starvation, hard marching and fighting, and bare footed and ragged half the time…"

SOJURNS OF A PATRIOT The Field and Prison Papers of An Unreconstructed Confederate by Richard Bender Abell & Fay Adamson Gecik pub by Southern Heritage Press Murfreesboro, TN 1998

Pg 213 Camp, 30th Ga.Regt. Near Dalton Ga. March 20th, 1864 "…I also wanted to have sent some clothing by him (a neighbor) but, owing to the drill on that day, was prevented from doing so. I shall probably send by express on Tuesday morning, if not prevented. I have a shirt, two pairs of drawers, pants, two coats, overcoat, and likely some little things to send. There will be others who will send with me but the things will be marked so they can be known. I think that we will start it about Tuesday, so Pa may look out…." In a letter the same day to his sister, he writes "…We have been getting plenty of clothing of late. I have drawn two coats, two pairs drawers, one shirt and a pair of pants, most of which I will send home…"

The army is getting the much needed clothing now, though he doesn't mention shoes. This was probably the resupply that Gen. Johnson initiated when he took over command.

"DEAR MOTHER: DON'T GRIEVE ABOUT ME. IF I GET KILLED, I'LL ONLY BE DEAD." ed. by Mills Lane pub by The Beehive Press 1977

Pg. 285 A.J. Neal to his Sister Dalton, Georgia March 23, 1864 Dear Emma: "….I had an order this morning to have the artificers make a flagstaff for the new battle flag which was given to us. I hardly know what to do with our flag, and from its reminiscences and associations I dislike to give it up. I think of sending it home for safekeeping. I intend in a day or so to send my saddle and bridle, also a bag of clothes. I know it will be news for me to send clothes home, but I have several articles of no value to me which you might give the Negroes. I have about as much as I care to be bothered with. I bought two nice shirts from the quartermaster last week for $18 apiece, which will do me 'till this war is over…"

Another example of the care and concern for the servants; Pvt. Neal was sending clothing home for them.

NO SOAP, NO PAY, DIARRHREA, DYSENTERY & DESERTION ed by Jeff Toalson pub by iUniverse Inc. 2006

Pg. 72 March 23, 1864 Camp-Army of Tennesse-NW Georgia Major Willis H. Claiborne Jeff Davis Legion Mississippi Cavalry; "…It is astonishing what a revolution Genl. Johnson has produced in this army. When I left for Virginia (on a 30 day furlough) it was little better than a mob-demoralized in sentiment (after the defeat at Chattanooga). Besides this, the men were ill-clad and worse fed. Many of them were without shoes and hats…"

Pg. 76 March 25, 1864 Newnan Georgia Miss. Kate Cumming, Nurse, CSA Hospital, Army of Tennessee: '…I have bought a number of home-mads socks and stockings (probably for her patients-ed.) The socks cost two dollars per pair, and the stockings five dollars. Many of the poorer class of country people round here earn their living by knitting articles and weaving cloth…"

WALKER'S TEXAS DIVISION, C.S.A. GRAYHOUNDS OF THE MISSISSIPPI by Richard Lowe pub by La. State Univ. Press 2004

Pg. 181 March 23, 1864 retreat up The Red River, La. Pvt. Samuel Farrow wrote "We have had nothing to eat except bread since we left Simsport and we have been without even that for two days twice. We hardly get more than one meal a day," he complained to his wife. "As to myself both legs of my pants are nearly torn off at the knee, and my drawers get the very mischief, though it is the best I can do."

REBELS VALIENT-SECOND ARKANSAS MOUNTED RIFLES (DISMOUNTED) by Wesley Thurman Leeper pub by Pioneer Press 1964

Pg.212 Gen. Joseph E. Johnston wrote from Dalton, Ga. Early spring, 1864 "…There is a great difficiencey of blankets, and it is painful to see the number of bare feet in every regiment. …There is also a great deficiency of small arms among the men…"

Pg. 214 Feb. 7, 1864 "Upon his arrival in Dalton (Ga), The general issued the following memorandum: "We have a few unarmed men in each brigade, about half of whom are without bayonets.

Many of the men are barefooted-the number of the latter increasing rapidly.13,300 pars of shoes are now needed for the infantry and artillery…The troops are very healthy and in fine spirits….A barefooted soldier in February was not unusual in the Confederate Army at that time, but it was not a thing to be proud of.Truly, "men were men in them days!"

Pg. 224 May 1864 "…When Gen. Joseph E. Johnston took over the command of the Army of Tennessee, one of the young officers of the Confederacy wrote home to his wife: "I doubt whether a volunteer army could be more perfect in its organization than the Army of Tennessee.

General Johnston seems to have inspired a new spirit into the whole mass, and out of chaos brought order and beauty.

Our men are better clothed than at any previous time, while their food is better than one would have anticipated two months ago..."

UNIFORMS OF THE CIVIL WAR by Lord, Wise, pub by A.S. Barnes & Co. 1970

Pg. 86 spring, 1864 "Clothing was sparcely issued...Shoes were scarce. I do not remember the issue of a single overcoat, and but a few blankets." J. Caldwell, 1st S.C. Infantry

Pg. 90 "Each man in Johnston's army, later Hood's army, for the summer and winter of 1864-65 would receive but one jacket (maybe), two pairs of pants, two or three pairs of shoes, maybe one blanket, if lucky, one hat or cap, one or two cotton shirts, two pairs of drawers, and one or two pairs of socks for five monthes of hard service."

Website Refence Publications A Brief History of the G.M.I. (Georgia Military Institute) and a Study of its uniform 1851-1864 David Wynn Vaughan Oct. 2004

"...In the spring of 1864, as Sherman's advancing army reached Dalton, Ga., G.M.I. cadets were reassigned and started their service as soldiers of the Confederate Army. They were organized into two companiesand designated "The Battalion of the Georgia military Institute Cadets" or G.M.I. and were assigned to Walker's Division, Army of Tennessee. They received grey jean militia field uniforms, canteens, cartridge boxes, knapsacks, and .69 Cal. Belgian muskets..."

Hey! Here's those damn Belgian muskets again!

TRUE TALES OF THE SOUTH AT WAR Collected and Edited by Clarence Poe pub by Univ. of N.C. Press 1961

Pg. 90 This reminiscence was handed down to Mr. Lance J. McLeroy of Natchitoches, La., by his grandmother, Mrs. Harry Higgenbotham, "...Twas now Saturday afternoon of April (1864) ...The children ran to the house from the bend of the road excitedly telling us, "There they ncome-there come the soldiers!" Just as they told us we saw a column of ragged, weary, grey-clad men marching in columns of fours, coming around the bend in the road. Walker's Texas Infantry Brigade had fought at Moss' Lane and the Bridwell place the afternoon before..."

Pg. 110 Diary of a Soldier's Wife on Looking Glass Plantation Catherine Deveroux Edmonson "...May 1 Hard at work all day cutting fatigue jackets. Had the women (Negroes) at work in the piazza-and through the open widow could hear their comments on the war-and the "cloth house" they were making for their master to sleep under!"

UNIFORMS OF THE CIVIL WAR by Lord, Wise, pub by A.S. Barnes & Co. 1970

Pg. 78 "Privare S.W. Holliday of the 55th Tennessee Infantry, writing from Camp Cummings, Mobile, Alabama, on April 1 1864 states, "We are stationed at this place and doing guard duty, but getting good rations and are very well clothed..."

Benefits of Gen. Johnson's re-equipping the troops.

KEEP ALL MY LETTERS The Civil War Letters of Richard Henry Brooks, 51st Ga. Inf. ed. by Katherine Holland pub by Mercer Univ. Press, Macon, Ga. 2003

Pg. 117 Camp near Bristol Tenn. April the 1st 1864 "...My Dear I want you to wash that old overcoat an mend it an dye it black some time this summer an if I have to stay in this cold county next winter it will do me a great deal of good if I can get it to me next winter..."

A civilian overcoat, but much better than none, or waiting for the government to issue him one, which is the same as none.

NO SOAP, NO PAY, DIARRHEA, DYSENTERY & DSERTION A Composite History of the Last 16 Monthes of the Confederacy ed by Jeff toalson pub by IUniverse Inc.2006

Pg.82 April 1 1864 Bristol, Tn. Cpl. Milton Barrett Co.-A 18th Georgia Inf. "...we all have tolerable close and shoes Our close is a very corse material of a dingi white sent to us by the State of Georgia. We call them our Joe Brown close..."

Dingy white? More of those undyed wool unforms that the Company of Military Historians class as "drab," which was more widely issued than previously supposed.

Pg. 87 April 9, 1864 Tunnel Hill, Georgia Captain Thomas J. Key Key's Arkansas Lt. Artillery; "...I called at the tailor's shop and had to pay $130 to have coat and pants made-I to furnish the cloth and trimmings except buttons, which were $4 each. Oh; how this world is given to extortion! I purchased some coffee for which I paid $25 per pound..."

The Captain says it best when it calls it extortion.

THE CIVIL WAR REMINISCENCES OF MAJOR SILAS T. GRISAMORE, C.S.A. ed by Arthur W. Bergeron, Jr. pub by La. State univ press 1991

Pg. 144 April 2nd, 1864 "The troops came over to the wagon train, and such a general changing of clothes had not been seen for many a day, as they had not seen their knapsacks for more than three weeks. Some of them, who had like Flora McFlimsey no changes, pulled off those they had on and put them on again, being carried away from strict rules of propriety by the examples around them…'

UNIFORMS OF THE CIVIL WAR Lord, Wise, A.S. Barnes & Co. 1970

Pg. 71 "Another change in officer's uniforms was noticed in the Wilmington Daily Journal of April 3, 1863. It seems that the white and buff facings on some coats "were easily soiled, and so difficult to clean (were) fast going out off use. In defiance of the regulations our officers were having their coats made plain without any facings."

WALKER'S TEXAS DIVISION C.S.A. GRAYHOUNDS OF THE MISSISSIPPI by Richard Lowe pub by La. State Univ Press 2004

Pg 199 Battle of Mansfield, La. April 8, 1864 "If some Federal staff officers were contemptuous of their scruffy opponents, the grimy Greyhounds returned the favor, especially when they beheld the exotic and colorful uniforms of some Federal Zouave reigiments. A captain in Randal's brigade laughed to his sister, "It is the most ludicrous costume, for a civilized man to wear, one could imagine. "Confederates in the 18th Texas were equally scornful:" their red, uncouth, unmanly looking uniform excited much laughter among out men, and many jokes were created at the expense of these "Jaobs," as they were called." Some of the Greyhounds swore theatrically in the presence of passing Zouave prisoners that Texans would have to stop fighting now; they "had too much honor to fight women." Some assured the Zouaves that they would be released when they reached Mansfield because the Confederacy had "scarcely provisions to feed their own troops, without providing for women prisoners." Even fellow Yankees, especially westerners, sometimes snickered at the expense of the Zouaves. A soldier in the 77th Illinois repeated a story later told around Federal campfires when the subject of Mansfield came up:' It is said that when the Zouaves came to the front and then fell back, a rebel was in pursuit of a retreating zouave, and another rebel drew his gun to shoot when the first rebel said, "don't shoot, I want to catch the thing alive."

This last story is very entertaining; who knows, it might be true.

Pg. 206 April 9, 1864 Battle of Pleasant Hill, La. "…A New Yorker, watching from a distance had to admire the Rebel charge: "It was a sight worth seeing that long line of butternut uniforms advancing slowly at first, then, as if gathering momentum, faster and faster, until with a yell they charged upon, and entirely enveloping the Third Brigade, swept it along as if it were but chaff…"

THE JOURNAL OF ELDRESS NANCY: KEPT AT THE SOUTH UNION, KENTUCKY SHAKER COLONY AUGUST 15, 1861-SETEMBER 4, 1864 pub by Parthnon Press 1963

Pg. 196 April 14th 1864 "…To day 4 very suspicious looking men called at the office and said they wished to purchase some cloth, leather, garden seeds &c to the amount of fifty dolar's worth. They first asked for grey cloth, black cloth. Fustic drab cloth, blue jeans, and silk for dresses…"

Basically any cloth they could get.

RELUCTANT REBEL The Secret Diary of Robert Patrick 1861-1865 ed. by F. Jay Taylor pub by La State Univ. Press 1959

Pg. 155 same camp April 15th, 1864 "Mother sent me one pair of pants, three colored shirts and one white one, one silk handkerchief and three or four white ones, three pair of cotton socks."

UNIFORMS OF THE CIVIL WAR by Lord, Wise, pub by A.S. Barnes & Co. 1970

Pg. 78 Dalton Ga. April 27,1864 Private Samuel Ketterick, 16th South Carolina Infantry

Dear Wife

We are expecting something to do here before long. We have received orders to move all surplus baggage to the rear. We have boxed our heavy and surplus baggage to be sent off for home. The box sent to Mr. Burditt you will find I have sent home a pair of shoes and my old pantaloons. I can draw plenty of clothing here and if we have to march I cannot carry it. I wish I had not brought so many (clothes) from home."

"Other soldiers writing from Dalton described the Army of Tennessee: We are in the finest trim. The men throughout are in the finest spirits that I ever saw and have no other idea that we will be in Middleton, Tennessee, this spring…I have about everything Ma that I need. I have uniforms enough to last me until next winter at least, but would like to have a few brown linen shirts. The greatest privation we have to endure now is doing without coffee."

Gen. Johnson's resupply efforts are bearing fruit.

THE CONFEDERATE VETERAN VOL.XII

Jan.1899 Pg. 12 May, 1864 Daring deeds of a Confederate Soldier by J.J. Montgomery "…I rested two months in North Alabama. In May I recrossed in a skiff, about dark, and walked back to Giles County, where I was soon remounted, and returned to North Alabama with a complete outfit of everything the U.S. government issued its cavalry…"

Gee, I wonder where he got his outfit?

U.S. ARMY HERITAGE & RESEARCH CENTER History & Memoirs of the 1st Georgia Regular Infantry by John Porter Fort

May 1864 Atlanta Campaign "…I was in the rear of the line, and as we were leaving I felt a musket and cartridge box leaning against a tree; and from its position I knew it belonged to one of the reserves who had abandoned it. I took about a half dozen cartridges from the box and put them one after the other in the musket and rammed them down, then threw the ramrod away. I leaned the gun up against a tree saying to myself, some Yankee soldier will find this gun in the morning, will probably shoot it off, and if he does how surprised he will be at the way the Rebels load their guns. I do not know the fate of this musket…"

If it was fired, it would have gone off like a shell.

ALL AFIRE TO FIGHT-The Untold Tale of the Civil War's Ninth Texas Cavalry by Martha L. Crabb pub by Avon Books 2000

Pg. 214 May 15, 1864 Retreating from Rome, Ga. "…Rome's merchants, the few who had not fled, opened their doors to the troopers, telling them to take what they needed. A.W. laid in a stock of tobacco while others helped themselves to "a great amount of things that were of no possible use," including stovepipe hats. The men also broke open an army depot and supplied themselves with clothing and commissary goods. When they marched out of Rome, their saddlebags and haversacks were stuffed…"

Resupplied by opportunity.

THE COLONELS DIARY: JOURNALS KEPT BEFORE AND DURING THE CIVIL WAR BY THE LATE COLONEL OSCAR L. JACKSON, SOMETIME COMANDER OF THE 63RD REGIMENT O.V.I. ed by David P. Jackson Privately Pub. 1922

Pg. 123 "…Army of the Tennessee Dallas, Ga. May 27th, 1864 "…Heavy skirmishing. The rebels are said to have been dressed in our uniforms and surprised our Grand Guard this morning who mistook them for friends…"

DIARY OF A CONFEDERATE SOLDIER John S. Jackman of the Orphan Brigade ed. by William C. Davis pub by Univ. S.C. Press 1990

Pg. 132 May 28, 1864 Atlanta Campaign after Battle of Dallas, Ga. "…There were some old smooth-bore muskets left lying around by the Tennessee Troops, also a box of buck-and-ball cartridges, and our boys have been trying to see who could shoot the largest loads out of them, directing the fire down through the woods, at the Federal Sharpshooters. Some have shot a handful of buckshot, and several balls, at a single load…"

A MEMOIR OF CAPT C. SETON FLEMING of the Second Florida Infantry C.S.A. by Francis P. Fleming pub by Times-Union Pub. House 1881

Pg. 131 May 30th 1864 Camp Hospital Newnan Ga. My Dear Aunt Tilly: "…Your revelation in regard to my coat did not surprise me. If you have not already done so, please don't send it on until we are stationary again. I do not need it now, and it might be lost if brought on while we are on the march…"

SOLDIERING IN THE ARMY OF TENNESSEE by Larry J. Daniel pub by Univ. of North Carolina Press 1991

Pg. 33 Summer, 1864 "A common complaint as the army moved toward Atlanta was the lack of opportunity to bathe and change clothing. "At times we are the dirtiest and filthiest creatures you ever saw," confessed a lieutenant, while a canoneer remarked that "I am as dirty as a hog-no clean clothes-all used up." William Stanley admitted to his wife in Alabama: "I have not changed my clothes in nearly five weeks. You may draw an idea what fix my clothes are in." Even on those rare occasions when there were opportunities to wash, there was little soap."

Kentucky Cavaliers in Dixie-Reminiscences of a Confederate Cavalryman by George Dallas Mosgrove pub. by Bison Books 1999

Pg. 188 Summer 1864, "…A soldier receiving new clothing from the quartermaster would carry them to a certain spot in a field, walk away from them a distance of probably fifty yards, divest himself of his old clothes, "graybacks and all," and then, being nude as nature made him, he would run to the pile of new clothing, put them on and-by the next morning be as full of graybacks as ever…"

Pg. 190 A Man in A "Fit" And A Fight. "Mrs. Stout, a Virginia lady, saw a great deal of the fourth Kentucky, and tells the following on Henry Razor and Jerry Leggett: Razor had "drawn" a new suit of clothes, which, as usual, were a "misfit." The trousers especially were ridiculous-the waist being about four sizes too large, and the legs only reaching a short distance below his knees. While Mrs. Stout was busily baking biscuits for them, which they were rapidly and voraciously devouring, Leggett slipped one of the hot biscuits down the bulge in Razor's Falstaffian trousers, and she says that right then and there occurred the most vcious fight she ever saw…"

Pg. 195 "An old gentleman wearing a high-crowned hat enters the camp.

Soldier-"Say, mister, where did you get that hat? Have you got a rammer for it?"

THE CONFEDERATE VETERAN VOL.1

Oct 1893 Pg. 309 Humors of Soldiers Life by Rev. J.H.M'Neilly summer 1864 "In our marches he had frequently called my attention to a very tall, slender, red-headed man, over six and a half feet high, belonging to one of the regiments of our brigade. Looking along the line, this figure, wearing a little skull cap, a jacket and trousers both too short for him, and often barefooted was certain to be seen either before or behind us…."

DIARY OF LT. SPENCER TALLY-28th Tennessee Infantry

Summer 1864 wounded and recovering at a relatives home in Georgia "…Aunt Pansy had plenty of gray cotton cloth that her Negro woman had woven for Confederate clothing; and was making me a new suit while Mr. Crutcher was daily telling me of the pretty girls to see as soon as my new suit was made…"

THE LOYAL, TRUE AND BRAVE ed. by Steven E. Woodworth pub byScharlarly Resources Inc. 2002

Pg. 162 Summer 1864 "…Despite wear and tear, clothing supplies appear to have remained adequate throughout the Atlanta Campaign. A Georgian indicated that he had "clothes a plenty," and a Mississippian revealed that he could "draw all kinds of Clothing from the Government." Writing from Atlanta in August 1864, one Southerner admitted that some of the men were "in rags," but he wondered "why they cannot get clothing from home as I do?" Shortages were often the result of the men's carelessness. On the march, veterans were quick to toss away unwanted items. "there is a great many men in so large an army who neglect themselves and throw away their clothing. This necessarily looks shabby," observed a cavalryman. A Georgian remarked that "as to Co. G being naked that is not so all have got clothes that would carry them some threw (away) their clothes but all have got clothes and shoes…"

Here's some reasons the Rebs were short of c;lothing, what clothing they did get they either didn't keep it mended or tossed it aside during a march.

KENTUCKY CAVALIERS IN DIXIE-Reminiscences of a Confederate Cavalryman.by George Dallas Mosgrove pub by First Bison Books 1999

Pg. 140 June 1864 Mt. Sterling, Ky. (after a retreat by the Federals) "…In the tents we found a number of officer's trunks filled with "biled shirts," fine clothing, etc. In common with others, I found a trunk, and without any conscientious scruples jumped upon it with both feet and smashed the top into smithereens. That was the only way to get into it, and, of course I was bound to "get there." The owner had the key in his pocket and was probably miles away with General Burbridge. The officer who owned that trunk must have been a dandy, a gentleman of exquisite fancy. I forthwith discarded my "old clothes" and "dressedup" in the elegant habiliments found in the trunk and, as luck would have it, they fitted me to a t-y ty…"

U.S. ARMY HERITAGE AND EDUCATION CENTER

June 15, 1864 Major John T. Carson 12th Georgia Infantry Regiment Parkhurst, West River (Ga?) to a fellow officer (unnamed) in the 127th Georgia Infantry: "…Please let me know your height and about your weight as my sisters wish to prepare a box for you of garments that I fancy will be acceptable in your present condition herein to suit also…Let me know in your letter what you are most in want of? If I could get your measure I could send you whatever you stand in need of from my own tailor and the girls would furnish the rest…"

A truly generous friend.

16th TENNESSEE VOLUNTEER INFANTRY REGIMENT: Clothing, Arms and Equipment (website)

Confederates captured near Atlanta, in (June) 1864, are described by a Sergeant-Major from Ohio, "Those brought in yesterday were veterans of Hardee's Corps…they wear grey pants, grey jeans "roundabouts." With blue cuffs and collars" the grey ran from a very brownish color to a very dark color.

Pants were made of wool, although the use of brown jean cloth was widespread These were to be seen patched in all colors and "any material they could get, One man had the seat of his pants patched with bright red, and his knees patched with black. Another used a piece of grey or brown blanket…"

Apparently they had uniforms, but they showed some wear.

THE LIFE OF CLARA BARTON; FOUNDER OF THE AMERICAN RED CROSS vol.1 by William Eleazer Barton pub by Houghton, Mifflin& Co. 1922

Pg. 362 June 5, 1864 "…On the plantation which from the site of this hospital is a colored woman, the house servant of the former owner, with thirteen children, eight with her and five of her oldest taken away. The rebel troops had taken her bedding and clothing and ours had taken her money, forty dollars in gold, which she had saved, she said, and I do not doubt her statement in the least. I gave her all the food I had that was suitable for her and her children and shall try to find employment for her…"

TRUE TALES OF THE SOUTH AT WAR Collected and Edited by Clarence Poe pub by Univ. of N.C. Press 1961

reminiscences of Barry Benson

Pg. 130 June 5 1864 "…Grant has been taught such a severe lesson by Lee and his ragged rebels that he is the most cautious man to be found…"

Gen. Grant didn't have the sense to be cautious. After Lee's ragged Rebels kicked the guts out of the army of the Potomac during the Spring Campaign of 1864, He was able to draw many more men, so why be cautious?

BLOODY BANNERS AND BAREFOOT BOYS-A History of the 27th Regiment Alabama Infantry C.S.A The Civil War memoirs and Diary Entries of J.P. Cannon, M.D. Compiled and Edited by Noel Crowson and John Brogden 1997

Pg. 74 June 15, 1864: Near Kennesaw Mountain. Ga. "We moved to the foot of Kenesaw. Our brigade was placed on a hill and ordered to hold it at all hazards. Here we have a splendid view of both armies. On the right and left can be seen the Confederates, clad in many colors, butternut jeans predominating, all more or less bespattered wth the red Georgia mud from the fresh ditches."

LETTER FROM ROBERT RANSOM in Andersonville Diary Dec. 3 1863

Pg. 304 June 17 1864 "…Some one stole my cap during the night. A dead neighbor furnished me with another, however. Fast as the men die they are stripped of their clothing so that those alive can be covered. Pretty hard, but the best we can do. Rebels are anxious to get hold of Yankee buttons. "Buttons with hens on," they enquire for. An insult to the American eagle- but they don't know any better…"

"DEAR MOTHER: DON'T GRIEVE ABOUT ME. IF I GET KILLED, I'LL ONLY BE DEAD." ed. by Mills Lane pub by The Beehive Press 1977

Pg. 306 Hamilton Branch to his Mother Kennesaw Mountain, Georgia June 19, 1864 My very dear Mother: regarding the battle "…I then found out that we were preparing to fall back and, as I was barefooted, thought I had better go ahead, which Sam and I did. We went until we arrived in Marietta…Hearing that Lieutenant Falligant was wounded I thought that I had better go back to my company, which I did, but found that Leiutenant Falligant did not have to go to the rear. If I had known this I would have stayed and tried to get me a pair of shoes in Marietta. I have been barefooted for two days, and it is pretty hard, although by the time you get this, I will have received a pair (of shoes). If it were not for the rocks, I would get along better…"

Lt. Branch states he will get a pair of shoes soon, but he doesn't tell us where he is planning to get them.

"DEAR MOTHER: DON'T GRIEVE ABOUT ME. IF I GET KILLED, I'LL ONLY BE DEAD." Ed. by Mills Lane The Beehive Press 1977

Pg. 308 Blanton Fortson to his Father Kennesaw Mountain Georgia June 24, 1864 Dear Pa: "…I have not yet received my box from Atlanta. I sent yesterday for it. I do believe I will get completely naked before I can get a rag. I now have on no shirt, having stripped to wash mine and have it now drying. I could not wash my drawers, for my pants was so holey I was ashamed to go without (them)…"

RELUCTANT REBEL The Secret Diary of Robert Patrick 1861-1865 ed. by F. Jay Taylor pub by La State Univ. Press 1959

Pg. 186 June 26th, 1864 "The infernal Yankees have plenty to eat and that of the best quality, and heavy blankets, and good oil clothes to protect them from the weather. Not so with our men. If they have one blanket they are lucky and oil clothing is rarely ever seen except in the possession of some officer."

Website: Tennessee Vlounteer Infantry Regiment: Clohting, Arms and Equipment: Part 1 Clothing

Pg. 3 "About 27 June, 1864, Kennesaw Mountain?: 'We were getting ragged and never got a chance to wash our rags except to wade into Creek, River or pond, pull off, rub and scrub without soap, rinse as best we could, wade out, put them on wet, and be ready for any order…"

For all of Gen. Johnson's good intentions to keep the army in uniform, it seems they had the same trouble as the Army of Northern Virginia, the clothes wore out faster than they could be replaced.

WORD FROM CAMP POLLARD C.S.A. by William H. Davidson pub by Hester Printing 1978

Pg. 273 "The troops stationed at Camp Pollard stood brigade inspection on June 30, 1864 "The brigade was composed of the 15th Confederate Cavalry, the 22nd Louisiana Infantry, and Tobin's Battery Artillery, Pollard troops were under the command of Colonel I.W. Patton.

No attempt was made to list clothing deficiencies. The inspecting officer drew a wide, wavering line down the list of overcoats, coats, trousers, shirts, drawers, shoes, boots for cavalry, spades, camp kettles and mess pans, under the camp and garrison equipage heading…."

THE CIVIL WAR REMINISCENCES OF MAJOR SILAS T. GRISAMORE, C.S.A. ed by Arthur W. Bergeron Jr pub by La. State Univ. Press 1993

Pg. 163 July, 1864 Camp on McNutt's Hill "Whilst at this point, Capt. Sanders, Chief Quartermaster at Alexandria, promised me if I would furnish two good wagons to be sent into Texas they should be returned to our division loaded with clothing. Two of my best teams were fitted up and started off, the prospect of a supply of clothing considerably brightening the hopes of our soldiers…'

That seems like a long way to go for uniforms, but that might have been the only place to get uniforms at all.

SOLDIERS' LETTERS FROM CAMP, BATTLEFIELD AND PRISON pub by Bunce & Huntington 1865

Pg. 472 Letter from John E. Whipple July 1864 Elmira Prison N.Y. "as a general thing, the prisoners are very destitute of clothing; many being barefoot, and destitute of pants and coats. Some of them had nothing but shirts and drawers on, when they came; and when they essayed to wash their linen, they were obliged to adopt the costume of our first parents- a very close-fitting suit assuredly! As for blankets, they have not enough of them to render themselves uncomfortable by any means, and with most of them, going to bed is a very simple process in deed, as they are saved all the trouble of shaking up smoothing down, and tucking under of bedclothes. In fact, they have nothing to do but select the softest board in their bunks, and stretch themselves out upon it. Whether they have the ability to determine the exact shade of difference between the softness of a pine or hemlock board is, as yet, unknown to the writer."

THE CONFEDERATE VETERAN VOL.XX Oct. 1912

Pg. 475 July, 1864 "THE STAMPEDE AT LA FAYETTE, GA by Charles Gore Joy, Company C, 14th Tennessee Cavalry"...The last two years of the war the Confederate government furnished guns, ammunition and rations only when they could be had, the men furnishing everything else-clothing, horses, saddles, etc.-much of which was contributed by the enemy. Many a blue overcoat did we have dyed black, and we sometimes threw away an old blanket upon getting a better one. We would not have their sabres. We did not receive any pay from the government, nor did we have any tents; but with a pole, a couple of forks, blankets and oilcloths we could make "dog" tents that protected us from the severe weather. However, we did not use these except in the event of rain, or when very cold, preferring to sleep in the open air; and this; with coarse food and exercise, gave to many a delicate boy bone and muscle, health and strength. The only kind of rations ever issued to us was flour or meal and beef or bacon and salt. Sugar and coffee were unknown. Our only cooking utensils were frying pans, tin buckets or cans, tin cups. We made "good coffee" with parched meal. If we had bacon and flour, we fried the bacon and mixed the flour with the grease; if beef and flour, we used water. We sometimes had to wash the dirty rock salt broken up. We ate bacon raw most of the time, many preferring it that way,especially in winter. A strip of bacon, "streak of lean and streak of fat," was greatly enjoyed after a hard day's march. We had no plates, cups, saucers, spoons, knives or forks, yet every man had a pocketknife. Occasionally some fortunate boy would have a tin pie pan. Our company officers fared just as we did. Sometimes we imagined they had it better at headquarters, but I douby if they fared as well. We were better rustlers and at times had things not on the regular bill of fare, not issued by the commissary. Maj. J. Gwynn Thurmond, once our captain, often came to our mess for a meal. We sent for him if we had anything extra. When our wagons were up, we got along some better, as some of us had ovens...We did not have uniforms. Among the officers there was some attempt to wear the Confederate gray, and the private did too if possible; but we were a motley crowd and wore whatever we could get. It mattered little about color, quality or fit, and it was nothing uncommon for those who had been immaculate in their dress at home to be wearing pants several inches too short, without socks, shoes too large and hats with holes in them. Our guns were all muzzle-loading, with different kinds in a company.

The first gun I had was a double-barrelled shotgun. I swapped it for the long Enfield rifle with which I was told I could kill a Yankee a mile off. It was long and unwieldy, and I was glad to exchange it for a Sharps rifle. They were little short breech-loaders, the first we had ever seen, and they were "dandies." After using them a while we exchanged them for short Enfield cavalry rifles, muzzle-loaders, and these we had when we surrendered at Gainsville, Ala. In May, 1865. We all had pistols. I had one that was issued to me by the government that looked as if it had been made in a country blacksmith's shop…"

This soldier gives a good overall description of conditions in the Confederate army in the Middle South.

"DEAR MOTHER: DON'T GRIEVE ABOUT ME. IF I GET KILLED, I'LL ONLY BE DEAD." ed. by Mills Lane pub by The Beehive Press 1977

Pg. 309 John McCorcle to his Wife Atlanta Georgia July 2, 1864 My dear and beloved Wife: "…I had to throw away my knapsack and everything in it, so I have no clothes, only what I have on and they are very dirty. But I would have thrown them away if I had have to have went naked 'till Christmas rather than be captured, though I reckon I can draw some (more clothes) soon…."

Pg. 313 William Jewell to his Sister (Chattahoochee River, Georgia July 8, 1864 Dear Sister: "…I lost my haversack and carpetsack and my socks. Tell Ma to send me a pair by Brother when he comes…"

Pg. 318 Jack King to his Wife Atlanta Georgia July 19, 1864 My darling Wife: "…My dearest Wife, I want a suit of some sort, a dark one if you can get one. The one I have is in rags. My pants are out at the seat and knees, but I have not worn my summer pants yet on account of getting washing done. I have washed my shirts twice since I have been here. They were not washed very nicely, but it was better than a black shirt…"

CIVIL WAR MEMORIES OF ROBERT C. CARDEN

Co. B 16th Tenn. Inf. July 22 1864 Atlanta "I ventured out in front of our line to see what I could find and run up on a dead Rebel and got me a good hat and a few shirts out of the Yankee knapsacks and then went back into our lines…"

First-hand account of plundering the dead, both friend and foe.

LIFE IN DIXIE DURING THE WAR ed by Mary A.H. Gay J.H. Segars pub by Mercer Univ. Press 2001

Pg. 140 Battles around Atlanta 22nd of July 1864 "…I had seen a splendidly equipped army, Schofield's division, I think, ignominiously flee from a little band of lean, lank, hungry, poorly-clad Confederate soldiers, and I doubted not an overruling providence would lead us to final victory…"

THE CONFEDERATE VETERAN VOL.II Dec. 1894

Pg. 357 he Borrowed Trousers From A Negro "Rising generations should have some idea of the straitened circumstances of a Confederate soldier. I was wounded near Atlanta, July 22, 1864, and sent to a hospital in the woods, in tents near Forsythe. On arriving at the hospital, I was divested of all my wearing apparel, and the hospital authorities gave me a receipt for my wardrobe, consisting of pants, one roundabout coat, hat, shoes, and shirt and drawers. I was taken from this hospital in the woods to the college hospital at Forsythe, where I remained several months and endured three courses of gangrene. From the college I was sent to Macon and from there to a "college" hospital, the Cuthbert. After several months at Cuthbert, when I had gotten almost well, the nurses brought me a pair of crutches and would come to my room occasionally to practice me in learning how to use them, so he concluded after awhile that I had learned enough about them to risk myself out on the ground. So he brought in my knapsack; but lo! To my surprise and sorrow, on opening it, I found I was entirely destitute of pants. Some good fellow, in the rounds I had taken, had confiscated the only trousers I possessed in the world. I didn't have a cent and couldn't draw any. What was I to do? The little town we were in had some fifteen hundred wounded and disabled soldiers then, but I could learn of none with more than one pair of pants, and I couldn't get out to beg the good citizens, and what should I do? For about nine months I had been confined to my bunk and room, and now I was physically unable to paddle my own canoe. I was heart-sick and had well-nigh given up ever getting another pair, when a negro boy named Byrd, serving his young master, Ridley Jackson, in an open-hearted way, proposed to lend me a pair until I could do better. I gladly accepted, put the negro's pants on, and felt as big as a king. I was soon out on the ground, down in town, at the depot, at the Alhambra, and around generally.

But alas! My joy was soon ended. After I had worn the pants five or six days, my benefactor came to me one morning, just after I had donned his trousers, and said to me that he had just received orders to go to the front, and unless I could pay him three dollars and twenty cents for his pants he would have to ask me to vacate and turn them over to him. With a heavy and sorrowful heart, I gave them up and stretched myself out on my bunk, where I mused over the trials and tribulations on a Confederate soldier."

A good account of the absolute destitution of the Rebel soldiers.

CIVIL WAR TIMES ILLUSTRATED April 1964

Pg.33 Brigade ordinance officer Robert M. Gill Co. H, 41st Mississippi wrote to his wife on July 23, 1864 about his fighting in the Battle of Atlanta.

"Being in advance we were ordered to fall back to the Yankee works which we did. I never saw the like of Knapsacks, Blankets, oil cloths and Canteens in my life. Our men supplied themselves. What do you suppose I got? I took a canteen as I had none, and it was a very good one. One of the men gave me a rubber cloth and a small blank book and being too heavily loaded I had to throw away the rubber."

I,personally, would have hung on to that rubber cloth, not being fond of sleeping in the rain.

HANCOCK'S DIARY, OR, A HISTORY OF THE SECOND TENNESSEE CONFEDERATE CAVALRY by Richrd Ramsey Hancock pub by Brandon Print co. 1887

Pg. 644 August 1864 "...The women and children and some of the men were screaming with affright, or shouting and clapping their hands and waving their handkerchiefs with joy as they recognized the mud-bespattered uniforms of the Confederate cavalry in their streets once more. Soon, indeed, the scene was one of memorable excitement. Memphis was the home of many of those grey-coated young riders who thus suddenly burst into the heart of their city that August morning, and the women, young and old, forgetting the costume of the hour, throwing open their window-blinds and doors, welcomed their dear countrymen by voices and smile and every possible manifestation of the delight inspired by such an advent..."

THE JOURNAL OF ELDRESS NANCY: KEPT AT THE SOUTH UNION, KENTUCKY SHAKER COLONY AUGUST 15, 1861-SETEMBER 4, 1864 pub by Partyhnon Press 1963

Pg. 218 August 4th,1864 "...Jefferson S. informs us that on Tuesday night a company of guerillas or night robbers dressed in Federal uniform went to Auburn and robbed the stores of the town to the amount of near four thousand dollars worth. They broke open doors and split open fresh boxes of goods and rifled them of their contents-packed them in sacks and carried them off...."

CANNONEERS IN GRAY-The Field Artillery of the Army of Tennessee 1861-1865 by Larry J. Daniel pub by Univ of Alabama Press 1984

Pg. 163 August 18, 1864 Gen.Hood's Artillery around Atlanta Ga. "...The August 18 report listed a dearth of 1,935 coats, 1,974 blankets, 1,651 pairs of shoes, 4,564 pairs of socks, 1,710 haversacks, and 1,288 canteens. The inspecting officers reported that "on very few occasions have I seen articles of clothing issued to the artillery with the proper (red) trimmings for that branch of the service. In nearly every instance it has been the uniform of the infantry, although occaisionally I have seen jackets with artillery trimmings in the infantry..."

CELINE-REMEMBERING LOUISIANA 1850-1871 Celine Fremaux Garcia ed. by Patrick J. Geary pub by Univ. GA Press 1987 "The war in Baton Rouge"

"...By morning there were twice as many and every boat that landed brought in companies. To be sure, they were not equipped and in some cases the uniformity was only in hats or caps or shirt sleeves. One company had jeans pants, common75 jeans pants over their tailor-made trousers, but all wore a determined look..."

Pg. 134 "...on the 1st of September, 1864, Ma let Leon start for the army. He was nearly 17. The C.S. law took the boys at 17, and Ma was willing she should obey the law but would have reproached herself if any thing should happen before the law claimed him. She made him promice not to join scouts or guerrillas but to go on to Mobile, meet Father, and follow his advice as to which corps to join. He was to be 17 on the 14th of September.

It was quite a business to fit him out for the trip. He left with one suit of unbleached under-clothing on and one in his bundle, his pair of college blankets, the top shirt he had on (made of mattress ticking) pants of Pa's surveying suit, and a coat of cotton wool bed spread (grey) He was also in possession of: three pairs of home-spun and knit socks, some lint, some old linen bandages, 3 needles, 6 bone buttons, about on third of a spool of good thread; an old but sharp pocket knife, an old flint-liock musket, some powder and balls that he and I has molded from an old black tin syringe and a piece of lead pipe; and spent bullets that we found in tree bark, sides of houses, or on the ground. At every place where a fight had taken place, we had been gathering them since the first days of the War. He also had a little cracked skillet. Leon was considered well-equipped for a volunteer of 1864..."

Leon was as well equipped as a volunteer in 1861.

ARMY LIFE OF AN ILLINOIS SOLDIER by Charles Wright Wills pub by Globe Print Co. 1906

Pg. 284 Sept. 9 1864 Atlanta "...Captain Smith mentioned some heavy skirmishing in our rear...and from our works we could see exactly in our rear a body of grey coats advance..."

I include this as the soldier mentions the Rebs as "grey coats," though whether out of habit or actual observation, we can't know.

FROM THAT TERRIBLE FIELD-CIVIL WAR LETTERS OF JAMES M. WILLIAMS, Twenty-First Alabama Volunteer Infatry ed by John Kent Folmer pub by Univ Al Press 1981

Pg 141 Sept 10 1864 Mobile (Al) Dear Lizzy,"...You can probably do one thing for me that is quite urgent, that is procure me two or three pairs of socks the Fort Powell misfortune has left me almost destitute (Lt. Williams and the garrison had to abadon Ft. Powell)"

RELUCTANT REBEL The Secret Diary of Robert Patrick 1861-1865 ed. by F. Jay Taylor pub by La State Univ. Press 1959

Pg. 227 Sept. 17th, 1864 Griffen, Ga. "The morning is quite cool and regular fall weather is here now I am very anxious to obtain some winter clothing. I will need my over-coat and I need woolen under clothing, for I am entirely out as the clothing I have now is worn out."

THE REGULAR CONFEDERATE ARMY by Richard P. Weinert, Jr pub by White Mane Pub Co. 1991

Pg. 42 Sept 1864 New Hope Church, Ga. "...Armstrong reported that out of one officer and forty men of Company A, thirty men were barefooted..."

That's three out of four men barefooted.

ALL AFIRE TO FIGHT-The Untold Tale of the Civil War's Ninth Texas Cavalry by Martha L. Crabb pub by Avon Books 2000

Pg. 255 Sept. 30, 1864 "With the onset of fall and another rainy season, officers and men began scrounging for boots and clothing. Tha officers sent a lieutenant south to buy new uniforms, and Ross ordered fabric from Macon (Ga). John Dunn was nearly barefoot. He hurried to a location where a few shoes were for sale, but the place was surrounded by soldiers and John gave up. He later learned the location of a tan yard, but again was too late. Some men were reduced to making moccasins out of hides freshly stripped from beef cattle."

A HISTORY OF THE SECOND TENNESSEE CONFEDERATE CAVALRY by Richard Ramsey Hancock pub by Brandon Print co. 1887

Pg.644 Oct. 1864 "...A daring feat was performed by Claib West, of Company G, Second Tennessee. Getting on a slab and using a chunk for a seat, he crossed the Tennessee by aid of a paddle which he had made with his knife (in anticipation for this trip), and was lifted on board by the captain, who had remained with his boat; and thus West was the first Confederate who boarded the Mazzeppa. The captain, by order of West, immediately crossed to the west bank in a yawl, in which General Buford, and a party of men,at once repaired to the Mazzeppa, and taking possession, she was soon brought across to the west bank of the river. She proved to be heavily freighted with flour, hard bread, shoes, clothing, axes, and other military stores, and by five P.M. the greater part of these were safely discharged upon the bank of the river.

At this juncture, however, three Federal gunboats came upon the scene, and taking position out of range of our guns, shelled the landing and the Mazzeppa with such vigor and precision, that Buford found it expedient to burn the steamer, and address himself at once to the security and removal of the stores already landed. Setting the Mazzeppa on fire, she was soon consumed, and shortly after sundown the gunboats withdrew down the Tennessee. Thus left in possession of the field, our division worked all that night in hauling the captured supplies to a place of safety, with wagons and teams mainly impressed for the service from the neighborhood...."

Why didn't the Yankee gunboats come further down and shell the landing? That would have dispersed the raiders, but the raiders would also have been able return fire on the Yanks.

THE CONFEDERATE VETERAN VOL. VII 1899

Pg. 359 August 1899 Oct. 1864 Pathetic burial at Midnight by Col. J.W. Simmons "... When the sun was setting that afternoon, as we were passing an old-fashioned farmhouse, a farmer hailed us and said one of our men was in the house, dying. We found him to be intelligent-looking, of middle age, and probably five feet eleven inches high. He wore a suit of home-made Confederate gray jeans. An examination of his effects failed to disclose his identity other than that by the Palmetto buttons we we supposed he was from South Carolina..."

UNIFORMS OF THE CIVIL WAR by Lord, Wise, pub by A.S. Barnes & Co. 1970

Pg.91 reporter from the Cincinnati Commercial of Hood's Army of Tennessee as it passed through Dalton, Ga. In October 1864 "They were ragged and thinly clad, having, as a general thing pantaloons, shirt and hat in their inventory of clothing; the first, greasy and tattered, the last, shocking affairs in multitudinous variety.

As a general thing they were tolerably well shod, though in one of Stewart's Divisions, one of our officers counted over three hundred barefooted privates...

Not more than one in ten have blankets…In the line, the distinction as to apparel between the officers and men was entirely obliterated!"

The Rebels are ragged once again, or still.

THE CIVIL WAR REMINISCENCES OF MAJOR SILAS T. GRISAMORE, C.S.A.ed by Arthur W. Bergeron jr. pub by La. State Univ. Press 1993

Pg. 171 Oct. 1864 "…Since the first of July we had marched over 500 miles without being at any time within 100 miles of any enemy. Our division was in a deplorable condition, not less than 200 men were barefooted, 100 had no pants and were marching in their drawers, others had no coats, some were without hats, and some had no signs of a blanket, yet we had been kept on this long march and hurried about the country at the rate of 15 to 25 miles per day…As soon as we went into camp, attempts were made to procure clothing for the more destitute soldiers, and a fair supply of shoes, pants jackets and blankets were issued to us by the post quartermaster.

It was during our stay at Camden that two or three boxes of clothing reached our quarters for the use of the 18th regiment, which that noble and patriotic man, Governor Henry W. Allen, had sent to them; these, with what we had received from the post at Camden, put our men in a tolerably comfortable condition again…."

Both issue and supply from home folks.

UNIFORMS OF THE CIVIL WAR by Lord, Wise, pub by A.S. Barnes & Co. 1970

Pg. 92 October 2 1864 a Federal soldier, private Aaron Smith,of the 14th Illinoois Infantry, captured in northern Georgia said: "As we marched out of the stockade…we found ourselves …surrounded by a howling mob of Confederates who unceremoniously relieved us of our watches, etc., and made all kinds of one-sided trades for clothing, hats, boots, and shoes.

At the time the Johnnies were robbing our effects they found me rather poorly clad. My pantaloons and blouse were quite threadbare, being considerably soiled, but I had on a good black hat which seemed attractive to them…A Johnnie jerked it from my head and handed me his old quilted one. I had no sooner got this old quilted rag placed on my head when another Johnnie jerked mine off and handed me his own broken-down broken-billed grey cap…and before I had gone another ten steps, another Johnnie (snatched) off my cap and handed me his hat! When I examined the old black and blue limp thing he handed me, I found the crown was an old piece of blue army overcoat which had "wanged on" with cotton cord, and the limp black rim was looped up to this on all sides with the same kind of cord."

Sorta a hierarchy of hats, from bad to terrible.

THE CIVIL WAR YEARS-A Day by Day Chronicle by Robert E. Denny pub by Gramercy books 1998

Pg. 467 Fighting near Ackworth and Lost Mountain, Ga. Barber, Sgt. Co. C, 15th Illinois Volunteer infantry captured at Ackworth "...After stacking our arms and delivering up our accouterments and stores, he (Gen. Loring) kindly permitted all to get their breakfast and such articles of clothing, etc., as we wished to take with us. He also ordered his men not to molest our private property without our consent but permitted them to purchase of us. This kindness was duly appreciated and we acted in a straightforward manner that won his confidence. This treatment was in striking contrast to that received by our comrades at Big Shanty and Moon Station. The rebels there stripped our boys of almost everything, even to their boots and hats, barely leaving them with their shirts and drawers..."

While I won't defend this practice, I can sure understand it, and, if I was in that situation, I probably would have stripped the prisoners also.

ALL AFIRE TO FIGHT-The Untold Story of the Civil War's Ninth Texas Cavalry by Martha L.Crabb pub by Avon Books 2000

Pg. 257 Oct. 7, 1864 "The fall rainy season continued with a vengeance. Tremendous storms pounded the thinly clad Confederates and turned the rutted roads to deep mud. John was still hunting a pair of boots, and Ross still had not received his cloth from Macon (Ga.) when a frigid north wind blew in the night of Oct. 7. Frost decorated the tree and sparkeled on the muddy fields the next morning. Men hovered near their fires, dreading their turn on picket duty..."

PASSAGES FROM THE LIFE OF HENRY WARREN HOWE pub byCourioe- Citizen Printers, 1899

Pg.170 Oct. 9 1864 "...Leiutenant Clinton E. Page has started for Boston today with the body of Lieutenant J.P. Haley. We obtained a metallic coffin at Harrisonburg, where a number had been stored by the rebels...Last night some of our Company K, went into the woods to see if they could find one of our men who was killed in the charge the day of the fight. They found him stripped of everything and buried him. It is said that the citizens of the town and all the prowlers round here did things of that kind after we went on in pursuit of the enemy. These guerillas show no mercy. On our return a signal officer was shot who was with the rear guard, and his throat was cut. We ascertained this as we drove the devils back, when his body was found. Many of them dress in our uniform, and thus elude capture..."

When you wage war by scorched earth policy, it is going to get this viscious.

NO SOAP, NO PAY, DIARREA, DYSENTERY & DESERTION A Composite History of the Last Sixteen Monthes of the Confederacy by Jeff Toalson pub by iUniverse Inc. 2006

Pg. 235 Oct. 9, 1864 Near Cedartown, Ga. Sergeant Archie Livingston, 3rd Florida Infantry "…I think my clothing-jacket, pants, socks, gloves, overcoat, scarf, 1 shirt, 1 drawers and shoes should be sent as early as they can reach me. Hope they will be sent by some trusty, safe hand…"

Sgt. Livingston needs everything it seems.

CONFEDERATE ECHOES A Soldier's Personal Story of Life in the Confederate Army From the Mississippi to the Carolinas by Albert Theodore Goodloe-First Lieutenant Company D Thirty-Fifth Regiment Alabama Volunteer Infantry C.S.A. pub by Zenger Pub. Co. 1897

Pg. 150 "…While the flesh of the ox was a success (let us admit) as army diet, his hide, untanned at least, was a failure as foot-covering, called at the time "moccasins." This was tested while on the march northward through Georgia on our way to Tennessee. The night of October 11, 1864, we camped just twelve miles northeast of Rome. Just after we had eaten our supper and jerked our beef for the next day, orders came for all the shoe makers to report at army headquarters. The presumption was that they would be sent to the rear to make shoes for the soldiers, many of whom were barefooted and many poorly shod; and never before was it known that the shoemaker's trade was so largely represented in the army. And those that were not shoemakers that night seemed to regret that they had not learned the trade. "Anything for a change" was the idea which sometimes pervaded the ranks; and so shoemaking just then was thought to be much better than marching, with those who professed to be qualified for such work. But late in the night came the shoemakers back to their respective companies in droves, disgusted with themselves and Gen. Hood and with ox hides. Instead of going to the rear to make shoes out of leather, as the order was very naturally interpreted to mean, they were required to make rawhide moccasins that night in camp and report back to their commands for duty at daybreak the next morning. The returned ones vowed, when they learned the real meaning of the order that they knew nothing about making moccasins, and furthermore they had never before heard of such things. That we enjoyed their discomfiture when they returned from their shoe-making expedition need not be stated.

But some of the shoe makers-how many I could never learn- toughed it out and made moccasins of the hides of the beeves that were slaughtered that day. They were made with the flesh sides out and the hair next to the bare feet of the soldiers who wore them. Before being put on the feet they looked like hideous pouches of some kind, but no man could have conjectured for what purpose they were made. However, there was much bragging on them the next day by those to whom they had been issued. But the next day and night following it rained, rained, rained and alas for the moccasins and the men who wore them Just such shapes as these moccasins assumed, and such positions as they occupied on the feet, as the men went trudging along through the mud and water, can never be told; nor can any imagination, however refined, justly depict them. The pioneer corps were ahead of us putting poles and rails across the numerous little branches which the rain had made, for us to walk over on; and whenever a moccasin-footed soldier would step on one of these poles or rails into the branch the moccasin would instantly conduct him. Ludicrous remarks and ludicrous scenes without number characterized that day's march, which were as cordial to us in our weariness, and long before night the moccasins and their wearers forever parted company…"

Another example of extreme misery, not only are you marching in the rain, through streams, but those moccasins couldn't be trusted not to dump you into the creek.

THIS WAR SO HORRIBLE-The Civil War Diary of Hiram Smith Williams ed by Lewis N. Wynne & Robert A. Taylor pub by Univ Al Press 1993

Pg. 118 Hiram Williams, 40th Alabama Infantry Oct. 12th, 1864 "…Drew Clothing of which I was in much need…'

Can't thise soldier give a better description of this clothing?

RELUCTANT REBEL The Secret Diary of Robert Patrick 1861-1865 ed. by F. Jay Taylor pub by La State Univ. Press 1959

Pg. 238 Oct. 20th, 1864 Gadsden, Al. "Weather clear and cold. I have found a plan by which I can sleep very warm the coldest night that comes. As it would be a difficult matter to explain the "modus operandi', I will simply say that it is made by leaning 5or 6 rails near the fire at an angle of about 45 degrees, and laying upon these rails a sufficient number of blankets to cover the rails. An old tent cloth that is worthless in its legitimate use serves the purpose admirably. This concern is placed on the side of the fire whence the wind blows, and prevents the wind from carrying away the heat of the fire. Under one of these things a man can sleep quite comfortably on a very cold night."

Ingenious

ALL AFIRE TO FIGHT-The Untold Tale of the Civil War's Ninth Texas Cavalry by Martha L. Crabb pub by Avon Books 2000

Pg. 259 "The Army of Tennessee reached Gadsden, Alabama, on October 20, 1864 where they found abundant supplies waiting, including shoes and clothing. When Ross's Brigade reached the same town, five days later, they found only scanty rations for themselves and their horses…"

Pg. 265 November 22, 1864 Skirmish near Cambeltown "…The Texans gleefully gathered in their spoils:200 fully equipped cavalry horses, 125 prisoners, 4 stand of colors, 65 cattle. And several pack mules laden with provisions. The provisions included great treasures-overcoats, blankets and coffee…"

FROM THAT TERRIBLE FIELD-Civil War Letters of James M. Williams, Twenty-First Alabama Infantry Volunteers ed by John Kent Folar pub by Univ of Alabama Press

Oct. 23, 1864 Mobile Al. Dear Lizzy; "…Mr. King says that Mr. Hazen will soon be sending him a packageand if you have no other opportunity you can send my socks with it-the Coquette does not run to this city now but the "Virginia" does; and if you will leave them with the warehouse man at your landing marked "care of Mr. Woodruff on steamer "Virginia" they will come soon: I need them very much as also the shoes…"

A CONFEDERATE SURGEON'S LETTERS TO HIS WIFE Spencer Glascow Welch pub by Neale Pub. O. 1911

Pg.127 Oct. 25, 1864 "…Your brother had received his new suit from home. Billie is well and hearty, but he needs a new coat. These government coats are too thin for exposed duty.

I have a nice little Yankee axe, which is so light that it can be carried in a knapsack, but just suitsa soldier for use in putting up his little shelter tent or for making a fire. All the Yankees have these little axes, and many of our men have supplied themselves with them, as they have with almost everything else the Yankees possess…"

NO SOAP, NO PAY, DIARRHEA, DYSENTERY & DESERTION A Composite History of the Last Sixteen Monthes of thew Confederacy ed by Jeff Toalson pub by iUniverse Inc. 2006

Pg 243 Late Oct 1864 Gadsden, Alabama Colonel Ellison Capers 24th South Carolina Infantry "...At Gadsden received for 285 men/20barefoot: 21 blankets 112 pants, 74 pair shoes, 44 jackets, 82 pairs socks, 37 shirts and 46 drawers. This issue by no means supplied our necessities but supplied our most needy...At Tuscumbia (as the march continued) received 64 jackets,16 pair pants, 38 pair socks, 24 blankets and 28 pair of shoes. (Lastly) At Florence another 45 pants, 50 pair of socks, 26 shirts, 34 drawers, and 16 pair shoes..."

Pg. 247 Oct. 29, 1864 Near Columbia, Tennessee, Sgt, Archie Livingston, 3rd Florida Infantry; "...Snow, ice and mud so freezing and cold that it (seem) to me ...I could not stand it. Amid all this some of the Army of Tennessee are barefoot. Hundreds indifferently clad, without good blankets..."

Starting the Nashville Campaign, but, as always, the men are poorly clad and shod.

UNIFORMS OF THE CIVIL WAR by Lord, Wise, pub by A.S. Barnes & Co. 1970

Pg. 92 Oct.-Nov. 1864 "An artilleryman on Guiber's Battery, while encamped at Tuscumbia, described his fellow soldiers as "having a rather ragged, dilapidated appearance, and many were barefooted."

THE CONFEDERATE VETERAN VOL.1

Pg. 312 Nov.1864 Hood's Campaign Through North Georgia by Col.R.H.Shotwell "...I stepped over to see the prisoners, and to my amazement found there were seventy-four of them, mostly dressed in Conferate attire, and about the same number of Confederates, dressed in Federal uniforms, guarding them. They had almost completely swapped clothes with them...."

The weather's starting to get cold, and the soldiers cannot rely on government supply, of course they're going to help themselves to Yankee uniforms whenever the opportunity presents it self.

THE CONFEDERATE VETERAN VOL.1

Pg. 307 Humors of Soldier Life by Rev. J.H. M'Neilly "Originally I enlisted as a private, and for a long time served as chaplain by detail, so I got to feel easier in the jacket, trousers and brogans of the private soldier than in the regulation uniform; and then, as I had no money to get a uniform, and as we had no chance to get anything from home, my plain apparel was a necessity.

From long esposure to the changes of climate and scene, my uniform became more picturesque than elegant. As we came into Tennessee, the nights were often quite cold, and I stood around the blazing camp-fires a sudden change of the wind would sometimes whip the blaze about my legs and scorch the lower extremities of my trousers. In the battle (Franklin) I had thrown off my jacket, and a shell exploding just over it had dropped a spark of fire in the middle of the back, which gradually spead until it burned a hole perfectly round and about four or five inches across.

Dressed "cap-a-pie", the following was my outfit: A hat made of brown jeans, quilted, and which when soaked took in half a gallon of water; a check cotton shirt that would not meet about my neck and had no button on the collar anyhow; my jacket, with the ventilator in the back; my trousers, fringed with scorched strings from the knee to the ankle; socks, with no feet but sound legs; shoes, in which sole and upper were only held together by strings.

My hair hung on my shoulders, and bleared eyes looked out from a long and scraggy beard that covered all my face."

He was probably dressed no better or worse than the rest of the army at this time.

NO SOAP, NO PAY, DIARREHA & DESERTION A Composite History of the Last Sixteen Monthes of the Confederacy ed by Jeff Toalson pub by iUniverse 2006

Pg. 254 Nov. 3, 1864 In Northern Alabama with the Army of Tennessee Prt, B.P. Weaver 42nd Georgia Infantry; "...This march has nearly worn out my shoes. Do not knoe what I will do if I get barefooted for I could not march at all then..."

Pg 255 Nov 1864 Near Bell Buckle, TN Private James F. Anthony, Co. B, 28th Tennessee Cavalry "...I enlisted in the Confederate army (18 years old) in November, 1864...Our uniforms were ragged! There were no 2 suits alike. We had rags of all sizes, shapes & colors, textures & makes..."

Pg. 260 Nov13, 1864 Near Florence. Alabama Sgt. Archie Livingston 3rd Floida Infantry; My dear Sisters; "...The troops all need clothing, shoes and blankets, yet they appear ready for any move to increase our supplies...Suffering and hardship is befre this army because of the inclement season and scarcity of necessary supplies of every description...send me a pair of suspenders..."

The soldiers all believe an advance will enable them to capture quantities of Yankee supplies.

Pg. 264 Nov 20, 1864 Florence, Alabama Sgt. Archie Livingston 3rd Florida Infantry My dear Sisters; "…I am almost barefoot, and have suffered some from cold and wind. Many of the Army are yet unshod. I don't know how they can stand cold and marching…"

Website: Tennessee Volunteer Infantry Regiment: Clothing, arms and Equipment

Pg. 3 "On the 13th of November,1864 Thomas Head wrote, "winter was now setting in with its severest rigor, and many of the men were …destitute of many other articles of clothing.' Ressinoretter noted, "we are looking for some clothing they are much needed. The men are in destitute circumstances…and have no pants." On the retreat from Nashville, (Tn) Jan. 1865, we find that the "clothes worn out."

Pg.3 "Due to the shortages of material,uniforms worn by Confederate soldiers was single-breasted, short-waisted, with low standing collar, the "shell" jacket. The buttons varied from five to nine, although eight has been claimed for the Army of Tennessee. About a third of the jackets had shoulder straps, some would have had belt loops, with most having a pocket inside the left breast pocket, some had pockets on the outside. These could be made of wool, satinette, kersey, cassimere or jeans cloth.

About 30% of the troops wore frock coats, either single or double-breasted, while others wore captured sack coats which had been bleached and then dyed.…The gray ran from a very brownish color to a very dark color,…"

DARK AND CRUEL WAR by Don Lowry pub by Hippocrene Books 1993

Pg. 544 Nov. 1864 Spring Hill, Tn. "The ground was planted in corn and very muddy and if the Johnnies in grey were not hit with artillery missiles, they were covered in mud.…"

Pg.559 Franklin, Tn. Confederate assault."…Now the confederates marveled at the spectacle of over 20,000 men in grey and butternut brown and bits of captured blue uniforms forming for the attack with fixed bayonets…"

That would have been a grand sight.

THE CONFEDERATE VETERAN VOL. XVII 1909

Pg. 448 Sept. 1909 A Confederate Is Grateful by J.D. Harwell Nov. 1864 "…I state I was a private in Company I, 20th Alabama Infantry…When we reached Gadsden Ala., I was barefooted; and although we waited there some days for shoes, clothing and blankets, we did not receive them, and I started into Tennessee barefooted. My only covering, a blanket, had been cut to pieces by a cannon ball, tearing it from my back as I made my way from a charge after being wounded in my left shoulder by a grapeshot…"

DIARY OF LT. SPENCER TALLY-28TH TENNESSEE INFANTRY

Nov 1864 march into Tennessee-"It was now about two monthes since we started on the raid, and many of our boys were barefooted, their shoes having worn out and the weather was now getting cold. One night when our poor cattle were being slaughtered, barefoot boys were thick around the carcusses for the skins which they would wrap around their feet with the hairy side next to the foot and ankle.

This was a severe test of Southern Patriotism, and as an illustration of the optimistic spirit which pervaded the army will say that on the 27th of November1864, I had charge of the advance guard. A cold, drizzly rain fell until about noon when it began snowing and continued all night. I was halted just before night for camping and while waiting for my company to come which was far back in the rear, I sat on a fence corner and was watching the hundreds and thousands of poorly clad and many barefooted soldiers spashing through the mud and slush which was now from four to six inches deep. A big Irish fellow, with pants rolled up to his knees in passing bellowed out "Oh, how glad I am to live to see it snow one more time!"

This optimistic soldier probably had everyone laughing, or at least smiling.

THE CONFEDERATE VETERAN VOL.XVII 1909

Pg. 164 April, 1909 From Nashville To Tannery On Duck River by Capt. A.C. Danner "When Hood's army arrived before Fanklin in November, 1864, it was by reason of its long, hurried marchfrom Atlanta poorly equipped, especially as to clothing and shoes. Those who went through and survived the terrible battle of Franklin were indeed ragged, worn out, and suffering in body and mind, but still had the spirit of fight in them.

When the army arrived before Nashville, General Hood learned that down near the mouth of the Duck River on the opposite side from his army there was located a large tanneryand shoe manufacturing establishment operated by the United States Government. As his army was suffering terribly for the want of shoes, it was very desirable to get hold of this factory and any leather and shoes that might be there before the Union forces abandoned and destroyed it. At that time it was expected that the Confederate army would capture and occupy Nashville.

Immediately on learning of the existence of this big tannery a young staff officer was detailed to go down and try to secure the tannery and leather that might be there and, if possible, start to making shoes. A company of cavalry was selected to go on this expedition, and splendid fellows they proved to be-young, but veterans in service, well mounted, and used to hardships.

A guide was procured and the company started at once; no wagons, no artillery, simply what they could carry on their horses in the way of rations, arms, and ammunition.

Arriving at the Duck River somewhere near its mouth, the river was found to be greatly swollen by reason of heavy rains. No ferryboats or means of crossing could be found. The people in the neighborhood welcomed the Confederates and did what they could for them. They told the young men that it was absolutely impossible to cross the stream in its present condition, it being so high and the current so strong and swift. Their advice was to go back; but the Confederates were not going to do that. They could give up their lives in doing their duty, and the young staff officer in charge of the expedition proposed that they swim the river on their horses. The natives said that it was impossible, that they would be swept out through the mouth of the river and drowned. Nevertheless volunteers were called for to go into the river, and every fellow went. It was a perilous undertaking; but the horses as well as the men were used to dangers and difficulties.

Success crowned the efforts of the little company. They landed, but were scattered about along the bank of the river from a quarter to a half mile below where they went in, the swift current having swept every horse down the stream; but at last all landed safe, with guns and cartridges dry.

The tannery was soon located. Many rumors were heard about it, such as it being strongly guarded with a large force of Union troops, while other reports were to the effect that it had been abandoned. The little command of Confederates, however, rushed on, really hoping to find some troops still there on guard. It was believed that if the tannery had been abandoned it would also be destroyed. They preferred to fight and capture it rather than get there too late. It was but a few miles to the tannery, and it was found to be complete, having just been abandoned. No shoes were there, but there were many pieces of leather, and steps were being taken to begin the manufacture of some kind of foot covering to answer as shoesfor the barefooted boys in front of Nashville. Before this was actually begun, however, orders were received to return immediately and join Hood's army as it fell back. The battle of Nashville had been fought and lost, and the army was in retreat. With grief and sorrow we prepared to go.

A roll of leather was tied to each saddle, knowing even this would be of immense value to the men if time could be found to turn it in to shoes of some kind."

They gave it a try

FROM THE FLAME OF BATTLE TO THE FIERY CROSS-The Third Tennessee Infantry by Jame van Eldik pub by Yucca Tree Press 2001

Pg. 251 Nov. 8th 1864 Captain Walter S. Jennings, Co. C.,"...I saw but yesterday the captain commanding his regiment barefoot..."

Pg. 254 Bivouac near Florence Alabama "...It has been a long weary march of nearly five hundred miles, still the soldiers have stood it nobly. Many of them marched barefoot, both officers and men..."

THIS BAND OF HEROES-Granbury's Texas Brigede, C.S.A. by James M. McCaffery pub by Texas A&M Univ. Press 1996

Nov. 13, 1864 Tennssee Campaign Florence, Al. "...General Forrest's tired troopers arrived, and on the 15 the Texas Brigade followed them across the pontoon bridge. Shoes, clothing, and other essential supplies had finally arrived..."

FROM THAT TERRIBLE FIELD-CIVIL WAR LETTERS OF JAMES M. WILLIAMS, Twenty-First Alabama Volunteer Infantry ed by John Kent Folmer pub by Univ Al Press 1981

Pg. 149 Dear Lizzy, "The shoes, socks &c. came last night, they were very acceptable and were needed very much. The shoes do very well, they are rather large but comfortable and good enough for a Confederate soldier I wish every one of my militant bretheren had each such a pair-

Do not worry yourself to make me any more clothing I have enough for present wants, and don't want to accumulate anything to be lost at the next move of the military chess board..."

DIARY OF A SOLDIER AND PRISONER OF WAR IN REBEL PRISONS-Diary of Eugene Forbes pub by Murphy & Bechtel Printers 1865

Pg. 68 Nov. 17, 1864 Andersonville, Ga. "...Some three or four hundred "galvanized Yanks," clad in Rebel uniforms, were turned into the stockade during the morning. They had taken the oath, and done duty in the Rebel service, and gave various reasons for their being re-transferred. The general opinion is that an exchange is about being effected, and the Rebels prefer having their own men back..."

I have read very little about the service record of these "galvanized" Yanks.

TWO WARS: AN AUTOBIOGRAPHY OF GENERAL SAMUEL G. FRENCH The Confederate Veteran, Nashville 1901

pg. 404 November 19, 1864 I remonstrated with Gen. Hood at a meeting of his officers, against taking so many pieces of artillery with the army unless we had a full supply of horses for the guns. But he insisted that, once in Tennessee, men would join us, horses could be obtained, and the men would be supplied with shoes and clothing…"

Just like in the Antietam invasion, men were supposed to flock to the colors, but it was all wishful thinking.

"DEAR MOTHER: DON'T GRIEVE ABOUT ME. IF I GET KILLED, I'LL ONLY BE DEAD." ed. by Mills Lane pub by The Beehive Press 1977

Pg. 336 Felix Pryor to his Wife Macon Georgia November 23, 1864 Dear Nancy: John says you may make his overcoat as he may need it after awhile. The government has furnished him one suit. My leggings are useful (in) this cold weather…."

THE CIVIL WAR YEARS-A Day-by Day Chroncle by Robert E. Denney pub by Randomhouse Books 1992

Pg. 492 November 25, 1864 "…George W. Nichols, Major, U.S.A. Sherman's Hdqtrs., Sandersville, Ga.:

"…Here they met with a force under the command of General Wayne, which was composed of a portion of Wheeler's cavalry, militia, and a band of convicts who had been liberated from the penitentiary upon the condition that they would join the army.The most of these desperadoes have been taken prisoners, dressed in their state prison clothing. General Sherman has turned them loose, believing that Governor Brown had not got the full benefits of his liberality…"

Convicts serving in the ranks dressed in prison clothes, now that's a challenge for re-enactors!

THE CONFEDERATE VETERAN VOL. XX Aug. 1912

Pg. 358 "Did Gen.Pat Cleburne Give His Boots? By Col. J.A. Watrous of the U.S. Army

Nov. 30 1864 Battle of Franklin TN. "General Cleburne died barefooted. While riding along his division from Spring Hill a few hours before the battle of Franklin, where he was killed, General Cleburne saw several soldiers trudging along with nothing on their feet. Coming to one who was leaving blood in each track, the General stopped, swung his right foot to the side of his left, and said:

"My man, take off my boots.'

"Why, General?"

"Never mind why, take them off."

'The private with bleeding feet obeyed his general's command reluctantly."

Put them on, you need them worse than I do," said the division commnder.

"And you barefooted, General?"

"Do as I tell you, and at once, and catch up with your command."

"General Pat Cleburne, of Cheatam's Corps, Hood's army, fought his division in his last battle and died, with his men, at the forefront of that awful battle of Franklin, where several general officers were killed.

It is said that General Cleburne had a premonition that he would be killed in that battle"

THE CONFEDERATE VETERAN VOL. XXII 1914

PG. 452 Oct 1914 Battle on Honey Hill, S.C. (November 30, 1864) by Capt. John J. Abercromie (Illinois Inf) "Out of the shadows of the misty past comes ever a ghostly figure, bronzed and gaunt, uniformed in a ragged butternut suit, with limp-brimmed slouch hat turned nondescript in color from exposure to the storms and suns of the four year's grinding campaign…"

THE CONFEDERATE VETERAN VOL.XII 1904

Pg. 540 Nov. 1904 A Boy's First Battle by Prof. H.M. Hamill "…I belonged to Finnegan's Brigade, made up from the odds and ends of the last crop of Florida soldiers, chiefly boys, and enrolled in the winter of 1863-64. After organizing and drilling for several months in Florida, we were hurried to the front of the Army of Northern Virginia, and given a place in Mahone's Division, along with the veteran soldiers of Lee. I can remember how the old soldiers made mock of our green and unsoldierly looks and ways, and dubbed us with nicknames that made us for a time the jest of the army. I cannot blame them. Falstaff's variegated soldiers would have put us to shame. I remember that, for lack of better guns, some of us were equipped with ancient big-bore Belgian muskets. If there was one decent uniform in my regiment, other than those of the officers, I fail to recall it. Some of us had brought along our neckties and handkerchiefs, and dazzled the eyes of Lee's clay-colored veterans for a season with our nicely laundered white shirts. I can recall the day when, under the laughter of the old soldiers, I bundled up my gala day toggery and cast it feelingly in a nearby thicket…."

UNIFORMS OF THE CIVIL WAR by Lord, Wise, pub by A.S. Barnes & Co. 1970

Pg. 79 winter 1863-64 A soldier from the 12th Louisiana appealed: "Many of the soldiers are desparate of socks. Many more have not a single blanket, quilt, or coverlet of any kind to preotect them from the chilling blasts of winter which has already lowered her heavy mantle around us, and the sad condition is representative of the brigade, Buford's, to which I belong. This Government no doubt has been doing all it could to meet this exigency, but as yet little has been done to alleviate the suffering.

While thousands are given for the distribution of tracts and other religious literature, which without contradiction is noble work, I think something can be done to alleviate the suffering of your noble soldiers. Come forward and clothe your soldiers, and they will defend your country."

Even with everyone sending what clothing they could spare, the army remained ragged.

UNIFORMS OF THE CIVIL WAR by Lord, Wise, pub by A.S. Barnes & Co. 1970

Pg. 93 return from Nashville, winter, 1864-65 "An artilleryman in Lumden's Battery, encamped at Iuka, Mississippi, dscribed the appearance of the typical Confederate soldier of the Army of Tennessee: "Recrossing the Tennessee River near Bainbridge, we camped a few days near Iuka, Miss., for rest and general cleaning, but many soldiers had no clothing except the rags they had on.

A Confederate private at the time consisted of a pair of old shoes or boots, soles gaping, and tyed to the uppers with strings, no socks, threadbare pants, patched at the knees burnt out at the bottom halfway to his knees, his calves black with smoke from standing with his back to the fire, his shirt sticking out the holes in the rear of his pants, a weather beaten jeans jacket, out at the elbows and collar greasy, and an old slouch hat hanging about his face, with a tuft of hair sticking out of the crown. The officers did not show up much better."

I still wonder how they could have carried on.

SOUTHERN INVINCEABILITY by Wiley Sword pub by St. Martin's Press 1999

Pg. 305 winter, 1864-1865 The reorganization of the Army of Tennessee after the retreat from Nashville-46th Mississippi Infantry "The regiment numbers about 150 men, about half of whom are barefoot. All are ragged, dirty and covered with vermin, some not having sufficient clothing to hide their bodies."

And this in the winter!

THE CONFEDERATE VETERAN VOL. VII 1899

Pg. 266 December 1864 Hard Times on Hood's Retreat by Sam B. Dunlap "...The weather was cold for the climate, and many of our men were without shoes and thinly clad otherwise. I had on a pair of old boots full of holes, and when marching, would frequently stop and empty the gravel that intruded on my toes.When the break in our lines at Nashville occurred, we were at Murfeesboro, and our route of exit by the main pike was cut off. After a very circuitous march over some of the roughest country I ever saw, attended by severe hardships, we arrived at Columbia December 19, 1864, and made a junction with the main army. Two days previous to our arrival my old boots had entirely deserted my bleeding feet, and my barefoot track was plainly visible in the snow.

A short time after we arrived at Columbia one of my comrades (Taylor) and I, by permission, crossed the pontoon bridge in advance of the company. Arriving at a livery barn filled with soldiers trying to dry themselves around some smokey fires, I asked if anyone in there had a pair of shoes to sell or give away. A boy of about fifteen years standing in the office door said: "Yes, Come In." He produced a pair of half-worn cloth shoes and priced them at fifteen dollars. I gave him a twenty-dollar bill, and while he was out hunting change I spied a pair of heavy leather shoes partly covered up by an old Federal overcoat under a bunk in the corner, and when he returned they were changed from that hiding place to one under a coat of the same color worn by the writer. The boy soon returned with two ten-dollar bills, and said I could have the shoes for one of them, as he failed to get the change desired. Taylor and I left the barn with a step somewhat faster than when we entered. I told Taylor he could have the cloth shoes, as they were about two numbers too large for me. We were both shod. The leather boots were just my fit...."

Another first-hand account of cloth shoes.

SOLDIERING IN THE ARMY OF TENNESSEE by Larry J. Daniel pub by Univ. of North Carolina Press 1991

Pg. 36 Winter Dec. 1864 "During the Tennessee Campaign, issues of winter clothing and shoes, which were by then in great demand, were made at Gadsden, Tuscombia, and Florence, Alabma. Shoes, however, remained in short supply. B.P.Weaver of the Forty-second Georgia wrote on November 3: "This march has nearly worn out my shoes. Do not know what I will do if I get barefooted for I could not march at all then." Another Georgian was even more desperate: "Father, I am plom barefooted. I hain't got a sine (sign) of a shoe on my foot nor don't know when I will hav." The men were ordered to sew shoes of beef hide, putting the hair next to the foot. This makeshift arrangement apparently worked well but caused a terrible odor after the first day or two. Clothing picked up on the Franklin battlefield proved adequate to get the army through, most of December. "I cant scarcle see a man but what has a good Yankee blanket," observed G.W. Athey. James Lanning of the Eighteenth Alabama noted that after Franklin he gave away much clothing because he could not carry it all. "I could have gathered a thousand Dollars worth of clothing etc," he boasted. Yet by December 9 he was writing "many a poor soldier is suffering for want of shoes and other clothing."

Major General Bate reported that his division was well shod when they departed Florence. "I pressed (confiscated) every pair of shoes which could be found for them, which partially supplied the command," he related. Yet before the division reached Nashville, he estimated that one-fourth of his men were shoeless, "many with bleeding feet," in the sleet and snow…"

THE STORY OF THE GREAT MARCH, From the Diary of a Staff Officer pub by Harper & Brothers 1865

Pg.100 Dec. 1864 Diary of George Ward Nichols Millien, Ga; "…A space of ground about three hundred feet square, enclosed by a stockade, without any covering whatsoever, was the hole where thousands of our brave soldiers have been confined for months past, exposed to heavy dews, biting frosts, and pelting rains, without so much as a board or tent to protect them after the rebels had stolen their clothing…"

THE CONFEDERATE VETERAN VOL. XI 1907

Pg. 508 Nov. 1907 Tennessee, A Grave Or a Free Home by H.K. Nelson Dec. 1864 march towards Nashville "…One evening after having bivouacked General Cheatham ("Old Frank," we called him) came along and called to the "barefooted Boys." He went with them to the slaughter pen and had them take the beef hides and whang them on their feet, turning the hairy side in. However ridiculous it may have looked, those moccasins served a good purpose…"

Pg. 32 "The veterans dispensed with many nonessentials on the march, resulting in a stripped-down, less polished, but more practical look. Explained a soldier in July 1863: "We got orders yesterday to throw away all our clothing but one suit (.) We aren't allowed to have but one pair of pants and have them on, one pair of drawers, two shirts, and one pair of socks…"

DON TRIOANI'S CIVIL WAR INFANTRY-Text by Earl J. Coates, Michael McAffee and Don Trioani pub by Stackpole Books 2002

Pg. 62 Dec. 1864 "…Descriptions of Hood's Army of Tennessee for late 1864 are many. Because Hood continually changed directions as he moved North, few supplies reached his army By necessity, the Confederates were forced to use the food and captured clothing of their enemies. They had bare feet and ragged uniforms for much of the campaign. A Union Private in the 14th Illinois captured near Moon's Station, Georgia, made note that the

Confederates "made all kinds of one-sided trades for our clothing, hats boots and shoes." From Big Shanty, the same Union prisoner watched as Hood's entire army marched past him on the way to Dalton, Georgia. He described the Confederates as "poorly clad in grey and brown cotton suits, and but for the flags that they carried, might have been a section of the old Continental Army." A Union Captain captured at Dalton also remarked as Hood's entire army marched by: "They were ragged and thinly clad, having, as a general thing, only pantaloons, shirt and hat in their inventory of clothing. Their pantaloons were greasy and tattered, the shirts, shocking affairs in multitudinous variety. As a general thing, they were liberally shod, though in Stewart's Division…over three hundred were without shoes. Not more then one in ten had blankets."

By the time Hood's Confederates reached Tuscumbia, Alabama, on October 31, an artilleryman in Guiber's Battery found his comrades to be "rather ragged and many… barefooted." To cover their feet, some soldiers began to make moccasins out of rawhide from slaughtered cattle. To add to their discomfort, a cold, chilly rain began to fall, turning the roads to slippery mud. "The boys who wore moccasins had a good deal of trouble keeping them on when they got wet," remembered an Alabama infantryman.

After the retreat from Nashville, at Tupelo, Mississippi, on January 3, 1865, "A Confederate officer in Whitehall's Division wrote home that "the army cannot muster 5,000 effectives (out of 17,000). Nine-tenths of the officers and men are barefooted and naked… and many go home every day never to return…"

Pg. 68 Descriptions of the appearance of Confederates in the closing days of the Civil war are many. A Union soldier remarked that the rebel soldiers that he saw "were mostly in homespun butternut jeans cloth, with no semblance of uniform (it was) hard to distinguish betwixt the officers and the privates as they were all dressed alike." Another Federal remembered the soldiers of the Army of Northern Virginia as a collection of "dirty, battered ranks of soldiers, none of them well clad, and nearly all the officers in fatigue dress."

Pg.69 "…A Confederate staffer described their dress toward the end of the war: "My equipment was a blanket rolled up and carried across my shoulder, and it contained a change of underclothes…Towards the last days we were almost barefoot…As to hats, their variety and material was marvelous…When it came to jackets and trousers, the least said is the easiest understood. They were conspicuous by their fluttering raggedness…"

THE DECISIVE BATTLE OF NASHVILLE by Stanley F. Horn pub by Univ. of Tenn. Press, Knoxville

Pg. 43-44 Dec.1864 "This abrupt and unseasonable change in the weather was a tremendous handicap to the Confederates. Not only did it put a stop to their vitally important work of entrenchment, but it was a source of the most intense suffering to the shivering, poorly clad men in the ranks. Hood was far from a source of supplies, with an attenuated line of communication. There was a sad lack of shoes, clothing, hats, and blankets. Occasional trains from Decatur brought in food supplies and some dribbles of jackets, breeches, and even underwear, but shoes were a virtually unknown luxury and so were hats and caps. A large proportion of the men were barefooted and many were bareheaded. Such tents as they once possessed were now mostly left far behind, but those of them who had blankets or oilclothes used them to improvise shelter which they shared with their less fortunate fellows. When beeves were butchered the raw hides were issued, as far as they would go, to those most in need. Where cobblers could be found in the ranks, it was possible to procure some makeshift kind of shoes; otherwise, the soldiers wrapped the pieces of hide around their raw and bleeding feet and were thankful for even that protection. But only a fortunate few were able to get even such crude footwear, and thousands of Hood's men remained barefooted as the sleet and snow pelted down on their bare heads and froze their thread-bare ragged clothing."

All this and it didn't accomplish anything.

CHRONICLES FROM A WAR PRISONER IN ANDERSON-VILLE AND OTHER MILITARY PRISONS IN THE SOUTH IN 1864 Diary of John Worrell Northrop Wichita, KS, 1904

Pg. 228 December, 1864 "...During the night a squad of 170 men had arrived from Sherman's army; they were drawn up in single files, submitting to a rigorous search. While awaiting the process of paroling I watched the proceeding, and it is more particularly worthy of note because of the season of the year, and the fact that there might be a possibility of their release. They were forced to undress, stripping off even their drawers. Tents, overcoats, blankets, all extra clothing was thrown in piles, and then they were roughly ordered to dress hurriedly, and were marched into the prison from which we had just escaped, leaving blankets and changes of clothing. It seemed to us that nothing but a merciless, hellish feeling of revenge could have prompted such an inexcusable action on the part of the Rebels..."

You damn Yankee, how about all the homes, barns, and towns burned and people made homeless from your wanton, senseless and cowardly destruction?

Pg. 228 Refering to the new guards-"...They were fine looking men, in neat gray suits, round-abouts, and caps, all South Carolina boys, sons of wealthy merchants and planters, apparently well bred and educated. They had never seen service in the field and thought their duty here extremely hard. They knew as little of the merits of the issue as innocent children;

appeared to be as free from partisan principles, but actually supposed they were on the right side, because on the South side…"

THE DECISIVE BATTLE OF NASHVILLE by Stanley F. Horn pub by Univ. Tn Press 1956

Pg. 155 Dec. 1864 retreat from Nashville- Hood's defeat-shocked army was on short rations- mostly parched corn, with an occaisional feast of corn pone and fat bacon or perhaps a pilfered pig or pullet. A fortunate few had blankets or overcoats picked up on the battlefield, but most of them had only their thread-bare uniforms to protect them from the icy rain that seemed to pierce to the very marrow of their bones. Many had no hats to cover their heads; but it was the scarcity of shoes that presented an especially acute problem. The number of men who were wholly or partially barefooted is almost unbelieveable; and Hood's weary veterans literally left bloody footprints in the roads as they stumbled over the frozen ruts. Major James D. Porter, of Cheatham's staff, relates that at one point on the retreat, when the tired and underfed horses were unable to pull a wagon train up a steep hill covered with ice, Cheatham ordered him to get a hundred well-shod men from the ranks to help push the wagons up the hill. After diligent search, Porter says, he was able to find in the whole corps a total of twenty-five men who had whole shoes on their feet…"

Twenty-five men in the whole Corps? Incredibly amazing.

SOLDIERS BLUE & GRAY by James I. Robertson Jr. pub by Univ. of S.C. Press 1988

Pg. 155 "…Late in 1864 after the Confederate army retreated from Nashville, Resinor Etter of a Tennessee regiment stated: "It snowed very hard and the ground was hard froze my feet suffered much as I was barefooted… It was so cold I came nigh freezing…"

Hey, Resinor, I would have froze—to death.

THE WAR-TIME JOURNAL OF A GEORGIA GIRL 1864-1865 Eliza Frances Andrews by Spencer B. King pub. by Appleton-Century-Crfts 1908

Pg. 27 Dec. 1864 "…The first to climb in was a poor sick soldier, of whom no pay was demanded. Next came a captain of Texas Rangers, then a young lieutenant in a shabby uniform that had evidently seen very hard service…"

THE CIVIL WAR INFANTRTYMAN-In Camp, on the March and in Battle, by Gregory A. Coco pub by Thomas Publications

"...In December 1864 John Green told how the 9th Kentucky quartermaster, had brought out of Savannah suits of "cotton underclothes& gray Jeans Jackets & trousers...for the men..."

THIS BAND OF HEROES-Granbury's Texas Brigade, C.S.A. by James M. MCCaffery pub by Texas A&M Univ. Press 1996

Pg. 142 Confederate troops surrounding Nashville, Tn "...The Texans worked hard to make their position as secure and as comfortable as they could. They dug a small ditch in front of their works and also made use of stout head logs. Their sleeping quarters were anything but elegant. Some of the men built small huts with fence rails covered with dirt and others improvised shelters from cornstalks. Some of the men who were without shoes wrapped their feet in rags or pieces of blankets. Brigade shoe shops were established, but because of the scarcity of leather about all that could be done was repair work. No new shoes were made. A soldier with worn-out shoes could go to the cobblers and have pieces of green cowhide stretched over the shoes with the hair to the inside. The soldier would then be forced to wear the shoes until the hide cured somewhat and shrank tightly to his foot. Another reason for leaving the shoes on all the time was so some less fortunate fellow soldier wouldn't steal them. Rations were typically poor and firewood rapidly became scarce..."

THE CONFEDERATE VETERAN VOL. IX 1901

Pg. 72 Feb. 1901 Southern Crosses Of Honor Bestowed-Remarks of Gen. George W. Gordon Dec. 1864 "...The suffering and destitution of the Army of Tennessee, during General Hood's ill-fated campaign to this state in 1864, was scarcely less severe. The hardships of that army, especially on the retreat from Nashville, were grevious in the extreeme. There were occasions on that retreat when comrades quarreled and almost fought each other for raw beef hides with which to clothe their bare and bleeding feet..."

THE CONFEDERATE VETERAN VOL. XXII 1914

Pg. 202 May, 1914 Rank And File In The Confederate Armies by Miss Hortense Herman Mongomery, Ala. December 1, 1864

"As chief quartermaster of this military division, I respectfully request that five thousand bales of cotton be turned over to Maj. L.Mims. There is now the most pressing need for blankets, shoes, axes, stationary, medicines, hardware, leather, horses and mules, bacon and salt to meet the immediate wants of the army. I have ascertained that prompt payment in cotton will readily secure adequate supplies, and in this manner a considerable quantity of cotton may be utilized before it becomes worthless

E. Willis, Chief Quartermaster"

He means to trade it to northern merchants in exchange for much-needed supplies, actually a very good idea.

YANKEE IN GRAY-The Civil War Memoirs of Henry E. Handerson pub by The Press of Western Reserve Univ. 1962

POW Pg. 108 Fort Puaski, Ga. December 4th, 1864 Dear Father; "…I am also getting in bad condition as regards outer clothing and enclose my measure for a suit of clothes. If the Exppress Company will engage to deliver them to the commandant of this Post, Col, P.P. Brown, it will doubtless be best for you to procure them in Cleveland and and forward them; but if not, I presume I shall be obliged to call upon you for money enough to purchase them of the sutler at this post. If purchased here they will cost, I presume, about $50.00. What I need is of course something serviceable not elegant;-a plain frock coat, vest and pants. If you conclude to purchase the clothing yourself please send also a good blanket, dark-colored…"

U,S. ARMY HERITAGE & EDUCATION CENTER

Dec. 5, 1864 Sergeant Major A.D.Craver, 26th Georgia Infantry Battalion-North-East corner of Mississippi, near the corner of Alabama "…We are in charge of the captured Negroes and have got them at work on the Railroad between Corinth and Cherokee, Alabama. We are near a little town Iuka but the Negroes are dying here very fast. We have buried 9 here in two weeks…"

NO SOAP, NO PAY, DIARRHEA, DYSENTERY & DESERTION ed by Jeff Toalson pub by iUniverse Inc. 2006

Pg. 279 Dec. 8&9 Nashville Tennessee Capt. Thomas J. Key Key's Akansas Lt. Artillery; "…This morning (8th) the northern blast swept chilly over the hills and the soldiers suffered greatly for comfortable clothing. The weather is cold and sleet is falling (9th) fast and thick. The sleet obliterates our fire and keeps us wet, and if we go under our little fly we suffer with cold so that our teeth chatter. The only alternative is to pile up under our blankets to keep warm…"

ONE OF CLEBURNE'S COMMAND-The Civil War Remini-scences & Diary of Captain Samuel T. Foster, Granbury's Texas brigade, C.S.A. pub by Univ. of Texas Press, 1980

Pg. 41 Dec. 12 1864 in trenches around NashvilleTn.-"…Still froze up. We are suffering more for shoes than anything else, and there is no chance to get new ones. At Brigade Head Quarters there has been established a Shoe Shop, not to make shoes, for there is no leather, but they take an old worn out pair of shoes and sew moccasins over them of green cow hide with the hair side in. The shoe is put on and kept there, and as the hide draws it draws closer and closer to the old shoe. I am wearing just such foot coverings now, and they are about as pleasant to the foot and about as comfortable as any I ever had..."

THE CONFEDERATE VETERAN VOL. XX OCT. 1912

THE STAMPEDE AT LA FAYETTE, GA by Charles Gore Joy, Company C, 14th Tennessee Cavalry Dec. 15, 1864 "...About the middle of December commenced the great battle of Nashville; and after two day's hard fighting against a force of fresh troops well-armed and well-fed fully three time as great, Hood's army was completely routed. It was very cold, still raining and snowing, the roads heavy with mud, the men suffering from hunger, cold, and exhaustion. Their clothing was ragged, often exposing the flesh. They looked like an army of tramps. Many were barefooted and had cut their feet on the ice and frozen ground, leaving blood marks in the snow. Hundreds of them whose feet became sore and inflamed were hauled in the wagons, as were some of the sick and wounded..."

ALL AFIRE TO FIGHT-The Unold Tale of the Civil War's Ninth Texas Cavalry by Martha L. Crabb pub by Avon Books 2000

Pg. 275 Dec. 15, 1864 Murfeesboro Tn. "the elated Confederates tore open the cars, which they foung loaded with 200,000 rations of sugar, coffee, hardtack, and bacon, plus clothing and all manner of tempting supplies. After plundering the cars and carrying off everything possible, they set fire to the train and retired with their booty and prisoners. The booty included enough overcoats to suppy the entire brigade. And Coffee! The Texans hauled off enough to supply themselves for three weeks, some men carrying away two or three bushels."

Pg. 281 Dec. 25, 1864 rearguard action for Hood's retreating army "...The most valuable capture of the day was 300 overcoats..."

AN ARTILLERY MAN'S DIARY by Jenkin Lloyd Jones pub by WN History Commission 1914

Pg. 395 December 18 1864 "...Griff and I visited a squad of 2,800 prisoners this morning, of which Nashville is nearly full. They look as well as any I have ever seen, clothing not as bad as I expected to see. Could not converse with them for the guards..."

How bad did he expect? Let him trade clothes with one of those prisoners and stay in a trench, without shelter, poor and inadequate food, then fight a battle against overwhelming odds.

CHARLOTTE'S BOYS-Civil War Letters of the Branch Familty of Savannah ed.by Mauriel Phillips Joslyn pub. by Rckbridge Pub. Co. 1996

Pg. 294 1 Lt. Hamilton Branch to Charlotte Branch Dec 19th/64 Columbia Tenn. (Retreat form Nashville) "…in the 3 days we made 60 miles over the worst roads I have ever seen. About 200 of our brigade were barefooted. Gen. Forrest made his escort take up barefooted men behind them. Our army is now on the retreat…"

Pg. 297 Dec26/64 Stegar (Sugar) Creek 20 miles from Pulaski (Geo)"…we crossed, that is we waded, about 20 creeks and went into bivouac in a mud hole at this place. It had been raining for the last two days but as I had captured a rubber cloth on Christmas I managed to keep pretty dry. I also captured a shirt and testament off the gun we captured…."

THE CONFEDERATE VETERAN VOL. XII 1904

Pg. 389 August 1904 Missouri Battery in Tennessee Campaign by Sam B. Dunlap 19 Dec. 1864 "I was a member of the first Missouri Artillery…The weather was very cold for the climate. Rain, snow, and sleet were severe. Many of our men were almost without clothing and shoes. I was one of the "shoeless Confederates."

REBEL PRIVATE FRONT AND REAR-Memoirs of a Confederate Soldier by William A. Fletcher pub by Dutton Books 1995

Pg. 171 William Fletcher was with the First Texas captured during retreat from Nashville, escaped and now making his way South, near Murfeesboro. "…Day was approaching. I had about retraced half my steps when the sole of one of my boots came loose from toe to heel. I tore a strip off of my blanket and hurriedly tied it in place. This soon worked loose; I tied it again and fastened the ends around my ankle; then it worked back to the instep, and from the noise it would make on the macadamized road a clod dancer would have thought he was not in the kerflop class. It was a cold clear morning. I did not think any of the surrounding natives were awake, and I wanted them to sleep on until I found hiding. I cut the sole off near the heel and started with the inner sole under foot. It was soon loose from the uppers and I had always thought the boots were too large; but I guess I was mistaken, for the inner sole was not large enough to keep the side of my foot off the cold, hard ground. After the sole had turned back a few times and let the ball of my foot on the ground, I tore another strip and took a few turns around my foot and sole by pulling back the upper. This was an improvement and I trotted on…

Pg. 175 (led to a house of a Southern sympathizer-a shoemaker- William enters), "…When I received an introduction I did not hang my head and blush on account of my unkempt appearance-in fact, I guess at the time I made no note of it, as I was well trained to not allow clothing to be a bar to evening callers. The only article of necessity that I thought I needed was shoes and the landlord and I were understood on that point, as he had the material and was going to devote the next day and part of the night, if necessary, to make me a pair, and possibly after taking measurements, he had a pair under construction. I told him that anything would fit my foot that was large enough. The ladies showed good common sense and were free to talk and did not seem to be inspecting me closely to get up the giggle; nor did they speak words of sympathy. They acted the true definition of friendship, which is: "He who comes in when the world goes out." After they had well looked me over they made their mission known which was to get me, as they said, much needed clothes. The older one knew of a good coat a few miles off that she would ride out and get the next day; the younger made several suggestions of places of probable finds. I said: "Anything will fit me that is large enough." They laughed, and said the man of the house (calling his name) was safe as he was too small and would not I look funny in Papa's clothes? They had mentioned over all the different items that I needed, including underclothes. When they got through I expressed my appreciation and said: "You can leave off the underclothes and socks, that is asking too much." They soon gave me to understand that they had my order booked…

Pg. 180 (He falls in with a Confederate cavalry goup out recruiting and hunting deserters) "…The greatest trouble was for man and horse to eat, and we seemed to have no connection with the supply train. Therefore, drew nothing. I was so hungry one morning when I struck where the infantry had camped for the night, I got down and threw some smoldering chunks together and had a fire started and threw on such bones and cow's heads as were handy to roast. The boys who had camped there had roasted the most of the bones once, but were not unto their job as well as one who had served a time in a Yankee prison; so I scraped and sucked hot bones until I appeased my hunger, and after that I had better luck in foraging…"

An amazing young man.

REMINISCENCES OF A PRIVATE William E. Bevins of the First Arkansas Inf. C.S.A. pub by Univ. Ark. Press 1992

Pg. 219 1864 "…December 20th we marched all day on the pike to Pulaski in a cold rain-a rain that froze on the trees. We had to sleep on the wet ground. Many men were barefooted and marched over the pike with bleeding feet" A driving snowstorm hit the column on December 21st and added to the misery of thousands of Hood's men who marched without shoes. General Smith complained about the "ill-provided for condition" of his division, "many being barefooted and otherwise badly clothed."

VOICES OF THE CIVIL WAR by Richard Wheeler pub by Meridian Books 1976

Pg. 434 Dec. 21, 1864 relief efforts for the citizens after the fall of Savannah, Ga., Federal newsman Charles Coffin reports: "...There was a motley crowd. Hundreds of both sexes, all ages, sizes, complexions, and costumes; gay-hared old men of the Anglo-Saxon blood, with bags, bottles and baskets; colored patriarches who had been in bondage for many years, suddenly made freemen; well-dressed women wearing crape for their husbands and sons who had fallen while fighting against the old flag-[all] stood patiently waiting their turn to enter the building, where through the open doors they could see barrels of flour, pork, beans, and piles of bacon, hogsheads of sugar, molasses and vinegar.

There were women in tattered dresses,-old silks and satins, years before in fashion but laid aside as useless, but which now had become valuable through destitution. There were women in linsey-woolsey, in Negro and gunny cloth, in garments made from mealbags; and men in Confederate gray and butternut brown; a boy with a crimson plush jacket made from the upholstering of a sofa; men in short jackets, and little boys in long ones; the cast-off clothes of soldiers; the rags which had been picked up in the streets and exhumed from garrets; boots and shoes down at the heel, open at the instep, and gaping at the toes.

[There were] old bonnets of every description, some with white and crimson feathers and ribbons once bright and flaunting; hats of every style worn by both sexes: palm-leaf, felt, straw, old and battered and well-ventilated. One without a crown was worn by a man with red hair, suggestive of a chimney on fire and flaming out at the top. It was the ragman's jubilee for charity..."

I've included this to show it wasn't just the soldiers who were ragged.

THE DEATH OF AN ARMY: The Battle of Nashville and Hood's Retreat Paul H. Stockdale pub by Southern Heritage Press 1992

Pg. 144 Dec. 25, 1864 Retreat from Nashville "...When the main army approached Pulaski, the weather became most severe. Rain fell in sheets and froze in a layer over the mud...The infantry found marching next to impossible. One member of the retreating force recalled in later years: "Heavy rains alternating with snow and ice now set in. To add to our suffering our clothing was worn threadbare and many were actually without shoes. These constituted the barefoot brigade, and were compelled to cover their feet with rawhide that being the only material at hand...'

Pg. "Private Nelson Rainey of Gen. W.H. Jackson's cavalry division was with the rearguard on the retreat southward and described conditions: "The weather was very cold...rain, half sleet, then snow half sleet on the rocky frozen roads. We all suffered. The infantry most of all. Not half of these poor boys had blankets, very few overcoats.More then half were without shoes, their feet tied up in gunny sacks or old cloth. We have all raed in history that Washington's barefooted soldiers left bloody tracks on the ground. I saw such instances, plenty of them, on this retreat…"

NO SOAP, NO PAY, DIARRHEA & DESERTION A Composite History of the Last Sixteen Monthes of the Confederacy ed by Jeff Toalson pub by iUniverse 2006

Pg. 292 Dec. 26, 1864 Savannah-Private Johnny Green 1st Kentucky Mounted Infantry "… We never had our clothes off and no clean clothes until now. The quartermaster brought clothes out from Savannah to issue to us; they would otherwise have been burned (to avoid falling into Sherman's hands)

I got my piece of soap and took a bath in the Savannah River. Lathered well and then soused in good & took a swim. It was pretty cold too. I donned my new clothes…and washed as best I could my old clothes, dried them and put them in my feed sack…"

New clothes, it seems, are only obtainable through accident.

Trans Mississippi

KIRBY SMITH'S CONFEDERACY

Pg.380 After the beginning of 1864, the most successful of all the industries in Kirby Smith's Confederacy were those overseen by the Clothing Bureau, which, under the able and efficient of Major W.H.Haynes, actually managed to satisfy many of the army's most pressing demands. Using cloth woven at Huntsville, at a new military mill near Tyler, or at one or another of the privately owned factories in East Texas, the Clothing Bureau's many plants, at Washington, Shreveport, Jefferson, Tyler, Houston and Austin, made thousands of hats, shirts, jeans, blankets, tents, and other textile products each month, while the bureau's shoe factories, located in the same towns, reported a monthly output of 10,000 pairs of army footwear. Haynes's various enterprises were so successful that, when it came time for the South to surrender, Kirby Smith's soldiers were probably the best dressed troops in the Confederate army. Their uniforms were seldom uniform, but, in general, their clothing was at least sufficient to keep them decent and warm. In late September, 1864, for instance, one of the ordinary infantrymen camped near Monticello was able to tell his wife:

"You need not send me any socks. I got two excellent pairs from [G.B.Lyon, a messmate]-he wanted to give them to me but I would make him take pay- I have enough clothes to last me through the winter & can always get them cheaper here than they can be bought at home. -My wardrobe consists of 3 pairs of pants a 4th not made up-1 new home made shirt 1 new calico shirt 1 new white shirt linen… & 1 old white shirt (the one Capt. Thompson gave me which will last a long time yet-) 2 pairs of drawers-31/2 pairs of socks-4 neck ties-2 woolen overshirts- 1 uniform coat- my old overcoat & one elastic waterproof overcoat- 1 pair shoes & one pair boots- The uniform coat I wrote to you about some time ago was too small & I have bought another one from my friend D. Head…so you see I am well fixed."

Yet neither trade, nor smuggling, nor industry, alone or in concert, enabled the Trans Mississippi's supply officers "to treat every soldier …as "some one's absent darling.'" Despite Major Haynes's best efforts, many soldiers continued to wear rough homespun, and some companies still depended on shipments of clothing parcels from their home districts."

Gen. Kirby-Smith has turned things completely around since the sartorial chaos of 1861.

VAQUEROS IN BLUE AND GRAY by Jerry D. Thompson pub by State House PRESS 2000

Pg. 121 Jan 1864 "…In January many of the Tejanos were reported to be "without pants" and were "going about camp in their drawers."

NO PARDONS TO ASK, NO APOLOGIES TO MAKE-The Journal of William Henry King, Grat's 28th Louisiana Infantry regiment ed by Gary D. Joiner, Marilyn S. joiner, and Clifton D. Cardin pub by Univ. TN Press 2006

Pg. 143 Jan 8th, 1864, Shreveport, La. "Maj. Schaffer is having the post guard uniformed. Perhaps his pride will result in some good, one time. All of us are in need of clothing, & some are in great need, and the Government has not given us any for a long time, neither has it paid our wages. Spur up, Major, we will not owe you any thanks for the clothing if we get it; for it is our due & you are promoted by no principle of justice, but by an ambitious pride; but let us have the clothing & we will applaud you a little."

Pg. 144 Jan. 29th, 1864 A.J. Groves-He was a messmate of mine from the first. (on furlough) For some time previous to his leaving, I had loaned him different articles of clothing when he went on guard; for he was so destitute of clothing he could not have possibly bourne the intense cold without additional clothing. A few days before he left, he made efforts to obtain clothing & money; the Gov't being considerably behind with him, both in clothing & money; but he failed in every attempt. He stated to the officials that he had no money, and was almost destitute of clothing; that he had no relations to furnish either…"

You'd think they could do something for this soldier.

Pg. 149 Feb. 15th, 1864 "Drew a jacket & a pair of pants to-day for a uniform..."

LONE STAR & DOUBLE EAGLE- Civil War Letters of a German-Texas Family ed by Menetta Altgelt Goyne pub by Texas Christian Univ. Press 1982

Pg. 121 Camp on the Colorado Saturday, 5 March 1864 Rudolf to family "...Thursday we left Camp Sidney Johnson. The trip was divided into two day-long parts, each of about fifteen miles... I found the walking rather difficult. My feet are completely soft from lying around so much, and then I drew new shoes that I had to put on right away, because my old ones were so torn up I couldn't wear them anymore. My feet got swollen and got lots of blisters. They are better again today, only I am still somewhat sore. The shoes we drew are quite good... They are English ones again, but a different kind than the last ones..."

The Trans-Mississippi Dept. is receiving English shoes, I guess through Mexico.

BLESSINGTON 1875

Pg. 115 May 1864 survivers of the Greyhound Division Walker's Division after the Red River campaign: "...It is impossible to point out the variety our division presented. Here would be a fellow dressed in homespun pants, with the knees out of them; on his head might be stuck the remnant of a straw hat, while a faded penitentiary cloth jacket would perhaps complete his outfit. His neighbor very likely in breeches made of some castoff blanket, with a dyed shirt as black as the ace of spades and no hat at all..."

VAQUEROS IN BLUE AND GRAY by Jewrry D. Thompson pub by State House Press 2000

Pg. 123 May 1864 "...In May a near riot broke out in the Confederate command at Rio Grande City. Part of Benavides' regiment had gathered around the commissary warehouse at Ringgold Barracks "demanding clothing and making threats." Captain Crystobal Benavides, in command of the post, strode onto the scene, assured the men they would get their clothing if they remained calm, and quietly turned to Captain Callaghan and ordered that the clothing be distributed in an orderly manner..."

Capt. Benavides certainly quelled that riot. The source doesn't say how badly these men were clad.

GRAY GHOSTS OF THE CONFEDERACY Guerrilla Warfare in the West by Richard S. Brownlee pub by La. State Univ. Press 1858

Pg. 189 1864 June 11 "…On the morning of that day, Anderson (Bloody Bill) and his men, all dressed in blue uniforms, approached and suddenly fired into a squad of the First Missouri Cavalry led by Sergeant J.V. Parman, which was scouting between Holden and Kingsville. Only Parman and two of the men escaped alive. The guerrillas stripped the Union dead to obtain additional items of uniform…."

Pg 194 "…A great deal of the failure of Egbert Brown's cavalry to exterminate the guerrillas in the spring of 1864 lay in the fact that most of the partisans were now dressed wholly or partially in blue Union uniforms. Early in April General Brown had informed departmental headquarters that nearly every guerrilla he killed was dressed in blue and that it was imperative that this should be known by all soldiers and civilians in the department."… "… No person, regardless of his sympathies, could any longer be certain whether he was meeting or conversing with legitimate Union soldiers or masquerading guerrillas. A good many men were pistoled down when they guessed wrong. The partisans obtained their uniforms from the bodies of the soldiers they killed, and prisoners were forced to strip before being shot. Naked or nearly naked corpses littered the woods and fields of Missouri during the summer and fall of 1864…."

The Guerilla War here is getting more and more viscious.

Pg. 194 1864 some of the methods used by the Yankees to distinguish between guerrillas and themselves "…The following signals and pass words for July, 1864 will be transmitted by sub-district commanders to the commanding officer of each scout,. Detachment, or escort detailed from their respective commands, every precaution being taken to prevent their being known to unauthorized persons: During the daytime the commanding officer of a scout, detachment or escort, upon observing the approach of a party or body of men, will ride a few paces in advance of his command and raising his hat or cap, with arm extended at full height, will lower it slowly and place it on his head. The commanding officer of the party thus challenged will immediately answer the same by raising the hat or cap from the head and extending the arm at full length horizontally, bringing the arm back slowly and replacing the hat or cap upon the head. The signal to be given and answered, where the nature of the ground will permit, before the parties have approached nearer than from 300 to 350 yards.

At night the party that first discovers the approach of another, when within challenging distance, will cry out loud and distinctly, "Halt!" and the party thus challenged will immediately answer, "Lyon," to be followed by a counter challenge of "Who comes there?" to which the party last challenged will answer "Reno." The failure of either party to answer promptly and correctly will be the signal to commence firing. The badges to be worn during the month of July will be as follows: On the odd days, as the 1st, 3rd, 5th, 7th,&c., a red strip of cloth fastened around the hat or cap, and on even days, of the month, as the 2nd, 4th 6th 8th,&c., a white strip will be worn in the same manner, the colors alternating each day.

Special care will be taken to avoid mishaps though negligence or the failure on the part of the men to change the badges as herein directed...."

This seems to me a lot of bother and a lot to remember, but a soldier's life could depend on it.

LONE STAR & DOUBLE EAGLE- Civil War Letters of a German-Texas Family ed by Menetta Altgelt Goyne pub by Texas Christian Univ. Press 1982

Pg. 137 Osburn's Mill, 7 July, 1864 Rudolf to Family "...We aren't very well provided with clothing anymore, either. Many have only the suit of clothes on their backs. I am still so fortunate to posses two shirts, a pair of trousers, and a pair of underpants, so that I always still have something to put on while my clothes are being washed; so does Carl. We usually have our clothes washed on farms, because we do not draw any soap. We have to pay $1-2 for a piece..."

THIS INFERNAL WAR by Edwin Hedge Fay/Bell Irvin Wiley pub by Univ. of Texas Press 1958

Pg. 399 Lewinville Ark. July 17 1864 My Own Dear Wife "...I wish I had my woolen clothes for I verily believe they are cooler. I heard from Shreveport that in about a month "they" would have the best article of Confederate Gray ever bought there. I want Mr. Black to buy me enough for a fine suit for I do think I am entitled to something from C.S.A.... Don't forget the Gray Cloth before it is all gone. I want a vest too...See if you can get a dressed buckskin from somebody (for) Dr. Patillo to make me a pair of gauntlets. I need them and will more when cool weather comes..."

LONE STAR & DOUBLE EAGLE- Civil War Letters of a German-Texas Family ed by Menetta Altgelt Goyne pub by Texas Christian Univ. Press 1982

Pg. 143 No Place-(plantation twelve miles from Alexandria) 1 September, 1864 Rudolf to Family "...Wednesday evening H(erman) Conring came and brought us the lovely things that you sent us by Wolfshol. Carl had gotten a bit of rest, which made it possible for him to be pleased about them too. The things had been as nicely selected as though you had known what we need. Our trousers had met their end on the expedition, so that we both had to go about in underpants. We had been out of tobacco for three or four days. We hadn't any handkerchiefs in a long time, and no soap either. But you thought of absolutely everything that we needed. Now we can keep clean, dress decently, and smoke tobacco. What more can a man want, except to be at home, and one simply has to put that out of his mind now..."

Supply from home folks.

Pg. 144 McNutt's Hill (Magnott's Hill) September, 1864 Rudolf to family "...Our clothes are very simple. We still have two shirts each, two pairs of underpants, and the trousers you sent; also rather tolerable shoes. Carl has made himself a straw hat, and I still have the felt hat I drew in Houston, which is still good too. Carl still has a good jacket; mine is a bit torn but it will still make it quite well till winter. Carl has an additional pair of torn trousers, which we want to patch so that we do not always have to wear the new ones right away.... We usually wash our laundry a couple of times in cold water and then hand the things over at a farm to have them washed, because we aren't supplied with soap and seldom have a chance to buy any..."

PRICE'S LAST CAMPAIGN by Mark Lause pub by Univ Missouri Press 2011

Pg. 59 Sept. 1864 "...Once outside, they forced the prisoners to "trade' their coats, hats, shirts, pants, boots, and shoes, leaving the line of prisoners to assume the trappings of the most ragged of the rebels...."...The army again reunited at Union,' recalled Major Edwards, and what a collection it was. Louisa Volker had described them as "barefooted but spured; others clothed in gaudy-colored curtain damask; all manner of hats and caps; some in federal uniform and strapped to their saddles was all kinds of plunder-calico, domestic, shoes, boots tin pans, bed quilts, etc. Of an earlier encounter with John S. Marmadukes' men, slaves remembered their tall hats and one said "most of 'em was a-wearin coonskin caps with de tail a-hanging down." Another Woman assured her cousin, "you never saw such a looking army as Price had. They were not half clothed, and not over two-thirds of them armed, but O there was so many."

Here we see the sartorial chaos again.

CIVIL WAR IN THE INDIAN TERRITORY by Steve Cottrell pub by Pelican Pub. 1998

Pg. 103 1864 capture of a Union wagon train at Horse Creek on Sept. 11 "...Heavily loaded with clothing, raw foodstuffs, ammunition and accouterments, the captured supply train transformed the ragged, half-starved Confederate force into a well-fed, properly equipped, and nearly uniformed little army..."

NO SOAP, NO PAY, DIARRHEA & DESERTION Composite History of the Last Sixteen Mothes of the Confederacy by Jeff Toalson pub by iUniverse Inc. 2006

Pg. 239 Oct. 1864 Near Camden Arkansas Major Silas T. Grisamore. AQM Co.G 18th Louisiana Infantry "...Our division was in a deplorable condition, not less than 200 men were barefooted, 100 had no pants and were, marching in their drawers, others had ne coats, some were without hats..."

Evidently, despite the informantion contained the first quote, there remained a severe clothing shortage in the Trans-Mississippi

THE CONFEDERATE VETERAN VOL. XVII 1909

Pg. 454 Sept. 1909 A Unique Trouser Trade by J. Mont Wilson "In the fall of 1864 General Price made a raid through Missouri. After continuous marching and fighting for weeks, a great many of the boys had trousers only in name. Kenneth Monroe, a short little Scotchman about five feet two inches high (but a good soldier all the same), orderly sergeant of a company in Col. D.C. Hunter's regiment of Missouri Cavalry, was one of the boys whose trousers did not permit him to go into polite society. He went to Col. Hunter and said: "Colonel, I want a furlough." "What for?""To get me a pair of trousers. I have the money to buy them; and if I cannot buy them, I will beg them." The Colonel asked: "If you do neither, will you steal them?" Kenneth replied quickly: "Yes sir." The Colonel said: "Hand me those saddlebags." He pulled out a fine pair of new blue trousers made for a man over six feet high. These he was holding as a reserve for his own wardrobe. Handing them to Kenneth, he said: "Sergeant, put these on till you can get you a pair."

In three minutes Kenneth was in the brush getting into his new possession. When dressed he had the "dude" roll at the bottom of his trousers and the waistband buckled up close under his arms. He quickly hid that by buttoning his jacket close. One of the new recruits who had on a nice brown pair saw Kenneth strutting around in his good clothes and conceived the idea that if he just had those blue trousers he would look like a soldier. This was the snap Kenneth was watching for. In five minutes after the trade was proposed, they were in the brush changing clothes.

A short time after this Colonel Hunter was badly in need of his reserve trousers. Meeting Kenneth, he said to him: "Orderly, if you are through with my trousers, I would like to have them." "Your trousers?" he replies, "I haven't got your trousers." The Colonel, seeing he had brown ones on, said: "You did not trade mine off?" "I certainly did, Colonel." Kenneth answered and marched on. The joke was one-sided and all on the Colonel; but he accepted it and the incident closed...."

I would not have been quite so understanding.

NO PARDONS TO ASK, NO APOLOGIES TO MAKE- The Journal of William Henry King, Gray's 28th Louisiana Infantry Regiment. ed by Gary D. Joiner, Marilyn S. Joiner, and Clifton D. Cardin pub by Univ TN Press 2006

Pg 199 Arkansas Oct. 24th 1864 "yesterday I visited General Polinac's Division, and found many of his men in destitute condition-some without shoes and many very thinly clad. Winter is close at hand, and if something is not done to relieve the wants of the men, many will suffer greatly…"

Pg. 203 Nov. 10th, 1864 "Yesterday, our detail who have been gone to Shreveport for blankets returned and the blankets are now issued. I have drawn one, the first one I have drawn since I have been in the army service…"

1865

EAST

GRANDFATHER'S JOURNAL (Franklin Lafayette Riley) Company B Sixteenth Mississippi Infantry Volunteers Harris' Brigade Mahone's Division Hill's Cops, A.N.V. May 27, 1861-July 15, 1865 pub by Austin C. Dobbins Morningside Press 1988

Pg. 227 Sunday-Tuesday, Jan. 1-3, 1865 Petersburg "...Our supplies are inadequate, but since Sept. 1 Lieut. Arnold-who is sick- has requisitioned for us 33 pr. Of shoes, 39 pr.Of pants, 44 pr. Of drawers, 19 shirts, 6 jackets, 36 pr. of socks and 12 blankets. So far as clothing is concerned, we are doing well..."

This company seems to be well supplied.

THE CONFEDERATE VETERAN VOL. XVII 1909

Pg. 436 Sept. 1909 The Men Of The Ranks-From An Address At Hollywood Cemetary "These men of the ranks were soldierly men. True, not so as to dress! Ah, comrades, shall I set you forth before the people as you were in '65? The crown of your dingy old cotton-felt hat had an ample hole at the top through which a tuft of hair waved gently to the breeze, and its limp rim generally flopped down along your cheeks; your gray jacket was dirty, brown, and ragged, likewise your trousers which were also burned or worn to frazzles; your shoes were often minus, and instead thereof your feet were wrapped in rags!..."

Once again, a Confederate veteran speaks of the destitution of clothing in the ranks. He is not trying to create a romantic myth regarding the Ragged Rebel, he is merely telling it like it was. See below.

CONFEDERATE VETERAN VOLUME XX num.4 1912 Confederate Gray Uniform-Roanoke Va. News

Pg. 157"Towards the last the Confederate soldiers wore anything they could get to cover them, whatever they could buy or pick up or capture from the enemy. Probably the clothing in most general use in the ranks was butternut homespun dyed at home with butternut or walnut shells."

WEBSITE-55thva.org/article00001

Pg. 4 "In Jaunuary 1865, Allen Redwood, then serving in the 1st Maryland Cavalry Battalion paid a visit to his comrades in Co. C, 55th Va., then stationed at Chaffin's Bluff on the Richmond lines. He described their apparel thus: "A few old uniform jackets, once gray, but now stained by dust and faded by sun and rain to a dingy yellow, still hold out against the vissiturdes of war, but the garb is uniform no longer: garments of civic cut and color prevail, interspersed with others, the dye of which proclaims them the spoil of the battlefield, stripped, under the prompting of hard necessity, from those who would never again need them…"

Ragged Rebels

MANASSAS TO APPOMATTOX The Civil War Memoirs of Pvt. Edgar Warfield 17th Virginia Infantry pub by EPM Pub Inc

Pg. 166 January 1865 "…For some time it had been the custom with us, when we had clothing to issue, to give the preference to arms-bearing men. Consequently those who did not bear arms were in a sorry plight. Tip Smith, the leader of our "band" which consisted of a small drum, a fife, and a bass drum, thought this was a good time to get even with those higher up and arranged matters accordingly. What he did was not made evident, at least to the colonel, until the regiment was lined up and the band passed down the front of it and reached the colors. And then it was promptly halted and ordered off the field. Tip and his men had already been ragged enough in their own right. But in addition they had borrowed freely from the rags of other boys in the regiment, and when they came marching bravely down the line playing their instruments they were a sight to behold! Needless to say, they were promised that when the next issue of clothing was to be made they would not be forgotten…"

VOICES FROM COMPANY D Diaries by the Greensboro Guards, Fifth Alabama infantry Regiment, Army of Northern Virginia ed. by G. Ward Hubbs pub by Univ. of Ga. Press 2003

Pg. 340 Jan. 4, 1865 ANV Va. SP "…John returned from Richmond to-day with some of the other Baggage of our Co.blankets, overcoats-woolen underclothes &c.-&brot my mess a little oven, Dutch pot and axe-things much needed- also my wax taper wh. Mary & all the children made for me the morning of day I left home, soap, red peppers etc-wh. Have increased our comforts greatly. I got worsted drawers & under shirts & my big lined blanket that Mama sent me the winter of 1862-invaluable. Peter H got N.C.O. coat too, so we'll now sleep warm…"

These men are finally able to retrieve their belongings from storage- they're lucky, a lot of stored itrems were never seen again by their rightful owners.

"DEAR MARTHA…" The Confederate War Letters of a South Carolina Soldier Alexander Faulkner Fewell compiled and edited by Robert Harley Mackintosh, Jr. pub by The R.L. Bryan Co. 1976 17th South Caroline Inf. Company E

Pg. 184 Entrenchments Jan. 6th 1865 Dear Martha"…if you could see me now the position I am sitting on a round log four inches high a little fire you could hold in your two hands, yet I am not cold having a good overcoat warm clothing. I have not worn my brown pants any yet and the gray ones I have never had off night nor day since the first day of October. My woolen drawers are very warm & comfortable. I intend trying to send my gray socks home with Dan to have you put a toe to it. I never put them on until last week and the second day I wore them I had been on duty and coming to the fire very cold pulled off my shoes to warm my toes burnt the whole bottom of the foot out of one and never felt the heat of the fire and did not know my sock was burnt…"

This soldier also seems well-equipped.

LETTERS TO AMANDA-The Civil War Letters of Marion Hill Fitzpatrick, Army of Northern Virginia ed by Jeffery C. Lowe & Sam Hodges pub by Mercer Univ Press 1998

Jan 7, 1865 Camp 45th Ga. Near Petersburg, Va. (Letter No 95) Dear Amanda," "…I am glad you are supplied with shoes and if I had known it would not have traded for them old things for you (shoes he traded for in Nov. '64), however take them as you may need them yet before the war ends and they are the best I could do for you away here in the war. I am sorry you are making me a coat and heartily wished you had used the cloth for Henry and yourself. Do not make me any more. I want you to have it for I can draw here and you have a hard task to cloth yourself and family without me…"

This writer seems confident he can draw clothing from the government, or is he just trying to ease his wife's mind?

CIVIL WAR REGIMENTS- A Journal of the American Civil War: Treasures from the Archive; Select Holdings from the Museum of the Confederacy

Pg. 147 Jan 7th, 1865 4th Co. Battalion, Washington Artillery Petersburg, Va. "Mr. Frederick Ames has gone from here on furlough, and I think he may go to N. Orleans if he should; I wish you would get him to fetch me a hat. (Soft felt, about Pa's fit) and get him to take it as I am very much in need of one-Brother Frederick"

Pg. 150 Jan'y 29th '65 Fort Louisiana, Petersburg Dear Sister, "I am and have been working at my old Business (printing) since the 13th of Sept. I got permission from my Capt. And Col. I told them it was for the purpose of buying myself some clothes. But everything is so high here, it would take a cart load of confederate money to buy a suit of clothes…"

A good comment on the runaway inflation

VOICES FROM COMPANY D Diaries by the Greensboro Guards, Fifth Alabama Infantry Regiment, Army of Northern Virginia ed. By G. Ward Hubbs pub by Univ. of Georgia Press 2000

Pg. 342 January 9 1865 SP"…Waddell, McD. & all the men left at camp on account of bad shoes…"

Pg. 345 January 16 1865 SP "…An unusually large lot of clothing, blankets, & shoes issued to-day. I drew a pr. Drawers & no. 1 pr. English shoes for John.…"

The government is attempting to issue needed clothing to the troops-especially shoes.

CIVIL WAR LEGENDS OF RICH MOUNTAIN & BEVERLY, WEST VIRGINIA by Mary Genevieve Ward pub by Mcclain Printing Co. 2004

PG. 19 Jan 11, 1865 Gen. Rosser's Raid Told by Mr. Clay Fitzwater "…Rosser did not give the prisoners time to dress but forced them to march a distance of several miles almost naked and barefooted in the snow. In the meantime, Rosser's soldiers, who were badly in need of shoes, had gone into the federal camp and donned the shoes of the prisoners…At Huttonsville, they were given scant clothing and then taken to Staunton, Virginia…"

Pg. 101 A Joke On Some Yankees told by Mr. John Channall "It is said that one hundred Yankees made camp for the night at the "Old Brick Presbyterian Church" near Huttonsville, and after they went to sleep, about the same number of Rebels came along the highway and learned of their hiding place. The Rebels advanced very quickly upon the Yankees and took them prisoner. Then, in order to play a joke on the Yankees, they striiped their clothing from them and sent them on toward Beverly. As the weather was cold and blustery, those who saw them say they went along humped up like turkeys."

I find it hard to have any sympathy for these Yanks.

NO SOAP, NO PAY, DIARRHEA, DYSENTERY & DESERTION ed by Jeff Toalson pub by iUniverse, Inc. 2006

Pg. 308 Jan 12, 1865 1st Lt.Tinsely Allen, Co. F- 58th Virginia Inf. College Hosp. Petersburg, Va. My Dear ma "…I purchased cloth enough for coat pants and trimmins which I gave the rise of seven hundred dollars, and by the time they are maid they will cost me the rise of nine hundred dollars…"

This is an outrageous example of inflation.

LIFE IN THE CONFEDERATE ARMY: Being Personal Experiences of a Private Soldier in the Confederate Army:And Some experiences and Sketches of Southern Life by Arthur P. Ford and Marion Johnstone Ford pub by The Neale Pub. Co. 1905

Pg. 103 Jan. 15, 1865 (Marian Ford) Otranto plantation "All the white men are in the army and some women are nervous, but we do not feel so. This intensely cold weather makes us feel wretched about our poor bare-footed soldiers. Mother can knit a pair of socks a day. Maun Martha spins the wool. I can only do one sock a day. We are fortunate to have so much lightwood. It is the only source of light we have, but we can manage our knitting and Annie even reads sometimes, but the paper is so bad it is hard to read the printing on it."

DIARY AND CORRESPONDENCE OF SALMON P. CHASE pub by American Historical Association, 1903

Pg. 526 Letter from Daniel Amnento Salmon Portland Chase, January 16, 1865 "Mohican" off Fort Fisher N.C.

"…In the fort today I saw a soldier picking up some rebel dirty clothing and advised him to let it alone as he would get lousy. A wounded rebel sitting near immediately spoke up and said he was not one half as lousy as our Gen'l Butler and then went on to say that he himself had not changed or taken off his clothing since the 27th of December. Pardon my introduction of so coarse a subject but I did so to show how thoroughly he had the hatred of the people of the South. I do not think any military ability that he has shown will compensate for the Phrenzy with which he inspires them…"

Way to go, Johnny!

FOOTPRINTS OF A REGIMENT-A Recollection of the 1st Georgia Regulars 1861-1865 by W.H. Andrews, 1st Sergeant, Co. M pub by Longstreet Press 1992

Pg. 160 Jan 20, 1865 Fighting in N.C. "As we charged, Sgt. Bruce and myself got within 20 yards of a man behind a tree. I called Bruce's attention to him telling him it was one of our men. Bruce said not. I then told Bruce to look at the light-clored overcoat he had on and the Confederate canteen hanging at his side. Still Bruce refused to be convinced. "Well, Bruce," said I, "if nothing else will convince you, I will shoot him and pressed the trigger. My gun being wet, failed to fire. Just at that time, the regiment that was charging in the rear of the skirmish line dashed up with Bruce and myself. The soldier with the light overcoat on blazed away at the regiment and beat a hasty retreat...."

This source never reveals who that guy was.

NO SOAP, NO PAY, DIARHHEA, DYSENTERY, & DESETION ed by Jeff Toalson pub by iUniverse Inc. 2006

Pg. 313 Jan. 20, 1865 Staunton Vindicator, Staunton, Va. Article of Appeal to Ctizens: "They (The Stonewall Brigade) are in need of clothes to keep them warm. They do not complain but we understand they suffer...The men...are from our midst-our own friends and relatives-and can be supplied with many things needful to them by use. If our people will but make the effort...these gallant men...in a few days...may be made more comfortable for the winter..."

It goes without saying that any clothing donated at this time was civilian, there was no time to dye cloth nor supplies of uniform cloth.

"DEAR MOTHER: DON'T GRIEVE ABOUT ME. IF I GET KILLED, I'LL ONLY BE DEAD." ed. by Mills Lane pub by The Beehive Press 1977

Pg. 339 J.H. Jenkins to his Wife, Coosawhatchee, South Carolina January 21, 1865 My Dear Wife: "...Sallie, I drew a shirt and a pair of drawers but could not draw shoes. If you ever do get the chance, I want you to send me a pair of shoes....Sallie, tell Mother that William says not to send his fine uniform coat..."

NO SOAP,NO PAY, DIARRHEA, DYSENTERY& DESERTION A Composite History of the Last 16 Monthes of the Confederacy ed by Jeff Toalson, pub by iUniverse Inc. 2006

Pg. 317 Jan. 27, 1865 Henry's 5th Battalion Virginia Reserves Lt. Col. A.S. Cunningham Adj. General's Office Inspecting Officer "Very deficient in clothing, shoes, &c., many men being entirely barefooted, and much sickness caused thereby…"

This group poorly supplied, and, once again the absolute dearth of shoes. See below

THE CIVIL WAR INFANTRYMAN, In Camp, on the March, and in Battle by Gregory A. Coco pub by Thomas publications, Gettysburg, Pa

Pg 81 By January 1865, Williams Chambers of the 46th Mississippi perceived that the end was near long before actually giving up. Expounded Chambers:

"I find my regiment, the whole army in fact, in a deplorable condition. Twenty besides myself of Company B are here, but there is not a gun in the company. The regiment numbers about one hundred and fifty men, about half of whom are barefoot. All are ragged, dirty and covered with vermin, some not having sufficient clothing to hide their bodies. There are perhaps twenty guns, but not a single cartridge box in the regiment. The men are jovial enough… (but) fully convinced that the Confederacy is gone."

GENERAL LEE'S ARMY-FROM VICTORY TO CALLAPSE by Joseph T. Glattharr pub by Free Press a div. of Simon and Schuster

Pg. 445 In late January 1865, Quartermaster Genral Alexander Lawson reorted that over the last seven months, his office had allocated enough supplies for each soldier to have received approximately two pairs of shoes, two shirts, two sets of drawers, ywo pair of socks, two pair of pants, one blanket, and more than one jacket. Yet inspection after inspection uncovered a lack of shoes and clothing in serious, often critical numbers. "The men are suffering for clothing," relayed an inspector in late 1864, "Many are ragged and some instances, strickly speaking, unfit for the field." He considered the delay in delivering clothing "inexcusable." Late in December, some men of the 9th Alabama attended inspection with no pants at all, and fifteen men in the 10th Alabama were barefoot. The same was true in Kershaw's division. "Some of the men are without pants and others nearly so," an inspector reported.

In mid-March, Lawton insisted that "a larger supply of clothing has been issued to the armies in the last three months than in any similar period during the war," yet men in Lee's army still suffered severe shortages. According to an inspector, "Experience has shown that the semi-annual allowance of clothing which would be sufficient to clothe men comfortably in less onerous duty will last scarcely three months in the Trenches, from the greater wear of material in rubbing against the sides of the ditches." During January and Febuary, inspectors uniformly determined the condition of clothing as poor. In Robert Ransom's Brigade, at the end of January, one in every six soldiers had shoes that were irreparable, and others were barefoot. Pickett's Division needed 757 jackets and 1,359 pairs of pants. Rufus Barringer's Cavalry Brigade had a "large number of the men" barefoot. As late as the end of March, soldiers like Pvt. Peter Cross complained, "I can tell you I am naked fur pants you oit (ought) see me then you would see a raged (ragged) man."

The quality of the material tended to be poor. For a long time, brigades and divisions had manufactured their own shoes, which by all accounts were superior to what the government issued. As an officer commented on the inspection report of Lane's Brigade at the end of 1864, "it has been satisfactorily demonstrated after a year's experience that better shoes can be made in camp than are suppled by the Q.M. Dept." Both Rode's and Early's Divisions ran shoe and tailoring shops for the men, something their commanders would never have established if the clothing and shoe shortage had not reached a grave status. To be sure, the problem at any given moment varied by unit and even state. In Wilcox's Division at the end of November1864, the two North Carolina brigades had received clothing allotments from their state and were "much better supplied" than the other two brigades, from Georgia and South Carolina. At the end of Febuary 1865, the quartermaster of Georgia had issued clothing to Anderson's Brigade, while the Texas Brigade, Bratton's Carolinians, and Law's Alabamians endured serious clothing shortages…"

Here is another mention of shoddy government issue clothes and shoes, which further reduced the lifespan of the article issued. Due to the increased wear & tear from duty in the trenches, supply could not keep up with demand.

PERSONAL RECOLLECTIONS OF PRIVATE JOHN HENRY CAMMACK: A SOLDIER FOR THE CONFEDERACY 1861-1865 pub by Pargon Printing & Pub. Co.

Pg. 105 Feb. 1865 after the repulse of the Kilpatrick/Dahlgreen Raid "…The raid made by the enemy was successfully repulsed. We were ordered back next morning about ten o'clock. I think it would have been hard to find a more wet, muddy and forelorn command than we were as we marched back that day to our camp. Some, like myself, were actually barefooted, dragging along throught the mud and water.

I made a request for a pair of shoes that day, but Capt. Barlow said none would be issued me because I had just had a pair. The next day I was ordered on guard duty up the line about a mile I refused to go unless shoes were issued to me or that I be sent in command of the guard….but the shoes were again refused…During the afternoon of that day the Colonel in command came as was the custom to make an inspection of the redoubt. The Colonel rode up and after the salute by the sentry, he asked for the officer in command. I immediately stepped out of the hut, dressed as follows: I think I wore a home-made straw hat, but do not know what sort of shirt, a pair of old gray trousers with one suspender and barefooted. I carried an Enfield rifle, which I very properly brought tp Present Arms. The Colonel returned the salute and said, "I want to see the officer in command of this redoubt." I kept my face perfectly straight and answered, "I have the hinor, sir, to be in command here." I could see that he was very amused at my appearance as an officer, but we went through with the inspection, the Colonel remaining as dignified as only an Old Army officer knows how to be.

When the inspection was over, the Colonel saluted and started away. I stopped him and said I had a small matter to talk about. He graciously gave me permission to talk and I explained my appearing before him barefooted, because my Captain declined to issue me a pair of shoes. The Colonel did not interupt until I was through, he then said, "I will see, sir, that the shoes are issued to you."

NO SOAP,NO PAY, DIARRHEA, DYSENTERY& DESERTION A Composite History of the Last 16 Monthes of the Confederacy ed by Jeff Toalson, pub by iUniverse Inc.2006

Pg. 323 Feb. 1865 Shenandoah Valley, Va. Private Jerrill Robinett Co.F-45th Va. Inf. "I am nearly barefooted but hope to draw shoes....the worst is I can't forage about over the country to get something to eat...I am sending my measurements home for shoes. Make a neat pair, longer than my foot. Make them round in the shank so I can get them off and on easy"

Pg. 326 Feb. 6, 1865 Wilmington, N.C. Seaman Robert Watson Fort Campbell "Drew one pr pants, 2 pr cotton drawers, 2 cotton shirts, and 2 plugs tobacco and 2lbs soap."

We see from this last quote that the Navy still had ample supplies.

THE CONFEDERATE VETERAN VOL. XXXII 1924

Pg. 301 August, 1917 Incidents of the Fighting at Aiken, S.C. (Feb.1865) by D.B. Morgan "...Near where my mule lay dead, I saw a dead Yankee trooper, and, being poorly shod, tried to get his shoes off; for some reason I do not now recall, I did not take them. He also had on a nice watch and chain, which I did not want, so allowed a fellow soldier to possess himself of them. However, I did take his nice overcoat and cape, almost new, and it did me good service in the days to come..."

I wonder what in the hell kept this soldier from getting those shoes?

LIFE IN THE CONFEEDERATE ARMY: Being Personal Expe-riences of a Private Soldier in the Confederate Army: and Some Experiences and Sketches of Southern Life. By Arthur P. Ford and Marion Johnstone Ford pub by the Neale Pub. Co. 1905

Pg.42 Feb. 1865 evacuation of James Island "Our men had started on this march with as much baggage as they thought they could carry, but they soon threw aside their impedimenta, and each settled down to his one blanket and such clothes as he actually wore. This march across the Carolinas was a very hard one. Our feet soon became blistered and sore, and many of us had no shoes, but trudged along in the cold and mud barefooted as best we could. As I have already said, this was a cold winter, and it seemed to us that it rained and snowed constantly. Not a particle of shelter did we have day or night. We would march all day, often in more or less rain, and at nightfall halt, and bivouac in the bushes, with every particle of food and clothing saturated…"

Notice that even the garrison troops were short of shoes.

A TRUE HISTORY OF COMPANY I, 49TH REGIMENT NORTH CAROLINA TROOPS by W.A. Day Printed At The Enterprise Job Office 1893

Pg. 93 Feb 1st, 1865 Petersburg, Va. "It rained almost half the time, sometimes it would freeze and everything would be covered with ice. The weather was very cold, and our uniforms and blankets worn out, and our Government too poor to furnish us new ones, but our people at home sent us clothes which kept us from freezing to death and boxes of rations which kept us from starving…"

Thank goodness for the folks at home!

THE CONFEDERATE LETTERS OF BENJAMIN H. FREEMAN Compiled & Edited by Stuart T. wright pub by Exposition Press 1974

Pg. 59 Feby 1 1865 Petersburg, Va. My Dear Farther: "…We get here some days sugar flour and polk (pork) "nassan"(?) and some molasses. Then again corn, Milk and few Peas. I drew some tobacco day before yesterday I drew a fine blanket the other day my little one was to(o) light this cold seasons…"

LIFE AND LETTERS OF ROBERT E. LEE, SOLDIER AND MAN

Pg. 486 Letter from Robert E. Lee to James Alexander Seddon, Feb. 8, 1865 Headquarters Army of Northern Virginia Sec. of War, Richmond, Va. "Sir, All the disposable force of the right wing of the army has been operating against the enemy beyond Hatcher's Run since Sunday. Yesterday, the most inclement day of the winter, they had to be retained in line of battle, having been in the same condition the previous two days ans nights. I regret to be obliged to state that under these circumstances, heightened by assaults and fire of the enemy, some of the men had been without meat for three days, and all were suffering from reduced rations and scant clothing, exposed to battle, cold hail and sleet."

I wonder how these men survived at all, much less performed their duty.

UNDER THE STARS AND BARS-A History of the Surrey Light Artillery pub by Press of Morningside Bookshop 1975

Pg. 231 Letter # 45 Feby 10, 1865 Camp Henrico, Va.My Dear Friend, "...There is an old English saying that, "God tempers the wind to the shorn lamb," and perhaps he has tempered the winter to the thin-clad soldiers, for many of our men are but sorrily clad, and few of them have overcoats. And good shoes or boots, and woolen socks are greatly needed. Such a thing as a dress parade would be out of the question now. The officers would be ashamed to exhibit such a rag-a-muffin, tatterdemalion set as the average private would make. Such a thing as a whole uniform is rarely to be seen.

Yet the boys do not take it much to heart because of their rags, but sing their songs and have their sports and fun, just as earnestly as though they were the best clad fellows in the land. Many of them have learned to patch quite neatly, and we have some men who could pass an examination for tailors. In fact, one of our boys has had his wedding suit of Confederate gray made for him by one of the company. And it was pronounced by all to have been a good job. But I reckon you would laugh heartily if you were to see some of the odd patches that some of the boys stitch on. The most of them never think of cutting out the old rent to set in a patch, but they stitch the piece on over the old cloth, which, of course, makes a bundle of it all. They say it makes the clothes warmer to set the patches on top the old cloth, and it is easier work....[Perhaps my old comrade and warm friend, John W. Ell, will bear me out about that nice tailor-built suit that he made for M.A. Delk, some time during the war-and how proud Matt was when it was finished and he got his furlough to go home]..."

Another witness of the "Ragged Rebels."

U.S. ARMY HERITAGE & INFORMATION CENTER

11th Feb. 1865 M.L. Wilson Co. E, 10th Alabama Infantry Regiment Petersburg, Va. Dear Marcas: "I understand Gen. Green H.M. for our state is now in Richmond with a quantity of clothing for the troops of Ala.

Since my entering the service (4 years past) I have never been able to draw, buy or have issued to me anything in the clothing line. Now I am cut off from home and can have nothing sent me. This is to ask you to procure me a full suit of everything he has & more especially an over coat. You well know my size.

Use my name in any way that may be necessary to obtain me something to hide my nakedness.

If it becomes necessary to advance money, please do so & let me know by return mail and I will forward any thing now to procure something to wear."

It seems this soldier can't get a uniform for conections or money

REBEL PRIVATE FRONT AND REAR by William A. Fletcher pub by Dutton Books 1995

Pg. 192 Feb. 17, 1865 After the fall of Colunbus, S.C. "...In our rambles we struck a man who asked if we could use some cotton or woolen cards, as he did not want them to fall into the hands of the Yankees. We accepted, as we knew something of their scarcity and value, so he gave us two pairs of cotton cards—one of my cards proved to be wool, but it was too late to correct...Pard and I had a good dinner for the cotton and woolen cards, and the woman who furnished it thought she was fortunate, and said she had fed a good many Rebs that day and the cards were ample pay for all, if one was woolen. One rarely sees cotton or woolen cards now, but they were a great factor during the war, and how the South would have kept clothed without them would have been a serious question, and would have added far greater suffering. I traded my pair of cotton cards for a good pair of pants and both the receiver of the pants and the cards were made happy..."

The Young Lions-Confederate Cadets at War by James Lee Conrad pub.by Stackpole Books 1997

"...VMI's condition was best illustrated by the requirements levied on the cadets for the spring 1865 session. Each cadet had to furnish his own underwear; a gray jacket; one pair of gray pants; an overcoat; two pairs of shoes; a mattress and beding; four towels; a comb, hairbrush and toothbrush; a knife and fork; and one hundred pounds of bacon. The cadets were also requested to furnish their own textbooks..."

At this point in time, what family could afford that kind of outlay?

THE CAVALRY AT APPOMATTOX by Edward G. Longacre pub byStackpole Books, 2003

Spring 1865 Col. Thomas Taylor Munford observed: "The trusted veterans of a hundred Battles. Their countenances were cheerful and bright, though their rations were pinched and scanty, their blankets thin and worn, their clothing tattered and of various colors. Many were shod with moccasins, fresh from slaughtered cattle. Some were housed in patched tents, and others in daubed huts, through which the cold winds might whistle…notwithstanding all, they hopefully awaited the dawn of a brighter morrow. The old Confederates knew that it was their own fight, and they felt sure that those of their old comrades who acted as spies and scouts…would keep their general accurately informed as to every movement of the enemy."

Here's a mention of cavalry wearing moccasins of green cow hide, still valiantly performing their duties.

A CONFEDERATE SURGEON'S LETTERS TO HIS WIFE Spencer Glascow Welch, Surgeon Thirteenth S. Ca. Vols., McGowans Brigade pub by Neale Pub. Co. 1911

Pg 125 CordeliaStrother Welch to her sister, Miss Georgia Strother, Fruit Hill, Edgefield, S. Ca. Petersburg, Va. March, 1865 "…You know I brought a quantity of woolen yarns from home. I wish I had kept an account of the number of pairs of socks I have knit for the soldiers. Then, too, I have done lots of patching and mending for them. It takes a good deal of work and planning to keep our clothes presentable."

An unending task.

LETTERS AND PAPERS OF AN ARTILLERY OFFICER A.N.V. IN THE WAR FOR SOUTHERN INDEPENDENCE 1861-1865 Capt. John Hampden Chamberlain-Virginian pub by Dietz Printing Co. Pub. 1932

Pg. 312 March 1865 My dear Sister "…You must have omitted sending the blank-book, as it was not in the bundle with the collars…"

Collars? Really? At this state of the war?

NO SOAP,NO PAY, DIARRHEA, DYSENTERY& DESERTION A Composite History of the Last 16 Monthes of the Confederacy Jeff Toalson, pub by iUniverse Inc. 2006

Pg.339 Early March, 1865 West of Petersburg, Va. Private David E. Grable Co. A-17th Tn. Inf. "Our clothing was thin…we wore them until they were old dirty and ragged. One would pull off our shirts and go naked until we could wash them. We could do very little washing in winter. I marched barefooted on the frozen ground, snow and frost. The sergeant had orders to detail the best shod boys for picket duty. The sergeant came along and said Dave you will have to go out…and I did not have a particle of shoe under the bottom of my foot."

Pg. 342 March 8 1865 Near Petersburg, Va. Ord. Sgt Nathaniel W. Watkins CoK-34th Va. Inf. "…send my trousers & cotton shirts as soon as you can safely send them…"

HAM CHAMBERLAYNE-VIRGINIAN Letters and Papers of an Artillery Officer in the War for Independence 1861-1865 with introduction, notes and index by his son C.G.Chamberlayne Richmond, Va. pub by Press of the Dietz Printing Co. Publishers 1932

Pg. 312 J.H.Chamberlayne to L.P. Bagby March 5th, 1865 My dear Sister, "…I will, on reflection, keep the hand trunk, only sending back the blue flannel suit, my jacket, and some useless shirts.…"

This officer acts like he is more than adequately supplied with clothing, in fact, not suffering at all.

AN IRISHMAN IN DIXIE-Thomas Conolly's Diary of the Fall of the Confederacy ed by Nelson D. Lankford pub by University of South Carolina Press 1988

Pg. 36 March 7th, 1865 "…We started out for a walk thro' Greensboro (N.C.) wh is a rising little Place where 4 lines of railway meet & where even now they are building largely-whole place full of soldiers in all manner of garb. Prisoners returning on parole & all the strays & waifs of war. Wagons with mule teams and black drivers & soldiers on duty keeping order &(regularity?) & the big blunderbuss funneled Engines booming & ringing their alrm bells at all hours-cars full inside with motley troops armed & covered with picturesque crowds camping on the top & rolling themselves in their large blankets with nothing but beards &sloughhat& rifle protruding &-&c-& Such all covered and spattered with red mud wh marks everything & everybody here was the scene as we left Greensboro.…"

8 March, 1865 Richmond Va. "…pickets of mud stained-slough-hatted rawboned cavalry-Every species of gray, brown, threadbare, jaunty & ragged uniform, or rather multiform here & there with smart officers & grisely hard lined determined veterans always neat among their rough and uncouth comrades (as yet untutored in the ways of war) mud, mud, mud everywhere, even thro' the halls and corridors of the hotel whch are a babel of chatter & oaths the word Yankee or Yanks issuing from every group…"

This man was not a soldier; so we havs an independent witness of the Rgged Rebels.

LETTERS FROM A PENNSYLVANIA CHAPLAIN AT THE SIEGE OF PETERSBURG 1865 Privately Pub. 1961

Pg. 47 Letter from Halleck Armstrong to Mary Armstrong March 7 1865 "…Did I write about seeing 500 Rebels at once? Oh what a dirty, greasy, filthy set. Many of them had pieces of carpet for blankets. Some were grey headed, some were little boys…."

Notice the last two quotes refer to the destitution of clothing in the Southern ranks.

A HISTORY OF THE SOUTHERN CONFEDERACY by Clement Eaton pub, by The MacMillan Co. 1954

PG. 259 March 10-11 1865 The Quartermaster General-"…Particularly significant was his remark that "a larger supply of clothing has been issued to the armies in the last three months than in any similar period og the war." The Army was better supplied with shoes than with any other article, and he was confident that there would be no serious lack of clothing…."

Maybe he should visit the front lines and inspect the troops himself.

NO SOAP, NO PAY, DIARHHEA, DYSENTERY & DESERTION ed by Jeff Toalson pub by iUniverse Inc. 2006

Pg. 345 March 14, 1865 Pvt. Joseph F. Shaner Rockbridge Artillery, Near Petersburg, Va. "I bought myself a good pair of shoes this morning. I had to pay $60 for them but I was oblige to have them as I have bin nearly bare footed for sometime."

$60 is not too steep a price for shoes at that time, I guess he couldn't get any from the government or from home.

WELCOME THE HOUR OF CONFLICT-William Cowan McClellan & the 9th Alabama ed by John C. Carter pub by Univ Al Press

Pg.273 March 18 1865 Petersburg, Va. "…Rations were scarce, and clothing was greatly needed by bthe troops, although most men had shoes…"

At last, a mention of adequate shoes!

THE MEN- 49TH VIRGINIA VOLUNTEERS C.S.A.

Pg. 232 March 18, 1865 HdQrsAof the P
Maj. Genl. Humphreys
Comdng 2 Corps

"A rebel scout captured by two of our scouts from Genl. Sheriden's Army escaped from him at 9PM. His description is, Franklin George, 49th Va. Inf. 25 years of age, 6 feet high, slim, dark long hair, heavy light colored mustache, lives in Faquer County. Dressed in a new blue blouse, blue overcoat and butternut trousers. Let the pickets watch for him."

S. Alex S. Webb
Chief of Staff

Sounds as though this scout had helped himself to some Yankee clothing.

VOICES OF THE CIVIL WAR by Richard Wheeler pub by Meridian Books 1976

Pg. 446 March 25, 1865 night assault on Fort Stedman, Petersburg entrenchments General Gordon-"All night my troops were moving and concentrating behind Colquitt's Salient. For hours Mrs. Gordon sat in her room in Petersburg tearing strips of white cloth to tie across the breats of the leading detachments, that they might recognize each other in the darkness..."

Once again using strips of white cloth to identify themselves

NO SOAP, NO PAY, DIARHHEA, DYSENTERY & DESERTION ed by Jeff Toalson pub by iUniverse 2006

Pg. 353 March 27, 1865 Pvt. Walter Clark, 70th N.C. Junior Reserves Camp near Smithfield, North Carolina Mother-"...I suppose Neverson told you that my shirts suited me exactly. They...have been much admired..."

Boxes from home were still getting through, though his mother may have lived close-by.

THE CONFEDERATE VETERAN VOL.3 FEB. 1895

Pg. 36 Last Battles of the War B.L. Ridley's Journal March 29, 1865 "...Maj. Hooper, Quartermaster, was exceedingly kind, and permitted me to buy an overcoat and a suit of gray clothes. Returned to camp, only to be scolded by Cols. Sevier and Gale, because I neglected them..."

THE CONFEDERATE VETERAN VOL.III 1905

Spring 1865 by A.E. Jenkins Greensboro, N.C. Gen. Wheeler, "...He had on a brown jeans overcoat of the cavalry pattern..."

SOUTH GEORGIA REBELS by Alton J. Murray 1976

Pg. 195 April 1865 Petersburg to Appomattox "...Lee's army was starving to death. General Gordon stated that it was not an uncommon sight to see soldiers gather grains of dry corn dropped from the mouths of the ill-fed horses while they were eating, pick it up from the ground around the horse's feet, wash and parch it, and eat it. Amazingly enough, the soldiers for the most part, did not loose their spirit or sense of humor. If one became sick overnight from eating the hard, dry corn, the next morning he would most likely say to Gordon, "Hello General; I am all rightr this morning. I ate a lot of corn last night and if you will have the commissary issue a good mess of hay for my breakfast, I'll be ready for the next fight." Another soldier would advise a companion to take his month's pay in Confederate money and but a bottle of strong astringent to draw up his stomch to the size of his ration...."

More than mortal man.

FOUR YEARS UNDER MARSE ROBERT by Robert Stiles pub by Pelican Pub. Co. Gretna 1998

Pg. 333 Sailor's Creek April 1865 "I had cautioned my men against wearing "Yankee overcoats," especially in battle, but had not been able to enforce the order perfectly-and almost at my side I saw a young fellow of one of my companies jam the muzzle of his musket against the back of the head of his most intimate friend, clad in a Yankee overcoat, and blow his brains out....I well remember the yell of demonic triumph with which that simple country lad of yesterday clubbed his musket and whirled savagely upon another victim."

PARKER'S VIRGINIA BATTERY by Robert K. Krick pub by Va. Book Co. 1975

Pg. 284 April, 1865, the beginning of the final retreat-"The Federal prisoners were brought up over the works around Parker's battery. The ragged canoneers marveled at their good clothes and equipment. Gibson Clark helped himself to a fine felt hat worn by one captive, giving in exchange his old and tattered hat. Clark also appropriated seventy-five cents from the prisoner before the captives were herded to the rear to the "bull pen" stockade where they were to be held while they were awaiting transportation.Thisthieveryu began to weigh on Clark's mind at once. He rationalized his action on the basis that he was "ragged, almost shoeless, dirty, hungry, penniless and exposed to the storms. "Within a short period, his conscience drove Clark back to the "bull pen," where he returned the stolen goods over the protestations of the prisoner. Clark explained his actions with a mixture of good character and terrible prophecy: "I felt not only ashamed and humiliated, also thjat we could expect no help from god for our cause, if the soldiers of the South did such wicked things." It was soon to become apparent that god didn't pick a winner on the basis of looting and destruction, or else he preferred to reward the practitioners of those trades…"

There is much evidence to support this man's claim.

THECONFEDERATE VETERAN VOL. XX NOV. 1912

Pg. 520 April 1865 "A Gossipy Letter From Georgia by Edward S. Lathrop Fayetteville, N.C. "…Things were so mixed in the town by the unexpected coming together that little fighting could be done. But the saddest yet most laughable sight was to see our poor boys as the women came to their front doors to feed them. The boys would hold the rags over their nakedness and sidle up to the ladies, grab the food, and get out of sight. I was almost naked myself but had a piece of cloth on my saddle. I heard of an old Savannah friend who was a tailor. I put spurs to my horse and found him at his front door. "Will you cut these out for me?" "yes, come in." And soon he did it.…My tailor was thoughtful enough to put in thread and needles…"

PARKER'S VIRGINIA BATTERY by Robert K. Krick pub. by Va. Book Co.1975

About mid-afternoon on April 2, a flag of truce was approved to allow the Federals to bury their numerous dead from the morning fight. The confederate officer accompanying the truce burial parties blushed deeply, it was said, when it was discovered that most of the bodies had already been stripped of their clothing by destitute Confederates…"

Blushed? I'd have been proud of the industriousness of the men.

THE HASKELL MEMOIRS-A Personal Narrative of a Confederate Officer by John Haskell ed by Gilbert E. Govan and James W. Livgood pub by G.P. Putnam's Sons 1960

Pg. 85 April 2, 1865 retreat through Richmond "I had some time before been fortunate enough to find a bootmaker in Richmond who had gotten some very fine leather through the blockade. He had made me a pair of boots, although refusing to let me have more than one pair, for which I paid him twelve hundred and fifty dollars. They were so new that they were not very comfortable, and I took them off when I reached camp. I then put them with some other valued possessions in an ambulance. I sent it with a battery of Armstrong's gun, which had been assigned to me but never put on the permanent line, as they were held too valuable and were only sent out for some special service where their great, accurate range and

English ammunition could do work that justified risking them. *When the Hell is an appropriate time? After the Yankees take them?*

The battery's captain had ordered us to cross the river at Richmond and wait on the other side, but when he got there he decided to follow his own lead. He went off after some infantry to find a better place and drove straight into the enemy's lines, losing my cherished Armstrong guns and my twelve hundred dollar boots…"

At this point I'd have been more concerned anout my boots, they were never going to use those guns, it seems.

UNDER THE STARS AND BARS-A History of the Surrey Light Artillery pub by Press of Morningside Bookshop 1975

April 2, 1865 Retreat through Richmond "At last a courier arrives, and we dash forward through Rocketts, where the wildest confusion prevails-on along Main Street, where numberless women, reckless of personal danger, were tugging and pulling at parcels and goods thrown out from the depots where supplies had been stored-on by the Government shoe factory, just in time to secure a supply of new shoes…"

A REBEL WAR CLERK'S DIARY AT THE CONFEDERATE STATES CAPITOL, vol.2 1868 pub by Lippencott& Co.

Pg. 482 Retreat through Richmond April 2 1865-"And some of the shops gave clothing to our last retiring guards."

NO SOAP, NO PAY, DIARRHEA, DYSENTERY& DESERTION A Composite History of the Last 16 Monthes of the Confederacy Jeff Toalson, pub by iUniverse Inc. 2006

Pg. 362 April 3 1865 Chester Station Va. Sgt. J.E. Whitehorne Co.F-12th Va. Inf. "We heard that a great quantity of Quarter Master stores were destroyed at Chester Station and Dunlops Crossing, at the latter place a quantity of clothing. What a pity clothing was not given to the ragged soldiers. One of our men, Horse Taylor,…went to Dunlops Crossing as the clothing were being burned and snatched 33 pairs of pants and 1 jacket…he gave me the jacket, kept one pair of pants for himself."

It is indefensible that these clothes weren't given or made available to the soldiers.

THE COMANCHES WHITE'S BATTALION, VIRGINIA CAVALRY LAUREL BRIGADE by Frank M. Myers pub by Continental Books 1956

Pg. 372 April 5, 1865 Amelia Springs Va. "…the 11th Virginia, under Lt. Col M.D.Ball, leading most gallantly, and being supported by the remainder of the division, and by a portion of Gen. Fitz Lee's division, they whipped the enemy's cavalry handsomely, killing and wounding nearly as many as were engaged on the Confedewrate side, and driving the remainder back upon their infantry.

The affair did more to revive the drooping spirits of the Cavalry Corps than anything else could, but it is doubtful if they would have fought so fiercely if they had not been so hungry; and the first demand, on taking a prisoner, was "hand me your haversack, quick, or I'll blow your brains out."…"

Now, that's hungry!

TO APPOMATTOX-Nine April Days, 1865 by Burke Davis pub by Rinehard& Co. Inc. 1959

Pg. 24 April 1865 Beginning the retreat from Petersburg Sharpshooters of McGowan's Brigade of South Carolinians. "A company of Federal cavalry, mistaking us for their own men, rode up within twenty yards from where we stood. A single volley from my line unhorsed nearly the last man of them, and in a few minutes my barefooted crowd were up to their knees in cavalry boots…"

Pg. 135 Monday, April 6 Semmes saw the absurdity of the sailor's appearance. "Loaded down with pots and pans and mess kettles, bags of bread, chunks of salted pork, sugar, tea, tobacco, pipes. It was as much as they could do to stagger under the load."

Another quote illustrating the well-supplied status of the Navy.

Pg. 281 Friday, April 7 General Wise "We were overcome by exhaustion, and without food. There was no water but the pools, as red as brick dust, in the soil of that region. Colonel J.Thomas Goode and myself washed our faces in the same pool, and neither of us had a handkerchief or towel to wipe with, and consequently the paint of the red water remained on our faces at the edges of our hair…".Wise said of his entry into Farmville: "With a face painted like an Indian, with the grey blanket around me, and with the Confederate Tyrolese hat on, and muddy all over, I put myself on foot at the head of the two brigades and marched…across an open field to where General Lee was sitting in his saddle, with General B.R.Johnson on his horse a little in the rear…"

Pg. 291 Friday, April 7 regarding a flag of truce Colonel Herman H. Perry was sent to investigate ...AFederal officer approached: "My worn Confederate uniform and slouched hat, even in the dim light, could not compare favorably with his magnificence," Perry said, "But as I am six feet high I drew myself up as proudly as I could and put on the appearance of being perfectly satisfied with my personal exterior."

Good for you, Col. Perry!

LETTERS FROM A PENNSYLVANIA CHAPLAIN AT THE SIEGE OF PETERSBURG 1865 Privately Pub. 1961

April 7, 1865 "...You can pick up muskets etc. almost every where thrown away by the Rebs. Nobody would touch one of their cast-off garments with a ten foot pole. They are alive with little "greybacks." Besides they have few garments to throw away. Their destitution is pitiful. Many are bare footed. Our boys have thrown away thousands of blankets and overcoats. Many of the Rebs have picked up something of these to cover their nakedness..."

RECOLLECTIONS OF AN OLD DOMINION DRAGOON The Civil War Experiences of Sgt. Robert S. Hudgins II Company B, 3rd Viginia Cavalry ed. by Garland C. Hudgins and Richard B. Klees pub by Publisher's Press, Inc. 1993

Pg. 99 Appomattox April 9, 1865 "Sometime later that after noon I caught up with our ragged column west of Amelia. As I sat on my horse and watched them file past I was almost moved to tears at the spectacle passing before me. The infantry looked like scarecrows in rags, with either no shoes or shoes so full of holes that they might as well have been barefooted...."

Ragged Rebels

THE CIVIL WAR INFANTRYMAN, In Camp, on the March, and in Battle by Gregory A. Coco pub by Thomas publications, Gettysburg, Pa

Pg78 Private Fisk described Lee's infantrymen he observed on April 9, 1865 "Large squads of the prisoners were taken by here...I thought they looked remarkably well, considering what had been said of their condition. Their faces looked grim and dusty, of course, but I couldn't see any sign at all of their having suffered from starvation. And their clothes and general appearance were as good as ours generally are, after we have been marching and fighting for some length of time. Great, long legged, hearty fellows-they looked as if they might fight with a vengeance, if they were where they could, and thought it would be of any use."

I wonder what units this Yank was observing.

THE HASKELL MEMOIRS-A Personal Narrative of a Conferate Officer by John Haskell ed by Gilbert E. Govan and James W. Livingood pub by G.P. Putnam's Sons 1960

Pg 95 April 9 1865 an incident with Custer "When I got back Longstreet was standing just where I had left him. I gave him General Lee's message to act on his own judgement in any emergency. Just then a Union officer came dashing up with Major Gibbs. He was a most striking picture: a rather young man, dressed in a blue sack with the largest shoulder-straps of a major-general I ever saw; with long, red hair hanging in oily curls down near to his shoulders, a gorgeous red scarf in which there was a gold pin, nearly two inches in length and breadth, with big letters, "Geoge A. Custer, Major-General."

As Custer swaggered up to Longstreet, he called out so loud that all around must hear, "I have come to demand your instant surrender. We are in position to crush you and unless you surrender at once we will destroy you."

Longstreet said: "By what authority do you come into our lines? General Lee is in communication with General Grant. We certainly will not recognize any subordinate."

Custer immediately swaggered out, "Oh, Sheridan and I are independent of Grant and we will destroy you if you don't surrender at once.'

Longstreet answered: "I suppose you know no better and have violated the decencies of military procedure because you know no better. But your ignorance will not save you if you do so again. Now go, and act as you and Sheridan choose; and I will teach you a lesson you won't forget." Then raising his voice and shaking his finger, he repeated, "Now, go."

If I ever saw a man with his tail between his legs, it was Custer. He asked for a safeguard back to his own lines, and someone pointed to Colonel Osmun Latrobe, Longstreet's adjutant general. Custer came up to him and asked him for a guard.It appeared that when he came into our lines with a handkerchief in his hand, some of our men pulled him off his horse and handled him rather roughly, though they did not injure him…."

I'd have shot him and saved Sitting Bull the trouble.

RICHMOND BURNIG-Last Days of the Confederate Capitol by Nelson Lankford pub by Viking Penguin Press 2002

Pg. 34 "The black Confederates drilled every day at their rendezvous point at the center of Cary and Twenty-first streets. Recruiting noticed encouraged owners to out fit their slaves who wished to join up with gray jacket and pants, an good pair of shoes, and a cap and blanket. About a third of the first batch of recruits were free, the rest slaves who had volunteered with the permission of their owners. Other patriotic Viginians offered money to purchase slaves willint to go into the army."

Only three years too late to do any good.

THE CONFEDERATE VETERAN Vol. XIII April 1905

Pg. 163 "The Prodigal's Return-Jack Moore"

"As a member of the gallant old 7th Tennessee, Archer's Brigade, he had followed the banner of that incomparable leader, Gen. Robert E. Lee, for four years, and when surrender came he was confined in one of the many hospitals of Virginia. It was customery on entering the hospital to take the patient's clothes, and give him instead a long shirt and a pair of woolen socks, until he was convalescent. Shirts were scarce in those days, and the material out of which to make them was scarcer; but the noble women, God bless them! Had given up their gowns and chemises to supply this defiency, and one of the latter had fallen to Jack. When it was learned that Gen. Lee had surrendered, he decided he would make an effort to go home; but when he was ready to give up his hospital toggery, none of his old clothes could be found. Even his hat and shoes were missing, and his entire wardrobe consisted of this low-neck, sleeveless garment and a pair of woolen socks. It was rather an airy costume, even for one of Lee's veterans to start with on a four-hundred-mile march, so Jack appealed to one of the Lady patrons of the hospital, and when did a Confederate soldier ever appeal to one in vain? She replied that she would go home and see what she could do. She returned with a pair of blue cottonade pants and a wide-brimmed straw hat. The pants belonged to her little fourteen-year-old brother, and the hat was her Sunday one. She had plaited the straw and made it herself. After a hard struggle Jack managed to get himself inside the pants. They struck him just a little below the knees, leaving exposed a liberal suppy of bare legs and feet. They "fit like wall paper."..."

Imagine being reduced to this state of sartorial poverty.

RECOLECTIONS OF A MD. CONFEDERATE SOLDIER AND STAFF OFFICER UNDER JOHNSON, JACKSON AND LEE by McHenry Howard pub by Press of Morningside Bookshop 1975

Pg. 386 April 9,1865 The surrender at Appomattox "...The Union were greatly astonished at the miscellaneous uniforms in our small division and under other circumstances we would have found amusement in listening to their comments. One of them pointed out an officer in a naval uniform with wide gold lace on it and asked me who he was. When I told him he belonged to the navy, his jaw dropped and he said," Good heaven, have you gunboats way up here too?" I might have answered, as someone said ealier in the war, that we had them wherever there was a little dew on the grass had I not been in too serious a frame of mind..."

Those spare Naval uniforms should have been issued to the army about six monthes before.

RECOLLECTIONS AND LETTERS OF GENERAL ROBERT E. LEE by his Son Capt. Robert E. Lee pub by Garden City Pub. Co. 1926

"Swintin, in his "History of the Army of the Potomac," after justly praising its deeds, thus speaks of its great opponent, the Army of Northern Virginia:

"Nor can there fail to arise the image of that other army that was the adversary of the Army of the Potomac, and-who that once looked upon it can ever forget it?-that array of tattered uniforms and bright muskets-that body of incomparable infantry, the Army of Northern Virginia, which, for four years carried the revolt on its bayonets, opposing a constant front to the mighty power of concentration brought against it; which receiving terrible blows, did not fail to give the like, and which, vital in all its parts, died only with its annihilation."

Yes, this quote brings trears to my eyes. This historian describes Lee's soldiers as Ragged Rebels.

LIFE IN THE CONFEDERATE ARMY by Arthur P. Ford pub by The Neale Pub. Co. 1905

Pg 53 April 19 1865 Near Bentonville, S.C. "… I had not owned a pair of socks since I left James Island a month before, and my shoes were in such tattered condition that I could keep uppers and soles together only by tying them with several leather strings, but most of my toes stuck out very conspicuously…."

I wouldn't even call those a pair of shoes.

NO SOAP, NO PAY, DIARRHEA, DYSENTERY& DESERTION A Composite History of the Lasr 16 Monthes of the Confederacy ed by Jeff Toalson, pub by iUniverse Inc.2006

Pg. 385 May 9 1865 Washington, Ga. 2nd Lt. Andrew K. Miller Co. D-7th Tn. Inf. "…I lived the life of the average infantry soldier. Sometimes we had tents and commissary…sometimes we were without shelter or rations. At times we suffered intensely from cold and hunger. My mother made all my clothes until I was promoted to Lieutenancy, after which I bought my own uniform. On return I resumed farming…."

OFFICAL RECORDS Series I Vol. 49

Pg. 755

Strawberry Plains, May 13, 1865

Maj. G.M. Bascom,
Assistant Adjudant-General:

Wheeler turned in thirty-four carbines and thiry revolvers. He says that his officers have no clothing except their uniforms. I stated to him that General Orders, No. 31, would be enforced. They murmered a little last night about turning in their arms. I presume as many were thrown into the river as were turned in.

I.C.Smith

Lieutenant-Colonel and Acting Assistant Inspector-General.

What in the hell did this Yankee expect? I'd have thrown my weapons into the river also, and laughed about it.

LAW'S ALABAMA BRIGADE IN THE WAR BETWEEN THE UNION AND THE CONFEDERACY by J. Gary Laine& Morris M. Penny pub by White Mane Pub. Co. 1996

Pg. 337 1865 "Of the 4th Alabama all but Scruggs, Karsner and Coles chose the land route home. (They went from City Point to Baltimore) There was much relief among the Alabamians when the boat docked the next morning. The recent parolees were a motley looking bunch. All but the doctor was dressed in dark grey jeans which had not been cleaned in some time. Dement's uniform was cadet grey; his major's bars were prominately visible on his collar. Scruggs and his companions were among the first Confederates from Lee's army to reach Baltimore, and there presence drew considerable attention as the walked along in search of lodging. As the group walked past a clothing store an old man beckoned from the shadows and led the men to the back of the store. They were quickly informed that a new Baltimore ordinance forbid Confederate soldiers to wear their uniforms in public. The old man gave each a duster to wear over his uniform."

A good samaritin

Middle South

DIARY OF KATE CUMMING in KATE: THE JOURNAL OF A CONFEDERATE NURSE ed. by Richard Barksdale Harwell pub by LA State Univ. Press 1998

Pg. 321 January, 1865 "…We have very excellent home-made cloth for gentlemen's clothing. I have seen some, made with a mixture of cow's hair and cotton, which was really nice, and I am told that it is water proof. I had no idea our people were so ingenious. A friend showed me a nice pair of gloves she had made from the ravelings of scraps of silk, worked in with a little cotton. The same lady makes all the shoes worn by her household. Dying old clothes is about the most fashionable thing done, those that can not afford to pay for it do it themselves. The materials used are to be found in the woods. Gentlemen's and ladies hats are made out of saw palmetto. The ladies braid it, and use it to trim their dresses, and it makes a very pretty trimming. We have any amount of shoe establishments, and very nice boots and shoes are made in them. An excellent pair of ladies' calf-skin booties can be bought for one hundred dollars, and men's are one hundred and fifty…"

Cow's hair and cotton? I'd like to try and weave that just to see how durable it is. These ladies are absolutely ingenious.

ALL AFIRE TO FIGHT-The Untold Tale of the Civil War's Ninth Texas Cavalry by Martha L Crabb pub by Avon Books 2000

Pg. 287 Jan. 1865 Egypt Station, Miss. "…the Texans were approach-ing a state of nudity. They had been unable to replace their boots or clothes and none had been issued. The officers, who usually managed to stay reasonably dressed, were as destitute as their men. When the brigade left Mississippi for Georgia, scarcity of transportation forced the officers to leave their trunks and valises containing their best clothes. A detail of two men, soon reduced to one, had faithfully guarded the baggage for nine months. While the brigade was moving out of Tennessee, the soldier took the baggage north by rail to meet them. "Just before we reached it,"

Sam Barron wrote, "a small scouting party of the enemy's cavalry swooped down, fired the station, and all our good clothes went up in smoke."…"

That wouldv'e been a terrible blow. Damn Yankees!

THE DEATH OF AN ARMY: The Battle of Nashville and Hood's Retreat by Paul H. Stockdale pub by Southern Heritage Press 1992

Pg. 171 "Private Emmett Hughes, Company E, 7th Tennessee Cavalry,…wrote to his sister from Rienzi, Mississippi, on January 4, 1865 "…I send you a few lines to let you know that I am unwell and barefooted and no chance of getting anything. If Billie Myrie don't start before you get this send me a pair of boots if you can get them if not a pair of shoes. If you can't get any new ones send me some old ones…anything to keep my feet off the ground…"

Shoes again

FROM THAT TERRIBLE FIELD-Civil war Letters of James M. Williams, Twenty-First Alabama Infantry Volunteers pub by Univ of Alabama Press1981

Pg. 152 Jan 11, 1865 Dear Lizzy; "…In have borrowed $350 which I am selfish enough to use for myself-as I cannot let the opportunity pass to buy good clothing from the State which I need so badly that I can hardly appear in church…"

THE SOLDIER'S PEN-Firsthand Impressions of the Civil War by Robert E. Bonner pub by Hill & Wang 2006

Pg. 184 Camp Near Tupelo Miss. Jan the 16th 1865 "…Dear Mary, I will tell you as near as I can what wee gand & what wee lost while wee was round & about Nashville…I can tell you it was the worst defeat ever befallen our army during the war. The army is in very bad condition al the men is nearly naked & barefooted…"

THE DEATH OF AN ARMY: The Battle of Nashville and Hood's Retreat by Paul H. Stockdale pub by Southern Heritage Press 1992

Pg. 172 "Kate cumming, the famous Confederate nurse, in her journal entry for Jan. 20, 1865 wrote:"…I have heard nothing to equal the sufferings of the men on this last retreat. Many of them were without shoes, and the snow was lying heavily on the ground. The flesh actually dropped from their feet. I heard of one man who has been compelled to have both feet amputated from this cause…"

I can't imagine how they manged. They were more than mortal men.

LETTERS OF A CONFEDERATE SURGEON 1861-65 pub by The Hurley Co. 1960

January 25, 1865 Letter from Anna K. Josephine Goddard Bragg to Julious Newport Bragg "…Charlie has gone to Fulton to work in a government shoe shop. Anthon is having a coat and pair of pants made this week also some underclothing and a pair of shoes…I am delighted to hear you have got cloth for a coat and pair of pants. Please do not forget to cut off the buttons on Joe's coat. He left it in camp and bring them home with you as you will need them to go on your new coat. I wish you could get a nice hat and then you would have a comfortable outfit…"

THIS INFERNAL WAR by Edwin Hedge Fay/Bell Irvin Wiley pub by Univ. of Texas Press 1958

Pg. 421 Opelousas La. January 29 1865 My Own Darling Wife "…I am sorry I cannot get any shoes. Maybe I can draw some from Govt. as I have to make a requisition for clothing for my men before long. I hope alas one of these days to get me a suit of gray.…I wrote enclosing a requisition for clothing for my men at Maj. Oliver's suggestion and I hope soon to get some. I included in it a suit for myself and Capt. McCandless says he will get me one in Shreveport and send it to you, so I hope to get two suits of grey…"

THE CONFEDERATE VETERAN VOL. XOV 1906

Pg. 211 Late Jan. 1865-retreating around Columbia, Ga. "…The weather was extremely cold, sleet and rain falling nearly all the time. In trying to get warm when we had the opportunity to stop by a fire, we would get so close to the fire that when the wind would shift about us the fire would be fanned against us and would burn our scant clothing, so that from above the knees to the feet we were barelegged. Very few of us had socks, and our shoes were little better than none. I have seen hundreds of poor, half-naked barefooted Confederate soldiers tramping along on the frozen ground, and ever ready to make a stand and hold the enemy in check until the wagons and other vehicles could get out of danger…"

I can't imagine how they stood it.

ARMY LIFE OF AN ILLINOIS SOLDIER Diary of Charles Wright Willis pub by Globe Print Co. 1906

Pg. 383 February 5 1865 twelve miles south of Johnston's Summit Augusta and Branchville Railroad "…Our men killed two and captured four Johnnies, all dressed in our clothing…"

FROM THAT TERRIBLE FIELD-CIVIL WAR LETTERS OF JAMES M. WILLIAMS-Twenty-First Alabama Volunteer Infantry ed by John Kent Folmer pub by Univ Al Press 1981

Pg. 153 Feb 8 1865 Battery C Near Mobile (Al) Dear Lizzy,"…My clothes came in good time, and I have hardly laid off my overcoat since it came. It looks very nice and is as comfortable as a good-good-well I don't know what to compare it with-I was going to say a good wife-but that is not so-there is nothing in the world so comfortable as she…

I occasionally spend the night in the city with John (King), but generally I sleep on the floor of my quarters rolled up in my blanket with a coat for a pillow-and dream of Lizzy and George…"

FLORA AND FAUNA OF THE CIVIL WAR-An Environmental Reference Guide by Kelby Ouchley pub.by La. Univ. Press 2010

Early 1865 "However, in at least one instance sweetgum logs were actually used as barrels of functioning cannons.The "Sweet Gum Battery" comprised six 6-pounders and one 12-pounder and was manned by the 33rd Missouri Volunteers at Spanish Fort, Alabama, in early 1865. A description cites: They were made of sweet gum wood, and banded at the muzzle and breech with a band of iron about one inch wide and one quarter of an inch thick. The gun and carriage were separate, the carriage being a block of wood with a socket for the breech of the gun, giving the gun an elevation of about 45 degrees. The ordinary 6 and 12 pound shells were used, the surface being coated with turpentine to secure ignition of the fuse.…The men became so expert as to be able to burst a shell within the size of an army blanket at 500 to 600 yards distance."

Amazing ingenuity

REMINISCENCES OF A PRIVATE William E. Bevins of the First Arkansas Inf. C.S.A. pub by Univ. Ark. Press 1992

Pg. 232 Augusta, Ga. Feb. 9 1865 "…The soldiers were thinly clad and few of them had shoes. One or two men froze, riding on the top of the cars. We travelled to Milledgeville Georgia, and from there we had to march over a forty mile gap to the Augusta road. I found my friends…They got me a new grey suit with a long tail coat. I sure was dressed in the height of style, but my shoes hardly corresponded to my suit. They were not very stylish… When we went back to Belair that night my uncle presented me with a fine pair of boots which cost $100. Then my stylish outfit was complete.

I got to Forty Mile Gap. I had more than when I went down. As I marched along one of the drivers of the four-mule wagon asked if I wanted to ride. A web-foot never refused. He said he would walk if I would ride and drive, but I told him I had never driven a four-mule team in my life.

"Oh, that's all right," said he," the mules follow the wagon ahead without a driver."

I rode his mule and drove his wagon, stylishly dressed, as I have said, in my long-tailed coat and fine new boots. The Virginia soldiers going on foot to their command, guyed me greatly. "When the war is over I bet that fellow will never tell that he drove a wagon train." Then others would yell, "Don't that guy look fine with his gay clothes on!" General Walthalarg came along and attracted by my dress, eyed me muchly…"

He states "gray long-tailed coat." I wonder, did he mean a swallow-tailed coat or a frock coat?

A SOUTHERN SOLDIER'S LETTERS HOME The Civil War Letters of Samuel Burney Cobb's Georgia Legion, Army of Northern Va. Ed. By Nat Turner pub by Mercer Univ. Press, Macon Ga.2002

Pg. 288 Wooten's Station, Ga. Feb. 13th, 1865 "…I have swapped off my overcoat for a Yankee one. It was blue but is dyed a dark brown. It is very long, almost new and very warm. The man was batty that traded with me, for I had worn mine a long time and it was wearing out. My Dearest One, I want you to make me one more shirt like those you made me with homespun muslin; also to knit me some cotton socks, not to fine and large every way. I know you say, "Well what would Mr. Burney do without a wife." I fancy I can see you now saying that and cutting a shy glance of love to me out of the corner of your eye…"

'WARE SHERMAN-A Journal of Three Month's Experience in the Last Days of the Confederacy by Joseph LeConte pub by Univ. of Califonia Press 1937

Pg. 106 refugeeing from Columbia South Carolina during Sherman's advance "we left the camp-fire about 9P.M. We had nothing in the world in the way of clothing except what we had on our backs. Fortunately, when the wagons were captured I had on my overcoat and Captain Greene a blanket arranged with a draw-string so as to be worn as a cloak and hood…."

THIS INFERNAL WAR by Edwin Hedge Fay/Bell Irvin Wiley pub by Univ. of Texas Press 1958

Pg. 427 Opelousas La. Feb. 19th 1865 My Own Dear Wife "…My coat is wearing out and I expect you had better make a tearful appeal to Maj. Heard and see if you cannot get me a suit of Grey or trouble Capt. Black with it as he is the Agent for foreign Supply…I need a suit and must have it somehow or other…."

BROTHERS IN GRAY-The Civil War Letters of the Pierson Family ed. by Thomas W. Cutrer& t. Michael Parrish pub by La. State Univ. Press 1997 Ninth Louisiana

Pg 250 James F. Pierson to Joseph Pierson Shreveport, La. Feb. 20th, 1865 Dear Joe "…I am very sorry to hear you had not received the cloth that I sent. You must make some inquiry about it for me. I will write to Mr. Simmes to know where he left it…"

Pg 151 James F. Pierson to William H. Pierson Dear Father "…I have been a little afraid that you would not get the cloth that I sent by Mr. Simmes' to Henry's about the first of this month. There was about 43/4 Yds. Of double width blue cloth. I would not take anything for it if I can get it. I will write to Mr. Simmes in a few days to know where he left it, and then, if I find out, I will write to you where it is.

I am very much in need of that hat that you promised me when I was at home. But you need not put yourself to any extra trouble about it, for I can do very well for sometime yet. I have drawn a full uniform since I left home. The uniform consists of a gray jacket, blue pants, and then I have drawn one undershirt net, one top shirt, one pair of drawers, and a pair of socks so I am very well off in the way of clothes. I also drew a pair of brogan shoes. I will watch the auctions here, and if I can I will buy you and me some shirting to wear next summer.... Tell Aunt Nan that her pants will be very thankfully received, as I do not want to wear my pretty uniform every day..."

Another mention of blue pants being issued. The auctions James speaks of were the auctioning of a dead man's clothing and belongings. He seems well equipped, and was able to draw clothing.

TRUE TALES OF THE SOUTH AT WAR Collected and Edited by Clarence Poe pub by Univ. of N.C. Press 1961

reminiscences of Barry Benson

Pg.136 Feb. 25 1865 "...I hard at work alone all day turning one of his thick overcoats! Think of it! Did I ever in former days think that I would come to sewing or he to wearing a turned coat. However it looks nice and I am thankful it is worth the labor..."

U.S. ARMY HERITAGE & RESEARCH CENTER History & Memoirs of the 1st Georgia Regular Infantry by John Porter Fort

Headquarters First Georgia Regulars In The Field March 1865, "It was not an infrequent custom with our poorly clad and ill-fed soldiers to require Yankee prisoners to disrobe for our benefit. He was made to take off his overcoat, blanket, or other extra accouterments that he might have, they word given was known as "shuck." As far as our men when captured were concerned they had no "shuck" upon them worth the taking. In the first days charge at Bentonville we captured two or three hundred of Kilpatrick's cavalry. We had a very large man in the regiment known as Sergeant Copeland of Company "F." He was six feet and a half tall, had enormous feet and was proportionately large, and was barefooted. I saw him go down the line of these prisoners walking in the ice and mud, trying to get a pair of shoes or boots from one of these troopers, but none could be found large enough for him. I recall the reluctance with which these prisoners held up their feet for inspection.

When we left Fayetteville there was issued to our regiment about a dozen pairs of inferior shoes, that had been brought through the blockading fleet at Wilmington. These shoes were given only to barefooted soldiers, and while I was not barefooted our negro cook Willis was; I wished to curconvent the Quartermaster and get a pair of shoes for Willis, I felt sorry to see him wading through the rain and mud barefooted with his long slue feet and jay bird heels. I put on some worthless shoes and went up to see Capt. W.W. Paine, our worthy quartermaster. The officers gave him the nickname of "Daddy" and so called him when not in his presence, I suppose in derision as he had been married many years but had no children. I applied for the shoes, he said he had but three pairs left, that they were for the barefooted men in the ranks, and I could not get them. I nexhibited my old shoes and eventually he relented and issued me a pair. I then informed him that I had good shoes and wanted these for my negro cook who was barefooted and entitled to them. The kind old fellow was furious at me but I laughingly kept the shoes (very shoddy shoes they were), and gave them to Willis with instructions to take the best care of them. A morning or so afterwards I saw Willis standing by the camp fire boiling a skillet of mush, his feet were pushed in the shoes over the vamp untied, with his long heels protruding. I was indignant at the sight and seizing a long hickory switch lying near, as Willis was stooping over the fire his tight pants presented a fair mark, and I gave him one cut, a good one, that caused him to jump over and into the fire, I pointed at his shoes. After this, Willis was careful of the said shoes. I mention this as the last and only whipping I ever gave a slave and he deserved it."

First of all, this shows again the care given to the "servants" in the Confederate army. On the second hand, I think he was justified in swatting Willis' rear after all the trouble he went to to obtain those shoes.

FROM THAT TERRIBLE FIELD-CIVIL WAR LETTERS OF JAMES M. WILLIAMS, Twenty-First Alabama Volunteer Infantry ed by John Kent Folmer pub by Univ Al

Pg. 156 March 10 1865 Dear Lizzy, "…I am thinking of sending you all the clothing I can dispense with-not much to be sure, but it may be the means of saving it from loss in case the coming campaign should be disasterous to our army…"

THIS INFERNAL WAR by Edwin Hedge Fay/Bell Irwin Wiley pub by Univ Texas press 1958

Pg. 436 Opelousas La. March 13th 1865 My Own Dear Wife I wonder if there is no chance for me to get a pair of shoes made up there somewhere. Ditmer has my measure. My boots have given out and I am reduced to my old shoes. I will buy some specie and then I can get shoes…Saturday I had a present of 3 linen collars that fit me tolerably well. I shall need some more socks some of these days and if you can make a trade with old sister Jones have me a couple of undershirts knitted.…Please tell your Father that as he controls old Ditmer to please have him make me a pair of Shoes of light Kip. Ditmer has my measure. I want them sewed-you have the thread I bro't from Arkansas but it must be boiled in weak ley (lye) before it is fit to use. I want them made with bottoms just like boots and nails on the outside of the heels if some of those 8 penny in the Dairy house have to be broken off-I want them made with Scotch bottoms and thick double sole.

What with all the trouble to get a decent pair of shoes or boots, he's still apreciative of linen collars.

THE CONFEDERATE VETERAN Vol. XIII Nov. 1905

Pg. 491 "Thrilling and Horrible Event Recalled" by W.M. Long

"Near Bentonville, N.C., March 19th, 1865, Johnston drove Sherman back three or four miles. I was detailed as one of a party of scouts to find out the location of the Yanks. We were riding very cautiously, expecting every minute to be fired upon. When nearing an old-fashioned Southern home we heard women screaming. We at once spurred our horses and charged upon the house. The family consisted of a mother and her three grown daughters. The Yankees ran out of the house, but the mother of the young ladies in her desperation ran ahead of them and appealed to us to shoot them down, as they were outraging her daughters. With the Rebel yell we killed all five of them. One of the dead was about my size, so I took his coat, hat, and boots.

The next day I was captured by members of the dead Yanks' company, who recognized the clothes. They were about to hang me to a tree. A rope was at hand, and I thought my time had come, but concluded that I would make an appeal to them, and said: "Gentlemen, think of your own fireside in your distant homes, and ask yourselves what you would do to men under similar circumstances." I could see a change in their faces, and one of them said, "Boys, we will not hang him, but we will strip him of John's clothes." So they left me without coat, hat and barefooted. You can imagine my condition on that bitter day in March, 1865, with the winds whistling through my ragged shirt. You may well imagine how the blood ran from my bare feet in walking from Bentonville, N.C., to Savannah, Ga., where we were put in a hull of a vessel, crowded like sardines in a box.

In passing through Cape HattererasLieunt. Pope invested his last money (fity cents in United States silver) in a coat for me, which was worth its weight in gold at that time.

We were all taken to Hart's Island prison, in New York harbor, and remained there until about June 20, 1865."

I'm surprised they didn't hang him. Custer's men in the Valley would have in a heartbeat.

BROTHERS IN GRAY-The Civil War Letters of the Pierson Family ed. by Thomas W. Cutrer& t. Michael Parrish pub by La. State Univ. Press 1997 Ninth Louisiana

Pg 253 David Pierson to Mary Catherine Pierson Shreveport, La. March 20th, 1865 My Dear Sister "...Well, sister I must tax your kindness for a pair of gloves. My buckskin ones are nearly worn out. Let them be plain and thin-no gauntlets to them. Another article I will want early in the spring-my mosquito bar. Send it by first opportunity. They are terrible here, and they say, as soon as the river falls, which is now receding very fast…"

Pg 253 David Pierson to William H. Pierson Shreveport La. March 25th, 1865 Dear Pa, Mr. Bob Key informs me that his wagon is going to start to Mt. Lebanon tomorrow and will return to this place in a few days. Please send my mosquito bar and summer pants when it returns…"

CONFEDERATE VETERAN VOL XI 1902

Pg. 281 The Capture of the Katydids "It was in April, 1865. The Confederate forces, Jackson's division of Forrest's command, had camped for a few hours on the Black Warrior (River), just across from the beautiful little town of Tuscaloosa, Ala.

These men were worn from months of fighting, foot-sore, poorly clad and they were ill-fed.

Across the bridge from town came a party of boys, evidently to visit the camp. They were fine young fellows, and manly, but all under fifteen. They were trimly dressed in cadet uniform of gray cloth made in Georgia, and looked like "carpet knights" when compared to Jackson's weary veterans in their cheap, dingy gray jeans…."

Eyewitness-The Civil War As We Lived It-The American Iliad by Otto Schmiml& Ralph Newman pub by The Universal Library 1947

Pg665 April 4, 1865 A young aide to Gen A.P. Stewart-Bentonville, N.C. "I witnessed today the saddest spectacle of my life, the review of the skeleton Army of Tennessee. But one year ago replete with men, it now filed by with tattered garments, barefooted, and with ranks so depleted that each color was supported by only thirty or forty men …"

This is a good indicator that Hood's Tennessee Campaign was a extremely costly idea.

THE LAST CAMPAIGN: A CAVALRYMAN'S JOURNAL by Ebenezer Nelsin Gilpin pub by Press of Ketcheson Print co. 1908

Pg. 59 April 9 1865 "…At the appointed time we met at the Mont Ford residence. I, in a blue jacket and gilt saber-belt, grey trousers above my cavalry boots, and wearing a secesh cap…"

THE WAR-TIME JOURNAL OF A GEORGIA GIRL 1864-1865 Eliza Frances Andrews pub by Appleton-Century-Crofts 1908

Pg. 233 May 1865 "…He was young, I could see, through all the dirt and grime on his face, so I suppose "Sally" was either his sweetheart, or the young bride he left when he went away to the war. Some of our Confederates wear a dark, bluish-grey uniform which is difficult to distinguish from the Federal blue, and I live in constant fear of making a mistake. As a general Thing our privates have no uniform but rags, poor fellows, but the officers sometimes puzzle me, unless they wear the Hungarian knot on their sleeves. It makes the letters C.S.A. but one would not be apt to notice the monogram unless it was pointed out to him. It is a beautiful uniform, and I will always love the colors, grey and gold, for its sake-or rather for the sake of the men who wore it. There is a report that Confederate officers are going to be ordered to lay aside their uniforms. It will be a black day when this habit that we all love so well gives place to the badge of servitude. There is nothing in the history of nations to compare with the humiliations we southerners have to endure…"

I agree, their valor earned them better treatment.

DIARY OF A CONFEDERATE SOLDIER-John S. Jackman of the Orphan Brigade ed by Williiam C. Davis pub by South Caroline Univ. Press 2000

Pg. May 3rd, 1865 Washington, Ga. "I believe it was in the afternoon of May 3rd "Uncle Jeff" rode into town escorted by Co. B of the 2d Ky Cavalry-Geo. Duke's old regiment He had on a broad-brimmed light colored felt hat which had a wide stripe of black around the crown and the brim turned down. He wore a gray coat without any gold lace on it (but was cut in a military style) and he had a pair of gray pants which stuffed in a pair of cavalry boots…"

THE STAR CORPS; or Notes of an Army Chaplain, During Sherman's Famous March to the Sea by William Bones, pub by Jerman&Brightman Printers 1865

Pg. 304 Letter from William Bones, May 13, 1865 "You have been apprised, by a far more able pen than mine, of the particulars of that terrible fight and its results, (note- no information as to what battle-ed.) as well as the sufferings endured by us on the march from there to Richmond prisons; in fact, no human power can tell all we suffered. Robbed of everything, stripped of our clothing and blankets, exposed to the severest weather, compelled to ford streams, where the water came up to our armpits, and forced to lie in the mud. I only wonder that any lived to tell the tale…"

Yeah? Well, turn-abouts fair play, Yank.

Trans Mississippi

The Civil War Reminiscences of Major Silas T. Grisamore, C.S.A. ed by Arthur W. Bergeron Jr pub by La. State Press 1993

Pg. 179 Jan 1865 Pineville, La. (near Alexandria, La) "One day I received from the Quartermaster Department in Shreveport about 3,000 yards of calico, with directions from Majoe Haynes, Chief Q'r-M'r, to exchange the same with the people about the country for homespun. I endeavered to get permission to go down in the praries about Opelousas to effect the exchange, without effect, and made preparations to distribute the calice among the troops for them to manufacture into shirts.One morning I received a letter from Major Haynes notifying me to send the calico back to Shreveport, as they had made arrangements to exchange it for other material in that vicinity.

Knowing that that "other material" would never gladden my eyes, I did not feel in the proper mood to return Major Haynes anything more substantial than my compliments. After breakfast I went over to Gen. Thomas' office, and upon his enquiry if there were any news, I handed him my letter. Those persons who had the pleasure of his company know that the General had a very peculiar way of expressing his thoughts in a manner that was easy to understand.

After reading the letter, he remarked, "Well, that's Hell," which was a peculiarity of the letter that I had not perceived but kept silence however. "Well, Major, what are you going to do about it?"

"General, will you give me written orders to return the calico to Shreveport?" "No, I'll be d-d if I do." "Well then, General, I will be under the disagreeable necessity of informing you that Major Haynes will never see these articles of femimineappaeral again. Good morning, General."

In less than three hour the calico was in wagons and on the way to the command, with written orders to the quartermasters to distribute it forthwith. If General Thomas should have been seized with a fit of repentance, I was determined that it would have to get hold of him quickly to do any good. The next morning, the General asked, me what I was going to do with my calico, I told him I did not have any, but could show him receipts for it if he wished to see them..."

LONE STAR & DOUBLE EAGLE- Civil War Letters of a German-Texas Family ed by Menetta Altgelt Goyne pub by Texas Christian univ. Press 1982

Pg. 161 Camp two miles north of Bellrue which is eight (illegible) miles north west of Henderson Rudolf from Hermann Kamerling 5 February 1865 "...My gray trousers, dear

Rudolf, just aren't going to make it after all, so it would be very agreeable to me if you could bring me down another light-weight pair of durable pants…"

WEBSITE OF THE 7TH TEXAS CAVALRY

"We went through the war without a uniform. We were lucky to keep our bottoms covered. When we got into the war, we wore overalls, and when we surrendered in 1865, I didn't even have a pair of shoes.

Notice the reference to overalls. Probably farmer's overalls. Unfortunately no reference to color. This is probably a good overall picture of the typical Trans-Mississippi soldier.

THE NAVY

WEBSITE-**Georgia C.S.M.C. Company "C" Uniforms**

Pg. 2 "...Before the war, the United States Marine Corps had been an exceptionally fine and well-disciplined organization, but from it came the corresponding establishment of the Confederate service, The Confederate States Marine Corps. The C.S.M.C. was modeled after the United States Marine Corps, but there were some differences. The Confederates organized themselves into permanent companies, replaced the fife with the light infantry bugle, and wore uniforms similar to those of the British Royal Marines..."

THE CIVIL WAR READER by Richard B. Harwell pub by Smithmark Pub. 1957

Pg. 259 "...at that time (1774) the great staple in the Southern States was indigo, the cultivation of which is now so entirely discontinued that they were not able to make the naval uniform of the Confederacy blue, as everyone knows a naval uniform ought to be. It is now the same color as the military uniform. I believe the reason that seamen dress in blue, is because it is the only color which is not stained by salt water..."

I didn't know this was the reason for blue naval uniforms.

THE NAVY AND MARINE LIVING HISTORY ASSOCIATION-Clothing, Pay and provisions for the Savannah River Squadron

"...The riverine sailor might not have been as well dressed as his "deep water" counterparts, but he was much better off than his army comrades. The paymaster issued uniforms to sailors upon induction and promised them a substantial clothing allowance to maintain their kit, but the pressing need for funds elsewhere in the Confederacy deprived the enlisted men of their much needed allowance. Robert Watson wrote in his diary that "we are not allowed any clothing money but have to pay for everything we draw out of our wages." Deficiencies resulted in the issue of new clothing to the sailor and the cost was deducted from his pay account. Clothing priced would range from as high as fifteen dollars to as little as ninety-five cents. A landsmen's (raw recruit) pay was $16.00 a month. The cost of the initial uniform was $100.12. It would take a new sailor, barring any other expenses and devoting his entire pay to the task, a little over six months to pay for his uniform. After deducting the clothing issue from their pay and forwarding any allotments to their families, many sailors were without money and would probably not see any for the entire war.

WHAT THEY WERE SUPPOSED TO LOOK LIKE

Regulations established in 1862 for the enlisted personnel of the Confederate States Navy were the same regulations adopted by the U.S. Navy in 1859, except that the Confederates replaced all references to blue with steel grey and changed the U.S. Navy's rating badge, the eagle and anchor surmounted by a five pointed star, to a fouled anchor.

The regulations described clothing for petty officers, firemen, coal-heavers, seamen, ordinary seamen, landsmen and boys at muster as steel gray cloth jackets (round jackets) and trousers and steel gray wool frocks (jumpers) with white duck collars and cuffs, black hats, black silk neckerchiefs and shoes, or boots in cold weather. In warm weather, the uniform was to consist of white jumpers-collars and cuffs to be lined with blue cloth-white trousers, black or white hats as the commander may direct, black silk neckerchiefs and black shoes. Thick gray hats without visors could be worn at sea when not at muster.

The gray jacket, known as the round or monkey jacket, was a waist length, eighteen button, shell jacket with a rolling collar. There were usually three buttons on the cuff...Enlisted men were not expected to maintain their uniforms to the standards of the officers and the color and button style could vary radically. The frock, or jumper, resembled the modern naval jumper with a few minor exceptions. Shoulder seams dropped off the shoulder, giving a more bloused appearance. The yoke-the joining of the upper part of the jumper to the lower-was of no set pattern or non-existent. The trousers of the enlisted sailor varied in pattern as much as the other articles of clothing. Clothing records indicate that blue trousers were issued throughout the war. Gray trousers did not become an item for issue until 1863. The Confederate government issued trousers in three different pattern: fall front, seam pocket, and mule ear. Government records did not distinguish which type of trouser was issued. Fall front trousers were the "traditional" sailor pants with seven to thirteen button, bib front enclosure. The legs and seat were full to allow free movement and the leg cuffs were open so that the pants could be rolled to the knee. Located on the waist band seam was a drawstring for size adjustment. There are no existing records, photographs or drawings indicating that Confederate sailors wore this type of trousers. It is unclear if this type of trouser was part of the captured stores from Norfolk. Clothing manifests do not indicate the trouser type. Seam pocket trousers appear to be the most common trouser type. These trousers are characterized by a four-button fly and seam pockets. The trouser cuff covers the top of the shoe and the waist had the same style drawstring adjustment as fall front trousers. The round hat, or pork pie, a blue or gray cloth cap, was the common hat style for the mid-nineteenth century sailor. Regulations called for sennet hats (a straw or grass braid for hats-ed) -white or japanned black, straw hats-for dress wear; there are no records of sennet hat issue.

The shirt, as issues from 1861 to 1865 was an off-white or cream colored flannel with reinforced shoulders and slit head opening. The shirt had a square collar closed with a metal button, tapered sleeves, closed with a single button, and a full cut body. Confederates issued this type of shirt, in wool or cotton, throughout the war. Confederate sailors supplemented their shirt issue with civilian clothing from home adding various color and style differences.

Shoes were the most serious problem for sailors.…Naval agents had to scramble to fill their shoe orders and, as a result, most of the shoes purchased from the navy came from England. The Office of Provisions and Clothing sent each squadron a pattern for canvas shoes and asked them to try to get them produced locally.…The C.S. Navy apparently never solved the "shoe problem." In November, 1864, the men of the James River Squadron stood watch on freezing decks without shoes, coats or blankets.

Yeah, the shoe problem was never solved by the army either. If they're speaking of canvas shoes with wooden bottoms, I think those would be fatally slippery on a wet or ice-covered deck.

Early clothing issues to Savannah River Squadron sailors were almost entirely blue in color. The uniform consisted of a blue cloth hat, blue jumper, blue trousers, blue shirt, blue round jacket, a black silk neckerchief, and shoes. Issues of gray overshirts occurred regularly in 1861 and by 1863, the Department issued gray cloth, gray jackets. And gray trousers to most squadrons.…despite efforts and issues, the Confederate sailor looked more like a merchant seaman than a naval sailor

The regulations described clothing for petty officers, firemen, coal-heavers, seamen, ordinary seamen, landsmen, and boys at muster as steel grey cloth jackets (round jackets) and trousers, or steel grey wool frocks (jumpers) with white duck collars and cuffs, black hats, black silk neckerchiefs and shoes, or boots in cold weather. In warm weather, the uniform was to consist of white jumpers- collars and cuffs to be lined with blue cloth- white trousers, black or white hats as the commander may direct, black silk neckerchiefs and black shoes. Thick grey hats without visors could be worn at sea when not at muster.

www.csnavy.org**ORGANIZATION OF THE CONFEDERATE STATES NAVY & REPORT FROM SECRETARY MALLORY TO THE PRESIDENT AS OF 26APRIL 1861**

"…In addition to guns you will purchase 1,000 navy pistols, revolvers, with 100,000 rounds of fixed ammunition, and 500,000 percussion caps. One thousand navy carbines, with 100,000 rounds fixed ammunition, and 500,000 percussion caps. The proper supply of appendages (bullets, molds, wipers, etc.) and also spare parts for pistols and carbines must be provided and also 1,000 navy cutlasses.

A supply of the ordinary marine fireworks for each vessel must also be obtained and 10,000 pounds of cannon and 2,000 pounds of musket powder.

The following articles of clothing you will also purchase:

For Marines-Two thousand pairs of pants, 2,000 jackets, 1,000 overcoats and watchcoats, 1,000 pairs of shoes, brogans, 2,000 flannel shirts, 2,000cotton flannel drawers, 2,000 pairs woolen socks, 1,000blankets, 1,000fatigue caps, 1,000shirts(linen and cotton).

For Seamen-Two thousand pairs pants, cloth or cassinette, 2,000 jumpers, 1,000 round jackets, 2,000 pairs duck pants, 2,000 blue flannel overshirts, 2,000 blue flannel undershirts, 2,000 blue flannel drawers, 2,000 pairs of shoes, 3,000 pairs of socks (woolen), 2,000 blankets, 2,000 blue cloth caps, 1,000 pea jackets, 2,000 barnseley shirting frocks, 2,000 black silk handkerchiefs, 1,000 yards of bunting divided into red, white and blue. (to be similar to the clothing use in the British navy without any designating marks.) I am, respectfully, your obedient servant, S.R. Mallory, Secretary of the Navy.

A CONFEDERATE MARINE-Excerpts from the Graves Family Correspondence Confederate Centennial Studies #24 ed by Richard Harwell Confederate Publication Co. Inc. 1963 Iverson D. Graves, Confederate Marine

Pg. 37 Sewell's Point, Va. Aug. 21, 1861 "I wish that Ma would send me a coat; let her make it of that gray woolen cloth she once made me a hunting coat from, of something of the same color. The cloth war furnished to us in Macon and it only cost 3 dollars for me to have a suit made. I had the pants made but not enough money for the coat. Ma can fit it by any of my coats. It must be a jacket, buttoning all the way up front, military fashion, with a short collar designed to stand up; buttons either brass or silver, oval shape, nearly half inch in diameter; put a short piece of white taps ¼ inch wide upon the shoulder, running from front to back. Let it be warm; pockets inside and on both sides.I wrote to Aunt Libbie to make Knox make me a pair of shoes. Please send them at the same time."

Pg. 40 Camp Huger near Norfolk Va. Sept. 13, 1861 Miss Cora Graves "...I will be free now from all duty till "dress parade," which comes off every evening at sundown. I wish you could come and witness our dress parade-you would be delighted with them I know. The whole battalion have to appear on the ground dressed up in their dress uniform and after forming what is called a "line of battle" go through with various forms in the manual of arms, with music, etc...."

Pg. 54 Drury's (Drewery's) Bluff, Va. June 6, 1862 Iverson L. Graves "...I left my knapsack in Richmond, taking nothing with me but my blanket oil cloth to sleep on. When I wanted clean clothes and to wash up I took off my shirt, put on coat, and washed the shirt and hung it by the fire to dry; then took off socks and proceed in the same way. It is my first experience at washing. I like the excitement of the life very much..."

Savannah, Ga., Feb. 5, 1863 Mrs. Sarah D. Graves "...Last night I had my cap stolen from the rack of the house where I eat. Unfortunate in the cap line, ain't I? Common gray caps are worth 12 to 14 dollars here. I got one this morning, a simple glazed cap worth 30 cents, but I paid $2.50 for it..."

Pg. 101 Savannah, Ga. Apr. 22, 1863 Mrs. Sarah D. Graves "When we get regularly into Barracks. I will have to go to some room, so I have commenced to prepare for it now. Have succeeded in getting a room in the same building as the Commodore's office, a single room; went around and purchased me a bedstead and table for which I had to pay 20 dollars. I will now have to get me a bowl and pitcher, counterpain and some sheets, one or two chairs, and I will be fixed. The room itself cost me nothing as the whole building has been rented by the Navy, and the Commodore allows me the use of mine free. I have a mattress, you know, so if you could find me some sort of a spread and a couple of pairs of sheets (for single bed 3 ½ feet wide) I would be obliged. The coat you sent me the sample of I shall like much, but am yet in doubt whether I want it made sack or like my dress military: Just wait and I will write to you when I am in need of it, and then how to make it. I have some hope of being able to come up sometime during the summer. I got me a coat and pair of pants the other day, made out of a sort of blue flannel, which is light and will do for the weather for a while yet...The white vests made military-I should like very much..."

Pg. 107 Steamer Savannah, Savannah Ga., Nov. 3, 1863 Mrs. Sarah D. Graves "I enclose by express today the butter bucket with the patterns for duty coat and pants and some buttons for my overcoat and I send 18-you can use them as you think best. If you have not already cut the overcoat, please cut them a little longer than Pa's coat (that black sack-looking overcoat of the raglan style is the one I mean) but I wish them cut exactly [like] in every other respect. I believe I told you about the cape; make it to meet in the front, under the throat to be held up by buttons under the collar of the coat. Please make button and eyelet holes to the number of six at regular intervals down the front of the cape so that it can be buttoned up and worn at times by itself; I have buttons for the cape. If you can get it, I would like much to have enough of the cloth for a sack coat and a pair of pants. If you have the cloth to spare now and will send it in the same bundle I will get it cut and made here. If you haven't it on hand, we will wait till I get home if I succeed in that. There is something I want very much now, and that is some part of cloth to make me a vest. Have you any remnants of black cloth of casimer or indeed anything that will make a vest? Or have I any winter vests at home? If not, please send me enough jeans, if you have it, for a vest. I would also like a piece of Tomesia's loop, or some like hers. Loop here is exorbantely high. Also please send me a little bottle of hair grease. This winds up my wants, I believe. Does that list overcome you?"

Steamer Savannah, Savannah Ga. Dec. 26, 1863 Mrs. Cora Graves, "...The package of soap, socks etc. came safely through. I am very much obliged for them. Please say to my father that I will have to get a pair of shoes here at once, and have no money to pay for them. They will cost me 60 dollars. If he has 50 he can spare now and will send me I can make out to pay the other ten and be very much obliged to him. My part of $80 per month barely pays my mess bill and contributes almost nothing towards my clothing. Shoes, and inferior ones at that, are selling in town for 125 dollars; boots from 175 to 200. If the government doesn't raise my pay soon, I can't imagine how I am to get along. I am almost persuaded to get married here and go and live with the girl's father..."

Savannah, Ga. March(?) 1864 Iverson L. Graves "...Cpt. Pinkney, the commander of the ship, is a friend of mine and made application for Dutt to be sent to his ship as a special favor to me. Dutt will need a uniform suit. A dress suit here would cost him about $500. If Mother can get some nice light gray jeans made, and send the cloth down, it will do very well, and he can get it cut and made here for a moderate sum…"

Savannah Ga. Aril 29, 1864 Mrs. Sarah D. Graves "Now of Dutt and his clothes-I wrote Pa a day or two since about getting the appointment of midshipman. I wish the name and addresses of the Congressmen from our district. I think by a little interest and perseverance in the matter we can secure the position for Dutt. The striped cloth would not do well, especially as it is getting quite hot here. He needs gray. The check you send is very pretty and if you have enough for coat and pants would make a beautiful suit. It would not do however, to make into pants and wear with a uniform coat. You had best send the cloth by all means as I can have it cut and made here comparatively cheaply, and besides saving you the trouble it will be certain to fit. If you can get some light material, jeans, or something else for a summer coat I will be obliged. I gave Dutt my cloth and cassimere sack I had so that I now have nothing but my heavy uniform coat…."

CONFEDERATE PRIVATEERS by William Morrison Robertson pub by Univ. S Ca. Press 1990

Pg. 64 Quoted in Mercury July 26, 1861 crew of the privateer Jefferson Davis.The N.Y. paper described them "No two of the men are dressed alike. Many have on loose "jumpers" or shirts made out of blue denim, similar in texture, quality and color to the overalls worn by laborers; others wear coarse shirts, made of yellow flannel, such as may be seen in the South, while others had nothing on the upper part of their bodies but their undershirts. Their nether garments, the extremities of which are, in many cases, pushed into their boots-are of every imaginable color and quality, rivaling in diversity of hues, the variegated tints of Joseph's coat. The majority wear ordinary cloth or glazed caps, but some have on black felt hats with high sugar-loaf crowns, resembling the Spanish sombreros, or the hats of Italian Brigands."

DEAR SISTER-Civil War Letters to a Sister in Alabama ed by Frank Anderson Chappell pub by Branch Springs Pub 2002

Jas. B. Branscomb was a private in the Southern Rifles of Union Springs, Alabama, which was part of the Third Alabama Regiment.(Infantry) stationed near Norfolk, Va.

Pg. 39 August 13, 1861 Dear Sister; "…They are building a floating battery here in the Gosport navy yard, that will make the blockade tremble when it is finished. It is the shape of a weaver's shuttle lengthwise, the machinery is worth $500,000, there is to be an iron cutter attached to the end, 12 feet long, pointed with steel. They say they can cut any vessel half into. I seen it last Saturday…"

Pg. 40 Auguast 24, 1861 "…We are having a new uniform made which will cost between $15 and $20 but we are to get money from the government to pay for. I reckon we will get them next week…"

PG. 46 Oct. 1861 My Dear Brother; "...I was at the navy yard last Friday and seen the floating battery. It will carry 13 guns I believe. It has a prow in front so that if she runs against a vessel it knocks a hole in it. I am satisfied that it is cannon proof and it will run like a top. It will be finished in about three weeks then look out Yankees..." Jim Branscomb

Pg. 55 December 27, 1861 Camp at Mosebey's Church near Norfolk Va. dear Sister; "... a few days ago my patriotism, or a want of something new, I tried to get aboard of the floating battery (Merrimac) and thought at the time I would succeed. There was a call on the different regiments here for men to form a crew for six months. Myself and ten others of the SR (Southern Rifles) sent in our names, but have failed to make the trip. I think our officers was the cause of our defeat. It is a great piece of mechanism. I think it will clear the Hampton road of the Federal fleet ..."

Pg. 61 Third Alabama Regiment Camp at Moseby's Church (Va) Feb. 7 1862 Dear Sister; "...You recollect I was speaking of going on board the Merrimac several weeks ago. I was at that time rejected. About three weeks age one of the officers of the same came to see if we were still in the notion to go. We all rejected him that, but McAlewit, he is now in the naval service, and I thought I was clear of the (undeciferable) but yesterday orders came to the Col. to send in all that had sent in their names, myself and 11 others of the S.R. to be sent to the navy yard this morning with all our clothes. I can tell you sister, I was much opposed to going, but I thought go I must, so this morning I packed up my duds, ready to tramp, but it was a hard trial. My mess mates are almost like brothers, and hated to leave them, but to my grat relief, (lat me here deviate from the subject a little. Lt. Col. Battle is the best man I ever saw, he is more like a father than an officer.) Capt P. told us that he and Col. Battle would go up and try to get us off, and therefore I was in great suspense all day, when he got back, he told us by the skin of his teeth got us off..." Except for the intervention of his Col. Battle, Jim would have ended up in the navy.

I had always wondered about the uniforms of the Virginia's crewmen. This proves they would have worn army infantry uniforms, as the navy would not have had the time or equipment to re-equip these soldiers. Also, remember he wrote they were supposed to report with all their clothing. The officers of the C.S.S. Virginia would have been too busy getting the last minute arraigements completed to have replaced perfectly good army uniforms with naval uniforms, even if they had them. Remember, they only had about a month before she steamed into Hampton Roads. From Jim's letter, it seems he didn't want to break his friendships in his mess, rather than any uneasiness regarding the C.S.S. Virginia.

CAPITOL NAVY John M. Coski pub by SavasBeatie 2005

Pg. 93 1862 "...The supply system was also efficient enough to supply officers and sailors with regulation uniforms. Despite the persistent image of Confederate soldiers and sailors dressed in makeshift, often mix-and-match uniforms, sailors in the squadron received issues of regulation Confederate naval uniforms. The Confederate Navy in late 1861 adopted a regulation uniform of steel grey. Depending on the occasion, officers were to wear grey frock coats or grey jackets, and steel grey or white vests and pantaloons. Sailor's uniforms were to consist of "grey cloth jackets and trousers, or grey woolen frocks with white duck cuffs and collar, black hats, black silk handkerchiefs and shoes, or boots in cold weather." During the summer, the sailors would wear white frocks and commanders were instructed to prescribe uniforms with "proper regard for the comfort of the crew..."

Navy blue was the traditional color for seamen the world over, and Confederate officers were reluctant to depart from it even in the name of Southern nationalism. Officers "kicked like steers when they were afterwards compelled to don the grey, contemptuously demanding to know, "Who had ever seen a grey sailor, no matter what nationality he served," remembered Midshipman James M. Morgan. As early as 1862, sailors in Richmond were nevertheless wearing the grey. Upon joining the navy in Richmond in June, 1862, Francis Dawson described his uniform as "grey, with any quantity of buttons, gold lace band, etc." Dawson's brother-in-law, Midshipman Morgan, received a cold welcome when he arrived in Richmond in May 1862 still wearing blue. As late as February, 1863, the government still issued blue jackets to men in the James River Squadron. However, an April 1863 order from the office of Orders and Detail forbade officers in Richmond from departing "from the prescribed uniform" without "sufficient cause."

Pg. 179 "There are also indications by the final year of the war that the Navy Department was having difficulty supplying crews with adequate clothing of any description. In appealing to the Office of Provisions and Clothing for pea jackets and blankets, Captain Mitchell reminded the paymaster in Richmond:

An adequate supply of winter clothing is all important at this time to make the men comfortable, and unless they are made so they must become discontented and unreliable in health and loyalty. It should be remembered that exposure to bad weather on shipboard is worse than in camp life, where the men can have the advantage of exercise and cheerful fires; hence the wants of the sailor in clothing are greater than those of the soldier in the field.

Sailors on the James were reportedly wearing English-made clothing. A deserter from the" Virginia II" reported in January, 1865 that the fall of Wilmington, North Carolina, the Confederacy's last port open to blockade runners-and thus to English clothing supplies- had created fears of a fabric shortage. Clothing, he said, was being issued very sparingly. Clothing records for the "Richmond" in 1864 reveal only blue and duck (white) cloth issued to the crews, but the ship's commander, John Kell, in January 1865 managed to draw seven yards of double-width grey cloth from the ship's supply."

REMINISCENCES OF CONFEDERATE SERVICE 1861-1865 Francis W. Dawson ed. by Bell I. Wiley La. State Univ. Press 1980

Pg. 8 An English subject preparing to become a crewman of the C.S.S. Nashville "I returned to London and began at once to make arrangements for my departure. My friend from Arkansas told me that the one indespensible thing was a Bowie-knife, and he explained the diverse uses to which this weapon could be put, assuring me that I would have no difficulty in seizing the gun of a Yankee soldier by the muzzle and, with one dexterous blow, severe the barrel in twain. Another way of using it was to attach a cord to the handle of this Bowie-knife and, with a skillful throw, to drive the blade into the heart of the advancing foeman, and, when he should have fallen, to haul it back by the string, and repeat the operation on another enemy. I had not much faith in my ability to use the Bowie-knife in this fashion, but I ordered one to be made by a surgical instrument maker, according to a pattern given me by my Arkansas friend. A sanguinary looking weapon it was. The blade was fifteen inches long and three inches wide at the broadest and a third of an inch thick at the back.... At Southampton I purchased a sailor's outfit, and, when I had rigged myself out in what I considered the proper style, I went down to the vessel. I wore a blue woolen shirt open at the neck; a black silk handkerchief, with ample flowing ends, tied loosely around the neck; blue trousers, made very tight at the knee and twenty-two inches in circumference at the bottom, and on my head a flat cloth cap ornamented with long black ribbons. I had besides, in the famous sea chest, a pea jacket, sea boots, and the necessary underclothing. As a reminder of my former estate, I retained a suit of dress clothes, and a black Inverness cape, which I had been in the habit of wearing..."

GRAY RAIDERS OF THE SEA Chester G. Hearn International Marine Pub. 1992

Pg. 166 Sept. 7, 1862 initiating the cruise of the Alabama "The next day, Semmes held the first of many Sunday Musters. Semmes wrote: "With clean white decks, with the brass and iron work glittering like so many mirrors in the sun, and with the sail neatly trimmed, and the Confederate States flag at our peak, we spread our awnings and read the Articles of War to the crew. A great change had taken place in the appearance of the men...Their parti-colored garments had been cast aside, and they were all neatly arrayed in duck frocks and trousers, well-polished shoes and straw hats..."

http://membres.multimania.fr/cssalabama/page/0-0html**NMLHA Navy & Marine Living History Association Clothing, Pay & Provisions for the Savannah River Squadron 1861-1864 by John Kennington**

Pg. 2 "The task of clothing and feeding the new navy was daunting. The need to maintain the navy's personnel grew as quickly as the navy grew. Initially congress authorized the C.S. Navy only 500 men. The bureau clothed these men by using existing stores captured at Norfolk and Pensacola in 1861. By late 1861 congress authorized the navy to increase its strength to 3000 men and the need to find other sources of supply was increasingly paramount. Stephen R. Mallory, Secretary of the Navy, sent naval purchasing agents throughout Europe to acquire the necessary supplies. James D.

Bullock, commander, C.S.N. was the chief procurement officer in Europe. Under his guidance the navy never wanted for adequate equipment and clothing; however, supplying clothing to the vessels of the Savannah River Squadron was a different matter.

The Navy Department instructed Bullock, in May1861 to purchase, without insignia, "cloth or cassinette pants (a lightweight twilled trousering usually with cotton warp and wool filling-ed), shoes, cloth jumpers, woolen socks, cloth round jackets, blankets, duck pants, blue cloth caps, blue flannel overshirts, pea jackets, blue flannel undershirts, barnsley sheeting frocks, blue flannel underdrawers, and black silk neckerchiefs." Some of these items made it through the blockade, several did not, Apparently much British uniform material reached the Confederacy. Supplies reaching Savannah, Georgia on the "Fingal" were issued to Savannah Squadron crews. Evidence of this is the issue of "blue pea jackets," "English clothing," and "blue satinette trousers (a thin silk satin or an imitation satin usually of silk and cotton or wool and cotton used chiefly for clothing-ed)." The "Gray Navy" that Secretary Mallory and Commander John M. Brooke envisioned was slow to come about because the army utilized most of the gray cloth and the Department continued to issue blue clothing captured at Norfolk."

This speaks for itself. Of course they are going to issue the captured blue naval uniforms until the supply wears out, especially as the gray naval uniforms were unpopular and slow to be supplied.

Pg. 12 "…James H. Tomb, of the Torpedo Bureau, recorded that, in 1865, seamen lying torpedoes at Shell Bluff below Augusta found two soldiers sleeping by a fire. The soldiers "surrendered" because "when they saw our men, who had on blue uniforms-clothes taken from the Water Witch-they thought we were Yanks, and said they were tired of war and going home…"

This shows that seamen were still wearing blue uniforms in 1865

http://historysites.com/cgi-bin/bbs53x/cwnavy/webbbs_config.pl?noframes;read=2983 Re: Confederate States Naval Uniforms "…The following passage is from page 632, volume IV of the volume **CORRESPONDENCE CONCERNING CLAIMS AGAINST GREAT BRITON, TRANSMITTED TO THE SENATE OF THE UNITED STATES IN ANSWER TO THE RESOLUTIONS OF DECEMBER 4AND 10,1867, AND MAY, 1868**, published by the Government Printing Office, Washington, which is the testimony ofCSS ALABAMA and CSS SHANEDOAH sailor Henry Alcott:

"…We all went on board in private clothes-the uniforms were in the trunks on board the LAUREL. They had been made in London and Paris. They were conveyed in boxes from the LAUREL to the SEA KING…"

NAVY GRAY by Maxine Turner pub by Mercer Univ. Press 1999

Pg. 81 the gunboat "Chattahoochee" on the Apalachicola River, fall 1862 "...In continued efforts to shape up the crew, Jones ordered the conscripts into Confederate gray uniforms so that they would "look a little more sailor-like." In Horry's view, it was a losing battle: "I never saw such a ragged and worthless set of men in my life. They are the very scourings of Florida."

Pg. 207 late 1864, Columbus Ga. & Selma, Al. re; shoes "...He had tried (McLaughlin) in vain to get 50 pairs from the local quartermaster in a faltering system slowed almost to a halt. A circular order from the quartermaster general left the sergeant without discretion to act unless he had approval from his commander. The quartermaster advised McLaughlin to advise Jones to apply directly to Gen. A.R. Lawton for an issue of shoes; two cases at the time (120 pairs) could be had, but not 50 pairs, unless Jones had the proper authorization from the quartermaster general himself..."

http://georgiacsmccompanyc.webs.com /uniforms.htm "...Brief history of the C.S. Marine Corps Uniform "...It is clear, however, that the marines were often equipped out of the stores of whichever garrison was closest their location. One description has the Marines dressed in frock coats of a particular (and undetermined) shade of gray and dark blue or black trousers. It appears the Confederate States Marines wore forage caps although it is unclear if there were any ornamentation on the cover. Much of the gear of the C.S.M.C. was imported from the United Kingdom and its empire, namely Canada, and Russia creating a fairly unique look...and wore uniforms similar to the British Royal Marines..."

DEAR MOTHER: DON'T GRIEVE ABOUT ME. IF I GET KILLED, IU'LL ONLY BE DEAD. ed by Mills Lane pub by The beehive Press 1977

Pg. 277 Henry Graves to his Mother; Steamer Savannah, Savannah Georgia, Nov. 3 1863 My dear Mother; "...I enclose by express today to Social Circle the butter bucket with patterns for duty coat and pants and buttons for my overcoat and hat. I send eighteen. You can use them as you think best. If you have not already cut the overcoats, please cut them a little longer than Pa's coat (that black sack-looking overcoat of the Raglan style is the one I mean) by which I wish them cut exactly in every other respect. I believe I told you about the cape. Make it to meet under the throat to be held up by buttons under the collar of the coat. Please make button and eyelet holes to the number of six at regular intervals down the front of the cape so that it can be buttoned up and worn at times by itself. I have buttons for the cape. If you can get it, I would like (very) much to have enough of the cloth for a sack coat and a pair of pants. If you have the cloth to spare now and will send it in the same bundle I will get it cut and made here. If you haven't it on hand we will wait 'till I get home, if I succeed in that. There is something I do want very much now and that is some sort of cloth to make me a vest. Have you any remnants of black cloth or cassimere or indeed anything that will make me a vest? Or have I any winter vests at home? If not, please send me enough jeans if you have it for a vest. I would also like a piece of soap. Soap here is exorbitantly high. Also please send me a little bottle of hair grease. This winds up my wants. Does the list overcome you?"

Yes, looking at this list overcomes me. He really expects a lot from his mother, he doesn't say why he cannot get clothing from the navy.

Midshipman in Gray-Selections From Recollections of a Rebel Reefer by James Morris Morgan pub by Burg Street Press 1917

Pg. 159 Aug 1864 (James Morris Morgan was a midshipman on the Confederate raider "Georgia") "At Wilmington I went to a wretched little cottage which sheltered several naval officers who were stationed in the town. I thought our condition in the Confederacy was bad enough when I had left its shores two years before, but these officers had literally nothing in the way of clothing besides their shabby uniforms, threadbare and patched. I felt ashamed of my new uniform, made by a fashionable London tailor, and my well-laundered white shirt, so I moved my trunks into the center of the room and insisted on a divide of its contents…"

Pg. 164 Sent to Naval School aboard the "Patrick Henry" in the James River, just in front of Drewry's Bluff "There were about sixty young midshipmen on the "Patrick Henry", varying in age from fourteen to seventeen. Their jackets were made out of very coarse gray cloth and the food they had to eat was, at first, revolting to me. The menu offered little variety. If it was not a tiny lump of fat pork, it was a shaving of fresh meat as tough as the hide that had once covered it, with a piece of hardtack and a tin cup of hot water colored by chickory or grains of burnt corn, ground up, and brevetted "coffee." But no one kicked about the food, it was as good if not better than that the poor soldiers in the trenches received…"

Supplies to the navy were as scarce as those sent to the army

Pg. 181 Fall, 1864 Going to a ball in Richmond, Va., attempting to get a suit "…To attend this ball, it was necessary for me to have a new uniform. With any amount of Confederate money at my disposal, the modern man might ask why I did not go to the tailor and order one, but that was not the way we did things in those days. In the first place, there were no stores, and had there been there would not have been anything in them for sale. I had to search the town before I found a man who possessed a few yards of gray cloth and willing to part with it for several hundred dollars in Confederate money. I finally found such a man; and also bought from him a pair of boots made out of thick, half-tanned cowskin for which I paid three hundred dollars. I looked so nice in my new togs that I was immediately asked by an army surgeon to be one of the groomsmen at his wedding, and I also attended the wedding of the beautiful Miss Hetty Cary and General John Pegram which had so sad an ending a few days afterwards when General Pegram was killed…"

Midshipman Morris was lucky to have gotten a suit and pair of boots for any price in Richmond at this time.

NO SOAP, NO PAY, DIARRHEA, DYSENTERY & DESERTION ed by Jeff Toalson pub by iUniverse 2006

Jan. 16, 1865 Seaman Robert Watson, Wilmington, North Carolina "Started at daylight (abandoned Battery Buchanan 1-15) and arrived at Wilmington at 11A.M. very tired and sore, drew a pair of shoes and went to the navy yard…Drew some rations and remained there all day and night…The place was overrun with lice…they were running over and biting me all night…the proper name for them is "soldier bugs."

POW

MY DIARY OF RAMBLES WITH THE 25TH MASSACHUSETTS VOLUNTEER INFANTRY
King & Billings Printers 1884

Pg. 37 Diary of David L. Day Feb.10 1862 "…The prisoners are a motley-looking set, all clothed (I can hardly say uniformed) in a dirty-looking homespun grey cloth. I should think every man's suit was cut from a design of his own. Some wore what was probably meant for a frock coat, others wore jackets or roundabouts; some of the coats were long skirted, others short, some tight-fitting, others loose, and no two men were dressed alike. Their head covering was in unison with the rest of their rig; of all kinds, from stovepipe hats to coonskin caps; with everything for blankets, from old bed quilts, cotton bagging, strips of carpet to buffalo robes. The Wise Legion are a more soldierly-looking set; they wear grey cloth caps of the same pattern, and long sheep's grey overcoats with capes. Most of the officers were smart, good-looking young men, wearing well-fitting grey uniforms, not unlike those of our own officers…"

Here the Yankees are confirming the "multiform" among the Rebs, see below.

LIFE AND LETTERS OF JUDGE THOMAS J.ANDERSONAND HIS WIFE James House and Nancy Anderson Press of F.J. Heer 1904

Pg. 198 Letter from Nancy Dunlevy Anderson to Princess A. Miller Anderson March 17, 1862 "… Mrs. Senator Hood, who was in Columbus and watched the 800 march through town to Camp Chase, said they were a motley set, dressed in garments of every conceivable style, material and color: yellow, red, blue grey, butternut, etc. Around some, dirty old bed quilts were thrown, pieces of carpeting, ragged blankets, etc.…"

THIS BAND OF HEROES-Granbury's Texas Brigade, C.S.A. by James M.McCaffery pub by Texas A&M Univ Press 1996

Pg. 55 April 1862- "the officers captured at Arkansas Post, about three hundred in number, were sent to Camp Chase…In their first full day in prison the inmates were given back their money, if it was less than one hundred dollars, and their pocketknives, if they were small enough. They learned that they could patronize the sutler's store which was located against the outside of one of the walls with a small window cut through to the prison yard. Those who had been carrying more than one hundred dollars had it placed to their accounts with the sutler. This arrangement was very favorable to the Confederate officers as they usually either had money or had friends or relatives who would send them money. Their spending habits were so lavish as to [prompt the prison commandant, Captain Edwin L. Webber, to write to Washington for instructions. "There are many of them who wish to purchase uniforms…and large supplies of extra clothing that they cannot obtain in the South; also the best quality of boots. I am at a loss to know where to draw the line in this respect." Within a week a reply came which stated that the prisoners should only be allowed enough clothing and shoes for their immediate needs and that these items "must be of a quality such as to insure its not lasting for any length of on their return to the South."

Of course these men wanted uniforms; that quality uniform would be several times as expensive in the Confederacy if it were even obtainable.

CAMPAIGNS OF A NON-COMBATANT and his Romaunt Abroad During the War by Geo. Alfred Townsend pub. By Blelock& Co. 1866

Pg. 103 after Battle of Hanover Court House May 27, 1862 "…It was evening, as I hitched my horse to a stake nearby, and pressed up to the recepticle for the unfortunates. Sentries enclosed the pen, walking to-and-fro and loaded muskets; a throng of officers and soldiers had assembled to gratify their curiosity; and new detachments of captives came in hourly, encircled by sabremen, the Southerners being disarmed and on foot. The scene within the area was ludicrously moving. It reminded me of the witch-scene in Macbeth, or the pictures of brigands or Bohemian gypsies at rendezvous, not less than five hundred men, in motley, ragged costumes, with long hair and lean, wild, haggard faces, were gathered in groups or in pairs, around some fagot fires. In the growing darkness their expressions were imperfectly visible; but I could see that most of them were weary, and hungry and were depressed and ashamed. Some were wrapped in blankets of rag-carpet, and others wore shoes of rough, untanned hide. Others were without either shoes or jackets, and their heads were bound with red handkerchiefs. Some appeared in red shirts; some in stiff beaver hats; some were attired in shreds and patches of cloth; and a few wore the soiled garments of citizen gentlemen; but the mass adhered to homespun suits of gray, or "butternut," and the coarse blue kersey common to slaves. In places I caught glimpses of red Zouave breeches and leggings; blue Federal caps, Federal buttons, or Federal blouses; these were the spoils of anterior battles and had been stripped from the slain. Most of the captives were of the appearances denominated "scraggy" or "knotty." They were brown, brawny and wiry, and their countenances were intense, fierce, and animal. They came from North Carolina, the poorest and least enterprising Southern State, and ignorance, with its attendant virtues, were the common facial manifestations. Some lay on the bare ground, fast asleep; others chatted nervously, as if doubtful of their future treatment; a few were boisterous, and anxious to beg tobacco of coffee from idle Federals; the rest-and they comprehended the greater number- were silent sullen and vindictive. They met curiosity with scorn, and spite with imprecations. A child-not more than four years of age, I think-sat sleeping in a corner upon a older comrade's lap. A gray-bearded pard was staunching a gash in his cheek with the tail of his coat. A fine-looking fellow sat with his face in his hands, as if his heart was far off, and he wished to shut out this bitter scene. In a corner, lying morosely apart, were a major, three captains, and three lieutenants,-young atheletic fellows, dressed in rich gray cassimere, trimmed with black, and wearing soft black hats adorned with black ostrich-feathers. Their spurs were strapped upon elegantly fitting boots, and they looked as far above the needy, seedy privates, as lords above their vassals.

After a time, couples and squads of the prisoners were marched off to cut and carry some firewood, and water, for the use of their pen, and then each Confederate received coffee, pork, and crackers; they were obliged to prepare their own meals, but some were so hungry that they gnawed the raw pork like beasts of prey. Those who were not provided with blankets, shivered through the night, though the rain was falling, and the succession of choking coughs that ran through the ranks, told how ill they could afford the exposure..."

Here's further evidence of multiform in the Rebel ranks, from a union observer, so the "Ragged Rebel" isn't just a romantic myth dreamed up by Southerners after the war. These men sound more like refugees than soldiers.

Pg. 134 after a battle during the Seven Day's campaign, in a Union hospital summer, 1862 "...Oh! You Rebil! You, with the butternut trousers! Say! Wake up and take some of this (soup)! Hello! Lad, partner. Wake up!

He stirred him gently with his foot; he bent down to touch his face. A grimmness came over his merriment. The man was stiff, and dumb..."

Pg. 268 after the Battle of Second Manassas "...As a rule, Northern and Southern troops have the same general manners and appearances. These were more ragged than any federals I had ever known, and their appetites were voracious..."

Pg. 272 after The Battle of Cedar Mountain, a scene of Confederate retreat summer 1862 "...Beyond, the road and fields were strewn with knapsacks, haversacks, jackets, canteens, cartridge-boxes, shoes, bayonets, knives, buttons, belts, blankets, girths and sabres..."

Pg. 326 after the Battle of Five Forks "...They were fine, hearty fellows, almost all Virginians, and seemed to take their capture not unkindly. They wore the gray and not very attractive uniform of the Confederacy, but looked to be warm and fat, and passing along in the night, under the fir trees, conveyed at most a romantic idea of grief and tribulation..."

DEFEND THE VALLEY Margaretta Barton Colt Crown Pub. 1994

Pg. 176 Memoir of Randolph Barton summer, 1862 "...One of the military companies in charge was a volunteer company made up largely of young gentlemen from Philadelphia. When they learned that Willie Barton and myself were receiving presents (which we did most bountifully, choice eatables and clothes) from the Ettings, Moncure Robinsons and others most favorably known in Philadelphia, their native civility seemed to increase, and we at least had nothing to complain of so far as discipline was concerned. Major Gibson, a regular army officer, was in command of the fort, and permitted my father and mother, visiting (the Shields) in Cecil County, Maryland, to come and see me.

Some unknown friend in Philadelphia asked permission of the Major for the army tailor to take my measure for a suit of clothes and soon I received from that intensely Union city a splendid grey uniform, perhaps the only rebel uniform made in that city. Who the donor was, I never discovered, peace to his or her ashes…"

LIBRARY OF VIRGINIA Box# 38559 Adeline Egerton Johnson's Island 20th July 1862

Dear Madam, "…The box to my care for the (Pt. Coopee?) Artillery and the First Alabama was rec'd yesterday & distributed by Major Knox. The private packages to Capt. Meadows, Col. Steadman& Henderson I delivered. The parties who rec'd them will appropriately acknowledge the favours.

The Box Contained

12 pairs shoes	26 pair pantaloons
14 vests	6 coats
18 shirts	18 undershirts
2 blankets	4 pair slippers
6 slouch hats	51 pair socks
18 pair drawers	1 bundle cravats
6 needle books	1 bundle pipes
1 package tobacco	2 packs soap
Books	sugar & preserves
1 box suspenders	cravats 20

Signed J. Gordon

This is one of many life-saving boxes sent to Rebel P.O.W.s by Northern people.

SOLDIERS BLUE AND GREY James I. Robertson Jr. Univ. of S.C. Press 1988

"…Inadequate clothing was also a widespread source of misery. Most soldiers were wearing lightweight summer issue and were unprepared for the frigid gales of winter in open and drafty stockades. One group of Confederate prisoners arrived at Rock Island Prison, Illinois, on a wintry afternoon. A cold wind was whipping across the Mississippi River compound. The new arrivals spent the next hours pounding themselves to keep warm as they trotted back and forth through the drafty barracks. In the days that followed, several comrades dozed off from coldness and quietly died. Topcoats were rarely in evidence, and as a rule only one man in three would possess even a scrap of a blanket. The need for clothing became so acute that the rags of dead comrades were eagerly seized by those still living...."

2. Pg. 34 Corinth, Miss. Oct. 3&4 "The Southern prisoner's escort consisted of men from the 28th Illinois Infantry. One Union private referred to the Confederates as : "butternuts, miserable; shabby, dirty and all but naked." ..."Nearly eight hundred Rebel prisoners passed by late in the afternoon. They were nearly all clad in butternut suits with a grey cap. Their knapsacks were made of rawhide with the hair on the outside."

2. Pg. 42 A New York paper reports on captured Confederates, as reported by the Richmond Examiner on May 14, 1862 "The New Yorker referred to the captured Rebel soldiers as being outfitted in a "peculiar uniform of a dirt-white color (drab?), covered with dirt and filth. It is far from attractive."

2. Pg 43 Battle of Hanover Court House, May 27-28 1862 Prisoners were mostly men of the 28th North Carolina from General Branch's North Carolina Brigade "...civilian clothes, but the mass adhered to homespun suits of grey or butternut, and the blue kersey common to slaves. Some were wrapped in blankets of rag carpets, and others wore shoes of rough, untanned hide. Others were without either shoes or jackets, and their heads were bound with red handkerchiefs. Some appeared in red shirts; some in stiff beaver hats; some in shreds and patches of cloth. In places I caught glimpses of red Zouave breeches and leggings; blue Federal caps, Federal buttons, or Federal blouses...

In a corner lying morosely apart, were a Major, three Captains, three Lieutenants-young atheletic fellows, dressed in rich grey cassimere (sic) trimmed in black, and wearing soft black hats adorned with ostrich feathers. Their spurs were snapped upon elegantly fitting boots..."

2. Pg. 71 "The following description of a group of some 460 captured Con federate officers illustrates the diversity of uniforms being worn:

"there among them were tall, lank mountaineers, dark, long-haired and fierce of aspect, and a lesser number of city men of jauntier appearance. The major part were common looking, evidently of the poorer class of Southerners, with a spreading of foreigners, principally Germans and Irish. Hardly any two dressed alike. They wore suits of blue jeans, homespuns of butternut, and a few in costumes of grey more or less trimmed. Upon their heads were all sorts of covering, straw and slouch hats, and forage caps of grey, blue, or red, decorated with braid. Cavalry boots, shoes and bootees, in all stages of wear on their feet. Their effects were wrapped in rubber sheets, pieces of carpet, or parts of quilts and comforts. Some had sacks of ancient make. Haversacks of waterproof cloth and cotton hung from their shoulders..."

2. Pg. 86 "Longstreet's Corps was re-uniformed in April 1864, a gift from the state of North Carolina. One Ohio lieutenant wrote immediately following the Battle of the Wilderness how he :...had the pleasure of seeing about 4,000 prisoners passing on their way to the rear. They seemed completely surprised, which is a wonder for old troops. As to their appearance, they were all clad in neat grey jackets and pantaloons with entire seats...."

CIVIL WAR SOLDIERS Reid Mitchell Viking Press, 1988

Pg. 39 "Union soldiers commented most often on the appearance of the Confederate prisoners they met. Confederates were ill-clothed poorly fed, and hard looking. Caleb Blanchard thought the Confederate prisoners brought to Fort McHenry after Antietam "the worst looking set I ever saw." "Some were shot through the head some in the leg I saw one who had one side of his face shot off several with their arms off and a good many on crutches." Despite their misery, the prisoners still said "they were fighting for their rights."

In September 1862, Allen Landis watched twelve or more Confederate prisoners pass through his camp in Fairfax, Virginia. He decided that they were happy to have been captured by the Federal pickets. "They looked tolerably well, though none of them were dressed in military clothing." Other Union soldiers commented as well on the "rag-tag" nature of Confederate clothing. One wrote, "I do think that the most forlorn picture of humanity is a Rebel Soldier taken prisoner on a very wet day."

Multiform predominates.

DIARY OF A SOUTHERN REFUGEE DURING THE WAR J.W. Randolph & English 1889

Pg. 184 Diary of Judith White Brockenbrough McGuire, Jan. 1863 "...Several friends have just arrived from Yankeedom in a vessel fitted out by the Northern Government to receive the exchanged prisoners. About six hundred women and children were allowed to come in it from Washington. They submitted to the most humiliating search...Some trunks were sadly pillaged if they happened to contain more clothes than the Northern Government thought proper for a rebel to possess. No material was allowed to come which was not made into garments. My friend brought me some pocket handkerchiefs and stockings, scattered in various parts of the trunk, so as not to seem to have too many. She brought her son, who is in our service, (soldier) a suit of clothes made into a cloak which she wore. Many a grey cloth traveling-dress and petticoat which was on the boat is now in camp, decking the person of a Confederate soldier; having undergone a transformation into jackets and pants..."

Once again, we see how the Yankees are very brave when confronted with women and children.

Pg. 296 **U.S.** **Quartermaster's Dept**.

Springfield, Ill., Feb. 24, 1863

Col. William Hoffman,
Commissary General of Prisoners, Washington, D.C.

COLONEL: I have received no instructions from you concerning issues to the Arkansas prisoners now confined at Camp Butler, near this city. I have a quantity of grey clothing on hand unfit for issue to volunteers which might answer for the prisoners if desirable. Please forward copies of any general regulations concerning prisoners which may have been recently adopted and oblige,

Very respectfully, your obedient servant,
W.H. BAILHACHE,
Captain and Assistant Quartermaster.

Pg 305 **HEADQUARTERS COMMANDANT OF PRISONS**

Camp Chase, Ohio, February 28, 1863
Capt. H.M. Lazelle,
Assistant to Commissary General of Prisoners, Washington
CAPTAIN: I have the honor of addressing you for the purpose of asking information on several subjects:

1. The rebel commissioned officers confined here are receiving large remittances of money from their friends and as the money costs nothing but the asking for it they are very lavish in expending it. There are many of them who wish to purchase uniforms; expensive cloth that would be readily turned into uniforms when they get back to the South, and large supplies of extra clothing that they cannot obtain in the South; also the best quality of boots. I am at a loss to know where to draw the line in this respect. My judgment is that they should be permitted to buy sufficient to keep them comfortable and nothing to carry away with them. Should a man who has a comfortable suit and a change of underclothing be permitted to buy extra clothing? Shall I permit friends to furnish unnecessary articles of clothing to prisoners? Also, should the prisoners be permitted to purchase any articles of food or should any delicacies be given them by their friends? There is much talk upon this subject and I should be thankful for your opinion and instructions.

... Very respectfully, captain, your obedient servant,
EDWIN L. WEBBER,
Captain Commanding Prisons

Pg306

Camp Chase, February 28, 1863

Col. William Hoffman,
Commissary General of Prisoners, Washington City

SIR: I have the honor respectfully to call your attention to the following statement: On the 23rd of October, 1862, I was appointed by the direction of Captain Freedley, assistant commissary-general of prisoners, provost marshal of prisoners in this camp. In such capacity I have acted as such, without any specific instructions being given to me that would guide me in the performance of any duty that might arise of an extraordinary nature incident to the confinement of such a large number of prisoners as are now here. In view of the above fact I would respectfully ask you to give me instructions on the following points viz.:

1. Would it be my duty as provost-marshal to permit friends or prisoners themselves to purchase such articles of clothes that would on their return to the South answer for a uniform in the rebel army?

2. Would it be inconsistent with the dignity of the United States to require every person who has interviews with the prisoners to take an oath of allegiance previous to the interview?

To the first question I would state that numerous friends of the rebels in the North send here daily large boxes, trunks and packages of clothing and other articles that cannot be purchased in the South except at a large sum. To my second question I state that of the numerous interviews held with the prisoners but few who desire the interview are in speech and actions any more loyal than the prisoners.

In view of the above facts and as a loyal officer striving to aid his Government be kind enough to give me the necessary information that I may be guided hereafter.

I have the honor to be, very respectfully, your obedient servant,
JAMES C. HENLEY
Lieutenant, Company A, Battalion Governors Guards.

Pg 317 **OFFICE COMMISSARY-GENERAL OF PRISONERS**

Washington D.C., March 4, 1863

Capt. Edwin L. Webber,
Commandant of Prison, Camp Chase, Ohio

Captain: Your letter of February 8, 1863, addressed to Capt. H.M. Lazelle, assistant to commissary-general of prisoners, was received, and I am directed by the commissary-general of prisoners to say in answer to same that the indulgences therein mentioned should not be allowed. Rebel officers are not to have any more clothing than they actually require for immediate and actual use and which must be of a quality such as to insure its not lasting for any length of time on their return to the South. As to their boots or shoes, they may be of the commonest quality or rather of a quality that will suffice but for immediate use. They are not to be allowed to purchase uniform clothing of any kind or have it or anything in that line furnished by their friends. They will be allowed to purchase a moderate or reasonable allowance of food or delicacies, and those that are too poor to purchase may have it furnished by their friends in reasonable quantities. Regulations made by the commissary-general of prisoners in June last show under what circumstances money may be received and expended.

THE COLOR-GUARD: BEING A COPORAL'S NOTES OF MILI-TARY SERVICE IN THE NINETEENTH ARMY CORPS Walker, Wise and Co. 1864

Pg. 134 Diary of James Kendall Hosmer April, 1863 La.

"...Prisoners come by in squads-sometimes five or six, sometimes twenty or thirty; some in grey, some in blue, some in faded brown...."

ARMY LIFE IN VIRGINIA -Letter from George Grenville Benedict Burlington VT. Free Press Association 1895

Pg. 159 April 9, 1863 writing about deserters-

"…Three of them came in today, one of them a pretty intelligent young man of 25, the other two bright-eyed & good-looking boys of 17, all members of the 5th Virginia Cavalry. They are clothed in the coarse cotton and wool butternut colored jackets and trousers which commonly form the uniform of a rebel soldier when he has one, and tell the often repeated story of scanty rations, hard treatment, and poor pay. The twelve dollars a month which they are payed barely cover the cost of their clothes, at the rates at which they are charged to them, so that the rebel soldier in fact works for his food and clothing, and not over much of either…"

Smith, Adelaide W. Reminiscences of an Army Nurse during the Civil War N.Y. Greaves Pub Co. 1911

Long Island - "David's Island, on the Sound, had a finely conducted hospital, with a diet kitchen in charge of ladies. There I saw hundreds of well-fed, happy Confederate patients, so many, indeed that they could not be supplied at once with proper clothing, and so made a unique appearance as they walked about in dressing gowns, white drawers, and slippers…."

Pg.462

Headquarters Commandant of Prisons,
Camp Chase, Ohio, April 10, 1863.

Col. W. Hoffman,
Commissary General of Prisoners, Washington, D.C.

COLONEL: I have respectfully to state that since the receipt of your instructions of the 4th ultimo concerning the uniform and clothing of prisoners a considerable amount of clothing has been received here for prisoners in boxes and other packages, sent to them by their friends and acquaintances. As much of it was superfluous above the necessities of the prisoners while here in confinement what they did not need has been withheld and turned over to the keeping of the prison provost marshal. On searching the baggage and persons of officers destined for Fort Delaware it was found that in many cases they had managed to purchase by some means more clothing than under your instructions was proper for them to carry off toward the point of exchange. In such cases a portion of the clothing was taken away and placed in charge of the provost marshal of prisons. I respectfully ask your instructions as to the disposition to be made of such clothing, blankets, &c.; also of surgical instruments, arms and other articles deemed contraband. In regard to the contributed clothing in a number of cases instead of distributing large packages to but two or three individuals as originally intended it has been distributed to destitute prisoners.

I am, colonel. Very respectfully, your obedient servant

Pg.509

Headquarters of the Army,

Washington, D.C. April 23, 1863
Fort Monroe

It has been officially reported that on the arrival at Tullahassee of prisoners of war of the twenty-second Wisconsin Volunteers, captured at Thompson's and Brentwood Stations up in Tennessee, they were by order of General Bragg stripped of their overcoats and blankets.

You will at your next interview with the officer appointed by the enemy for the exchange of prisoners present him with a copy of this letter and ask an answer whether this allegation be true and whether the Confederate authorities approve or disapprove the act alleged.

Very respectfully, your obedient servant,
H.W. HALLECK
General-in-chief

Hey, Gen. Bragg's troops need those overcoats and blankets.

Headquarters Department no.2

May 21, 1863

The complaint is true; my action was retaliatory. Prisoners captured from this army have not only been stripped of overcoats and blankets but money, watches and even small articles of priceless value to them, though of no earthly use to the robbers who took them.

I informed Major-General Rosecrans when I first gave the order early in December last and expressed my regret that the conduct of the officers of his Government imposed this unpleasant duty upon me. The staff officer of the general who received the prisoners with this notice acknowledged the precedent and told his men in the presence of my representative that he regretted the act but would not complain, the example having been set by them. Instead of checking such outrages the general has permitted them to a greater extent, and has recently by general orders required the uniform pantaloons to be taken from my men when captured. He has even pronounced the death penalty against prisoners who may be taken wearing the uniform prescribed by our Government and ordered that no quarter shall be shown them on the field. There is not one of us from the private up but will come within the terms of this general order.

BRAXTON BRAGG,
General Commanding

Another example of the extremes the Union army exerted towards unarmed men.

HDQRS. EIGHTH REGT. CAV. MISSOURI STATE MILITIA,

Lebanon, Mo., April 28, 1863

Maj. James H. Steger,
Assistant adjutant-general, district of Southwest Missouri

Major: I telegraphed to the colonel commanding Southwest District of Missouri on the 23rd that seven men were taken prisoners on their return from Springfield as escort to paymaster. They were taken in Dallas County, carried about fifty miles into Cedar County, stripped, murdered and thrown into a heap like so many hogs. Three of the soldiers thus murdered belonged to Company D and four to Company E of this regiment. The rebels were dressed in Federal uniform, and the men rode up to them as friends, when they were captured and most cruelly murdered. The three men of Company D were as good soldiers as ever shouldered a musket, always obedient, but on this occasion had straggled behind the command. Major, I respectfully inquire of the colonel commanding district whether any rebel wearing the Federal uniform should be treated as a prisoner of war? If I capture any rebel thus attired, I will have him shot unless otherwise ordered.

I have the honor to be, most respectfully, your obedient servant,

J.J. Gravely
Colonel, Eighth Regiment Cavalry Missouri State Militia

Here's an example of the war's brutality in the Trans-Mississippi.

SOLDIER BOYS LETTERS TO HIS FATHER AND MOTHER 1861-5 News Office 1915

Pg. 34 Letter from Chauncy Herbert Cooke May 12, 1863 Columbus somewhere in Tn.

Dear Mother "...We have some rebel prisoners down town and they have been talking pretty saucy to the guard. They say one butternut (that is the color of their uniform) is good for four Yanks..."

VOICES FROM COMPANY D

Pg. 166 exchanged prisoners in Petersburg 1863 May 14 SP

"...Returned to Camp & found giving Out clothes & as was much in want of change under clothes tried to get some but none could be had as such crowd gathered round place ahead of us...."

Pg. 366 April 4 1865 SP

"...Landed 2 or 3 P.M. Divided into Cos. About 100 each-names taken searched & marched into the enclosure- acres plank fence 15ft. High. Took tents, oilclothes& all blankets ex. I hid my knife in one sock & my pocket spoon in other, old letters in shirt pockets & Portfolio down my back. $300 Ala money sewed in lining pants-& 40 Confed. in lining hat. So nothing taken from us. One of Co. H (...) gave up 10 gold pieces-which he'll never see again..."

LETTERS OF TWO BROTHERS SERVING IN THE WAR FOR THE UNION TO THEIR FAMILY AT HOME IN WEST CAMBRIDGE, MASS. H.O. Houghton and Co. 1871

Pg. 74 Letter from warren Hapgood Freeman to J.D. Freeman May 18, 1863 after Chancellorsville

"...Our papers speak about the prisoners that we take as looking half-starved, ragged, etc. Now I could never see this. Those that I saw, and I think there were 2,000 of them, were fully equal in looks and condition to the average of our men; they sat we can never subdue them, that they will fight till there is not a man left. Their grey uniforms give them a kind of dirty appearance, and they nearly all wore felt hats, but some of them had on very neat and handsome uniforms…"

THE ADVENTURES OF A PRISONER OF WAR; AND LIFE AND SCENES IN THE FEDERAL PRISONS : JOHNSON'S ISLAND, FORT DELAWARE; POINT LOOKOUT; by an escaped prisoner of Hood's Brigade 1865 summer 1863-prisoners from Gettysburg passing through Baltimore, Md.

"…We were in a sorry plight; our wounds had not been dressed for forty-eight hours; our clothes had never been changed since the battle-thus, bloody, dirty, ragged, bare-footed, bare-headed, and crippled, we marched through the streets of the monumental city, a spectacle of fiendish delight to some, but one of sympathy and pity for thousands of true subjugated Southerners, who inhabit the city…"

THE CONFEDERATE VETERAN VOL.XXX 1922 June 1922

Pg. 223 The Record That He Made by D.B. Easley, Company H, 14th Virginia Infantry

"I went into the charge of Pickett's division on July 3, 1863, stripped to my shirt sleeves and in due time landed at Fort Delaware with my entire worldly possessions, consisting of shoes, socks, pants, drawers, shirt and part of a hat.

As long as it was warm, I borrowed a roundabout occasionally, and washed my shirt in the moat; also my drawers and socks, without any borrowing, but I could not see that I improved them much. Along toward October it was getting cool, and roundabouts were hard to borrow."

(On a detail at a storeroom) "I dived in first and got an assortment of clothes that they must have captured on a blockader, and struck out down the hall, but cast my eye back at "Hike Out" till he dived into the storeroom: then I went down the steps beside a wing and under the house, slipped a shirt over mine, a pair of pants over my old ones, also a roundabout, then walked out to where one of my regiment had a detail cleaning up around the hospital, told him what I had done, and asked him to pass me into camp that night.… Shortly after that, they sent us to Point Lookout. Somebody stole my hat on the boat while I slept. They put us in Sibley tents, sixteen to a tent. We slept eight on a side, and sewed our blankets together; four to go under and four over us. I forgot to say that the Yankees stole the patent right on the tents from General Sibley, as he was in our army. …I enjoyed my clothes probably half the winter; then some one cut the tent and stole my clothes from under my head as I slept. This left me with a shirt, drawers, shoes and socks, and I had gotten some sort of hat, but no coat or pants.…I missed my breakfast next day, but some unknown friend at the hospital sent me a pair of pants and a Yankee coat with the tails cut off, making it a roundabout. I swore-this to be taken literally-"that I wound starve and freeze before I would wear that coat." So I gave fifty crackers to boot for a Confederate roundabout, and lived on three crackers a day, the little piece of meat, and some hot water soup till I paid it."

WRITING & FIGHTING FROM THE ARMY OF NORTHERN VIRGINA-A Collection of Soldier Correspondence ed. By William B. Styple Belle Grove pub. 2003

Pg. 160 Fort Delaware "...One day, in consequence to the men crowding about the dining room floor, I failed getting my allowance of grub. I was very hungry. I asked a Yank if he wished to but a knife. He looked at my knife and inquired what I asked for it. I told him I would take a piece of bread for it. He asked me if I had nothing to eat that day. I told him I had not. Said he, "you are a liar; the prisoners have all been fed and better than they deserve; and you are a fool. Why don't you take the oath, throw aside those dirty, filthy rags, put on a decent suit and come under the glorious stars and stripes?" I replied, every star has been blotted out, and every stripe turned into a serpent; moreover, I owe no allegiance to any government that will deny a prisoner food and water; and furthermore, I will perish before I will forsake our glorious little Confederacy, the land of my father and my mother. "Upon this he drew his sabre and said if I did not leave his presence immediately, he would run it through me-a damned impudent rebel...."

SOLDIERS BLUE AND GRAY by James I. Robertson Jr. pub by Univ of S.C. Press 1988

Pg. 200 "...One group of Confederate prisoners arrived at Rock Island Prison, Illinois, on a wintery afternoon. A cold wind was whipping across the Mississippi River compound. The new arrivals spent the next hours pounding themselves to keep warm as they trotted back and forth through the drafty barracks. In the days that followed, several comrades dozed off from coldness and quietly died. Topcoats were rarely in evidence, and as a rule only one man in three would possess even a scrap of a blanket. The need for clothing became so acute that the rags of dead comrades were eagerly seized by those still living..."

Pg. 205 Elmira Prison "...On one occasion, over 1600 half-naked Confederates, lacking any semblance of a blanket or tent, stood ankle-deep in the snow to answer a morning roll-call..."

LETTERS OF JOHN HAY AND EXTRACTS FROM DIARY VOL.1 Henry and Hay, Clara Louise Adams Privately Pub. 1908

Pg. 164 Diary of John Milton Hay Feb. 1864

"...They soon came, a dirty swarm of grey coats, and filed into the room, escorted by a negro guard..."

LIBRARY OF VIRGINIA Archives file #38559 Adeline Egerton

Johnson Island Ohio

Feb. 16, 1864

Mrs. A. D. Egerton

"...As I am in need of a suit of clothes and without means to purchase with... If you can conveniently you will please send me pr. (? Gloves) one pr. Pants size 32.32 on (?) vet 21/2 one hat 71/8 one pr. Drawers a shirt or two pr. Socks also a few shirt collars. By so doing you will oblige a friend in need..."

Very Respectfully,
A. A. Moffett
Capt. 18. NC

Point Lookout
Feb. 27th /64

Mrs. Egerton

I receives your kind token of rememberance yesterday which I am very thankful. You spoke of a coat which I did not receive the pants I received this morning. The coat I suppose was lost on the way. I am very much in need of a coat shoes also No 7 if you can supply me with them - you will oblige me very much in deed Capt. Little sends has very kind regards to you. I remain yours very respectfully,

Capt. W. E. Oriley

Cag(?) 9 Regt. La.
Hammand General Hospital

Point Lookout, Md.
March 13th, 1864

Mrs. Ada Egerton

"...The coat shoes etc. are an excellent fit and I could not have been suited better had I made the selection myself. The articles contained in the package were one coat, one pair shoes, two shirts, one pair drawers, two pair socks..." Hugh L. Barn Lieut. Co. "B" 2nd Regt. Miss. Inf.

Fort McHenry April the1/64

Mrs. Carr

"...Dear Madam I am very much in need of some clothing and if you can through your friends help me in any way I will be very much indebted to you. The articles that I am most in need of are shoes and shirts that is outside shirts and some kind of a coat as it is getting warm weather any kind of light coat will be very thankfully received no. 8 shoes are the size I wear I will mention to you that I wrote to Mrs. Fairbanks three weeks ago for the above articles but think she did not get my letter and if I was not much in want I would not trouble you with this..." William Givins a Confederate Prisoner

LETTER FROM BENJAMIN FRANKLIN BUTLER, MAY 1, 1864

By Telegram from Fort Monroe, May 1, 1864

To: Com'g Officer, Point Lookout

By the direction of Col. Hoffman, Commissary of Prisoners, you will direct all surplus clothing in the possession of rebel prisoners, issued to them by the government, to be taken from them on flag-of-truce boat, and return to be issued to other prisoners. They are not permitted to take with them either blankets, caps, shoes, or great-coats, and the Commissary of Prisoners thinks it would be advisable to take their coats from them. This order is rendered necessary for the reason many have taken away a complete outfit to the rebel service…" PRIVATE ANDS OFFICIAL CORRESPONDENCE OF GEN. BENJAMIN F. BUTLER, DURING THE PERIOD OF THE CIVIL WAR Plimpton Press 1917 Pg. 628

AN ARTILLERYMAN'S DIARY Wisconson History Commission 1914

Pg. 213 Diary of Jenkin Lloyd Jones May 22, 1864

"…A train of thirty cars loaded with "grey backs" captured by Sherman passed North; very dirty and filthy-looking clothes…"

REDCLAY TO RICHMOND by John J. Fox pub by Angle Valley Press 2006

Pg. 327 "…Rigby had been captured at the beginning of Grant's Overland Campaign in May 1864. He endured the harsh New York winter of 1864-65 at Elmira only to succumb to disease les than a month after the Appomattox surrender. Federal officials logged, "One blanket, one vest, one shirt, one pair of pants," as his remaining possessions at his death. Rigby had used these few items for protection during the previous winter when the thermometer frequently dropped below zero degrees…"

KATE: THE JOURNAL OF A CONFEDERATE NURSE Kate Cumming La. State Univ. Press 1998

Pg. 321 April 1864 "…Dr. Hughes proved himself a very good singer. He is an enthusiastic southerner, over sixty years of age, and has left wife and home for the cause. He tells me that his daughters in Kentucky are indefatigable in working for the southern cause. They are very kind to our men who are in the northern prisons, as I am told that nearly all the women of that state are. They and many other ladies have made up thousands of suits of clothing for them, and taken them to the prisons in person…."

HANDLEY LIBRARY ARCHIVES, WINCHESTER, VA DIARY OF James McGowan Co K, 5th Virginia Infantry Stonewall Brigade

Pg. 3 May 21, 1864 Point Lookout Md. "…Met with A.R.Varner who is much depressed in spirits although is well dressed, having some friends in the Northern States, who have sent him clothes…"

Pg. 4 May 22, 1864 "...So much suffering, some of the men have scarcely enough clothes and they were eaten up by scurvy, very common to all who are here any length of time. The whole place is alive with body lice-no one being exempt..."

Pg. 4 June 1, 1864 "...The prisoners, many of them are catching rats and are eating them. Those who eat them say they are as nice as squirrel. I see them cooked but can't quite go the rates. May do so yet. They look nice enough. Oh for one good square meal..."

Pg. 5 July 10, 1864 "...In their search of the quarters, some rafts were found with canteens attached ready to float, only awaiting a dark night to make the venture. Some, am told, have gotten away in this manner..."

Pg. 6 July 20, 1864 Good for your uncle. My name being called by a pompous looking Sergeant was informed there was a box for me and he would take me out to get it. After taking me out was ordered to strip myself of old rags and get into the new ones. Was soon off with them. The pants are six inches too long, shirt fits well enough and shoes splendid. Socks knit by Aunt Adeline Bass, my own dear mother's sister, and a nicer pair I never saw. My hat is very nice and fits. A nice jelly cake and a package of sweet cakes. We all feasted and thought many kind thoughts of my good old uncle..."

THE PRIVATIONS OF A PRIVATE by Marcus B. Toney pub by Univ. of Alabama Press 2005

Pg. 79 Summer, 1864 Point Lookout, Md. "...I was at the Point for five weeks without a change of clothing. I would go into the bay, wash my clothes, hang them on sand to dry, and go into the water up to my chin to keep from getting sunburned. At the end of five weeks I resolved to get some clothing, so I denied myself a ration a day, and after the two day's fast I sold my two rations to a fellow prisoner for five cents, and with the money I purchased from the sutler one postage stamp, in those days three cents, and one cent each for sheets of paper and envelopes; and as soon as my letter reached a friend in Baltimore ha sent me a package of clothing and a ten-pound package of Killikinnick smoking tobacco..."

LETTERS FROM TWO BROTHERS SERVING IN THE WAR FOR THE UNION TO THEIR FAMILY AT HOME IN WEST CAMBRIDGE MASS. Eugene Harrison Freeman to J.D. Freeman and Mrs. J.D. Freeman Houghton & Co. 1971

Pg. 126 June 1864

"...We soon received orders to proceed to West Point and take a load of prisoners and carry them to Point Lookout, Maryland, so we took on ninety men of the invalid corps for guard, and started at one P.M. and arrived at West Point at four P.M. then went up the Mattapony River a few miles and saw the cavalry approaching; they soon came in; bringing any number of negroes, wagons, etc.... They brought in 355 rebel prisoners, twenty-three of whom were officers, these we took on board, and Monday morning, at four o'clock, started for Point Lookout, where we arrived Monday afternoon at half past four. Landed the prisoners, and this (Tuesday) morning left there at two o'clock, bound for Washington. The prisoners were hard-looking customers, clad in the universal dirty grey uniform worn by the rebs,- not much of a uniform either; some had on one thing and some another; some had on Kossuth hats (a hat with a flat-topped crown and a rolled brim, looks something like the Iron Brigade's hats-ed.), some straw hats, some old oil-cloth caps, but no two alike. There were old men and young men and a great many boys; dirty, dusty, filthy and ragged; and the officers looked almost as bad as the men. They belonged to South Carolina and Georgia regiments…"

CIVIL WAR MEMOIRS OF TWO REBEL SISTERS-ed by William D. Wintz Pictorial History Pub Co. 1989

Pg. 61 June 29th, 1864 Prisoners camp Point Lookout, Maryland
My Dear Sister (Vic) "I am in a bad fix here having no money and no clothes except those I have on…"

AUTOGRAPH AND DIARY, J.R. Michael's Book: Bought July 15th, 1864 at Fort Delaware Del. Privately Pub. 1889

Pg. 35 Letter from Alice Buchanen to J.J. McDaniel, August 2, 1864
Dear Friend

"I received your letter yesterday and we were delighted to hear of the arrival of the "box," but imagine our surprise and concern to find that you received so few of the contents. We were very particular in sending such things as we were assured were not contraband; so can not imagine why you were not allowed to receive them. It must indeed been tantalizing to receive (comparatively) empty "box", for after putting in the clothing we could not get in as many eatables as we wanted to. The articles of clothing: three shirts, two pairs of drawers and socks we made with our own hands and marked your name on them and sent four "needle cases" directed to each of the officers of your mess with handkerchiefs and socks tied to each package, and the "needle cases" filled with stamps and pens, as well as other little things that would be useful in "prison", so I am sure you did not receive one half of what we sent: the smoking tobacco was something very superior. We regret the loss of the things exceedingly on your account, as we hoped the contents of that "box" would make you very comfortable for the present…"

March 23rd, 1865 "…Received a letter from Miss Alice Buchanon containing five dollars with the request for me to obtain a permit for her to send me clothing as she already had them ready…"

PRISON ECHOES OF THE GREAT REBELLION-Diary of Daniel Robinson Hundley S.W. Green 1874

Pg. 235 Sept. 1864 "…One hundred men, prisoners of Camp Chase, all privates, arrived here today. They look very yellow, sickly, and woebegone, with wool hats and ragged clothing, bearing the outward marks of having seen much hard usage, but they have already given evidence that they are not yet "subdued."..."

DIARY OF WILLIAM J. THOMAS, 2ND MARYLAND BATTALION Point Lookout, Md.

Sept 6 1864 "...weather rather unpleasant for a man without a jacket..."

Sept. 17, 1864 "...received a box of clothing, also tobacco an d some small affairs which I needed..."

Nov. 28 1864 "Had inspection and a grand search for blankets, it being the intention of the Provost Marshal to allow but one to the man. In the 10th Div. they secured a good many. But in the rest of the Camp I think Mr. Yank was decidedly euchered..."

Dec. 22, 1864 "...Received a nice pair of gloves from Miss F. McD...."

THE STORY OF THE GREAT MARCH, From the diary of a staff officer Diary of George Ward Nichols Harper & Brothers 1865

Pg. 100 December 1864 "...the hideous prison-pen used by the enemy for the confinement of Federal soldiers that had become prisoners of war. A space of ground about three hundred feet square, enclosed by a stockade, without any covering whatsoever, was the hole where thousands of our brave soldiers have been confined for months past, exposed to heavy dues, biting frosts, and pelting rains, without so much as a board or a tent to protect the after the rebels had stolen their clothing..."

Hey, Yank maybe the Rebs wouldn't be so angry if you all hadn't burned everything you could reach in the South.

CHRONICLES FROM THE DIARY OF A WAR PRISONER IN ANDERSONVILLE AND OTHER MILITARY PRISONS IN THE SOUTH IN 1864 J.W. Northup 1904

Pg. 184 Diary of John Worrell Northup Dec. 7th1864 (the Guards)

"...They were fine looking young men, in neat grey suits, roundabouts, and caps, all South Carolina boys, sons of wealthy merchants and planters, apparently well bred and educated. They had never seen service in the field, and thought there duty here extremely hard..."

PRISON ECHOES OF THE GREAT REBELLION Diary of Daniel Robinson Hundley S.W. Green 1874

Pg. 235 September, 1864

"...We have had several excitements in the bull-pen today. In the first place, the Rat Club (which is now a recognized institution, on an equal footing with our Chess Club, our Base-Ball

Club, Cricket Club, and numerous others) are much exercised-that is, the members of it-over the fact that Nellie has given birth to four puppies. It is expected now that next winter will afford a splendid opportunity for training these juvenal terriers to hunt the much-coveted game. Rats are now all the rage, and, next to rats, Nellie and her terrior pups…"

December 22, 1864 "…Over three hundred officers, recently captured in Tennessee, reached here tonight. They were in a sad plight, having been nearly starved on their way here, besides being nearly frozen, owing to the coldness of the weather and their lack of necessary clothing. Some of them are badly frost bitten; most of them are more or less demoralized, and their doleful accounts of Hood's mismanagement have terribly demoralized the bull-pen…"

NO SOAP, NO PAY, DIARRHEA, DYSENTERY & DESERTION ed. by Jeff Toalson pub by iUniverse 2006

Pg. 286 Winter, 1864 Camp Douglas, Ill. "Note of Reply on a "Lost Dog Poster" posted by a Union prison guard…" For Want of Meat, That Dog was Eat."

PRISON ECHOES OF THE GREAT REBELLION S.W. Green 1874

Pg. 193 Diary of Daniel Robinson Hundley Dec. 1864 (after Battle of Nashville)

"…As a good many of the officers recently brought in have on Yankee pants, I think I can now manage to secure me a Yankee suit out and out. At all events, I shall try. Captain McGibbon, of my regiment, has again secured himself a full suit, making accouterments also out of black oil-cloth, and intends attempting to pass out with the roll-callers to-morrow morning…"

CONFEDERATE LETTERS AND DIARIES 1861-1865 by Walbrook D. Swank, Colonel, USAF, Ret. Pub by Papercraft Printing & Design Company, Inc. 1988

Pg. 167 "Letters and Diary of a Confederate Prisoner of War, Private William W. Downer, Co. I, 6th Virginia Cavalry

Camp Chase Ohio, Prison #2, Barracks 15 Jany 24th, 1865 Dear Lucie, "…I am not in need of clothes. Cousin Tavener Goodloe has just sent me a full suit of clothes from Baltimore. I am in need of tobacco and money and could get it if I could get the offices of those I have mentioned…"

NO SOAP, NO PAY, DIARHHEA, DYSENERY & DESERTION, ed by Jeff Toalson pub by iUniverse Inc. 2006

Pg. 314 Jan. 20, 1865Sgt. Archie Livingston, 3rd Florida Infantry Camp Chase Prison, Ohio

"…Freezing weather is severe on Florida prisoners. There is considerable want of clothing and blankets…We hear you may be permitted to send us clothing…"

Pg 23 **HEADQUARTERS DEPOT PRISONERS OF WAR**

Brig. Gen. H.W. Wessells
Commissary-General of Prisoners, Washington, D.C.

General: I have the honor to state that I forwarded from these headquarters December 1, 1864, a requisition for clothing for issue to prisoners of war. About December 7 we received a quantity of clothing, partly filling the requisition, which was issued to the prisoners. December 12 we received a communication from Brig. Gen. H.E. Paine, U.S. Volunteers, inclosing communication from Brig. Gen. Beall, agent for rebel authorities, by which each was to supply its own prisoners with necessary supplies, and issue to them the supplies on their arrival. This request was complied with and report forwarded though General Paine December 17. December 14 we received a communication from your office advising us of the fact that, by a mutual agreement between the United States Government and rebel authorities, a large amount of cotton had been shipped for New York to be sold, the proceeds to be applied to the purchase of clothing for prisoners of war, and that in view of this fact it was not deemed advisable to provide any more clothing to prisoners than was absolutely demanded by the ordinary dictates of humanity. December 18 we received a communication from your office directing that, in pursuance of the arrangement between the United States and rebel authorities, commanding officers of military prisons will afford every necessary and proper facility for the purpose upon the request of Brig. Gen. Paine. We have heard nothing further in relation to the subject since. A number of prisoners will soon be destitute of trousers and other articles of clothing. They are still due upon requisition of December 1 1,000 jackets, 2,500 shirts, 3,000 pair trousers, 8,000 drawers, 4,000bootees, 7,000 socks, 1,500 caps and I would respectfully request that these amounts of jackets, trousers, shirts, bootees, socks, caps and 4,000 pair of drawers be furnished immediately for issue to prisoners unless the Department is advised that supplies will be speedily forwarded by the rebel authorities.

I am, general. Very respectfully, your obedient servant,
B.F. Tracy,
Colonel 127th U.S. Colored Troops, Commanding Depot

Pg36

"While it is true that the clothing of the prisoners in prison on the day of inspection was good, as reported, it is also true that very many of the prisoners recently received at and forwarded from this prison were in a very destitute condition. No arrangements have been made for distributing any portion of the "Confederate fund" at this prison, and General Hoffman, Commissary-General Prisoners of War, having issued instructions in communications dated December 22 and 23, 1864, to issue no more clothing from the supply furnished by the United States Government, many prisoners must suffer severely. All of which is respectfully referred to the Commissary-General of Prisoners.

Stephen E. Jones,
Captain and Additional Aide-de-Camp, Comdg. Military Prison

Pg. 166 (inclosure) Richmond, January, 1865

General Grant, Commanding U.S. Army:

Sir: We have the honor to announce to you that the Legislature of the State of Alabama has appropriated $500,000 for the relief of the prisoners of the State held by the United States. The undersigned have been appointed by the governor to carry out the object of this appropriation, most respectfully ask through you permission to proceed to the United States for this purpose. Having obtained permission from the Confederate Government to carry out cotton to the amount of this appropriation, we are instructed by the Governor of Alabama to ask permission to ship this cotton through the blockade for the purpose of supplying the prisoners from that state with blankets, clothing, and such other things as may be necessary for their comfort. We beg leave to suggest Mobile Bay as the point from which this cotton may be shipped. We would further state that it would be agreeable to the Governor of Alabama if a vessel belonging to the united States, or citizens thereof, should be permitted to carry this cotton from Mobile Bay to the port of New York; to be sold there for the purpose already indicated. We deem it proper to say that our mission is con fined strictly to the object stated in this communication; it embraces nothing of a military or political nature. If permitted to carry out the object of our mission we will cheerfully submit to such rules, regulations and paroles as are usual in such cases. We well know how a gallant soldier must feel for the conditions of those brave men who by the fortunes of war are held as prisoners; exposed to the rigors of a climate to which they are not accustomed, the severities of which are augmented by the privations necessarily attendant upon their condition. We make this request in confidence, assured that your sympathies for the unfortunate brave will lead you to do all in your power to promote the benevolent design entrusted to us by the State of Alabama.

We have the honor to remain, very respectfully, your obedient servants,

M. Lehman

CONFEDERATE VETERAN VOL.XIII June 1905

About Some "Galvanized Yanks"

(regarding Jan. 1865) "Replying to an inquiry in the Veteran for May by Comrade Case, of Prospect Tenn., Mr. L. McLendon, of Rison, Ark, says that the "galvanized Yanks" referred to were sent to Memphis, and from there to Alton, Ill., and arrived there a short time before any of the Confederate prisoners were sent on exchange to Richmond. Comrade McLendon states further: "I do not know how the boys found the name "galvanized Yanks", but found it was very quickly, and it was not resented. Our boys were continually fighting them with rock and fist. I talked with a number of them who were from the northeastern part of the United States and had been captured in Virginia and sent to Andersonville, and from there joined the Confederate army. They told me they fought as hard at Egypt Station (Jan. 1865) for us as they did in Virginia against us. When I left prison, they were still there..."

I wonder whatever happened to these "galvanized Yanks."

The following is from the "Official Records," and details an ingenious plan to clothe the Rebel P.O.W.s.

Pg. 63 **Fort Lafayette**, New York Harbor, January 13, 1865

Brig. Gen. H.E. Paine, U.S. Volunteers, New York:

General: I have the honor to enclose a slip from the Richmond Examiner of the 6th instant, which shows that the cotton has been shipped from Mobile," and I presume will be here in a day or so.

Pg. 67 **Fort Morgan**, January 13, 1865

Maj. James E. Montgomery:

Major: I respectfully state that I reached this post this evening with the rebel steamer Waverly with the 1,000 bales of cotton which I am to take to New York under orders of the major-general commanding.

Captain Jenkins, U.S. Navy, commanding naval forces Mobile Bay, having stated to me this evening (upon my reporting to him) that he could furnish no men to transfer the cotton from the Waverly to the Atlanta, I immediately endeavored to raise a gang of stevedores form Captain Dunham, assistant quartermaster, and failing that (as the men had been worked very hard), I obtained from Colonel Clarke\, commanding post, an order for thirty teamsters fromCaptain Dunham, for whom I am now waiting. This haste is necessary from the fact that the rebel steamer is a very frail, light vessel, and in the event of much wind would be obliged to seek shelter in a safe harbor until calm weather, and this is the season of "Northers."

I shall use all my exertion to forward this (already too long delayed) business with as much dispatch as possible, and keep you promptly informed of my actions.

Very respectfully, Your Obedient Servant,
Frank G. Noyes,
Captain and Commissary of Subsistence.

Pg. 90 **OFFICE COMMISSARY-GENERAL OF PRISONERS**

Washington D.C., January 19, 1865

Col. B.F. Tracy,
Commanding Depot Prisoners of War, Elmira, N.Y.

Colonel: Your letter of the 5th instant, requesting that the balance of the requisition for clothing made by you on the 1st ultimo may be forwarded to Elmira, has been received. The requisitions were held awaiting your reply to letter of the 12th ultimo from this office, which explained the necessity of strict economy in the issue of clothing to rebel prisoners at the present time, and requested that you would report your views on the necessity of such issue at Elmira N.Y. No reply to this letter has been received, and the requisitions are still in this office. The clothing received by you was sent to Elmira by mistake, and was no part of that required for by you. It was reported as issued before the error was discovered. As the cotton from the South referred to in my letter of the 12th ultimo is daily expected, you will please make immediate requisition for such clothing as may be absolutely necessary within the next three or four weeks, after which time it is hoped clothing from the rebel authorities may be ready for issue.

Very respectfully, your obedient servant,
H.W. Wessells,
Brig. Gen., U.S. Vols, Inspector and Com. Gen. of Prisoners.

Pg. 105 **HEADQUARTERS DEPOT PRISONERS OF WAR**

Elmira, N.Y. January 21, 1865

Brig. Gen. H.W. Wessells,
Commissary-general of Prisoners:

General: I have the honor to acknowledge the receipt of your communication of the 19th instant, calling attention to the fact that I have not reported my views (as requested in communication from your office dated December12, 1864) as to the necessity of issuing clothing to prisoners of war at the present time. I would offer in explanation that about the same date (December12) we received instructions from Brigadier-General Paine, U.S. Volunteers, to forward immediately through him, to the agent of the rebel authorities, a report from the prisoners of war at this depot of the supplies necessary to render them comfortable. This report was forwarded at once, and inasmuch as we had just received a partial supply of clothing (sent by mistake to this depot), I did not deem it necessary to make any further report before the arrival of the supplies from the rebel authorities. In obedience to your instructions of the 19th instant I have forwarded this day requisition in duplicate for such clothing as will be absolutely necessary within the next four weeks.

I am, very respectfully, your obedient servant,
B.F. Tracy,
Colonel 127th Colored troops, Commanding Depot.

Pg 137 **OFFICE COMMISSARY-GENERAL OF PRISONERS**

Washington D.C., January 27, 1865

Col. B.F. Tracy,
Commanding depot Prisoners of War, Elmira, N.Y.

Colonel: I have the honor, by direction of the Commissary-General of Prisoners, to acknowledge reciept of requisitions for clothing forwarded by you for approval on the 21st instant. As the cotton for the purchase of supplies for rebel prisoners has arrived ay New York, it is supposed that clothing will be forwarded by General Beall nearly or quite as soon as it could be furnished by the Quartermaster's Department. The requisitions will be held for the present.

Very respectfully, your obedient servant,
G. Blagden,
Major, Second Mass. Cav., Asst. to Com. Gen. of Prisoners

Pg 139 **48 BLEECKER STREET**

New York, January 28, 1865

Maj. Gen. H.W. Halleck, Chief of Staff, U.S. Army

General: General Beall has again asked for permission to receive and forward to prisoners of war contributions from friends resident within our lines. I replied that this application had already been twice made at headquarters, and was doubtless finally disposed of in the absence of an agreement between Mr. Ould and General Grant covering the case; that while the General Order 299, of December 7, 1864, would seem to justify a claim to receive contributions from Southern friends, properly forwarded, the case of aid from residents of the north was quite different, but I promised to advise him promptly if any new arrangements should be made applicable to this case.

I have the honor to request that you will inform me if any such arrangement is affected.

Most respectfully, your obedient servant,
H.E. Paine,
Brigadier-General of Volunteers.

(1st indorsement) January 31, 1865

Respectfully referred to Lieutenant-General Grant.

The secretary of War knows of no agreement authorizing our people to send presents to rebel prisoners of war.

H.W. Halleck
Major-General and Chief of Staff

(2nd indorsement)

HEADQUARTERS ARMIES OF THE UNITED STATES,

City point, Va., February 7, 1865

Respectfully returned.

No stipulation has been entered into between judge Ould and myself authorizing contributions to Confederate prisoners of war from friends within our lines, nor would I consent to such an arrangement.

U.S. Grant, Lieutenant-general.

Pg151 Washington, January 30, 1865

Brig. Gen. H.E. Paine, 48 BleeckerStreet, New York:

How soon will the clothing to be bought with the rebel cotton be forwarded to the prison camps by General Beall?

H.W. Wessells,
Commissary-General of Prisoners

Pg 163 **HEADQUARTERS DISTRICT OF SAVANNAH**

Savannah, Ga., February 1, 1865

Assistant Adjutant General
Headquarters, department of the South:

My medical director yesterday inspected the conditions of the rebel prisoners confined at Fort Pulaski, and represents that they are in a condition of great suffering and exhaustion for want of sufficient food and clothing; also that they have the scurvy to a considerable extent. He recommends, as a necessary sanitary measure, that they be at once put on full prison rations, and also that they be allowed to receive necessary articles of clothing from their friends. I would respectfully indorse the surgeon's recommendation and ask authority to take such steps as may be necessary to relieve actual sickness and suffering.

C. Grover,
Brevet Major-General, Commanding

Pg 166 Richmond, February 1, 1865

Lieutenant-General Grant:

General: We had the honor to forward to you on the 14th of January, by flag-of-truce boat, an application for permission to proceed to the United States for the purpose of supplying the wants of prisoners from the State of Alabama. The closing of that mode of communication by the ice in the river has induced our government to grant us permission to communicate with you by another channel. We enclose a copy (substantially) of our former letter, and as it is a matter of the highest interest to the Government and the people of our State, most respectfully ask that we may be permitted to confer with you in person in regard to it. If such an in review should be deemed by you inconsistent with the interests of your government or inconvenient to yourself, we would be pleased to receive your decision on our application of the 14th ultimo.

We have the honor to be, most respectfully, your obedient servants,

M. Lehman
I. T. Tichenor,
Agents of the State of Alabama.

Pg. 180 **OFFICE COMMISSARY-GENERAL OF PRISONERS**

Washington, D.C., February 4, 1865

Brig. Gen. H.E. Paine, New York City, N.Y.

General: your letter of the 2nd instant, requesting to be informed of the number of prisoners at the several stations, to enable General Beall to distribute his supplies judiciously, is received, and in reply I have to inform you that there is an average of about 8,000 at the following stations, viz: Point Lookout, Fort Delaware, Elmira, Camp Chase, Columbus, Ohio; Camp Douglas Chicago, Ill.; about 3,000 at Johnsons Island, 1,200 at Alton, Ill. And about 1,500 wounded men in and near Nashville, Tenn. There may be about 500 at and near New Orleans.

I am, general, very respectfully, your obedient servant,
W. Hoffman,
Bvt. Brig. Gen. U.S. Army, Commissary General of Prisoners.

OFFICE COMMISSARY-GENERAL OF PRISONERS

Washington D.C., February 4, 1865

Brig. Gen. H.E. Paine, U.S. Volunteers, New York, N.Y.

General: I have the honor to inclose herewith requisition for clothing required for prisoners at Fort Delaware, Point Lookout, Camp Chase, and camp Douglas. As under the recent understanding these articles are to be furnished by the rebel authorities through their agent, general Beall, I send you the estimate to show what quantities should be furnished. Please notify me to what prisons supplies are forwarded, and when.

I am, general, very respectfully, your obedient servant,
W. Hoffman,
Bvt. Brig. Gen. U.S. Army, Commissary-General of prisoners.

Pg. 189 **75 MURRAY STREET**

New York, N.Y. February 6, 18

Brig. Gen. H.E. PaineU.S. Volunteers, Present

General: I have the honor to ask that you make, if there is no objection, an arrangement with the Quartermaster's Department to furnish transportation on requisitions made direct from me for supplies to go to the several prisons. This, if done, will save much time and will save you the work of forwarding my requisitions. Please inform me if you have received any notice from Washington that officers have been transferred to the several prisons. I would respectfully ask that Brig. Gen. R.B. Vance, who is to be my assistant, be permitted to visit such prisons as I may desire, to look to the distribution of supplies. This priveledge is, I see from the papers, granted to the U.S. officers in the South. I inclose a letter from General Vance. Please write an d telegraph General Schoepf at Fort Delaware. If the arrangements can be made to ship on my requisition made direct I can report to you each day the shipments made the previous day. On Saturday I shipped to Point Lookout 2,000 blankets, 1,000socks; to Elmira 1,000 blankets 1,000socks; have also supplies to ship to-day to Fort Delaware. I purchased 15,000 pair socks and 7,000 pair shoes on Saturday. The delay in the cotton transshipped by Captain Noyes will cause me great inconvenience, I fear. Can he not hurry it up?

I am, very respectfully, your obedient servant,
WM. N.R. Beall,
ier-General, Provisional Army, C.S., Paroled Prisoner and Agent to Supply Prisoners of War.

FORT DELAWARE, DEL.
February 6, 1865

Brigadier-General Paine, New York

Dear Sir: I am satisfied there is some mistake in reference to my aiding General Beall in his purchasing supplies for Confederate soldiers prisoners of war. If correctly informed my government made for me to join general Beall. The order came here from Washington to that effect and my parole was made out, notice to be given General Schoepfby you when the cotton arrived in New York. I desire to call your attention to the facts, feeling assured that a mistake has been made in the matter. Justice to the agreement with my Government would suggest that it be carried out.

Very truly yours,
Robt. B. Vance,
Brigadier-General and Prisoner of War.

37 BLEECKER STREET
New York, February 6, 1865

Brig. Gen. W.N.R. Beall, 75 Murray Street, New York:

General: I have the honor ti forward for your information papers this day received from Brevet Brigadier General Hoffman, Commissary-General of Prisoners, viz., (1) requisition and letter og Capt. Charles Goodman, Assistant Quartermaster, Camp Douglas; (2) letter of general A. Schoepf and requisition of Capt. S.R. Craig assistant quartermaster; (3) letter of Alonzo Morgan and requisition of Alonzo Morgan, and others, Point Lookout, and (4) requisition of Capt. T.J. Kerr, assistant quartermaster, camp Chase. These requisitions were drawn on U.S. officers, except that of A. Morgan and associates.

I will endeaver to make the arrangement referred to in communication of this date.

I have received no notice of the transfer of any officers. Will communicate by telegraph and mail with general Schoepf, as requested, and obtain from the War Department information as to the functions of General Vance.

Very respectfully, your obedient servant,
H.E. Paine,
Brigadier-General of Volunteers

Pg. 180 **HEADQUARTERS FORT COLUMBUS**

New York Harbor, February 6, 1865
Commissary-General of Prisoners, Washington City, D.C.

Sir: In compliance with paragraph 12 of circular from the Commissary-General of Prisoners, dated Washington D.C. April 20, 1864, I have the honor to submit for your approval the inclosed special estimate of clothing required for the use of prisoners at this post, and to state that although all of the amount specified is not now actually required, yet it is deemed necessary to keep a small quantity on hand to meet the frequent demands for clothing consequent on the liability of having the class of prisoners for whom it is intended for issue sent to this point at any moment, many of whom are entirely destitute of bedding, and in a great measure of the necessary clothing to insure cleanliness and comfort.

Very respectfully, your obedient servant,
J.M. Bomford,
Colonel Eighth U.S. Infantry, Commanding Post

Received February 1, 1865, of Brig. Gen. W.N.R. Beall, paroled commissioner for supplying Confederate prisoners, the following named articles: Twenty-five pair pants, 25 pair shoes, 25 blankets, 3 dozen pair woolen socks.

Respectfully referred to the Commissary-General of Prisoners.

A. Chapel,
Surgeon, U.S.Volunteers, Commanding Hospital.

Pg195 **GENERAL ORDERS,** **HDQRS. C.S. MILITARY PRISONS EAST OF MISSISSIPPI RIVER,**

No.3 Columbia, S.C. February 7, 1865

Sutlers at various prison camps are the only persons authorized to trade with the prisoners. The commanding officers at the various prisons will grant them the permission to purchase U.S. Treasury notes from the prisoners for the use of the Government at the rates to be established by the Quartermaster-General, which until further orders will be $5 in C.S. notes for $1 in U.S.Treasury notes. All trafficking and trading by unauthorized persons must be stopped. Commanding officers will use stringent measures to prevent it, and all persons so offending connected with the post will be placed under arrest and brought before a court-martial. Others will be turned over to the civil authorities for trial.

Jno. H. Winder

WASHINGTON, D.C. February 8, 1865

Col. B.F. Tracy,
Commanding Depot Prisoners of War, Elmira, N.Y.:

Colonel: The Quartermaster-General has referred to this office a letter from Capt. J.J. Elwell, assistant quartermaster at Elmira, in which he reports that he has been obliged by your order to issue U.S. clothing to prisoners of war in consequence of there being no clothing on hand furnished specially for prisoners. The regulations, to which your attention has before been called, proscribe the mode of procuring clothing for prisoners, and if at any time there was an insufficiency on hand to meet the demands, it must be attributed to want of attention on the part of the commanding officer whose duty it is to see that timely requisitions are made for such clothing as may be required; and when, to meet demands which are occasioned by his neglecting this duty, he takes upon himself to order the clothing in a mode not authorized, he commits another error. I call your attention to this subject again in the hope there will be no recurrence of similar irregularities. See my letter of October 5 1864.

Very respectfully, your obedient servant,
W. Hoffman,
Bvt. Brig. Gen., U.S. Army, Commissary-General of Prisoners.

Pg. 199 **MURRAY STREET**, New York, February 9, 1865

Brigadier-General Hunt, U.S. Volunteers, Present:

General; I have the honor to state that since nothing has been heard from the 170 bales of cotton received by Capt Frank G. Noyes, U.S. Army, under the late agreement between General Grant and General Ould to supply prisoners of war and transshipped as per remarks on bill of lading:

"U.S.S. Transport Atlanta, Mobile Bay, January 16, 1865.

Owing to the incapacity of the steamer Atlanta to carry all the articles named within, 170 of the bales mentioned have been transferred to the assistant quartermaster, U.S. Army, Fort Morgan, Ala. For shipment to at New York.

Frank G. Noyes,
Captain and Commissary of Subsistence, U.S. Army"

I would respectfully ask the honorable Secretary of War give an order to have the same quantity of cotton turned over to me at this place and that the cotton turned over to the quartermaster at Fort Morgan be kept by the United States. I have in my possession the weight and classification of the cotton shipped from Mobile. I make the forgoing request from the fact that till the cotton is received and turned into funds it is impossible for me to arrange and make purchases of supplies under my instructions.

I am, general, very respectfully your obedient servant,
Wm. N.R. Beall,
Brigadier-General Provisional Army, C.S.
Paroled Prisoner and Agent to Supply Prisoners of War

NEW YORK CITY, February 10, 1865.

Honorable Secretary of War, Richmond, Va.:

I have the honor to report that 830 of the 1,000 bales of cotton which were to be sent to this city, sold, and the proceeds to be expended to supply prisoners (of) war, under the late agreement between General grant and Col. R. Ould, arrived here on the 24th of January. The remaining 170 bales, on account of the incapacity of the vessel, the U.S. transport Atlanta, to bring them, were left with the U.S. Quartermaster at Fort Morgan, Ala., and are daily looked for. The cotton reached this place in very bad condition and the bill of lading shows it was received in this condition. It had to be repacked and rebaled and was sold at pub lic auction on the 8th; averaged 82 48/100 cents per pound, which is considered by the best judges to have been a remarkably good sale. The long delay in the arrival of the cotton has caused it to bring much less than was expected at the time of the agreement. The waste in transporting the cotton, which was in a very bad condition, was considerable. The proceeds of the cotton will furnish but a small portion of the actual wants of the prisoners, and some arrangement should at once be made to send an additional quantity of cotton under the agreement, and I would respectfully suggest that it be sent from a convenient point, and the delay be as little as possible. I have purchased 16,983 blankets, 16,216 jackets and coats, 19,888 pair of pants, 19,000 overshirts, 5,948 pair of drawers, 10,140 pair of socks, 17,000 pair of shoes, and have since the 4th instant been sending the supplies to the different prisons daily. I take pleasure in stating that the U.S. officers in Boston, Philedelphia, Baltimore and this city have treated me with courtesy and given every facility in their power to enable me to carry out the agreement. I visited those cities for the purpose of examining the market and to make purchases.

A few days since a large number of packages principally: tobacco, arrived via flag of truce for the prisoners and are being sent forward as fast as possible. My assistant adjutant general, Capt. Beall Hempstead, who is a prisoner of war at Johnson's Island, could be of great assistance to me, and I respectfully ask that an arrangement be made that will permit his being paroled and permitted to join me at this place.

I have the honor to be, very respectfully, your obedient servant,
WM. N.R.BEALL,
Brigadier-General, Provisional Army,C.S.
Paroled prisoner and Agent to Supply Prisoners of War

This is a vast amount of clothing purchased with the proceeds of the cotton.

33 BEEKMAN STREET, New York, February 13 1865

The within communication having been shown me by Brigadier-General Beall, with a request that I indorse the same, I respectfully state that the only objection I see to making the arrangements asked for hearin by Brigadier-General Beall is the difficulty of ascertaining the correct weight and classification of the 170 bales of cotton turned over by me to the assistant quartermaster at Fort Morgan for shipment to me at this city.
The cotton received by me from General Maury January 1, ultimo, in mobile Bay, was in very bad condition, many of the bales open, the roping broken, and there being consequently a large quantity of loose cotton. The marks on many of these bales were illegible. I was therefore unable to sign bills of lading for a stated number of pounds of cotton, but only for a certain number of bales in bad order and condition and with marks illegible. I loaded the transport Atlanta to her full capacity, and in addition to her cargo of whole bales put all the loose cotton from the entire number of bales received by me from general Maury on board of her, and turned over the remaining 170 bales to the assistant quartermaster at Fort Morgan, for shipment to me at New York, through Captain Perkins, Assistant Quartermaster, in charge of in charge of water transportation, New Orleans, La. It is therefore probable that the average weight of the 830 bales brought here by me on the Atlanta (arriving at New York January24, ultimo) and turned over to Brigadier-General Beall is greater than the average weight of the 170 bales yet to arrive. It also seems probable that the bad condition of the cotton when received by me, and its frequent handling since it was invoiced to Brigadier-General Beall by General Maury, may have reduced its classification and consequent value. If these difficulties can be obviated, I respectfully recommend that the request of Brigadier-General Beall be granted. It may be proper for me to state that the 170 bales of cotton were loaded at Fort Morgan on the U.S. schooner Highlander, and the master of that schooner had received his sailing orders for New Orleans on the day I left Mobile Bay, to wit, January 16, ultimo, and that the same day I wrote Col. S.B. Holabird, Chief Quartermaster, Department of the Gulf, New Orleans, explaining to him the whole matterand requesting him to see that the 170 bales were forwarded to me at New York without delay.

Frank G. Noyes,
Captain and Com. OfSub., Major-General Granger's Staff.

Pg. 202

Richmond, February 10, 1865

Lieut. Gen. U.S. Grant, U.S. Army:

Sir: The Confederate authorities desire to send from Mobile an additional supply of 1,500 bales of cotton, to be disposed of by our agents in New York for the benefit of our prisoners. The cotton will be ready for delivery at an early day. I will thank you to instruct your military authorities near Mobile to notify Major-General Maury of the time when they will be ready to receive it.

Respectfully, your obedient servant,
Ro. Ould,
Agent of Exchange.

Pg. 204 **Confederate States of America, War Department,**

Richmond, Va., February 10, 1865.

General D.H. Maury,Mobile, Ala.:

Under the arrangement with General Grant, send out, through N. Harleston Brown, 1,500 bales cotton on notice of Federal authorities of readiness to receive. Allow no delay.

J.C. Breckinridge,
Secretary of War.

Inspection report, February 12, 1865, Leiutenant James R. Reid stated

"Clothing-decidedly deficient, but is now being corrected by the distribution of clothing from the Confederate authorities." Pg.208

Pg. 221-222

Inspection by Gust. Heinrichs,Leiut. Col., Forty-first Missouri Regiment and Inspecting Officer, at Saint Louis, Mo.,February 14, 1865, in his remarks and suggestions, stated "At my recent inspections I have observed that prisoners of war coming from the smallpox hospital are furnished with clothing exactly the same as that worn by our own men. Paragraph XII of the commissary-General's circular of April, 1864, directs that the skirts of the coats will be cut short, but these are jackets such as many Western regiments have received and still wear. I have, of course, ordered the buttons to be cut off, but I still believe it to be dangerous to issue that kind of clothing, because prisoners will be very easily mistaken for U.S. Soldiers. I would respectfully suggest that only grey clothing (which is often confiscated on prize vessels) be issued, or some other mark, such as replacing the blue collars or part of their sleeves by grey ones, which the prisoners can do themselves, to prevent such mistakes." There was an indosement, written by J.H. Baker, Colonel and Provost-Marshal-general, Commanding, "Approved, with the remark that I have directed that grey cloth be provided by sutler, that part of the sleeve may be marked as recommended by Colonel Heinrichs."

Can you imagine a large group of prisoners dressed exactly like your own soldiers? This officer was right to be concerned.

Pg. 226

HEADQUARTERS OF THE ARMY

Washington D.C., February 15, 1865
Lieutenant-General Grant, City Point:

General: Information has been received here from various sources that the proceeds of the 1,000 bales of cotton sent from Mobile are to be used to supply the rebel prisoners of war, now being exchanged, with new uniforms and blankets, so that they can return to the field fully clothed and supplied in the United States. By direction of the Secretary of War I enclose herewith a copy of a letter referring to a contract by the rebel General Beall in New York for 20,000 grey coats and pants and 20,000 blankets. The Secretary of War does not see how, under the agreement between yourself and Mr. Ould, this can be prevented, and directs me to refer the matter to you for your actions or suggestions.

Very respectfully, your obedient servant,
H.W. Halleck,
Major-General and Chief of Staff
(inclosure)

NEW YORK, February 10, 1865
Hon. Charles A. Dana,
Assistant Secretary of War, Washington D.C.:

Dear Sir: I am this morning informed that the rebel General Beall has contracted with one of our clothiers (John F. Martin) for 20,000 grey coats and pants for the purpose of clothing the Confederate prisoners, and that he has also contracted for 20,000 blankets for same use. From the fact that these prisoners are soon to be exchanged, as I am informed, and that the clothing ordered is in every respect the Confederate uniform (save as to buttons), that they can be readily changed (grey satinets), will not this, if permitted, place 20,000 men in the confederate ranks, uniformed and with blankets, ready for active service? I have felt it my duty to call the attention of the Government, through you, to the above facts, &c....

Truly, yours,
Henry E. Clark

That Mr. Ould is a genious; imagine buying gray uniforms for the prisoners from northern merchants, using the money from the cotton exchanged. I'd like to have seen Gen. Grant's face when he found out about these "goings on."

Pg. 241 **HEADQUARTERS OF THE ARMY,**

Washington, D.C. February 17, 1865.
Lieutenant-General Grant, City Point:

General: Iam directed by the Secretary of War to forward the inclosed letter of General Beall, and to say that General Vance has been released on parole to assist general Beall, and also that three officers have been sent to the prison depots as agreed upon. It will be seen from this letter the all the proceeds of the rebel cotton are devoted to supplying the rebel prisoners with new clothing, shoes, and blankets. Not a cent is expended for provisions. The result is that we feed their prisoners and permit the rebel Government to send cotton within our lines, free of all charge, to purchase and carry back the means of fitting out their own men for the field. Under these circumstances the Secretary of War is not disposed to sanction the admission of any more cotton on the same terms.

Very respectfully, your obedient servant,
H.W. Halleck,
Major-General and Chief of Staff.
(Inclosure)

Pg257 **HEADQUARTERS ARMIES OF THE UNITED STATES**

City Point, Va. February 18, 1865

Maj. Gen. H.W. Halleck,
Chief of Staff of the Army, Washington, D.C.

General: Your communication of the 15th instant, with inclosure, calling my attention to the fact advantage is being taken by General Beall, Confederate agent, of the recent agreement between Judge Ould and myself to supply rebel prisoners with new uniforms and blankets, is received.

The arrangement for the relief of prisoners of war was made at a time when exchanges could not be made, and under it I see no way to prevent rebel prisoners from being clothed. Having, however, a very large excess of prisoners over the enemy, we can in making exchanges select those who have not been furnished with new clothing or blankets. By this means but a very limited number of rebel soldiers will be returned with new uniforms.

Should it become necessary prisoners for exchange can be required to turn in their blankets to their comrades who remain.

Please give orders to General Hoffman accordingly.

Very respectfully, your obedient servant,
U.S. Grant,
Lieutenant-General.

Pg 258 **37 BLEECKER STREET, NEW YORK**, FEBRUARY 18, 1865.

Maj. Gen. H.W. Halleck, Chief of Staff, U.S. Army:

General: General Beall informs me that the officer commanding Fort McHenry has suggested to him that it might be convenient to make a depot of clothing at Baltimore for distribution to rebel prisoners in transit to our prisons, and asks leave to send General Vance thither to attend personally to such distribution. It is obvious that the method adopted at the prisons of intrusting this duty to officers confined in them is impracticable at Baltimore, the prisoners being all transient.

I respectfully recommend that this request be granted, and am of the opinion that no harm will result from permitting General Vance to deliver the clothing directly to the prisoners in the presence of our officers, but if that is deemed inadmissible he can be instructed to avoid personal intercourse with the prisoners.

Most respectfully, your obedient servant,
H.E. Paine,
Brigadier-General of Volunteers.
(Indorsement)

February 20, 1865

Respectfully referred to Brevet Brigadier-General Hoffman.
The Secretary of War directs that the recommendations of Lieutenant-General Grant be carried out.

H.W. Halleck,
Major-General and Chief of Staff

Pg 282 **37BLEECKER STRET, NEW YORK**, FEBUARY 21, 1865.

Maj. Gen. H.W. Halleck, Chief of Staff U.S. Army:

General: I have the honor to forward the petition of General Beall to be relieved from the internal revenue tax of 2 cents per pound on the cotton received from Mobile under the arrangement between Lieutenant-General Grant and Judge Ould, with the correspondence of Mr. Commissioner Lewis and Messrs. Duncan, Sherman & Co. on that subject.

Very respectfully, your obedient servant,
H.E. Paine,
Brigadier-General of Volunteers.

(Indorsement)

Submitted to Secretary of War. No Action.

H.W. Halleck, major-general

Pg 289 **OFFICE COMMISSARY-GENERA;L OF PRIOSONERS**,

Washington D.C. February 22, 1865.

Maj. Gen. H.W. Halleck, Chief of Staff, Washington, D.C.:

General: In reference in the matter of supplying clothing to rebel prisoners by General Beall, as mentioned in the letter of Lieutenant-General Grant, referred to me on the 20th instant and received last evening, I have the honor to state that the rolls of those prisoners who desire to be exchanged at the several camps are already far advanced, and those who decline to be exchanged have already so expressed themselves, and it is not therefore probable that clothing will be distributed by General Beall's representatives to any but those who are to be immediately exchanged.

The number who decline to be exchanged will, I think, more than balance the excess of prisoners in our hands over those held by the enemy, and I presume Lieutenant-General Grant's is not to be understood as directing that blankets shall be taken from prisoners who wish to be exchanged and given to those that desire to take the oath of allegiance.

As far as practicable the instruct\ions of Lieutenant-General Grant shall be carried out.

I am, general. Very respectfully, your obedient servant,

W. Hoffman,

Bvt. Brig. Gen. U.S. Army, Commissary-General of prisoners.

Pg 356 **HEADQUARTERS, DISTRICT OF THE GULF**,

Mobile, Ala., March 4, 1865.

Major-General Granger,

Commanding U.S. Forces, Fort Gaines, Ala.:

General: I have the honor to in form you that I have received orders from the War Department to deliver to the U.S. commander in Mobile Bay 1,500 bales cotton, to be applied toward relief of the C.S. prisoners of war now in the hands of the U.S. authorities.

Please inform me at what time and place you will receive the above-stated cotton, as it is now ready for delivery.

I am, general, very respectfully, your obedient servant,

Dabney H. Maury,

Major-General, Commanding.

FOUR YEARS IN THE CONFEDERATE ARTILLERY The Diary of Pvt. Henry Robinson Berkely Ed. By William H. Runge Univ. of N.C. Press 1961

Pg. 130 March 21 1865 "…I also saw Gen. page, who recently commanded the defenses in Mobile Harbor. He and Lieut. Anderson are on a committee of Confederate officers to divide out some blankets and clothing among Southern prisoners of war at Fort Delaware. These blankets, shoes and clothing have been bought with the proceeds of a cargo of cotton, which the Yanks permitted the Confederate Government to send to New York City and sell there for that purpose. Gen. Page gave me a new blanket. Our rations are tolerably good…"

Pg. 130 March 22 1865 '…Bev. Tells me, in his note, if I am much in need of clothes, shoes, etc., to apply to Mrs. S. Dickson of Philadelphia for anything I may need. This good woman, it seems, is at the head of an organization to relieve southern prisoners of war; but behind her is Mr. Henry Turner, Bevs uncle, and some other Southern sympathizers who furnish the money to carry on the good work. I am very much in need, but I hate to beg…"

Pg. 137 May 7 1865 "…Mrs. Dickson sent me five (dollars) and informed me that she had sent me by express a suit of clothes and a hat and a pair of shoes…"

A CIVIL WAR MARRIAGE IN VIRGINIA: REMINISCENCES AND LETTERS Carr Pub. Co. 1956 Letter from Green Berry Samuels to Katheleen Boone Samuels March 7, 1865

"…Do not give yourself any uneasiness on my account. I have met with, many kind friends, who have furnished me with good warm clothing and from time to time with small remittances of money, which has prevented me from suffering either with cold or hunger.…"

MEADE'S HEADQUARTERS 1863-1865 ED. George R. Agassiz Atlantic monthly Press 1922

Pg. 324 Letter from Theodore Lyman to Elizabeth Russell Lyman March 26, 1865

"…Then there was a lull, filled by the arrival of a long, grey procession of some 1500 prisoners from the 9th Corps. Really these men possess a capacity for looking "rough" beyond any people I ever saw, except the townsmen of Signor Fra Diavolo. They grew rougher and rougher. These looked brown and athletic, but had the most matted hair, tangled beards, and slouched hats, and the most astounding carpets, hose-sheets, and transmogrified shelter-tents for blankets, that you ever imagined. One grim gentleman, of forbidding aspect, had tempered his ferocity by a black, broad-brimmed straw hat, such as country ministers sometimes wear-a head-dress which, as Whittier remarked, "rather forced the season!"

Well, one expects to find the Rebels in rags this late in the war, though, as we've seen, this is a continuance of their usual raggedness.

TO APPPOMATTOX Burke Davis Rinehart & Co. 1959

Pg. 26 March 26 1865 "Colonel Theodore Lyman of Meade's staff thought the prisoners the most disheveled he ever saw: "They grew rougher and rougher. These looked brown and athletic, but had the most matted hair, tangled beards, and slouched hats, and the most astonishing carpets, horse-sheets, and transmogrified shelter-tents for blankets."

WAR HISTORY OF THE OLD FIRST VIRGINIA REGIMENT ARMY OF NORTHERN VIRGINIA William Ellis Jones Book & Job Printer 1884 prisoners from A.N.V. retreat from Richmond April, 1865

"...The majority of the prisoners were sent to Point Lookout, I among this lot, where they arrived on the 5th (April) after a wearisome march of over sixty miles to City Point, and thence by boat. What we here suffered cannot be described. When we landed we were stripped of our overcoats, blankets, oil-cloths, and most of our baggage, which was kicked into the water by the Federal Sergeants who searched us, for the reason it was United States Property, which was true in most cases, for we were armed and clothed by the Federal government by the battles we had won. After being deprived of nearly all we had to keep us warm, we were put into the bull-pen, as it was called..."

I find this action totally unnecessary.

THE DIARY OF PRIVATE HENRY ROBINSON BERKELY-ed by William H. Runge pub by Univ of North Carolina Press1961

Pg. 137 May 7 1865 Fort Delaware "...Miss Evie sent me five dollars. Mrs. Dickson sent me five and informed me that she had sent me by express a suit of clothes and a hat and a pair of shoes..."

THIS WAR SO HORRIBLE-The Civil War Diary of Hiram Smith Williams ed by Lewis N. Wynne & Robert A. Taylor pub by Univ Al Press 1993

Pg. 131 April 26th, 1865 Point Lookout Md. "...Had I a wood house as some have, with money enough to buy what I dearly need, food and clothing, I could content myself, but instead, not a dollar have I got as yet...Had I ten dollars in greenbacks I could get along very well, as I could but as much clothing and foods I wanted. Even had I something to read I could get along very well, but even a paper is a rarity..."

Pg. 329 Point Lookout, Md. "...One of the gates opened to the bay and some of the prisoners were allowed to wade into the water to bathe. Edwards watched one day as a man waded too far out and suddenly was pulled under water. He thrashed back to the surface and screamed as a large shark dragged him back under..."

THE STAR CORPS; OR NOTES OF AN ARMY CHAPLAIN Jermain and Brightman Printers 1865

Pg. 304 Letter from William Bones, May 13, 1865 about being captured in the spring of '65

"...You have been apprised, by a far more able pen than mine, of the particulars of that terrible fight and its result, as well as the sufferings endured by us all while on the march from there to Richmond prisons; in fact, no human power can tell all that we suffered. Robbed of everything, stripped of our clothing and blankets, exposed to the severest weather, compelled to ford streams where the water came up to our armpits, and forced to lie in the mud. I only wonder that any lived to tell the tale..."

You don't like it Yank? Then go home!

REMINISCENCES OF THE WAR OF THE REBEELLION1861-1865 Memoir of Jacob Roemer Estate of Jacob Roemer

Pg. 316 June 1865 "where 273 rebel prisoners of war were confined. All these were dressed in rebel grey uniforms or what was left of them, and some were literally in rags, and very many looked as if a little soap and water would be beneficial to both faces and clothes...."

LETTERS FROM A PENNSYLVANIA CHAPLAIN AT THE SEIGE OF PETERSBURG-1865 Mary Bronson Armstrong Privately Pub. 1961

Pg. 25 Letter from Halleck Armstrong to Mary Armstrong April 10, 1865

"...They seem able-bodied and healthy, and are quite as large and stout as the same number of our boys. In short, in a good cause, they are excellent material for soldiers. Many of them had picked up our cast away blankets and overcoats. Nearly all had shoes. Our boys let them pass in silence, none being disposed to taunt them. A few of the officers rode wretched horses or mules. It was a motley group; there being no pretence in uniformity of dress. Dirty grey and butternut were the prevailing colors. Most of them wore old, seedy, slouched hats of brown color..."

Elmira Prison N.Y.

"On account of the waste from the commissary a great many rodents from Elmira ran into the prison. As there were not any holes in which they could hide, it was an easy catch for the boys by knocking them over with sticks, and there was quite a traffic in them. As there were very little currency in prison, tobacco, rats, pickles, and light bread were mediums of exchange. Five chews of tobacco would buy a rat, a rat would buy five chews of tobacco, a loaf of bread would buy a rat, a rat would buy a loaf of bread, and so on....On the 29th of January,(1865) so my diary reads, I was ordered to the cook house for a bath, and my nice suit of gray was burned.: and as the authorities did not keep any uniforms of gray, I donned a suit of blue, so in the picture I do not resemble "the boy in gray."

(there is a photo in the book, Pg. 105-ed.) I buttoned up my coat and was feeling comfortable as “the boy in blue,” when the sergeant, who was robing me, took out his knife and commenced to cut off my skirt. “Hold on, sergeant,” I said; “don’t disfigure my uniform in that manner.” He continued to cut until my skirt was gone, and then replied: “If I had left that frock intact, you might have walked out as one of our guards.” And I guess I would have attempted it…”

EPILOGUE

OK, I have included here a few closing quotes to illustrate what the participants hed to saw about the Southern Struggle.

W.C. Ward, Private of Co. G, 4th Alabama Regiment, Law's Brigade, on Sat. may 5, 1900 to Camp Hardee in Birmingham, Al.

"To make grander men, God must create a new world."

THE LOST CAUSE, by Edward A. Pollard 1866

"The Confederates have gone out of this war, with the proud, secret, deathless, consciousness that they are THE BETTER MEN, and that there was nothing wanting but a change in a set of circumstances and a firmer resolve to make them the victors."

THE CONFEDERATE VETERAN

THAT OLD GRAY COAT
Ragman, leave that Old Gray Coat,
Touch not a single fold,
It served me well when it was new,
I'll save it, now 'tis old.
Through sunshine, storm, and battle's rush,
Where shell and shrapnel flew,
In camp where slumber gave sweet rest,
When winter's tempest blew;
In hospital where anguished groan,
Expressed the sufferer's pain;
On firing-line where death came near,
And deep wounds left their stain-
It was to me protector, friend,
A comfort, shield, and joy,
And 'though 'tis torn and tattered now,

You shall not it destroy.
So keep it well, save the skirt and sleeve,
From dust, and moth, and gorm,
And when in death's cold arms I lie,
Just wrap it round my form.
-James Edward Payne, Dallas Texas

THE CONFEDERATE VETERAN VOL. XIII 1905

A TATTERED REMNANT.

"The Albany (Ga.) Herald tells a pathetic story of the Memorial Day service in that city:

"The conclusion of the Memorial Day exercises was marked by an incident which brought tears to hundreds of eyes....The Veterans were attentive auditors to the music, prayers and address. The speaker had concluded his remarks, the closing anthem was sung, and the final announcements made. Then the audience heard a husky voice issue a command. There was a stir at the front of the auditorium, and from their seats uprose a handful of Confederate veterans. Only a handful! Fifteen or sixteen in that Memorial Day audience of many hundreds.

"Right Face! Forward column right march!"

Down the aisle they started, a corporal's guard of that magnificent army of forty years ago. Every head was white of streaked with gray and nearly every form was bent. Here was an empty sleeve, there a leg of cork. As they moved down the aisle, this scant handful of heroes, the great audience, by a common impulse, rose and stood in reverant silence. It was a spontaneous tribute of a Southern audience to Southern heroes. But, simple tribute though it was, it touched the hearts of those white-haired veterans, and as they moved on down the aisle tears-grateful tears-fell from the glistening eyes of every man of them. And the members of the younger generations present, thus suddenly brought face to face with the fact that we now have with us but a tattered remnant of that glorious army of the sixties whose undying fame is burned into the pages of history, mingled their own eloquent tears with those of their heroes.

"Do we love our Confederate heroes? God bless them, yes!

A thousand times yes! They are enshrined in our hearts, and to love them less would be to dishonor Southern manhood and womanhood."

THE AMERICAN CIVIL WAR: LETTERS AND DIARIES

Diary of Judith White Brockenbrough, Randolph & English 1889 Pg. 360

April 28, 1865 "...We have no mail communication, and can hear nothing from General Johnson. We go on as usual, but we are almost despairing. Dear M., in her sadness has put some Confederate money and postage stamps into a Confederate envelope, sealed it up, and endorsed it "In memory of our beloved Confederacy." I feel like doing the same, and treasuring up the buttons and the stars and the dear gray coats, faded and worn as they are, with the soiled and tattered banner, which has no dishonoring blot, the untarnished sword, and other arms, though defeated, still crowned with glory. But not yet-I cannot feel that all is over yet…"

THE AMERICAN CIVIL WAR: LETTERS AND DIARIES

The Wartime Journal of a Georgia Girl 1861-1865-Diary of Eliza Francis Andrews ed by Spencer B. King, pub by Appleton-Century-Crofts 1908 Pg. 392
May 27, 1865 "…One of the latest proposals of the conquerors is to make our Confederate uniform the dress of convicts. The wretches! As if it was within the power of men to disgrace the uniform of Robert E. Lee and Stonewall Jackson! They couldn't disgrace it, even if they were to put their own army into it…"

About the Author

Kenn Woods lives in Front Royal Virginia with his wife of 26 years and daughter. He has had a lifelong interest in the American Civil War. He attended Frostburg State University and earned a BS in Fisheries/Wildlife Biology and is currently a mental health nurse with the state of Virginia.